My Double Life 2

A Rainbow
over the Hills

The Vision of Unity

Episodes and Pattern in a Writer's Life

First published by O-Books, 2015
O-Books is an imprint of John Hunt Publishing Ltd., Laurel House, Station Approach,
Alresford, Hants, SO24 9JH, UK
office1@jhpbooks.net
www.johnhuntpublishing.com

For distributor details and how to order please visit the 'Ordering' section on our website.

Text copyright: Nicholas Hagger 2015

ISBN: 978 1 78099 714 8

A CIP catalogue record for this book is available from the British Library.

Design: Stuart Davies

Printed and bound by CPI Group (UK) Ltd, Croydon, CR0 4YY

We operate a distinctive and ethical publishing philosophy in all areas of
our business, from our global network of authors to production and
worldwide distribution.

My Double Life 2

A Rainbow
over the Hills

The Vision of Unity

Episodes and Pattern in a Writer's Life

Nicholas Hagger

BOOKS

Winchester, UK
Washington, USA

Books published by Nicholas Hagger

"Our structure is very beautiful. DNA can be thought of roughly as a very long chain with flat bits sticking out.... The beauty of our model is that the shape of it is such that only these pairs can go together."[1]

Francis Crick, Letter to his 12-year-old son on the double-helix structure of DNA, 19 March 1953

'Double' (adj): "consisting of two, usually equal parts"; "having twice the usual size, quantity or strength"; "having two different roles or interpretations" (*Concise Oxford Dictionary*). And: "consisting of two combined"; "forming a pair, coupled"; "acting in two ways at different times" (*Shorter Oxford English Dictionary*).

*

The vision of unity
Graeco-Roman bronze of the Titan Atlas holding the unified world, showing Africa misshapen (in accordance with the geographical knowledge of the Graeco-Roman time), by a sculptor who grasped that the earth is round. (*See* pp.539, 759, 864.)

A Rainbow over the Hills
"I can't think of any other person on this earth who could take nearly 5,000 years of writing and unite it with a single overarching vision, like a perfect rainbow."

Charles Beauclerk, letter to Nicholas Hagger about
A New Philosophy of Literature, 26 May 2012

"We sit in a small boat which dips in a high
Sea against the tide and, the sun behind, flips wet.
All huddle under oilskins to keep dry
But I, salt on my cheeks, ignore each jet
And think of how I breast a tide each day
And sometimes glimpse a vision as I go.
I look and see a rainbow in the spray,
An arch in the flicking foam of a glimpsed rainbow!"

Nicholas Hagger, 'Staffa: Wind', 1984

"The hills are shadows, and they flow
From form to form, and nothing stands;
They melt like mist, the solid lands,
Like clouds they shape themselves and go."

Tennyson, *In Memoriam*, CXXIII

* * *

To the memory of Ted Hughes, who wrote "I read your books with a sort of automatic assent" and "I'm sure you've seen a genuine historical pattern and law"; to Christopher Ricks, who witnessed the long-drawn-out birth of my literary Universalism; to John Hunt, who immediately grasped the unity behind seven disciplines and the seven bands of my rainbow; to the literary authors, philosophers and historians to whom I described the unity of the universe as I toiled within the seven hills; and again to my family, and in particular to Ann, who travelled with me.

CONTENTS

Table of Contents

Summary of the story through section headings

Part One: Towards the Shimmering Rainbow

1. Through a Mist of Unknowing: Dark Night of the Spirit and Infused Powers

Episode 1: Remarriage and Comprehensive Education
I start as Second-in-command in English Department at Henry Thornton School. Jim Doolan, Head of English. Lyric poems, influence of Roman poetry. 'In Marvell's Garden, at Nun Appleton'. *The Gates of Hell*: Catullus and Ovid. Idea of 'The Night-Sea Crossing'. *The Pilgrim in the Garden*: Elegies 1–10. Sale of Flat 6, 33 Stanhope Gardens and purchase of Flat 5, 10 Brechin Place. Wedding: I marry Ann. Interview for new job. New flat: move to 10 Brechin Place. Poetic technique. Satire, *The Fountain*. Stress metre. 'The Night-Sea Crossing', final version. New stress metre. Leaving Henry Thornton.

Episode 2: Lyric Poetry and Administration
I continue writing lyric poems: Elegies 11–20. Satire, *The Garden*. I start as Head of English and Senior Teacher at Garratt Green School. Birth of Matthew. Elegies 21–23. Two Dark Nights. *The Gates of Hell*. 'The Flight'. I share a room with a nun: illumination and nuns. Outpouring of lyric poems: "volcanic eruption". 'The Four Seasons'. Second Dark Night leads to the Unitive Way. Poetic forms. 'Lighthouse'. Idea of 'The Weed-Garden'. Idea of 'The Labyrinth': odes. 'The Weed-Garden': culture and civilization. Sonnets. World history: Toynbee. Overworked at Garratt Green. Christening of Matthew in High Beach church, Epping Forest. Finishing 'The Weed-Garden'. Idea for epic poem: *Overlord*. 'The Labyrinth'. *Whispers from the West*. At the D-Day beaches for *Overlord*. 'The Fall of the West'. The West must toughen its attitude to survive. Kingsley Shorter on the Light. Visit to Wandsworth prison: Hell, Balcombe-Street terrorists Harry Duggan and Joseph O'Connell. Interested in Harbour-master's House at Charlestown. *Locusts upon the Earth* and work on *Overlord*. Classical style: "Baroque *Gates of Hell*". I write a paper, 'The European Resurgence'. I talk with Margaret Thatcher on liberating East-European nations. Opposing post-Renaissance European philosophy: bringing the metaphysical Light back into philosophy. Parenting: medical issues. Research on the Light: *The Secret Light*. Search for a larger home: move to 100A Stapleton Road. Dinner with

Donald Maclean's son. Birth of Anthony. School in Epping Forest. Retreat from becoming an MEP. Light-seers.

Episode 3: New Powers and Dogmatic Authority
New unitive vision brings with it new powers. Egyptian temple-dancers and healing. Rev. John Jewsbury. Research into the Light. Miss Lord offers Oaklands School at christening of Anthony. Receiving new powers in sleep. Thinking about neo-Baroque poetry. Reading by David Gascoyne, and Kathleen Raine. Keith Critchlow on Chartres. Kathleen Raine's neo-Romantic view of poetry versus my neo-Baroque view. Seeing the One revealed in the new physics: Fritjof Capra. Finding a larger home: sale of flat 5, 10 Brechin Place and purchase of 46 Ritherdon Road, SW17. Perception of energy, and healing. I am regressed to two 'past lives'. 'Life' as John Barfield in Lake District. 'Life' as consort of Ramesses II in Egypt. At King's College, Cambridge: with Colin MacCabe and Bernard Williams. I meet Colin Wilson again. Asa Briggs urges me to write on Libya and my double life. ILEA inspection. Peace and sanctions. Healing at Bruce MacManaway's Centre. New understanding: Christopher Ricks and me as a Metaphysical poet, content versus technique. Metaphysical Kabbalah: Warren Kenton. Matthew Manning healing cripples. Experience of Hermeticism and beginning of Third Mystic Life (13 May 1979–31 October 1981). Universal gardener. Still overworked at Garratt Green, illness: Matthew and Anthony have measles and then whooping cough. Dinner with Colin MacCabe, Frank Tuohy. New observation: Invisible behind the visible. Inspiration in sleep and view of world history: I receive idea for The Fire and the Stones – civilizations as Light-bearers. Struggling with authority: overwork and bronchitis. I revise Elegies for The Fire-Flower – gardener's pruning. Dogmatic authority and disharmony. More revising for The Fire-Flower. 'The Fire-Flower': yugen and Reality. I revise all my poetic works and embrace discipline of rules. New power of hypnosis. Independence: I explore small school in Cranleigh. Finishing The Fire-Flower. Perception of the metaphysical universe. The ILEA's Trotskyite exam policies. The Brain of Britain, opening to the Universal Mind. Jill Purce: I belong to no 'school' and reject the New Age's unevidential dogmas. Research into ancient cultures: The Sun-Hawk and chaos.

2. Ordeals of Independence: Trials of the Dark Night

Episode 4: Baroque and Egalitarian Socialism
Miss Lord agrees to sell Oaklands School. Mysticism: I attend four conference retreats. High Leigh. Hawkwood. Kent House. St Peter's Convent. Negotiating Oaklands, family. Four quartets, Beauty and Angelhood.

Baroque Age. Operation on varicose veins. In hospital I work on five Universalist poems: 'Night Visions in Charlestown'; 'Iona: Silence'; 'Staffa: Wind'; 'Crab-Fishing on a Boundless Deep'; 'Cambridge Ode: Against Materialism' – and Orpheus. Garratt Green, running Oaklands: Geoff Hurst opens Oaklands fête. In the Dordogne: Cro-Magnon man, 'In Périgord'. Idea of *The Fire and the Stones* received in sleep: the Light shaping civilizations of history. Flurry of poems. In York, 'At Dark Age Jorvik: the Light of Civilisation'. Cosmology: star-gazing. Des McForan's book on terrorism. Paul Gorka's book on Hungarian uprising. The future growth of the West. At Frankfurt book fair with Trevor Maher. Caroline's dark news. *The Executive Intelligence Review* on Philby and the US-Soviet 'Trust'; the Duke of Grantmesnil and Victor, Lord Rothschild as the fifth man. Tomlin's book on philosophy. Asked to run *The Salisbury Review* by Jillian Becker. Tomlin and A.L. Rowse. Voluntary severance from Garratt Green. Oaklands: Len Murray. Jack Wood's book on unions. A new group, 'Heroes of the West', and McForan. *The Fire and the Stones*. In the Cotswolds: 'Winter Four-Sidedness'; 'Oxford Revisited'. 'Heroes of the West': *The Executive Intelligence Review* again on Philby, the US-Soviet 'Trust' and its Head Victor, Lord Rothschild. Lord Whitelaw at dinner. 'Question Mark over the West'. Poems written in Stratford-upon-Avon and Warwick. 'Heroes of the West': eliminating Gaddafi's missiles near Sebha. In the Lake District: news of the raid on Libya, Universalist poems. Confirmation that evidence in McForan's book caused the US raid on Libya. Kathleen Raine and Tomlin. 'Heroes of the West': discussion with Lord Whitelaw on Victor, Lord Rothschild as fifth man, Thatcher uses my Recommendations on terrorism to end Soviet-inspired terrorism. "I had wounded the chimera." Raine and imagination. Book on Epping Forest. News of Argie's birth found under church foundation stone. Garratt Green. Duke of Grantmesnil again on 'The Trust' (Force X) and its Head Victor, Lord Rothschild. Launch of McForan's *The World Held Hostage*. Norris McWhirter investigates and reports. I buy a computer. Valerie Eliot's nephew. Return to Stratford-upon-Avon: Shakespeare. Tour of Western Europe: 'A Pilgrim in Europe'. Fishing in Cornwall. Launch of Tomlin's *Philosophers of East and West*. Nature walk along the Roding. Preparing for launch of Gorka's *Budapest Betrayed*: Jessica Douglas-Home and Roger Scruton, Krassó's petition for democracy, Bukovsky. Launch of *Budapest Betrayed*: my live broadcast into the USSR on FREE, Prime Minister of Polish Government-in-Exile, Sabbat, on my challenge to the 1943 Tehran Agreement on Soviet sphere of influence and to British foreign policy since the war. Thatcher outs Victor, Lord Rothschild as fifth man, his denial. I visit 10 Downing Street to discuss publishing Thatcher's speeches: Whitelaw. Implementation of FREE in committee of exile representatives of Captive Nations. I leave publishing to become an author, the monstrous chimera mortally wounded. A vision like a rainbow: seven bands, seven hills.

Part Two: The Unitive Way: the Seven Hills of Achievement

3. Arrival in the Hills

Episode 7: Metaphysical Poetry and World History
The Fire and the Stones: the Light behind all cultures. Margaret Riley's last visit. Universalist perspective and Oaklands. In the Lake District: Wordsworth places. Symbolism and healing society. Tomlin's illness. Poems written in Denmark: Viking roots. Fishing in Cornwall, 'Out on the Alone'. Donald Wilhelm, satellite dishes and the Soviet Union. Auction of Charlestown. Wilhelm and FREE. Frankfurt and Universalism. *The Fire and the Stones* as a study of civilizations, storm. I buy Harbour-master's House at auction. Death of Tomlin: Kathleen Raine, memorial service. Oaklands and law of history: overwork and suspected TIA. Finding Coopersale Hall. Finishing 61 stages in 25 civilizations. Village plan and collapse of marquee at Charlestown. Death of Biggs-Davison. Eliot's centenary service, Laurens van der Post. "Get on with your work." I found and establish Coopersale Hall School. I influence choice of Tony Little as Head of Chigwell School. Free will in history of civilizations. I open Coopersale Hall School. Finishing *The Fire and the Stones:* 'Introduction to the New Universalism' received in sleep. Steve Norris becomes our tenant. 'Tablecloth' of seven years of projections, seven-foot-long chart of 25 civilizations. Asa Briggs. Orpheus in the Underworld. Kathleen Raine invites me to be metaphysical historian in *Temenos* Academy. Cornwall and the universe, Preface to *Selected Poems*. Full opening of Coopersale Hall School. Steve Norris burgled. Building Coopersale Hall extension: Paul Gorka architect. With Laurens van der Post. With Kathleen Raine. Fire and storms. Metaphysical vision. Essex and Cornwall: opposites – action and contemplation. *Selected Poems, A Metaphysical's Way of Fire* and beginning of Fourth Mystic Life (8 April 1990–6 December 1993). In Hungary, declining a castle. Schools and poems: "Ambassador to Hungary." Tebbit formally opens Coopersale Hall School. I work on *Selected Poems*. Kathleen Raine and Laurens van der Post. In Czechoslovakia – Otto von Habsburg and Pan-Europeanism. I am put in touch with Element, temple-dancer. Preparing for the launch. Cosmology and Theory of Everything: with David Bohm – the infinite and Metaphysical Revolution. Cosmology: Edgard Gunzig and Light. Launch of *The Fire and the Stones* and *Selected Poems, A Metaphysical's Way of Fire*. Speeches by Asa Briggs, Kathleen Raine and David Gascoyne. Starting the *Temenos* Academy.

4. Hard Slog: Contemplative Works

syndrome diagnosed. *Overlord* books 8–9. An afternoon with Svetlana Stalin. Earls and endings: at Hay-on-Wye, the Earl of Burford, Asa Briggs, Ted Hughes. In Greece: Helen of Troy's palace and Kazantzakis's house. *Overlord* books 10–12. I am asked to acquire Normanhurst School. In Rome: drinking from the spring at Horace's Sabine farm in Licenza. Finishing *Overlord*; Normanhurst's Founders Day, Nasser Hussain.

Episode 11: Verse Plays and Tudor Knots
Purchase of Tudor Otley Hall. Transforming Otley Hall: classical odes. Death of John Broadley V. The pro-Nazi Sherstons and Mrs. Schofield, Godolphin House. Otley Hall: knot-garden. Otley Hall: more transforming and delving. My lecture at Aldeburgh, 'Revolution in Thought and Culture', and *The One and the Many*. My talk in Cambridge, 'In the Garden of the One'. Screenplay about Bartholomew Gosnold, *Gosnold's Hope* (later *The Founding of America*). Death of Ann's mother. *Collected Stories*, vol. 3, *Wheeling Bats and a Harvest Moon*. Otley Hall and Tudor knots; deaths of A.L. Rowse and Frank Tuohy. At Bourn Hall, seat of Haggers. At the Globe: Mark Rylance, Derek Jacobi. The Earl of Burford asks to work at Otley Hall. I am asked to house Shakespearean Authorship Trust and De Vere Society libraries at Otley Hall and to be a trustee of the SAT. *The Tragedy of Prince Tudor*. In the Lake District. Cast of the Globe's *As You Like It* stay and rehearse at Otley Hall; Jonathan Cecil. Visitors to Otley Hall. Second operation for varicose veins. John Southworth and Fools. Opening Otley village fête, John Michell. Robert Gosnold III secretary to the Earl of Essex. In Italy: Verona and Venice – Catullus, Dante and Shakespeare. Six forthcoming works: *Collected Stories*, vol. 4, *The Warm Glow of the Monastery Courtyard*; *Ovid Banished*; *The Warlords* abridged; *Gosnold's Hope*; *The One and the Many*; *The New Philosophy of Universalism*. Asked to arrange twinning between Jamestown and Ipswich. In the USA: my lecture in Richmond on Bartholomew Gosnold – Norman Beatty, Bill Kelso, Elizabethan values. Mark Rylance visits Otley Hall. Tebbit and the New World Order. Twinning: Ipswich and Jamestown, Lord Belstead and Bill Kelso. UK to be split into 8 regions. Martin Taylor and the earth-dollar. 'Plahouse'. Twinning with Jamestown, Lord Belstead, Gen. Knapp, sculpture of Gosnold. Death of Argie. Otley Hall and ghosts. St Osyth Priory. Anglo-Saxon Suffolk. Tudor houses: The Thatch, South Wraxall Manor. 'A Defence of Traditional Poetic Method'. *Ovid Banished*. *The Rise of Oliver Cromwell*. Cast of the Globe's *Julius Caesar* stay and rehearse at Otley Hall. Next works.

Episode 12: Classical Odes and Utopianism
Perfect utopias, and the classical tradition in *Classical Odes*. Work on *The Secret History of the West*. In Cathar country: Carcassonne, Rennes-le-

Table of Contents

Discovery of Bartholomew Gosnold's skeleton. Structuring *Classical Odes*: "three of space and one of time".

5. Final Ascent: Unitive Vision

Episode 13: Collected Literature and Secret History
US invasion of Iraq: 'Shock and Awe'. Writing *The Syndicate*: John Hunt. Disillusion with the Shakespearean Authorship Trust. At the schools. Finishing *Classical Odes*. Fall of Iain Duncan Smith. In Gran Canaria: Fortunate Isles. Finishing *The Syndicate*, radio. Sale of Otley Hall. At Cliveden. Upheaval. Travellers next to Coopersale Hall. *The Secret History of the West*. Medical. In the Scilly Isles: 'In the Brilliant Autumn Sunshine, Among a Thousand Islands'. In Brussels: "a top-down organisation". Leaving the Shakespearean Authorship Trust. In Stratford-upon-Avon. *The Light of Civilization*. In Egypt: charnel-house in Sinai, Bedouin and the universe. Collected literature. *Classical Odes*. *Collected Poems, 1958–2005*. *The Rise and Fall of Civilizations*. Christopher Ricks, Professor of Poetry. Shakespeare's bedchamber. Shakespeare's trunk. Charles Beauclerk and Nell Gwyn. Otley Hall top private garden in UK. Bill Kelso, Gosnold DNA and Shelley church. Family events. Connaught House. John Silberrad and Sisyphus. Death of Silberrad. Paul Doherty and Faustian striving. Christopher Ricks and plagiarism. David Cameron. Harry Beckhough, Montgomery and Ultra. Lindsay Jenkins and Germany. Hernia operation. *The Secret Founding of America* and steroids for insect bite. *Collected Verse Plays*. Working on ten books simultaneously. One-volume *Overlord*. Connaught House grounds, sale of The Bell. Schools. Ricks's lectures. Stories for *In the Brilliant Autumn Sunshine*. *Collected Stories*, including *In the Brilliant Autumn Sunshine*.

Episode 14: Order and Terror
Beginning of *Armageddon* as *Crusaders*. In Iran: machine-guns at Natanz and the Hidden Imam's well. *The Last Tourist in Iran*. In Austria: Waterloo ball, *The Lost Englishman*. Three novellas. Death of Ricky Herbert. 25 radio broadcasts to USA on *The Secret Founding of America*. Christopher Ricks. Eternity and Providence. Beginning of *The New Philosophy of Universalism*. In the Galapagos Islands: 13 species of finches, turtles' instincts and Darwinist evolution. In Peru: sun-centred Incas and Machu Picchu's Temple of the Sun. *The New Philosophy of Universalism*. In Argentina, Falkland Islands, South Georgia, Antarctica: Ice Ages and global warming. *The New Philosophy of Universalism* continued: synthetic method. Ken Campbell: reading of *The Warlords*, death and funeral. Shoulder operation. Ben and Chigwell. Matthew's wedding. Wilton House. Opening bank branch. Tony's award:

present. Universal intelligence. Distilling: Golden Age. 'Intellect'. Unified view of health. My garden and Paradise. Rainbow: vision of unity and unification, the One.

Epilogue: Rainbow over Hills

Episodes, structure, pattern and unity in double lives
My double life and episodes. Working and writing lives. Social and metaphysical worlds. My turbulent time: from post-imperial nationhood to Universalism. My task and mission? My ordinary and extraordinary double life. No duality. Episodes. Pattern and transformation in 30 episodes and pairs of opposites. Nodal points in 30 episodes. In all, 42 episodes and over 50 works. Universal double lives and the Universalist rainbow. Structure, pattern and unity in all double lives. Free will, chance and Providence in all double lives. Rainbow over the hills: visible and invisible rainbow in all double lives.

The Rainbow Portrait of Elizabeth I holding a rainbow, painted in the last year of her reign (c.1602, attributed to Isaac Oliver). The Queen is wearing an orange cloak decorated with eyes, ears and mouths, a sign that she sees and hears everything through her intelligence agents. On her left sleeve is a jewelled serpent. She holds a rainbow in her right hand (*see* pp.232, 351, 559, 841, 868, 869) and the Latin inscription on the painting, '*Non sine sole iris*' translates as 'No rainbow without the sun'.

Sketch for a portrait of Nicholas Hagger by Stuart Davies

"The unexamined life is not worth living."
Socrates, in Plato, *Apology*, 38a

Author's Note

My Double Life 1: This Dark Wood presented the first 15 episodes of my life. This book, its companion volume and sequel, continues the story and presents the next 15 episodes. They are numbered 1–15 to give this work the feel of a self-contained volume but they could have been numbered 16–30. *My Double Life 1: This Dark Wood* dealt with my travels in the Middle and Far East, including China, my work for British Intelligence in Europe and Africa, my emergence from darkness into Light and the birth of my vision of unity. This work deals with my emergence to Universalism (whose different activities, disciplines and *genres* are symbolised in the bands of a rainbow) and the gestation and production of my first 40 books. It deals with how the books came to be written, the pressures behind them, the processes that brought their Universalism to birth and their attempt to convey my vision of the universe as a unity.

My Double Life 1: This Dark Wood contains a very full Prologue, which deals with all the main issues, including the presentation of my life as a chain-like succession of episodes, in each of which there is a pair of conflicting sequences of events that resemble the pairs of opposites in the double helix of DNA and in the two spirals on a spruce cone. This book therefore does not have a Prologue, which is replaced by this Author's Note. *My Double Life 1: This Dark Wood* contains an Epilogue that looks back over the first 15 episodes. This work's Epilogue looks back over the next 15 episodes, and assesses all 30 episodes. Through their episodic structure the two books together convey the pattern in my life, and it is my contention that a similar episodic approach will reveal the pattern in all lives. I see both works as therefore being Universalist works.

In the Prologue of *My Double Life 1: This Dark Wood* I said that I have had four Mystic Lives. I wrote:

During my journey I had four Mystic Lives. These can be dated from the chronological list of experiences of the Light (*see* Appendix 1, p.903). There are 16 experiences of the *Light in My Double Life 1: This Dark Wood* and 77 in *My Double Life 2: A Rainbow over the Hills*, a total of 93 experiences of the Light, each of which is documented from *Diaries* written at the time. Between the First and Second Mystic Lives was my Dark Night of the Soul, and between my Second and Third Mystic Lives was the first part of my Dark Night of the Spirit, in which I was fed new powers. *My Double Life 1: This Dark Wood* ends near the beginning of This Dark Night. In *My Double Life 2: A Rainbow over the Hills* the story continues, and between my Third and Fourth Mystic Lives was the second part of My Dark Night of the Spirit in which I was confronted with ordeals. My Unitive Life began after my Fourth Mystic Life.

In *My Double Life 2: A Rainbow over the Hills* I narrate my progress into unitive life within seven disciplines.

Taken together, these two works recount how during my quest my glimpses of the metaphysical Reality known as the One inspired me to write Universalist works in seven disciplines: transpersonal psychology and mysticism, literature, science and philosophy (including cosmology), world history, international politics and statecraft, comparative religion, and world culture. They therefore narrate the development of my world view, Universalism, which focuses on the unity of the universe and the universality of humankind and seeks to bring in a harmonious world in the near-future; and which I have expressed in my 40 books.

In the Prologue of *My Double Life 1: This Dark Wood* I wrote the following regarding my method:

I have frequently quoted from my *Diaries* as they were written immediately after the events described and give 'at-the-time' authenticity to my recollection. 'At-the-time' wording bypasses fallible memory and inadvertent embellishing-in-hindsight. It adds vividness by recapturing long-forgotten details relating to the day on which events happened with precision, and reproduces how events struck me at the time. My aim has been to get as close to the original experience in the moment as is possible at such a distance, and my method has enabled me to achieve a fidelity to the moment which many memoirs that look back over decades fail to achieve. The moments all belong to a process, and my double life is a process life. My Diaries add immediacy and bring the past alive in the dynamic, baroque, process-led Universalist manner. I have sourced the quotations from my *Diaries* so that my memoir has the flavour of being evidential and objective as well as vividly detailed and 'at the time'.

As will be seen, the bands of the rainbow represent the disciplines in which I have worked (*see* pp.260, 873). It will become apparent that within each episode many of the italicised subheadings begin with one of the two 'opposites' of that episode, and as the episodes of Part Two reflect these disciplines many of the subheadings reflect one or more of these disciplines. The subheadings therefore connect the reader to the seven bands of the rainbow.

Finally I should add that, having finished *My Double Life 1: This Dark Wood* in seven months, I took longer on this work, which spans 40 years and 40 books. I completed the research and writing in eleven months (from 19

August 2012 to 7 September 2013), and amended both books for another seven-and-a-half months (until 25 April 2014, *see* pp.844–845 for further details). I would like to pay tribute to my PA Ingrid Kirk who helped me complete both books so quickly.

Nicholas Hagger

PART ONE

Towards the Shimmering Rainbow

"On a huge hill,
Cragged, and steep, Truth stands, and hee that will
Reach her, about must, and about must goe."
John Donne, 'Satyre III'

"A man can embody truth but he cannot know it."
W.B. Yeats, letter to Elizabeth Pelham,
4 January 1939

CHAPTER 1

Through a Mist of Unknowing: Dark Night of the Spirit and Infused Powers

"It is characteristic of the journey along the Mystic Way that those lost in its 'Dark Wood' and experiencing its Dark Night are unaware of the explanation for what is happening to them and what lies ahead; this is only grasped later when, from the serene calm of unitary consciousness, the self can look back and understand the detaching that suffering brought as a gift."

Nicholas Hagger, Preface to *Collected Poems*

From this sloping hill I look down on the dark wood spread out beneath and recall my journey to Kaseem's Iraq and to Japan, where I was a Professor, taught the Emperor Hirohito's second son, wrote my early poems, encountered Zen and was told the wisdom of the East by the poet Nishiwaki: +A + −A = 0; and experienced a First Mystic Life and contact with my imagination and my Muse. My journey took me to China, where I was the first to discover the Cultural Revolution, and to Libya, where I was an eyewitness of Gaddafi's revolution, became a secret agent and lost my marriage. I was now in a Dark Night of the Soul (or more strictly, a Dark Night of the Senses), and I began to undergo an inner transformation and purgation: a centre-shift. I returned to London, became Heath's 'unofficial Ambassador' to the African liberation movements and wrote for *The Times*. I recall how I was routinely followed by surveillance squads. Living in a boarding-house in London and helped by an Austrian artist, I experienced illumination and further purgation in a Second Mystic Life and renewed contact with my imagination and Muse. I had visions of the One, the Light, and instinctively came to see the universe as a unity. At the same time I monitored Soviet and Chinese activity in Africa, visited Tanzania and managed to get into a restricted section of the Chinese Tanzam railway. I recall how I severed connections with the SIS in 1973.

All this I narrated in *My Double Life 1: This Dark Wood*. I told my story in 15 episodes (or sequences of events), in each of which there was a pair of opposites. I ended that account with me still in my cover job at a school for educationally subnormal boys but having secured a new job in a new school. I had started a new relationship with Ann, a primary school teacher I had met in Greenwich, and I had just moved into a flat I had bought in Stanhope Gardens, near South Kensington station. I left my story with me clear of the dark wood, my finding complete, and sensing that I would complete innovatory works and projects of founding that would reflect my new sense of purpose. I sensed that in the next 15 episodes I would express the One in my works and convey a new sense of meaning.

But I did not know that before that could happen I had to undergo a Dark Night of the Spirit in which new infused powers would pour into my self and I would experience a Third Mystic Life lasting a couple of years. In the creative Night of Unknowing between illumination and the unitive life the spirit is covered as in a mist and is fed new energy, knowledge and powers by the enfolding darkness which acts as a Muse and often pours in inspiration during sleep. On the universal Mystic Way the Night of Unknowing is a final purification and infusing of knowledge in preparation for the unitive life along the Unitive Way. In this Night a 'Cloud of Unknowing' descends on the spirit and the Light is only experienced from time to time. I did not know that, while veiled by Unknowing and nourished with new powers and a Third Mystic Life, I would undergo further purgation and trials, ordeals in which I would find myself fighting Communism. I did not know that only after these ordeals of combat would I be able to emerge from my Dark Night of the Spirit, reach the beginning of the Unitive Way and create my works.

I stand just below the rim on the outer side of the crater that half-surrounds Loughton. On the inside of the crater seven roads wind up seven separate hills. On the outside each hill is interconnected by the crater's wall. As I look, between sunshine and cloud a rainbow gathers over the hills. It forms slowly out of nothing like the Light, at first a shimmering haze. An arch of seven symmetrical bands of different colours manifests into form from the cloudy sunshine. Slowly I identify the colours in the bands: red, orange, yellow, green, blue, indigo and violet. The rainbow straddles the crater that contains the seven hills of Loughton,[1] uniting them under the span of its arch.

The curved bands reflect the seven curved hills within the crater below its span. I now see each band as a discipline and *genre* in which I have worked. But then, emerging from the dark wood in mist and looking up at the hills and the side of the crater to be ascended, I had only a hazy idea of the disciplines and *genres* in which I would work. I just knew my illumination had marked me out to complete a number of works and projects.

Now I look down on the young man who emerged from the dark wood with a vision of the unity of the universe and a determination to make use of the knowledge he had found. He was constricted by having to earn a living, and had little time to produce works that would convey his vision. He was hoping the way would open. I find him near the beginning of a new episode. His mystical Light is behind him, and a fog has enfolded his soul, like a mist that rises from Connaught Water and enfolds the Ching valley, a mist of Unknowing that pours in infused knowledge and gives the spirit new powers which pass into works.

Now my theme ceases to be one of finding and becomes one of founding: the process of implementing what I found in the course of my journey in a succession of works. I continue the story that began in *My Double Life 1: This Dark Wood* and present a new series of 15 episodes. I will then lay out the pattern of my life, an approach that can be applied to all lives.

Episode 1:

Remarriage and Comprehensive Education

Years: 1973–1974
Locations: London; Hastings
Works: *The Gates of Hell*; Elegies: *A Bulb in Winter*; *The Pilgrim in the Garden*,
nos. 1–10; *The Night-Sea Crossing*; *The Fountain*.
Initiatives: Metaphysical poetry; neo-Baroque poetry

"We begin to live when we have conceived life as tragedy."
W.B. Yeats, *Autobiography*, 'Four Years', 1887–1891, chapter 21, 1922[1]

When the moon's upset, he doesn't fret
He doesn't sit around and cry
He gets all dolled up in a sky-blue shirt
And a rainbow tie

Jack Berch/John Redmond,
'A Sky-Blue Shirt and a Rainbow Tie', 1954

In my new episode my busy life as an educator at a comprehensive school, whose daily obfuscation of work covered my soul like mist, was in conflict with my increasingly settled domestic life in whose peaceful atmosphere, in an unprecedented burst of creativity, I wrote hundreds of inspired lyric poems and stories.

Comprehensive education
I start as Second-in-command in English Department at Henry Thornton School
In *My Double Life 1: This Dark Wood* I described how I had to find a new job for September 1973 so I could leave my secret work as a British intelligence

agent, and how I was appointed Second-in-command of the English Department at Henry Thornton School.

Henry Thornton School faces Clapham Common. Founded in 1894 and located on its present site as a grammar school from 1929, it was now a comprehensive that combined grammar and secondary-modern intakes. Local boys of all abilities mixed freely in accordance with the comprehensive ideal. Every morning I drove from our flat in Stanhope Gardens, leaving Ann to go to work at St James Norlands, Holland Park, and returned each evening with piles of books to mark while Ann (who had less marking, teaching ten-year-olds) watched television, sometimes curled up in a chair beside a bowl of cherries.

Henry Thornton was ten times larger than Riverway, the ESN school in Greenwich I had left behind. I found it glassy, hectic and crowded. The playground was always filled with shrieking teenage boys playing manic games of football, and walking from the staff room to the English block involved running a gauntlet of flying footballs. The first few days I was rushed off my feet. The English Department had no syllabus. The elderly Head of Department, white-haired Jim Doolan, who wore a bow-tie and whose great joy was reading Chaucer in the original, did not believe in syllabuses. The Head of the school asked me to write one. I had to sort through the stockroom, which did not seem to have been touched since Henry Thornton ceased to be a grammar school – the old Honours boards from that time were stored up one end – and I had to hold meetings with the ten young teachers to co-ordinate what they were doing into a progression. They told me the only guidance Doolan had given them was: "You're an English teacher, teach." I soon discovered I was running the Department. From the outset I was courted as if I were Head of Department by both the English staff and the Head of the school.

The staff were very well-mannered, pleasant, urbane and well-spoken, and there was a great contrast between the civilised atmosphere in the huge staff room, where over 100 sat in comfortable chairs reading newspapers, and the confused and noisy congestion in the corridors. The Head of the school sat in his study all day, coping with paperwork, and discipline was left to his two deputies.

Soon after I arrived I encountered one of them, an ex-RSM (Regimental Sergeant-Major), Mr Nicholls, in the playground in a quieter moment. (He had brought the quiet with him.) He asked how I was getting on. I said, "Fine. How do you keep order in this place?"

"I'll show you," he said, and he bellowed: "Boy." About 200 yards away a West-Indian boy of about 11 cringed, turned and scampered up to us. "You keep a cane up your sleeve," Nicholls told me. He shook down from the right-hand sleeve of his threadbare suit a small cane. "Boy," he commanded, "put your hand out." Cowering and with his bottom lip out and quivering, the boy sulkily extended his right hand. Swish. The boy ran off, flicking his fingers. No one else was around.

"What was that for?" I asked, scarcely believing what I had seen.

"Oh, that wasn't *for* anything," Nicholls said. "That's how I keep order in this place."

While the senior staff, like the Head of the school and Jim Doolan, went gravely to and fro, carrying with them an oasis of untroubled calm amid the general chaos, one of the Heads of House, a small balding Welshman, Mr Daniels, patrolled my corridor waving a large cane to persuade the tearaways to line up. "You need a stick, Mr Hagger," Mr Daniels said with mock-seriousness at the beginning of one of my classes, and he presented me with a cane, which I theatrically locked away in my cupboard. I never used it, but when the high tide of turmoil outside my classroom rose to threatening proportions I appeared and brandished it, and the general rushing-about suddenly stopped.

I do not know how we got some of the boys to stay in their desks all lesson, let alone do the work we set. I took 1st and 2nd years, 4th, 5th, 6th and 7th years. There was an enormous range of ability, and some 15-year-olds could hardly write their name. I struggled on with *Macbeth* and *Brighton Rock*, and the dunces would say, "Oh sir, can't we play cards today?" Some of them handed in wretched work with a pleading "Sir, do you think you could give me an A?" Some just pushed their papers on the floor and stared out of the window. When they did this in other classes, the boys were sent to me and I had them sitting near the front as a punishment. "Sir, what's the use of teaching us?" one of the miscreants asked me. "We're not going to do anything that needs what we learn at this dump of a school." He had a point. I fairly soon realised that such pupils had been failed by their primary schools, that their English in our school was crippled by what they had failed to learn when younger.

I enjoyed the 6th- and 7th-year lessons most, the 'A'-level classes. A dozen intelligent boys sat down both sides of a long table in the calm of the long shelf-lined 'A'-level room, which had been an extensive 'A'-level library in the grammar-school days. Somehow these boys had survived the frenetic rushing-about and had come through with some semblance of literary criticism, although in their essays they needed to "tighten up", as Jim Doolan put it. They appeared generally interested in the Metaphysical poets which I had to read with them. I had first found out about the Light from the 17th-century Metaphysical poets I had read in Spain, and I greatly enjoyed combing their poems for references to it.

Jim Doolan, Head of English
In the calm atmosphere of this long room we had our Departmental meetings. As there was no pre-existing structure whatsoever, except for lists of class names, the classes teachers were taking and the exam set books, I had to start from scratch. Everything was new, and Jim Doolan presided over our deliberations at the end of the table, white-haired and horn-rimmed, with a disdainful, detached, sometimes scathing expression on his face.

As the term progressed and he and I talked more and more, he made no attempt to disguise his criticisms of the comprehensive system and of its uncaring attitude in lumping together the more able and the less able on one site. "The more able suffer because of the hooligans," he used to say to me, "and the less able feel inferior because of the more able. It doesn't work. And the meetings are all a waste of time. Yesterday they spent an hour discussing a one-way system to get the children to proceed in an orderly fashion in the corridors without mentioning once that they rush about as if they're on a football pitch." He aired his criticisms in the staff room, and they had not gone down well at the top. When there was a vacancy for Senior Teacher the previous term (a post rightfully Jim's by seniority) the post had been given to a young Head of Science who had been a pupil at the school under Jim. Jim had been bitterly hurt at the snub. Hence he had withdrawn from his role and had told me to run the Department as best as I could.

There was much talk of the Head not doing enough about discipline. One of the staff, an ex-commando who had lost fingers at Arromanches, 'Tug' Wilson, took a party of 5th-years to a *matinée* at the Royal Court in Sloane Square. A tall West-Indian with a boxer's physique was difficult outside the theatre and 'Tug' sent him home. The boy knocked him out with a right hook. The ex-war hero lay unconscious in the gutter and was taken to hospital by ambulance. The boy was suspended for a couple of days and then allowed back into school, where he boasted that any other master who crossed him would receive the same treatment. Appalled, the staff held a meeting and threatened to strike unless the boy was expelled. The boy remained in school but was not taught. Everyone said that the Head was too soft and ought to leave his room and tour the school.

Lyric poems: influence of Roman poetry
Teaching Marvell's 'The Definition of Love' and 'Dialogue of Soul and Body' in the long room took me back into my own poetry. In early October Margaret Riley, the artist at 13 Egerton Gardens who had induced my illumination (*see My Double Life 1: This Dark Wood*), arrived uninvited and stayed a night. I showed her Marvell's 'The Garden', which I was also teaching (and had read with Christopher Ricks). She said, "If you met Marvell you would

talk for a long time, you are on the same level." On 7 October I wrote in my *Diaries*: "Get back to poetry after 5 months." And on 11 October:

> I am a poet.... I write of the moment – in poems and short stories.... My journalism took me off on a different route.... I neglected my true way. I had it between 1965 and 1966.... 1967: that is when I went wrong.... I lost my way. And now I am finding it again. I must face up to the fact that I have had a false start.... My major work – which I described to [Ezra] Pound – is ahead. Images.... Jim on Eliot knowing his method is right because it was used [by] the Elizabethans, i.e. taking his strength from the past.... A new onslaught into poetry. Something original each day.... I must make poetry come across and give it a new philosophical dignity. The line: think. Old Norse. *Vers libre*.

And again: "Buy Catullus and Piers Plowman. Get back to poems... Get on to long poems.... Fulfil what I said to Ezra Pound."[2]

'In Marvell's Garden, at Nun Appleton'

Under the influence of Marvell (for which I have to thank my time at Henry Thornton), I returned to poetry in October 1973 and wrote many poems during the next six months. At half-term I went to Lincolnshire and Scarborough to visit the school Nadia might go to, and returned via Nun Appleton House, the site of Marvell's 'Garden'. The House had been rebuilt since 1650 when Marvell lived there and tutored Fairfax's daughter. I visited without appointment. Despite notices warning that I was on private land I was not challenged. Only a piano-tuner seemed to be in and he invited me into the House. I was able to wander freely into the grounds. I wrote bits of 'In Marvell's Garden, at Nun Appleton' (which I eventually revised and retitled 'A Metaphysical in Marvell's Garden') sitting by the pool, and I finished the poem on 28 October. Earlier I had written: "I am entering a new phase in my poetry. A new fusion of image and thought, a new freedom." (Later I reflected: "I would not have known of Marvell's 'Garden' if I had not read English at Oxford – and so I would not have written 'A Metaphysical in Marvell's Garden'.")

In November I was reading Donne with the 7th year. I loved 'Twicknam Garden'. On 2

The pool in Marvell's Garden at Nun Appleton House, Yorkshire where Nicholas drafted 'A Metaphysical in Marvell's Garden' on 24 October 1973

November I wrote: "Poetry is about the real world, novels are about an imagined one. I am interested in the real one…. The best poetry gives you something to dig out and the satisfaction is in getting there. That is how my poetry is similar to that of the Metaphysicals. I am in the Metaphysical vein…. I love the physical things." And again:

> I am undergoing an upheaval…. My voice that told me to give up alcohol tells me to concentrate on poetry…. My belated self-discovery. From now on I must not forget this. I swear: that as from 2 November 1973 I will be a poet, a whole poet, and nothing but a poet. So help me God. This night… I have made a decision from inside. I proclaim 1967–1972 my 'lost years' – when I was lost to poetry, save for the occasional poem. My Dark Night of the Soul. Five 'lost years' of objectivity and confusion. When I was lost.

And on 3 November:

> My lost years are over…. I must embody in verse the new Age ahead…. From now I will live by the spring of my Muse.

My talks with Jim Doolan were of great value. I noted that he had "revived the poet in me. With him I can discuss Donne in the staff room as I could not at Riverway." The next day he told me: "The longer I live, the more I am convinced that great poetry comes from the heart. You have to suffer. I've written but it's superficial, not a cry like a man in agony – Marvell or Donne." He wondered whether Marvell had to leave Nun Appleton because of Fairfax's daughter: "After 'The Definition of Love' what else can you do?" He observed, "Shakespeare was going through a hell of a time when he wrote *Lear*. It is black."[3] The next day, on 9 November, I wrote four poems.

The Gates of Hell: *Catullus and Ovid*

In December I returned to Roman poetry. I wrote: "Reading Ovid and Catullus until 1 a.m. as I could not sleep. The Ovidian couplet: dactylic hexameter plus pentameter with disyllabic ending. Or Alexandrine plus pentameter or two pentameters (the first with a feminine ending)…. Go into Latin poetry…. Catullus and Ovid. A third long poem about the modern equivalent of Gallus." And: "Write a group of poems which are dramatic monologues, which together form 100. Do them in the new flat (the Poem Factory or Workshop). Communicate the times. The Roman vision: a time of promiscuity and decay, like ours. Catch the life and times of today in 100 linked poems in the Catullan or Ovidian manner." This was the idea for my sequence of poems *The Gates of Hell*, which looked back to Catullus and Ovid.

In December I found a flat off the Gloucester Road. It comprised the top two floors and roof garden of 10 Brechin Place (flat 5), and there was a "cabin" where Nadia could sleep. It had more space and a longer lease than my flat in Stanhope Gardens. To buy it I would have to sell both 33 Stanhope Gardens and 9 Crescent View, Loughton (which I had bought before going to Japan and now rented out). Four days later I met the owner's wife 'by accident' in the street, and carried forward my negotiation. I met her 'by accident' again the day I broke up. I had the feeling Providence was intriguing a purchase in Brechin Place. On Christmas Eve I agreed to sell 9 Crescent View to my tenant for a good price. (Contracts were exchanged on 8 March 1974.)

During the Christmas holidays I associated Brechin Place with remarrying. It would be a perfect place for a new marriage. Ann went down to her mother's in Cornwall and I buried myself in Roman poetry in Stanhope Gardens. I noted I was "on the side of the well-wrought urn, against self-expression". I read Catullus and noted: "'The calm of mind, all passion spent.' Catullus's only hope with Lesbia was complete renunciation." I reread the Latin elegiac poets who wrote between c.60BC and c.20BC and reflected on their heroines: Catullus's Lesbia; Gallus's Lycaris; Tibullus's Delia; Propertius's Cynthia; and Ovid's Corinna. I wrote:

Ladies began to lead an independent life; traditional ideals of marriage lost their meaning, men and women alike sought love outside marriage…. Love-elegies…. Later the Christians took the elegy over…. Eros became Agape. In his *Odes* Horace adapted Greek metres to the Latin language, e.g. Alcaics, Sapphics, Asclepiads…. If Pope can begin an Augustan period, why can't I revive the elegy? Augustus in tranquillising the world, tranquillised letters. A poetry of peace attained.

And again:

Track down: why was Queen Anne's reign called 'The Augustan' age? Find Goldsmith's essay, find what Augustan qualities Pope took. For sure, it was not the elegiac. Write an elegy in stresses: hexameter and then pentameter. In short, adapt the heroic couplet. Go back to Horace's source in Alcaics etc., but do them in terms of stress. Think: the couplet gives the "rise and fall of the jet of water" (Ovid) but should it rhyme? Think: blank verse. What about ON [Old Norse] narrative poetry? Tell a story through a sequence of elegies? A Golden Age can take place now. Our time is very near to that of the Roman Augustan period…. The new Golden Age.[4]

At the end of the year I looked back on a year of reordering and renewing myself. I had left behind Riverway, my Volkswagen, my African journalism and 9 Crescent View, and would soon leave behind 33 Stanhope Gardens. I had given up alcohol for nine months now, and had done five months of exercises and got rid of my paunch. I had rebuilt myself. And I had finished 100 stories, and was looking towards poems.

Idea of 'The Night-Sea Crossing'

On 7 January I had the idea for a poem, 'The Night-Sea Crossing', and made notes for it during the next few weeks. On 18 January I wrote of the Light: "The Light comes as naturally as the flower blooms or the wind blows – it comes to rich and poor alike, king and peasant, master and servant. All are heirs to it." And on 24 January: "I saw a great fire in a grate.... From now I will 'ponder' night and morning, i.e. lie in bed in the dark and look for the Divine illumination. Night-Sea Crossing, a crossing of the night-sea of the mind. From now, I must journey in the mind. Be a mental traveller."

At the end of January I was sent to Stoke D'Abernon on an ILEA course on how to run a Department. We stayed in a country house by the River Mole. On the first night John Welch, the Chief English Inspector, talked to about 50 of us and told us, "Everyone here has made it." I thought: 'This isn't making it, I haven't even begun.' On the Saturday night I went for a walk by the weir and the church, and when I returned there was a commotion. The Chief English Inspector was being carried to his room, drunk. On the Sunday morning I wrote five poems: "My five poems, before and after breakfast in the sun. Now I feel refreshed. I could be a Head of Department without too much difficulty."

On my return I wrote an elegy on the Pelagian heresy, the point of view that asserts that we are all perfect and do not have to rise to standards and that writing is self-expression. On 27 January I "wrote six poems and saw a wonderful blue light. Very limpid." And the next day: "Saw a sunflower in my secret journeying."[5]

The Pilgrim in the Garden: Elegies 1–10

I now focused on Elegies. I was obsessed by a tapestry of Burne-Jones's, and noted, anticipating the title of a collection of poems, "*The Heart of the Rose, or: The Pilgrim in the Garden*." Soon afterwards I wrote:

> Consider setting out my reflective poems as elegies or odes.... The difference between the Classical ode and the Romantic ode – both of which were forms of address. Horace wrote for the people, like Catullus, whereas Keats addressed things, birds, etc. (like Shelley). I will be Classical.... To belong to the English poetic tradition I should try elegies and odes and the other verse

forms that the poets tried – not the dribbling non-metre, not-rhymed free verse of the poetasters.... I have revived the elegy and the ode. I am in a Classical period now – the mature man. Not the youthful Romantic in his twenties.... I have turned the elegy into a form of struggle through to a victory, a joy, after a tussle, an argument. Through me speaks an Infinite depth.

Soon afterwards I recorded:

1st, 2nd, 3rd, 4th elegies and titles. I have ten elegies altogether. They express an attitude.... All should be rooted in specific days between the autumn of 1973 and the summer of 1974. These elegies have just 'come', of their own accord.

And again:

'A weekend elegist.' This weekend I have done the 4th, last weekend the 2nd and 3rd. For an introductory note on the elegy. It is not associated with grief in Roman times – the couplet. Marlowe began the heroic couplet. Dryden and Pope, using the classical model. '*Annus Mirabilis*' and Gray, untypical offshoots. Regular or irregular paragraphing. Rilke. How it is an ideal form for reflection (Coleridge). Claim Marvell's 'Garden' as an elegy. The heroic couplet. A provisional title for the elegies: *Pilgrim in the Garden*. From the Burne-Jones tapestry, *The Heart of the Rose*.[6]

Remarriage
Sale of Flat 6, 33 Stanhope Gardens and purchase of Flat 5, 10 Brechin Place
In the third week of February I sold 33 Stanhope Gardens and was all set to convert my two flats into the larger flat 5 in 10 Brechin Place. On 6 February there was snow and I had stayed away from school and thought about the future, and the prospect that my new flat should coincide with a new marriage. On 10 February I wrote of "the Tudor images I saw in my looking last night".

On 16 February I visited Nadia with Ann. We took her to Tattershall Castle, where I drafted another elegy. On the way back I had a long discussion with Ann. I wrote: "On the journey, discussed wedding with Ann. Finally decided that we should be married quickly, with just her mother and my mother being told." It seemed a natural step to take in view of the property changes, and (to avoid clashing with and upstaging my younger brother's long-announced marriage in April) one that ought to be got out of the way quickly; one that would bring peace and sincerity of heart.

Wedding: I marry Ann
The wedding took place that Thursday – it was half-term at both our schools – with just our mothers present. There was time to go to Oxford for a day. I bought Ann a ring. Thursday was wet. We all wore carnations. We were married at the Register Office at 46 Cheniston Gardens, W8. We lunched at the Hilton, and then Ann and I drove to Hastings for our honeymoon and stayed at the Royal Victoria Hotel (room 82 on the 4th floor). Queen Victoria's name was displayed in the visiting-book: she stayed in 1875. Outside there was a wrinkled sea, sand, rocks and the cry of gulls. I quoted Matthew Arnold's 'Dover Beach':

> Come to the window, sweet is the night-air!...
> Listen! you hear the grating roar
> Of pebbles which the waves draw back, and fling....
> Ah, love, let us be true
> To one another! For...
> ...we are here as on a darkling plain
> Swept with confused alarms of struggle and flight,
> Where ignorant armies clash by night.

I was pleased to see the sea again as I had begun to write 'The Night-Sea Crossing'. I had with me *Thought Forces* by Prentice Mulford, and I reflected its view in my *Diaries*: "If you want the new, you must not cling to the old, like a bird clinging to its old plumage, a tree to its old fruit."[7]

We spent our short honeymoon touring the south coast. We visited Hastings Castle and cave, Battle Abbey, Beachy Head, Bognor, Felpham (where I saw Blake's house again), Arundel, Dunford House in Midhurst (which I had not seen since the course I attended in 1961 and which represented, like Oxford, a time before Caroline), Merrow Downs and Shere church (with its 14th-century anchoress's cell). I wrote eight poems. It was hot, and I returned bronzed by the sun and, flushed with my new status, immediately applied for a job which offered a post of Head of English and Senior Teacher two rungs up the ladder.

Interview for new job
On 18 March I was interviewed at Garratt Green School in Wandsworth. It was a glassy comprehensive. The Acting Head of Department was not a candidate, but the Second-of-Department was interviewed ahead of me, a fellow approaching 60, Bob Leach. He told me after his interview before I went in that the Governors had asked him, "Why do you want the job?" and that he had replied: "Because it's on my railway line. It's easy to get here." One is supposed to talk about one's mission to improve the education of the

pupils, and I smiled at his honesty and practicality. I was grilled by 15 Governors for 50 minutes and offered the job from September. Within nine months I had progressed from Scale 2 to Scale 6, Head of English and Senior Teacher, a meteoric rise up the teaching ladder.

I told Caroline I was married and was a Head of English. She said, "You married out of spite." But how wrong she was. She told me she and her husband were going abroad, to live in Germany. Nadia had been accepted by Hunmanby Hall, near Scarborough, and we would pay half the fees each. On Malta she had said to me, "You can't get a permanent home in London and a job and stay in England." But now she was unable to stay in England, and I had a place and a better job than her husband had. The wheel of Fortune had turned remarkably quickly.

New flat: move to 10 Brechin Place

Ann and I moved out of Stanhope Gardens on 20 March and stayed at my mother's house – my childhood Journey's End in Loughton, Essex – until we moved to 10 Brechin Place on 4 April. The pear and apple-trees began to blossom and rabbits ran round the lawn. I took the tube from Loughton to Clapham and went up to the Forest each evening on my return. There were many practical arrangements as we prepared to begin our new married life in our new flat, but I managed to write some poems. Caroline rang to say she would be going to Brüggen, Germany in May, and that I would have to look after Nadia until she started at Hunmanby Hall in September. My mother offered to have Nadia at Loughton, which meant that she could attend Oaklands School (my old school) for the summer term and be with her former classmates from before we went to Libya. This would be a better arrangement than for her to attend a school in central London where she would know nobody. She would come up to us for weekends in Kensington.

We moved into Brechin Place. It had thick piled carpets, brocade curtains with tassels, expensive wallpaper, a bathroom with many mirrors and a bedroom with soft lights behind a pelmet over the bed. I had to put up shelves for my books, and my mother provided Jack Skilton, who had looked after 6 Warrington Gardens for my father. He spent a day doing carpentry and electrical work, and would not hear of being paid. "Your father would have wanted me to do it," he said.

I settled into married life. It was a joy to return to stability and tranquillity after nearly five disturbed years. I was still writing elegies. In mid-April I was on the 8th elegy. I wrote:

Should all my elegies be in heroic couplets and not alternatingly rhymed? Except the first and the last? Will it make for monotony as opposed to a style? A fusing of thought, feeling, place, symbol, my own life – and old forms. That is what *The Pilgrim in the Garden* stands for. In the Garden of Eden. A fixed rhyme appeals to my new thinking: the tranquillity of order, discipline. Against revolutionary freedom. Traditional poetry. Strict.[8]

We collected Nadia from Peterborough and drove her down to stay in our new flat. I changed my MGB GT for a Lotus Elan S4, a royal blue, white and gold racer with a bonnet that sloped to the ground. I had central heating installed in the flat. A lot was happening, and it was now increasingly apparent that Ann was pregnant, and that a new baby would join us in our new home.

Comprehensive education: poetic technique
Satire, The Fountain
In the new stability of my marriage I became more measured, more classical in my literary approach. I had been interested in the follies and vices of society, and had explored whether I could write a satire.

I was interested in classical satire: "Read Horace's *Satires*.... I am going through a Classical phase. What unites me with Marvell and Horace, not to mention Pope, is the form[s] we are trying: the elegy, the ode, the satire.... Bought Horace's *Satires* and his literary criticism. Horace's advice in the *Art of Poetry*: 'Choose a subject within your powers.'"

On a Friday at the end of April, the day before my younger brother Jonathan's wedding, Ann, Nadia and I drove to Packfords Hotel, where we had booked to stay a couple of nights, and joined some of my family at The Roebuck, Buckhurst Hill. We dined looking out on Scotch pines and a sunset while cows horned round the cars, and my family were able to catch up with my remarriage. The next day I put on morning dress and a top hat and drove with Ann and Nadia to St Mary's church, Loughton in an Austin Princess, white streamers flicking on the bonnet. Jonathan's bride came down the aisle in white. Later we threw confetti and I walked with Miss Lord, Headmistress of Oaklands, who said, "We're very glad to have Nadia back at Oaklands." The reception was at Theydon Bois Golf Club.

While returning my morning dress to Alkits I bought Juvenal's satires and wrote: "Do a series of satires next. Cf Horace's satires." I was still writing stories, and had the idea for making some of them satires of "vices: greed, adultery, unfairness, ambition, gluttony". I wrote:

'Satire' comes from '*satura*' or 'medley', or from '*lanx satura*' or 'dish full of first fruits (offered to the gods)'. According to the OED [*Oxford English Dictionary*], a 'satire' is a poem or prose composition in which 'prevailing vices or follies are held up to ridicule'. ('The Rape of the Lock' is quoted as an example.) So in my stories or satires I am ridiculing certain vices or follies of our times, i.e. these people are suffering from vices of these permissive, materialistic, spiritually-enervated times. My standard, by which I judge their vices and follies, is therefore one of enlightened human nature.... My view of human nature must be that it needs a great effort of will for it to approach perfection. My stamp in all these stories must be: look, this man is ridiculous because of his vices (sex) and his follies (money) – this is how our society expects us to live.

I discussed satire with Jim Doolan, who said: "Swift stood for commonsense – the territory of his belief is small." I added: "Departures from common-sense are his excesses. The golden mean of moderation and commonsense." In May I groped towards a blend of Classicism and Romanticism:

> Classicism is simply impersonality – in the sense that I concentrate on the object of my attention and leave myself out of it. I paint the person as he is, without investing the situation with any of my hopes and fears.... If man is the measure of everything... then what of the universe? What of mysticism? What of the Light in the mind? Of God? Cannot Classicism be – is *not* Classicism – reconciled with subordination to divine standards?... Turn against Romantic excess, yet have a Baroque sense of life with a classical attitude.... If I am destined to be a classical... I must discipline myself. I must get up early in the morning to compensate for these worldly goods which come too easily: power, money, material prosperity – things which sap the soul.

I was still fascinated by satire and wrote a satirical story in which everyone shrank, so that "size was now an indication of inner stature". This became *The Fountain*. I wrote: "Do a satire in verse: ridicule vices and follies by exaggeration."[9]

Stress Metre
I was now thinking about poetic technique and wrote: "I am starting a search for a new kind of poetry – a new development of a traditional form. A new line." I was looking for an experimental, innovatory metre that would be effective in catching the thoughts and felt thought I wanted to convey. I turned my thoughts to Churchill and wondered if I could write an epic poem about his role in the war: "I can write a visionary poem about Arthur, but can I about Churchill? To what extent does the historical become legendary?" I also sketched out a structure for *Life Cycle*. In June I devised an accent metre:

> Since the 16th and 17th centuries exhausted blank verse, and the 18th

century the heroic couplet, I must use a 20th-century line for my epic: and it can only be accent metre – after Hopkins and Eliot – i.e. 4 stresses (for meaning) or accents (natural stress of the word) in mixed metres with no rhyme. This will be the basic line…. In the elegies, use a Modernist accent metre, i.e. modernise the traditional form.

Of my coming epic I wrote:

"My whole life has been a preparation for this: for this I read Homer and Virgil at school and English at Oxford (Milton in the holidays, having given up Law). For this I went to the Middle East and Japan – [to] Hiroshima and to El Alamein. Now it is all to come together."

I wrote 'Blind Churchill to the Night', "some 90 odd lines exploring the accent metre I am developing for my epic." (Looking back, I can see that even then I was feeling my way into the story of *Overlord*. When I came to write it Churchill was prominent but I did not use accent metre but blank verse.)

I had doubts about accent metre. I talked with Jim Doolan and wrote:

The accent metre is saved from being the first thing that comes into my head (the fírst thíng that cómes into my héad) by devices, e.g. alliteration, internal rhyme. There must also be "a ghost of a regular form behind the arras of free verse". So I must strive for a line that is sometimes blank verse, sometimes stress-verse, i.e. metrical verse rather than accent…. A blank-verse line in which there are 4 stresses and devices."

I was still pondering the line while thinking of my mist of unknowing. I wrote: "The barriers that cloud perception – spiritual perception – are self-righteousness, avarice, lust, gluttony, envy, inertia, and they must all be burnt away by the divine fire…. The Cloud of Unknowing pierced with light."[10]

'The Night-Sea Crossing', final version

In early July I was off work with a painful knee, which was diagnosed as "housemaid's knee" or "muscular rheumatism", and between 4 and 16 July I wrote the final version of "The Night-Sea Crossing', which sees life and death as being reconciled in a greater whole and overcome by eternity. I used sonata form. I had considered how musical form might work in poetry, and this was a symphonic poem. I wrote in my *Diaries*: "Both life and death are reconciled in the idea of eternity as a fountain that reduces all to dust and goes on reusing the same in new forms…. So *Tao* contains life *and* death."[11]

New stress metre

My solution to the line came in a blinding flash: a new 'stress-metre' line. I wrote: "Was substituting today in Room 14, with an awful class, and was pondering my first elegy and the tension between scansion and stress, and suddenly it hit me – I had a system of primary and secondary stress. In white-hot heat I scribbled out some pencilled notes on a piece of paper about library books, and put it to Jim, who opposed it: "Overtechnical", "the natural voice". But I wasn't quite there! I found it in Hopkins, the ☐, and then I realised I had a system of primary stress – a 4-stress line. All that remained was to check the rules of primary/secondary stress in word-combinations from my days of teaching English as a Foreign Language. It was in the file I made up, my Prosody Notes. So there we are. I have my line. 4 stresses, 4 primary stresses. I used to sit on a garden seat on Lower Field at Chigwell and read Hopkins in the *Faber Book of Modern Verse*. I did not know that he held an insight for me.[12]

Leaving Henry Thornton

The end of term approached. Jim Doolan felt sad that I was going. It was poignant that I would be leap-frogging him to the rank of Senior Teacher, which he had been denied. He spoke of the rising tide of yobbishness in the school. "We're a dying breed," he told me. The day before we broke up he asked, "What do you think I should do?" I said, "If the tide of mindlessness and ignorance is coming in, you should get up and move your deck-chair higher up the beach." He said: "Yes, but where? Where can I get a job at 56? I can't go anywhere where I'd lose my pension. I'm trapped."[13] The next day he presented me with a copy of *The Tempest* and said: "Further to our conversation yesterday, I find myself going back to *The Tempest* more and more."

I felt genuinely sad to leave Henry Thornton. The reason I had been there, it seemed to me now, was to talk poetry with Jim Doolan. I was moving further up the beach to a girls school as a Senior Teacher with reduced teaching commitment, an administrative role that Jim had sought, and I was sorry to leave him exposed to the tidal waves set off by the tempest of inner-city comprehensive education.

I had found that remarriage had brought new domestic serenity and creativity but had been in conflict with the increasing demands of my salaried work in a chaotic comprehensive. The next episode ratcheted up this conflict.

Episode 2:

Lyric Poetry and Administration

Years: 1974–1977
Locations: London; D-Day beaches and Normandy; Chartres; Versailles;
Paris; Rouen
Works: *The Gates of Hell*; Elegies, 11–23; *Visions near the Gates of Paradise*; *The Four Seasons*; *Lighthouse*; *The Weed-Garden*; *The Labyrinth*; *Whispers from the West*;
short stories; satire: *The Garden*
Initiatives: Classical poetry; European resurgence

"Young man everywhere, profit from the fact that nobody knows you."
Rilke, *Malte Laurids Brigge*

My next episode involved a conflict between my growing roles as a poet and parent and as an administrator within a huge school bringing work home each evening. Again, the obfuscation of my more responsible and better paid work blanketed my soul in mist for much of each term-time week, and I wrote during the weekends and school holidays.

Lyric poetry
I continue writing lyric poems: Elegies 11–20
I continued writing lyric poems. In the summer holidays I explained my stress metre to Tuohy when he came to a salad lunch at 10 Brechin Place on his way to Brighton. I traced it back to Coleridge's 'Christabel', which has 4 stresses in a line. He spoke of Yeats as the best poet of cadence after Shelley, and said: "People legislate for their own systems – that's what Hopkins did. You do it first, then make the rules afterwards."[1] Doolan had said something similar. Tuohy said that Milton was the turning-point in the elegy, and insisted that poets need a disciplined form to work against.

I began to revise my poem 'The Silence'. Ann and I took Nadia to Sompting for her children's holiday. I wrote my 11th elegy, 'Sompting Abbotts'. We went on to Brighton, where Tuohy cooked us a chicken dinner and we talked until 2 a.m., during which he expressed his social, political and aesthetic attitudes. He argued that the autobiographical must be generalised by being distanced, as in Donne and Yeats. He said that a poem is an objective correlative: as in a sausage machine, experience goes in one end and comes out as a generalised object which then passes on to a reader. I wrote a 12th elegy about him, 'Chester Court, Sussex Square', which later became 'An Aesthete's Golden Artefacts'. I sent this to him, and he rang to say that he liked my poem on him and offered me the use of his flat in August. He said, "Your broken metre [i.e. stress metre] works very well." I had written: "I am a symbolist, using traditional symbols (e.g. alchemy). And uniting the traditions of statement and image." I reread some of my lyrics and wrote: "They are fresh.... The feeling is there. An urgency." Thinking of my 11th and 12th elegies, I wrote:

> I am like a furnace. The base experience comes into me and comes out as an artefact, an object. This is what Tuohy meant by the sausage machine. The [raw] meat goes into the machine and comes out as sausage.... The artist turning people into stone, experience into ingots. The artist as Gorgon, or as alchemist.... The dual nature of the artist. He has to turn living experience to stone in his art, but is apt to turn real people to stone in life.... My growing Platonism: turning experience into ingot/stone – turning an idea into a form.[2]

I was also thinking about the source of my inspiration, my Muse: "Inspiration comes from the Universal Mind... which the superconscious can join to – the Muse. This Universal Mind is the reality behind the universe."

The day before Nadia was to leave to go to Germany I took her up to the Strawberry Hill pond, the one that had a fallen tree jutting out across the water, and watched her skip round the gravel. We walked back to the pond by the road, Earl's Path. I looked into the pond and saw its reflecting surface and its ground at the same time. Seeing the reflected clouds above the gravel ground in the same moment revealed the fundamental Oneness of the universe. That evening I wrote my 14th elegy, 'Strawberry Hill', and tried to catch this Oneness.

Nadia went to Germany. I drove her to Gatwick and put her on a plane. Then Ann and I took the train to Cornwall to stay with her mother. I wrote a Postscript to an earlier essay: 'The Mystic Revival'. I wrote:

> No illumination for a long time, yet I am purposive.... Is this my second Dark Night? If so, what is its purpose? Think. If the first Dark Night was 1967–1971 [in retrospect, 1965–1971], when the senses had to be burned away after the first illumination (1965/6) [in retrospect 1965], this second Dark Night is a final purification – now that I have given up drink.

I was still writing stories and I revised my poem 'Archangel' and some of the elegies. We went to Porthleven and saw the traditional carrying of torches. I wrote: "The procession around the harbour, then the field where they

21

threw their flaming brands onto the bonfire. The burning fire – the sparks. Red smuts, white stars. A village as a whole." I later wrote my 15th elegy, 'Sea-Fire', about Porthleven. We drove with Ann's mother to Newlyn to see Ann's cousin's boat, and to Pendeen lighthouse, where Ann's mother's mother had lived, and to Geevor mine where her husband had worked, and to Cape Cornwall. Of my elegies I wrote: "They use personal experience to forge a symbol that is not autobiographical....The personal tradition goes back to Marvell."[3] We went to Caerhays to see the castle Byron's grandmother lived in, fairytale battlements and towers amid windswept trees by the sea.

Back in London Margaret Riley arrived unannounced, clutching a plastic bag from which she laid out a round pottery halo broken in three places: the Light in red enamel. She said: "The centre is empty and yet it isn't." She spoke of the Holy Spirit as "the inward surge of the tide into a Cornish harbour, when the heart and soul are at peace". She said of my suffering: "It deepens you, it releases the feelings, it makes you *alive*. Before you suffer you are dead. It brings you alive deep down. You could never have created what you are doing now if you had not suffered."

She returned to Shoreham, where she had a small art gallery in the High Street, and put her enamel halo in the window. Sometimes it was broken, sometimes it was whole, depending on the state of her peace of soul. I wrote a 16th elegy about her visit, which became 'A Mystic Fire-Potter's Red Sun-Halo'.

Margaret had urged me to accept all my past works: "No one can correct your work. You have done it. It is yours. No one can say, 'You should have made this more light, more dark.'... If you don't like it, don't look at it." I surveyed my poems and concluded: "A pear-tree does not hawk its fruit. It is there to be picked and eaten if people want it. If they don't want it, they needn't [eat it]. The wasps will get it when it is windfalls."

Ann and I drove to Hill Place, East Grinstead, the 13th-century home of Gwen Broad who had written to me on the day of my christening and who had died in 1972 (*see My Double Life 1: This Dark Wood*). We went on to Brighton and spent a couple of days in Tuohy's empty flat in Sussex Square. I wrote my 17th elegy about Hill Place, which became 'An Obscure Symbolist's Rock-Tree', within its snow-white walls. Margaret visited us there from Shoreham and enjoined me as she left: "Accept. No rebellion any more. Accept." I was aware that she was speaking of the Catholic Church, and I applied my acceptance to the universe rather than a corrupt institution. I accepted my family's origins in Methodism, against which I had rebelled in my 19th elegy, titled 'Loughton Methodist Church'.

The Light returned: "Last night, Light again, after a long dark. Not as brilliant as usual, but still enough. I buried my face in my pillow, then put my pillow over my head, the better to see." A couple of days later I recorded: "In touch with my imagination again. Saw flowers, a guitar, a host of strange images."[4] My acceptance of the universe had filled me with a deep calm, the "peace that passeth understanding", and I felt that I was filled with knowledge from the Light, a wisdom that seemed to be hatching into my soul as if it was cocooned in cloud.

Satire, The Garden
I was nearing the end of my elegies. While writing my 20th elegy on Chigwell School I had sketched out details for a satire on the theory of mixed-ability teaching in comprehensive education, which became *The Garden.* My *Diaries* catch the tone: "Selectivity is not fair. All seeds should have an equal chance. There is no difference between roses and weeds except for environmental differences. In fact the roses will help the weeds to become more rose-like."[5] With the idea of this satire still fresh in my mind I began my new job at Garratt Green School.

Administration
I start as Head of English and Senior Teacher at Garratt Green School
Garratt Green was a glassy comprehensive set in green grounds with many shrubs in Burntwood Lane, which runs between Wandsworth Common and Garratt Lane. It has since been amalgamated with another school and renamed Burntwood School. In September 1974 it had getting on for 2,200 girls and 140 mainly female staff, and an English Department of 26. It was a well-run school – it had none of the manic rushing-about of Henry Thornton – with a relatively new Head, Mrs. Kay, who was finding coping with so many pupils a handful. A German Jew rumoured to have survived the severity and regimentation of Auschwitz as a child, she ruled autocratically, often interrupting lessons on the tannoy, and enforced strict adherence to the running of the school system. The corridors were crowded, and at break and lunchtime the staff withdrew into a cramped staff room. I had a classroom of my own and taught 'O' and 'A' levels. I found my Departmental staff – all of whom were women except for Bob Leach, the fellow who had chosen the school because it was on his railway line – very courteous, respectful and eager to please.

There were many meetings – House meetings, Departmental meetings which I took (seating the staff at desks in a classroom), Heads-of-Department and Heads-of-House meetings (nicknamed Hods and Hohs) and Senior Management Team meetings (when the three Senior Teachers met with the two Deputies and Head) – and I never left school until after 5 and always had work that took all evening: planning meetings, preparing classes, marking essays, and typing reports on unsatisfactory pupils for the

Head.

Every day I collected sheaves of papers from my pigeon-hole which went into a bulging file I carried about. Each day I tried to empty the file. But as fast as I dealt with papers, more appeared in my pigeon-hole. I worked incredibly hard but always ended each day with as fat a file of papers as I had started the day. It seemed I was running very hard to stand still. Administrative work took up much of my evenings. I wrote: "After my first week at Garratt Green School: much battered by all the questions and problems I had to answer and sort out. Am drawing up a syllabus to put a stop to such questions."

Nadia arrived at 9.30 p.m. (after her bedtime) to spend a night with us on her way to Scarborough and then to spend her first night at boarding-school, Hunmanby Hall. There was little time to see her as I had to be up at 6.30 a.m. the next morning and off early. Ann, who had now begun maternity leave, drove her back to Dulwich to be taken to Yorkshire. I slogged away at the Departmental syllabus and finished it: a fat wodge of closely-typed sheets of A4 clipped together, covering every English class and directing teachers and supply teachers what to teach. At the end of September I wrote: "Living at work. A shadow of my true self." Being an administrator removed me from my remarriage each weekday and burdened me with typing, tasks and marking for much of each evening. There was little time to relate to Ann or write. But I was able to spend a weekend writing *The Garden*, and turning back to poems: "Poems of London. The sun shining through, the light. Ghosts, skeletons underneath. The rain. Huge Nature, tiny man. The city as it is. The beauty of London."[6]

Birth of Matthew

On 2 October a tannoy message asked me to contact the Head. She told me, "Your wife has to go to hospital." I drove home and learned from Ann that her blood pressure was up and that she might be induced. I drove her to Queen Charlotte's Hospital and stayed with her until late, then returned home to sleep.

I was woken at 5 a.m. Ann was on the phone from the labour ward. She said, "I've started." I immediately went to the hospital. I wrote: "My heart was in my mouth because the baby was 'very tired', struggling to get out the wrong way – and [its] heart stopped and I was sent out of the room. I returned later and a forceps delivery was set in motion, me staying. The 'fetal heartbeat' kept going nil and it looked stillborn but was revived. High blood pressure makes a baby very tired."[7] The baby was delivered success-fully in a ventouse-and-forceps delivery at 7.07 a.m., weighing 6lbs 11ozs, a little boy. We called the baby Matthew.

There was no paternity leave in those days, and I had to go straight from the labour ward to work and apologise to the Head for being slightly late.

Lyric Poetry: eruption
Elegies: 21–23

I wrote about the birth in my 21st elegy. That day there was an article on Ken Campbell, with whom I had visited the Partisan, who had written a "fantasy" about his friend Ion Will – none other than the Will who ran behind me on Belgrade Station in 1958 and just missed the train. It was about telepathy and another planet.

Ann came home with Matthew and I tried to reconcile my role as husband and father with my administration, which seemed endless. There was a general election. Prime Minister Edward Heath, whose 'unofficial Ambassador' to the African liberation movements I had been, had taken on the National Union of Mineworkers whose action had led to power cuts and a three-day week, and had been advised to go to the country on the issue by the Head of his think-tank, Victor, Lord Rothschild. I managed to write my 22nd elegy about voting at Our Lady of Victory's School. Later it became clear that Heath had been voted out of office. I was very tired at half-term. I recorded: "A blue light again, glowing like a stone. A wonderful blue. I lay in the bath and peeped for it and saw it. A wonderful, wonderful blue."

On 23 October I drafted my 23rd elegy, 'Brechin Place'. This completed my cycle of elegies. It combined the domesticity of my remarriage and illumination with my daughter's visit for half-term. She brought with her the Hunmanby School magazine, called *Flame-Bearer*, which contained a song and a prayer about the Light.

I drove my new family to lunch with my mother in Loughton. Ann had a sleep after lunch alongside Matthew, who was in the Moses basket. I took Nadia and my sister Frances (who had also been invited to lunch) up to High Beach church and the two ponds. I wrote: "The golden, rust and orange-copper leaves, we scuffled and shuffled."[8]

Two Dark Nights

At half-term I identified two Dark Nights that I had experienced:

The Dark Night of the Senses was when the divine intelligence detached my soul from the web of the lower senses,... which left the lower senses in emptiness and darkness. In this, spiritual knowing and illumination were imparted (in September 1971) and my high spiritual state with its emotional ecstasy led to fatigue (May 1972, my exhaustion). The Night of the Spirit was an exhaustion that followed from that. Now I am emerging into the unitive life, my self remade.... Giving up alcohol in 1973 was... part of my Second Dark Night, of the Spirit. Union is ahead.

In fact my emergence into the full unitive life was still two decades away. I thought about the unitive life:

> The self desires nothing, and has nothing, is passive. A state of equilibrium, at one with the Absolute life – not perceiving it; a state of purely spiritual life, characterised by peaceful joy, enhanced powers, intense certitude. So when did this calm come upon me?... I would date its onset to September 1973, when I started at Henry Thornton, having finished my purgation. Certainly since October 1973 when I started my elegies.... I had it with 'The Night-Sea Crossing' and throughout the summer, when I worked really well.[9]

These *Diary* entries record how my Dark Nights appeared in 1974. With hindsight, my Dark Night of the Soul or Senses ended in September 1971, and my Dark Night of the Spirit began when my Second Mystic Life ended in April 1972 and lasted until May 1979, when my Third Mystic Life began. (*See* Appendix 1, pp.903–904 and *My Double Life 1: This Dark Wood*, Appendix 1, p.489.)

The Gates of Hell
I now returned to lyric poems, *The Gates of Hell*. I wrote:

> *The Gates of Hell*. These should not be in the order that they were written but in the order in which they "happened" – to overcome the sort of confusion we experience when we go to Donne, whose chronology is unknown. Also, I should not force the irregularities of the originals into a tight metrical form. They begin in regular metre and become irregular as the feeling of disintegration proceeds.

On 3 November I wrote: "This weekend I have typed up 40 lyrics. 21 yesterday, 19 today." And I reflected: "When I was smashed in 1969/1970/1971, I found my wholeness again by associating with the meek and the maimed, the insulted and the injured, the boys of Greenwich, the wretched of the earth." Again: "*The Gates of Hell* poems 'happened'. In that dark night...they wrote themselves without any pushing from me." And again: "I grew *The Gates of Hell* effortlessly in two years (after 6 November 1972), like a tree putting out leaves." And again: "I have not bothered to type out my 110 short lyrics before now – they are too small – yet each one is more significant than the Movement poems in *New Poetry*." I went on:

> What a pity I didn't write these short poems in Libya. I clung to prose, having to... preserve my sanity.... I can do it now, recollecting emotion in tranquillity.... It is as though only now I have found my material as a poet:

26

the situation that engulfed me.... "Emotion recollected in tranquillity." Yet [you] can't write when you are disturbed, you can only write when recollecting.

On 10 November I wrote: "I typed 31 poems yesterday, and another 31 today, and have now finished transferring them from the green manuscript book."

I was living with great energy, and asked:

To what do I attribute my tremendous energy? For I have twice the stamina and energy of most men – ... this spring. This quantitative energy which contains quality. Perhaps the disciplines of my childhood – the hard work I put in then. The Latin, the homework. Eruption year, 1974 – this must be connected with my marriage. I have so many works to do: 'Flight', 16 sonnets, 12 odes (Pindaric odes) on the months, the Cromwell poem, my *juvenilia*, the 80-odd poems I wrote in Japan before I met Tuohy. Not my greatest work, but certainly some should be printed.... Then my epic. Pound, I think of him so often, and of my evening with him. I have a destiny ahead of me. It is there, all I have to do is to follow footsteps.

I reflected on Wordsworth whose *The Prelude* books 1 and 2 I was teaching my 'A'-level class, and saw how the order in the universe and the calm in the spirit reconciled opposites:

Wordsworth's two passages in *The Prelude* about how the mountain moved – once when he was rowing, once when he felt giddy. His attribution of unknown "modes of being" to Nature and mountains, which "do not live like living men" – but which live. The wisdom and spirit of the universe which breathes through all things; the eternity of thought. The order in the universe reconciles the contradictions (storms, wars, killings) and the calm in the spirit that reconciles the passions, e.g. terror. We are purified until we recognise "the grandeur in the beating of the heart" – i.e. we have reverence and are always capable of greatness. This wonderful calm! The Spirit gives "to forms and images a breath and everlasting motion". Images can be trees etc. – things seen – but also mental pictures of things which have excited feelings of love, joy, fear, wonder. These images move through our minds like living things; they grow and are linked with our earliest and strongest feelings. "If the images are great, beautiful and mysterious, the feelings themselves will be purified and sanctified." Then the terror is ennobled by the image of the mountain. A child's wonder at a rainbow remains a beautiful feeling which grows in spiritual strength each time a rainbow returns. So it is image–feeling–purification when it returns....The unity of creation: the Zen Stone Garden in Japan.[10]

'The Flight'
I began typing out 'The Flight' while Ann took Matthew to a reunion of her antenatal class. I wrote:

> The metaphysical flight. If there is one Spirit in the universe, which breathes life into all forms, then all images in Nature are part of a unity and all images in the mind are too. Strong feelings see into the unity of life in the universe and are remembered and derive a living power of their own. They purify our clogged-up feelings. If the universe is all one, then images are a revelation of the One. They are not just intense memories, but chinks into the unity of the universe, glimpses of the Power which have a metaphysical sense.

I felt that I would move back to Epping Forest. I wrote:

> I am unable to tear my soul away from the [place] which has so inspired me: Epping Forest. I have moved away… but my heart is still there. And I can see myself moving back…. I am a child of Epping Forest, and should find a good place near it – in it, or on it – to live. Or else I should stay within reach of it in anonymous London, where I can avoid the people of Essex but go down and savour her beauty, and observe the changing seasons.

On 14 December I wrote: "What I want to do with the rest of my life. Live quietly in the Forest where there is peace. Go for walks among leaves and living things. Grow things. Contemplate. Get away from the stress of the city and its unreality. Live the stylish life of a country squire."

Meanwhile I finished 'The Flight' and had ideas for writing *haiku*s, my epistle to Cromwell and further revisions of 'The Silence'. I wrote: "I must write, in addition to my epic: odes, epistles (to the living and the dead), satires, etc. I need to make a study of Roman poetry." And: "If I have 100 good lines among 4,000 average ones, that is enough…. I have retrieved 'I skulk under the rim of my collar'. I must not forget to salvage 'While hostesses serve drinks and pickled prattle'."

The Light had returned on 1 December. I wrote: "The Light returned several times today, a mirror for my soul. Lightly bluish."[11]

I share a room with a nun: illumination and nuns
At Garratt Green I shared a room with another Senior Teacher, the Head of Science, Sister Hurst. She was a nun with La Retraite for 30 years and was transferred to their Clapham branch, told to live out in society and find herself a job. For the first time for over 30 years she had to think about the

practicalities of maintaining a home, and she used to ask me about rates and drainpipes. One lunchtime she described how she got up at 5.30 a.m. to contemplate before coming into school for her active life. I told her about Margaret and asked her: "To what extent is she – and her illumination – normal in a convent, and to what extent is she different?" Sister replied: "Oh, no, she's a leader. It's [i.e. illumination's] not mentioned in our convent. That's what we are praying for but it never comes. Only the saints have that. You have to shout for the Lord." Here was a nun living the devotional life who had not been told what Margaret and I knew, that illumination is normal, and I was shocked that the nuns were not experiencing the One.

Outpouring of lyric poems: "volcanic eruption"
Nadia came to stay for the Christmas holidays and I continued working on my poems. I wrote:

> Today I finished the 'Epistle to His Imperial Highness, on his Birthday', which I only started yesterday – 150 lines – and did 'Winter in Nara'. At present I can do anything I want. I pick up works that defeated me 10 years or less ago, and do them straight out on the typewriter, and so true is my ear that out of 150 lines there was only one tetrameter – all the rest were pentameters when I wanted them to be. I have mastery of my subject, I am on top of my material. It is a wonderful gift, I am using it to get ready a considerable body of material. A lot of this newly-won confidence must come from my settled family life – my marriage to Ann. She has provided settled conditions.

Looking back on 1974, I wrote: "This year has been poetry, poetry, poetry, ever since July, which reopened the spring. ('The Night-Sea Crossing.')" I echoed the settled conditions on Boxing Day: "I am surrounded by a family again, am settled and happy." Two days later I added: "At present am doing a sonnet a day, the October-1970 material."

In early 1975 I felt overworked but I was still writing poems and recorded:

> Wrote 'The Blind', 'Generations like Seasons' and 'Recurrence' between 7 p.m. and 11 p.m. after a hard day's work – and a fruitful assembly. My… idea of seasonal recurrence. Not eternal recurrence, just men and history turning through, and obeying the same law as, the seasons. I have written 192 poems in *The Gates of Hell* alone. Baudelaire only wrote 144 in his whole life…. In the last six months there has been a great outpouring, a volcanic eruption. Poems have shot from me like rocks of molten lava. I have typed up the equivalent of the entire output of Baudelaire in the last four months alone.[12]

29

The last poem in *The Gates of Hell* was 'The Code'. I first drafted the poem in 1969 and revised it in 1975 when I added the numbers: the code. Two columns of numbers supply two words that answer the question raised in stanza 2. The first of the numbers, "6 of 2", supplies the first letter of the first word which is in the left-hand column. The second number, "7 of 24", supplies the first letter of the second word in the right-hand column. The first number in each pair of numbers supplies the first letter of a line in a poem in *The Gates of Hell*. The second number in each pair of numbers relates to the number of a poem in *The Gates of Hell* where the line of the first number can be found. The code varies the number of each poem in *The Gates of Hell*. It is not as complex as the Enigma code in Bletchley Park, but there are 192 permutations for the first letter of each second number. Now my lips are sealed and my teasing is ended.

I was making arrangements to have all my poems typed and bound in chronological order. I saw my poems as being a record of my journey along the Mystic Way: "From now on I must unite all my works in the light of my mysticism. Each poem of any length must be a slim-volume part of a large whole, *A Mystic Way*." I was grouping my poems into volumes. I had not forgotten *Life Cycle*, the title I had received on a plane between Baghdad and Basra in 1962: "*Life Cycle* itself is to be 10 poems, of the length of Rilke's [Duino] Elegies." I was haunted by a line I had come across in Ovid's *Metamorphoses*: "When the sun rises I see that everything is modelled on his divine plane." I was still writing poems: 'Traitor's Gate', 'Flowers in the Soul' and 'A Sheikh in his Harem' (1 February) and 'Cherry Blossom' and 'Sunday' (9 February). At half-term I wrote: "Still the lyrics pour: 'The Gates of Paradise'…. 'No one is upset within the Gates of Paradise'." Two days later I wrote: "Have drafted some 10 poems in the last two days. Cannot stop them pouring up. About Paradise mostly at present. Are these poems part of *The Gates of Hell* or are they a separate work, e.g. *The Gates of Paradise*?"

At February half-term Ann and I spent nights at Folkestone – we stayed in Marine Crescent where the Channel swimmers I watched as a boy used to stay – and Margate, and I wrote "two stories and various poems". I gave Ann a poem, 'Keep', to mark our first wedding anniversary. 'Keep' referred to Dover Castle's keep as well as the idea of 'keeping for good'. Back at school I was teaching book 9 of *Paradise Lost* and considering Milton's Satan. I recorded: "Wrote another Divine Sonnet, 'The Seed of God'…. These Divine poems keep coming to me."

In March I defrosted the fridge. I wrote: "Slabs of ice, melted under the tap's jet. A fridge of memories. Wrote 'De-Frosting', then dozed off downstairs."[13]

When I came to I had a vision of ecumenical unity: the union of all sects of Christianity and the World Council of Churches, and of all religions, including Zen. I was groping towards religious Universalism, which I would develop in the future.

On 9 March I wrote: "Under my shower saw the Light – blue and round for a while.... 250 poems now." On 12 March I asked: "How to arrange these poems? *Pilgrim in the Garden* separately? *The Gates of Hell*, all 250 or just some of them? In 3 parts? Or separate 'volumes'? The answer came nine days later: "Got it: the whole work is *Sonnets and Lyrics from a Dark, Dark Night*, and Part One is *Inscriptions on the Gates of Hell*. Part Two: *A Bulb in Winter*, as I decided last weekend, and Part Three: *Paradise within the Cathedral*." I had not forgotten Epping Forest: "Though in London I am unable to forget Epping Forest, where my heart is,... where I will live until I die." And: "The Poet of Epping Forest – that is what I must become." I saw *The Gates of Hell*, which had looked back to Catullus and Ovid, as being "in the tradition of Wyatt, Shakespeare and Tennyson, all of whom wrote sequences of poems for people they loved". I later observed: "In my three collections of lyrics and sonnets I... express the mystical truths of the Mystic tradition through my experience."[14]

'The Four Seasons'
I began to think about *The Four Seasons* and wrote:

> Spiritual truths were traditionally conveyed by illustrations from everyday life. The earliest Mystery was an agricultural cult. All plants were sacred, possessed immortality exhibited each spring by the constant renewing of themselves. The unity of life – of man and plant – is manifested in myriad forms in Nature.... Man was taught to interpret Nature, to feel at one with it, to subject his soul to be cultivated by it. So if he shared in the agricultural operations he induced spiritual growth. Thus if I write about agricultural operations, I induce spiritual growth. In Dulwich Park I was the Wise Gardener – in the Garden of my Soul. So set one of the 12 Months there. Forests – Epping Forest (winter); crops and fruit trees (autumn); garden plants and flowers (spring and summer).

I spent a fortnight writing the poem in May. I had continued to think about applying musical form to poetry, and this poem was in sonata form with dissociation.

I was still thinking deeply about mysticism:

> The unitive Light brings new creative powers.... Works of art it produces found schools. If this hard work now is the Mystic Life, then the purgation began in 1964, when I defined the prison of 'I'hood as the Reflection.... [My] consciousness again unified itself and formed a new centre.... The

dethronement of the self.... Mystics come after the great intellectual, material and artistic periods – such as ours, which is coming to an end. The Mystic is the crest of the wave....

I was thinking about the Metaphysical poets and wrote: "The Metaphysicals use figurative language so that they can give abstract ideas a pictorial concreteness."

I was still pondering on mysticism in May and noted: "The blue light came last night, effortlessly." In June I took Ann and Matthew to Farm Street Jesuit Church in London, which had been associated with Hopkins. The centenary of Hopkins's death was being celebrated there, and we heard Robert Speight (the actor I had met in Japan) read 'The Wreck of the *Deutschland'* and then an address by Father D'Arcy, who had converted Graham Greene in the 1920s and was now a wizened, stooping, frail, greying man who still retained his intellectual vigour. I had heard my Call to be a poet while reading 'The Wreck of the *Deutschland'* on a bench in Lower Field at Chigwell School in 1957 (see *My Double Life 1: This Dark Wood*).

I recorded that my work as an administrator left me little time: "Now I am working hard – running to stand still. Meetings, timetable, 4th-year list – every day is taken up with practicalities. And [in] the evenings I am tired."[15]

Second Dark Night leads to the Unitive Way
In June 1975 I read St John of the Cross's *The Dark Night of the Soul*. I read that the soul enters the Dark Night gradually and emerges in degrees. At first there is the Night of Sense when the soul's lower nature is purified and united to the spirit, and then, when the soul has been blinded by Light, the Night of Spirit, in which the spirit is purified in the spiritual Night and prepared for union. I pondered the difference between the Dark Night of Sense and the later Dark Night of the Spirit and applied them to my experience:

My self-division in 1971 was sense v. spirit.... My problem: Cold War (i.e. my journalism) did not admit the tastes of the higher self.... [The] Night of Sense [, the Dark Night of the Senses,] is a bridling of a desire rather than a purgation, which happens in the Night of [the] Spirit. Night of Spirit purges sense and spirit together, a sharper purgation after the tranquillity that follows the Night of Sense.... The Dark Night of the Spirit is an inflowing... into the soul which cleanses it of its ignorances and imperfections, i.e. 'infused contemplation'.... "Clouds and Darkness are round" our under-standing. Divine contemplation in impure soul – two contraries.... My Dark Night of Sense began in 1968 [, in retrospect, 1965,] and ended in 1971. My

Night of the Spirit followed in... 1972, May [in retrospect, 29 April]. Once sense and soul were united it was impossible for me to continue in the Cold War, which conflicts with the divine laws.... My subject in all my work is this Dark Night.

I considered purgation and the suffering of the soul as "Purgatory":

The cause of Purgatory is therefore the weakness and imperfections of the soul. When these are all burned away, the suffering ceases, and joy takes it place: it glows with love.... All art is a cheat – if written or made by people who have not been through the Dark Night. It is a waste of our time consuming it, for it is an error.... The quest I set off on in 1961, an incomplete soul.... The pain of the Night of [the] Spirit is "beyond comparison greater" than that of the Night of Sense.... The soul... sees nothing at first but what is within itself – its own darkness. The supernatural Light gives light to the understanding.

I thought again about my sensual and spiritual parts and the dates of my own Dark Nights:

The tranquillity of my lower and sensual part was not complete until 1973.... The soul is struck unexpectedly by a ray of divine grace, as I was in 1965. A new chord was touched... (e.g. my 'Archangel'). Now I am in the Dark Night of the Spirit, which will lead to ascent,... beatific vision. This did not begin before September 1971. April 1973 I stopped alcohol. Illumination was strong from 1971/2.... The Night of the Spirit comes after... the illumination – and is a swing back to darkness. In my case it was after the ecstasies of May 1972. The confusion of 1973.... It is the end, before the Unitive Way, in which sense and spirit are united. Ahead, the dawn of a new and glorious day. Perhaps my Dark Night [of the Spirit] was *A Bulb in Winter*, and the Unitive Way emerged with [*Visions near the Gates of*] *Paradise*? In which case I have emerged from the Dark Night, or am emerging?

I was trying to understand the mystic life as a process. I felt that I had been through a Dark Night of Sense from 1968 – which I now believe began in early 1966, after my First Mystic Life in 1964–5 and my first illumination in 1965 – to 1971 and a Dark Night of Spirit from 1972 onwards, beginning with my illness on 17 May 1972. (*See* Appendix 1, p.903 and *My Double Life 1: This Dark Wood*, Appendix 1, p.489.)

The Night of Unknowing within the Dark Night of Spirit was pouring knowledge about our civilization into me while my bodily health was temporarily suspended. At the end of term I was ill. For three days I had a temperature of 103°F, a viral illness. I wrote: "Several times when I got the shivers my entire hands went that same deathly numb and cold, the fingers white, the knuckles a strange blue." A few days later I was diagnosed as having neutropenia – too few white blood cells (leucocytes) in the blood.[16]

Poetic forms

I had been thinking feverishly about the form in my poems. While under the weather I wrote: "The line goes from Shakespeare–Donne–Tennyson–Hardy–Hagger;… stemming from Catullus and Ovid (Shakespeare's inspiration). The sonnets [of Shakespeare] are sincere, not a technical exercise…. My poems are often in unfamiliar forms, but the form can be justified: go and look at the symphony, the fugue, and see how traditional ideas can be reapplied in a seemingly unfamiliar way. And so I am an innovator."[17]

'Lighthouse'

I had broken up now and battled with my illness. On my first day in Cornwall I wrote: "In spite of being persistently tired I have completed 'Lighthouse'."[18] 'Lighthouse' was a fugue, the contrapuntal form catching the self-divided mind, and I later thought of calling it 'The Dark Night Easter Temptation of a Somewhat Saintly Man, or a Formerly Derelict Lighthouse'. In the event, I dropped the last five words and the rest became the poem's subtitle. It drew on the Dark Night of St John of the Cross. I made notes for several poems including one about the 12 months, and one to be called 'The Labyrinth'.

Idea of 'The Weed-Garden'

I was also pondering a new symphony I thought of as my 'Heroic Symphony', which eventually became 'The Weed-Garden' (originally 'The Cockleshell Weed-Garden') with a subtitle 'A Heroic Symphony drafted in Cornwall'. On this poem I wrote:

> Bear in mind my lecture to the Garratt Green 6th form about man being a bud and a bloom, the purpose of education being to unfold, "explication". Education is an explication…. A poem about all man in all time showing that the unfolding of the soul contributes to civilization (art and religion), and when it does not unfold we have the decline of civilization and religion, expressed in materialism, outer-technology as opposed to inner spirit and mysticism and art, i.e. today we have a culture that is "unexplicated", i.e. no unfolding has taken place, and that is unnatural, for all flowers unfold naturally. We have thus "gone against" Nature. This… is about all men's search for civilization (and truth and human wisdom). See Spengler, the decline of the West and the flower in the meadow. Because it is about all men,

there must be a protean theme, and the one hero must stand for all great men, and be interchangeable with them, cf Ovid's *Metamorphoses*. So this is a statement about the great men, how their souls unfold and they pour their "explicatedness" into their civilization and religion and renew it.... Also put the decline of civilization and religion – caused by failure to unfold into "12 experiences that sum up the culture of the last 30 years" (my conversation with Ezra Pound in 1970).

In the poem I was seeing civilizations and cultures in terms of "unfolding of the soul":

There are three themes.... Can they be woven together into a design, like the flowers on Miss Barron's curtains? [Miss Barron had looked after Queen Mary in Buckingham Palace and had given me the curtains from her room in Buckingham Palace.] Answer: yes, if I take the form of a symphony and have the odes within it, each ode as a thought-block, i.e. a *strophe*, containing its own *strophe-antistrophe*, to be balanced against another thought-block, the antithetical scheme being a contrast... between past and present. On these lines the main thread is the unfolding of the soul/rose, which can take place in a great man's life... and often did in the past – and so lead to civilization and art and religion... but which today all too often does not take place because of the new world we live in, so that men live without seeing the *flora* and *fauna* which feed the soul..., and concentrate on outer things which brings down civilization and religion and art.... Have one cyclic heroic symphony weaving all these thought-blocks into the "curtain".

I wrote:

Suggested movements for my symphony: (1) The unfolding of the soul which can take place, and which in the past often did; contrasted with its all too often not taking place today.... (2) How the great men evolve this unfolding, which is seen in terms of life cycle, i.e. between birth, death and suffering, and a definition of man as he can be. Spiritual gardening (ABA). (3) How new men live without seeing the *flora* and *fauna* that feed the soul (ABA). (4) A restatement of how the soul can unfold (ABACABA), and examples from the heroic men of history and [from] eternity.... A definition of greatness.... If a great man is a flower bloomed, then history is a flower-garden. The soul is a living part of the human organism, and it contains the creative powers of the mind, which unfold like a bloom from the human stem.[19]

Idea of 'The Labyrinth': odes

Now I temporarily pushed 'The Weed-Garden' aside for I had had the idea of writing a poem in odes: "Also do the 12 odes of a dying man – intensity – and 'Labyrinth'."[20]

We toured Cornwall. We spent a hot day in Porthleven and visited Gunwalloe beach. We went to Fowey and looked at Sir Arthur Quiller-Couch's ivy-creepered house and crossed to Polruan. We went to Tintagel and took a Land Rover to the castle and Merlin's cave. We went on to Boscastle and Slaughter Bridge, where according to one version of the legend Arthur is reputed to have fought his last battle, and we found what local legend calls Arthur's tombstone on the bank of the River Camel, near Camelford.[21]

The next day I wrote: "Trees. The lime, oak and yew can live to be 800–1,000 years old…. My images are like acorns on an oak." I was still groping towards 'The Weed-Garden' and latched on to the idea of the Forest.

In my *Diaries* I wrote out all the Epping-Forest places I might draw on for this work, and also the exact course of two streams through Epping Forest. I added:

> For my odes I need to link the months that flow by and the seasons of my life. These can be measured against the Forest, which measures the months and is a time-keeper (changing of colours of leaves, etc.), and against whose years… I can measure myself….The odes: the year in the Forest. How it turns – and I will not be there (*strophe*). The years, my life (*antistrophe*)…. A symbol to unite the two as I pass into the Forest through the graveyard: from life to eternity, my body a part of the Forest, my soul like a willow-warbler.

I concluded: "Man has to subject his soul to be cultivated in the same way as Nature, by sharing the various agricultural operations, thereby inducing spiritual growth."

It was an exciting time intellectually: "Every day I take a different topic. Yesterday King Arthur, today wild flowers, tomorrow – who knows? Stars? Before I came away there were *strophe*s in Greek choruses, and then the *Odes* of Horace. Every day is therefore an adventure, and there is no knowing what tomorrow's studying will bring. My garden, my soul, has neat flowers."[22]

'The Weed-Garden': culture and civilization

Ann and I walked to the end of the Black Head of Trenarren, the headland in St Austell Bay on which A.L. Rowse lived, and I picked ragwort, sheep's bit scabious and woodruff. On my return I thought about our culture and civilization:

A culture takes its tone from its leaders. If the leaders' souls are unfolded, it will be an explicated culture. If not, a materialistic, technological culture….Culture comes down to the arts: paintings, cathedrals, books from libraries, concerts. What Clark calls "civilization"…. A 'culture' is within 'a civilization': 'a civilization' has 'a culture' – and 'civilization'. 'A civilization' suggests organisation, the Roman civilization; 'civilization' (=reclaiming from a savage state) is the opposite of barbarianism, i.e. being civilised, as the arts can show…. A 'culture' is a geographical homogeneous mass, the total output of its cultivation or civilization, e.g. 'Western culture'; 'culture' (= cultivation of the mind, educated and refined) generally is the opposite of 'primitive'…. It is the ideas of the Age as expressed in the arts…. So when a number of souls in a culture, i.e. in a civilization, unfold, then civilization (as opposed to barbarism) and art and religion flourish…. If 'civilization' = soul-unfolded, it is the idea of the Age as reflected in art that is important…. If 'civilization' = soul-not-unfolded, then we get seeds and husks and socialism…. Change the tone of the culture and the notion of civilization…. My purpose – my mission – is to draw attention to what is happening to our culture, and therefore to our civilization.

This concern with culture and civilization was to come out in *The Fire and the Stones*.

We went to Roche Chapel, which is perched high on a rock and where a hermit lived in the Middle Ages, and then to Castle Killibury, the Kelli Wic of the Welsh Triads, where Arthur was reputed to have lived. It was a circular mound on a hill, an unexcavated hill-fort. We went to St Michael's Mount and I visited Trevarthian, where I had stayed in 1955. Many of these Cornish places found their way into 'The Weed-Garden'.

I thought again about our culture for 'The Weed-Garden', and wrote:

Our culture is the idea of the Age given in the arts, painting, sculpture, music, poetry and novels, i.e. a mass age in which there are no heroes and no grand themes…. Now we are part of European culture…. There has been a levelling since 1940….There is now something of an inner Hell: materialist sloth and ease, low spiritual tension….In place of the old self-discipline, moderation and restraint – the traditional virtues – the 7 Deadly Sins are now worshipped, the weeds called by the names of flowers which choke the growth of flowers in our outwardly well-organised, 'no-growth' garden: pride…; avarice…; lust…; anger…; gluttony…; envy…; and sloth…. All these choke, i.e. impede growth…. Today we have… a waste land of weeds choking flowers inside, i.e. a culture like a rubbish dump in which no discrimination exists in the gardener's mind as to what is a weed, what is a flower…. Our culture needs weeding, because our flowers are choked by weeds.[23]

I began writing 'The Weed-Garden':

> A wet morning. Wrote my spider's-web poem and then finished the first movement of my cultural symphony, and decided on the title: 'The Cockleshell Weed-Garden' [, now 'The Weed-Garden']. I will quote 'Mary, Mary, quite contrary' and dedicate the poem to Harold and Mary Wilson. I am saying to our Prime Minister that all the well-organised outer life has overlooked the fact that we have a cultural weed-garden. Eliot is a flower, his soul unfolded. Weeds are too numerous to recall. I can make the lilies of light the "silver bells" – the heroes, i.e. there should be more lilies. The "pretty maids" are the weeds.... The cockleshells are all the outer decorations of the garden. This is my appeal to our Government for more lilies and fewer weeds in our culture.

I wrote about the myth of Arthur and the legend of Christ's visit to Britain and again thought about culture and civilization for 'The Weed-Garden':

> Toynbee and Eliot are agreed that religion is the centre of a culture and of art.... To Toynbee, art serves religion or it becomes vulgar and barbarised. Eliot insists that in a healthy culture religion and philosophy and art are all united. Bring this into 'The Weed-Garden'. What was a whole is now divided up into fragments. Think, a garden as a whole, a garden of allotments.... Civilization.... Our ideal of perfection today should be the mind at peace, illuminated, confident in the face of all outer conditions and uncertainties... that there is permanence and stability ahead.... What a muddled, confused society I grew up in. I am moving towards a classical period, in which permanence and stability and peace and light and confidence dominate and the powers of fear, barbarism and darkness are routed. The triumph of civilization over barbarism.

I asked about the future of Western civilization:

> Can the West be optimistic and have a sense of permanence and stability in the bastion of Europe?... Can it have a post-imperial life?... The surrounding conditions suggest that the West is doomed.... On the other hand, within the united West material conditions and prosperity look hopeful. There is *limes* (frontier), that is the point, and though the barbarians are massing they do not threaten yet. Our generation, and the next generation, will probably survive intact, but the West is on the slide.... My commitment was for light, against the dark represented by Communism; for the West and against the successor; for the West against the enemy in the Third World War. It has to be seen in these terms, and not in liberal terms.... I defended the West against

the barbarians. I was fighting for a culture of flowers, not a culture of weeds.

I finished the first draft of 'The Weed-Garden' on 18 August. I also researched my epic in the library: read books and typed out notes. I wrote: "My Heroic Symphony was conceived – in the shape it is in – in Cornwall. Before I went to Cornwall I did not know it would be a symphony."

We returned from Cornwall and I looked towards Essex. I rang the vicar of High Beach church (church of the Holy Innocents), and arranged for Matthew to be christened there. I instinctively knew that I was heading back to Essex: "The London years are drawing to an end. What I need is somewhere like Pound's house, on top of a mountain in Rapallo. Get to know the woodlanders of Essex." My intuition that I would live in Essex was right, but my timing was out: it was too soon. And: "We must live in the Forest.... I must work over in Essex somewhere." We visited the vicarage at High Beach and visited the Essex villages.

We visited Tuohy in Brighton and sat in his garden for two-and-a-half hours after Matthew had been sick on his sofa. He said memorably, "Disintegrating societies produce the best art," as in such societies the artist is detached. We went on to visit Margaret and sat in the "weed-garden" at the back of her Shoreham shop, and I realised it had given me the idea for the title of 'The Weed-Garden'. I told myself again that I should live "surrounded by beauty, not ugliness – ... the countryside of Epping Forest".[24]

Sonnets

Back at school I began writing sonnets. I wrote: "The sonnet line: (Ovid)–Wyatt and Surrey–Shakespeare–Donne–Milton–Wordsworth–Hopkins–me. Hand on the sonnet in good health. I am the custodian of the sonnet, and must hand it on." I read Shakespeare's *Sonnets*, and observed: "I have sonnets inside me. They are going to pour out. I drafted, I scribbled out, two today." Being an administrator was again cutting across my family life and writing. I also wrote: "My solitary struggle. Between visits to school, I struggle to set down a vision, a vision of growth." I had to produce a document for the other Heads of Department, proposing a policy for Language across the Curriculum. Soon afterwards I wrote: "At 36... I feel worn out. I long to retire, and sit under an apple-tree and read the classics I have no time to read."

I discussed the order of Shakespeare's sonnets with my 6th-form class. I wrote that the order of the sonnets "is not necessarily the order in which they were written – as I well know from *The Gates of Hell*. A poet writes what is on his mind and arranges his offerings in order later on, or else leaves them in the haphazard order in which they were written." I was clear on the provenance of *The Gates of Hell*: "My *Gates of Hell* are in the *genre* of Catullus, Wyatt and Surrey, Shakespeare, Donne, Tennyson, Hardy."[25]

World history: Toynbee

In October Arnold Toynbee died and I wrote an appreciation of him in my *Diaries*, which began: "I am sad, for Toynbee has died, and I never met him." I noted the contrast between his progressive view, that *hubris* leads to *nemesis* and destroys civilizations, and my traditional view that questioning traditional values destroys civilizations. I noted: "I have stood for the oppressed victims of Western *hubris*, but I have also stood for the West – purged of its *hubris*..., reformed from within." I was aware that my role in Western civilization was deeply connected with my poetry: "The poet is an oracle, a speaker of truth."[26]

Administration: system

Overworked at Garratt Green

I had embarked on my second academic year at Garratt Green. I was even more busy than the previous year. The bulging file I carried about with me was permanently fatter than the previous year. In it were minutes of meetings to digest, recommendations to implement, and always two dozen case histories on which to adjudicate. I had to know about the progress in English of about 2,200 pupils, and there were daily notes expressing concern for some of the less able and whether individual pupils should have remedial supplementary work (which I should set). Whenever I walked into the staff room I had three or four of the 140 members of staff trying to tell me about specific problems. The system required any girl singled out for discipline to write a letter of apology in triplicate, a copy of which was sent home by post. I had to supervise the writing of such letters. The writers did not want to admit to the offence they were apologizing for as they knew their parents would soon be reading their admission in their own handwriting, and I had to use all my diplomatic skills of persuasion to cajole them into confessing in writing to whatever misdemeanour they were alleged to have committed.

I held weekly Department meetings and was responsible for putting full minutes in the Head's basket. As a Senior Teacher I was in charge of exams, including the security of all exam papers which I kept in a locked filing cabinet in a locked room. I had other duties delegated to me by the two Deputy Heads. Every evening I had to mark work, especially the 'O' level and 'A' level essays which had to be turned round within 24 hours. I would go to bed at midnight having worked non-stop since 7.45 a.m., having run very hard all day without reducing the number of outstanding tasks. Each day made no impact on the width of my bulging file. Even though I turfed out a hundred of yesterday's papers, a hundred more of today's flowed in. Any lyric poems I wrote were in hasty snatches at lunchtime or after dinner when I should really have been doing schoolwork. I was one of the main administrators in the school, but I was one of its biggest slaves.

Lyric and reflective poetry
Christening of Matthew in High Beach church, Epping Forest

Ann had returned to St James Norlands after her maternity leave. Matthew, still under one, was left with the wife of a local vicar, whose vicarage was in Westway. The vicar's wife was heavily involved in the local community, and Matthew spent time in the church playgroup and in local pensioners' gatherings, where he would crawl round the old folk. He sometimes came back with the pockets of his blue baby-grow filled with pennies they had given "the angelic little boy".

At the end of October Matthew was christened in the church in the Forest, High Beach. Tuohy and Margaret were godparents. They both came to Brechin Place, and I drove them out to Loughton, passing leaves turning red and gold. We all had lunch at Journey's End with my mother and my brother Robert, the other godparent. Tuohy said of me, "He doesn't like our society, whereas I am fairly friendly towards it." I maintained: "There is a case to be made out for seeing the artist as outside his society and judging it." Then I took Tuohy and Margaret for a drive to Clare's madhouse at Lippitt's Hill and Tennyson's coach-house at High Beach.

Two babies were being baptised. The vicar, a white-haired, deaf man, gave us a talk about "our perilous times", which Tuohy later criticised ("he shouldn't bring politics into it"), and Matthew was baptised with a scoop of holy water from a scallop shell and signed with the cross. There was a tea party at my mother's, followed by evening drinks. Tuohy and Margaret returned to London. Margaret (who had not met Tuohy before that day) told me, "Tuohy felt 'I am nothing' during the service, I was watching him."[27] Tuohy later sent me a card: "The origin of Christianity is esotericism – why should the Church have anything to do with society?"[28] I believe his comment was as much a criticism of Margaret as of the High Beach church. After they had left I walked on the lawn under the pear-tree with John Ezard.

A few days later Ann and I visited Worthing and had dinner in the Amsterdam with Margaret. I had a disagreement with Margaret which began a widening between us. She showed me a painting of three chrysan-themums "which represented purity". The three flowers may have been Ann, Matthew and me or the three godparents, but they looked ragged and I pointed out that they looked past their best. She said that they came from her heart, but I pointed out that the heart and head should be mixed as in

Donne. She then said that art is unimportant compared with business. Again I disagreed and pointed out that Yeats wrote, "The intellect of man is forced to choose/Perfection of the life or of the work." Margaret had chosen perfection of the life; I had chosen perfection of the work, the most recent work being 'The Weed-Garden'.[29]

Finishing 'The Weed-Garden'

I at last finished my long poem 'The Weed-Garden'. I wrote: "Today, 2 November, I finished 'The Weed-Garden', once through. It comes to 30 pages and I am too tired to count lines." I wrote about the theme of the poem: in some detail. I ended:

> Overall argument. The soul must be treated like a plant or it will not unfold; in which case civilization, art and religion decline…. The soul *can* unfold and renew, it has a future, our culture can be saved.

This thinking would find its way into *The Fire and the Stones*. I was still revising the poem at the end of November, when I wrote: "Am ill. Fever, temperature, but it is going. Finished Part One of '[The] Weed-Garden' yesterday, rewriting, but too ill to touch it today. I have no stamina any longer."

I revised 'The Weed-Garden' throughout December. I wrote entries in my *Diaries* regarding my attitude and settled the titles of the four parts of the poem. I wrote: "When souls do not unfold, civilization declines." And: "The 14th century was the blossom time of Western civilization." On 22 December I "finished '[The] Weed-Garden' which was first drafted in Cornwall".[30] 'The Weed-Garden' had taken me over four months to write (18 August–22 December 1975).

Idea for epic poem: Overlord

I had been thinking about my poetic epic. On 6 December I wrote, "Decided to call my epic *Overlord*." And: "I travelled to prepare for *Overlord*." On 28 December: "It is my destiny to write a 12-book epic about the Second World War. Now I have finished '[The] Weed-Garden', finally and irrevocably, I have planned the 12 books [of *Overlord*], and must now fit in the Christ-Devil theme and get the form right…. I am afraid in case my other project, which seems tame by comparison, will interfere with this my main work." My "other project" was a book about the Light in relation to 25 civilizations, which eventually became *The Fire and the Stones*.

The Christmas holidays had come. I had been overworked throughout the year but noted: "I have much to be grateful for. A little boy who walks!"[31] In early January Matthew climbed out of his cot, and throughout the coming months he plodded round the flat, crawling into my study and sitting back, one leg under the other, and beaming at me while I wrote, and I would smile happily back at him.

'The Labyrinth'
On 22 February I returned to 'The Labyrinth'. I recorded: "Wrote to an end my 16-page draft for 'The Labyrinth'.... I am very tired within. Have not been away this half-term. Would like some sea air, but too tired to get it.... This morning wrote 'The Moon' for Ann, on our second anniversary today, using the image of the Apollo 10 Command Module, which we saw at the Science Museum yesterday [with Nadia]."

'The Labyrinth', subtitled '(Images from a Dying Mind)', was set in a large house in Epping Forest. I had met the Godfreys by accident at Matthew's christening. They were in the congregation for the other baby being christened. They were converting Warren Hill House, a large house in Manor Road, Buckhurst Hill which they were renaming Warren Hall, into apartments, and they invited me to look at a ground-floor apartment that was ready, which could be ours if we paid a 10-per-cent deposit. I had asked my mother if she would consider selling her house and moving into Warren Hall along with Argie and ourselves, and we had taken a look. It had been owned by the Lustys, and I had been to tea there when I was an Oaklands pupil. The apartments had high ceilings and retained many of the 19th-century features. Nothing came of our interest as my mother was not interested in selling immediately – it was too far from the shops for her – and Ann and I would need to sell our flat first and I would need to find work closer to Epping Forest. I had written on 21 February, "I move in the labyrinth of my mind." 'The Labyrinth' was set in Warren Hall and embodied the ideal of returning to live in Epping Forest. I had written, "Like the Reeve [in Chaucer's *Prologue*] I will live on a heath."[32] (This I would do, half a mile from Warren Hall.)

Whispers from the West
That day, 22 February, began a period in which I wrote lyrical poems, and was transformed back to being a reflective and lyric poet. In this period I wrote much of what became *Whispers from the West*. On 26 February I noted: "Type up the 3 poems I drafted yesterday: 'Angels near a Fairground Hell'; 'Love like a [length of] Cloth'; and the other one. ['Lament of the Cast-off Shirt'.]... I am a poet of domesticity: of domestic things." And: "Wrote another poem, 'Like a Tin of Fly Spray'. (Or rather, drafted it late last night; polished and typed it this afternoon.)... My Head-of-Department job is speeding me up. My brain is becoming more complex as I have to cope with more complex things, and consequently it is easier to write poems."

I was still being overworked, and there was never enough money from Garratt Green to finance my mortgage and family. I observed wryly: "I get £356 a month and am still £20 down on the first day, once the overdraft (£200 currently) has eaten into my salary. Running hard to stand still or fall behind." But still the lyrics came. On 1 March as I was writing, a bomb went off around 7, with an echo like thunder: an IRA bomber had blown himself up. I wrote a poem 'A Boo-oom and an Undeaf Ear'. On 13 March I wrote: "Yesterday and the day before scribbled half a dozen poems, which just came by themselves. Domestic situations, everyday experience, 'making the familiar strange'. I put them down hastily, and to my astonishment three of 6 stanzas rhymed without my realising it, so deep were the words.... I make poems out of little things." Later I noted: "Today have drafted some 10 poems."

In March my mother's health deteriorated. She reported to different members of the family that on the night of Saturday 10 March she had a cramp in her leg which paralysed her right side for ten minutes, and that the same had happened again on the next two mornings. My aunt Argie took her to the London Hospital on the Monday afternoon and she was categorised as having had a "small stroke". In fact she told my brother Jonathan that she had had three strokes on the Sunday morning and had 'spaced the strokes out' so we would not worry. Later my sister Frances phoned. She said that my mother had had *five* strokes (affecting a leg, a hand, her speech, and two more affecting a hand) and had managed to deceive Jonathan so as not to alarm him. I visited her a couple of times in the London Hospital. She lay in bed connected to the tube of a drip. She seemed to make a good recovery but it was agreed by all that Journey's End was now too much for her and that she should move to a smaller house.

I was still writing poems. On 27 March I typed up another two poems and felt I had recorded the spoken voice naturally, like Herbert and Donne. I wrote: "Ideas no longer seize me. I can cope better, i.e. get them into poems better. This is being a poet. Ideas/images come, then I am blissfully calm and can write them up.... The more the work, the more the mind races and makes you creative." On 4 April I wrote: "My ten lost years, when I could not finish anything to my own satisfaction. Now I have a spring of images that bubbles from me, and that is my feeling – whatever comes out of this spring. Feeling/spring, i.e. what strikes me strongly, what comes out of my flow." I was still in my Night of Unknowing. I had seen the blue light in my bath on 21 December 1975, and on 11 April recorded: "A blue light when I close my eyes in my bath."[33]

At the D-Day beaches for Overlord
I interrupted *Whispers from the West* as I wanted to see the D-Day beaches for

my poetic epic *Overlord*. I took Ann to France from 12 to 15 April while her mother looked after Matthew. I summarised my impressions very briefly in my *Diaries*:

> From Cherbourg to Valognes and St Mère-Eglise – the church in the deserted square, the museum with the WACO plane/glider; the tank. On to Utah beaches. The monuments and American flags, the German bunkers and film. The sea defences. The yellow sand. Primroses in the hedgerows, fields and cows. (France is agricultural whereas Britain is industrial.) The Omaha beaches. The cliffs, the part where so many died. The American Military Cemetery. Nearly 10,000 crosses. On to Bayeux – William the Conqueror's Cathedral, the tapestry and the war…. Arromanches and the Mulberry. Juno and Sword beaches, then on to Pegasus Bridge, all iron, and the first house to be liberated. On to Cabourg – Le Home; the antelope statue; then Deauville, Trouville. Back to Caen. Then Ouistreham. Stayed at the Hotel Le Chalet, having found Caen full…. On to Boron next morning, which we never found; but did find hill 112. Also Falaise. The wader's fountain. The Castle. The gap – the road. On to Chartres [Cathedral]. Heaven in the stained glass…. The light changing. On to Versailles. Trianons. On to Paris. This morning Rouen. Joan's tower, the place where she was burned; the Cathedral bells – the service. The Abbey sanctuary we never found.

In Chartres Cathedral I watched the sunlight illumine the stained glass and observed: "How the Light affects the soul…. A soul like this glass. So Heaven can be in the soul."

Back in England I was "rapt" on Easter Sunday night. I wrote: "Rapt…. Lay down on my bed, saw the white light – also the rose-light through rings and the shield of God and Kandinsky-like patterns and squiggles. See [C. Day] Lewis's *Poetic Image*: does the poet fish for this?... Now feel tired. This is the first time I have seen the rose-light, so far as I recollect." I wrote a poem, 'Rapt'. On 19 April, Easter Monday, after visiting Loughton I observed: "My poetry has to be scanned like Latin verse…. And there may be 3 syllables (or even, on occasion 4 syllables) to a foot. These poems are not addressed to the public; they are private poems on which the public is allowed to eavesdrop…. They catch a tone of unaffected simplicity."[34]

'The Fall of the West'

I returned to *Whispers from the West*. We went to Lincolnshire to see Nadia in her new red-brick house, which had a green lawn in front of it. We went to Grantham and saw Newton's school. Back with my poetry I reflected: "In a poem, go for the image and for the eternal." On 28 April I wrote:

Worked on school business until 6, bathed, typed up last night's draft of the [then] last poem in my book, 'Wistful Time-Travellers'. At 10.35 p.m. the title [of the volume] came to me: *Whispers from a Wistful West* – which I changed to *Wistful Whispers from the West*, then to *Whispers from the West*.

The next day I wrote:

I live near my "Pierian" spring: I have built my house near it and I drink from it each day. I was about to do the washing-up and my fourth poem came up like being sick – gold prospector. [('Gold').] 60 something poems in 9 weeks (since Feb 22nd)!

And: "The poet as gargoyle – spouting grotesquely, projecting from gutter, carrying water away from wall; with a grimace on its face."

I thought I had finished *Whispers from the West* but I was still adding poems. On 5 May I observed: "Matthew with a daisy-chain in his hair." I saw each daisy as a poem held together in a chain or volume. The next day:

Tired today. Then, after finishing my reports, I wrote a poem – and immediately I felt all right. I sometimes wonder how I would be if I had to earn my living at writing. Dead, probably. In 1970 I vowed I would turn with a savage fury. Now, after 17 volumes of poetry, I have turned with a savage fury. All the strictures of the Movement break down over Catullus and Horace, who had a personal, 'egocentric' outlook. The 'I' in Horace and Catullus. The Romantic 'I' in Keats's "I stood tiptoe".[35]

I was now writing 'The Fall of the West', which was about terrorism. I noted in my *Diaries*:

I am saying (1) intellectuals are opting for Tyranny as opposed to democracy all over Europe; (2) this is a disease within... which saps the health of the West; (3) the germ began with the Nihilists and can lead to revolution; (4) it can also lead to our being overrun by Russia...; (5) final passionate appeal: let us not go Tyranny, so that democracy dies.... The West may fall unless we crush the [pro-tyrannical] left.

And again:

Title: 'The Fall of the West'. Will the West fall? My attitude must not be Yes, must not be No. I must warn of the danger like an *Old Testament* prophet. Decided to make it 3 parts: symptoms, the disease, the cure.... Our disease is only a neurotic figment of the imagination – if we see things correctly.

My thinking about terrorism set me thinking about the future of Western civilization, and I found I needed the *Encyclopedia Britannica* to clear my thoughts. I needed to consult it for *Overlord* as well. I ordered a set.

Meanwhile the poems continued:

> *Whispers from the West* has taken me over. I began to clear up some 10 poems and have now done getting on for 100, and these new poems are holding me up. In one week I have finished 'Fall of the West' which began as 4 stanzas and ended as 140 lines. In this collection I am speaking to a later Age in the future, and so I am able to generalise the present.

At the end of May I slipped a disc. The pain came on as I was driving home from school. I could not get out of my car. I drove straight to my doctor in Hereford Square. He lay me face down and pulled my left leg and right arm back as if he were handling a bow, and then my right leg and left arm. He told me to do an exercise that involved holding on to both handles of a door and rising on tiptoe on first the right and then the left foot. I took to my bed. I "had a slipped disc... and have spent 3 days in bed.... The other day I saw the red light for the second time, like a stained-glass window, when I was on my back. Ever since that time I have had sporadic trouble with my back."

At last I finished *Whispers from the West*. On 5 June I recorded: "Have finished my poems.... All my energy has been going into my poems. *Whispers from the West* was written between 22 February (about) and around 22 May (most of it). I used to write so much in my *Diaries*; now it goes into my work – my art."[36]

The West must toughen its attitude to survive

But I felt uneasy about 'The Fall of the West'. Line 2 of that poem recorded: "Thirty civilizations have tumbled to dust." Was it exactly 30? And (in 1976) the poems spoke of "An enemy within the heart of the West" long before the politicians used that slogan in the 1980s. The end of the poem pronounced "the fall of West" a "delusion". I was not saying that the West was about to fall, but that the West must toughen its attitude if it was to survive. The pressing question was: would it survive? I knew I would have to research into civilizations.

On 19 June I took delivery of the *Encyclopedia Britannica*. I could now begin my research. This effectively put an end to my outpourings of short lyric poems as I began a switch of my energies from poetry to history. The poems would continue, but at a more reflective level while I explored Western civilization. Meanwhile I wrote a short essay on the imagination, the faculty that forms images of external objects not present to the senses.[37]

Kingsley Shorter on the Light

I had been living intensely finishing my poems and I welcomed distractions from the outer world as I wound my effort down. My old Oxford friend Kingsley Shorter came to dine at Brechin Place. He lived in Scotland with his actress wife and was on one of his rare forays to London. He was still pale and lean, and still went to Subud, which he described as a sect of Islam. ("I observe Ramadan".) I told him about my experiences of illumination, and he said: "My *guru*, Pak Subu, had a similar experience at the age of 24. For him it was the great experience of his life."

Since Oxford Kingsley had worked with the UN as a Russian interpreter and had made a lot of money. He was now freelance and earned more than my annual teaching salary for three months' interpreting a year at the disarmament talks. He spoke of the UN's bureaucratic nature and told me that the Russians would not invade the West but would "nibble away gradually".[38] He gave me news of our mutual Oxford friends, "the comrades" as he laughingly called them. Perry Anderson had written a book, *Lineages of the Absolutist State*; Adrian Hohler had left the Foreign Office and gone into banking; Erica Cheetham had written a book on Nostradamus; and James Greene (son of Sir Hugh Greene, Director General of the BBC, and a nephew of Graham Greene) had sent me his best wishes. We had a very pleasant evening but I did not see him again.

Visit to Wandsworth prison: Hell, Balcombe-Street terrorists Harry Duggan and Joseph O'Connell

The next day I visited Wandsworth prison as the guest of the father of a pupil, the Czech Mr Burdysek, who worked there as a warder. I had taken his daughter for 'O'-level English Language – she later heard that she had got an A – and he had invited me at a parents' evening. Driving to and fro past the prison I had seen it as a Hell of smoky black towers with an enormous clock, and I had written in 'A Vision near the Gates of Paradise': "Hell is a dungeon like Wandsworth prison,/With a portcullis and gate clock." I knocked on the "studded gates of Hell".[39]

He was waiting for me in uniform and took me to meet the Deputy Governor, who told me: "You can't see the gallows." Wandsworth prison maintained a gallows in working order. I was taken to A, B, C and D blocks, passing netting over gates and arches and prisoners in dungarees, and we came out through E block. I passed the room with the gallows (where Derek Bentley, with whom I had played as a child, was hanged on 28 January 1953). It was next to the Censor's Office.

We walked to the hospital section and passed padded cells with spyholes. We went back to the cells and Mr Burdysek pointed out a staircase and said, "Look, Balcombe siege." Up the stairs, carrying buckets and mops, walked two of the IRA Balcombe-Street-siege terrorists who had been arrested, hands up, on television at night on a London balcony, one with a longish wad of hair. They wore open-necked shirts and trousers, and I recognised them instantly: Harry Duggan, alias Michael Wilson, once the most wanted man in Britain, who was supposed to have shot Ross McWhirter, the twin brother of Norris McWhirter, as he opened his front door; and Joseph O'Connell. Duggan was not in the least threatening, he was much smaller than me, rather weedy, very inoffensive and had no presence, and I immediately knew that Ross McWhirter would have opened his front door and not been at all afraid in the second or two it took this mild man to produce a gun and shoot him.

As they passed me they gave me a courteous half-smile and nodded, and I had a split second to decide my attitude. Should I cut them dead and freeze them out as IRA murderers?

Social etiquette took over, and I half-smiled and nodded back, addressing the soul rather than the murderer in each of them, being aware of their potential rather than of what they had done. On reflection I was glad that I had acknowledged them and felt that my instinctive decision was right.

Soon afterwards Tuohy looked in unexpectedly. He had met the poet Donald Davie in the US and found him "very dry". He was set to go back to Japan the following April. Matthew was in his lobster-pot (as I called his round netted play-pen) and he stood up and held on to the round rail and grinned at his godfather.

Interested in Harbour-master's House at Charlestown

Ann and Matthew drove to Cornwall. Nadia was staying with me in London. I returned her and then joined them by train. Ann and Matthew met me on the platform, and on the way back we stopped to watch the Carnival at the end of Ann's mother's road.

That evening Ann and I went down to Charlestown, the local harbour, and I wrote: "I would like to live in the Harbour-master's House." This was the most seaward house that had a view of the harbour, the beach and the entire bay. I had already sensed that this was the house that I had 'seen' when I was at Oxford as being where I would write many of my works.

Charlestown's harbour

Locusts upon the Earth *and work on* Overlord

Feeling a need to understand the period of my secret work, I wrote a plan for *Locusts upon the Earth*, a study of my life as a secret agent what I described in *My Double Life 1:This Dark Wood*. (The 'locusts' referred to the spreading plague of Communists.) I had related myself to history and society, and had thought about the coming Europe. This was part of my emerging unitive vision. I now entered a time when I was groping towards new developments in my way of seeing new angles in literature, philosophy and history.

I had been reading about the war for my epic. I now planned my epic and worked out its metaphysical superstructure, which involved Christ and Satan. I was absorbing the physical structure of Cornwall for this work. On 2 August, "we went to Polkerris, and Matthew and I looked in rocky pools". On 3 August Ann and I returned to Charlestown in the evening. I wrote: "The moon was over the headland, and a wriggling eel of yellow light in the harbour." The next afternoon we "went to Trenarren and lay down on the top of the Black Head among burnt gorse.... We also saw Portmellon, Mevagissey and Gorran." We went to Fowey and Polruan and looked at Tristan's stone. In between I wrote and sunbathed in the garden of Ann's mother's house. We went to the Scilly Isles and saw Sir Harold Wilson walking towards the harbour walls with his wife and entourage. I wrote a story, 'A Wag in Lyonesse'. On 13 August I wrote of Charlestown: "The moon on the sea last night, the triangle and causeway of moonlight, the two night anglers." I went to Charlestown again and wrote: "Bats, dripping stars, no moon. On Charlestown harbour I felt giddy, lost among so many stars, some bright, some not. My feet on my world, and so many other worlds. The vastness of the universe, which I felt so often in the desert."

We drove back to London via Longleat. We stood and looked at

Tumblers Bottom, where Tuohy had lived – it was now a herb farm – and visited Bath. On our return I visited Churchill's war rooms below the Treasury in London, for my epic. Soon afterwards I went to Churchill's home at Chartwell.[40]

Classical style: "Baroque Gates of Hell"
I now saw my literary work as a combination of Classical and Romantic approaches. On 29 August I watched a programme on television about Betjeman's *Summoned by Bells* and wrote: "The line goes from Wordsworth's *Prelude* through *Summoned* to my *Silence*." Of Betjeman's style I wrote: "Few metaphors, few similes; a plain, flat, almost prosaic style of everyday reflection." I was exploring classicism:

> In the cycle of styles,... pre-classical... leads to classical (harmony and proportion), which is [the style of] my epic. I have finished my Baroque *Gates of Hell* and am now concerned with balance and proportion – the classical values.... I am on the side of the poem as image and organic form (the Coleridgean imagination) but I am also on the side of the Journey, the mysticism, the Baroque.

In this 1976 *Diary* entry I saw *The Gates of Hell* as a Baroque work. I now saw Modern Art as a mannerism that would lead to a new Baroque period, but also wondered if "Modern Art was a Primitivism preparing for a Classicism".[41]

Administration and Europe
I write a paper, 'The European Resurgence'
I had been an administrator in my school and now turned my management skills and leadership to advancing the revival of Europe.

I had been thinking about the European civilization. Intuitively I sensed that a revitalising European renaissance was taking shape. I had worked on this in the course of September and sensed that a European Resurgence was ahead, which I connected with the United States of Europe I had first anticipated as far back as Festival of Britain year, 1951. I had been an administrator in my school and now turned my management and leadership skills to leading forward the revival of Europe. I was away from school for two days, having been giddy, on 4 and 5 October, and wrote 'The European Resurgence'. I recorded: "Am exhausted from writing 'The European Resurgence'. I have got to the end in draft.... I must rest, i.e. go back to school tomorrow and relax.... I started 'Resurgence' when I finished my syllabus two weeks into this term." My paper (*see* Appendix 5, p.925) envisaged the collapse of Soviet Communism; a European superstate, a

United States of Europe that would include the UK; and an eventual world government – a vision of which I had had in the Cathedral of the Archangel in Moscow on 9 June 1966 and reflected in my poem 'Archangel' (lines 276–300).

I had not formalised the end of one historical stage in the European civilization and the beginning of another – that did not happen until I codified stages in *The Fire and the Stones* – but I now saw history in terms of Light: "The Light being the Catholic, mystical tradition of the Church in the West from 550 to 1150 at the beginning of the Holy Roman Empire." In early November I began a draft for what eventually became *The Fire and the Stones*: "Fireworks yesterday in the gardens for Matthew; and now to my amazement I have a 12-chapter book.... My destiny has been to recall this generation to the Light.... I am merely an agent of the Divine will – an espionage image."[42]

I talk with Margaret Thatcher on liberating East-European nations

I was clear that the obstacle to a new United States of Europe and to a European Resurgence was the Soviet Union's occupation of Eastern Europe. In November I was invited to hear Margaret Thatcher, then Leader of the Opposition, address the Conservative Group for Europe at the Waldorf Hotel on 24 November. Dinner was in a large room and I was on an outside table. I was told that if I had a question I could write it down and Margaret Thatcher would include it in her speech. I wrote a question on my place card about the Soviet occupation of Eastern Europe and asking for a more fundamental British link with the European Christian Democrats to encourage the collapse of Soviet Communism. I sent it in.

Margaret Thatcher spoke with impressive fluency, wearing a pale floaty-green dress, and much of her speech was devoted to the Christian Democrats. At the end I went across to where she was standing near the table and thanked her for her answer to my question, and again stressed the need for the East-European nations to be free.[43] I asked her, "What are you going to do about the half of Europe that's occupied?"

We stood in a furniture-free area, and a crowd gathered round us almost immediately. Douglas Hurd (Edward Heath's Political Secretary in 1970 and later Margaret Thatcher's Foreign Secretary) was by her side. Mrs. Thatcher said to me: "You must remember that they [i.e. the Soviet Union] are used to living under a vast government, psychologically, they are not used to freedom. You have to do it through propaganda, radio broadcasts."

I told her "It needs more than propaganda." I said it should come from the European Parliament, and that there should be a movement to liberate the East-European nations from the USSR – a liberation movement.

She gave me a long look. I did not then know what her true views on

Europe were: that she was as anti-Europe as she was anti-Soviet.

Then Douglas Hurd took me aside and said, "Come and have a drink." He bought me a drink at the bar and said: "You are quite right, we should mention Eastern Europe much more in our speeches than we do." I half-wondered whether I should become a European MP and proclaim the European Resurgence, and freedom of Eastern Europe, from within the European Parliament. I wrote Mrs. Thatcher a letter and enclosed my essay on the European Resurgence, and this act would have repercussions in the mid-1980s. (*See* Appendix 5, p.925.)

Opposing post-Renaissance European philosophy: bringing the metaphysical Light back into philosophy
I had also turned my attention to philosophy. I thought my way back to the time of the Renaissance and considered the tradition of multiplicity in philosophy since that time in contrast to the previous unity made possible by the metaphysical Light. I wrote:

> Today, Friday, after a hard week at school, I overthrew the whole of modern philosophy since the Renaissance – both Rationalism and Empiricism, and the isms that follow from them.... I have been working on the essay ['The European Resurgence'] until midnight every night for the last three or four weeks, and my overthrow follows quite naturally from my earlier findings. I have just demolished the whole of philosophy.... Unity, not multiplicity, is my love.... The point is, all the 'isms' of post-Renaissance philosophy came from the pre-Christian Greeks. Now is the time to sweep the lot aside as partial truths by returning to the vision of Fra Angelico and his predecessors, and to the early Renaissance and Classical man.

It is worth noting that the day before my "overthrow" I had more visions: "Two nights ago I saw fine old masters and brilliant visions of patterns, like the inside of a richly-domed Cathedral. (Heaven.) I have not seen the Light recently."

I thought again about my search. I wrote of my time at Oxford: "I regarded as a search what Ricks and others regarded as a science. I went through literature seeking while Ricks had different criteria; he measured. I was sent to Oxford and to the finest tutorial mind of our time (in literature) so that I would search." I reflected on Libya: "I went to Libya to connect myself to the tradition of Cassian: the desert vision and Ghadames spring."[44]

Parenting: medical issues
There were now family medical issues to manage. At the end of September

I had heard that Ann was pregnant: "The news today; Ann is 42 days pregnant with what will be our second (my third) child. I had suspected and was not overly surprised when she told me by whispering as a secret in Matthew's ear, 'Having a baby.'" She would be on maternity leave again and I was now clear that we needed more room. "We need a minimum of four bedrooms, and could do with five."

On 12 November Matthew fell down the stairs and had a bump on his head. The next morning he was flushed. He slept from 10.30. It was a Saturday and I went to the Kensington library to research into the Grail for my poetic epic, leaving Ann to watch over Matthew. I was set to work until 5 p.m. but around 3 I had a strong feeling that all was not well at home. I suddenly knew I had to get home. As I turned into Brechin Place I saw an ambulance scream up to our front door. Two men ran out, threw the door open and rushed upstairs. I followed them, very concerned, to see Matthew in a sort of coma, deathly white, the life gone out of him. Ann, pregnant and distressed, said that he had slept until 2.45 and had then had convulsions. He twitched and had a fit, with slight bubbling.

The ambulance men took him down to the ambulance and we accompanied him to St Stephen's Hospital. We sat with him and I expected him to stop breathing at any time. I turned myself into a healer and asked for the Light to come through while I put my fingers on his forehead and healed him in the hospital cubicle, and within a minute there was a surge of life and Matthew came round, the colour back in his cheeks. I was drained and felt sick. I had to sit down. He had X-rays on his head, which showed no fracture or bleeding, and had tonsillitis diagnosed, which he had had before his fall. His temperature was brought down by a fan.

The next morning, a Sunday, Ann visited the hospital at 7.30. She found that Matthew had had another fit at 6 and yet another as she arrived. He had a fourth fit when I arrived. The doctor said that fits breed fits through the trigger mechanism. He was concerned as Matthew had a low temperature during one of the fits. He had a lumbar puncture, which was clear. There was no haemorrhage. He had to lie flat for 24 hours. There was a yellow stain on his back and a plaster. All day his temperature fluctuated, going up, coming down and going up again. All day a fan whirred to keep his temperature down.[45]

In the afternoon, when I was back at home, Tuohy came. Coincidentally, he had been visiting someone else at St Stephen's Hospital and was looking in on his way back without realising that Matthew was in St Stephen's. He talked about his book on Yeats.[46] He said: "Yeats was a Freemason. Hence 'Sato's ancient blade' – the Freemason's sword."

The next day Matthew began to improve. He had a temperature of 103 during the night but it was down in the morning. He was grizzly but sitting up and playing with books. He was well enough to eat at the table with the other children in his ward, and the next day he was better again.

In early December I was diagnosed as having poor blood flow back to my heart, caused by valve failure. The pooling of my blood gave me varicose veins and a tendency to dermatitis on my ankles.

Ann stopped working at St James Norlands to go on maternity leave at the end of the autumn term, 1976. She was now obviously pregnant. We went to Loughton the first weekend in December. We attended a morning service at High Beach church with Matthew to inform the vicar that there would soon be another christening. It was frosty, and I noted the "crisp" graveyard, "last year's oak leaves covered with wonderful patterns, a blue sky" and "the sun in the evergreen". We walked in the Forest after lunch and passed holly with red berries. There were a dozen skaters on the iced-over pond, and the ice was nearly an inch thick.[47]

Research on the Light: The Secret Light
I thought about the physical field of the manifesting Light: "There is surely a spectrum of light as there is a frequency of sound – from invisible (high frequency?) to visible (low frequency?). The invisible light streams into the body cells and is stored and can be seen psychically, but cannot be seen by the naked eye; it is red, blue, white. The visible light – sunlight – has a different wattage per metre. This may activate our matter – our bodies – with energy and keep us going."

I now worked on a tradition of the Light in dead cultures. By the time we spent Boxing Day at my mother's in Loughton, I was researching into dead cultures – into Egypt and then into Druids and sacred circles – and took Ann to an exhibition on them. I prepared to write a book titled *The Secret Light* (which eventually became *The Fire and the Stones*). I noted of my Mystic Way: "Illumination is a stage, between Purgation and Union. So my Illuminative Way is over."[48]

Search for a larger home: move to 100A Stapleton Road
With a new baby coming I had to manage a move to a larger home. We would need more space, and I was aware that we should move out of Brechin Place, which was up several flights of stairs, into a larger house within reach of my work. However, in early 1977 my overdraft had risen and I was over my bank limit. My account needed an injection of cash. In early February, Ann, Matthew and I moved out of Brechin Place, which we let furnished to an American Professor whose rent went into my account. We moved to a ground-floor flat in an Edwardian terrace near Garratt Green, at 100A Stapleton Road, which we rented for much less than the rent we had received. An old lady lived above us, and there were night-storage

heaters. Here we brought our main possessions and camped. It was only an interim measure – it was not the larger house I was seeking – but the move benefited Ann, who no longer had to cope with flights of stairs, and I endeavoured to write on the sitting-room table.

The move unsettled my writing. I considered how I could make writing instantly commercial and dashed off a couple of pot-boilers, one about a school and one set in Libya. Neither advanced my work, and I could not bring myself to admit to having written them. They were not typical of my writing. I had to recognise that I could not change the writer I was trying to become. A month on, I wrote: "I am a discoverer, a seeker of truth…. I am a solitary, a loner; an explorer; a Captain Scott."[49]

Dinner with Donald Maclean's son

There were complications with Ann's pregnancy. She had high blood pressure. In April Tuohy invited us to a dinner he was giving in London. It was at the house of a relative who kept the Berlin desk at the Foreign Office, but who could not attend herself. Tuohy had invited a relative of his publisher's, Fergus Maclean, the 33-year-old son of Donald Maclean, the British diplomat who defected to the USSR after betraying Western nuclear secrets to Stalin. Donald Maclean's younger brother, Alan Maclean (A.D. Maclean) had been Tuohy's friend at Stowe before becoming his publisher at Macmillan. Fergie Maclean was over in England with his Russian wife Olga and his son, and he seemed to have lost his job as a translator. Ann had been advised to rest, and her doctor advised her not to attend this dinner, so I went on my own.

There were just six of us that evening: Tuohy, me, Fergie and Olga Maclean, and Tuohy's cousin Lady Flavia and her pro-Communist boyfriend, Dr Colin MacCabe, who then taught in Christopher Ricks's English Faculty at Cambridge. Fergie Maclean turned out to be an extremely nice young man. In Moscow he had lived in Philby's household from 1966 to 1968: Fergie's mother Melinda Maclean had left Donald Maclean for Philby for two years and had taken the children with her. I realised the reason Philby had escaped detection so long was such niceness. I sat next to Fergie's Russian wife, a short dark-haired attractive woman, over dinner, and I remember MacCabe saying, "I'd love to live in the Soviet Union," and Fergie saying that Braine's *Room at the Top* had been translated into Russian as *The Attic*. As I had been told that Philby had been on the verge of exposing me in September 1971, I was keen to know what life was like in Philby's household.[50] Fergie was reluctant to talk about Philby. I wondered what Tuohy was doing inviting me to an evening with a Soviet citizen who had lived in Philby's household and who could be expected to return to Moscow and communicate to Philby what I had said. The thought briefly crossed my mind that Tuohy had been a Soviet agent all along.

A few days later Fergie rang me and asked if I could find him a job in the ILEA. (Perhaps I had been invited so that I could find him a job.) Soon afterwards he rang Garratt Green at break when I happened to be in the staff room and said that Olga had gone back to the USSR with his son, and that he would have to return to Moscow, otherwise he would not see his son again. He said over the phone, "I am in effect being blackmailed from Moscow." I stood a few paces from the teachers in my Department and bizarrely talked Moscow with a recent member of Philby's household at the height of the Cold War. Fergie returned to Moscow and I never saw him again.

Birth of Anthony

The diagnosis on Ann was not good. She had mild toxaemia, and had to be admitted to Queen Charlotte's Hospital until the birth, which was officially still six weeks away. I would have to look after Matthew. Ann's mother would come up from Cornwall and mind Matthew during the day at Stapleton Road. I took Ann into hospital, and while I was arranging for her mother to come, she had a crisis. Her blood pressure rose to 140 (bottom line) when the normal is 80, and there was a danger that the baby might be born prematurely. She was taken to intensive care. She said to me when I visited her with Matthew: "You may have difficulty in finding me tomorrow. They may have put me in the garden."

Ann had an ultrasound, which showed the baby had not grown as much as it should, was not being fed through the placenta and was starving to death. The decision was made to induce. On 26 April I arrived at the Labour Ward and sat with Ann, who was plugged into a cardiotachograph, which showed contractions and the zig-zag fetal heartbeat. She had an epidural and I put on a white mask with loops round my ears, a white shower-hat and a white gown that tied at the back of my neck. A nurse said, "The fetal heartbeat is distressed." I tensed. But Ann was calm when the baby's head appeared, covered in green puss: a boy. Ann held him and then I held him and looked with relief at the blood in his eyes mixed with tears as he gave healthy cries. A nurse took him to Special Care. Later I saw him in an incubator: a slim little thing just 4lbs 12ozs with screwn-up eyes and a pink nose, lips and chin and a greeny forehead.

For several days there were bulletins: "Causing anxiety but prospects satisfactory", "improving". I visited and saw him in the incubator, his head in a box with an oxygen tube nearby, a drip and monitor from his tummy. His breathing was very laboured and his breaths were quick; he had been sick and some of what he had brought up had gone back into his lungs. His little fingers closed briefly round mine as I put my hand through the round rabbit-hutch hole. Soon afterwards he developed jaundice. He had a collapsed left lung and had air round his lungs which was being absorbed. But then he began making progress and I knew little Anthony, as we were going to call him, was going to be all right. On 2 May Ann came home. Anthony had to remain in hospital. He came out of his incubator on 6 May and breathed air in his cot. He came home on 15 May.

I was exhausted. I had not slept properly for nearly four weeks, and had been working. I had a bath and noted: "Saw the blue light yesterday. Very vivid. While sitting in my bath. I suddenly felt rapt, and I looked and there it was, round and luminous blue, a deep turquoise. It gathered and formed in a circle and I felt charged through with life afterwards."[51]

School in Epping Forest
As a way out of the financial crisis Ann and I had explored the possibility of buying a small private school which Ann could run. It made sense: I had traced mistakes in university students' English back to their secondary schools, and had now traced mistakes in secondary schoolchildren's English back to their primary schools. It was in the primary schools that mistakes could be prevented. A school in Streatham, Somerville, was on the market for £60,000, and we met the Head, who was keen to sell to us. To buy it we would have to sell Brechin Place. Garratt Green was beginning to pall. I had written: "I do not want to continue at Garratt Green; it has become petty, endless duties and no inspiration.... I only derive satisfaction from my Blake and *Coriolanus* and [Shakespeare's] *Sonnets* classes.... Aimlessness and frustration working for the State. Meaning and fulfilment at growing a family business in education and educating the family [i.e. Matthew and the unborn baby] well."[52]

I looked ahead and felt drawn to Epping Forest: "I have two sons, and I may become rooted in Somerville School. This is all happening away from Hagger country, where my heart is, to which I would love to return." I received a letter from Mabel Reid, my Oaklands teacher: "These have been such anxious days for you both, life weaves such strange patterns.... I know both of you will have faced the challenge with great courage."

Our offer for the school in Streatham turned out to be not enough, and I wrote: "The answer on the Streatham school is No. Now buy one over Epping-Forest way, e.g. start a school.... Start a private school as competition to Oaklands; on the edge of the Forest."[53]

Retreat from becoming an MEP
I had spoken to my MP, John Biggs-Davison, about my encounter with Margaret Thatcher and about liberating Eastern Europe from Communism. He arranged for me to have a preliminary, exploratory interview with

Marcus Fox to see if I should become an MEP (Member of the European Parliament) to work for this liberation of Eastern Europe. I had written a paper entitled 'The Development of the European Community' to state my position. However, I was dubious about becoming an MEP as I wanted to be at home helping with my two boys.

Fox was a bit like a tortoise, lined, creased and swarthy, and he asked what committees I would work on. The idea of being a committee man was not appetising – it made me feel weary and it would take me away from Ann and my two boys, and my poems – and I backed off from becoming a European MP while retaining my commitment to a United States of Europe. I wrote: "Action tempted Rimbaud away from poetry, and did for [i.e. killed] T.E. Hulme. It cut short the literary career of Sheridan. Yet I must act. For actions speak louder than words – and actions give backing to words. A whole man expresses himself through words... and actions."

Soon afterwards I visited Biggs-Davison at the House of Commons and endeavoured to extricate myself from progressing with the idea that I might become a European MP. We had a drink on the terrace and we talked about the political scene. I told him I had sent my essay, 'The European Resurgence' to Margaret Thatcher. He said that she had spoken of a European *'Risorgimento'* ('Resurgence') in Rome, and that the concept may have come from her copy of my paper. He asked me to send him 'The European Resurgence'.

In early July I met the MP for Kensington (Brechin Place's constituency) at the House of Commons, Sir Brandon Rhys Williams, at his invitation. He was a tall ex-Etonian of 50 and he spent some time giving me his left-wing Conservative views on how there was no harm in Eurocommunism as it was democratic Communism and might make the Iron-Curtain countries democratic.[54] He was favouring the *status quo* in Eastern Europe, and I wondered if an organisation had put him up to dissuading me from becoming a European MP (which I had already decided I did not want to be). I profoundly disagreed with his view: Communists had always locked up the opposition, Communism was the enemy of democracy. I had taken a Churchillian path towards Europe – Churchill had advocated a United States of Europe in a speech in Zürich in September 1946 – and I now wanted to see a United States of Europe that included Eastern Europe.

Light-seers

Ann had been looking after Matthew and Anthony throughout the second half of May and June. In July she was ill for two weeks. She had nervous exhaustion after the birth, and glandular fever. She took the two children down to Cornwall to stay with her mother and rest. I stayed in London to look after Nadia, who was visiting.

The summer holidays had begun and I continued my research on the Light. I was reading books for references to the Light: Langland, Bunyan and Dante's *Paradiso*. I took Nadia to see Nelson's *Victory*, and on our return did more research into Boehme and the *Upanisads*. At the end of July I read all Pope. I drove Nadia to Loughton and wrote: "Took Nadia for a walk in the Forest. The lilies on the ponds. The grasshoppers on the Stubbles. The meadow browns and copper browns and ghost moths. Read all Rilke between 6 and 7, had supper, then came home by tube.... Read all Milton save the last nine books of *Paradise Lost*." I read Emerson and Thoreau. I wrote: "Plato affirmed absolute values and a reality that is independent of sense-perception. All Light-seers are therefore Platonists; or (in the Plotinan sense) Neoplatonists."[55]

My poetry and parenting had increasingly come into conflict with my work as an administrator within a school and a revitalised Europe, and this conflict took a new twist in my next episode.

Episode 3:

New Powers and Dogmatic Authority

Years: 1977–1981
Location: London
Works: *Whispers from the West*; *Lady of the Lamp*; *The Fire-Flower*
Initiatives: Third Mystic Life; Metaphysical Revolution

"Myself when young did eagerly frequent
Doctor and Saint, and heard great argument
About it and about: but evermore
Came out by the same door as in I went."
Rubaiyat of Omar Khayyam, trans. by Edward Fitzgerald,
second edition, 1868

I have said that between the Illuminative Way and the Unitive Way there is a further purgation of the spirit in which new powers are received, inspiration seemingly from the cosmos (the ordered universe). In my next episode the tension between new inner powers and the dogmatic authority of the controlling organisation I worked for became acute.

A 'dogma' is "a principle, tenet or system laid down by the authority of a Church", "an arrogant declaration of opinion" (*Concise Oxford Dictionary*). I was under the often dogmatic authority and control of the left-wing system that emanated from the Inner London Education Authority at County Hall, its inspectors and my Head, and the obfuscation of implementing the ILEA's policies in my daily work immersed my soul in thickening mist for long stretches of each day.

New powers
New unitive vision brings with it new powers
I had begun to live through a new centre in my consciousness which instinctively saw the universe as a unity. New unitive vision brings with it new powers. I now found that I was given inspired powers of healing which the cosmos supplied without my really seeking them, and I was drawn to explore the New Age, some of whose tenets resembled unbelievable and controlling dogmas.

Egyptian temple-dancers and healing
I was made aware of these powers and dogmas at a conference on the ancient Egyptians and the Essenes which was held in St John's, Smith Square, London on 30 July 1977. I had been sent a leaflet about it by Flavia Anderson. I had written to her in Edinburgh about her book on the Grail, *The Ancient Secret*, and we had corresponded. At the conference Sir George Trevelyan talked about the Essenes and Denis Stoll about the ancient Egyptians. At regular intervals during the day there was a dance from his five Egyptian temple-dancers to music he claimed had been used in the Egyptian temples.

The day was a revelation. To my recollection I had not encountered the Essenes before, the gentle people who lived on the edge of Lake Mareotis from the 3rd century BC and who peopled the Qumran caves where the Dead Sea Scrolls were found, which I had visited in 1962. I had not properly grasped that the Egyptian *Book of the Dead* was full of experiences of the Light. And throughout the day the five temple-maidens dressed in white moved in trance, striking slow and graceful hand postures, replicating over 900 hand- and foot-poses found in murals in the Egyptian tombs in synchronised movements. Denis Stoll claimed to have received the music from the beyond and to have researched it for accuracy, and he explained that the maidens became "*khus*" – he meant "*akhs*" – or spiritual souls, "Shining Ones". There was a pale, ethereal beauty about the measured dance of these temple-dancers. Watching them, I was aware of a spiritual, occult tradition that had flourished before the Christian tradition, which was in contact with the Light and rejected the materialistic point of view.

Rev. John Jewsbury

At lunch in the crypt I found myself sitting next to the Rev. John Jewsbury, a Unitarian minister from Sketty, Swansea. He conducted services of mass-healing at his church through the laying-on of hands, and he took part in a group for absent healing. He looked at me and said quietly, "You have the power to heal." I said I was going down to Cornwall the next day, where Ann had a bad headache (a prolonged consequence of her toxaemia) and we arranged that I would heal her that first evening at 9 p.m. and then ring him. He gave me instructions: I was to become a channel for the healing power, and his group would be backing me up.

The next day I travelled to Cornwall and sat with Ann at 9 p.m. I "felt a surge of power that left me cold – it hit my back and ran through my arms and out, at 9. I tried again 5 minutes later and felt power sweep through me again. Ann felt an accumulated warmth from my fingers, but not a sudden burning…. I felt two different surges." Afterwards I rang Jewsbury, who saw the rushes as 'spirits', in which he dogmatically believed. But I did not think I had been invaded by spirits. To me, a power from the beyond had surged through me, entering my back and coursing along my right arm into my little finger and out into Ann.

The next day I tried again at 9 p.m. I wrote: "[The power] came through me, entering my back and sweeping along my arms and out into Ann,… making me shiver and tingle, four times. Then there was a massive [surge] which lasted twice as long. All were different: each different in character. A tingling sensation." I rang Jewsbury, who told me that Mrs. Jewsbury received a headache in the middle or back of her head around 9.05. Jewsbury reckoned that Ann's headache had been transferred to his wife.

Now I think energy flows through me like water through a pipe. I have to empty myself of any obstructing ego which can block the flow. The ego blocks the pipe like a lump of Plasticine. I have to pack the Plasticine round the pipe to let the water flow through. If I can do that, I can channel the healing energy, which is independent of human beings.

I healed Ann again the next day: "9.45 p.m., Tuesday…. I burned and was cold at the same time in my back and was very restless, then four waves came through me. Ann said my hand was cold. She burned at the 4th wave…. The cold rushes through me were felt as burning by Ann." The next night I healed Ann again, and "was hot and cold at the same time and my fingers burned". The following night there were "four rushes, followed by another four. All more gentle than before, each different. The 3rd of the second lot was very strong. Ann's forehead burned, my hands felt hot. I had power in me. My hair sparked to the comb later."[1] The following night I had six rushes, the next night three and the next night four. Jewsbury then suggested that I discontinued for a while. By now Ann's headaches had been completely cured.

In Cornwall we spent days in Charlestown on the beach below the Harbour-master's House, the most seaward house, where in *The Eagle Has Landed* Col. Radl (played by Robert Duvall) was shot against a breakwater. I digested the Essenes, and realised I had made my first contact with the New Age movement. The New Age was a movement of heretics who challenged the Church with their belief in spirits – like Jewsbury's – and in reincarnation, angels and higher intelligences. It was a new heresy whose worldview had drawn attention to my new healing powers, and so I was interested in it – and in the Essenes who lived close to the Earthly Mother in fields, aware of the sun, air and water. I thought of the sea-eagle's domain in the invisible spirit-like air, above the shark's domain in the tangible, material sea. I wrote four stories, seeking to understand my new experience.

The Light returned and I wrote:

I saw glimmerings, the celestial curtain, the star, the dawning, but not as yet the round sun – all pale white. And between times I saw my imagination, a lovely 'carpet' full of colours, a perfect pattern; and a stained-glass window of breathtaking splendour, with a red saint on it. O, and I saw a cloud over a sun with lines of gold finely wrought all round it. I need leisure for these visions, I need to be unwound, and Charlestown can do it. I could sit on my cliff and look down on the harbour from an eagle's height and feel the peace of sea and country and town and sky, a great oneness from my eagle's eyrie.

I saw a house on the Cornish cliffs as an eyrie, home of the eagle, and I wrote: "I look forward to a quiet, retired life on the cliffs of Charlestown."

Meanwhile I revelled in the physical world of the beach at Charlestown beside my wife and two sons: "Sunday, on Charlestown beach. Distant thunderings, the gull gleaming against the black sky. The green water and limpid, translucent rocks."[2]

We returned to London. Soon afterwards we sunbathed in Hereford Gardens (to which we had a key), and Matthew crawled away across the lawn and hoisted himself up by a man lying on a sunbed stripped to the waist and reading, and tickled his toes. The man put down his Parliamentary report, and I realised it was Biggs-Davison, our MP at Epping Forest, who then lived the other side of Hereford Square. I put my book up and hid my face, pretending that Matthew was nothing to do with me. Eventually I had to retrieve him and sauntered over to say hello to Biggs-Davison.

Research into the Light
I had written no poems since 1976. I was unearthing the occult stream which

preceded Christianity and flowed alongside it, and I was doing research into the New Age universe and into the mystic tradition over 5,000 years for *The Secret Light*. From the reserve stock of the larger London public libraries – for which my time in Kingswood library, Dulwich, now seemed a preparation – I found Friedrich von Hugel's *The Mystical Element in Religion* and Anna Kingsford's *Clothed with the Sun*. I saw the Light as a spiritual sun. This work that would portray a universe into which the healing energy could pour would become Part One of *The Fire and the Stones*. Back at school I taught D.H. Lawrence's *The Rainbow* for 'A' level, time spent on a symbol that antic-ipated the title of this work. I did not realise that I was resting before a new, intense outpouring of poetry, and I longed to be independent of my London school.

Miss Lord offers Oaklands School at christening of Anthony
Whether openness to one's future destiny is a new power I do not know, but I was now approached with a life-changing offer. In September our second son Anthony was christened at the High Beach church in Epping Forest. After a family lunch at my younger brother's and the afternoon ceremony involving the same scallop shell that had christened Matthew, there was a gathering at my mother's house for tea. Two long-standing friends of my mother's were present: my Oaklands Headmistress Miss Lord and co-owner Mabel Reid, who immediately invited me to go for a Nature walk in the Forest with her.

Standing on the lawn under the pear-tree holding a cup of tea near where I sat with my Oaklands classmates on my sixth birthday and saw my mother pour salt on the stain of spilt damson jam (*see My Double Life 1: This Dark Wood*), Miss Lord, proud, erect and thick-nosed, asked, "What are you and Ann doing?"

I told her that Ann had been teaching at Blackheath and was now teaching at Holland Park, and that we had considered buying a school in Streatham for Ann to run.

"Blackheath?" Miss Lord said. "I came to Loughton from Blackheath. You mustn't go to Streatham, you must have Oaklands." She said: "I'm looking for an Old Boy whose wife is a trained teacher and can be Headmistress, and you fit the bill perfectly. As an educator you'll under-stand the problems of teachers while you run the financial side. I won't go on for ever. Tell Ann to ring and make an appointment to come and spend a day with us."

Her reaction took me completely by surprise. I had a sense that my destiny was contacting me. It had not occurred to me that I could afford Oaklands, the school I attended from the ages of 4 to 8. Only an independent school would give me the independence to spend more time on my writing for which I craved. Ann did later spend a day at Oaklands, but with Anthony so small and with my being immersed in my school activities in Wandsworth, we did not follow the visit up and the situation was left unresolved.

John Ezard, *Guardian* journalist, was a godparent at the christening and stood near Miss Lord under the pear-tree on the Journey's End lawn. I told him I "was on a search till 1971" and that I was researching the tradition of the Light.

Soon afterwards I had further experiences of the Light: "5.30. Relaxed on bed when I got home. I had seen the Light in the bath and all the Paisley colours of my soul, on water as it were, for ripples now and again disturbed them; the Light was blue and very powerful." Again: "After midnight (2 a.m.). Clairvoyant pictures. Can't sleep. Kandinsky scrivenings (*sic*) deep in my mind. An effect of space, me floating through these lovely patterns towards a sunrise. The golden 'cauliflower'. Beautiful detail. Gold light with a gold coin of a primitive emperor on it – who was that emperor?... Beautiful monsters, Tibetan-like, on the floor of my mind."

As I researched the Light I felt I was being introduced to people who would become significant in my life like Miss Lord, and to ideas that would influence my destiny, and I wondered if I was witnessing the workings of Providence.

I was looking for an alternative to my Wandsworth school and had half-wondered if I should go into politics. I had sent Biggs-Davison my essay on the European Resurgence (*see* Appendix 5, p.925) which predicted a unified Europe liberated from Soviet Communism in which all the nations would be federal states under a European Parliament. Now he sent me a pamphlet that made it clear that Conservatives regarded Europe as a cluster of nation-states with no federal links. Biggs-Davison was a nationalist regarding Europe, and my unitary vision of Europe was out of keeping with his Party. But in 1984 I would draw on this essay for my paper, FREE, Freedom for the Republics of Eastern Europe. My essay on the European Resurgence could be seen as Providentially leading to FREE.

I was wondering how I could afford to escape my Wandsworth school for Oaklands when I bumped into the ILEA inspector who had interviewed me for Riverway, Mr Lewis. He had come to see my Head and he knew I was now at Garratt Green. He told me that Riverway School had closed and that all the staff were "supernumerary". "You got out at the right time," he said,[3] and he made me feel glad to be holding the Headship of English in my Wandsworth school.

Receiving new powers in sleep
I carried on my research into the Light by going to hear Paul Solomon in

November. I had been given a leaflet at the conference on the Egyptians and Essenes, and had noted that he had founded the Fellowship of the Inner Light. There was a huge queue, and I was given the last seat. Those behind me were turned away.

He was a large ex-Baptist minister who, like Edgar Cayce, had contacted a source within himself which he regarded as his inspiration. It gave life-readings, predicting people's futures, and he claimed that it always came up with the right answers. Sir George Trevelyan set him in context by speaking on the New Age. At the end I went up to Solomon and asked him, out of curiosity, to describe the inner Light he knew. He said it was a point of reference that gives guidance – enlightenment – when it's needed. I came away not sure that he had even seen the Light I knew.

I read the psychic Edgar Cayce, who had received prophetic visions in sleep, and I knew receiving ideas in sleep would be another 'new power' I would experience. The following August I would receive the view of history I put in *The Fire and the Stones* in my sleep in Cornwall. (*See* p.86.) Looking back, I see my visit to Solomon, when I was the last person to be admitted, as Providential, for it familiarised me with receiving ideas from the beyond in sleep and let me know that I was not alone, that others had also received the 'new powers' I was experiencing in myself.

Thinking about neo-Baroque poetry
While I was researching the occult tradition and the New Age I was thinking about my new Baroque age in poetry. In November 1977 I reflected deeply on my poetic method, and wrote Tuohy a letter about my deepening metaphysical view.[4]

Reading by David Gascoyne, and Kathleen Raine
In response Tuohy proposed that we should go to a poetry reading in a meeting room below a pub in Hampstead. Kathleen Raine was to chair a reading by David Gascoyne. Tuohy said to me in the upstairs room in a loud voice, which the nearby Gascoyne could hear, "He's very dotty, he's been in bins." We shook hands with Mrs. Gascoyne and the bard, a tall distinguished grey-haired man who (I recorded) "looked like a cross between Yeats and Lord Shackleton".

We went down to the cellar and sat at the back. Some 30 were gathered – mostly Hampstead people from the 1940s, we judged – and Kathleen Raine, a small woman with an imperious demeanour and a confrontational manner, spoke against the "journalistic" poems of Auden and the Movement. I observed in my *Diaries*: "Kathleen Raine introduced Gascoyne, who read bad poems (received diction, verbal fustian and monotonous iambic rhythms – a dead language, too little experience, the interior not exteriorised; only one about a field was any good). 'Christ of revolution and poetry' – read in a nonconformist preacher's tone." In the interval I spoke to Kathleen Raine about Flavia Anderson, whose out-of-print book on the Grail I had been reading, and she immediately said, "It's Providence, you can come to RILKO [Research Into Lost Knowledge Organisation] and hear a lecture on Chartres."[5] I noticed that she did not speak to Tuohy at all; they had been together on a summer school in Sligo and had quarrelled. Tuohy had sent me a card saying, "It rains here, and I quarrel with Miss Raine, who is illuminated, while the rest of us are lit up."[6] After the interval Gascoyne read George Herbert, a fellow Anglican. We left early and stopped the reading when Tuohy could not open the door. We had an Arab meal of *kebab* and garlicky lettuce and talked of mystic illumination.

Looking back on that evening I am aware of the workings of Providence – as Kathleen Raine had remarked. For in 1991 my book *The Fire and the Stones* and my *Selected Poems, A Metaphysical's Way of Fire* would be launched by the same two, Kathleen Raine and David Gascoyne (who Durrell called England's foremost metaphysical poet, which was true although I felt he had "never exteriorised his interior"). On Tuohy's initiative I was shown Raine and Gascoyne in 1977, and the reason for my being shown them only became apparent over 13 years later. Often in life a seemingly accidental encounter later becomes significant and with hindsight seems not accidental at all but Providential.

Keith Critchlow on Chartres
On 8 December I attended the lecture on Chartres. It was given at the invitation of RILKO by Keith Critchlow, who Kathleen Raine had told me was a 'genius'. I stood in the foyer of the theatre and bizarrely Kathleen Raine appeared from one side holding a book by Keith Critchlow, and Keith Critchlow appeared from the other side, holding a book of poems by Kathleen Raine. They stood together, face to face, pointing to each other's books. No words could have revealed more clearly that I was in on a mutual-congratulation society. In 1991 Critchlow would give me advice over the telephone on how I should announce *The Fire and the Stones*.

I was yearning to escape Garratt Green: "Am below par in my health. Am tired inside. Too much external distraction…. I have a lifetime's work ahead and I am held back by that… school." Then at the end of term I was asked to take on extra responsibilities at Garratt Green: "Mrs. Kay asked me to join the hierarchy [share the management] and have responsibility for internal and external exams. I groaned within at the work I am being dumped, but smiled and simulated enthusiasm even though it costs me valuable time which should be spent on my books." Again I longed for independence.

Kathleen Raine's neo-Romantic view of poetry versus my neo-Baroque view

I had sent Kathleen Raine some of my poems in the belief that she knew about the Light. To my surprise she replied completely misunderstanding the Light. Not realising that I was trying to unite the Classical and Romantic tradition in neo-Baroque poetry in which the rational 'I' of Movement poetry would experience Reality, the Romantic Light, that in a Universalist work the 'I' of the poet can peep round the objective poem and make contact with the reader, she wrote that "my work is a record of my thoughts about experiences, i.e. the rational intelligence working on the data of the sensible world – not from the 'other mind' from which is born poetic speech. My 'virtues' are articulacy, honesty and discrimination – not luminous vision." She did not seem to recognise my Light as 'luminous vision', and she wanted me to describe it as a neo-Romantic without reference to the classical world of sense-experience. She had not understood that my work fuses thought and feeling. I wrote: "What she overlooks is that mystical Light is, for me, a sense-experience…. I do not like Gascoyne because he ignores the sense-world; she does not like me because I put the sense-world in, and make it symbolise something else." (The Neoclassical Christopher Ricks would omit the neo-Romantic Raine and Gascoyne from his edition of the *Oxford Book of English Verse*.)

I wrote: "I am a Movement poet who has the mysticism of an Eliot…. I am an Elizabethan poet – but a mystical one (not a poet of high dream)." I knew I had been "finding a way back from material sense-experience… to the One, in the rational speaking voice of the Donne–Eliot–Movement tradition, plus Wyatt–Shakepeare's sonnets–Tennyson–Hardy". I wrote of my neo-Baroque approach which was more classical than Raine's neo-Romanticism: "I may receive poetry from… the unconscious,… the symbols of imagination…. My epic will be 'received' like my healing powers. A Classical manner (rational intelligence) balancing inner and outer; a Romantic manner, allowing the prophetic voice to speak through me."

I found Kathleen Raine's *Defending Ancient Springs* in the library at Garratt Green (which was next to my Departmental room, Room 64). The essays in it, on Blake, Coleridge, Shelley and Yeats and on her contemporaries Edwin Muir, Vernon Watkins and David Gascoyne, set out a Romantic tradition of the imagination that drew on the occult tradition from Neoplatonism and the Kabbalah and attacked materialist, secular culture. I agreed with her anti-materialism and anti-secularism and associated the tradition of the imagination with the images I had experienced during my contemplation. However I felt that she had neglected the mystic tradition of experiencing Reality as Light, which was equally anti-materialist and anti-secular. Mystics did not only draw on her occultist tradition. Full of my new Baroque, I felt that she was too severe on realistic art. I wrote: "If a painter paints the outside world (Nature), then is that painting worthless? What about portrait paintings? A painting does not come from the imagination, always. So it is with a poem. Not all poetry can be received in inspiration; that is only one way." In short, I was in a contemplative tradition that included Classical realism and the Romantic imagination – the sense-world *and* imaginative experience beyond it – and was not in an exclusively Romantic imaginative tradition. I noted that in my writing of *The Secret Light* "each time I need to delve into something I am presented with the right person.... It is not I who am writing this book but a power writing it through me." I felt I was discovering new powers within myself that were similar to Yeats's discovery of automatic writing.

I had little time for writing that spring but at weekends I typed up stories I had drafted. I wrote a story about a funeral I had attended of a boy I had taught at Henry Thornton who had been killed on a railway line in November 1976, which I entitled 'The Clear, Shining Sunlight of Eternity'. *The Clear, Shining Sunlight of Eternity*[7] would become the title of Part Two of *A Smell of Leaves and Summer*, my second collection of stories.

Seeing the One revealed in the new physics: Fritjof Capra
During the planning of our move I had researched the One, and I see the hand of Providence in the way I came to attend a Mystics and Scientists conference in Winchester in mid-April. I had been sent a leaflet about it by the organisers of the conference on the Egyptians and the Essenes, and (as I would be hearing him speak) had read Fritjof Capra's *The Tao of Physics*, a book about how the new physics revealed the One of the mystics. The conference was put on by the Wrekin Trust in conjunction with the Scientific and Medical Network. Weirdly, the next time the SMN were involved in this annual Mystics and Scientists conference would be in 1992, when I would give the first lecture that would later form part of my book *The Universe and the Light*.

The conference was at King Alfred's College. There were 400 registered, and there was an overflow hall with televised covering of the lectures, which I was in. I was staying off site in a student's room in Winchester. The discomfort was considerable, and it was cold, but I spoke to Capra, who looked like a tousled-haired pop star. He told me he had obtained his mysticism from Stace's *The Teachings of the Mystics*, and I knew from our conversation that he did not know the Light. I later read Stace and confirmed that the Light is not mentioned in the excerpts he chose.

I also spoke to Pir Vilayat Inayat Khan, the bearded and ancient Sufi leader who in 1975 had led a large Cosmic Mass at the Temple of the Understanding (an inter-faith organisation founded with 'Rockefeller' money). He was the brother of the British agent Madeleine (Noor Inayat

Khan). I asked him how he thought the Light is received, and he told me it comes in at the base of the spine, into the *chakras*, and that it is conveyed to the head. His account differed from the Christian mystics' view, and my view, that the Light enters the head first – it is the healing energy that comes in at the base of the spine – and accorded more with Tantric Kundalini and psychic practices. I distinguished the mystic and the psychic very firmly.

On the Sunday I meditated in the conference hall before breakfast and saw "a nuclear explosion". Back in Tooting I wrote: "I am radioactive since the Light on Sunday, and ought to be evacuated…. I glow with Light. I can see the Light in my fingertips. I need to measure myself on a Geiger counter." (I believed that the Light contained ionising particles.)

Two days later Matthew had more febrile convulsions as a result of another high temperature which was again caused by tonsillitis, and he was admitted to St James's Hospital, Balham. I visited him every day, and on the way back from hospital the following Saturday, still seeking to understand my new powers, with Ann I looked in on the Mind Body Spirit Festival. I saw very clearly that psychic abilities may be a bridge to spiritual truth but are inferior to it. I noted: "The New Age (our Renaissance) has unearthed the Light."

In mid-May my research on the Light inspired an insight that would become the main idea of Part One of *The Fire and the Stones*: "My theme is: all the Lights are one… and can be the basis of a world religion." I was determined to make notes for a critique of 'isms': "State the problem: the waste land of 'isms', which have been compounded by the modern science." I thought of the 'isms' that Tuohy and Kathleen Raine stood for: "Kathleen Raine and Tuohy represent rival traditions which they embody well…. [Raine] is wrong to espouse the way of erudition as a means to a rational metaphysical knowledge…. The Raine tradition approaches the unconscious through Platonic scholarship."[8] More and more I saw the necessity to include both the world of sense-experience (Tuohy's world) and the metaphysical world (the mystic's rather than Raine's scholarly Platonist world).

Finding a larger home: sale of flat 5, 10 Brechin Place and purchase of 46 Ritherdon Road, SW17
My new powers included a drive to find a larger home that had more room for our two boys and would improve my family's lot.

We had moved to Stapleton Road and rented out the flat in 10 Brechin Place as an immediate response to my growing financial crisis. However, my salary at Garratt Green, though one of the highest as teachers' salaries went, still did not cover the expenditure of running a family home with a wife and two children and paying half my daughter's boarding-school fees. To start afresh I had put the flat in 10 Brechin Place on the market and had begun looking for a more spacious house in Wandsworth near Garratt Green. In early January 1978 I had had an offer for my flat in Brechin Place. Contracts were not exchanged until March. The sale went through, and we moved our furniture into storage on 25 April.

Meanwhile I redoubled my search for a house in Wandsworth. I wrote: "I have so little time these days. Being in the hierarchy now, I have been at three meetings with the Head as part of our policy group of six, taking decisions about school matters, being a managerial executive."[9]

After much house-hunting and pursuing false leads I had put in a bid for the former Vicarage of St Mary's, Balham, a six-bedroom double-fronted house at 46 Ritherdon Road, London SW17. The bids were all to be opened at the same time at a local estate agent's, and after researching the amount to offer I managed to offer £500 more than anyone else, and so acquired the property. I could now see my way of moving the Brechin-Place furniture out of store into this property and leaving the rented flat in Stapleton Road.

We would move into 46 Ritherdon Road on 15 August after more than three weeks of decorating, laying carpets and taking delivery of a gas stove and beds.

In August we stayed in Cornwall with Ann's mother. I recorded: "Went for a glorious walk at Charlestown. Blue calm sea…. Sunwashed cliffs, the old 1790s harbour wall." The same day I recorded: "David Gascoyne called brilliant by Philip Toynbee in today's *Observer*. What a joy to have the time to reflect. I will now return to a life of quiet reflection, as I pursue my Gascoyne-like destiny. Gascoyne's *Journal 1937–9*, cf mine 1964–7." (My journal would become *Awakening to the Light*.) And: "Wrote 'A Causeway of Light'. [A story.] Am vibrant within…. The spring of creativity is flowing." During the last week in August I redrafted my plan for *The Secret Light* "following a shandy in the Rashleigh Arms garden, Charlestown last night, under brilliant stars." I added: "We are shadows on the wall of Light."[10] I was thinking of the pier wall in that sunlit Charlestown. This concept later passed into *The Fire and the Stones*.

Perception of energy, and healing

All through that summer term I was still pondering new powers. There was social reality and absolute Reality. I told Margaret Riley when she visited me on my birthday,

> A work of art is a model of Reality. Tuohy's Reality is social reality, and he sees a work of art as being absolute in itself, instead of Reality as being absolute…. There is a variety of realities. A tree can be a social thing or a being full of energy.

It was a question of perception. I had become aware of globules of energy in the air as I sunbathed – "vitality globules dancing in the blue sky" – and as I squinted I wondered if they were blobs within my eyeballs, a trick of my sight. I heard Paul Solomon again, this time on mystery schools. He described his Zen teacher in Japan, a servant who swept a tea-house with a broom, which Solomon took as an image for keeping one's own soul clean, the way I had taken it. Solomon raised another new power. He told how his son had got straight As in his college work by going "to the window in my mind" and looking through it to see the answers.

As I investigated new energy – the tree, globules and the window in the mind – the school was sapping my physical energy. Over half-term I was ill with a fever. In mid-June I wrote: "Am really tired. Slept all yesterday afternoon and am finding it hard to stay awake this afternoon. Am drained."

It was exam time at school, and besides coping with 'O'- and 'A'-level classes and marking, running a Department of 26 teachers and daily rounds of meetings before school, at lunch-time and after school, I now had to run the public exams in the school's hall. Sometimes 350 took different exams at the same time. For a month I was in charge of the security of exam papers, getting in very early and taking them to the hall, distributing them on the desks along with the correct place numbers of the candidates, co-ordinating the invigilators and making sure each exam ended at the right time while teaching. Then I collected the papers and sent them off after school. The ILEA had decided that Garratt Green would be inspected that autumn, and there were reports to the Inspectors to write and I was asked to do the early-morning coverage from the coming September, the worst job in the school as it meant taking the staff's free periods. I was still teaching my usual timetable with all the marking and meetings involved, and I was in daily negotiations about the arrangements for 46 Ritherdon Road.

While all this was going on I was exploring my new powers of healing. I healed Anthony, who had just stood for the first time, "and felt cold". I found the healing surges came into my meditations now: "Later meditated towards the Light and again felt shivers up my spine." I attended a Wrekin-Trust course on healing and met Bruce Macmanaway, a tall, seemingly military man who had a great reputation as a healer and knew about my "waves" that came from the beyond, and said of them: "They are very strong." He invited me to his clinic in Lupus Street, London to heal some of his patients. I also met Edgar Chase, an ex-Naval buffer in a tie and blazer, and described my surges to him. He also told me I was a healer. Thinking of my healing in relation to *The Secret Light*, I wrote,

I am saying that there is a sun, and in the Kingdom of the Blind this is shattering news. I am saying 300 people have seen it. I am seeking nothing....

I have a mission to tell people about the sun.... It is the sun's rays that heal....
The sun breaks the seedcase of one's destiny and enables the vine to grow.
The vision of love: every man is my brother, for he has a spark of the... Light.
Therefore I must act out my love – in the form of little "unremembered acts"
of kindness.

I was critical of "making the Light available to those who can afford fees....
Christ did not charge an entrance to the Sermon on the Mount, and nor do
the mystery schools. Healing is a tributary of the river of Light."[11]

I am regressed to two 'past lives'
While I decorated Ritherdon Road I had been thinking about reincarnation.
I had attended a Wrekin-Trust conference on it in mid-July. At the healing
conference I had met Maurice Blake, who regressed people to past lives like
Arnall Bloxham. He was elderly and offered to regress me if I visited him in
Norwich. School had broken up and I was organising work on the new
house, which was now festooned in scaffolding and was like a building site
inside. A team of men I had found had tea several times a day in what
would become our living-room, and there was always a full skip outside.

I was apprehensive: could I be sure there would be no ill effects, no
dangers from being hypnotised? I decided to go to Norwich, aware that like
Faust I was seeking "beyond the threshold of death".[12]

I got up at 6 a.m. on 2 August and drove to Norwich. I lay down on the
sofa in Maurice Blake's sitting-room. He switched on a tape-recorder and sat
near me. He made me raise my left arm and counted to 10. I have the tape
of the next hour and-a-half. I was not aware that my arm was raised
throughout: both it and I had "gone to sleep".

'Life' as John Barfield in Lake District
He took me back to when I was 16, then 10, then 5, then to my birth, and
then beyond my birth to a previous life in the 19th century. Blake asked me
question after question, and after each a clear image rose in my mind, which
I can still remember, and I then, slowly and haltingly in my hypnotised
trance, looked at the image and tried to provide an answer.

In "my" 19th-century childhood I saw a valley and pronounced it
Esthwaite. I was among trees, wearing boots with large black toecaps. I saw
"myself" crossing the sea on a four-masted ship in a storm. I was among
religious people who sang hymns on deck, going to New Brunswick. I saw
myself as a priest – I seemed to be a Jesuit priest called *Abbé* ("abbot" or
"priest") – among tree-fellers, 'lumberjacks', in woods in a "Sirioux"
settlement in Canada. The loggers wore white shirts with short braces and
high trousers and boots. I saw their log-cabins, brown mud and a camp-fire,

and I had the feeling that the settlement was near a river. I was 26 and I saw the boat in a yellow newspaper: 1829.

Then I saw my last hours in my own log-cabin. Looking down from the ceiling I saw myself on a bed in a corner of the room, near a woman with a white bonnet who was rolling pastry with a rolling-pin. I told Blake that I was dying of cholera as a result of water-contamination, and that the woman was Esmé, a French-speaker. She called me John or Jonquil. A rush of feeling came into my throat, for I knew we had had a liaison that no one knew about, and the emotion at seeing her again across lifetimes was uncontainable.

Blake made me relive my death at 33. I was on a single bed with a black cover in the shadowy log-cabin. My lips and tongue were parched, my breathing was noisy. The woman was stooping over me. I wanted a drink of water, but there was no water. It was difficult to breathe. I was going to sleep, I was growing cold, my right hand was cold and numb, my little finger had gone numb and was almost paralysed. I took my last breath, then there was relief and peace without any sensation in my body, and I was in a mist of colourless light. From a great height I saw the woman stooping near my body, and then I was floating with a buoyant feeling and I looked down on the log-cabin settlement from a great height.

I saw my funeral. There were people present. A logger in a white shirt and braces with high trousers leaned on the long handle of an axe near a fire that glowed through white ash. I saw my tombstone, which was two feet high and like a rough, uneven milestone. Blake told me to look at it, and I read: 'John Barfield, d.1836'. The loggers were not aware that I was there and I observed them from head-height. Afterwards I found I was in a mist and feeling very peaceful.

Blake brought me out of my hypnotised state for a discussion. My left arm was still raised. On the way home I pondered what I had experienced. Did I really die in 1836, and had I had proof of an immortal spirit that can survive death with memories intact? Were the images far memories? Or were they just personal memories or imaginings, at the level of wish-fulfilments or waking day-dreams, elaborate fantasies? I was not sure that I believed in reincarnation. In 1836 there had only been about 1 billion bodies in which to reincarnate, and now there were 7 billion. I was not sure about the mathematics of reincarnation. At the same time I could see how I might have had far memories. I wrote: "The poet sees images from within which link him to past lives and far memory, the collective unconscious, healing forces, the imagination whose source is the Light, and the mystic Light, most supreme of all; also to meditative images."

For several days I was filled with sadness for the woman. I wrote: "A great sadness all day, for *Abbé* (me) and Esmé. When I was a priest in

Canada, I was very alone and grew fond of Esmé, and she had a soft spot for me and was with me when I died, though she pottered about, turning her back. *Abbé*. I am consumed with sadness for a life that has gone. I have been haunted by my life in Canada in a way I have never been haunted by a dream."[13] My relationship with Esmé felt real and I accepted the images as a possible far memory while leaving open the possibility that they had been thrown up in the course of a waking hypnotised dream.

I later wrote to the parish of Esthwaite and enquired about Barfield. They had no record of that name on the parish register.

'Life' as consort of Ramesses II in Egypt

I was still contemplating my latest new power, contacting a previous life. On 31 August I returned to Maurice Blake and was regressed again. I revisited my life as John Barfield. I confirmed that I was in a relationship with Esmé when I died, that I was a Jesuit priest and that there were 100 other Jesuits on the ship crossing to New Brunswick. Then Blake took me back a long time and I surfaced under a huge temple statue of a man I pronounced to be 'Ramesses the Second as a Sun-god'. I was a woman and lay a garland at his feet at the top of the steps. I lived in the temple. Outside the temple a philosopher sat on a stool, naked above the waist and sporting a black beard, before a group of ten temple-maidens who sat on sand before him. One of them was me. I wore a dress with one shoulder bare and sandals with a twined thong between each big and second toe. The image of the philosopher and his class was so vivid and colourful that I could almost put my hand in and grab a handful of sand. It was like seeing a scene from c.1300 BC on live TV. I knew the philosopher was a healer and taught occult arts, and that the maidens made the Nile flood by taking part in a public ritual involving the Sun-god.

This ritual involved Ramesses II coming into the temple and choosing one of us for ritual love-making. I saw the beginning of such a ceremony. It was a hot day with a blue sky, and all those who lived in the temple were on parade. The young Ramesses arrived with a tall and shining gold head-dress and gold armour. He was surrounded by his entourage and we were thrilled to see him. He looked magnificent. He came down the line and stopped at me and touched his heart. Recounting this to Blake under hypnotism I dissolved into tears, which can be heard on the tape. I was choking with emotion at the honour, for I was the "Chosen One" and he would take me within and make love to me and make the Nile flood. My name was Nebhotep, and I was ecstatically happy.

Blake brought me out of my trance. In the ensuing discussion I recalled having seen the mummy of Ramesses II in the Cairo Museum. I had looked at the mummy for a long time without realising that I was gazing at the corpse of my former boyfriend. Later I wrote a poem about my two visits to Maurice Blake: 'A Temple-Dancer's Temple-Sleep'. I again pondered whether I had a spirit that can survive death and take memories with it. Had I had far memories or just day-dreams? I knew that if my spirit had lived many times before and brought memories of past lives with it to my present life, then I would want to know this and know my past lives as such knowledge would affect my view of what a man is and of his place in the universe, which would have to be measured over many centuries and not just one lifetime. I knew that if this was the case I would have no fear of death, and that after dying I would be conscious in a mist of light. If, on the other hand, I had merely been day-dreaming then I received some very vivid poetic images which had the force of memories.

After this last regression I renewed my research into ancient cultures and new powers with zest. My research took me to the Buddhist Society and I meditated. I observed that the seekers were "twisting their body into cramps" whereas "enlightenment happens to one and changes one within".[14]

At King's College, Cambridge: with Colin MacCabe and Bernard Williams

My research was countered by a view of social engineering. The ginger-haired post-structuralist Colin MacCabe, who had been at the dinner for Fergie Maclean and was militantly pro-comprehensive, had invited me to take a party of senior girls to King's College, Cambridge. He gave us lunch. I remember an African girl breaking away and buying an ice-cream just as we were about to enter the college gates, and I had to explain to the group that it was bad form to arrive at a Cambridge college licking a cornet. It was a sunny day and I loved the open spaces at King's and felt relaxed among staff and students in casual dress, and dons who told me they championed social engineering.

During lunch in the college hall I encountered the Provost, Bernard Williams, who was in a suit. I spoke of his kindness to me on my first day at Chigwell School in 1947 and said I remembered him as a tall boy in long trousers (see My Double Life 1: This Dark Wood). Speaking as an equal, he told me that if our parents had really wanted us to get ahead they would have sent us to a school like Radley. He implied that we had progressed to where we were in spite of rather than because of our schooling.

I thought of my writing as reflecting these new powers and toyed with seeing poetry as a form of healing: perhaps inspiration entered like the Light and came out in stanzas like rushes of healing energy.

I meet Colin Wilson again

I see the hand of Providence at work that October. I was somehow put in touch with figures who would help me bring works to birth.

I had heard that Colin Wilson would be signing copies of his latest book *Mysteries* in Watkins Bookshop, and for old time's sake I looked in and joined the queue. He sat behind a desk in his old sweater and jacket, and I said, "Hello, Colin, do you remember me?" He said in a very loud voice so that 60 in the queue could hear as he signed my book: "Hello, Nick. You helped me with an article and stayed at the Savages." The encounter was a bridge for I would take up with Colin Wilson again. And Watkins would publish two of my books.

Asa Briggs urges me to write on Libya and my double life
Then in mid-October I returned to Worcester College, Oxford to attend a Gaudy: a reunion for graduates who started in 1924 and in 1958. The evening began with chapel, where the new Provost, the historian Asa Briggs, a small bespectacled man with a mop of hair, read the lesson. I dined in Hall (where I had taken the entrance exam in late 1956) with a third of my year, but no Ricky Herbert or Kingsley Shorter. After ten minutes the wrinkles fell away and we were back in 1960. A.B. Brown, my old Law tutor, made a witty and fluent speech that raised many laughs, and the sconce came out and there was an Old-English *camaraderie* as we banded together against the dark world outside.

Afterwards we drank in the Buttery and I found myself talking at some length to Asa Briggs. We discussed Libya and I told him that I had been involved in a pro-Western *coup* that had been stolen by Gaddafi, who had posed as its implementer, Col. Saad eddin Bushwerib, and that Gaddafi's *coup* had been accepted by the West in the belief that it was ours. Asa Briggs said: "You must write a book about your experiences. You have told me something I have often wondered about and did not know, you must write it down. You have just explained how the West came to accept the Gaddafi revolution. I have not seen this written anywhere else. You must write the full story. It is of historical importance." I did not know that he had worked in Bletchley Park for two years from 1943 to 1945, and would write *Secret Days* about his time there. I left about 2 a.m. and slept in a room in the Main Terrace. Briggs followed his urgings up with a letter: "I feel that you ought to write up your experience, and I am sure that it would be of very wide interest."[15] In due course I would write *The Libyan Revolution* and later still *My Double Life 1: This Dark Wood* in response to his urging.

The experience of that weekend made me wonder if I should return to academic life. I knew I should research into Classicism and Romanticism, and possibly also Modernism, the ground of Kermode's *Romantic Image*. Connecting my new powers with poetry, I wrote to my English tutor Christopher Ricks about my poems, and he replied that we would meet.

After teaching Wordsworth's 'Tintern Abbey' for 'A' level I had an experience of the Light: "The Light came again in my bath, a blue sparkling diamond, beautiful to look on. I gazed in deep contemplation for a good half a minute." I saw it in poetic terms and saw myself as first and foremost a Metaphysical poet: "By returning to Ricks I am defining myself as I really am.... I am a Metaphysical poet writing a book about the Light. This [book] is my 'second string'.... My one-man campaign to rediscover enlightenment as a literary subject.... Enlightenment is the 'one word' Ezra Pound spoke to me about: the one theme I could put on half a side of a postcard, in T.E. Hulme's words."[16]

Dogmatic authority
ILEA inspection
My new powers and poetry were swept aside for a month. The time for the ILEA inspection had arrived. For three weeks there was a team of authoritative Inspectors looking at every aspect of the work at Garratt Green. I gave ten interviews of an hour and-a-half each and had little time to think about my true work. I wrote: "I am totally uncreative.... At present I am in a fallow time.... I keep falling asleep in the evenings... because of overwork at school." I wrote of the Inspectors: "Dry, ageing men with lined faces and moustaches and joyless eyes; men who have become social personas, wrongly living as social identities."[17]

Peace and sanctions
Towards the end of the Inspection I attended the Chelsea Mayor's reception for the two softly-spoken Irish housewives who had won a Nobel Peace Prize. I met a relative of Biggs-Davison there, Mrs. Ewart-Biggs, the wife of Christopher Ewart-Biggs who was to be murdered in Dublin.

A few days later it was announced that Biggs-Davison had been sacked from his job as Shadow no. 2 in Northern Ireland for voting against – rather than abstaining from – the governing Labour Party's continuation of sanctions against the black internal settlement government of Rhodesia which had put Bishop Muzorewa (who I had interviewed twice) in power. Biggs-Davison said on the morning news about his rebellion against Thatcher's authority: "I cannot explain Mrs. Thatcher's inexplicable instructions." (Winston Churchill, Churchill's grandson, had been sacked at the same time.)

New powers and Third Mystic Life
Healing at Bruce MacManaway's Centre
At the end of the inspection, in mid-November, the healing session at Bruce MacManaway's 'surgery' at 13 Moreton Terrace, Lupus Street took place to

measure my potential as a healer.

I was given a stand-up 'buffet lunch' of orange juice. I was wired up to Cade's 'Mind Mirror' by his wife, and spent an hour 'healing' a young boy with a damaged brain, Geoffrey Stewart. When the four rushes came through Geoffrey had the best brain rhythms he had had for two years – even though the power did not feel as great as usual because of the hairnet, and the public spectacle. I later helped with an old man and a boy who had a blood clot in his artery by his right ear. I left just before Lord Hailsham arrived for his 5-o'clock appointment. "The brain machine showed I have a deep, deep calm. I calm my patients back to health."

The experiment had been a success and had confirmed my healing powers, but I did not want to become a healer. I wrote of the poet as healer: "Keats on healing and the poet. 'The poet and the dreamer are distinct..../The one pours out a balm upon the World,/The other vexes it.'... My healing powers come from the same source that my images come from." I later wrote a story, 'Christmas-Tree Patterns on the Lunatic Fringe'.

The Inspectors had now left us in peace and I had more time to spend with my young family. We were still working on 46 Ritherdon Road. The scaffolding was now down and outside painting took place between torrential showers. I had let our top floor to a succession of tenants at the request of the British Council. The most recent was the nephew of the Kurdish resistance leader Jalal Talabani, who would become President of Iraq in 2003 after the overthrow of the regime of Saddam Hussein. Talabani's nephew was studying in the UK for three months. I always put the two boys to bed and read to them. Later I carried forward my research into the Light, drafting what would become Part One of *The Fire and the Stones*.

In mid-December I returned to Bruce MacManaway's healing centre. I wrote: "Healed Bruce MacManaway, the maestro himself, who suffers from insomnia. Pumped in a lot of delta sleep rhythms while Cade scribbled, bending over his Mind Mirror.... Lunch with Bruce and Cade; while the others ate downstairs. We were in 'Rosalind's' bedroom."[18] I now knew the experiment was over and that I should devote my energies to poetry.

I spent much of the Christmas holidays unpacking after the building work, sorting books in the library and organising my study. We went to Loughton for Boxing Day and there were party games for the children: bagatelle, jigsaw cards, dice and *charades*, in which Matthew took part. I learned from my mother of the deaths of some of the stalwarts in the Methodist church of my childhood: Mr Llewellyn (a local preacher who often visited us just after we had started Sunday lunch and sat in a chair and watched us eat), Mr Yelland (who wore bifocals) and Mr Bedwell (the sidesman who generally forgot to take off his cycle clips); and Ebenezer

Occomore (the bald organist who had cancer of the spine and was crippled). We were now in the throes of Callaghan's 'winter of discontent'. Towards the end of January there was a strike by ancillary staff at my school and I had to cross a picket line of lorry drivers, cleaners and lunch staff to do adminis- tration. We did not teach during the strike. This gave me more time to write during term time than I had had for a long while.

New understanding: Christopher Ricks and me as a Metaphysical poet, content versus technique
By January 1979 I was writing a sequence of sonnets, *Lady of the Lamp*. At one level they were about Orpheus entering the underworld to find Eurydice, whose lamp is the Light. At another level I was trying to find Universalist symbols for the Light in everyday situations. I wrote: "Aleksander Blok wrote a Beautiful Lady mystical sequence ['Verses about the Lady Beautiful'].... I am a metaphysical poet, and am therefore a Symbolist; not a Symbolist who is therefore metaphysical."[19]

I had sent some of my poems to Christopher Ricks. Knowing I would be seeing him soon I went to Foyles and found his book on Milton and took stock of his tradition. I wrote: "He is the Empson of the 1970s: in the Empson tradition. His verbal approach: word-play: what is successful and what is an unsuccessful metaphor (Milton's delicacy rather than grandness): his 'embarrassment' – sensitivity. He has antennae for embarrassment.... Ricks's theory that art is a way of coping with embarrassment. It can be. For me it is a means of searching."[20]

I took stock of my own poetry. I wrote:

My strengths are: metaphor, verbal play, wit. They are Metaphysical strengths; which blend in with my metaphysical search for reality or enlight- enment, and symbolism. Love is a theme for me as it was with the Metaphysicals (Marvell's 'Coy Mistress').... I am more of a Metaphysical than a Romantic.... I am interested in the symbol in so far as a Metaphysical poet is interested in symbols.... This also explains the reflective autobiographical interest as opposed to the imaginative... and the insistence on learning.... What is the Metaphysical imagination (as opposed to Romantic image)? This coming contact with Ricks has got me away from *Romantic Image* to the Metaphysicals. I go back to Empson's ambiguity.... Kathleen Raine... is not a true Metaphysical.

On 18 February 1979 I wrote the first of three letters to Ricks in which I attempted to define my place in the tradition. This letter saw myself as a Metaphysical. (*See* Appendix 6, p.929.)

I visited Christopher Ricks at Christ's College, Cambridge, on a snowy day, 20 February. I passed the mulberry tree Milton knew when he was a pupil there. Ricks was waiting for me in his large room, dressed in a blue denim shirt and trousers. We walked to the Buttery and there, dome-headed with round spectacles and wispy grey hair, he gave me a tutorial whose brilliance took my breath away. He made 16 technical points about my poems[21] one after the other with great rapidness, declaring that they were not Metaphysical in the sense that the Metaphysical poets' poems are Metaphysical. He was not thinking of their metaphysical content at all (for me, the central issue), but purely of beginnings and endings, syntax, imagery and such matters. He launched into a long monologue while I listened, saying Marvell had done this and Hagger that; Milton and Tennyson had treated a particular theme one way, Hagger another; Keats and Eliot had done such-and-such, while Hagger had done so-and-so. For a good hour he related my work to the highest standards, and I felt as though I was listening to a tutorial in which my work had already joined the canon.

We had lunch in the Senior Common Room at Christ's. I sat next to Ricks and in between making general conversation with the other dons I said to him at one point that Coleridge distinguished imagination and fancy to which Ricks replied: "I've never found that distinction particularly helpful." (Being a Neoclassical critic he disagreed with Coleridge's Romantic view of the imagination.) We had coffee in a snoozy room aglare with snow, and Ricks suddenly said, "You're very learned," which I took as a compliment rather than as a criticism. Being learned was a characteristic of the Metaphysical poets. (My mother's reaction to this comment was, "The more learned you become the fewer people you can write for," to which I retorted that the important thing was to be right, not to have mass appeal and be wrong.)

I had tried to place myself in the tradition as a Metaphysical poet, and I would make a further attempt to place myself in the tradition as a Romantic poet and then as a Baroque poet (*see* Appendix 6, p.929). (In October 1982 he would tell me, "I think your work is Baroque." *See* p.127.)[22]

Looking back, I now believe that I am more of a Metaphysical poet than Ricks gave me credit for. He approached what I sent from the point of view of technique, ignoring similarities in content between the poems of Donne and Marvell and some of my poems. This view can be tested by reading through my recent *Selected Poems: Quest for the One*.

I was still thinking about Ricks when a few days later I took a party of seven girls from Garratt Green to Worcester College, Oxford. We were given sherry in the Cottages on staircase 8 by Michael Winterbottom, who said: "Do you know whose room you're in?" There were girls sitting in all the chairs and even on the window-sill, and I looked again and said, not having realised until then: "It's Christopher Ricks's room, but it's been changed."

"That's right," Winterbottom said.

It was an eerie experience, sitting where I had had so many tutorials with seven girls sprawling everywhere.

Later I had lunch with the dons in the Senior Common Room. I sat next to Francis Reynolds, who had briefly taught me Roman Law, and I was struck by how they all treated me as an equal, without any sense of superiority or of my being an outsider. I experienced the truth of what Asa Briggs had said at the Gaudy: that to be at a college is to belong to it for life. Afterwards we had coffee up the stairs where I had Collections (examinations after each vacation) and where I had my interview the day I talked about my Corinthian coin. (*See My Double Life 1: This Dark Wood.*)

Metaphysical Kabbalah: Warren Kenton

My research into the metaphysical took me to a conference on the Kabbalah at Ammerdown in Somerset. It was taken by Warren Kenton, a young bearded man, who taught the names of the 10 *sephiroth*, the centres which form the Kabbalistic diagram, the Tree of Life. Knowing that Shakespeare, Blake and Yeats were all influenced by the Kabbalah, I found the weekend very helpful. At one point Kenton put 10 chairs in a hopscotch pattern to reflect the *sephiroth*, and we took it in turns to sit in chair 2, the rational social ego which looks out at the world, and chair 5, the new centre Tepheret or Beauty, where the inner psychological, spiritual and divine worlds can be contacted. He invited us to see our soul as a bird, and I had the image of a huge brown and white eagle with a hooked beak and tawny eyes; not at all fierce. He said later, "Your bird shows how you view your soul." Kenton told me: "You have been posted at your school to bring Light to the place."[23]

Matthew Manning healing cripples

The Kabbalah gave me an insight into balancing within, and balancing Classicism and Romanticism on either side of the Tree of Life. The routine of school was even more irksome than usual. To the Head's annoyance the English Department had come out of the inspection well. She increased her attempts to control me. She encouraged factionalism, and was ever-ready to stir up my Department.

I was relieved to be able to return to my research in the Easter holidays. I wrote: "It is as though I am being guided at present. I go to a book and it falls open at a certain page and a quotation I need leaps up and hits me."[24] I visited the Mind Body Spirit Festival and saw Matthew Manning heal. It was very dramatic. A line of cripples limped up to the platform and after receiving healing moved on without their crutches. I knew that I should not do something similar. I knew I had to write books and keep my healing private, to be used on members of the family. I had strengthened my resolve to avoid returning to Lupus Street and to concentrate on being a writer.

Experience of Hermeticism and beginning of Third Mystic Life (13 May 1979–31 October 1981)
Still researching ancient cultures, in May I attended a conference at Hoddesdon on the *Hermetica*. It was taken by Frederic Lionel, a Hermeticist and French ex-intelligence agent who spoke on the Egyptian mysteries and in particular on the 'spiritual sun'. On the Sunday morning I had an experience of the Light. I wrote: "Sunday morning meditation, and the 'spiritual sun' broke as the ancient bearded face of God, looking down and to the right, a great matted beard…. I tingled all over from the scalp to the backs of my ankles and felt a great power flowing through me, and the tingling and sensation of higher energies went on for a minute or two…. All through breakfast, I could not speak for the tingling and prickling on my skin." However, I was perturbed by the interest in astrology on the course, and the talk of magic. I saw the New Age in a new light. It was a vehicle for the occult, and I knew I did not want to become too involved in it.

This experience of the Light began my Third Mystic Life (*see* Appendix 1, p.903).

Universal gardener
I now saw myself as a gardener. In May our gardener brought a pyracantha, a firethorn, on his bus and planted it in our front garden. I dwelt on the image of fire consuming thorns. Suddenly I grasped what I was doing at Garratt Green: "the Light – all creatures are made of it and from it, and so it is the living proof of the brotherhood of man which transcends racial barriers and power politics; and I am at Garratt Green serving Asians and West Indians so that I can learn this truth." I had a chat with the school gardener about rhododendrons, and wrote: "I am a universal Gardener, and at my school I have 1,800 flowers, and I look after each with loving care. They all grow and bloom."[25]

Still overworked at Garratt Green, illness: Matthew and Anthony have measles and then whooping cough
Suddenly life became stressful. In June I was again organising the public exams, and controlled by my job. Ann and the two boys returned from spending four days with Ann's mother in Cornwall, and I noted: "Matthew laughed with excitement and ran and jumped around my neck and hugged me, delighted to see his Daddy again…. Matthew has had a bad cough." Four days later he had convulsions in Whitechapel lasting two minutes as the result of another sudden high-rising temperature caused by a virus. Ann

drove him unconscious to the London Hospital and he was unconscious for half an hour.

I was rung and immediately left school (passing my Head at the gate and ignoring her order to return to class). I travelled to the hospital by tube and helped him back to consciousness. He was transferred to St James's Hospital, Balham and Ann stayed the night with him. I visited him the next day, and he was sitting up and pleased that he had been brave and not cried when given an injection in his arm. That same day Ann's car battery went dead, our upstairs' tenant's fridge broke down and my electric typewriter packed up. Matthew now developed measles.

The next fortnight was chaotic. I wrote of my busy life: "I am amazed at the load I carry, at the active life that is the context for my contemplative life. Everyone depends on me. At work I have done the timetable for next year, the coverage for all this last week – 25 teachers away on Wednesday, 16 today – and I am doing the 1st-year placing and the inductions course, as well as trying to mark two more sets of exam papers…. On top of all, Anthony now has measles – Matthew having finished it – and I have to go to the chemist for medicine and help clear up vomit. And we have a change of tenant tomorrow."

Soon afterwards Ann was ill, which meant that I had to take Matthew to his school on Tooting Common and do additional chores. Then Anthony, having weathered measles, was taken to St George's Hospital, Tooting, with bacterial pneumonia. He looked bedraggled, but he picked up after I sat quietly with him and put healing surges into him. When Matthew and Anthony both developed whooping cough I wrote: "They have been ill for the whole month, non-stop: convulsions–measles–measles–pneumonia – and now whooping cough, which they had before the convulsions, though the hospital would not believe us."[26] Somehow in June and July I had managed to get 145 pages of my research typed. These would pass into Part One of *The Fire and the Stones*. I had also managed to visit Glastonbury for lectures on Arthur, and had sat in the garden of the chalice well and written a poem, 'By the Chalice Well, Glastonbury', within view of the house once occupied by the occultist Tudor Pole.

Dinner with Colin MacCabe, Frank Tuohy

In the middle of all this I managed to attend a dinner party at Colin MacCabe's. He had rung me to say that his wife Lady Flavia had applied to teach Italian and French at Garratt Green and asked me if I could help.[27] It now transpired that she had toyed with the idea of teaching there, and had changed her mind. The dinner party was at Flavia's house in Islington, and we sat in the unkempt garden near an overgrown lily pond and drank wine. Tuohy was present. We came in when Colin was bitten by gnats. I wrote:

"Colin, unkempt hair and open-necked shirt, somehow like his untouched garden, and with a soft dream in his eyes, somehow rather Brooke-ian." In the middle of dinner, at which the drink flowed very liberally, the post-structuralist MacCabe attacked the traditionalists in Cambridge's English Faculty, which was then run by Christopher Ricks. He left the table and the room and came back wearing a plain sweatshirt on which was printed: "More P – ks than Ricks?" I was an eyewitness of the beginning of the trouble that was brewing between the traditionalists and the dogmatic modernists in Cambridge English circles, that would spill over into the press.

New observation: Invisible behind the visible
As soon as the boys were fit to travel Ann took them down to Cornwall. I joined my family in August. The two boys had now recovered their health. The next day I "took Matthew to Charlestown: skimmed stones, fished, watched the gulls round the harbour, found some pink valerian (or all-heal) at the top of the cliffs". I noted: "In the last three years I have demonstrated a tradition in which the Invisible is behind the visible; and I have therefore weakened scientific materialism and Humanism."

We went to St Michael's Mount "which hung in mist when we arrived, but cleared as the tide went out". We passed the imposing grey Trevarthian House where Robert and I stayed as children, and walked along the causeway, looking up at the obsessing Castle. We climbed the stone path to the steepling height where a beacon was lit for the Spanish Armada and where terraces jutted out over thin-air and overhung great drops to the rocks below.

We went on to Newlyn and Mousehole and returned to Penzance and Porthleven, where we walked in mist among the fishermen on the pier. That night I went down to Charlestown. "It is very dark. A few late-night fishermen by torchlight. The tide is in. Out at sea a lightship flashed and beamed its light off the low cloud."

The next day it rained and we could not go out:

I played Matthew snakes and ladders and lost.... Then, around 9.30 p.m. the rain stopped and we went down to Charlestown. Leaning against the wall under the Harbour-master's House I felt 'The Sea is Wild' come, a lyric, and came home and wrote it out, rhymes and all.

The rest of my time in Cornwall I looked for things the boys would like. We took them to watch the Red Arrows at the Charlestown Regatta – "the Red Arrows in their Gnats; zooming and looping and making steeples of smoke over Fowey" – and we danced the Floral Dance at the Carnival. We went to

Bude where there were "wild Atlantic rollers"[28] and we had our lunch on Chapel Point. We went to Clovelly. A few days later we went to the Fowey Carnival. We gave Matthew and Anthony a ride on a little train and walked them round the model railway museum.

Inspiration in sleep and view of world history: I receive idea for The Fire and the Stones – *civilizations as Light-bearers*
I had been sleeping well – I had been to bed before midnight for two-and-a-half weeks. I had been reflecting on how the life of the ego can give way to the life of the Self, the soul, and universal consciousness.

One morning I awoke from sleep with the view of history that became Part Two of *The Fire and the Stones* lodged in my mind by infused contemplation (*see* p.66):

Aug 24th. Again, a morning inflow around 5.30 a.m., when I was too tired to do anything, though around 6.15 I woke up and wrote it down. It is a new [view] of history. The idea I received in sleep is: that civilizations are 'Light-bearers', that their initial *élan* reflects the active values of the Self (not the ego), and that civilizations last as long as the Light lasts: hence the Egyptian civilization lasted 3,000 years. While the Light lasts, the ego is not pandered to, and there is a national Self with military and national values ('the Lord Mighty in Battle'). But when the ego predominates and Welfare States pamper it and it gets used for luxuries, then the Light goes.

I was aware that I was becoming a writer of the Self – or, as I had put it in 'The Silence', "Poet of the Self" – and that my research into the ancient Egyptians and the Egyptian mysteries was actually a research into the Egyptian civilization.

Back in London I leafed again through my 12 volumes of Toynbee's *A Study of History* "and saw him admit to drawing a blank as to why civilizations spring up…. Toynbee has been 'all round the houses', analysing each civilization in detail and drawing conclusions from each, and seeing what each has in common. I have started with the answer and am working backwards. It was like a jigsaw puzzle: Toynbee didn't know the picture, I have been given it in my sleep from a source that is *always* right."[29]

Struggling with authority: overwork and bronchitis
In September we went to Loughton for family tea. We went up to High Beach church and to the Strawberry Hill pond, which was green round the fallen tree. There was a tufted duck on the Horseman's Pool.

Those moments of peace were set aside when I went back to school for the autumn term. I had been given the coverage full-time and some day-today running of the school, and the CSE entries. One day I wrote: "What *am* I doing at Garratt Green?" The same day it was announced that Wandsworth's schools would be reduced from 17 to 8 in 1982, and I resolved to leave secondary-school teaching and take on a primary school which Ann could run as Head.

The strain of being controlled – regimented – took its toll. In October I was off work for ten days with bronchitis. I wrote: "Oct 7, coughed blood. Oct 8, X-ray clear. So I am not seriously ill, not got lung cancer. Have had a cold for the last 3 or 4 weeks, and it went to my chest: a virus, not bacterial.... The dark-red blood I coughed up in clear sputum was similar to a nose-bleed, only in the lung (right lung).... I have been unwell for a month.... Oct 10. Have spent all day lying at the bottom of the sofa, unable to move. Am exhausted.... Because of this medicine to dry up my right lung, in which I have bronchitis, I am so tired and drowsy, and slightly trembly. I feel as if my energy has gone, and will not come back." Overwork had reduced me to a state of exhaustion. This was the beginning of my later-to-be-diagnosed bronchiectasis.

When I returned to school I found a fierce debate going on as to whether language is acquired or innate. One of my staff, who espoused socio-linguistics, insisted that Plato was wrong. I took Plato's side and said that language is both innate and acquired. I loathed being controlled by the Head – "I am discontented at Garratt Green, I am now too much of an administrator and too little a teacher of Milton" – and remembered "the great appalling truth, which I stumbled on in 'The Riddle of the Great Pyramid' that people come to love Hell. They like its routine, like men who miss the security of a prison." I added: "But I am going over the wall. I am going to escape and fulfil my vision and destiny."[30]

At the end of October I finished my account of the vision of the Light. It had taken me from 5 March to 22 October – seven-and-a-half months. It would eventually form the basis of Part One of *The Fire and the Stones*. And I was again aware of the link between philosophy and the New Age.

I revise Elegies for The Fire-Flower – *gardener's pruning*
I was on the verge of one of my most creative poetic periods, in which I discovered I had new poetic powers. It began in October with my feeling that I should accept Ricks's advice to be like Tennyson and revise my past poems, replace experimental long lines with heroic couplets or pentameters. I wrote: "Tidy up my past poems – do away with the long lines and put them into heroic couplets, which are the traditional memorable lines for all time.... Cf Ricks: 'Revise them, like Tennyson.' Get a scheme going for revision. Especially for the elegies. Prune. Ricks advised me to revise and improve, and so I shall.... A system for improving them. Especially,

pentameters." I reflected: "Garratt Green has enabled me to prune my talent. I had a wild talent that grew like a summer garden; it needed me to act as gardener, edge the lawns and generally keep it under control, and prevent it from getting overgrown." Having jibbed at the control of the ILEA's educational system I now proposed to apply greater control to my poetic works.

I now began revising past poems. I recorded: "Am revising 40 poems." In fact I was working on the volume that would become *The Fire-Flower*: "Revised 'Rubbish Dump' and saw that my present… 'selection'… [should be titled] *Firethorn*, too poetic a title not to use on these poems. I must depict existence as a crackling, blazing fire…. I must show it full… of hidden energies." (In the event, I stuck to *The Fire-Flower*, and 'Firethorn' became one poem within it, see below.) I wrote: "In poetry I used to aim for roughness – a ghost of pentameter behind a longish line – but now I aim for perfection…. Garratt Green has 'de-egoed' me, got me to eliminate the personal 'I' and its distinctive metres and to 'die' into the tradition and obey rules. Mrs. Kay's rulebook has taught me to write in… strict pentameters." On 29 November I finished the draft of 'Pear-Ripening House' and spent a fortnight polishing the poem that would become 'The Obscure Symbolist's Rock-Tree'.

Before Christmas I wrote: "Starting six major new poems. The first on Ricks. [Later titled 'The Tree of Imagination'.] Language and symbol. To the verbalist language has a social reality only. But to the mystic, language… communicates Reality, and symbols express visible spiritual Truths, the invisible as the visible…. I am all set for putting down these six…. Strict metre and clarity of image." I added: "I have alienated all: Movement by being too metaphysical, Raine by being too rational-contemplative. I have to journey alone. The modern Metaphysical poem must be ruminative. The old certainties (soul, e.g.) have to be re-established, whereas Donne, taking these for granted, could be immediate and momentary."

Matthew had not been well, and I had been healing him with four surges. I wrote: "Dec 23. Matthew has been 102.5 – for 4 days. I healed him at 6.30, and by 8.30 his temperature had dropped to under 97 – 6 degrees. Eight surges went into his stomach, a double dose. A dramatic drop."[31]

I reflected on the symbol:

Reality is layered, language is capable of approaching each layer, including the topmost spiritual layer, whose truths come down as symbols…. Reality sends pictures from the spiritual dimension which are framed in language – or painted in words. Language is the paint, the symbol is the picture…. Blake, 'The Imaginative Image returns by the seed of Contemplative Thought'…. The imagination or image-making faculty – image-seeing faculty – of the soul perceives symbols which contain truths.

And again:

> Ideas manifest into forms, innate ideas manifest into language which bears symbols as a tree bears fruit from the Idea of fruit.... I have... rediscovered the imaginative symbol (as opposed to the fanciful metaphor). Fancy is a matter of memory and association.

On Christmas Eve I went to church at All Saint's, Tooting, Graveney, and recorded observations that would lead to 'Firethorn'. I noted that "all prayers to saints are openings of oneself to a higher world": the Truth of the Light. I wrote:

> The poet receives the symbol from the spiritual world and beams or channels it into the material world. His is therefore a holy occupation, and Movement poetry has abdicated this holy function in favour of an enfeebled secular *frisson*, a pleasurable massage of the spine.

On Boxing Day we visited Loughton and I visited the church in the Forest, the church of the Holy Innocents, High Beach. I wrote, "The stile with stone steps. I am a symbolist now, and cannot help myself." I was building up to 'A Crocus in the Churchyard'.

'The Tree of Imagination', started on Christmas Eve, began six creative weeks in which I wrote 'Firethorn', 'A Temple-Dancer's Temple-Sleep', 'A Metaphysical's Light-*Mandala*' and 'The Fire-Flower' between Christmas 1979 and February 1980. This was achieved despite colossal distractions at school. In early January 1980 I opened the way to 'Firethorn' with this entry:

> Symbols are in the collective unconscious – ocean of Light... – that is all around us, and which flows into us.... Just as I channel healing powers..., so the poet channels symbols from outside. It is a blinkered psychological heresy that symbols exist only in the mind. They flow into the mind from the collective unconscious, and filter their universal qualities into the individual... recipient.... The symbols raise consciousness, transform it into a higher form.... Nature is a symbol that points to metaphysical truths.... Symbols and the language of image and emotion reveal transcendent truths external to man, i.e. the cosmic order in which everything corresponds and everything is related.... Symbolic analogy demonstrates the unity of the universe.... The poet as a medium for symbols.

I also wrote: "Symbols reveal One."[32]

In the middle of this intense contemplation of symbols my mother had heart failure. She woke up short of breath as if she had asthma, her lungs full of fluid. I visited her at Journey's End the next day and found her in the room in which my father died, sitting up in bed very rosy-cheeked. She told Ann that she had had angina for two years and had kept it from her sister Argie. She had tried to sell Journey's End, the family house of 35 years, and move. She said that this plan was so she could live on a ground floor and avoid stairs. She later rang to say that the ECG had confirmed that she had had a heart attack. She had shed some of her violin pupils and the schools where she taught the violin.[33]

Dogmatic authority and disharmony

At school the Head's control of us all had intensified. There had been a succession of incidents in which the overstressed and overworked Head had irritably confronted members of the staff and exhibited bad temper. She had shouted at the nun, "Read the bulletin," and the nun had been too Christian to do anything except retreat, apologising. Most Heads of Department had been confronted, and there was resentment. The school had become a place of stress and someone had to speak up.

At a Heads-of-Department meeting the Head asked what was to prevent us from becoming an excellent school. Someone asked, "Why are we so demoralised?" I then spoke. My *Diaries* record: "I told them. For five minutes: there is too little stillness and tranquillity, too little friendliness, too much 'professional' criticism…, too many meetings which are enervating,… and the Head must create conditions in which there is more trust. On the way out, in rain, the Head of Geography said, 'Your speech was so brilliant, it said everything I was going to say but you articulated it and formulated it better than I could, so basically there wasn't anything left to say after-wards.'"[34]

I had felt impelled to speak out against the excessive control the Head was exercising and I knew I would be singled out. Two days later I was put in sole charge of the coverage, which I had hitherto done in conjunction with the two Deputy Heads. In other words, I had to be in even earlier and write out the list of substitutions for absent teachers, which in such a large school sometimes meant filling in 150 slots for periods with the names of teachers who had spare time. It was the most unpopular job in the school. Each morning 25 copies of the coverage sheet were posted in different parts of the school and 110 staff looked to see how many of their free periods had been taken and complained that they had been picked on unfairly. (With the falling roll in Wandsworth which was causing schools to amalgamate the staff had dwindled from 140 to 110.) I countered by saying that I could only perform a limited service as Head of Department because I was now doing the Deputy Heads' work as well.

A few days later at a Senior Teachers' meeting with the Head and two

Deputies I urged the Head "to improve the vibrations in the school". I said: "Professional courtesies are very important, and the senior six don't shout at each other." I wrote: "I am taking the disharmony of the school into my soul and then purging it to leave the school tranquil and whole, healed."

New Powers
More revising for The Fire-Flower
Nevertheless, that weekend I wrote 'A Temple-Dancer's Temple-Sleep'. I wrote: "Jan 27, Sunday. Finished 'A Temple-Dancer's Temple-Sleep' around 12.45 p.m., having done it since yesterday morning (late). Went downstairs to make coffee, touched Ann who jumped and said, 'You've given me a shock.' I am so electric after typing it up that I crackle when people touch me."[35]

'The Fire-Flower', yugen and Reality
Two days later I had a profound experience of the Light and finished another poem. I wrote: "Jan 29. 9 p.m., nearly. A 'brainstorm', and stanzas 4–11 of 'The Metaphysical's Light-Mandala' wrote themselves. Around 6.45 I looked for the Light.... I sat with the light out and felt the surges coming into me, and my quickening heart – all the healing symptoms – while I put my hands over my eyes and looked for the Light in a kind of trance. And it was there: silver in water, as fire, as rose, as reflected moon,... but when Fire, full of hints of the face of God.... Now I am tired, drained, a little shaky from the massive discharge of energy. My body is silky-smooth with Light." I finished the poem next weekend.

A Japanese tenant, Kyoko Sato, took the top-floor room at 46 Ritherdon Road, having been introduced by the British Council. She was studying drama, and I used to go up and discuss the Japanese "yugen" (the Flower), a symbol that referred to an unparaphrasable glimpse of Reality, a hint of "what lies beneath the surface". (My Fire-Flower included the idea of the yugen.) She gave me a Japanese fan as a present. It was covered with wispy clouds, foaming waves and flickering fire (Taoistic Oneness), but also with a mesh of chains suggesting atoms and social organisation. The fan was to be held by a Noh dancer, and on her return to Japan Kyoko became Japan's best-known Noh dancer. The fan lay on a shelf unlooked at, until one day an art teacher at Garratt Green, who had got to know me through my new coverage job, asked if I had a "Japanese male fan" she could paint. I found it and looked at it and saw I had another poem.

I took the fan to school for her, and wrote the poem on February 5, 9 and 10. It was about the yugen or Zen flower of Noh, which I saw as the Light, whose dawning is received with a satisfied "Aaaaaaaaaaaaaah!" I wrote: "Feb 10. Am tired for I have spent the weekend, polishing, rewriting and typing up 'A Fan of Swirling *Tao*' [later retitled 'The Fire-Flower'])." I wrote: "It is 11 stanzas long, was drafted on Feb 5 and not touched until Feb 9. I spent all day yesterday on it, and was really tired after typing up 5 stanzas. I started early on the remainder this morning and finished it before lunch at 1.40, but had to type from 2.45 to 3.15. Then after reading the Sunday papers (3.30–5) and having my bath and giving the two boys their bath, I polished further, and am now leaving it at 8.45."

I added: "I have written 5... poems since Christmas: 'The Tree of Imagination', 'Firethorn', 'A Temple-Dancer's Temple-Sleep', 'A Metaphysical's Light-*Mandala*' and now 'A Fan of Swirling *Tao*' ['The Fire-Flower'] – all in a spell of six weeks. January and February 1980 are for me what May 1819 was to Keats, when he wrote those Odes. I am tired, but pleased."

I had not finished the volume that would be called *The Fire-Flower*, but I was now "about to fold myself down like a radio station in a hostile country" [, the school].[36]

I revise all my poetic works and embrace discipline of rules

Christopher Ricks (whose complete edition of *The Poems of Tennyson* in 1969 consisted of 1,812 pages with a full note on the genesis and variant textual readings of each poem, and all Tennyson's many revisions at the bottom of each page) had urged me to follow the example of Tennyson and revise my poems. I now felt that all my poetic works should be revised, that long lines should be replaced with strict, disciplined pentameters. I began my revisions on 16 February 1980. Over half-term I revised 'A Metaphysical in Marvell's Garden' and 'A Crocus in the Churchyard', relating them more to the soul and eternity. We went to Worthing, where I noted: "Wind, sun, sunlight on the water by the pier, gulls hindward hovering, flying into the wind, great foam as the breakers crashed on stones, wagtails,... gabled tops of the boarding-houses." I worked on 'Fire-Void', which showed eternity as a Buddhist void that is in fact a fullness, and then on 'Sea-Fire'. While I worked on this poem back in Ritherdon Road, Ann's car was stolen from outside our front gate. I telephoned the police, and police stopped the driver ten minutes later. Ann, returning from private tuition in my car, passed her car surrounded by police, stopped and said in astonishment, "That's *my* car." I revised 'A Mystic Fire-Potter's Red Sun-Halo' and then 'An Aesthete's "Golden" Artefacts', which is about the artist's development to a "gold" soul. (In this I drew on a visit I made to the goldsmiths of Hatton Garden.)

I now saw that the control of Garratt Green had had the disciplinary effect of a monastery:

It took me 20 years to accept the discipline of the Rule.... Where some men would have sought a monastery, I sought the discipline of the tannoy in a large school, where a different kind of silence, and self-abnegation, was possible. No one there knows I am a poet, not one soul of the 110 teachers there. This is my penance and sacrifice: to hide my true profession, as Hopkins denied his for 7 years, in the name of discipline. I have disciplined myself and can now write within the rules.

I knew that I needed to be disciplined to develop as a poet.

In March I carried on revising my poems. I "wrote the 'theodolite' stanza into 'Crocus', thereby purging the haunting, surprised image that seized me as I walked with Richard [Moxon, the surgeon] in the churchyard...a couple of weeks ago on March 8". On 23 March I revised my 14th elegy, 'Strawberry Hill', as 'Clouded-Ground Pond'. Again I was dwelling on the fusing of the surface reflection of the clouds and the ground of the pond beneath. In a few seconds I could be simultaneously aware of the cloudy reflection and the ground, which to me symbolised the Oneness of time and eternity. I wrote: "The pond symbolises the self... which is united with Oneness (*Tao*)." On 23 March I wrote:

Have had a good Sunday morning typing up 'Clouded-Ground Pond' and revising 'Pear-Ripening House'. At the end the question 'Why be ripe?' lodged itself in my mind. Shakespeare did not explain this in *King Lear* ('ripeness is all') and immediately a stanza welled up and I grabbed paper and wrote out stanza 6, the rhymes virtually perfect, which relates the whole poem to the metaphysical view and contains the idea that pips are future lives.... Soul has genes which are passed on to the next life.

I was mulling over the concept of the Fire-Flower when I attended another Mystics and Scientists conference on the theme of consciousness. I wrote: "A new way of seeing Reality and the universe has been made possible by post-Newtonian physics. Reality is a swirl, there is no distinction between mind and matter, consciousness flows in and 'thinks us', and the vanguard of the movement is the enlightened poet, for his image comes from a sea of consciousness." Pir Vilayat Inayat Khan was present. He took a meditation on the Sunday morning, and I saw the Light as a collapsing black hole: "March 30. In meditation this morning under Pir, saw a collapsing black hole of Light." I was aware that the universe, including its black holes, was ultimately composed of the Light. Later I realised: "'The black hole of Light... was the Fire-Flower' of course, the petals were of white fire."

I now saw perfection in a new light: "The outer eye sees the form, the inner eye of the mind or self sees into the form for the Idea, sees the oak-tree within the acorn, feels the sap rising. The imagination is the eye of the mind which can see the Eternal world working out at the level of Idea, which is living and real." I related this kind of perception to my poetry: "The language of poetry: catch the living Idea and image, and fix it in its outer form (rhyme)." I also saw the relationship between the part and the whole in a new way: "My body is a wave (particle) in our universe and therefore *is* our universe…. There is no more 'a part of', only an indivisible unity which is the 'part'." A work of art "should be a dynamic canvas in which there is transience and eternity at the same time, but perpetual transformation".[37]

In April I continued revising 'Pear-Ripening House' after we all visited Journey's End for the last time before it was sold. I then continued revising 'Sea-Fire'. I felt in harmony with Nature – "a host of birds picking among the flower-beds" and "my 45 fish" in the aquarium in the sitting-room – and, now the school holidays had arrived, wrote an essay on the Metaphysical Revolution, an introduction to the poems in the *Fire-Flower*. I continued revising the other poems in that volume to "blackbirds piping in trees, sparrows chattering". I was so hard up I could not afford to get my car through its MOT, but then the British Council sent me a Turkish tenant who paid a deposit and I could relax again. I recognised that "six years of pursuing threads of essays [at Garratt Green] have been a good discipline, and I now work a central idea to its conclusion" and that "Garratt Green has been the teaching-school for my soul".

On 5 May I wrote: "Am a bit tired, having checked and typed out 3 poems in the last two days. Now 'The Fire-Flower'. I worked on, writing about the "rose-tree of Light" which I wrote into 'A Metaphysical in Marvell's Garden', and after spending a day moving my mother from Journey's End to her new, smaller house at 54 High Road, I wrote: "I sit looking down on this old vicarage garden [in Ritherdon Road]. Roses pour up at me, yellow, pink and red, and it seems so natural that I should be writing of a flowered soul as a rose."[38]

I felt even more controlled at school. The day before my birthday I wrote: "Eve of my birthday and I'm so cluttered with school work (for my staff meeting tomorrow) and car trouble that I have not been able to touch any poems all day." I was teaching 'The Waste Land' again to a sceptical Lower 6th and "thought again what an overrated work it is. It rings very hollow in places, e.g. the fishermen lounging at noon – couldn't they just be having lunch?"

I did more work on 'Pear-Ripening House' and 'Fire-Void' and after a brief visit to Worthing (where hot sun left my face red), I finished my Preface on the Metaphysical Revolution. I noted: "Found that 'meta' of 'metaphysics' can mean 'behind' as well as 'after'." The metaphysical is what is 'behind' the physical. In early June I finished 'A Metaphysical in Marvell's Garden' and observed: "I have 16 poems of the length of Larkin's best-known two, 'Church Going' and 'The Whitsun Weddings', both of which have social themes." My Third Mystic Life was reflected in *The Fire-Flower*.

I added: "I charted the mystical tradition of the Light... and have now put it with modern physics and transpersonal psychology into a Metaphysical Revolution. My next work must give the model for this Metaphysical Reality, i.e. include physics – and biology – and psychology."[39] This entry anticipated *The Universe and the Light*.

New power of hypnosis

About this time I discovered another new power: "My additional powers include my ability to hypnotise my children to sleep. Two nights running I have taken Matthew down the (imaginary) flight of stairs, and on the bottom stair he has slumped into sleep, and I have touched Anthony on his head three times, and each time he has got more sleepy until he is off."

Independence: I explore small school in Cranleigh

I was desperate to give myself more time for writing, and I returned to the idea of buying a school which Ann could run. I saw an advertisement for a small school in Cranleigh, Surrey in *The Times Educational Supplement*. It was going with a 5-bedroom house, and I took Ann to see it and felt that very soon I would be running a school and escaping from Garratt Green. I would of course have to sell 46 Ritherdon Road, and I was not in a position to go ahead on the school in Cranleigh. But the model seemed right. I wrote: "My poetry now needs the freshness of the countryside... the bees humming among the flowers by the orchard." On a second visit I wrote: "In the heart of lovely countryside: Cranleigh. Winding road, cows, sheep, farms, foxgloves growing wild, a flower-watcher's Paradise."

Finishing The Fire-Flower

I was still polishing some of the 16 poems. Redrafting 'The Bride of Time' left me exhausted, and the next day I "awoke unwell and by 10 a.m. had a migraine, my first since I was 14 or so. Had blotches in front of my eyes.... Stayed in bed all morning and made corrections to 'The Bride of Time' in a near-blind condition."[40]

In early July I finished revising 'The Fire-Flower'. I had a vision: "Saw a wonderful, elaborate blue light 6 inches x 4 inches (down) with sparkling 'beads' across it, a beautiful... heavenly vision, as I lay totally relaxed." I thought that the beads might symbolise my poems. A couple of days later I wrote: "I am tired from 10 months of work on the 16 poems, and the Metaphysical Revolution." I added: "The closest parallel to *The Fire-Flower* is *The Duino Elegies*, for Rilke wrote: 'We are the bees of the Invisible'." And "My journey has been from the anti-metaphysical to the metaphysical.... All my works should at the end of my life add up to one unified statement of a metaphysical nature." (*My Double Life 1* and 2 contain such a unified statement.)

In Cornwall at the end of July I researched the local china-clay industry. We went to Porthleven, and Wheal Martin china-clay mine, and a fête at Caerhays Castle. We visited the Gweek seal sanctuary and returned to the 17th-century church on Gunwalloe beach, and I wrote of "beautiful country hedges full of wild flowers and butterflies and birds" and "slugs on the grass, Cornish mists, damp". We went to Plymouth and visited Mount Edgcumbe and Cotehele, and went up Smeaton's Tower on the Hoe.

But I was still thinking about *The Fire-Flower*. Back in Ritherdon Road and still looking for sun in a year when there was very little sun, I wrote: "Sunbathed in the only patch of sun, under our pear-tree. A bird – a speckled thrush – was pecking at pears, and I thought that my image of pears falling round a poet's head, i.e. images, could have been...dislodged by the bird (thrush) of the soul which, hawk-like, flew into the boughs. I was lying on my front on my sun-couch, and at that moment... there was a 'spat' on the canvas by the back of my leg."[41] The thrush had done a dropping by my leg. So the physical world interacts with poetic musings.

Somehow (via Tuohy?) *The Fire-Flower* found its way to Lord Longford, who sent me a letter saying that the poems are "beautiful" and "moving" and have "many merits", while the introduction is "impressive". He was an ally of the metaphysical as distinct from the secular.

Perception of the metaphysical universe

I pursued the metaphysical idea in different disciplines. I "tubed" into town, went to Watkins and bought Bohm's *Wholeness and the Implicate Order*, which confirmed an idea I had been groping towards, that "language fails to reflect reality, it fragments reality [i.e. the whole] and distorts philosophic thought with its 'I-you', subject-verb-object-structure". I went to a recital at Christ Church, Streatham (the church of the Harding branch of my family, where my father had sung) and regarded the "music as a soul-releaser, as it used to be, rather than as a language to be listened to with the mind". I was also researching into the metaphysical philosophers. I wrote: "I am a process philosopher who is developing the metaphysics of Bergson, Whitehead and Heidegger.... Also Bohm, who adds to their work.... [I] must unfold the metaphysics of light."

I was in an unsettled time. Trying to set up an escape from the control of Garratt Green, I had had 46 Ritherdon Road painted and had shown it to an estate agent with a view to selling it to fund a private school such as the one in Cranleigh. There had been an offer for more than double what I paid for it, but (having nothing to buy) I was in no position to sell and after some weeks the offer was withdrawn. I had been briefly ill: "Sep 19. Chest pains began at 8.20 and by 9.15 at St James's [Hospital] thinking I might die of a heart attack: feeling giddy and faint, being ECG-ed and then X-rayed, being wheeled about the corridors with my feet over the end of the trolley, in my white 'paper' short-sleeved gown." Matthew had thoughtfully said, "I hope you don't die." I was diagnosed as having a lung infection which had caused the pain.

In October we celebrated Matthew's sixth birthday with a party for 29 at which Lawrence (a boy in his class) "wrecked the garden and broke the cricket bat and took the wheel off the tricycle and bent the whirligig for clothes and was frequently ordered out of the room where films were shown". I was now determined to get Matthew away from his school.

I marvelled at the way our pear-tree seemed to be feeding us: "The mystery of the pears. Since July the pear-tree has been dropping a few pears each day: four or five, at the most six, never less than four. I pick them up each morning.... Four or five a day, by staggering its dropping, the pear-tree is almost trying to keep us provided. No matter what wind or storm, no more than six pears come down a day, and now, in October, it is still dropping." Trees seemed to co-operate with the scheme of the universe to provide wasps, birds and humans with fruit.

I attended a gathering for my mother's 70th birthday at my younger brother's. There was a discussion of Europe, and I shared "my vision of a unitary European state with one currency, leading to world government which will hold wars in check, and be a part of the disintegration of Western civilization".[42]

Dogmatic authority
The ILEA's Trotskyite exam policies

The following week I had to attend a course on 'The English Department in the 1980s' in Dartford. About 30 actual and would-be Heads of Department stayed at Thames Polytechnic, and during the day there were long sessions which went on into the evening, after which we were free. I went to my room and sat at my desk and pored over the *Encyclopaedia Britannica*'s entry for 'Metaphysics'. I wrote ironically: "14 Oct. A day at my typewriter on metaphysics, punctuated by visits to the course."

The course seemed to be run by controlling Trotskyites who were ideologically against all examinations and wanted teachers to take the place of examiners. It was said more than once that pupils and teachers were equal and that pupils should therefore not be subjected to outside examination boards or repressed by teachers' standards. But their revolt against authority created a new elitist authority: they had now become very influential; indeed, powerful. I noted: "This course is run by a bunch of Trots, and everyone is creeping and crawling up to them because of all the amalgamations; and expressing interest in 100% course work even though they have already admitted to me that they are on the side of examined 'A' level." Soon afterwards there was a Divisional Heads-of-English meeting, at which the Trotskyites' attitudes were put forward, and I was in a minority of one in opposing the revolutionary changes and speaking out for the retention of 'A' level in the name of preserving standards.

When Ann went into hospital in Wimbledon for a couple of days to have a bone cyst removed I looked after Matthew and Anthony and nursed Ann when she came out, "sick and dizzy all day", making meals and drinks for all of them at different times. I was in "domestic chaos".[43]

To get Matthew away from the local church school, where Lawrence's influence was worrying and he had left everyone else behind with his reading, I had arranged for him to be interviewed at Dulwich College Preparatory School. We had had a meeting with Mr Woodcock, the Head of the school, and to our surprise and delight Dulwich Prep offered Matthew a place immediately, to start the next week. There were school fees to afford and more of a journey to school to cope with but Matthew was now being stretched and writing at length, and had the prospect of avoiding the dreadful policies being inflicted on London's State secondary schools.

New powers: Universal Mind and research into ancient cultures
The Brain of Britain, opening to the Universal Mind
At Garratt Green I became aware of a new power. I had met Tom Dyer, who was Brain of Britain. He was now a supply teacher at our school, and I had gone into his class in search of his Head of Department, and saw him standing on a chair and being lapped by a sea of moving girls. "Sit down," I bellowed, restoring order, and he got off the chair and muttered his thanks. He was fairly corpulent with an old face, spectacles and a convict's crew cut, and he wore an old raincoat round the school. He was seeing if he wanted to become a mature student and train as a teacher, and had concluded he was not suited to the teaching profession. Then it was announced in the staff room that he had just become Brain of Britain in the BBC radio's knock-out competition. He now latched on to me and sat with me at lunch, asking me to test him for a quiz he was going in for.

I was fascinated by where he located his knowledge. I would say, "Name me six ecclesiastical characters in Chaucer's *Prologue*," and he rattled them off without hesitation. Then I asked, "How do you know that?" He would shrug and say, "I don't know, I just do, the answers float through the air." "Name me Amenhotep IV's family," I said, and when he did that I probed further – and found he believed in a Universal Mind that he was somehow able to plug into, a kind of Collective Unconscious of information all round him which channelled in the answers with unerring accuracy. It was like the Light flowing into him, except that it was a stream of accurate historical knowledge. In spite of his gift he was unemployable. "I have no imagination," he would say, "I couldn't write a letter or an essay to save my life. I can only be used for retrieving information – in a library, and libraries now have computers."

Tom took to calling at 46 Ritherdon Road on his late-night walk so that I could test him from my *Encyclopaedia Britannicas*. We talked about the universe. We went out into the street and gazed at the stars, and he would identify each and tell me its age, size, composition and special features.

Jill Purce: I belong to no 'school' and reject the New Age's unevidential dogmas
I had been in touch with Jill Purce, the author of *The Mystic Spiral*, about my research into ancient cultures and the possibility of my presenting the metaphysical Light in an illustrated Thames & Hudson book, the series for which she was an editor. She invited me to her Hampstead flat. I found myself in an enormous room with books and whorled shells, and the beautiful blonde appearance I had seen on television talking about mystical art. Jill quickly made it clear that she was pulling away from Thames & Hudson and wanted to be my agent. She signed my copy of her book and said, "I want to know where you are coming from. To what school [i.e. tradition, group] do you belong?" I told her I was independent of all approaches so that I could view all objectively. Nothing came of our arrangement as she married Rupert Sheldrake soon afterwards and held seminars in Tibetan chanting.

Before I left she said, "You must always have an interdisciplinary theme," advice I have taken. Her question as to what "school" I belong brought me face to face with the New Age, and I knew I would never belong to any New-Age school. I did not believe some unevidential New-Age dogmas such as the one that held that a change in all human consciousness was imminent, and I was not keen on the occult. I was clear in my mind that I had now rejected the unevidential dogmas of the New Age.[44] It had served its purpose in introducing me to ancient cultures and symbols I could use in my poetic works.

Research into ancient cultures: The Sun-Hawk and chaos
One such symbol was "the image of flight,... the Flight to the Sun.... The Sun-Hawk is the soul journeying to the sun." I now thought of my book as *The Sun-Hawk* and tried to make time to research into ancient cultures, which I planned to cover near the beginning.

However, at Garratt Green I had been equipped with a bleeper and was now on call like a hospital consultant for any emergency. More and more of my time was being taken. In November 1980 my 'A' level pupil at Garratt Green, Razia Iqbal (who was also Head Girl and later a television presenter), sensing the gulf between my love of literature and the prevalent philistinism, had asked me perceptively, "Sir, why are you here?" I increasingly asked myself that same question. I wrote: "I have so much to do, and such a short time in which to do it."

Caroline's father, the Group Captain, had died aged 85. I was invited to the funeral but did not attend as he had been obstructive during our separation and it would be hard to take time off work. The Christmas holidays came as a relief, but now I was preparing for the boys' Christmas, and my family came on Boxing Day.

I was pondering on how to unite the way of action and the way of contemplation when I went to Worthing in January 1981 and visited Margaret Riley in nearby Shoreham. She had her painting of St Thérèse of Lisieux propped on a chair, and Margaret drew my attention to her eyes. I wrote: "One eye (the right one) focuses on time and on the world (the way of action of Mother Teresa of Calcutta), and the left eye looks far into eternity, the white being a circle of light in the centre of the pupil, a deep contemplative look that is lost to its situation." Her painting united the two ways. She described to me again the vision she had of Christ in St Ives in October 1974. She woke and saw him in the corner of her room, and he said, "Here I am, I am with you." There were many visions of Christ in past centuries but this is the only one I know of in the 20th century.

While Ann was at a course on dyslexia I saw the Light in terms of a seed: "The Seed-Light means that the Light is the source of everything.... The seed contains the tree, so there is a parallel upwards movement, from seed to root/trunk, thence to branches and fruit.... A sea of seeds from one seed or point (*cornucopia*)."[45]

Suddenly my life became chaotic and events seemed to conspire against my writing. A thief loaded a Mercedes onto a stolen trailer and ran into 20 cars outside our house. Ann's car suffered a slight knock. An upstairs tenant dislodged a pipe which caused a flood. I was just starting to rewrite my book on ancient cultures, *The Sun-Hawk*. "Wrote the first paragraph... and before I could type it the bedroom ceiling began to leak. Water poured down the light flex, flashing the light bulb on and off." Luckily I was in the room at the time and averted further damage by asking the tenants upstairs not to run their water and by catching the cascade in buckets. But a ceiling had to be redecorated and a pipe refitted. I began to write my first paragraph again "and there was a sizzling from the bedroom flex (the light was off) and a major fire risk glowed with a spark". So I again abandoned my attempt to write and spent an hour-and-a-half avoiding a major fire. I "turned off the electricity at source in the cellar, unscrewed the white disc by torchlight, undid the screws in the ceiling to let the cable hang out, emptied it of water, then turned on the electricity and heated up the sizzling wires with the hair-drier". My provisional title for Chapter One was 'The Spark and the Fire'. Somehow the metaphysical meaning of the words had turned social.

The dispute between Ricks and MacCabe at Cambridge University surfaced in *The Guardian* a few days later when Ricks blocked MacCabe's promotion for wanting to teach grammar, psychoanalysis, linguistics, sociology and Marxism at the expense of the 600 years of English Literature, including the metaphysical tradition. Ricks stood for the tradition, and although he was a secular sceptic he included the metaphysical line within the tradition. MacCabe stood for change, linguistics, structuralism and post-structuralism. I sided with Ricks. A few days later still it transpired that MacCabe had been sacked.

I was now doing further research into ancient cultures for *The Sun-Hawk*. I read widely on Egypt and the *khu* or *akh*, the spiritual soul which was at the centre of Egyptian life. I researched into bull-cults, Zoroastrianism and ancient religions. I discovered that the man I was introduced to in the Dulwich library when I worked there, W.B. Emery, was the first to discover evidence of the bull-cult. I learned he had discovered the Iseum (a place linked with Apis bulls) while I was in Egypt in 1970. I researched into the Kurgans and realised I had met one of the authorities, Leon Stover, in Tuohy's room in Japan. I realised that I had been shown two people I would need. I warmed to the Puritan in F.D. Millet's c.1892 picture, *Between Two Fires*, which shows him sitting between two women, and when I found a print in an antique show I bought it.

I was still thinking about the universe. Tom Dyer came round in February and we "went out star-gazing with his binoculars on the frosty grass. Saw Orion of course...; the red bull's eye (Taurus); the nebula of the sword; Gemini; Capella [within] Auriga; Regulus; Algol 4 (Perseus); Cassiopeia; Ursa Major and Plough – trapezoid 6 including two pointers to the North or Pole Star; the Lion, Leo...; Rigal in Orion; and Sirius (8 light-years away)."

We went to Loughton at half-term and visited my aunt Argie "who moves slowly after her heart attack and is slightly dazed with a strange smile". Back at school I used humour to wreck serious meetings. In early March I demolished a meeting of the Heads of Department: "I use humour as an anarchic weapon.... I use jokes like bombs. I creep into a meeting and lay a joke like an IRA bomber, crouch down and put my fingers in my ears and bang! my Headmistress's policies have a gaping hole in them and the atmosphere has been spoiled, for no one can concentrate on her words any longer."[46]

I continued my research into Buddhism and then Judaism for *The Sun-*

Hawk. I reflected on the Kabbalistic Tree of Life. I realised the true nature of "the experience by the Worcester College lake, when I gave up the Law to read English: the trees reflected in the water, a tumbling chestnut – upside down: the Tree of Life (rooted in the sky)". I wrote of the Essenes: "The Invisible Light (Heavenly Father) and the visible reflection, Darkness or outer Darkness (Earthly Mother), live in harmony with the Law through the Tree of Life, so all energies flow in and one is... at one with the Light."

I saw that the Great Pyramid represented "the Tree of Life, inverted from seed/golden apex of Light to base on Earth". Later I added, thinking of the shape of the Great Pyramid rather than the reason it was built: "When I was writing 'The Riddle of the Great Pyramid' in Dulwich in 1963, I stopped W.B. Emery to obtain his view – without success. It was still a riddle. Now I have solved the riddle. It is the Tree of Life, from a point downwards, creation coming out of Light."[47]

I had channelled my new powers into disciplined poetry, and moved away from the unevidential New Age while continuing my scholarly research into the ancient cultures and religions it had rediscovered. I was determined to escape the Head's stifling control, and a new episode would bring this about.

CHAPTER 2

Ordeals of Independence: Trials of the Dark Night, Battles against Communism

"The Final Ordeals: The hero has to undergo a last series of tests (often three in number) to prove that he is truly worthy of the prize. This culminates in a last great battle or ordeal which may be the most threatening of all."
Christopher Booker, *The Seven Basic Plots*, p.83, 'The Quest: Summing up'

After the illumination I described in *My Double Life 1: This Dark Wood* there were raptures and visions, recollection and contemplation. New works came out of my new consciousness, but the Dark Night was still with me. My Dark Night of the Soul (or Dark Night of the Senses) had detached my soul from the web of the lower senses. My Dark Night of the Spirit was a further purgation which had poured new powers and knowledge into my soul and spirit and united sense and spirit, a reconciliation that is a hallmark of the neo-Baroque vision. Now I was confronted by new challenges in the outside world, trials, ordeals of combat that tested my determination to be independent. The ordeals were political, and they were all battles against different forms of Communism.

In the German medieval vehmic courts an ordeal was a test of guilt or innocence: an accused person was subjected to severe pain or torture, and survival was taken as divine proof of innocence. My three Communist-related ordeals were not about guilt or innocence, but about coping with extreme difficulties. Looking back, I see my survival as winning my independence and indicating my suitability and readiness – my worthiness – to enter unitive life.

Episode 4:

Baroque and Egalitarian Socialism

First ordeal: many-headed hydra (egalitarian socialism of ILEA)

Years: 1981–1983
Locations: Loughton; Winchester
Works: *Beauty and Angelhood*; *The Wind and the Earth*; *A Rainbow in the Spray*

Initiatives: Third Mystic Life; identification as neo-Baroque writer; acquiring Oaklands School

"Nor is there singing school but studying."

W.B. Yeats, 'Sailing to Byzantium'

"The Baroque writer combines Classicism and Romanticism by reflecting both the social ego of the Classical writer and the mystic infinite spirit of the Romantic writer…. The [Baroque] language combines Classical statement and Romantic image."

Nicholas Hagger, 'Preface on the
New Baroque Consciousness and the
Redefinition of Poetry as Classical Baroque'
Collected Poems, 1958–2005

"I have seen Classicism as a movement of felt thought and the social ego, and Romanticism as a movement (as in Wordsworth and Shelley) of the soul, spirit and the One. And I have called for a poetry that is a mixture of sense and spirit, of Classicism and Romanticism. I saw this mixture of sense and spirit as 'Baroque'."

Nicholas Hagger, Preface on *Classical Odes*

In my next episode my new powers had blossomed into my Baroque principle and poetic style (blending the sensual and spiritual, Classical and Romantic), and I yearned for time to write new literary works, I longed to become an independent Principal and escape from the ILEA Inspectorate whose new egalitarian policy deprived London children of marking. My first ordeal was my struggle to be free from the many-headed hydra, the ILEA.

Egalitarian socialism: escaping Garratt Green, securing Oaklands School
Miss Lord agrees to sell Oaklands School
I had become increasingly demoralised at Garratt Green, which was waiting to be amalgamated and I saw as a "dying school". I wanted to escape the distractions from learning and the Trotskyites and create a Centre of Excellence where learning and standards would be encouraged. I had not forgotten Miss Lord saying to me at Anthony's christening: "You'd better have Oaklands." I had written: "Shall I risk going to see her? Do we want it?

Probably. Ann could be Headmistress and I could do the administrative side and write…. Buy over in Epping Forest?" One morning, standing in the window of our large bedroom in Ritherdon Road, Ann prompted me: "Go and ask Miss Lord if you can have Oaklands." I telephoned Miss Lord, "and will see her at 5 on Friday".

I visited Miss Lord and toured an empty Oaklands School. It was homely with many nooks and crannies, but evidently needed a lot of decoration and renewal. She said to me as we returned to the study, "I've often thought about you and wondered if you still wanted it." We arranged that Ann would visit the school and have a look. I wrote: "So as my beliefs deepen I turn towards infancy: from university to secondary school and now primary school…. I shall live among the innocent in green fields…. Back in Epping Forest I shall create again." It seemed that going to Oaklands would solve all our problems in one go: "School fees, the Head taking too much of my time, the impending closure of Garratt Green, escaping an urban setting for the countryside and a place with more sense of a community."

In April I heard from Miss Lord. She wrote that she would let us have Oaklands in 1983 at a valuation to be agreed. I was elated. I wrote: "So I may end up with the… school I went to in the war…. The seed (acorn) I planted just down the road from Oaklands in the 1960s has grown into the great oak of Oaklands."[1]

I turned against Garratt Green: "I have had enough of civilising Caliban at my unruly State school. Like Prospero, I will retire from the civilising process and bury my [staff], but enjoy the magic of enchanted Oaklands in retirement. Long summer days in the green fields and the buttercups."

My imperious aunt Argie, who had been Assistant Matron at the London Hospital, was full of the abuses of the State system and she told a gathering at my brother Rob's large house near Tunbridge Wells about a conversation she had had with Len Murray, the local Secretary-General of the TUC, in her newsagents. She had taken him to task for the widespread breaking of the 5th commandment, "Thou shalt not steal", which was then costing the National Health Service a quarter of its annual budget. Murray protested that the unions did not approve of stealing, to which Argie said, "Come off it, Lionel."

Argie had very definite ideas. She was driving near the London Hospital when a foreign-looking gentleman stepped into the road in front of her car. She stopped (holding up the traffic), got out and said to him, "In this country we cross on a pedestrian crossing." She led him to a nearby crossing and escorted him across the road so he would know what to do next time. One day she went into the Loughton delicatessen and was greeted with "Oh, Miss Broadley, I've got some nice French cheese and I've saved you some. Would you like it now?" Argie replied, "No, thank you very much. I don't like cheese and I don't like the French, and no, I won't have your French cheese, thank you very much."

At the beginning of May we went to Loughton and met Miss Lord, who was "determined" we should have Oaklands and was moving towards a price. We went to the Strawberry Hill pond and looked at the tadpoles, and

to Connaught Water and noted the coots and catkins, and then went on to Queen Elizabeth's hunting lodge.

My research had been continuing, and at a Mystics and Scientists conference in Winchester I had chatted with Dr Peter Fenwick, one of the country's leading experts on the mind-body relationship. I asked him, "Do you still believe that mind is dependent on brain, or could mind

Ann and Miss Lord in 1982

transcend brain?" He replied, "I increasingly feel that mind may be a universal phenomenon interpreted by the brain." (The Brain of Britain would have agreed with that.) I had gone into Gnosticism and church architecture, and had "realised that a church spire is... an apex down which creation manifests into spirit and psyche and matter, or into mind and soul and form".[2]

Baroque
Mysticism: I attend four conference retreats
Between May and July 1981 I attended four conferences or weekend retreats, on which I drew for the four poems of *Beauty and Angelhood*. Like *The Fire-Flower* these poems came out of my Third Mystic Life.

High Leigh
The first was a conference on esoteric Christianity at High Leigh, Hoddesdon, Herts, where I heard an inspirational talk by the young canon Peter Spink of Coventry Cathedral, an Anglican priest who had founded the Omega Order. He sought to revive practical mysticism and recover the "divine indwelling Light" in accordance with the work of F.C. Happold and Teilhard de Chardin. He stood and talked fluently without notes, and I recorded: "He said many of the things that I have said, e.g. the old forms are dead and the upsurge of the spirit requires new forms." Afterwards I walked with him in the maze and he urged me, "Come and join me, leave your school and work with me." It felt like a call but I knew I could not work within Christianity.

The next morning there was a meditation based on the Christian Lord's

Prayer in the library, taken by Kenneth Cuming, a former Warden of Burrswood Healing Centre, Kent:

> The Hoddesdon 'library'. Sitting...by the second door to the right... – Light! For at least three-quarters of an hour.... I gazed at the Light all the time.... Pow! Light almost blew my mind, and I had a tremendous tingling all over and my hair prickled and stood on end for three minutes.

The next day I wrote:

> All day I have shone with the Light. My skin has a glow, I can see reflections in it. My body is so full of Light that I am almost transparent in profile.... The Light... has made my skin immensely soft, my flesh very pliant.... My skin is more 'oily' as though it is permeated by dew. The Light is in every pore of my skin.

I now began typing notes for my coming epic poem. I recorded that the last time I tried to begin it, I "realised" that "I would have to reflect the new scientific discoveries and spirituality in my poem".

I thought intensely again about the connection between the decline of Western civilization and the absence of the Light:

> What I am essentially writing is my anatomy of the Decline of the West.... Our rubbishy culture and civilization, and the misery of the Seeker... who grasps the significance of living by the Light, his higher purpose.... How the enlightened Seeker... can contribute to the salvation of his culture and civilization, by de-Humanism.... When Seekers cease to be enlightened, they lose their aim and purpose, and civilization (which they lead) loses its aim and declines.[3]

Hawkwood
At the end of May I attended a weekend course on the Kabbalah at Hawkwood, Gloucestershire. I walked in the beautiful grounds – "birdsong, cows, horses, hundreds of daisies, railings" – and encountered Warren Kenton, the informally-dressed, small man with a beard I already knew, who was taking the course.

The course proved disappointing. We had to ask the inner teacher a question and were encouraged to visualise images. The visualising of images we practised seemed shallow. I wrote that they are "not as deep as what is received during contemplation". Conscious retrieval of images seemed a form of magic I was not interested in. I wrote:

My images. Peacock/lyre/hopscotch/Tree of Life in mosaic. Then a Christ upside down on the temple floor.... The ark in a black cloud with flames. Angels as white brightnesses instead of faces, and folded robes or veils, five or six approaching, heavenly hosts.... A chariot in a dark crowd. High priest with hands raised.... A large ring of celestial beings with a dark centre, like folds in veils. [My] Shadow as a black-hooded monk, no face at all.... A traveller in rags, dishevelled, dusty clothes, naked. Deep eyes of high priest.

On our free Saturday afternoon I visited the nearby monastery of Prinknash, a worldly monastery with a shop for food produced by the monks. On the Sunday I saw more images: "Rose, golden flower, veil with patterns over Light, the waters of spirit, an angel in a cloud. Divine Fire. Levels as water-falls or terraces with gardens."

A week later, after attending my nephew William's christening, I experienced: "Pow! A flood of consciousness filled me, so when I lay down to sleep I saw Paisley patterns from the unconscious and was filled with consciousness on a different level. Sleep was hopeless." The next weekend, after writing some stories, I "cut the lawn briefly, and imagined myself into birds and daisies and thirsty flowers, which I had to give a drink. I find that more and more I feel into the being of leaves and growing things, and am still as a stone, and just listen to everything. I have a poet's imagination of entering the inner essence, becoming the sap rising."[4]

After a tour of Kent, I took the boys to Canterbury Cathedral and showed them the place where four knights killed Becket. We encountered a priest in black. Later Anthony went missing. I eventually found him sitting on a step in front of the small shut door in a wall near where Becket was murdered. Aged four he said, "They're in there. The knights. They can't get out. I've caught them. I will take their swords and kill them for killing that kind man in black." I was amazed at his courage in capturing four knights armed with swords without any weapon of his own.

Kent House

I attended the third of the four weekends on 20 June at Kent House, near Tunbridge Wells, a house Peter Spink had taken over as a near-ruin and restored by hard work. I stayed with his wife and walked to Kent House, where Spink held court at the end of a long room which had a carpet, comfortable chairs and a table. There were about 20 of us. We were put into silence for the weekend and told that we should hoe weeds in the grounds (as in a Zen temple). In the first session Spink emphasised contemporary mysticism among the working classes and impatiently brushed aside any references to the mystic tradition of the last 600 years. I wrote: "The mystic way of life of silence, which accords with my poem 'The Silence', is a necessary base for Spink's movement." I wrote that his direction was to "remysticise Christianity, provide a new ecumenical impetus on the basis of the Light, transform Church services into meditations and contemplations".

Spink held himself back from us during this weekend. On the last day he performed a Mass based on the Light, a Light Eucharist. Everyone spoke of him as a *guru*, a leader of a cult, a Steiner. I saw his religious community as being like "[Thomas à Kempis's] Windesheim or [Pascal's] Port Royal or [Nicholas Ferrar's] Little Gidding".[5]

St Peter's Convent

The fourth conference was again with Peter Spink, a day at St Peter's Convent, Woking. Spink wanted to change the direction of the Omega Order and had invited about 60 people to hear a proposal that it should become a teaching order with modules on education, healing and counselling. We ate packed lunches in the sisters' garden, and I sat next to Betty James who was making the proposal. After Eucharist in the chapel and then *Feria* (Divine Office) she gave her talk. I talked of remysticising Europe: "This led to a heated discussion outside with Spink.... He said: 'I want communities everywhere, throughout England. Europe is further ahead.'" He wanted to secure his flanks against the Church and other religions, while I emphasised the experiences of the Light of the great mystics. "Spink: 'We're not ready for that yet, I'm not ready, none of us are ready.'"[6] I decided to have no more to do with him.

Negotiating Oaklands, family

At school I had been running the exams for a month and had internal exam papers to mark. I was still negotiating Oaklands, with regular visits to Miss Lord's house. The thought of creating a Centre of Excellence that would implement everything the ILEA was obstructing had taken hold. In July I spent several days going through the Oaklands books and negotiating where we would build our new house, whether in the kitchen garden or (as we eventually decided) on the site of the Art Room next to Miss Lord's own house. On 11 July I was able to report: "Finished with Miss Lord. It is all sewn up now." We would be taking over in September 1982, a year earlier than originally planned. I began to design the house I would build within the grounds and recalled 1968, when I used to walk Nadia past Oaklands to see the cows at the top of the road and say jokingly "I will buy Oaklands one day." I wondered if

Providence marked me out in 1968 as the future... Principal of Oaklands, and did its upmost to put me in the position of being able to take over:... got me away from the wife who was 'no good to me', in Libya; got me attached to the wife who would be Headmistress; got me into the schools and a salary that could sustain Oaklands; got me Ritherdon Road to improve so that I could buy Oaklands; and blocked all buyers of the house until I was ready to convert it into Oaklands. It was for that that I had to become a Head of Department at Garratt Green.

I had seen much less of Nadia since she moved to Edinburgh in view of the distance involved. I now heard that Caroline's husband had been unemployed since leaving the RAF in March 1981, that he had found a job in Brussels and that Caroline would join him there in September. Nadia would live in a flat in Edinburgh.

My sister Frances bought a house in Wimbledon. She was in competition with an unknown buyer who turned out to be Biggs-Davison. Frances and her husband secured the house, whereupon Biggs-Davison bought one two doors down and moved in, and soon Frances had one of Biggs-Davison's children as a babysitter. Immediately he moved in, Biggs-Davison went to the Palace to collect his knighthood; he forgot his top hat and had to return for it. I had written to congratulate him on his honour, and a week later he invited me to the House of Commons for a drink. We "drank on the terrace overlooking the river. Shook hands with [Mark] Carlisle [, the Secretary of State for Education,] and Winston Churchill [i.e. Churchill's grandson], whom I liked. Churchill asked me, 'Has my grandfather's statue on Woodford Green been blown up during the disturbances?' Had a talk with Carlisle."

I briefed the Minister on the ILEA's egalitarian socialism and Trotskyites. He said, "Good Lord, I did not realise it was that bad." I had cut off one of the hydra's many heads. I did not know it but I had mortally wounded the hydra, the water-monster that each time a head was cut off grew two more and lived in poisonous fumes.

Before I went to Cornwall Tom Dyer, the Brain of Britain, came round and sat in our front room. He suddenly swooped on the carpet. "A flying ant," he said, holding it in his hand, "a female," and to our astonishment he ate it. "It tastes acidy like formic acid or vinegar." He explained that it was protein. "Had it been a male it would have been poisonous rather than protein."[7]

Four quartets, Beauty and Angelhood
I spent much of the summer in Cornwall working on the four poems that became *Beauty and Angelhood*. After a morning on the Charlestown beach, "drunk with the drugged air", and an evening watching the local carnival with our two boys, I worked on the first of the four poems that became *Beauty and Angelhood*: "I woke in a poetic mood, and, unable to get the

papers because of the rain, sat and assembled the four poems just like that. Now have 'High Leigh' behind me." Then: "Aug 1. Rhymed the draft of, and typed up, 'Hawkwood', which I consider one of my most successful poems…. Did this before and after attending the Charlestown Regatta with the children – Punch and Judy, a Nimrod flying low, water polo, raft races in the harbour."

Soon afterwards: "Drafted the third poem, first six or seven stanzas until it was time to walk to Charlestown at 11 p.m…. Walked to Charlestown pier late at night and looked at the stars above and felt a part of them, standing above the sea." Then: "Aug 2. Typed up 'Kent House'. A hot summer's day and cloudless sky, so sunbathed and read the papers from 11 to 1, and spent the afternoon on Par beach, where the final wording of the last 3 rhymes came to me, sitting on my blue sun-couch gazing at the sea, hills and blue sky all round…. Re-drafted the fourth poem which now has to be rhymed." The next day I wrote: "Cooler. Stayed in and re-drafted the fourth poem, 'St Peter's Convent'. Was taken over near the end and got a last line that pleased me without really realising the ambiguity until it was done…. Typed up the fourth poem and went to Mevagissey."

In the succeeding days we went to Pendeen, where several of Ann's ancestors had lived, including her great-grandfather who had become a coastguard there and had six children including her grandmother, Vera, who had married a Pendeen tin-miner. (He had gone to mine in North Rhodesia and had been killed in a car accident when Ann's mother was 15, and Vera had returned to Par.) We went to Golant, then to Perranporth and sunbathed on the sand and watched the donkey rides. Then we went to East Wheal Rose mine.

I recorded: "A hard struggle, making sure the crescendo of the fourth poem is properly motivated in the third poem." Soon afterwards Ann came in and found me tapping out metre and said, "It's like living with a Morse code agent."[8] (Wordsworth "bummed and booed"[9] his metres, whereas I "tee-tummed or tapped the third finger of my right hand on my desk".)

We went to Charlestown again (from 12 till 3.30) and lunched on the beach. We watched a large Irish china-clay boat manoeuvre into the harbour. All day, blue sky and warm sun. In the evening we went to Mevagissey, Portmellon and finally Gorran, "where we had a drink in the garden of the Hotel. Thought a lot about Colin Wilson at nearby Tetherdown. Would like to visit him, but have nothing to say at present."

Two days later I wrote: "Worked all day on the fourth poem, to secure the Angels = Flames image, and on the first poem, to unify it. Am pleased with the shape of the 4 [poems] for they reflect the new definition of man I was after in Libya – body, mind (including soul), spirit and Angelic flame. A mackerel sky tonight after a hot day."

I went fishing with Ann's cousin, a professional fisherman who owned his own small boat. We left Newlyn and fished all day from 7 a.m. till 3 p.m. We steered out about eight miles and hauled up crab-pots and then winched up nets with large fish, including monkfish. I stood at the back of the boat and generally helped, and mucked in with the crew of three at meal times. I wrote a story about the experience. ('A Sea with Potted Crabs'.)

Near the end of our time in Cornwall I recorded:

Finished the notes to *Beauty and Angelhood* yesterday, went to bed with only two 'Cornish' images and woke up with four – refined the crab-pot idea and got Smeaton's lighthouse, which is perfect (having been behind Britannia on the old penny).... Smeaton had other lighthouses in Cornwall, e.g. St Ives', [and] Smeaton's Pier.... Tonight I looked at the stars.... Must include the shower of stars in the poems." I wrote: "I have spent the whole of my holidays on *Beauty and Angelhood*, which came unplanned.[10]

Metaphysical generation, poetic spring

Looking back I thought again that "I belonged to the Metaphysical generation at Oxford – those who were deeply interested in metaphysical issues, Buddhist truths as well as Donne and Marvell". I had written again of a Metaphysical Revolution that has changed everything and destroyed Humanism. Of my poetic gift I wrote: "I am such a good spy that I am careful to give no indication of it in ordinary conversation, for hoarding it makes its springs flow more abundantly."

I am announced as Principal of Oaklands School while still working at Garratt Green

Back in London there were further negotiations regarding Oaklands, and a meeting was set up by Mabel Reid with Elizabeth Lord and two of her advisers. We went to Oaklands, and later I told my mother and Argie that Oaklands was in the offing. My mother was very much in favour, and Argie reminded me that mother's great-grandmother, Hannah Comfort, had run a school in Croydon. I noted that my mother looked "pale".[11]

Miss Lord now said she would tell the Oaklands' staff that I was buying the school, and I rejoiced in the prospect of having the Oaklands' grounds and garden as a backdrop to my poems. After having an ingrown toenail cut out at the Royal Masonic Hospital in mid-September, I learned that Miss Lord had told the staff. Then a letter came from the vendors containing detail that required further discussion with Miss Lord's advisers.

Eventually the day came in October when I appeared at a packed Parents' Association Annual General Meeting. I sat in the bay window for the formal part of the meeting, and waited while Miss Lord coped with some sharp questioning. Then Miss Lord announced that she would be retiring the following July, and that I would be taking over. I stood in front of the parents and made a short speech, which was greeted with applause. Then I was surrounded by a throng of many wives, all eager to have a word. I went on to my mother's new house in the High Road. She looked very satisfied, if slightly pale and drawn. A few days later Miss Lord rang her bell and said "Well, what do you think of Nicholas taking over at Oaklands?"

Death of my mother

My mother's end came suddenly, little more than three weeks after that evening. At the end of October she was unwell as if she was starting a cold, how she felt before her first heart attack two years previously. She had another turn at 8, gasped for breath and went grey and rang my younger brother, Jonathan, who was living in Loughton. She said, "Can you come now?" And put the phone down. The doctor arrived as my mother was taken by ambulance to Princess Alexandra Hospital, Harlow. I went and sat with her in Casualty while she waited for the X-rays. Her thin face had a very rosy complexion round her cheeks and slightly blurred eyes. Lying back she gave me a number of instructions concerning the house and several messages. That night she had another tightening across her chest, her third heart attack.

On Hallowe'en there was a phone call from Jonathan's wife Anne, saying my mother had had another heart attack (her fourth). It was four days after her third attack, the most dangerous time. I rang the hospital and was told: "She has suffered irreversible heart damage, her lungs have filled with water, her kidneys have packed up, her heart is worn out." We put the boys to bed, arranged a babysitter and drove to the hospital. She was in Harvey ward on the third floor, in a private room with a view over the lights, where my two brothers and their wives had gathered. Jonathan said, "What a lovely surprise, Nick is here."

My mother was conscious. She had an oxygen mask over her nose – the oxygen unit hissed – and she was attached to a drip, a tube to drain off her water and an ECG, which indicated her heart rate in beats per minute and a zig-zag pattern. I sat with her and said, "It's Nick." She smiled. "Is there anything I can do?" She shook her head three times as if to say 'No, I'm beyond help', and attempted to lift her arm which was bandaged to a board to secure the drip, to remove the oxygen mask. Then she let her half-raised arm flop limply down. I warmed her arm and conferred with my brothers.

We split the time into shifts. Jonathan and his wife went home to sleep. At midnight Robert went off to sleep and I sat on with his wife and Ann. Nurses came to take my mother's blood pressure and temperature at regular intervals, and periodically she had crises and showed signs of distress, trying to sit up and still attempting to lift her arm which was still bandaged to the board, to reach the oxygen mask and tear it off. She did not speak, but the message was clear: 'Don't keep me alive, let me die.' She dozed frequently, and then surfaced, whimpering with some of her breaths, something that almost sounded like, "Oh dear." Her chest heaved with bronchitis, her breaths were laboured and there was an echo from each breath like a baby crying in a different ward. I sat and, holding her hand, healed her without speaking. There was a great surge of energy up my back and down my arm, but there was no more, for the power told me it was useless and it was not the will of the Light that there should be any more. One of the nurses opened a window. It was a blustery night and the wind moaned all round Harlow as if Hallowe'en spirits were gathering outside in the dark.

She barely spoke, but there was one exchange. Surfacing, she got out, "Hot." I asked, "Are you too hot now?" "No." "Are you too cold?" "No." "Are you uncomfortable?" "No…. So tired." At one point as the wind moaned two nurses came and stood each side of the bed, bent and sat her up, puffed up her pillows and gave her a drink of water which she sipped while I stood, watching hauntedly at the end of the bed, and as her night-dress rode up her legs I thought of how I had crawled from her to give my first cry, and there was something very elemental in seeing her flesh so close to returning to the earth.

Hallowe'en had now become All Hallows or All Saints' Day, and the moaning died away. Robert returned from his sleep and we sat on either side of the bed, and talked quietly across her, recalling in whispers the family holidays we had had as children, evoking over her dying body scenes of the family life she had had while nurses came and listened with a stethoscope. The oxygen unit hissed and we whispered and waited, having subcontracted to the hospital the business of coping with the physical side of death. Slowly she became more comfortable and sank into sleep.

Under the shift system we had all worked out, I was to be present from 12 noon and with Jonathan due at 6 a.m., Robert urged Ann and me to go and get some sleep. We had a babysitter, there were two young boys to think of. So I stooped and kissed her forehead and left. We drove home to Wandsworth and slept. I was woken at 8 by the telephone. It was Robert. He said, "Mother went just after 7."

After I had gone, Robert had sat with her, squeezing her hand and talking to her. She had asked for her white pills, and said, "Tired." At one point she said, "If only they'd let me die." Apparently she said of the dawn, "It's lovely, look at it." At 6 Jonathan took over. Robert said, "Jonnie's here," and she said: "Oh, is he? Oh, where? Oh, yes, there." Just after 7 Jonathan went down the corridor to speak to the staff nurse. When he returned a student nurse was fiddling with the oxygen mask and my mother said, "I think you'd better get the staff nurse." Two minutes later, at 7.12, she suffered her fifth heart attack and died. Her crisis lasted a very short time, she was too tired to fight. Jonathan later told me, "She went out like a light. Her heart couldn't stand any more." She had wanted her body to be used for medical research but this was not raised until 40 minutes after her death, too late to be acted on.

I felt drained and numb, a blank exhaustion and relief that her suffering had been removed from her. I experienced a mixture of feelings. I was half sad that she had not lived to see me return to the area and to Oaklands, and part of me wondered if she had moved on as a self-sacrifice because I was returning, selflessly thinking that it was time I had my share of her estate. I kept remembering certain days, like the one when she walked me to my first day at Chigwell School, pushing her bicycle with my kitbag on her front basket.

At 12 that morning I visited my mother in the Chapel of Rest, intending to send her soul on its posthumous journey. (From my researches into religions, I understood that a newly-released soul often does not realise it has died.) The Chapel of Rest was downstairs along a corridor, and an attendant showed me to the door and said I could be alone with her. She was on a raised bier with two candles, a *Bible* and a prayer-book. She lay with a veil over her white face, the frill of her shroud under blue satin. I forced myself to stoop and kiss her cold forehead. Her eyes were closed, her mouth tight, peaceful, a slight frown above her hooked nose, her white hair and the whitish pallor on her cheeks. Through the open window there was a hint of a breeze and I thought once or twice she breathed as *rigor mortis* stirred the satin. I talked to her: "It's Nick. You're happy now, for you are dead. I know you can hear me. Thank you for all you did for us. We can look after ourselves now." I actually spoke aloud, looking up at the ceiling. I felt an immense peace, and then suddenly the candle nearest me flickered and guttered as if in answer. It flickered several times and nearly went out, and I wondered if her spirit, realising she was dead, had rushed out of her body, guttering the candle, and moved on to the next stage of her life. Can a spirit make a candle gutter? At that moment the attendant tapped on the door, and it was time to go.

I looked in on the ward to thank the nurses for their efforts. Bizarrely I found them clowning around holding a wooden leg. The day sister had taken over from the night sister and said, "You are a very loving family, she had her family round her to the end," words that would haunt me.

There was a family lunch at Jonathan's, which used to be my grand-mother's and then Argie's home, 20 Brook Road, Loughton. Over lamb and *rosé* Robert sat at the end of the table and made arrangements, speaking in a loud voice. The men were matter-of-fact, the women were quiet and subdued. Keeping quiet about the guttering candle, I pointed out, "She may be there at the funeral, able to see" – a metaphysical perspective lobbed into all the organising. I was an executor along with my two brothers and had a quarter of her estate.

Now the letters came in, over a hundred. They were addressed to me. It was apparent that my mother had collected people and was a semi-public figure. She had a gift for making people feel they were important and for giving them the whole of her attention and being enthusiastic about their plans. Her friends all commented on the enthusiasm she put into life, how she really cared about people and was greatly liked and respected. I reflected that that same enthusiasm had brought us, her children, all forward, made us strive to achieve gold stars. She had cared about all our problems, and there was no one who would care in the same way now, and the world was a colder place.

I grieved gently and tenderly. I was deeply affected by my mother's death and felt the poignancy of little Anthony hugging me "because I'm here and not dead like Grannie".

The funeral was on a Monday, just over a week after she died, at St Mary's church, Loughton, where my father's funeral service was held. I went straight to the church, where I encountered Robert, to check the arrangements, and we then all met at Jonathan's house. There were a lot of flowers in his porch. I talked to my Aunt Flo and her husband until the hearse and limousines arrived. I sat in the first limousine with my mother's two sisters, and the rest of the family travelled in the second one. With the funeral director walking in front, we drove slowly past Journey's End to the church. The coffin was carried in by the pall-bearers. I followed down the aisle with Ann beside me. Could my mother see us as I had seen my funeral service in 1836 under hypnosis?

It was a poignant service: a hymn 'To be a Pilgrim', psalm 84 and then the eulogy. The Rector, the Reverend Price, described how she was originally a Methodist, and he dwelt on her warm and outgoing personality and her courage in coping with the deaths of six children. He described how the association with the Church of England at Chigwell School had brought her to St Mary's. He commented on "her gifted family" and her triumph over suffering. "She died on All Saints' Day," he said, "and in view of what she did for others, she was a saint. God has a new saint at His side."

I led the way back down the aisle and Robert and I stood at the door and shook hands and thanked people for coming. Lucy's son John now arrived, representing the Hove branch of the family, red-eyed and trembling, having lost his way and full of profuse apologies for missing the funeral service. The family limousines then drove past ploughed fields to Parndon Wood

Crematorium, near Harlow, and we stood while the Rector said a prayer ("Go forth upon your journey from this world, o Christian soul") and we watched the curtains draw so we could not see the coffin sink down. Outside, feeling some relief, I turned and looked at the chimney and its wispy smoke – did some believe that a warm, gentle person really became nothing in thin air, gone up in smoke? – and wanting to leave it behind we went on to lunch at Jonathan's. My sister Frances asked me: "Why did she die just now? Just after I've come from Shrewsbury to Wimbledon and you are set for Oaklands? Why now?" And I wondered if there was something Providential again, for my share of her estate would help with the purchase of Oaklands. Or was it just an accident?

I returned to Garratt Green to find the staff in uproar. Mr Dowley, the school keeper who had kept me informed of the summer Test-match scores, had died of a brain haemorrhage the previous Friday. Twenty-four hours earlier he had been carpeted by the Head, and it was widely said that her dressing-down had triggered the death. The Head denied any responsibility. She had heard that I was taking over at Oaklands, and during Part Three of my Departmental review she belaboured me for purportedly being about to take on a private school. I gave back as good as I received and ironically thanked her for being considerate during my bereavement. Col. Sir Stuart Mallinson, the local worthy who had provided cricket nets during the Easter holidays when I was still at school, had also died. I reflected that my mother was in the queue for the next life along with my school keeper and the Colonel.

In July 1983 a Fire Officer in uniform came to inspect Oaklands. He told me he had known my mother. He said: "I remember passing your dear mother's house in the week she died. She was in the garden, very busy, very serene. I stood and watched her and thought she was working hard because she knew she hadn't got long. Strange, isn't it? Strange." (In mid-February 1988 I went to St Mary's church and he served me communion, saying, "The Blood of Christ, Mr Hagger," a phrase that haunted me as catching the "enmeshing of community and spirit in Essex".)[12]

Sonnets: The Wind and the Earth
I found myself drafting sonnets about my mother's death. (The series was entitled *The Wind and the Earth*.) My mother's possessions had to be sorted through. I arranged to meet Robert and Jonathan at her house one weekend in November, but Robert rang to say that they would not be there. On the Saturday evening he rang me and said they had been at the house all day. "I've thrown away 12 black bags of her stuff and I have another 12 bags in my car." I immediately said, "What happened to my letters to her from abroad and the family photos, the ones she had of our childhood and the

19th-century family figures?" Robert said he did not know, and it was possible they were in the bags in his car. I said I would like to look through the 12 bags. I insisted that as my mother's eldest son and executor I should have been involved in the sorting. Robert had to ring off as he was beginning to have a diabetic reaction, and when I next rang I found myself talking to his wife, who said I had no right to sort through any of my own mother's possessions.

I will skate over the negotiations, but I went down to my brother's house in Tunbridge Wells. He gave me a friendly welcome, provided a ground-sheet and (much to his wife's disapproval) I sat on the front lawn and sorted through the 12 bags in the open air. I retrieved many of my letters and many photos, including the (then) only surviving photograph of Hannah Comfort, later Mrs. Burton, who opened a school in Croydon and lived to be 100. I later compiled the photographs in three albums, and Frances's husband has since loaded some 200 scanned photographs on to a family website. It was right to retrieve this family history.

I scrutinised the facial similarities between members of the family and wrote of "the 'enmity' in the blood between the brown-eyed Broadleys, who are practical, from Yorkshire, and the fair-eyed Hardings – and Haggers – who are not Broadleys at all and have different values".

Matthew, who was six, volunteered his opinion on his grandmother's death: "Grannie came down to teach the violin…, and she finished it so she had to go on to what she had to do next. We're all here to do something, and when you're little you don't know what it is but when you're bigger the idea is there in your brain." I knew then he would go far.

I did more work on Oaklands. I met my new accountant, who had been recommended by my Loughton solicitor, near Chancery Lane, and somehow we walked past Bedford Row, where I spent a troubled year as an articled clerk who spent all his time reading literature. The solicitors' building I was then in looked as black as ever. In December I took a day off school, saw my accountant again and took my bank manager, Mr Cannon, round Oaklands. (When I first visited him to explain that I wanted to buy Oaklands he was sitting back at his desk, which was where the mound of foreign coins had been in 1946, reading the broadsheet *Times*, immaculate in a formal dark suit, white shirt and tie, and as he carefully folded his *Times* and placed it reverentially on his desk I felt I was intruding on his important considering of stocks and shares with my less important plan to buy a local school.) We walked together from the bank. From Albion Hill Oaklands looked massive, and I was reminded of what the clairvoyant in the Markham Arms had said in 1971, ten years earlier: "You're going to buy a big house, I can see it, but there's sadness on the way, a death."

In the Christmas holidays I "drafted ten poems on mother". Early in the new year I recorded: "Wrote 'Wind-Chaser', one of my most metaphysical... sonnets." I had returned to *The Secret Light* (as the book that would become Part One of *The Fire and the Stones* was now called) and, thinking ahead to my poetic epic, I described it as "a prolegomena to my epic [poem] and the philosophy of my metaphysical poems". I was steeped in the Kaballah, and wrote: "I have to reflect the Kaballah as much as Blake or Yeats because I happened to live in the same metropolis as the greatest Kaballah teacher of this century – Warren Kenton."[13]

Egalitarian socialism: acquiring Oaklands

It had snowed again and there was a slight thaw with "jagged icicles, and everywhere dripping". I went to Oaklands and walked round with a surveyor, then sat in Miss Lord's house at 4 Albion Hill. Soon afterwards there was a letter from my bank manager challenging the figures I had done for him and saying we could not afford Oaklands. For a whole weekend I did revised figures for him: "Have totally redone all the figures. Spent all weekend as an accountant.... Have just finished copying out the projections. It took me from Friday afternoon till now, non-stop except for sleep, and I have... made Oaklands possible."

At the end of January my family gathered at my mother's house to remove effects. Robert presented his fees for winding up the estate and then disappeared for lunch with Jonathan while Frances went to Argie, leaving me to ruminate alone in the dismembered home. I studied my mother's small round metallic Chinese table, which I had always called a "metaphysical" table and which I had requested. It showed a Chinese labyrinthine maze, the *Tao*, with a snake, a wasp, a dragon and a dung-beetle on it. It was a *yin-yang* table, a Chinese *mandala*. Robert returned from lunch full of beer and insisted on wanting the metaphysical table as he could do jigsaw puzzles on it. I let him have it and later wrote: "Let the *yin-yang* table go to... Rob who has not been to China and does not know.... I had the most perfect *Tao* on a table and I gave it away. I suppose because I understood it I did not need it." I added:

> I went to the East to get the *Tao* into my work.... I looked at a thousand books for an illustration of what I understood by the *Tao* and it was under my nose all the time [i.e. on the Chinese table].... I went to Oxford in order that I might get to Japan so that I could go on to China and know the *Tao*.[14]

I had tracked the history of the Light back to Central-Asian shamanism, whence it passed through Egypt and Palestine. I was aware of treading in the footsteps of Robert Graves's *The White Goddess*, and wrote: "My wide reading is *unifying* reading." I was deeply immersed in sun- and moon-cults:

> Today worked out the ceremony in the Great Pyramid, from King's Chamber to Queen's Chamber, the sacred ceremony of marriage; and that Stonehenge and other megaliths were used for sacrificing bulls to the sun-god.... Got the bull's horn/cusped moon – the link is the moon 'on its back' I saw in Iraq.... Graves's [*The*] *White Goddess* – the moon and poetry.... Graves's feeling that ancient knowledge and mysteries were being thrust upon him.

By March the Head of Garratt Green had informed the ILEA Inspectorate that I was proposing to take over a private school while continuing as a Senior Teacher. The State ethos was opposed to independent education, and I was visited by a left-wing inspector who proposed heaping half the Deputy Heads' workload unto me, but not on the other Senior Teachers. I pointed out the inequity in her proposal and saw her off.[15]

Meanwhile Miss Lord wanted me to attend a policy-meeting on a Wednesday. I arrived at Oaklands to find a packed hall with some 150–200 parents in every available inch of space. Miss Lord and I sat at the table on the low stage and I spoke, promising the continuation of the Oaklands that I had known as a boy, with its emphasis on the 3 Rs, and defused their worries. What I said was very well received, and two days later I returned for a cheese-and-wine gathering to meet 80 more parents.

I had persuaded my new bank manager to give me a bridging loan so that the purchase of Oaklands could proceed before I sold 46 Ritherdon Road, which was sticking, and in June I was organising an exchange of contracts, which happened on 26 July. It was agreed that Ann would be Headmistress from the beginning of the autumn term and that we would collect the fees from September in return for completing the purchase of Oaklands in October. I reviewed the staff's pay structure. A neighbour offered us the top floor of 15 Albion Hill from September, where we could live while I built a new house in the school grounds.

We went to a Parents' barbeque at Oaklands. At one point my aunt Argie sat in the study with Miss Lord while I was asked questions about next term's arrangements by several parents. A fortnight later in July we lunched with Miss Lord and stayed until sunset, when there were drinks on her patio. On 17 July Miss Lord officially retired. Many people gathered in the Oaklands' tennis-court and there were balloons.

My Third Mystic Life, which was reflected in *The Fire-Flower* and *Beauty and Angelhood*, ended with my growing involvement in taking over at Oaklands and with the death of my mother.

Baroque

Romanticism: Christopher Ricks and me as a Romantic poet

I had suggested to Ricks that my poems were the work of a modern Metaphysical poet, but he had argued against this interpretation of my work. I now began to think that they might be the work of a modern Romantic poet.

I had been delving into Romanticism. My Romantic perspective began at the Mystics and Scientists conference of 1982 which was held in Winchester. Speakers attacked Darwinian biology along with Newtonian physics, arguing that a directing, purposive intelligence holds creation in balance. Sir John Eccles, the Cartesian dualist (who believed that mind and matter are different) and Nobel-Prize-winning scientist, was one of the speakers. He was of very advanced years, white-haired and bespectacled, and I encountered him at the top of the steps outside, and asked him about Descartes's theory of perception. I said, "If I look at that flower, where is the mind that is doing the looking?" He said: "If I look at that flower, my mind is outside my skull between me and the flower. The mind is in a relationship between head and flower, it is outside the skull." I was reminded of Donne's view in 'The Extasie' and also of Coleridge's view of perception. The brain physiologist Peter Fenwick was nearby, balding and bespectacled, and I turned to him for his view after Eccles had walked on. He said, "OK, mind acts on brain but is not dualistically different from it but is all one. Eccles needs to modify his view. Eccles has said nothing. He has just pushed the mind further back." Soon afterwards Sir George Trevelyan approached and shook my hand, gazing deep into my eyes, and then shuffled off without a word.

I realised that the Romantic poets were aware of the invisible world and of an infinite universe. Arguably, the New-Age vision was a late flowering of Romanticism. I wrote: "I am one of the last Romantics." I thought it was Romantic to see a "new Baroque age", as I had done in Japan. Romantics saw the One and were not dualists. "The way forward" from *Beauty and Angelhood* was "through Romanticism". I "wrote 'A New Romanticism' [a first draft of a poem later titled 'Garden of Organism'], a poem about Oaklands. And then a short essay on the new Romanticism." I wrote that my stories were "Romantic stories, full of the throbbing cosmos, teeming with the unity of life, and my poems about my mother are also Romantic poems". I wrote that "Tuohy tried to 'Neoclassicise' 'The Silence', which was really my *Prelude* in Modernist technique". I also observed that "Ricks is a Neoclassical critic, applying Neoclassical attitudes to my organic form and image".

I discussed my kinship with the Romantics with Tuohy, who I encoun-tered at a memorial service in Brighton (for the wife of my British-Council colleague in Japan, Alan Baker). I wrote: "Tuohy… was in good form, challenging Romantic views with Neoclassical positions." He told me: "The English feel contempt for foreigners and the working class, and the Empire held so long as the contempt was there; it is all snobbishness and class-based." And: "[The Romantics] are making propositions which are unanswerable." I had greater success with the Chief Examiner of 'O' level English Literature, who came to Garratt Green. I told him: "Set books grow in the mind like trees, they take on an organic shape in the mind as image. They have an organic form." I recorded: "He agreed with this Romantic view of set-book teaching."[16] Having tried to see myself as a Metaphysical poet on 18 February 1979 and found that label inadequate (*see* p.81), on 1 May 1982 I wrote a second letter to Ricks, seeing my work as Romantic (*see* Appendix 6, pp.930–932).

Looking back, I can see that I was groping towards a balanced view between Romanticism and Neoclassicism, the view of the Baroque and of Universalism which I have set out in detail in *A New Philosophy of Literature*. Looking back, I can see that I was strengthening the Romantic half of the balance by focusing on Romanticism so intensely.

'Cambridge Ode: Against Materialism'

My focus came out in poems. I went to Cambridge and visited Grantchester: "Tea at the Orchard and then a look at Mill House, where Whitehead lived. The apple blossom and breakfast in the garden in 1910. Brooke moved before Christmas 1910. He was all that was golden and good about the Edwardian time." During the next few weeks I ruminated, and slowly 'Cambridge Ode: Against Materialism' took shape about this visit.

I had written a *Preface to my Selected Poems* and shown it to Sir George Trevelyan, who had written: "Now I have read the Preface with delight and excitement. It is a splendid statement and it is fine to have it made by one who has the authority of the scholar and poet. I gained a lot by reading it." I reread Whitehead and wrote: "My Preface… echoes Whitehead's *Science and the Modern World* – the chapter on the Romantic reaction." Whitehead had lived in Grantchester just before Brooke. He had championed

a philosophy of organism, with organism in a vitalist organic theory replacing material in the materialistic theory. No bifurcation of Nature…. The unity view of today… goes back to Whitehead and Brooke – Grantchester – and from there to the Romantic reaction against materialism which presented Nature alive, as a living thing, of which Grantchester is an image and Oaklands too…. Oaklands, the living rejection of materialism, a garden where everything is organism.

Out of this perception I glimpsed 'Cambridge Ode'. I thought I had three Odes: "A reflective Ode on Grantchester in Keatsian form, and a Pindaric Ode on the Pope, and a Wordsworthian Ode, an 'Intimations of Immortality' in irregular lines on mother's death." A day later I wrote: "June 15. Have planned 3 Odes, two smallish ones on the materialism of today (Grantchester) and on the Pope; and one extended one on mother's death. Have worked out strophe, antistrophe and epode in each." In fact I used the strophe-antistrophe epode form in 'Cambridge Ode' and wrote *The Wind and the Earth* about my mother's death.

The visit of Pope John Paul II to Britain at the end of May had made a great impression on me. We got up at 6 a.m. and saw him drive from the Papal Nuncio's residence at Parkside, Wimbledon, towards Roehampton. He stood, wearing white, in his Popemobile, and the road was lined with people on both sides. He went on to Canterbury to advance the ecumenical movement.[17] The image of a Polish Pope reuniting Christendom, and the mystical tradition of St Augustine, Pope Gregory the Great and St Bernard which he embodied, against Communism was a further blow to materialism.

Preparing for Oaklands

There had been developments within the family as we approached the take-over of Oaklands. I had helped to prepare Matthew for his entrance exam to Chigwell School, which he took while suffering from the after-effects of chickenpox. He had had an interview and done well. I had recorded: "[He] spoke of Agrippa and Augustus and Tiberius, though only 7." When we heard that he had a place I arranged for him to have a "family clap" at tea-time. I went to see Mr Woodcock of Dulwich College Prep to explain that we would be withdrawing Matthew, and I told him that we were taking over at Oaklands. He was very helpful and gave us some advice – and at an evening for parents "in the fading light of the hall" he "mentioned us in his address – 'among you are some parents who are even opening their own school'".

In April we had had Nadia to stay. Ann and I collected her from Caroline at The Crown and Greyhound, the scene of my despair in 1970, and I again had the sense of events gathering round places like different tides washing flotsam round the same breakwater. Now that I was about to be the only parent of Nadia's living in the UK, Caroline had mellowed. I wrote:

> [Caroline] is tall, willowy, blonde, well-groomed, slightly ravaged-looking, with the old glint in her eye. Slightly more relaxed and happier than when I last saw her, more at ease with herself socially. A lot of questions, good feeling. I sat at the end of the table in the large 'snug' in The Crown and Greyhound, the children drank two coca-colas and ate crisps, Nadia had a lager, Caroline and Ann dry martinis and I drank my shandy.... Nadia was

pleased we were together and kept smiling at me…. My strange family… two halves now reconciled and in balance; a format I like.

Caroline said that she did not like Belgium much and planned to return to the UK during school holidays to see Nadia.

In May I had happened to drive past Riverway School, where I had taught from 1971 to 1973, and saw from the board that it was now East Greenwich Christ Church C of E Primary School, and also Thameside Adult Education Institute.

Kyoko Sato, who had been our tenant upstairs at 46 Ritherdon Road, made contact and came to tea on 11 July. I wrote that she "is now a *Noh* dancer in Japan, in the 'sect' of Tamura in Kyoto; the third woman to do it in Japan, and the youngest".

After the end of term at Garratt Green Ann and I spent ten days decorating the most essential parts of Oaklands. Ann's mother took the two boys to Cornwall and Ann and I stayed with Argie, who told me that my aunt Flo had secondary bone cancer and had been in bed for a month. Ann and I worked from 8 a.m. until 10 p.m. each day, and averaged a room a day: two coats on ceilings and walls and doors. Exhausted, we then drove to Cornwall in the middle of the night and soon I was walking across the Charlestown rocks with the boys, stepping carefully over slimy green weed.

Romanticism and Classicism
In Cornwall I realised that my interest in Romanticism was only part of the story, and that I was really combining Classicism and Romanticism to bring to birth a new Baroque poetry.

I had sent some poems to Ricks with a letter about Romanticism and he now replied that Romanticism was the "right context" for my work, and he cited W. Jackson Bate on the essential continuity of Augustan poetry into Romantic poetry, as opposed to a confrontation between the two. (This perception had opened the way for Ricks to see Keats as an Augustan in his book, *Keats and Embarrassment*.) He felt Romanticism pays a price, meaning that it forfeits the social world of the ego.

On 11 August, after visiting a house in Polruan whose normally private garden was open for visiting for one day, I drafted the poem that became 'Cambridge Ode: Against Materialism' at Ann's mother's house in St Austell (4 Manor Close, Fairfield Park): "This evening shaped 'Against Materialism: A New Renaissance' into 16 stanzas of 10 lines each having sketched 3 or 4 stanzas in the course of the day. At 11.50 p.m. finished – feel very alive…. The force seized me and made me shape my poem and would not let me rest until I had done it."

I was diverted into carrying forward my book on the Light: "Typed in the correct version of Zoroastrians and Essenes... and refined shamanism. That evening I took Ann for a drink at Charlestown and we walked, hand in hand, down to the harbour under a starlit sky, no cloud and lo! across the moonlit sky like a firework rocket trailing yellow as on a bonfire night and falling, from right to left, sped – what? A meteorite re-entering the earth's atmosphere? A comet? A shooting star?" A shooting star *is*, of course, a burning meteorite, but I had a wider meaning in mind. I added:

Nicholas with Matthew and Anthony in Polruan, Cornwall in 1982

"But afterwards it seemed as if no star was secure in its place and Newton was all wrong and any star might suddenly hurtle towards us and fall into Charlestown harbour."[18]

Artistic styles and the Baroque principle
I was still pondering the differences between Romanticism and Classicism. I wrote:

> The ego of the Classicist writer hides behind the ego of man – but it is ego, social ego, that he writes about.... A Classicist's work reveals very little of the writer, and he creates a world to be shared by all, whereas the Romantic creates a world that is different from anyone else's.... Whereas the Classicist hides his ego behind the ego of Man, the Romantic reveals his ego – and it is only the new Romanticism that seeks to relate that ego to the core behind it.... My whole life-style has been a Romantic one: living in the solitude of a foreign city – Tokyo – and writing these *Diaries*, observing, delving, remembering. To be a Classicist I should have obtained a social position at Oxford and observed others in their social positions.

I came up with a definition of Baroque (and therefore of Universalist) poetry:

> [Baroque] poetry is the opening of the social ego to the core, and the outpouring of the soul's delight when, in the course of contemplating the natural world, it opens to Reality and perceives the infinite and eternal world of Light which is immanent in creation, and whose symbols control the imagination.

I felt I should return to lyric poetry: "Get back to writing more lyrics – only with the infinite and eternal world peeping through. Pope: 'Most souls, 'tis true, but peep out once an age.' Show the infinite peeping through the finite, the eternal peeping through the temporal."

I felt that European civilization had one artistic style, a Classical style, which went through a pre-classical archaic phase (medieval art); a classical phase (the Italian Renaissance); a first post-classical or Neoclassical academic stage (the 15th-16th-century academy); a first Mannerist or pre-baroque stage (El Greco); and a first baroque stage (the historical Baroque, c.1600–1750).

I wrote that after a civilization had broken down and lost its Light there is a renewed struggle between Neoclassicism and Romanticism – whose classical phase of 1798–1830 passed into an academic phase (Matthew Arnold and the 1890s poets), Modernism and Neo-Romanticism – and that out of the conflict between these repeated stages comes a new Baroque stage, a mixture of Classicism and Mannerism (or Neoclassicism and Neo-Romanticism, of Movement form and universal Romantic subject matter) – of sense and spirit.

In my *Preface* I saw my work as bringing in this coming stage. I felt that work from the new Baroque Age cannot be judged by Neoclassical or Neo-Romantic standards or criteria, but must be judged by standards or criteria that have not yet come into being, which do not now exist but which must now be devised. My "new Baroque Age" was therefore a final stage in the second repeated cycle of our civilization. It would mark a unique and quite distinct stage in European civilization and would develop from the academic, social perspective of Neoclassicism, which was an art of reaction as in Larkin, and from the more individual perspective of Neo-Romanticism of such poets as Dylan Thomas and Kathleen Raine. I added:

I am right to oppose Neoclassicism because I belong to a coming Age.... Each year brings me nearer to it.... I found my voice late because it is the voice of the next Age.

Later I recorded that this theory of cycles may have come from the Light itself:

12.15 a.m. on Aug 22.... I woke early and looked for the Light, and spent an hour with faint Light playing, swirling through water.... I felt very calm and tranquil and very charged.... The theory of cycles I have come up with on this important day may well have come from the Light that filled my mind... this morning.

Later that day I recorded my disagreement with Coleridge:

> I have knocked down Coleridge. Instead of Platonist Ideas flowing into the higher Reason and thence to the imagination as symbols, and the phenomena of the natural world in turn being regarded as symbols of the Ideas (Coleridge); the eternal symbols flow into the core – the soul and spirit which awaken when the reason and social ego slumber – as the Light and proceed thence to the imagination, while the phenomena of the natural world are 'symbols' for the eternal world of the Light.

(I noted that the Light is Hindu *prana*, an immaterial substance that pervades the universe, and that the Light is also the Romantic Infinite.[19])

Baroque principle: Christopher Ricks and me as a Baroque poet, "I think your work is Baroque"
I had finished my *Preface* on 17 October and sent it to Christopher Ricks with a letter seeing my work as Baroque, a combination of the Romantic and Classical (*see* Appendix 6, pp.932–934). To put it in algebraic terms, $+A + -A = 0$ (Classicism + Romanticism = neo-Baroque).

Ricks invited me to meet him at Christ's College, Cambridge on 29 October. I went up to B6 and saw him through the open door, wearing jeans, and immediately warmed to his endearing smile beneath his bald head and small round spectacles. "He said I had sharpened up my essay, 'I believe in the Baroque, but though everything that is Baroque is Classical and Romantic, not everything that is Classical and Romantic is Baroque.'" I replied that the Light is central to the new Baroque. He said: "The proof of the pudding is in the eating. I think your work is Baroque. You got there, even though your itinerary surprised you." I told him that until recently I had been unwilling to select some poems because they did not fit in with Romanticism, but they all "fell within the Baroque".

He nodded. Ricks had skilfully diagnosed the position ahead of mine and was moving me forward. Of Oaklands, he said, "It's Providential," an adjective I did not expect to hear from him.

He discussed his role as Faculty Chairman. He said, "I'm not Leavis yet. I want to unify the Faculty." He came downstairs with me and as we trotted in the Christ's quadrangle I asked how he would unify the Faculty. Without hesitation, with impressive alertness and fluency, he quoted Dryden's 'Absalom and Achitophel':

> And David's mildness managed things so well
> The bad found no occasion to rebel.

I marvelled at the exactness and appropriateness of Ricks's spontaneous use of Dryden's words to convey his attitude. I did not know that "the bad" – Ricks was referring to Colin MacCabe – had already violently rebelled and split the Cambridge English Faculty, and that Ricks, Frank Kermode and MacCabe himself would all leave their jobs soon afterwards, Ricks for the USA. He shook my hand and dived across the road to attend a lecture. I went on to Grantchester to stand by the Old Vicarage and think of Brooke, and my musings were disturbed when Jeffrey Archer, the then owner, got into a new car and drove out.

Soon afterwards Ricks was on television. He was in dazzling form and glittered with his distinctions and attitudes, dwarfing the other guests and saying memorable things that lingered in the mind long after the programme was over.

I had shown Ricks *The Fire-Flower* and *Beauty and Angelhood*. He wrote to me that he had read them "with some awe at your energy of mind and synthesising… aspirations. The Notes are I think a genuine help, and done (both proffered and enacted) with tact and modesty. Touches of the best of Empson in them – and in some things in the poems (that despair/rare rhyme, for instance)." I noted: "As Ricks was on TV recently saying that Empson is the only living 'genius', that is praise enough."[20]

Principal: running Oaklands

We began moving from 46 Ritherdon Road to Loughton at the end of August. We filled the car, took the stuff in to 15 Albion Hill, then had lunch with Elizabeth Lord and tea with Mabel Reid. We lived in the two upstairs rooms at our new address now, and while Ann took over as Headmistress at Oaklands, immediately across the road, I got up at 5.45 a.m., ate a silent breakfast I had made overnight, crept out of the house without waking Matthew (who had started at Chigwell School) and Anthony (who had started at Oaklands), lingered to admire the dawn over the Oaklands' grounds, got into my car and drove to Wandsworth in time to do the coverage. When I got back in the evening there was money to organise and there were accounts to do, and I worked flat out coping with both schools. Still trying to control me, the Head heaped additional work on me at every turn as if trying to take what time I had in the evenings. I did no writing for the first two weeks, but took to looking in on the empty 46 Ritherdon Road after school and began typing up my *Preface* in my study before locking the house and returning to Loughton.

Following the announcement that Miss Lord was retiring the Oaklands roll had fallen to 156. Now that we were in place and demonstrating an intention to renew the building and syllabus, the numbers began to creep up, and it was soon clear that confidence had returned and that Oaklands was in demand. To cut costs while the roll was built up again I mowed the two fields each weekend – it took two-and-a-half hours on the ride-on mower, starting on the outside and making ever-decreasing circles to end in the centre – and every Friday Ann and I shopped for 200 lunches a day for the next week. We bought the ingredients for 1,000 lunches and I carried them down the old cellar steps to the Oaklands storeroom.

Oaklands School (left) and Oaklands under snow (right)

In October Matthew had his birthday lunch in the Oaklands hall. We then took him and his Chigwell friends to the Tower. We "saw the Crown Jewels, the axe that killed Lord Lovat (two chops on the block) in 1747, the ravens, the armour in the White Tower where the princes were murdered, Raleigh's place of imprisonment and the site of the scaffold".

It soon became apparent that Miss Lord had run Oaklands in a particularly idiosyncratic and somewhat Irish way. She was 81 when she handed over, and she had a habit of collecting cash and tucking it behind a cushion in one of the study chairs. Parents spoke of sitting on the settee and becoming aware of a wad of notes beside them. On one occasion she collected getting on for £1,000 and hid it in the gas oven, a place where no one would think of looking. The cook arrived and began to light the gas for lunch. Miss Lord cried "No" – and removed the notes before they were roasted. I insisted on all cheques and cash received being banked the same day.

We were asked to meet the Oaklands' Parents' Association at a parent's house. We rang the bell one evening, were shown in and found ourselves being interrogated in interview chairs in the middle of a circle of some 30 parents about what we would do with the funds they raised for the school. I quickly gathered that with Miss Lord approaching 82, some of the parents had in effect run parts of the school on her behalf and resented our arrival, which threatened their empire. I made a low-key impromptu speech, and one of the parents, who came from Cornwall, said afterwards: "We thought you might be an ogre. You laid a lot of dust. You're not an ogre."

Soon afterwards I held an evening meeting for the local residents about the parking at Oaklands. I invited local councillors and a policeman, and we made Albion Hill unofficially one way at peak times to ease the flow of the traffic. On the following day, 29 October, I completed the purchase of Oaklands. I still had not sold 46 Ritherdon Road but gambled on selling it once the property market recovered.

In November we went for a Nature walk with Mabel Reid. We left her house in Albion Hill, Elm Cottage (since demolished), turned left into Nursery Road, plunged into the Forest before the track to the Warren and walked to sweet chestnuts. She talked all the way, striding along with her stick and her eye-shield while the four of us struggled to keep up. We walked round the gravel pits and returned through the Stubbles while she reminisced about "the unwashed" who used to come out from the East End during her childhood.

Towards the end of November I visited Tuohy at 13 Ladbroke Grove, London. We sat downstairs in Sophia's room among old masters, marbles, African eggs, leather chairs and a grandfather clock that was inscribed *Dum dormiunt vigilo* ("I keep watch while they sleep") until a Foreign-Office Arabist came in. We then went round the corner to a pub.[21]

The Oaklands term had come to an end and I was somehow able to attend the staff lunch on the last day. I sat next to the Dickensian odd-job man, a red-faced octogenarian called Mr Burns. We could not go to Edinburgh to see Nadia during the Christmas holidays. There was too much to do around Oaklands. I had to do paperwork for the accountant and the staff's salaries, and Matthew and Anthony needed my full attention.

At Cramond with Nadia

After going to Norfolk to buy some school furniture and visiting Cromwell's home, we drove up to Edinburgh at the February half-term. I was shocked to find Nadia in a caravan in Cramond, having fled a man who was sharing a very large flat she had been in. She had left school and after a spell at Edinburgh airport (whose shift work cut across her social life) was working with a music publisher, having got a job for which there were 252 applicants. The caravan was in the garden of a lady Caroline had known, but I felt she had been abandoned. I wrote after a night tour of the village we all made: "Cramond, where Nadia was brought by Caroline, and left, and where she has taken root among her friends. It is a backwater.... The sea runs inland, there is a 10p ferry and a boat-house and 3-storey fishermen's cottages and stepped paths that climb steeply up to hidden cottages. There is a pub, a phone box and the café where Nadia worked. There is a quarter where Caroline and David lived, now empty and looking like a council house, very functional. There is the house where Nadia lived..., and the terrace just off it where her caravan is.... Her caravan... is in the grounds of the house of the café-owner['s parents]. Nadia... has booked us into the Barnton Hotel up the road from her, where the social life is…. Feel sad. Nadia was dumped here all alone, and is now fending for herself without much money, and I have to save her from the place – or she will be hobbling along the Cramond water-front at the age of 80."

The next morning we went for a walk with Nadia on the Cramond waterfront and took in the islands of muddy sand and many birds, white cottages and woods. Mist obscured the Firth of Forth. We visited the café and the caravan. It was cosy enough: a double bed, a well for logs, a loo, a kitchen, an electric fire, a hot-water bottle. We lunched with Nadia, and I determined to get her out of the caravan, explained to her how she could set about buying a flat. Nadia had to go into work in the afternoon, so I took Ann and the boys to Holyrood Castle and toured where Rizzio was murdered. We returned to Cramond where the birds were pecking among the mudbanks: "oyster-catchers (white underbelly and bar on wing, curved long back and curious running head-nodding walk), terns, curlews, snipe." Cramond was as old as AD142 and Severus. In the evening Nadia brought a friend to the Cramond Inn and we all had dinner. Later we went back to the Barnton Hotel and met other friends.

The following morning we met her in Cramond. She wore a donkey jacket and plimsolls and carried an ex-army bag over her shoulder. She gazed across the weir and low tide towards Forth Bridge, which was hidden in the mist, and I left her to brave the world and to her lonely life trapped in a caravan among her friends. I urged her to move into a flat and again explained the steps she would have to take, and I stressed that I would help her. I made arrangements for her to come and see Oaklands. Then we all waved goodbye and I drove my family home via Hadrian's Wall, a "grey-green wall overlooking plunging green fields of Cumbria".[22]

David Bohm at Winchester
The sale of 46 Ritherdon Road was dragging on. In April I attended the 1983 Mystics and Scientists conference at Winchester to hear David Bohm, the physicist who had had discussions with Einstein and had proposed that the universe is an implicate or unfolding order that is whole, keen to absorb the physics of the One. He stood rather wooden-faced and mumbled at the lectern – he was not the best of speakers – and later, finding myself standing beside him waiting for rain to cease, I had a short discussion with him. He told me, "These are just some ideas I've got, that's all. Just some ideas." And I warmed to his modesty as he had put the evidential basis for his work in a very truthful perspective. I did not know I would get to know him.

Norman Rodway buys 46 Ritherdon Road
I was supposed to drive from Winchester to 46 Ritherdon Road to show

round a prospective buyer. On the way home my car broke down and I was late. I met the prospective buyer the next day: the Shakespearean actor Norman Rodway, a likeable silver-haired, thin-bearded, silky-looking man who spoke scathingly of the lack of professionalism of the young actresses he had to rehearse with. We had tea together, sitting in the dining-room and talking about the theatre, and the following Sunday he came by appointment with a younger, thin, quiet man in jeans with a bookish brow and thick-lensed spectacles who seemed shy and wandered round on his own. Eventually when we all stood together, Rodway said, "Nicholas, have you met Alan Howard?" I realised I was standing with one of the great Shakespearean actors who would later play all the kings of Shakespeare's histories. He could hold a theatre spellbound, but was unassuming and retiring in my house.

Rodway made an offer for the house, which I accepted, thereby very belatedly – over six months after the completion of the school – confirming the last condition for the purchase of Oaklands and the start of the building of our new house. I had taken a huge risk in proceeding with Oaklands before selling the house, and the gamble had paid off, vindicating the old adage that one must speculate to accumulate – or, in the words of *Beowulf*: "*wyrd oft nereth/unfaegne eorl thonne his ellen deah*", 'Fate often preserves the undoomed warrior when his courage is strong.'

Over the next few weeks I saw quite a bit of Rodway. He wanted to alter the kitchen and make one big open-plan area at the back of the house, and he would ring and ask if he could meet me in the afternoon on my way home from school to measure this or look at that, and I always enjoyed our chats. He always had an interesting theatre story, and much of what he said confirmed my view that acting standards were falling. He was a very well-read actor, who enjoyed discussing the interpretation of the classics. On one occasion he rang me at 3.50 and asked to come round. I put the radio on while I waited and heard: "Monday's play is Gorky's *Enemies*. Here is the star of the play, Norman Rodway, to tell you about it." For five minutes Rodway talked, slightly inarticulately, fumbling for the occasional word, and as he finished the doorbell rang and there stood the bearded Rodway.[23] I exchanged contracts with Rodway on 46 Ritherdon Road on 3 June and moved our furniture out into store the same day.

Egalitarian socialism
The ILEA's egalitarian 'no marking' policy: English inspectors ban marking in ILEA English Departments
I spent half-term week redecorating around the Oaklands hall and on 5 June I hosted a family gathering at Oaklands for Argie's 80th birthday. Aunt Flo came, looking swollen and bloated. The secondary bone cancer Argie had

told me about the previous summer was now very advanced. Nadia had come down, and in her old school I urged her again to leave the caravan and apply for a mortgage to buy a flat. I made a speech. The next day the builders started building our new house in the Oaklands grounds.

I had opened negotiations to buy the two fields, which we were renting. I had thought of the rooted Essex life, of how my father had come to Essex in wartime and become established and put me through the local private school, and now I had come back and acquired it I realised that Voltaire's advice to "dig your garden" was only partly correct. It was also to "get your land, make a garden and become rooted".

That summer Matthew had riding lessons at the Nightingale stables, down a lane off the Epping New Road. After one lesson I was able to collect him. I wrote: "18th-century buildings, horses, two dogs playing and Mr Robinson in riding breeches, and Fairmead Bottom all round: green fields and countryside. As the light faded and a bird sang and the moon came up, curved and on its back, and the evening star shone above it, I was happy, and I wanted to devote the rest of my life to my writing." I did not then know that one day I would be living in a large house in Fairmead Bottom that was distantly within view from where I was standing, and would spend my last years writing there.

I was planning my escape from the control of the ILEA, but I was not in a position to 'go over the wall' yet. I would have to continue commuting to and from Wandsworth each day for at least two more years while I turned Miss Lord's *laissez-faire* school into a more viable business. At Garratt Green I found myself in conflict with the ILEA Inspectorate, who had been encouraged by my Head to identify me as a traditionalist who might resist the new anti-traditional English policy of no marking. One of the Inspectors (Geoffrey Thornton) told Heads of English that he wanted to abolish detailed marking as it suggested "the teacher snarling in the margin" and the children should learn their mistakes for themselves. It was not explained how the children would learn their mistakes without guidance and I thought the view crazy and said so. Pupils should learn from their teachers, not claim an equality of standards with them that in reality did not exist.

There was a doctrinaire egalitarian socialism behind the ILEA's no-marking policy: pupils and teachers were equal, and so teachers should not assert their inequality by marking. The Inspector responsible for this 'no marking' policy (Thornton) shouted at me in front of the other Heads of English – [24] ten times louder than a snarl – as if the rightness of not marking children's work could be demonstrated by the volume of his voice rather than by logic. I struck back by recommending at the next Garratt Green Senior Teachers' meeting with the Head and her two Deputies, which was considering how to raise awareness of language across the curriculum, that the school should forthwith cease all marking in all subjects in accordance with the new ILEA policy; and succeeded in dividing the Head and the Senior Teachers from the Inspectorate.

A teacher with whom I was friendly, John Cameron, was so disgusted by the new policy that he wrote to Stuart Sexton, special adviser to Education Secretaries Mark Carlisle (who I had already briefed) and Keith Joseph in the late 1970s and early 1980s. Shortly afterwards it was announced that the Inspector in question (Thornton) was retiring. I attended his farewell party, staring at him in silence. Glaring at me, he issued a defiant call to carry on with the 'no marking' policy. But the policy was weakened with his retirement and would soon be abandoned. I had seen the policy off and cut off another of the already wounded hyrdra's many heads.

Principal: escaping to Oaklands

I was teaching Matthew Arnold's *Culture and Anarchy* for 'A' level, and wrote of "Matthew Arnold, the Inspector of Schools who was never himself – taken away by a thousand railway lines, and feeling the 'melancholy' of a starved, neglected soul". I taught 'The Scholar-Gipsy' and understood that the Scholar-Gipsy represented Arnold's dream of escaping from the Inspectorate: "The escape: the Scholar-Gipsy." I, too, had dreamt of escaping to become a Scholar-Gipsy in a life of greater leisure, but unlike Arnold, the Inspector of Schools, I was doing something about it. I would become a researching Scholar-Gipsy while running an educational institution that would set the highest standards in marking.

The annual Oaklands fête was held in June. I wrote: "Glorious sunshine and a family atmosphere, traditional dancing – and today, lay in the sun and watched the swifts skim and dart." Soon afterwards Mabel Reid invited us for tea and told us about the Loughton families at the beginning of the 20th century and the decline of their houses: the Warren Hall of the Lustys, which was now flats – the setting for my poem 'The Labyrinth'; the Palladian house of the Buxtons near High Beach church; the Pollards she took us to at the end of our Nature walk, which had a Roman-inspired mosaic and was now gone (except for a magnificent fountain near the Oaklands second field); the Dragons, which had been built on; Jacob Epstein's house, which was now in two; and Oaklands – then Firbank – which was now a school, and mine.

In July the Garratt Green 6th-form conference had an outing down the Thames on a boat, *The Marchioness*, which would collide and sink in 1989. We passed Dry Dock where Fagan lived and chugged all the way to the Woolwich flood barrier, seven futuristic curved ovals protruding from the water like gigantic floats from a hidden net.

Our new house was almost waist-high now. We had moved the Art Room and tacked it onto the Garden Room (a garden classroom) to clear the base for the new house, and we now had to move the flight of Yorkstone steps that had led down to the Art Room and now led down to the side of our house. We decided to transport them twenty yards and turn them at 90 degrees, so there would be a direct route from the school entrance down to the fields. I employed the husband of one of our staff and his son and son-in-law, and we discussed how we would move the largest half-ton slab of Yorkstone in the middle of the steps. We wondered what the builders of Stonehenge and the Great Pyramid would have done. I borrowed pipes and a board from the building site and we raised the slab onto them by primitive leverage: the husband dug and raised the garden fork and his son-in-law prised with a pickaxe, and the slab was moved 20 yards on our makeshift rollers.

At the same time I restored the school's original front-door opening, which had been converted into a window. I found two doors at London Architectural Salvage, which was housed in a disused church. They were the original doors for Christopher Wren's St James's, Piccadilly; the vicar had sold them to fund some lectures. I tied them to the open boot of Ann's Spacewagon and drove them back to the school and had them fitted. [25]

Baroque
Death of Aunt Flo

We spent a week painting Oaklands, and then went down to Cornwall, where almost immediately I "wrote 3 poems, all very metaphysical".

On 4 August we visited the unspoilt beach at Hemmick where I saw "4 kestrels hovering over the hill, looking for mice; absolutely still while all around them moved". That evening I heard that my Aunt Flo had died. The cancer had spread to a breast and leg, and as her kidneys failed her water seeped into her body. She had had a bad night and slipped into a coma that morning and had died at 7 p.m., alone. I went to Charlestown and there was a bright evening star. I wrote: "Two shooting stars right down the sky, one after another, like bright angels." I noted: "Aunt Flo went to sleep last night and is dead tonight. I am alive and can go to sleep tonight with this large moth circling under the light."

The next day I plunged into thoughts about the materialist old Age and the metaphysical new Age. I wrote:

> This probing, this spirit of metaphysical inquiry which is the spirit of the new Age now emerging from the Elizabethan Age – is fascinated by the findings of the ancient wisdom, the soul and spirit, higher intelligence, the new horizon and perspectives of space, the dynamic nature of the moving universe and the still centre which is illumined by the Light..., the movement against the ego and materialism, and by the fact that the Dark Ages are near, only a bomb blast away.

I noted: "In Japan… the words floated in 'a new Baroque age is born', and my task now is to bring this into the arts." I wondered: "Perhaps I have trodden my lonely path so that I can come up with the idea for the next Age, and so lead the West on."

I "coped with Aunt Flo's death: wrote 5 poems with images of death". I wrote to the bereaved and made arrangements to attend the funeral, then "spent the day at deserted Hemmick beach and looked at Vault, then drafted a poem 'Night Thoughts in Charlestown' [later retitled 'Night Visions in Charlestown']. (Charles' Town is the Carolingian age which is waiting to burst out of the Elizabethan age.)" I was fed much of this poem in my sleep:

6 Aug. Awoke with 12 stanzas latently (implicately) in my mind; did my exercises and then, before breakfast, with Ann asleep at first, wrote them straight out, some 100 lines about the spirit of the new age, 'Night Thoughts in Charlestown'. When I got to stanza 4 Ann awoke and got up…, and it required all my concentration to ignore her presence and get what was in my soul down on paper. But I did it, writing on my knee, sitting on the side of my bed in my bedroom at 4 Manor Close, Fairfield Park, the window on my right letting enough light through the drawn curtains for me to see.

That afternoon I went to Charlestown for the Regatta, and the next day we visited Poldark mine: "The hellish tunnels, the caverns of granite with lodes and stopes where minerals (copper, quartz, tin) had been; the water trickling down the walls which would become a torrent bursting over the miners. The hellish ghostly voices of men working, on tape, as it used to be." The following day I drove up from Cornwall for Aunt Flo's funeral. I had to go home to Essex first to change into a dark suit and black tie, and then I drove to Merrow, near Guildford and put the car into a car-wash. The brush would not stop rolling, and the spraying of water somehow got into the engine. I was trapped, and after the machine was turned off I could not start the car for a while and only just got to Merrow church in time.

The coffin was on two stands with two wreaths on top, and the eulogy mentioned Aunt Flo's "puckish, irreverent sense of humour" along with her "commitment, cheerfulness and courage". It occurred to me that the soul is like grain, that the stalk (body) grows so that the grain (soul) can be garnered, after which the stalk is useless. After the service we drove through Guildford High Street and then on to the crematorium and witnessed the committal. Then we drove to a reception where my Uncle Reg poured drinks for everyone. I drove back to Cornwall and stopped at Plymouth. I "dashed off the poem on grain ['Grain'] in 2 minutes sitting on the grass overlooking Brunel's bridge at Plymouth, doing in 2 mins what it would have taken me 7 days to do in the 1960s". (I added later: "Some people are taken short and have to go to the lavatory; I am taken short as I was at Plymouth and have to write a poem." The same happened five minutes before an appointment with my bank manager, *see* pp.466–467.)[26]

Literary Baroque
In Cornwall I had pondered the contradictions in my make-up:

> In some ways I am an ultra-radical – the Light and anti-Newtonian anti-materialism challenge the *status quo* – and in other ways I am a reactionary, in my sense of the importance of preserving the social structure and the Englishness of our life. In poetry I am a radical... in going for a new view of human being as Light-bearing... which is traditional in terms of the tradition (back to the 14th century).

My sonnets combined Classical Renaissance emotions and Romantic medieval Light, radical stress metre and traditional pentameters, and "being a neo-Baroque writer I fused the two traditions". I enjoined myself:

> Identify the spirit of this Age – what it is preoccupied with – and, as the highest expression of the Age leads to the next Age anticipate what the next Age's spirit will be. Think: space; scientific inquiry into the origins of life (DNA, cancer);... the spirit and soul. Put all this together, and do we not have a new metaphysical age ahead of us? A new Baroque age."

I saw myself as combining Classicism and Romanticism: "I synthesise all – medieval, metaphysical, Romantic, Classical, and all religions."

In Cornwall before Aunt Flo's death I had focused on my life and my works in relation to the Baroque:

> My life has already been given to me, like jigsaw-like bits of mosaic – the Far East, the ancient world of Egypt and Babylon, the classical world, the Renaissance, the medieval Light, etc – and I have to piece them all together to make a – Baroque – picture that defines me.... The spirit of our Age: a dynamic moving universe, stillness.

(I saw the Baroque as combining movement and stillness.) In search of the Baroque, I revisited the originally Baroque Lanhydrock House and Restormel Castle. I read into the historical Baroque, how it emphasised one moment and the conflict between appearance and reality. I had given the Baroque conflict between sense and spirit a new twist by focusing on the conflict between appearance and Reality.

Back in Cornwall from Aunt Flo's funeral I tried to characterise "the

Anti-Materialist Age which will replace the Age of Materialism which has lasted 300 years (Descartes, Newton and Darwin), and which produced the Space Age and the Nuclear Age, i.e. outer things". I saw the Anti-Materialist Age as "the Age of Reunification (= oneness),... or Age of Oneness". (It would be an age that aspires to abolish wars, famine and disease.) It would be the time of "the European Resurgence", an "Age of Baroque", a "Metaphysical Age". Two days later I received another poem. I went fishing with Ann's cousin:

> Up at 4.40 a.m. and out fishing in Mount's Bay, on a sunny day and calm sea; hauled up 300 crab-pots.... Drafted [the outline of] a poem. The outing, hauling up crabs – the sea, indivisible (*cf* Stone Garden, non-local theory) – the world as an ocean of being ruled by tides.... This is another metaphysical poem.

The poem itself came to me in my sleep: "Awoke at 7.30 a.m. and wrote an 8-stanza poem, 'Crab-Fishing in a Boundless Sea' [later retitled 'Crab-Fishing on a Boundless Deep'] by 9.15."[27]

I pondered the literary Baroque. I was sure it began with Shakespeare.

> His great theme, appearance versus reality, illusion versus truth, is the Baroque theme. Hence the mistaken identity in *Twelfth Night*... and in *Measure for Measure*.... Also the exposure of those who seem more virtuous than they are (Malvolio, Angelo). What seems versus what is. There should be a book redefining Shakespeare as the first Baroque writer.

I wrote:

> The whole period 1600–1700 in literature should be redefined as the Baroque Age, to show the connection between Shakespeare, Donne, Marvell, Milton, Dryden (and through Dryden, Pope). Shakespeare is the founder of literary Baroque. But so was Marlowe, e.g. in *Dr Faustus*. The ornamental metaphor or simile – Baroque.... It is the amount of decoration that counts.

My book *A New Philosophy of Literature* would state the fundamental theme of world literature as having metaphysical and secular aspects from 2,600BC to the present time, and my view of the Baroque Age in 1983 should now be seen within this wider context.

I now wrote a Baroque story. It grew out of my questioning of the idea of Providence:

> The Providence idea can be egocentric: the whole universe revolves around

little 'me', and even Hell is conspiring to make me avoid accidents, to jog my memory, to contrive my good, like the sylphs around Belinda in Pope's 'The Rape of the Lock' – proud Belinda.

Two days later I went out fishing with Ann's cousin again and got the idea for the story. The next day:

Wrote 'Light in the Storm', a short story which expresses a great truth and is perhaps my first genuinely Baroque short story.... It wrote itself effortlessly. I did it at two sittings, this morning and afternoon, and the draft was finished by 7 p.m." Later I wrote of Cornwall: "Every year I come to Cornwall and return to the elemental world, the world of sea and sky and fish and shooting stars and seaweed and crabs, and I come extra-specially alive. It is the intensity of the elemental world which I need as an artist, that makes each visit worthwhile.

The rest of the time in Cornwall I had to work on the wages book and the fees register for Oaklands. We went to Charlestown and the Fowey carnival with the boys, and to Golant and to Penquite House, which Garibaldi visited because Peard had fought, Byronically, in Italy. I reflected that Miss Attwood, mother's neighbour at Journey's End, had Garibaldi's bed in her house. We returned home to Essex and almost immediately took Miss Lord to Heathrow as, at 82, she was flying to see her relatives in Australia. I had to spend long hours with my bank manager and accountant. We went to Guildford for the day, and to Shere, where I again looked at the 14th-century quatrefoil and squint of Christine Carpenter, anchoress, who had herself walled up inside the church so that in her enclosed cell she could contemplate Reality.

To my delight Nadia rang in early September to say she had found a flat and needed the deposit to make a conclusive offer. I had said I wanted her to have the security and rootedness of a flat. She said, "I want to get out of the caravan.... I've often wondered how I was going to get out of the caravan."[28] I told her that the family would not abandon her.

Egalitarian socialism: the hydra slain

The time was approaching when I would have to return to Garratt Green and to the oppression of the wounded many-headed hydra, the ILEA. I wrote: "I would rather go to prison for a year than go back to Marxist Garratt Green." And: "I need to get away from the Garratt Green world which is removed from Nature."[29] I had planned my escape and was still waiting for the day when I could 'go over the wall' to my independence, which promised to give me the leisure I needed to deliver the works I carried within me.

It was now announced that the Greater London Council (GLC) was to be abolished, and there was a move to abolish the ILEA. The London boroughs were not ready to take over the education of London children, and the ILEA survived until 4 February 1988, when it was announced that it would be abolished in 1990. But the process of abolition had been begun. Like Heracles in his Second Labour, I had been fighting the hydra. I had assisted the Government in slaying the many-headed monster.

I had fought off the ILEA's Trotskyite control and had channelled my new powers away from the New Age into a new burst of activity. I had become a Principal and had sharpened my Baroque principle. But now a new conflict arose as I found myself drawn into the national political scene.

Episode 5:

Vision and Subversion

Second ordeal: gorgon (subversion of Soviet-supported Scargill)

Years: 1983–1985
Locations: Loughton; London; Paris; Frankfurt
Works: *A Rainbow in the Spray*; *Scargill the Stalinist?*
Initiatives: FREE (Freedom for the Republics of Eastern Europe); 'Heroes of the West'

'Vision': "statesmanlike foresight, sagacity in planning; imaginative insight" (*Concise Oxford Dictionary*)
'Subvert': "to bring about the overthrow or ruin of (a person, people or country, a dynasty)" (*Shorter Oxford English Dictionary*); "overturn, overthrown, or upset (government)" (*Concise Oxford Dictionary*)

"*Qui desiderat pacem, praeparet bellum.*"
"Let him who desires peace, prepare for war."
Vegetius, *De Re Militari*, bk 3 (4th century AD)

A new episode now began in which my new vision came into conflict with an attempt to overthrow the British Establishment, an uprising I defended like a Crusader and subverted – and found myself on the receiving end of, and grappling with, subversion. My second ordeal was my struggle against the subversion of the dreadful gorgon Scargill who had turned a Prime Minister (Heath) to stone and terrified all with totalitarian deeds like venomous snakes.

Vision: call to politics

In early September I returned reluctantly to Garratt Green and to a tirade against the staff by the Head. Much to her chagrin, the English results were very good. All were reeling at the announcement that the ILEA was to be abolished and at the first Heads-of-Department and Heads-of-House meeting I spoke out indignantly against the anti-marking Inspectorate and regime "whose dubious ideas may have contributed to the abolition of the ILEA". A generation of London children were to be deprived of marking, of being shown their mistakes. The next day Sinclair, the Deputy Head, said: "That was your most spectacular yet, yesterday. It had everything: variety, riposte, humour and anger."[1]

Offer to make me an MP: National Council for Educational Standards

John Cameron, who had political connections, heard about my blast and invited me to the National Council for Educational Standards, who were meeting at the Mostyn Hotel, Bryanston Street, near Marble Arch. I was met by Prof. C.B. Cox of Black-Paper fame, who invited me to lunch with him.

The lunch introduced me to a political circle I would encounter a year later. After speeches from Bob Dunn, MP for Dartford and a junior education minister to Sir Keith Joseph and from Harry Greenway MP, I sat next to Cox and opposite Dunn, and the conversation included the ILEA's attempt to ban marking. They knew about my stand against Thornton. At one point Cox said: "Did I hear you tell Greenway you want to become an MP? Because I can get you on the list, so long as you help me on the secretarial side, send out three letters a year to our 255 members and take cheques." I was to be secretary and treasurer. Cox said: "It will be a deal, you help me and I'll make you an MP." And, "I'm corresponding with Ted Hughes at present about writing, which ought to feature at 'A' level, and I edit *Critical Quarterly*." Cox explained: "We are a pressure group and need to keep in the headlines to make Ministers' tasks easier."

Stuart Sexton, who had helped defeat the ILEA's "no marking policy", joined Cox and me after Dunn and Greenway had left. He said, "Dunn was appointed to be tough with the DES, you should hear the rows we've already had." After lunch Baroness Cox, a nurse who had been elevated to the peerage by Margaret Thatcher, and Dr John Marks, director of the Educational Research Trust, who had written an educational paper, spoke.

Later I had a long talk with Baroness Cox, who was opposed by the ILEA and DES Inspectors but supported by Tory ministers and advisers within the DES.

I left the lunch with a promise from C.B. Cox that he would make me an MP. I wrote: "So my public career as an MP has been launched; Cameron will be my agent and will be my political adviser when I am a Minister."[2]

Why did I not keep my side of the deal, and act as Cox's honorary (unpaid) secretary and treasurer? Partly because I was already doing two jobs – being a Senior Teacher and Head of English during the day, and Principal of an independent school in the evenings – and was just too busy to take on extra work. Partly because I was propelled into more prominent political circles and partly because I was wary of his Black-Paper extremism. And partly because I needed to hoard as much of my spare time as I could for my family and writing. Also because the NCES were waiting on an application for money, as Prof. Cox told me in a letter of 20 January, saying he would come back with a "definite proposal", but he never did.[3]

Pneumonia: sinuses washed out

I was unwell. I wrote: "I have pneumonia; have had it for months." I was referred to the local ear-nose-and-throat consultant Mr Morrison, who had had children at Oaklands. He requested an X-ray of my chest and sinuses and referred me to David Hughes of the London Hospital. "There will have to be a general anaesthetic to wash sinuses out and suck out the mucus following a bronchoscopy." I recorded: "My pneumonia is taking hold. I have a cough and my left lung hurts – today for the first time." I visited Hughes, "a dapper, bespectacled little man", who looked at my X-ray and said: "You've had pneumonia but you've thrown it off." He showed me my lungs on the X-ray, which should be dark, and the inflammation that still showed up light. "You've had a very bad bug in the dry hot summer.... You must have your sinuses drained as sinuses and lungs are interconnected and an infection in one infects the other. Take Erythromycin the morning you have your sinuses done."

A week later I went into Holly House, Buckhurst Hill, Oak ward. I was "given a pre-med and was later wheeled to the lift and went up. Male nurse in shower-hat [i.e. theatre cap]. Two other nurses put on 'shower-proof' booties and masks and shower-hats.... The masked anaesthetist came in, and a masked Morrison, and they attempted to give me an injection in the back of my left hand. 'You haven't got a good vein there, can you give me a good vein.' (As if it was my fault.).... They whopped the back of my hand yet again and then injected it. I felt the cold run up my arm. 'You'll be out in a few seconds.' It seemed like an eternity, and then I drowned."

Several people were "shouting at me, 'Mr Hagger, wake up, wake up' and I slowly came to in the recovery room and asked, 'What did they do?' 'Washed your sinuses out, did an antrum puncture on each side and got rid of a cyst.' A cyst.... It had been there a long time, Morrison said, and it was under my right eye; if undetected it might have pushed the right eyeball out.... Morrison: 'I removed a lump of puss which I've sent to Dr Hughes for a culture. You've still got some pneumonia, he may want to see you again.'" The cyst was in the antrum. Later I commented: "Still in Holly House with its routines of tea, temperature-taking, pulse-taking and sunny nurses; still sore-throated and stiff-backed from the hard narrow bed that works from a side-brake and moves into a sitting position. I still have a snuffle of blood which I must not blow down, and a deeply sore throat, and don't feel up to too much work."[4]

While I convalesced out of hospital I saw the Oaklands staff for 10 minutes each. Then we went to Worthing and walked on the front and I got the pneumonia out of my lungs. In November we exchanged contracts on the Oaklands fields.

I oppose Communism in Europe through FREE (Freedom for the Republics of Eastern Europe)
In the summer the Soviet writer Solzhenitsyn had attracted publicity by raising the spectre that if Western civilization did not find the spiritual strength to resist, Communism might end it. I did not believe that Communism would win the Cold War, but became aware that if the West were to survive and come through then Communism must be resisted. I returned to the idea I had put to Margaret Thatcher in 1976 that the Eastern-European nations should be free. Europe was half-*occupied* by the Soviet Union, and Eastern Europe was constantly being described as Communist. I felt there should be a liberation movement against Communism to free the Eastern Europeans from Soviet tyranny.

In the presence of Lord Whitelaw John Biggs-Davison asks me to write a paper on FREE, I revise 'The European Resurgence'
On 11 November 1983 I was invited to Thatcher House in Loughton, the constituency office of John Biggs-Davison MP, for a reception for Willie Whitelaw, later Lord Whitelaw, Margaret Thatcher's number 2. I chatted with Biggs-Davison and told him that there should be a liberation movement to free Eastern Europe. I said it should be called FREE (Freedom for the Republics of Eastern Europe). He looked startled and said, "The Americans would be against it. Kissinger carved up the world and agreed not to interfere in the Soviet sphere of influence."

I was taken aback. It was the first indication I had had that there was more to the Cold War than met the eye, and that the Soviet presence in

Eastern Europe was the result of a deal of which I had not been aware. Biggs-Davison was tipping me off that there was a deal between Western and Eastern leaders involving spheres of influence. The deal went back to the wartime meetings at Tehran and Yalta.

I said, "If what you say is true, that's terrible. It means that the Soviet Union is allowed to continue its occupation of Europe by Western lack of will to roll it back to Russia."

At that point Biggs-Davison went to Whitelaw and brought him over to meet me. I noted that he was "huge and jowly and eyebrowed and bloodshot-eyed". Biggs-Davison asked me to explain FREE to Whitelaw. I outlined my idea of the need to liberate Eastern Europe regardless of the spheres of influence, and said: "I can't think why it isn't happening."

Whitelaw had listened intently. He said, "Now you put it in those terms I can't for the life of me think why it isn't happening either, and I will ask upwards why it isn't happening and let John know." "Upwards" meant Margaret Thatcher, to whom I had first revealed the idea.

In front of Whitelaw Biggs-Davison asked me to write a paper on the subject and send it to him. It was clear that I would be writing the paper for Biggs-Davison to pass to Whitelaw, who would pass it to Thatcher.

I wrote my paper, 'The European Resurgence', along the following lines:

> Europe has been occupied since 1945 yet everyone pretends this is not so. The future of Europe will be good if Eastern-European states throw off the Soviet yoke and join the Western democracies.... The idea of our century [is] the European resurgence, the resurgence of Europe against the Communist advance, pushing back the tide, by a London-led encouraging of liberation movements. Someone outside the Government, but linked, should... organise 'governments in exile' for these liberation movements.[5]

(*See* Appendix 5, p.925.) I followed this paper up with a draft paper on 'The FREE (Freedom for the Republics of Eastern Europe) Movement' on 12 November. (*See* Appendix 7.) Headed 'Highly Confidential', it would go through five versions during the coming months.

I was ill before Christmas. I visited my consultant, David Hughes, and learned: "I have another patch on my lungs... this time on the right lung." We had Christmas lunch in Theydon and Christmas tea with Miss Lord, and soon afterwards went to Cornwall. I spent a couple of days on the Oaklands accounts, and on the Saturday morning "awoke early... and looked for the Light and saw it, was filled with it. Then opened myself to healing energies and felt them lodged in the middle of my spine for a while until they finally moved up and made my little finger glow. Healed my sinuses and my right lung and my varicose veins with my little finger and then got up, at 9."

We went to Porthleven – "a green sea with sea horses... and a stormy petrel sweeping round the cliff in the wind", "the sea splashing over the harbour wall". Then: "Got back to the 3 odes I drafted in the summer.... 3 Metaphysical odes." These were 'Crab-Fishing on a Boundless Deep', 'Cambridge Ode: Against Materialism' and 'Night Visions in Charlestown (An Ode)'. The next day I typed up a longish story I had written, 'Light in the Storm', of which I wrote, "The precise details of crab-fishing at the beginning are authentic, and say 'Trust me'... to make more credible the blatantly metaphysical end." I wrote to Tuohy: "It is to some extent a deliberate sleight-of-hand as it starts with the firmly physical – precise authentic details of crab-fishing – and leads the reader into the possible, the blatantly metaphysical, without letting on what's happening."

The next day we went to Mevagissey – "a fresh wind whipping across the waves" – and on my return from Cornwall saw David Hughes again. He diagnosed thrombophlebitis in my right ankle. According to Dr Hughes "I have been living on the verge of a coronary thrombosis." I later found out, while "struggling with 5 sets of exam papers and reports" that I was "ill with bronchiectasis" as well as post-thrombophlebitis".[6] It was not an auspicious beginning to 1984.

Biggs-Davison puts me in touch with Josef Josten
On 19 January I received a letter from Biggs-Davison, saying he had taken part

in a private conference of the Committee for the Defence of the Unjustly Prosecuted which helps... political dissidents and other victims of Communist oppression. The organiser was Josef Josten whose letter to me about your proposals I enclose. I suggest that you should get in touch with Josten and let me know how you get on. Josten is in touch with Michael Alison, Parliamentary Private Secretary to the Prime Minister, so I will not, at this stage, trouble Whitelaw.[7]

The enclosure was a letter (3 single-spaced pages of A4) from Josten to "John" broadly agreeing with each of my 8 headings but concluding that the movement should be fronted by someone with a higher profile and proposing that I should "prepare a new paper which could be discussed by a group of British politicians who show a well-known interest in the problem, e.g. Sir Bernard Braine, Sir Patrick Wall, Lord Chalfont" and others. "Then their findings could be discussed with... free statesmen from East Central Europe, e.g. the Free Polish Premier Mr Sabbat.... Only then their common findings, embodied in a final Memorandum, should be presented to the Prime Minister's office and to the Foreign Office. All these steps should be undertaken in absolute secrecy."[8] The intervention of Josten marked the beginning of his attempts, which lasted several months, to slow down, delay and obstruct the implementation of FREE.

Battle to secure planning permission for Oaklands' extension
Meanwhile I was involved in local politics. I had put in a planning application to build a three-classroom extension at Oaklands. It had been opposed by the Loughton Residents Association at the instigation of the man in whose house we had been living, an LRA councillor, and had been recommended for rejection by the Planning Department. I had been asked if I would stand as a Conservative councillor in the May elections for Roding ward, the most Labour ward in the area. It included the path I took when I cycled to Chigwell School across the River Roding, as a schoolboy. I had invited the Leader of the Council to Oaklands for a briefing visit, and he told me that if I beat the Loughton Residents Association in the election it would strengthen the councillors' hands to go against the recommendation of the Planning Department. I knew that I would have no chance of winning but agreed to stand so that I could outmanoeuvre the planning recommendation.

I wrote to Biggs-Davison on 22 January with news of my adoption, and told him about my meeting with the Deputy Leader of the Christian Democrats in the European Parliament, Siegbert Alber, who had visited Thatcher House to speak and had agreed with me that the Soviet occupation of Eastern Europe should be opposed. Over a cup of tea after his talk I pointed out to him that atlases now labelled Eastern Europe as 'European Russia' rather than 'Russianised Europe', a measure of the permanence which the Russian occupation of Eastern Europe had come to have.[9]

Subversion of FREE
In a subsequent letter I asked Biggs-Davison to confirm that he had vetted Josten: "Experience has taught me to be cautious in matters that may involve the KGB, and although I know you would vet wisely and carefully before passing my proposal on, I would be very grateful for a few words about the... pre-1956 background of Josten, and for a few details about the FCP News Agency, together with the basis on which he is in touch with the Prime Minister's PPS."[10] Biggs-Davison replied that "such as Sir Bernard Braine and Winston Churchill would be prepared to vouch" for Josten, who "was a Czech who had to emigrate after a brief incarceration".[11]

Biggs-Davison puts me in touch with Brian Crozier
I had written a second version of my paper on FREE, and on 29 January sent it to Biggs-Davison. I told him that this second version "incorporates some

of Josten's points and generally toughens the argument", and I enclosed copies for him to send to Josten and to Brian Crozier, who Biggs-Davison wanted me to meet.[12] On 31 January Biggs-Davison sent me copies of his letters to Josten and Brian Crozier, that enclosed my revised paper.[13]

The progress of FREE was interrupted as my wife and I moved into our new house across the road in Albion Hill in early February. It was a brick building with aluminium windows that nestled under the listed blue acacia cedar some twenty yards from the Oaklands main entrance. It had a rear view across the tennis-court and fields, and from my study at the back I could watch squirrels and magpies settle on the Victorian iron railings. There was much to do, and I could now recover the furniture from 46 Ritherdon Road, which had been in store since the previous July. We all relished the space of a house after living in cramped conditions on the top floor across the road for a year-and-a-half, and our two boys loved having their own bedrooms.

Crozier asks for a new paper on FREE
On 20 February I met Brian Crozier in his Regent-Street office. I knew little about him beyond what Biggs-Davison had told me. (In those days there was of course no internet and we were dependent on books like *Who's Who*.) I knew that he had started a private intelligence agency and in 1977 become Mrs. Thatcher's adviser on security and intelligence. I did not know that he was an Australian who had believed in Communism in his early life and spent the rest of his life opposing it. I knew he had founded the Institute for the Study of Conflict, a think-tank devoted to studying terrorism and subversion, but I did not know that he advised the SIS, the Information Research Department of the Foreign Office and the CIA. I knew he had worked for *The Economist* but I did not know that he kept his best stories for the SIS. ("I know a number of reputable journalists of various nationalities who have done as I did," he later wrote.)[14] I did not know that he had interviewed more heads of state or government than anybody else: 58.[15] He greeted me warmly, silver-haired and bushy-eyebrowed, 67 years old, and gave me a copy of his book, *Soviet Imperialism, How to Contain It* (previously titled *Strategy of Survival*). It was one of the few books about the Cold War which faced up to the Soviet Union, and I had considerable sympathy for Crozier.

I said that I had come to discuss the liberation of Eastern Europe a~ eventually of the Soviet Union, and that those who have a belief in We~ values should act. I told him I wanted to "build a Greater Europ~ strike a blow for Western values against Communist values. Crozi~ with me – everyone I met from Whitelaw down agreed that it~ idea – but he said that it must be proceeded with cautiously. ~

to have a chat with the Russian George Miller, who happened to be in the next room. Miller, a youngish handsome man who did not look unlike Che Guevara, was holding a copy of my paper. He told me that one day we would ride together through a Moscow liberated from Communism.[17] With hindsight, both Miller and I have been proved right. Back with Crozier, I pointed out that the African liberation movements I had covered for *The Times* did not win by being cautious but being bold. Crozier asked me to revise the paper to include George Miller's and his own points.

FREE in competition with European Liaison Group

Crozier said that my idea cut across the work of the European Liaison Group, whose leading light was the MP Sir Bernard Braine. He said that the ELG was not very active, and that he hoped that FREE could be more dynamic than the ELG. It so happened that the ELG had a meeting the next day. Crozier gave me an invitation addressed to him. He scribbled on a printed card saying "With the compliments of Brian Crozier": "Mr Marcetic [the ELG Chairman]/Sir Bernard Braine, I have suggested that Mr Nicholas Hagger should attend the meeting – as I cannot to my regret. Brian Crozier."[18]

The next day, 21 February, I went to the Grand Committee Room at the House of Commons at 5.30, showed the invitation sent to Crozier and his compliments card at the door, and heard the Senior Counsellor to the US Permanent Representative to the UN speak on 'The Problem of Totalitarianism – a view from the United States'. The invitation stated in small print at the end that the ELG co-ordinated the activities of exile communities from 14 East-European countries: Albania, Bulgaria, Byelorussia, Czechoslovakia, Estonia, Georgia, Hungary, Latvia, Lithuania, Poland, Romania, Russia, Ukraine and Yugoslavia. At the end of the meeting I shook hands with Sir Bernard Braine, who was portly and said little. There was a reception and cold buffet at Latvia House, Queensborough Terrace, W2. I met Josten briefly, who told me he "had a network behind the Iron Curtain". He was bald, sallow, withered, bespectacled and just turned 70. I did not know that he had been a journalist in Prague in the 1930s, had fled the Gestapo to France, joined the Czech Brigade and that he had been in the team that assassinated Heidrich. He had returned to work in the Czech Ministry of Foreign Affairs after the war, but had refused to join the Communist Party in 1948 and had fled to England. Afterwards I met Lady Olga Maitland, who told me that she was launching a new movement, a pro-NATO campaign against CND, and reckoned it would take five weeks from ˹ to press conference.[19]

˹ring the next two days I revised my paper to include Crozier's and ˹ points and added numbered paragraphs. On Friday 24 February I took the revised paper to Crozier, who said he would take it to the US the following week and that he would send a copy to George Miller. I told Crozier that I proposed to start a small publishing company that would strengthen the resolve of the West by publishing appropriate books. I told him that I would gather a group of people who would be the opposite of the Cambridge Apostles – Donald Maclean and others – but would be 'Heroes of the West': counterbalancing the 'Martyrs of the East'. Crozier nodded in approval. He had my paper on FREE in front of him and was leafing through it. He asked me to reduce it to 15 points on 1 or 2 sides of A4 to make discussion of the idea easier.

I struggled on with my school work in deteriorating health. On 12 March I attended another meeting at the House of Commons and sat next to Biggs-Davison and Josten, and spoke again to Lady Olga Maitland at the end. Josten invited me to visit him, but the next day I had a slipped disc and was off work for the rest of the week. I felt tired as if I had a patch on one of my lungs. On Monday 19 March I revisited Crozier and gave him the shortened version of my paper. (*See* Appendix 7, p.935.) For an hour-and-a-half he opened up to me. He told me

> that in 1977 he started a private intelligence agency which is now repre-
> sented in 11 countries, and that he funds 15 organisations; that in 1977 he
> became Mrs. Thatcher's adviser on security and intelligence, and held the
> position until 1979, and that now the SIS and MI5 point to him. How he can
> go to the White House whenever he wants and also to Chequers. He is on
> Ron/Margaret terms with our leaders…. The whole point of Crozier's organ-
> isation is that there are no Philbys and Blakes in it. Clearly, it is a
> Communist-proof organisation, starting again with conviction people and
> not having the risk of career diplomats.

While I was with him Crozier rang Josten and arranged for me to meet him on 22 March.

I was unwell. I was off work for another week with a slipped disc and suspected bronchiectasis. But I dragged myself up to London and spent three hours with Josten. I wondered if he was more committed to the ELG and Sir Bernard Braine than to my idea for FREE. I asked him of Crozier, "He is a supremo?"

"Yes. He is too busy. Mrs. Thatcher has been let down so many times by the Foreign Office and others. He is her right-hand man. He is ill. He will soon be having an operation."[20]

I gave him the latest version of my paper and he said he would write comments, after which we should meet again. We discussed his reservations on "revolutions behind the Iron Curtain", an idea that was not in my paper.

He worried about the dangers to people behind the Iron Curtain and that we would be penetrated and our efforts exposed as American imperialism.

I wrote a letter to Biggs-Davison the next day, 23 March:

We have devised a formula to cope with this: a top-secret and impenetrable Directorate of 5 utterly reliable people, each of whom would have an adviser. The 5 would be behind the Co-ordinating Council, who would not even know of their existence. If I were on the Council, I would be the point of contact between the 5 and the Council. The *émigré* advisers to the Council, the Advisory Committee would all have to be publicly vetted by Special Branch… to minimise penetration. Crozier is very keen on the idea as it will be the first instance of the West going on the offensive in the last 40 years. He told Josten on Monday in my presence that he is very interested indeed. Josten is now happy that we should proceed to the politicians. He suggests that you, Crozier and Sir Bernard Braine should hold a tea at the RAF Club, Piccadilly… for some 15 MPs and others: Sir Patrick Wall, Lord Chalfont, Dickson Mabon, Lord Cameron, Winston Churchill, Julian Amery, Jo Grimond, Sir Victor Goodhew and others.

At this meeting I would hand out a sanitised version of my paper, which would contain no references to Josten and Crozier or to the Directorate of 5. I pointed out that I should meet Sir Bernard Braine in advance of the tea.[21]

My letter was headed "Most Confidential". I handed the letter to Biggs-Davison personally on the platform at Lopping Hall, Loughton after a constituency Annual General Meeting attended by only 50, to which he had invited me. He read it and said: "Shall I burn it?"

I met Biggs-Davison at a dinner-dance the following day. He told me: "'I'll have nothing to do with the tea as I'm busy, let Crozier do it, he knows Julian Amery, and I'll speak to Braine and say, "Do you remember Nicholas Hagger?" And if you need anything, come back to me.'"[22] I wondered why Biggs-Davison had suddenly pulled away from the tea, why he was putting distance between himself and the setting-up of FREE. On 26 March he wrote a handwritten letter: "I've destroyed the letter you gave me dated the 23rd and the previous correspondence. As I explained, I can't add to my commitments but am ready to make contacts for you."[23] I wondered whether the activities of FREE, in leading a Western offensive for the first time in 40 years, were at variance with the activities of an MP and had strayed into the intelligence zone sufficiently for him to destroy all the previous correspondence.

Meanwhile Josten had been in touch again, recommending that there should be no tea but that I should contact the politicians individually. I reported this in a letter to Biggs-Davison, saying that I would "discuss a purged version of my paper with each. This was a better idea than holding a tea as in a group each politician can be expected to uphold an image in relation to each of the other politicians, no matter how sympathetic they might be privately. The priority now is to get the Co-ordinating Council established so that funding can commence. I need to make a start with Sir Bernard Braine."[24] I received a reply from Biggs-Davison saying that he had written to Sir Bernard Braine to ask him to see me.[25]

I wrote to Crozier at the beginning of April enclosing a version of my paper purged of all names. I pointed out that the first three pages were the same as in the previous version, only the last five pages were different. I drew his attention to the more structured financing and launching arrangements, which included the idea that I would start a publishing company.

Idea of setting up Oak-Tree Books and of taking voluntary redundancy from ILEA
I was determined to found a new publishing company, which I thought of as being called Acorn Publishing Limited. In my letter to Crozier I said: "The imprint of 'Acorn Books' will be an oak-tree."[26] Later I decided: "My publishing house should be called Oak-Tree Publishing Limited or Oak-Tree Books."[27] I spoke of applying for voluntary redundancy from the ILEA to take effect in August 1985 as I would need my salary until then to afford the school's extension. I spoke of being funded to work full-time on the FREE Movement on the equivalent of my ILEA salary. On 13 April I wrote to my accountant asking him to set up a publishing company.[28]

Subversion of FREE by Josten: Baroness Cox, Roger Scruton; Oaklands' planning permission secured
I now received Josten's critique of the shortened version of my paper. It began "Dear Colleague" and was signed by "You know who" with copies "to those two persons who advised you to contact me". It raised questions on minutiae and came across as an attempt to delay, indeed obstruct, my proposals. I contacted him. He told me: "You are trying to do in a few weeks what it would normally – if you were in the Foreign Office – take one year to do."[29] Again, he seemed to be putting a brake on my activities. Immediately afterwards I received a letter from Crozier: "I have discussed your ideas with Baroness [Caroline] Cox and with Roger Scruton, both of whom are already involved in compatible activities concerning Eastern Europe. Before we go any further, I think it would be very useful for you to meet them. Roger has gone away (to Prague), I believe, for a week or so. Please ring Lady Cox, or write to her." He provided their addresses and phone numbers.[30]

I visited Caroline Cox on 17 April. I found her at the NCES office and she took me back to her house in Stag Lane, Kingsbury, NW9. I explained the

FREE idea. She spoke of how she could help: "The points of contact: organisation behind the Iron Curtain, which can be activated in the future; publishing; and the line to Margaret Thatcher. 'As one of her peeresses I can ask for an interview and get it, and take you along.'" She said she was very excited and enthusiastic about FREE: "I am 100 per cent enthusiastic in principle. I find it very inspiring. Let us drink to the success of your idea."[31] We had sherry.

Soon afterwards I visited Roger Scruton, columnist for *The Times*, later Professor and writer on philosophy, who received me in his flat in Linden Gardens, Notting Hill, W2. The floor was awash with books in all languages, and I paddled through them to sit on the chair by the mantelpiece that faced his. He listened but said very little. I told him that the end of Soviet Communism was in sight and it needed one more push. He countered this with a faintly depressed air. (In fact, although the USSR was in a hard-line phase under Yuri Andropov, former head of the KGB, the Berlin Wall would begin to come down five years later, in late 1989.)

The obstruction became more pronounced. I had sent version 5 to Josten, and on 18 April he wrote to me as "Dear Arthur", saying that the envelope had been opened, suggesting that postal communication was no longer safe.[32] Then Biggs-Davison's Private Secretary wrote: "Sir John, who is in the country for a few days, has asked me to let you know that Sir Bernard Braine feels that there is no point in creating an additional organisation and suggests that you should discuss your ideas with the European Liaison Group, whose Chairman is Mr R Marcetic." His address was given.[33]

I wrote to Crozier on 24 April enclosing a final version of my paper. It incorporated Josten's points and Braine's point about the ELG not needing another organisation. I drew his attention to Baroness Cox's offer to take me with her to meet Mrs. Thatcher. I wrote: "What is now needed is a discussion on the idea in principle; agreement on the immediate priority and the way forward."[34] I wrote to Josten on 26 April and again on 30 April, when I reported that my accountant had the Articles of Association to set up my new publishing company.

The Council elections now took place. I had been taken for a tour of my ward on Sunday morning by Councillor Ann Miller, and I had canvassed by knocking on doors and asking how each household would vote. The response was heavily pro-Labour. On polling day, 3 May, Biggs-Davison came to give me his support. I toured the area, speaking through a car loudspeaker, wearing a blue rosette, and Biggs-Davison attended the count. To my relief I came 2nd. Labour had retained the seat in their stronghold, and I did well to beat the Loughton Residents Association (LRA) when planning permission for Oaklands was an issue that divided us. The tide was generally out for the Conservatives, and even the veteran Mrs. Scott and

Doug James, the Leader of the Council, had come 2nd, beaten by the Residents. Seen within that perspective, my victory over the Residents had been excellent. The Conservatives were so angry at the defeat of James by the LRA that they forced through all the policies that the LRA had opposed. The Residents had organised 30 letters against the Oaklands extension and I had mustered 45 for, and now my victory over the Residents in the election added democratic weight to my numerical advantage. My strategy had worked: to fight the Residents by allying with the Conservatives on the hustings and so defeat the LRA's political campaign against Oaklands. On 22 May I celebrated my 45th birthday with the news that we had now been given planning permission for the Oaklands extension of three classrooms.

I now received a letter from Crozier saying that there would be a fairly lengthy delay on FREE, and that I should stay in touch with Josten. Crozier wrote:

> The consensus which has emerged is that any plans need to be handled with great care and delicacy, not least because of the susceptibilities of East-European exiles in this county, who already have their own organisations and offices, together with the overall 'Liaison Group'. I really believe a fairly lengthy period of study is going to be required before I feel sufficiently confident to raise money for the project. I know I may have given you a more optimistic reading at an earlier stage, but I feel bound to take the opinions of the various people consulted into serious consideration. I suggest that from this point on, you may care to liaise from time to time with our friend Josef, who has much experience and wisdom on such matters.

This meant that Josten and Braine were opposed to FREE. Biggs-Davison told me that Sir Bernard Braine of the European Liaison Group (ELG) had said that FREE was pointless as the ELG (which was widely known for being ineffective, Biggs-Davison had said) was performing a similar role. Biggs-Davison wanted to see FREE implemented as soon as possible.

It was clear that Josten somehow had the power to decide the next move. Josten assumed an authority over me he was not entitled to have. I was not working under anybody and it would not matter to me if I never saw Josten again.

On 15 June Josten sent me a revised version of my paper with some deletions and insertions.[35] Bizarrely he again gave me the code-name "Arthur", having told me that the paper was deemed too important to be under my own name. (He saw me as King Arthur and himself as Merlin.) I considered that he was diluting and threatening my "ownership" of FREE along with the message itself. I replied on 24 June telling him that he was diluting and watering down the idea and that he gave the impression of serving the interests of the KGB.[36] I told him that my publishing company was now incorporated and that I was looking for my first book. I sent copies of my letter to Crozier and Biggs-Davison.

On 27 June, after school and at his request, I visited Josten at the F.C.P. News Agency (Directors Sir Bernard Braine MP and Mrs. Josten, Editor Josten) at 38 Tregunter Road, SW10 (a room at the top of stairs) to talk through my letter. He said that to get some experience I should do some letter-writing to make contact with MPs to raise money. He tried to marginalise me into letter-writing. When I pressed him about Crozier, he said that Crozier had run out of money until next year's budget. He said that he was to advise Crozier when – not whether – he should go public, and that the paper would ultimately go to Mrs. Thatcher.

I had seen that it was possible to get rid of Communism in Eastern Europe and the Soviet Union. The low-level activities Josten wanted me to undertake were not what I had in mind. I told him I would not be doing letter-writing and that I had started a publishing company and would express the idea of FREE in books.

Material on the miners' strike
Josten looked shocked as I seemed to be outmanoeuvring his delaying tactics. He said he would put me in touch with someone who would give me some sensational material for a first book. "What material?" I asked. "Material that makes it clear that the miners' strike, and therefore Scargill's role in it, is linked to the Soviet Union."

The miners' strike had begun in March 1984, and for several weeks the news had been dominated by flying pickets who travelled around the country to blockade different mines.

At first I thought Josten was deflecting me from FREE into the miners' strike. I thought that if he were in the KGB he would divert into an alternative project that would absorb my energies and keep me quiet. I was cool about the idea. But, having been a journalist, I knew when to follow a lead. I agreed to *rendezvous* in London with his source on 12 July to take delivery of the material. I would take a look at it and evaluate it without promising anything.

On 2 July Josten wrote[37] rebutting my letter of 24 June. I replied on 4 July standing my ground[38] I sent copies to Crozier and Biggs-Davison.

Josten had begun to irritate me. But I was in favour of defeating Communism and freeing Europe from the Soviet Union, and if the Soviet Union was behind the miners' strike then I was certainly in favour of defending Britain from Soviet involvement – if that was what was indeed happening. So it was that my anti-Soviet outlook and link with Biggs-Davison over FREE had swept me into involvement in the miners' strike.

So it was that I found myself in the thick of the Thatcherite revolution. The radical Margaret Thatcher, practising conviction politics in place of the old 'post-war' consensus politics of both left and right, had come to power after the 'winter of discontent' when trade-union activity prevented rubbish from being collected and the dead from being buried. Britain's finances had been taken over by the IMF and Britain had come to be regarded as 'the sick man of Europe'. Thatcher had set about crushing the power of the unions so that swathes of the State could be privatised and share-holding could be spread among the British working class. She had taken back the Falklands Islands from the Argentinians and was working to end the Cold War. The biggest union challenge had come from Arthur Scargill, the President of the National Union of Mineworkers, who had brought down the Heath Government in which I had been involved and wanted to bring down Thatcher's. Scargill was reputed to have Soviet backing and in his revolutionist speeches spread revolutionary principles to subvert and overthrow the Thatcher Government. Margaret Thatcher had built up coal stocks and skilfully manoeuvred Scargill into calling a strike – the Chairman of the National Coal Board Ian MacGregor closed a Barnsley pit as a provocation – at the beginning of the summer rather than at the beginning of winter.

Diagnosis of bronchiectasis

Meanwhile as if reiterating Western values at the end of May I attended the Passion play in the Chigwell car parks of first the William IV pub and then of the King's Head, and finally in the churchyard "with Jesus up a huge cross, bloodstained and nails in his hands, after carrying his cross... as I stood among the graves". I had also visited Copped Hall. I recorded: "Wrote 3 poems in draft: 'Passion Play', 'Copped Hall', 'Oaklands: Oak Tree'.... They need a lot of polishing, but it is a start.... Back to poetry."

The same day I was ill: "May 31, I felt exhausted since last Thursday. Came off antibiotics 9 days ago on Tuesday, and have undoubtedly got lung patches.... 1 June. I have bronchiectasis again, and am back on antibiotics.... I am very inflamed in my lungs; the X-ray shows all the 'veins' white. Normally you do not see them." I saw David Hughes who confirmed that I had bronchiectasis permanently, and would continually have lung patches, a melancholy development. He said that if I had been alive in Keats's day I would have died of it: "The cure is to cut out the patch, but we can't do it if you've got it in both lungs, as you have. We can only give you antibiotics to prevent patches and keep you well."

Death of Phil Tribe

My own ailment was overshadowed by the sudden death in early June of a youngish teacher I lunched with every day, Phil Tribe. Garratt Green was notable for the calibre and quality of the staff one could lunch with: the likes of Cameron, Dyer (the Brain of Britain), Mike Winch (the Olympic shot-putter) and Tribe. Tribe had been educated at St Paul's and had lived in the medieval Paycockes in Coggeshall for some years as a tenant of the National Trust with an obligation to open the house to the public at certain times, and we often discussed medieval history. He was yet another victim of the stress at Garratt Green. As Chairman of the Staff Association he had taken up the "derisory pay offer" (his words) and other matters at a meeting with the Head immediately before half-term. He told me that Friday that she had shouted at him and that he was going to see her again before he left school. The following Sunday he had read the papers in Brighton where he lived with his wife and three children and from where he had been commuting. He complained of a headache, went to get an aspirin, cried out and died of a brain haemorrhage.

The public exams were immediately after half-term, and as usual I was running them. The Head refused to allow me to attend Tribe's funeral, although I was the closest to him on the staff, and, saying it was in accordance with Mrs. Tribe's wishes, she limited attendance at his funeral to two staff representatives, one from the academic and one from the pastoral side. As a result two relative strangers saw him buried and, deprived of that therapeutic experience, I kept expecting to see him turn a corner in the corridors. I asked, "Why did it have to happen to him?" and wondered if he "had nothing more to do, and had lost his way".[39] I wrote to Mrs. Tribe, explaining that she had apparently requested that only two of the staff should attend the funeral and that I had not been chosen, and I had a letter back, thanking me for my "beautiful" letter and stressing that she "did not mind how many came" to the funeral. She had not restricted the number who could attend. The episode increased my determination to escape the unhealthy atmosphere at Garratt Green and intensified my sense that time was short, that one should get on and fulfil one's destiny as soon as possible and not shelve it as death could intervene at any time.

Vision: opposing Communism in the British miners' strike
Vernon Davies

In mid-June I attended Chigwell School's Speech Day and was astonished to hear an Old Chigwellian, Admiral Gerkin, say in his speech in a marquee on Top Field, echoing William Penn, "Chigwell gives a foundation of the Inner Light." There was a ball in the marquee that evening, and we joined the party of a parent multi-millionaire I had been at school with, Vernon Davies, and drank champagne all evening. He was younger than me and had made his money out of the sale of his computer company, Atlantic, and he had bought a large house in Pudding Lane with 100 acres of fields. I told him about FREE. He invited me to visit him, and on 28 June I spent two-and-a-half hours drinking white wine in his large house under a beautiful clock. He wanted to be involved in my dealings with Josten.

He was an Oaklands parent and a few days later he came to Oaklands early before picking up his children. We had a chat at the sunny end of my sitting-room with the patio doors open. He told me: "I've got a problem, I've got £6million in the bank and I don't know what to do. Should I retrain as a doctor?"

I told him he should consider politics. He thought that a good idea. He said he would put up the money and with my contacts we could make inroads into politics. He asked to meet Josten. I told him Biggs-Davison was coming to Oaklands in July to attend a garden party. He said: "Who?" I explained that Biggs-Davison was his MP, which he did not know. Within a short time (and after donating some money) he would be Constituency Chairman.

Josten hands me a file of cuttings on Scargill

On 12 July I kept my *rendezvous* in London. Josten met me alone and handed me two files of material on Scargill. They were buff files in slightly tattered condition. He would not say where they had come from. I peeped inside and immediately saw that the papers traced Scargill's sayings back over many years. There were many newspaper cuttings, some original clippings and some Photostats.

I reckoned the files were indeed sensational, but I was still cautious, suspecting that Josten had pushed this material my way to head me off FREE. I took the material home and spread it out on my dining-room table. There was no pattern in the material, it was just a sheaf of cuttings, broadly chronological. I wondered how I could use it.

That evening there was an Oaklands Open Evening. Vernon Davies attended as an Oaklands parent. I met him in the school hall and took him down to my house and showed him the material. I told him there was enough material for both an article and a book. He repeated that he wanted to be involved in the launching of my publishing company and to meet Josten.

Article for The Times, Charlie Douglas-Home

Within a week I had written an article for *The Times*, which was now edited by my old Features Editor, Charlie Douglas-Home. (*See My Double Life 1: This Dark Wood.*) I told him: "A very interesting file of cuttings and background material on Arthur Scargill has come into my possession from a very reliable source. It is full of information on Scargill's Communist links (actions, visits, friends, sayings etc.), and if the right tapestry is woven it will undoubtedly raise questions about the Communist role in the current miners' strike…. The material is so topical now that *The Times* may like to take an abridged version in the form of an article. The perspective needs to be made generally available while the miners' strike is still on, and it may be settled by the time I can get a book out."[40] I had a message from Charlie saying he wanted to see the article "in the raw". I wrote: "I have broken up, having taken July 18 and 19 off to write an article on Scargill for *The Times*, who want to see it 'in the raw'. It is all about how Soviet money is funding the miners' strike, from Ponomarev to the *Morning Star*…. Am back in touch with Charlie Douglas-Home after 12 years."

On 26 July Charlie telephoned me. He said: "Your article is formidable and should be published, but my problem is how to project it at Scargill through the medium of a freelance contribution. Could I buy the material from you for a professional journalist to write it, or for an editorial?" I said no, I would see it through as it was within my interest in resisting Communism. He said he would pass it to Features for the centre page.

Two days earlier, on 24 July, I had taken Vernon Davies to meet Josten at the Polish Air Force Club. Josten tried to get Vernon to spearhead a "Buy British" campaign along with Tebbit and Frank Chapple, past President of the TUC and former electricians leader. Again, this was far removed from the original idea of FREE.

Baroness Cox keen for me to set up FREE
I began to suspect that someone did not want me to pursue FREE. In the afternoon I took Vernon Davies to have tea with Baroness Cox in the House of Lords, and explained the difficulties I was having regarding FREE and Josten to her. She was very keen that FREE should be launched. I did not ask her to take me to Mrs. Thatcher as she had volunteered the previous time we met: when I first raised the idea of FREE with Mrs. Thatcher in November 1976 she had wanted the BBC World Service to project the idea, and I did not think she would budge from this position in a discussion with me.

The next Saturday there was a garden party at Oaklands. It was very hot and Biggs-Davison and our MEP were present, along with John Cameron and Vernon Davies. I introduced Davies to Biggs-Davison, who asked me to arrange for him to meet his Constituency Chairman "so we can get him involved in the constituency". I told Biggs-Davison that Davies and I had lunched with Josten.

Biggs-Davison said of FREE: "I can't understand it, it seems a total *impasse*. It's exasperating." Standing in the Oaklands tennis-court, I told Biggs-Davison that Josten seemed to be obstructing me, and that I wondered if he was acting in the interests of the Soviet Union as an agent of the KGB. Biggs-Davison looked thunderstruck and said quietly, "I hope not." "I hope not too," I said. Biggs-Davison had introduced me to Crozier and Josten so that FREE could happen swiftly, and he could not understand why the idea was being obstructed, or who was doing the obstructing.

In early May David Hoppit, with whom I had gone to Italy in 1957 (*see My Double Life 1: This Dark Wood*), turned up in the Oaklands hall to officiate at his sister's party. I wrote: "The years have greyed him and thinned him, but underneath he is the same." He invited us to dinner in July. I wrote: "1424 house, built round; patio with telegraph pole bringing electricity and telephone; pond and ducks and ducklings; hedges and a lane and brambles all round. A greenhouse.... Roman and Iron-Age vases, archaeology is his hobby; his Roman coins."[41] He was writing on property for *The Daily Telegraph*, and would have been extremely interested in my material regarding Scargill. Richard Fradd was present, the boy who played marbles in Chigwell church (*see My Double Life 1: This Dark Wood*), now a grown market gardener.

We were away for the next two weeks. On 30 July we set off for Liverpool to see a relation of Ann's and then drove to Staveley, where we stayed in a guest-house kept by a former Oaklands girl and saw my Uncle Reg who had returned to his roots in the Lake District.

In the Lake District
We then crossed Windermere on the ferry and drove to Beatrix Potter's house, the setting for *Samuel Whiskers* which the boys enjoyed, and drove past Esthwaite, where I was supposed to have lived in a previous life and where Jeremy Fisher lived and Wordsworth skated. We went on to Hawkshead, where I visited Wordsworth's school. We saw where Wordsworth lived with Ann Tyson at the Friends' Meeting House, and then drove on to Langdale Fell and Blea Tarn House, which the Wanderer visited in Wordsworth's 'The Excursion'. We went to Ambleside and then Rydal Mount, Wordsworth's last house which Keats visited. We went on to Dove Cottage and found the Leech-gatherer's pool nearby. We went on to Grasmere to see where Wordsworth is buried and where Michael lived. Then we drove to Ullswater and saw the daffodils under the trees near Gowbarrow. We saw St Sunday's Crag, which rises as you come from Glenridding and lowers as you go towards it, as Wordsworth experienced when he stole the boat and rowed on the lake. We spent that night at Watermillock overlooking the lake.

I wrote:

What I admire about Wordsworth is his insistence on tranquillity at the expense of the newspapers' sound and fury (e.g. his letter to Beaumont of 3 June 1805), something I would do well to consider as I prepare to take on

Scargill; and the way they all formed a group, so that Wordsworth wrote: 'The Immortality Ode', to which Coleridge wrote 'Dejection', and Wordsworth wrote 'Resolution and Independence' as a reply, urging the need for the artist to be like the Leech-gatherer gathering poems but not being depressed if it went badly – an excellent reply for Wordsworth to write to Coleridge. I also appreciate his countryside, and the solitaries and their shepherd huts, and consider Wordsworth now less of a revolutionary than a regional poet who reflected the spirit of lakeland. They were all a group, Wordsworth and Coleridge married sisters (Sara and Mary) and they made a cult of their feelings and thoughts – had the leisure to do so. It was very creative.[42]

In Scotland: draft poems for A Rainbow in the Spray *–'Greenfield', 'Iona: Silence', 'Staffa: Wind', 'Ben Nevis: Cloud of Unknowing'*
The next day we drove to Scotland and had tea with Nadia, having met her at the music publishers where she was working. We visited Cramond and saw her new flat, which was in an 1823 house that had a beautiful frieze. She told me she planned to become an air hostess. We booked in at the Dean Hotel, Edinburgh. There she gave me a belated birthday present: a broken eggshell-like sculpture with sea urchins and sea anemones growing on it. I said, "It symbolises our family." She agreed and said: "You're the biggest flower, I didn't think you'd see the symbolism so quickly." We ate at the Peacock Restaurant near Leith docks and then returned to our hotel.

The next day we drove into the Scottish Highlands, past Bannockburn and through Glencoe, past Fort William and Ben Nevis, to an isolated house near Invergarry, which Argie had taken. She had invited my sister Frances and her family to take one half and us to take the other half. Argie, Frances and her family greeted us at the gate. We were in deep countryside, with mountains all round, green hills, black-faced sheep and cows which nuzzled against the windows. The lawn was covered with lesser celandine and harebells, and swifts swooped and dipped and flitted. There was rose-bay willow herb in the hedgerows and on the moors. There was no water – we were supposed to draw water from the burn but it was dry, so we had to drive containers to a petrol station – and the loo was bracken at the back of the house. There was no Scottish doctor or nearby hospital. It was brave of Argie at over 80 to put herself in such an isolated situation, even though Frances's husband was a doctor.

I put a chair and table on the lawn, stripped to my waist in the warm sun and wrote with black-faced sheep to keep me company in the clear mountain air, and in the evenings, when midges gathered at dusk, I worked upstairs on the second version of my article for *The Times* and sifted the material with a view to working on a short book about the miners' strike.

The others gossiped fitfully or read and I realised we had slipped back into the 19th century and that I was living through my soul, not my social ego, measuring myself against mountains rather than social groups, against Nature rather than man. I wrote: "The stillness of the country.... The shepherd driving the sheep. The two horsemen. The two hikers. Otherwise nobody. Just the bees humming in the climbing roses. And a drowsy silence on which voices murmur from afar." I wrote two poems, 'At Greenfield Farmhouse' and 'Greenfield'.

We went to Loch Ness and visited Castle Urquhart. We went into Inverness and recoiled at the crowded streets. From Fort Augustus we cruised on Loch Ness, and saw some glass-blowing. Back at Greenfield Matthew played 'Over the Sea to Skye' on his ocarina. Ann and I left the boys behind with Argie and Frances and toured Skye, crossing from Kyle of Lochalsh. We drove among mountains and mists and saw the Outer Hebrides, and then followed Bonnie Prince Charlie's journey in 1746 as he escaped to France with the help of Flora MacDonald. It was still light after 11 p.m.

The next day we took the children fishing in Laddie Wood. Richard Moxon and I stood near waterfalls, "probing the pools with a rod and line and worm, like a poet probing the depth of the unconscious for a swish of a tail". We caught nothing. Later I wrote a story, 'Trout-Fishing and a Severed Worm'. The next day we took the boys to Mull on the ferry from Oban, and were soon in mountains with a swooping golden eagle for company. We stayed at Bunessan with a view of the sea. There were "oyster-catchers with red beaks", and there was "a yellow and green sunset over islands".[43]

The following day we took the ferry to Iona from Fionnphort. From the sea I had a breathtaking view of the ancient Iona, where St Columba, who converted Scotland to Christianity, had his cell: a green hillock rising out of blue waves and the ancient Abbey standing alone with no enclosing walls, a part of the rugged scenery. I spent a profound day there:

A day of contemplation close to St Columba. Through the nunnery to the ancient St Oran's chapel (12th century) and on to his cousin St Columba's cell and shrine, outside which stood St John's cross. Then to the Abbey, and the oldest Benedictine bit, where I meditated.... The Light came and went and came again, and I felt wonderfully peaceful.

We went on to Staffa on a small boat that dipped and tossed and rolled. Many of the other travellers vomited over the side, but not my intrepid family. There was too much of a swell to alight at the usual landing area, so we were put off at the other end of the island and had to walk the entire length of the island back to Fingal's Cave. I wrote:

Heard the piping, like woodwind – the ghostly sound of the wind – inside the organ-pipe rock formation. This must have been what Mendelssohn heard. The boom of the sea and a frail pipe…. Back to Iona, after which I meditated again until the Light poured up me, and St Columba came into me to heal my bronchiectasis. The circular cross over the door of St Columba's shrine in shadow from the evening sun, as I meditated inside [the shadow of the cross] was on my back.

Back at the Argyll Arms, Bunessan I recalled "the rainbow in the spray as the boat sped against the tide, the sun on my back, to Staffa…. Have written a poem on Iona (9 stanzas) and am nearly asleep after the effort. I am so full of fresh air I can hardly think, but I am glad I've got it all down while it is fresh in my mind. The Plough is very clear in the night sky almost overhead, and there is light blue sky on the horizon. A lighthouse pulses regularly from the island in the dark. Existence is good!"

The next day we left Bunessan for Salem and caught the ferry from Craignure to Oban. We meandered back to Greenfield. I spent some of that evening "polishing my poem on Iona"[44] My poems 'Iona: Silence' and 'Staffa: Wind' came out of this.

Frances's doctor husband Richard had said he was climbing Ben Nevis the next day alone. On impulse I said I would go with him even though I did not have appropriate footwear and there was not time to drive to a shop. The following day I wore flip-flops. We left at 7 a.m. and drove to Ben Nevis. I wrote:

Climbed Ben Nevis, although suffering from bronchiectasis, and earlier this year from phlebitis. Did 4,400 feet in 3 hrs 15 mins, stayed on the mountain for 45 mins as a cloud (of unknowing) cleared, giving views of precipitous drops into green glens, and then took over 3 hrs coming down, with many rests as my legs went. At 45 I gave Richard (34) a good 10 years but matched him for heart and lungs to the top, and only flagged on the way down. Saw the ascent into cloud, which lifted giving visions and then the sun, as a parable for the Mystic Way, and wrote a poem about it [, 'Ben Nevis: Cloud of Unknowing'].[45]

The descent was truly awful, as Keats found in 1818: "I felt it terribly – 'twas the most vile descent – shook me all to pieces."[46] Several times I felt I would not make it, but Richard encouraged me and, reassured by having my own personal doctor accompanying me, I got down in the end.

The next day we went to Culloden and found the stone Cumberland stood on behind the enemy's rank. We drove on to Findhorn and found the caravan park and Caddy vegetable garden which the New-Age community had gathered round. We wandered among the huts. I had written 'Greenfield' on 3 August, and later that evening I copied the poem into Greenfield's visitors' book.

We left Scotland the next morning and drove the 590 miles in just under 10 hours. We shared the driving, and when I was in the passenger's seat I "wrote poems on Wordsworth ['Letter to Wordsworth'] and Beatrix Potter ['Letter to Beatrix Potter'] in the car".[47]

Subversion
Josten blocks Times article
At Greenfield I had spread out the miners' material on the floor of a room at the top of the house. There was a telephone in the room, and I had been rung by a fellow in *The Times* Features, who told me he was making very heavy weather of editing my article. He said he was "defeated by the material". Perplexed, I rang Josten, who said that *The Times* was "penetrated" and that the journalist in question had "Trotskyite" leanings. Josten urged me to send a copy of my article to *The Daily Telegraph* (the newspaper for which David Hoppit wrote on property).

Charlie Douglas-Home had rung me to ask for my next (i.e. Cornish) telephone number so he could ring me from his holiday. I explained that I was having difficulty with Features and he urged me to deal directly with Peter Stothard (Features Editor) from now on. I was aware of the Civil-War-like in-fighting between two factions within *The Times*: those who were pro-Scargill and those who were pro-Government like the Editor and his nominee.

I knew that my article was still encountering opposition within *The Times*. I decided to take Josten's advice and submit a copy to *The Telegraph*.

I spent a day in Loughton on the Oaklands accounts and then we left for Cornwall. I went round to Vernon Davies's house and picked up a copy of *The Times* article which he had had typed out. I had a couple of glasses of wine with him. The next morning we left for Cornwall via *The Telegraph*. I handed the article in with a covering letter to Bill Deedes, the Editor.[48] I drove on to the Polish Air Force Club to deliver a package to Josten, and he came downstairs and introduced himself to Ann and the boys: "I am the terrible Josten who takes up so much of your husband's time."

In Cornwall we spent a sunny, windless day at Charlestown where Matthew and Anthony played on a dinghy in the calm shallows. Both sat in it while I read on the beach and Ann sunbathed. Suddenly I heard a scream and looked up. The dinghy was drifting rapidly out on unseen currents towards the rocks and rougher sea. Matthew had dropped his oar and Anthony had screamed in terror. I quickly undressed to my pants and half-ran, half-waded in and as I was about to go out of my depth and the first rocks scraped my feet I managed to grab the dinghy and lead it in. I had saved my two sons from being swept out to sea.

After that we went to Par and spent golden days under a blue sky and yellow sun. I sat and pondered Scargill's Communism and wrote headings for a revised article: "The CPGB's (Communist Party of Great Britain's) three definitions of what a Communist is, how Scargill looks a Communist despite his denials, and [perhaps] a Stalinist one at that, how his background reinforces this view, how he left the YCs (Young Communists) for political expediency, how he continued to work for their goals at home and how the CPGB supported him, both in becoming President of the NUM [National Union of Mineworkers] and in the present strike, how the CPGB supported him through Watters, how Moscow is behind the CPGB, his visits to Moscow,... and finally revolution through coal."

That night the second version of my article "came to me... whole after I saw the CPGB's 'The British Road to Socialism', and I drafted it hastily on my knee around midnight and began typing it [the next] morning".

I was still open to poetic inspiration and forgot about Scargill that afternoon. We went to Gunwalloe, "where the sea was full of surf and several bathers were in difficulties and had to be rescued. I wrote two poems, 'Sea-Rescue'... and 'Sea-Force', a sonnet which answers Keats's 'It keeps eternal whisperings around' and tackles the fundamental – elemental – question about the sea: what is the cause of its energy? Which I see as emblematic of the ebb and flow of the life-force. A poem Wordsworth would not have minded owning up to. I am so creative at present."

The next day I "spent all day typing the second version of my Scargill article, with 'The British Road to Socialism' thrown in and a new opening".[49] I wrote to Charlie Douglas-Home saying I had not received a reply from Stothard by the time I left for Cornwall, and that "the article now concentrates on establishing the link between Scargill's pronouncements about his beliefs and the CPGB's programme, with which they accord". I said that the overall title 'Scargill's Revolution through Coal' should cover the two pieces, and that the first piece should be separately called 'Scargill's Stalinism?' and the second piece 'The Communist Role in the Miners' Strike'. I said I felt the article was now much firmer and more solid. I wrote along the same lines to Bill Deedes, the Editor of *The Daily Telegraph*, and sent a copy of the new article to Josten.[50] Just before I posted the letter to *The Times* I remembered that Douglas-Home was away until 10 September, and I sent the letter to Stothard. I included my Cornish phone number. Soon afterwards I had a call from a journalist in Features. He told me *The Times* had received a call from Josten on 9 August. "He told us to hurry up with the publication of the article. He accused *The Times* of being 'penetrated' and told us you will be proceeding with *The Daily Telegraph*. He asked us to send the article back. So we sent the article back to you to send to *The Daily Telegraph*. It's already in the post."

I was stunned. "Did he really say that I was proceeding with *The Daily Telegraph*? Did he really ask you to send the article back?"

"Yes," the Features journalist said.

I said that I had not fixed up anything with *The Daily Telegraph* and had not asked that the article should be returned to me.

I rang off and considered what Josten had done. He had obstructed FREE, and now he had obstructed my article. He had supplied the material on which it was based, and now he had interposed himself between me and *The Times* and asked them to return the article. Why did he want to obstruct the article? Was he acting for the European Liaison Group, and attempting to annihilate all my attempts to oppose the Soviet Union over FREE and the miners' strike, so I would not hijack the work of the ELG? Or had he worked with the Soviet Union against the Nazis during the war and in the Czech Foreign Ministry until 1948, and was he a long-term KGB agent? Was he obstructing my article on behalf of the KGB? Or on behalf of another intelligence agency? Who was behind Josten's attempt to subvert my opposition to the Soviet Union?

Vision: exposure

I could not do anything until I was back in Essex, so I pushed the miners' strike aside and concentrated on poems. Ricks had suggested that I should select 30 poems.

Mystic poems

On 5 August I worked on "a selection [of] 30 poems which tell a story and catch the focal points of the new Baroque age, whose characteristics I am endeavouring to chart". That evening I noted, "I am still effortlessly writing poems." A couple of days later I sketched out a selection of my poems, which

> should proceed from Awakening to Silence to Transformation to Illumination to visions of Paradise, Self-Surmounting, Creativity, Sense and Spirit and Dynamic Nature (the Unitive Life) – reflecting the Mystic Way. So there are stages along the *Tokaido* road..., a journey showing progress to mysticism, a strong collection that characterises the Baroque.... The Mystic Way – Way of Fire.

The selection (many more than 30 poems) appeared in 1991 under the title *A Metaphysical's Way of Fire* and reflected these "stages along the *Tokaido* road". I was still thinking about the selection the next day: "When Ricks said 'choose poems that are technically accurate' he was judging as a Neoclassical."

I was back into poems. We went to Tintagel where I "drafted a poem on St Juliot ('At Tintagel: St Juliot and Merlin')…. Returned and finished typing up my introductory essay on the New Baroque, which is now finished." This essay can be found in my *Selected Poems: A Metaphysical's Way of Fire*.

I went out fishing with Ann's cousin. We left at 5.45 a.m., and I deputised for one of the crew whose wife had had a baby at 4.30 a.m. I pulled in nets with a fisherman called Kingsley. There was "little wind, although there was a south-easterly for a time which made the sea choppy as we went east". I remember Kingsley standing legs astride on the dipping boat, cigarette in mouth, fisherman's apron on, sharpening a huge knife on a carving sharpener, cutting forward and back and just missing his own knuckles each time. Two days later I wrote a poem about the experience: 'Hauling up Nets in Mount's Bay: Divine Plan'.

We returned home through Dorset via "Clouds Hill… and Moreton cemetery to pay respects to Lawrence of Arabia, and via Wool (Tess's honeymoon house with its forbidding 1631 chimneys and Tess's grave in the grounds of the ruined and now privately-owned Bindon Abbey) and Bere Regis (the Turbeyville church window and vault [which became the D'Urberville tomb in Kingsbere church]). Passed through Lyme, which was unspeakably crowded." I noted: "Drafted 3 poems on the way home: one on Charlestown calm (a sonnet) ['Quiet'] which I experienced on my last visit there; one on Lawrence ['Clouds Hill']; and one [since lost] on Hardy places and the Turbeyvilles."[51]

Back in Essex, I found the letter from Stothard, dated 10 August: "I learned last night from the Editor's office, that you have had an offer to publish the material in *The Daily Telegraph*. Although I still think that there are some interesting aspects to the work that you have done, I think that from your own best point of view you would be better to take *The Telegraph*'s offer. We would need a good deal more work to fit it into the pattern of our coverage of the miners dispute and, since this is a fast-moving story, I suggest that you accept the more immediate offer – even it is from our rival."[52] There was a second letter from him dated 23 August, reiterating that "I am perfectly happy for *The Telegraph* to make quick use of this material in line with the wishes which you have expressed".

On 1 September I had an insight. I grasped very clearly that the Government did not want negotiation, they were committed to smashing the NUM and breaking the coal industry. I wrote: "It came to me while I read the papers after mowing and painting, at 11.45 p.m.: the Government do not want the miners' strike to end. Hence the reluctance of *The Times* to publish my material. They want the strike to continue, because it can discredit

Labour [which supported the strike]. It is dirty, it stinks, but no other explanation fits the facts."

I wrote, feeling shackled to my article, "I am now in an Underworld.... And I, Orpheus, with my poems, sing in spite of my chains." A few days later my wife and I attended a dinner at Chigwell School for 'feeder' schools and I spoke with my classics master in the 1950s, David Horton, "about classics – how Alcestis's Underworld is resonant, and Greek history vis-à-vis Toynbee (Scargill/Cleon) and how Thucydides and Tacitus relate to the modern world".

I was diverted from Scargill by the West Ham goalkeeper, Tom McAlister, who was an Oaklands parent. He gave us all complimentary tickets in the stand for the match against Watford on 8 September. He brought them round to our house and I asked him what he would do if there was a penalty. He said, standing in our porch: "If he takes it with his right foot I'll go to my right." Twenty minutes into the game there was a penalty against West Ham just under where we were sitting. I wrote:

> Tom's great save from the Watford no. 8, [Mo] Johnstone. He went the way he said he'd go. Then after half-time West Ham scored twice. And I am left with a moment that is eternal: Tom saving the penalty – the ball in mid-air between boot and goalposts and Tom will dive and save it and the whole stand will rise to its feet and shout 'Yes'. A moment frozen for all eternity.... These sporting images – memories mixed with emotion which revives when the image is recalled.

I wrote a poem 'At West Ham: Saved by an Artist'.

The following Wednesday Tom started as my football coach at Oaklands. He took the six-year-olds for football, and when I did not have to go to Wandsworth I put my track suit on and played up one end while he played at the other. I recall him diving too slowly and deliberately letting in a goal so a six-year-old could celebrate.

I am urged to write a political pamphlet

Charlie Douglas-Home returned from his holiday, and I rang him very belatedly to ask what had happened about my article. He was embarrassed. He said, "Unfortunately Josten made threats and Features won't be intimidated by anyone. So they sent the article back to you." I told him I would be bringing out a book on the miners' strike. "Keep me informed," he said.

The next day I took Vernon Davies to lunch with Josten again at the Polish Air Force Club. I remonstrated with Josten for ringing *The Times*. Josten insisted that he had complained that *The Times* was "penetrated" by an agent of the Soviet Union. He again tried to persuade Vernon to launch a campaign on unemployment, emphasising "Buying British". He said he had been in touch with the Prime Minister's PPS about "Eldon Griffiths's secret document on psychological warfare".

It was now clear to me that Josten was involved in some kind of psychological warfare for someone other than himself. How had Biggs-Davison got me mixed up with this?

Josten tried to persuade me to use the material he had given me to ridicule Scargill. Josten wanted me "to pretend that Scargill is writing 'quotations from King Arthur', e.g. 'My dream' and 'My *guru*'; but this will detract from the straight, academic nature of the work and it will take it into 'dirty tricks'. It is better to get the point across straight, and not to scorn Scargill too much." I told him in no uncertain terms that I was not a scurrilous pamphleteer.

I was aware that we were being spied on. My work in the early 1970s had given me a sixth sense that instantly recognised surveillance. I noted: "The van outside with packing-cases in the back, probably disguising electronic equipment, and two well-dressed drivers who sat outside the conference room where we met for one-and-a-half hours without moving, and were there when we left." (According to Vernon, who was watching from his car, they drove off as soon as I had driven away.)[53]

I write a booklet on Scargill in the tradition of Dryden, Swift and Pope: help from John Cameron
I had set up my small publishing company to bring out books on the Western ideology and attacks on it by revolutionary or Communist sources. I was now clear that I should write a short book on the miners' strike, using argument and reason to devastating effect within the tradition of the literary exposures of the 17th and 18th centuries: Dryden's exposure of Lord Shaftesbury in 'Absalom and Achitophel'; his cousin Swift's political pamphlet 'The Public Spirit of the Whigs'; and Pope's exposure of Lord Hervey as Sporus. I would also apply techniques of literary criticism to a living person in an 18th-century-style social criticism that went back to Marvell's 'Horatian Ode'. I wrote: "The book must be straight, not ironic."

I had now done enough digging into the Scargill material to be able to start a book for my publishing company. I had decided that Part One would consist of quotations from his own mouth. John Cameron came to my house and I spent the whole weekend of 22–23 September writing it. We worked at the dining-room table. Cameron sifted the material while I wrote. I worked all day on the Sunday. I wrote of Part Two: "The theme, 'The Communist Role in the 1984 Miners' Strike'…. The CPGB programme, and how Scargill reflects it…. The Soviet involvement in the strike (and past strikes)…. How Scargill['s]… aim is revolution."[54] I decided to call the book *Scargill the*

Stalinist? after the Bishop of Durham spoke of rejecting Scargill's "apparent attachment to a Stalinist type of Marxism".[55]

Organising my new publishing venture was now taking all my time. I was in touch with designers, printers and distributors. I found a libel lawyer, Edward Garnier, who later became a Conservative MP and Shadow Attorney General and Solicitor-General. I found a consultant, Trevor Maher, a well-known figure in the book trade. I met him several times to learn what percentages to let bookshops take and how to calculate the number of copies a book must sell before its costs are covered. He fixed me up with distribution and hired office space where a live telephonist took messages in Rosemont Road, Hampstead. He said I should do my own warehousing and invoicing. I chose a Yugoslav printer, Dusan Plenicar, a former Yugoslav guerilla who believed that Christianity was at the centre of Western ideology and would defeat Communism. At the end of September I wrote: "I am so besieged with publishing phone calls these days – designer, printer, distributor, etc. – that, with my two jobs [Garratt Green and Oaklands], I have not been able to do any creative writing… for the last month."[56]

Brighton bomb

While I was to-ing and fro-ing to bring out the book in November, on 12 October 1984 a bomb exploded at the Grand Hotel, Brighton, the scene of the Conservative Party conference, and Norman Tebbit was pulled out of the rubble. At the time I connected this outrage to the IRA. It was only in 1986 that I learned of Gaddafi's involvement as revenge for the humiliation of the Libyan People's Bureau siege following the murder of WPC Fletcher. The Brighton bomb was intended to wipe out the entire British Government, and I wondered if the Soviet Union was involved. At the time it seemed inconceivable that the Soviet Union could plan to seize the UK, Bolshevik-style, and install a puppet who could call in Soviet troops. In 1986 I came to believe that my book could not have appeared at a more timely moment.

Subversion of Scargill the Stalinist?

Josten demands money

I received a letter from Josten, dated 17 September, that attempted to put our arrangement onto a business footing. He said that he had put a lot of work and time into giving me the cuttings and other material, and that I should discuss "the professional side of this co-operation" with Vernon Davies. The implication was that I should send Josten some money.

Once again he seemed to be obstructing me: first he had obstructed FREE, then my article on Scargill and now he wanted money from my new publishing company, which was struggling to establish itself amid numerous set-up costs. Was some organisation using him to attempt to smother Oak-Tree Books with high costs while it was still recovering from its birth?

Josten had written to me on 9 October, asking for the return of "all the material, including books and cuttings, that were put at your disposal".[57] He wrote again on 31 October, saying: "Your delaying a proper business arrangement and commitment in respect of the material for the Scargill book and the service we have rendered is unacceptable.... Unless we receive satisfaction by Monday November 5th I shall have to seek legal advice."[58]

On 4 November I received a phone call from Josten. He asked me for money: £400, for supplying the Scargill material. I bluntly told him he was undermining me, that I had started a new company as a kind of self-funding crusade to implement the FREE idea and that he was just concerned to extort money from me.

To my amazement he admitted torpedoing the FREE idea: "'It would have been a disaster, you were not ready.' I: 'I am no less capable of doing it now than I was then. Your refusal had the consequence of doing what the KGB wanted.' He: 'I've pressed my record button: you are accusing me of being in the KGB, that's libellous.' He now tried to resurrect the FREE idea: 'I did not know you had set up your limited company during the first idea as opposed to the second one.... We'll open discussions on the first idea immediately this is finished.' I: 'No, I was as expert then as I am now, if it wouldn't work then it won't work now.'" I repeated that the KGB would be delighted and relieved that FREE had not been implemented, and that he had done them a service.

My book was progressing. I had written laconically: "Too busy to go to work."[59] I had visited my printer several times and advised on the cover. W.H. Smith had ordered 4,000 copies, and I elected to print 10,000. John Cameron drove around with me, acting as my chauffeur and endlessly giving me support as I did a radio interview for LBC and kept my evening appointments. The book was available from 1 November and one of the first members of the public to buy it was Vic Allen, an associate of Scargill's (*see* p.172). Crozier had three of the first copies to be received and sent two of them to Mrs. Thatcher and Peter Walker, who was in charge of the miners' strike. He asked if I would contact his friend Julian Lewis (later an MP and Shadow Defence Minister). At Crozier's request I arranged for a consignment of early books to go to the Freedom Association. I visited the Association's offices in Oxford Street and found a team of volunteers, including Julian Lewis, putting books into envelopes to be sent to purchasers who had placed orders via the Association. I sent copies to Ian MacGregor, the Head of the National Coal Board; Norris McWhirter; David Owen; Peter Walker; and Edward Heath, whose 'unofficial Ambassador' I had been in the early 1970s.

I asked if he would attend the launch on 29 November.

Crozier claims ownership of the Scargill file
On 9 November I visited Crozier, who had now read the book. He was sheepish, not having seen me since his failure to go ahead with FREE. He told me, as if making up for letting me down, "You had *my* material on Scargill." I said caustically that in that case Josten was trying to charge me £400 for looking at his (Crozier's) material. Crozier said: "Your book is extraordinarily effective." I asked him to write to Peter Walker, the Secretary of State for Energy. Crozier told me he was writing his memoirs, which became *Free Agent: The Unseen War 1941–1991*. (Interestingly, my acronym FREE is in his title.)

Josten wrote to me on 9 November asking for the first 20 copies of the book. He was more than a week behind the times. He added: "I have not had from you confirmation of the arrangement I made with Mr Davies which I should like to have in writing."[60] Josten said that he had discussed the matter with Crozier. Again he was well behind the game. A few days later I received a photocopy of a letter written by Crozier at my request to Peter Walker, the Secretary of State for Energy, dated 12 November:

> Some friends of mine have just produced a most useful book on Scargill, which condemns him out of his own mouth. I gather the launching is to be in the late morning of 29 November, and it would help the cause if you felt able to attend it…. As I am about to go on holiday, until the 26th, I should be grateful if you could get in touch during my absence with Mr Josef Josten, who took the initiative in compiling the book. Mr Josten, who is of Czechoslovak origin, has a long history of devotion to the defence of our freedoms.

Josten had *not* taken the initiative in compiling the book. There would have been no book unless I had written it, and the material only came my way to obstruct me from carrying FREE forward. Crozier was clearly siding with Josten, perhaps fearing to lose him as Josten had made an issue of receiving money from Oak-Tree Books.

Wounding the gorgon: Scargill at the Soviet Embassy
On 15 November *The Times Diary*[61] broke news of the book on the centre page of *The Times*. The short article mentioned Frank Chapple as writing a Foreword and included some of my quotations from Scargill's own words. The next day, 16 November, the *Daily Mail's* front-page headline was "Scargill Goes to Russians for Help".[62] I was told by Josten that Scargill heard about the book in Yorkshire on Thursday 15 November and drove

straight to the Soviet Embassy in London, where Oleg Gordievsky (a British agent) was then employed. This was confirmed to me later (*see* p.251) by an ex-Communist contact of Scargill's, Tony Murphy. He said that Scargill was given an early copy of my book by Professor Vic Allen, (*see* p.170) an associate of Scargill's who had worked closely with the NUM, and that, shocked, Scargill took it to the Soviet Embassy. According to *The Sunday Times* of 18 November Scargill left Sheffield by car at 1.30 p.m. and arrived at the Soviet Embassy at 7 p.m. He spent 70 minutes there.

Crozier and Biggs-Davison gave me a slightly different account of what happened on 15 November: Scargill was apparently called to the Soviet Embassy and briefed about the book. But whether Scargill chose to visit the Soviet Embassy or was summoned, even before my launch I had struck a blow and wounded the terrifying Soviet-supported gorgon who turned his opponents to stone. Like Perseus, I had kept my eyes on the reflection of his own words in my shield, so I would not be turned to stone.

Shortly afterwards a shadowy pro-Soviet figure, who may have been sent out by the Soviet Embassy, went up and down the Charing Cross Road warning bookshops not to stock my book. Foyles would not be intimidated. The Yugoslav senior manager gave the order for an entire window to be cleared of Alistair MacLeans and Agatha Christies and filled with my book. At the same time he doubled Foyles' order.

Josten blocks serialisation
The Sunday Express had agreed to serialise the book. However, also on 16 November an article appeared in the *Daily Mail* with a picture of Scargill giving a Fascist salute with 16 quotations taken from the book. This was a leak. Someone leaked the text to the *Daily Mail*. As a result of the leak *The Sunday Express* withdrew its offer to serialise.

I rang Josten. He admitted organising the *Daily Mail* article. He had torpedoed a large publicity spread over weeks for a small-publicity, one-hit. Once again he had obstructed the message. I expressed my irritation that he had made an arrangement without consulting me and lost me my serialisation, obstructed my publicity. It was clear that he regarded the book as *his* property.

I was still assembling a guest list for the launch. I rang Harold Wilson. "'Lord Wilson?' 'Yes.' I did my spiel. 'I'm sorry, I have an engagement in Oxford on the 29th.' And he rang off."[63]

Peter Walker, Secretary of State for Energy, asks me to visit him
Following Crozier's letter to him, Peter Walker had asked to see me. I told the Head at Garratt Green that I would be late in as I had to see the Secretary of State, and received a dark look that suggested my dreadfulness now knew

no bounds: not only was I Principal of a private school while working in the ILEA, which opposed private education, but I was now consorting with a Conservative Minister when the Trotskyites in the ILEA were supporting the miners.

On 20 November the book was discussed on the *Today* programme. I learned this when I received a letter from a publisher's agent who asked if he could represent me to the book trade in the North of England and Scotland. He wrote, "As the book is topical and of urgent interest it would be feasible to get your agents to carry car-stock in order to supply the nation's bookshops quickly."

On 23 November, in a suit as ever, I met Cameron who was acting as my chauffeur and was driven to the Department of Energy. I signed in to see the "SoS" (Secretary of State), was given a tab, went up in a lift to the second floor and then progressed to the waiting-room which overlooked the river. Peter Walker appeared to meet me, the man in charge of opposing Scargill for the Government, grey-haired and in a light suit. "Hello, how is Britain's newest publisher?" "Feeling like a one-man band at present," I replied. He laughed. I followed him past secretaries in two outer rooms to his huge inner sanctum, where papers were spread in two dozen piles in neat rows on the carpet near an open red box. "You work on the floor?" I said. "Yes," he said.

We sat side by side and he asked about the publicity and distribution of the book. He gave me "a quotation for the launch". He was very easy to talk to, and there was laughter. I recalled how he had visited Loughton and addressed the Young Conservatives in the Hideaway café in 1957. We talked about Scargill's 1972 strike, and I mentioned the Brighton bomb. I raised the Soviet connection in the current strike.

Walker told me: "There's a very strong Soviet connection. I have held back on it because I don't want people to think of Reds under the beds. (In her autobiography Margaret Thatcher would write that the British Government's first "confirmation" that the Soviet Union had given financial aid to the NUM took place in November 1984.[64] Cabinet papers released 30 years after 1984 revealed that MI5 informed ministers in November 1984 that the Soviet Union were funding the NUM.[65] This information coincided with revelations in my book.) I said, "But as there *is* a strong Soviet connection, it's time to put the boot in." He said, "No one has stood up to Scargill yet." I said, "That must have been said of Lenin in early 1917. If you were in the Tsar's Russia and Bolsheviks were rioting in the streets and a building had been blown up, we would be saying it was time to stand up to Lenin."

He thought hard and there was a silence. He seemed to decide something (perhaps not to press the Soviet connection) and then said,

"Good. Good luck with the launch." Smiling, he shook my hand and then I was out among the secretaries and being taken downstairs in the lift.[66]

I reflected that my emphasis on "the Communist role in the miners' strike" (the book's subtitle) and my stance had been vindicated. I had heard at the highest level that there *was* a very strong Soviet connection. Walker's quotation for the launch, "Compulsory reading for anyone who wants to have a clearer understanding of the political objectives and methods of Mr Scargill", appeared, blown-up, in Foyles' window alongside my books.

Josten leaks guest list for launch

Josten asked for a list of invitees to the launch so that he could prepare himself. The launch was to be held in the Connaught Rooms, Holborn with Lord Orr-Ewing in the chair and Sir John Biggs-Davison and Sir Bernard Braine in attendance. I had invited numerous people, including Edward Heath (whose government had fallen as a result of Scargill's militant action), David Owen and other prominent politicians and journalists. I was pleased that Winston Churchill, Churchill's grandson, had accepted.

The Sunday before the launch Atticus, the diary column in *The Sunday Times* wrote a short piece about the guest list, which had been leaked. It made out – because someone had steered the column into thinking this – that the list of those invited was being passed off as the list of those who had accepted. It was a facetious piece deliberately misunderstanding the list, making out that all the great and the good would be present. This was another example of the "Civil War" within institutions caused by the miners' strike as pro-NUM and anti-NUM journalists produced copy on the same page. The piece undoubtedly turned some acceptances into absences.

Josten rang on the Sunday morning and congratulated me on the publicity. He admitted to leaking the list. I remonstrated with him in exasperation. His action obstructed the launch.

Launch of Scargill the Stalinist?

On the morning of 29 November *The Sun* published an article about the book, which Josten took the credit for organising. There was a three-column editorial in *The Times*, entitled "We have been warned", written by Charlie Douglas-Home. (In a rebuke to the 'Trotskyites' on the paper, including the journalist who was "defeated by the material", Charlie had written that the book was "ably presented".) In those days editorials did not mention books. At the bottom of the fourth column there was a four-line note: "*Scargill the Stalinist?*, discussed in the leading article on this page, is published by...." (My publishing address and the price of the book followed. *See* Appendix 8, p.938.) There was a stampede to buy the book. People went to Hampstead to try and buy a copy from my telephone-answering service.

When Biggs-Davison arrived at the launch he reported that he had been at a dinner the previous evening and those present had talked about nothing other than the book for the whole evening. He said that Norris McWhirter had described it as "devastating" (a word McWhirter repeated to me over the phone later). "May I have your autograph?" Biggs-Davison asked as we waited for the guests to assemble, standing in the York Room near a pile of books and sipping wine. "You've done yourself a lot of good by doing this." Once again for a few hours I could probably have arranged to become an MP. Lord Orr-Ewing said to me: "I want to build you up."

But it was already apparent that the reverse was happening. Messages were being received of last-minute cancellations. ITN had rung twice to make arrangements to be present, but did not turn up. Liz Forgan and Gus McDonald, both of Channel 4, were present, along with representatives from *The Sunday Times*, *Daily Mail*, *The Financial Times*, *The Daily Telegraph*, and LBC. One of those present said he had been rung up by an anonymous caller earlier that morning and advised not to attend the launch. Winston Churchill did not appear, presumably having been advised not to attend. Lord Chapple, who had written the Foreword to the book, was unexpectedly absent. There were no pickets outside the Connaught Rooms, as had been feared, but only about 40 turned up.

Lord Orr-Ewing spoke first. Sir Bernard Braine, who had obstructed my interest in FREE, spoke next at the insistence of Josten. Josten then made an unscheduled speech at the invitation of Braine. I spoke last and at some length. In my speech I talked about the intense interest generated by the book up and down the country, how I had got the book out, the perspective on Scargill, Scargill's links with the Soviet Union and the totalitarianism of the dictatorship of the proletariat.[67] Josten was beside himself with rage as I spoke, for my narrative did not ascribe any role to him.

The journalist from *The Telegraph* then took me to one side and asked, "What's a nice, decent young man like you doing mixed up in all this?" I described how I came to be involved, beginning with FREE and ending with the files of material I had been given. No article appeared in *The Daily Telegraph* about this interview.

I found myself standing beside Biggs-Davison. I told him that an anonymous caller had rung invitees that morning and advised them not to attend. I said, "The question is, who muzzled my launch?" He nodded but said nothing, looking uncomfortable.

Who was the anonymous caller working for? A benevolent organisation? One that helped the Government? I was sure that the Government was committed to playing the strike long, wearing the miners out and waiting for them to cave in. Peter Walker had been happy for my book to embarrass Scargill but he did not want to provoke the miners or worry the British people about the Soviet connection. Could the anonymous caller have been Josten? Surely not, his voice would have been recognised. Was the organisation malevolent? Was it the shadowy pro-Soviet figure who had gone up and down Charing Cross Road warning bookshops not to stock my book? Was I being muzzled – obstructed – by our side or by the Soviet Union and the KGB? Or both?

Later I wrote: "Who muzzled – and why? This muzzling. Either it's benevolent (my security...)... or it's malevolent."[68] I felt the operation was malevolent rather than benevolent.

Silence

The reality was that a screen of silence had been thrown around my book; a dead silence, given the stampeding interest only a day previously. I suspected that Josten had been involved, but I had no proof.

His attitude to me hardened, and at the end of the launch he again asked me for money and requested me to agree in writing that his company would participate in the financial results of my publishing the book: a further step in obstructing me. On 16 November before the launch he had put a draft agreement before me, listing all the services he provided. He claimed he had supplied the idea; hundreds of press cuttings; indexes with quotations; a printer; Frank Chapple's introduction, of which he claimed he owned the copyright; and "much expertise and constant advice".[69]

On 2 December I wrote Josten a long letter. I itemised what he claimed to have provided: an embryonic idea for the book, which envisaged a book of quotations without any interpretation, "an idea... my publishing consultant found to be uncommercial in the sense that it would not be self-financing"; Crozier's press cuttings; index cards that could not be used; a printer I could not use as he would have had to subcontract the book to another printer; a Foreword by Frank Chapple, "on which you claim copyright (at present unconfirmed by Frank Chapple)"; "advice which... ran counter to the professional advice of my designer, publishing consultant, distributor, printer and marketing expert"; the embargo-breaking article in *The Mail*, which "torpedoed serialisation of the book in *The Sunday Express* and weakened the impact of the launch in the media"; and Sir Bernard Braine's presence. Josten provided no risk of any capital or dangerous involvement of his name.

I said that I had provided: "the successful realisation of the idea, turning a newspaper article's statement of the theme into an interpretation that is both controversial and marketable"; "a combing of the press cuttings and material to provide the interpretation" and 89 per cent of the quotations in Part One (135 quotations in all); corrections to Chapple's written English; professional advice "at my expense" from a publishing consultant, a marketing consultant, a designer, a printer, three distributors, a financial adviser, a specialist libel solicitor and counsel – all of whom collectively created a cover design and packaged book of sufficient quality to be accepted by Smiths and Foyles; the title; a secretarial, clerical and courier service to over 30 booksellers, over 35 newspapers and journals, over 55 radio and TV programmes, and to Parliament; and my name. I had greatly risked my capital as in September I had taken the decision to print 10,000 copies of the book without knowing that the miners' strike would still be continuing at the end of November.

After discussing the situation with Vernon Davies I said Josten would receive 15-per-cent participation in verified net profit, accounts to be produced three months after the date of the book's publication, and a 50-per-cent non-transferable discount on books he bought from my company. (Davies felt the discount should be 40 per cent in view of the great risks I had taken.) I pointed out that the aim of publishing the book was "not to make a fortune. The book is the product of my political sincerity. From the outset, the book has been a non-profit-making, and probably loss-making, enterprise to warn the British people of the totalitarian threat to democracy, and neither my printer, nor my research assistant, nor I have expected to make any financial gain from it." I said, "Of all the many people involved in the production of the book, you are the only one to have mentioned money; the… professional advisers involved have all delayed presenting their bills because they sympathised with what I was doing in this national crisis." I said that I had removed myself from the company's finances, and he should reply to "my financial adviser, Vernon Davies".[70]

I sent a copy of my letter to Crozier. I told him that Josten had been writing me letters about his terms and pointed out that the launch had had no publicity. I suggested that there had been "malevolent (as opposed to benevolent) muzzling of the press and media that kept them away and converted Winston Churchill's acceptance (for example) and ITN's promise to be there into absences". I said that "someone well-placed should find out who was doing the muzzling" and confirm that the muzzler was not "pro-Soviet". Crozier did not reply.

Josten rang me and asked me to visit his office in Tregunter Road and return the material. I carried the files up the stairs. He was sitting at his desk in a room cluttered with papers and files on shelves. Bald-headed, hook-nosed, beady-eyed behind spectacles, he gave me a piercing look like an angry bird. He had been working with Evelyn Le Chêne (a name which means "oak tree"), the widow of an SAS hero. She had attended my launch. She did his secretarial work, and in her presence Josten rose as I sat down to remove the files from my bag and suddenly flew into a rage. He bellowed at me, as if volume could vindicate his argument, because I would not do what he was asking: write him an immediate cheque for several hundreds of pounds.

I stayed calm and told him gently that although my publishing venture had a commercial aspect, it was also for the good of the cause. As I had said in my letter, the accounts in three months' time would show if there was a net profit, and he would be entitled to 15 per cent if there was.

He was quivering with fury. I was sitting near Evelyn Le Chêne, and he came and stood over me and raised his hand as if to hit me. I was very calm and just looked at him. Slowly he calmed down and lowered his hand. He said, "This cannot be, I am getting excited. I will telephone Sir Bernard Braine. You will never work again. You will be *persona non grata*." Evelyn Le Chêne looked aghast. I withdrew.

The next time I was in touch with him, he repeated over the telephone, "You will never work again. I have put you on a list. You are now blacklisted. Whatever you write you will never receive publicity. I have fixed it."

Once he had shouted at me and told me he had put me on a list so that I would never work again I was adamant that he would not receive a penny from me. I stood firm on the principle that I would not give in to extortion. On 13 December I signed an agreement undertaking to pay him 15 per cent of my net profit, but I knew I would never pay him anything. There had been subversion before his 'blacklisting'. I was sceptical about his claim to have blacklisted me, and suspected that subversion would have continued anyway.

My books in Foyles' window, NUM invade Foyles
The book was still selling well. New orders were placed every day. There had been a demonstration against the book in Foyles on 13 December. The NUM had invaded Foyles and taken it over. They had stuck 'Coal not Dole' stickers all over the display window off Charing Cross Road so that the public would have difficulty in seeing the book. The miners sat on the floor and chanted, demanding the withdrawal of the book. The Foyles manager, Vic Stymak, told me that Foyles had not known anything like it since the war. A snippet appeared in *The Times Diary* the following day saying that Foyles had been threatened with broken windows unless the books were removed, and that Foyles had defiantly ordered more.[71]

An ex-Communist's material in Hull
Meanwhile I had been rung up on 5 December by an ex-Communist, Tony Murphy of Hull. He promised to give me details of how the miners' strike was being organised from Moscow. He asked me to visit him at his home in Hull. I had to wait until both schools had broken up. It was a busy time. On 6 December I attended the farewell to John Welch, the Chief Inspector of the

ILEA, who was retiring. On 9 December my son Matthew was invited to tea at Vernon Davies's house, swallowed a peanut which lodged in his bronchi and was rushed to hospital and operated on for an hour-and-a-half.

I went up to Hull on 22 December. I travelled by train from King's Cross, ignoring Baroness Cox's warning that the invitation might be a trap to attack me with a baseball bat or kidnap me. I was met at the station by Murphy's wife who took me home on a double-decker bus in the rain. Murphy lived in a terrace. He was "black-haired…, darting to his books, each of which [was] heavily scored and underlined". He told me in detail about the Moscow-Scargill link, the role of the *World Marxist Review* and of Bert Ramelson. He told me that when Scargill read *The Times Diary* report about the book he "took the book (Vic Allen's copy) to the Soviet Embassy, who advised 'ignore and… leave it to us'".[72] He said that he feared a Scargill victory in the strike would trigger a military *coup*, and he told me that Robert Maxwell (originally a Czech like Josten) was definitely a Soviet agent. He showed a diagram of the Soviet subversive apparatus that purported to represent the structure of government in the Soviet Union, on which an apparently new and top-secret "Foreign Department" played a key role.

I returned safely by train. The Christmas festivities included a gathering at Paddy Manning's in Moreton, where I ate opposite Patrick Griggs, my contemporary at the old (and later the new) Oaklands, now a solicitor, who, when I had said at school soon after D-Day that there had been a knocking under my iron bed (which had metal springs), that had alarmed my childish imagination, had told me, "I was under your bed all last night, I was doing the knocking." In early January, aware that I might have been fed disinformation, I sent to Crozier: the diagram; Murphy's letter; and additional material on *Scargill the Stalinist?* which I planned to include as a new section in a second edition.[73]

Crozier informed me that the 'Foreign Department' was known as the 'International Department', which was under Boris Ponomarev. He said that I was in "the Soviet minefield".[74] Three weeks later he wrote that his expert had confirmed that the 'Foreign Department' was simply one of the earlier names of the 'International Department', and that Murphy was out of date. His expert's opinion was that the additional material I had written would "largely negate the impact of the first edition".[75]

I sensed another attempt to obstruct and muzzle my work. I had no more to do with Crozier after that. Crozier had been a patron who had got me to Peter Walker but had not funded me with one penny.

Thrombophlebitis and creativity: decision to leave Garratt Green
In mid-January I had health issues. I had thrombophlebitis again in my right

leg and ankle. The strain of running both the English Department at Garratt Green and Oaklands while being involved in the miners' strike was beginning to tell. I made the decision to leave Garratt Green in the summer. I wrote: "I am experiencing what my father had at not much greater than my age.... I leave Garratt Green in July this year – before my health is damaged any further. This will mean depending exclusively on Oaklands." I showed my phlebitis to David Hughes, who had just told me that my lung was clear. I wrote: "But there are degrees of clearness which show up on an X-ray, and I still have bronchiectasis, and ought to have parts of both lungs cut away. If I were to have a thrombosis in my lungs – a pulmonary embolism – it could be very dangerous, and so now I have had two attacks of thrombophlebitis... I must have the superficial veins removed like twigs from a tree." David Hughes sent me to a consultant, Mr Maclean, who took one look at my thrombophlebitis and said: "You need an operation. Your blood is flowing the wrong way in your right ankle. I need to cut it and clean it up. There will be a risk of post-operational thrombosis." He would do this in April, during the Easter holidays.

In February I was working hard in the two schools and publishing company. I lamented:

All weekend on money – doing the Oak-Tree accounts..., coping with Oaklands payments, totalling etc. All weekend I was an accountant, and where was my creativity? Then went for a walk on the estate [i.e. the Oaklands fields] and saw the sun on the snow, with Oaklands sheltering under the big tree along with my house, and I felt at peace. Ice on the pond, and an awakening spirit.

I wrote a few days later: "Most of all I loved the physical things: the pyramid of Miss Lord's roof against the golden dusk and dark silhouettes of trees. I am a poet with too little time."

The nearest I had come to being creative was when I gave a class on Shakespeare "in which I said (to my own surprise) that the centre of Shakespeare is that ambition leads to murder and disaster, and that revenge for the murder is futile and not as good as forgiveness. Hence *Macbeth*, *Hamlet*, *Measure for Measure*, *Romeo and Juliet* (the futile feud) and *The Merchant of Venice* (Shylock's revenge), and *Twelfth Night* (Malvolio's self-assertion being revenged in the sub-plot). I would expand this theme in *A New Philosophy of Literature*. I continued: "It occurred to me on the way home that my ambition–revenge–forgiveness theme is actually what I am about in my epic: Hitler's ambition–Churchill's revenge (including Dresden)–and the forgiveness of the European Community."[76] I would work this theme out in *Overlord*.

In France: guillotine

At the February half-term I took my family to France by hovercraft. I slept for much of the train journey, having congestion in a lung and pain in my right leg from thrombophlebitis. We skimmed through spray across a mill-pond sea to Boulogne and took the train to Paris, where we stayed at the Brochant des Tours. We visited the Arc de Triomphe, the Champs-Élysées, Notre Dame and Saint-Germain-des-Prés, passing the Café Bonaparte where Sartre wrote some of his books in public. I revisited the Île Saint-Louis in the Seine where I spent much of the Easter holidays of 1959 reading Milton's *Paradise Lost*. The next morning we had a coach tour round Paris, "stopping at Notre Dame – the sunlight through the reds and blues of the stained-glass windows at the prow end of the sailing-boat (flying buttresses = sails on the Seine) – and at Napoleon's tomb". We took a train to Versailles and "visited the State apartments, including the Queen's bedroom and the Hall of Mirrors, a dazzling experience of light and gold.... Back to 'Le Caveau des Oubliettes', 11 St Julien le Pauvre, a... cabaret housed in an ancient dungeon [which held prisoners awaiting the guillotine] with the only surviving guillotine (1793)."

We went up the Eiffel Tower to eat. I was "confronted by a childhood phobia" (my fear of heights) when "I saw the ground disappear through glass in the floor of the lift". We took the lift again and "dined [in] white-tableclothed splendour, waiters, manager in evening dress, and drank red burgundy, while I felt the plates creak and groan and shudder in my imagination each time the lift crashed to a halt the other side of our plate-glass window, all Paris spread underneath, lit up, and the floodlit top of the tower rising above us like some great giant's Meccano set."

The next morning we visited the Conciergerie: the 14th-century kitchen and guardroom of the old palace, then the prison rooms: the Rue de Paris, where M. le Paris, executioner, collected his victims; the room where the condemned had their heads shaved, sitting on a bench, in twelves – 42,000 were guillotined; Marie Antoinette's two prison cells, the first with four holes in a diamond through which she handed a note with a lock of hair, and the second (now with an altar) from which she was taken to execution; and Robespierre's cell, and the guillotine blades and ladder which victims mounted. Outside we saw the courtyard of women, where families came to say goodbye. The prison was on the isle with the Seine all round it for security.[77]

We ate at L'Espérance, a restaurant near Gare du Nord, and caught the 2.20 train to Boulogne, whence we went to Caen and the Hotel Central and dined by prior arrangement among noisy Normans. We saw William the Conqueror's grave and returned via Rouen past the spot where Joan of Arc was burned.

End of miners' strike

Back in England the miners' strike ended abruptly in early March 1985. I wrote: "Scargill, the tribune of the people, being hauled down by his own supporters."[78] It had been a long and exhausting struggle, and the Government had waited for Scargill to be beaten. My role had been to express the Soviet involvement in a limited way as the Government did not want to blazon it too strongly. My book had been widely read and had influenced the strike. I had mortally wounded the gorgon, who had failed to turn Prime Minister Thatcher to stone and was now slain.

It came out in 2014 from the Cabinet papers for 1984 that the Government had taken the decision *before* the strike to close 75 mines over three years (not the 20 claimed), as Scargill had correctly announced. Scargill had not been scaremongering despite his revolutionary agenda. In due course a Rothschild Report would recommend the effective closure of the British coal industry, and 170 pits were reduced to 12.

I had sold 8,000 of my 10,000 books, and had easily covered my costs and had made some profit. I was determined that Josten, who was now claiming to have compiled the book, should not receive a penny of this.

Death of John Cameron

Almost immediately I had a letter from John Cameron, who was still the Oak-Tree Books' Secretary. He was ill with pernicious anaemia, myocarditis and haemorrhages.[79] Towards the end of August I found another letter from him dated 12 August, resigning from his position as Secretary to Oak-Tree Books due to "pressure of work".[80] I later heard in a letter from his brother-in-law that he died on 12 August and that the funeral was on 23 August at Putney Crematorium. He had been found in his flat in Dulwich. He had been dead a week.

I telephoned the police, and was eventually put through to the policeman who found him. He said there was a stench as they broke open his door. I said I was not convinced he had died of natural causes, but the policeman said there was no evidence to suggest foul play. He said there was speculation among the police that he might have been murdered, but he would not give me details as to why they thought that. I wondered if someone had stood over him and dictated his resignation letter addressed to me. Did someone want to eliminate the knowledge he had acquired in the course of the miners' strike?

The inquest took place on 27 September. I rang the Southwark Coroner's court and again spoke to the policeman who had found Cameron. He said that the inquest had reached an open verdict: "In other words, suspicious circumstances exist." I asked, "What suspicious circumstances?" He said that the body had been highly decomposed and had smelt because the windows were closed and the weather was hot; and that the pathologist was unable to determine the cause of death, but there seemed to be no bruises or signs or any blow.[81] "That's all I'm liberty to say."

John's brother-in-law rang me soon afterwards and said there had been a dozen pill-bottles around his bed, that all the pills were for anaemia or his heart, and that the open verdict suggested he had taken an overdose. I asked if someone could have forced him to take an overdose. His letter to me of 12 August was forward-looking and not suicidal, and it was strange that he had resigned as Secretary to Oak-Tree Books after all the enthusiastic support he had given me.

I knew I would never know the full truth about what happened. For at least two years, Tribe, Cameron and I had sat together for lunch at Garratt Green, and now I was the only survivor.

Death of Josten

Josten had written on 1 April demanding to see my accounts, and continued to write me letters until May 1985, demanding money for "copyright material". I replied on 4 April informing him that the ledger and files had gone to the accountant, and that so far the accountant had produced a draft which showed that the book was struggling to make a net profit, partly because there were still some 2,500 copies unsold (taking the most recent returns into account).

Meanwhile Josten took the credit for my Scargill book. He made out that it was all his conception and that it was ghosted by him. He was awarded the MBE for his "initiative" in the Queen's birthday honours in June 1985.

He died on 29 November 1985, on the first anniversary of my Scargill launch, and I have often wondered if someone had paid him back for hijacking my book and subverting my launch. He was 72, and *The Daily Telegraph* obituary described him as a "Foreign Office adviser". Biggs-Davison said to me perceptively: "Sometimes a Crusader can be jealous of another Crusader." He said that Josten had always been very difficult to deal with and was "a jealous man".

Josten had misrepresented himself as the author of my book and had been awarded an MBE while I was being obstructed and muzzled and Cameron was dying. I wondered again what organisation had instructed Josten to obstruct me, gain access to my publishing accounts and attempt to extort hundreds of pounds from me. I had contributed to the thwarting of Scargill's ambitions, but had received no gratitude from the Government, apart from Peter Walker's endorsement; only vilification and suppression.

Death of Douglas-Home

My book was very influential in high places. Charlie Douglas-Home had been terminally ill for more than a year and worked to the end in a wheelchair. He died at the beginning of November 1985. In 1986 his widow Jessica told me: "Your book was permanently on his desk, much thumbed and with comments written in the margin and many underlinings. It was his Bible. He based so many *Times* editorials on it."[82] So my stand had influenced the Thunderer. I also heard that it was a much-used reference book on the shelves of the Chairman of the Conservative Party, when Tebbit held that position.

An episode had come to an end. I had asserted the ideology of the West by calling for freedom for the republics of Eastern Europe. I had exposed the Soviet involvement in the miners' strike at a crucial moment, and had drawn attention to Scargill's revolutionary aims. I had defended the West. I had stood up to be counted. I had been obstructed, subverted, and now I turned my attention to being a publisher.

A new episode began. I still had literary books to write, and I came to regard the book that had warned the West, and resonated in *The Times* first leader, as political journalism and uncharacteristic of my literary work. For many years I would leave it out of my canon. However, it was a bridge to the writing I would soon be doing: it was in the tradition of the exposures of Marvell and Swift. I now see that I should not disown this work. It is now apparent that the Soviet support for the miners' strike was Soviet Communism's dying aggressiveness towards the West, and I am now proud that I issued a public warning against an intention to impose a totalitarian state on my England.

Episode 6:

Universalism and Expansionism

Third ordeal: chimera (Soviet expansionism and its mouthpiece Gaddafi)

Years: 1985–1987
Locations: Essex: Loughton;: Paris; Rouen; Dordogne; Frankfurt; Belgium; Holland; Germany; Luxembourg; France
Work: *Question Mark over the West*
Initiatives: Oak-Tree Books; 'Heroes of the West'; challenging 1943 Tehran Agreement; Universalism

"Come said the Muse,
Sing me a song no poet yet has chanted,
Sing me the universal."
                    Walt Whitman, 'Song of the Universal', in *Leaves of Grass*

In my next episode, my poetry embraced Universalist principles and was in conflict with my work as a publisher of books on the Western ideology that opposed Soviet expansionism. Universalism enfolds a World State that is above all empires; expansionism is imperialist and serves the interests of a nation-state's empire and so opposition to it is sub-Universalist.

My third ordeal was my struggle against the monstrous fire-breathing chimera of Soviet imperialism and its fiery mouthpiece Gaddafi. It had Gaddafi's lion's roar; a Soviet body that had devoured Eastern Europe; and the KGB's terrorist serpent tail.

Universalism: Universalist poems announcing a Universal Age
It seemed that I had been pushed into being a participant in the miners' strike and was now pulled away to block Soviet expansionism in Europe and the wider world. I had not liked what I had seen of the British political Establishment, which was full of patronage, vested interests and inflated egos. I was disillusioned at the pettiness, financial self-interest and personal advancement that had thwarted an important idea: FREE. I had achieved my aim in blocking Communism within the UK and was now happy to turn my attention to international terrorism, then an instrument of Soviet expansionism. Meanwhile I continued thinking about the Baroque and the coming Age, and completing my more recent poems.

I was inspired to be a Universalist poet again at the end of March when I again went to Winchester for the Mystics and Scientists conference (or mystery school) and heard Sir George Trevelyan on the New Renaissance in the arts. Jocelyn Godwin and Keith Critchlow spoke on how the universe obeys mathematical and musical number, a sound. I listened to Jonathan Harvey's neo-Baroque music. We were invited to listen within and for 12 seconds I heard a majestic symphony that had not yet been written: "The experience in Winchester of hearing a symphony (clairaudience), which I have written into 'Staffa Wind' [, the last stanza].... I heard the most majestic sound in the King Alfred's College hall..., a large part of a symphony. Cf my 'nocturnal travels' and painting – I often see paintings that are better than most I see in art galleries." I thought deeply about Orpheus and how poetry is given from the beyond, and wrote of artists who "who do not reflect their age but create the next one".[1]

Cornwall: 'Lock-gate', Baroque Age

I returned to my poetry in Cornwall a week later. I "walked by the Charlestown sea on the pier in the fading light. Fishermen lit a lamp on the end of the pier, and it was high tide, and the sea smashed against the stone breakwater above the beach. Looked at the lock-gate and mourned my poetic life, at present held dormant." I went again to Charlestown

> between the showers on a cold, damp day.... And I watched the sea pushed in across the moist sand. Wind-beaten trees, smoke-like clouds, a green sea. Art reveals higher worlds – or the Underworld (Homer, Virgil).... Imagery that reveals higher worlds is from pure imagination, imagery in terms of other objects in the natural world, unless it is suggesting inter-relatedness and variety, is decorative fancy.

I added:

> My search for meaning – man in the universe being fed by the universe – begins in the world of the senses and breaks through (in my late poems) into the beyond the senses.... Life has meaning when we are aware of our connection with everything and everybody and with the universe, with the power that fills us with wisdom and Light.... Wrote 'Lock-Gate' in draft during a wet afternoon.... Soul and body together – the very essence of Baroque.

I thought about the pattern of my life. Oaklands would give me the time to write, and my thrombophlebitis would detach me from Garratt Green. I observed: "A part of reflecting Western civilization has been the international political theme of Grivas–Kaseem–Mao–Gaddafi–African liberation movements–ILEA extremists–Scargill etc. While I had also been shown the ancient world of Babylon–China–Egypt–and... ancient wisdom."

I was receiving intense impressions:

> Being a poet is so exciting, it is constantly having a diary or notebook ready at hand in which to record ideas and observations.... Back to Charlestown. High tide. The sea crashed in, sending fountains of spray across the break-water. It boiled and foamed and boomed and surged and poured and thudded against the wall by the 'sleep tunnel' [a tunnel half-way down the steps to the beach which I described to the boys at their bedtime, taking them down ten steps and into deep sleep] and foamed back up the steps, and a mist of spray drifted landwards like smoke. The boys ran from the waves as the surf frothed round their ankles and Matthew got a bootful and squelched in his wellies and tipped a lot of water out in the sleep tunnel. The sheer

power and the energy of the sea, drawn by the moon, hurled by the moon, and the great hissing back-drag of the pebbles on each out-draw.

In Charlestown I pondered the next age:

Artists create the next stage, which will be a Baroque one, uniting Classicism and Romanticism.... It is an Age of Soul, an Age of Ancient Wisdom, of New Science. It is anti-Humanist and counter-Renaissance, but should have a positive name of its own and not be defined in relation to other ages. Make up a word, a stronger word than Holism?... A new flowering of the Romantic age amalgamated to Classicism.... The philosophy of the new Renaissance, which I must define in an essay. An Age of Transformation?

These thoughts anticipated the coming Universalist Age.

In Charlestown I saw my *Diaries* as catching the truth of the "sum total" about me: "We are at present cross-sections of ourselves, but at the end of our lives we will be all our time, our true selves are all our time. Something like this is the theory behind these *Diaries*, but I am the sum total of all my thoughts and images and events, which these *Diaries* get nearer to catching, in their fragmentary diversity, than any other approach to me. I am in these *Diaries*."[2]

I was coming to see the age as a Universal Age, and myself as a Universalist. I visited Charlestown again:

The Cornish air aerates my consciousness. 7 p.m. Went down to Charlestown after spending all day on end-of-year returns and April salaries – figures – with the exception of visits to Charlestown harbour in the morning and afternoon with the boys.... Wrote a poem this morning ['Time Compressed (or: A Universe like Sparkles from a Wave)'], sitting on the harbour wall in the sun. Now in the evening the sea turned calm... and it was a lovely satiny, silky blue, like shot silk, and barely a wrinkle. I stood on the harbour in breathless quiet, listening to every lapping sound, totally at one with the sea. Wrote a poem about it.... I have discovered new beauties in Charlestown harbour at low tide: two headlands of a small bay, rocks and seaweed, sand and higher-up shingle, a view of green-clad cliffs – and a lock-gate and chimney.... Tonight the clear sky, no light on the end of the harbour wall, on which I sat and looked up, and all round me on all sides were stars, I was under a tall tree with round apples, a large apple-tree.... Then I saw the Big Bang above my head, and the stars blown outwards and frozen in time in mid-fall, like a shower burst from a firework frozen in its explosion outwards. This was the second time today I felt frozen in time, for I wrote a poem this morning [*see* above], also on the harbour wall (pressing on my knee, sitting half-way along up on the edge) in which the sparkles on the waves are the same as the glowing stars, only time is longer and is compressed in sparkles. My feeling that time is on our scale, but that if it were compressed, the whole time-scale of the universe from start to finish would appear like – a sparkle from a wave, which is gone.... Read this in conjunction with 'Night Thoughts [in Charlestown', later retitled 'Night Visions in Charlestown'].... Forests, seas, mountains... – these are the places where I can recover the elemental.... I see so clearly from a Cornish cliff, and *that* is why I must buy a cliff-top house in Cornwall, e.g. Charlestown.... My 'trademark' is man in the universe, against the stars, not the social man.... I see a man against the stars, a frightening vision that permeates my '[The] Silence' and which should still permeate my work.... I am a Universalist – a word that has the idea of Holism, the whole, i.e. all universes, and all that is universal; while going for the Light which permeates the universe. Universalism.... That is the new philosophy, which has characteristics of the Baroque. Especially if Universalism includes soul and spirit, 4 levels of man's being.... A Universal Age. After Realism and Nominalism came Humanism, the human stage (mind and body, not soul). Now Universalism, the scale of the universe, which includes the soul, for entry into the soul takes us out into the universe. The Universal Age.... There are as many stars as sparkles, and they fade and form like the jumping lights on a sunlit sea – one perception I have had which takes me to the truth about the universe – "bunches of grapes of 5,000 galaxies each". An age that raised its eyes from the street and social concerns to its place in the universe.[3]

After a few days of intense thought I now regarded myself as a Universalist announcing and heralding in a Universal Age, in which Universalism would succeed Humanism. I wrote that any selection of my poems "must go with the Universal Age" and that I should write "an essay on our Universal Age which has Baroque features: on communications, the global view, but also on man's role in relation to the universe, which the new Renaissance is making possible.... The new science has opened up the stars and enlarged the soul, and my work must respond to this."

I was moving towards a poetry of the open air. I wrote:

This visit to Charlestown I have sat on the harbour wall at night and measured myself against the stars, against the universe.... 10 Ap. Stayed at home in morning and typed up 'Time Compressed', a metaphysical poem of the Universal Age.... Open-air poetry, poetry written in the open air – which lets in the universe. Try to write in the open air whenever possible – at least first drafts. I write my poems in the Charlestown harbour, in the Oaklands fields.... 11 Ap. Awoke and saw raindrops on the window-pane and wrote another of my 'Time Sequence' poems, 'Raindrops like Stars (or Warmth)' lying in bed, with Matthew lying in the other bed beside me.... Typed 'Raindrops like Stars', went down to Charlestown the third or fourth time today, and saw 'still clouds' and 'moving stars' in a high wind, sketched the ideas for 'Still Clouds and Whirling Stars' in the dark, in the frosty open air and half-light on the harbour wall, then came home and wrote the poem at 11 p.m.[4]

Operation on varicose veins
But almost immediately I went to the London Hospital to have my varicose veins stripped from my right leg. The surgeon, David Maclean, came and drew on my legs in black "magic marker". He told me my operation would last an hour and a half, 8.30 to 10, and that he would start in my right groin and strip me from the knee down. He would wear microscopic glasses and make about 15 small cuts. Later I wrote: "I am serene.... 12.30 a.m. Basked in the Light."[5]

The next day I was given a pre-med of three green pills, which sent me to sleep. I was woken as stretcher poles were being pushed into the side of my 'sheets'. I dozed again and awoke outside the theatre to see the anaesthetist give me an injection in my left hand, which bruised me. I did not remember losing consciousness or even waking up. Mr Maclean visited me and told me he had tied off a vein between my groin and knee, leaving it in case I ever need it for my heart. He had tried to remove a vein between my knee and ankle but as it would not come out (because of the 1978 injection of the vein) he rendered it non-working and left it in. He had dealt with two perforating veins, which, he said, had caused my thrombophlebitis. Now the blood was circulating the right way.

In hospital I work on five Universalist poems: 'Night Visions in Charlestown'; 'Iona: Silence'; 'Staffa: Wind'; 'Crab-Fishing on a Boundless Deep'; 'Cambridge Ode: Against Materialism' – and Orpheus
During my convalescence I plunged back into poetry:

In hospital, working on 'Night Thoughts [in Charlestown', later retitled 'Night Visions in Charlestown']. From the night thoughts (what is space, what is life/death) I see the stars as blossoms on a Tree, and the new science unfolding it all out of nothing, both in physics and biology, and show that a new Baroque Age has grown out of seeing in new dimensions, in terms of the universe.... The new age of (Charles' town) v. the Elizabethan materialism, anti-materialism v. materialism, the spiritual resurgence coming as I sit in the Charlestown dark having night thoughts. Characteristics of the new Baroque Age, oneness, the pastoral.

I was visited by Argie, and Frances ("a gale of fresh air and humour"). I wrote of a picture on the wall "of a house mirrored in a lake, blue sky representing health and the mirror image of brown suggesting ill health".

I was writing poetry. The next day I wrote: "2.30 p.m. Tea has arrived and I sink back exhausted on my hospital bed to drink it, having redrafted in bold rhyme 14 stanzas of 'Night Thoughts [later, Visions] in Charlestown' so that there are 3 sections, 'Dark Night', 'Flight of the Soul to the Next Age' and 'The Soul Aglow' – 14 x 8 lines, i.e. 112 lines…. I have earned my tea after two days' redrafting with my bandaged leg out and a heat outside in the early summer." Later I added: "The silver pot held 4 cups of tea, and I wrote 'Blue Up, Brown Down' between the third and fourth cups. This is living! Having time to follow my impressions. Worked on the Iona poem ['Iona: Silence'] in evening."

Mr Maclean came in to sign my insurance form: "Varicose veins right leg/bronchiectasis. 16 April 85, right Trendelenburg multiple avulsions and ligation of perforators." That evening I picked up Nona Coxhead's *Relevance of Bliss*: "It fell open at the page on which she admitted she had never had the full Bliss Experience. She wanted me to contribute my experience to it."[6] I had met her at one of the Mystics and Scientists conferences and she had pleaded with me to tell her my experiences of the Light, but I had declined, feeling it would not be right to present the experience out of context and in abridged form, knowing I had to save it for a fuller account like that of *My Double Life 1: This Dark Wood*.

Later that night I was in contact with my imagination. I wrote: "Couldn't sleep, was filled with imaginative patterns like old masters, incredibly detailed – if only I were a painter. So now have had from higher worlds, part of a symphony and part of an art exhibition." I "sat bolt upright here in hospital, switched on the light, and wrote that in 'Night Thoughts [later, Visions] in Charlestown' my soul flies… to an historical Caroline (as opposed to Elizabethan) Age of Anti-Materialism, which accords with traditional mysticism…. This is pro-Western, very much so – a new development." I wrote: "Bring out the most recent poems, from 'A Metaphysical [in Marvell's Garden]' onwards – with an introductory essay on the New Universal Age and Baroque Age…. Call it *The Rainbow in the Water Spray*." A later volume was titled *A Rainbow in the Spray*. I wrote of "the shift in perspective caused by going into space, a new perspective" and that "in my poetry I am a lover of beauty, and… carry on the Romantic tradition". I was "bringing out a body of Nature verse".

I worked on my poem 'Staffa: Wind' and observed: "I now have a distinctive poetic style…. One of my strengths as a poet has been the background reading I did in my youth, which I have been forced to add to at Garratt Green, which in itself has been a mystery school to throw me onto

my own resources and teach me that only I can... get myself across....
Another hallmark of my work is the carefully-worked-out image which
reverberates like thunder and echoes through the poem, taking on (like
'Staffa's' 'wind') new shades of connotations in each stanza."

My bandage was removed. I wrote: "My leg looks as if it's been through
a barbed-wired fence. Yellow all round, jagged black stitches and several
small cuts, while the sore area, where he went 1 inch in, looks like raw
meat." I was told that my valve failure at the top of my right leg and in the
region of my right ankle, which had caused my blood to circulate the wrong
way and leak and jet, was hereditary. My family came to see me: Matthew
and Anthony looked sunburnt and freckled.[7]

I turned to my next poem, 'Crab-Fishing [on a Boundless Deep]', and the
next day noted the importance of the sea in my work. "I am... a Nature poet,
with mystical interpretations of Nature." I reflected that my life had been
lived in a mystery school:

The school theme in my life (Riverway–Henry Thornton–Garratt
Green–Oaklands) must now be seen as a life-apprenticeship at a mystery
school.... Definition of a mystery school: where you go and develop qualities
in yourself which you need in order to perform your mission or destiny.

Later I "closed my eyes... and saw a stained-glass window of Chartrean or
Notre-Damean majesty". (A stained-glass window from Notre Dame later
formed the cover of *The Fire and the Stones*.) I reflected: "The mystery of the
creative act comes into my poems, e.g. 'Staffa [Wind]', '[Crab-Fishing in a]
Boundless Sea'. Like the Romantics I cannot help bringing the creative
mystery into my poems." I was feeling energetic: "11 a.m., still on Ap. 20,
have finished 'Crab-Fishing on a Boundless Sea'.... I will now read the
papers, then tackle the big one, 'Against Materialism'. Four poems [, Night
Visions in Charlestown', Iona: Silence', 'Staffa: Wind' and 'Crab-Fishing on
a Boundless Deep',] have escaped me for some 2–3 years, and they are now
finished in the 'poetic white heat' since my operation.... Perhaps the correct
circulation of the blood has been restored, and I now feel more vigorous and
fresh, my creative energies functioning fully?"[8]

I now tackled 'Against Materialism': "3.15 p.m. I have had tea, have
made a plan of 'Against Materialism'.... 6 p.m. Drafted the first part of
'Against Materialism', then stopped to untie and learn to tie my blue-line
bandage.... 11.50 p.m. Have written out a reasonable draft of all of 'Against
Materialism' – at present one stanza too long at 22 stanzas of 8 lines each....
The temptation is to write it in blank verse, but it needs the polish and
accomplishment of rhyme, which binds ideas together. I'll rhyme it fully
tomorrow, but it stands up now as argument. Have been on it all day.... The

5 hardest poems to do, done in 4 days! What a 4 days!... I have just physically written out some 250 lines of poetry, but so effortless has it been that I am not exhausted."

The next day I wrote: "My 'Cambridge Ode [Against Materialism]' will have taken me three years to finish. I drafted it, I believe, in April [in fact, 11–12 August] 1982, and I hope it will be finished in April 1985 – three years for ideas (e.g. about Newton) to mull around and sort themselves out." I reflected:

> My early writing career was but an apprenticeship in technique, using observation. I then had to open a pathway to my true inspiration, the 'Shadow', which in my 'Silence' I succeeded in doing.... I have had some of the greatest tranquillity in years in the past 5 days – most unexpected.... I tried to define my poetic self first in relation to the tradition (the Metaphysicals first, then the Romantics, and the Modernists) before coming to the reluctant conclusion that I was doing something new.... I came to hospital to repair and improve my body, but found contact with my soul.... The last 5 days I have actually been in pain, which I escaped by concentrating on the poems.

I wrote: "9.20 a.m., still on April 21. I have finished collapsing 3 stanzas into 2 (about Newton) and am now 7 x 3, i.e. 21 stanzas, and am ready to start tinkering. The structure looks good. Higher thought and feeling combined in a new way. The 'Cambridge Ode'." I reflected on my support for rhyme: "Marvell's 'The mind, that ocean where each kind' demonstrates the polish of rhyme in metaphysical writing at its best. How dreary the same stanza would be without rhyme!"

I had my stitches out and aired my legs. Maclean visited me and said I would not have a thrombosis now. I left hospital and was soon sitting looking out "at my green fields, shimmering in the sun". Ann's new car arrived, another Rancho, "a red gleamer", whose delivery I had organised from my hospital bed. The next day I returned to 'Against Materialism': "It is a 10-liner, ABABCDCDEE – the last two encapsulating the central idea, and pointing forward. An Ode should be 10 lines rather than 8, it gives it more of a 'rolling-downhill' effect, not to mention philosophical weight." A few days later I wrote: "Ap. 29. Have nearly finished 'Against Materialism' – four stanzas more to do, having rhymed most of it on Saturday evening, all day yesterday (Sunday) and this morning, very slowly.... I have taken up where later Newton left off. I am sure he was right, and that rays of light contain 4 sides.... Have finished 'Against Materialism'! Completed the last stanza as the light faded about 7.30 p.m."[9]

From my convalescence I rang Garratt Green, which had restarted on 22 April. Mrs. Kay had left, and Sinclair was now Head: "Is that the

Headmaster?" "In person." He said: "I've rearranged the desk so I've got a better view out of the window, and of the rhododendrons. I'm actually looking for things to do. A lot is going in the waste-paper basket." At the end I said, "It's a breath of fresh air being able to get through to the Head's room for the first time in 10 years." He said: "Yes, I have got the window open and there is a lot of fresh air in the room." I warmed to his infectious, boisterous good humour.

While I continued to convalesce I reflected on Orpheus: "I saw Orpheus as an embodiment of the Baroque:... The poet has to enter Hades and experience it." I reflected that "the Hell he entered to bring Eurydice back" proved the existence of the soul and gave him secret knowledge; that the artist is aware of the soul as well as the body. The fate of Orpheus repre-sented the destruction of the artist by a harsh world and the artist's world of imagination. My Orpheus continued to sing though torn to pieces by the Maenads of Garratt Green. Orpheus reveals "the Baroque spirit and sense, the higher inspiration and erotic Eurydice, and how they are separated".

While I was still reflecting on Orpheus's visit to Hades and confrontation with Eurydice's soul I had a report about my mother's life beyond the grave. Anthony had a party at Oaklands and my brother Jonathan's wife, Anne, brought my nephew William, who was a pupil at Oaklands, and told me about a visit she had made to a medium in Harlow. She reported that my mother came through. "She is living with my father and they are very happy now.... Talk of an RAF wedding (mine).... She thanked Jonathan for being with her when she died – said it was heart trouble and painful, and that my father had something in his brain which led to his death." I record what was reported to me without making any judgement on whether it was really my mother.

That evening I "typed up 'Crab-Fishing [in a Boundless Deep]' and 'Staffa [: Wind]'. Am at the height of my powers now. And fuse thought and rhyme and metre effortlessly, having learned my trade with great sweat and application, on and off – in solitude. I carry my knowledge in silence."

My convalescence was over and I was back at work and around Oaklands in the evenings. The following Sunday I "finished the notes to 'Against Materialism', played some cricket with the boys in the tennis-court, then [went] to the Mind Body Spirit Festival, where I bought... a crystal that fills my room with rainbows when hung into the sun (cf the Light on the soul)". I hung it on my study window-catch. Sometimes there could be between 20 and 30 rainbows in my study, on the carpet, on the wall, on the desk and my hands. The rainbow parabola for each civilization in *The Fire and the Stones* came from this crystal.

I reflected on 'Cambridge Ode: Against Materialism': "In my 'Against Materialism' I have come nearer to the truth than in any poem I have written. A poem… creates an idea in beauty which the mind can hold and respond to and which has resonances and is evocative…. The idea I have created in that poem is near the Truth, and Newton's four-sided ray of light is very much a part of it…. I am not a dualist, but monist – I see a single, unified system which includes mind and body – and soul and spirit." I added that Colin Wilson's *Religion and the Rebel* "gets to the starting-point of 'Against Materialism'" as his rebel had rebelled against both the Church and materialism. I observed: "Wordsworth's Leech-Gatherer was the artist – like my crab-fisher, my Fisher King. Wordsworth saw in him the revolution and independence an artist needs in gathering leeches/poems." I saw the same qualities in my crab-fisher. I noted the tradition that Pythagoras wrote under the name of Orpheus, and that he had travelled for 20 years and then climaxed his training with lonely contemplation. I wrote: "Compare my 10 years' travels."

I looked back and observed that "the last fortnight, a week in hospital and a week of convalescence at home, have seen the completion of 5 solid works spanning three years". The five works were 'Night Visions in Charlestown' (first drafted on 6 August 1983); 'Iona: Silence' and 'Staffa: Wind' (both drafted in August 1984); 'Crab-Fishing on a Boundless Deep' ("boundless deep" "to emphasise the width and depth of the divine mind", first drafted on 24 August 1981); and 'Cambridge Ode: Against Materialism' (first drafted on 11–12 August 1982). I now "took up the Ben Nevis poem".[10]

Garratt Green, running Oaklands: Geoff Hurst opens Oaklands fête
I was trying to extricate myself from Garratt Green. I was told that it might be possible for me to have voluntary severance – early retirement – from the ILEA on favourable terms in December.

Life had eased following the departure of Mrs. Kay, and the atmosphere under Martin Sinclair was far more benevolent. I was now keeping the register and marking in everyone else. Looking back in the register I was astonished to see that I had been marked late four days in five some weeks, when I had arrived soon after 7.30 for an 8.45 start. Mrs. Kay had regularly marked me late in the register when I was early, very often the first in the school as I was doing the coverage. I reflected that I had been marked late for owning a private school and visiting Peter Walker. I wrote: "Deliverance is at hand! I will have served a fifteen-year sentence [January 1971–December 1985]." But it was still not clear that I would be allowed to leave in December.

I had explored the possibility of starting an English Language school in Rouen, which I saw as a return to the Normandy I visited as a boy. I explored the tax implications of starting a French company and found a fellow who would run it in France for me as director. I met him at the Grosvenor Hotel,

Victoria (which I had used to give surveillance squads the slip in the dark days of the early 1970s, entering by the front door and leaving by the back door into Victoria Station and then plunging down into the underground). I flew to Paris for a day and met an accountant for three hours in Rue la Fayette to discuss the costs of starting a French business. I lunched at a restaurant near the Opera and then flew back ("descended out of the sun into a cloud of unknowing"). A fortnight later, at half-term, I took my director to Rouen, I found two possible properties where a language school could be based. I went off the Rouen idea when my director changed his mind about living in Normandy and said he would commute from Brighton, where he lived.

After dropping the director off in Brighton I went on to Shoreham and visited Margaret on 30 May. She sat in her "little weed patch" (at the back of her shop) which contained a few pansies and forget-me-nots, and called it her "Paradise". "Flowers, children's laughter and stars are a Paradise, a priest said to me." I sat with her in her garden of her soul.[11]

Back in Loughton, I mowed the two Oaklands fields, stripped to the waist and driving round and round in ever-decreasing circles, a practice I found very therapeutic. Everywhere there was "large cow-parsley, gnats dancing under a blue sky, fountains of late may, burgeoning hawthorn – early June is here, and a heat". Miss Lord invited us in for a drink. Afterwards at bedtime Anthony complained of a bruise on his head. I put my finger on his head and gave thanks for the healing power. "Immediately there were four surges, each punctuated by 10 seconds, and then (most unusual for me) a final half-surge. Anthony immediately relaxed…. My little finger burned. Now I am shiny, having been a conductor for the healing Light."[12]

I had my hands full with the two schools and my family, and there was little time to advance the publishing. The 1985 Oaklands fête was opened by the footballer Geoff Hurst, who had scored a hat-trick when England won the World Cup in 1966. He had a daughter in Ann's class, and I stood with him and chatted during the country dancing, and then I introduced him to the crowd. He said a few words and judged a contest. Then I took him on a tour of the school grounds, and in the second field we discussed his hat-trick. He said: "It's a 20th-century record that looks safe. I can't see England getting to the Final again before the end of the century, let alone anyone scoring a hat-trick in a World Cup Final." (His prediction turned out to be right. In 2014 I spent an evening with him, and he told me he could still see the moment of his third goal in his mind, and that he had tried to hoof the ball over the bar to waste time and was astonished when his shot went in.) He told me he had walked away from football without any difficulty. In the evening Ann and I went out with Tom McAlister, the West Ham goalie, and his wife. I found him more articulate than many footballers.

The next day Ann and I were talking with Argie. She told us that High Beach church was to be uncoupled from St Mary's Loughton and attached to Waltham Abbey. She surprised me by saying that she saw me in terms of the pre-First-World-War generation, that of her elder brother Tom who had been killed in 1918: "One million men were killed in the First World War, and we have been ruled by a generation of weaklings. Tom was 19 when he was killed, it is their grandsons who are now asserting themselves, like Nick, and doing what Nick is doing and standing up to those who are causing trouble, and making us strong." I smiled at being considered an Edwardian, but I had always got on well with Edwardians such as Sir John Masterman. Soon afterwards my brother Jonathan rang me to announce that he had made an offer for a house in Tunbridge Wells, that they were selling their house (my grandmother's and then Argie's home) and joining Robert in Kent.

I met my publishing consultant Trevor Maher at Brent Cross. We drew up a timetable for the next four or five books, which would come out in 1986. Trevor said he was trying to get me to achieve a list approaching 50 books. One of them would be a world best-seller, and I would then be able to expand – and spend more time writing.

I was working incredibly hard. Each school day at Oaklands we still put on nearly 200 lunches. We still shopped for these at Makro and a frozen-food store every Friday evening, and I still carried the tins down to the cellar storeroom. I cut the two fields each summer weekend and did the staff salaries and accounts and paid the bills. I was still commuting to Wandsworth, running the public exams and marking exam essays. I was still coping with the aftermath of *Scargill the Stalinist?* (At Garratt Green I was teaching Dryden and wrote: "Dryden's 'Absalom and Achitophel', c.1681, is a Baroque work.... Dryden, pro-Tory and anti-Whig, ripping into the Scargill of the day, Shaftesbury and his mob, supporting the Establishment. Verse satire defends the Establishment by lampooning ambition.") I was running the publishing company and exploring the French market. Looking back, I am amazed at how much I managed to pack in that summer after my operation.

I had a strange experience listening to Matthew (flushed from success at coming 1st in his class in Science) play in a summer concert at Chigwell. I wrote:

Three Renaissance tunes.... Henry [VIII] himself composed the middle one ('*Schiarazula Marazula*' by Giorgio Mainerio). [The tune has been attributed to Henry VIII although it was officially composed by Mainerio.] As I listened I had an image of people dancing, right hands out, two paces forward to join tips of fingers in fours, two paces back, then forward again, wearing red and yellow, a red cape to the base of the back and a yellow 'tunic' underneath, with black decorations, and 'tights' on the legs. The one I was looking at had dark hair and a beard, and this image – memory from a past life? – was accompanied by emotion which was not entirely positive, some form of aggression or dislike for him. Who was this bearded man dancing with his lady, who looked like portraits of Anne of Cleves? And who was the lady? Mine? Or even – me?

Somehow I knew that the title of Henry's piece '*Schiarazula Marazula*' caused great mirth among the Tudor courtiers, and even now I can see bearded Renaissance men laughing and repeating the play on 'Zula'.

We were breaking up at both schools. At Oaklands there was an Open Evening and wine flowed. Between 300 and 400 parents looked in, and the drinking went on until 11.45 p.m. Tom McAlister stood by the door in an open-necked shirt, examining the sunburn on his arms with admiring ladies standing round. Soon afterwards there was a barbeque on a hot Sunday. Wearing a French apron McAlister cooked sausages on our improvised barbecue of half an oil drum on a stand with a grille over it. Many people came and there were rounders in the field. I chatted to Geoff Hurst.

By contrast the Garratt Green English Department's party took place at the house of one of the staff. I noted: "The house with the broken front door, faded carpet, peeling paint, flaking walls, broken fence in garden.... The curtainless windows, so the street can see, the poverty."[13] The teachers at Garratt Green came from a different region of society from the affluent middle classes I saw at Oaklands, and which I was now used to.

In the Dordogne: Cro-Magnon man, 'In Périgord'
As soon as Garratt Green broke up we all left to spend a week near the River Dordogne in France, where I could confront human origins.

We drove to Dover, caught a hovercraft to Calais "turbulent seas after a storm, spray whipping past the window" and found a roadside hotel. Next morning we drove via Orleans, Blois and Périgueux to Les Eyzies, passing through the Valley of Prehistory and glimpsing the cliffs which contain the caves where Cro-Magnon man replaced Neanderthal man c.35,000BC, and where Magdalenian man flourished c.16,000–11,000BC.

We found the yellow cottage we had rented. It was on the edge of a farm in the countryside and surrounded by scented pines. There was no electricity and lamps worked from bottled *gaz*. We were high up in a wooded area with chalk cliffs. It was very hot and the stone floors were wonderfully cool. Immediately I was back in the life of the 18th century, quiet, peaceful, only a yellowhammer disturbing the evening quiet: the depth where Cro-Magnon can be found. Drunk with fresh wooded air, that

Saturday night I slept 10 hours. The next morning we sunbathed among wild flowers, cicadas and butterflies. A brownish-grey snake slithered past the front door and a lizard lived under the bathroom window-sill.

It was extremely hot. We dragged ourselves round Les Eyzies, which contains most of our knowledge about the development of man from c.100,000BC, and then to the Grand Roc caves, which had watery passages and stalagmites and stalactites. We went on to Sarlat, a round medieval and Renaissance town where I was fascinated by the Lantern of the Dead behind the Cathedral where St Bernard's bread cured the sick. The Lantern was built in commemoration of the event: a beehive pyramid with windows and a winding path leading down its outside, representing the divine manifesting into human affairs and a lantern at the top, the Light which cured the sick and looks after the dead who have been laid beneath it for hundreds of years.

The next day we went to St Cyprian and Beynac, and to the château that overlooks the Dordogne where there were brimstones, a swallowtail and lizards on high-up stones where the lords tyrannised the villagers. We went on to La Roque and then Domme, a medieval town with a panoramic view of a bend in the River Dordogne. We went on to Gourdon and Rocamadour's steps up a gorge to its miraculous chapel and blackened Madonna, and then on to the Padirac chasm. We forded the underground river on a boat, passing stalactites and stalagmites and ferns growing underground. We returned via Souillac to Les Eyzies and ate at the Hotel Centre.

The following day we drove to La Madeleine and saw the cavemen's shelter which gave its name to Magdalenian man, and to the Château de Losse by the River Vézère. That afternoon Anthony developed tonsillitis and ran a temperature of 103°F, and so I walked up to the farm and called a doctor, who arrived after 11 p.m., a young man who spoke no English. He got his syringe out and advanced on Matthew, who had woken up and was sitting on his bed. Matthew backed away and the doctor pursued him round the cottage until I interposed myself and explained in French that he was trying to inject the wrong boy. He gave Anthony an injection in his bottom (for 200F), and his temperature soon came down.

The next day we visited Les Combarelles, which had a tunnel that was an underground river millions of years ago. Here Cro-Magnon men did their wall-engravings, which showed up best in the half-light, the oil-lamp or torchlight by which they worked. I saw a squinting face, an elongated Egyptian-type man, various female forms stressing fertility, and many animals – horses, reindeer, deer, a bear and a lioness – all done in lines, using the rock so a natural line was the base, a relief, and a bulge suggested a swelling of pregnancy. We went on to Cap Blanc and saw a relief of seven horses. I related the cave-paintings to shamans' magic. The caves and their tunnels were entrances to the Underworld and the shamans entered them like Aeneas and gained power over the spirits of animals, who could then be more easily hunted and killed. We went on to Font de Gaume, where black- and red-oxide paints were used, and to Lascaux, where we saw the wall-paintings of bulls, and then on to Montfort on the River Dordogne.

After a week we left the Dordogne and drove through vineyards to St Emilion, a Roman and medieval town where we tasted the red wine in two châteaux. We went on to Bordeaux and then La Rochelle, where we found a hotel with a view over the two 13th-century towers in the harbour. The following morning La Rochelle was a sleepy town above fishing-smacks, and I described the salmon roofs and smell of salt on the breeze under a grey sky, and the grey battlement walls of the two castle towers at the mouth of the harbour... and wrote: "Here I sit,... an inveterate painter in words." We drove on to Nantes and arrived at Mont St Michel, where we found an apartment with a sea-view on the battlements of a 13th-century building. We walked along the main street, which was full images of St Michael killing the Dragon, and we walked "back across the battlements where house martins squeaked and dived and squealed, zooming low and flitting high".[14] The next morning we toured the Abbey of Mont St Michel. We went on to Rouen, made our way to Boulogne and returned by ferry.

After seeing my bank manager we drove to Cornwall and the next afternoon went to Charlestown and climbed round the rocks with the boys. We returned at 10.30 under brilliant stars, and watched the *Mary Coast* leave for Guernsey. The massive boat manoeuvered through the inner and outer harbour necks with taut ropes and rubber tyres that squeaked and squealed as she slowly wheeled. We went to Fowey past Tristan's stone and over to Polruan on the ferry by Quiller-Couch's house. We took the boys to Fowey's aquarium and saw wrasse, conger eels, dogfish, plaice, and pollack. We went to Mevagissey and watched the foam on the rocks.

My visit to the Dordogne now expressed itself in poetry: "Aug. 11. Slept after lunch." This was the fourth successive afternoon I had slept, and I had had long sleeps at night as well, having been exhausted. "Suddenly tonight, at 10.15 p.m., I sat down without intending to and drafted 12 stanzas, 'The Purpose of Périgord' – on the purpose behind evolution." I noted that creativity was latent in me, buried, and just waiting to fountain out when the moment was right. "It is now 11.13, and within an hour I have put Périgord into perspective. I can work on this draft, which must sum up the purpose of the evolutionary drive, which is to a new consciousness." Matthew had stirred me to write the poem by asking for where we went in the Dordogne for his diary. The poem had four parts: "Pt 1, the physical side of the Dordogne; Pt 2, the prehistory and the caves; Pt 3, Sarlat and the Lantern of the Dead; Pt 4, the motive force behind evolution."[15] This poem became 'In Périgord'.

Idea of The Fire and the Stones *received in sleep: the Light shaping civilizations of history*
Early next morning, 12 August (the day Cameron died) I received, again in sleep, a strengthening of the idea that Light shaped the civilizations of history, and recorded the theme of *The Fire and the Stones*:

> Awoke with the idea: do a Toynbee and 'rewrite' history, showing that it is the Light that makes civilizations grow, i.e. that the Light is... present at the growth of civilizations – and at their high points. (The Light of the World through Christian civilization up through the Dark Ages – it is always a metaphysical idea that makes civilizations grow, for it energises with its purpose.)

I saw the overall movement of history as a spiral: "Man spirals up, from prehistory via Graeco-Romans and medievalism to now. So too do we spiral. My life as a spiral from Loughton in the Law, to Loughton after losing my marriage, to Loughton under Oaklands: unhappiness, pain, contentment, the soul ascending... in a spiral (cf the Milky Way and galaxies, and all oceans, e.g. the Gulf Stream).... And civilization too is a spiral?... From growth, through breakdown, to disintegration, but spiralling upwards.... Life is a spiral, and I am now higher than them but in the same place."[16]

Flurry of poems
I was too busy visiting Cornish places and coping with new poems to advance my publishing. I took the boys down to Charlestown: "The sea smoothed away their footprints." We drove to St Michael's Mount on a misty day and walked across the causeway. The Mount was hidden in low cloud, but we climbed to the top and toured the Castle and church and "lingered before the picture of Lettice Knollys" (the wife of Leicester and mother of Essex, who was blamed for turning the two men, the two crushed flowers she held, against Elizabeth I). We looked at Trevarthian, where I stayed as a boy: a grey Georgian house with clusters of palms on either side of the veranda.

We drove on to Pendeen and visited the lighthouse, which was shrouded in fog. We saw the coastguard's house where Ann's mother once lived and the final house, rented, from which Ann's grandfather went to Rhodesia. We went to Geevor Mine, Cape Cornwall and then Land's End. I drafted poems on Trevarthian ('Trevarthian Revisited'), St Michael's Mount ('Rough Stones like Monks'), and Lettice Knollys ('Lettice'), and the Geevor Mine ('At Geevor Tin-mine'). Another day we went to Goonhilly, dishes of skyscraper size that tracked satellites on the Lizard cliffs, one of the marvels of the 20th century.

We went on to Gunwalloe, where it was hot. We sunbathed on the beach under the church as the sea raced in and dashed on the rocks. We walked to Dollar Cove. Then we went to Porthleven and walked along the pier. I wrote poems on Goonhilly ('The Wonder of the West: At Goonhilly'), Gunwalloe ('At Gunwalloe') and Porthleven ('At Porthleven: All One') – and on infinity and eternity beyond space and time ('The Divine').

I thought about the coming Age and again reflected on the theme of *The Fire and the Stones*:

> Aug. 20. The Universal Age.... The immensely creative 20th century – our creativity has not broken down, we have not begun to disintegrate?... The Universal Age is a time of creativity.... We are parallel to the Roman age of Augustus, for our creativity has enabled us to Westernise the whole world. TV, telephone, aircraft, space rockets – all Western creations that are global. We are a rally, a Golden Age... It can see off Communism and bring universal benefit to all mankind.

The contrast between our Golden Age and the tyranny in Libya was starkly evident when an anti-Gaddafi student was hanged near the entrance to the University of Libya, where I often walked. The hanging, which led to the demonstration outside the Libyan People's Bureau in London, the Libyan retaliation for which killed W.P.C. Fletcher, was shown on television. I watched in appalled fascination: "The balding, moustached student in an open-necked shirt stood by a noose while someone read accusations in Arabic to a chanting crowd. Then the noose was put over his head – he co-operated by extending his neck – and he was then pushed and you saw him dangling and turning, head bent, while the crowd of students chanted with raised fists. He died to hysterical chanting."

Still the poems came. There was a wet day, and I went to Charlestown for half an hour. Four poems came to me, 'Rod-Fishing', 'Words spent like Waves' (on the harbour wall), 'Moments like Waves' and 'Cerberus' (on the sea-barrier, watching the children play on the rocks). "Half an hour and effortlessly, four poems.... A phrase, 'I, the Poet of the Sea.'" I wrote: "I dream of typing up all my poems and publishing them like Wordsworth, to be known and bought as those of a moderate, Nature-loving mind in touch with deep reality. I am quivering with poetic inspiration. The longer I leave my talent for the everyday, the more the spring flows when it is contacted. It gushes." The next morning was fine. We took a picnic lunch to Par and played football and then cricket on the sand with the boys until rain came, leaving distant Trenarren in a mist. I reflected on how we have two consciousnesses: the personality, which is mechanical, robotic and lazy; and the real one, which is full of freedom, energy and power, pure consciousness. The next day I taught Anthony to bowl at Par and wrote three poems, about a kite ('Will like a Kite'), two consciousnesses ('Consciousness') and wild ponies ('Tamed Ponies').

On my last night in Cornwall I thought again about Western civilization: "The civilization keeps the culture going," and for Western mysticism to be kept going "the civilization which has respected mysticism must be kept going in spite of and against its enemies (Communists, terrorists who would destroy real consciousness)". I felt that my Baroque Age "is a rediscovery of the Western mystic tradition", and "my book on the Light is a definition of the next way of looking which is really a revival of an old way of looking in a new guise".[17]

In York: 'At Dark Age Jorvik: The Light of Civilisation'
At half-term we drove the two boys to York and stayed at the Viking Hotel by the Ouse. We walked in the 14th-century streets and the Shambles (the butchers' street) and visited the minster. The next morning we visited Jorvik and were taken through an underground reconstruction of a Viking settlement of thatched houses and farmyard smells. (The original Viking village was destroyed by a Norman fire in 1069.) Later we toured York and saw Dick Turpin's condemned cell with its iron bed, and Clifford's Tower, where the 1190 massacre took place. On our return I started a poem, 'At Dark Age Jorvik: The Light of Civilisation', which I finished in draft the next day.

Cosmology: star-gazing
I was extending my knowledge of cosmology while I advanced my publishing. I took ten Oaklands girls to look through the Chigwell School telescope. After a talk from Mr Sizer in front of charts, we went down to the bottom of the field and squinted through the telescope's 10-inch eyepiece at Halley's comet, a fuzzy smudge above. The comet glowed between the Pleiades and the V of the Hyades. Jupiter was in the trees with its moon Io. Looking at the starpoints in the black sky I went back into the ancient time when the first geometers began to solve problems, and I knew that Pythagoras's theorem, and other discoveries in geometry were made by gazing at stars.

A few days later I studied Jupiter's four moons at an evening class Sizer gave at Loughton High School, and thought about moves towards a Grand Unified Theory. Anticipating Universalism, I noted that "there has been a revolutionary shift in consciousness from earth-centred to galaxy-centred consciousness" and that "the new man is aware of Jupiter's four moons… and this adds to his ecstatic joy at being here on the earth".[18]

Expansionism: 'Heroes of the West', Gaddafi's missiles and terrorism
With some reluctance I had applied myself to my publishing and to the cluster of books by other people which I was preparing for publication in 1986. I had been heating my publishing irons in the fire.

Des McForan's book on terrorism
I had been sent a book about terrorism by Dr Des McForan. I knew it would be Oak-Tree Books' next publication. McForan had read *Scargill the Stalinist?* while sheltering from the rain in Birmingham and had decided I was the right publisher for his book. I also received an illiterate book on trade unions by Jack Wood, which would need rewriting.

Paul Gorka's book on Hungarian uprising
On 3 May I had lunched with the Hungarian Paul Gorka – the Hungarian representative of the European Liaison Group and Deputy Leader of the Hungarian Freedom-Fighters' Association – at the Polish Centre, which he had designed as an architect. He told me he had worked for British Intelligence from 1948 to 1951 during the Stalin years. He had reported on Soviet tank movements in Hungary, and told me that he had been betrayed by Philby and Blunt. Philby recruited British spies, his wife Litzi informed her lover, Gábor Péter, the Head of Hungary's Secret Police, who arrested and imprisoned them. Gorka had been arrested and imprisoned under the Russians, and heard the leader of his group being hanged in the prison courtyard through a high-up grating in his cell. He had been released during the Hungarian uprising, when the prison was briefly liberated, and with his family had fled to Britain where he had practised as an architect. He was a podgy, bespectacled man in his fifties. He had written a rare eyewitness account of life in a Stalinist prison. I knew immediately that I would publish his prisoner's story of the betrayal of the Hungarian resistance movement to the Russians, which became 'Budapest Betrayed'.

Along with Gorka I had met Morris Riley, a lean, craggy, northern accountant who was writing a book on Philby, which contained some extremely interesting insights; including (he claimed) the identity of the fifth man. I met Gorka and Riley together in the King Street Polish Centre on 25 May and heard details of the Vatican. Gorka wanted to write a book about the role of the KGB inside the Vatican. Somehow I had attracted two writers from the intelligence world. Both had come to me because I seemed fearless in bringing out *Scargill the Stalinist?*

The future growth of the West
In Essex I edited the book on terrorism that I was publishing: *The World Held Hostage*. I knew I had an important subject. Terrorism was out of control.

There had been 50,000 acts of terrorism in 15 years, 2 million terrorists were being trained in more than 220 training camps, and 50 terrorist groups were centrally co-ordinated by Palestinians for the Communist nations. Standing up to the terrorists would keep Western civilization going against its enemies. I was thinking about the future of the West, and while it was necessary to stand up to terrorism. I wrote: "Future history can be understood by careful study of the past and identifying the seeds of what is to come."

I took on an editor and met her at the Athenaeum Hotel. I showed her my books about the fate of the West. She asked, "Why a political start when publishers avoid a political list?" I recorded my reply: "It's a look at the future of the West – what prospects have we? The plight of the West is more desperate than we realise." I said: "Western civilization... has been a good civilization and brought freedom, democracy and justice to victims of tyranny; and art, music and literature of the highest quality and a spiritual vision; and I must defend it against the forces that are massing against it."

I developed this crusading thinking. I spoke of "my essential vision of order and harmony". I saw myself as "a kind of Rambo, conducting a one-man war on Communism to strengthen the spiritual force of the West". I still saw my fight in terms of Western values rather than in global Universalist terms (as I do now).

I wrote about the "future growth of the West which will counter and arrest the disintegration for a while – see two forces, growth versus disintegration". I observed:

The West is still growing or still capable of growing although the force of disintegration is widespread.... Communism has broken down, and it is itself a symptom of a disintegrating and broken-down society.... Yeats's Chinamen... are wrong to be detached while civilization sinks.... What is needed is commitment, a crusading spirit... and a determination to fight for the West to help its growth, to strengthen it for survival.

I was obsessed with Western growth:

The Oak-Tree idea.... Is Western civilization disintegrating? It is the idea of Gibbon, Spengler and Toynbee that needs scrutiny, and Solzhenitsyn. According to Gibbon Rome fell because of barbarism and religion. According to Spengler because it grew old like a mallow in the field. According to Toynbee it had stopped growing and lost harmony between its parts. The Islamic and Soviet cultures are the enemies to Western civilization.... Western civilization is like an oak-tree, it will go on growing so long as the sap is there.

I told Dusan: "My mission is to give the positive side of Western civilization." I saw the process in terms of healing: "Oak-Tree is healing the nation,... pouring... energy into the nation."

My concern with growth affected my view of a work of art. I wrote: "The cessation of a traditional artistic style is a breakdown symptom.... Eliot's '[The] Waste Land' is therefore a sign of a breakdown as is the Modernistic music and art that broke with tradition, i.e. our Western breakdown happened in 1914.... The fracture, then is reflected in art, which goes off tradition and the spirit." A growing civilization therefore has a continuity of artistic style, and I was determined to see my own work as a continuation of the tradition, not as a cessation of it; to return to the position in 1910 and grow it from there.

My view of growth also entered my outlook on current affairs: "I will call for a Universal State in Europe as that is a rally.... I will call for a new universalised religion" that "will universalise... the tradition of the... new religion of Light." I saw both Europe and religion in Universalist terms. I wrote: "The conflict between the end of the Humanist breakdown and the new spiritual religion that will replace materialistic Christianity... will... produce great art."[19]

I was now doing as much as I could to advance my publishing, bearing in mind that the new year had begun at Oaklands and I had started what was to be my last term at Garratt Green. Towards the end of September Trevor Maher took me to the English-speaking Union for an introductory talk on the Frankfurt Book Fair, to which we would be going. I encountered Bob Leach, my number two at Garratt Green, who had retired following a heart attack and had written a couple of books. The next day I spoke for an hour on the phone to Des McForan about how to present and improve his book. The following day I had a further meeting in the Athenaeum Hotel with my editor, and spent four hours going through Jack Wood's illiterate manuscript. On Saturday 21 September I rang Wood and then met Gorka and Riley in the Athenaeum Hotel. I discussed their books.

The following Wednesday I met my editor on the St Paul's steps to carry forward the next stage of the work she was doing, and then went to Vernon Davies's house in Chigwell. He was fund-raising for the Conservative Party by starting a Patrons Club. Some 140 local people were invited, to be addressed by Norman Tebbit. I arrived at the same time as Biggs-Davison and Tebbit. We joined the queue to get in, and Biggs-Davison introduced me to Tebbit and talked about the Scargill book. Tebbit said of Scargill, "He's well and truly in the Soviet camp now," but otherwise listened in silence.

As a birthday outing, I took Matthew and five friends to see Churchill's War Cabinet rooms. What we were allowed to see was now protected by glass, and I was not able to sit in Churchill's chair as I had the previous time, when I had walked underground as far as Trafalgar Square through grimy, dusty rooms. The rooms were a time capsule. Everything looked antiquated and out of date – all the booklets, newspapers and lettering – and yet this was the most modern and well-equipped place in the early 1940s. There was a hotline to the president of the United States behind a loo door. I looked in on the world of my childhood, a world that had passed, and noted details for *Overlord*.

At Frankfurt Book Fair with Trevor Maher
A week later I went to the Frankfurt Book Fair. I took Trevor Maher to show me how the Frankfurt Fair worked. Trevor arrived late at Heathrow, realised he had left his car in the short-stay, expensive car park and disappeared again, leaving me to ask the air-hostesses after we had boarded to delay the take-off, which they did. Trevor arrived out of breath, having kept the passengers waiting, and to speed things up was shown to the first available seat, which was in Clipper class. He was then told he could stay put. He removed his jacket and hung it up, and when we were airborne came down to the economy-class section in his shirtsleeves and said (I having paid for his ticket): "Just seeing how the underclass are getting on. Bit cramped for space here, aren't you. I must go back to my champagne now." It was not until we were by the taxi-rank at Frankfurt that he tapped his breast pocket for his wallet and realised his credit card and money had been stolen from his jacket while he was talking to me.

We drove straight to the Messe, left our luggage in the cloakroom and walked the coconut matting. Each floor was as large as Olympia, and there were many floors with labelled booths for different companies on both sides of each aisle, all heaped with books. It seemed that everybody present knew Trevor. There were shouts of "Trevor, nice to see you, how are you keeping?" Trevor introduced me to each acquaintance, explaining he was showing me Frankfurt so I could take part next year, and then told the story of how he lost his wallet on the flight. "I haven't got any money, could I borrow ten quid in marks?" After an hour he had a fistful of German notes. "I've done far better than if I'd gone to the bank," he chuckled.

We made appointments to see American companies, lunched on a long frankfurter sausage from a fast-food place at the end of one of the floors, and from the Messe hall booked accommodation in a private house in Durkheim Strasse half an hour to the east of Frankfurt near the Main. We took a tram out there and then went out to eat. Next morning, after a huge breakfast served by an old lady who spoke no English, we returned and visited the Americans, often seeing the top person, attempting to sell the rights to the books we were planning to bring out. We had a drink and a long chat with Bill Campbell and Peter MacKenzie of Mainstream, and then attended a drinks gathering run by a remainder man on the 40th floor of the Canadian Pacific building. The next day we visited British publishers and then caught the plane home We discussed the Oak-Tree authors' contract and the presentation of the coming catalogue during the flight (a come-down for Trevor as he had to sit in economy class).

When I got back I saw Des McForan in the Athenaeum Hotel and we went on to the Shepherd Tavern and drank upstairs in the Sedan Room. I told him: "A group is gathering around Oak-Tree that is determined to shield the West from the neo-barbarian menace: Westerners who have the courage to tell the truth and stand up to the might of Communism and reverse it, the Crusaders."[20]

Caroline's dark news

In early October 1985 I received a letter from Caroline: "David has left me – in fact he has undertaken a new life for himself: new job, new home and new woman.... It is as you predicted." So came this dark news that I wanted to hear so much 15 years previously, but which now left me – sad for her, a little, but otherwise unaffected. I had grown so much in the last 15 years, and was now so purposive. A 15-year-period was coming to an end for both of us, and I was struck by the strange pattern life weaves, a strange spiral: "Life is a spiral and similar situations return to haunt us."

I heard the details. Caroline told me over the phone: "He went to Australia for a few weeks and didn't say when he was coming back and I found out by accident by ringing work that he'd sneaked back and was living with another woman nearby." He had lived with Vivien until October. During that time his parents had her to stay in Scarborough although Caroline and David were still married. "I've seen him since. He doesn't talk. He's just thinking about his job and nothing else. He hasn't thought about Damian or any of the consequences." I pointed out that he had not thought of the effects on other people's lives on Malta, and that to be so blind to the lives of others revealed "a lack of sensibility, a terrible coldness, an inhuman lack of feeling".

On 19 October Nadia came to stay. I met her at Heathrow and drove her back to our house next to Oaklands. At the end of her visit she rang Caroline briefly, and I had a word. Caroline said: "I feel such a failure. I've messed up everyone's life, yours, Nadia's, Damian's. I don't see anyone for days, and go out walking and thinking. I'm in pieces. Moods – up and then down." She said he had told people that he was going deaf flying Phantoms, and was discontinuing to save his hearing. They had moved to Edinburgh in 1978 when it was apparent he would not get promotion within the RAF, and he had worked away from home. There had been phone calls from him following his spells of work in Oxford, America and Scandinavia. Caroline had moved to Salisbury on 17 July and it was there she had found out he was seeing Vivien. He had taken Caroline out to dinner on 27 July and had complained that she had wrongly accused him of improper relations with women. He had not mentioned at the dinner that he had filed for divorce earlier that day, 27 July. She had received a letter offering her a divorce in return for not naming Vivien. Some years earlier he had bought Caroline's parents' house in Dulwich (177 South Croxted Road) cheaply as it had sitting tenants (Caroline's parents), and, to cover his American-Express debts for his overseas trips, he had sold a half-share in the house to friends of his who now wanted to put the property on the market so they could maximise the half they owned. Caroline's father had died in November 1980, and her mother was still living in the property. Caroline was trying to salvage a very difficult situation for her family.[21]

The Executive Intelligence Review *on Philby and the US-Soviet 'Trust'; the Duke of Grantmesnil and Victor, Lord Rothschild as the fifth man*

The publishing put me in touch with *The Executive Intelligence Review*, a weekly news magazine founded in 1974 by the American Lyndon Larouche, who had founded a private intelligence network in 1971. I was taken by Riley to their seminar at the Foreign Press Association in Carlton House Terrace. Someone read a paper saying that the Soviet Union was aiming for a first nuclear strike in 1988/89. It was said that the Warsaw Pact had a plan for a *Blitzkrieg* of Western Europe in 35 days, using tactical nuclear weapons in four areas.[22] (*See* p.216.) Riley mentioned his book on Philby to one of the EIR staff, who said: "Philby wasn't a traitor, he worked for 'the Trust'. He was between the West and the Soviet Union, helping to manage the Cold War."[23] I connected what he had said with what Biggs-Davison had told me about Kissinger's "spheres of influence" – Philby was moving between spheres of influence.

Riley introduced me to Kenneth de Courcy, confidant to the Duke and Duchess of Windsor shortly after the Duke's abdication as Edward VIII and promoter of the Duke as Regent to his niece, later Queen Elizabeth II.[24] De Courcy, self-styled Duke de Grantmesnil (and descendant of the Norman Ducs de Grandmesnil), was an untidy-haired, pot-bellied man with a coronet and G on his shirt. I interviewed him before a huge fireplace. Our conversation turned to the fifth man, and he told me, "The fifth man is Victor, Lord Rothschild. When I worked for Lord Halifax, the British Foreign Secretary, just before the war, I would often look out of my window and see Baldwin walking with John Buchan. Baldwin wouldn't take any decision without Buchan. Lord Rothschild has taken Buchan's place." (He was Head of Heath's think-tank.)

Tomlin's book on philosophy

While I was supervising a bonfire night at Oaklands – 500 people standing behind the rope watching a large fire shooting sparks into the night, rockets, Roman candles shooting green and red balls into the air ('phut'), mortars, fountains and later drinking soup in the tennis-court which was hung with fairy lights – there was a call from Tomlin, my boss in Japan, friend of T.S. Eliot and metaphysical philosopher. I returned his call, and he offered me two books, one on Cornwall and the possibility, which I jumped at, of reprinting his 1950s works, *The Western Philosophers* and *The Eastern Philosophers* as *Philosophers of East and West*. He told me, "In May I tour the whole of Japan, lecturing." The great man was now leaning on me to publish his works, depending on me.[25]

Asked to run The Salisbury Review *by Jillian Becker*

I thought more about the Oak-Tree magazine. I had had the idea that Oak-Tree should publish a monthly, bi-monthly or quarterly magazine, my *Encounter*, and that the editor should be someone other than me. I discussed this with Gorka in Ealing Broadway, and the following Saturday attended a conference on Marxism–Leninism with Des McForan, on his invitation. We discovered after our arrival that it was run by the Moonies (under the name Causa UK). The writer and adviser to the British Government on international terrorism, Jillian Becker, was present. I did not know that she had just founded the Institute for the Study of Terrorism with Baroness Cox and Lord Orr-Ewing, who chaired the launch of *Scargill the Stalinist?*; or that Ted Hughes's wife, Sylvia Plath, had stayed with her during the last weekend of her life. (She later wrote *Giving Up: The Last Days of Sylvia Plath*.) She targeted me, having read my book on Scargill, and came and sat beside me.

She proposed that I should run a magazine similar in concept to the idea I had already formed, and that I should share the running costs of *The Salisbury Review*, which since its founding in 1982 had been edited by Roger Scruton (who later wrote in *The Spectator*[26] that the editorship had cost him "many thousand hours of unpaid labour"). She wanted me to take over *The Salisbury Review* and bring to it some of the effective communication skills she had detected in my book on Scargill. She suggested that Roger Scruton should be my editor. McForan sat in silence, not trusting her Thatcher-like strength. I drove her home and met her Polish business partner Bernhard Adamczewski and daughter in an expensively furnished flat in Maida Vale.

I soon gathered that I would be expected to pour a lot of money into *The Salisbury Review*. At present neither the editorial board nor the contributors were paid. I was in two minds for a while as I thought I could rename it *The Western Review* and publish articles on Western ideology. Then McForan rang and urged me to decline as the publication was too "far right", and I backed off.

On 4 December I visited Jillian Becker's flat in Little Venice within Maida Vale. Trevor Maher was supposed to accompany me but was late. There were no mobiles in those days. I left a written note with the ticket-collector at Warwick Avenue station, and he gave it to Trevor half an hour later. Trevor arrived on a rain-sodden evening while I was in the middle of my preamble retitling *The Salisbury Review* as *The Western Review*. She tried to turn my No into a Yes and offered Trevor a distributorship.[27] But I would not be swayed. I did not want to take over *The Salisbury Review*, but I might be interested in turning it into *The Western Review*. We had a long talk during which I referred to Toynbee and Spengler. She said, revealing her Thatcherite connections, "We don't like Toynbee or Spengler, we believe individuals can shape history, not events." On the contrary, I held, the stage of one's civilization shapes events and events shape individuals who in turn influence events. (The context of the coming European Union would be responsible for Thatcher's ousting in 1991.) I told Becker that I was interested in starting a *Western Review* that would include philosophy and literature – today I would call it a *Universalist Review* – but that would be all.

Tomlin and A.L. Rowse

The previous day I had met Tomlin at the Athenaeum Club, and enlisted him as an Oak-Tree author. He was waiting inside the door, talking to A.L. Rowse, a white-haired bespectacled elderly man, the historian of Shakespeare and poet who lived on Trenarren, near Charlestown in Cornwall. Tomlin introduced me. Rowse smiled and shook my hand, then turned and disappeared. Tomlin was very dressed up in a dark suit and in a good mood below the stairs where Dickens was reconciled with Thackeray. We dined near Michael Meacher, MP, John Cole of the BBC and the new Head of the Foreign Office, and Tomlin advised me steer clear of *The Salisbury Review* because of its right-wing associations. As business could not be conducted inside the Athenaeum we signed contracts in a café playing muzak (recorded background music) round the corner in Waterloo Place.[28]

Voluntary severance from Garratt Green

I was now, very late in the term, offered voluntary severance from the ILEA. There would be a lump-sum payment, and it was said that I might have no pension unless I waited until I was 50, in over three years' time. I could not wait. I was aware that my father had died at 57, and that I had to get on and complete the writing I had to do. I would have completed 15 years in the ILEA by December. My prison sentence was coming to an end, and I longed for release. London education had become even more ideological with calls from the inspectors to root out "Eurocentricity" and to teach all history (and aspects of English literature) from the "multiracial" point of view of the Third World. I was a Universalist and wanted to take a whole view, but I was not interested in replacing the tradition of English Literature with contemporary African and Caribbean literature. I made arrangements to leave.

I signed the voluntary severance form on the penultimate day of term, a Thursday evening (19 December), at County Hall by the Thames, and only revealed my departure to the school the next day, the last day of term, deliberately keeping the news quiet until the final revelation for dramatic effect. Sinclair said to me: "Just how I'd like to go…. I'm so envious." Mrs. Kay, the ex-Head of Garratt Green, had returned for the last day's buffet lunch, and in front of her, called by Sinclair, I made a farewell speech to the staff, who were totally taken by surprise.

I told the staff I would concentrate on my private school – there was an audible gasp of outrage from the ex-Head – and publish books on the theme of arresting the decline of, and revitalizing, Western civilization. I reviewed the changes in the ILEA from 1974 to 1985, and, thinking of the Trotskyites and the no-marking and anti-Eurocentricity policies, I quoted Yeats's lines: "The best lack all conviction while the worst/Are full of passionate intensity." Aware that Garratt Green was facing an amalgamation and would become a new school, Burntwood, I said that I hoped "there will be, among the staff and therefore among the pupils, the consequences of some conviction: inner calm, good humour, amused erudition, intellectual and spiritual grooming, and a sound belief in the merit of Western civilization – amid the Brave New World of mixed ability, Foundation Courses and anti-Eurocentricity which passionate, intense people will no doubt urge on the Steering Committee". I was getting near the ideological bone, and Sinclair was trying to stop me. But I said, "I haven't finished," and continued with a prison image: I told them I was being "released". I had defined my attitude and stance and there was a fair bit of applause at the end, some clapping over their heads at what they regarded as an act of courage, and some ignoring me in disapproval of my message.[29]

Oaklands: Len Murray

That Christmas I savoured my retirement and looked forward to becoming a publisher and eventually a full-time author. Now that I was not commuting to Wandsworth, I was able to keep an eye on the changes we were making to Oaklands. Having been granted planning permission for the Oaklands extension, I had asked the husband of one of our staff to build it in the course of the coming year. He had dug the foundations and was progressing to the brick walls. Each morning I continued to liaise with my authors so that their books would appear on time. I was able to see more of our children. Each night they had stayed awake until I was back, and I had always read them a bedtime story.

Now I was able to share a car-run to school. On one occasion I was standing with the two boys waiting for their lift to arrive when Lord Murray – Len Murray was now Lord Epping Forest – plodded up Albion Hill, silver hair flopping above his red cheeks. We chatted. We talked about Scargill. He said: "He hasn't the discipline to be a Stalinist and to say 'This is the bottom line'." Matthew was holding a violin case. The car arrived as we talked, and Murray helped him in and said (thinking of my mother), "Playing the violin is a Hagger thing". I found him a nice fellow, craggy-faced and creased and seemingly broken-nosed.

I was still carrying forward my poems and was interested to read in an *Essex Countryside* of 1977 in a doctor's surgery an article, 'Has Essex a Housman?' It was by Frederic Vanson, and said "that Lakeland has Wordsworth, Suffolk Crabbe, Wessex Hardy, Ayrshire Burns, and Glamorgan Dylan Thomas. 'Who is thus to be identified with Essex?' So far there has not been produced a distinctive Essex poet who can encapsulate the character of the county, its great fields, enormous skies, forgotten villages, low estuary coastline, busy Thames side, and windswept hamlets. This is the Essex I now need to reflect."[30] I was aware that I had an opportunity to reflect Essex in my poetic work.

Jack Wood's book on unions
I applied myself to my publishing. I went up to Manchester to see Jack Wood, formerly of the Transport and General Workers Union, who had a plan to revive British industry, was in touch with Tebbit, and wrote Tebbit's Law. Jim Prior, Secretary of State for Employment from 1979 to 1981, against Wood's advice left out a "six-pickets-only" clause and let in the mass picketing of the miners' strike. Wood had a rugged face with a red wound under an eye from a fall, and I noted he had a craggy honesty and integrity and a Cromwellian drive against financial corruption: "A fearless Cromwellian bruiser.... He knocked [Frank] Cousins out at a meeting.... A Cromwellian who has found his way back to the forces of the King."

I also visited Tomlin at 31 Redan Street, London W14. He was sitting in his study at the top of his house with his leg up, suffering from phlebitis, and I sat with him and discussed the one-volume edition of his two works on philosophers. I met John O'Sullivan, who was writing eyewitness material about Mao's expulsion of the Chinese missionaries from China. I also met Gorka, whose book on Hungary dealt with Philby. I spent time editing Tomlin's and Gorka's books.

A new group, 'Heroes of the West', and McForan

But my most pressing book was McForan's *The World Held Hostage*, which dealt with international terrorism and Gaddafi. I spent a day, 20 February 1986, with the moustached and bespectacled McForan in the Charing Cross Hotel's Rendezvous lounge on the first floor, which I called "the Oak-Tree office". We could arrive soon after 10 and have regular coffee, a sandwich lunch, and then tea, and stay until 3.30, talking confidentially at tables while the likes of Roy Hattersley came and talked nearby and went. I combed through McForan's book. It had many revelations, including Gaddafi's attempt to build rockets with a nuclear warhead near Sebha by hiring ex-Nazi V-1, V-2 and V-3 rocket scientists from Argentina, which was prepared to sell plutonium.

McForan had been and asked the terrorists who funded them and had come up with some original answers, quite different from the answers offered by columnists who had not left their newspaper offices. McForan told me that Pope John Paul I was murdered to keep the power of the left in the Vatican; and Pope John Paul II had been shot as a warning following his letter to Brezhnev. He told me that Gaddafi had organised the attack and got Carlos to spirit Agca away.[31] He told me that an intelligence agent, code-named 'The Babysitter',[32] was supplying Gaddafi and the international terrorist movement with arms through Heathrow and bringing them through customs to pass on to terrorists. That was what he had learned from some of the terrorists.

I was concerned to extricate Universalist ideas from Communism. In "the Oak-Tree office" at the Charing Cross Hotel I told McForan, reiterating the idea I had put to Crozier, "There should be a new group like the 'Martyrs of the East' who will stand up to the enemies of the West. The group might be called the 'Heroes of the West'." The name stuck. I told him, "The Oak-Tree authors are Universalists who stand for freedom from the Soviet menace. The 'Heroes of the West' stand up to Communism and dicta-torship, which plan to subvert the Western way of life."

I spoke of our operation to defend the West as a 'Heroes of the West' operation. I told him: "The 'Heroes of the West' will counterbalance the 'Martyrs of the East'. We are trying to put an end to terrorism, to end the 50,000 acts of terror.... We need some recommendations for Reagan." I said that his book was a call to end international terrorism. And off the top of my head I dictated a dozen headings (such as "Airports", "Airlines", "Exit visas"), which he scribbled down. I told him to flesh the headings out into a programme for action. (*See* p.223.) They appeared in Appendix VI of his book as 'General Recommendations'.[33] (*See* Appendix 9, p.941.)

The Fire and the Stones

I now returned to my book on the Light. I was clear that I had to consider the Light in relation to civilizations: "The Light is a phenomenon which is found in all religions from 3,000BC to today. It is found in all civilizations and has assisted their growth and survival. We need it in Western civilization today. So a full study is not just of the experience of the Light… but of the Light in its civilization, proceeding civilization by civilization, and then seeing what happens to each civilization as the Light disappeared, and… what is happening in Western civilization/European civilization today." I would focus on "the separation of European culture from the Light and its consequences".

I considered that all living civilizations may flow into "a world-wide civilization", and drafted a "flow-chart of all civilizations, their offshoots and affiliations, from 3,000BC on". I wrote of "the coming Universal Age" and said:

> I have to prove a connection between the growth of civilizations and the flourishing of the Light, and the collapse of civilizations and the disappearance of the Light…. The Light gives energy, which is poured into a civilization…. My world view is of a coming Universal Age, in which there is a world-wide oecumenical-based civilization.

In a tree image, I wrote: "The Light is the sacred sap which was in the arts and withdraws as the civilization becomes brittle…. The Light spurts a civilization into energy and action (growth) and it dwindles when the Light dries up in its higher religion." My very full *Diary* entries at this time anticipated this theme of *The Fire and the Stones*.

I also thought hard about culture:

> Culture ('self-cultivation') of the individual is dependent on that of the group (arts/science), class and that of the society, the total being civilization. Cultural disintegration is disintegration of the classes, i.e. separation of strata… and fragmentation of culture at the… group level so that the artistic sensibility and religious sensibility are divorced from each other and impoverished. Culture is all the activities and interests of a people, and religion and culture cannot be separated…. Excessive scepticism can cause a civilization to die…. An excess of cultural unity is barbarism; [an excess] of disunity is decadence, *élites* being isolated from each other and departmentalised (*Two Cultures*)…. The unity of European culture (i.e. Western civilization) is when artist, poet, politician, labourer have a culture in common in a healthy society/civilization…. When a culture is healthy there is a healthy contemplative life…. In the disintegration phase it is the rebel against scientific

materialism who keeps the civilization growing.

I wrote of "the long tradition of the Light which has shaped Western civilization and contained it.... Contact with the Light is contact with the metaphysical purpose."[34] I worked on the connections between ancient religions and the Light, exploring how the Light began in shamanism and moved from culture to culture, and I traced the classical thread of Western civilization from classical Rome through the Renaissance to the 18th century. This theme can also be found in *The Fire and the Stones* and its updating, *The Rise and Fall of Civilizations*.

In the Cotswolds: 'Winter Four-Sidedness'; 'Oxford Revisited'
More poems came. We spent a weekend with the boys in the Cotswolds at The White Hart Royal, Moreton-in-Marsh, a pretty village full of Regency windows where Charles I stayed in 1644. We drove through drifted, impacted snow two feet high in the ditches. Bounded by Stratford, Gloucester and Oxford, the Cotswolds nuzzled peaceful, rural villages, quaint buildings and antiquity. We had dinner at the hotel overlooking a fountain of icicles.

The next day we drove from Moreton to Broadway, a picturesque 18th-century village with an enormously long street, on to Evesham and across the vale to Winchcombe, Chedworth Roman villa (which had a mosaic of cloaked Winter with a Roman-British hare) and the wild-life park at Burford, where we saw penguins being fed. We went up to Bourton-on-the-Water, whose petit-Venetian bridges were low over the Windrush, and then on to Stow-on-the-Wold, a wide square with a medieval cross and stocks and a church where Cromwell locked up a thousand Royalists in 1646.

Soon after, a blue car in front of us swerved across a red car, careered into a stone wall, flew through the air, turned over three times and ended up in a ploughed field, its windscreen smashed, steam rising from the battered bonnet. The driver lifted two pieces of wall from his lip while his wife sat, stunned, bleeding from her nose. Meanwhile the red car swerved towards our car and in a split-second-decision I continued my course, and he swerved back and avoided me. We were within inches of being wiped out. I parked, ran back and encouraged the injured couple while the ambulance came and their hideous wounds congealed.[35]

On the way home we went to Oxford and walked round Christchurch and then the Worcester College gardens. We skated on the lake and went on to Port Meadow beyond Southmoor Road in a biting east wind that froze our cheeks, noses and ears. People were skating where the Thames had overflowed onto the grass, and Binsey Green was visible from the tow-path. We lunched in the Randolph. I later wrote 'Cotswolds: Winter Four-

Sidedness' and 'Oxford Revisited'.

'Heroes of the West': The Executive Intelligence Review *again on Philby, the US-Soviet 'Trust' and its Head Victor, Lord Rothschild*
I was invited to lunch by the fellow from *The Executive Intelligence Review* who had told me: "Philby was a Trust man." We discussed this further over our one-to-one lunch. He told me: "Ever since Lenin, the US-Soviet alliance, 'the Trust', has carved up the world – hence Yalta. Force X [another name for 'the Trust']... brought down the Macmillan Government through the Profumo affair.... The Head of Force X is Victor, Lord Rothschild.... There has been a US-Soviet alliance to run the world since Sidney Reilly, and... confrontation is phoney.... [There was] co-operation between East and West all through the Cold War, to maintain spheres of influence.... Fleming fictionalised the Trust as Spectre (James Bond's Third Force, Force X)."[36]
As Head of Heath's think-tank Rothschild was instrumental in handling Heath's response to the miners' strike of 1973–74 and in mistakenly choosing the election date which lost the Conservatives the election. If he was the fifth man, there might have been a Soviet role in Heath's fall from power.

Lord Whitelaw at dinner
I now met Lord Whitelaw again at a dinner at the Commons. Lord Whitelaw, Mrs. Thatcher's no. 2, was the guest of honour. He arrived and stood near Ann and me. When any famous person first arrives there is a general stand-off until the ice is broken. That is the time to have a chat. So I asked him what he would like to drink and bought him a Cinzano. I reminded him about my FREE idea, told him about my publishing programme, about the Scargill book and my call for an end to international terrorism through *The World Held Hostage*, and described the work of the 'Heroes of the West'. I said I had been told who the fifth man was. He immediately invited me to see him in Downing Street. Biggs-Davison approached and said he wanted me to visit him at the Commons. Later, after Whitelaw's speech, seeking to clarify the US-Soviet alliance run by the Trust, I asked a question, "How does the Government perceive the Soviet Union under Gorbachev?"

'Question Mark over the West'
I thought deeply about the Soviet Union. I had heard at *The Executive Intelligence Review*'s conference that the Soviet Union was planning a *Blitzkrieg* in Western Europe in 1988/89. (*See* p.208.) I had also heard that the Soviet aggression was phoney. The snow was thawing and huge drips splashed down from the gutters. At night there was a slight frost, and "a question mark in the heavens (the Plough)".[37] The Plough looked like a question mark amid the stars. On 15 March I spent a night staying with my

cousin Richard and his wife in the large house to which they had just moved in Haslemere in Surrey. We walked to Birchhill Copse and the next day to Henley Common. I wrote 'Question Mark over the West'. The question mark "like a sickle" in the night sky in that poem catches the worry I felt about the true role of the Soviet Union and the future of the West, in view of 50,000 acts of terror and Gaddafi's Soviet-backed hostility towards London.

Poems written in Stratford-upon-Avon and Warwick
Poems were still coming. In May Ann and I went to Stratford-upon-Avon for a weekend. We stayed at the Moat House Hotel across a strip of water from the theatre. There was morris dancing on the green. Some 250 morris dancers had gathered and different groups cavorted and leapt and twirled, flapping white handkerchiefs and looking intent in their fine clothes and flowered hats. Walking among a stag, a badger, a bear, I "felt the writer in me stir, a buried, forgotten life under all this outer organisation of letters and phone calls".

I went in search of Shakespeare, who allegedly left Stratford for poaching on Charlcote Estate – Sir Thomas Lucy may have been satirised as Justice Shallow – and was away from his wife until his return in 1610, when he wrote *A Winter's Tale*, which we saw. We visited the house of Shakespeare's mother Mary Arden, his birthplace, his school, his wife's house, New Place where he retired, his church, his daughter Susanna's house and the house of Nash (who married his granddaughter). I saw the death of his son Hamnet as beginning a dark phase in 1596 and wondered where his papers went after his death. I wrote 'In Shakespeare's Stratford: The Nature of Art'.

I look back on this visit with affection as I did not doubt that the author of Shakespeare's works was Shakespeare of Stratford, and this instinctive belief was unpolluted by claims that one of more than 70 others had written the works, a confusion I would have to work through in the late 1990s. On the Monday on our way back from a visit to Warwick Castle, on which I wrote another poem 'Castles in the Air', we went to Lucy's Charlcote and looked through railings at the "beautiful Avon-side house".[38]

'Heroes of the West': eliminating Gaddafi's missiles near Sebha
Gaddafi had been involved in the miners' strike. Roger Windsor, the NUM's Chief Executive, had secretly visited Libya between 22 and 26 October 1984 to discuss Libyan support for the British miners,[39] and Libya was close to the Soviet Union, having received a US$12 billion arms contract from Moscow in 1976 along with 12,000 Soviet military advisers. McForan's book revealed that Gaddafi had installed the West-German company OTRAG

south of Sebha which since 1979 had tested missiles that could reach London, Paris and Bonn; while since 1975 Pakistan had been making an atomic bomb at Chasma which Libya would own. McForan and I, the two main 'Heroes of the West', were appalled at Gaddafi's ability to strike at London, Paris and Bonn with potentially nuclear weapons, and at Gaddafi's involvement, along with the Provisional IRA, in the Brighton bomb of 1984 which was intended to wipe out the entire British Government. (In February 1985 Gaddafi had attempted to blow up the entire Chadian Cabinet in much the same way as the Thatcher Cabinet.) I had ended my editing of McForan's book by writing in: "The West must stand up to the anti-Western terrorists."[40]

At the Charing Cross Hotel Des and I discussed what to do. We agreed that we must get the book to President Reagan through a correct channel. Des had a contact, Shmuel Moyal of the Embassy of Israel in London, who could act as a conduit.

He made the arrangements. We met one morning in London (on 24 March) and went to Swiss Cottage Holiday Inn. We took great care to ensure we were not being followed. We walked past and then into our rendezvous, met our contact, explained and handed over an early copy of the book with the pages on Libya's rockets flagged. Our contact assured us that it would be on Reagan's desk within 24 hours. We were escorted out by an armed girl in her twenties who walked half a mile with us to make sure we were safe.

I was full of foreboding that my defence of the West might lead to my death: "If there is a Providence that sees the civilised world through, my death will have been an unnecessary waste. But if there has to be a struggle on the part of human agency to preserve the spiritual values, and if one has to take risks because nothing is guaranteed, as I believe, then my death will have been necessary, for my generation must not fail.... I will have died for the preservation of Western civilization.... It is a mixture – a partnership – between Providence and human agency that keeps civilization going."

I was waiting for something dreadful to happen. On 4 April I went to the Mystics and Scientists conference at Winchester and busied myself with my publishing. I had coffee with the biologist Rupert Sheldrake and his wife Jill Purce on the Saturday morning. I showed Sheldrake the typescript of Tomlin's book, which became *Philosophers of East and West*, and after lunch he came back to my room and for one-and-a-half hours we discussed a book I might publish, to be entitled *The New Teleology*. It would include "Tomlin, Sheldrake, Bohm, astronomy, art, cultural movements, politics, educational theory, theology, technology, medicine, literature... and the common ground, *telos* being 'end', 'goal' or 'purpose', a synthesising of all the disciplines".

Immediately afterwards that Saturday afternoon I went to Winchester

Cathedral, which I had briefly visited on my way in, and I wrote a poem, 'Ode: Counter Renaissance'. I wrote of the "tradition of the secret Light" and of "the world-wide Baroque culture". I was feeling my way from a pro-Western position to Universalism: "It is not a civilization but the whole world that needs to be unified – we are shifting our perspective from Europe to the whole world, which is embraced in one unitive vision and common culture."[41]

I did not realise it but my poetic vision was being proclaimed at the Winchester conference. I left the conference early on the Sunday to call in again at Winchester Cathedral, to hone my poem, and I missed Sir George Trevelyan's winding up. He quoted my essay on Romanticism. He wrote to me: "I used a fine quotation from you in my final talk at Winchester. I had at some time copied it into my little book of quotations and it said exactly what I wanted about the real significance of the Romantic Movement. I was sorry you were not there but I acknowledged it to you."[42]

In the Lake District: news of the raid on Libya, Universalist poems
I still had a sense of foreboding that bringing Gaddafi's rocket terrorism to Reagan's attention would result in dreadful consequences. On 14 April we went to the Lake District to stay with my Uncle Reg in High Newton, a grey village with grey stone walls, grey slate roofs and grey curling smoke against a sweep of green hillside and crows. We drove to Grange-over-Sands, to the house of a friend of his overlooking the quicksands of Morecambe Bay, a 1750 coach-house from when the coach crossed the sands. We drove on to the Cumbrian hills, past a Roman fort and Scafell to

Blea Tarn House, where Wordsworth's Solitary lived. Ann took a picture of me sitting with Blea Tarn House in the background, a Solitary sitting on rocks where Wordsworth's Solitary used to sit. Minutes later I returned to the car, switched on the radio and heard news that American F-111s based in Suffolk had bombed Libya. I described this in my poem 'At Blea Tarn House'. After hearing the news I was more solitary than ever.

Nicholas with the cottage of Wordsworth's Solitary in the background minutes before learning of the bombing of Libya on the radio, 14 April 1986

We went on to Langdale and Grasmere, visited Wordsworth's grave and then drove on to Dove Cottage (*see* my poem 'At Dove Cottage'), and then walked up to the small tarn where the Leech-gatherer sat. We drove to Rydal and the stream with stepping-stones on the way to De Quincey's Fox Ghyll, which Wordsworth stepped across when he went to Ambleside. We returned home via Kendal and Kirkby Lonsdale, a grey granite village under green hills.[43]

When we got back to High Newton I was shocked to see pictures on the television news of America's raid on Libya. According to the television reporter Israeli intelligence had helped to plan the attack and the American F-111s had taken off from Britain with Mrs. Thatcher's support. I stared at the ruins on Uncle Reg's screen and knew immediately that McForan's book was the cause of the raid, that F-111s had flattened the base near Sebha besides bombing Tripoli and Benghazi.

That night I thought deeply about the West: "Paint the treasures of Western civilization, the Ionas and abbeys, the Marvell and Wordsworth places – the heritage of values, so that true values can be found in the *corpus*." This was the embryonic idea for *Classical Odes*.

The extreme situation inspired a flurry of Universalist poems: "April 16. Awoke early and sketched, sitting on the edge of my bed in the large front bedroom upstairs at Reg's house, stanzas 3–11 of a poem I had started yesterday ['At Blea Tarn House'], on the active and contemplative life: the way the two can be united in art as the Solitary... [writes a contemplative] poem on terrorism and therefore acts against Gaddafi". I also wrote 'The Artist' after seeing W. Heaton Cooper in his studio: a "Lakeland artist who relates earth and sky and gives what we see a pattern of relationship – and therefore a meaning".

We went to Ambleside, passing the stepping-stones by the Rothay near Rydal; and to Cockermouth where the end of Wordsworth's garden overlooked the Derwent. We visited Aira Force waterfall. We went to Ullswater – Place Fell or St Sunday's Crag – and passed where Wordsworth saw daffodils (Glencoyne Park) and where he stole the boat (Devil's Chimney [or Stybarrow Crag]). We crossed Kirkstone Pass through cloud.

The next morning I "awoke early and wrote two poems, 'Inner Power' about the Rothay stepping-stones near Rydal;... and 'The Power Within the Mind' (or: 'At Aira Force Waterfall'), which is my 'Kubla Khan' – a metaphysical Baroque 'Kubla Khan', not a dreamy (opium-dreamy) Romantic one".

My foreboding about the raid on Libya had turned to a nagging sense of dread, which I expressed in 'At Cartmel Priory: Taming the Unicorn'. April 17: "Began today... by going to meet Cedric Robinson, the guide of the quicksands... at his 700-year-old farm... and then went to Cartmel Priory Gatehouse, Hawkshead (Wordsworth's school), Grasmere... and Ambleside, where I saw the grim office where Wordsworth was distributor of stamps 1813–43, wasting all those great energies – his Garratt Green." We returned home after climbing Jenkins Crag above Ambleside with Anthony. The next morning I wrote: "April 18. Awoke early to write 'At Cartmel Priory: Taming the [Unicorn]', with the image of Gaddafi the unicorn caught by an oak-tree."

Confirmation that evidence in McForan's book caused the US raid on Libya
It was confirmed that the 'Heroes of the West's' initiative in bringing out McForan's book had caused the attack on Libya and Gaddafi's nuclear plans when, on 17 May, McForan and I "met Moyal of the Israeli Embassy at the Swiss Cottage Holiday Inn". A 4-man surveillance team scrutinised McForan and me before 10.30. During our meeting in the foyer of the Holiday Inn Moyal told us that while 40 planes were publicly admitted to, 55 planes were involved in the total operation: 20 went to Tripoli and 20 to Benghazi, while another 15 had gone to the base near Sebha and set back Gaddafi's nuclear plans. I wrote: "It is now confirmed.... Des's book caused the raid on Libya, I have struck a blow against Gaddafi and the anti-Western forces."[44]

According to Brian Davis's 1990 study, *Qaddafi, Terrorism and the Origins of the US Attack on Libya*, which does not mention Sebha, there were 77 planes, a mixture of F-111s and A-6s, and the cause of the attack, which may have been a pretext, was the Libyan bombing of a Berlin nightclub, La Belle, where US military personnel were present. Nine F-111s each dropped four 2,000-pound laser-guided smart bombs on the Bab al-Azizia compound, and Gaddafi was lucky to survive.

Gaddafi claimed that his adopted daughter was killed in one of the raids on Tripoli. There is no doubt that the planes were trying to kill Gaddafi but it subsequently came to light that his adopted daughter was still alive in 2014, having lived out of the public eye since the raid. At the time I felt that although Gaddafi's revolution had taken my daughter from me, I had not wanted him to lose *his* daughter. Nevertheless, he could not be allowed to threaten the West with nuclear rockets. The 'Heroes of the West' had again influenced world events and struck a blow against the centre of international terrorism. I had wounded the fearsome fire-breathing chimera from the air, like Bellerophon on Pegasus, and had stopped Soviet expansionism's mouthpiece Gaddafi from terrorising the West with nuclear fire.

Kathleen Raine and Tomlin
I was still waiting to see Lord Whitelaw. I was now immersed in my publishing. I had sent Tomlin's book, *Philosophers of East and West*, to Kathleen Raine in the hope that she would write a Foreword. She rang and said: "I find the book brilliant but deplore the omission of Plotinus, Eckhart and Schelling, the Neoplatonists." She said: "I am on Yeats's side, not Eliot's. The only traditional thinkers are Dante and Blake, for they used tradition as

'truth absolute' – Blake was a traditional thinker in a heretical age – whereas Eliot's alternative view of tradition is of a row of statues to which the artist adds himself. European Christendom is a strait-jacket, and although Tomlin reflects the East he wears the strait-jacket as Eliot did."

She agreed that Tomlin is the Whitehead of our time, a teleologist. I wrote: "He puts down all that philosophy has been, and does not select like Leavis in accordance with his own way of looking. Kathleen Raine lives in an intensely abstract world of traditions and theories – for someone who believes in the 'other mind'."

I visited Tomlin on 25 April. I found him sitting dome-headed in his high-up study in Redan Street. We discussed Reality. "The philosopher must get out of his study among organisms," he said, "for we are animals rather than Raine's spirit." At that point we were disturbed by the reality of a gasman. (The previous time I had visited him, the great philosopher had been unable to decipher a telephone message from the London Electricity Board and had to get his wife to hear the answer to his question, "Yes, but can an electricity man come round in 15 minutes?") Tomlin's theme was that "our sense of mutability gives rise to a sense of immutability, the many give rise to the One, multiplicity is multiple organisms.... We are part of Nature." Tomlin said he was Aristotelian (like Sheldrake) whereas Raine is a Platonist, and he agreed with me that the metaphysical "beyond" is "behind", behind Nature. He said: "The rehabilitation of metaphysics depends on its new alliance with the new biology.... There must be an after-life, otherwise there is nothing."[45]

I worked from 10 to 2.30, sitting at his desk while he sat in an easy chair with his leg up. We stopped for chats about his reminiscences of Eliot and Toynbee over coffee, over a working lunch beautifully arranged and served by his wife (who used to work with Crozier on *The Economist*), and over tea. At the end we discussed the fifth man and, speaking as a 'Hero of the West', he said: "You ought to see the Head of MI5. Whitelaw will arrange it, I have no doubt."

'Heroes of the West': discussion with Lord Whitelaw on Victor, Lord Rothschild as fifth man, Thatcher uses my Recommendations on terrorism to end Soviet-inspired terrorism

I visited Lord Whitelaw in the Lord Privy Seal's office, 68 Whitehall, on 30 April to tell him about the fifth man. I waited in a waiting-room of law reports and green chesterfields, having entered from Downing Street, and was shown through ante-rooms to the Holy of Holies. "Very nice to see you again," boomed Lord Whitelaw, huge, stooping, jowly and bloodshot-eyed at 10 a.m., having just finished a meeting. He had commanded a tank in Normandy and had a powerful presence. We sat in huge chairs and I talked, and he sat and listened and made a note, dealt with it, then attended to my next item. "Des's book is going to the Cabinet Office Intelligence Unit, I am being put in touch with someone high up in the intelligence services."[46] This was the equivalent of Tomlin's "Head of MI5", and the person I would see would cover MI5 and the SIS so that I could go into detail regarding the fifth man. I discussed with Whitelaw the whole question of the fifth man and the information I had been given that he was Victor, Lord Rothschild, who, I had been told by my contact in *The Executive Intelligence Review* and by the Duke of Grantmesnil, had tipped Philby off.

I drew Whitelaw's attention to the 'General Recommendations' at the back of *The World Held Hostage*,[47] and he said, "Can I take a copy for Margaret?" I said without hesitation, "Yes." He left the room to photocopy the Recommendations for Margaret Thatcher, the Prime Minister, and returned later.

On 6 May 1986 I looked at the front page of *The Times* and nearly fell out of my chair. For there was an account of how the World Summit leaders in Tokyo, including Reagan and Margaret Thatcher, who was personally representing the UK at the Summit, had adopted a British plan to control terrorism. The itemised points echoed those I had dictated to McForan at the Charing Cross Hotel (*see* p.213). They were presented in a different order. (*See* Appendix 9, p.941.) I realised that an idea cuts across all classes and power barriers, and is a passport to the highest places.

"I had wounded the chimera"
The Moscow-inspired international terrorism of the 1960s, 1970s and 1980s more or less ended with the summit leaders' adoption of this British plan, partly because Gorbachev's attempted reforms had produced a less aggressive and hard-line Soviet approach to the world. It could be said that from that moment on Moscow-inspired international terrorism abruptly ended. Islam-inspired terrorism would resurface, but the Moscow-inspired phase had come to an end. I had wounded the chimera in its serpent's tail.

Once again the 'Heroes of the West' had intervened at a critical moment to change history. FREE, Scargill, Libya, the fifth man, terrorism – on so many burning contemporary and topical issues we had made a contribution. And though the politicians liked it, officialdom did not, as I would discover in July.

Raine and Imagination
I was still advancing the publication of Tomlin's book, and Kathleen Raine had agreed to write the Foreword. She wanted me to go and see her. On 1 May at 1.30 she received me at 47 Paultons Square and led me into a front-to-back ground-floor room. I could see the trees of the summery square

through the front window and, through an open window, camellias at the back. Her typewriter was on a table by the window. There were paintings and etchings on the tastefully-furnished walls and *bric-à-brac*. She made me coffee (herb tea for herself as she was not allowed to drink coffee) and I picked up Tomlin's proofs and put them in my plastic bag of butterflies. She wore a pleated skirt and had her hair done up. She had penetrating eyes, but there was a softness about her. She was not the imperious woman of a few years ago. *Temenos* had made her more tolerant.

We chatted about Barkingside where she lived, Cumberland, Oak-Tree, values, banks, how she was selling the furniture for *Temenos*; she wanted to bring out ten issues and then stop. Eventually I showed her my book about the Light, *The Fire and the Stones*. She said: "This is very important." I said it presented the tradition of those who had seen the Light, that they couldn't all be wrong, that it was something I had come across in poetry. She said: "Autobiography. I've had a similar experience and made it the basis for my autobiography. I call it Imagination." She saw her Imagination as the Light, but the Light that permeates the universe is more than the imagination. She had firm views: "The great shift that is required is against materialism." "The worship of technology is all wrong." I found her a very clear lady with a great softness, and an enchanting manner. I left at 2.30.[48]

Book on Epping Forest

I was thinking of bringing out a book about the Essex landscape: the Thames Basin, the Roding tributary, Clay Country, the ploughed fields, open spaces and rape-seed fields round the Rodings, the marshes, the Stour valley, the pretty villages, the farms. I would include the historical places: Greensted church, Queen Elizabeth's hunting lodge, Copped Hall (a ruin); Loughton camp with its pollards, Lippitt's Hill, the Strawberry Hill ponds, High Beach church, Waltham Abbey and Harold's grave; Chigwell School and the King's Head; Boadicea's (Boudicca's) Ambresbury banks. The trees were like roots in the mind. Epping Forest was a region of the mind.

I wrote: "Essex is different from the mountainous Lake District or craggy, country Cornwall. [It] is foresty (the Royal Forest and Willingale). We are all woodlanders at heart with our love of *flora* and *fauna* and our walks in the woods. But [Essex] is also flat, open, ploughed and marshy.... Loughton with its oldest house [nearly] 400 years old (Beech House) and 16th-century pottery near the Gardeners.... Get the area into poems: Oaklands as microcosm. Constable's Essex, the heart of England. Industrialised, commuter Essex and a wild Forest (murders, rapes and excitement). Catch the feeling and the atmosphere of the place – man alone in the Forest, man in a rural setting, the antiquity of history (Greensted and Waltham)."[49] All these places would come into my poems, and many of them were covered in

A View of Epping Forest.
News of Argie's birth found under church foundation-stone
One of these places, on which I wrote a poem, was Loughton Methodist
church, which I had attended as a boy. Argie rang to say that the
foundation-stone of the church had been lifted and a copy of the *Methodist
Recorder* was found with an announcement "To Mrs. G.H. Broadley…
twins" – the announcement of Argie's birth and the news that she had a
stillborn twin. Argie did not know of the existence of the church until my
father came to Loughton in November 1942. She told me: "I feel I was meant
to come to Loughton, it is all Providential."[50] She meant that her path was
preordained to lead her to a place that had been founded on the
announcement of her birth. Once again I detected a strange pattern in the
lives of the close members of my family.

Garratt Green
I had been so absorbed in advancing the publishing that I had barely given
Garratt Green a thought. I had to ring Martin Sinclair to make a request, and
he told me a new Head had been appointed from September. She apparently
came in and spoke to the Senior school for 50 minutes and was anti-racist,
anti-sexist and anti-classist, and the girls could go in for coffee on arrival.
She was applauded. She was pro-NUT. Sinclair told me: "I have an illness,
a disease – self-doubt and shyness about ILEA principles." He told me there
were tensions in the English Department, and that Mr and Mrs. Kay were
training lunch supervisors at £50 an hour at County Hall.

*Duke of Grantmesnil again on 'The Trust' (Force X) and its Head Victor, Lord
Rothschild*
There had been discussions among the 'Heroes of the West' about Force X,
and Riley and Gorka arranged for us all to find out more by driving to
Moreton in the Cotswolds (a return visit for me) to speak at greater length
with the Duke of Grantmesnil, the tousle-haired patrician and nobleman
who claimed to be descended from forebears going back a thousand years.
The whole conversation was connected with intelligence matters. He told
me that we went to war to stop Hitler from having nuclear weapons. He told
me that Gaddafi had threatened Britain and America with nuclear bombs
unless his demands were met: a unified Ireland, a dismantled Israel, and a
South-Africa surrendered to the guerillas. He said that Force X – Victor,
Lord Rothschild's force – was "the Third Force" that was neither Capitalism
nor Communism but a form of Fascism in which "far-right and far-left
meet".[51] He reiterated that Force X was behind the Profumo Affair – it
wanted to change the British Government – and was responsible for Philby.
Philby was pursuing the policies of 'Rothschilds' for Victor, Lord

Rothschild, who had been behind his defection to Moscow. Victor, Lord Rothschild was the fifth man.

I came away from our discussion pondering Philby's intention to name me in 1971. If Philby was so close to 'Rothschilds', had Victor, Lord Rothschild been in on the plan to name me? I resolved to research into Force X and my findings later appeared in *The Syndicate* (2004).

Launch of McForan's The World Held Hostage

The World Held Hostage was nearly ready, and the launch loomed. Towards the end of May Evelyn Le Chêne rang. I had last met her when she was an eyewitness of Josten's shouting at me. She said she was interested in *The World Held Hostage*, and might be able to arrange for the launch to be held in the Special Forces Club, of which she was a member. It had been founded in 1945 by surviving members of the SOE (Special Operations Executive) and had a close relationship with European resistance organisations, FREE being the latest. Biggs-Davison, who was also a member, had suggested that the launch should take place there, and I wondered if she had rung at his instigation.

We talked about Josten, and she said that after he had raged against me and after I had left he had asked her to sign the form he had wanted me to sign – I understood that she was being asked to sign my name – and she had refused. He had then made a number of vitriolic calls, notably to Crozier and Sir Bernard Braine, in the course of which "he got me into trouble with the Palace and reduced me to a typist". She had been reduced to a typist to punish her for not signing the form, and I presumed that he had further punished her by involving Buckingham Palace. She said: "You handled a very difficult situation – an unprovoked attack – with aplomb. Everyone says now, 'Here comes the lady who should be in the *Guinness Book of Records* for surviving 11 months with him.'" She said of FREE: "'Le Chêne' means 'oak' – from which our battleships were made. Josten started enthusiastically [with regard to FREE] but along the line the project changed and he ended discouraging." So now Oak-Tree's launching of a book to oppose international terrorism was supported by an 'oak'.

Evelyn Le Chêne asked me to preview the Special Forces Club for the launch. Biggs-Davison had reckoned that with its SAS connections it would be safe from terrorist attack. The Club was in a back street (Herbert Crescent) not far from Harrods, and there Evelyn Le Chêne introduced me to Clive, who had masterminded the SAS operation to end the Iranian siege. I had watched the ending of the Iranian siege with admiration for the daring of the masked SAS special forces, and now I was with their ringleader. I also met Mike, who had been blown up and was now in CI3. I examined the Staircase of Heroes, framed photos of legendary faces up the stairs which included (as she pointed out) her husband, a war hero.

I met Biggs-Davison to discuss the invitations to the launch. He insisted that Ian Greig should be invited, a name that meant nothing to me. I did not know why Biggs-Davison wanted him there. We discussed Josten. He spoke frankly about him now that he was dead. He told me that Josten had received £3,000 from Crozier as a retainer for obtaining material from behind the Iron Curtain, including translated material from Radio Free Europe. We agreed that Josten had obstructed and torpedoed my Scargill launch and was linked to Winston Churchill's cancellation, and we wondered if he had turned up along with Braine to save it to make me see how much I needed him.

I said I thought Josten had been working for the KGB, having allied with Russians against the Nazis. I wrote: "Biggs-Davison, embarrassed by all that happened and all the State's efforts to crush me…, is now seeking to make amends following Josten's death." We discussed the idea that the Babysitter was the sixth man and linked to the Soviet Embassy.

I had given Evelyn Le Chêne an early copy of *The World Held Hostage*. She rang to say she had read the book, and that its blaming of Gaddafi for the Brighton bomb could be used by the IRA defendant who was about to be convicted and sentenced for the explosion. She said the case was *sub judice*, and that I should withdraw the book to assist the conviction. My Scargill launch had been subverted and torpedoed in suspicious circumstances, and now there was an attempt to subvert and torpedo a second launch. I rang Des, who said he would go to prison rather than withdraw the book.

I left a message for Biggs-Davison with his secretary, saying there was an issue and I did not want it to precipitate his resignation from the Special Forces Club. I visited Biggs-Davison in the House of Commons the next day. He had been up all night and his eyes were bloodshot. He greeted me with: "What's all this about *sub judice*? Is she mad or something?" I reminded him that one of the book's revelations was that Gaddafi was being sent arms for Carlos and other terrorists through Heathrow in the operation code-named 'The Babysitter', and that I thought forces who wished to keep this operation in place were discouraging the book. I pointed out that the attitude behind such an operation had already kept Gaddafi in power and lost Libya to him while I was there. I pointed out that torpedoing a second launch of mine would contribute to perpetuating Gaddafi's international terrorism, which Philby for one would want.

I did not then realise that powerful forces within the West connected with Force X and what I later called the Syndicate wished to do just that; that international terrorism, which was organised from behind the Iron Curtain and based in countries like Libya, had its conception and funding in the West.[52]

I was waiting for the launch of *The World Held Hostage* but school and family life went on. I held the Oaklands fête, which Vernon Davies and David Hoppit attended. I gave Hoppit a copy of the book to take back to *The Daily Telegraph*. I monitored my distributor. I gave tea to my new bank manager. I mowed the school fields and saw my two boys collect prizes at Chigwell School's Speech Day. I took them to watch Essex play Hampshire at Ilford, and they got Alan Border's autograph when he was fielding on the boundary near us. I had another patch on a lung and took antibiotics to fight off tiredness. An ex-Oaklands parent, Mrs. Clauson, had hired the Oaklands hall for a healing course on 21 June. It was taken by Matthew Manning, a well-known young healer, and I looked in on his sessions and was invited to have tea with him the next afternoon at the Clausons' huge house (since demolished) in Loughton High Road. We sat round the fireplace while Clauson ostentatiously mowed the lawn outside, demonstrating his practical priorities, leaving me alone to talk with Matthew Manning. I found him fairly monosyllabic. We had a discussion on energy and he commented on my *chakra*s, which he described as "red-hot". I wrote: "My own energy level is very great. I have red-hot *chakra*s, and need someone of less energy to neutralise me and relax me – but I also need great energy."

While I waited for the launch of Des's book, I pondered the source of the Light. I saw it in terms of the River Roding, across which I drove the boys to and from school. I wrote: "This part of Essex is lowland river valley with flower-rich flood meadows and marshes, flooded each winter…. Snipe and redshank…. The Roding flows into the Thames…. Where is the Roding's source?" The answer was: near Dunmow. I was tracking back the Light to its appearance in history "behind so many Western traditions and Eastern traditions": "[It] is superbly there in every man's consciousness to form the basis of a world-wide Western civilization that is moving against materialism…. Whatever tradition Westerners embrace… the Light is at its source." I had unwittingly laid down the spiritual basis for a coming Universalist World State.

While I worked on the launch – arranged to liaise with a police inspector at the Special Forces Club, organised the guest list and talked through the aftermath with Trevor and others – I heard a scream from next door, 4 Albion Hill, and went round to investigate. I entered Miss Lord's sitting-room. A colony of bats had somehow got into her house, and several bats were wheeling round and round the room: "Bats, wheeling and dipping and darting outside, and squeaking…. Miss Lord had five bats flitting round her sitting-room. They had come down the chimney." I grabbed a copy of *The Times* and rolled it into a tube. I "flapped them… and in a combination of forearm tennis smashes and cricket hooks stunned them and lifted them outside her glass patio doors with the newspaper and a cushion, little blind pipistrelle mice with folded-umbrella wings. As fast as I got them outside more came down the chimney and squeezed through the fireguard and got behind a picture, under a bookcase, in a chair – or just incessantly wheeled. It was an hour later, after midnight, when I got away to have my supper, her house clear. We had been investigating the crack in the fascia board under her eaves where they all lived and where they could be heard squeaking and chattering at night."[53] The next day I wrote a poem 'Bats'.

On 1 July I launched *The World Held Hostage* at the Special Forces Club. I put on wine and a finger buffet and with an SAS defensive presence the road outside was sealed off by the police "because Whitelaw's coming, the Government's number–2". The policeman repeated: "We've had instructions from Downing Street that he's coming." The invitations had gone out in Biggs-Davison's name and Julian Amery MP (who had intelligence links) had been secured to speak.

I greeted the legendary Lt. Col. Neil ('Billy') McLean, a former British Army intelligence officer who had led an SOE operation in Albania in 1943 and had returned in 1944 on a secret mission with a small team: 'The Musketeers' who included Major David Smiley, a regular soldier frequently seconded to MI6, and Capt. Julian Amery. The Musketeers attempted to overthrow the new Communist regime of Enver Hoxha by liaising with royalist guerilas loyal to King Zog. More than 100 agents sent into Albania at this time were betrayed by Philby, and are believed to have been killed. McLean and Amery had put into practice in Albania an operation parallel to the one I had proposed should take place in China, as I told them.

Many of those who had accepted my invitation to the launch did not appear, including Whitelaw. It was now clear that the launch had been subverted. It was a re-run of the Scargill launch – only Josten could not be held responsible this time as he was dead. Had he fixed it so I would "never work again" as he had told me he had? I wondered if Josten had not been responsible for subverting the Scargill launch.

Biggs-Davison introduced me. I spoke, detailing the revelations and called for the West to halt the Babysitter, subvert Gaddafi and snuff out international terrorism. (In fact, following the summit of world leaders in Tokyo which had implemented the Recommendations at the end of Des's book, international terrorism was already being snuffed out.) Then Julian Amery spoke, and finally Des McForan, moustached.

In the Special Forces Club with Des McForan (left) on 1 July 1986

Gorka, a fellow Hero of the West, lurked in the background. After the speeches McLean came across to me and congratulated me on my stance, as did one of my SAS minders. McLean died three months later, in November. I overheard Biggs-Davison and Amery agreeing that the book "sailed very close to the wind", that there were "too many revelations for officialdom's comfort", and that there would have to be official investigations into some of the allegations. The four or five journalists present interviewed us. I chatted to Andrew Lownie, a sharp, incisive literary agent who had said he might become an agent for Oak-Tree's books. I remember Des standing with Trevor Maher, Klaus (my East-German office manager who had a bookshop in Wembley), and me.

Des and I had allocated the rest of the day for interviews. We began with *Time Out* and shortly afterwards went to *TV AM* for a pre-booked interview. We sat in a glassy foyer with a garden outside, and the producer came and greeted us warmly, but then had to leave to take a phone call. He returned, upset, to say that he had orders from higher up not to proceed with the interview and that he had to comply. It was apparent that a similar operation to the one that threw silence round my Scargill book was at work, and that there was subversion. In spite of interviews at the launch by journalists representing several national dailies no article or reviews appeared, and I knew there had been interference from higher up. But who from?

Des now received two death-sentences from the IRA, both on the telephone. The 'Heroes of the West' had risked their lives to improve things for the West, and had been rewarded by being told in effect: "We don't want you to recoup your investment in your book." Determined to get to the bottom of the subversion, I made phone calls.

The first to report back was Paul Gorka. He said: "I lunched with someone from the British intelligence services who said, 'The intelligence services are engaged in damage limitation, in other words a cover-up following the raid on Libya [which had been precipitated by the book], while at the same time investigating the Babysitter [who was supplying arms to Gaddafi from Heathrow]. The instructions for the scandal-limitation were issued by middle-ranking officialdom.' It is like John Dean [who was involved in the Watergate burglaries and the subsequent cover-up] after Watergate, if you get any more publicity for the book it will expose the cover-up which could bring the Government down. There is gratitude for the revelations, and they are being acted on, but the cover-up must continue."[54] He made it clear that what was being covered up was the involvement of the author and publisher (McForan and me) in the bombing of Libya, including the bombing of Gaddafi's rockets near Sebha.

Norris McWhirter investigates and reports

I then received a call from Norris McWhirter, twin brother of Ross McWhirter who had been shot by the IRA man I had encountered in Wandsworth prison, Harry Duggan. Norris McWhirter said that Lord Whitelaw had asked him to see me. McWhirter was the "someone high up in the intelligence services" with whom I should discuss the fifth man.

I visited McWhirter at his office. He had enthusiastically praised my Scargill book and advertised it in his Freedom Society's publication, *Free Nation*. Now he told me, "I've made enquiries about *The World Held Hostage* through contacts, and the order has gone out to 'kill the book with silence'. The German word is *'Totenstille'*, 'death by silence'." (A better translation might be "deathly silence", which amounts to the same thing.) "Nikolai Tolstoy's book [*Victims of Yalta: The Secret Betrayal of the Allies – 1944–1947*] about the Cossacks being handed over to the Russians has had the same silent treatment." (Nikolai Tolstoy was the great-grandson of Leo Tolstoy.)

I protested that this was a wrong policy, which was against the West's interests. I said we were living in a democracy, and a publisher had every right to publish books on the state of Western civilization. I said it was undemocratic for hidden forces to be subverting my books when my books were standing up to the enemies of the West. I said the situation was outrageous and demanded an investigation into who was doing it and the immediate suspension of their policy which had resulted in the phone call to *TV AM* and the denial of publicity for McForan's book. I said it was simply not good enough to express gratitude for my stance and then to make it impossible for the books I published to sell, involving me in potential financial loss. That was a very strange way of being grateful. I was with him for two hours – and he listened intently while he sat at his desk and made extensive notes.

McWhirter then asked me if I knew who the fifth man was. I gave him a detailed account of all I knew and made a case for the fifth man's being Victor, Lord Rothschild. I pointed out that he had been at Trinity College and had known the Cambridge Apostles, including Philby. He had worked in MI5 during the war and had been in charge of Heath's think-tank when Heath was Prime Minister and I was Heath's unofficial Ambassador. (Rothschild presumably knew about me through that role.) I wondered whether he had been behind the subversion of Oak-Tree's books.

McWhirter recorded every detail of our conversation and promised to pass it on. He promised to go away and negotiate with "them" and report back to me.

A few days later Norris McWhirter rang to say he had negotiated a "deal" with the intelligence services. They would "neither confirm nor deny" that the publicity ban had happened; but would now allow "limited publicity" for the book. He said he was proposing to run a story in *Free Nation* that the intelligence services "would neither confirm nor deny that the Babysitter tried to suppress publicity for the book", and Eddie Shah, owner of the *Today* newspaper, would run a story. McWhirter said: "The Babysitter is now being smoked out." He had nothing to report on the fifth man.

McWhirter had reminded me of the Rainbow portrait of Elizabeth I (*see* p.xxii) in which the Queen holds the rainbow of the literary disciplines. The State held sway over all literary endeavours, and in some cases writers were only allowed to operate if 'deals' were negotiated. To me, the rainbow of seven disciplines straddled the sky, high above the puny affairs of state.

At first I was pleased at his call. By forcing the intelligence services to act against the Babysitter, I had secured the objectives of the 'Heroes of the West'. The 'Heroes of the West' had been responsible for the bombing of Libya, and were now exposing the secret British channel that had been supplying Gaddafi with arms. However, the book would still have to operate in handicapped circumstances of silence, and would be lucky to cover its costs. In the event, nothing appeared in *Free Nation* or in *Today*. The "deal" that we had done with the intelligence services did not seem to be operating.

I reported the "death by silence" to Biggs-Davison and to Julian Amery who, between them, reported it to the Prime Minister's office. I was rung up at 6.30 p.m. on 16 July by Christopher Monckton (later Viscount Monckton of Brenchley), an ex-aide to the Prime Minister who was now no. 2 on the *Today* newspaper. (He was the son of Sir Walter Monckton, adviser to Edward VIII during the abdication, Director-General of the Ministry of Information during the war and Eden's Minister of Defence during the Suez crisis.) He wanted to see Des and me urgently. Could we be at Brooks's, St James's Street at 7.30 p.m., in one hour's time? We could, and at this club I told him the story from start to finish until 9.45 p.m., in the course of which we moved to The Ritz. Then he abruptly looked at this watch and had to leave, I understood for 10 Downing Street. He wanted to meet us for breakfast at The Ritz at 8.30 a.m. the next morning.

He arrived bleary-eyed, having read *Scargill the Stalinist?* And *The World Held Hostage*, and placed his bowler-hat on the table until our breakfast arrived. He then took us back to his office, which was completely empty, no paper anywhere. He again put his bowler-hat in front of him, this time on his bare desk, and made a phone call. He said: "I shall write an article about it for the front page and I will get it through the editorial conference."

He rang Des at 12 to say he had got it through the editorial conference and that he would be visiting 10 Downing Street that afternoon. We could expect the front-page story within the next couple of days. I noted:

"Somehow, we are in the number–10 network."[55] To what extent this was due to Biggs-Davison and Amery rather than McWhirter I did not know.

Nothing appeared in *Today*. When I rang him to find out why, Monckton's attitude had changed. "The story was without foundation," was all he would say. He was implying that McWhirter's "deal" was without foundation. I did not believe this. The story clearly had *considerable* foundation. Clearly someone had countermanded the "deal" McWhirter had spoken of, and had subverted publicity in *Today* in the same way that it had been subverted at *TV AM*.

I now accepted that there was no more I could do. The Babysitter, the fifth man (possibly Victor, Lord Rothschild), an official in the intelligence services or perhaps even the Prime Minister herself (though I am satisfied from Monckton's initial reaction that 10 Downing Street knew nothing of the order to "silence", and was, indeed, shocked by the muzzling) – *someone* had ordered silence. Someone was grateful to the 'Heroes of the West' for their revelations but was concerned to reduce their impact and squeeze their financial position in a policy of subversion.

Eighteen months later *The Times* used "The Word Held Hostage" as a headline for their first leader,[56] demonstrating that the title had quietly passed into the English language, and there was a very favourable review of the book by Lord Chalfont, who worked with Jillian Becker. He said that it should be on the shelves of every military academy. But by then the early-sales drive was at an end.

Two launches of mine out of two had been muzzled and subverted, and I now knew that the time was coming when I would concentrate on being an author rather than a publisher walled round by silence.

I buy a computer

Before I could cease to be a publisher I had to bring out Tomlin's book, which was being launched in September. I spent another day with Tomlin and mentioned my relief that a book on philosophy would give me some respite from tangling with the affairs of State. Sitting in his upstairs room in Redan Street, we drew up a list of 70 guests, and I suggested Tuohy, who had known Tomlin in Japan. Tomlin immediately vetoed him. "He knows Skeffington-Lodge [a Labour MP in Atlee's post-war Government] in Brighton. With all the difficulty you've been having it would be unwise to have him." I wrote: "Then discussed traitors. Tuohy's name came up. I will feel sad if this was so." I did not believe that Tuohy was a Soviet agent, but felt that if he *had* developed warm feelings towards the Soviet Union (a British ally) during the Second World War, then the allegedly pro-Soviet Wittgenstein would have been more of an influence in trying to persuade him to work for the Soviet Union than Skeffington-Lodge.

Computers were now on the market. At Vernon Davies's barbecue for his 40th birthday at his great house where a cover had been thrown over the swimming-pool to keep out the rain, a live band thumped and the champagne flowed all night. I stood in the long queue for the gargantuan feast (salmon, prawns and many meats) behind Ian Bennett, an Oaklands parent who ran DPS Computers in Basildon, and Vernon, who commented that I was doing some publishing. Bennett asked, "Why don't you buy an Apple Macintosh computer from me, employ a typist to work at your dining-room table and run the Oak-Tree accounts and key in some of Oak-Tree's books?" The proposal seemed revolutionary as no one else I knew did this, and the accidental nature of the conversation seemed Providential. I said it seemed a good idea.

Later I went to the bathroom and found Vernon sitting alone nearby. I said, "You remind me of the Great Gatsby." He did not understand the reference, so I explained that in Scott Fitzgerald's novel Gatsby threw lavish parties and absented himself from his many guests. Towards midnight the 120 beautiful people at Vernon's cavorted and milled about, many inebriated, and several fell into the swimming-pool, including Vernon himself. He had gone from sitting alone like Gatsby to being the centre of attention in the floodlit night.

I came away from the barbecue with a completely new method of working. I duly bought a computer from Ian Bennett, and used it initially for Oak-Tree work but very soon worked with my typist as an author to key in the book that became *The Fire and the Stones*.

I was able to take up the 'death by silence' of McForan's book with Biggs-Davison at a ceremony at Loughton Methodist church. The old Methodist church which I used to attend had been demolished, and on Ann's birthday, 19 July, Argie laid a time capsule – I believe, including the copy of the *Methodist Recorder* with the announcement of her birth – under the new foundation-stone of the new Methodist church in the presence of an open-air audience seated on chairs. Matthew was at camp at Llandudno, but Ann, Anthony and I sat in the front row alongside other members of my family, including my sister Frances and cousin Richard. Biggs-Davison came and had a chat, and I told him: "There's a deafening silence around the book. It's not fair on Des, he's risked his life for the West." Biggs-Davison said he would speak to Amery. Nothing happened. I wrote a week later: "Why hasn't Amery got back? It's a deafening silence out there."[57]

Universalism: more Universalist poems

One half of me – the half that included my soul – was still literary, and I was delighted when we were visited by a friend of Ann's, Tanya, who had married T.S. Eliot's nephew by marriage (Valerie's nephew, Graeme

Fletcher). They both had tea on our patio looking up at Oaklands, and Eliot's nephew told me how he burned down his prep school at 13, and reminisced about Eliot.

Valerie Eliot's nephew
He said Eliot had a reserved pew at St Stephen's, Gloucester Road, and had bought him a James Bond car. "Eliot was fascinated by James Bond, and played with the car on the floor with me. He kept saying, 'See if its boot opens, see if guns appear.'" He recalled a conversation about *The Family Reunion*: "He said, 'I don't know if Harry pushed her, I only wrote it.'" He told me they lived in Kensington, and Eliot's idea of a treat was to take him to Dino's by South Kensington tube station, where I had often had coffee or lunch. "We'd sit in Dino's and he looked after me, made sure I had what I wanted." I said that Eliot was great because he embodied the European tradition and stood for the wisdom of past generations. He said: "He was a hypocrite, he was sentimental."[58]

Return to Stratford-upon-Avon: Shakespeare
While I waited to launch Tomlin's book in early September we returned to Stratford to see *A Midsummer Night's Dream*, and I intuitively grasped that the new bride of Copped Hall had commissioned Shakespeare's *Sonnets*:

> Theseus and Hippolyta being Heneage and Mary, Countess of Southampton whose marriage was celebrated in the Long Gallery at Copped Hall in 1594. The vision of spirits in the woods, i.e. Epping Forest: the Forest flowers including the blue "love-in-idleness" which influences sleeping eyes, and the musk-rose and eglantine.... 1594, Southampton became Heneage's stepson. The sonnets were written 1592–1594 according to one dating, so who put Shakespeare up to urging Southampton's marriage in the sonnets? Surely his mother? That is the key – 1594. After the wedding, Shakespeare was commissioned to write poems by Henry Wriothesley's mother. "Thou art thy mother's glass and she in thee/Calls back the lovely April of her prime"(sonnet 3). The idea that Shakespeare lived outside London during the plague [in] 1591–1593. How he lived in Silver Street..., with a Huguenot family.[59]

I did not check the dating of the sonnets in Stratford, I merely recorded the perception that came to me that Southampton's "onlie begetter", his mother, urged Shakespeare to write the early sonnets. Once again I came away from Stratford feeling closer to Shakespeare the Stratfordian.

Tour of Western Europe: 'A Pilgrim in Europe'
I knew I had to write a poem about Europe about a journey along a modern Pilgrim's Way, contrasting the spiritual depth of the past with modern noise. The same journey would take in many of the contested towns and battle-grounds of the Second World War and would be preliminary research for my epic poem *Overlord*.

And so in early August I took Ann and the two boys on a whirlwind tour of the Continent. We drove to Ramsgate and crossed to Dunkirk, where the sun glinted on abandoned cranes and water where our army waded out, and we drove through Flanders' poppied field to Brugge, or Bruges, which by night was magical: full of canals, moated medieval walls and Baroque buildings. There Carolus Haggar may have lived before he settled in Chelmsford in c.1366.

We found accommodation near a windmill, drank wine in the main square and looked at the 'Halles' (market halls) and Belfry. The next morning we walked to the Basilica of the Holy Blood: we started downstairs in the 12th-century chapel of St Basil amid chanting and I gazed for a long time at the Grail cup on two flagstones. We went upstairs to the Chapel of the Holy Blood, and in an ineffable atmosphere as Mozart played softly I sat and gazed at the altar of the Holy Blood which contained the phial of blood reputedly collected by Joseph of Arimathaea and brought back by Thierry of Alsace from the Second Crusade. I felt sublimity and peace and a sense of my spirit free and soaring, having progressed from earth downstairs up to these heights in this double chapel. I pondered the Holy Blood upstairs and the Holy Grail downstairs. We walked by weeping willows to the Church of Our Lady, as the Belfry gave us a carillon of 47 bells, and saw the spoked Light above the altar.

We drove on to Ghent and St Bavo's Cathedral, and I looked at Hubert and Jan van Eyck's *Mystic Lamb*, the Light rays streaming from Heaven. I felt close to the vision of the Light during the Crusades and in van Eyck's day.

Next we arrived in Holland. Amsterdam was full and we somehow stayed with a family in the Consulate of Madagascar in Rooseveltstraat, and ate between Dam Square and Centraal Station. We took a canal trip in a glass-topped boat and passed many Baroque fronts and visited Anne Frank's house and her hiding-place behind a movable bookcase. We went on to Rembrandt's house where he lived from 1639 to 1658, the years of the English Civil war; and went bankrupt in 1656/7. I detected the start of the Baroque in his portraits and dynamic life. We went on to the van Gogh museum and I saw *Wheatfield with Crows* (1890) in the original.

We drove on to Germany and stayed in Bonn at the Hotel Beethoven by the Rhine, near Kennedy Bridge. We ate in the open by the Town Hall. There were swarms of midges on the outside of the hotel windows, and swarms of birds flew down the Rhine. Next morning we walked to Minster Basilica where I saw Christ on a rainbow above the altar and spider-web-tracery stained glass. There was a great silence before the monstrance. We went on to Beethoven's House and saw Beethoven's personal musical instruments and learned about his growing deafness from 26 to 47.

We went on to Luxembourg. We stopped at Echternach and visited the tomb of Saint Willibrord, the first Anglo-Saxon to missionarise and evangelise the Germanic tribes. We went on to Luxembourg City, which rises round a ravine, and stayed at the International Hotel opposite Central Station. The next morning we toured Luxembourg, a city built on a gorge, fortified over the years with beetling walls that make it impregnable, and riddled underground with 17 miles of tunnels (the Bock) so that troops could be moved around in huge quantities without the enemy seeing, which we visited.

We drove via Bourscheid castle in the Ardennes and to Brussels. We stood in the Grand Place and looked at the nearby Manneken Pis, and then stayed at Waterloo. Next morning we toured the battleground: the Wellington Museum, where Wellington heard news that Blücher would join him and resisted Napoleon's advance on Brussels near Waterloo, held the line until Blücher arrived. We stood by the lion of victory, the mount near where Gordon fell, where Wellington surveyed the battlefield amid the shells, and by the monument to Lord Uxbridge's amputated leg. From the lion I could see that the English, Dutch, Belgians and Prussians were on the left and that the French advanced up the road from the right. We visited the house where Napoleon spent the night before the battle in a green bed; the headquarters he used; La Belle Alliance where Wellington and Blücher met (100 metres to the south). I absorbed the images of futile wars. We then drove via Lille to Dunkirk and caught the 5 p.m. ferry.

I again had the idea for the poem that became 'A Pilgrim in Europe': "In the car queue, waiting to drive onto the Sally Line ferry, had the idea for a great poem on Europe: on the past and present." I added: "A poem to be drafted on the meaning of Western civilization in Europe. Through juxtaposition of images, contrast the town non-values with the enduring heritage to be found in Cathedrals and the countryside – the true values which have nothing to do with profit-making or wars." I noted images I would use: the Holy Blood, something preserved (Bruges); the Mystic Lamb – Light from Providence (Ghent); also the Light above the pulpit (Bruges). The Baroque (Amsterdam canals); and the vision of Rembrandt and van Gogh (energy in fields, swirling stars, flaming cypress etc.). The creative force was contrasted with the opposing destructive force of wars: Arnhem, where the Cathedral was destroyed; Echternach (Luxembourg), where the top was destroyed during the Ardennes offensive; and the Bock, where troop movements fended off the invader. Finally Waterloo, the destruction of so many fine people. I identified "two forces: the creative, healing, enduring force of Christ and the Light ('*Lux*'embourg) and the destructive, assertive force of wars, money-making, the newspapers; and of the darker forces". I wrote: "Christ and the Devil represent these two forces. Overall image for Europe: St Michael v Dragon (in Luxembourg)".[60] The two forces symbolised by Christ and the Devil found their way into *Overlord* nine years later.

I had deepened my knowledge of European culture and moved further towards Universalism. 'A Pilgrim in Europe' would not be written until 6 November.

Fishing in Cornwall

Back in Essex, we went straight down to Cornwall and stayed with Ann's mother. I threw myself into the book that would become *The Fire and the Stones*. The air relaxed and energised me, and I read up on megaliths, Eleusis, Pythagoras and Scandinavian mythology. I wrote: "Have been to Charlestown twice – calm seas, mist, familiar setting – and to Par beach yesterday, where I was windburnt.... Mornings work, afternoons beach." I read on *yin* and *yang* and Taoism and observed:

> Balance and harmony, in a garden. I have the Taoist Garden and an awareness of opposites (cf my 'Silence'), and I deplore the lack of balance and lack of harmony with Nature in Western life: the hurry, the industrialisation that takes away from Nature, the unbalancing power-seeking and time-taking and influencing people. I would like to live like a hermit in my garden.... This is why I like Cornwall: as soon as I arrive there, the balance and harmony return.

I observed: "Civilization has lost its true balance, because it has lost the value of being close to Nature and is too materialistic." I wrote of "my sense of opposites in 'The Silence' and my reconciliation of them: "*yin-yang-Tao*.... The Taoist ideas in 'The Silence'."

I had to spend days on figures and spreadsheets, but I knew poems were imminent. We went to Mevagissey and I noted "the calm sea, boys plunging into the harbour" and received pleasure from "branches against the sky and twigs". We went to Fowey and Polruan and walked to the 15th-century castle. We had tea in the Singing Kettle and I wrote: "A tortoiseshell strayed in and I caught it in my hand and let it go outside, bringing all conversation in the full café to a halt and leaving many smiling." We returned to Fowey and took the boat from the main square down to Golant. I wrote: "Passed the ferry and Daphne du Maurier's ivied house, to Golant, and the church of St

Sampson on the brow of the hill, behind trees."[61] I would set the title story of my collection *Wheeling Bats and a Harvest Moon* there. The next day we went to Gunwalloe and I "wrote 'At Gunwalloe: the *Tao*' during a golden day sitting on the beach near the church; watching the waves break on the distant rocks". I was still writing the beginning of the book that would become *The Fire and the Stones* and noted, "I am progressing towards a whole vision of civilization."

The next day at 6 a.m. I went out fishing from Newlyn with Ann's cousin Stephen, his business partner Anthony and the fisherman Kingsley. We dropped two nets off the Lizard and another four in deeper water, 17 miles from Newlyn and 6 from the Lizard: three-quarters-of-a-mile-long tennis nets of Japanese mono-filament with floats at each end and weighted with chains to suspend them seven feet above the bottom, which was 35 fathoms deep (210 feet). I saw a pilot whale with a curved fin humping up and down seven times 50 yards away. We caught 30 or 40 monk, 20 ray, turbot and brill (both brown, spotty and flat), 4 lobsters and a crayfish: some £500 worth of fish at the present good prices. Anthony had a very swollen knee and felt giddy, and lay down. I put on oilskins and took his place, hauling the top part of the net – Kingsley did the weighted bottom – over the bar after it coiled off the winch. We threw the offal out into the sea for the common gulls, a Manx sheerwater, a shag, three fulmers, a kittiwake and many scavenging black-backed gulls.

The fishermen gave me tips: "Monk drown in the nets if the tide is high: not enough oxygen to flow through their gills." "The sail keeps the boat steady, keeps its head to the wind so it goes up and down and not from side to side, and gives a better platform for working." "Ray will bite your finger and suck it in." "The old fishermen steered by course and time and the sun to find their nets." Kingsley told me: "Always look the way of the wind, Nicholas." He said a shower was coming, and he was right. I steered back to harbour, turning now to leeward, now to windward (now to port, now to starboard), now to left and now to right. "Don't fish when there is a tide as the currents at the bottom flatten the nets, which only stand up 6 or 7 feet anyway. They get full of seaweed and contain no fish, and they foul through being dragged along the ground." When I returned home "the floor was lurching like a boat" and I observed that "I totter and stagger like a sea dog". I drafted a poem 'The Fishermen: God's Plan'.

While I waited for Tomlin's launch I carried on my research for what became *The Fire and the Stones*. I worked on the early Church in Britain and the Grail, and considered the early Gnostic belief that we have been sent down from "a world of light into an inherently evil world". I wrote: "Oak-Tree's image should now be one of restoring a purpose in religion and philosophy, i.e. bringing about a Metaphysical Revolution." I took this aim upon myself as I moved towards becoming an author instead of a publisher. I wrote an introduction to the metaphysical Tomlin's *The Tall Trees of Marsland* (which I never published) and then went for a walk by Charlestown harbour. "The tide was very high, at least seven feet, and the sea crashed onto the shingle which gave a displeasing hiss while the boys threw stones at each dark curl of a wave. Water lapped up to the harbour stones which stood opposite the pier." I took Ann and the boys to visit Marsland where Tomlin had lived, and found Tall Trees at Gooseham Mill: up a muddy lane beyond a stream, and empty. I wandered round Tall Trees peering through windows at where my boss had lived in Cornwall. "We went on to Morwenstow, and visited the churchyard and found the eccentric Parson Hawker's hut on the sea-cliffs."

I had been thinking about the need for a Metaphysical Revolution: "Get the metaphysical idea into our culture." The next day "on a rainy day, without undue preparation 'out of nowhere' [I] typed the last part of the conclusion to my book on the... Light.... The secular and metaphysical." Now I had to "take each civilization in turn and prove the life cycle of the... Light within it".

On our last day in Cornwall I went to Charlestown at 7.30 p.m. "A green sea, stormy, and huge rollers that washed over the pier and crashed onto the shingle, dashing spray over our rocks and up the cliff and smashing against the concrete breakwater at the top of the beach. All action and movement and dynamic energy – so different from the calm of two nights ago, the still." I made one last visit to Charlestown at 11 p.m.: "Still a hugely high tide – still up to the wall. I was the only human around (drizzle in the wind) and the light on the pier was out and as I walked to the end, braving the spray, I could not see farther than 40 yards into a dark sea (no moon, no stars, no light) and on the large moundy rocks which I could hardly make out the white foam was luminous – all I could see in the dark as I peered was the breaking white foam across the bay. A very exciting elemental prospect."[62]

Launch of Tomlin's Philosophers of East and West
On 2 September I held the launch of E.W.F. Tomlin's *Philosophers of East and West* at the Athenaeum Ladies' Annexe, downstairs among the sofas. About 40 attended. I spoke for 10 minutes, about Oak-Tree's probing of Western values and Tomlin's contrast of 5,000 years of a metaphysical tradition with the anti-metaphysical Vienna Circle and called for a change in philosophy, for a Metaphysical Revolution, to achieve which was part of the work of the 'Heroes of the West'. I compared Tomlin's role to Whitehead's as an original philosopher to have written about other philosophers: "This book is his *Science and the Modern World*." Tomlin, who was very fidgety, spoke next. He went off to his briefcase to look for his speech and returned without it. I said

to him, "You must speak without notes as I did," which he did. Then Kathleen Raine spoke, mentioning Plato's Philosopher-King. The guests included Kathleen Nott; the Chinese Cultural Attaché; Andrew Lownie, the budding literary agent who sat on the sofa beside the Attaché; and John Ezard.

The next morning Kathleen Raine rang ("It's Kathleen"). She repeated that politics cannot solve our problems, that it all comes down to value-systems:

Nicholas at the Athenaeum with E.W.F. Tomlin and Kathleen Raine holding books and John Ezard between them at the back on 2 September 1986

"Plato in the *Republic* asks, what is good for society? It isn't materialism and computers and atom bombs – that's not what's good for society. We have to start again." She said that all the political parties are wrong. Ezard rang and said, "All our bureaucrats read Plato at school, and they still get it wrong." I was clear that the West is living by wrong values, but that Communist values are worse.

Nature walk along the Roding
The following Saturday was warm, and I took Ann and the two boys to walk by the River Roding with Mabel Reid. It was a glorious late summer day, not too hot, and we walked two miles from the bridge in Roding Lane past the humped-back bridge to the bridge near the end of Oakwood Hill. On one side of "our Avon" were "willows; on the other, thistles with bearded seed, and purple loosestrife and nettles. A flock of whitethroats, a pipit." I saw viper's bugloss, teasle, burdock and purple mallow, which reminded me of Spengler's comparison between mallow and a civilization, and many red haws on the hawthorn bushes. We went back to Mabel's house in Albion Hill for tea and a walk in her walled garden. "Eight newts in her pond (one great-crested), no walnuts because the birds had eaten them (shells underneath), one quince on her quince tree but many mulberries on her mulberry bush – we all ate one. 'Lovely jam.' 'Yes, but actually it's a year old.' (My face set the boys into giggles.)"[63]

Expansionism: challenging Tehran Agreement on Soviet sphere of influence
Preparing for launch of Gorka's Budapest Betrayed: *Jessica Douglas-Home and Roger Scruton, Krassó's petition for democracy, Bukovsky*
I now had two books to distribute, one on international terrorism and one

on philosophy. Much of the day-to-day Oak-Tree effort on these books was laid at my door. Addresses were keyed into the computer I had bought for a mail-shot, and I personally tramped round the London bookshops, delivering copies of McForan's and Tomlin's books to Foyles and Waterstones and other booksellers. In early September my compilation of Jack Wood's papers (extensively rewritten by me) came out, *Union for Recovery*, a radical plan based on his experience in the Transport and General Workers Union for workers to work fewer hours, achieve greater productivity and reverse Britain's industrial decline by having harmonious industrial relations. I spent hours on the telephone organising the transfer of books and liaising with my distributor.

I now threw myself into launching Paul Gorka's *Budapest Betrayed* (Hungarian English edited by me), which stood up to Philby and the KGB he represented. The book narrated how Gorka was betrayed, tortured and imprisoned prior to the 1956 uprising, which allowed him to escape to the West. The Hungarian resistance network (like the Albanian resistance) was betrayed to the Soviet forces by Philby (with help from Burgess, Maclean and Blunt), who caused 45 victims to be executed between 1949 and 1953. All had been involved with the Western intelligence agencies, and their association with the West resulted in their execution. (Their names were listed in an appendix.)

Biggs-Davison booked the launch in the Palace of Westminster and arranged for Julian Amery, who was known to have links with the SIS, to speak again. I had agreed to bring out a Hungarian version of the book to implement the idea behind FREE: to reach Hungarians behind the Iron Curtain and call for Hungary to leave the Warsaw Pact and join the European Union. Not speaking Hungarian, I left all questions regarding the accuracy of the language in the Hungarian version to Paul Gorka. Nevertheless, I found that bringing out a book in both English and Hungarian was time-consuming.

About six weeks before the launch Jessica Douglas-Home, Charlie's widow, rang and asked if she could join "your Hungarian day, to give advice". I knew of her interest in Iron-Curtain countries, and I wondered if she had been put up to ringing me by someone like Crozier and was acting on behalf of an organisation. She invited me to dinner at 63 Hillgate Place, Notting Hill Gate, the family home she had shared with Charlie before he died in a charming road of 1850s houses built for railway workers, each painted a different colour.

She arrived from Oxford at 7 just as I arrived, and I spent an hour with her drinking white wine and discussing the guest list. She proposed two or three Hungarians, who Gorka vetoed later on security grounds. I said I would invite the Prime Minister. She said, "Yes, invite the Prime Minister, but I don't know Julian Amery – can you ask him to invite her?" We discussed *Scargill the Stalinist?* And she told me that her late husband had kept the book on his desk at *The Times*, and had written many leaders from it; that the book was underlined and much-thumbed, and had comments in the margin. Eventually we went downstairs and ate beetroot soup, meat casserole and rice, followed by cheese and red wine.

At 8 Roger Scruton appeared, open-necked shirt and in rimmed spectacles, and we talked at length. I raised the question of FREE with him, and of sending 'freedom-fighters' into Eastern Europe. He said: "Unless they're parachuted in, they'd be betrayed. It is so well sewn-up they'd be betrayed and killed." I thought this conclusion unnecessarily pessimistic and defeatist, and told him that his reservations had helped prevent FREE from happening. Scruton asked if I would bring out a book he had compiled about the thinkers of the left, and said that I should reach a decision soon before he and Jessica offered it to Sherwood Press. He said, "It will get you a lot of publicity, for it will be attacked." Meanwhile Jessica brought in a pair of hens and nursing them in turn cut off their wing feathers with scissors. Scruton said: "You're mad, Jessica." She said, "They're pets, now they won't fly over the wall." Later her son rang and asked about Fascism for an essay. Scruton briefed him, *in loco parentis*. I left them to it as they had an hour's work to do.[64]

I took my publishing drive to Frankfurt on my own. It took me all day to arrive there because Gatwick was closed due to fog and the company I was flying with had ceased trading. I was reallocated to Heathrow and eventually flew Pan Am. I arrived at the Messe at 5.30. There I booked accommodation in a flat. Later I walked through the dark to a nearby restaurant that served magnificent steak and peppers under swords on the walls. Next morning I went to the Messe by tram. By the end of my stay I had interest from 35 different companies in the US, South Africa, Israel, Australia and Singapore, each of which wanted a copy of one or other of the books I had published. As a result of this visit there were American and Singapore editions of *The World Held Hostage*. But I had to send 35 letters or parcels. I was too busy with publishing chores and longed to get back to my own writing.

I returned to England and attended an Oaklands parents' annual general meeting. The next day I had an unexpected visit from Nadia, who was staying in Dulwich. She looked relaxed and glamorous, and we walked round the grounds. She came again the following day, a sunny, golden October day. We drove and walked to the Strawberry Hill pond with sandy gravel banks and an uprooted tree in whose network of roots she once crouched. The water was still rather dank. We drove on to High Beach church, the church in the Forest. I noted the neo-Gothic medieval style of its spire and hammerbeam roof. We looked at the runic stone, which quotes *Beowulf*.

One of my ideas for implementing FREE had been to petition the Eastern-European governments for democracy. After my visit to the Duke of Grantmesnil in Moreton I had said to Paul Gorka at one of our 'Heroes of the West' meetings in his house: "I don't see why someone doesn't organise a petition of Iron-Curtain names calling for democracy." I said: "Whoever does it should act as if they are free and move freely and blatantly collecting signatures from key people in the Eastern-European regimes." Paul Gorka had put this to one of Hungary's leading dissidents, György Krassó, who had subsequently organised a petition from 122 Eastern Europeans from Hungary, Poland, Czechoslovakia and East Germany without being betrayed or killed (contrary to what Roger Scruton had told me).

I attended a press conference at which a Hungarian-Romanian accord was announced (Paul Gorka representing Hungary) and met Krassó. I wrote: "My idea got across to Paul after we visited the Duke, and Paul got it across to Krassó…. Krassó, white-haired, smiling-eyed, a believer in his cause, a latter-day Lenin. At one level, the overt, there is a declaration, a demand for democracy. At the covert level he can organise disturbances and resistance. He has the eyes of a revolutionary. He is a Robespierre." In Krassó I saw that my FREE idea could still find some expression, and I put the idea of FREE to him. He reacted very favourably and enthusiastically, and said he would introduce me to the leading Soviet dissident, Vladimir Bukovsky, who was based in France where he was engaged in stockpiling arms to subvert the USSR.

The next day Vernon Davies invited me for lunch and proposed a restructuring of Oak-Tree Books with a role for him. We had a glass of wine in his huge sitting-room overlooking the lawn and were then chauffeured in his new BMW to the Chinese restaurant in Abridge, where we were the only lunchers: crispy duck rolled in pancakes eaten with fingers, sauce dripping through; sweet and sour pork; chicken and cashew nuts; and prawns – and Chablis. Vernon suggested that I should go in with another publisher to profit from their distribution. He would be Chairman of a company that published "less sensitive" books. I wondered if Oak-Tree could be converted into a trust into which American money could to poured, with Vernon as Chairman, and could launch a new magazine, *Western Review*. (In the event, he did not become Chairman and I had to pay for the lunch as he had forgotten his wallet.)

I was still writing poems, and the latest poems came out of a weekend we all spent in Glastonbury. We had a long drive through lashing rain and did not arrive at Street until 11. We were fed soup and a cold salad (the night porter huffing and puffing). The next morning we drove through rain to

Glastonbury and thence to Wookey Hole, the model for the geography of the Roman Hell. We saw the papermill and went on to Cheddar Gorge, In Gough's cave we saw many stalactites and stalagmites. We drove on to Priddy, where Jesus reputedly spent time at the Roman lead mine. We went on to Wells and visited the Cathedral, and had tea at the place where William Penn addressed 3,000 from a window. I drafted 'In Gough's Cavern, Cheddar' and 'Paper like a Tongue'.

The next day, 26 October, was fine. After breakfast we went straight up the Glastonbury Tor. It was very windy, and we had a spectacular view. We descended to the Chalice Well. I felt very poetic and scribbled images sitting in the shade, looking up at the Tor. I was invited to look over Tudor Pole's house, including his 'Last Supper' room. We went on to Gog and Magog: we walked down a track and climbed over a stile and saw the two surviving 2,000-year-old oak-trees with very wide trunks. We went on to Joseph's Holy Thorn on Wearyall Hill. Joseph of Arimathaea landed by boat, and from that spot (where he was weary) one gets a good idea of the isle of Avalon: Wearyall Hill, Chalice Well, the Tor and sea-water all round. (I thought there must have been a semi-submerged causeway to Pomparles Bridge.) We lunched in Glastonbury, then hunted in vain in the churchyard of the parish church of John the Baptist for Joseph of Arimathaea's tomb, and then went to the Abbey, where I dwelt on the Lady Chapel and Arthur's resting-place. We went on to Bridgewater and thence to Nether Stowey. I saw the house where Coleridge wrote 'Kubla Khan' and 'The Ancient Mariner'. We went on to Watchet, a port on the Bristol Channel, the setting for 'The Ancient Mariner' with its lighthouse, hill and Methodist church. We returned via Alfoxton House (now a hotel) where Wordsworth wrote *The Prelude* and lived with Dorothy on the legacy from Raisley Calvert. We returned with reddened faces from the wind and sun.

That night I drafted three poems: 'By the Chalice Well, Glastonbury', 'The Romantic Revolution' and 'Gog and Magog'. I also researched into Joseph of Arimathaea's tomb and established that it was inside the church. The following day we found Joseph of Arimathaea's altar tomb (with the initials J.A.) in St Katherine's chapel in the Glastonbury parish church of John the Baptist, called Christendom's biggest secret. It had been moved into the church from the churchyard in 1928, having been removed from Mary's chapel in Glastonbury Abbey some time after 1662. We went on to Templecombe Templar Church and saw the medieval face of Christ on a wall. [65]

The 'Heroes of the West' had stood up to Scargill, international terrorism, Gaddafi and Philby, all enemies of the West. But their independent stand had not been supported by the State. Each book had involved an ordeal in which the State, at the very least, was an accomplice of the Soviet Union, concerned not to offend the Soviet occupiers of Europe who had been given Eastern Europe at Tehran during the Second World War. There had been obstruction and subversion.

On 2 November I talked with Sir Bernard Braine. Gorka took me to 55 Exhibition Road for a "solemn commemoration" of the 30th anniversary of the Soviet crushing of the Hungarian Revolution. I sold copies of Gorka's book at the door. Then "Sir Braine" (as Gorka referred to him) and Winston Churchill spoke. A fire-alarm of great stridency went off, which threatened to drown the speeches, and there were mutterings that deliberate sabotage – subversion – was at work. Later I shook hands with Churchill and noted that he "gripped my hand hard and said 'Nice to meet you'". I sensed that Biggs-Davison had briefed him on the difficulties I had had. I discussed the US and Soviet spheres of influence with Sir Bernard Braine, who confirmed that the superpowers had reached a deal in Kissinger's day that the world should have "spheres of influence" and that the US would do nothing to disturb the *status quo*. (This was what Biggs-Davison had told me when I first met Whitelaw.) "Any attempt to do that would be obsolete and dangerous," Braine told me in an obvious echo of Josten's position, abjectly bowing to the Kissinger deal and to the wishes of the KGB. I found this position unnecessarily defeatist, and said so. I sensed that Josten's secrecy regarding FREE and his addressing me in letters as 'Arthur' were to contain me and prevent me from challenging the Soviet rule in Eastern Europe.[66]

Afterwards I talked with Krassó, and he asked me to obtain a travel document (in lieu of a passport) for him, and political asylum. I duly wrote a letter to the Foreign Office on his behalf, pointing out that his 122 signatures for democracy in Eastern Europe might have put his life at risk. A few days later I heard the news from Gorka that Bukovsky was founding an East-European Resistance Movement – inspired by my idea of FREE – and that Gorka and Krassó would be the Hungarian representatives.[67] FREE was becoming a reality to Eastern-European dissidents introduced by my 'Heroes of the West' author Gorka.

Launch of Budapest Betrayed: *my live broadcast into the USSR on FREE, Prime Minister of Polish Government-in-Exile, Sabbat, on my challenge to the 1943 Tehran Agreement on Soviet sphere of influence and to British foreign policy since the war*

On 4 November I launched Gorka's book in the Jubilee Room at the Palace of Westminster. The Hungarian flag was draped over the front table and Ann was at the books table. The 60 guests included representatives from every Iron-Curtain country, and there were two bearded Afghans, one of whom looked like the youthful Osama bin Laden, who was then fighting the Soviet occupiers of Afghanistan and had visited London with his half-brother

Salem in mid-1986 (staying at the Dorchester Hotel) to purchase anti-aircraft missiles.[68] I spoke at some length with both of them. (It would indeed by bizarre if Osama bin Laden had attended my anti-Soviet launch as he would be a main character in my poetic epic *Armageddon*.) The leader writers from *The Daily Telegraph* and *The Times* were present, together with a specialist at *The Guardian*, Jessica Douglas-Home, Ian Crowther (representing *The Salisbury Review*, which I had been asked to run the previous December) and Vernon Davies.

The five speeches were broadcast live behind the Iron Curtain by the BBC World Service. This was the approach Margaret Thatcher had outlined to me in 1976 when I briefed her on FREE. Biggs-Davison spoke first about my "campaign", meaning FREE. Then I spoke directly to the Eastern-European and Soviet audience about the need for resistance to the USSR, and called for a free Eastern Europe and a reunified Eastern and Western Europe. I broadcast FREE into occupied Europe and called for a revolution to liberate the oppressed from tyranny. I called for FREE, Freedom for the Republics of Eastern Europe. I entered into combat with the frightening chimera.

I denounced Philby's betrayal of British agents in Hungary and drew attention to the list of 45 who were executed as a result.

In the Palace of Westminster (left) Nicholas proclaiming FREE behind the Iron Curtain on the BBC World Service on 4 November 1985, challenging the 1943 Tehran Agreement with a worried John Biggs-Davison looking on; and (right) with Paul Gorka on the same day

I found it exhilarating to denounce Philby live when he might be listening – he did not die until May 1988 – to pay him back for planning to name me in September 1971.

Julian Amery, Churchill's son-in-law, then supported my vision of Europe. Then I introduced Krassó, "the Leninist genius", and, live in a broadcast that was reaching into the Soviet Union, described his petition of 122 calling for democracy, which had implemented my FREE. (In my thinking, it was right to apply Leninist tactics to overthrow Soviet totalitarianism and the Gulag for British-style freedom but wrong to apply Leninist tactics to overthrow British freedom for Soviet totalitarianism.) When Krassó had spoken I introduced Gorka.

As usual several MPs who had accepted did not turn up, including

Winston Churchill. However, Virginia Bottomley MP came; her father, John Garnett had written the Foreword to Jack Wood's book. We had not invited Sir Bernard Braine as he would have regarded the occasion as too "dangerous". The Prime Minister, Margaret Thatcher, did not attend, but that morning she had sent me a message of support. I was rung by Julian Amery's secretary, who told me that the Prime Minister had rung her to say she was sorry she could not attend but that she sent her best wishes.

Did our broadcast behind the Iron Curtain contribute to the fall of the Berlin Wall? Who knows.

The Prime Minister of the Polish Government-in-Exile, Kazimierz Sabbat, was present and as I helped him on with his coat at the end he said to me: "When I became Prime Minister of the Polish Government-in-Exile [on 8 April 1986] I had the intelligence services under me and I found out something which is not in the history books. Near the end of the war there was a deal between the superpowers in Tehran – it was confirmed at Yalta – involving the present Winston Churchill's grandfather. It condemned the East Europeans to slavery, and the West abided by the deal when Hungary was invaded by the Soviet Union in 1956 just as the other side abided by it in relation to Suez. You are to be congratulated. You have just challenged that deal and the entire British foreign policy since the war, which has been wrong. I want to shake your hand." Sabbat left. (He died in 1989, still Prime Minister of the Polish Government-in-Exile.)

Sabbat had confirmed the deal that Biggs-Davison and Braine had mentioned. I had struck a blow at the chimera's belly, which had devoured Eastern Europe. It dawned on me that the reason my books were surrounded by silence was that I had challenged the Soviet sphere of influence in my Scargill book and, through McForan's book on international terrorism, the British Foreign Office and its hidden apparatus.

I was shocked – if it was true – that Churchill had *given away* Eastern Europe to Stalin rather than grudgingly put up with its occupation. But the deal cannot be laid at Churchill's door alone. It was more Roosevelt's doing. I glimpsed why Winston Churchill MP had not attended, for I was challenging his grandfather's order. (I had admired – indeed hero-worshipped – Churchill during the war and had been proud to implement his vision in Iraq, and I believed that after 40 years of 'spheres of influence' Churchill himself would have been on my side and on the side of change.) FREE had subverted the Establishment's legalistic, unvisionary determination to hold in place the Stalin–Churchill–Roosevelt agreements in Tehran and Yalta and perpetuate the past rather than bring change.

Gorka was delighted with the evening and said he would introduce me to Otto von Habsburg, the heir to the Austro-Hungarian and Holy Roman Empires. Ann and I took the Gorkas to dinner. Mrs. Gorka understood our stand against Philby and the KGB. She said to me: "You will now be on a [Soviet] blacklist, you will be the first to be hanged when the Russians come to London. You are exposed now. Your children will never get visas to Hungary or Russia." Although it was only three years before the dismantling of the Berlin Wall in 1989, it seemed – not just to Mrs. Gorka, but to Sir Bernard Braine and Roger Scruton as well – that Communism was unassailable. I said: "When, not if, *when* Communism falls we will have red-carpet treatment there." The Gorkas left the restaurant hand in hand. Later I wrote: "I have done my duty…. I may now be allowed to get back to my own work…. I have challenged the division of Europe by the two super-powers, and want to see a reunited Europe re-emerge."[69]

I had expected to pay for the drinks consumed at the launch, but the account was never presented. Somewhere out there I had an ally, a friend, who would not declare himself or herself, who picked up the tab without letting me know. I wondered if it was Crozier, or Sabbat; or Margaret Thatcher, who approved of my use of radio to challenge an old order that had lasted 40 years. It is worth noting that after my stand Mrs. Thatcher made letting Eastern-European nation-states into Europe a part of her European policy, and introduced a number of Eastern-European leaders from the platform at a Conservative Party Conference.

Once again the book was surrounded by silence. Despite the presence of the leader writers from *The Daily Telegraph* and *The Times*, and the *Guardian* specialist, no reports or leaders appeared. I received a letter from Andrew Lownie defending the role of the British intelligence service and stating there was no evidence that Philby had belonged to it. I saw his letter as a British denial of responsibility for the 45 executed Hungarian British agents. I wrote back defending the position of the book, and forfeited Lownie as Oak-Tree's literary agent.

I looked at the state of Oak-Tree's finances and the prospect of further silences round my 'Heroes of the West' books, and resolved to return to poetry and my book on the Light. An insurance man had visited the Oaklands estate and valued it, and I discovered that I was now a paper millionaire in the course of pursuing my path. I had had more trouble with my lungs, and I wrote: "The Light will look after my lungs and my bank balance if it wants me to do its work – something I believe implicitly which is akin to trust in God. For the Light *is* God."

But there were repercussions from my talk with Sabbat. I had often told Gorka that we needed a meeting of exile representatives of all the Captive Nations, and following the launch and my rapport with Sabbat I urged Gorka to convene a meeting. With the approval of Sabbat Gorka and I went to the Polish Government-in-Exile, 43 Eaton Place, London, for a gathering of exile representatives that included the Head of Radio Free Europe. I was the only Briton present. Thinking of the 122 East-European democrats, I asked the leaders present: "What can Radio Free Europe do to help *them* [i.e. the 122 democrats] liberate themselves from the Soviet, occupying power?" I was again challenging an old order that had dominated Europe for 40 years. The Head of Radio Free Europe spoke of non-interference and non-liberation, of presenting "facts" and not propaganda. The real answer to my question was 'very little, under the present policy'. I again urged the formation of a committee that would implement FREE under Polish super-vision. I was attempting to turn the passive outlook of members of the European Liaison Group into a more proactive, revolutionary force, taking advantage of Sir Bernard Braine's absence.

I met Bukovsky on 27 November. He, Krassó and Gorka were at 55 Exhibition Road. Bukovsky had been one of the first to expose the use of forced-treatment psychiatric hospitals for special prisoners in the Soviet Union. He had spent 12 years in Soviet prisons, labour camps and psychi-atric hospitals, and had been exchanged in Switzerland in 1976. I found him an immensely likeable, straight-talking Russian who spoke fluent and excellent English and thought about a number of points I raised. I wrote: "As a result of our meeting, which I chaired, Krassó's dissidence will flow into Bukovsky's Resistance International, which is to have a new initiative, the FREE movement." If Biggs-Davison or Crozier had introduced me to Bukovsky at the outset, the idea of FREE would have spread through Eastern Europe in the late summer of 1984. It so happened that on that very day there were questions in the Commons about Victor, Lord Rothschild's being the fifth man.

I now heard that Tomlin was in the Charing Cross Hospital in Fulham Palace Road after having a prostate operation. He sent me a message: "I miss my sherry." He asked if I could bring him some. I was surprised that the great philosopher should be dependent on alcohol, but he had been my boss and was now an author of mine, and so I took him a bottle. I wrote: "He looked flushed, with a fever from an infection which gave him a thrombosis that morning, the day after his prostate was removed; it was dispersed by water poured down his tube, which was sticking out of his pyjama trousers. The great philosopher sitting up in bed with a tube sticking up between his legs." I "put the sherry bottle I had brought in by his bed".[70] He hid it under his pillow so the nurses would not see. I recalled first reading his two books on the great philosophers while I was at Oxford. It was unthinkable then that I would smuggle a bottle of sherry to his bedside and watch him hide it under his pillow.

Thatcher outs Victor, Lord Rothschild as fifth man, his denial
There were repercussions following my naming of the fifth man. On 3

December 1986 I was astonished to read a public letter by Victor, Lord Rothschild to Mrs. Thatcher, the British Prime Minister, in the newspapers. It was carried on many front pages with banner headlines: "I am not, and never have been a Soviet agent."[71] This was a direct response to what I had told Whitelaw and McWhirter and followed a lengthy interrogation of Rothschild by Scotland Yard. Mrs. Thatcher at first publicly declined to give him the ringing endorsement he sought. The 'Heroes of the West' had again stood up for what was right by not tolerating the influence of someone about whom allegations had been made.

The furore over Victor, Lord Rothschild's public letter was intermingled with the outcry caused by the British Government's decision to ban the publication of *Spycatcher* by the MI5 official Peter Wright. It was being said that the Government had decided to suppress 'sensitive' books like Wright's. It seemed that Gorka's book may have been put on a 'sensitive' list. Gorka had told me that he was allowed to write about events before 1956, so I could not attribute the "stay-away" from the launch to the Government's decision. It looked as if Gorka's book had been wrongly placed on a 'sensitive' list.

The following October both Ivor Stanbrook, MP, and my contact in the Cabinet Office gave me the impression that my 'Heroes of the West' books were victims of the Government's drive against Wright, and that this was the reason for the silence surrounding them. I did not believe this as my Scargill book had come out long before Wright's book had been brought to the Government's attention.

I now read that Mrs. Thatcher and Peter Wright together cleared Victor, Lord Rothschild, of being the fifth man. I was puzzled, and happened to speak about it to Andrew Lownie. Lownie, who was very well informed, told me that Rothschild had confessed to being the fifth man and was offered a deal, and turned. Wright's friendship with Rothschild was based on this confession, and (from Rothschild's view) on Wright's being used to clear his name. So Wright and Thatcher had cleared Rothschild to confuse the Russians.[72] This was further confirmation that what I had told Whitelaw about Rothschild was right. I had again slashed the chimera's serpent's tail.

Although it appeared that Victor, Lord Rothschild had fended off the accusation that he was the fifth man, in 1993 six retired KGB Colonels in Moscow confirmed Rothschild's identity as the fifth man to author Roland Perry.[73] According to these six ex-KGB front men I was right. Meanwhile (in 1989) John Cairncross had been identified as the fifth man by the KGB defector Oleg Gordievsky (who had been in the Soviet Embassy in London when Scargill visited it in 1984). (*See* pp.171–172.) Cairncross was undoubtedly a Russian spy who handed over more than 5,000 documents, but he always said he was unaware that Burgess, Maclean and Philby were doing the same and therefore could not have been the fifth man who recruited them. Later still Andrew Gow of Trinity College, Cambridge (and later King's College) was identified as the fifth man. He too was a Soviet sympathiser but may have been one of a dozen pro-Soviet members of the intelligentsia at Cambridge during and after the Second World War, and not the fifth man who recruited Philby.

I had a 'Heroes of the West' meeting with Des McForan at "the Oak-Tree office" in the Charing Cross Hotel. He confirmed from his enquiries that the intelligence services had blocked his book, and he named four people involved in the operation, who, one way or another, had done nothing. I disputed his names as all four had tried to help in their own ways. I said we had been let down by our marketing: by our inactive distributor. But privately I knew that my 'Heroes of the West' books were being stifled by silence, and I was not keen to take on any more books. Sheldrake had urged me to reprint and republish Sir George Trevelyan's book on architecture, and Trevelyan had written to me along these lines. Trevor Maher was urging me to buy (through Vernon Davies) a retail store in London, but I was rethinking the future of Oak-Tree Books.

I mulled over my publishing while Oaklands broke up for Christmas. Nadia visited on Christmas Eve. After Christmas with the boys there was a family gathering at The Roebuck, where we had a long table in the Beech Room and all wore paper hats and drank sparkling wine. I visited Mabel Reid, who was in St Margaret's Hospital, having dropped a gatepost and taken the skin off her shin; and then white-haired Miss Root, my old maths teacher at Oaklands, who lay in bed, "a bag of skin and bones", a lamp with a naked bulb on the floor, and an electric fire on.

Soon after the new term began there was heavy snow two days running, and both days I went out and swept the paths in the school and came in glowing for breakfast. Matthew was doing a jigsaw on Bruges, where the Haggers had originated, and I was happy and wrote: "These wonderfully heavy snow days."[74] I was inclining towards ending my publishing very soon.

I visit 10 Downing Street to discuss publishing Thatcher's speeches: Whitelaw
In the middle of the snow the 'Heroes of the West' came up with the idea that the way to challenge the silence surrounding my books would be to publish a book containing the Prime Minister's speeches for the coming election. Trevor Maher said that no secret organisation would dare to subvert a book containing Margaret Thatcher's speeches. I made an appointment to meet Michael Alison, the Prime Minister's PPS (and a contact of Josten's), in the Central Lobby of the House of Commons on 21 January. I arrived punctually despite the snow and filled in cards for the police, but Alison did not appear.

I waited from 4 p.m. until 5.30. Eventually he rang and said there had been a mess-up: "I thought it was tomorrow." He said: "Can you come straight over? Walk over and be here by a quarter to." He was inviting me into 10 Downing Street.

I paddled through the snow and thick slush to the policeman at the end of Downing Street, who radioed to check that I was authorised. I strode up to the front door where I had seen Eden receive Bulganin and Krushchev and a policeman said, "Mr Hagger?" He opened the door and I found myself in the lobby, where one of two policemen said, "Mr Alison is on his way." I stood and waited near the picture of Downing, holding my briefcase and drinking in the spaciousness, the fireplace filled with flowers, the pictures, and then Alison's secretary came and led me into a corridor, past three or four doors and into a room on the left where someone was on the phone by the table. He put the phone down, pushed magazines in my direction and withdrew.

Soon Alison entered, a tall and gangling man in a suit. I discussed the publishing idea with him, and he was receptive: "I shall put the idea to the Prime Minister, but I can't guarantee her reply. It's a good idea." The Prime Minister's speeches were collected and published after I ceased to be a publisher.

On the way out I passed "a gaggle of suited men in the corridor of power waiting to go into a ground-floor room" – it was the 'A' team waiting to meet the Prime Minister – "and greeted one I recognised without stopping: 'Hello, Lord Whitelaw.'" He ran along beside me as I walked to the front door. "Very nice to see you again, nice to see you, nice to see you, very nice to see you."[75]

The number 2 of the Government was trotting along behind me and indirectly recognising the work I had done, including identifying the fifth man, while indirectly apologising for two lots of plagiarising (Recommendations on international terrorism and the fifth man) and for three lots of muzzling (my launch for McForan's book, the book itself and now Gorka's book). I swept out, feeling full of the power of Downing Street.

Looking back, I can see that at that moment I could have chosen a political career. With Biggs-Davison's support and my links with Lord Whitelaw and Margaret Thatcher I could have applied to contest a seat. But my direction was literary, not political. A political future had loomed like a turning off my main path. I knew I would remain on my main path as I had pressing things to write and did not want to be diverted into full-time politics.

Implementation of FREE in committee of exile representatives of Captive Nations
Ironically, now that I was taking a step back from politics, FREE was imple-

mented in exactly the way my paper had proposed. The Polish Government-in-Exile and Gorka had between them at last implemented the Committee of Exiles for which I had so long pressed. Between a dozen and twenty now met monthly in the Free Polish Headquarters at 43 Eaton Place, just as I had proposed. Gorka was in the chair and sent out the agenda, and every Iron-Curtain nation was represented, including the Baltic Captive Nations, and I was the only non-East European present. We discussed how to overthrow Communism in Eastern Europe and the USSR, and I frequently spoke strongly in favour of resistance and urged unrest. I found the representatives very reluctant to plan anything insurrectional, not least because they did not trust everyone at the table and feared the KGB, but after each meeting we all felt progress was being made.

I leave publishing to become an author, the monstrous chimera mortally wounded
The books had been selling but not in as many numbers as if there had been publicity. The idea had arisen that I might take over another publisher. Colin Walsh of Book Production Consultants, Cambridge, who had prepared *Budapest Betrayed* for me, invited me to Emmanuel College, Cambridge for a publishers' dinner. Over sherry I met the new Earl of Stockton, the new head of Macmillans following the recent death of his father, Harold Macmillan: a large, bearded, big-shouldered man. I sat next to John Murray of the oldest publishing firm in town (1768), Byron's publisher, who I "liked very much". (John Murray Publishers had also published Jane Austen and Coleridge.) He invited me to his office, the room Byron visited, for a chat.

At the dinner I had spoken to a dozen other publishers, including Penguins, and wrote that they were "all into marketing, hyping and turnover, and only secondarily interested in the content of their books". They all had "an endless round of small talk and laughter to cushion themselves against embarrassment, which they know better than most".[76]

I was in among the publishers and thought I would go to Frankfurt once more while I made the transition from publisher to author for another publisher. In February I met Biggs-Davison at a dinner at the House of Lords. He insisted on buying me a Scotch and soda and then asked if I would publish a book he was writing on Ireland.

But I had had enough of political publishing and being subverted. I had mortally wounded the monstrous chimera with several savage cuts, and I had achieved what I had set out to do. I knew that I would not be bringing Biggs-Davison's book out as an episode had come to an end. By now I was already preparing myself to be an author in my own right and project my vision like a rainbow over hills in a cluster of books.

*

A vision like a rainbow: seven bands, seven hills

I saw a rainbow shimmering like a vision, overarching in the sky. And I saw my vision as a rainbow with seven bands that shone tremulously before fading from view. I saw the bands – red, orange, yellow, green, blue, indigo and violet – as the disciplines in which my vision would be expressed. The rainbow called to me, and I knew what the bands signified: transpersonal psychology and mysticism (transforming ego to self and perceiving unity); literature (reflecting the Age in lyric and epic poetry and other forms as a man of letters); philosophy (approaching the One through science, cosmology and philosophy); history (discovering a pattern in civilizations); international politics and statecraft (investigating who is running the world and secret history, and proposing the ideal World State); comparative religion (perceiving the unity of world religions); and culture (re-establishing the metaphysical alongside the secular).

The seven-banded rainbow shimmered over the seven hills of Loughton. Each hill, to me, represented one of the seven disciplines I had to ascend. Each hill represented a band in the rainbow. Plodding up each would be hard work but I could take heart from the rainbow, whose arch reflected my finished toil in the hills.

The rainbow was an image, a symbol, of a perfected journey. It symbolised the completion of an ascent of the seven hills of achievement, where many have toiled in past generations. It shone out in light as an example to me and to others. The rainbow that appeared at intervals was a symbol of the work I had to complete and of my completed life and work.

The iridescent rainbow shimmered over the hills like a vision promising works to come. It called me to ascend each hill. Among the seven hills I could achieve personal growth. I could know truth. I could discover the order within the universe. I could perceive the pattern within world history. I could contribute to bringing in a political World State. I could know the unity of world religions. And I could glimpse the true, unified culture of the Age. To complete all seven ascents would take a lifetime of research and experience and could result in many works.

The rainbow came and went. For long spells it was not there, out of mind. Then its seven bands shone out proclaiming an overarching vision of unity. It was always present like the Light, but, like the Light, it came intermittently, sometimes after a gap of a year or more. It was a universal rainbow proclaiming activities, ascents and goals for all, and each person interpreted the bands in his or her own way.

The universal rainbow called me to be an author and reflect its vision of unity in my works. My books would appear intermittently and each would reflect a band in the rainbow for a while. Each work would bring the rainbow into view again for a while until it faded again, and then disappeared. The vision of unity would reappear in my next book like the rainbow materialising out of mist.

I had finished with State education and publishing. They had served their purpose: I had stood up to ideologically-driven egalitarian socialism, subversion within the UK and Soviet (and Libyan) expansionism, three different forms of Communism, and I had got to know the world of books. I was going to be a writer now, ascend to a perception of oneness and operate within the seven hills of achievement where so many had toiled and left traces of their work. I would quest on my own, confident in my own judgement. I would progress on my own initiative, ready to innovate and to found or renovate institutions that would assist me along my way.

PART TWO

The Unitive Way: the Seven Hills of Achievement

"The seven hills of Loughton are the slopes up the three-sided crater to the rim. They are: The Crescent/Spring Grove; Buckhurst Hill; Manor Road/Warren Hill/Albion Hill/Ollards Grove; Robin Hood Lane or Earl's Path/Strawberry Hill/Staples Hill; York Hill/Woodbury Hill/Baldwin's Hill/Church Hill; Sedley Rise/Golding's Hill; and Trap's Hill/Alderton Hill. The Forest curved like a bow from the Roebuck on top of Buckhurst Hill, round the Epping New Road to Baldwin's Hill at the top of Golding's Hill and round to the top of Trap's Hill. The Forest enfolded the village on three sides and could be seen above the rooftops, in some places looming large on the skyline, and well before the Second World War roads up the seven hills of Loughton connected the High Road to the Forest's curved ridge."

Nicholas Hagger, *A View of Epping Forest*, p.101

"Wisdom hath builded her house, she hath hewn out her seven pillars."
Proverbs 9.1

(Quoted in T.E. Lawrence, *Seven Pillars of Wisdom*)

"You'll never finish your work. You'll be like Sisyphus who rolled his boulder up to the top of the hill – and then he was fated to have it fall down again and go back to the beginning."

John Silberrad, in conversation with Nicholas Hagger, 24 April 2005

CHAPTER 3

Arrival in the Hills

"Operations of thought are like cavalry charges in a battle – they are strictly limited in number, they require fresh horses, and must only be made at decisive moments."

Alfred North Whitehead, *Introduction to Mathematics* (1911)

The Unitive Way unites sense and spirit, a reconciliation that is a hallmark of the neo-Baroque vision. The seeker approaches the One through learning and knowledge – as Yeats remarked in 'Sailing to Byzantium', "Nor is there singing school but studying" – and begins an ascent of the disciplines, toils in the seven hills whose ridge is bathed in sunlight. All paths up the hills of achievement lead to this same sunny prospect. From its eminence the seeker sees the world as a unity and all disciplines – including philosophy, science, history, literature – appear to be reconciled.

Now I had arrived among the seven hills, my Second Dark Night and its purgation of my spirit behind me, I was aware of what mystics have called "the fruits of the spirit": a tireless energy that pours in and demands the incessant production of unifying works. My broadening vision of unity intensified my awareness that the Light is behind the universe and is central to all civilizations, and demanded works that showed the Oneness of the Light and the unity behind multiplicity. My task hung before me like an intermittent seven-banded rainbow.

During my Dark Night of the Spirit the Light had shown itself to me from time to time sometimes as a blue Light (8 April 1972–12 October 1977) and then as white Light during my Third Mystic Life (13 May 1979–31 October 1981, *see* Appendix 1, p.903.) The Light returned at various times between 1981 and 1987 and then in April 1990. This began my Fourth Mystic Life (8 April 1990–6 December 1993, *see* Appendix 1, p.903). The Light showed itself in April 1991, at the time of the publication of *The Fire and the Stones*.

Episode 7:

Metaphysical Poetry and World History

Years: 1987–1991
Locations: Loughton; Epping; Charlestown; London; Denmark; Frankfurt;
Hungary; Prague
Works: *Question Mark over the West*; *A Sneeze in the Universe*; *The Fire and the
Stones*; *Selected Poems, A Metaphysical's Way of Fire*
Initiatives: founding Coopersale Hall School; Fourth Mystic Life; Metaphysical
Revolution

"Wer immer strebend sich bemüht, den können wir erlösen."
"He who strives without ceasing/We can redeem."
Or: "He who exerts himself with constant strivings, he we can save."

Goethe, *Faust*, V, 11936–7

"History is a pattern
Of timeless moments."

T.S. Eliot, 'Little Gidding'

In my next episode there was an underlying conflict between my writing, which resulted in two books being published, and my running and expansion of my school business. On top of this conflict there was a more prominent conflict between my two very different books: my metaphysical poetry and world history.

In the course of this episode I began a new career as an author writing in seven disciplines. Now my writing to some extent became my work, and from now on the conflict in each episode would be between different *genres*, as from now on I was always simultaneously writing two books reflecting different disciplines: conflicting bands of the rainbow. (*See* p.xxvi.)

World history: the tradition of the Light
The Fire and the Stones: the Light behind all cultures
Something had happened to my energy flow. It was as if I had permanently opened to a movement of energy from the universe into my universal being, and now had permanent unity of being. On 7 December I received many surges from the Light after asking for wisdom as opposed to healing:

Dec. 7. Sunday evening…. Asked the Light to send its wisdom into Matthew and immediately received not the usual 4 surges but 8 – the first time the 4 barrier has ever been broken, surges into Matthew's head via my spine, arm and finger (little finger of right hand)…. Have just asked for wisdom [for myself] and have had another 10 surges – in fact they could go on coming…. My spine is a-shudder, and I can see the Light like the sun in a puddle; as I gaze at the reflection…. I am filled with power – there has been a break-through today: many surges, over 30 so far (10.35 p.m.) from before 10 p.m. and the power is still coming through as I write…. Dec. 7 still, 11.05. Only now is the power abating, partly because I want it to. Have been sitting on the bed in the bedroom, feeling the power pour up my spine and prickle my scalp and swirl fire-like Light in my soul. My third eye. Saw the universe as an eyeball with a million mottled stars like flecks. This was a 'shewing'. Something extraordinary has happened to me today…. The Light poured in as I have described, and kept going for over an hour, so I felt floating on it, sustained by it, encouraged. This is the best 'encouragement' for my Light book that I could have had. Now I glow all over. All my fingers shine. I am full of Light. And still it surges up my spine and into my head…. At 1.50 a.m. it is still there and able to sweep up my back in waves and tingle my cheeks; and I know that my energy-circuit is complete.

I returned to the Light book and wrote: "What I am saying in the Light book: the Light is behind all cultures, and is common ground for a world-wide culture; it reconciles all faiths and is a new metaphysical vision." I had already decided that the title of my book would be *The Fire and the Stones*, and I had told Sir George Trevelyan in a letter I later wrote: "A card from Sir George Trevelyan… showing a gateway and a spire, and quoting (in response to my *Fire and Stones*) Teilhard de Chardin's 'for the second time in the history of the world, man will have discovered fire'." I continued: "I who am so good at identifying the starting-point of other people's books need to ask myself: what is the starting-point of *The Fire and the Stones*? Logically it is the one-world vision, for that is the exoteric theme. Emotionally it is the Inner Light, for that is the esoteric theme."

I was now using the computer to work on the beginnings of *The Fire and the Stones*. My typist came each Tuesday and worked on the dining-room table and I tackled the world's cultures and all experiences of the Inner Light. I had found evidence that a civilization starts with a metaphysical vision which turns secular, and I wrote of "a metaphysical path which our world culture needs" and of "the need for a mass return to the Inner Light in our world-wide civilization". I continued that there was a need for "one world-wide religion whose ceremonies draw on the Inner Light…, a new universalism. The Universalist movement within the Church as Christians move out and find common ground with non-Christians in the Light." I found I was writing effortlessly, and wrote after Christmas: "I effortlessly edited and cut…. It is all coming through from elsewhere." I was aware of infused knowledge as I worked: "The wisdom is pouring in, tingling my spine, involuntarily as I work on editing *The Fire and the Stones*."

In early January I wrote: "My *Fire and the Stones* – the Light manifesting in culture or the Light contrasted with materialism. I am giving evidence for what I assert, and if the tradition is accepted the next stage is to write Part 2 on philosophy explaining what the implications are for all the anti-metaphysical creeds."

I realised that if I had not taken over at Oaklands and started Oak-Tree I would not have had the computer, and *The Fire and the Stones* would be a very different work. I also saw that "in *The Fire and the Stones* I am ploughing back my individual experience of the Light into my culture and civilization". I restated my task with a new confidence: "My purpose… is to state the Light, and… get it out into society, reflect it to others as a symbol, so that my life is a symbol for the Way of Illumination." I felt I had "to live up to Ezra Pound's handing-on of the energy of the Muse" and that "*The Fire and the Stones* is my *White Goddess*, and like Robert Graves, I have to write some poems to go with it". It was allowed for poets to write cultural works: had not Eliot, a poet and publisher, written *Notes towards the Definition of Culture*? I wrote: "I must walk in the tradition of Graves and Eliot…. I must become a man of letters."[1]

There was more snow and each week I prepared a new section of *The Fire and the Stones* for the typist to key into the computer. I was researching world history but everyday life continued. We were taken to the Barbican by a member of staff to see her son, Bramwell Tovey, conduct a Tchaikovsky concert, which included the 1812 overture with cannon-and-mortar fire. (We were taken to the dressing-room afterwards, where he sat in evening dress, broken-nosed, a shock of hair and self-effacing, almost depressed: the conductor after the applause has stopped ringing in his ears. I saw him as an artist without his audience and realised that as an author I should be as much of a performer as he was.) Nadia came and we scooped frog-spawn from the Strawberry Hill pond. It was like a jellyfish.

Margaret Riley's last visit
Matthew's confirmation at St Mary's church, Loughton on 22 March, at which the Bishop of Chelmsford wore his mitre, carried his crozier and laid his hands on the heads of those being confirmed, was followed by a buffet lunch in the Oaklands hall. This was notable for Margaret Riley's appearance at the end of lunchtime. She had travelled by taxi and lost her way and completely missed the service and the lunch. Margaret riled the guests,

including Miss Lord and Miss Reid, the ex-co-owners of Oaklands, by chain-smoking. She was the only smoker there. A dozen guests came down to our house for tea, including Tom McAlister, the West Ham goalie. Margaret told him he was like a cardboard cut-out, which caused some offence. Then, catching sight of the painting of Manarola in Italy she gave me in 1971, which I had subsequently framed at my expense and put on a wall, she loudly demanded it back. "I want my work back," she kept saying, "I want it back." She had always advocated "not wanting", and I was sad at the change in her outlook. I took the picture off the wall and put it in her arms, frame and all. I took Nadia to the car as she had to be driven to the station to catch her flight from Heathrow to Edinburgh. Margaret pursued us, wanting a bag for the painting and wanting to come with us to the station. I went back for a bag and as a result Nadia missed the tube she needed to catch and therefore her flight from Heathrow. While I negotiated the time of the next tube with the ticket office, Margaret wandered up onto the platform without saying goodbye. Nadia went up a different flight of steps and travelled on her own, greatly inconvenienced.

I did not see Margaret Riley again. I did not feel moved to invite her – what else might disappear off my wall and what other scenes might be caused – and she never made contact. But her Zen-like wisdom had helped me at a very difficult stage in my journey (see *My Double Life 1: This Dark Wood*), and she had introduced me to the Austro-Hungarian Habsburg Light from a Vienna that preceded the anti-metaphysical philosophers of the Vienna Circle. And for that I will always be grateful.

Universalist perspective and Oaklands
I had nearly completed Part One of *The Fire and the Stones*, and while I was immersed in my universalist perspective Tomlin invited me to lunch in the Athenaeum, and I discussed it with the secretary to the Archbishop of Canterbury's inter-faith committee who joined us for port in the morning room, sitting in green leather chairs by a log fire. (Later that night Matthew had so bad a headache he could not move, and I "healed him with *six* surges of energy. The headache totally went.")

I took up my metaphysical mode of thinking at a dinner given by our neighbour Mrs. Clauson to introduce me to her relative Norman Franklin, who was about to retire as Chairman of Routledge. After dinner we talked metaphysics and I said, "Darwin left the idea of purpose out of the universe." I developed the argument at some length and then appealed to the Routledge Chairman to publish a book, *The New Purpose*, that would bring the universe back into philosophy and reinstate the One behind the senses. Soon afterwards I received a letter from Franklin saying he had stayed awake much of that night thinking about what I had said. He sent me a copy of *Dialogues with Scientists and Sages* which, he claimed, was the book about the purpose in the universe I had been calling for. It wasn't, and I would eventually write it (*The New Philosophy of Universalism*).

At the 1987 Mystics and Scientists conference at Winchester Kathleen Raine, maintaining her anti-Christian line, said to me of Tomlin, who had written an article for *The Tablet*: "*I* wouldn't write for *The Tablet*." Sir Fred Hoyle spoke, and I later had a talk with him about his steady-state theory, pointing out that the Big-Bang theory had general prevalence. He told me: "Every universe begins with a big bang, and all universes maintain themselves with steady state. It's regional and global. At least, that's how the maths look." I meditated with Lawrence Freeman, a Benedictine who looked back to the 4th-century Cassian, and I "saw fire within which were words in Islamic, then Hebrew, then Latin…, the Islamic, Jewish and Christian traditions, all of which are One". I wrote the Hebrew word in my Diary entry for 4 April without knowing that it meant Yahweh: יהוה. What I had seen seemed to be telling me that in *The Fire and the Stones* I should treat the Fire or Light of Islam, Judaism and Christianity as one and Universalist.

Back in Essex I had a strong sense of the One on Easter Sunday, when Ann, the boys and I walked with Miss Reid to the Strawberry Hill pond via Warren Hill. The wood was full of birdsong and we identified a willow warbler and chiff chaff (two summer visitors), a wren, a green woodpecker and a reed bunting. The hornbeams were out, with catkins; and the poplar catkins were on the ground. We saw pussy willow with yellow and green 'cushions' and millions of tadpoles among starwort pondweed. We went back to tea with Miss Reid for scones, butter, home-made crab-apple jelly, flapjack, cake, chocolate biscuits and many cups of strong tea. We talked overlooking the green Forest.

I drew inspiration from the Oaklands grounds. I worked on the Islamic Paradise, which was a garden, and I raised my eyes to the Oaklands greenhouse and saw two bullfinches flying in and out of the yew hedge and perching on the freshly-budding apple-tree. Gazing across the Oaklands grounds, with its trees and many birds, I had no doubt that this was a Paradise, with every kind and colour of tree and bird, every bit as enticing as Arabi's or the gardens shown in illustrations to Persian poems: "I must recreate this Paradise or vision, using the Paradise that is round me. I, who have known Hell, or at least, the Gates of Hell, am now living in Paradise." There were bees round the rotten tree by the log shed. The gardener's son caught one in a glass and we took it to Derek Balls of Balls Brothers who lived up the road. He had hives, and we thought it was an escaped 'honeybee' of his. Derek put it on his finger, and as it crawled, pronounced it a "tree wasp". I watched fascinated. It did not sting him. I told myself: "Reread *Georgics IV* on bees. Virgil's Paradise in the country is no different from the

Oaklands fields."

My publishing was petering out, but from time to time I was pressed to revive it. Oleg Gordievsky had defected from the Soviet Embassy in London and gone into hiding. There had been a proposal that Oak-Tree should publish Gordievsky's memoirs, and through Julian Amery's secretary I sent a half-hearted message to his hide-out. Nothing came of the idea. Gorka invited me to the House of Lords to have tea with the elderly Lord Bauer in the Peers' Guest Room bar, trying to arrange for funding for Oak-Tree.

I had seen little of our MP Biggs-Davison, but as I introduced Geoff Hurst, the star of England's World Cup soccer final in 1966, near the hall windows at the Oaklands summer fair five days before the 1987 General Election he unexpectedly arrived. While Hurst was speaking about Oaklands Biggs-Davison walked to the middle of the steps wearing a blue rosette and holding an umbrella, trying to upstage him and canvass votes from his constituents. A few days later I went to the Council offices to collect dustbin bags from the receptionist, who said: "I used to work with your father. I can see him now, walking in with his stick, hopping." On the way back I nearly ran Biggs-Davison over. He was in a dream and did not see me, walking slowly, carrying the umbrella. I congratulated him on his election victory. He came out of his dream. At Chigwell School's Speech Day the prizes were distributed by John Garnett (Virginia Bottomley's father), who had written the Foreword to my author Jack Wood's book. He sat behind me in the ancient church and talked about Jack Wood with me in the porch. These events echoed a past I had left behind.

At a craft exhibition in Epping I encountered a group of Hesychasts from Woodford Green who lived metaphysics and made a living out of icons. From one I bought an icon showing Christ with a huge halo of Light and a book, a 6th-century Byzantine image from St Catherine's monastery, Sinai. The balding thin-lipped man who sold me the icon told me that he meditated each day on the Being behind the image.

While I wrote about world history, I was absorbing the local East Anglian history. I took my family to Stansted Mountfitchet to see the reconstruction of an 11th-century Norman castle. We visited the nearby windmill "which ground corn and made bread out of the wind – like the sails of my creative imagination blown by... inspiration, producing poems. I have been a disused windmill of late, but will begin to grind again." I climbed the wooden stairs of the tower mill to the top. And on a rainy day, dressed as a 1520s friar, I accompanied a group of Oaklands children to Kentwell Hall, Suffolk, which was peopled by volunteers in 1520s dress, for an immersion experience in Tudor England.

John Dutchman, the Pegasus footballer and Chigwell School master was now taking football at Oaklands in place of McAlister (his Chigwell hours having been temporarily reduced). He played for one side and I played for the other side in my track suit. He told me, "Johnny Haynes was the best passer I have seen." Dutchman must have been the second-best passer. He nicknamed David Hoppit's six-year-old nephew "Daisy-picker" as he was more interested in the flowers than the ball – he went on to own his own nursery – and I recall an inch-perfect pass from 40 yards that cannoned off his foot into the goal as he headed towards some flowers so he scored without realising what he had done.

There were events to cope with. My Uncle Harold, the youngest son of John Broadley II, had died: my grandfather's brother John's son, who had run the Bromley family business. I drove to Barham for the funeral and went back to the house of his eldest son John, John Broadley IV, at Bishopsbourne. John was now a consultant at Canterbury Hospital, and he lived overlooking the sheep in the valley. I wrote: "Death is the perfection of a life, so that all the life's achievements can be measured finally. It is a looking-back on a life, a time for assessment." I later wrote a poem, 'Near Barham'. Nadia had visited. She had at last become an air hostess with British Midland. After her training she would fly, being based at Edinburgh. She said: "I'll have to learn to put out a fire and cope with a terrorist emergency." Matthew, having recovered from breaking his arm when he fell off his skateboard in the Oaklands tennis-court, spent a night sleeping rough at Waters Farm, Hatfield Broad Oak. Two days later I lunched with the artist Gwen Broad's two daughters, Gwen and Flinders, at Argie's and it turned out that Waters Farm was owned by their father Nanscawen's brother. "What an amazing coincidence," Gwen said.[2] It was extraordinary that of all the places in Essex and East Anglia that Chigwell could have chosen to give their boys the experience of sleeping rough, they should choose my Aunt Gwen's brother-in-law. Again I had an eerie feeling that there is an underlying pattern to our lives.

I plodded on with *The Fire and the Stones* and oversaw the running of Oaklands. I put my foot on the bottom rung of the ladder while Les, our odd-job man who was over 65, painted the highest back gable above the third storey. He had been used to running up the rigging in the Navy during the war, and he scampered up the ladder. He wanted me to go up and have a look, and when I had climbed about 15 feet high the top of the ladder moved away from the wall into a vertical position. For a few moments I clung on, and it seemed I might swing backwards and land on my back in the rockery and rose-bushes beneath. Les struggled to push the ladder back towards the wall and eventually succeeded. Had I gone backwards I might have broken my back or my neck.

There was a dancing display at Oaklands on the grass under the apple-trees. The parents sat facing the back of the school in the tennis-court, which melted in the scorching sun. Some of the benches and chairs became buried in the tarmac, which I had to get repaired. Soon afterwards Oaklands celebrated its 50th anniversary with a barbecue run by the parents in the main field. Some 500 attended, including past staff and pupils. I put on an exhibition of Oaklands memorabilia (old photos and registers) from 1937 to 1987 in the hall. The Labour politician Jack Straw had been a pupil – his mother had been a teacher at Oaklands[3] – and he sent me a hand-written letter wishing Oaklands well on its 50th birthday. It was a golden day and the field was full of sitting parents.

Metaphysical poetry: **Selected Poems**
While I was working on *The Fire and the Stones* I was deeply involved in assembling my *Selected Poems*.

In the Lake District: Wordsworth places
Another visit to the Lake District had brought some poems. Matthew was staying on a school trip at Murton, near Appleby. Ann, Anthony and I stayed with my Uncle Reg, who reminisced about my grandmother: "She sat erect on the edge of her chair, hand on a thick stick, and told George [her son] 'No more coal on the fire' (and George was ill afterwards)." He talked about the walks he took me on over the Downs, and I recalled "lying in the long grass below the first tee, azure blues fluttering everywhere, under a blue sky – my first hint of a mystical experience, the stillness and harmony among the summer butterflies and flowers, the sense of a One... that throbbed through everything" (*see My Double Life 1: This Dark Wood*). He was a Freemason, and after dinner he put on his Templar knight's costume: a white cowl and tunic with a red cross on the front, a belt and sword. I was interested in his Crusader costume but wary of the Templars.

I wanted to visit places associated with Wordsworth. The next day we toured the western lakes: from High Newton to Wast Water, and the smallest church, St Olaf's. I wrote a poem, 'St Olaf's Church'. We went on to Buttermere, Keswick and Grasmere, where we had tea at The Swan. We went to Allan Bank, where Wordsworth had been unhappy, then to the Rectory, into which he moved. We went to Dove Cottage, and we walked to the Leech-gatherer's pond. I stirred it but found only frog-spawn. We went on to Rydal and the stepping-stones across the Rothay which Wordsworth crossed when he walked to work in Ambleside. We went on to Fox Ghyll (De Quincey's house) and then Coniston Water; along past Ruskin's house (Brantwood) and then home. It was a day full of lakes and mountains, some snow-capped; and huge rocks and boulders.

The next day we went (past Barnard Castle and Dotheboys Hall) to High Force, a cascading 70-foot waterfall near its cousin, Aira Force. We crossed the Pennines on a clear evening to the 1653 converted barn where Matthew was staying. He was up Great Gable – we could see the climbers. There was a full moon over the Pennines as we drove back, and I wrote a poem, 'Full Moon on the Pennines'.

The following day we returned to Grasmere. We went on to Great Langdale and Dungeon Ghyll, and up and over to Blea Tarn. I sat by the stream and went into the house and saw where the Solitary entertained Wordsworth. We went on to Little Langdale and to Hawkshead. The school keeper told me that Wordsworth snared woodcock above Ann Tyson's house, and searched for ravens' eggs at Tilberthwaite, two miles outside Coniston on the road to Ambleside. We went on to Esthwaite, where Wordsworth skated and Jeremy Fisher fished, and on to Beatrix Potter's house. We drove up Gummer's How, above Windermere, "incredibly high on a lovely evening. Skylarks, a peregrine falcon, two ravens and tame chaffinches which sat by me on the wall and nearly ate out of my hand."[4] I came away with a renewed sense of the One.

Symbolism and healing society

I was thinking about the metaphysical significance of images and symbols in poetry:

> The Guénon view of the symbol – everything corresponds as everything is a oneness, a unity…. The poet speaks to the inner man in a language of images… which communicates to the inner imagination. The artist ideally at one with his society but in a violent time at odds with his society…. Images of calm for a violent time, images of peace for an alienated time. The artist living close to Nature. I go further and suggest that images are in fact symbols, with a plurality of meaning as lower and higher domains corre-spond. Symbolism is… a metaphysical philosophy. Art mirrors the disease of society, but if it is to save it it has to heal it with a flow of Light and symbolism.[5]

Tomlin's illness

At the end of July I visited Tomlin in Redan Street. At the front door his wife Judith, who had worked with Brian Crozier on *The Economist*, told me of his declining health. In his study upstairs Tomlin told me that cancer had been found in his bladder in June. He had had an operation and might lose a kidney. He said that he had tuberculosis and was going to bed at 7, exhausted; also that he had had a headache for a month. He said he would look at my book for mistakes. (He was very interested in my metaphysical side.) He showed me his essays on the Sacred, on Ruskin and on Guénon. He said, "Kathleen Raine is not a Guénonist, she says he ignores emotion." He passed judgement on his fellow philosophers: "Russell's *History of Western Philosophy* is a poor book, poorly written. He said logic ruined his brain." "Wittgenstein's been hijacked by the sceptics. He asked for a priest when he died and said 'Don't let him be a philosopher.'" "Husserl – he's unnecessarily complicated: intentionality." "I had lunch with Gabriel Marcel, I spoke in French. He raises metaphysical questions, that's why they don't like him." And so on. I did not know that the previous month, in June 1987, his memoir, *T.S. Eliot: A Friendship*, had been handed over to Routledge for publication the following year, or that the book was addressed to Eliot's widow, Valerie Eliot. Nor did I know that this would be the last time that I saw him. Later I wrote a poem 'Visit to a Philosopher'.

On the way home I recalled my poem 'Twilight', which I had written in June 1964 and which appeared in the Japanese magazine, *The Rising Generation*. I had seen a prophet "squatting in twilight" in a "flickering cathedral square", and I now thought the fire image in that poem was both symbolic and prophetic. I had wanted to call my *Collected Poems* at one time *The Death-Fires*, and 'Fire' had been a constant theme in my work. I later observed:

My *Death-Fires*, then my *Fire-Flower*, and eventually *The Fire and the Stones*. But what I have in common in all my work is a concern for, a search for, metaphysical truth.... The personal is subordinated to that. Ironically, it is self-stripping which produces it. I also have a 'Metaphysical Diary' (Journal) and letters on metaphysical subjects. Anthologise... a metaphysical theme, with excerpts from diaries and letters, all dated; presenting metaphysical reality.... 'The Silence' – a search for metaphysical reality that succeeded.[6]

Poems written in Denmark: Viking roots

I had long wanted to explore the Haggers' Viking roots. In August Ann and I took the boys and our car to Denmark, where the Haggers may have originated before they went to Bruges (perhaps via Normandy).

We caught a ferry from Harwich, slept on board and docked at Esbjerg next morning. We drove to Legoland. There I had chest pains – "acute pains in my heart, sharp stabbings" – and had to sit in a café while the boys went on their activities. At one stage I thought I might be dying from an extended heart attack and wrote 'Reality in Legoland or Sudden Confrontation with Death'." We drove to Odense, and I corrected the poem at the Hotel Windsor "until late at night". At 2 a.m. I woke with the idea firmly in my mind that "there should be extracts on my poetic method from these *Diaries* over the years, and some letters". (The idea was partly implemented in *Awakening to the Light*, with *Selected Diaries* and *Selected Letters* to come.)

The next day, with the boys in mind, we went to Hans Christian

Andersen's alleged birthplace and to his childhood home. We went on to Rynkeby church, on whose walls Erik Hardenberg's murals expressed the Reformation ideal he learned at the house of Luther's friend Philipp Melanchthon: a choir of 31 angels with bobbed hair playing 17 different instruments, conducted by Christ. I drafted 'The Metaphysical Conductor' in room 305 at the Hotel Windsor, Odense. Earlier we had gone on to Ladby and saw how the *fjord* near Kertminde acted as a harbour with sheltered waters for the Vikings.

We sought out the Vikings the following day. We took a ferry and drove to Trelleborg, where Svein Forkbeard set sail to conquer England. We visited Lejre's Kurgan-style Funnel-Neck Beaker c.3,000BC long barrow for a chieftain (with 11 upright megaliths and capstones) and Iron-Age village. We went on to the Viking ship museum at Roskilde and saw a long warship for 50–110 men. I wrote more poems: 'A Viking Inheritance', 'Long Barrow at Lejre' and 'Centre of the Maze'.

I had a hunch that "my family came from Aggersborg, 'a town of Aggers', with Svein Forkbeard c.1013, and sailed for England or the Continent to plunder and travel under the protection of Odin". I later wrote and asked the local Historic Bibliothek: "Is there any record of a Hagger or Agger leaving the Viking settlement at Aggersborg, perhaps for England, c.1000?" I received an inconclusive answer. I should have asked if a Hagger or Agger left for Normandy *en route* for Bruges.

We went on to Nodebo and tried to find an intersection where eight roads meet in Gribskov Forest, not far from Copenhagen, which Kierkegaard described in *Stages on Life's Way* and which inspired *Either/Or: A Fragment of Life*. The intersection is now in beech woods and can only be reached on foot. (Kierkegaard, a late Romantic, like Goethe's Werther, Wordsworth and Shelley walked in forests alone.) I wrote a poem, 'At Gilbjerg: Kierkegaard the Romantic'. We went on to Gilleleje and Gilbjerg Hoved, and found where Kierkegaard's stone monument stands in a small forest. We went on to Helsingor (Elsinor) to see Hamlet's castle, but it was closed due to a museum strike. We then drove to Kobenhavn (Copenhagen): Tivoli Gardens and the royal palace. We left at 8.30 and drove 103 kms in time to catch the return ferry with only half a minute to spare.

From Odense we went to Jelling, the royal capital of Denmark in the 10th century under the rule of Gorm and his son Harald Bluetooth, who made the Danes Christian. I saw the two stones they raised (one with Christ on it), which I would put into *The Fire and the Stones*. I wrote a fragment of a poem, 'At Jelling'. On the way back to England there was a great swell and the boat rolled. The following morning I drafted a poem, 'Vikings and the Sea', and "jotted for a philosophical sequel to *The Fire and the Stones*".[7]

Fishing in Cornwall, 'Out on the Alone'

We drove to Cornwall and after visiting Charlestown I wrote to Tomlin. I held up Socrates as an example of a philosopher who calmly discussed and planned his end. I sent him a copy of my draft of *The Fire and the Stones* in the hope that he would find some comfort by being confronted with the workings of the Light. Then I wrote to Kathleen Raine about Tomlin. I received a letter from her in reply lamenting that Frederick must now leave "this dark world".[8]

I proof-read Part One of *The Fire and the Stones* on Sunday on Par beach. We spent a day on Charlestown beach and ate pasties for lunch. The boys "boated in their rubber dinghy, snorkelled, crabbed, swam". I sunbathed and drafted poems: 'At Charlestown' and 'Gravity'. I knew that the Charlestown harbour was for sale for about £2.5 million, and I wandered up and looked through the windows of the Harbour-master's House, the most seaward house, which stood above "the sleep tunnel" and which I was now certain was the house by a harbour where I had seen myself writing poetry while attending lectures on Yeats in Oxford. I looked in on Stratton and Holborow (as it was then) and established that the property would be auctioned along with the harbour in September.

The next day we went to Porthleven. I sat on the rocks and wrote the third of my Gunwalloe Metaphysical Sonnets ('Time and Eternity: A Cross of Light'), and polished the rhymes. I visited the church on the beach and returned to walk under the stars at Charlestown.

The following day I returned to Porthleven and slept at Ann's cousin's house. At 4 a.m. I went out with the fishermen on a clear blue day. We fished for cod, hake, guernard and pollack off the Lizard. I wrote 'Out on the Alone (or The Mystery of Being)', a metaphysical poem. I introduced the idea of 'Amness' or 'Isness' (an idea which first surfaced in my Japanese *Diary* 20 years or more previously), suggesting a separation between things that have being and things that have existence (for example, fish and waves). I took up the distinction in 'Spur Dog and Philosopher', a poem on Tomlin. I reflected: "I am becoming a Metaphysical poet in the sense that many of my poems now have metaphysical echoes or work out fundamental metaphysical problems related to Being…. My contact with the sea (including Charlestown) has deepened my poetry: it has stressed the metaphysical 'alone' at the expense of the social vision."

The next day I went to Charlestown, after typing up 'Out on the Alone' and my Gunwalloe poem. There was a breathless calm. We also went to Fowey and to Mevagissey.

Back in Loughton there had been a violent storm. A fir-tree across the road had been struck by lightning and split in two. Much of Loughton was flooded, including the school staff room. I mowed wet fields, avoiding the frogs that leapt out of my path. A harvest mouse swung on some long grass in the second field, and many butterflies, moths and beetles fluttered or crawled out of my way.[9]

World history: integrating 25 civilizations while founding a second home and school

I had still been attending the monthly meetings of the Committee of Captive Nations, which was implementing FREE and calling for an end to Soviet occupation. The live broadcast I had made into the Soviet Union at Gorka's launch had attracted American attention, and there was a plan to follow up my broadcast with a programme to sell dishes that could receive anti-Soviet programmes from satellites behind the Iron Curtain and link this to a broadcasting network based on FREE. The innovatory plan aimed to use satellite technology in July 1987, over three years before the founding of BSkyB in November 1990.

Donald Wilhelm, satellite dishes and the Soviet Union

An American, Professor Donald Wilhelm, had asked to see me. I met him at the Charing Cross Hotel, "the Oak-Tree office" on 22 July. He gave me an article on satellite technology and suggested that we should found a company, Satellite Consultants Ltd, which would share its address with Oak-Tree, and that we should tie in two technicians he named to act as consultants to companies, raise funds, make programmes and supply satellite channels, to make films of books about the ideology of the West and to co-ordinate global broadcasting and my challenging of the Soviet sphere of influence for the first time in 40 years. I was to be assisted by being offered satellite dishes that would be transported behind the Iron Curtain so that broadcasts like the one I had made at Gorka's launch could be more widely heard behind the Iron Curtain. Money would come in from venture capital, and he and I would be directors. The income in the first year would come from three sources: production contracts (with advances), global link-up through satellites, and charity payments.

This was not the first time that an American had contacted me out of nowhere to put me in touch with advanced technology. The previous time, in Libya, had been disastrous, and I was wary of this approach. Satellite technology was of the future as was the computer, and the idea was very attractive. He would present FREE – and the representatives of the Captive Nations – on film.

But his approach had come too late. A year earlier I would have jumped at it, but now I was on a new course, having made the decision to write books for another publisher. Wilhelm was very determined. He attached himself to me and kept making contact, and I wondered if Satellite

272

Consultants Ltd was a CIA idea.

Curious about his motivation, I met Wilhelm for lunch at Kettners in Romilly Street on 7 August to be introduced to the two technicians who would act as consultants for the new company. Both technicians were imposing characters. Professor Wilhem, hook-nosed and whiskery, smilingly asked their attitude to the military use of satellites.[10] He wanted to send satellite dishes behind the Iron Curtain so that East Europeans could receive insurrectionary broadcasts. He had secured an office in Knightsbridge. He wanted to meet my Committee of Exiles as they could put us in touch with our market. Wilhelm was fomenting insurrection in just the way I had envisaged in my papers on FREE.

Auction of Charlestown
The auction of Charlestown, our local harbour in Cornwall, took place in September in a London hotel (the Crystal Room of the May Fair InterContinental Hotel, Stratton Street). Donald Wilhelm wanted to meet me that afternoon and said he would tag along and talk to me before Charlestown came up.

There were 800 people in the large room, and I could not see who was bidding. The auction of the port ended in confusion as it was not clear whether the reserve price had been reached. Together with many others I milled around at the front (Wilhelm at my elbow) and found myself being interviewed by *The Times*, who thought I had bought the harbour. A small, podgy man with a handlebar moustache and wrists that bulged at his cuffs whispered to me out of the corner of his mouth, "Don't say it's me," and I found myself speaking to Stephen Lucas. We all stood around, and I said to him, guided by my intuition: "If you're borrowing £2.6 million for the harbour, the interest could work out at £4,000 for a weekend. You'll need to sell something to reduce your borrowing. I'm interested in the Harbour-master's House. Here's my card." He said "Right," and disappeared to sign the auctioneer's papers. He bought the harbour on an overdraft for his brother's BOM Holdings.

Wilhelm and FREE
Wilhelm and I went on to the Great Western Hotel, Paddington and met a representative of Keston College, which had been founded by Dr Michael Bourdeaux in 1969 to promote religious freedom against Communism. Wilhelm proposed that members of the College would courier satellite dishes into the USSR. The response was inconclusive. I then took Wilhelm on to address representatives of the Captive Nations on satellite technology. Some 20 Exiles sat round a rectangle of tables in the Polish Government-in-Exile headquarters in Eaton Place, and he asked if *they* would send satellite

dishes into the USSR. The atmosphere was strained. I said the idea would implement FREE, but the Exiles were suspicious. Two days later Gorka rang me and said, "Professor Wilhelm was with the CIA during the war and later in Geneva, where he worked with Michael Bourdeaux of Keston. He was a scientific adviser." He said that the Exiles did not trust him.

I was now sure that my paper on FREE, my urging of a signed petition for democracy in Eastern Europe, my broadcast at Gorka's launch, my meeting with Bukovsky and the creation of the Committee of Representatives of Captive Nations had come to the attention of the CIA, who were trying to help FREE by expanding freedom of speech via satellite dishes in the Soviet Union.

I was invited to Cambridgeshire to lunch with Donald Wilhelm and his wife in their new house near the Gog-Magog hills. I went to see what the Americans were trying to do with me. Wilhelm took me to the Cambridge office and we met two of the personnel who had leased it. In my presence Wilhelm rang the Head of the British National Space Centre and tried to persuade him to meet us to discuss the transmission of broadcasts into the USSR via satellites in space.

On the way home I made a conscious decision to pull away from Wilhelm, and later wrote: "To be a poet is to be fully aware of Nature, and one's surroundings and have the time for verse – i.e. to have no projects, to run no empires or do any of the things that take one's time." In my mind I had also ceased to be a publisher when on 2 October Vernon Davies held a gathering and I chatted to Ivor Stanbrook MP about Oak-Tree Books' difficulties and he remarked that in his view I had been wrongly put on a list.

I was still meeting the Committee of Exiles at the Free Polish headquarters, under Gorka's chairmanship, and at the beginning of April the group adopted my acronym, FREEDOM (Freedom for Eastern Europe from DOMination). So the ideas, expressed in my paper for Biggs-Davison had now been implemented even though I was distancing myself from political activity and satellite transmissions.[11]

Frankfurt and Universalism

I went to the Frankfurt Book Fair to announce that I was winding down Oak-Tree Books to become an author. I took a taxi straight to the Messe and my heart sank as I entered the familiar glass buildings with their escalators and unpacked my books at my stand for the last time. In the evening I went back to the apartment I had taken at Ronneburgstrasse 11. The next day I interviewed the American and English publishers, and when the Book Fair became oppressive I visited Goethe's house, basking in the tranquillity, allowing my soul to breathe. The visit would find its way into an invocation in *Overlord*.

I talked with some of the German publishers, most notably with a German representative of Fischers, Reiner Stach. I told him about *The Fire and the Stones,* and said that just as Einstein had a hunch lying in a meadow and looking at the sun and mentally travelling back up its ray, so I had had a hunch about the cause of civilizations. He said: "You have developed a universalist theory of world civilizations." His use of the word "universalist", coming from a German speaking in what was for him a second language, chimed with my own earlier focus on the word, and spurred on my choice of the word "Universalism" for my own philosophy.

The Fire and the Stones *as a study of civilizations, storm*
Back in England I moved my study into the extension I had had built onto the back of our house (6 Albion Hill) and, despite the distraction, tackled Part Two of *The Fire and the Stones*: my view that 25 civilizations passed through parallel stages during their rise and fall. I wrote: "Of all the theories for the growth and decay of civilizations... the secular ones don't explain the idea that gave rise to the civilization. The idea behind a civilization is always a metaphysical vision." Soon my desk was covered with 'post-its' containing dates of stages of civilizations.

The great storm of October 1987 swept in. After the Oaklands parents' Annual General Meeting Vernon Davies, his wife and chauffeur found the battery of their new Jaguar was flat, and I drove them home through driving rain. When I returned our road was like a river. I slept soundly through the ensuing hurricane. The eye of the storm passed over the Roebuck, cut a corridor twenty feet wide through the Forest to our second field and then drove on, demolishing everything within its path including a large chestnut tree that fell across the netting of our tennis-court, up and over the school, just 20 yards from where we were sleeping. It crossed the Oaklands roof, ripping out many tiles. When I woke the grounds were in chaos: several trees were down, branches were strewn everywhere. For days afterwards woodsmen sawed branches and trees for logs as we cleared up round the school, and there were ladders up to the school roof. At home I was still moving rooms and carried on tussling with civilizations.

In the midst of the outer chaos I glimpsed the underlying pattern of history:

America is a growing civilization with little history – the Rome to our Greece. We are old and declining and decaying, we British; we have had our history, like 4th-century Greece.... Thatcher believes our decline has political causes (socialism) but she is wrong; it is historical, and irreversible, and will accelerate once she has gone, taking her archaistic attitudes with her. Russia is old and European, and also in decline. America's rise will go on happening long after Russia has joined Europe. America will introduce a world civilization.

The turbulence in our house continued round work on our extension and I wrote: "Nov. 2. Workmen all round me – painters, carpenters, hammerers by day, gas-central-heating mechanics by night – and I am just pouring data on world civilizations, none of which I 'know', all of which seems to present itself to me of its own accord, leaping off books' pages that fall open; I record and list, and lo! The evidence is assembled as I prove my hunch." Again: "The house is nearly clear as the extension comes to an end. We are carpeted upstairs now. Have got to know: 4 plasterers, 2 carpenters, 2 plumbers, 2 painters, 4 bricklayers, 3 labourers, the supervisor and others who have been daily visitors while I tabulated my Universalist view of history." I now found myself trying to retain data from several civilizations simultaneously during the noisy upheaval around my study.

I struggled on:

Clear thoughts on Russia and China, and the West. The point is, Western civilization is an amalgam of European and American civilizations, both Christian but both separate, one growing and religious (America) and the other old and secular (Europe). The same tension as is found between Rome and Byzantium.

I was working on the pattern of civilizations. Over Christmas I wrote: "The Fundamentalist Islam is a greater danger than Soviet Communism." I was sure that was why I had lived in Iraq and Libya. The family gathered at the Roebuck (at a long table with place cards, crackers and hats), and a couple of days later the last piece of my law of history fell into place:

A brainwave. I see that my... law of history... has a *second* period of expansion before the civilization ends. I have now got the chronology right, I think, and I'm doing a spreadsheet to end all spreadsheets. Every civilization listed down, every stage with dates... listed across.... All the facts will be accurate.

A day later I wrote: "I have seen (been given?) the law of history, and will be able to predict international relations by the time the chart is finished." In January I worked on the stages in civilizations. I worked civilization by civilization: "Jan. 2. Gales. Did India and finished the Arabs."

All through January I worked on my law of history, comparing and contrasting the evolution and development of different civilizations, adapting to historical ends the model of the spreadsheets I did for the bank manager. Transcribing information from the 'post-its' that covered my desk, I compared the Egyptian, the Tibetan, the Syrian, the Mesopotamian, the Greek and the Roman civilizations. I saw a link between Anatolia and Syria:

> Then at midnight, not having eaten, after perseverance of many hours, I saw a whole civilization based on Baal: Ugarit–Philistines–Phoenicians–Aramaeans – and so on, down to the Roman emperor Elagabalus who took his name from Baal. Now it is clear. The answer is there in history; I have to worry away to find it. Mounting excitement. I have done, what, 16 civilizations, and it works for each of them. I am the first man to have discovered the Law of history, and as each day confirms it I get tingles up the spine.

I pressed on with my comparative study of civilizations: "Two for the New World, Celtic and Irish Celtic dovetail, Oceania includes Australia."

I was thinking deeply about civilizations and found one problem solved in my sleep:

> This morning woke up with the solution to the Israelite civilization in my mind: David's time is *not* the unification but the expansion, and by putting the unification back to the tribal league I find that everything fits perfectly. The Law is there and it's like a breakwater perceived through a wobbling surface of water: you have to peer to see it, and it is not always visible at once. But on a clear day it is.

A month later I wrote: "The most important thing is to define, and state in writing, the long-term context in which we live, i.e. the point which our civilization has reached. Everything then becomes clear and is seen as a temporary, a local manifestation of specific historical conditions within the universalist 'plan'."[12]

Nadia came, very much the glamorous and well-groomed British Midland air hostess now. And I encountered Lord (ex-Len) Murray, the ex-TUC Secretary-General, on Loughton station and travelled to Leytonstone with him. I asked if he was writing his memoirs. He said, "No." I said he should write a reflective book that sought to understand our time. He said with intense interest, "To understand oneself might be a good start." I said, "You should write a book that seeks to understand your times and your role in them – and your self." I am partly following my own advice in *My Double Life*.[13]

I buy Harbour-master's House at auction

While I worked on world history I was following the sale of Charlestown and the status of the Harbour-master's House, which commanded a view of the harbour very similar to the view I had glimpsed at Oxford. My talk with Stephen Lucas at the auction of the village had led to a call from his estate agent, who asked if I would pay £150,000 for the Harbour-master's House in its dilapidated condition, an idea on which I was cool. I then received a circular informing me that several properties (including that House) would be auctioned in London on 15 December 1987. I asked a surveyor to look at the property, and on 1 December had a phone call: "It's Lucas. I'm doing you the courtesy of phoning. You'll know the properties are being auctioned." I pointed out the disadvantages of the Harbour-master's House and that his reserve price should be low, and interviewed him about his future plans. "Charlestown will be better, not worse." My bank agreed to fund my purchase and improvements as a retreat every half-term and school holidays. After that I had a deep inner feeling that in some strange way the Harbour-master's House was being given to us to restore: "The harbour property I dreamt of in Oxford may soon be mine."

The auction of properties within Charlestown took place at the location of the original auction: the May Fair InterContinental Hotel, Stratton Street, near Green Park. There were getting on for 800 present, and the auctioneers made the mistake of putting the one with the best view, the Harbour-master's House, first, before the ice was broken. I let two bidders make the running and came in towards the end when it was less than two-thirds of what I had been asked to pay. There was a long pause, and I knew I would be doing future writing there and that no one else would come in. The hammer fell. Stephen Lucas came and shook my hand. Compared with what the other properties fetched I had a bargain.

We drove down to Ann's mother's house and went to nearby Charlestown to view our purchase: a listed building in a conservation area with a view of the sea on two sides: St Austell Bay and Charlestown harbour. I met the surveyor and building engineer who would modernise the House. It was very spacious with excellent views across the soothing sea. Back in Essex I returned to world history: "A day of pondering the Judaistic stages."[14]

Death of Tomlin: Kathleen Raine, memorial service
A few days after my return from Denmark I had received a call from Judith Tomlin: "The news is bad. Frederick has cancer in both lungs and in his brain and has not long to live. He wanted you to know." All day I "felt sombre". There was personal sadness after nearly 25 years of knowing him, but also a rage that a philosopher with so much in his head had to stop before his time.

He had chemotherapy, which was very painful and gave him a temperature for about 6 weeks. He could not see anybody and was very low. He worried about trivia which played on his mind. He had not accepted his impending death; he was fighting it – and so he could not see those he should be bidding farewell. His death was far removed from Socrates's with his friends round him.

Tomlin did not eat for a fortnight to starve his dividing cells. He was given blood, and had sores in his mouth from the chemotherapy, and a cough. Judith said, "He is coughing his lungs away, each time he coughs the disease is advancing. It's dreadful to watch." He had a headache. Judith said he was fascinated by *The Fire and the Stones* but had queried my phrase "Christian Neoplatonism", by which I meant Christianity's drawing on the pagan Neoplatonist tradition. The phrase was justified in its context, but it was kind of Tomlin to express concern when he was so ill.

He was moved to Trinity Hospice, Clapham. No one told me and I did not visit him. He died peacefully on 16 January. I found out from an obituary in *The Daily Telegraph*. I felt sad that he had suffered dreadfully. Towards the end he kept trying to get out of bed to attend a meeting. The funeral was at Hawker's church of St Morwenna in Morwenstow, Cornwall.

Kathleen Raine was asked to write an obituary for *The Independent* and she rang me to check some points: "It's Kathleen Raine, we are both grieving for Frederick Tomlin." We had an hour on the telephone, ostensibly about the obituary... but more on the TLS's book review of *Temenos* ('Élitist and esoteric'). I explained my work. I said Toynbee had been unable to find what differentiated civilizations and that it was the metaphysical Fire. She said: "Of course it is; you can't find it in history, it's not in history." I said: "So he went all round the houses." She suddenly said, "Perhaps Prince Charles would like *Temenos*. I shall ask my good friend Laurens van der Post to give him a set, all the back numbers." We discussed C.S. Lewis; Blake and Yeats; India; America holding the future; and Europe being in decay. We were in accord, and she agreed with all my ideas. She said she would use some of my points in her obituary: that Tomlin was at Eliot's church before Eliot, and was at home in every culture. She said: "Come and see me."

I attended Tomlin's memorial service in St Stephen's, Gloucester Road: T.S. Eliot's beautiful church with red and white arches and gold 'paraphernalia' at the front. Some 200 people attended and the address followed Kathleen Raine's obituary. A small choir sang medieval music in Latin, and there was a High Mass: ringing bells, sung responses, much crossing. The hymns were all Metaphysical poems. Afterwards in the hall behind the Lady Chapel near the T.S. Eliot memorial I spoke to a white-haired man who was at the church in 1947 and said of Eliot: "He was a gentleman. You wouldn't think he was a poet, you'd think he was in the City. He always wore a bowler-hat and carried a furled umbrella when he was church-warden. He was always interested in what you said, very modest. He was very tall, and he bent down to you." I saw Kathleen Raine, attempting to get a cup of tea in the scrimmage and got her one. She told me: "Tom Eliot said to me here that there could be nothing worse than an Americanised Russia." She left to lunch with Laurens van der Post. I sketched a poem on the Eliot tradition within which Tomlin wrote: 'On Eliot's Church'.[15]

Shortly afterwards Kathleen sent me a card saying of authors' works, "We can only scatter seed for future harvests."[16] Which is what I am doing in this work.

Oaklands and law of history: overwork and suspected TIA
After Tomlin's memorial service I met Gorka. I now approached the Byzantine-Russian civilization through world history, and, viewing the Soviet Union in terms of my law of history I told him: "The USSR will break up because of *glasnost*, as economic weakness and loss of central control combine to create revolts in the Soviet empire." I am struck by the accuracy of my interpretation of the Soviet Union.

I had attended an Epping Forest Centenary Trust evening at Queen Elizabeth's hunting lodge and met Sir William Addison, the author of books on Epping Forest who had sold me my *Observer's* books just after the war. He was in a wheelchair, and very interested in my return to Oaklands. Sitting grandly with sticks at 82, he talked about his ailments and his 17 books including *Epping Forest*. He invited me to visit him at home. I did not take his address, and to my regret I never took up his invitation. He died in 1992.

Two days later I talked about Oaklands with Robin Parfitt, Head of the Chigwell Junior School, when he and his wife invited us to dinner in Harsnetts, the 1485 house where my earliest Chigwell teacher Arnold Fellows had lived while he wrote *A Wayfarer's Companion* (*see My Double Life 1: This Dark Wood*). Robin told me about his brother Tudor, an explorer who was currently up the Zambezi in Mozambique, looking for an African tribe that follows Judaism, the lost 12th tribe.

I now learned about Oaklands' past. Around 1900 it was called Fir Bank (or Firbank) and owned by the Sturges, whose daughter Florence married the son of the Harris family who lived across the road in Albion Park House (demolished in 2013). Before the First World War Fir Bank passed to the Howard family who gave their name to the Howard League for Penal Reform and also to Howard's aspirins, in whose Ilford factory one of the Howard boys was killed during the Blitz.

Mabel Reid brought two of the daughters of Bernard Howard (who had been on the platform at Chigwell when I received a prize in 1949). They had lived at what is now Oaklands during the First World War, and as we wandered from room to room they reminisced. They had played records in the cellar, dined in the library (where there was then a door to the garden), used the study as a den and slept up in the right-hand attic, lighting their way with candles as there was no electricity and gas stopped at the first floor. They said that their parents' bedroom was at the top of the first flight of stairs on the right and had a nurses' room next door. The nursery was the large room towards the other end of the first floor. They recalled a fire-drill out of their top-floor bedroom window during the First World War: they had to abseil down on ropes, a terrifying experience from such a great height for small girls. The Howards were at Fir Bank until 1929.

As I worked on world history the Light continued to pour through. There was a play at St Mary's church, Loughton, *Papa Panov's Christmas*, which was based on a story by Leo Tolstoy, with Matthew narrating and Anthony singing a solo. A few days later there was a carol service at St Mary's. I greeted the parents outside in a cold wind. Uniformed children sang in the choir with bright little faces, and there were readings and carols. There was a prayer that gave thanks for Oaklands, for "the one who founded it" and for "new skills", and there was a democratic prayer for the teachers and caretakers. I sat and asked the Light (the Fire) to come into me, and it poured into me and up my spine, filling me with peace as the vicar prayed.

I attended a Christingle service. Matthew and Anthony alternated in reading the lesson, Anthony from the pulpit, Matthew from the lectern. Then the children took Christingles ('Christ-lights') – oranges with lit candles – and stood in the side aisles with them; and when they were snuffed there was smoke in the sunshafts. I gazed at the smoke for a long time, for I had lit my own candle and was ecstatic, the power pouring through me."

That evening I went to Chigwell parish church for their carol service, the fourth time I had been to church within a week. Anthony sang the choir solo. At 5.30 the lights were switched off, and in the dark from the porch door He sang '*Hodie*' and a clear, piping, unaccompanied 'Once in Royal David's City', so loud it filled the church like a blackbird's song, moving me. Afterwards there were mince pies in school.

At the end of January it was reported that record numbers of 11-year-olds (510 to be exact) were sitting for the local independent schools, Bancroft's, Forest and Chigwell, who between them had only 115 places. The idea surfaced that I should start a new school to take some of the 300 who would be unsuccessful. A similar shortage of places was facing younger pupils. I was too involved in my study of civilizations to do anything at the time, but I carried the idea round with me at the back of my mind as I studied each civilization.

I was doing a colossal amount – running Oaklands, calculating salaries, paying invoices and listing every transaction in the accounts while retaining all world history in my head as I went to and fro, pondering on the minutiae of the patterns of world civilizations and overseeing the two boys when Ann had to be in school – and I had wondered if overwork would make me ill. In early February I woke one morning with a loss of grip in my right hand and persisting pins and needles. Ann persuaded me to go to the doctor. I was referred to a neurologist at the National Hospital for Neurology and Neurosurgery in Queen Square. I could not feel pinpricks in my right fingers. I was aware this temporary disability coincided with intensive work (often to 2 a.m.) and the exceptional brain power I had had to draw on as I contemplated my Grand Unified Theory of world history. The demands over two years on my body had been very great, and my poor body was also a pathway for the metaphysical Fire.

In Queen Square I was sent for an MRI brain scan. I was slid into a magnet like the inside of a washing-machine, and the clicking, grating sound reminded me of a tumble-drier. I lay still for two 20-minute spells, a band on my forehead. In due course I was pronounced clear, my brain was not damaged in any way. My consultant, Morgan Hughes, said, "You had a microembolus, a tiny blood-clot. It came from the fatty deposit on the inside of the arteries. You were part-paralysed on the right-hand side. So your leg and arm muscles were weak."[17] He wrote in his report that I had had a "transient ischaemic attack" (TIA). He told me that the blood-clot could have been caused by the overloading of my brain due to the sheer complexity of retaining hundreds of dates and details relating to my Grand Unified Theory for days on end as I compared each stage of 25 civilizations and sought a pattern while running schools, and that it was a warning. I have taken aspirin 75mg prophylactically every day since then. The experience left me aware of what it is like to have a stroke and I wrote a poem, 'A Stroke from the Dark'.

I was thinking about poetry. Matthew had had to read 'Auguries of Innocence' by Blake, and he asked what I thought of the poem. I told him: "The central idea is that there is an invisible world behind the visible world, which looks after all natural creatures and takes revenge if they suffer. Blake wrote this poem in the 1780s; within 10 years or so Coleridge was putting forward the same idea in 'The Ancient Mariner', for the invisible world looks after the albatross and takes revenge against the crew of 200 sailors. Romanticism identifies an invisible world behind the visible." I resolved that my poems "will assert a metaphysical invisible world behind the visible – a Romantic depth". I was aware that I must work in isolation, eschewing all groups, in Charlestown, close to the waves.[18]

We all went to Cornwall at half-term and I had another meeting with the building engineer at the Harbour-master's House in Charlestown. There was now a hole in the front-room floor and much débris off the wall. It was a fine day and the sea sparkled. We went to Cornwall again at the end of March and chose a new kitchen and bathroom and furniture from local stores.

My law of history showed that in the European civilization an imminent stage 44 was one of syncretism and universalism. I attended the Mystics and Scientists conference in Winchester and saw the speakers – Sir George Trevelyan, Lyall Watson, Brian Goodwin, Rupert Sheldrake and Paul Davies – as mainstream figures in the budding universalist 'Renaissance' rather than as New-Thought-type figures of a movement that would soon be forgotten.

From Winchester I joined Ann and our two boys at Lyme Regis's Bay Hotel between the Cobb and the Charmouth cliffs. We hunted for fossils and I bought a 150-million-year-old Jurassic and a 500-million-year-old Cambrian trilobite. We walked along the deserted Monmouth beach before breakfast, and then walked to the end of the Cobb. I wrote a poem, 'From the Cobb, Lyme Regis, 1988', 400 years after the Spanish Armada.

Back in Essex I was aware that my right (writing) arm was now slowly becoming paralysed. I forced it to do things – to twist and push – but it was painful and preferred to hang limply by my side. I kept it writing but it would rather not write.[19] I was battling a physical disability of my right arm to complete my study of world history.

Finding Coopersale Hall
Soon after Easter a doctor approached me on the Oaklands steps and said that he had two children on the Oaklands waiting-list of 150 and that all the local schools were full. He asked, "Couldn't you start a new school somewhere nearby, teaching the same as you teach at Oaklands, and fill it from families like mine?" He revived the idea I had had earlier of starting a new school. I decided to ignore my alleged TIA.

I did not find Coopersale Hall; it found me. I looked at what was on the market and saw three or four properties: Oak Grove, New Barns Farm, Hainault Hall – and Coopersale House, Rupert Murdoch's old house. It had a lake that children could fall in and no assembly hall, and I was not sure I could obtain planning consent: change of use from 'residential'. I considered making an offer for Buckhurst Hill County High School, which Essex County Council were considering selling, but it was snapped up by Sikhs before any advertisement. In early May I happened to be in the Oaklands main field one afternoon when parents were rounding up children at the end of the school day. I was approached by Alan Fordham, an Oaklands parent and property developer, who told me he had heard I was looking for a site on which to start a new school and would I consider his property, Coopersale Hall?

I visited Fordham on 18 May and was immediately impressed by the property's suitability. It was a Georgian building, Fordham said c.1776, set in eight acres of beautiful grounds which had been stocked from Kew Gardens and had been opened to the public during the First World War, and it had an orangery/ballroom that could be converted into an assembly hall that would seat 250. It was near the M11/M25 interchange, and I felt I could secure change of use – planning consent – on the grounds of motorway noise. I talked with Fordham in the oak-panelled dining-room (now the library) before a barley-twist wooden fireplace; the first room that Churchill had known in Epping when he visited its then owner Lord Lyle, MP for Epping, to arrange the transfer of the MPship to himself in 1924. Fordham worked out that I would have to buy Coopersale Hall, the neighbouring Orchard Cottage and the private drive from three separate vendors and put them together in order to found a new school. I wrote: "Coopersale Hall is in my grasp, together with Orchard Cottage.... I must be courageous.... Like Brutus, I feel 'There is a tide in the affairs of men/Which, taken at the flood, leads on to fortune.'"

I was aware that an economic phase was coming to an end and that there would be a recession, but reckoned that if I went ahead a new school would be in place for the next mini-boom, when the expansion of nearby Stansted Airport might bring 50,000 more families into the area. I had obtained planning permission to develop the Cornish house, which would require an outlay. But I knew that Oaklands had 150 on its waiting-list and that there was a shortage of places in the locality. We decided we would do our best to found a new school in Epping at Coopersale Hall.

We hosted a reception in the Oaklands hall on a Sunday for Argie's 85th birthday. It was attended by 34 relatives and 15 friends, including Lord Murray. I greeted him and his wife at the door, and Lady Murray's first words to me were: "You taught in the State system, now you're in the private system. You were with the deprived and now you're with the privileged – how do you square that, how do you justify it?" Amused, I said that the ILEA had degenerated in my time. She asked: "What do you mean, degenerated?" So I explained that academic content and standards had been sacrificed to political initiatives. Lord Murray listened in uncomfortable silence. He was not confrontational, and I had a couple of pleasant conversations with him. I made a speech about Argie. I had a long conversation with Nadia, who had come down from Scotland for the party.

A fortnight later I watched Anthony receive a prize from Edward Heath at Chigwell School's speech day. Heath made an amusing speech but then refused to conduct the orchestra in which Matthew played in the open air, the wind blowing the music about. I had risked my life to supply him with intelligence about Communist intentions, and I saw him as a pro-European universalist. I stood beside him but did not speak to him, walled in by silence, unable to declare my service.

The bank agreed to advance what I needed to buy Coopersale Hall and Orchard Cottage from two separate vendors, and later in the month contracts were exchanged on condition that planning consent was given for the Hall to become a school. I now opened negotiations with a third vendor (a local called Hammond) to buy the private drive. I barely thought of the risk I was taking. I knew within that the idea would work.

I had learned more about Coopersale Hall. Having visited Lord Lyle there in 1924, Churchill stayed there in the war when it was a rest home for civil defence wardens. He slept in the classroom we would call 'the Churchill room', and he retired to the air-raid shelters in the cellars when there was an air raid. He would leave Downing Street and in 24 hours he would visit Blake Hall where the Battle of Britain was being planned, visit the pilots at North Weald and then spend the night with the civil defence wardens at Coopersale Hall before returning to Downing Street, having had 24 hours of country air. In those days the Coopersale Hall estate was over 150 acres and stretched to the hills.

In due course I met a former owner of Coopersale Hall, Peter Norman, at a Chigwell Speech Day (where I was seeing Anthony receive the Governors' Prize) who told me that the thick wall in Orchard Cottage was 14th-century.

Finishing 61 stages in 25 civilizations
In early July I finished the 61 stages of the life cycles of civilizations. I had spent nine months turning my inspiration into perspiration. I was now writing about the American civilization: "The Achaemenian [Persian] and American civilizations and empires are in the same stage regarding expansion.... Perhaps a world order is ahead, as regional power blocs (Africa, Asia, etc), under American leadership (the nuclear superpower)."[20] I placed Britain's imperial decline in the pattern, and Britain's colonial conflict. I pinpointed the growth of the British Empire.

Village plan and collapse of marquee at Charlestown
We returned to Cornwall and visited Charlestown. I wrote: "A rough sea after rain, misty spray over the rocks and the house has been gutted: old plaster out, stripped back to red bricks, slate walls, beams and joists. Two skips of plaster outside." I met a sea captain who lived next door, Ken Gowsell, whose house was the only building in Charlestown in the 1770s, where fishermen brought their pilchards and loaded them onto carts. There were holes in the wall for levering on the tops of the pilchard barrels. According to the received view our house followed with a few others soon

after 1790.

At the end of July we were back in Cornwall. The Harbour-master's House had scaffolding round it, having had the seaward wall replaced as it was made of porous shale. BOM Holdings had sold Charlestown harbour on and the new owners put on a presentation in a marquee in the cobbled car park. There were wooden seats for 285 within scaffolding, and the new owners – bow-tied, dapper, dark-haired Barry Williamson and (incredibly) Stephen Lucas – spoke to the village, trying to create a favourable reception for a massive planning application to build 94 new houses. They showed maps and charts to the villagers and planners. There were questions. The chief planner asked a question about sewage. A woman from the local Residents Association near me asked a hostile question on parking. Then I heard a crack behind me, and we sank. It was like going down in a lift and stopping with a bump. The scaffolding on which the floor and seats rested caved in and we dropped four feet. The marquee's 'tent pole' swayed. Then there was a silence.

No one took charge and said, "Stay in your seats, ladies and gentlemen." There was no panic, but while Williamson stared, hypnotised by the awfulness of what had happened we all rose and made our way out to the cobbled car park. The spread of food, which had cost £10,000, was brought out and we tucked in, venting our indignation at the plan to overdevelop the port while we munched.

We drove back to Essex to oversee work in the classrooms and carry forward the purchase of Coopersale Hall. I did further work on the stages of civilizations, and found that my unconscious mind was solving problems for me while I mowed the Oaklands fields: "The mind is amazing. Sat on the mower and worked out a revised Russia [i.e. Byzantine–Russian civilization] without any notes, and retained it all."

In early August we returned to Cornwall to supervise the building work at the Harbour-master's House. The boys went canoeing to Silver Mine cove, beyond Gull Island. Our near neighbour, Arthur Hosegood was very welcoming and told me, "It's a wonderful place for a writer down here. You can walk on the cliffs and on the beach and think, and you see everything clear." A few days later I recorded: "A scorcher yesterday; hazy today. Spent both days on Charlestown beach, sunbathing. Corrected proofs. Today, redid Japan; suddenly saw it…. The boys in their dinghy and [on their] raft, paddling round the rocks in their wet suits."

We heard that Williamson and Lucas had been denied planning permission for 94 houses. The collapse of the scaffolding in the marquee round the planning officer had anticipated the collapse of the planning application.

The secretary of the Cornish Buildings Group and a man from Truro

County's Archaeological Department, came to look at the open walls of the Harbour-master's House and the neighbouring buildings and concluded – in a minority view – they may all have been built before 1790: "In our case, the fireplace on the back wall (i.e. our middle wall, which was the original back wall) is a sign of the 17th or early 18th century, as is the granite pillar [now on the outside of the most seaward wall]." There were cobbles under our kitchen floor, which could have been a yard or a kitchen. They concluded that the house was probably not a boat-house but a domestic residence with a stud wall. They said that pilchards were exported from the beach, and that the shingle on the beach was ballast from foreign shores, dropped by sailing-ships. The holes in the Gowsells' wall were where levers squeezed the oil down in the pilchard barrels. The two historians challenged the idea that Charlestown had only four houses in 1788, and said that Charles Rashleigh would have built the harbour in the 1790s where there were houses.

During my walks by the night sea at Charlestown I thought about the Grand Unified Theory the physicists sought (the union of all four forces) and wrote:

> The Grand Unified Theory of the universe which physicists seek in the phenomenal world is to be found in the Fire (as Heracleitus probably foresaw). Like the historians looking for their Grand Unified Theory in history books, physicists seek it in physics books.[21]

This perception anticipated my coming work, *The Universe and the Light*.

Back in Essex I was getting a new classroom ready at Oaklands. The work had fallen behind, and I painted it all day until midnight, working with our in-house general builder. The first day of term began without a pane of glass in the new door. The children came into their new classroom, left their bags and went to assembly. The glazier came, and, under my supervision, when they returned the door contained glass and the room was finished. I had cut it very fine.

Death of Biggs-Davison

In February 1988 I had attended a dinner at the House of Commons and I had been shocked by Biggs-Davison's appearance. He had lost his hair, having had cancer and chemotherapy, and was reported to be considering giving up his MPship. Douglas Hurd, now Home Secretary, who had bought me a drink after my public debate with Margaret Thatcher regarding FREE in 1976, was the guest of honour. To my surprise I found that Ann and I were on top table – it was as if Biggs-Davison were indirectly recognising the work of the 'Heroes of the West' – and I chatted to him and to Hurd before the meal. I said I was investigating world history, and Biggs-Davison said: "Both Toynbee and Spengler were wrong about Western civilization, it's not in decline." I was seated next to Tim Pratt, Biggs-Davison's constituency chairman, and was surprised to be sounded out as to whether I would be interested in replacing Biggs-Davison. With hindsight I can see that he had told Pratt that he was about to retire due to ill health, and had suggested that I might replace him. I said I was not interested – my priority now was world history and metaphysical poetry – and that there would be "a flood of applications", as he agreed. As he left after his speech, Hurd stopped and said to me, "Good luck with the books." He was speaking of my turning to authorship. Looking back, I wonder if I turned my back on a career in the House of Commons that day.

In mid-September 1988 I learned that Sir John Biggs-Davison had died (on 17 September) after being taken ill while visiting Angola. I read in the press that he had survived cancer and was cleared after chemotherapy in July. He had gone to Angola with Sir Anthony Buck MP, where for some of the time they slept in a tent. He had returned to Taunton Hospital with viral pneumonia and suffering from jaundice, and had died. The virus was a mystery. He was 70, and I had known him for over 32 years. He had not lived to see the successful outcome of my idea of FREE in 1989–1991: the fall of the Berlin Wall and the collapse of Soviet Communism.

I thought of his role in the 'Heroes of the West'. He had first gone to Angola in 1961, long before I had worked with Africans. His recent visit to Angola was at a time when hostilities between South Africa and Angola had just ceased and UNITA was supported by the US and in alliance with South Africa. An accord was being negotiated between Angola, Cuba and South Africa that would lead to the withdrawal of Cuban and South African troops from Angola. There was a timetable for Cuban withdrawal from Southern Africa. In a sense Biggs-Davison was making a visit like the one I had planned to make with Sartre.

I wondered whether there was more to his death than pneumonia. Could he have been poisoned? I then read in an obituary that he had been a Marxist at Oxford. I was astonished. He had always been too right-wing to be in the company of Maclean and Philby. I read that he was being buried at St Petroc's church, Timberscombe, near Minehead, Somerset, and sent flowers. Vernon Davies (who now knew who Biggs-Davison was) attended the funeral by helicopter, which, I was told, landed in the churchyard.

The more I thought about Biggs-Davison's sudden death, the more I thought it suspicious. Angola was ruled by the MPLA, a pro-Soviet organisation with links with the IRA (as I knew from McForan's book). He had been associated with Airey Neave, who had been killed by the IRA. All it would take was one telephone call and a doctored ham sandwich. I wrote: "I am in Hamlet's situation. Intuitively, I know Biggs-Davison was murdered, as Hamlet knew his father was murdered. The question is, how do I bring it out?"

The situation bothered me, for the 'Heroes of the West' should not simply accept the murder (if that was what it was) without protest. A father, Mr Fisher, came to watch his son play football at Oaklands, and as I walked back across the fields with him in my track suit I asked him where he worked. He said, "It's secret, but in Stormont." I immediately asked: "What did you think of Biggs-Davison's death?" He countered by asking my view. I said: "I think it stinks. He's cured of cancer, goes to Angola, contracts a mystery virus and dies on his return. I think he was murdered." The parent said, "I'll think about that."

The next time I saw him, standing outside my house near the school, he said: "I stopped an important man in the corridor at Stormont [Tom King, then Secretary of State for Northern Ireland] and told him what you said. He stood and said, 'No, no, I don't think so.' I left it at that, and next day he stopped me and said, 'You know, I couldn't sleep last night, I was thinking about what you said, and I think, Yes, yes, there may be something in it. So I've launched an investigation. Both intelligence services have launched an investigation. It's gone to the top in Northern Ireland, it's now in Curzon Street."

I felt relieved. There was no more I could do. I had raised this at the highest level, and if the professionals found nothing, then I would never find anything. I never heard the outcome, and officially Biggs-Davison, ally of the 'Heroes of the West', died of a mystery virus, to the consternation of Taunton Hospital.

I went to the memorial service for Biggs-Davison at Waltham Abbey. The Abbey was packed. There were chairs all down the side aisles, and even then there was not enough room to seat everybody. It was an ecumenical service, taken by the Bishop of Barking with a Catholic representation under the Bishop of Brentwood. I shook hands with all his family afterwards. They greeted me very warmly. Lingering in the porch of Waltham Abbey I thought it a good place for the service to be held.

The following February I dined at the Carlton Club and sat next to a local American, Harriet Pratt, the wife of Biggs-Davison's constituency chairman. Biggs-Davison often stayed with her and her husband. She said to me: "He only left £20,000. It was Pamela's parents' money, the house in Hereford Square was her parents'. He lived on his MP's salary and his writing. He always liked meeting you, he said you were the most intelligent of his constituents. He liked the intellectual discussions with you." I asked, thinking of his involvement with Crozier and of his death in Angola: "Do you think Biggs-Davison was involved in intelligence work?" She said without hesitation, "Yes. I'm cynical – everyone who's worked abroad has been."[22] And I fell silent and went over a chain of events that had affected my life from a new perspective, and wondered how he, a right-wing MP who had supported South Africa, could, if what I had just heard was right, have made himself vulnerable in a country like Angola which opposed everything he had stood for.

Eliot's centenary service, Laurens van der Post
I attended Eliot's centenary service in a packed St Stephen's, Gloucester Road. I passed blind Heath-Stubbs on the pavement and spoke to him. I sat across the aisle from Eliot's widow Valerie Eliot and next to Judith Tomlin in the Tomlin pew. Tomlin's book on his friendship with Eliot had just appeared posthumously, telling the story of his long relationship with Eliot through Eliot's letters to him and saying that Eliot was the greatest man he had ever met, and that he regarded Eliot's poetry "the most powerful counterweight in my time" to the "ugliest of trends" that led poetry to reflect the violent and erotic rather than the sacred.[23] Sir Laurens van der Post spoke brilliantly about Fire. Leaning on the lectern (which collapsed after loud knockings, causing him to say "It's done this because I'm going to talk about thunder"), he said that Eliot was the greatest religious poet in the English language, that he first read Eliot in 1953 in Africa, while caring for flocks. He said that Eliot unswervingly stood for the Fire and that the poems grew naturally like roses. I spoke to Valerie Eliot and van der Post afterwards. Van der Post invited me to be in touch with him about my own work on the Fire and civilizations. I was extremely impressed by the fluency and force of van der Post's Fire sermon.

On the way back I passed Francis Bacon, the artist, who I had met and spoken with in the Colony Room. He was wandering along Harley Street towards Oxford Street, looking upwards, barely looking where he was going; aged yet handsome.[24]

"Get on with your work"
I was under my own shadow of death. I had a health check, and the consultant told me after I had been ECGed and tested: "The TIA [transient ischaemic attack] you had is the most serious thing. There could be a second TIA at any time; alternatively one may never come. Do what you want to do now." He told me, "Get on with your work." I had already made the decision to concentrate on the books I had to do. On my bronchiectasis he said: "You had TB in 1947, which probably came from the milk." (The milk delivered by the milkman to our home and the crates of free third-of-a-pint bottles of milk we drank through straws in school at break?) "The milk then was not treated and there were no antibiotics. TB as a child leads to bronchiectasis later."

I sensed that I would soon be writing poetry again. In October I made a couple of flying visits to Cornwall to supervise the work on the Harbour-master's House. I drove "through storm and spray" and stayed at the Pier House Hotel and wrote: "The sea has been over the road up to the [Pier House] hotel wall: trails of seaweed, and shingle. Feel flinty and pre-poetic. Am ready to rejoin the [poetic] road I left in 1976 to report the history of the Fire and of civilizations. A poetic output is ahead. I wrote a poem, 'A Home like a Nest'." A fortnight later I joined Ann and the boys, who were already in Cornwall. I wrote: "The house began like a building site, but now that the carpets are down and all the sofas are there it is turning into a very good house."[25]

I found and establish Coopersale Hall School
I had had meetings with Epping Forest District Council officials and planners about the private road to Coopersale Hall – I had reached a semblance of agreement with Hammond after tortuous negotiations – and as I progressed to the planning decision there was news that Bancroft's would be opening a new prep school in 1990, and would be in competition with what I was trying to do. On 3 November the planning committee reached a decision allowing Coopersale Hall to become a school. At 8.30 p.m. Ann Miller, the Chairman of the Council, rang to tell me I had received planning permission. I knew within that the new school would be supported. Now I regularly interrupted my work on my study of civiliza-tions to complete the purchase of Coopersale Hall, Orchard Cottage and the private road – the exchange of contracts had been conditional on my obtaining planning permission – and to present news of the new school to parents. I told the Oaklands staff after a fire-drill. There was applause.

Soon afterwards my wife and I were invited to dinner by Chigwell parents, the Thoms, and the only other guests were Dr Southern, Head Master of Bancroft's School, and his wife. As the six of us dined, Dr Southern said, "May I take this opportunity to tell you that we're opening a new Junior School, Bancroft's Prep, in September 1990." I said, "May I take this opportunity to tell you that we're opening a new Junior School in Epping, Coopersale Hall, in September 1989." There was a stunned silence. Later we agreed that there was room for both of us. (Our hosts had no idea we were both starting new schools at the same time.)

Having declined to be considered as Biggs-Davison's successor, in November I took Matthew to Waltham Abbey Town Hall to attend the adoption of Biggs-Davison's replacement. Steve Norris was adopted: a forceful 43-year-old with definite opinions and fluent articulacy on a platform, who went to my College. I met him on the platform afterwards. He said: "We must talk." In fact, I had quite a discussion with him – he was

Nicholas shortly after purchasing Coopersale Hall, November 1988

younger than me and we had not overlapped at Worcester College – and I told him about my time as a publisher and how I now ran two schools.

On 17 November I completed the purchase of Coopersale Hall and there were articles in the local press. The Oaklands secretary had taken 70 applications for the new school. The idea was clearly working. I immediately began to organise work on widening the 450-yard private road, which involved building an embankment, doubling the width of the front gate, widening the internal drive, converting the downstairs of the school into classrooms and installing fire doors.

I was still working on my study of civilizations and during this time I heard Anthony sing a solo in Mendelssohn's *Elijah* at St John's, Epping. Half the church held two huge choirs (which included the Old Chigwellian Richard Leng), and the other half held the audience. Anthony, the youth, sang in a Chigwell blazer, a boy of eleven among professional singers in DJ, and received loud applause.

On 9 December Hammond exchanged contracts on the road after I had done most of the widening. I took him to meet my solicitor. As I introduced him Hammond produced a mobile phone and began a shouted conversation with his ex-bunny girlfriend while my solicitor looked on in speechless horror. By mid-December 200 applications had been received for the new school.

We held the Oaklands Christmas gathering at Coopersale Hall, which the Fordhams had now vacated. There was no furniture in the building, but there were expensive carpets and curtains and we managed. In candlelight I served wine from packets in the hall. We had wooden chairs in the Jacobean/panelled room and the Adam room, and some sat under the frieze and in the bay window. Many were quite overcome by it all. Many said that the school would last a very long time. After Christmas we went to Tunbridge Wells and lunched with the family at the Spa Hotel.

In January 1989 I supervised a JCB and a 10-ton lorry to widen the internal drive at Coopersale Hall. We doubled the width of the private road at the bottom of Flux's Lane by creating an embankment. I changed the contour of Nature, applying the thinking I had observed during the creation of the Tanzam railway. I organised the delivery of a septic tank, which was installed with the help of the local fire brigade. I coped with the safety requirements of the Fire Officer. I held interviews for the new Headship and appointed Frances Best (deputy head at another local independent school, Woodford Prep) as the first Head of the new school. At an event at St Mary's church, Loughton I ran into Ann Miller, the Chairman of the Council, who said, "I want to come and teach at your new school."

Following publicity about the new school I had received 60 letters of application from local teachers. I set up interviews in the inadequately furnished and heated building and the new Head and I saw the applicants in batches of four or five. We appointed twenty. Ann Miller was appointed to teach the oldest children. At a gathering I met Steve Norris, the new MP who had won the by-election caused by Biggs-Davison's death. He said he would be putting his second son Edward's name down for Coopersale Hall, and agreed to open the Oaklands fête. The new school's secretary was in Mensa and a long-standing friend of the Oaklands secretary. (They had been in the same class at Woodford County High School and the Oaklands' secretary's hair was set alight from the Bunsen burner they shared in science.)

I always talked to my two boys at bedtime, and in the course of asking Anthony to visualise the Charlestown steps down to the beach I put him in touch with a part of his mind that was new to him. He said he could see a cobbled street bustling with people in Victorian clothes and a sign swinging in the wind over a vegetable shop. Then he was in a wooden room with a bare wooden bed and a blanket, wearing a nightshirt. He went downstairs and a woman in black wearing a Victorian hat said, "Why, Master Edward." Later he looked at his black front door and read the number: 17. I wondered if he had had a far memory of a previous life or located his imagination. His vivid description of what he saw was an indication that he would become a film director.

At half-term I took Ann and the boys down to Cornwall to stay for the first time in the Harbour-master's House. We walked up to The Rashleigh Arms, Charlestown and chatted to the barman, who told me that BOM were in difficulties, that Lucas was £1.8 million in debt and that Williamson and Lucas's planning application for 94 new houses would never happen on appeal. A couple of days later a friend of the barman told me that Lucas had been in prison, and that his brother was being investigated by the Department of Trade and Industry.

The son of Dr Southern (Head Master of Bancroft's, now Coopersale Hall's rival), Tom Southern, a friend of Matthew's, came to stay. It is my recollection that the arrangement was made during our dinner with the Southerns in November, and that he was brought by Dr Southern, who was staying in Falmouth. I can recall talking to him on the green before our house. We watched a Dutch boat leave. It was manned by Dutch Calvinists who would not work on a Sunday. It got stuck on the beach in the harbour entrance and took an hour to refloat. Williamson called across to Graham the Harbour-master, "I want this boat away," not realising that high pressure and wind compress the water downwards, so that a depth of two feet swiftly becomes six inches. Soon afterwards Dr Southern became Head Master of Christ's Hospital, on which my father's Bluecoat school was based.

I worked on *The Fire and the Stones*. I "proof-read stages 35–47, and checked them against the chart of all stages. Corrected the Germanic pattern which somehow had a couple of wrong dates. Made adjustments." In between times I walked by the sea. From the pier I saw my boys near Gull Rock, "standing like sea-birds silhouetted in the twilight: dark outlines against a calm sea. Now hear the breathings of Nature outside. All is energy, and so am I." My energy flowed into stories, and also poems: "Feb. 13. Wrote 'The Artist and Fame' about 'shotgun Tommy'.... Wrote 'Maturing Love and Vision'.... Feb. 14. More poems: 'Shingle Streaked with Tar', 'A Business Walk by the Sea' (having observed Barry Williamson in consultation with his adviser this morning) and 'Chain and Padlock: Time and Forgotten Years'."

Easter was in March that year. Back in Essex I noted: "Easter Sunday. Wrote two poems. 'Toil' and then 'Easter Sunday', in the middle of which I saw a woodpecker tapping on the elm by the gate from my study window; and put it in the poem."[26]

I influence choice of Tony Little as Head of Chigwell School
David Evennett, MP (later Lord Commissioner of HM Treasury), a Chigwell School parent, one of whose sons was a friend of Anthony's, had us to dinner at his home, and I told him about my study of civilizations. He expressed concern at the leadership and standards at Chigwell School. The Head was retiring and we discussed how we could influence the choice of successor. I had heard that the interviews would soon take place, and that there was a short-list of three: two economists and a young Head of English from Brentwood School. Evennett asked me if I knew any of the Governors, and I replied that Colin Wilcoxon, then a Cambridge English don at Pembroke, had been Head Boy when I was at school. It was agreed that I would go up and see him in Cambridge to reflect concern in a number of areas on behalf of several parents.

I accordingly rang Colin Wilcoxon and visited him in Pembroke for a couple of hours. I got my message across that there should be a return to academic standards. I said Chigwell should go for the Head of English who would emphasise the right things despite his relative inexperience, rather than for an economist who might emphasise the wrong things. Colin Wilcoxon took note of all I said and thanked me for reflecting the views of a number of parents. Soon afterwards the Governors duly appointed the Head of English from Brentwood, Tony Little, who went on to become Head Master of Eton. If I had not visited Wilcoxon, would Chigwell have appointed Little and would he have gone on to be Head Master of Eton?

Free will in history of civilizations
I was reflecting deeply on my study of civilizations and the principle of free will:

> There is no determinism in history or religion. Civilizations move through stages because human free will (of contemplative mystics and leaders) takes them from stage to stage. Nothing is written in the stars. There are possibilities or tendencies only, which human effort brings to being – like my struggle to found and grow Coopersale Hall School.

I had been scrutinising different civilizations – the American, Russian and Japanese – and had gone through Turkish history when, at the end of January, my Turkish ex-tenant Jalal rang from Germany to say that his wife and niece would be arriving the next morning. They stayed for a short while, and a conversation I had with his wife strengthened my feeling that both Gibbon and Toynbee were wrong about the Byzantine civilization, which neither continued the Roman civilization (as Gibbon had claimed) nor passed into the Ottoman civilization (as Toynbee had claimed). The Byzantine civilization had passed into the Russian civilization: "The Byzantine civilization had not become the Ottomans; rather the Russians with the Arabs passing under the Ottomans." Jalal had made contact at just the right time. I had seen the European civilization was about to pass into a conglomerate, a United States of Europe, ending a colonial conflict. All through Easter I wrestled with the role of the conglomerate in all 25 civilizations.

I now took a new look at Ezra Pound's question to me in 1970: "Have you had 12 experiences that sum up the culture of the last 30 years?" I boiled the 12 experiences down to 10:

> Answer: (1) Chinese cultural revolution; (2) Libyan Revolution; (3) Iraq, Arab revival (cf Iran); (4) USA – world dominance; (5) British decline; (6) Japan, industrial miracle and Zen; (7) Vietnam; (8) European reunion (Brussels bursting into light); (9) Far East tour, coming Pacific 'Eastern' civilization; (10) Russia, 'Archangel' (Byzantine identity v Communism). They are all there. Already done [in poems]. Just simply order and organise them.

The experiences of the culture of the Age that Pound had asked me about were already in my poetic works. I knew that I would be making a selection of these as soon as I could get clear from world history.

At the beginning of April we went to Cornwall and I sat in the sitting-room of the Harbour-master's House, which now had central heating. There was a view across St Austell Bay to the Black Head of Trenarren and down to the harbour where long china clay boats came and went, manoeuvring through the narrow neck, their sides squealing on hung tyres. I was able to sit on the sofa surrounded by my work, and watch the dramatic changes to the sea. I wrote: "The sea is booming and crashing, the rain is lashing." I walked in "a blustery wind, worked at figures as in a chamber of Hell, totalling, doing end-of-the-year returns for the taxman, all essential yet isolating and what I wanted to be doing, my history, lying nearby. Wrote a poem, 'Charlestown in Motion'." More clear, I reflected that in the 1960s I had "rejected the armchair mind for *experience*".[27] Now I found the peace to reflect on my study of civilizations.

I open Coopersale Hall School

Towards the end of February I had announced Frances Best as Headmistress of Coopersale Hall School to the local press, in the presence of Pam Giblett of the *West Essex Gazette* (who as Pam Humphreys had worked for my mother and bathed me) and a journalist of the *Epping and Harlow Star* who also interviewed me on local radio and filmed me for 20–30 minutes. I designed a new uniform in conjunction with the new Head. I designed the School badge, which showed the evergreen holm-oak on the lawn that was reputed to have been planted by Elizabeth I. I improved the heating and furnishings. A local road company widened the private drive, and snow fell the day after the workmen finished. Soon a blizzard was raging. I had announced that I would open Coopersale Hall School for 35 very young children in April and 40 parents turned up for the School's first Induction Day in March.

In April I opened Coopersale Hall School for two classes downstairs while we carried on getting the upstairs ready for September when the roll would increase to 150. That summer the children spent golden mornings sitting at tables on the terrace or on the lawn under the holm-oak. Every morning I organised the workmen who were converting different parts of the building and improving the grounds, and I would always look in on the two classes, which were often out of doors.

We attended an event at St Martin-in-the-Fields to commemorate the 360th anniversary of the founding of Chigwell School, at which Anthony sang a solo, 'O Sing unto the Lord', to a packed, ticket-only congregation. His solo to a packed church was confident and clear, under the sun-burst over the altar.[28] In the aisle I met Tony Little, the new Head at Chigwell

School. In the crypt I met Tudor Parfitt, the explorer, who was with his schoolmaster brother. Afterwards I wrote a couple of stories: 'A Sunburst in St Martin's' and 'Tombstones and a Good-looking Explorer'.

Finishing The Fire and the Stones: *'Introduction to the New Universalism' received in sleep*
I was working hard on my study of civilizations and again received inspiration in my sleep; this time on Universalism:

> Ap. 29. After ten days of working late on the book; slept fitfully.... Woke with the beginning of my 'Introduction to the New Universalism' in mind and wrote it in vest and pants before doing exercises. I believe I have devised a new discipline. As Sartre redefined Existentialism, I have devised Universalism.

I finally finished *The Fire and the Stones*. "11 May. After a week-and-a-half of daily revision amid Coopersale Hall, have finally finished my revision.... I predict that European civilization will end AD c.2610. It has taken me a year to establish the details."[29]

I was relieved to have unburdened myself. On a sweltering Sunday, 21 May, I celebrated my 50th birthday at Coopersale Hall. More than 80 family members and friends arrived and a buffet lunch was served in the incomplete assembly hall. There were staff from both Oaklands and Coopersale Hall Schools. David Evennett stood alongside my old cricket captain Alan Lavers and the Essex cricketer David East (whose wife was joining Coopersale Hall School). My brother Rob made a speech about my experience as tutor to Hirohito's son and as eyewitness of Gaddafi's revolution, and about my "achievement" in having two schools. There was a game of cricket on the lawn for the children, watched by the guests sitting on the terrace, and Anthony hit lustily. One ball just missed Miss Lord's head as she sat snoozing under a tree.

Steve Norris becomes our tenant
The following week the new Epping Forest MP Steve Norris and his wife looked round Coopersale Hall for their son. I showed them Orchard Cottage, which was standing empty while waiting to be converted into classrooms, and Steve said: "I'd like to live there." "Why don't you?" I said. "We're not ready to use it yet. You can live there until we're ready. You could have the run of the grounds at weekends and the squash court and tennis-court." The idea lodged. Ann and I put on tea in the study.

Steve Norris MP opened the Oaklands fair. I greeted him and his wife outside the gate in Albion Hill and he immediately raised the possibility of renting Orchard Cottage, with parents queuing near our elbows. Before we walked through the front gate he asked how much I would charge. As we sauntered down to the main field I said it should be a fair rent, at the bottom end of the scale to compensate for building work we would do if we received planning permission to build an extension behind the hall. A thousand people were waiting for the fair to be declared open. I mentioned a figure and then introduced him, microphone in hand. I pointed out that he had just monitored the unfairness of Noriega's election in Panama, and that he would be bringing the same critical skills to his judgement of the 'bouncy castle drawing competition'. He congratulated "Nick and Ann" on another successful fair and declared it open. There was then a falconry display. A kestrel called 'Lady' sat high up in the oak-tree and swooped to take food from the handler's gloved fist. The Norrises walked round all the stalls and I saw them to their car at the end.[30]

'Tablecloth' of seven years of projections, seven-foot-long chart of 25 civilizations
We had been down to Cornwall for half-term. I revised *The Fire and the Stones* on "a hot sunny day. In the evening a calm sea." I immediately wrote three poems: 'Dancing Universe', 'Silence' and 'Under the Stars'. On 1 June I "finished the substance of Part Two of the book on a fine but chilly day. Sat in the sun during the afternoon.... Have done the 'Rainbow' chart [i.e. the parabola of the rise and fall of a civilization]."

I had been working on the seven-foot-long chart of 25 civilizations that accompanies the book. It grew out of bank projections on the schools' income and expenditure I had done all through the 1980s. I had begun to apply the principle of bank projections to history at the end of the 1980s, and now I had 25 civilizations down, each with 61 parallel stages across. The chart was entitled 'Chart summarizing 61 stages in the Life Cycle of 25 civilizations' and included projections for living civilizations. I noted: "Life cycle. The words came to me on the plane between Baghdad and Basra, and now they are in the title above my history chart." They had lodged in my mind back in 1962 high above Ur, the site of the first Middle-Eastern civilization, as a call to study the life cycle of the civilizations, and again there seemed a certain inevitability about what I had done.

I took Ann and the boys to hear the evangelist Billy Graham preach at West Ham football stadium. I had not seen him since 1954. He called for people to declare themselves for eternal life, and members of the crowd came forward onto the pitch in silence. I wrote 'An Evangelist's Instant Salvation' about the event.

I was overdoing it. I was putting the finishing touches to *The Fire and the Stones* while doing the latest figures for the bank manager: *seven* years of forecasts for Coopersale Hall on a long sheet of stuck-together pages that folded out, carrying dozens of costs across and forecasting anticipated inflation increases for each year. (I was expected to predict the level of inflation each year for the next seven years and build it in to each successive cost.) I had a lot in my head and had toothache which was diagnosed as "neuralgia". Three days later at an Open Evening at Oaklands I felt giddy but forced myself to serve wine for the 400 parents and talk from 7 p.m. to 10 p.m. I wrote: "Felt myself passing out. A woman talking at me going round and round. Said 'Excuse me' and dashed out to the kitchen, went out to the house, lay down with feet up for 5 mins, then returned via the kitchen to resume the conversation."

The schools required my constant attention. At Coopersale Hall the work upstairs was progressing. A fire door had to be knocked into a very thick wall. (Two of my in-house builders found an 1817 shilling of George III which had dropped down a flue. One of the fellows told me authoritatively that a shilling was three hours' work in 1817.) I was transforming the garage-like orangery into an assembly hall with a stage. I personally designed the panelling, which was fitted by our in-house carpenter. We had found some Jacobean carvings in the loft, including a coat of arms which showed a knight's armorial helmet, and we fixed it over the fireplace, where it can still be seen. We had Sports Day at both schools, and the Oaklands swimming gala took place at Loughton Pool. I was on the microphone for all three events.

Soon after the schools broke up the bank staff came to play rounders on the Oaklands fields: twenty cashiers in singlets and shorts. I served wine and orange and left them to their game. There was much shouting and cheering from the field. The deputy manager told me of my seven-year projections, "Ken [Jones, my bank manager,] is always poring over your figures. He calls them 'the tablecloth' because when they are folded out they cover the entire table." My running of Oaklands throughout the 1980s influenced my presentation of world history in stages, and without the bank's 'tablecloth' I might not have had the idea for the seven-foot-long history chart on the 'life cycle' of 25 civilizations.

At Coopersale Hall the work had intensified. To cut costs I took water and gas up the 450-yard private drive myself. I bought the pipes and hired a digger and driver. We dug a long trench: "July 20 and 21. Battled with the road. Tony gouged…, then we lowered blue 125mm MDPE water-pipe in and knitted the six-metre sections with electrofusion equipment. Mick did the fusing."[31] At the same time I was building and tarmacing a playground with tennis-court netting in the 18th-century walled garden.

Asa Briggs
I had rung Asa Briggs, the Provost of Worcester College I had spoken with

in 1978, and he had kindly agreed to read the book. I arrived early and sat by the Worcester College lake "and reached out to the ghosts that flitted by from the lost days – the canal behind me, sitting as I was on the stone seat with the lion and sphinx – and pondered that day in 1959 when I gave up Law, 30 years ago, and never dreamt I would be returning with a finished book for the Provost to read". I took *The Fire and the Stones* to the Provost's Lodging. I knocked loudly and waited for the Provost's secretary, and had a telephone conversation up to the Provost. He said: "I'm so glad you brought it in and that you've got the support of Kathleen Raine. She's a wonderful woman."[32]

Metaphysical poetry: assembling A Metaphysical's Way of Fire, *Fourth Mystic Life*
Orpheus in the Underworld

The first version of *The Fire and the Stones* was now finished. Almost immediately I resolved to bring out a selection of my more metaphysical poems at the same time as *The Fire and the Stones*. I wrote:

> Feel liberated after my book, and have returned to my poems (after preparing the Oak-Tree accounts for the accountant). On a sweltering day, stripped to the waist and in shorts, rediscovered my own poems.... The theme of Orpheus in the Underworld struck me. Orpheus in the Coopersale [Hall] drive. The poet in the middle of all these practical things.... The importance of having something else to do besides poetry. The world – the Underworld – *feeds* a poet. The greatest poetry is written by men who are living first and foremost, and who occasionally stand back from their lives, to reflect on its contact with Reality, to reflect the metaphysical.

I was aware of the conflict between the part of myself that had uncovered the pattern of world history and the part of myself that had written Metaphysical poetry.

I was now almost constantly aware of the tension between the poet in me and the historian. Towards the end of July we went to Cornwall. We had to collect Anthony from Waterloo on the way. (While we waited I bought coins of Shapur I and Ardashir I, Persian Sasanians, both with fire-temples, both silver.) It was hot and sweaty in London, but there was a cooling breeze in Cornwall. My sister Frances and Richard and their children stayed with us. Frances entered the village donkey derby and came a creditable second, smacking the back of the donkey to keep it running. Four parachutists then landed in the field, trailing smoke from their ankles. I wrote poems about both these events.

Richard asked me what I was writing. I showed him my history chart, and a few poems. I told him I had "found a form, in the reflective poem, which enables me to include biology and physics and other disciplines, i.e. to take a whole view of everything; and that my poems have to hint at a metaphysical Reality". I also said that the poetic activity has to take place alone and in silence, and that a poem is also a record of a particular day, "better than a photograph because it includes thoughts and feelings and images". I showed him the revised poem, 'Ben Nevis: Cloud of Unknowing', which I was then reworking, as he had climbed the mountain with me. He liked it. I explained that the greatest poetry is not about the physical world only, but about the metaphysical world, too; that it hints at a different order of Reality. "The great poets are those who combine the sensual-tactile with the eternal, and corrections can take place 20, 30 or even 40 years later, as you get the poetry right." I explained that I had always been careful to get my rhymes right, and "that I am not a hasty, doodling sort of poet; I have always made poems to be well-wrought and to last".

We all walked to Porthpean to look at the coffin cave and the waterfall, on which I wrote a poem, 'Spring, Brain', We went on to Fowey and had a cream tea in the Singing Kettle, Polruan.[33] The Charlestown carnival satirised the sale of Charlestown, featuring a group of Chinamen pushing a rickshaw with signs saying "I bought village", "Chinese take-away". We went to St Mawes castle, which was built by Henry VIII, and to Mevagissey. After Frances and Richard left the four of us watched the competitive games in the Charlestown Regatta: water-races, crawling out on a greasy pole and outlasting a pillow fight with a rival, team races in the harbour with tyres. And the boys canoed on the calm sea with the Canoe Club.

Kathleen Raine invites me to be metaphysical historian in Temenos *Academy*
At the beginning of August I rang Kathleen Raine from Cornwall and told her about *The Fire and the Stones* and my *Selected Poems*. She immediately tried to typecast me as a historian rather than as a poet who happened to have studied civilizations, and attempted to hijack me into her Platonic Academy. She said: "You will be my metaphysical historian in the Academy we want to set up. This must be Providential. Sacred history – you might teach at our Academy. We want £2 million to build it. It will be in London. Laurens van der Post is involved and is seeing the Prince of Wales. Keith Critchlow is involved. David Bohm is doing physics – the philosophy of science. But we haven't got anyone who is covering the philosophy of history. I thought it might give you a platform. If I can widen from history to poetry, have you read Yeats's *A Vision*? What do you think of his view of history?" Yeats's *A Vision* was based on the automatic writing of his wife George, whereas *The Fire and the Stones* had a more academic provenance. She said, "Tomlin would have been so good doing philosophy." She added

of Tomlin's widow, "Judith is someone who will make a man happy, I never had that quality, it wasn't to be my destiny." (She had left her first husband Hugh Sykes Davies and married Charles Madge. That marriage had broken up and she had an unrequited passion for Gavin Maxwell, whose otter, which she lost, featured in the film *Ring of Bright Water*, a title taken from one of her poems.) She invited me to tea: "At 3 on August 10th there will be a cup of tea. I don't know what I can do for you, but do ring Laurens van der Post." She gave me his number.

Knowing that I was a poet who had temporarily diverted into world history to see the present Age within the context of the flow of 25 civilizations, I duly rang van der Post, who I had met at Eliot's centenary service. He said: "What a wonderful idea, the Fire. And *The Fire and the Stones*, what a wonderful title. I'd like to hear you on it, but I'm just going away. Can you ring me in mid-September and come and see me?"

I reported back to Kathleen Raine, who said: "The mantle is passing to you. Toynbee would have written you a Foreword if he were alive." We talked about how a book is never really finished, and she said: "When you've finished a book you think it could be better, and certainly 20 years later you see things you could have put in, but it was the best you could do at the time, quite simply you couldn't have done better at the time." I have come to see the wisdom of these words. We discussed Tomlin, and Ayer's claiming to have had an illumination. She said: "He needn't have said that he'd seen the Light. Indirectly he was saying his work of 50 years was wrong." I told her: "The poet's aim is to receive the vision and hand it on to the next generation," to which she said, "Yes."

I returned to Loughton from Cornwall for a few days as Steve Norris had signed the contract to move in to Orchard Cottage and I had to get the place ready for him besides monitoring the work on Coopersale Hall and getting the new gas and water supply ready before opening in September. I was still writing cheques for all bills to the two schools, along with paying the staff and keeping the accounts, and the mound of post was so high that I nearly needed to shovel it off the floor, like frozen snow. Nadia, now a Flight Supervisor with British Midland, visited me for a few hours.

Back in Cornwall we all drove to Porthleven and attended the christening of Ann's fisherman-cousin Stephen's daughter at Kenneggy Methodist chapel. It was hot. We waited outside in the sun. There was a long service, and we returned to a roomful of chatty women and silent men. During the sweltering afternoon I took Matthew to Porthleven harbour. Back in Charlestown I read Anthony and Matthew (in Ant's bedroom) Coleridge's 'Kubla Khan', Tennyson's 'The Splendour Falls' and Kathleen Raine's 'Seed of Creation'. I surprised myself by telling the boys that Kubla Khan's sunny dome and caves were a metaphor for the Platonist view of creation, with life ("the sacred river") coming out of nothing and turning to nothing; the nothing of course being a Platonist something.

Matthew and I went for a walk under the stars and saw an enormously long shooting star. Later we took a rug and lay in the back garden and saw another shooting star. A couple of days later I reflected that there are "1,000 million [(100 billion)] galaxies of which ours is one, in which there are 1,000 million million [(100 billion)] stars of which ours is one.... The immensity and smallness." (Estimates of the size of the universe have greatly increased since then. A German supercomputer estimates that the universe consists of 500 billion galaxies and the Kepler space telescope site estimates that our galaxy consists of 500 billion stars. *See* p.712 and ep.13, note 30.) I sunbathed and wrote a poem, 'House Martins in the Dock' following my early morning walk to but the papers.

I drove back to Essex and on 10 August I visited Kathleen Raine in Chelsea at 3 p.m. I sat in her aesthete's room in Paultons Square with a picture by Æ on the wall, an original Cecil Collins, Indian heads and old books in 1930s jacketless boards, all rather dusty. A garden was visible through the back window. She offered me cake she had specially baked, sandwiches she had specially made, and Darjeeling tea while I spread the chart out on a table. After leafing through the Fire of Part One, I talked her through all the stages. She asked a lot of questions: "Where's India?" "What will happen in China?"

Her historian friend Dorothy Carrington (who had spent half her life living in Corsica) came in for tea and talked about Napoleon. Kathleen seemed to understand about the Fire and said: "It's a great work or it's nothing. It's a great work. Sacred history returns in our time, secular events being within a context of what is sacred." I gave her food for thought: "Michelangelo had to operate within the context of a civilization, he couldn't have done it outside." She took down Yeats's *A Vision* and read passages showing Yeats knew the Fire. "Yeats was groping towards what you've done; the diagrams. You've seen the pattern of history. You are a historian.... There's no need to write poems about the Fire. Leave that to others. Poetry is the language of the soul speaking to the spirit. It comes to the poet, who waits for it. You can't write *about* the Fire." But you can! Wordsworth wrote *about* the unseen power in a language that appealed to the common man.

Raine said: "TV has corrupted the language poets use, the soul's language has gone." But life is about more than the soul, it includes the world and social activity, and poetry can catch the soul *and* the world. She was too 'other mind' and not enough social ego.

I told her: "A poetry as language of the soul is too etiolated." The soul should look at Nature but incorporate the social ego as well. Raine said: "A poet channels images from another world, from a higher world, but is different from the priestess in the Delphic oracle. Poetry is not mediumship: there is metre and technique to consider." She said: "David Gascoyne is the last great poet. There are so many great poets of my generation: Yeats, Pound, Watkins (Yeats's disciple), Gascoyne, Muir, Eliot, Thomas. But now there is no one." She meant that no poets wrote exclusively in the language of the soul but included social ego. "I started *Temenos* in the hope that it would throw up new poets. But it hasn't." I stayed until 9 p.m., longer than I intended. She ended by saying: "It's a long time, many years, since I had such an interesting and memorable afternoon."

Later I reflected: "She looks like Blake. Sits alone in her Chelsea flat with her definite opinions about the imaginative world, and is opposed to the social world. A liver in the soul who rejects the social world." I noted that she had visited an art gallery with "Bill Empson" – "Ricks," she said, "I don't care for his criticism at all", for it includes the social ego – and that she had visited Ezra Pound at St Elizabeth's. She told me: "Yes, Pound said the same to me that he said to you. He said, 'I like your poems, but you must learn not to waste any words.' I've never forgotten that advice." She said: "Eliot didn't have the vision, as Yeats did; only allegiance to a moribund Church of England which has lost its vision." But how wrong she was.

As I pointed out Eliot *did* have the vision of the Light, the "fire and the rose", which is not a moribund vision but a Universalist vision that is superior to Yeats's vision in *A Vision*, as Auden recognised when he said to Andrew Harvey, "Eliot was so damn lucky, he had the mystic vision." (I have combined Eliot's mystic vision of the Light with a development of Yeats's universalism. In *A Vision*, a text largely received by his wife as automatic writing and edited by him, Yeats gives no dates and lacks precision; his vision is more mythological and derives from the Hindu *Kali Yuga* and Great Year.)

Kathleen Raine had told me: "Imaginative poetry is in decay, therefore civilization is about to collapse." I wrote: "My history demonstrates that this is not so. She needs to revise her poetic attitudes in the light of my history." I also wrote: "Poetry is not exclusively about the social world" (like the Movement's) "or exclusively about an imaginative world; it is about both." I recalled a remark of Tomlin's, "There's something very virginal about Kathleen Raine," meaning: 'She doesn't live in the social world, she's a nun, she lives apart with her gift of imagination.'[34]

Cornwall and the universe, Preface to Selected Poems
I returned to Cornwall on a windy fine day. I settled to the Preface to my *Selected Poems*:

With my curtains blowing, worked on my Preface which is now entitled 'On the New Baroque Consciousness and the Redefinition of Poetry'. I've declared how I see poetry – its language being a language that appeals to the common man…. Smash the view, "It's got to be waited on, the other mind of the soul opens to inner imagination." This happens, e.g. my "string of images" in 'The Silence' and [*The*] *Gates of Hell*, but it is how the images are presented that is crucial.

I had pulled away from Kathleen Raine's view of poetry as exclusively the language of the soul from within. Poetry also included the outer world – hence my Baroque. Kathleen Raine was a neo-Romantic poet, I was a Baroque poet. Later I wrote a poem, 'Charlestown, Moon and Meteorite Trails'.

The next day we took a boat trip up the Tamar from Saltash. We passed wooded hills, shingle beaches and sedge and reached Calstock. We went on to Morwellham Quay. I saw the Tamar as a frontier, its mouth as wide as the Thames, its source little wider than the Roding's but turning Cornwall effectively into an island in Saxon times. I wrote some poems: 'Up the Tamar', 'Two Swans' and 'Universe'.

Some international cricketers came down to play on the St Austell cricket field with local cricketers at the invitation of Stephen Lucas, and the boys and I watched Lucas open the batting with Chris Broad. There was a hospitality tent. It was rumoured that the cricketers were not paid at the end of the day. That night there was an eclipse of the moon. I set the alarm and woke in the middle of the night to watch the eclipse. The earth's shadow and curve took three-quarters off the brightness of the full moon, which earlier had illumined the entire sea and beach. Everywhere was a glory in pale moonlight. Ann and I spent time among the Charlestown rock pools. Little sandfish darted out of our way among mussels, limpets, barnacles, bladderwrack, shrimps, a few crabs. I saw the cliffs and our house and lamppost from a new angle, across rocks and sand. Our house looked set in Nature.

The next day we went to Gunwalloe: I sat on a rock and wrote another metaphysical sonnet, 'The Church of Storms'; then walked to St Winwaloe, the medieval church, in which I wrote a poem, 'At Gunwalloe: Light'. A very high tide came in very quickly. As I scrambled to safety Anthony lost a shoe – which was swept away and which the sea returned to him an hour later. The rollers crashed in and foamed and climbed the cliff. Back in

Nicholas writing 'The Church of Storms' at Gunwalloe

Charlestown the next day we went round on the rocks past Gull Island to where there is a view of Duporth slope and sat on slate while our two boys fished in rock pools for transparent shrimps, mini-'sticklebacks', 'weavers' and 'tropical fish'.

Back in Essex I thrilled to pictures from Neptune 2.8 billion miles away, which confirmed "that this solar system of ours is devoid of life – is barren and icy – and that only on earth do human things happen." I thought about the vastness of space and the tininess of earth – the uniqueness of life on earth that strengthens the metaphysical position. I pondered the symbol's link to this uniqueness and a few days later wrote:

> The symbol transmits an esoteric metaphysical Reality by expressing the inexpressible in terms of the expressible.... What is the link between metaphysical Fire and the vast interstellar spaces? Quite simply, the one manifests into the other, as Bohm has set out in *Wholeness and the Implicate Order*. The Fire is implicate.

I was reluctant to be associated with Kathleen Raine's Academy, which she regarded as a revival of Plato's Academy: "Raine states the tradition through Plato's Academy (c.385BC–AD 529) and its revival in Florence which (she asserts) influenced Michelangelo and Blake; and [she] wars with Christianity as Justinian destroyed the Academy." The idea of a university that is close to the Light is a very appealing and attractive one. In fact, her *Temenos* Academy would not emphasise the Light at all.

At half-term we went to Cornwall, where an energetic, dynamic sea flung spray halfway up the opposing cliff. I wrote of "the amazing clarity of vision" I had in Cornwall. We went to Wheal Martin to see the clay dries. Back in Charlestown there was a wonderfully clear night, a "huge apple-tree with white fruit", "the apple-tree of stars". I did further work on my Preface, went to Mevagissey and then we walked on the harbour "under a reddened sky, with birds skimming low over the silver waves and a group of yellowhammers pecking round the front doorstep. Arthur Hosegood watches from dawn to dusk, watches the progress of each day and marvels ''Tis beautiful.'.... My heart lifts at the thought of seeing my beloved Charlestown again, the front steps guarded by yellowhammers." Later I had a final walk under the tree of stars, and encountered Capt. Gowsell, my neighbour. He pointed out Orion's belt and said he could steer by the stars if his compass failed. He had been taught the old sea lore that had applied in Chaucer's day.

I had kept in touch with events in London. I encountered Philip Mawer, who was then in the Cabinet Office (and as Sir Philip Mawer has since been Parliamentary Commissioner for Standards), at my brother-in-law Richard's

40th birthday party. He asked if I would like to become an MP and what my policy would be.

Tomlin's widow remarried a former British Ambassador, Sir Peter Marshall, and became Lady Marshall. I attended her marriage reception at the Commonwealth House, Northumberland Avenue and sat with Kathleen Raine (who told me she wanted me to meet Prince Charles), and David Holbrook.[35]

Full opening of Coopersale Hall School
At the beginning of September I installed the Norrises as tenants in Orchard Cottage and carried tables and chairs into new classrooms and arranged them while workmen cemented the courtyard and bricklayers cemented bricks. In the room where Churchill slept I thought of my 1974 poem 'Blind Churchill to the Night'.

On 10 September I opened Coopersale Hall upstairs as well as downstairs and accommodated 150 pupils as we had planned. At the staff meeting I stressed the historic nature of our presence, pointing out that our new school was the largest independent school to have been founded in West Essex of its kind since the Second World War. On the first day I acted as a traffic warden to impose a pattern on the cars and harangued the new parents from the fire-escape.

After my long dealings with Biggs-Davison, it was extraordinary that his replacement should be my tenant, and that Coopersale Hall, which had been associated with two past Epping MPs in Lord Lyle and Churchill, should now be associated with the present MP for Epping Forest. What other school had its own resident MP living on site? Norris was good value as a walking advertisement, for when his constituents asked where he was living, he would say, "At Coopersale Hall. Don't you know about the new school there?" He spread the word of my founding of a new school. I recorded that I visited Steve Norris and his family to discuss his waste-disposal system, which had gone wrong, and ended up discussing Africa and Communism.

I was now in overall control of two up-and-running schools five miles apart. Every morning I left our house next to Oaklands and drove to Coopersale Hall and helped Mrs. Best sort out the teaching problems there while Ann looked after Oaklands as Headmistress. I returned home to the house next to Oaklands for lunch. I had engaged Compass Services to run the lunches at both schools, and so Ann and I had shed food-buying. I still retained the day-to-day accounts, staff salaries and writing cheques for all invoices and bills. I had fully opened Coopersale Hall a year before Bancroft's Preparatory School which still had to be built, and so I had a year's start on the market. Two HMIs (Department of Education Inspectors) visited Coopersale Hall to start the process of official registration, and reported that it felt like a school that had been open three years rather than three weeks. The Headmaster of Chigwell, Tony Little, came and lunched with me at Coopersale Hall soon afterwards, and made a similar remark. All in all, we had a very smooth opening.

I was a central authority for the two schools. I helped with insurance, legal advice and financing. I did the banking. I negotiated with Tom Hammond, who did his best to interfere with free passage up the private drive he still owned, often obstructing the area near the gate with farm equipment.

The costs of opening a new school proved heavy. The council exacted an improvement to their public road at the end of Flux's Lane as the price for planning permission (£30,000) and the fire officer had imposed an automated system of fire doors (£20,000). I had to raise fees more than I would have liked to cover these set-up costs. I at last secured an agreement to buy a 6-metre corridor up the private drive to the school from Hammond. The Oaklands Parents' Association's Guy Fawkes night was attended by 600. The great fire leapt up, there were orchestrated fireworks and there was food on the floodlit tennis-court. I wrote ironically: "Yeats's 'Flames that no faggot feeds' (art) and my big fire yesterday (life). Which was more important? To write a line that is occasionally read, or to make a fire which 600 people watch, with glowing sparks, glowing the cheeks red? I would once have replied, 'Art.' Now I am not so sure. Life! Art reflects life and is only relevant as a comment on life."

Two days later I set up the Coopersale Hall Parents' Association. I convened a meeting of interested parents and dictatorially persuaded three to volunteer for the role of Chairman and make a speech saying what they would do. I made them leave the room, and organised an election. Having forced through democratic structures I then pulled away to allow them to operate without interference. Towards the end of November we had the bespectacled and moustached Head of Chigwell, Tony Little and David Evennett MP and their wives to dinner. Little, slightly awkward but with a quick wit and considerable humour, said he had been showing his wife "your empire, the fields", and Evennett confirmed my view of politics by saying he loathed the drill halls and gang shows and the wasted time. It was a frosty night and there was a spitting fire.[36]

Coopersale Hall's end-of-term nativity play was attended by the new Chairman of the Council, the Mayor of the Town Council and our local councillor. I was able to tell them that I was putting in a planning application to build a six-classroom extension at Coopersale Hall. There was an exhibition in the staff room, which I made sure they all saw. We broke up the next day and soon afterwards there was a reception for the combined staffs and spouses at Coopersale Hall.

Steve Norris burgled

After Christmas I heard that Miss Root, the Oaklands teacher who taught me maths when I was a boy, had died of bronchial pneumonia in Forest Place. I had visited her and found her very respectful, but she had become cantankerous towards others. When the vicar came and preached to the inmates she called out, "What about the Buddha?" And she sent back the harvest gift from the church. When the Oaklands children went to sing carols to the inmates she refused to leave her room and listen.

Before the new year we had Steve Norris and his wife for a long talk. He spoke at length, and it was hard to interrupt him. Four topics in two hours was good going when Steve Norris was in full flow, whereas with David Evennett it was possible to cover 40 in an hour. I described my view of history. "He said: "If I become Foreign Secretary, I will ask you to be an adviser on a discussion panel." He criticised Thatcher's dictatorial approach to her MPs: "There is a Presidential Ceauşescu syndrome: decrees are handed down from on high and we have to accept them or we're out." (The Ceauşescus had been shot in Romania on Christmas Day.)

In January the Norrises were burgled. Steve's wife lost some jewellery given to her family in imperial times, worth perhaps £90,000. The CID had visited Hammond, who had volunteered before being told that there had been a burglary, "Where was the burglary then, at the MP's?" Hammond seemed to know that there had been a burglary, so (having finally bought the road from him) I visited him and explained that it was in all our interests to keep the Norrises happy. I asked him if he would help me recover the jewellery by putting word out in the East End. Hammond said, spreading his hands wide in an innocent shrug, "You've come to the wrong man, you might as well ask that tree." Soon afterwards his girlfriend sent me a card from the Seychelles. Amid exotic stamps she wrote that she and "Tom" were enjoying a surprise fortnight's break. The Norrises never recovered their jewellery.

Building Coopersale Hall extension: Paul Gorka architect

My architect had applied for planning permission to build six classrooms at Coopersale Hall. He then convened a meeting of four "experts", which I attended. Each spoke of conducting preliminary tests on the soil behind the school's assembly hall, and each costed the tests at getting on for £5,000. I would have to spend £20,000 before work had even started. I said I did not think the tests were necessary. "What happens if you build the extension in the wrong place and its back breaks?" the architect asked, and I could see cash-signs in four pairs of eyes waiting for my answer. "I'm going to build it anyway, and on the only available site," I said, "and if its back breaks, it breaks."

I recounted this to Paul Gorka, my author who was by profession an architect, and he immediately said he would take over on an at-cost basis in gratitude for my bringing out *Budapest Betrayed*. In early February Gorka took over as architect of the extension at Coopersale Hall, and at a time when Gorbachev was making concessions in the Soviet-occupied states of Eastern Europe, I was able to urge him to tell Bukovsky and the Exiles on the Committee of Captive Nations and others to redouble their efforts to win freedom. Gorka made regular visits to Coopersale Hall and we would stand in the foundations a stone's throw from Norris's Orchard Cottage, and in the same meetings discuss technical building problems and fulfilling the work of FREE. I would say what should happen next and Gorka would relay it to the Exiles on the Committee of Captive Nations. Articles appeared in the press describing Roger Scruton as a 'Scarlet Pimpernel' who had smuggled printing-presses into Eastern Europe, and I now grasped that he had felt that FREE might lead to his exposure.

It was now clear that the Soviet Union was collapsing. At half-term on the way down to Cornwall I saw that Eastern Europe was changing:

Why is the West victorious in the Cold War?... Is the Fire being renewed in Russia, by the Russian Orthodox Church? Ponder on... the renewal of Eastern Europe's central idea which... has resulted in the end of the Cold War.... It is not what the West has done but what Eastern Europe has done. The Fire is the central idea of all civilizations including European civilization, which has thrown off its semi-occupation by Russia through Eastern-European Christianity (Polish and Hungarian Catholicism under a Polish Pope and a resurgence of Russian-Orthodox rule, i.e. their Fire). The West's Cold-War victory is thus a victory for Eastern Europe, which the Western Europeans and Americans have watched from outside; [at the same time as] Russia's admission of her own difficulties and abandonment of the Communist position. An expanding Europe must therefore take up the Eastern-European initiative.

I observed: "The thinking of 'Wistful Time-Travellers' began my history book [, *The Fire and the Stones*]; and the above vision has come out of it."

It was very damp in Charlestown. We went to Porthleven. We lunched at Gunwalloe church cove and I wrote another metaphysical sonnet, 'Being as a Ripple or Two'. The Cornish damp reactivated my bronchiectasis: "Very weak from bronchiectasis this evening. Could not stay awake, very unsteady on my legs and short of breath."

Back in Essex I went up to Coopersale Hall and encountered Steve Norris washing his wife's car. We chatted on the green sward, sometimes leaning on my car, he in sweater and boots. He told me he was getting Tebbit to perform an official opening of Coopersale Hall School. At a gathering at the Carlton Club – at which Norris had brought the Home Secretary (David Waddington) over to shake my hand before I realised who he was – I had encountered the Chairman of Planning and engineered a conversation about Coopersale Hall. On 6 March I heard that planning permission had been granted for Coopersale Hall to expand by six more classrooms as educational use was permitted development within London's Green Belt. I now formally sacked the previous architect and formally employed Gorka, who promised the buildings regulations drawings would not cost more than £3,000. Gorka urged me to buy a castle in Hungary and open it as a European centre to coincide with the renewal of Eastern Europe's central idea and the implementation of FREE. FREE would have its headquarters in a Hungarian castle which he would find.

But now I was establishing myself in Epping Forest. I did not want to move away. Anthony was confirmed in the chapel at Chigwell School by the Bishop of Barking. The Bishop sat in red and faded gold robes with his mitre on and intoned "Confirm O Lord your servant Anthony with your Holy Spirit", his hands on Ant's head. I accepted that I would never leave Epping Forest: "I will never leave it. The pear-tree, hollies and silver birch have informed my poetry." I was particularly pleased that I had seen a firecrest in the blue Atlantic cedar.

A couple of days afterwards I spoke to McForan on the telephone. He had just returned from a month in Russia, living in a hotel by himself and meeting Russian miners, who told him they subscribed one rouble (£1) each to help British miners, and one pit sent 1,500 roubles. He said that my book on Scargill was right, Soviet funding *was* sent to the British miners. McForan said: "I've read many books about events in the 1980s, but yours and mine stand head and shoulders above the rest because we saw the scenario."[37]

With Laurens van der Post

I visited Sir Laurens van der Post at 27 Chelsea Towers, off Chelsea Manor Street as he had proposed. He was good for 82. I was pleased to have the opportunity of conversing with the man who had spoken so authoritatively about the Fire at Eliot's centenary service. He was a significant 20th-century figure: he had come from South Africa to London, had known T.E. Lawrence, had been published by Virginia Woolf, had known Jung, had spent two years in a Japanese prisoner-of-war camp, was a friend of Margaret Thatcher and a close friend of Prince Charles. We had Japan and Africa in common besides Eliot and the Fire.

On a windy day I rang the bell, went up to the top floor in the lift and puckish Sir Laurens met me, shook my hand and took me into his flat and upstairs to his study. "My beloved," he said to his wife, "you write your book, we're here with the door open." Throughout our conversation his wife, Ingaret, interrupted several times asking for a sharpened pencil, and I was struck by how patient he was with her, giving her what she wanted, humouring her. She had Alzheimer's disease and he was a gentle and caring guardian.

I spoke of myself and showed him the contents of Parts One and Two of *The Fire and the Stones*, then the chart. He said: "It's very impressive. This is a work of immense importance. I can see that just from your headlines." He was wearing a monocle in one eye, and I could see the Chelsea skyline behind where he sat. He asked questions. He told me that Jung had discussed the Fire with an Austrian, who did not know what it was, and had then turned to van der Post to discuss it. "Jung was a confirmation rather than a revelation." He spoke of the Kalahari bushmen making fire by clapping hands and exorcising dreams before fire. "There's a metaphysical Fire behind actual fire in the bushman's consciousness." He was sure I would not find a historian to write a Foreword: "There are no Universalist historians, Toynbee was the last and he funked the irrational at the end and never explained the genesis of civilizations." (Toynbee's books were on his shelf.)

I said I could explain that my vision was of the future, not of the past, and should be seen in terms of the new Baroque of the coming Carolingian Age. Van der Post said: "You can see the direction, I don't know what I'm about but you can see the way forward. You could not do that without knowing the Fire. You must have known it to write at such length. If it is going to happen it will happen, yes, but you have to push at life a little, knock on the door, and then it opens to you." He told me, "What a pity Eliot, Toynbee and Jung are not here, sitting with us now. They would be so interested in what you have said and in this book. The mantle has passed to you. Now that Toynbee is not here no one else is writing about the Fire." He hinted that I should be the Prime Minister's history adviser. He told me, "The Prime Minister's history adviser doesn't know any history. I said in front of him and her, 'Why do you have him as an adviser?'" His wife had wandered in and out and asked several questions about "Mr Hagger" to which he replied patiently, "I'm just talking to Mr Hagger, I'll be with you very soon." I left after one-and-a-quarter hours (4.45–6.00).[38]

With Kathleen Raine
From Sir Laurens's flat I walked to Kathleen Raine's house. She immediately began discussing the role of her Academy. I said it may hand on the vision and therefore bring about a Renaissance of the arts, and I spoke at length

about my Baroque age in poetry. She concurred with my Baroque analysis (my Preface), but said that poets have the imaginative vision and cannot be taught it. I said the imagination is not Neoclassical fancy, it is either images from the 'other mind' or it is the Fire (Coleridge's "esemplastic power"). She had a more scholarly approach, that of Thomas Taylor the Platonist, who gave Keats 'Beauty is Truth, Truth Beauty' (which she said Keats got from Bailey who read Thomas Taylor while staying with him). She said that Yeats's "golden bird" was a present from the caliph to the Byzantine Emperor (and can be found in Gibbon). She said that few poets have the vision, which churches are supposed to hand on, and that the Academy would not produce a Renaissance in the arts because the artist "will appear". She and Gascoyne are in Paris as *classiques vivants* (living classics). Raine said: "Gascoyne and I are part of the European tradition, we are closer to the European tradition than to the English tradition." I noted: "Kathleen Raine is a scholar rather than a mystic: she has gleaned the knowledge from books." She said: "Five of us should have a meeting: you, the Prince, me, Keith Critchlow and Laurens."

I came away from Kathleen Raine's feeling the rigidity of her position regarding the Academy and aware that she was manipulating me into promoting her dream of an Academy in relation to the five. I left after spending three-and-a-quarter hours with Kathleen Raine (6.30–9.45).

Following my talks with van der Post and Kathleen Raine I wrote: "We're part of the contemporary scene and part of the eternal mosaic at the same time."[39]

Fire and storms
I had continued to work on my *Selected Poems, A Metaphysical's Way of Fire*. I had made a connection between the Fire and the cosmic background radiation from cooling after the Big Bang, which appeared in some of my later poems and in my 'Preface on the Metaphysical Revolution' for *The Fire-Flower*:

> Nov. 21. On Sunday morning… I woke and made the link between the Fire and its manifestation (Bohm-like) in cosmic background radiation…. The three families of particles in cosmic rays after the Big Bang…. I got up, and still in my pyjamas, scribbled the connection…. The Fire of eternity preceded the Big Bang, which began time, and will succeed time.

I also "connected my work on the symbol with Guénon's law of correspondence".

I was revising some of my poems, and after hearing Anthony sing a solo 'In the Bleak Midwinter' from the choir at Chigwell church, I "did the figures... then worked on 'Old Man in a Circle'".

We spent a few days in Charlestown before Christmas. We arrived to mountainous seas, the combination of an exceptionally high tide and a hurricane which gave the largest seas for 50 years. Spray dashed on our upper windows, and Ann got soaked as a wave came through our upstairs window. The sea broke over the harbour wall making it into a waterfall. "Wrote 'Elemental' and 'Invisible Foam', the first on Saturday night with the storm raging, the second on Sunday (yesterday) morning." The weather cleared and on a clear night I star-gazed with Ken, the bearded sea-captain. He pointed out Orion's belt, Betelgeuse and Rigel on either side (shoulder and knee), the triangle of Sirius (the brightest star), Procyon, Pollux, Aldebaran (an Arab name, like Algol), and the two pointer stars of the Plough (Ursa Minor) which lead towards Polaris. Cassiopeia and the Pleiades, and the bright stars in between. "Am picking up Ken's knowledge of winds, tides and stars – his old seaman's lore handed down over the generations." A couple of days later I wrote a poem, 'A Man of Winds and Tides'.

We went to Truro and then to Gunwalloe, where I found shingle had been washed by the sea into the church, and then to Porthleven, where I inspected the storm damage: high seas had broken away part of the harbour wall. We returned to another storm and a dark Charlestown:

Sat alone by nightlights while the storm raged and wrote 'Candleflame Storm', a very metaphysical poem. When I finished polishing the last rhyme at 8.30 exactly, the lights came back on. I realised how Wordsworth and Coleridge lived in the 1790s, when this cottage was built, and how natural it was for people to think of themselves as being candles, and how people have forgotten this today. The anti-metaphysical outlook of today is largely a forgetting. A forgetfulness of Being. Also wrote 'Stillness and Tides'.

The next day there was more rain and another power cut in the afternoon (our third in 24 hours); mist on the horizon and white surf. I revised 'The Silence', placing it in the canon of my work. In it I laid the foundations for my present development, and my poetic work belongs as a whole. "Can see Trenarren out of the window as I write. Trenarren begins and ends 'The Silence', and now I have a house within sight of it."[40]

Metaphysical vision
We returned to Essex for Christmas. I went to Foyles and bought some American books on astronomy, which showed that cosmology is not a speculative hobby any more but an observable, empirical science. I thought that the same should apply to metaphysics. There should be "a practical

metaphysics of Being and its relationship to the structure of the universe (for Being as Fire controls the post-Big-Bang radiation)". I thought about metaphysics on and off all through Christmas:

> Being,... together with Non-Being, makes up infinity. Non-Being envelops Being, but is itself enveloped by Supreme Being/Reality/infinity, i.e. there are three levels or stages above the physical level. A system based on experience of the Fire. I have reached a unity of vision. My metaphysical vision has taken shape this Christmas Day.

I wrote that in Japan "I got behind existence and detected Being, the one sea of Being or unity of Being in the Stone Garden.... The closing vision of 'The Silence' is the fourfold vision." On Boxing Day I wrote:

> The family still asleep at 11 a.m. Have been up three hours. Want to write essays on the Existentialists – exposing those (like Sartre and Camus) who remained at layer 4, the world of the senses, and approving of those who progressed to Being; but evaluating their use of Being. Also on the Metaphysical philosophers of the past, again rejecting those who did not go far enough.

I was "against rational and speculative metaphysics" and "for Metaphysical Existentialism or Existential Metaphysics. The world of the senses prevents you from rising to Being. So the poems of *The Gates of Hell* must be seen as a dying of the clinging senses and an unfolding of Being."

I now focused on Being:

> How when you look at existence are you aware of Being? Through [perceiving] its unity as opposed to its multiplicity, i.e. the unitive vision of the Stone Garden, the oneness of all manifestation below which are the particulars. (The [poetic] image shows the particular existence and the universal Being.) Behind Being are the Forms in Non-Being, the Idea, all the latent potentialities of the Void which have not come into creation. And through the Void is the Fire. So how does Existence differ from Being? Existence is the disorderly, chaotic, apparently random world of phenomena. Being is the sum total of all manifestation, perceived as a whole in the poetic vision: the glimpse in the [reflecting] pond. The poet humanises Being, trans-lates the abstract into a concrete. Being in the abstract is no use at all unless it can be experienced. That is why I am a Metaphysical Existentialist. Being is the... unity or oneness behind manifestation (as opposed to the ultimate oneness behind non-manifestation as well).... Being controls the cosmic background radiation, one of its principal manifestations.... The Fire is

beyond Being because it has not come into form although it manifests in our soul.

I was still working hard on my poems, and on New Year's Eve I referred to my two forthcoming books by the titles under which they appeared: "I must… revert to the role of writer-poet by getting *The Fire and the Stones* and *A Metaphysical's Way of Fire* placed."[41]

Essex and Cornwall: opposites – action and contemplation
I was now acting as site foreman and supervising the building of the extension of Coopersale Hall. I noted: "All weekend, digging trenches. But not fast enough. Will not be able to pump concrete until Thursday." I understood that Essex was one pole of my being: "Amid the hurly-burly of life in Essex, paying people, directing building work, acting like Zorba the Greek, I caught sight of a picture of the house in Charlestown and was transported to a world of simplicity and peace, where it is possible to dwell on poems and Being…. It is a place of stillness and simplicity and peace, it satisfies one pole of my soul; but I will always need the moving, dynamic, whirling rush of a hectic, exciting life. I could not retire to Charlestown for good, but will always have to return to Essex or London regularly, to satisfy the other part of my being. Charlestown and Loughton – contemplation and action. It is from Loughton that my action has been planned; from Charlestown that I have made the greatest gains in contemplation."[42] My double life was lived between active and contemplative opposites as well as between Existence and Being.

Selected Poems, A Metaphysical's Way of Fire *and beginning of Fourth Mystic Life (8 April 1990–6 December 1993)*
Towards the end of March I was revising my poems for the *Selected Poems* I was preparing: "Mar 20. Worked late on my poems last night…. All day on poems…. A poet suffers and wins through to the vision of the Fire, and that is what gives his poems quality."

The hectic lifestyle in Essex was making me ill. Concrete was pumped into the footings and the work was progressing well, but I felt giddy: "Mar 23. Giddy…. Two days of rushing about, paying people, negotiating between architect and structural engineer…. Mar 25. Giddy. Several times have nearly keeled over." I talked at length with Norris on the phone that evening while giddy, and he said "I'll make a speech tomorrow evening defending the poll tax, and I'll incorporate some of your points." I wrote: "Mar 27. Still giddy. Nearly fell out of my chair when I spoke with [Steve] Norris, nearly keeled over when talking to Ginger, so went to doctor, who prescribed something for giddiness but said it is cerebrovascular." I was still giddy on 28 March: "Can at least work on my poems while the desk moves up towards me and I lurch sideways." I was still "giddy at times" on 1 April. The following day Elizabeth Lord complained of being giddy, of the "furniture coming up – I've never felt like this before" – and I recorded: "[She] had a cerebral stroke in my arms, paralyzing her legs." It later transpired she had had a blot clot which had deprived her brain of oxygen. She was taken by ambulance to St Margaret's Hospital. I recorded: "I was giddy while holding her. She nearly died in my arms."

After hectic days of organising bricklayers, I went to Winchester for the Mystics and Scientists conference. There I saw Coopersale Hall as a "mystery school... in which life brings on the souls of all who work under me...; building a kitchen can be building round your soul". I spoke with Peter Fenwick about the subject of the conference: the nature of the self, "which is a droplet of Being...: we are body-mind-soul-spirit". The four worlds of the Kabbalah all contribute to the self, and four parts of the self correspond to the four worlds. The next day I meditated at 8 and noted: "A round of white light exploded and shot power from my head throughout my body. All day felt the after-shock. Could dip back into Light during the lectures at will." I "felt a lightness of being" in my self and was "full of Light and power".

From Winchester I drove to Cornwall, passing Wylye and Steve Norris's old house. That night I walked by the sea after dark. The moon was on the water and in the curl of each wave and I reflected: "'Universe' means derivatively 'combined into one, whole'." I slept deeply and "have gone to the Light *three* times.... The sea out of my window is sparkling. It is a 'one': an image of Being, not existence." I drafted a poem, 'Gnosis: The Nature of the Self (or: Brain, Mind; Heart, Soul; Spark, Spirit)', "a very important poem in my metaphysical canon". I gazed at a full moon on dark water at 1 a.m. The next day I "added the penultimate stanza of [my poem] 'Out on the Alone', about the Negative Way". In the afternoon I "went to the Light again between 3 and 3.30. Am going through an intense period of the kind I went through in 1971."

The next day I worked on 'Night Visions in Charlestown' and recorded: "I had earlier been to the Light." As I worked on my *Selected Poems* I noted a new sense of meaning: "The healing of peace as I distil my life's vision into one selection of poems, gather them together and make sure they are internally consistent. Meaning." That night I went for a walk with Matthew to the end of the pier and later sat in the darkened living-room, "closed my eyes, stilled my body and mind and went to the Light.... There was a great surge of power from the back of my skull, prickling me all through, moving from scalp to toes. It is still pouring through me, mildly, as I write." And again: "Wave or power, less intense than last night, lasting some minutes."

We went to Porthleven and I sat in the church of storms and wrote my fourth Gunwalloe metaphysical poem, 'Skylark and Foam', after seeing a skylark high up outside and "after receiving a number of strange images – of extraordinary architectural detail from a bygone age, quite indescribable but paintable". I later recorded: "Have had no giddiness since the influx of Light last Sunday morning [8 April]. The power has healed my inside." I added a scheme of the self to my 'Preface on the Metaphysical Revolution' as "we need a clear chart of the structure of the self.... I woke with a model which I wrote into the Metaphysical Revolution essay."

We returned to Essex and the schools restarted. Again I supervised building work. On a day when a concrete pump arrived at 7 a.m. we concreted the extension so that the bricklayers could start on the following Monday, dug up the private drive and laid pipe. I mowed the Oaklands fields, then went back to Coopersale Hall to see how the work was progressing and "had tea with Steve Norris, who was in an open-necked shirt and jeans".[43]

My intense experiences of the Light from 8–11 April 1990 began my Fourth Mystic Life (*see* Appendix 1, p.903).

International politics: in Hungary, declining a castle

Gorka and his wife were taking a party of student architects who were studying under Mrs. Gorka to Hungary, and asked me to tag along to look at two castles Gorka had earmarked. I had already decided I would not buy a castle, and went along to see a bit of Hungary.

We flew to Budapest and were driven by coach through the centre of the city. Gorka sat near me and pointed out places associated with *Budapest Betrayed*, in particular every prison. We arrived at a hostel on the outskirts overlooking the blue-tinted Danube. I was allocated a tiny heated room with a balcony. We dined in the Citadel, a floodlit fortress overlooking Budapest. Four gipsies serenaded diners, for money.

Gorka hoped that my experience of Hungary would make me want to buy a castle. The next morning we walked along the Danube to where we were to have breakfast. We had a long wait because we were expected an hour later. We visited the Old City with a guide: the prison, three churches, Turkish baths and the Communist Party HQ. I found a baroque coffee-house, in which I drafted a poem, 'In Budapest Old City'. We visited the Roman ruins of Aquincum in the Roman Pannonia. We encountered 15 Russian soldiers, and through our guide I asked them when they were leaving Hungary. We went to the Hotel Gellert, which Gorka's uncle used to own.

After dark, Budapest became like East Berlin. Many streets were dingily lit, and, looking for an international phone, I walked down dark streets with houses still chipped from the war and with bullet holes from the 1956

Revolution. I found Budapest slightly menacing and depressing. Next morning the Danube was misty with trees reflected in its grey. I drafted a poem, 'Danube: Ball and Chain'. My basin had no plug and I shaved in cold water.

I tagged along on the students' architectural tour. At the Technical University we were addressed by a Professor. We visited Markowicz's mortuary. Lunch took two-and-a-quarter hours. Later we had drinks at the University of Architecture and went on to Vaci Street and ate at the Apostolou, where nothing I wanted was available. Gorka's son Sebastian (who would work for NATO) went out with some of the students and they returned noisily at 2.15 a.m.

We went by coach to the Danube bend via Szentendre and the church of St Andrew. The pulpit had an eye with a triangle in it, and spokes of Light, the symbol of Weishaupt's Illuminati. We went on to Visegrad and the anti-Tatar castle high above the Danube. Lunch took two-and-a-quarter hours. Gorka sat in silence, privately aware that the service was bad. We went on to Esztergon and looked across into Czechoslovakia. We returned past four Russian camps and Aquincum, its amphitheatres and thermal baths.

That night the students came in at 4.30 a.m. and talked noisily. Mrs. Gorka told them off angrily over breakfast. Gorka had been deputed to stay at a different hostel with the worst-behaved students so he could control what time they returned at night.

At last it was time to look at the two castles. In the morning I walked to Gorka's hostel: "Walked along the 'tow-path' by willows, and wrote a poem, 'Willow Warblers', sitting in the sun by the Danube." A Hungarian builder and lawyer turned up with a girl who spoke no English, in anticipation of my buying a castle, and we all drove in a rented car to Tura, 40 kms outside Budapest. We saw the first castle. It had been built in 1883 by Baron Schlossberger. It looked splendid from the outside, but was a ruin within. We had lunch at a petrol station and then drove to Castle Acsa, which was already a hotel that slept 62 and a further 27 in the grounds. It was not a ruin, and was on the market for nearly £1.5 million. I could not see it being a European centre for FREE. I was not going to buy a castle.

We drove back to Budapest and visited Gorka's wife's cousins in a flat in one of Budapest's central streets pocked with bullets. I had a conversation about Hungarian history with two Hungarian men: one a fierce general's son who showed me the medal he received for destroying a Russian tank during the Uprising, and one quiet. They rejected Hungary's position in a coming United States of Europe and wanted a revived Austro-Hungarian empire. Gorka sat in dignified silence. Only a twitching at his eye revealed his disapproval of what they were saying. Here I felt close to the heart of traditional Hungary.

The next day Gorka revealed his plan for me. On the coach as we went to Kocskemet, south of Budapest, to see ethnic architecture at the Town Hall and to Paks to see Markowicz's Roman Catholic church, which had "a heart at the top to attract God's attention", he pressed me to set up a company with the Hungarian builder, and then employ him. The lawyer would arrange the details. I made an excuse. In a market I bought Red Army hats for the boys and an Austro-Hungarian Marie-Thérèse coin of 1763.

Gorka had another plan for me. He and I ate with the Deputy Secretary-General of the Hungarian Chamber of Commerce and a Professor at the College of Foreign Trade, who both urged me to found a new British Council to teach English and know-how skills to Hungarians. Again I made an excuse. Afterwards I went to the Gellert and wrote some stories. Then I went to Vaci Street and ran into Gorka. We encountered two Russians in leather jackets who, seeing that I was holding two Russian Red Army hats, confronted me indignantly in Russian. Despite their dress they seemed to be in positions of authority, and I thought I was going to be arrested.

The Russians had not yet left Hungary, and their presence was still resented by the students and all Hungarians. The students were pleased to be flying back to Britain. As we took off, I put one of my Red Army hats on and saluted, and there was a cheer from the students on either side of the aisle, followed by applause. Several hurled anti-Soviet slogans down at Budapest as it receded below us.[44]

Schools and poems: "Ambassador to Hungary"
I returned to a heatwave and was soon coping with Coopersale Hall's being without water for a whole day – I managed to avoid closing the school – and moving Oaklands sheds. I saw a pheasant and a nuthatch. A blue tit was nesting in the Oaklands tree stumps near the new shed. Kestrels were nesting in the poplar in the Gates' garden. I learned from our neighbour, Gates, that the 'Roman' fountain that stood not far from our second field was built by 14 Italians c.1850.

At half-term I supervised the completion of a new path at Coopersale Hall and then joined Ann in Charlestown. I heard from the Harbour-master that the harbour had been repossessed as interest payments had not been made, had been sold to Target Life Insurance Group and was being run by Peter Clapperton. On "a magically still evening with an orange sunset and a twilight part clear, part overtaken by creeping sea-mist" I "stood breathless".

I spent three days "combing the poems, checking proofs, amending the notes" in "a terrific flow. I haven't touched any of the school work – the bank figures I should be doing – but I have made terrific gains on the poetry anthology, *Selected Poems, A Metaphysical's Way of Fire*, which is now nearly finished." My aim was to bring "English poetry... back to its true metaphysical roots". I had written a stanza into 'Night Thoughts in Charlestown', and worked on 'A Temple-Dancer's Temple-Sleep'.

In June I was dealing with parents' problems in the schools. I counselled two who had been bereaved, a bankrupt, two had been made redundant, the wife of a prisoner, a husband about to be bereaved and a wife who had received a black eye. At the same time I was revising my poems and grappling with 'The Silence', "my *Portrait of the Artist as a Young Man*". I wrote that "the silence as eternity is the source of mysticism and of creativity and therefore of art" and that "'The Silence'... contains all four worlds, the physical, psychological, spiritual and divine". I wrote that the Shadow is "an artist with a metaphysical vision". Between June 8 and 10 I "polished and typed up 'By the Chalice Well, Glastonbury'". Three days later Nadia came, I took her up to Coopersale Hall and we sat by the pond and talked, looking at the carp and golden orfe.

I had invited Steve Norris to open the Coopersale Hall fête. I wrote: "June 20. A day sorting out the building work.... *Zorba the Greek* considerations again (only my building won't collapse). Vicky [Norris] was on the lawn so went and had a chat.... Then Steve rang." Vicky took the call and said I was with her. He said he wanted to speak with me. It was an odd conversation. "Nick, I apologise if it's crackling but I'm speaking from the Central Lobby of the Houses of Parliament. Something's happened. Your ears will have been burning, I was with our Leader [Margaret Thatcher] at 4 and we were discussing you. It's far more important than if I were ringing you to give you advance information of an honour [i.e. for me, not him]. I can't be with you on Saturday for the fête. I've got to do something for the Government. It'll take Friday and Saturday and it won't finish until 4. After that I can try and get to the fête. Could Vicky open it on my behalf? I really am sorry, but if you could do that for me I'd be very grateful. It won't be forgotten." He said, "I'm seeing mother [i.e. Margaret Thatcher] on Thursday, a five-minute interview."

Gorka had visited me to look at the progress of the extension, and he was standing to one side and had overheard my end of the conversation. Gorka said, "I was speaking to someone very well-informed in the Government. He said you're going to be the new Ambassador to Hungary."

I smiled. I remembered hearing that I would be Ambassador to Libya. A new Ambassador to Hungary had been appointed the previous year so Gorka could not be right. Whatever was being discussed that was more important than an honour never happened.

Before the fête I saw the last piece of the jigsaw of my history book and wrote it in: the table of winners in stage 43 and the age of their civilization, and how that indicates the strength and vitality of their Fire and their potentiality to renew the declining civilization.

I was thinking about the Fire and my attention was drawn to a picture in the front hall of our house, 'Between Two Fires'. It showed a Puritan seated between two women and the 'Fires' were of course the two women, but also the inner Fire of his Puritanism and the outer fire of their sensuality. The picture hung near another picture, 'Checkmate', of a Roundhead standing by a fire after checkmating a Cavalier, as happened historically. I noted, "Symbolism and realism together."[45]

Vicky Norris duly opened the Coopersale Hall fête. The afternoon was notable for an auction conducted by the Essex cricketer David East, who auctioned a cricket bat signed by the Essex team for £400 to swell the Parents' Association's funds. Graham Gooch had sent me this bat via East to thank me for trying to place the Essex cricketer Alan Lilley at Chigwell School. East had first mentioned that Essex were seeking a job for Lilley the previous summer. As one of the first acts of the 'East-Hagger Placement Organisation for Retiring and Deserving Cricketers' I had rung Tony Little. It was the first phone call he took after moving into the Head's house and he told me it had taken him some time to locate the phone (which was on the floor behind the sofa). I put it to Little that he might like to employ Lilley. It was the first decision he had to make in his new job. The negotiations had almost been completed when Lilley accepted the top job of coaching the county's children. My initiative did help Chigwell, however, as Gooch (accompanied by Lilley) opened the school's new Sports Hall.

Tebbit formally opens Coopersale Hall School
Norman Tebbit, a victim of the Brighton bomb during the 1984 miners' strike when Secretary of State for Trade and Industry and MP for Chingford, had agreed to perform a formal opening of Coopersale Hall School. I had met a Chief Inspector of Police at the bottom of our private drive to plan the security, which would include a helicopter hovering at the back. The Chief Inspector considered where the IRA might infiltrate, but he was mainly concerned about Hammond. He told me: "I knew him ten years ago at Wickford when he was in… a gang of robbers. He was the safe man. He may still be active." At 1 a.m. on the morning of the formal opening the burglar alarm went off at Coopersale Hall, and Matthew and I got out of bed and drove to the School. To seize a psychological ascendancy I flung open the front door in the dark and shouted, "Armed police." It was a false alarm.

Tebbit (now Lord Tebbit) was the last to arrive on 9 July 1990 to unveil a plaque at the successful end of our first academic year. He came across as a gentle man, who got out of his car amid intense police security (passes, men in the grounds and the hovering helicopter) and I showed him round with the Chairman of the Council and his wife, the Mayor, the MP and his wife

(Steve Norris and Vicky), Ann and Frances Best. We then went out on to the terrace where there was a table between PA-system boxes. It was flanked by seated guests, many of whom were councillors. The children and parents were on the lawn before us. I spoke for nearly ten minutes, introducing everyone, dwelling on Tebbit's local connec-tions and describing the evolution of our school, and then spoke of four MPs – Lord Lyle, Churchill, Norris and now Tebbit himself – who had been associated with Coopersale Hall in the 20th century.

Tebbit began, "Hello kids." He spoke directly to the children, saying that adults were "funny" to have openings when the school had already been open, and that private education is a good thing. He unveiled the plaque, drawing the curtains (which had been lent to me by an Old Chigwellian, Doug Sweet). Mrs. Best thanked him, we had our photos taken and then

Norman Tebbit formally opening Coopersale Hall School on 9 July 1990

repaired inside to the hall. There was an iced cake that was a model of the school, which Tebbit cut, and I took him round the parents. Eventually I announced that he was leaving and there was applause. We went off to the study. There I asked him if he might become Prime Minister if anything happened to Thatcher. He said: "It would probably be a younger man, such as John Major."[46] I asked him, "Do you see Rupert Murdoch?" "Yes." "Often?" "Yes." "He's local, and he was an Oaklands parent who lived at Coopersale House nearby. Could you tell him you were here and tell him about me?" "Yes." I escorted him to his chauffeur-driven car and he spread himself over the back seat with his briefcase and papers and left.

On the same day, 9 July, Tebbit was quoted in the *Epping and Harlow Star* as not believing that maintained schools should opt out of local authority control. Soon afterwards I was startled to read a change in Tebbit's views. He called for all maintained schools to be allowed to opt out. I was sure that his impression of Coopersale Hall School had changed his mind, and his call was taken up by John MacGregor, the Secretary of State for Education and Science, and then by Mrs. Thatcher. My decision to found Coopersale Hall was soon reverberating round the nation.

So it happened that after resisting Scargill and opposing those who had organised the Brighton bomb that had blown Tebbit up, I had my new school opened by the Government's leading victim of international terrorism.

I work on Selected Poems

We travelled through great heat to Cornwall and arrived as the *Maria Asumpta* (1858) was about to sail. I climbed aboard and spoke to the owner, Mark Litchfield, who had owned the ill-fated *Marques*. He told me her sinking within the Bermuda Triangle had nothing to do with the Bermuda Triangle itself. The hatch was off-centre and flooded, and the boat was heavy and in the squall she went down. I returned to land and we watched the *Maria Asumpta* go, bobbing offshore in the dark, led by the pilot boat.

I settled at my desk overlooking St Austell Bay to revise my study of world history. I revised chapter 14 with the wind howling and the sea pounding. I ironed out contradictions. Europe's conglomerate was imposed by the winner of the colonial conflict and no one else. The USSR would be federalist and would not enter the United States of Europe yet. I finished the last chapter and walked under the stars, having smoothed out the end wrinkles.

Two days later I hurt my back while exercising. My back stiffened. I worked on Appendices One and Two twisted with pain; concentrating by will-power. I spent an agonising night on my bedroom floor, then proof-read upside down, lying on my back. I went to the doctor – a *locum* who said I must stay in bed all week – and then Ann drove me to an osteopath in Falmouth, a youngish man with a beard who manipulated my back and said: "The muscle has gone into a spasm." He told me to lie on my back and draw my knees up to my chin every hour. I carried on proof-reading.

I had to return to Essex for a day with Matthew, and as I drove I heard that Saddam Hussein had invaded Kuwait. At a service station on the M4 I got out of my car and lay on my back on a grassy knoll, now an abiding memory of Matthew's. I had to pick up what we had acquired at auction on the closure of Loughton School. (One of the two owners had rung me and asked if I would rescue the school before the closure was announced in that week's local paper, and he warned me that my offer would have to exceed an inflated developer's offer for it as building land. The school would be pulled down.) I collected a load of television monitors he had secured for me, and bought a human skull for £10. It had belonged to an Indian woman who died in the 1940s, he told me, and had been used as a teaching aid. It is now in an alcove in my study as a *memento mori*, a reminder of my mortality.

Having installed the television monitors in the schools, I returned to Cornwall. The papers were full of Mrs. Thatcher's Aspen speech in which she followed the policy of my FREE paper on the Eastern Europeans, welcoming them in from the cold of Soviet occupation, but said she did not want a centralised European Union. My comparative study of 25 civilizations showed there would be a centralised European conglomerate and that history was against her. At night there was a full moon and a shimmering causeway under water as I walked with my boys. I drafted a poem, 'Metaphysical-Physical'. A few days later my back was in discomfort. I returned to the osteopath who said that the spine area between my shoulder-blades was rigid and had not moved for years. The next day I finished proof-reading *The Fire and the Stones* and drank elderberry wine with Capt. Gowsell. I saw three shooting stars.[47]

I returned to my *Selected Poems* and worked on 'The Silence'. I wrote: "I have not been able to get 'The Silence' fully ready until now. First because my metaphysical vision has been developing and the poem is coloured by it, and secondly I needed the grasp and sweep… to be able to explain in notes that there are two voices which are sometimes in dialogue."

I had to go back to Essex again for a couple of days to pay staff and cope with problems. I returned and we all joined the Gowsells for a two-hour walk on the Black Head of Trenarren. We passed A.L. Rowse's smoking chimney and closed high black gates and went down to Ropehaven, where there were cormorants on a rock. We walked a mile to the end of the Black Head of Trenarren past sloes, campion and viper's bugloss and through thunderflies. I sat and looked down on the rocks below and watched "The sea boil from the angry years" (line 7 of 'The Silence').

We all returned to Essex. I had figures to do for the bank manager but also reflected on my work. The new Baroque reconciled all my contradictions:

> The new Baroque makes all my work of a piece. *The Fire and the Stones*, the metaphysical and the social; the Silence, the Shadow and the Reflection, one being an amorphous principle, the other a manifestation…. Spirit and sense, the erotic and the spiritual. All of a piece, a complex whole.

I visited Miss Lord (whose niece Zena had left her soldier-husband and was with her) and learned that Mrs. Macy, an ex-teacher at Oaklands, was in Claybury Hospital having nearly gassed Mr Macy absent-mindedly two weeks previously. A paper-boy smelt gas and Mr Macy was unconscious. (Soon after I left Wandsworth in 1985 I was chatting at 10.45 a.m. to a grim-faced inspector outside the Oaklands front door – he was holding a one-metre ruler to measure every classroom and telling me he was not allowed to accept coffee as he should not be beholden to the school – when Mrs. Macy bustled through the gate from two years of retirement and casually said, "I'm sorry I'm late, I'm just going to the staffroom." As he questioned her lack of punctuality I quickly explained that she was no longer on the staff.)

I continued work on 'The Silence' and did not understand lines 162–163, "After confirming the 'approximate' acreage/Of the pre-1810 unregistered estate." I rang my solicitor, Ian Hawthorne, and asked what I meant by... "pre-1810, unregistered estate". He could not remember what happened to estates in 1810 and said: "You're in good company. Browning was asked what he meant and said 'Only God and Browning knew, and now only God knows.'" (I now recall that an estate in existence before 1810 escaped the need for registration, which applied to all post-1810 estates, and therefore its acreage and annual rents were merely estimated, allowing room for tax evasion.)

A new three-year arrangement with my bank began for the schools. The bank's Head Office (whose adviser, I was told, was Nigel Lawson) made the new LIBOR arrangement and changed its basis without informing my bank manager. I discovered from my bank statement that without our bank manager knowing we had been surcharged £16,000 a quarter – £64,000 per annum – in capital repayments we had not expected to make, on top of our interest. Over the next three years we would be repaying £192,000 I had not included in previous projections. I found the lack of explanation for the new arrangement strange, but it could not be reversed and had to be absorbed. If I had planned to continue Oak-Tree's publishing, the surcharge would have prevented me from continuing. The surcharge had the effect of killing off Oak-Tree Books and ending the work of the 'Heroes of the West'. As it was, I was confirmed in my decision not to publish any more books through Oak-Tree. Everything was now clear-cut: I was an author and concentrating on the two schools.[48]

Kathleen Raine and Laurens van der Post

In Frankfurt I had passed the stand of HarperCollins (owned by Rupert Murdoch, with whom Tebbit was in touch) and had been stopped by Barry Winkleman, who had invited me to dinner at Oxford and who I had seen at Pinter's *The Caretaker* in early 1961. He was now Murdoch's Managing Director and had brought out reference works. I had subsequently sent him an early version of *The Fire and the Stones*. There had been a lengthy delay, and there was talk of cutting the book to 600 pages, omitting the chart and not bringing out the book until after October 1991. I rang Kathleen Raine (who was about to leave for Switzerland where the Millennium Trust had claimed to be raising £2 million for her revival of Plato's Academy in October 1991). Wanting me to have the book out before the opening of her Academy, she said: "The chart *must* exist, and in March 1991." She advised me to ring Laurens van der Post. She thought he might write a Foreword and said: "Tell him I want you to lecture at the Academy in October 1991."

I duly rang Sir Laurens, who said: "I've often thought of you. How is the work? I've got a few people here now, please ring me at 4.30 tomorrow, between 4.30 and 5." I rang him the next day. His wife was in the background. "Dearest, I am taking a business call in the other room." I heard her ask: "Is it Mr Hagger? Give him my love." He agreed with Kathleen Raine's view that the book should not be cut and said he would write to his American publisher. He said: "My heart goes out to you. You are doing wonderful work, and the book is of great importance." He ended: "I am not important. I don't regard myself as important or as a link to the Fire. A link to Eliot, Toynbee and Jung, yes, but not an important one. You are the only one alive who is continuing the tradition of Eliot, Toynbee and Jung." After speaking with van der Post I resolved to find another publisher.

Kathleen Raine invited me to her home in Chelsea on 13 September. There was no answer at her door so I waited and saw her plodding along from the King's Road, holding her stick and two large plastic bags. I advanced, kissed her and took the bags and walked back to the house. She said: "I have *angina* in the afternoons, and I sit and wait for the pain to go before I do what has to be done, the shopping." Inside she sat and chatted, and confirmed that she had funding to open her Academy in October 1991.

Then "Lady Rose" came in, alias Dorothy Carrington, who I had met at Kathleen's before, and talked about the Cathars and Corsica. I spoke, and they cross-questioned me for three hours about *The Fire and the Stones*. I kept my end up. Kathleen's questions were coloured by her anti-Americanism: "Where's the American Fire?" And: "Universalism, what sort of religion is Universalism? All religions are one – if it's just a background for American imperialism, it won't do." She said: "People are interested in predictions." I said: "In physics physicists pursue a Grand Unified Theory, and I have endeavoured to do the same with religion and world history." Lady Rose said: "This is grandiose. Mine is tiny in comparison." Kathleen persisted in her anti-Americanism: "I'd rather be Islamic than American because they believe in God. Nicholas sees what is there, he does not say whether it is good." I said, "The 14th-century mystics couldn't have happened in the 10th century because history was not ready for them, their stage had not come. There is a right time for everything to appear on the pattern." Kathleen said: "Am I right in thinking that the genesis of civilizations is caused by something outside history?" When I said "Yes", she said "That is where you will be criticised by historians." I added, "The central idea of each civilization is outside history."

Generally Kathleen Raine approved of my scheme. She said of *The Fire and the Stones*: "It will come out and the Academy will happen." She signed her book, *India Seen Afar*, for me: "For Nicholas Hagger, Servant of the Sacred Fire." I kissed them both twice on their cheeks and left to struggle to a Coopersale Hall parents meeting.

Soon afterwards I met Trevor Maher in the Charing Cross Hotel, "the Oak-Tree office". He had flown British Midland from Edinburgh and had identified Nadia from her name-tag and had introduced himself. "I had wonderful service because I know you," Trevor beamed. We reviewed the length of the book and the HarperCollins delay, which he pronounced unsatisfactory. It was clear again that Kathleen Raine did not want me to go ahead with HarperCollins as she wanted my full-length book and the chart ready for her Academy's opening in October 1991. We agreed to wait a little longer, and then he would implement an idea he had.

The next day I attended the launch of Kathleen Raine's book on India, *India Seen Afar*, at India House, the Adelphi. I climbed the stairs past a bust of Tagore to a room with pictures of Nehru, Gandhi and an enlightened Buddha, where an audience waited. Satish Kumar of Green Books entered with Kathleen and gave an enthusiastic view of Kathleen, rather like Dr Aziz in *A Passage to India*. The Indian High Commissioner spoke without notes. Kathleen read her speech, ending with the words that she was pleased to pour back a drop from the cupful she had taken. We helped ourselves to wine and spicy Indian food and I spoke with Keith Critchlow and Warren Kenton, who asked me about my book and when I told him said, "You've just spoken me your blurb. What you've just said is your blurb." He told me, "I'm working in the same area."

I encountered David Gascoyne, as always in a bow-tie, looking pale and aesthetic at 74, and frail, and I asked, "Do you write poems now?" He said: "No, I haven't written for many years. I had an amphetamine dependency which blocked off my inspiration." His wife of 15 years told me that Kathleen had written to her telling her Gascoyne did not need the worry of a wife, it would depress him." Gascoyne's wife said, "I didn't show David the letter. I received it the day before we were married. I loved him so much." Gascoyne looked rather pathetic and I thought of Wordsworth's lines, "We Poets in our youth begin in gladness;/And thereof comes in the end despondency and madness." Gascoyne did however see the poet as a seer, as I do. Kathleen Raine looking serene and with a transparent, beautiful smile, contrasted with the shuffling, awkward Gascoyne in whose presence she was so imperious at the poetry reading Tuohy and I attended some years back. I met James Madge, her son by Charles Madge, a silky-haired architect.

I felt I should "write a book about poets, defining the Metaphysical line," tracing it through Marvell–Donne, Milton, Blake, Shelley, Eliot–Yeats and resurrecting poets that conform to the Metaphysical Baroque vision. I should include European poets from Germany and France. And "go for metaphysical Reality (the Fire) at the expense of imaginative vision unless Imagination = Fire (as in Coleridge)". I would state the Metaphysical line in *A New Philosophy of Literature*, and include examples in its Appendix.

I subconsciously looked out for a London building of the Metaphysical time of Donne and Marvell that could stand for Universalism where I could hold a launch for *The Fire and the Stones* and *Selected Poems*. I spent an afternoon rooting around the Temple church and the Middle Temple – where there are Elizabethan rooms, including the hall where Shakespeare reputedly acted in *Twelfth Night* in 1602 and a room overlooking the Middle-Temple garden where Shakespeare set the quarrel that led to the Wars of the Roses. The Temple had many literary and historical associations with the likes of Goldsmith, Johnson and Lamb.

Trevor Maher had asked me to find out who would be available to launch *The Fire and the Stones* in April. He needed to know this to help him find an alternative to HarperCollins. I rang Asa Briggs, who said he would attend "and say a few words". I rang van der Post and reminded him that I wanted to call for a Metaphysical Revolution across disciplines at the launch of *The Fire and the Stones*. He suggested that I should ask Keith Critchlow ("who is in dialogue with him about the origins of culture and sees a lot of him") to approach Prince Charles. I rang Kathleen Raine, who gave me Critchlow's phone number and advised: "All you can do is plant a seed and let it grow. Those who have ears to hear, let them hear. Those who have eyes to see, let them see. Don't have a wider and wider circle of people knowing about the metaphysical. You will never persuade the opposition; they are happy the way they are. They have power and influence and don't want to change. I don't want anything to do with Antonia Fraser."

I rang Critchlow, who (according to his wife) was "exhausted, lying on his bed". He came to the phone and listened intently and asked me to send a synopsis of my work. He suggested I rang Warren Kenton. Kenton said: "You will not convert anyone over 40, but the metaphysical work is aimed at the under-forties. The thing to do is to minimise the hostility. Don't rush, you are aiming at the next three centuries. Be careful how you expose yourself. The work is happening anyway. In a hundred years' time they will say, 'Oh, this happened in the 1980s.' Leonardo said, 'Never was there bright light without shadow.'… Leave your brick in the wall, your capstone in the temple, and then move on to the next thing. Don't attract hostility. Don't expose yourself." I replied: "Do you remember the Angry Young Men and how they all contributed to *Declaration*? There should be another *Declaration* about the Metaphysical Revolution."

Getting people together for a hypothetical launch was proving difficult, and I rang Kenton and presented all the options. He insisted on taking an astrological viewpoint and said: "Go for April 22nd. The moon in Leo – a grand entrance. But there is tension and conflict. A risk worth taking. The moon is more favourable than on the 10th. The book will become famous and as the sun is in Taurus it will make money. Go for the Museum of London as it is of more general appeal. The university suggests something more narrow. Don't try to convert or get approval from the academic world.

Just sow your seed and move on. Plod on." It was a prediction that was to prove strangely accurate.

I was torn between world history and metaphysical poetry. I fell asleep downstairs, woke and went to bed. I could not sleep because I was pondering whether David Gascoyne had the Universalist vision:

Oct. 6th. 3.30 a.m.... Got up and read Kathleen Raine's essay on Gascoyne, Hölderlin and Hölderlin's madness." [Gascoyne had written *Hölderlin's Madness*, and I was seeing him as afflicted with the madness suffered by Hölderlin.] "His [Gascoyne's] paradisal world of the poet-seer; going mad through too much Light. He lacked the grounding of the historical vision and of a grounded social life. I, too, am in the seer's tradition. Like Prometheus, I stole the Fire from Heaven, but so far I have not gone mad. The weakness in Raine's view: it isn't only poets who have tasted the Light, known the Fire; as *The Fire and the Stones* shows, it is religious peoples.

I considered her "imagination" and concluded from *In Defence of Ancient Springs* that it meant "divine inspiration from the Muses: receiving dictation from a voice beyond, the words of which the poet barely understands". I pinpointed Plato's doctrine of inspiration and what it does not mean. "It does not mean exclusion of the social world, or receiving dictation.... Kathleen Raine is against Eliot because he was not inspired." I noted: "I have remade myself. The Egerton Gardens mysticism and metaphysical inklings are now fundamental to my outlook."

I had the idea for splitting the *Selected Poems* into social and metaphysical poems and wrote: "Does the social/metaphysical split help the Baroque idea or hinder it? The metaphysical and the social, they are together, not in opposition." I implemented this idea: Part One of my *Selected Poems* had 'Social World' in its title, and Part Two had 'Metaphysical World'. And the contradiction between the social and metaphysical can be found in the theme of *A New Philosophy of Literature*. In Foyles by accident I found the last copy of Frank Warnke's *European Metaphysical Poetry*, which is on the Baroque and Metaphysical tradition, and bought it.

Meanwhile I was working on the index of *The Fire and the Stones*. I knew deep down that there would be a launch in April, but I was still waiting for a publisher to commit to publication. As I waited I had further corroboration that my view of contemporary world history was right when Des McForan rang me three times from Bulgaria, where he was advising the President. He wanted me to go to Sofia for a fortnight "and meet the Government". He said I could give a lecture on FREE. He told me: "Our interpretation *was* correct, the terrorists *were* hiding in Eastern Europe. Your letter to Julian Amery was prophetic, there will be a United States of Europe." (When silence had been thrown round McForan's book, I had written to Amery explaining that the United States of Europe that I had foreseen was in the best interests of the UK, and I had asked what people saw wrong with the context of my vision that would make them want to block it.)

We briefly visited Cornwall – "a high wind, an energetic sea, white waves racing and the wind whistles round the chimney, blown spume drifting through the air like smoke" – and I wrote: "Somehow I must launch a Metaphysical Revolution in 1991, as predicted (in The Markham [on 26 July 1971])."

Back in Essex I spoke to Steve Norris at the Coopersale Hall fireworks party when 300 parents stood in mild, cloudy weather on the terrace and the tree-end of the lawn and watched as a bonfire shot a cloud of sparks and fireworks went up all at once. Thatcher had been challenged by Heseltine and Conservative MPs had to vote. Norris had changed from anti-European to being pro-European after a talk with Heseltine: "Mother (Thatcher) is a drag-anchor. We need a winner. Heseltine will challenge." A week later I met Norris again at a reception, and he invited Ann and me to join him for dinner at a Chinese restaurant in Loughton with two or three others. I travelled alone with Steve. He told me he received 50 letters a day.

Steve drove us home and as Ann got out I asked him which way he would vote for Thatcher's successor. He said, "I won't mess you about, Nick, I will tell you, I shall vote bat." I looked blank. "Cricket bat?" I ventured. "Straight bat?" "I shall vote for the old bat [i.e. Thatcher] because she should win well; and Hurd in the second round." Which was what happened. He offered to invite the Minister for Arts to attend my coming launch. (When David Mellor was replaced as Minister for Arts by the Chief Whip, Tim Renton, he later told me he would invite Renton, with whom he had bad relations.) I spoke to David Evennett at Chigwell School's Dr Faustus, in which Anthony was a demon, and he told me he would be voting for John Major.

I had looked in on HarperCollins. Barry Winkleman's secretary had said: "Excellent work. The chart ought to be compulsory reading for everybody, everybody in the world ought to learn it from birth. And Barry sends his love." But there was still no progress with a publication date, and there was still the prospect of shortening. I was confident that something was about to happen and that my two titles were right: "The Light has been pouring in, answering Yes to The Fire and the Stones and A Metaphysical's Way of Fire, a getting-across of the Metaphysical Revolution,... to something being about to happen."

Nearly a week later I met Trevor Maher, who said that the HarperCollins delay was increasingly unsatisfactory. He proposed that Weidenfeld or Mainstream should be approached to take the books over.[49] We had had a drink with the two Mainstream fellows at Frankfurt, and as they were Edinburgh-based like Trevor, he said he would speak to them.

International politics: in Czechoslovakia – Otto von Habsburg and Pan-Europeanism

In *The Fire and the Stones* I had predicted a coming United States of Europe. Gorka had invited me to attend the Pan-European Union congress in Prague from 7 to 9 December. It was a good opportunity to monitor the emergence of the new superstate.

The Pan-European Union was the oldest European unification movement, and had begun in 1923. Otto von Habsburg, the heir to the Austro-Hungarian Empire and the Holy Roman Empire, had become its President in 1973 after the death of its founder Count von Coudenhove-Kalergi. He would be there, and Gorka, who regarded him as Emperor-in-Exile (much more than an MEP) said he would introduce me. We flew to Prague with a director of the anti-Communist Western Goals, which had produced a very interesting leaflet saying that the decision to overthrow Thatcher had been taken at a meeting in May at La Toja, where Kissinger of the New-World-Order Bilderberg Group had called for a more rapid movement towards a European Central Bank, which Thatcher was opposing.

The three of us drove to Prague's Hotel Dlabacov in a temperature of minus 8, with Adam Ferguson, ex-MEP and Vice-President of the Pan-European Union. We registered and learned we were in the House Mickel (Michael House), a cab ride away. We found our room, and then returned to the Dlabacov where, in a huge reception room, among tables with white tablecloths, ham rolls and wine, we attended a reception and spoke with Otto von Habsburg. Gorka bowed and kissed his hand, renewing his fealty to the old Austro-Hungarian ideal. I recall a small, ageing, balding figure who avoided all eye-contact to preserve the distance required by his royal pedigree. He had the air of an emperor and spoke all the European languages. He listened to what I said about FREE and the coming United States of Europe, which my book had predicted, and said I was welcome.

We walked to Wenceslas Square in a temperature of minus 10 or 11, our ears stinging and noses numb. We ate in the Beograde restaurant.

Breakfast next morning was in the Pan-European Union's room. Otto von Habsburg's step-by-step approach to a United States of Europe had rather got lost amid shambolic organisation. No one introduced anyone to anyone.

I encountered Adam Ferguson, who had been personal adviser to Sir Geoffrey Howe, and asked him if there would be British funding for a British branch of Pan-Europe. He said, "There won't be any funding," and I gathered that his role was to keep a brake on Pan-Europeanism. In the main hall we were given earphones and heard simultaneous translation, and I listened to speeches by Sir Tom Normanton, a former MEP and friend of Thatcher, and Valburga Habsburg, Otto's daughter. Adam Ferguson spoke and mentioned us as the British delegation. There seemed to be a contradiction between his public enthusiasm for Pan-Europe and his brake on funding.

After lunch we toured Prague. We went to the castle, which towered over the city, and walked among the palaces and churches of its squares and streets. We then took a taxi to the crowded cobbled Charles IV bridge over the river Vltava, which had 31 statues. We walked to the other side and were driven to Old Square. Round the corner, within sight of the sunburst high up on the church, the significance of which he never discovered, was Kafka's house, shut up. Down a side street there was a view of the spires of the castle complex.

The next day was a Sunday morning. We were up early and breakfasted in the same room as Otto von Habsburg and then went by coach to Holy Mass in the church of the Order of Malta in Mala Strana, near Charles IV bridge. The white interior had gilt figures and a pulpit. There was a packed congregation and people were standing in the aisles at the sides. There was singing and kneeling on one knee. There was an address about Nazism and Communism, and then Mass. Otto von Habsburg went up first. I went up about 20th, and took the wafer dipped in wine, standing, from a priest. I pondered the significance of attending Mass with the Head of the Habsburgs in an ancient centre of the Holy Roman Empire. I felt I had been passed on to a Central-European Light tradition embodied by the Habsburgs, a tradition that was in waiting for the coming United States of Europe.

Otto von Habsburg made the final speech at the conference. He spoke without notes, a current flowing through him. He made a plea for more recognition of Central Europe and for a Continent at peace without borders. He called for a new European language. I was listening to the translation through my earphones, and I understood that he wanted to revive the Holy Roman Empire with himself as Emperor and with German as its main language. I could understand why Britain might want to contain this idea rather than encourage it. I flew back with Adam Ferguson, who waited for us at Heathrow and sat next to me in the tube, and I said as much to him.

I had liked Prague. It was the baroque capital of Europe because it was little war-damaged, because so much had survived. Understanding Otto von Habsburg's view of a unified Europe had given me a great insight into the coming United States of Europe.[50]

World history and metaphysical poetry: launching **The Fire and the Stones** *and* **A Metaphysical's Way of Fire,** *bringing in a new Universalist Age*

I was now ready to be "an Ambassador for the Fire". I was in dialogue with the Light about *The Fire and the Stones*. I asked the Light if I was on course:

Dec. 19. Went to the Light twice. The first time, meditated and asked if I am on the right track regarding the Metaphysical Revolution and got surges in reply.... The second time, several hours later, had huge surges and am filled with the Light. The second surge was enormously powerful, went down my back and through my legs and feet. It confirmed that there will be a Metaphysical Revolution.

On Christmas Eve I "went to the Light. Many answering surges.... The new direction is inevitable". On Christmas morning an idea lodged in my mind: "An insight at 7.45 a.m. as I lay in bed. If all goes well there must be a Foundation to promote the ideas of the Metaphysical Revolution.... A Foundation of the Light."[51]

Over Christmas I talked with my younger brother Jonathan, who had been appointed Finance Director to the Duke of Westminster and would be managing the Grosvenor Estate in Davies Street, where he would have a staff of 50. I also heard that Margaret Shubber of Iraq had died in March.

I am put in touch with Element, temple-dancer

After the lengthy delays the way suddenly opened. In early January Trevor Maher rang me. He had made use of his copies of my two books. To unjam the HarperCollins delay Peter MacKenzie of Mainstream had rung a contact of his in Element Books and as a result I was to send *The Fire and the Stones* to Michael Mann. This duly happened. There was swiftly a message from Michael on my answerphone asking me to ring before he went to Switzerland. I rang and arrangements were made for Element to take over both *The Fire and the Stones* and *Selected Poems* without cuts and with the chart, and by the end of April. I had always known that if I got the books ready the right publisher would appear, and I was not really surprised. I was relieved for I would now be a published poet and cultural historian and the Metaphysical Revolution would be marketed and spread. I had become the author I planned to be.

In mid-January, a few days after the Allies bombed Baghdad (leaving me feeling sombre for the Iraqis there I used to know) I went to Shaftesbury, Dorset, to visit Element. I entered a pleasant old grammar school, an ancient building with many staircases, nooks and crannies, and a warren of rooms. I met Michael Mann, followed him upstairs and took in his sweater and tie, and his soft look. He smoked filter tips throughout our one-and-a-half hour chat, first on practicalities – he took notes while I freewheeled – and then on the Fire generally and on my poems. He turned out to be a relative of Vicky Norris's through a cousin. He said *he* told Kathleen Raine about the Millennium Trust, which he founded – "It hasn't any money and Kathleen Raine has little business sense" – and that he was publishing a book about Colin Wilson. He knew Warren Kenton and had been a pupil of his. He said that in religion, "Universalism cannot be absolutist, it will always be regional," to which I replied: "In the Roman times, regions had Mithras and Isis, but they synchretistically merged with the Roman gods without losing their separateness." He took me on a tour of the building and introduced me to several of his 40 staff and we made arrangements for the launch, which he said he would be running.

We had agreed that the launch should have a central event that should be Universalist, and latched on to the Egyptian temple-dancers, who Michael had seen. They brought down the Light of Amun-Re. A week later, taking time off from my frantic work on the two books, selecting illustrations and writing captions, at the Museum of London, which was to be the venue for the launch, I met Christine Finlayson, then Klein (her married name), one of the Egyptian temple-dancers I had seen in Smith Square. She said she would dance the Descent of the Light of Amun-Re. We chose a setting with a column behind her. Ever since my second visit to be regressed by Maurice Blake I had been haunted by an image within. I was in a large Egyptian garden of about two acres with a high brick wall all round, in the middle of which was a round lotus pond. Standing by it, looking into it with her back to the house, was a slender Egyptian lady with black hair wearing a long white dress. Seeing Christine with green Egyptian eye-liner under her eyes, I had a sense of *déjà-vu* and the image of the lady in white came into my mind – from a past life? I described my memory of the lotus pool and she said quietly, "I remember that lotus pool." She said she would dance to "water-music" and wear a white dress with gold and use green eye-liner. She said: "I will reflect and project. Reflect the Light of Amun-Re, and project it. I mirror the Light and become a Shining One and dance with the Shining Ones and project the Light onto the audience. I get a flow. I do it by feeling. I don't like to put a date on it. It's early." Amun-Re was strong from c.1990 BC. "I create a stillness." Christine later told me that at bedtime that night she had had "a rush of images", all from the Egyptian days, in which she saw herself in a life with me.

I was working on both books simultaneously. I had the idea for calling the notes to the poem 'A Metaphysical Commentary'. On the same day I spoke with Keith Critchlow over the telephone. He said: "Do send Prince Charles an invitation. He might be able to come if it's near Kensington Palace."

At Coopersale Hall I got the concrete floor laid just before it snowed. Snow fell for two days – eight inches on the last night – and the two schools were closed and I could not move my car. I was snowbound in a magical world of white, everything clean and pure and the familiar made wonderfully strange. I wrote a poem, 'Snow Peace'. During the break from rushing about I recorded the idea for a future work:

> My next work will be excerpts from my *Diaries*, focusing on my metaphysical development and the bits that support the poems…. Had this idea two or three days ago, but know it is next.

This idea became *Awakening to the Light*.

A week later we drove to Cornwall at half-term and I proof-read my two books. I heard that Stephen Lucas had gone bankrupt the previous July and that he was in prison for fraud. While in Cornwall I read obituaries about György Krassó, the Hungarian dissident. He had been given a British passport in 1985 but returned to Hungary in 1989 to set up the Hungarian October Party. He had apparently died after suffering a heart attack and was in a coma for a long time. The obituaries described how he was among the first who fired at the secret police units during the Hungarian Revolution of 1956. I wondered whether he had in fact had a heart attack or whether he had been assisted to have one, following his petition for democracy. He had been a strong supporter of the ideas of the 'Heroes of the West'.

Preparing for the launch
Back in Essex I continued working on the books and preparing for the launch. I had a startling experience of synchronicity, which made me ponder the powers of the human mind:

> I was thinking that I should write to Valerie Eliot and [was] looking for my *Diary* entry for my visit to Ezra Pound when Valerie's nephew's wife, Tanya, rang from Sunderland saying she had been trying to get Valerie, who was not in, and asking about my visit to Pound [so that she could inform Valerie]. Extraordinary telepathy.

In early March I began setting up my launch. I rang Warren Kenton in the evening, around 6. He had just moved to a new flat and was among packing-cases. "If he is not in America – and his diary is packed – he will be pleased to speak about the Fire." I rang David Gascoyne in the Isle of Wight. "He is very interested in my *Selected Poems* and will be honoured to say a few words at my launch."

Four days later I rang Kathleen Raine. I told her about Element and the

Metaphysical Revolution. She happened to be writing to Michael Mann (another example of synchronicity). She was very excited. I said: "The Revolution was prophesied by David Gascoyne in the late 1930s, and has been worked for by you and others for decades... and has now happened." She said she felt the *Temenos* Academy would happen. She had seen Prince Charles twice – she was consulted by him about his own work. She said, "Tomlin foresaw all this." She, Gascoyne and Warren Kenton now subscribed to the idea of a Metaphysical Revolution. She said: "The bullets will fly on April 22nd." She said she would invite Bohm. She added a word of caution: "People won't say, 'Oh good, Nicholas Hagger has told us the truth.' They will be snide and will reject it, as they did my book on Blake. But out of it will come your immortality."

Kathleen Raine was like Mrs. Thatcher: "You're one of us." She said, "I shan't be able to be present if the Poet Laureate [Ted Hughes] is there." I said: "It's like a relay race. You've held the baton for one lap and you're handing over to me. But there are several runners in parallel lanes." (I meant that Hughes was one of parallel runners.) She widened our discussion. She said: "I'm writing an essay, 'On the Vertical Dimension'." I said: "In a poem of transformation I wrote in 1966 [, 'The Silence',] I wrote of 'the vertical vision' as opposed to 'the horizontal vision'." Kathleen said: "Eliot never had the vision." I said to her once again: "He knew 'the Fire and the rose are one'." She said grudgingly: "Yes, but he never had the vision. I write Valerie as she's a sweet person."

I saw the Metaphysical Revolution, to be proclaimed at the launch, as signalling the end of an Age of Materialism, Scepticism and Humanism that had lasted 300 years and bringing in a new Universalist Age that would emphasise the oneness of all creation in accordance with the new physics and have a profound impact on art. And so I spread awareness of the launch. I rang Rupert Sheldrake, the biologist, and spoke with his wife Jill Purce, who I had visited in Hampstead. She explained they would be in Devon on the morning of the launch. "I'll be coming up from Devon on that day to give a lecture at St James's, Piccadilly, I have a one-year-old child. Rupert will be looking after him in Devon." Later I spoke to Rupert, who said: "Your books look very interesting. I want to read them. The Tomlin book is one of my most thumbed ones. I often refer to it and recommend it. The one you published. It's a very good book." "I said: "Tomlin... never came off the fence." He: "You must. You must declare yourself."

I rang David Bohm, who arranged to see me the following week. He asked: "You don't want me to speak at the launch?" I said: "No, just to be there." I said Sheldrake's morphogenetic field goes with his (Bohm's) implicate order which goes with my Void/Non-Being. He said: "Huh huh." I said we should meet "to agree [that]... the Fire... is behind the oneness of creation and history, and the mysticism of poetry".[52] I had a letter from Dr Brian Hanson, adviser to the Prince of Wales, saying he (Hanson) would attend the launch. Had he heard about it from Laurens van der Post or Critchlow?

I had two letters from Kathleen Raine. She had received an early copy of *The Fire and the Stones* and said she would speak about the Fire at my launch. She was desperate to organise the *Temenos* Academy, and asked if I could raise funds for her: "You as the High Priest of Fire, I entrust with my last hope."[53] She had clearly given up on the Millennium Trust. I offered my schools at weekends and in the school holidays as temporary accommodation for her Academy to help her get it off the ground.

Cosmology and Theory of Everything: with David Bohm – the infinite and Metaphysical Revolution

I visited David Bohm, who had discussions with his friend Einstein at Princeton and had been a devotee of Krishnamurti (who saw Reality as mental), at Birkbeck. He could not be found. I was early and waited, I was then sent to PE 40, and found him opening letters. He said, "It's just the right time," but he carried on opening mail and seemed to forget that I was there. Then he took me to a small room he shared with an Asian, who asked: "Do you mind if I stay?" We stood without saying anything and he took the hint and left. Then Bohm changed his mind and said we should sit in another room. He led me to where six people were standing by a computer and sorting through a thesis. They switched off, packed up and left. He closed the door, still opening and reading a letter, and then said, "Sit down." I did so and looked deep into his eyes and he into mine, and then we got on fine and the words came.

I talked for 40 minutes about how he had stood for the whole and a Theory of Everything must include a Grand Unified Theory of physics as well as of history, and how metaphysics looked as ontological theory, Being, and I spoke of the significance of the Fire. I did not have the chart – that would have led to a five-hour conversation – but I gave him my 'Preface on the Metaphysical Revolution' and talked him through the paragraphs. I pressed him, creased-faced and rumpled-looking but strangely innocent. Some of the things he said reverberated through my consciousness. He asked, "Have you seen the Fire?" I said, "Yes." He said: "Good." I put it to him that physics is within metaphysics. He said: "You can't have a vision of the whole. It's infinite." I said: "You can interpret it simultaneously through different faculties, vision, imagination, reason." He said: "The universe is infinite," meaning 'Our vision is finite'. I said: "Is that what your equations and calculations tell you?" He said: "Yes. It's infinite, and our universe is a local event, an area within the sea of energy." (He wrote as much in

Wholeness and the Implicate Order.) I pointed out that the self has an infinite part to it, a spark in the soul, and that by journeying from the ego to our universal being we *can* have a vision of the infinite.

I tackled him on what he thought. He said on the Metaphysical Revolution, "I'm not optimistic, I think everything's in decline. Ecologically, for example." I said: "History shows that there are young civilizations with a vision still ahead of them. The North-American civilization is young and it has not found its orthodoxy yet – which may be a Universalist metaphysical vision." I pressed him on the Metaphysical Revolution. He said: "There is something cosmic, which is behind physics." I said: "That's what I mean when I say the Fire manifests into Void and Being and Existence." I added: "The Fire is a sea of energy. What about the Big Bang?" "A local event, a ripple." "And cosmic background radiation (CBR)? Penzias and Wilson?" "The residue." He said, "I wish I had your enthusiasm. We're not near a Unified Theory of physics. Different physicists have different views." I asked him, "Do you feel out on a limb or in the mainstream of physics?" He repeated: "Different physicists have different views." I said, "Any new idea is always opposed and you must have felt opposition." "Yes." He asked, "What do you want to say at the launch?" I told him. "I'll go along with that. Send me your work." With that he stood up and held out a hand, and I wished him goodbye and said I hope he'd be at the launch. "I may be in Israel, but if not I'll be there."

I came away knowing that the concept of the universe we had been discussing would pass into my future poems. I observed:

> This great man has seen matter and consciousness as a unity… and he has confirmed the vision in my poems…. The universe is infinite. We are finite minds – which can receive the infinite vision and therefore we take part in infinity. Part of us is of the infinity in the universe. I have a new poem about this and about CBR…. There is a sea of souls in the infinite sea of energy, and we are a local surfacing of minds too finite to grasp it, but we partake of infinity. My insistence that the metaphysical Fire unites everything – physics, history here in this tiny local corner. We see it, not the whole of it but part of this vast cosmic Fire for it manifests into Void and fullness.

Pondering on the infinite, I drove with my family to Cornwall, where the air was drugged and I slowed down. I went for a walk under a full moon with a haze-corona. The tide was out, the moon shone in the curl of each wave.

The next day I thought about the coming Metaphysical Revolution. The social poetry must go on – the sunny scene of *Love's Labours Lost*, of young lords renouncing love for studies but ending up with girls. But the infinite universe which has no beginning and no end, in which we are a local event and the cosmic Fire from infinity which manifests – this must also be stated. I watched the sea from my upstairs writing window: "A curl of sunlight in the gentle waves at low tide, a sparkling on the water, two birds flew across it. Then the sun went in. A Metaphysical sea. Trenarren visible to the right from my window as I lean, chin on fist."

Still pondering, I wrote:

> The Metaphysical Revolution boils down to the benefit of man in relation to the cosmic Fire, a beneficial relationship; and of a universe which is local in relation to an infinite and eternal vastness which the Fire pervades. It is the extra dimension that makes the Metaphysical Revolution.... We are of the infinite, we can see the Fire, there is that in us which is of the infinite sea.

I was glad to be back in Cornwall. As I went to get the papers I heard a bird singing from the wall, by the car park where the ruined boat stood, and saw a small fat wren. It sang and flew. I loved the Cornish walls: old rocky walls exposed at low tide, and granite walls that protect the land from the sea. And grassy hills, a land-and-sea landscape in one view, under a vast sky that at night sparkles with thousands of stars.

The next day was sunny. I felt the hot sun on my cheeks. There was a sparkling tranquil sea and in the evening a full moon and a causeway of moonlight on a low tide. The moon was in rock pools and in the harbour, and everything was bathed in a glow, a wonderful moonlight: "The universe has no beginning and no end, is infinite and eternal; and we are a local happening within its diverse immensity." On 2 April I "sat at peace and drafted seven out of an intended eight stanzas of a poem about the finite mind contemplating an infinite universe. Bohm comes into it. I have left a stanza for Gunzig. Called it 'Our Local Universe in Infinite Space' (later retitled 'Ode: Spider's Web: Our Local Universe in an Infinite Whole')." I carried straight on and from 9.45 p.m., drafted my address for the launch. I finished working at 1 a.m. (2 a.m. in effect, allowing for Summer Time). This effort was the result of "a surge of energy".

The next day I was "awoken at 5 by howling winds and crashing seas. I tried to sleep, but gave up before 7 and got up. I was set to pack the car but the raging wind was filled with clouds of spray blowing in them and I waited for the storm to abate. Am close to the elements: the wind, the rough seas and blown spume." On our return to Essex I heard that Caroline's mother had died. She had sat down at her dressing-table and slumped forward from a heart attack.[54]

Cosmology: Edgard Gunzig and Light

I attended the Mystics and Scientists conference at Winchester to hear

Edgard Gunzig, the Belgian cosmologist, who was to speak first on the Saturday morning. I found myself being charged up with Light for my launch. On the Friday evening there was a film on fractals and I noted that when I got into bed, "The Fire poured in as I lay down."

Gunzig was a small Frenchman with curly hair and a beard, wearing brown, and his talk was entitled 'Cosmos out of Chaos: Why there is a Universe rather than a Vacuum'. It was the clearest explanation – in a foreign language for him – for the quantum vacuum and creation that I have ever heard. As a three-time winner of the Gravity Research Foundation's International Award he was in the Hawking league. He spoke of curved space, how space is curved because objects make pathways, not because of gravitation or variables; and then of how the universe expels pairs of particles, positive and negative, and sucks them in again, and how these virtual particles can be made real by energy from the geometric background, negative energy, which was known about a long time ago.

After his lecture I talked with Gunzig and got his phone number. I asked him about Bohm and the infinite universe, and he said, "Bohm is very important." I asked him about CBR (cosmic background radiation): "It is not important, the Big Bang too, not important." I asked him if there is something metaphysical behind the physical world. He replied: "No, there is just the world of physics.... Mysticism is not my field, I do not know." He spoke warmly of Bohm to me, and wanted to meet him, but would not be drawn on Bohm with others around. Similarly he would not say, 'There is infinity behind the world of physics.' Gunzig was close to Bohm's position but would not affirm it.

In the afternoon I visited Winchester Cathedral's Saxon kings in mortuary chests and medieval knights. I sat in the Venerable Chapel twice and "had two great surges of Light". Later that night I received an influx of Light:

1.15 a.m. Light still pouring into me. Making my fingers shiny, tingling my spine. I am filled with Light. The last two days I have taken in a huge dose which will get me past April 22nd.

And:

After lunch [the next day] meditated in my bare room. Much Light. Many tingles. I offered the two books, the launch and the Metaphysical Revolution to the Light for the greater good of the Light, then received answering currents and many symbols in code, which I could not decode.... Then a terrific white pillar of white Light that made me gasp. I nearly lost consciousness. Slowly came to. Am writing this in the car park three-quarters of an hour later as I set off to Cornwall, filled with the Light, serene.... I nearly choked, my chest heaved up and down as I fought for breath as it cascaded in like a waterfall.... An influx full of coded wisdom which will hatch like caterpillars.[55]

I joined the family in Cornwall for a couple of days.

Launch of The Fire and the Stones *and* Selected Poems, A Metaphysical's Way of Fire

Back in Essex I drove to London to deliver some early copies of *The Fire and the Stones* and called in on Kathleen Raine. She said: "You must come in for tea, it's just made." John Matthews, a writer on Celtic mysteries, was with her. Kathleen focused on my history book. Matthews said: "This is right up my street. This is a very important book. I shall buy this. I can't come to the launch, I'm lecturing in America."

Another chamberlain from St James's Palace rang me, Rasmussen, wanting an invitation to the launch. "I'm very interested, I'm working in that field." I rang blind Heath-Stubbs, who told me he would not be able to attend the launch. He said, "I am read to on a Monday." He wanted to send Eddie Linden. I rang van der Post, who said he would be on "Royal command" during the launch, but told me: "Excellent work." Roger Scruton told me he would be in Hungary for the launch, "but the books are very interesting. I will review them for *The Salisbury Review.*" I rang David Gascoyne, who fell upon me over the phone: "I was expecting you to ring. You've put me in. Did you know I wrote 'The Sun at Midnight'? I was in a lunatic asylum three times you know. Let's go out to dinner afterwards." I rang Bohm. "I won't be able to come. I'll be in Israel. Yes, I got the book." I rang Valerie Eliot. She had had teeth out. "I've a pile [of correspondence] several feet high and no secretary. I'm going to Oxford on Monday, if I'm back in time I'll come straight in." Valerie Eliot's nephew rang soon afterwards, and told me how Eliot always walked through Stanhope Gardens, where I had lived, to go to Dino's. Sir Tom Normanton, the ex-MEP I had met in Prague, said over the phone about the two chamberlains: "That's very interesting." I received an unexpected letter from Rupert Murdoch, ex-Oaklands parent, wishing the book well.

I was still coping with building work at Coopersale Hall – joists and joist-hangers – but I noted: "There is a tremendous feeling of expectancy in the air. The Metaphysical Revolution is possible and can happen. All day, influxes – while driving, while waiting for the photocopier, while on the telephone." The next day Andrew Lownie rang: "I saw your book on sale in Scotland. You've got a book out, poetry." I told him about my history. I noted: "This excitement. Gascoyne, according to Durrell 'one of the finest and purest metaphysical poets of our age'." I booked the restaurant at the Barbican, then rang Gascoyne. He said: "Oh, there's a nice French restaurant in Priory Square. In the north, a Mews." His wife came on: "It's in Charterhouse Square and it only opens for lunch. I think stick to the Barbican, the French *brasserie*." I rang Gascoyne again. He said: "There are two fires, there's Pentecostal Fire and Luciferian Fire, Hell Fire." I said firmly: "It's the first we're talking about, not the second."

Later that night I wrote: "Swept with tides of Fire again. Three times between 11.30 and 12.30 a.m..... Eliot is near me. Each time I think of Eliot I pour with Light; I am filled with an influx." The next day Eddie Linden rang, saying he would represent John Heath-Stubbs, who had written me a letter. I rang Kathleen Raine. She said: "You are the first since the *Old Testament* to write of sacred history." But had not Yeats written, "There is only one history and that is the soul's"? She said she would wear red for fire.[56] I was aware that she was pigeon-holing me into sacred history because it suited her scenario regarding her Academy.

My launch took place at the Museum of London on 22 April. Some I was expecting did not turn up, including Jessica Douglas-Home, who had written me a very polite note of acceptance. Sir Tom Normanton did not turn up but I received a letter from Douglas Hurd, the British Foreign Secretary, saying he was reading the book on planes. Philip Mawer was stuck in traffic trying to reach the launch. (He was then Secretary-General of the Church of England Synod, and he later wrote that he had been given a brief by the Archbishop of Canterbury which had held him up.) Drinks were served among the exhibits, and I encountered Asa Briggs grinning to himself among the glass cases. I introduced him to David Gascoyne and Kathleen Raine. Through some mismanagement on the part of the Museum there was no microphone, but the launch was filmed.

Speeches by Asa Briggs, Kathleen Raine and David Gascoyne
Michael Mann spoke first. He said that bookshops were already taking *The Fire and the Stones* without hesitation, despite its price, in fives and sixes and tens, and that the first impression was already sold out. Asa Briggs spoke brilliantly. He described my 30 years of research and how he had recon-structed my poem about the Worcester College lake by walking under the stone arch and finding the stone seat I had sat on in the Worcester College gardens. He described how he found a letter connected with the Fire. He said, "*The Fire and the Stones* is the most powerful *tour de force* I have come across in my entire academic life." He said how proud he was to be at the same College as me, perhaps an indirect reference to the work I was doing in Libya which he had known about in October 1978.[57] He said that although books had dealt with why civilizations declined, there was very

little about what made them grow, and he strongly recommended my poems. He said he had found the groupings under headings showing progress along the Mystic Way very interesting. David Gascoyne read a few texts about the metaphysical Fire. Kathleen Raine spoke of the Pentecostal Fire and said again that it was the first time since the *Old Testament* that sacred history had returned.

Asa Briggs (left) and Kathleen Raine (right) speaking at the launch of Nicholas's two books on 22 April 1991, with David Gascoyne sitting

I spoke of Gascoyne's *Journal 1937–1939* (written in France at the same time as *La Nausée*) having predicted that the future of the 20th century would burn with an "extraordinary, unseen and secret radiance".[58] Then I declared

Nicholas with David Gascoyne on 22 April 1991

the Metaphysical Revolution, calling on the west wind of Shelley's 'Ode to the West Wind' to "scatter, as from an unextinguished hearth/Ashes and sparks, my words among mankind!" Ronald Lello, who was associated with the Millennium Trust and had pushed Kathleen Raine's wheelchair, then made an impromptu and unscheduled speech relating my Revolution to what Prince Charles was doing, with one eye on the two chamberlains present. The two chamberlains Prince Charles had sent both asked me to sign the two books for Prince Charles. Christine, the temple-dancer, then performed a stunning dance of the Descent of the Fire and the inauguration of the Revolution, combining stillness and beauty. At one point her hand movements suggested scooping the Light and pouring it over herself and opening doors. (There are 900 different hand gestures in Egyptian temple-dancing, of which Christine told me she used about 100.)

I remember Steve Norris, who was representing the Minister for Arts, speaking to Asa Briggs and to his wife's relation Michael Mann. I remember Eddie Linden, who was representing John Heath-Stubbs, talking to Steve Norris about "this Philistine Government", and getting progressively drunk until John Ezard took him away at the end as he wanted to join the speakers' dinner. I remember Sebastian Barker, the poet George Barker's son and Chairman of the Poetry Society, telling me he would "follow me", and Peter Donebauer of Diverse Production helping my boys with their camcorder.

Afterwards I took Kathleen Raine, Michael Mann and David Gascoyne to eat, and Ronald Lello tagged along, uninvited. (Because he pushed Kathleen Raine's wheelchair seemed to give him a right to voice opinions at our table.) I sat next to Gascoyne, who told me, "I'm an autodidact" ('self-taught'), and heard about his meetings with various poets, including Eliot, and his wish to know the Fire. I said that one day we would sit together and bring it down, and he said "he would like to sit and meditate to feel the influxes which he has not felt since his youth". I noted: "He is a shell of a man, looking to me to revive his experience of the beyond." Kathleen Raine said: "The poets I have written about have all lasted: Vernon Watkins and the rest. The 1950s poets haven't lasted."[59] Lello questioned the basis of my study of world history, and Kathleen turned and said to him in an almost scolding voice, "Nicholas is going to lecture in history at the Academy." Soon afterwards a printed leaflet appeared with names of all lecturers in all the subjects, and (although I had not given my consent) my name was in the History slot.[60]

There was very little publicity about the books. John Ezard told me that *The Guardian* had a backlog of 37 book reviews it could not use. The 'Heroes of the West' had folded themselves down, but I was saying through my world history that a United States of Europe was approaching (not a popular idea in some quarters), that Communism was about to end (as it did), and that America was poised for a world role as the only superpower (as happened). I could imagine that some might want to stifle these predictions. The day before the launch a British tabloid newspaper, *The People*, had published a story associating Steve Norris, my tenant, with a *Times* journalist. Ann and I took him and Vicky out to dinner in Epping High Street to show our solidarity, and I remember Norris telling me he thought the Far Right pro-Thatcher wing were behind the smear.[61] Privately I wondered if the revelation had been timed to coincide with the publication of my books, to discredit them by association in some way.

Warren Kenton had predicted that I would make a "grand entrance". There were some indications that he may have been right. I received a letter from Sebastian Barker, Chairman of the Poetry Society, saying: "You are the nucleus of a comet of history trailing a wonderful vapour-trail of poetry. My profound respect and wonder before your achievement."[62] I replied wondering if I was not rather a comet of poetry trailing history, but the truth was that I was a metaphysical Fire trailing both history and poetry.

I wrote to various people, including Frank Kermode (about 'the dancer' in his *Romantic Image* and at my launch, among other things); Valerie Eliot; St James's Palace; Sir Laurens van der Post and Sir Tom Normanton while running between the two schools and solving problems. I rang Gascoyne, the author of "Christ of Revolution and Poetry." He said: "I'm disillusioned with revolution. It's interior revolution. I tried to tell the Royal family about the revolution and was put in a lunatic asylum. My life has three periods: my early precocity, 10 or 15 years when I was mad, and some rehabilitation under Judy." I told him: "A sea-change is happening and people will respond more to metaphysical poetry, including yours." He said: "I wish I could believe that. That's what surrealism tried to do." He told me: "I can only think of one thing at a time. I've got to finish the Introduction to Elizabeth Smart's work." Elizabeth Smart was Sebastian Barker's mother, and Gascoyne was attaching great importance to the promised fee of £100.

The launch over, I was able to relax a bit. On the May Day Holiday I slept late "and pondered on Prince Charles, who was calling for European cultural reunification in Prague". I had discussed the cultural revolution that a United States of Europe would bring when I was in Prague. I "sat and let the Fire come through. It surged into me, glowing my fingers." I began a selection from my earlier *Diaries*, which would become *Awakening to the Light*. I visited Mabel Reid and discussed 'Clouded-Ground Pond' and the resemblance between mind and pond: "You can see the surface and depth at the same time." She asked me about the Metaphysical Revolution and I told her that "the anti-metaphysical philosophers shut out the universe and confined it all to their room, but now the American spacecraft were flying round the planets and we know it is vast out there and infinite".[63] I watched Anthony play cricket and stood on the boundary with David Evennett.

I received a letter from Frank Kermode, the influential literary critic, referring to my "scholarship and gifts as a writer, both expository and poetic" which exacted "my tribute of respect" as my mind "embraces huge masses of apparently disparate material in the service of an idea" which "speaks of a great renovation". His own sceptical, materialistic mind resists as "the unification is too much for me" as he endearingly described himself as a clerk and sceptic. He said my "notable statement" deserved to be "intelligently opposed rather than neglected". He valued my ideas "without being able to accommodate their arguments". He wrote, "I am a sincere admirer."[64] I wrote: "I put forward a unification and have announced a Revolution. I stand like a mountain… peak round which clouds will gather, as critics obscure me. But at the end the clouds will pass and the mountain will be there." I also noted, "Frank Kermode is unillumined."[65]

There was a Quiz Night at Coopersale Hall, put on by the Parents' Association, that included the question, "Who is the author who spent 20 years writing *The Fire and the Stones*?" One parent answered, "Harold Robbins."

Starting the Temenos *Academy*

Kathleen Raine wrote and asked if I would start the Academy with a series of lectures in Great College Street, near Westminster Abbey. She said: "Something happened at your launch. You changed the atmosphere."[66] I told her that Kermode had written, and she said: "All the people who have important positions seem to be there without the knowledge. The idea of the sage has gone. They're not sages." I wrote to Kermode "presenting the artist as solving his isolation by renovating his civilization, and suggesting that he should write a sequel to *Romantic Image*, on the metaphysical line in English poetry and how it finds a solution to the isolated Romantic predicament".

I was invited to the consecration of the *Temenos* Academy at All Souls', Margaret Street, a Tractarian Victorian church. I was greeted by Kathleen Raine, Critchlow, Matthews, David Cadman, Lello and John Allott, who accosted me: "I recognise you from the photo in your book. It reflects what I have thought over 20 years." We sat for the ceremony, which was conducted by wizened, white-haired Father Slade in an inaudible voice that was lost in the echoing acoustics. Music, including a violin; a chant; a Vedic meditation; the consecration in Latin, and finally a reading from Dante and a reading from Plato. I talked in the aisle, with John Matthews, who said he had just returned from Seattle and had been staying with David Spangler and had told him about the book; and with Critchlow, who said, "I was weary and could not come to your launch."

We went to the vestry for wine and I encountered Kathleen, who told me that the housing of the Academy in Great College Street had "fallen through. We have no home. Father Superior says we will disturb his sleep. I wish he'd drop dead." A friend of John Allott's asked: "What would you put on in June if you had a choice?" I said: "A lecture on the Metaphysical Revolution, preferably in Cambridge, saying that the wrong people occupy British literature and philosophy and should move over." Allott asked: "What next?" "A book of essays next, on the Metaphysical Revolution." Brian Goodwin said: "It's political and dangerous. That's not to say it should not happen." I now believe that Kathleen Raine was later told that I'd planned to take over her Academy and make it a mouthpiece for the Metaphysical Revolution.

I was taken away from the *Temenos* Academy by half-term. I attended an evening of Baroque music at Chigwell, at which Vernon Davies came and sat next to me, and Mrs. Dutchman came and had a word about my double life: "You've had several careers – lecturing, *The Times*, publishing, writing and owning prep schools – whereas most only have one. You've been very fortunate." I could not but agree. The next day I took my family to Cornwall and we watched gig-racing. Almost immediately I wrote a poem, 'Sparkles in an Infinite Sea'. I wrote: The Charlestown gig went out with raised oar blades. The gig was the old lifeboat of the kind Grace Darling rowed and possibly the traditional Viking boat, long and narrow with curved ends like the boats in Roskilde, which survived in the Scillies from the 11th century until the 19th century and now.[67]

Autobiographical literature: Diaries, Awakening to the Light
That night at 11.45 p.m. I walked on the Charlestown pier, "utterly alone", and had the idea of handing over the running of the schools to a Bursar "so that I can concentrate on getting out the *Collected Poems*, the *Collected Stories*, my autobiography and of course my *Selected Diaries*". The next morning I went to get the papers on foot and paused under a tree near the Visitors' Centre. A nightingale was singing. I manoeuvred until I could see it on a bough. I listened transfixed for five minutes, then walked on. I could still hear it after I had turned the corner.

I returned to Essex full of my *Diaries*. I hoped that the many impressions my *Diaries* reflected would help future people understand our Age. I wrote: "Like Donne I reflect the Age, so that in 400 years' time people [will] know what it was like to be in our Age." I wrote

The philosopher is part of what he is observing, he is not detached from it; he is in the process and is transformed.... So my *Diaries* are an Existential Philosophy – a Journal, in which the philosopher is involved in a dynamic process. This is Baroque philosophy. Kierkegaard and Marcel linked philosophy to Journals, and there is Rilke's *Malte Laurids Brigge*; and Wittgenstein wrote snippets. But otherwise no philosopher has used the journal form.[68]

I was already some way into *Awakening to the Light*.

Break with Kathleen Raine and Academy
There had been several letters from Kathleen Raine. She wrote to me on 21, 25, 26 March and again on 7 and 29 April. On 1 May she wrote again and "formally asked whether you are prepared to give a course of lectures or seminars on your metaphysical reading of history" as it would "be a rich contribution to have a series from you on this new and important view of history".[69] She wrote on 12 May, repeating her request. I was wondering

how to decline so soon after she had spoken at my launch. Many of the letters dealt with her problems in setting up a *Temenos* Academy. On 12 May she wrote that "Prince Charles has given *Temenos* permission to print his Shakespeare lecture. That is tacit support to [*sic*] the whole *Temenos* idea." I gathered that Prince Charles was considering housing the *Temenos* Academy in his Institute of Architecture, which was run by Keith Critchlow, in Regent's Park. I do not know whether the two chamberlains had spoken to her, or whether someone else (like Lello, who had turned up at Coopersale Hall, sent by her, to see if the site would be suitable to house the Academy in the school holidays) had drawn her attention to a page in *The Fire and the Stones*, but now on 31 May she wrote withdrawing her invitation (to my relief) because I had referred (on p.61) to the "descent of the reigning House of Windsor from the Kings of Israel, and… the mysterious journey of the Coronation Stone which according to legend had been Jacob's pillow".[70]

I saw immediately that the connection between Prince Charles and *Temenos* had made her edgy about my reference to the House of Windsor (for which there was a body of tradition). I saw that her public support for *The Fire and the Stones* a month previously could not be allowed to hinder a Royal connection. At the same time, as a mystic poet stating the tradition of the metaphysical Fire, I reserved the right to mention legend and tradition in my whole perspective that included history and religion.

Though I was relieved to have escaped the drain on my time I wrote expressing surprise at her sudden change of attitude. I appreciated that finding sponsors for *Temenos* must be her most important consideration.[71] She wrote again on 7 June, and I wrote back at greater length, rebutting her points, and saying, "when you warned me the bullets would fly when I launched my Metaphysical Revolution, I did not expect that you (or one of your advisers) would be squeezing the trigger".[72] I insisted on my right to be cross-disciplinary and rejected her implication that disciplines must be kept separate for academic reasons. She wrote back on 13 June insisting that legend, myth and "mystical insights" have no place in history, a reversal of her position. I wrote back rejecting her "separatist system of scholarship in which disciplines are kept separate" and I defended my view of history as "precisely-dated 'wave'-like patterns rather than 'particle'-like events". I said that the difference between Rank and Jung now seemed to involve a "shade, an emphasis, within a broad agreement",[73] and that our difference was a question of such emphasis. At this point there was a public announcement that her *Temenos* Academy had been given accommodation by Prince Charles, and I did not see her after that.

I was relieved to have extricated myself from the Academy so easily. Looking back, I see that, quite simply, my Fire threatened to take over her academic tradition, as did my Metaphysical Revolution, just as the Fire in my poems challenged her poetic tradition, which fails to mention it; and that she wanted me out unless she wanted to house her Academy at Coopersale Hall, and the House of Windsor was as good a pretext as any. By insisting on publication in April rather than October she had been instrumental in taking my books away from HarperCollins and getting them to Element, who understood the One; and for that I would always be grateful. But I now think that Kathleen Raine's sponsored lectures about Islamic and other specialised and élitist subjects belong to the past. They preserve a tradition of academic scholarship and keep it alive for a future generation, but they make no mention of the Fire or Light or of mysticism and involve no existential or experiential component. She was all along more interested in the vision of the imagination than in the more powerful mystic Fire or Light.

I was especially relieved that I did not have to prepare lectures she would typecast as history rather than as the cultural reflections of a mystic and poet, and I could now concentrate on offering the Fire to those in whom it resonated. Warren Kenton had warned that my grand entrance would be accompanied by tension, and he had been proved right.

Aftermath of launch, Sebastian Barker

After the launch, healers, filmmakers and poetry organisers wanted me to embody the Fire or Light, and the Metaphysical Revolution. I was invited to talk to Anthea Courtenay's group of lady healers in Hampstead. After visiting the Keats museum (and walking "by the replacement plum tree where Keats sat on a chair and wrote 'Ode to a Nightingale'") I explained the Fire, the stones and the chart, read some poems on the theme of the Fire and held a candlelit meditation. Peter Donebauer, the Managing Director of Diverse Production, who was at the launch, invited me to lunch near Olympia and proposed filming three one-hour programmes on *The Fire and the Stones* to cover the Fire, unity and pattern and the history of Western civilization. Patricia Dawson, who I had met in Dulwich in 1963 and told about the Dulwich Group of Poets, had (unbeknown to me) come to run the Group while I was in Japan. She wrote that she had tried to contact me to read some poems then, and that she had tried to contact me in Japan, in May, after the launch.

I returned to poetry. I had read Herbert Read's essays, especially 'Surrealism and the Romantic Principle' in which he associates Classicism with Renaissance dictatorships and capitalism, and Romanticism with the inspiration in Plato's *Ion*, where lyric poets are said to be "not in their right mind" and "possessed". I reflected on the exact relation between metaphysics and poetry. Poetry is inspired from sensational awareness of the objective world or from the promptings of the unconscious, but poetry may be generated by discursive reasoning or metaphysical speculation. I saw Metaphysical poetry as "felt thought". Soon after I "went to the Light, sitting alone in my study. Many tingles as it poured in." The next day I went to Cambridge's Science park to attend a food-seminar for the schools. I sat outside Trinity House by the lake at 1.50 and returned at 2 to begin the seminar with a poem, 'Rippling One'. I later drafted a poem about a tinkling bell ['Tinkling: Being like a Breeze']. I was returning to poetry and felt "very poetic".

I was running events at the schools. I was at the microphone for the Oaklands fête and again at Sports Day at Coopersale Hall, when the fathers' race was won by David Seaman, the England goalie. He was very tall with a slight crew-cut and had a Rotherham accent, and we chatted easily. He opened the Coopersale Hall fête on a hot day. He arrived before 2, "the international goalie in a sweatshirt and track-suit bottom, moustached. Immediately an autograph queue formed. I introduced him at 2.15 over the PA system. The Epping Town brass band played outside the hall." Hammond approached me when I was with Vicky Norris and asked me to introduce him as a farmer, so I introduced him to PC Sims, who was standing by his police car.

The Fire and the Stones was selling in the bookshops but there had been no publicity. On 2 July I rang Gorka and asked him to investigate. Gorka rang back and confirmed that there had been "an operation" against my book. I thought of Elizabeth I holding the Rainbow. (*See* p.xxii.)

After many end-of-term events – a barbecue, prize-giving, Oaklands rounders (staff v. school) – the schools broke up and I met Nadia at Heathrow and drove her down to Cornwall. A boat went out at 11 p.m. Under floodlights, held by a taut rope, the boat swung round and then inched out backwards and left for Holland. Graham the Harbour-master stood with his pipe; a "gnarled weather-beaten man with a face like a walnut". I negotiated to buy the green sward in front of our house from Peter Clapperton. We went to Fowey and Polruan and clambered on the rocks by the blockhouse.

When I got home, I wrote 'At Polruan: Soul and Body', setting down an idea that came to me as I sat by the blockhouse:

A poem comes to you like a butterfly and you sit and work it out – see what the butterfly does. I saw the butterfly, herring gull and bumble-bee this afternoon. My poem also incorporated my reading of Michelangelo's poem last night. Hence the words 'Renaissance' and 'skull' – and possibly the unconscious focusing on a 'bumble-bee'.

(I had read one of Michelangelo's poems from 1546/50: 'I've got a bumble-bee inside my jug/Some bones and strings inside my leather bag.' The context makes it clear that the jug is his skull, and that he has a buzzing sound inside his head or ears.) The next day "three green woodpeckers visited our lawn". Two of them passed into my poem, 'Tall-Masted Ship and Woodpeckers'. From Cornwall I rang Sebastian Barker, who had planned to give me an evening at the Poetry Society. He said: "Because of the politics of the Poetry Society nothing can happen quickly. On Friday the decision is being taken to fold down the Poetry Society."

Nicholas writing 'Calm and Serene' at Gunwalloe

The next day there were more poems. After lunch Ann, Nadia, Ant and I went to Gunwalloe, leaving Matthew to learn the French subjunctive. Rain spattered the windscreen as we approached Gunwalloe and suddenly there were patches of blue sky and I sat on the far rocks and with a calm sea beneath my feet composed another metaphysical sonnet, 'At Gunwalloe: Calm and Serene', writing on paper on my knee. I like Gunwalloe because all life "can be seen from those rocks – sea, shore, universe, church, farmhouse, representatives of all species, all in just enough economical detail to make the point. Nowhere else can you find graves on the beach." We went on to Porthleven and had a cream tea, then walked to the end of the pier, where a fisherman had caught a conger eel. On the way back I was "dazzled by sparkling water and wrote a quick poem (eight lines), pressing on the granite harbour wall before walking fast and catching the others up". (They were not aware I had scribbled an eight-line poem, 'At Porthleven' while they were walking.)

We went on to Marazion where the tide was going out and the causeway to St Michael's Mount was nearly uncovered. Ant changed and splashed across to the Mount, and then returned, running both ways. The rock my mother used to sit against put me in mind of Trevarthian, where my brother Rob and I stayed, and on the way back I stopped, walked to the House and peered through the windows where we slept. The library had gone and it had been converted into apartments. I walked round and entered the present hall and then lingered on the sloping lawn outside, recalling my parents and the time I cycled up to a Bronze-Age tumulus in the hills.

Two days later we lunched at the Rashleigh, Polkerris and saw Kerris, the artist. After a week we returned and I took Nadia to Heathrow. I had found her a nice girl, good-tempered, agreeable and agreeing, and ever-ready to offer me tea and coffee; a nice laughing girl with a great sense of humour.

Sebastian Barker invited me to his home in Lawford Road, London. We sat in the garden drinking jasmine tea at a table he had made himself. We talked for two-and-a-quarter hours quite effortlessly. He showed me his long poem on Nietzsche – 245 pages. We agreed that the Metaphysical Revolution must be a 'showing' rather than a 'saying'. He called Kathleen Raine an "intellectual snob" and *Temenos* "a nothing project". He agreed there is no Fire or Light in any of the *Temenos* volumes. He had edited his mother Elizabeth Smart's journals, vol. 1. The trick, he said, is to get a good thread by editing. He agreed the Metaphysicals will solve problems the Romantics did not solve and that Dryden and Pope hang onto the coat-tails of the Metaphysicals. He said of me, "You have been in the furnace and you've survived, but only just. The pressure must have been enormous." He advised me, "Once you've finished a work, pull away from it. It becomes someone else's. My mother said that works she wrote 40–50 years before were by someone else."

At Asa Briggs's request I visited Johan Goudsblom, a Dutch Professor of Sociology from the University of Amsterdam, who had finished a book on physical fire, *Fire and Civilization*, at All Souls, Oxford that morning. I sat with him in his room with a yellow-stone view from his window and drank bottled water. We were the only two in All Souls. He had a balding head and wore glasses, and he told me, "Asa Briggs said, 'Nicholas Hagger was a pupil of mine.'" He spoke of when physical fire was domesticated and when old towns and temples guarded fire. I noted his secular, sceptical position: everything was human and within society and social organisation. Briggs had said to me that I was writing history in terms of an idea that is outside history, echoing what I said to Kathleen Raine in the vestry at Eliot's centenary service.

I rejoined Ann in Cornwall. There were two tall-masted ships in, the brig *Maria Asumpta* and the rigger, the *Astrid*. These two ships passed into my poem, 'Tall-Masted Ships and Woodpeckers'. Matthew rang from Tours, where he was learning French grammar for a month. I listened to the first part of Betjeman's *Summoned by Bells*, which I found "in the idiom of *The Prelude* but without the metaphysics; pure memory and association and reflection on social situations, naming shops and places; the stuff of minor poetry despite the bulk". I rang Sir Tom Normanton from Cornwall, who said: "Your book is very interesting as you spell out our decline very clearly."[74]

Future works

Now I was clear of the aftermath of my launch and of distractions such as the Academy. I could focus on my future works: philosophical essays on the Metaphysical Revolution and more autobiographical writing in the tradition of Laurens van der Post, beginning with what would become *Awakening to the Light*.

I was working on my *Diaries* from the 1970s and 1980s and saw a work ahead, *The Metaphysical Journals* or *A Metaphysical Journal*. (This anticipated *Selected Diaries*.) I saw ahead: "My *Prelude* [*Life Cycle*]; Essex poems; epic [, *Overlord* and *Armageddon*];... Metaphysical Revolution [, *The One and the Many*]; *Collected Poems*; *Collected Stories*; and an autobiography [, *A Mystic Way*]." These were works that would keep me busy during the next 20 years.[75] I was now a published poet and cultural historian, at odds with the social-materialist literary world, yes, but strong in my belief that my Light-led Baroque was a way forward for my Age.

An episode had now ended. My world history had been in conflict with my metaphysical poetry, and now a new episode brought a new conflict.

Episode 8:

Philosophy and Practical Mysticism

Years: 1991–1992
Locations: Loughton; Epping; Charlestown
Works: *A Sneeze in the Universe*; *A Flirtation with the Muse*; *The Universe and the Light*
Initiatives: Fourth Mystic Life; Universalist Philosophy Group; Foundation of the Light; Mystic revival; Universalism

"The purpose of philosophy is to rationalize mysticism."
Alfred North Whitehead, *Modes of Thought*, 'The Aim of Philosophy'

In the next stage of my journey I turned to philosophy after being invited to give a lecture, and the prominence of my lecture and my two books led to invitations to conduct sessions of practical mysticism. My next episode involved a conflict between philosophy and practical mysticism.

Philosophy: unification of mysticism, cosmology, physics and history for Winchester lecture

Preparation for Winchester lecture
I returned from Cornwall to find a letter from David Lorimer inviting me to address the 1992 Mystics and Scientists conference at Winchester. I commented, "So I went to listen and ended up teaching."[1] Colin Wilson had sent me a letter, saying that "the book looks fascinating".[2]

I saw how to present my Winchester lecture. It should be a philosophical unification of mysticism, cosmology, physics and world history:

> It should be entitled, 'The Metaphysical Revolution: The One Unifying Fire or Light behind Nature and History', which is known to (experienced by) mystics and poets, and which is the central idea of civilizations.... Cover what the Metaphysical Revolution is, how it's inter- or cross-disciplinary.... How the quantum void is behind it – the One, Non-Being or Void, Being, Existence. Guénon. The rational, theoretical basis of traditional metaphysics, the practical experience of Light-based metaphysics. The experience of the Light. How it is known by mystics and poets.... How it is the central idea of 25 civilizations. Back to the Fire-based common basis of all cultures – pattern, not accident.... The Theory of Everything it makes possible. A Grand Unified Theory of Religion and World History.

(The sub-title of *The Fire and the Stones* was 'A Grand Unified Theory of World History and Religion'.)

I had also begun a new poem about the universe, "shaping it here and there, tying in stanzas. Part One is the case against a GUT [Grand Unified Theory], a metaphysical reality... other than the human and social. Part Two is the vision of the One Fire or Light which is behind Nature and History, which can be known through vision, existentially."[3] I would expand this poem during the next week.

Three visits to Colin Wilson on consciousness: 'Reflection and Reality', death of Margaret Taylor, Smeaton's Tower
Colin Wilson rang me in Charlestown on 6 August: "May I speak to Nick Hagger, please." "Speaking." "Oh, hello, it's Colin Wilson." He invited me to visit him that same day. "We see people 5.30 to 7.30, then we throw them out so we can have some dinner. We always watch the news at 6, come at 5.30."

I was pleased to go for I could run aspects of my unification of mysticism, cosmology, physics and history past him. I drove to Tetherdown, Gorran Haven up a lane with brambles scraping the side of my car. The chalet where I stayed in 1961 was in the orchard, but what had been a cliff-top view had been obscured by a building. I walked in through the back door. Colin was making plates of smoked salmon in the kitchen, wearing an open-necked shirt, sailing dungarees and his 1950s-style spectacles dangling on a cord from his neck. He welcomed me warmly: "Come in, Nick." We talked in the kitchen about Husserl. I said his recommendation gave me my method for *The Fire and the Stones*, then went through to the sitting-room and sat beside his mother (who was about 80). She had been living there about two years. (While Colin was out of the room I asked what he was like as a schoolboy, and she said: "He always had his nose in a book, even walking down the road. I was surprised he didn't get run over. He was always reading." The news was on TV.

He poured large goblets of wine and we spoke at some length about my book. He said: "It will be a cult book. But what I'm interested in isn't there." I said: "Faculty X." He said: "Yes. I'm deeply suspicious of the right brain." I explained that my Baroque is both left and right brain, that the experience I had in Japan and then in London in 1971 is tempered with left-brain presentation. He said: "It's like wine, having a drink." Joy, his wife, said: "I disagree, it's religious."

Wilson said: "It's pressure. If you pump up the brain and increase the pressure you have this sort of experience. It's intensity. Pascal was exhausted before he had his experience of Fire, you did not say that." I said: "It didn't matter that he was ill, the illness had the same effect as Zen, blanking out the left brain." He insisted: "William James described his three mystical experiences as pressure." I said: "Photism." He said: "I'm deeply suspicious of everything right brain. You've gone the way of Yeats. Left brain is the way." I insisted: "Wholeness demands both." He said: "Left brain can be intensity in the Naafi, Tolstoy's two Hussars in step, finding it's marvellous. I'm delighted you've written this, I'm glad you've said what you have but it only goes halfway." I said: "Perhaps the Light is the end of the Outsider's vision." He said: "No, it's just a moment of intensity or pressure. Faculty X is better, read *Beyond the Outsider*." I was surprised by Wilson's 'suspicion' of illumination.

I said on the Metaphysical Revolution: "Metaphysics are no longer rational and speculative but experiential." He said: "I'm deeply suspicious of that." I was asking him to be more right-brain, he was asking me to be more left-brain and saying again that poetry and mysticism are a wrong way. I told him about some of the sceptics I had encountered. He said: "Kermode attacked me years ago. Ricks, Kermode, Larkin and Goudsblom don't matter and needn't be mentioned. Scepticism of their kind is not the way. Larkin referred to 'that toad' work and then elsewhere said he liked work." We talked about the 1950s – the Fleet Street coffee-house – and I told him: "You were a role model for a generation." I told him to return to *The Outsider* and *Religion and the Rebel* and to state a unified vision of everything. He said: "That's what I have done at the end of *Beyond the Occult*." I said: "*Beyond the Outsider* and *Beyond the Occult* – you need a book beyond both, confronting the metaphysical. You were the first I heard say that Humanism was a bad thing, I'm only reminding you, not telling you." I fought well, and it was all very friendly and a draw. He invited me to go back in a fortnight for round 2.

I mulled over my encounter with Colin Wilson the next day. On reflection

I particularly took issue with something he had said: "The vision of the Fire is half-way to a peak experience." On the contrary, the vision of the Fire *is* the supreme peak experience, and because he had not had it, he did not recognise this. I found myself drafting a poem on this theme. It reconciled our two conflicting positions in the Universalist manner. On 7 August I wrote: "Finished the poem about Colin Wilson in draft: 'Peak Experiences and Consciousness' [later 'Reflection and Reality: Peak Experiences and Tidal Consciousness']. Am polishing the rhymes. Went for walks in Charlestown, including one late at night. Vivid stars. Three shooting stars, one over Fowey a finger down the night sky."

The next day I took Anthony to the Charlestown Carnival – he was dressed as a convict with a moustache – and there was a Floral Dance through the village. Later I walked out onto the harbour wall under brilliant stars. A pear-tree above me dripping with fruit, and the streak of one windfall bursting through the branches: a shooting star.

The next day I realised what both Colin Wilson and I had in common. We were two Existentialists. For my Universalism was a post-Existentialism. I rang Wilson in the early evening. He said: "We're just about to catch the news." I said I had mulled over my visit and we ought to meet again because I could see his next book. "We're both Existentialists with different emphases, like Marcel and Sartre. Let's revive British Existentialism." He said: "Fine. Great." I said: "My next book should be on Existentialism, and yours should be too." We settled on Thursday 15 August at 5.30. I asked: "What wine do you like?" He said: "Beaujolais. What's your address? I want to send you *Access to the Inner Worlds*." I said: "I've written a poem called 'Peak Experiences and Consciousness', it's in three parts."

I attended a falconry display on the village field, during which the trainer flew a tawny eagle, a barn owl and a Harris hawk, holding bits of raw rabbit in a gloved hand. Later I added a final stanza to my poem and noted: "My poem assimilates Colin Wilson's peak experience to my vision of the Fire."[4]

We had to return to Essex. I had encountered our gardener, Margaret Taylor, in a card shop in Loughton with her doctor husband at the end of March. I had heard her coughing and said to her, "*You*'ve got a cough." She had said, "Yes, I've got two secondaries in my lungs. I have chemotherapy from next Tuesday for eight months. They can't operate." I noted that she enjoyed having a dramatic effect on everyone. She had visited me in May and was overtaken by uncontrollable coughing, sitting in my window. She talked in a desperate, breathless, wheezy whisper. Chemotherapy every Thursday left her down and it took her a week to get back up, then she was down again. She had said, "I must think positive. Otherwise I might as well curl up and die." She had died the previous Sunday.

Christ Church, Wanstead was half to three-quarters full for her funeral. Her husband Graham was on the verge of tears. The coffin was on high under a covering. The vicar wore a biretta (a square black hat). Afterwards we followed the *cortège* to City of London Cemetery and were present for the committal. I cast a handful of dust on what had once been Margaret. The priest had said, "Acceptance of suffering ennobles." Her Calvary began in March. I would soon write a poem, 'Calvary: A Pure Being goes under the Earth' (*see* p.360).

We returned to Cornwall. At 2.45 on 14 August Ant came in holding *Access to Inner Worlds* and said, "It's from Colin Wilson." It had been put through the letterbox with a note saying could I come that day as a Japanese girl, Sai, was staying with them. She was writing a book on mysticism and was very interested in *The Fire and the Stones*. I rang Wilson and said I would bring my poem about him "as it could be that we are nearer than we thought". He said: "Read *Access* before you come, it's all about this." He was saying in the book that peak experiences can be summoned at will when left brain says 'All's well' and right brain responds with a glow of warmth, sheer joy. I was saying that right brain is filled with the Light and responds with rapture and that everything has meaning afterwards as right brain filled with vision passes meaning to left brain.[5]

Colin had been swimming and was preparing smoked salmon in the kitchen. I sat with my wine, his mother came in, and one of the dogs jogged the table. "It's a f—ing nuisance," Wilson shouted. "I'm going to kick it, it's always f—ing well doing things like that." His mother said, "No, don't speak to him like that." Each time I visited him there was an obligatory breaking of the taboo "f— " word in front of his mother. (The previous time he had spoken of "that f—ing girl of Stuart Holroyd's".) Then the dog knocked the wine decanter off.

Wilson sat and poured the three bottles of Beaujolais I had brought into decanters and we talked about Existentialism, and whether our next books should be on Existentialism. He said: "The trouble is, Existentialism's old hat now, it's been replaced by structuralism, post-structuralism and deconstructionism, which has to do with language. Derrida." I said: "They can be ignored." He said: "I agree, but Existentialism was about physical reality – Kierkegaard – whereas what you're talking about is something beyond, not pessimism, but optimism." I said: "Yes. Sartre and Camus were wrong." He said: "I said that to Camus. We were talking and I said 'Your reality is material, material reality' and he pointed and said 'My reality has to be the same as that Teddy boy's', and I said: 'I don't see why it has to be. Einstein would never have discovered the atomic secret if he had thought that.' Most established writers are trapped within their obsessions and don't communicate: Sartre, Camus, Toynbee and Eliot. Shaw believed socialism would be the answer, and now it's gone both as Communism and over here. He was a genius but he was wrong." I said: "Genius is a spring that is within you. You turn away from society and sit beside it." He nodded. I said: "You will find my poems repay study." He said: "I can see that." I said: "There will be quotable lines. If there are 200 lines in my work – one per poem – I will be happy." He said, agreeing: "I only know 200 lines of Yeats and of Eliot." He told me: "My essay on Husserl is one of the best things I've ever written. I cringe when I look back at *Religion and the Rebel*. I can see why people said it was bad." I said: "The new Existentialism is to do with Being, the Fire and freedom." He said: "Perhaps it should be called something else."

I was on the verge of bringing Universalism to birth, a new philosophy that is not handicapped by the errors of Existentialism, and knew I would continue to call it Universalism even though it was an offshoot of Existentialism and that I would not work for an alliance with Colin Wilson. I said: "Bohm subscribed to the Metaphysical Revolution." He said: "I'm interested in metaphysics, it's mysticism I can't stand. I'm not interested in unity, the unified vision of mysticism." (The rational, social ego cannot bear to subordinate itself to a higher unified scheme.) He continued, surprisingly: "I've misjudged you, we *are* close."

Then the Japanese girl, Sai, returned with Joy and asked me if the Japanese imperial chrysanthemum came from Judaism along the Silk Route in the 3rd century BC. She asked if she could take my photo, and so Colin Wilson and I

Nicholas with Colin Wilson on 14 August 1991

stood together and were photographed side by side. Supper was prepared and I left. I left my poem about him for him to read.

I reflected later: "Who else can I discuss Husserl and Heidegger with?... We are a second generation of Existentialists, as the second generation Romantics (Keats and Shelley) looked back to the first generation Romantics.... [Wilson] and I differ because he is sceptical, I am a Metaphysical.... The Metaphysical Revolution... carries forward Romanticism and Existentialism, being optimistic whereas they are pessimistic.... The vision of the Fire is higher than his peak experiences."[6]

That night in Charlestown there was swimming in the harbour until long after dusk. There was a Wordsworthian feeling as the village leapt in and out, all friends together, one with the sea. The next day I wrote another stanza into 'Reflection and Reality: Peak Experiences and Tidal Consciousness'. I had now written four more stanzas since leaving a draft with Colin Wilson. I finished that poem at lunch-time and launched straight into revising the poem on the universe, 'Ode: Spider's Web: Our Local Universe in an Infinite Whole', and "went straight through it; finished it by 10.30 p.m., every rhyme; and wrote in 2 extra stanzas. An immensely creative session." I had "even drafted a poem on Margaret Taylor: 'Calvary' [, 'Calvary: A Pure Being goes under the Earth']: 9 stanzas. An immensely creative day…. My spring is gushing. I am completely whole: left brain and right." (*See* p.358.)

We went to Plymouth, where I walked down Armada Way to the Hoe and went up Smeaton's Tower and had a good view of the sweep of the bay. I drafted a poem on the coach back from Plymouth, 'Smeaton's Tower and Western Civilisation', which I added to and polished later. I had forgotten that Smeaton's Tower has a spiral staircase. The next day we lunched at the 15th-century St Benet's Abbey, near Lanivet, which was probably built by the Hospitallers for lazars: lepers. I wrote "'Lepers' Abbey' and 'Bumble-bee [: Correspondence']", which came to me as I sunbathed that hot afternoon; and I polished 'A Shooting Star'." Two days later I wrote 'Polkerris-Kerris' straight out, all done from start to finish within half an hour. "It says something about being an artist that is important."

On 19 August I rang Colin Wilson and told him we needed one more discussion on the Metaphysical Revolution. I arranged to see him on 22 August. There was a beautiful moon above Gull Island and a causeway of moonlight between the harbour and the Battery rocks.

The next morning was misty and we went to the Scillies for the day. We took the *Scillonian* and reached St Mary's about 12.45. We walked to the square and caught a bus round the island. I "reflected on Lyonesse" and wrote two poems, 'Lyonesse: Being like Submerged Land' and 'Gulls: A Cloud of Being'. I began a book of images for my epic. I took many visual images from St Mary's, especially the islands being mountain peaks of Lyonesse. On the journey back I wrote: "Gulls, waves, winds, skies, fields – Cornwall has everything a poet needs…. Have lived as a poet for the last two weeks, and have loved it." I loved focusing intensely on the present moment.[7]

I visited Colin Wilson for the third time. I arrived at 5.30 and was given smoked salmon, one slice of rivita, gherkin, lemon and a huge glass of white wine followed by Beaujolais. Joy asked me about my schools while Wilson listened. We watched the news and he dried his hair under a hair-drier that looked like a tea cosy with a Hoover lead going to it. Then we got on to metaphysics. Earlier that day he had talked about Mozart and the Steppenwolf at Dartington. He said, "I was asked about metaphysics and I talked about Leibniz and Kant, and the occult."

I defined metaphysics to include "beyond the five senses" and asked if that was his definition of metaphysics. He did not really answer. One of his sons interrupted to ask if Wilson would take a phone call, and he said sternly: "I'm talking metaphysics with Nick, I'm not to be disturbed. I don't care who rings." I asked: "Are you Humanist or metaphysical?" He said: "It's a problem of language. You make it sound so difficult. It's simple. What do I do? What do I do with your view?" I said: "Read the poems: you transform your ego into self, personality into essence, shift your centre and receive the Light." He said: "It's more simple than that. When I wrote *The Outsider* I had glimpses of the vision but couldn't hold to it for more than 12 minutes." I said: "I've ransacked the history of the last 5,000 years for the vision." He said: "Peak experiences. Never have I been so aware of the limitations of language as when I listen to you. You're trying to put the unsayable into words." I said: "Agreed."

"He said: "When I was at Dartington I was asked, 'What will the new man be like?' I said, 'He's never depressed, he's interested in everything – in all disciplines – and he's competent in everything.' Someone said, 'Such a person would be boring.' I said, 'You find it boring, you're not a new person, you have old consciousness.'" I told him: "I'm never depressed, I'm interested in all disciplines in my poetry, and whether I'm competent is for others to judge. I'm not depressed because the Fire or Light has cleaned it up at source, as Jung says. What can I do? Go to the Fire or Light, at will. Open a pathway from left brain to right. I live and concentrate for greater parts of the day, editing journals, writing poems, reflecting, with meaning and purpose." He said: "Kierkegaard said 'Subjectivity is Truth' and he meant: 'Go within and take out what's within and express it well in a lecture.'" I said: "But Objectivity is Truth – the objective One, the metaphysical context in which we live."

But Wilson stuck to the way he had always thought. He said: "I'm impressed by what you've achieved. But I have reservations about *The Fire and the Stones* because I'm not sure what I can do." He paid me the compliment of telling me that he had given me half a page in his "permanent book", and he agreed that one day we might write a book together. I said, "I can see a new *Declaration* on the Metaphysical Revolution with you, Sheldrake, Bohm and others, and me." He said: "Yes." I said: "As I'm going to be in Charlestown on and off for the next 40 years, we'll meet again." He said: "Come before 25 October. You make me laugh when you say 'One more time'. It'll take years to conclude our discussions." I said: "I like to set an agenda, it's positive and meaningful discussion." Wilson said: "I'm not against what you're doing. I want to make that clear. On the evidence of the poems, there are three great poets of the 20th century, Eliot, Yeats and you. No one else is tackling these important themes." Then his chicken was served and I drove home.

When I got home I looked out of my bedroom window. Anthony and his friend were surfing in the moonlit curl of the waves. I pondered something Wilson had said: "It's a language thing. You and I aren't communicating sometimes, because I don't understand your language and you don't understand mine." I had spoken of a 'club' of the 600 greatest cultural figures of the past. He had said, "The 600 in your Club, Shakespeare wouldn't communicate with Horace. They've all got their own way of looking." I had disagreed, holding that the language of truth is a universal language.

We went to Penwith to see ancient stones. I tried to find the chamber tomb near Marazion. We went on to the Merry Maidens in brightening weather: 19 stones near Lamorna. I saw the Tregiffian chamber tomb, 3rd millennium BC; and the Merry Maidens, a Beaker stone sun circle c.2000 BC (like Stonehenge). We drove on to Sennen, and the Manor House opposite the church (founded 520) and a small cove near the Brisons and lunched to dashing sea. I wrote a poem, 'Dandelion'. We went on to Carn Gluze on a cliff top near a tin-mine chimney, a chamber tomb from the Middle-Late Bronze Age, c.1400–600BC. I wrote another poem, 'At the Ballowall Barrow'. We drove on to Cape Cornwall, the setting for my aunt Gwen's painting, 'Dusk at Land's End', the chimney being by the Carn Gluze tomb (or Ballowall Barrow). We went on to St Just and Pendeen, where Ant and I walked to the lighthouse, and on to Zennor and the mermaid. We visited Chysauster, an ancient British village, probably 1st–3rd century AD, of seven huts with thatched corners round a central courtyard. We saw plenty of montbretia, green hedgerows with yellow and orange flowers and narrow lanes. We returned via Penzance.

I wrote another four stanzas of my poem about Wilson during our tour. It was now about a collision between creeds. There was a full moon. I wrote a poem, 'A Gold Being Glowing' and two more poems: 'Ancient Village: Our Skilled Tin-Mining Ancestors' and 'Mermaid of Zennor'. I wrote: "I am so clear and elemental and sharp, so close to Nature down here in Cornwall. I must… get out among the 'stones' more." The next day, thinking about Lyonesse, I met Dick Larn (an authority on wrecks) on the harbour wall. I said I had been in the Scillies and at Sennen, checking the Lyonesse legend. He spoke of the Scillies and said, "Peat has been found between the islands, and tree stumps, showing they were once connected, and it's true that if you took 30 foot of water out they would all be joined."

The next day I rang Colin Wilson to check a quotation from Whitehead. (My copy of Whitehead was in Essex.) His son said, "He's cleaning his teeth." Colin, "I'm in the bathroom. If it's short do it now, but if it's ten minutes, later. I hate the telephone. It's all right for 'Meet you then'." I asked for the Whitehead quotation about movements of thought. Wilson said: "Whitehead says that movements of thought are like movements of cavalry in a battle, one movement too many and you lose the battle. There must be economy of ideas." He said he would ring me. I pointed out: "On language, further to our discussion, the commentary to the poems does some useful defining." (He said: "Good.") "And on 'What do I do?', you open yourself to the Fire or Light and get infused knowledge and energy which renews the civilization and contributes to evolution." He said: "Yes, that's right."

Later Colin Wilson rang me back when my telephone ear was full of Cerumol. He said: "The Whitehead quotation is from *Introduction to Mathematics*: 'Operations of thought are like cavalry charges in a battle – they're strictly limited in number, they require fresh forces and must only be made at decisive moments.'" I said I would do the poem out and send it to him. He said: "Have a good trip." I reflected:

> I am a fresh horse, and the decisive moment is now. There hasn't been a movement for 35 years. My Metaphysical Revolution is the next one.

That night I walked on the harbour wall under a moon with a halo in a slight mist. I wrote a poem, 'A Moon with a Halo'.

Back in Essex I thought about the philosophy of history and its role in the unification of disciplines. I dismissed Yeats's *A Vision* as automatic writing. I bought William McNeill's diffusionist *The Rise of the West* which challenges Spengler's and Toynbee's view that separate civilizations pursued independent careers. But cultures have different religions, and "I am a believer in civilizations and in the pattern they have". As I wrote in *The Fire and the Stones*, diffusionism is less complete than Universalism as it avoids defining each civilization's central idea.[8]

Dream: on clouds
The night of 1–2 September was very hot and I slept with the fan on. I had a very memorable dream:

> Dreamt I was on a mountainside with clouds beneath me. Saw a poem I was writing, the first 20 or 30 lines about the meaning of life. Remembered the lines "I went for a walk on the clouds. My Shadow in the moonlight/Lay beneath me on the clouds." Actually saw my shadow on the clouds below as I moved.... I woke with a start, convinced I knew the meaning of life. Came and wrote this. I can see the clouds rolling away beneath me: I am higher than the clouds and have transcended material reality.... The time is now 4.39 a.m. I woke around 4.30 a.m.... Perhaps this is a stanza for the poem on Colin Wilson, this dream.

I wrote the words about my Shadow into 'Reflection and Reality'.

Later I "polished the rhymes of the two stanzas I drafted... at 4.30 a.m.

and which I have pondered all day…. Also polished a stanza of [my poem on] the poet as a spider [, 'Ode: Spider's Web: Our Local Universe in an Infinite Whole'], the one now beginning 'Like God, the poet sits in a spider's web'."

That evening I made some changes to the poem on Colin Wilson and wrote the notes. I wrote: "It is a very deep poem with all levels of reality reflecting each. It is now one of my most philosophical poems." I received a massive letter from Sai, who was now in Japan, describing how the Japanese chrysanthemum originated among the Hebrews c.2000BC and enclosing a photo of Colin Wilson and me.[9]

Pattern

I was thinking about the pattern of our lives and I bought Marcus Aurelius's *Meditations* for his insight into pattern. I leafed through his Stoic reflective Journal written among barbarians such as the Quadi and tried to find "If aught befall thee it is good, it is all part of the great web", consoling wisdom I had heard in Libya, but was defeated by the modern translation. (The Penguin edition has: "Whatever may happen to you was prepared for you in advance from the beginning of time. In the woven tapestry of causation, the thread of your being had been intertwined from all time with that particular incident.")

Pondering my philosophy, I turned to Derrida to see what Colin Wilson had seen in him, and noted that he took the term 'deconstruction' from Heidegger's *'Destruktion'*, a term Derrida used during his call for the destruction of ontology, the branch of metaphysics that studies the nature of Being. I, a re-stater of ontology in terms of the Fire, was therefore ideologically opposed to deconstructionism.[10]

Grounding philosophy

While I prepared a statement of my philosophy for my Winchester lecture the schools and everyday social living kept me grounded. The schools fed me images and poems.

I took delivery of six loads of crushed concrete and widened the internal driveway near the front door and the car-parking area to cope with the extra pupils in the substantially-finished extension at Coopersale Hall. I now had an accounting assistant, Jeremy Miller, a retired bank manager with Victorian whiskers and an enormous bushy moustache who worked in our dining-room a day each week keeping accounts, writing cheques and calculating salaries, and I had many sessions of talking figures. Oaklands had an open evening and an inspector visited Coopersale Hall, an HMI from the Department of Education with whom I talked economics. I returned for lunch. Our tenant Steve Norris rang our doorbell wearing wellies after visiting a sewage works – I asked, "Would you like a bath?" – and we talked politics in our sitting-room. After the Oaklands Harvest Festival I wrote a poem, 'Children like Fruit'.

Chigwell School held a dinner for Heads and teachers of 'feeder schools'. A couple of State-school teachers on my table attacked the "privileged life of Chigwell" and its "pressurised approach" to children (while eating the Chigwell food). I leaned forward and said: "Listen, every child has a human right to be taught to read and spell by the age of seven, so they can have the skills they need to survive in this society. The unpressurised methods used in State schools are wrong and conflict with the children's human right." I was supported by an Archdeacon and the teachers had no answer.

Two days later I encountered the Japanese *yugen* when a Japanese parent took Dr Southern of Bancroft's, his wife, Ann and me to see *kabuki* at the National Theatre. In the third piece, *Sagi-Musume*, which is about a heron-girl, the musicians played *samisen*s (3-stringed instruments) and beat *yin* shoulder drums and *yang* masculine stick drums, stamping with *yang* feet, and the *yugen* (Flower) was revealed when Tamasaburo leaned back and held an impossible pose, head near the floor. That evening I wrote two poems, 'At *Kabuki*: The Flower of Culture' and 'Flower (*Yugen*)'.

I went to the Frankfurt book fair at Element's request, to spread awareness of my books. I met Michael Mann and various American publishers at the Messe and stayed with a *Grossvater* who got me slippers and insisted on pouring me the best Bavarian beer. I dreamt I had slugs in my lungs, coughed and spat twice, and each time a yellow slug came up, wriggling and alive – how my dreaming brain saw my bronchiectasis.

Back in Essex I heard that Hammond's son had committed suicide in a car outside one of his corrugated-iron barns near the Coopersale Hall School gates. He had left a note saying nobody loved him – a criticism of his father – and there was an emotional East-End funeral with two hearses, one filled with flowers, and everyone wore black. A plainclothes policeman stood and filmed the visitors.

At half-term Oaklands was under scaffolding: half the roof was being retiled and there was dust and débris (broken rafters and tiles) everywhere. I climbed the scaffolding to inspect the tiles and battens and was met with a *crescendo* of hammering and answering banging, the dialogue of men working. I was only thirty feet up but I felt vertigo as strongly as if I was up the Eiffel Tower and had to hold on to scaffolding poles.

While I was working on my philosophy for my Winchester lecture I heard Seamus Heaney read some poems on television and wrote:

They were unmemorable and unprofound; mere observations of the visible world and childhood memories and no hint of a metaphysic or of the invisible…. The image reveals the unseen world behind the seen. That is now my considered view of the image, after 25 years of development since 1966. The images I am most attached to hint at the world behind, which for a second peeps into creation, the phenomenal world, and is nearly caught.

I saw on the television news that Harrington Hall in Lincolnshire, the home of the ex-Loughton Maitlands I had visited, had burned down, and was sad as it had associations with Tennyson and had been home to Nadia for a while. I watched a football match in the field at the bottom of the Coopersale Hall drive and stood on the touchline beside a parent, Patrick Clark, who had been tried for his role in the Brink's-Mat gold bullion robbery. £4 million had been laundered through his son's bank account, and he told me, "I'm innocent, Mister Hagger." Six months later he received six years. I oversaw Fireworks Evenings at Coopersale Hall, during which I chatted with Steve Norris, and at Oaklands, at which a bonfire shaped like a wigwam shot flames 30 foot into the night.

Ann and I then travelled to the Carnarvon Hotel, Ealing for a Masonic dinner at which my brother-in-law Richard and Frances were the President and President's lady. We sat at top table among these latter-day builders of Solomon's Temple and revivers of the secret they found – of the Light (darkness visible) – and then joined a table set aside for our family. I did not know that I would be writing a book on Freemasonry (*The Secret Founding of America*).

Matthew did weekly broadcasts at St Margaret's Hospital radio, and interviewed Steve Norris. Off air Norris asked him about our Lexus and said truthfully, "I recommended Nick to buy it." We were invited to a gathering at a large house in Roding Lane, Chigwell. In front of Tim Yeo, a Conservative Junior Minister, Steve Norris said of *The Fire and the Stones*: "I'm reading your book in the loo. I was discussing it with Douglas Hurd [, the Foreign Secretary,] last week. He is very interested in it. I've been trying to decide if Nick's a genius." Yeo said: "I'll read your book."

Ann and I stayed at my cousin Richard's house in Haslemere to celebrate his 50th birthday. There was a drinks gathering and we then drove to The Holly Tree Inn, Easebourne for dinner, at which I made a speech. I said that Richard enjoyed life in a particularly English way – with his infectious sense of humour, his quick remarks, banter and repartee – and that "quite simply he's a jolly good fellow", whereupon all sang 'For he's a jolly good fellow'. We drove back across the Cowdray Estate in moonlight.

Chauffeuring my two boys to and from their leisure activities kept me grounded. I collected Matthew, who was rising in *Choi Kwang Do* – a Korean martial art introduced by the Chigwell chaplain that used unchaplain-like Korean punching, kicking and blocking techniques in street self-defence – and would become a black belt and instructor; and Anthony after he came

5th in a cross-country race for the Federation of London Boys' Club, which meant that he would run for London. I saw Anthony play a hunchback, silent but watchful and disdainful in *A Child's Christmas in Wales*, a play about Dylan Thomas's memories of Christmas.

I attended the Oaklands carol service and the Coopersale Hall nativity play. I attended Coopersale Hall's carol service at All Saints, Theydon Garnon. I sat in the empty choir pews near the altar in the 700-year-old church. During two moments of quietness the Light came, shivering my spine; once when I was sitting, once when I was standing. I talked at length with one of the churchwardens, a Foreign-Office adviser on Defence, and urged the FO to contact Kazakhstan and tie it into the new federal structure in Russia. After a staff lunch in the hall I visited Marion Lord in the Herts and Essex Hospital. The previous day Miss Lord's niece Zena had come in to say that Marion had inoperable cancer. Zena said: "She's never been able to control her life, and now cancer's controlling her." Marion was pallid-white and had her death upon her. I made her laugh a lot.

Our tenant Steve Norris invited me to dine with him in the House of Commons dining-room. We sat near Bob Dunn and Neil Kinnock and discussed Maastricht. He surprised me by asking me to be his constituency chairman, after being deputy for a year. He told me that in his interview he had said: "The most important quality for an MP is to like people. I get on with people. They all wave at me, they all know me. That counts for votes." He spoke of his agent Tricia Gurnett as having enjoyed being Ambassadress for the irascible and absent Biggs-Davison, who didn't like people. He told me, "You are quality, a quality person." As we parted at midnight he told me, "I'm now going to speak in support of Government housing policy and Tim Yeo even though I privately don't believe in it." He told me prophetically: "I'll be a Minister next time."

I attended a lecture on Lucien Pissarro by Nicholas Reed. Pissarro lived at 44 Hemnall Street, Epping in the 1890s and painted several pictures of Coopersale Hall. Reed visited Coopersale Hall and found that one of Pissarro's paintings was of a path between Orchard Cottage and the walled garden in the Coopersale Hall grounds. We stood together on the path at the back of Orchard Cottage by the squash court (now the studio), and he told me he had been at Worcester College, Oxford like Steve Norris who was renting Orchard Cottage from me. It was bizarre that all three of us passed through the same college and arrived here at Coopersale Hall. The three of us were held together round Pissarro's path to the walled garden. I was again struck by the concealed pattern in life.

I was grounded in Cornwall. There was a blood-red sunset and Charlestown was deserted, the tide out. A round, nearly-full moon was reflected in the water. The stars were out and moonlight silhouetted the

Battery hill. The next morning I breakfasted at the Pier House Hotel and a dozen fishermen gathered outside. I wrote four poems: 'Mechanised Motion and Nature', 'Fire within the Globe', 'Harvest Moon and a Cheer' and 'Image and Reality: Street-Lamp and Sun in Mist'. Charlestown's 200th anniversary was celebrated. Crowds poured into the village, there was a shire horse and Clapperton patrolled the tall ships in the inner harbour like a small boy playing boats in his bath.[11]

Orpheus among green apples

In a letter T.S. Eliot told Colin Wilson that it is better to come in quietly and grow from there than to come in in a blaze of publicity which is then doused by critics:[12] "It seems to me that the right way is first to become known to a small group of people who can recognise what is good when they see it; next to become known to a slightly larger group who will take the word of the others on what is good; and finally, to reach the wider public. To do it the other way round could be disastrous."[13] I hoped that Eliot's prescription was applying to me.

A few days later I had a haunting dream which hinted at my poetic identity: a "large face of Orpheus with dozens of green apples in front of it…, as tall as the trees and orchard…. I knew it was Orpheus because of the Thracian hat." The image, received in sleep, of Orpheus among green apples was a powerful one. I assumed that the apples symbolised poems.

Three days later John Ezard rang and surprised me by saying in the course of our conversation: "I often read your poems. Some are very good."[14]

Arrangements for Winchester lecture

David Lorimer rang to make arrangements for my Winchester lecture the following April. I was to speak on the Friday evening of the 'Nature of Light' conference, with Bede Griffiths, John Barrow, William Anderson, Brian Hicks and others speaking later. I would speak on the philosophical unification of mysticism, cosmology, physics and history. My title began as: 'The Metaphysical Light that Permeates History and Nature: Mystical Illumination, The Vision of God as Fire or Light in Civilizations, Cosmology and Everything.' I revised it to: 'Illumination and Metaphysics: The Light and Mysticism, History, Nature, Cosmology and Everything'. It ended as 'Illumination and Metaphysics: A Grand Unified Theory of the Mystic Light in History, Nature and Cosmology.'[15]

I had to summarise my talk in 200 words, and the conflict between my philosophy and my mysticism was very apparent. I knew I would state my philosophy, which was influenced by mysticism, rather than describe my mysticism in terms of the Foundation of the Light. I would project myself as a writer rather than as a New-Age *guru*.

Universalism, a metaphysical movement, Romanticism and Colin Wilson
Towards the end of October we returned to Cornwall in the Lexus I had just acquired. We arrived on a brilliant day, blue sky, sun and a sparkling, calm sea. The *Maria Asumpta* was in together with three ships whose ghostly rigging was part floodlit, part in darkness at midnight. The following evening I went for a walk with Matthew under a cloudy sky. It was eerily light and Trenarren was clearly reflected in the calm sea, all the way down to Gull Island, which was also reflected down to the beach, just as I put in 'Reflection and Reality'.

I talked philosophy to Matthew on the harbour wall:

There are two views of the universe: one is Beckett's that we're waiting between birth and death and that the universe is material and nothing survives our end; and there is the more metaphysical view that there is an invisible reality behind the visible reality, the view of Blake, Shelley, Coleridge and Wordsworth that all the vast universe is One and that we're a tiny corner of it, that there is a spiritual reality which is alive. With the first we survey the dead universe with passive consciousness; with the second we gaze at it with active consciousness.

We returned yawning from the fresh air.

I had rung Colin Wilson, who answered the phone. "Yes, that's fine. I've my secretary coming so we'll throw you out at 7.30. I liked the poem very much." I said: "Good. It attempts to catch the invisible behind the visible, the unseen behind the seen. It's different from the first draft I gave you, that's how it should be, written in layers." He: "Yes, I've got the first draft." I rang off, my spirits lifted.

We lunched at Polkerris, in the restaurant section of the Rashleigh and then walked to the end of the harbour pier. I had a fleeting 'memory' of being 300 feet up in Ancient Egypt, above a statue of a face, a head. I was terrified of falling; perhaps I did fall. I held onto the wall by an iron ring. There were three cormorants on a rock. That night I took a late-night walk on the harbour. A full moon was reflected in the pool below the pier. The Pier House Hotel reflected perfectly in another low-tide pool. A nightbird fluted from the water. There were moonlit lines of gentle waves. I woke in the night from a dream and saw streaks of red and orange in the sky above the sea and breathless panting as the sea flowed in, a silver calm with almost imperceptible ripples.

The question in my mind was: could Colin Wilson and I belong to a metaphysical movement? The main task was to clarify his, and my, overall aim, and to consider whether we were working along parallel lines, within the same movement:

I am writer of the Light, in both my history and my poetry, and I am restating a metaphysical reality in our time. He is seeing how human beings become truly human through an extension of consciousness which makes an evolutionary leap. Do we meet? Yes, if my experience of illumination is his experience of consciousness; and if he agrees that the problems of the Romantic (and Modernist) poets are solved by my Metaphysical approach.... I must produce another... book soon, *Illumination and Metaphysics*. This can be published as an essay; my equivalent to (Sartre's) *Existentialism is a Humanism*.

This 'essay' became my Winchester lecture, which was eventually published as: 'The Nature of Light: Illumination and a Metaphysical Theory of Everything'. The new movement would be a revival of the metaphysical vision, of what is, reality; and should be called Universalism.

My meeting with Colin Wilson turned out to be a collision. I arrived at 5.30 and was given smoked salmon and wine. In came his secretary and her boyfriend Paul Newman, who compiled *Abraxas*, a regular newsletter-cum-magazine on Colin Wilson. We started on the Sparticans and Bill Hopkins, then got on to Japan. He had shown me a fragment of his autobiography: "Here, Nick, read this. It begins with my hand up a girl's knickers." Joy, his wife, looked with disdain. Colin said Buddhists need "more words, not less" (his rationalist criticism of Zen). We got on to books. During the second wine (after Paul had "broken the f – ing corkscrew" – Wilson) I said, "Like Goethe you've been through your *Sturm-und-Drang* period and are approaching maturity." He said: "You're still in *Sturm und Drang*, the right brain, that's the trouble."

Now we collided head on like two *sumo* wrestlers. I rebutted this, and Paul and Joy took my side. (They were very interested in my two books, which Wilson had produced.) I said: "My Fire is your eighth state of consciousness." (He had called his Faculty X the seventh state of consciousness.) He said: "The Fire is like alcohol or mescaline" and: "Why did the Romantics and [David] Gascoyne smash? Because they weren't strong enough. Nietzsche's 'will to power' and '5,000 feet up' are reality – the peak experience." I said: "The Fire cleans up all problems. It is about inner purification of consciousness. If the consciousness is impure it will not happen." He said: "But what does one *do*?" I said: "Next Wednesday, for example, I'm going to Hampstead and I'll sit with a group of healers at their request and bring it down for them in a safe way, and those who are ready will see it and those who aren't won't." He said: "But it causes cancer and the two are connected." There was a chorus of dissent.

I said: "I don't know about that. But what I do know is that I have forged an Existential Metaphysics through it, and that a new Existentialism is wrong because it focuses on existence rather than Being, and that the new movement may have to be called by a new name, for example 'Universalism'. You're holding a book [, *The Fire and the Stones*,] that looks into the experience of Fire (*samadhi, satori*) from a scientific point of view, and possibly we write two halves of the same book and launch a new movement. Man in relation to the universe through consciousness." I said: "There needs to be a new movement to get that across. Will you think about this?" "Yes, I will, seriously." Pam said: "You must do it, it's the way forward." He said: "I don't object to the Fire as the central idea of civilizations, I object to the lack of strength it suggests. *The Outsider* was saying that in the eighteenth century man became too sensitive in the Romantic time and smashed, plain sick – and what was wrong? What is wrong with Gascoyne? He isn't strong enough. The answer is therefore in the will." I said, "No, in the metaphysical Romantic vision."

We had made contact. He said to Paul Newman: "And here's Nick's poem about Gorran Haven and me for the magazine." Paul said: "We'll put it in." I said: "I'm lecturing in Winchester in April on 'Illumination and Metaphysics: the Mystic Light in History, Nature and Cosmology'. Will you come and listen?" Colin said: "Yes. Send me details." Pam said: "I'd like to come." I said: "Think of illumination in terms of its effect on consciousness, not as a doctrine. It will repay you to go to comparative religion and consider whether it gives you your missing ingredient in consciousness." He said: "Can you stand up to them out there?" I said: "I can. I produced these two books and I'm strong enough to produce another on the Metaphysical Revolution." Pam said: "You don't have to justify yourself." I said: "If I was Stuart Holroyd and my *Tenth Chance* had caused that furore at the Royal Court, I wouldn't have slunk off." He said: "Stuart was a slinker-off. It's all a question of strength. You launch a movement and carry it through with strength." I said to Wilson: "I was too young to be an Angry. If I'd been a few years older you'd have had a fourth in the movement." He grinned. "You've made a hit with Pam."

I arranged to see him in the week after 13 December. He said: "We can have a reunion of the 1950s people at your school." Pam said: "Can I come?" I said: "Just as you said *The Outsider* was the most important book of its generation, and that you feel you have something more important to say than most writers, so I feel the same, and we can each pursue our vision separately or we can work in alliance, and I can see that an alliance could achieve much; it could bring in a new movement." He said: "I'll think about it." I said before I left: "You're the tutor and I'm the pupil and need to be deferential, but sometimes the pupil can be strong enough to express his ideas forcibly, and when two strong people express their views, sparks fly. But no offence on either side." He said, smiling: "No." Pam said to Colin:

"You're in danger of being all ego. I've been talking about this all the weekend, it's synchronicity." Outside, Pam said: "I've never seen him so animated. He loved that."

I had made contact at a real level. I had interrupted him and shouted him down when necessary. Later still I observed: "Why the Fire?.... To bring in energy from the beyond which dynamises and strengthens the soul, and unites action and contemplation.... The Fire as a purifying of consciousness, a heightened consciousness in the mystic progression towards a unitive vision, which is perceived by post-Fire consciousness.... When I speak to Colin Wilson about the Light those listening – his wife, his secretary, the editor of the newsletter about him – all recognise that I am speaking the truth and urge him to look at what I have done."[16] I was now determined to push Universalism through on my own.

Shaping my philosophy
I had been very interested in Michelangelo's metaphysical vision: his Platonic view of art, that it is preordained by God and implanted within the marble which the artist perceives and hews out.

Late at night I recorded the idea for a forthcoming book:

Part One, the Mystic Way, i.e. the Way to a Metaphysical Vision, the Unitive Vision. Part Two, the Challenge to Humanism, Rejection of 28 'isms' in terms of the Metaphysical Light which is Metaphysical Being. Part Three, the Metaphysical Revolution across all disciplines and resurgences.

This approach would surface in *The New Philosophy of Universalism*, which contains a list of 50 'isms'.

I was shaping my philosophy. I wrote of metaphysics:

An ontology of separateness needs to be replaced by one of oneness. An epistemology of sense data by one of inner vision of the Light.... An ontology and epistemology of the Light, which is Reality known within; the Light behind cosmology – the reunion between science and metaphysics.[17]

Practical mysticism: Foundation, bringing down the Light in Fourth Mystic Life
I start the Foundation of the Light, David Seaman plays football with Coopersale Hall boys
I had been contacted by a local mystic, Heather Andrews Dobbs, a founder of the Troward Society and editor of its publication *New Light* with a background in Science of Mind and New Thought. She rang me about *The Fire and the Stones* and spoke of levels of consciousness. "Your level of

consciousness is so great," she told me, "the spiritual is higher than the psychic or occult; now you have got the consciousness it can pass to the whole nation." She asked if she could be my research assistant, and she found me books and put me in touch with new sources of information. She helped me set up a World Metaphysical Foundation, which I eventually called The Foundation of the Light.

Heather saw its purpose as spreading mysticism: "You have spiritual charisma. No one else is combining the academic and metaphysical." I was clear that I should not become a spiritual *guru* but besides being a poet should be a philosopher and historian (writing the philosophy of history) whose works reflected mysticism. Should my metaphysical perception be my standpoint? Or should I be a mainstream historian-cum-poet who hides his metaphysics behind this *façade*? Tomlin had hidden behind a *façade*, and Sheldrake had urged me to come out into the open, and I knew I was going to be more of a spokesman for the metaphysical, not less. I saw the World Metaphysical Centre in terms of Coopersale Hall, as "a mystery school based on an invisible school", a "seed-bed for souls". Heather wanted to call the Centre 'The Nicholas Hagger Foundation', saying: "The Troward Society is not about Troward's ego, but what he stands for." I replied: "The Light would look at my name as bringing ego into it." I had been careful to call my new school Coopersale Hall School and to leave my name out of it. I wrote: "Metaphysics is the study of Reality and of Being, i.e. of the Light."

At the beginning of November I became convinced that the World Metaphysical Foundation should teach trainees to "experience the transcendental". I resolved to try this out in Hampstead when I spoke to the healers.

I went back to Hampstead to bring down the Light for Anthea Courtenay's healing group and to work out a way I could begin to bring down the Light for groups of would-be mystics. I spoke of the theme of *The Fire and the Stones* and of the unmetaphorical nature of the Light we were trying to see. I spoke of the Mystic Way. I read out St Augustine's and Hildegard's accounts of their experiences. I told them exactly what they had to do. Then the lights were turned out and we went to the Light with me leading the meditation – or rather contemplation. As the Light poured into me, I said: "Leave your body. Move behind your mind to the centre where you can open to the Light. Open yourself. Go deeper. The Light is in the room, open yourself to it. If it is your will [the Light's will], enter whoever you feel you want to. Not my will but thy will be done. Look at the Light with your inner eye, keeping your outer eye closed. It is the Light that manifested into the universe. It will soon be time to return to the world of time from this eternity. Close your new place, your new centre and return to your social ego. Reoccupy your body."

Back in the social setting I asked for feedback. One girl had been filled with a crackling Light that had temporarily frightened her. Another had glimpsed a dawning. Christine, the temple-dancer, remained silent. After a break for coffee or tea I told them about the healing Light and the surges, which I demonstrated later, quietly and unobtrusively. Throughout I emphasised that the ego is like a stone in a pipe, that the stone must be removed.

The next three days I heard tales over the telephone of what individual members of the group had experienced. The girl in red had the most intense Light she has ever had. Christine, the temple-dancer, reported that she did not sleep that night. She told me over the phone that she saw many things, including a Light coming out of a chalice, deep-blue, a tunnel, a Light, a monastery, a man in black in a cloak, a Light the other side. Christine also saw some personal things she would not talk about.

There was an interlude while I put energy into Coopersale Hall. I had consoled David Seaman, the Arsenal goalie who had just been displaced as England's goalie by Chris Woods. I said to Mrs. Seaman, "Perhaps Woods will break a leg or let one through his legs." On 17 November he *did* let one through his legs. Mrs. Seaman said to me: "You're clairvoyant." Seaman asked me: "When am I going to get back in the England team?" I told him he would get back in, and that prediction came to pass.

At my invitation he came and played football at Coopersale Hall, on the playing-field at the bottom of Flux's Lane, the touchline lined by parents, some of whom regularly watched Arsenal. I put on a track suit and played too. Seaman was on my side. At half-time we were losing 5–2. I said to him, "Come on, you may be an international but we're being trounced by nine- and ten-year-olds, we're going to have to put the ball in the air to keep our honour up. Get ready for some headers." We pulled back to 5–3 and then scored three goals. The opposing team equalised off a shoulder as the whistle blew. The match had ended in a 6–6 draw, and Seaman had scored most of our goals from my crosses. There was a report with a photo on the front page of the next *West Essex Gazette*, and applications to join the school rose dramatically.

One of the healers had a husband in PR, and there was a proposal that Universalism should be launched at Queen Elizabeth's Hall, and that I would explain the Metaphysical Revolution to 900 people. I said: "I will be a T.E. Hulme and deliver the theme: 'What is in common in the shift in the arts?'"[18] As her husband felt that the arts were in perpetual 'new movement' the idea was not implemented, but it surfaced in a strengthened form in my Aldeburgh lecture in 1997.

Philosophy: Winchester lecture and origin of the universe
Metaphysical Research Group and the Light
I had been invited to attend the Scientific and Medical Network's

Metaphysical Research Group in Oxford. The morning of the event I received a letter from Charlotte Waterlow, a historian, who in a review for the Scientific and Medical Network's *Newsletter* had seized on pages 708-15 of *The Fire and the Stones* and taken exception to my linking of the New World Order to a powerful shadow group who manipulated the US President and Western leaders as puppets. I had researched my information very carefully and concluded that this cabal, which I later called 'the Syndicate', aimed to take over all living civilizations and fuse them into a world government which it would control, looting the earth's resources. Waterlow enclosed an abusive letter from a United World Federalist and in her review set out her own idea: that civilization is about to undergo a mass leap in consciousness which will bring in a new stage in evolution, a highly optimistic New-Age view not shared by the findings of the mystics and for which there was no evidence.

I made my way to the house in Hinksey where the Metaphysical Research Group were meeting. I arrived after a drive through fog and talked to David Lorimer about Charlotte Waterlow. He said: "She is put out because she's a Federalist and she doesn't know about the conspiracy." I showed him *None Dare Call it Conspiracy* by Gary Allen. He had read it. The book had sold over 5 million copies in the US, and it was naïve for any historian dealing with the New World Order not to know about it. Lorimer said he would handle her. We then sat round a modern room overlooking a wooded garden and 9 of us gave presentations for ten minutes each, followed by 20 minutes' discussion. Most of them were sceptics who were seeing if there is anything beyond scepticism, including Max Payne, who used to lecture at Sheffield Polytechnic (now Sheffield Hallam University). I handed out notes and got my points across, the intuitive and inner being admissible.

I was asked to hold a meditation. For half an hour before lunch I had the philosophers sitting with closed eyes and brought down the Light. The soup was on the table with an inviting smell, and we were opening ourselves to the Light. The sceptics sat in a darkened room, and, after the Light had poured into me, discussed Vaughan's "I saw Eternity the other night,/Like a great ring of pure and endless light". The philosopher Geoffrey Read asked, "Why couldn't he just say, 'I saw a ring?'" At lunch the philosophers spoke about language and after lunch one of the philosophers said, "To a linguistic analyst there is no metaphysical Reality." I said: "The Vienna Circle said this in the 1920s and where did it get us? In *The Fire and the Stones* I show a thousand experiences of the Fire from all cultures, and they are all the same."

The next day I had a long talk with David Lorimer on the phone about the running of the world. I told him it may seem strange to do poetry and history but that in the 20th century some poets had written on cultural topics, hence Eliot's *Notes Towards the Definition of Culture* and Robert Graves's *The White Goddess*, next to which *The Fire and the Stones* was placed by Waterstones, Charing Cross Road. I compared our philosophy group with the Aristotelian Society that was founded in 1880 for the systematic study of philosophy, whose members included T.E. Hulme and Whitehead. (Whitehead would have been in his logical empiricist rather than his metaphysical stage.)

In spite of these ideas I was still grounded in practical reality at the schools. The Oaklands school keeper left and I interviewed (among others) Ernie Peake, a former caretaker at Holly House and an ex-soldier. He told me he had been among the first to enter Belsen with his Crocodile flame-thrower in 1945. We discussed his qualifications for being a school keeper. During the war he had been a sentry at a military base. A German Colonel wearing a peaked cap and looking like Hitler had failed to stop and Ernie had shot and killed him. He was court-martialled and acquitted, and put back on duty. He then opened fire on a car that failed to stop and killed an English Colonel, who was smuggling a German girl back into the base. He was court-martialled again and again acquitted. I said, "I reckon your skills will enhance the School's security," and appointed him. Having been among the first to liberate Belsen, he would now be patrolling the site of our wartime pretend concentration camp at the bottom of the main field.

Nadia visited. We went to Coopersale Hall and walked round the pond, and I was soon back in my sub-rational self. Later I listened to Elgar's *Enigma Variations*, which led me to contrast language and silence:

Language – the social ego's province. Silence – the universal ego's province. My [poem] 'The Silence' was about my contact with the universal ego.[19]

Universalism, structuralism and Colin Wilson

In December we drove to Cornwall and I rang Colin Wilson. "Why don't you come on Wednesday? Pam and Paul are coming then. They can give you a lift." I cast around in Wilson's writings and read in *Existentially Speaking*: "The very essence of my position is a belief in the power of reason."[20] I agreed with Whitehead: "The purpose of philosophy is to rationalize mysticism".[21] I was focusing on a deeper part of the self than the rational, social ego.

I was collected by Pam and Paul at 4.50. Colin was in a blue shell suit. He was still in his hair-drier. Two ladies came to the door, one of whom wanted to be Colin's research assistant. They joined the circle and talked with Pam, his mother and Joy while Paul, Colin and I talked about his filmscript on Atlantis. We got on to the successor to Existentialism. He said: "Stuart

[Holroyd], Bill [Hopkins] and I discussed what the sequel to Existentialism should be and decided it is Personalism." I explained why Personalism was inadequate to describe the universal energies pouring from the metaphysical beyond into the soul or self, at a sub-personal level, and he agreed.

Then he said the Fire is an inadequate substitute for conscious control. I said Hulme and Whitehead were the ending-points in philosophy and spoke of the revolution in philosophy the Fire offers. He said: "I don't want the f—g Fire. Hulme wouldn't have championed your Fire. He'd have described it as Romantic abandon. You and I are always at loggerheads." The 'adjective' he used to describe the Fire told me much about his soul. Yet he pressed me to go on Friday. In the car on the way home Pam said: "He's totally resistant to the Fire." Paul asked: "Do you have a view on murder in Colin Wilson?" I said: "It's the glee of the ego." He seemed to be on the side of the glee, and I was not impressed by his support for his correspondent Ian Brady's egocentric view of killing.

My encounter with Wilson had not carried my philosophy forward in any way. The next day I awoke early to a sea racing in over rocks. I had my world-view, which coloured my poems; Wilson had his, which coloured his works. "I am a Universalist, he is a Rationalist. With our different emphases, can we be in the same movement? Is it desirable for Wilson to be in a new movement? Probably not." I rang Paul Newman to borrow his typewriter so I could type a letter to Colin Wilson. He said: "Colin sees man as a self-charging battery, you see the energy as coming from outside." I said: "Yes."

I went back to Colin Wilson on my own at 5.30 on 20 December. His daughter Sally was there. We had ham, melon and white wine while we watched the news, a parrot perching on Sally's shoulder. Then he talked about his journals. He said, "I cringe with embarrassment every time I read them." Joy had told him he was rude to me last time and he said I talk over him. So after handing my letter over I listened.

He said: "To get a new movement off the ground, and I don't like new 'isms', you need to talk the language of Lévi-Strauss and Derrida. After Existentialism there was structuralism and then post-structuralism, and then postmodernism, showing it all ends in nothing. Derrida started from Husserl and showed him affected by deconstruction. The conclusion is that the 'I' of the transcendental ego is an illusion and there is no metaphysical reality, because they are concepts in language which are false. So start there." I said: "The starting-point is the 'I' behind the 'I think'." He said: "Yes, but you have to tackle the language. Deconstruction is anti-Marxism. It's like Heidegger, *Being and Time* contains 10 definitions of Existence, and you have to say Existence 1, Existence 2, etc. Read Christopher Norris on Derrida. Meursault's 'I was happy and am happy still'. How could he say he was happy? Answer that. When I started writing I had to refer everything to Sartre and Camus. It's all moved on since then. Now it's Derrida and Lévi-Strauss, and they're much harder to understand. Read Derrida in *On Grammatology*. You need to put the crowbar in at the right place. Otherwise you're rushing about waving swords and not getting anywhere. Derrida is the *Principia* of our time. Give one single proof that he's wrong and you're there. Your Fire is irrelevant. Anyone can have it. But what is needed is...." And away he went on conscious pressure. He concluded: "It's not the Fire, it's language." I said: "Spengler saw civilizations as passing from soul-power to intellectual power. And I am saying they pass from the metaphysical to the secular." He said: "Spengler said aqueducts were better than Renaissance buildings because they *did* something. So it is with [Ted] Hughes. When we met we talked about vole-traps. He's only got one poem in him, the violence and cruelty of Nature. He didn't want to talk about poetry, only about *doing*."

I said: "I will come up with 10 arguments against Derrida. Rejection of Derrida is the starting-point." His family came down while I was with him – the two boys joining their sister – but apart from pouring them glasses of wine he carried on talking to me and was reluctant to let me go. I was standing by the fire for 10 minutes while he ate his mussels, talking at me. I left arranging to see him in February, when the starting-point would be Derrida and Lévi-Strauss and the 'I' behind the 'I think' and metaphysical reality.

I returned to Essex and went to work on Derrida. In Foyles I bought 19 books related to structuralism, deconstruction and post-structuralism; and postmodernism. Also on the new historicism. It was a maze. Structuralism, which began in the 1960s with Saussure and Lévi-Strauss was over. Deconstruction – Derrida and de Man in the 1960s – criticised it by analysis and claimed to have destroyed ontology, saying there is nothing external to the text, which is evidently not true. However, borders were dissolved, and the mixture of linguistics, literary criticism and philosophy resulted in post-structuralism, a move away from the unified person. Post-modernism focused on how the author tells a story.

I wrote Colin Wilson another letter debunking Derrida in terms of the universal ego of Universalism, Kant's transcendental ego behind reason. The next day I revised my letter to include a 5-point proof of my 'non-competence principle' that debunks Derrida, structuralism, deconstruction, post-structuralism and postmodernism: (1) Derrida's theories about language are the province of the social ego rather than the universal (or transcendental) ego; (2) contrary to Sartre, the universal ego exists, the proof including a use of phenomenology, bracketing out the Cartesian 'I think' to reveal the 'I' behind it; (3) intuitive information received by the universal ego is admissible evidence for philosophers to consider (as supported by Willis Harman's article); (4) the territories of the social and universal egos are separate and distinct, and the social ego is not competent to judge what is or is not real outside its territory as language falls silent and the universal ego takes over the direction of consciousness (just as the Vienna Circle's verification principle is not competent to apply empirical standards to quasi-empirical intuitive experience); and (5) the universal energy called the Fire or Light which is received in the universal 'I' rather than the linguistic social ego is a reality outside language that has been experienced in all cultures at all times (*see* Part One of *The Fire and the Stones*), contrary to what Derrida holds. So Derrida is a trespasser who doesn't matter.[22] My 'non-competence principle' had much in common with Wittgenstein's later "Whereof one cannot speak, thereof one must be silent".

Unified view of the universe

I had now finished the Coopersale Hall extension of four classrooms, a kitchen and toilets in spite of the recession, and I applied myself to a statement of my unified philosophy. I did a draft of my Winchester lecture in four days (31 December to 3 January). It became the first part of *The Universe and the Light*. I wrote: "I propose the Light – spiritual *and* natural – as a Theory of Everything. I do it by adapting Newton's expanding force and reconciling it to Bohm and including Hawking."

At the end of the year I tried to sleep but at 12.45 a.m. had a slight pain in my heart, for the second time in three days. I got up. At 1.15 a.m. I got up again, suffering from severe pain in my heart. The pain did not recur the next day, and we had Miss Lord and Marion round from next door to see the New Year in. Marion "drank a little wine though she was supposed not to because of her pills [for cancer of the uterus], and, absorbed in laughter, forgot about her condition and enjoyed life for an hour-and-a-half. Miss Lord had four glasses of wine and rolled home on my arm (aged 91)."

On 5 January the local vicar visited Miss Lord's to anoint Marion with oil, and Ann and I were invited. On his own admission the vicar did not know how to heal, and he mechanically read from a book, devoid of inspiration or healing energy. Ten sat in a circle, including blind Judith, for the anointing. A grim Marion lowered her eyes and all hands were put on her head or arm. Judith prayed loudly, alone; the blind leading the sick. Later Marion visited a consultant with Zena, who told us: "He drew a diagram of the stomach and shaded it in and said: 'It's spreading. You're in the third stage of four stages. Have you any questions?' Marion asked, 'Where did you go on holiday?'" Had she not taken anything in – or was it bravura?

I continued work on my unified view of the universe and of thought: "To unite religion, mysticism, metaphysics, philosophy; mind, consciousness;

history, civilizations, cultures, world events; subatomic physics, biology; and cosmology, the macrocosmic universe." That was the task of my lecture. I had several telephone conversations with the physicist Edgard Gunzig in Brussels. In one call I "discussed the origin of the universe, which was from real nothing to a quantum vacuum (by quantum processes) and thence to a universe (by virtual particles becoming real particles)". Three days later I talked with him for an hour and ten minutes on the phone and he said several times: "You are asking the most fundamental question in theoretical physics." Gunzig explained how a real nothing or emptiness became a quantum vacuum through virtual particles, and how the CBR (cosmic background radiation) did not come from the Big Bang but from a cooling 300,000–500,000 years after the beginning.[23]

BBC

While my philosophical unification was taking shape, world history being an aspect, Peter Donebauer and his producer Roy Ackerman took me to the BBC to propose that a film should be made of *The Fire and the Stones*. We met Stephen Whyttle (the Head of Religious Broadcasting at the BBC) and John Blake and had a freewheeling conversation with sceptical probings from the two of them about the difference between a civilization and a culture; whether primitive religions belonged to a culture rather than a civilization; how comparative religion is "out" as it is "boring"; and whether we were being descriptive or evangelical. At the end Whyttle said: "'Are religions the dynamos of civilizations?' That is of interest. It's a six-parter. Consider how you can make it into six parts while we read the book." I went on to lunch with Peter and we drafted a "stages" model for our six parts – "beginnings, unifications, reformations, empires and religion, secularization and today"[24] – and also a chronological model splitting the spread of the Fire over 5,000 years into six parts. Peter and Roy put a lot of work into the project, which over the coming months went through four different phases as the BBC changed its perspective. These four phases can be found in the Appendix to *The Universe and the Light*.[25] After many months Peter was forced to admit that getting agreement for the project was more difficult than he had expected.

The TV presenter Michael Wood rang me. He said he knew of *The Fire and the Stones* and would do a series with me, and "a film on a brief history of God, showing all the gods from all the civilizations".[26] I had coffee with him and he met Peter Donebauer, but there was an unexplained delay and the idea was never implemented.

Russia

The news from the USSR had been exciting. There were remarkable scenes on TV as Moscow decommunised. Yeltsin ordering Gorbachev to sign decrees banning the Communist Party in Russia, and flew the Russian national flag over the Kremlin. A revolution swept away Soviet Communism. The next day Gorbachev resigned as General Secretary of the Communist Party. Soviet Communism had ended. All my FREE activities were vindicated. The USSR was breaking up – Armenia, Moldavia, Ukraine, Latvia, Estonia and Lithuania. Some of the republics would get together into a federation as I predicted in *The Fire and the Stones* with internal independence but external linking. The next day the USSR finally ended. Gorbachev resigned as the last President of the USSR. All the republics were now free. FREE had happened.

At the end of January a South-African Hungarian, Professor Elemer Elad Rosinger, Professor of Pure and Applied Mathematics in the University of Pretoria, flew from Johannesburg to London and stayed at the nearby Roebuck Hotel to meet me. He had read my two books and declared me in a letter "a great Old Master". He did not know Gorka. He had sideburns and a moustache, and over tea at the Roebuck he began by saying, "I am in the KGB. That is a joke." He said: "'Your two books are exceptional. What impressed me was the contrast between them. One was objective, the other subjective, they were from two opposite ends of the spectrum. The only other person I could think of who had done such a thing was St Augustine with *Confessions* (which is not as good as your poems) and *City of God*, but they were not published at the same time. Also, where is the middle between these two opposites?' On my poems he said, 'You write so objectively about yourself, that in itself is an indication of exceptional quality.'" We talked for three-and-a-quarter hours and Heather Dobbs entertained him for the rest of the week. She reported: "He is so immersed in what he has to say that he is not thinking about the Light."

Shortly afterwards I received letters and phone calls from Moscow inviting me to make an educational visit there. They were received at both schools. I replied that I would need "to discuss the coming Russian Federation with Yeltsin", and heard no more. I was aware that George Miller, whom I had met at the time of FREE in 1984, had been reported to be Yeltsin's secretary. In fact, as George Miller-Kurakin he was working under Anatoly Chubais, the privatisation minister under Yeltsin. (George died in 2009.)

The political world was suddenly everywhere. I went to the London Hospital in Whitechapel for a routine X-ray and sat next to Jimmy Denne (the Conservative who ran my election campaign in Roding) who was there, with his wife. He talked non-stop. He told me that Biggs-Davison always talked in code, that "I'm coming to Buckhurst Hill" meant "Meet me at Loughton station". He said, "Biggs-Davison used intelligence techniques."

He said he would melt away to meet Biggs-Davison, not telling anyone.[27] I wondered if this was when Biggs-Davison was Opposition Shadow Cabinet spokesman for Northern Ireland and was a routine precaution against the IRA, or whether there was another explanation.

My car is shot at twice
A week and a bit later I worked all day on the six-part TV project for the BBC and (having made the arrangement over the phone) drove to collect the work printed out in Barking. Just after the Loughton entry to the M11 at 4.45 I heard a crack, like a stone hitting my windscreen at great speed, but there was no vehicle in front of me. My Lexus windscreen was very thick, and I continued my journey and printed out. On the way back, at 6.05 in the same part of the M11 there was another crack and a star appeared on my windscreen. Again there were no cars or lorries in front of me or overtaking. I went to the police and they examined the car. A policeman said that someone who could hit a moving car and knew my Lexus, had shot at me at 4.45 and waited till I returned at 6.05 and had another shot, hoping to cause me to have an accident. The policeman said: "It wasn't casual or boys, they hit you in the dark, that's professional. Someone wants you out of the way." I had to replace the windscreen.[28]

Looking back, I am sure that the shots came from the undergrowth between the M11 and the River Roding, and I wonder if a tracking device had been fitted to my car so whoever was waiting for me to return knew I was approaching. I have no idea if an organisation was involved and there was no evidence for the motive for the shooting. (The incident took place more than four years after my involvement in destabilising the Soviet Union with satellite dishes, and I thought it unlikely that the two were linked.) Privately I reckoned that someone did not want the six-part filming of *The Fire and the Stones* to go ahead.

Philosophy of history: Francis Fukuyama and the end of history
Western civilization had lost the Toynbeean vision of civilizations and philosophy of history. Francis Fukuyama, author of *The End of History and the Last Man*, had come to London. I knew it was not history that was ending, even in the Hegelian sense, but a stage of history. I had written:

> Fukuyama says that history had been proceeding inevitably to its end when spiritual and material values create a Hegelian synthesis, a permanent world-wide American liberal democracy (American optimism). I say that history is composed of 25 civilizations which enshrine the vision of the contemplative mystic as the central idea and decay as they turn secular; and that world-wide democracy is merely a stage, like stage 15 of the Roman Empire, which

will pass when the phase moves on. The inevitability concerns the stage in the North-American civilization that North-America is in.... The world-wideness is a phase in a number of stages, not a permanent thing. (As was Communism.)

On 5 March I went up to London and heard Fukuyama, the neo-Hegelian and admirer of Kojève, at the Logan Hall. There was a highly-accomplished debate from a socio-economic point of view. Simon Jenkins, editor of *The Times*, spoke first and introduced Fukuyama, who spoke rapidly and fluently without notes, very impressively and clearly. Then the panel of two left-wingers and two right-wingers that included Ernest Gellner, Roger Scruton, and Norman Stone. Afterwards I had a word with Scruton and with Jenkins. I got Fukuyama to sign a book and gave him *The Fire and the Stones*, which I signed for him. I explained that in my view there are always civilizations undergoing different stages, and that history does not end in universal democracy. Fukuyama hailed a permanent universal democracy, a form of the New World Order, but it has to be said that tyrannies now abound.

The latest Scientific and Medical *Network Review* arrived with the review of *The Fire and the Stones* by Charlotte Waterlow. She wanted to believe in permanent benevolent world government and took me to task for drawing attention to a self-interested *élite* that sought to dominate all civilizations. I wrote:

It is Fukuyama's error to assume that a new phase of history is coming which will be final and forever. In New Age and holistic circles there is a desire to believe that there is going to be an evolutionary change in man. Waterlow says a new kind of civilization is dawning based on world co-operation to implement human rights.

I was realistic and had seen that each living civilization would develop within itself and perhaps consent to form a world union for a while. I had misgivings about the New World Order that encouraged wars, diseases and famines to maximise its own resources. I was pleased that Lady Astor had told Waterlow that she had missed the point of the self-interestedness of the 'Conspiracy'.[29] I wanted perpetual Universalism as much as Waterlow but I was realistic enough to know that in the immediate future it was not going to happen.

The Light had not deserted me. After I rang Michael Mann of Element "I had a great surge of Light which tingled my spine. The Eternal is pleased with what I have done, and is encouraging me."

I was soon grounded. My new bank manager, Ken Jones, rang and told me that his predecessor, who had backed my vision of Oaklands and had been interested in my book on the miners' strike and in the 'Heroes of the West' before he retired, had died in the Canary Islands: "He drowned. He seems to have had a heart attack while swimming. He was 57."[30] He had waded out to swim and would not be able to enjoy his early retirement. I saw his early death as a call to carry forward my works *now*.

Universalism and unified knowledge, Sir Philip Mawer
I had nearly finished work on my Winchester lecture and was editing my *Diaries* for what would become *Awakening to the Light*, tracing my mystical development in Japan. In Cornwall I returned to poetry. I "immediately settled to my poem on Bohm, 'Ode: Spider's Web: Our Local Universe in an Infinite Whole' and placed in a couple of stanzas". Later I walked with Anthony: "The moon was a day from being full, the stars were out, the air was cold and bracing, the sea was fairly low, the tide coming in. Spoke to a boy fishing at the end of the harbour. He had caught two small whiting and pollack and would fish all night."

The next day I went for another walk with Anthony: "A full moon, our shadows on the harbour wall. A shooting star. The moon in the curl of the waves. Returned and wrote 'Full Moon', about the Light in the waves of history." The next day I found an orange-tree in my *Diaries*: "Remembered the orange-tree by my gate in Libya and wrote 'Orange Tree'." I read that George MacBeth had died of motor neurone disease and recalled "the slim Edwardian dandy who read at The Crown and Greyhound, Dulwich, in 1963, and the dancing fop I went out to dinner with in 1970 and who skip-danced up Dean Street". Arthur Hosegood's wife had had a stroke, and died from pneumonia on 17 February. I wrote a poem, 'An Old Cornish Lady Glimpses Reality'.

A couple of days later I "stepped outside my front door and saw a rainbow..., and a black cloud and sea-mist over Trenarren. Took gulps of sea air in fine rain that moistened my cheeks.... Returned to our sitting-room and wrote 'Rainbow' straight out."

That night at 11.30 I went for a late-night walk with the boys. It was very cold and the tide was the longest out we had seen and the

Nicholas at Charlestown with a rainbow on 18 February 1992

waves were rough. "A full moon in the opening in black cloud. Returned... quite drunk with fresh air, cheeks and ears cold." The next morning I "went to get the papers, saw a bare tree with four birds in [it], and stopped and wrote a poem on my knee ['Bare Tree'], standing, at the top of the harbour". We lunched at Polkerris and "walked along the pier and again I felt I was about to be thrown off the high ledge of an Egyptian temple, and was quite panic-stricken until I could place my feet on the sand". Clapperton came to tea and stayed a couple of hours, "fulminating at dog-owners who mess up his harbour, and almost inconsequentially agreeing our offer... for the strip in front of our house here, and the green sward and water pump/tap".

I returned to Essex via Shaftesbury and lunched with Michael Mann in The Coppleridge Inn, Motcombe. We discussed the draft of my lecture. He said smilingly, "Unification of knowledge – those who are there know it already, whereas those who aren't there won't believe it." He said he was interested in my "book of essays" (*The Universe and the Light*). Back at home there was a letter from David Lorimer saying that the Winchester conference was oversubscribed and arrangements were being made to film the speakers in an adjoining hall – did I have any objection?

I was still working on my lecture. I intuitively felt that consciousness is

on the electro-magnetic spectrum. We all have an infinite part of ourselves that can see the whole, and which brings to us... a hierarchical vibrational level. The highest wave band for the highest level. Matter is frozen light.

I researched Bede Griffiths's equation of God and Darkness and grasped his distinction between transcendence and immanence:

The Godhead is transcendent in real nothing, latent Fire before the quantum vacuum. God is immanent as Fire or Light in the quantum vacuum, the universe of creation at both psychological and physical levels.

A few days later I lunched with Philip Mawer, the Secretary-General of the Church of England Synod, at Vitello's in Great Smith Street. We talked of Universalism and a Mystic Revival. He pointed out that some in the Church are against syncretism. He said he would see if the Archbishop would like 20 minutes about the Fire or Light. I knew this would not happen as the Church had lost its vision of the Light.

Following my talk to the Hampstead healers a dinner was arranged for the publicist Lynne Franks, who had a PR company, to advise on how to project Universalism. She advised holding an event that should be called 'Celebration of Light' at the Royal Albert Hall. Patrick Hamilton, who was present, visited Lord Palumbo of the Arts Council, who told him that it would take a year to put on a production at the Royal Albert Hall. The idea was shelved.

At another meeting of the philosophers of the Metaphysical Research Group at Oxford I laid down some Universalist principles: I referred everything to ontology and cosmology, epistemology and psychology, and Max Payne agreed. The only opposition came from Geoffrey Read. I sided with intuition against Read's reason, and distinguished the 'I' of the rational ego and the 'I' of the soul. I said: "When the Metaphysical Revolution happens, we will lock you up, Geoffrey," and everyone laughed. At lunch I talked of Universalism as the new movement. I found them attached to logic and sidelined it. I centralised the intuitional, marginalised the logical.

Reflection on Universalism took me back to Greek philosophy, and I recalled that "the Greek theatres were within the religion". At the Epidaurus theatre, the altar was in the centre of the stage, the temple of Aesculapius being nearby. In Athens the high priest of Dionysus was guest of honour at plays, and plays were part of the religious festivals of Dionysus. Athenian – and all Greek – history has been secularised, and the period we concentrate on (Herodotus and Thucydides) was a secularised time of decline. "Greek history has been presented in a secularised way."

Back in Cornwall I walked with my two boys and passed on the message I had given the philosophers: "Told them there are two selves and that my greatest gift to them is knowledge of their universal being, [which was] greater than a Chigwell education; for Chigwell doesn't teach the second self, only the rational social ego."

I worked on my lecture and Clapperton (the owner of the port) came round. He said to me: "I'm an asset-stripper, haven't you worked that out?" and asked me to buy the port for £250,000. He wheedled in my ear, tempting me like the Devil: "All this could be yours." I was not tempted, seeing expensive sea damage and little income. That night I went for a night walk on the harbour with Anthony. "Dark, no moon, bright, twinkling stars. Stood for a long time with Anthony, craning my neck and looking into the universe." I could have owned the harbour but I was more interested in the universe.

The next morning I woke early: "A glorious morning. Walked on the harbour, revelling in the early light on the calm sea.... Returned and sat quietly over my breakfast tray in the front room and wrote 'Sunlight' (a poem)." That night I "went for a late-night walk under bright stars, and wrote 'Mystery'". The next day I wrote: "A sunny morning, a tranquil sea, and a reflection. Even the Black Head is reflected."

I was waiting for my lecture now. I wrote:

Ap. 7. A green and choppy sea at high tide, white surf dashing against the rocks, and a roaring of wind and booming of waves, quietly, as a backdrop of consciousness. It is a tense time, waiting for... my [Winchester] lecture, but I am serene.... Awoke this morning with the idea that the Light – a fifth, expanding force – was responsible for inflation in the early universe.

I had received the connection between the latent Fire or Light and cosmo-logical inflation in sleep, like my Grand Unified Theory of world history and religion, and was in my consciousness when I woke.

Knowing I was thinking about my lecture, Anthony put on a video of 'Clockwise': of John Cleese as a Headmaster going to give an important speech. His speech is left on the train, and the lecture ends with his being arrested by the police. I laughed a lot. Anthony had brought joy to a careworn philosopher's heart.

The next day I left a calm sea and returned to Essex. On the way back I

had a new idea for the unification of consciousness and the spectrum. Our own brainwaves, 10–30 cycles per second, interfere with our contact with the spectrum, and it is only by going into radio silence and shutting down our own interference that we can open to the high frequencies higher up the spectrum, including the Light.[31]

I dream the date of the general election and Major's victory, Tebbit
Shortly after my visit to the BBC, the 'Muse' that gave me my Grand Unified Theory of world history had given me the date of the next general election, also in a dream: "Jan. 25. A long dream. I remember being in a room and watching John Major look at... a computer, although it looked more like an EEG (being flat and greenish – metallic), and a red line moved and he had found: growth! The news was delivered excitedly. I knew it was the end of January and there would be an election around April 9th." In sleep I was given the actual date of the general election and Major's victory. I did not want to believe that Major's victory was preordained but my confidence in the 'Muse' that had given me my GUT of world history was now increased.

I met Tebbit again at Garnish Hall, the 1750 timbered house of Diana Collins (*née* Padfield). There was a leaping log fire in the inglenook of the beamed main room, and I spoke with Bunny Morton (an old friend of Tebbit's), who told me Howe was put up to assassinating Thatcher by a group of senior Conservatives because Thatcher would not listen. I invited Tebbit to distribute some prizes and asked him how the coming election would turn out. Tebbit said: "The Conservatives will win by 20." I said that Thatcher had been ousted following a Bilderberg meeting at La Toja in the Canary Islands. Tebbit received this without comment.[32]

Election day was the day before my Winchester lecture and Major led the Conservatives back with a majority of 21 as Tebbit had more or less predicted at Garnish Hall – and exactly as I had seen in my sleep on 25 January.

My Winchester lecture, 'The Nature of Light'– Bronwen Astor, Bede Griffiths, John Barrow

On little sleep, I drove to Winchester for my lecture and arrived at 3.15. The speakers were housed in the Christchurch Lodge coach-house. There was a rehearsal in the main hall under a glaring light and then dinner, which was packed. I, a conference attender turned teacher, sat on top table with Sir George Trevelyan and other speakers. I had been allocated the whole evening for my presentation.

David Lorimer introduced me and spoke of *The Fire and the Stones* as a "monumental work". I then stood at the podium and delivered my lecture, dazzled in a blinding light as my words were carried by live TV to a different hall. There were nearly 500 listening, and I spoke for an hour and a half. My lecture was the first third of what became *The Universe and the Light*. I ignored Trevelyan's hearing-aid which whined intermittently, and described my approach to a Theory of Everything which included the metaphysical reality of the Light. I touched on the Metaphysical Revolution I had declared in 1991, and Universalism. With the octogenarian Father Bede Griffiths sitting in the audience with the straggly long hair and beard of a *guru* I insisted that God as immanent is present as Light, and that it is God transcendent who is Darkness, Non-Being. (Later in his monk's robe, Griffiths said God is beyond all imagery and symbolism, insisting that God is Darkness.) I also insisted that the future is American, that the North-American civilization will be strong and that there is not about to be a new Indian civilization (Griffiths being connected with India).

At the end a queue formed and I answered private questions. I was asked to sign a book by a lady who identified herself as Bronwen Astor: wife of Lord Astor and the chatelaine of Cliveden during the Profumo Affair. I recalled my visit to Cliveden before the Profumo Affair (*see My Double Life 1: This Dark Wood*). I spent five minutes asking her about her impressions of Stephen Ward and Profumo. (She said: "I married Bill in 1960, the autumn. Stephen Ward gave me the creeps, as soon as I saw him.")

The lecture seemed to go down well. Several said, *"Tour de force."* Two said, "Brilliant presentation." Several said, "How did you get all that together?" Peter Donebauer, who was in the audience, reported that a lady had said to him: "How did that nice Mr Hagger manage to speak so long without his voice being affected, does he do throat exercises?"

The speakers were invited to drinks. We all stood with a glass of wine in our hands – not Griffiths, who had gone to bed. Jacob Liberman was very positive and said he would speak about my account of the electromagnetic spectrum. He told me, "I haven't got anything prepared, I used to spend months writing it all out – for others, what about me?" Griffiths's German translator was present and chided me for going with the Light instead of the

Darkness behind the Light, which is filled with love. I challenged his ideas. Mark Lazarus, former director of the Wrekin Trust, told me: "I wondered why I have given 15 years to the Wrekin Trust but now I see it was to make you possible, to be a handmaiden to your Metaphysical Revolution."

The next day I meditated under Bede Griffiths and then breakfasted with Professor John Barrow, author of *Theories of Everything*. I asked him: "Where do love and order come into your mathematics?" John Barrow was not prepared to go outside his area of cosmology, the materialistic level. I commented: "He has defined his prison, and everything beyond that is speculative. He isn't interested in a theory of everything; only in a theory of cosmology." He talked about his visit to 10 Downing Street. Thatcher asked him about the fifth force.

That day Barrow gave a brilliant mathematical talk but it was all at one level: rational, not contemplative. Bede Griffiths spoke on unity. Over lunch many came and told me that my talk was comprehensive and clear. The evening session involved a poem by William Anderson, author of a book on Dante, *Dante the Maker*. Afterwards I spoke with some of the rank and file. One or two wanted me to preach the Light rather than describe how it works. I distinguished between being evangelical and being descriptive.

The next morning there was an indifferent meditation (Trevelyan relaxing all parts of the body and going into the stillness) and I breakfasted with Bede Griffiths. I discussed the Light with him. I said: "There are two traditions, an Eastern one of Gregory of Nyssa and Dionysius, which is yours, and a Western one of Augustine, Gregory the Great and St Bernard, which is mine. The first is transcendent, the second immanent." He agreed. I said: "Is there anyone else in the Christian tradition who is doing what you're doing, after Thomas Merton?" He said: "No." I said: "Did you think you'd end up like this when you went to India in 1957?" He said, shaking his head: "No." Later Griffiths gave another lecture "in which he repeated that God is behind all difference. He said that transcending dualism, getting behind good and evil, was not monism but non-dualism (*advaita*)." After lunch there was a question-and-answer session, and William Anderson said that my Grand Unified Theory is right. I had several discussions with different people and then drove to Cornwall.

In the practical sanity of Charlestown I asked myself: "What did I achieve at Winchester?" I sorted out the immanent and the transcendent and fixed a scientific theory. I was now identified with Universalism and the Metaphysical Revolution. I said to someone: "If we don't have a revolution in philosophy now, it'll be unchanged for the next 20 years." I was on the side of change. Bede Griffiths told me: "Get beyond all difference and conflict to the unity behind diversity." Which is what my reconciling Universalism does. I wrote: "Syncretism – the doctrinal coming together.

Universalism – coming together at a level behind the doctrine." At 8 a.m. the next morning I realised I had not been fully well during the conference: "Hawked and spat at 8 a.m., and coughed up a long trail of sputum that was filled with blood; a long line of blood." (A few days later Dr Hughes rang me at 11 p.m. to say that my bronchiectasis had flared up again.)

I reviewed the weekend conference:

It was unbalanced. I combined scientists and mystics; Barrow gave a view of cosmology in terms of advanced mathematical equations; Bede Griffiths saw science in terms of mysticism. But then (apart from Liberman's view of the Light as programming the pineal gland) it became unbalanced with two poetic offerings (Trevelyan and William Anderson) and more mysticism (Bede Griffiths) and art (Thetis Blacker) and it needed someone at the end to draw things together. The word 'vision' echoed through the conference, the vision of the Light, and Bede Griffiths confused it all by insisting that everything is imagery except for the Darkness, i.e. everything immanent is imagery in terms of the transcendent. We have to deal with the immanent, that is the point.

I was struck by references to the 'veil' or 'shutter' between rational ego and universal being. Goethe had written, "Open the second shutter so more light can come in." The eye of contemplation is higher than the eye of reason. I was clear that Universalism presents the unity behind all differences – syncretism is merely at the level of outer forms.

I again glimpsed a book that I might write on the Metaphysical Revolution:

Reconciling the immanent and transcendent and covering the various disciplines touched on in my lecture. Part One: overview of reality, how universal being connects with the ultimate reality beyond all personal Gods. Part Two: the differences, a survey of all the disciplines that are being affected by the letting-in of metaphysical reality, including the 'isms'. Part Three: the unity behind and how this renews the European civilization.

A similar three-part scheme (with different content) passed into *The Universe and the Light*.

On Tuesday 14 April I revisited a slightly careworn Colin Wilson with Pam and Paul. I told him about my Winchester lecture and gave him a tape. I did most of the talking. The moors murderer Ian Brady had written to Wilson, and Pam discussed Brady with him at some length, fairly obliquely. When we left Colin said, "I don't know how you think I've got an hour-and-three-quarters to listen to a tape, Nick. I write all day downstairs and then watch television." I said: "Perhaps in your bath."

My lecture was over, but its repercussions dominated my thoughts. After stumbling across the *Diaries* entry for 7 September 1963 which inspired 'The Silence', I had the idea for a new poem, which would be called 'The Second Coming', in which Christ comes down in human form, in a cloud to hide his brightness, to see his world and is appalled at humankind's egocentric pursuit of money. He concludes that man is not ready for his Second Coming. The poem was never written but it would colour my Christ in *Overlord*.[33]

Cosmology and the Theory of Everything – Rupert Sheldrake, Stephen Hawking; my essay 'What is Universalism?'
Then I was back in cosmology and philosophy, and suddenly approaching a Theory of Everything. If the Fire (F) manifests (m) at different intensities (i) according to the receptivity (r) of matter – and positioning of matter, $Fm = i + r$. So $i = Fm – r$. Variability (v) is to do with varying wavelengths (wl) of the Light (or Fire). If Light, L (high frequency) + wle (wavelength of electrons) = v (variability), then $v = L + wle$. "So it comes down to frequencies and wavelengths. Express the whole thing in one beautiful and simple equation." I saw the material world as permeated by a transcendent Reality – the *Tao, sunyata*, Brahman, *Al-Haqq*, Godhead – which is experienced at an immanent level as Light. The Light is universally present everywhere.

At the same time I was working on what would become *Awakening to the Light* (having begun work on my *Diaries* on 8 May). I wrote:

A bracing land-wind tugging at hair and bringing red to the cheeks. At 7.45 a boat came in. Knots of shivering people watched it. Having finished editing the first 100 pages of the *Diaries* (to 1965) [i.e. of *Awakening to the Light*] I watched…. Walked with Ant under a full moon. Pondered whether or not there is a singularity in terms of the Fire.

I answered Ant's questions: "'What's so special about Japan?' I: 'In India, China and Japan you can find the wisdom of the East, people who know that there is something invisible behind the physical reality; whereas in the West that knowledge has died out after the Romantics.' He: 'I don't know what I want to do.' I: 'You'll find it. It's a seed in you, it'll unfold.' He: 'I want to be happy.' I: 'You don't find happiness by seeking it. You find what you're here to do and what you like doing, and happiness is a by-product. That's the wisdom of the East.'"

I thought about the origin and creation of the universe. There was a pre-existing infinite and metaphysical darkness or quantum void with potentials of Light, out of which came one virtual particle or proton. This expanded by inflation in accordance with space-time laws which were (potentially) in the pre-existent quantum vacuum before the beginning. Once the beginning happened, all the particles were interconnected and entangled by Light. There was a unifying superlaw which makes the whole universe necessary and is consistent with quantum mechanics and relativity. I rang Edgard Gunzig in Belgium and he invited me to a conference on 'The Origin and Structure of the Universe' for 40 international physicists in a castle in Belgium. I was tempted to go to sort out the question of singularity and inflation and how galaxies formed out of the dark Fire in transcendent formlessness that manifested into an immanent fifth force, the Light.

However, I already had an understanding of the origin and structure of the universe, and did not need to go to Belgium:

An infinite Fire with transcendent laws created in one 'corner' of infinity a finite universe from the quantum vacuum in which souls could leave unity and take on the differentiation of bodies and tasks and grow. The pre-existing laws of Nature include a law of expansion or inflation, with a mathematical exactness for fine-tuned creation of the planets and stars; a law of microworld and macroworld gravity; three other forces; and various regularities. All this can be expressed in a simple formula, which includes constants for all particles and forces, and explains the hidden variability of the microworld; and the ratio of the mass of the electron to proton; and includes non-local superluminal particles which defy relativity theory, that nothing moves faster than the speed of light. The universe began, Dante said, in an infinitesimal point of light [, a singularity].... The singularity could be of infinite limit. The universe is a giant organism.

Soon after we returned to Essex news came through of the discovery of a wispy cloud, a ripple of matter, "on the edge of the universe", seen from the rocket looking for CBR [cosmic background radiation], cooling after the Big Bang that proved the Big Bang happened. I thought again about a Theory of Everything. I had been to see Norman Wisdom at Harlow, and marvelled at his affecting combination of laughter and sadness as he played the fool, and I wrote:

Laughter and sadness must be a part of the Theory of Everything. The discovery by COBE that there are ripples of matter in the universe, that the Big Bang led to primordial seeds of galaxies, to matter being attracted into stars by gravity.... My work has anticipated this. The CBR (cosmic background radiation) features in my poems as important.

I saw myself as a presenter of order in terms of the metaphysical Fire or Light behind the Big Bang.

I was aware of a conflict between my philosophy, which I defended at the Metaphysical Research Group of philosophers, and my mysticism, which I would soon be teaching at my new mystery school at Coopersale Hall. I had to do two opposite things at the same time. Be in the soul or universal being in Epping, and be in the contemplation-led reason, at the rational level among academics. I could do both but must clearly distinguish reason, contemplation and empiricism. My poetry bridged my soul and rational, social ego and created a oneness between the two: the wordless reception of the soul reflected in words. My Epping centre would be a base for soul and contemplation. Reason would be on the lecture platform.

I thought again about the Origin and Structure of the Universe: "The universe began from an 'infinitesimal point' (Dante), a pinhead, and inflation happened." There *was* an eternal, latent, invisible, metaphysical Fire without beginning and end that manifested into the visible:

Nothingness, the vacuum, before the Big Bang, out of which came a virtual particle that exploded. The Light is the temporal form of Dark Fire which is eternal; compare dark matter. +A (Light) + −A (Darkness) = Zero. Or +A (Nothingness, Void, Darkness) + −A (Light) = Zero. Nothingness as a womb. I think I have all the answers without needing to attend the conference on the Origin and Structure of the Universe [in Belgium], which will be at the materialistic level.

Word of my Winchester presentation and of Universalism had spread. The Scientific and Medical Network held a dining-club dinner at the Hale Clinic's premises, 7 Park Crescent in London, hosted by David Lorimer and Peter Fenwick. Some 25 were invited, rather like the 1890s poets' Rhymers' Club, only emphasising spirituality and science. I chatted with tousle-headed Rupert Sheldrake, who looked like a slightly-inebriated Romantic poet. He had heard about my Winchester presentation of Universalism, and when I spoke of revolution said: "I quite agree, I believe in hurrying it along. Your book is daunting." I said: "To make mystics the centre of history you need evidence." Arthur Ellison, formerly of the Psychic Research Society and friend of Arthur Koestler, came and had a long talk about the Light, knowing about *The Fire and the Stones*, and said he would like to come to Epping. He said: "We construct reality, arrive at our paradigm which perhaps does not correspond with what is out there, and we won't listen to anything else. There's still a lot I don't know. The dead are around like presences but not in space."

Two days later I was refuting the materialistic view of Hawking, who was present at a public debate at Logan Hall, Bedford Way, London, which I attended. A film on Hawking was shown and then Hawking wheeled himself on, a pale figure in his red chair, his head motionless, and made a pre-prepared speech from his voice synthesiser, welcoming the ripple discovery as confirming his no-boundary principle. Part of the film of his book was shown, and then he answered four pre-asked questions: the distribution of galaxies goes on forever; time-travel back in time doesn't work because the quantum fluctuations are too large; according to relativity we began in singularity but according to quantum maths there are no singularities, at least in imaginary time; and COBE has confirmed the inflation of the universe and his no-boundary principle. He was asked, "Do you believe in God or are you a Humanist?" He replied: "Like Einstein I use the term God in an impersonal sense, as an embodiment of the laws of physics or the answer to the question, 'Why does the universe exist?'" Then he wheeled himself off after final applause. It was like being in the presence of Galileo or Newton. (Penrose's final Big Crunch had given him the idea of reversing it to get back to the Big Bang.)

Hawking was a gentle, independent person with a delightful personality and sense of humour, still seeking to explain the universe, excited at the time we live in. But what has he explained? That the Big Bang came out of an infinitesimal point according to relativity, that the laws of physics operate without singularity according to quantum maths and space-time is finite without boundaries; that inflation made the universe infinite as it is curved; that black holes emit radiation; and that the Big Crunch is wrong. He was like an entertainer working an audience for laughs. He raised a laugh by saying that the Pope told him not to investigate the Big Bang as it was Creation.

His was a materialistic view that left out the Light. Two days later I saw Hawking as "a frail Beckett-character in a wheelchair, speculating about the universe, mighty reason in a jamjar." He was trying to prove our futility. Whitehead had remarked: "Scientists who spend their life with the purpose of proving that it is purposeless constitute an interesting subject of study."

I was working on 'What is Universalism?' (the second section of *The Universe and the Light*) and wrote: "A great energy. Worked to 1 a.m. Feel very well. (Brought the Light down this afternoon.)" That same day Kathleen Raine had sent me a leaflet saying that the perennial philosophy has been "the ground of all civilizations, including our own, until the last few hundred years", and that "Reality is always itself". I saw what she was trying to do, and could have retorted: 'The Fire or Light is central to the perennial philosophy in the East and the central idea of civilizations, and is Reality. The Light is always itself.' I had no further contact with Kathleen

Raine, and she died at the age of 95 in July 2003.

I thought about language in relation to the soul:

> Language is of the rational, social ego; the soul is wordless. So poetry is a recollection of soul experience, with contemplative use of language blending with images from the outside world.

I had an hour on the telephone with Edgard Gunzig about the Origin and Structure of the Universe. He laid out what he now knew:

> The discovery of CBR proves that dark matter is there, whose density is unknown. (10^{-6}, where the discovery was made, suggests dark matter.) Galaxies' seeds probably grew from inflation as microscopic seeds inflated to galaxies' seeds. "Everyone is working on this." There is increasing entropy within an increasing expansion. The universe is not a closed sphere as the Smoot and Mather picture showed but an open hyperboloid or plane. (There are three families in geometry: homogeneous sphere, hyperboloid or plane.)... I see an infinite quantum vacuum, open, not closed; instability which is bound to create virtual particles; real particles which create inflation...; small microscopic seeds becoming seeds of galaxies in the macrocosm; and endless expansion of dark matter. No closed universe like a balloon from an infinitesimal point, no Big Bang; just a hot beginning which can create inflation.

Like Bohm, Gunzig had moved away from Dante's initial point and Big Bang. He saw Existence beginning in a vast quantum vacuum, a sea of energy which I maintain was already filled with Fire or Light.[34]

Practical mysticism: mystery school
Mystery school lasting five days

I had been rung up by a Syrian lady. She said she had been reading *The Fire and the Stones*. She said, "I look for meaning, like Gilgamesh." I said: "It's to be found by making a transformational journey from the social, rational ego to the soul or inner being." There was a stunned silence. "No one ever told me that. You are right. My whole life has been searching for meaning."

As I worked on my lecture I had seen the need for a forum in which I could give practical demonstrations of the bringing-down of the Light. I saw that I could turn Coopersale Hall's assembly hall into a mystery school for five afternoons in May and June, and invite 35 to receive the Light on each of the five afternoons. It would be like my sessions with the Hampstead healers. I would do no more than five sessions, but that would be enough to write about practical mysticism in the essays that would form round my Winchester lecture.

I was now preparing to open Coopersale Hall for five days as a mystery school, "a school that guards a mystery, where a mystery is taught in an open and shared way – inner knowledge". I was clear that this inner knowledge, this vision, is needed by Western civilization. Universalism is a philosophy and new movement involving the opening of the soul, and my Epping school would be my "school for self-realisation", which I foresaw in 1966. The mystery school would open people to the Light and send them out to found their own communities of Light. I made it clear to my helpers that there were to be no New-Age dogmas: "There is not going to be a great change in human consciousness." We were renewing European civilization, and eventually our Universalism would go into the [North-] American civilization and become a world-wide movement. I also observed: "Kathleen Raine told me last year she separated her poetic and academic sides, so that no one could criticise her academic side in relation to her poetry. I have chosen to combine them; so that the Fire of my poetry is the centre of my academic side."

The first day of the Foundation of the Light's mystery school took place on Saturday 9 May. In the afternoon I received 42 people and spoke for half an hour, and then held a meditation to bring down the Light. It was a very successful meditation. As the Light came down into me, one from White Eagle Lodge went into the Light straightaway. Another, Susie, was opened very powerfully and had swollen fingers. I answered questions from 4.25 to 5.45. There were only two discordant notes. There was criticism from an intense young man who said I could be a *guru*, but I did not want to be; and there was criticism of one of the helpers who kept her eyes open during the meditation.

The day at Epping had led to further questions about our tradition. I said: "My tradition is that of St Augustine, Dante, Shelley and Eliot and many others; it is of the intellectual vision, which is the soul's union with the Light that opens the heart centre and fills the soul with love so it says 'Aah'. It is from the top down." (In the Tantric Hindu tradition it flows from the base of the spine to the heart, from the bottom up.) Later phone calls established that some had opened to the Light but said nothing. Heather Dobbs said: "Linda says she can read and understand better now, after Saturday." I said: "Remember [St] Hildegard, who could understand the breviary and the *New Testament*?" Heather said: "Yes. It's the same."

On 13 May there was another practical session in Hampstead for the healing group. In fading light at dusk I gave a talk and held a 50-minute meditation. Again the Light came into me. Several opened to the Light. After tea there was a discussion until 10.30. The whole evening was done without a note. I was totally unprepared and just let it come through. One of the healers, Susie, sat glassy-eyed and swollen-fingered (again), having hugely received the Light. One of the group said that the Light comes from "beings" and is a neutral, not a good force but an occult force. I rejected this: "The mystical tradition says it is good and safe." One of my helpers believed that purifying the body allowed the inner light to shine like a pilot light. I saw the inner universal being as a wick of a candle waiting to be lit by an influx of Light from the beyond.

The squabbling over how the Light works disillusioned me. I had got a movement going, and should return to world history and writing, leaving others to spread what I had begun as a movement and indulge in doctrinal differences. The Light is not the self. Rather the self is lit by the Light. We have a candlewick, and it needs to be lit by letting in the Light.

The second day of the Foundation of the Light's mystery school took place at Coopersale Hall on Sunday 17 May: "18 seekers this time; one from Brussels, one from Bristol, several from Wiltshire and Dorset. Susie opened to the Light for the third time in a week and had swollen fingers, as did Heather. Mona was radiant. I healed her painful back and head. Several had slightly painful areas of their bodies and Adrian Cairns (a Quaker Universalist who had attended my Winchester lecture) came. He told Heather, "I came to Coopersale Hall because I've never heard a presentation like Nicholas's before. He just stood up and did it. I was fascinated." He invited me to address a conference of Quakers in Birmingham in April. (Steve Norris, who had just been made Parliamentary Under Secretary for Transport, a Junior Minister, put his head over the gate as I locked up and told me the new Worcester College Provost was Dick Smethurst.)

The general consensus was that I had answered all their questions and that the session was very helpful and useful. Once again most regarded me as a *guru*, which I did not want to be. There was a line of people with problems who would have liked to depend on me if I had allowed them. As it was I had placed myself in the mainstream as the communicator and practical illustrator of an idea central to our culture and civilization.

The next day Coopersale Hall had reverted to being a school, and I talked to David Seaman, the Arsenal goalie. I invited him to open the Coopersale Hall summer fair. He had been named as reserve for the England football team, and we discussed his omission. He said: "I'm disappointed." I told him that he was number–1 under Robson and that he must play so well Taylor could not leave him out. "You believe in yourself, you're determined, so you must do it this season." "I will, I'm disappointed, but I must get on with it and make sure he can't leave me out." "The selection is wrong." "It is," he said, "yes."[35] It seemed perfectly natural to relate to the seekers on Sunday and Seaman on Monday in terms of what mattered most to them and carry them forward. I saw this as unitive living: to help all in so far as one is able to help.

Philosophy: Universalism

Forthcoming works, poem on Bohm, 'Ode: Spider's Web: Our Local Universe in an Infinite Whole'

My philosophy had progressed. The next day I "sketched the beginning of 'What is Universalism?', an essay" – the second third of *The Universe and the Light*, the book Michael Mann had asked me to get ready as soon as possible.

I was still combing my *Diaries* for what would become *Awakening to the Light*. Looking back at the early years of these *Diaries*, I was struck by how many advances in thought succeeded visits to the dentist and routine outings:

> I think I have captured the way the creative life works. One has to be alone and apart from one's contemporaries to produce such a body of work. One has to be unknown as well; otherwise one's life is an endless procession of meetings with people with names, and what one thought of them, not Yeatsian "remaking of self". I could now become a talker, holding court at Coopersale Hall every Sunday or every other Sunday, and answering questions every Monday evening like David Bohm…. But I am fundamentally a writer and poet who has created a new metaphysical being in myself by my existential action and re-formations of attitudes over the years.

I carried on with this line of thought in Cornwall, where I noted "small purple-violet flowers in the ivy on the port wall, singing birds. Saw it all with new eyes, and rejoiced…. The red-hot pokers are out." I wrote: "I played it long…. I have aimed at the highest: not to amuse or entertain, but to reflect the truth in all its guises. I have stuck to my task, despite distractions. Like Anthony completing a 48-mile walk in just under 20 hours, I have spent a long day trudging the Mystic Way to present eternity to mankind."

I was still collecting and revising my poetic works: "In the late afternoon and evening typed two-thirds of 'Spider's Web', my ode on Bohm and Gunzig" – 'Ode: Spider's Web: Our Local Universe in an Infinite Whole' which I had drafted the previous year, after my visit to Bohm. "My lyrics are numerous, I dash off two or three at a time with perfect rhyme. But the weightier poems get to the heart of the Age. Like… a Holbein, I paint the great men of our Age, showing the essence of what they stand for."

At the same time I continued to edit my *Diaries*: my Coleridgean *Literaria Biographia*, my Yeatsian *Autobiographies*, my Kafkaesque *Diaries* which move from a sceptical to a metaphysical position through my Journey into illumination and enlightenment, into wisdom and understanding. I saw that what distinguishes these *Diaries* from other works is their inwardness, their search within which eventually goes through to the Light.

I spent all one morning working on my *Diaries*, and from nowhere "decided to do a trilogy on the Mystic Way: three approaches to illumination: an awakening and purgation among the Sufis, and illumination [which would become *The Tree of Knowledge*]; Zabov's illumination as the Eternicide becomes an Eternity-preserver [which would become *The Soul-Destroyer*, later retitled *The Eternicide*]; and the lost Englishman ending up as a cosmologist after last being seen in Ghadames." (This would become *The Lost Englishman* but with a changed theme.) Looking back, I am astonished at the clarity of the ideas I received at this time, though the three novellas of the trilogy would evolve to focus on mind, body and spirit. My Winchester lecture seemed to have stimulated my inspiration.

I now began to recast my Winchester lecture for *The Universe and the Light*. Ann and I ate at the Rashleigh Inn, Polkerris, overlooking the sea. I returned and drafted part of the book's outline with bits of the second essay. I scribbled as it came through from the beyond. That night I went for a late-night walk and it hit me midway on the harbour wall as I walked back: I should reverse the sections on the new man and the new view of the universe in my second essay and that would be better. I took five deep breaths and was yawning, but an energy came through from the beyond:

> By 12.30 a.m.... I had written out a good part of the second essay, almost effortlessly; with a great flow from the beyond.... All week I have been connected to a current of thought. I put pen to paper and the thought flows and I have a paragraph. A whole essay has more or less been written in haste, chunks at a time; not in the order in which they will appear. Just sections I can see.[36]

Practical mysticism: end of mystery school

I returned to Essex to find the helpers squabbling about the Light. Heather Dobbs said that one of the helpers was too body-centred: "Yoga is getting up from the body. It is not the spiritual way down." I had said that the Light "must be from above down; it's dangerous if it's from the bottom up". The body-centred helper defended her earth-centredness and said that some of her invitees wanted me to demonstrate love to them. Again they were trying to impose on me the role and image of a *guru* just as Kathleen Raine tried to impose on me the role and image of a historian. My answer was: "The truth is, the psychic leads up to the spiritual, and the spiritual is superior to the psychic." Meanwhile a Colombian woman who had attended one of the mystery school's days at Coopersale Hall arrived at Heather's house in a desperate state. Following experience of Sahaja Yoga she had had rushings and tingling vibrations in her head and heart. I went round to Heather's and gave her healing – it all came out in a rush and she was "a new person" and slowly the tingling went. It was like casting out a devil. I said: "You've had the operation, now the convalescence."

However, four days later on a Friday she hitchhiked from Heather's house to Coopersale Hall and appeared in school in trance to announce to Mrs. Best, the Head, "Nicholas is the Messiah." I was called. When I arrived she prostrated herself at my feet with wild eyes, called me "Father" and said: "You are the infinite one on earth, Jesus Christ. Harmony. You are to write an important book by 1997. You must neutralise Saddam Hussein's power by 1997. *The Fire and the Stones* is the Bible of modern times, in our modern time. Universalism can go ahead. Nicholas is a new vibration." I wondered if she was on Colombian cocaine. She went outside and rolled on the lawn. Heather had arrived. She and I took a wrist each and led her firmly to Heather's car and Heather drove her away. She was socially disorientated with energy rushing about in her head. She was admitted to a mental hospital the next day. I felt sad. She was the victim of an episode of half-raised Kundalini (from the bottom up) within Sahaja Yoga. I now felt the mystery school should be outside Coopersale Hall, and my appetite to continue it had been diminished.

The Oaklands summer fair was opened by Nick Berry, an actor in *Eastenders* and *Heartbeat* and singer. He arrived late during the country dancing, and he brought another Eastender, Sid Owen, with him. They wore blue denim suits and several thought they were intruding hooligans. They opened the fair on the field. I stood before the caravan and spoke about the two of them. In the evening we went to dinner with Tony Little and his wife at Haylands, the 1820s Headmaster's house at Chigwell. We drank Pimm's in the front room with local Heads, and ate in the dining-room overlooking the rose-garden at the back.

The next day was the third day of the Foundation of the Light at Coopersale Hall. Just under 20 came. I greeted everyone and welcomed everyone officially. I delegated the morning session and went home to do some work. I returned in the afternoon for my meditation. I included the earth, and the universe; love, knowledge, understanding, and wisdom and healing. Many were opened up. Susie and Mona had swollen fingers. I spoke at length (and was taped) about Universalism: I said: "At the practical level it's a Mystic Revival. At the theoretical level it's a Metaphysical Revolution." I returned home to finish the second version of 'What is Universalism?'

From feedback it seemed that only about 20 of all who had come to the mystery school's days so far were "the right people". I had a discussion with Heather Dobbs about the guidelines of the Foundation of the Light, which, we agreed, are in the last paragraph of *The Fire and the Stones*: knowing the Light at the personal level (which we did in the meditation); understanding the Metaphysical Revolution at the theoretical level (which I did at Winchester and in *A Metaphysical's Way of Fire,* and in some of the talks); and understanding the Universalist common Fire or Light for all mankind between all religions (which I did after the meditation, in our question-and-answer session). We agreed that those who wanted a 'Foundation of the Earth' with barefootery to teach contact with Nature and make animal noises to feel one with the animal world should go away and found a 'Foundation of the Earth' and do their own thing.

The next day I felt at one with the universe. It was a glorious sunny day, and a woodpecker tapped in the elm; sudden staccato knockings, very rapid, drifting through the open, summery window. The sunlight on my hanging crystal flashed red, then green, then orange. A squirrel sat on the iron railings, then scampered across the field. I felt my oneness with Nature and the sun.

I was aware of my long-term task. I had finished work for the accountant in preparation for more work on Universalism. I had had the idea for an essay, 'The Rise and Fall of Civilizations', which would become *The Rise and Fall of Civilizations.* I reflected:

> June 13. I have turned my back on the possibility of a public life for a quiet, private life which is the only way to reach truth. Through my poems and writings and *Diaries* I may reach an international audience but my way is the way of the backwater (like Charlestown) or the leafy lane (like Coopersale Hall): of obscurity.

I added: "I lived in the Arab and Eastern cultures so that I could develop a Universalist vision, which is needed in our time."

The fourth day of the Foundation of the Light mystery school took place: "June 14. Another gathering at Coopersale Hall, on a hot day. A few seekers only, including Steve (HIV positive), who lay on a mat, having come from hospital for the day, and J, who is in a wheelchair, having thrown herself under a train and snapped her spinal cord.... (Steve broke down at the beginning of the meditation.)" The lady in the wheelchair had to return to her car, and I had to help lift her wheelchair over the low fence. Syrian Mona said: "Your voice is from the heart; it has vibrations."

I now had a day pursuing philosophy rather than practical mysticism. The Metaphysical Research Group of philosophers met at David Lorimer's flint-and-brick house at Alresford, near the thatched village of East Stratton, up a lane, near a cricket field, amid wheatfields and sheep grazing: a house, guinea-fowl, peacocks screaming and a turkey. Inside were many books, and pictures on the wall of Samuel Johnson, Schweitzer, Whitehead, Jung and others. After coffee we sat round on wooden chairs and discussed Willis

Harman's *A Re-examination of the Metaphysical Foundation of Modern Science*. I distinguished the rational from the contemplative approach and swiped jokingly at Geoffrey Read. In the afternoon after a buffet lunch (during which several sought me out about my books), we sat on the lawn in the sun, like those pictured breakfasting with Rupert Brooke and philosophised. I defended the Fire and the Light during a golden afternoon amongst screaming peacocks.

I returned with a slipped disc, initially caused by lifting the suicidal lady's wheelchair. I went to an osteopath in Buckhurst Hill, Robin Woodleigh, an ex-Coopersale Hall parent, who greeted me warmly. He lay me on his ironing-board of a table and arranged my arms and legs and massaged my back and then wrenched down and as I yelled said excitedly, "Ah, did you hear the click? One side's in. Now the other side." The other side was just as painful but I did not hear the click. He said: "The prolapse is in now." He ended by giving me the cup his son had won at Coopersale Hall to hold, and I left his room carrying the cup. I said to the next patient, "This is for being brave." He laughed. I noted my gift for spreading laughter along with wisdom: "I spread the Light but am at heart a clown, a jester, a court-fool."[37] (Laughter has always been an attribute of enlightenment: hence the figurines of the laughing Buddha.)

Canon Peter Spink

Chigwell's Speech Day began with a service in the parish church, which I attended along with many other parents after addressing 60 new parents at Coopersale Hall. The guest speaker was none other than Canon Peter Spink, on whose activities I had based *Beauty and Angelhood*. I sat near the door and (rising and sitting with difficulty because of my slipped disc) heard Peter Spink preach. The charismatic, inspirational young man had aged and now wore spectacles, but he still got across the message that 'God is Light' – compare Blake – and 'God is nearer to you than your breath', and put the boys into silence so that they could experience this practically. The whole of Chigwell School sat looking for the Light. Spink then spoke of the need to reject false images of God, including the one that excludes other religions.

Outside in the churchyard, near the door furthest from the road, I went and shook his hand and reminded him: "I was at St Peter's, Woking when you had your think-in, and before that was at Kent House." I talked of Happold and Teilhard de Chardin. I told him I now had two schools and had had two books published, one that includes the history of the mystical tradition, and had opened one school as a centre for Universalism to all mankind. He listened and said, "Send me your literature," and asked me to write my address on the back of his service booklet. Then he needed to get away and we walked side by side without speaking as he headed for the road. Later the school chaplain told me, over tea on the lawn, that Spink had described how he remembered me.

The next day was the last of the five days of the Foundation of the Light's mystery school at Coopersale Hall. I was short of sleep, having attended the Chigwell ball with Matthew. (We sat with Carolyn Ladd, Mephistophilis in the school's *Dr Faustus*.) Despite having a slipped disc I had danced from 11 p.m. to 2 a.m., and did not sleep until 3. I was still in some discomfort. Some people drove from as far as Littlehampton and Lincolnshire. In the morning I raised the possibilities ahead, now that we had got to the end of a cycle: meditation and study of Universalism, mysticism and metaphysics. After lunch I held a meditation in heat among 25 or 30 people, in which I went back from the rational, social ego to the soul, opened to the Light, brought down its powers of wisdom, understanding, guidance and healing to all the group, help for financial problems and creative energies and finally help for the planet.

After tea there was a heated debate as to what should happen next and I was aware of the doctrinal divide between some of the helpers' followers and mine. Anthea Courtenay (who had attended all sessions) said: "I don't want to be part of a Universalist movement, it'll happen anyway." I talked about movements and how to change things in the universities, what strategies have to be used and how movements in thought happen and Anthea was isolated. I said I stood for a three-pronged approach (or three-legged stool): a mystic revival, which the meditation was doing; a Metaphysical Revolution to speed a change in outlook; and Universalism, the common essence of all religion. A healer, Malcolm Southwood, declared that one of the helpers was "not of Light level". The crippled woman who had asked me to lift her wheelchair and slipped my disc told me: "Your 'top down' jars. The Light comes from the bottom up; the mind in your feet, earthy." She was back in the occult and I was relieved to have got to the end. I agreed with Mona that three-quarters of our clientele were the wrong people. I noted that from the five days we had raised £1,500 for the Foundation of the Light.

I was disillusioned with the outlook of some of our clientele. The idea that revolutions are unnecessary because it is all happening anyway from below was a nice thought but was not necessarily true. I had tried to share a fundamental perception: "The One is everywhere, behind Nature and consciousness. It covers all four levels (divine, spiritual, human, psychological) and all faculties: reason, emotions, intuition, instinct, the concrete. All is within this unity." And the Light of the One pervades our universal being. Three-quarters of our clientele still seemed not to get this. I had tried to teach them how to be a lighthouse. I reflected: "I have a poem 'Lighthouse' to write: the Foundation of the Light in terms of Smeaton's

Tower at Plymouth."

That same evening I resolved to terminate the activities of the Foundation of the Light for a while and concentrate on writing that would become *The Universe and the Light*. That would end the doctrinal disputes about the interpretation of the Light for the time being. I would be free to reopen on my own as a Metaphysical Centre if I wished.[38]

Philosophy: The Universe and the Light, *reductionism and Form from Movement Theory*

As if the universe had wanted me to move on, the next day I received an invitation to participate in a conference on 'Reductionism' at Cambridge, and to write a paper for it. (This would become the final third of *The Universe and the Light*, and would deal with the philosophy of science.) I wondered if I owed my invitation to John Barrow, a fellow speaker at Winchester who was to be a speaker at Jesus, Cambridge. I would be able to meet some of the key scientists of our time, including Roger Penrose. My fascination with science had begun with EEGs and DNA and had now spread to the universe. It was interesting to know that if one speaks at Winchester, one is 'heard' in Cambridge. I saw how it works in academic life and how a Metaphysical Revolution could be launched at Cambridge.

I worked on *The Universe and the Light* through many distractions. We went to the House of Lords for a reception in the Cholmondeley Room as the guest of David Thompson, husband of one of the Oaklands staff, who made a speech on housing for the disabled from his wheelchair after speeches by Lord Swinfen and Nicholas Scott MP. There was a letter from Geoffrey Read of the philosophers, who told me he had had an exchange about me at the end of a lecture given by Colin Wilson (which Read described as amateurish reflections with a marvellously professional delivery). He had raised me and my talk of throwing bricks through logical positivists' windows (a joke on my part about what the Metaphysical Revolution would do), and Wilson had said of me, "Nick is obsessed with the Fire or Light." I replied to Read, "So were Heracleitus and Plato, and many other cultural leaders of the past." Read mentioned holism. I wrote of "my Light-based brand of holism, Universalism. Holism has no Fire or Light." Read had also heard about me from Nona Coxhead: "I'm in her book, *The Relevance of Bliss*. I remember her telling me about a young man who had had Light experiences for two months. Now I've met him. It's you."

I was in a very hectic time. There was an Oaklands Sports Day in which the mothers' race was won by a Mrs. Bird who was a huge distance ahead of the rest of the field. I said to her, "You've run before." She said: "I was with the British relay team in the Los Angeles Olympics." I said: "If I'd known, I would have given you a handicap. You would have started outside the field." The Coopersale Hall summer fayre was opened by David Seaman. I rang salaries through to BACS and attended a reception at Bancroft's School followed by their prize-giving.

In the middle of this activity I focused on Hegel, who was more relevant to my thinking than I had realised. To him, as to me, reality can only be understood as a totality, and Being is contrasted with Nothingness as in Sartre's book, his synthesis implying Becoming. I see Being as contrasted with Non-Being (which has manifested from Nothingness) and producing Existence or Becoming.

I write a paper, 'Against Reductionism', for a Cambridge conference
A representative from Jesus College, Cambridge rang to discuss my paper for the conference on 'Reductionism'. Reductionism is "the principle of analysing complex things into simple constituents" (*Concise Oxford Dictionary*), making the complex simple, the scientific method followed by Hawking and many other scientific materialists. I relished the prospect of having a Cambridge platform for the Metaphysical Revolution. I confirmed that I would produce a 10-page paper "saying that holism is spatial, whereas Universalism is metaphysical and that Universalism, not holism, is therefore the true antithesis of reductionism in biology and the physical sciences". I was pleased to have the opportunity of writing the third essay in *The Universe and the Light*.

I decided on the title of *The Universe and the Light* on 1 July and provisionally had the subtitle, *Essays on the Philosophy of Universalism*. Later the subtitle was extended to: *Essays on the Philosophy of Universalism and the Metaphysical Revolution*. Later still, at the publisher's request, another subtitle crept in above it: *A New View of the Universe and Reality and of Science and Philosophy*.

While all this was going on, I had rung David Bohm and spoken to his wife. He was diagnosed as having had a heart attack on his return from Prague. He thought it was a chest infection, but he was kept in hospital and everything had been cancelled. His wife said: "Thank you for ringing, Nicholas. I'll tell him tomorrow." To cheer him up, I said: "Tell him his paper of January 1952 ['A Suggested Interpretation of the Quantum Theory of "Hidden" Variables'] is crucial. I've mentioned it in an essay I've written, and I shall mention it in a paper for the conference on reductionism at Cambridge."

I found myself talking about the parlous state of our culture. While I worked on *The Universe and the Light* I was invited to the home of a local Head and found myself sitting next to the husband of the Head of Braeside, who had run a British Council summer school for 24 years in Wales. He complained at how élitist Tomlin and Eliot were, and disparaged literary theory. He said: "The young want to know what's happened in the last 25 years, not the 18th century." I told him I objected to the secular literature of our time, which neglected the metaphysical. I said: "The Augean stables need clearing out. And there is great filth among them." I would take up this theme in *The One and the Many*.

Someone phoning from Russia made another attempt to contact me. After the Coopersale Hall swimming gala, at which I made announcements on the PA system, I was told there had been two calls from Moscow, one to each school: "Moscow calling, Moscow calling. Hagger. Moscow. Hagger." As the voice spoke no other English, it was difficult to know why it wanted me; whether I was being offered the meeting with Yeltsin for which I had asked.

There was another moment of synchronicity. At the Oaklands Open Evening (after I had been on the microphone for the Oaklands swimming gala at which a line of sitting girls screamed "Reds, Reds, Reds") I met a parent who was a British Midland pilot, who had flown with Nadia. The next day Nadia rang to say she was selling her flat and buying another one in Colinton, just outside Edinburgh. "It has a river (Dingley Dell) with ducks, a church and a pub."

I was approaching the end of my work on *The Universe and the Light*. I saw that besides being a revolutionary work that establishes metaphysics *The Fire and the Stones* had come up with a new and original conception, "that reality can be contacted behind the reason". I was "very close to understanding how the universe came to be, having finished *The Universe and the Light*". I was sure that "Universalism... will be the new orthodoxy of the North-American civilization, and a stage in the European civilization".

On the day Oaklands broke up I found a dormouse by my front door, shivering and quaking. There was a celebration of Steve Norris's election victory in Coopersale Hall's wooden panelled assembly hall in the course of which I drew his attention to an unwanted road that would bring noise to Charlestown in Cornwall: "Do you want to save £24 million and make the Government popular? The locals don't want it, it's a road to nowhere." He agreed and went off to make a phone call. He recommended the road should be scrapped, and it was.

I finished proof-reading the first two-thirds *The Universe and the Light* and drove to Shaftesbury in Dorset and handed an early copy to Michael Mann. We had a three-course lunch in the pub across the car park. Michael wore a blue-and-white shirt and spotted yellow tie. On the way down I had switched on the car radio and found myself listening to Sir Laurens van der Post describing a journey in Malawi, and a letter from him was waiting for me when I returned (another example of synchronicity that hinted at a hidden pattern).

I had written:

Reductionism: it is natural to go for the smaller (e.g. in genetics and medicine) but... the whole theory of everything must include everything, including the view of the universe as organic... and therefore the hidden reality that is behind the uncertainty principle, the cosmological constant and order and mass.... The whole vision includes mysticism and metaphysics.... There can be no materialistic Grand Unified Theory.

I now turned to my paper on reductionism. I dashed off a draft on a day when "flying ants hatched everywhere and the heat rose" and there was "a toad in our porch". The next day I typed up the draft and then drove to Cornwall through foggy rain. The following day I settled to my Cambridge paper in the Harbour-master's House, reading bits of metaphysics in the Charlestown front room, piles of books on the carpet at my feet, the three-seat sofa covered in papers and me sitting in the middle working from ten books at once and making notes, jotting on lined paper. At the end of my drafting the bank manager rang with a horrific figure-problem, and the next day I had constant interruptions from the accounting assistant and the phone. Practising philosophy today requires intense concentration in the middle of distraction. Despite the disturbances I was able to draw a distinction between the whole and every possible concept – the all, which is multi-level – and grounded holism and the metaphysical view.

In my Cambridge paper I distinguished "a 'within-Nature' organising principle and a 'beyond-Nature' organising force". My paper advanced my thinking. I saw reductionism as being within physicalist holism, which is in turn within non-physicalist, metaphysical Universalism. Besides distinguishing holism and Universalism, I introduced metaphysics from rational, intuitive and empirical positions. The next day I typed up 10 points for a metaphysical science and therefore a Metaphysical Revolution.

We toured the English China Clay works, starting at Wheel Martyn museum, and I took notes on many technical details, including how the Cornish beam engine worked by compressed air. After lunch at the Carlyon Bay Hotel for Ann's birthday I reflected:

I used to think that I would state the meaning of life.... I did locate the meaning of life in relation to the Light, and now I state the universe in terms of... Einstein, Whitehead and others. I was on the right lines in the 1950s, and have arrived at what I should be doing now.... I have written little poetry for the last 12 months because, after drafting my Bohm poem [, 'Ode: Spider's Web: Our Local Universe in an Infinite Whole'], I felt the need to find out what the current knowledge is about the universe; and *The Universe and the Light* shows my findings. It is worth sacrificing poetry for my Winchester lecture and my Cambridge paper as I shall have a total knowledge.

That night there was a "moon, not full, and a wide causeway of moonlight across the sea to Polkerris. Stars. A calm sea. A calm in me as I tackle the next stage of my Cambridge paper: editing and cutting to make room for the additions I have done today." The next day I "pasted and stuck bits together..., putting in the insertions written since I have been down.... I now need to edit. I have produced and added, and will now reduce." That night I "went to the bathroom, returned to the darkened bedroom and, standing, was filled with Light: oval and shining.... As I 'looked' a surge of power swept into my back, filling my fingers and body."

The next day was fine and I sunbathed while Anthony jumped into the harbour with his friends. The following day I "sunbathed and finished my Cambridge paper, except for a final read-through".

The next Sunday, after lunch at the Charlestown Rashleigh, I returned to Essex to put my Cambridge paper on computer. I rang Sir Laurens van der Post to tell him about it. He said affectionately, "Hello dear boy, nice to hear you." He said he would like to read my paper. The impression he gave was of having unlimited time for me. It took a couple of days to put the text on computer, and I printed out copies at Prontaprint, Barking. I posted my paper to Cambridge and drove to Shaftesbury to deliver a copy to Element. I had an hour's meeting with Michael Mann who (tall in a sports jacket, leather pads on his elbows, smoking) said he wanted endorsements: from Bohm, Penrose and van der Post. Hawking was mentioned, for an adverse reaction, and Gunzig.

Back in Cornwall I sensed Oneness: "Wheeling gulls. Bees, butterflies. And a strong sense that everything's a whole. Every species has its part to play within the metaphysical whole." The next day I wrote: "A day of sun. Dozed. Can't stay awake in the evening. Then the brightness of the stars. Surprised by beauty." I took issue with Karl Popper, whose 'falsifiability principle' – "if it can't be falsified by the reason it isn't science" – opposed Wittgenstein's 'verifiability principle' (that a statement is only meaningful if it is empirically verifiable or tautological in the sense of 'necessarily true', and that metaphysical statements are meaningless). I wrote: "My principle is a 'trespasser principle'": reason trespasses if it attempts to verify or falsify – pronounce on – metaphysical matters whose origin lies behind the reason. The next day I had a strong sense of the physical world as I walked "among the rock pools. Bladderwrack, sea anemones, limpets, strange seaweeds, and a tide coming in. Reality – physical reality." But the following morning I woke "with the phrase 'of Being' in mind – to go in after 'metaphysical totality'. The Universal Mind has considered my [text in sleep] and has added those two words, which I have put in. 'Man is a being within a metaphysical totality of hierarchical Being.'"

I had to return to Essex again to catch up with school administration and letters. On 7 August on my way back to Cornwall I met Michael Mann in Dorset from 3.15 to 5. *The Universe and the Light* was now complete save for the comments. I wrote: "Mann... feels I have an account of a Journey, which I should tell.... The Light should be central: from scepticism to a metaphysical outlook." So was born the idea of writing *A Mystic Way*, and in due course *My Double Life*.

Back in Cornwall again I dipped into van der Post's books, which I had brought back with me, and read that Ingaret Gifford, who was so friendly towards me when I visited van der Post, introduced him to Jung, urged him to go off on his exploring journeys and edited his works. I saw him as a writer of autobiographical adventure and thought him like Marlow in Conrad's *Heart of Darkness*. He drew heavily on the bushmen's sayings, which are evocative: "The story is like the wind, it comes from a far-off place and we feel it." Van der Post was a T.E. Lawrence of our time. Old enough to remember the outbreak of the Great War, he did a Rider Haggard in the Kalahari, discovered through exploration the original man and his mystic powers and brought news of him back to civilization. Round the Kalahari were SWAPO in what is now Namibia. His interest in a lost world of pre-history had done much to stimulate interest in the pre-civiliza-tional.[39]

Conference on reductionism
On 1 September I went up to Cambridge for the 'Conference on Reductionism'. I arrived at Jesus College by 4.30 and was installed in a 200-year-old building (staircase 5, room 6), where I looked out at battlements. There was a reception in the 12th-century convent cloisters, the oldest insti-tutional building in Cambridge. I spoke with a Jesus Fellow, Michael Sofroniew, then William Anderson, who was a fellow-speaker with me in Winchester and had hardly any voice. I spotted Roger Penrose, a small, dark-haired pleasant fellow in a red jacket, and introduced myself.

At dinner I sat next to Sofroniew, who said: "We are very near a mecha-nistic view of consciousness. Without the brain there is no consciousness, and without consciousness there is no mind. We have to be more reduc-tionist to understand the mechanisms. Reductionism has done great things, to criticise it is to pee on a bush. There is no evidence for anything else." We climbed up stairs to the lecture room. We heard the elderly, thinnish and besuited Freeman Dyson (the eminent space researcher who had lived below Wittgenstein in Cambridge in the 1940s) on the scientist as rebel. He answered the many questions with dry one-liners. David Lorimer recorded his talk with earphones on. Mary Midgley sat behind me. I came away from Dyson's lecture with Roger Penrose, who was still in a red jacket.[40]

Roger Penrose, Mary Midgley, John Barrow, Freeman Dyson
As we walked I began a conversation about the universe with Penrose. To me he was a legendary figure, a mathematical physicist who had made huge contributions to general relativity and cosmology. In 1965 he had proved that singularities such as black holes could be formed from the gravitational collapse of dying stars, work extended by Hawking, and was therefore an authority on the singularity from which came the Big Bang. We headed for the bar, chatting about metaphysics. He told me: "There's room for a non-local hidden variability, but not a local one." On Einstein, who had been attacked by Dyson for spending his last 20 years in reductionist equations, forgetting about the world of Nature which gave him his relativity theory, Penrose remarked to me: "It's odd that Einstein and Oppenheimer never met." (Oppenheimer and Sneider took black holes from Einstein's equation.) He said: "They must have met, it's odd they never discussed it."

The bar was full of noisy undergraduates on a bar-football machine, and Penrose excused himself to go and work. I said I was going to look for a telephone, he said he would come too, so we went in search of one and got totally lost, talking of Gunzig. In the end Jeremy Butterfield, a Fellow of Jesus, took us to his room which had a telephone, and showed me how to lock the door and went. Penrose went first and after a long time worked out the fact that he had to dial 9 to get an outside line. He came out and left me to it. I sat in a room with posters of Einstein on the walls and books on quantum mechanics and knowledge and mounds of exam papers on the bed and on the floor, and made my calls to Ann and Matthew. Then I found my way back to staircase 5. Midnight struck, on the college clock, time intruding on eternity, sending a medieval message into our monastic rooms. I wrote a poem, 'Midnight in Jesus College, Cambridge'.

The next morning I woke at 8.40 (having gone back to sleep after the alarm) and had to rush to catch breakfast, which finished at 9. I sat near Penrose for a lecture by Patricia Churchland on a reductionist view of the neurobiology of the mind. During coffee I spoke with David Lorimer, then returned to my seat for a lecture by William Clocksin. Penrose then moved up to sit next to me. After Clocksin's reductionist talk I engaged Penrose on his book on computers, on Gödel and on the 37 scientists he was replying to. I walked to lunch with him and sat with him. He was hook-nosed and intent-eyed with a faint smile; very clubbable, very easy to talk to, very approachable, not stuck up in any way.

I asked him about the singularity he had brilliantly calculated. He agreed with Gunzig that the universe began simultaneously across a surface and not from one point. He agreed that Smoot and Mather's discovery of cosmic microwave background radiation does not provide evidence for a Big Crunch: "You can't tell either way." He agreed a Theory of Everything must include consciousness, love and prayer, absolutely everything. He gave me an account of inflation: of the Weyl curvature hypothesis in which past and future are necessary. He said the Big Bang is very important; that Bohm was wrong to marginalise it, it is central. The expanding universe is explained by it. I asked him: "How, when you look in opposite directions, does the universe obey the same laws, for example of temperature?" He thought and suggested there *is* something real behind physics. I ended up asking if he would like a copy of *The Fire and the Stones* and suggesting we should collaborate on a cross-disciplinary study on the unification of all disciplines. I asked him Hawking's position. He said, "I don't know Hawking's position. I think he disagrees. I have difficulty talking to Hawking. You have to wait for him to reply and lose the flow. I spoke with him five years ago, in conjunction with others, but I haven't spoken to him properly for ten years. He allows speculation to be passed off as scientific fact."

On the Grand Unified Theory he said: "They're nowhere near it. When it comes, yes you are right, it will be simple, but only from the viewpoint of understanding it. When you don't understand it, it appears complicated, like relativity." Saying the theory may be nearer than he thinks I suggested: "Perhaps you should walk across the road and feel elated" (a reference to his walk in the 1960s which led to his understanding "the trapped surface" while in mid-road, then forgetting it, and then remembering it later when investigating his elation). Penrose laughed. I asked: "Shouldn't you make a statement of the whole position to date?" He said: "I don't know enough." Then he headed off to his room.

Penrose talked on maths that afternoon and said that consciousness is non-local, meaning that the answer to the question 'Where is consciousness?' is 'Somewhere other'. Afterwards I walked with him to tea and met Mary Midgley, who was very pro- what I stand for. We returned for Margaret Boden's talk on artificial intelligence (which contradicts Penrose's book) and then I handed my books and *The Universe and the Light* to Penrose, who left to take them back to his room. ("What time's dinner?" "7.30." "Oh, I've time to go back to my room.") I went to my car and saw David Lorimer running in a singlet and shorts. He stopped and chatted and then ran off into Cambridge. I had dinner in the hall with David Lorimer – we talked about Charlotte Waterlow – and Hao Wang, who had criticised Penrose over Gödel. There was then a lecture on psychiatry by Dr Fulford.

The next morning I heard Michael Sofroniew on the Neural Basis of Consciousness and Martin Davies on Neuroscience; and then Gregory

411

Chaitin on Randomness and Arithmetic, and Hao Wang on Algorithmism and Physicalism. I asked a question after Sofroniew's talk. I lunched with Butterfield, the don, and Penrose, and talked about Whitehead and the need for a more metaphysical philosophy at Cambridge. I teased Butterfield; he told me he would be putting up a poster of "Hume" on his wall, and I said, "You mean, of course, T.E. Hulme?" Afterwards I walked in the fields. In the afternoon tea-break I tackled Tim Smiley, Professor of Logic, about doing a critique of the premises of reductionism, which I felt I should do. My Zabov was such a reductionist. In the last session of the afternoon there was a dispute between Wang and Penrose, which I had fuelled on both sides. During supper Geoffrey Read (who was at a nearby, but quite different conference) turned up in hall.

Then Mary Midgley spoke, on 'Reductionist Megalomania', reading out adverse quotations on Atkins, being confrontational and lively and funny, debunking reductionism. She was attacked by John Cornwell, the convener, who perhaps wanted reductionism affirmed. Afterwards I talked with Mary Midgley. She asked: "Was he drunk?" I talked with Sofroniew, and Sofroniew said he was really studying Alzheimer's disease. I told him: "Use what you're doing for other people and don't have any truck with Churchland's philosophy." He said: "That's what I'm going to do." I said to Sofroniew: "'There are more things on heaven and earth/Than are dreamt of in your philosophy.'" He said: "I'll go along with the divine." In the evening I sat with Freeman Dyson.

The next morning I "woke at 7.40, then the fire-alarm went off on our staircase. All six of us gathered downstairs. Freeman Dyson put his head out of the top-floor window. I called, "Quick, get a blanket," and mimed a blanket for him to jump. He grinned. I called up: "This is called 'Disturbing the Universe'." (He had written *Disturbing the Universe*.) Again he grinned. After breakfast Lorimer and Anderson went off to the Fitzwilliam to look at art as a counter-balance to neurons; largely for effect, as a political statement. I talked to Phil Alport about CERN. He told me he sat in a hole watching a screen and occasionally had data meetings one week a month.

Penrose came and sat next to me again, and after a rambling um-and-er talk by Oliver Sacks Penrose said he was very interested in *The Universe and the Light* and asked if he could hang onto it and read more. I told him what I was about – that it was an Eliot view, as it were, reconciling the disciplines – and I said I was doing a Coleridge, reconciling physics and metaphysics. I spent the tea break telling Penrose about the history theory (until Cornwell took him away), and then heard Peter Atkins on 'The Limitless Power of Science', in which he described his atheistic materialistic view of the world "as a dung-heap". I said to Mary Midgley at the end, "'May God us keep/From single vision and Newton's sleep.'" Cornwell attacked Atkins for his fundamentalism. Science and mysticism happily co-exist in Capra and Zukav, but science and religion are enemies in Atkins whose reductionism simplified and unified (in Atkins's case by eliminating). I lunched with John Barrow, who was sitting on his own in a multi-coloured shirt a whole table away from the nearest person. He still affirmed inflation and did not see Penrose's 'ground-state' Weyl hypothesis as being necessary. "You can't observe or measure it." He told me, "I will explain why theories of everything don't have to include everything." He said he had a fellowship which saves him from working for a year, so he could do theoretical research in astrophysics. He had visited the Pope and he had been in Japan with Hawking but they did not communicate.

I sat back and asked myself: "How has this conflict of ideas affected my own view?" The answer was, "Not at all." I was in the position of Coleridge, reconciling physics and metaphysics. I had charted my way, and must continue it through English literature. Barrow gave a brilliant talk about the universe, why it has to be so large (because it took life 10 billion years to arrive) and why general principles cannot be applied as we only see part of the visible universe and not its related sections. In the break for tea I had a further talk with David Lorimer and Mary Midgley, and then heard Michael Redhead, who argued against reductionism.[41]

My Form from Movement Theory, drafted in Jesus College's hall with Henning Broten; David Bohm, Geoffrey Read's Leibnizian view of time
I was in among the leading scientists of the Age, and I had resolved to barnstorm a new view of the origin of the universe. It was at this point, in the early evening on 4 September 1992, that I met up with the young Norwegian mathematician who helped the mathematical side of my Form from Movement Theory (that physical phenomena emerged from a pre-existing, moving, latent Fire) which is in Appendix 2 of *The Universe and the Light*. He had come to my attention when Geoffrey Read appeared in hall at dinner the previous night: he stood up to greet Read.

I wrote:

Before dinner met up with Henning Broten, a Norwegian mathematician of 27 who is still an undergraduate of great creativity and brilliance, who told me he had just phoned Bohm and mentioned me [having read my paper], and who (standing in Jesus College's front quad near the statue of a horse and then in the cloisters) questioned me about how I got from the Fire to Existence and proposed that he do a new maths which could show how the universe was created.

He explained I would have to tell him very precisely and he would convert it into maths.

I told him as we sat together over dinner in the candlelit Jesus dining-hall. At the outset he said that Bohm could not come up with an imagine-first proof but that I could; and that he would do the maths to put it into stages. I talked and made notes, and he converted what I said into maths. As we progressed others, including several of the speakers, got up and stood near us to observe how we were getting on. Penrose was smiling. It was an event: I was describing the philosophical origin of the universe. Prompted by Henning's questions, I said the Fire or Light is a movement in all directions which is infinitely self-entangled and eternal. It created a vacuum in a point – a singularity – because the Fire was moving in all directions. This empty point was in the centre of a rotation of Fire and expanded in a pre-space regularity. The rotation provided a regular calm symmetrical field in an infinitely wide area (the pre-vacuum which surrounded this and envelops the pre-universe). In this calm field there was a disturbance, Prigogine's interplay between the infinite and the regular or regularity and randomness, which was the Big Bang. The first virtual particle produced Being, and locality, which was a factoralisation – or limitation or fragmentation or reduction – of the infinite self-entanglement. The virtual particle became real, the first proton, and the hot beginning or Big Bang took place. This went beyond Gödel's "Any finite system is incapable of complete self-awareness".

At each stage Henning told me the maths. I wrote the maths out on a scrappy piece of paper I had in my pocket and had finished it by the end of the third course. We sat on and eventually we were the only ones left in the dining-hall. We then went to the bar, where I talked with him, standing by the door, drinking orange and lemonade mixed.

I needed to clean up my tangled jottings. I had talked with Henning until 11.20, for four-and-a-half hours without a break. He said: "I like your passion. You're like Einstein, you attack the problem with imagination." He said we would write a paper and send it to Bohm and Penrose, Gunzig, Geoffrey Read and his friend in Oslo. Henning was three years older than Heisenberg was at the time of the uncertainty principle, and he would work through all my points in my metaphysical science. He quoted Geoffrey Read: "'Space is the order of co-existence of events; time is the order of succession of events.'" He insisted that the written proof was the result of my imagination.

Penrose and Mary Midgley had seen something in the paper I had written for the conference. I now saw that Henning and I were the significant event at this conference, producing the Form from Movement Theory now in the Appendix of *The Universe and the Light*, and only half a dozen saw. I was elated as I walked back from the bar. The stars were overhead, and my elation as I looked at my jottings found its way into a poem about my elation, 'Form from Movement Theory'.

The next morning, 5 September, I breakfasted with Henning and then heard Edelman on 'Memory and Neural Darwinism'. Mary Midgley sought me out and sat next to me at lunch. We formed an alliance and I promised to send her my finished book. I went on to the Old Library with Cornwell to see Coleridge's letter; his essay in Latin (1792) that "to long for posthumous fame is unworthy of a wise man"; his curled lock of hair; and an edition of the Notebooks which turned up in the 1930s and was taken to Toronto.

Looking back on the conference, I reflected that the Light had put me among the materialists and neural biologists and that I had carried its torch through my paper. The next day Henning rang me on his way home to Norway and told me he was improving the maths. His improved maths are in Appendix 2 in *The Universe and the Light*. A couple of days later Geoffrey Read rang, full of gossip, and advanced his theory of memory and time: "The past is overlaid by the present, a Leibnizian, Bohmian view that all is process, and time and space are to be defined in terms of the structure of a process."

I rang Bohm for 45 minutes. I told him about Henning, the conference and my theory of the beginning. Bohm interrupted: "Space-time have to be abstracted, the beginning was when time began, you can't talk of a pre-time." But you can. Time began with the Big Bang (which Penrose said Bohm had marginalised) and something pre-existed the Big Bang: Nothingness, potential Non-Being (a Plenitude). He said, "In the 19th century there was more hope of progress than today." I told him Redhead had said writers respect him but do not mention him in their indexes, and said: "I can't understand it." Bohm said: "I can't understand it either."

On the stranglehold of science, Bohm said: "It used to be the other way round. In Galileo's time religion was in charge." I told him of Barrow's criticism that the visible universe is a bubble in foam. Bohm asked: "How does he know that?" He asked, "What did Penrose say?" I told him Barrow said Penrose was wrong to have general principles. Bohm said: "He's just created a general principle by saying that." I said: "I agree." Bohm said: "Scientists don't know what metaphysics is, they think it's something flakey." I reminded him, "Einstein said physics inevitably leads to metaphysics." Bohm, who had held discussions with his friend Einstein, said: "Yes." I told him how Henning and I were left alone in the hall at the end of dinner. Bohm laughed. He said he would make a comment on my book to the effect that my "attempt to bring together physics and the philosophical view in a coherent whole is a worthwhile one" or something of the sort. He would sort out the exact wording if I rang him in two weeks' time. I told him about Geoffrey Read's view of space-time.

Then I rang Geoffrey Read and gave him feedback. Geoffrey Read said of Bohm: "He has sincerity. The one distinctive feature of genius is undoubtedly sincerity, and he has that. But I feel he is torn about Einstein. He knows Einstein was seriously wrong, as I believe, but is trying to make an apology for him, and so he stutters, for in his heart of hearts he knows Einstein was wrong." I was on Einstein's side and did not believe he was wrong. In March 2014 evidence was found that confirmed inflation following a Big Bang and also Einstein's gravitational waves, and it is now clear that Read was wrong.

I broke off my session on the phone as Anthony had a headache from being kicked on the back of his head during football. I healed him for a few minutes: "Surges came immediately and within five minutes he reported that the headache had gone."

I resumed my telephoning the next day. I rang Sir Laurens van der Post who listened to my account of Cambridge and said: "It's a hell-hole." He said, "They need to read more of your work. The universities are awful. Oxford as well as Cambridge. It's very distressing that they've gone like that." I told him about Atkins's view of "the dung-hill" and said, "They need to put just one of your books beside their vision." "Yes." I asked: "Is your present work about Africa?" He said: "No. I don't know what it's about. I don't let myself ask that. I haven't got down to your thing because I can't take my mind off the book I'm writing. One day I'll be useful to you." On my answerphone Mary Midgley said "she would be prepared to comment: 'challenging, serious and timely'." I rang her in Newcastle and she told me: "I wrote my thesis on Plotinus. I'm familiar with the concepts in your work." I noted: "Penrose, Bohm, Mary Midgley and van der Post – all allies of mine."

Two days later I wrote out the first version of my 'Form from Movement Theory' between 10.30 and 2. Ann and I then went to dinner with Clapperton via Flatford Mill, where I wrote a poem, 'Autumn at Flatford Mill'. We arrived at 7.15 at East Bergholt Place, which has a clock at the front; where Squire Heaney once lived. We dined with Clapperton, his partner, a GP and a farmer and his wife, and I was asked for my view of the universe. After I had finished explaining it Clapperton said, "We're Haggerists." I wrote a poem, 'Nature, Walled'.

On 15 September I dictated my 'Form from Movement Theory' and while I was talking about the creation of the universe two Jehovah's witnesses came to the door. One holding a book said, "Can I tell you how the universe was created?" I said: "I'm just dictating my theory on it now, you'll be able to read it before the end of the year." Startled, she said "Oh", and retreated abashed. (I noted another example of synchronicity: as if by telepathy we were both thinking about the beginning of the universe. Had my words, and the energy in my thought, telepathically attracted her to my door?) By the evening my 'Form from Movement Theory' was on computer.

I was preparing to send it out to all my allies (Bohm, Penrose, Read, Broten, Gunzig and van der Post), but the next day there was another distraction. It was Black Wednesday: the ERM crisis when interest rates were dramatically raised by 5%. I heard the news outside Coopersale Hall's front door and knew my projections would not be able to bear the unbudgeted increased payments on a permanent basis. I wrote a poem 'Five-Per-Cent Rise in Interest Rates'. Luckily the rise was cancelled soon after lunchtime and soon afterwards I sketched the outline for my next essay, 'Beyond Evolution and Neurons: Manifestation and Transmissive Consciousness', which became Appendix 3 in *The Universe and the Light*. This grew out of the discussion at Clapperton's dinner-table. I left a Coopersale-Hall parents evening early and wrote until 1.15 a.m. "though I could have written more. The sudden thunder, echoing through the night, startling me."

I finished work on Appendix 3 about 6 the next day, 19 September. I was now clear of the conference and relaxed with Anthony watching the end of Clint Eastwood's *High Plains Drifter*.[42] There was a cricket in the porch that night. I would soon be chirping again in my autobiographical work.

Comments on my work: David Bohm and his death, Laurens van der Post, Roger Penrose

But I still had to deliver the comments on *The Universe and the Light* that Element needed. A couple of nights later I made some telephone calls. I rang Gunzig, who told me he would comment: "An outstanding and unexpected marriage between cosmology and its metaphysical counterpart. Very impressive." I rang David Bohm, who it transpired had had a second heart attack: "I had another setback last weekend, another heart attack, only mild." We chatted about Gunzig and Hawking, who described himself in a letter to me as "a reductionalist" and wrote that holism – in terms of my paper, he meant Universalism – is mysticism. We discussed my theory of the universe, which would go through a second edition the following week as Henning told me over the phone from Norway he wanted to make some revisions to the maths. Bohm commented: "This attempt to bring together physics and the philosophical view of the cosmos in a coherent whole is interesting and worthwhile."

Five weeks later I read that David Bohm had died in a taxi on 27 October. He gave me a quotation for my book "just before he went". The day after I learned of his death I sensed him sitting near me. I was shocked to read that Robert Oppenheimer had asked him to work on designing the atomic bomb at Los Alamos in 1942 but that he had not been given security clearance because of his Communist sympathies. I was dismayed to read that he had left the US after refusing to testify against a colleague before Senator McCarthy's Un-American Activities Committee, and was consequently suspected of being a Communist. I learned that he had been born to a Hungarian Jewish immigrant father and a Lithuanian Jewish mother. Yet another academic who had befriended me, and had been my living link to Einstein, had possible Soviet links. The Cold War had ended but its impact was still pervasive.

I rang van der Post. "Oh, Nicholas, how *are* you? How nice to hear from you. Yes, I got your paper about the origin of the universe. You're doing something very important." I told him that I had begun the work that would become *A Mystic Way* and was drawing on the vividness of memory: "I want to show that someone born in ordinary circumstances in the 20th century can progress to a metaphysical outlook; and do it in everyday language that ordinary people will respond to." I then rang Sheldrake. He said: "I got your paper. It's very interesting. How was Cambridge? I'm not surprised, anything at Cambridge is full of reductionists…. I'm engaged in an academic dispute with Stephen Rose." I said: "I've ordered his book." "What book?" "*The Making of Memory.*" "Oh, I must read it, I didn't know he had a book out." I said: "The other book out is Richard Milton's *The Facts of Life: Shattering the Myth of Darwinism.*" He said: "I've been away, I don't know about these books. And I didn't know Bohm had had a first heart attack, let alone a second." I observed: "So in one evening [I] phoned Gunzig, Bohm, van der Post and Sheldrake."

Heather Dobbs rang me. I told her about my conversation with Sheldrake. She remarked: "Sheldrake is not on the metaphysical level, he is at a materialistic level. He is not drawing to himself the books he needs." I sensed that she wanted more Foundation days. I said: "I should not be doing the practical Foundation because I have to get the Appendices right and the endorsers and oppose materialism at Cambridge, and in 1993 found Universalism as an international philosophy." I received a long letter, five handwritten pages of A4, from Mary Midgley, and wrote: "What a fine woman and type of mind she represents: upright, forthright, fearless, intellectually honest, perceptive." She confirmed Heather's view of Sheldrake: "He is a materialist, who cannot help at the metaphysical level."

Matthew's 'A'-level results had came out in August and within a couple of days he learned that he had his first choice, to do a split English/French degree over four years at the University of Bangor, with a year in France. Towards the end of September we took Matthew to Bangor. He was only the second member of our family to go to university, I being the first. I drove through mist and then drove on through clear weather and stunning scenery via Llangollen and Llanberis pass, past the Betws-y-coed Swallow Falls and Capel Curig, to Bangor. The view of Snowdon on the way in elicited two poems which I wrote in the car: 'Being in Snowdonia' and 'Snowdon'. We put in at the Menai Straights Hotel and then walked round Bangor, which was in a valley with a skyline of trees. The university building was old and inspiring. We then drove through the dark to Llandudno, where, in the middle of the cream Belgravia-style hotels between the Great and Little Orme, I located the Hydro Hotel with the glass veranda where I kept my file of Suez cuttings in 1956 and received news of my 'A'-level results. We went in and looked round. Outside there were fishermen with lights – like souls showing their lights. I wrote a poem, 'Lights like Souls'. We went on to Conway Castle and then ate in the main square before returning to Bangor.

The next morning I woke to a view across the wooded valley and water to Anglesey, and was struck by the stillness. I wrote a poem, 'Stillness overlooking Anglesey'. After breakfast we transferred Matthew into the tiny room that would be his new home. It was soon cosy with a TV, music centre and computer. We visited the University's dining-hall and then I walked to the end of the pier, which had Victorian lamps and domes. I wrote two poems, 'A New Life' and 'Transient Existence and Lasting Being'. We left Matthew to his new life and then returned home via the coastal route and Chester, and went to Albrighton Centre to see where the Oaklanders would stay. I wrote poems, 'Rabbit: Self-preservation' and 'Ladybird'. Back home we already missed Matthew who had been a large part of our family. But he was having a good time. On his birthday, he rang and told us he had joined badminton, aikido, judo, parachuting, squash, fencing, snooker, golf and the real ale society.

Later I rang Sir Laurens van der Post, who said of *The Universe and the Light*: "It looks very interesting, I want to give you an honest opinion. But I haven't finished my 'thing' yet. One gets pushed oneself. And how is your autobiography going? How many pages have you done? How's it going?" He was taking a father's – a very benevolent, interested father's – interest in a son. I said: "Other things keep coming." He said: "If it comes from a deep place then it's to be considered very seriously." I told him: "The two go together: the reflective essay and the lightness of touch of a narrative; the one informs the other." He said: "Yes, that's true. I think that's right. I'm doing something similar now." I noted: "With Sir Laurens you feel... he has pushed everything to one side and is focusing on you and nothing else; giving you his undivided attention. He has great charm."

I learned from Michael Mann that Peter Roche de Coppens was reading *The Fire and the Stones*: "He is very enthusiastic about it; says it is right." (Heather Dobbs had told me she had received a letter from de Coppens, allegedly Head of the Templars, who wrote that he was "most interested in Nicholas Hagger", meaning *The Fire and the Stones*.)

The same day I attended Chigwell School for the local Heads' annual dinner. The Head, Tony Little, said that the Head of History (who had characterful Victorian whiskers) had insisted "he would only come if he sat next to Nicholas Hagger". I met an Old Chigwellian (Roger Hickling, whom I had not met since the mid-1950s), who recalled Thompson, our Head, asking him: "Do you come from the Isle of Dogs? I'd have thought so because of your dog Latin." David Ballance, who kept the library, told me he would be displaying my books alongside books by Bernard Williams at a forthcoming Open Day.

In mid-October, Sir Laurens van der Post gave me his comment on *The Universe and the Light*. He dictated: "'It is nearly 100 years since William James first warned against the reductionism which he saw increasing in the scientific and philosophic spirits of his day, the 'but only' element as he labelled it. Even he would have been dismayed at the extent of the empire the element has established in all the disciplines he valued, and how much he would have supported all those who value the quality and range of a truly comprehensive modern awareness as Nicholas Hagger does in all he has written with a rare intellectual passion in all his works since *The Fire and the Stones*.'" "Now will that help you?" he asked.

I rang Penrose ("Roger Penrose here") and he gave me his comment: "I read Hawking's comment about holism being mysticism and want to comment as follows: 'Holistic concepts have a profound role in modern mathematics and physics, and need not be mystical; Hagger's broad sweep over the holistic scene is not so constrained by scientific desiderata.' That answers Hawking." His concern was as much to answer – indeed, to correct – Hawking as to comment on my work.

The next day I visited Michael Mann. We walked across the car park to the pub and had steak-and-kidney pie sitting next to the log fire. We discussed our future roles. Michael said: "Yours is to oppose materialism: the Metaphysical Revolution, with all the conflict that brings."[43]

Philosophy had won the conflict with the Foundation of the Light, and though there would be a new round of philosophy and a reborn Metaphysical Centre before they finally fell away, I was already being pressed by my next episode and pair of opposites.

Episode 9:

Autobiography and International Politics

Years: 1992–1994
Locations: Loughton; Charlestown; Scotland; Florence, Pisa; USA

Works: *A Flirtation with the Muse*; *Sojourns*; *Angel of Vertical Vision*; *A Mystic Way*; *Awakening to the Light*; *A White Radiance*
Initiatives: spiritual autobiography; Universalist Group of Philosophers; research into New World Order; Metaphysical Centre

"Every artist writes his own autobiography."
Henry Havelock Ellis, *Tolstoi: A Man of Peace; The New Spirit*

In my next episode my autobiographical writing, which I had already commenced, was in conflict with my research into international politics and the New World Order for my poetic epic. However, the consequences of the last episode were still unfolding and there was a new minor conflict between philosophy and practical mysticism.

Autobiography: man of letters, future works and poems
Writing out of direct experience: A Mystic Way
I had written to Sir Laurens van der Post that I had finished *The Universe and the Light* and that I would be writing out of my own experience. I had taken up Michael Mann's suggestion on 7 August 1992 that I should write about my "Journey". In Cornwall before the conference I had thought about my impending autobiography: "My own journey – in relation to 'the Light'." I identified its aim:

> My autobiography tells the story of how I came to know the Light and to apply it internationally after national considerations, and to oppose the *status quo* in science and philosophy and to opt for the metaphysical. The emerging of my ideas from my life, the caption (*sic*) being +A + −A = 0, i.e. reconciliation of the opposites. +A = the world (scepticism, nationalism etc.); −A = the beyond (mysticism, the Metaphysical Revolution, Universalism).... The most remarkable thing about me is my contact with the Light and the new philosophy it has made possible, and the new literature and science. So the Light must be the theme.... Call it *A Mystic Way*.

This was the first time I had fixed on that title.

The same day I had ideas for other future works, which I thought of as 'essays':

> How the universe works as a whole, full of checks and balances, how everything needs everything else, i.e. the oneness of everything within the metaphysical scheme [which later became *The New Philosophy of*

Universalism].... Spiritual, religious and political Universalism, the philosophy of the coming supra-national state in Europe, its various layers [which anticipated *The World Government*].... Literary criticism and Universalism. The Light and literature, defining the tradition of literature [which anticipated *A New Philosophy of Literature*].

I was asked to address the Quaker Universalist Group in Birmingham the following April. (The QUG was linked to the International Society for Universalism, which politically sees Universalism as a metaphilosophy for the coming European supra-national state.)

I added: "The philosophy essay is about knowing true reality.... Call it *The One and the Many*. (Cf Shelley, 'Life like a dome of many-coloured glass/Stains the white radiance of eternity'.)" This anticipated my volume of philosophical essays, 'The One and the Many'. On 9 August I went for a late-night walk and

saw the full moon, slightly misty, emerge from behind the Battery cliff as I stood half along the pier... and under it a reflection of the cliff in the still sea. Gazed in some ecstasy and quickly returned and wrote [a poem,] 'The One and the Many', which is about manifestation of Reality through the Void into Being and thence into its reflection, Existence.

In 24 hours I had anticipated at least five forthcoming books and had the titles for two of them.

I was now defending writing from personal experience. After noting "the meadow browns" and "the bees nuzzling the pink blackberry flowers", I went to Porthleven to see the gig-racing. I wrote:

Imagination is day-dreaming, being apart from the worldly situation; the activity of the soul.... The whole basis of reading is being apart from the situation and the present moment, i.e. responding with the soul.... What I said in my Preface to my poems is that the beyond must be mixed with the worldly.... Why write for the imagination and not out of direct experience, like T.E. Lawrence and van der Post? Cannot the imagination make use of direct experience? Imagination: "Mental faculty forming images or concepts of external objects not present to the senses." (*Concise Oxford Dictionary*) Writing as recollection in tranquillity (Wordsworth) is the recall of 'concepts of external objects not present to the senses', so autobiographical writing can be imaginative.

(The imagination can also 'dream' events which have not happened.)

I had written 'Gig-Racing' and plunged back into poetry. The next day I sunbathed for an hour and read van der Post on his POW camp and the Kalahari. I wrote a poem, 'Moon and Tide'. The Regatta evening included a display of falconry: a tawny eagle, swooping, taking raw meat, then soaring effortlessly and gliding; a common buzzard and two Harris hawks.[1] That evening I "wrote the first four stanzas of 'Hooded Falcon' (my fourth poem in four days)". I typed it up "and added a fifth stanza which just wrote itself, 'the poet as falcon'". Matthew arrived back from his holiday, bringing a letter from van der Post which included the sentence: "I am glad that you are thinking of writing directly out of your own experience of travel and the world."[2]

We drove to Portloe, had a cream tea at the Lugger Hotel and went on to Carne beach and Nairn Head, to Pentire beach and then to Veryan with its thatched houses and four round houses – round so the Devil could not hide round corners. Back in Charlestown there was a barbecue on the quay as the *Maria Asumpta* came in, and gig-racing. Ann and I sat in chairs by the green sward and watched the sun set. Later I went for a walk after playing Matthew chess. The moon was a day after full but very bright. "It was as if we were walking on a winter's afternoon, the moonlight was so bright." I wrote a poem, 'Still and Moving: Moon and Eyes'. The next afternoon Anthony's friends took part in the Regatta festivities, in the raft race and on the greasy pole. I wrote a poem, 'Young and Old: Noise and Stealth'.

I had thought about my work and had resolved to be "a man of letters before a philosopher". On 18 August I picked up Paul Newman, Pam and a friend and drove to Gorran Haven to revisit Colin Wilson. Colin wandered in, hair all over the place, and handed me smoked salmon and poured wine. I asked, "What are you writing?" "*Space Vampires 2.*" After the news I told him about the symposium on reductionism. I told him I had pinned that label onto post-1900 philosophy, and told him about my book *The Universe and the Light* and how Universalism was proving a way of action. "I agree," he said, "that's why I have reservations about Universalism, it attracts followers." Then in came a lady from Bath and the conversation became general while Joy sat with the parrot on her shoulder. It asked: "What time's dinner?" Colin told me, "I go to bed at 9 and wake and think between 12 and 2 or 3. I do all my important thinking then." After the lady left to drive back to Bath I discussed Popper with Colin and he gave me an article on Gödel's Incompleteness Theorem, which we discussed.

As I left, Joy showed me the chalet where I stayed in 1961 (two rooms, then with a view of the sea, now blocked by trees). Pam said on the way back: "He's wasting himself on the vampires, but he's exhausted, it's easier than philosophy. And he's a law unto himself, he won't do otherwise. He needs the money. He's popularising." I wrote: "The Colin of 1961, eagerly talking of literature and philosophy, referring to two or three writers every

sentence, showing the baker the latest chapter – that Colin is out of reach....
I sit in the same place, near where the swivel arm and typewriter used to be,
and am separated from the person I knew then."

The next day I returned to Essex. On impulse I rang Andrew Murdoch,
who had helped me with my books, and told him I wanted to double my
literary output. He offered his wife, an ex-secretary to a solicitor, to type
from tapes on her machine. I wrote, "Got fixed up effortlessly for my
increased output." Without trying, I was set up to start my autobiographical
A Mystic Way, about my journey to the Light.

Towards the end of August I began writing a number of short poems. I
wrote: "Haunted by images.... Poems of place with a human dimension." I
was moving "towards a new symbolic verse". I

> excused myself from the accountant and wrote 'Time and the Timeless',
> about a juxtaposition.... Poems form in my mind and I write them to get them
> out of the way.... Wrote poems all evening until 1.15 a.m. (now).... 17 poems,
> wrung from me within three days.... 10.15 a.m. Now 20 poems in three
> days.... 10.35. Have just written 'Imagination: Spring and Sea', my most
> Platonist or Neoplatonic poem. I did not think it at the time but on reflection
> it is in the tradition of 'Kubla Khan'.

That morning I had dreamt there was a neap (spring high) tide in
Charlestown and the water came past our house. I wondered if a tide from
Nature would sweep away my academic side and wrote 'Spring Tide and
Academic Work'. I wanted to call my next volume of poems *"Smeaton's Tower*
and have a lighthouse on the front [cover]", but many of the poems were
about the connection between the Light and the imagination, and the Muse,
and the title passed into a later poem, 'Smeaton's Tower and Western
Civilisation'.

On 31 August I began dictating *A Mystic Way*. I reflected again on my
energy.

> Where I got my energy from, when did I have it?... I worked through to it....
> It was not the Light alone that gave me this universal energy. I knew it in
> Japan. Tony Rainer: "What is this energy you have, where does it come
> from?" (The energy to write.)... Somewhere along the Way I contacted a
> universal energy which worked through me.[3]

I was determined to start research on the poetic epic I had discussed with
Ezra Pound, which would be about the Second World War. Universalism
reconciles all opposites, and its biggest challenge is to reconcile the
conflicting ideologies of hostile belligerents in a war in accordance with its

principle: $+A + -A = 0$. I was concerned to establish the origins of the $+A +$ $-A$ (democracy and Nazi Fascism) that had led to the Second World War. I knew that the New World Order was involved in its outbreak and resolved to probe further.

International politics: global deception and the New World Order

I had stumbled across the New World Order and its role in the war while working out the 25 civilizations of *The Fire and the Stones*. Suddenly the New World Order was in the news. The closure of coalmines in the UK was dominating the headlines, following a report by 'Rothschilds', the Government's bank manager, recommending closures.

Musing on the war, I investigated the New World Order, which Churchill once called "a long-running Conspiracy". Churchill had bankrupted the UK by lend-lease in the course of opposing Hitler's domination of Europe. I wrote: "'The Conspiracy' [(Churchill's word)] want a United States of the World (as did Lenin) and a United States of Europe as a stepping-stone with its independent bank, the Bundesbank... to smash the nation-states' currencies." I told the Oaklands accounting assistant that a United States of the World (USW) would be created and that a United States of Europe (USE) would be "a stepping-stone" to a USW. Over Christmas I had worked on the Bilderberg Group's plan to rule the world and bring in its self-interested form of political universalism (world citizenship for all human beings). I saw that the Maastricht Treaty had been imposed on nation-states. A united world, the dream of political Universalism, was good, but when it was controlled by the leaders of the New World Order who had their own self-interested agenda it was bad.

'The Conspiracy' was behind the fall of Edward Heath, for whom I had worked, and the fall of Thatcher. Victor, Lord Rothschild, the head of Heath's think-tank (and fifth man, *see* pp.250–251) had led Heath into a miners' strike with Scargill and the ensuing three-day week lost Heath the election, and as a result Wilson held the referendum on Europe. Thatcher defeated the miners, and the Rothschild Report that closed the British mines effectively internationalised the UK's national mining industry. In 1985 Victor, Lord Rothschild had proposed that Thatcher should implement the poll tax and the ensuing riots undermined her and contributed to her fall, which was implemented after the Bilderberg Group, prompted by Kissinger, took the decision to overthrow her at the La Toja meeting. In 1992 Labour were supposed to win the election and ratify the Maastricht Treaty. The Conservatives' ratification of the Maastricht Treaty was fraught, and Black Wednesday could be seen as a consequence of Europe's demoting of nation-states' currencies.

I was clear that 'the Conspiracy', which I would later refer to as 'the

Syndicate', had been behind the outbreak of the Second World War, and it had supplied Hitler with oil. I knew I would bring the New World Order into my epic, and that it could have a role in the epic's mythological story. I wrote:

> This will be a Universalist epic. Compare Milton and Puritanism. Universalism is the new idea that impels me to write this epic. I could not do it before because I had to work out Universalism [first].... This idea has burst through from the beyond, like a windfall out of a tree, taking me by surprise when I was not ready.

I hastily drafted 10 of the 12 books within the epic.

At the conference on Global Deception: Mary Seal, Eustace Mullins

In early January 1993 I attended a weekend conference on Global Deception at the Wembley Conference Centre. I had rung the organiser, Mary Seal, who "said that the New World Order will be imposed if it is not achieved by co-operation – Kissinger had said this at the Paris Bilderberger meeting". I found a bookshop that supplied books about the New World Order and its offshoot agencies, the Bilderberg Group and the Trilateral Commission. I grasped that the UN war against Saddam was to demonstrate the New World Order's sovereignty against Iraqi national sovereignty. I wrote: "The Rockefeller–Rothschild (American–European) one-worlders are acting through American institutions...: e.g. through the President."

The conference was very poorly attended, partly because there was a mysterious problem with the computers that issued tickets. Some 200 people attended on the first day and there were 4,500 empty seats. Mary Seal, longish blonde hair, tightly dressed and chain-smoking, was around in the corridor. She had mortgaged her boyfriend's house to put the conference on and draw public attention to the global deception being perpetrated. The conference itself was a series of university-level lectures illustrated with slides or with snippets of video. The lectures suggested that the world's population would have to be reduced from 6 billion to 4 billion by the end of the 1990s (which has not happened), and that AIDS and 47 related man-made germs would contribute to that reduction. They suggested that when the time came for the world to draw together into a New-World-Order-dominated world government there would be sightings of flying saucers to unite the world against an invading enemy from another planet. These already existed on this planet, following Nazi discovery of their technology in the 1940s.

But I wanted to learn about the New World Order's role in the war, and I was especially interested in a lecture by Eustace Mullins, a *protégé* of Ezra

Pound's, who held that the global *élite* backed both sides during the Second World War. I spoke with Mullins at some length after his talk. He mentioned Ezra Pound and I said I had visited him. He said, "Everything in my lecture came from Pound. He was in St Elizabeth's Hospital because of 'Rothschilds' and while he was in there he funded me to research 'Rothschilds'." It had not dawned on me yet that Ezra Pound had been placed in the insane asylum at the instigation of 'Rothschilds', and had asked Eustace Mullins to expose this. I later wrote: "I now have a higher opinion of Pound, who, Mullins tells me, introduced him to [books about] 'Rothschilds' and the Illuminati. When I said to Pound, 'I feel that two halves of the 20th century are meeting', I did not realise it would be regarding 'the Conspiracy' as well as literature."

The next day Mullins spoke on the Baal/Christ split and how 'Rothschilds' are neo-Baalists. William Cooper, an ex-US naval intelligence officer, showed a hitherto unshown colour film of the assassination of President J.F. Kennedy that had been shot with a home-movie camera by a private citizen, Abraham Zapruder. This film has since been widely shown on television. Cooper claimed that it shows the driver turning round and blowing part of Kennedy's head off with a third and final shot. Kennedy's head jerks back and causes Jackie to scramble over the back of the car, Cooper said, to try and escape. In 2013 it was revealed that she was trying to retrieve a piece of Kennedy's skull that had flown through the air and landed on the flat back of the car. Analyses of the shooting in 2013 suggest that the third shot came from the back or the side if it did not come from Oswald's gun. I have no means of assessing the film's authenticity. (In November 2001 Cooper was shot and killed in the US as a "major fugitive" after being charged with tax evasion.)

The conference proposed a scenario which confirmed my view in *The Fire and the Stones* that America was poised for a global phase. It suggested that the Bilderbergers would take the world over and run it as a neo-Fascist totalitarian dictatorship on Baalist–Luciferian principles, and kill a third of the world's population to make the resources go round. I saw the Bilderbergers as a kind of advisory body or quango to the US Government, steering US policy so that a New World Order can happen under a US umbrella of implementation. I saw that it was vital that there should be a benevolent rule at the top in a world government, which could bring about a benevolent Universalism, and that on no account must there be a universal despot. I would deal with the self-interested, dictatorial New World Order in *The Syndicate*, and with the two – benevolent and malevolent – 'New World Orders' in my poetic epic, *Overlord*. The conference advanced my global thinking even though I did not believe some of its conclusions.

I wrote:

My epic will be like *Paradise Lost*, [and will refer] to the New World Order. This is a struggle between Christ, who wants it to be within the framework of civilizations...; and the Devil, who wants it to be a world-wide Baalite order.... There is... a struggle between two New World Orders.... The Christian view will include Universalism, a Light-based common ground for all cultures. The diabolical view will attack all religion.[4]

I brought this thinking into my poetic epic.

Autobiography: growing Universalism
Autobiographical literature: A Mystic Way; Collected Poems: A White Radiance; Awakening to the Light
I was still working on *A Mystic Way*, which I had begun on 31 August 1992, and on what would become *Awakening to the Light*, and I was thinking about my *Collected Poems*.

I was also thinking about sequences of events. At another meeting of the philosophers in Oxford a dozen philosophers were chaired by Max Payne. We went round clockwise, each speaking on what metaphysics is and what process is. I spoke of a Metaphysical Revolution, and David Lorimer asked everyone to refer to the "Metaphysical Revolution" in conversation to spread the idea. Geoffrey Read, who with Chris Macann (an ex-Lincoln Oxford don) and Alison Watson, was one of the main philosophers there, spoke of his theory of memory. He said: "Our memories are images in the past. Greece is in Greece. There is no memory in the brain." It was as if the present self were a tiny skiff on a vast ocean with all memories below the water (my analogy). Geoffrey Read insisted he was a reductionist: "I reduce the present to the past, time and space to events." Memories were past events. I pondered the strings of events in our lives. At the end there was a queue asking me to outline my philosophy.

While I mulled over sequences of events I reflected on my development and growing Universalism for *A Mystic Way*:

There is early Hagger, middle Hagger and late Hagger. Earlier Hagger is largely Existentialist and focuses on 'the Shadow'. Middle Hagger is illumined and focuses on the Light. Later Hagger focuses on civilizations and the universe.... The movement is [also] from individual to mysticism to science and philosophy. The movement is from Existentialism to Mysticism to Universalism.... My Existentialist concepts: the Silence, the Search, the Journey.... As an independent philosophy, [Universalism] emerges from Existentialism.

I was writing poems. I wrote 'Leaves like Memories' after a whirling wind had scattered the leaves on the tennis-court at Oaklands, blowing them up into a storm like snowflakes. Down in Cornwall I proof-read my 1966 *Diaries*. We went to Porthleven and I took Anthony on to the pier: "Sea was breaking over the end and flinging spray. Surf out beyond the cliffs, very windy. Came back with reddened face." The next day I woke to a brilliant sun and wrote a poem, 'Brilliant Sun'. Back in Essex I went to Parndon Wood on the anniversary of my mother's death and wrote 'Split Ash' and 'All Souls' Day' at midnight. I wrote of my mission: "My task and mission is to state how life connects with the eternal, in poetry, in novels, in autobiography and in diaries – and of course in history. I have to state how life links to the mystic Reality, indeed comes from it." The next day I "woke with an idea for a poem about our national decay into Europe and world government". Still in my pyjamas, I sketched crucial images, lines of Light: "Christ's visit… to Loughton and Epping, and he's disillusioned with what he has found." This idea would pass into my poetic epic, *Overlord*.

The report by the Government's bank manager Rothschilds recommending the closure of coalmines had reverberated. I had discussed 'Rothschilds' with Steve Norris, our tenant, now Parliamentary Under Secretary of State for Transport and Minister for Transport in London. He rang my Cornish number and for half an hour he questioned me about Rothschild connections. I spoke of Scargill being stirred up and Rothschilds' hand in the pit closures. Norris: "Very interesting. There's definitely someone else's hand in it. I don't think Heseltine just made a mistake." I said: "Heseltine overthrew Thatcher. They found themselves stuck with Major who very soon had to learn that he had to implement what Rothschilds say."

In November I escorted Norris round Prontaprint, Barking, having invited him to reopen Andrew Murdoch's redecorated office where some 30 local businessmen sipped drinks and munched nuts. I walked with him to Barking station. He said, "I told Heseltine about you. He's received the Scargill book and he said he'd look into it." I had seen the new Prime Minister John Major as being under orders, having found out fast the facts of life of being a Prime Minister or leader of any Western country, that you have to co-operate with your bank manager and do what he says – hence the ratification of the Maastricht Treaty which had astonished Norris. I wrote: "But, o the agony and uncertainty as the nation-states die away from their independence into a United States of Europe! I am the poet… of the transition, seeing the underlying historical movement." I wrote: "The whole Establishment in Britain is in decay…. The Government borrowing from the bank ('Rothschilds') and having to do what they say over the poll tax and mining…. How are the mighty fallen! The Age of Churchill has gone, the 1950s were a high point."[5]

Oaklands School: carol service

While writing *A Mystic Way* I had coped with the end of term at the schools. On 9 December there was a Coopersale Hall carol service at Theydon Garnon. I sat under a deafening organ. After a staff lunch in the assembly hall I hurried to St Mary's, Loughton for the Oaklands carol service. The church was packed and there seemed to be no seats anywhere. I asked Ann who was standing at the back, "Where am I sitting?" She said: "You're not. The vicar hasn't turned up, you're taking the service." So I went straight down to the front and welcomed everyone. The service then ran itself, with children doing readings and singing carols and parading to the crib. Five minutes before the end there was still no sign of the vicar, and the organist passed me a book and gesticulated that I should perform the closing prayer. "You'll have to do the blessing," one of the staff whispered as she handed the book to me.

So I went out to the front, went to the Light, extemporised about the meaning of Christmas for the children and read a collect. Then I made a split-second decision in front of the packed church and intoned: "May the Lord bless you and keep you...." Even as I said the words I realised I should be saying "May the Lord bless *us* and keep *us*", but I had started and had to finish, so I continued: "... and make his face to shine upon you and give you peace. Amen." As I made the sign of the cross I could see the Oaklands staff looking down, trying not to laugh out loud. There was a chorus of "Amen" and I then walked down the aisle to the porch to say goodbyes to my flock. The first parent to come out said, "I didn't know you did that," and I said: "I don't."

At that point the vicar turned up. "Oh," he said. "Oh. Who took the service?" "I did," I said. "And who did the blessing?" "I did," I said. Next day staff passing me said, "Good morning, Bishop."

That evening there was a candlelit buffet for the Oaklands staff, who gave Ann and me a large glass bowl engraved with an oak-tree to commemorate our 10 years at Oaklands. I sat with two Old-Chigwellian husbands, Tim Norris and Richard Fradd, who reminisced on the Chigwell masters Whitford and Lister, who had both recently died. Fradd had a pocket full of marbles: eighters, fourers and oners. I chalked out a gulley on the library carpet and the three of us played. Kneeling on the carpet, flicking and peering, we could have been back at the end of the 1940s among the gulleys at Chigwell School. Fradd and I won a game each.

We had a call from a friend that Mabel Reid's light was on. I went with Ann and found her lying in a hot, smelly bedroom, her electric blanket having been on all night and all day. I turned the blanket off and called to her. She opened an eye but could only move her arms. We called an ambulance. Two men lifted her into a portable chair and strapped her in. Her hairnet was still on, her spectacles were off her curved nose, her mouth was open. An ambulanceman said to me: "I think she's had a stroke." We were later told she had in fact had a stroke, and that we had saved her life.[6]

Death of Miss Lord

Miss Lord's niece Marion had gone to hospital to have a life-saving operation for cancer. She would still have to have chemotherapy. Miss Lord had put herself in a private nursing home, Marcris House, in Theydon Bois. We visited her there, in a room with an open window and blue tits, great tits and coal tits hopping nearby. I played dominoes with her, and she looked very old, her eyes itching, and kept asking, "Why am I here, how much longer am I here?" while saying, "Thank you very much for coming, you're a good-looking couple," and (to Ann) "You would have been a beautiful bride."

Miss Lord hated it in the nursing home, and even though Marion would soon be home to look after her she had refused food and water. On the morning of Saturday 2 January, the day Marion was due back, her niece Zena rang us to say she was only expected to live a few minutes. Shocked, Ann and I left immediately. We arrived a few minutes too late.

I was shown to her room. She lay on her back, a sheet and green bedspread up to her chin, her white-haired head well back on a low pillow, her mouth slightly open, her right eye half-closed. Zena was tearful outside. We talked softly about arrangements. I said I wanted to sit with her by myself. I sat with her, gave thanks for her life, and told her she had died. She had cared for so many small souls and I commended her soul to the Light. Two surges of energy filled me. I kissed her cold forehead. On my way out I spoke to the sister, who said: "She gave up. She had no will to live. She didn't take food or drink." (There was a packet of orange juice with a straw by her bed, which she declined as if on hunger strike.) "She was a very clever lady. Deep-down she knew Marion wouldn't be able to look after her, and she decided to go."

Miss Lord's cremation took place at Parndon Wood. It was a bitterly cold day, I tasted chimney smoke in my mouth as I walked to the entrance where the hearse with mourners and Marion's car waited. The vicar, David Broomfield, arrived and in the chapel performed a perfunctory service: two readings (both in modern English), a statement about how we are like grass in the wind. The curtains closed round "our sister", and it was all over without one mention of her name or why we were there. We looked at the flowers and then drove to St Mary's church, Loughton for the memorial service.[7]

The church was three-quarters full. We sang a hymn, 'Praise my soul'. I read *Matthew* 5, 14–16; 18, 1–5; and *Proverbs* 3, 13–18. I read slowly, pausing after the first word ('she', 'happy') and looking up at the congregation at each reference to Miss Lord ('hill', 'good works', 'child', 'length of days'). We sang 'All things bright and beautiful'. In his eulogy the vicar gave the bare facts about Miss Lord, and did not take up the stories I had mentioned to him. We sang 'Lord of all hopefulness' and finally, after prayers, 'Glad that I live am I' without reference to its being the school hymn. Then people came to me: Mark Liell (in whose solicitors' office I had spent a week), looking white-haired and old, no longer black-haired and bowler-hatted; and Mabel Reid, now recovered. Old Loughton had turned out and we went back to Marion's for a buffet lunch.

Metaphysical poems

I had written a batch of short poems just before the new year. I found poems coming by themselves. I had been down to Cornwall and had rung Colin Wilson, who could not see me. I had told him about my autobiography, *A Mystic Way*. He said: "It's a good plan." There was a night of storm and gales: a roaring in the chimney, a battering on the front door, a great buffeting all round the house. The sea fountained over the rocks, poured over the harbour wall and flung plumes of spray. Winds lashed and blew spume like driving rain, whistling round the house and rattling in the chimney. I wrote a poem, 'Flow and Flood', on how the body and Nature are at one and obey the same law; how wind and sea, and breath and blood are aspects of one flow.

We went to Gunwalloe. The whole sea was white with boiling surf, spray and flung foam. I scribbled a poem, another Gunwalloe metaphysical sonnet, 'Boiling Foam', standing by the stone steps that lead from the churchyard to the church and wearing my Guernsey fisherman's sweater. We went on to Porthleven and walked down to the pier and more boiling foam. I wrote another poem, 'Elemental', mist all over me, and later 'Royals'. I also overhauled earlier poems: 'War and Peace', 'Eternity' and 'Stepping-Stones'. I drafted 'Harbour-master'. The next day I went out into the rain and saw a black cormorant. I returned and in five minutes scribbled out 'The Workings of the Universe', which takes the reader very close to my poetic method: a small particular scene opens into something more universal, an image of an elusive truth about the universe.

Back in Essex I got up after a cold night between –6° and –9°C, went up to school to put the central heating on and saw the frost on my car: crystals out of last night's fog. I immediately came in and before making breakfast wrote a poem, 'Fog and Frost: The Universe'. On the night of Miss Lord's memorial service I wrote another four poems.

I had seen Ken Russell's film about Delius and had written that I

would love to live full-time for my art like Delius and catch the beauty of

Nature: the sweep of the gull, the majesty of the sun – but in relation to the metaphysical Reality of the universe. Delius's advice [was to] get away from other artists and out into Nature. That is what I've tried to do, in Cornwall and here, overlooking the fields of my childhood, in Essex, damp, drizzly Essex (as it is at present).... I need to focus on small things like a snail or drop of dew and embroider imagery, but I also take the reader to large things, literal things embodying or incarnating metaphysical things.[8]

With Christopher Ricks in the Turf

I had received a letter from Christopher Ricks, saying he was on sabbatical from Boston and staying in Oxford for six months. He rang towards the end of January: "It's Christopher Ricks here. I'm going out to dinner on Wednesday evening, but I can be outside Blackwell's at 5.15. I ought to be back by 6.15." This arrangement made, I said, "I hope you're well?" I thought I detected some doubt. "I've been lucky in my health and my life.... I'll be outside Blackwell's in my Robin-Hood hat. Don't laugh."

I had told him that I would be in Oxford for another meeting with the philosophers. The meeting was about consciousness and 20 wrong assumptions that scientists make, and Geoffrey Read spoke on Whitehead's refutation of materialism (which he called "undifferentiated endurance") in *Process and Reality* 2.2.5. I left the philosophers at 4.30, drove into Oxford, parked in Broad Street and waited outside Blackwell's for Ricks, who came out open-necked, grey-haired, round glasses, warm and smiling but very exact – and no hat. We walked to the Turf while he asked me about the philosophers and the schools, focusing warmly on me.

In the Turf I bought him a cider and myself an orange juice and we sat to the right of the bar on wooden seats. Leaning on the table, I talked about Ezra Pound, the Rothschilds, Mullins, Pound in Italy and my desire to write an epic in the tradition of Virgil, Dante and Milton (who were all in Italy). He asked, "What are you about?"

I said I had seen something that is widespread in the Metaphysical poets and realised it was the centre of religion and history's civilizations and also the Reality behind physics and philosophy. I said this was new and I was doing an interlocking jigsaw. He mentioned holism. I said I agreed, in the sense that everything is part of a whole. I spoke of my "close reading of the universe and what is hidden, [which is] perhaps in the tradition of the Ricksite way of looking". I said: "You taught me to read closely, and now I am reading the universe closely, for what is hidden behind Nature and Western civilization." But, I said, my base is literature and like a *Times* reporter or barrister mastering his brief I go out into disciplines. I said: "A poem is a wonderful medium for a cross-disciplinary approach. In Donne for example." He said: "It can be small in subject and huge in range.

Tennyson's library – there's a precedent for it. Tennyson was very interested in science." I said: "Darwinism in *In Memoriam*." He said: "Yes."

Then we got onto poems. I explained that my *Selected Poems* were thematically chosen. He said: "Like Wavell's *Other Men's Flowers*." I said: "There must now be a *Collected Poems*, perhaps with chronological selection." He nodded. I told him my output is that of a Tennyson or Wordsworth in bulk. He said: "You haven't done much about getting recognised." I said: "No, I'm not interested in self-promotion. I don't think about how good I am. That is for others [to judge]. I'm a factory. I just get on and do it." He said: "It's like Beckett. He was going to write anyway, whether he was published or not.... There are degrees of disinterest. There's not getting published and there's getting published and being ignored, and there's getting published and not being read very carefully (like me).... Empson told me that recognition of good new poetry is the first faculty to go. I can't recognise good new poets any more."

I said of his work: "You're the Leavis figure now." "I'm not." "*The Force of Poetry*" is his Great Tradition." "No, it isn't, it's just about those on whom I have something to say. I've got nothing to say about some writers. I love George Eliot but I've got nothing to say about her." I said: "Your next book should state the Tradition. Perhaps we can discuss that again. Come and see the schools one day and have lunch and we'll talk it through." "I'd like that." He said: "We both have confidence in ourselves, but you have faith in what you're doing, I don't have faith that anyone will read me carefully, that I won't be ignored. We could have disagreements, but these don't matter and we can still talk." I said: "We'll talk it through, with your scholarship and my faith we'll go far."

He quoted my poem 'Royals' with approval. Then we left and returned to the car and I drove him home. I asked him to sign a copy of his *The Force of Poetry*, which he did. He said: "Thank you for asking me to do that." He was a punctiliously correct man with perfect manners who always shut up when someone else spoke. I asked him: "Will you stay in Boston?" He said: "I'll be there until I die. I'm 61, and I have children of 10, 12 and 14 by Judith, who's American. Retiring is attractive, but I can't retire until my youngest is 20. At Boston they let you go on. There's no ageism in America, I can work until I'm 80."[9]

Process and inspiration, in Edinburgh

I was developing an autobiographical method that accommodated process, that allowed themes to surface, vanish and then surface again like distant waves in a sea's incoming tide.

I rang Geoffrey Read and discussed how present events are added to past events without obliterating them. Whitehead rejected undifferentiated endurance in which entities persist through time, the root doctrine of materialism. (According to materialism past events have to be obliterated to make way for present ones.) If time is a succession of events, nothing endures through time and there can be process. He surprised me by suddenly saying: "You are the greatest man I have ever met. You have a family and have earned enough money to take time off to write and have written your big book and your poems and now the one on the universe. That's an achievement. You are the greatest I've met. You have your health and your energy. You're the most remarkable. You're organised. You are sincere. Sincerity shines through." I record this unexpected eulogy as he would shortly turn against my philosophy.

The conversation left me reflecting deeply on endurance and process, and I wrote: "The universe is in process." I wrote a poem on Geoffrey Read, 'Not Endurance but Process: The Past Present'. And, following a quarter of an hour talking to Ernie, the Oaklands school keeper, at the foot of the Oaklands steps, amid birdsong, I wrote a poem, 'Rainglobes'.

As I wrote *A Mystic Way* I was keen to apply the Metaphysical Revolution to the arts as well as to philosophy: "If the Light is central to civilizations (as I have shown it is), then the artists who are illumined are leaders of Light in their civilization... [and] are central to our civilization." When the philosopher Alison Watson rang I told her: "I'm having a Metaphysical Revolution anyway. I'm going through the hole in the hedge and I'm going to stand on the lawn. You, Geoffrey Read and Chris Macann can follow me through the hedge." This anticipated *The One and the Many* and my essay, 'A Defence of Traditional Poetic Method or: Poking the Hornets' Nest'.

Des McForan, my Oak-Tree author, had been a surfacing wave in my process and had nearly vanished. He rang me from Bulgaria, where he was an adviser to the President, and again urged me to visit and meet the Government. He wanted me to buy a publishing company there for a nominal sum. But I was too involved in autobiographical writing to go to Bulgaria. Recalling how a Bulgarian had murdered a dissident (Georgi Markov) in a London street with an umbrella tipped with a syringe that injected poison, I said to him: "What about the brolly brigade?" "They're in the street. I see them every day." I said, "I hope you're wearing shin-pads."

I had a strange feeling that my epic already existed as a whole in the Universal Mind beyond my process, for I was receiving infused knowledge about it in my sleep: "Woke up in the night and realised that Hitler was an Illuminatist." The Light seemed to be urging me onwards: "To bed at 12.45 a.m. Put my head on the pillow and immediately saw a calm Light. Spent five minutes sunbathing in it before deciding it was time to sleep." My inspiration extended to my coming *Collected Poems*, the project I had mentioned to Ricks. Down in Cornwall I composed 'February Daffodils' and wrote: "I have another collection 1989–92:... *A Sneeze in the Universe*. It is a good title. A personal sneeze and the whole universe." I followed my inspiration and titled the volume *A Sneeze in the Universe*.

I wrote on in *A Mystic Way*, and my process took me back to Chigwell. I had been invited to give the toast, "*Floreat Antiqua Domus*" ("May the ancient house florish") at the Old Chigwellians' Shrove-Tuesday dinner, the highest profile speech in Old-Chigwellian circles. I was unwell in the afternoon. I lay on my bed and became nothing for an hour and a half, during which "the Light came in, unbidden, and I heard a voice telling me I would be all right.... Am in tune with the infinite, in harmony with the One." I revived and sat on Top Table with elderly ex-soldiers who fought in the infantry at El Alamein. At 10.45 Little, the Head, knocked the gavel, and I was standing holding a microphone and giving my address without notes: Harsnett and Penn, certain masters of the 1940s and 1950s, how the boys learned to be streetwise (the marble pitch, avoiding being beaten up), how dunces had become millionaires, how Chigwell was a different place now, and then, 15 minutes after beginning, the toast: *Floreat Antiqua Domus*. There were then speeches from Little, the President of the OCs and the Head Boy.

Like another wave surfacing with a place in the whole moving pattern I was invited back to Edinburgh to stay with Nadia. I flew on Nadia's flight. Nadia, waiting in a red-and-grey uniform, looked very demure and I was on the flight deck for take-off, among a maze of dials and switches. I was struck by the casualness of the take-off. I returned to the cabin to eat, and was served by Nadia. Then I was back onto the flight deck for the landing, harnessed with a seat-belt like a parachute over my shoulders, between my legs and round my waist. After lunching I drove with Nadi to Colinton, a pretty stone 1780s village in a valley, with the water of Leith running through it. I saw her flat, then walked to the church. I noted a mortsafe and skulls and bones on some of the graves, and a font with a dove on a pulley. We returned for tea and I wrote 'At Colinton', a poem about death and love (the two themes of major poetry according to Yeats).

We had dinner and the next day I wrote a poem, 'In Spylaw Street', "about love and pain but accepting there must be love". After lunch we walked to the churchyard and watched a dipper (or water ouzel). I flew back with Nadia's air-hostess friends. I was very pleased I had visited her. She was living alone and my picture was up more than anyone else's.

At Coopersale Hall School I became aware that my inspiration included premonition. A teacher, Ann Heald, had started with us in January. She had proved an excellent teacher and had conducted brilliantly at a concert at St John's Epping during which a butterfly had flown about, settled and been inadvertently trodden on by a Coopersale-Hall boy, and was then replaced by another butterfly. I had written 'Butterfly' about the event. After half-term she went missing and was not at home. She lived alone and she had a set of exam papers she had marked.

We became concerned. I rang the police on 3 March. The officer said: "I'm filling in a form and need to write a reason for your concern." Without thinking I said: "I have a premonition she will commit suicide." The policeman visited her house within the hour and reported she was there.

I drove straight round and found her being sick. She was in her dressing-gown and looked dreadful, very pale and shaky. I took delivery of the exam papers between bouts of violent vomiting, and tried to persuade her to visit her doctor. I telephoned the doctor from her house to make an appointment, but she insisted she was all right. The next day I called to try and take her, but she politely declined. On the evening of Sunday 7 March she drove to Knighton Woods 300 yards away and connected a lead to her exhaust. She was found dead the next morning with the engine still running, and there were three lengthy notes on the seat, none involving the school.

The policeman who visited her rang me and said he should have paid more attention to my premonition. With hindsight it seems he interrupted a suicide attempt and I witnessed its aftermath. I felt she had slipped through my fingers like a dropped catch in cricket, but I knew I could not have done any more. I was relieved to learn from her sister that she had made other attempts and that she had announced at Christmas that 1993 would be the year in which she finally "did it".

I was still spending whole days on *A Mystic Way*. I wrote: "My autobiography is a Universalist work. It could be subtitled 'The Birth of a Universalist'." I was pleased that Ted Hughes had written to my publisher and asked for my *Selected Poems*. The publisher sent me Hughes's card, which said: "I am extremely interested."

I was still pondering my coming epic. Back at Chigwell School to watch Anthony act in R.C. Sherriff's *Journey's End*, I spoke to my old Latin and Greek master David Horton (who had been present at my *Floreat* speech) about Virgil's not wanting to write the *Aeneid*, but being pressed by Augustus and Maecenas. I quoted the last line, in which Turnus's soul *"Fugit indignata per umbras"* ("Fled indignant through the shades") and asked, "Did Virgil write in code as Milton did?" He said: "Augustus's presence is everywhere in the *Aeneid*." This made me think again of the New World Order and of the moves towards world government in Hitler's time. Tebbit had been campaigning against the Maastricht Treaty, and I recalled that I had rung Steve Norris and asked, "Does Tebbit know about the Bilderberg Group?" Norris said: "Oh yes, he was associated with it in the past." I asked: "Is Tebbit's campaign against Maastricht to do with blocking the Bilderberg Group?" He said: "Yes. It's subtle." I knew that in my epic the

New World Order would be everywhere.

I was aware that my autobiographical writing followed in the footsteps of my aunt Argie, who as Margaret Broadley had written about her career at the London Hospital between the wars. I reckoned that I shared a gene of hers as we had both run institutions and written autobiographical works. And we both accepted our own deaths. Because of her prominence in nursing circles she had been interviewed at home by BBC Radio 4. She was asked: "Do you think about death?" She replied: "Well, I always leave the kitchen tidy in case I don't wake up."

My book *The Universe and the Light* was now out, and I was asked to write articles for several magazines, including *Radionic Quarterly*, and was interviewed on GLR (Greater London Radio, now BBC London 94.9) in Marylebone High Street late at night. I was led to the studio where Peter Curran was talking to a rock star. I sat at a table opposite Curran with a bank of equipment between us. He said he was going to start me with the Light, and history, then go on to the Metaphysical Revolution, then go into the countries I'd been to and ask about a Grand Unified Theory. We talked for about a quarter of an hour, live. My description of the Light went out across London.

Oaklands kept me grounded. Ernie found a long-tailed field mouse nesting in an old shoe in our porch. It jumped out and scurried under the wooden steps leading up to the school. There were four green woodpeckers in the main field. A fox sat in the sun in the second field. He found a toad sheltering under four pieces of bark. A walk with Ernie was a revelation. He showed me where there were green lizards, and where squirrels had hidden last year's acorns. But I lamented the lack of the metaphysical in contemporary English poetry. Larkin single-handedly ended Modernism with his anti-intellectualism, Little-Englandism and lack of experiment. It was on balance a regressive step. I saw him as a minor poet in theme, though accomplished in style. "He starts with 'I' and widens into a general truth." This was good, but "there is not much transcendental in him".[10]

In Winchester: Universalist metaphysics versus materialism, reductionism and Rationalism
I returned to Winchester in early April and discovered that for many Universalism had polarised metaphysics and materialism into a +A and −A. Before dinner several stopped me and said: "Your book *The Fire and the Stones* is very familiar." One said: "Your name has been the most mentioned in my household during the last year." I had dinner with Lady Astor. I heard Matthew Fox, who was steeped in Aquinas, Meister Eckhart, Hildegard and Julian of Norwich, but was at odds with the Vatican, who had expelled him. The next day I lunched with Fox and heard Kathleen Raine. At the end of the

day, "the Light poured in making my left fingers quiver".

On the Sunday I lunched with Adrian Cairns, who had attended my lecture at Winchester. He said: "It's the Fire versus materialism, you have polarised it in a new and exciting way." Fox and Satish Kumar had both read *The Universe and the Light* the previous night. Stephen Rose, a BBC producer, also read the book and told me: "Your ideas fit in with an ambitious project I've got. They fit in very well. I'm not at liberty to say more, but I'll be in touch." He did not get in touch.

The next day I attempted to convey the vision within my autobiographical work to David Hoppit (the *Daily Telegraph* correspondent with whom I had travelled to Italy in 1957). He invited me to his 1424 house at Curtis Mill Farm: beams and weatherboard standing by a lovely pond, alongside stables and a garden with a greenhouse. I had a long talk with Hoppit about how people rush about and need to become tranquil to feel calm. I explained +A + −A = 0. All contradictions are reconciled within my unity. Justice + injustice = the whole. Suffering + compassion; anger + love. Everything has its opposite and is part of a whole. I was content with 'polarised Fire versus materialism' but uneasy at 'metaphysics versus materialism' as materialism is one of the four levels of metaphysics and therefore a component.

I went to Cornwall that afternoon and was drunk with air after walking by the sea after dinner. I wrote two poems and "went to the Light. Like [the day before] it poured in, 9.45–10 p.m."[11] *A Mystic Way* was about my growing Universalism as is *My Double Life*.

Three visits to Colin Wilson

I wanted to collect Colin Wilson's view of Universalism as outlined in *The Universe and the Light*. I rang him. He reacted to my book with predictable coolness: "Universalism's too vague, you define it as being different from different movements but you don't say what it is. Derrida will say it doesn't exist. What is it that we've overlooked all these years?" I defended: he wanted to keep everything in the rational, social ego and was on Derrida's side in wanting to reduce Universalism to a text. I pointed out that a lot were reading the book. He said: "You'll be able to tell me what it is tomorrow."

I visited Colin Wilson the next day with Paul Newman. We sipped large goblets of white wine, ate dips and smoked salmon and started on Universalism. Colin said: "I don't see what the starting-point is. What is the application, what do people do, where's the crowbar?" I explained that the starting-point is the Fire or Light in many disciplines, that experiential metaphysics is different from rational metaphysics. He said: "But it's vague." I said: "Give us a chance. Existentialism was going for 100 years, this has only been going for a month, more thinkers will come along in the future." I explained about the energy of Light which can be seen. Joy and Paul were on my side. Colin, who did not seem to have had any mystical experiences, said: "Mysticism's wishy-washy. It's like a girl I know. She said, 'You are a Rationalist,' and I said, 'You're f—g right I am.'"

I said: "We're like a movement of post-Existentialists, and we have different emphases." He said: "Post-Existentialism was defining more clearly the concepts of Existentialism." I said: "Well, the Fire or Light is a post-post-Existentialism." He asked: "But what are you against?" I said: "I'm against the materialist universe." "So was Blake." "But he was then, I am now. Reductionism began after Blake – it's reductionism I am crowbar-ing." He said: "What do I do? I want to know what I should do in a seminar, the language is vague. Derrida will say it doesn't exist." I retorted: "Derrida says reality is within a text, I'm saying it's outside a text. The starting-point is the materialism of Dawkins, Derrida and Hawking." He said: "The unification of the four forces may get science forward but Universalism doesn't get philosophy forward." I said: "The starting-point in philosophy is Bergson, T.E. Hulme, Husserl, Whitehead and William James – going back to them, and using phenomenology to look at the Fire in the soul." He said: "Universalism is an everything-ism." I said: "No, it's an everyone-ism, everyone has access to the Fire or Light." He said: "The idea of *The Fire and the Stones* is very simple." I said: "It has a beautiful simplicity. It's as simple as $E = mc^2$; Fire." He said: "$E = mc^2$ is saying that something equals something." I said: "I'm saying the Fire equals the central idea of the universe." He said: "What are you saying?" I said: "We live in a universe of Light which flows into us, bringing supra-rational powers."

I said to him that in 1961 he had written *The Outsider* and *Religion and the Rebel* and that "what I am doing helps forward your vision". Joy agreed. I said, "I'm an Outsider and have ended with the Fire or Light, like some in your last chapter. I told you I would go abroad for ten years and this is what I've found. It's withdrawal and return. If I die tonight and am remembered by the poems, *The Fire and the Stones* and *The Universe and the Light*" – Paul interjected, "A considerable body of work already" – "I hope you'll look back and see me as an Outsider who did what the Outsiders in your last chapter did and became a mystic." He said: "You *are* an Outsider." I said: "If you're going to decide we're similar, don't leave it until you're 86 and I'm 79. Watch this space." He said: "I'm not against the space. I am interested in higher consciousness. I just don't think mysticism's the way of doing it." I said: "Let me rephrase it: higher consciousness and awareness of the reality behind the universe – you're in favour of that." He nodded. I said: "There's a constituency out there, my ideas have resonance. Those who have ears to hear, let them hear. I am not forcing it down anyone. But I should have thought you would have heard the echo, the resonance."

He said: "I discovered I couldn't change people and came down here and got on with limited things. You've turned Husserl upside down. I remember Stuart Holroyd and Bill Hopkins trying to persuade me I should believe in a philosophy called Personalism." I said: "Philosophers do found 'isms'. Bergson founded Vitalism." He said: "Why don't you call it Haggerism? Why don't you call Universalism Haggerism?" I noted: "[I was] with Wilson 5.15 to 8. At least two-and-a-half hours of philosophical arguments, mostly on Universalism."

I drove Paul Newman home. He said: "You kept your cool, you dealt with it very well. He's provincial and insider and involved in serial killers, you're global and more than he can cope with. You are multi-cultural. You are more pure than Wilson's philosophy, which is mixed up with serial killers. He's written about murders and glimpses of higher consciousness – peak experiences – whereas you are steeped in them, you're too much for him, you're transcendental. Language is a problem. He wants to reduce mysticism to a text, you're beyond language."

I wrote:

> What I must do: demonstrate the good things that flow out of the experience of the Light – wisdom, psychological problems resolved, peace, tranquillity, meaning, the unitive vision. Present the Light as a means of attaining higher consciousness.... In 1961 Wilson said, "I like metaphysical discussions, at a level." Now I am on his level or beyond it.... Colin Wilson's approach is psychological with spiritual glimpses. My approach is spiritual, at a higher level than his. He remained a psychological Outsider, I went on and healed my divided self.[12]

Two days later in brilliant sunshine, I wrote an a magazine article, 'Living in a Universe of Fire'. I started after gazing at the sea and watching points of light jump and dance for about ten minutes. I wrote the jumping lights into the beginning. The theme was: the Fire against materialism.

I had arranged to meet Colin Wilson in The Ship, Pentewan the next day, a Saturday, and Pam, his secretary, rang asking for a lift. She said: "Colin's lost his way into serial killing. I tried to tell him and his hackles rose. He's got an inferiority complex from when he didn't go to university. He's self-taught. There's fear at the bottom of it. He's afraid of you. I see letters that come in. Some are difficult and he never replies, he just says he's going to Poland and he'll write when he comes back and he never does.... Paul said there was aggression and anger. People who are no threat he patronises, like women. Anyone who's a threat he wards off. Your book is very interesting. Paul took it to a coffee bar and someone said, 'Could I look at it?' and ended up going off to buy it. It looks interesting. You offered Colin a share in the Metaphysical Revolution and he wouldn't do it. He's got to be Kingsy.... You tackled him in 1961 and he's never forgotten it."

Matthew joined us from Skye, where he had been mountaineering, hanging from ropes. I took the boys with me to meet Colin Wilson and Joy in the Pentewan Ship along with Paul and Pam. I introduced them. Colin gave them a glass of wine each and offered to help both of them. To me he said: "I'm going to write you a letter and set it out because my objections are not frivolous. An 'ism' doesn't get us further forward. Reductionism will collapse through experiments, not through a Metaphysical Revolution. It's individuals that count. I used to write of a religious Existentialism but I've left that behind." I stood my ground and argued back: "An 'ism' is a ladder. Universalism is a ladder you dispense with once you've climbed it." He said: "Perhaps the boat's going your way." I said: "The tide has turned. The tide is carrying the boat my way." Sitting next to Wilson in the Pentewan Ship I quoted my own lines from 'The Silence': "I cannot live by Freud,/There in his mirror I cannot create/A towering image of man against a void." Wilson said, "That reflects how I think." He told Matthew and Ant he wrote 1,000 words an hour, and that Stevenson once wrote 10,000 words in a day. He mentioned Shaw and other writers. He said: "I wrote *The Outsider* in three months – 110,000 words."

After he left Joy remained and gave Pam a *précis* of Colin's reaction to me: "He wants to keep his feet on the ground, he won't go to yoga when I ask him to, he's led people into things in San Francisco and is wary, he wants to keep rational control." I told Joy: "I am amazed that the philosophers – Kant and Hegel, for instance – by and large missed the Fire or Light. It was because they were Rationalists and looked out from their reason. Plato had it." She said: "Yes, Plato knew it. Colin believes in the will." I said: "There is the personal will and a deeper drive, the will of the unconscious strengthened from the beyond."

As Pam had predicted Wilson did not write me a letter setting out his objections to Universalism.

I briefly swung back into poetry. There was a dramatic sea with surf and foam. The next day a stormy petrel settled on the cliff and a greenfinch flew in trees near our garden. I went for a walk into the field, up past the gorse, and heard a nightingale sing. I stalked it from bush to bush until it vanished; a lovely evening walk. I wrote five poems: 'Car Park: Ascending', 'A Nightingale in the Mind', 'Soul like a Greenfinch', 'Stormy Petrel', and 'Sand-Hoppers', this last one after seeing a thousand sand-hoppers on our pink wall under the street lamp.[13]

The next day, 13 April, I visited Colin Wilson on my own for the third time within a week, and talked with him alone from 5.30 to 8 p.m. Bob, his odd-job man, sat with us and had an awkward drink. Joy remarked that Colin's socks had holes, and he took them off and threw them on the fire. He then said that we don't need Universalism or the Metaphysical Revolution, we need a precise refutation of neo-Darwinism through a proof that acquired characteristics can be inherited, and that we need a precise refutation of Derrida from the starting-point which is Husserl and Rousseau saying that "immediacy is not better than meaning-perception".

He gave an account of Derrida's refutation of first Rousseau, then Husserl on account of their language. I refuted Derrida for applying rational language to Reality which is beyond language. Wilson said: "It's immediacy versus meaning-perception. Does Universalism make for a better scientist?" I said: "Yes, because there are two kinds of scientists, one a separate observer and the other part of the whole and open to intuition and inflowings of wisdom and questions of metaphysical Reality." He said: "You're in the wrong direction." Wilson then asked his second question: "Could Universalism give you the mental muscle to switch from a vase to a face?" (He showed me a picture which could be interpreted as a vase or as a face.) I said: "Yes, through the inflowings of the beyond." Wilson argued that the self (meaning the rational, social ego) is the right direction, not the universe, and said: "You are systematising." I said: "Blake said, 'I must Create a System, or be enslav'd by another Man's.'" He said: "It's like Whitehead's philosophy of organism, too vague." He had blasted Whitehead to blast me but I was honoured to be in the company of Whitehead.

Joy brought in his meal and I again brought our discussion down to a more personal level. I said: "Don't leave it until you are 86 and I'm 79 to decide we form a corner. What will they say in 2005? 'Hagger and Wilson often met but could never get it together?' Think of Sartre and Camus in 1946, and Sartre saying to Camus: 'I don't like what you're doing, *L'Homme révolté* is too humanist and moderate.' I have will-power – I believe the will is energised from the beyond – and I carry things through like the school. Everyone said, 'It'll fail, you won't get the pupils or the planning permission, it'll be bankrupt within a week,' but it wasn't. I'm used to leadership, saying, 'This is where we're going and what we're doing.' It'll be all right. You see." He said: "You built the school the right way up. You're in the wrong direction with Universalism."

I asked: "Who else is sharing the consciousness concerns regarding mankind?" He said: "No one else. No one. Just you and me." I said: "Our intention is the same, our results may be different." He said: "You're going about it the wrong way." I said: "Let's see what happens, what the outcome is. I'm doing a jigsaw, all my works are jigsaw puzzles and they will make a picture. Wait till I've finished my jigsaw. If you were then to write about me like Whitehead and Toynbee, like Yeats's *Autobiographies* –" He interrupted: "Whitehead had no impact on philosophy at all." I said: "His time is coming. We need a Metaphysical Revolution to organise it." He said: "If I thought that we were going in the same direction, I'd be with you 100%. But we need more mental muscle, and how do we get that from Universalism and the Metaphysical Revolution?" I said: "Both the Mystic Way and the Dark Night end in a different kind of consciousness. I'm speaking of the unitive consciousness of all mankind. The way forward is not through language but into the Light." And I went, having had the last word while he ate.

After I left I reflected: "Colin and I are unique in being interested in a vision of meaning and purpose. My unitive consciousness sees meaning in a way the tepid everyday consciousness does not."[14] I was pleased at the outcome of our three-part discussion for I felt that Universalism had emerged from his hawkish interrogation unscathed.

Frank Tuohy

On the way home from Cornwall Ann, Anthony and I looked in on Frank Tuohy, who was living in Somerset. He had sent me a card, a map and directions to Shatwell Cottage, near Yarlington. He came to the door of his yellow stone stable block near the 1700 farmhouse of his cousin who lived there with his five children (his wife having died of leukaemia at the age of 55). Tuohy had converted the stable into a downstairs ('garage', entry, kitchen and loo) and an upstairs: a bedroom and a huge study/living room with foreign pictures, wall-hangings and numerous books. We sat on a sofa. Tuohy (the de Maupassant of our time) sat in a chair opposite. We talked of Japan. He had returned to Japan from 1982 to 1989 and when he left he got drunk, made a speech in which he told the *sensei* (professors), "Your students are better than you are," and fell into the *sashimi* (raw fish) and had fish on his shoulder. He had been given two Tibetan spaniels by the Warden of All Souls.

We lunched downstairs: ham, baked potato, egg mayonnaise he made during a thunderstorm the previous night with dogs yapping and had to remake that morning, followed by raspberries with cream and cheese. We drank soda and chattered about mutual friends such as Alan Baker, who had remarried, and the poetic views of Ricks and Larkin. He said: "Ricks carries things to extreme, he makes a word used accidentally appear deliberate. Larkin uses exclamation marks at the end of a poem to solve the problem of how to end strongly." Tuohy stooped and shuffled and appeared much older, with less of a memory. Upstairs, over bitter coffee, he spoke of Wittgenstein: "I can't remember what he said, I didn't understand much. I remember his German intonation and metaphors. I went to see a film, *Ladies Courageous*, with him. I remember his deck-chair and pile of detective novels. He liked Westerns and Betty Hutton." Tuohy told me: "I have arthritis and blood pressure." Later we toured the farm, met the five children and visited a barn where there was a barn owl. We ended the tour at our car.

My impression of Tuohy was that he was getting old and that his powers were failing. He was not as sharp as he had been and was not as used to focusing on writers. He wrote every morning. He did not want to talk about my books, and when I mentioned the "jigsaw [of interlocking works] I am doing" said, "Shall we look round the garden?" But mention of his own work was in order – as it was for Kathleen Raine and Colin Wilson.[15]

Quaker Universalists in Birmingham

While writing my autobiographical approach to Universalism I was still being invited to talk about *The Universe and the Light*. I drove to Birmingham to address the Quaker Universalists' annual weekend conference.

I arrived around 4 at Fircroft College, Selly Oak, a College of Adult Education with grounds including a pool, polyanthuses and daffodils. I noted a Quaker ambience of plainness about the place: there was no basin in my room, and the bathroom was across the passage. During a get-together on the first evening I asked the group sitting near me, "In the silence are you aware of the Quaker Light?" Eyes were in corners. The next morning I woke at 6.15 and went to the bathroom early and joined a man who was shaving. He said, "I'm putting on a cycle of 12 plays about the 20th century, based on *The Fire and the Stones*." It was linked to mythical themes such as the expulsion from Paradise, and the first was at the Birmingham Arts Theatre in July. I asked: "And you bring the Fire into the cycle?" He said: "Yes, we have a Greek chorus." And immediately I saw how I could do my own verse drama with a Greek chorus. The idea would surface in my *Collected Verse Plays*. "Our committee studied your book and the charts." At the end of our shaving together he said: "Thank you for your writings. You are making an impact because Fundamentalism is digging its heels in."

Before my talk I went to the Light: "First there was 'silent worship' from 9 till 9.45 during which the Light poured in, empowering me from head to foot, at 9.05 and about 9.20; enormous surges." I then spoke to 50 or 60 who sat facing me. I spoke on religious and spiritual Universalism, saying that there will be pressure for religious Universalism when there is a political Universalist New World Order. I used the overhead projector and stirred them up. There were many questions. I was controversial about the Bilderberg Group. My address can be found in *The One and the Many*, 'A New Mystic and Philosophical Universalism'.

At lunchtime I had finished. But at 2.15 there was a study group of 10 which went on until 4. They wanted me to join it and I spoke for most of the time. I said to them, they can be the Quaker Universalist Group, or they can network all the churches and take part in religious Universalism or they can form a Universalist religion. One of the Quakers asked me, "Can we really believe that the Light is the energy that keeps our civilization going?" I replied, "Yes, because it gets into the religion which is involved in the State. Mystics affect the State." I meant that the unitive consciousness the Light creates has infused wisdom and knowledge from the beyond which improves the civilization's government. I was talking about transcendence's concerned and involved action in the world: in everyday life and history.

The next day, a Sunday, there was a reply to my view of Universalism by Marcus Braybrooke, Chairman of the World Congress of Faiths and an authority on the interfaith movement. He said "there can be Universalism and diversity". I spoke with him at length over coffee – he had a shock of curly hair and was bespectacled with a lean, precise mouth – and he was extremely interested in *The Fire and the Stones*.

Back at home I realised I had the answer to Wilson's question, "What do I do?" I realised I had a new ethic based on the Light:

> Everyone has brotherhood in the Light, as in St Augustine's *Civitas Dei*. So all are responsible for all. So [an enlightened] World-Lord has a duty to help the poor, to spread resources…. Right action by all illumined people. Each day, help someone poor, help a child, help someone disabled, help a teenager, practising compassionate action in the world. Separate going to the Light in silence and 'What do I do out in the world?'… The duties involved in world government. An end to all war. Become an enthusiastic devotee of [non-New-World-Order] world government…. Show enlightened help and reverence for Light. Respect the Light in everybody…. My amelioration. The illumined make things better for everyone else.

I preferred to think of the metaphysical Reality as the One but I saw how it could be seen as the four aspects of God:

> The fourfold nature of God: as One – 'dark' Godhead (i.e. latent Light); as Non-Being – limitation of Godhead becoming involved in Creation; as Being – the Fire or Light; as existence – energy within form. It is all one manifesting process.

And I added: "All knowledge is a human construct. Mysticism is not, it comes into the soul and has not been constructed by humans, only received."[16]

Metaphysical Research Group renamed Universalist Group of Philosophers

I was certain about my presentation of Universalism in my autobiographical writing, and my new self-assurance may have been evident at the next meeting of the philosophers of the 'Metaphysical Research Group'. I drove to David Lorimer's house in Tilehouse Lane, Denham, near Uxbridge, Buckinghamshire. Max Payne chaired the philosophy group. There were papers on Bohm's consciousness and number. There was a disagreement between Max and Geoffrey Read regarding one of the papers. Max then attacked metaphysics and declared the Metaphysical Research Group at an end.

There was a stunned silence. I said very calmly: "We are finished with the caterpillar stage and must become a chrysalis before the butterfly emerges. This phase that has finished was necessary. But there is now a new phase. We must work in a latent movement, we have become a movement."

Peter Hewitt was appalled by Payne's decision and asked me (by writing on the back of our agenda), "Would you be prepared to act as Chairman?" I nodded. He proposed it, I came in and with Max looking deeply unhappy, it was agreed that the group should continue under a Universalist banner, to get across to those "out there" and study our own work as if we were Existentialists. I said: "It's as if we were Sartre, Camus, Heidegger and Jaspers – each will have a different emphasis but we're all one movement." Max said: "It's 'as if we were pre-Raphaelites'." Chris Macann (formerly a don at Lincoln College, Oxford) was very active in supporting our new direction. We had a vision to get across: "We are an anti-materialist alliance but we are under a positive banner." Satish Kumar, who had rung me the previous day, had asked me to explain 'What is the Fire? What is Universalism?' in an article for his magazine. I said: "We're like the Aristotelian Society, which had Whitehead and T.E. Hulme in the same room. One day it be will said: 'Just think, Max Payne and Geoffrey Read fell out, I would like to have been a fly on the wall; and David Lorimer was there – and Alison Watson!'" There were smirks all round.

I was now chairing the philosophers as Universalists. I started with my image of going through the hole in the hedge. Later, we talked on the lawn near the orchard of apple-trees in the evening sun, I in a long-sleeved shirt and tie. I told them that our Universalist group would reverse the work of the Vienna Circle (which had included Ayer and Wittgenstein). I said: "The bus is going, we just have to get on it. The Metaphysical Revolution has taken over."[17] We agreed to rename the group the Universalist Group of Philosophers. All members of the group now subscribed to Universalism.

Autobiography: glimpsing two new works in Pisa
In Florence: Villa Careggi and Ficino

A new phase in my autobiographical writing and work on my epic began immediately after the creation of the Universalist Group of Philosophers. I had a strong intuitive feeling I did not wholly understand that I should go to Pisa as my vision of the Light would be advanced there. I had decided to go to nearby Florence for a conference on Ficino, who translated Plato at the beginning of the Renaissance and integrated Plato's and the Christian concepts of love. He was on the side of invisible Reality and I was sure I had a poem about Ficino's role c.1450.

I flew to Pisa on my way to the conference in Florence. I took a bus from Pisa airport to the station, and then a number–1 bus that crossed the Arno's shimmering reflection of coloured houses. I got off at the Piazza, walked through an arch and was suddenly back in the Middle Ages: the round Baptistery, the rectangular Cathedral (Duomo), and the Leaning Tower of Pisa, very white and leaning much more than I had expected, and a 13th-century square with stalls. I caught another bus back over the Arno, near where Shelley lived, and returned to the station. I caught a train past mountains and Tuscan farms to Florence, took a bus out to Careggi and booked in at the Hotel Careggi.

I walked to the 15th-century Villa Careggi, where Cosimo Medici died and Ficino founded the Platonist Academy: a towering orange façade with arches at the top, and a courtyard inside. I made my way into the meeting-room, a hall with frescoes, where two dozen attendees were sitting. There were five red apples over double doors at the end (the Medicis' pawnbrokers symbol). I was slightly late. Linda Proud spoke on the Orphic and pagan background to Ficino, trying to make him out to be more pagan than he was. At question time I asked if she knew why he had become a priest in 1473, and held that he was endeavouring to reconcile Christian and pagan, as had Clement of Alexandria, that he was a reconciling Universalist rather than a neo-pagan. There was then a break, and I studied a fresco of Verrocchio's *Resurrection* in the next room and wandered out among orange-trees and wisteria in the gardens, and sat by a sculpture of boys riding on an owl and a tortoise.

The second lecture was on Gemistos Plethon and the Fire or Light. Chris Bamford traced the tradition of the Fire, and I was sure he had used my work as a source. I asked the first question at the end: "Ficino and Plethon were not typical Renaissance figures but were continuing the tradition of the Fire or Light, which has applications today in history, science and philosophy." I quoted Tillich on local traditions also being universal. I asked him, "Have you seen my book?" He said: "I've got it, Noel Cobb sent it to me." I said: "So you know about my interest in the Fire." He said: "Gemistos was not a Universalist but a localist." I said: "That's why I quoted Tillich. You can have your own local tradition but relate it to the universal religion of which Christianity and Islam are types." I said that Ficino and Plethon should not be seen solely as Platonists but as reconcilers of Platonism and the universal religion of Christianity. Later we all ate at the 15th-century Villa Cancelli.

The next morning I learned more about Cosimo's link with Ficino. I was collected by a minibus and driven to the Villa Careggi. I learned that Cosimo, a banker who managed the Papacy's finances and became the wealthiest man of his time, at 50 (in 1439) attended lectures on Plato and eventually invited his doctor's son, Ficino, to open the Academy. Ficino had been six when he met Cosimo through his father at a time when Cosimo was enthused by Gemistos Plethon to study Plato. The decision to found the Academy can be dated to 1462 (or 1468, *De Amore*) and began the Italian Renaissance after the fall of Constantinople in 1453 had sent a flow of ancient works from libraries to Italy. I learned that Ficino lived in the Villa La Fontanelle about two miles away, and that he visited Cosimo at Careggi in a room upstairs. There is a letter from Ficino to Cosimo thanking him for the "little house" which local tradition puts on the hill; and revealing that Cosimo had gout. Ficino's letters had influenced Botticelli regarding the divine Venus (Plato's divine principle). There was a lecture on Ficino's unified view of the universe and mention of "the supernatural Light".

In the early evening I went in to Florence on a bus to seek Ficino's city. Inside the Duomo I saw the picture of Dante and Ficino's bust. I "went to where (between numbers 12 and 13 outside) Dante sat in the evenings, and walked to the house of his birth and childhood in Via Dante Alighieri". I walked on to the Piazza della Signoria where Savonarola was hanged and burnt. I visited the Palazzo Vecchio where Cosimo was imprisoned and then the Uffizi and "saw Botticelli's *Primavera* (Plato's divine principle) and *The birth of Venus* – pagan images of Beauty and unity which Ficino influenced". I crossed the Ponte Vecchio, whose shops protrude over the Arno, to Santa Maria del Carmine.

I had grasped that the first Humanists such as Ficino wanted *more* Light, and that it was only later that they turned secular. I realised that the halo disappeared with Botticelli. It was in Fra Filippo Lippi, but had gone by Titian. It was still there in those who died c.1490. The great change happened about 1468: a new Age had brought geographical voyages, printing and a new interest in paganism. Ficino had combined Plato and Christianity in Venus as spiritual love. Those who died c.1510 had lost the halo.

I had grasped that the Light was central to Ficino. The next morning I sat and wrote three stanzas of the poem that would become 'The Laughing

Philosopher' in the courtyard of the Villa Careggi, amid tinkling birdsong. I then went into the grounds and wrote another stanza, sitting and writing on paper on my knee near the statue of a Greek goddess. After lunch there was a tour of the Villa Careggi: I climbed the stairs to the room where the Academy met, according to the nuns' oral tradition. It had a polished floor and red carpet. I wandered out to a *loggia* with 16th-century frescoes including the Medicis' pawnbrokers' symbol. Back in the lecture room I heard a talk on the sad smile of Aphrodite (because Adonis had left her) and scribbled more stanzas for my poem on the Renaissance. I listened to a paper on *De Amore* that claimed that to Ficino Eros was divine love. Then we all took the minibus to Villa La Fontanelle, the hilly site of Ficino's house, where the owner received us. I ate in a *trattoria* and reflected that the lecturers had a scholar's approach to the Light – "You can find out about the Rosicrucian Fire in Amsterdam," I had been told – whereas I approached it through experience as in 1971.

The next morning I explored the Florentine Renaissance in art. I went into Florence by bus and visited San Marco's Dominican monastery and saw in the upstairs monastic cells Fra Angelico's wonderful frescoes. I saw Cosimo's cell (where he went on retreat) and Savonarola's cell (and where he was arrested by the library). Downstairs in rooms off the cloisters I saw more Angelicos in which the halo and his view of man within a sea of Light were very pronounced. I then found the Medici chapel. I walked on to Florence's Baptistery and saw the 'Gate of Paradise' – so called by Michelangelo – that was crafted by Ghiberti (who died in 1452). Inside I saw the dome of 13th-century mosaics with Christ, which Dante would have known. I visited the Carmine – in the Brancacci chapel of which are Masaccio's frescoes with his wonderful shiverer, fishermen, aghast Eve and weeping Adam – and in the silence in the rebuilt 18th-century cloisters I felt the Light come through and wrote a poem or two. I went on to S. Maria Novella but could not see the portrait of Ficino as the central altar was cordoned off. I saw the frescoes, showing Dante as one of the blessed and Dante's Hell.

I was aware that the Renaissance under Ficino involved a fusion of the Christian and pagan. I was sure that the Renaissance effected a shift from Mary's halo to Venus's body, a paganisation of divine love. However, Ficino had shown Venus as spiritual love, and back in the lecture room I listened to Monteverdi's union of erotic and divine love. I should show the Virgin and Venus as a Universalist principle of Light. I reflected that Ficino and Botticelli had used symbolism similar to the symbolism I had used in two volumes of my poetry, *Lady of the Lamp* and *A Flirtation with the Muse*.

Later we were shown a picture by Bramante (1444–1514) of the two philosophers Democritus and Heracleitus, "one laughing and the other sad". I contrasted the laughing Democritus and sad Heracleitus in the last stanza of 'The Laughing Philosopher' and reflected that both Ficino and Heracleitus were sad because humankind does not recognise the Fire. I was now clear from my few days' contact with the Renaissance that the Light was central Western culture, although largely and wrongly ignored, and that my role as a poet was to bring back the experience of the Light and the vision I had had in Egerton Gardens in 1971 into my poetic work.[18]

Two finished works revealed in Pisa: Overlord *(poetic epic) and* Classical Odes
The next phase of my autobiographical writing and poetic epic was revealed to me the following morning. I paid my hotel bill and took a taxi to the station and the train to Pisa, where I

> left my luggage at the station and took a bus to the Arno and walked to where Shelley lived. The plaque on the wall, near Ponte alla Fortezza.... Here he wrote 'Adonais'. An emotional walk along the end of Lung'arno Galileo (via S. Sepolchro, a Templar church) across the river to Lung'arno Mediceo where, after looking at a Roman wall, I pondered my future.... I had written poems, and after being opened up by Angelico and at the Carmine yesterday, I was filled with higher feeling as I sensed my future and destiny, to write an epic as great as Homer's, Virgil's Dante's, Milton's, Pound's. I had done my basic work [in the footsteps of] Ficino – my history and cosmology – and only had political and religious Universalism to do. Like Virgil I had shelved the huge task for 20 years, having been caught up in worldly things, and now was the time to get on and do it. I could hide here in Pisa.... This was the Arno of Dante (in Florence) and of Shelley and Pound (who was detained here) – the medieval, Romantic and Modernist union, the tradition. I had to dare to be great. I had all the qualifications needed to write an epic: the Fire, history, cosmology, science. All, achievements in themselves, were but preludes to the epic, clearing my head for what is to come, a work that would plumb the height of goodness and the depth of evil, the struggle between the universal Christ and Lucifer whose Seven Deadly Sins are winning (Hitler, Stalin, Cold War, Conspiracy).[19]

What happened next I have described in *A New Philosophy of Literature*:[20]

> Sitting [in the open air] on the Lung'arno Mediceo by the Arno in Pisa in May 1993, within view of the wall behind which Shelley wrote *A Defence of Poetry* in March 1821 and spoke of poetry's lifting the veil from the hidden beauty of the world, I had a glimpse – a profound revelation – in which, for about ten seconds, I saw two vast finished works of mine in an image and knew that I should undertake them immediately: my epic poem *Overlord*, and

451

Classical Odes, a work of autobiographical literature. I had literally seen ten years' work in seconds. This revelation was a compelling instance of Romantic inspiration in the imagination, and I recorded it in two poems, 'By the Arno, Pisa' and 'After the Pisan Arno'. I had had the idea for a poetic epic for nearly 25 years, but this glimpse of the finished work had an intensity that brought with it a commitment to an immediate start.

It was typical of my double life that I had seen two works. At first I did not understand what was being shown to me. I misinterpreted what I had seen. I thought that the finished poems drawing on the classical tradition, the odes, were *part of* my epic. What I wrote later that day preserves this misunderstanding but catches the intensity of the inspiration:

> The elemental, high, pure feeling overflowed in me, and my eyes were wet, I trembled inside at the intensity of what I must do: to embody all the culture of Western civilization in a twelve-book poem. The exalted vision of perfection brought with it a sense of the inadequacy of my realisation of the vision (or so I thought). My vision was one of meaning and awe, of optimism, not despair. I was in [an open-air] bar on the Lung'arno Mediceo, drinking a cup of tea, and my eyes were filled with tears on and off for about ten minutes. I could not speak, blinking back the tears. I had found my next stage in my work.... I had had the equivalent of Dante's vision of 1301.... Now with awesome certainty I knew what I had to do.... I would... incorporate the Italian (and Greek) tradition into my epic.... In Pisa I discovered a spring of creative feeling and imagination.[21]

I returned to the station by bus and sat by the fountain until 7, then went by taxi to the airport. I flew home. I was full of the Renaissance and the whole of the Quattrocento. Geoffrey Read rang, supportive of what I was trying to do in philosophy, but under a large full moon I was only thinking of my vision by the Arno:

> I must return to Italy and Greece, where I began, and apply my Ficinian vision of oneness in a great epic. Virgil died at 51 having spent 11 years on his epic. It must be now. In two years' time [I must have finished my epic], at 55.... My difficulty has been in understanding my many-sidedness, in grasping that I had to express *all* aspects of my Ficinian unitive outlook. I was an all-rounder.... Me working on my epic among Italian stones, my Fire among Italian temples and cathedrals.[22]

Throughout May and June I thought about the epic while I worked on my autobiography and *Collected Poems* [later titled *A White Radiance*].

I dined with Steve Norris at the House of Commons. We discussed Maastricht and the committee to investigate MI5 and MI6, which was headed by Sir John Hoskyns, our dining neighbour. I said that a politician needs a vision: "There has to be a vision behind the words, as de Gaulle had, and then there is a strong projection [from the people]." He said: "You are absolutely right." He asked what job I would do if he became Prime Minister around 2000. I said I would be "roving Ambassador between world leaders". After dinner we "went to his room on the bottom corridor of the Ministers' block" and I showed him some material I had brought on the New World Order.

But I was planning to implement my vision by the Arno. I began looking for a bursar who would help me run the financial side of Coopersale Hall and take the daily visit to the bank from me. I rang Sir Laurens van der Post and "told him about... the Fire surfacing in Florence". He said: "It's confirmation. I did nothing except to give you some recognition, and you have provided confirmation."[23]

Then I attended a course on Goethe at St Catherine's College, Oxford. I passed the Eastgate, where Ann was having a reunion with her college friends. The lectures on Goethe were by two scientists, Arthur Zajonc (pronounced 'Zience'), author of Catching the Light, and Brian Goodwin (who I had met the last time I saw Kathleen Raine), and they focused on Goethe's biology and view of flowers. When I got home I realised that my epic "is like a plant – as a poem – a Jack-by-the-hedge or garlic mustard (or lily) with 12 leaves.... The theme and 12 books. Organic form for my epic.... My epic form must be transformative."[24] The image of Jack-by-the-hedge appears in book 1, lines 146–151 of Overlord.

The next day I had coffee with Ann and her college friends at their breakfast table at the Eastgate, and then had discussions with the two scientists about Goethe's observation of plants. For several days I had thought about my epic and I now wrote: "Call it Overlord, first after the D-Day operation 'Overlord', secondly [because of] the struggle between Christ and Lucifer, and finally because of the world government and Universalism, the defeat of Lucifer." Two days later I drafted an outline for Overlord.[25]

'The Laughing Philosopher', 'Epithalamion'
I was carrying forward my poetry. On 11 May I wrote: "Worked on 'The Weeping Philosopher'. Polished 6 stanzas." The next day I "finished my poem on Ficino. It is now called 'The Laughing Philosopher'. The emphasis on flux."[26]

Nadia had met a classical guitarist, Sandy Wright, who had "whisked her off her feet" and she said she would like to get married. I had said that I was delighted for her. She rang again – I could hear the classical guitar in the background sounding like "the play of light on the water outside her window" – to say that the wedding would be at Johnsburn House, Balerno, near Edinburgh. The next evening I "drafted an epithalamion about my daughter's marriage. Used Spenser's 18-line stanza and rhyme scheme, mixing modern realities with the traditional nymphs."[27] Towards the end of May I was revising sonnets written in 1979 for my *Collected Poems*.

Reversing the Vienna Circle, Willis Harman

While I wrote on into *A Mystic Way* I was sucked back into philosophy. I met the inner core of the philosophers in The Grosvenor Hotel, Victoria. Chris Macann immediately produced his tome for me to read, an awesome universal system after the manner of Hegel or Heidegger. I told him we are perhaps the first group to be considering the whole universe and universal systems since the Vienna Circle. Alison Watson arrived, and Geoffrey Read. We sat in front of the hearth in the tea-room, and considered *Declaration*-style essays with a possible manifesto at the end. Alison and Geoffrey had a bickering quarrel which Alison stood up to leave. I insisted she sat down. I said: "There's the work as an object but also there's how it is perceived and received, what interpretation the reader puts on it, and that's important. We must have an accessible general book." All agreed. Chris said: "The book can be called *Universalism: The Philosophy of the Future*." Later Alison rang me and said: "It's your drive that has got us together, it's your drive that's keeping us all to the point."

Three days later I went to Regent's College, London to listen to Willis Harman, author of *A Re-Examination of the Metaphysical Foundations of Modern Science*. I sat with him in Regent's Park where we took to deck-chairs for a picnic lunch. I put it to him that the revolution in philosophy will have useful consequences for science. He agreed. Later I walked to Baker Street station with William Anderson, author of *Dante the Maker* (who had been a speaker with me at Winchester). We discussed Italy. He recommended Lonsdale Ragg, *Dante and his Italy* on Dante's Italy and Gilbert Highet, *Poets in a Landscape* on the Italy of Virgil, Horace and Ovid. He said he would live in Vicenza or in the Tuscan San Gimignano, where Dante was sent as ambassador in 1300. Anderson was besuited with waistcoat and spectacles, and had hardly any voice because of a bad throat, but gave precise and considered answers to my questions. Then abruptly he said goodbye and disappeared in haste for an appointment.

Another three days later I attended the Universalist Philosophy Group at David Lorimer's house in Uxbridge. I spoke to the philosophers on tape for two hours on how wide Universalism is; on my central idea of the Fire as a first principle out of which the universe and evolution came; on how the vision of the Fire is central to history; on how the metaphysical view is of a totality that includes science and spirituality; on how there should be a metaphysical science and a metaphysical philosophy; and on how Universalism is happening anyway. There was universal agreement that my philosophy can be accepted. I wrote: "Whitehead's 'The purpose of philosophy is to rationalize mysticism'. That's how I see philosophy.... I have turned the Vienna Circle's principle back on itself and am reversing it."[28]

Back in Cornwall at the end of May I edited my Birmingham lecture for publication in *The Universalist*. I had to visit a Cornish osteopath, having strained a muscle in my left arm, and while he kneaded my muscle with his thumb, quite painfully, I drifted off and "was aware of the Light breaking through. I record this to show that it is possible to see the Light while you are having your arm (painfully) massaged."

We returned for my aunt Argie's 90th-birthday party at the Roebuck's Beech Room. I made a speech about her "two lifelong loves", her family and the London Hospital, on a warm summery night. Mabel Reid was moving for good into Forest Place, a private nursing home near the Roebuck, and she asked me to take any books I wanted from her library. I was surprised at the number of books on mysticism she had. Oaklands kept me grounded at this time: a week later I was announcing from the caravan at the Oaklands fête.

I had managed to find time to revise sonnets:

June 7. Ill: fell asleep three times this afternoon. In the evening stayed away from the Oaklands parents meeting and revised four sonnets from *Lady of the Lamp* ('Dustpan', 'Solitude', 'Door' and 'Stalemate')…. I know I am in the Catullus tradition…. I have a felicity of language I must not be shy about.

Later I "did 'Mutiny' (another sonnet)".[29] My "felicity of language" did not make me any more indulgent towards the Vienna Circle. I was aware that I was living a reversal of the Vienna Circle's outlook.

With Christopher Ricks all round Oxford, choice of blank verse for epic
Christopher Ricks rang, inviting me to Oxford where he was finishing his sabbatical to discuss my coming epic. I had told him in a letter that I was now aiming to be a man of letters and he said, "I like what you said. I want to see you but I've got to pack up a house by the end of June. I don't think I can get away, but you can come here and have tea." And so on 21 June I met Ricks outside Blackwell's at 3.30.

He was open-necked and in jeans material, and carrying nothing. I instantly warmed to his wrinkled, bald pate, grey hair, round glasses and kind smile. At his suggestion we walked to Worcester College. We sauntered to the Worcester Gardens past staircase 8 (which had housed his room), wandered through the tunnel and sat on a seat looking at the lake – the seat we sat on for our first tutorial, as he remembered and recalled – and towards the seat beyond the arch where I chose to be a poet, a neat twist on his part. I told him about my epic. He spoke on the difficulties. He said, "Your predecessors are Homer, Virgil, Dante, Milton and Pound. Don't be in competition with them, don't be hubristic, people will snipe, it is very ambitious of you. Second, are you Manichaean: dualistic? Is it good versus evil or are both reconciled in one? Thirdly, it is easier to do evil than good. Blake said Milton is of the Devil's party. Think about regicide, deicide, Heaven and Hell. There is something wrong with God that makes the poem *Paradise Lost* go wrong, as Dryden, Addison and Pope pointed out, and defeated Tennyson in *Idylls of the King*. The mightiest of your predecessors have failed in getting the art right; Milton's Heaven was not a 'glory'. 'Justifying the ways of God to men' (Milton) is not the primary poetic theme today; making 'friends with the necessity of dying' (Lear's words which Freud took up) is, to me. Empson, when he returned from Japan, once he had got his book on complexity done, said "*Nunc dimittis*" (loosely meaning 'Now I can die'). (*See* p.866.)

"Fourth, there is a problem regarding the future, which is left unrealised. A lump of futurity. Look at the end of [Marvell's] 'Horatian Ode'. What happens in the future?" I said: "I can show the future without predestination, and still believe in free will." He said: "Prediction and prophecy, or prescience, Eliot's distinction: be prophetic, don't predict. Fifth there is a moral position." He spoke on the difference between a religious position and a technical position or artistic problem. "And so, sixth, long poems tend not to be as good as shorter ones, for example *Paradise Lost*, books 11 and 12 are not poetically achieved, and Milton writes 'Egypt, divided by the river Nile' (a flat line). Learn the lesson of the failure of the geniuses of the past in respect of points five and six, for example *Idylls of the King* and the problems of the historical novel.

"Seventh, there needs to be a common belief or body of agreement or consensus, which (I assert) is not achievable as it's Christianity or nothing, and our multi-ethnic society and atheism deny consensus." I identified the problem and said it was solvable by Universalism and by Michelangelo's unitive vision in which everything is a hierarchy. He said: "Without a universal figure, and it can't be Christ, you're like Blake with a private mythology, for example Los. Eliot's objection to Blake was his lack of orthodoxy. Dante was the beneficiary of sustained and coherent thinking such as Aquinas – but Dante was Christian and not Universalist (although in his time Christianity covered the known world and so *was* Universalist). Look at Tennyson's 'Ancient Sage' and *In Memoriam* and consider what failed

Tennyson, the inner qualities of accomplishment. Tennyson's late poems are not as good as his early poems, for example 'St Telemachus' is not as good as 'St Simeon'. Eighth, religion still means Christianity and Christ cannot stand for holism, and homogeneity of culture is an assumption." He advised me: "Have a Hellish Council and a Heavenly Council." Ricks's posture was that he "is better than Homer, Virgil and Milton, who are 'geniuses' but made mistakes and failed in their efforts". I "must learn from their mistakes".

We then walked back to Worcester and peed in the Fellows' "lavatory" for guests near the chapel by staircase 2, which Ricks described as a "sump". He insisted I went first: "Guests first." It was very primitive and reminded me of Baghdad. We walked to Longwall Street, and I said to him as we walked round Oxford: "Tuohy went for walks with Wittgenstein. I have the feeling of what it was like when I walk with you." I thought of him as the Leavis of our time. Ricks said: "Yeats says we make poems out of the quarrel with ourselves and rhetoric out of the quarrel with others. Quarrel with yourself: art. Quarrel with others: rhetoric. Keats quarrelled with himself when he wrote: 'O for a life of ease.' He wanted a life he had not got. I hate Yeats but he said something that is true." He added, the Neoclassical atheist now: "Religions are bad things and there should be a Government health warning about holism and unity." I said of Yeats: "Kathleen Raine compared *The Fire and the Stones* to *A Vision* and phases of the moon, she got me wrong. I'm not as mad as Yeats." He laughed. We were near the Martyrs' Memorial, and he said: "Yes, there's a madometer (not a swingometer but a madometer)."

We passed his bike, which was propped against the wall outside Balliol, much battered, with a crossbar, and I asked what poetic line would be most appropriate for an epic. He said: "Blank verse is better than stress metre, 'Maud' is an alternative as it contains every known line except blank verse; but it lacks dignity. Look at *The Dynasts* again, Hardy's long poem. Don't have a stanza for an epic like Byron's *Don Juan*." I settled for blank verse but said there might be occasional lyrical bits (as in *Gawain and the Green Knight*). I later opted for exclusive blank verse. I raised similes and said I was looking forward to using Miltonic similes from everyday life. He said: "They can be slightly demotic." He quoted a couple of lines of Wordsworth which dwell on the smell of sewers and city fumes in the air.

I refilled my parking meter and we found a tea-room opposite Eastgate (where not long before I had visited Ann's friends, events again gathering round constant places). He ordered coffee and I ordered tea from a mini-skirted waitress and I showed him some of my poems: 'Epithalamion' (pointing out that I wrote an essay on Spenser's 'Epithalamion' for him in 1959, nearly 35 years previously) and 'The Laughing Philosopher'. (I said it was my 'Byzantium' or 'Sailing to Byzantium', and he looked at me very intently and with great alertness and when I said, "I hope that's not presumptuous," said "No, it's not presumptuous.") I showed him the red card in my Masaccio poem, 'Paradise, Red Card', which he liked.

I raised the Great Tradition and suggested he came up with a new criterion of maturity: inner and outer and the evolution of an individual style. He said: "I don't find the idea of a 'Great' tradition valuable. There are several traditions, not just one. There are vantage points. The top of University church enables you to see all Oxford but the view from the basement of the Ashmolean is better. Epics are necessary but so are limericks and sonnets. Compare first and third person, where the question is: 'What can an artist see and show?' The artist can't die in the first person. Roger Scruton, whom I've got to know and like, talks of 'hitting the target' but I talk of steering between Scylla and Charybdis." (These two opposites resonated with my view of $+A + -A = 0$.) "Leavis seizes on maturity and a particular kind of maturity, but freshness is also important. The Great Tradition is not a good thing to do."

Regarding my epic, he said: "The danger is that you will feel too strongly about the New World Order and will quarrel with others and not make art out of the quarrel with yourself." I replied: "I can paint my Sistine chapel. My art is not propaganda." I reflected that I needed to withdraw from quarrelling with others such as Colin Wilson and the philosophers to quarrel with myself. Ricks sneezed from hay fever and I was struck by his violent and loud blowing of his nose. I showed him the title of a volume of my poems: *A Sneeze in the Universe*. He smiled. He spoke of my "gigantism". I said I "have a gigantic theme, like Milton's *Paradise Lost*". He said: "Nothing's changed since Tennyson's *Idylls of the King* technically. Go back to him." He remarked: "We communicate through poetic and artistic ideas. You've done your thinking and thought it all out and so you can use it in an epic."

Suddenly at 5.45 he leapt up, said "I've got to be back by six", darted over to the counter and paid, and as I followed him out into the street, said, "I shall shake you by the hand and say goodbye because I'm going *that* way," and with a brief shake of the hand he had gone before I could properly thank him. Shortly afterwards Ricks was in *The Times*, speaking about Eliot's unpublished poems (which he was editing) which, he said, are not up to Eliot's highest standards but are "much better than any poems being written today".[30]

My walk round Oxford with Ricks had enabled me to fix on blank verse as the line for my epic, and provided me with fresh angles to consider during the last days of the summer term.

The hectic world of the schools closed round me, and I had little time to think about my epic. There were Sports Days in both schools and the Coopersale Hall fête was opened by Nick Berry, the police constable in British television's *Heartbeat*. Steve Norris's seven-year-old son had written a letter that won a national competition. He read it out at the Coopersale Hall prize-giving to considerable mirth. It described how his father, Parliamentary Under Secretary of State for Transport and Minister for Transport in London, had been wheel-clamped outside Sainsbury's and had tried to remove the clamp on hands and knees with a screwdriver.

International politics: poems on the New World Order
In the USA, 'American Liberty Quintet'

I knew that America and the New World Order would feature strongly in my epic, and I had arranged to take my family for a three-week tour of the East Coast, visiting cities and 18th-century sites. Our flight tickets did not arrive until half an hour before we left for Heathrow. We were compensated by flying Connoisseur class, and I was sipping champagne, eating steak and reading books on New York and Boston in comfort in the air when I

> had the idea for writing a... quintet of poems about America's world dominance, each one set in a different city or place: New York (the UN); Boston (the expulsion of the British); Washington (Kennedy and the founding fathers); Philadelphia (the origin of the US); and Florida.

In New York we walked among the towering buildings in a heat of 95 degrees and got used to the pedestrian lights saying "Don't Walk" and "Walk". I noted: "Everything here is better than in Europe: bigger, brassier and lasting longer." I asked: "Is America a different civilization from the European one? Undoubtedly.... A thrusting, money-making gigantistic civilization, where you express your individual wealth on a vast scale."

We visited places connected with America's world role and the New World Order. We toured New York on an air-conditioned coach. We went to downtown Manhattan, stopped at the Rockefeller building and went to the Empire State Building, Maddison Square and Avenue, Fifth Avenue and Wall Street. There was a clear blue sky and we had a good view of the Statue of Liberty "in the distance, like the Colossus of Rhodes, an Illuminati symbol from France guaranteeing liberty". We ended in the fragile UN building. We were taken round and I entered all the chambers, including the Security Council and the General Assembly. I then took a taxi to East 68th Street and gazed for a long time at the anonymous CFR (Council on Foreign Relations) building, centre of America's world ideal, the place where the UN was dreamt up. We toured Harlem, and passed the Rockefeller-backed non-denominational Riverside church. During the day I saw the Greek statues and images of the New World Order's rule: Atlas, Prometheus and Zeus. In the early evening I took a taxi to Washington Square and looked in vain for no. 38, where Eugene O'Neill wrote *The Iceman Cometh*. We went up to the 86th floor of the Empire State Building for the view. My perceptions would pass into my books on America and the New World Order: *The Syndicate*, *The Secret History of the West*, *The Secret Founding of America* and *The Secret American Dream*; and into my two epics, *Overlord* and *Armageddon*.

We flew to Boston and back the next day. We took the Freedom Trail in a great heat. We went over the *USS Constitution*, which was in dry dock, and then to the Old State House, Old South Meeting-House where the Tea-Party debate took place, Faneuil Hall and other buildings connected with Benjamin Franklin, and the *Beaver II*, a boat on which we witnessed a reconstruction of the 1773 Tea Party.

The next morning we were to go by coach to the Niagara Falls. I received poems in my sleep:

July 11. Woke before 6 to pack cases in time for 6.45 and 'saw' two of my American quintets. 'New York' to catch the thrusting economic growth of America, to be built around the Rockefellers, the dream of world government. 'Boston' to catch the separation from the British of the Boston Tea Party and Samuel Adams, a separation by separatists and dissenting Puritans: the dissenting spirit.

We drove through wooded Pennsylvania (founded by William Penn of Chigwell School) and I began what became my 'American Liberty Quintet', drafting the first two poems on my knee on the coach.

We ate overlooking the Niagara Falls and went on a boat, *The Maid of the Mist*, to get a closer look: "At the top of Niagara Falls... I had drafted 3 stanzas of 'Niagara Falls', and now, back on the coach, I polished them and added a 4th stanza, and also wrote 2 more poems as we continued our drive to Lake Ontario and the town Niagara-by-the-lake: 'A Floral Clock'..., and 'At Lake Ontario' as the four of us ate a picnic lunch with our feet near the water, lying on a grassy bank in bright sunshine." We enjoyed our brief visit to Canada.

We returned through the Appalachian mountains and farms. I "wrote 3 more poems: 'Rainbow'; 'Susquehanna'; and 'UN Security Council'". In Lancaster Matthew gave a *Choi Kwang Do* class. He was received like royalty by the Americans. The next day we saw the Puritan Amish, who wore plain black clothes (the women white bonnets), a Mennonite sect that had not changed since 1690.

I was impressed by Washington's huge Roman grandeur: wide open spaces and gigantic Graeco-Roman buildings, all white marble, well-kept.

We visited the Holocaust Museum and toured the FBI and in the evening ate overlooking the Potomac. We went to the Jefferson Memorial in a thunder-storm, then the Lincoln Memorial, the Kennedy Centre and the Watergate building. The next morning we visited Arlington Cemetery (and JFK's grave), the Capitol, the Vietnam Memorial and Mount Vernon, George Washington's estate. I went by car to the Washington Masonic Monument or Temple and I bought a book, *Washington, Master Mason*, which contained details of Washington's hostile attitude to the 18th-century Illuminati.

We went on to Philadelphia and saw the Liberty Bell, the Congress Hall and Independence Hall, with the half-sun on Washington's chair. I "saw that the original Fire or Light of the American civilization was a Masonic one – Washington's half-sun in his chair; that Washington's Masonry... operated within his Episcopalian religion".

We flew to Orlando in Florida, and I drafted a third poem of my 'American Liberty Quintet' on Washington. I went out to the Kennedy Space Centre to see the space shuttle leave, but the launch was aborted. We visited Disneyland and Universal Studios.

We moved on to St Petersburg on the Gulf of Mexico, where we spent nine days at the Dolphin Beach Hotel: by (and in) the pool on the edge of the beach, looking at the dolphins and bird life in the intercoastal waterway and seeing wild alligators in the Everglades swamps, the millionaires' colony in Naples and the shells on Marco Island .

We had hired a car and we drove to St Augustine, where I focused on Ponce de Léon's Fountain of Youth. We stopped at Daytona beach on the way expecting to see the Shuttle launch, but it was aborted two minutes before take-off with thousands on the beach, all looking in the direction of Cape Canaveral. We returned to Orlando and visited the Epcot Centre. At the end of July I went to the Kennedy Space Centre and drove round the launch pads and researched NASA's space station.

All the while I carried forward my 'Quintet', and by 20 July I wrote:

Call the 'American Quintet' the 'Liberty Quintet'. Liberty is the common theme: liberty for the world under a world government that must not be a slavery.

Soon afterwards I settled for 'American Liberty Quintet'. Somehow the poem wrote itself, between buffet breakfasts, lunches at the Dolphin beach and evening forays to local restaurants. I polished the sections, and on 28 July noted: "My poem was... unplanned and is... 'guided'." I completed the fifth poem of the 'Quintet'. I had dictated the earlier poems, and I wrote: "At both Tampa and Washington I dictated parts of 'St Petersburg' on to my hand-held cassette-recorder, and in the 747 going home I finished section 5

Nicholas dictating 'American Liberty Quintet' on the plane home on 29 July 1993

and dictated it. Worked until midnight."[31] The poem was dedicated to President Clinton and included an appeal to him to turn his back on the self-interested New World Order. I arrived at Heathrow with the whole poem, which I had not planned to write, completely finished and on tape for typing.

The trip had been so full of new impressions of the outer world that there was little time for the Light. I felt I had "seen" East-Coast America and its world role, and confirmed the vision I had had in *The Fire and the Stones*. I had written a poem that balanced 'Archangel' in my poetic work. I had many images to channel into my four 'American books' and my two poetic epics.

Autobiography: poems of the universe
Nadia's wedding

Soon after our return we flew to Edinburgh for Nadia's wedding. Nadia was on our British Midland flight and I was again shown onto the flight deck. We took off at 133 knots (taking the weight and temperature into account) and climbed to 35,000 feet. I unclipped my harness which was between my legs, round my sides and over my shoulders (5 straps into a central clip) and emerged from the flight deck dazed with instrumentation. I returned to the flight deck for the landing which was over Edinburgh's Forth Bridge and the Firth estuary. At the last minute the captain realised that he had not pulled down the second lever for an automated landing and our landing had to be manual. That was because I was asking questions.

From the airport we were driven to the Riccarton Arms, Currie, ten minutes away. We were collected by Sandy and Nadia in a car, with Caroline and Damian following, and driven to Johnsburn House for a rehearsal. Caroline was relaxed, and looked willowy and elegant, if weathered. In the evening I held a dinner party for 11 in the Kweilin, which had a round table that turned, and got to know Sandy's mother. There was a lot of merriment.

The next morning was wet and misty. We breakfasted in a beamy room, all yellow plaster, and I gazed at the doves on the dovecote outside my window and "wrote 'The Hills of Fife' straight out". We left the Riccarton at 3 in a taxi with Caroline, Damian and Nadia in her ivory dress. Nadia changed at Johnsburn House. We waited in an 18th-century room overlooking the lawn. A picture of Burns hung over the hearth to commemorate his visit 197 years previously. There were tears at 3.45 and I reassured her. The vicar arrived in a kilt and at 4 I led Nadia out to the lawn, and we took our place before a simple altar on which stood a cross near a rushing stream. Sandy was waiting in a kilt.

As the vicar married the couple midges bit and danced round our necks, and all the time I heard the stream bubbling. Afterwards there were photos, and there was champagne in the wooden panelled room. I spoke for five minutes about Nadia. I said "You've been a wonderful daughter and you'll make a great wife." I read my 'Epithalamion' – first the note and then the poem – which was received with thunderous applause. As it died down I said that I hoped my poem would last 400 years as Spenser's 'Epithalamion' did, and that this day would be remembered in 400 years' time, and there was more applause. Nadia was much affected by the poem; I think it touched her.[32]

The dance floor was soon crowded, and I danced with several of Nadia's friends. Several said to me, "I can see the resemblance between Nadia and you," and "She's got your eyes." Nadia and Sandy left at 11.45. A circle was formed, there was a long wait for Nadia, and she came to me first, tearful, and I told her, "All you've got to do is to hold yourself together for another two minutes." She went round embracing everyone, and then returned to me. As we drove away I was very aware that had I done what the SIS wanted me to do I would not have been present at Nadia's wedding and given her away.

Poems inspired by sea
I felt creative: "Aug. 9. Creative all day. The Light came in about 9 and my aura was visible out of the corner of my eye in the dark: white radiance. My Muse is back." Poems kept coming when I was back in Cornwall:

Aug. 12. Arrived under a cloudless sky and shooting stars like exclamation marks down the sky. It is the last day of the dog days.... Aug. 13. 21 poems on my Muse.... Went for a walk with Matthew and Ann.... Wrote a poem ['Trawling'] asking if the Shuttle was up there, a poem about the universe.... Aug. 14. Reflected and polished poems.... On the *Maria Asumpta* the rear sail is up and a man is singing sea-shanties to a crowd as evening closes in on the harbour. Wrote: 'Sea-Shanty'.

The next day I watched the *Maria Asumpta* leave port and wrote two more poems, 'Tall Ship' and 'Brig'. I then settled to the 'American Liberty Quintet'. I "went for a walk at 11.45 with Matthew and Anthony and returned and wrote 'Midnight Sky: Hawthorn and Almond'". The next day I reworked "the 'American Liberty Quintet' and dictated it. I wrote another poem about the sparkling waves, 'Dancing'. A beautiful late-night walk under vivid stars."[33] The following day Clapperton and his partner Susie visited me and said they had sold the harbour to Robin Davies of Bristol, who would use it for tall-masted ships.

Last visit to Colin Wilson
On 18 August I made one last visit to Colin Wilson on my own. I encountered him at 5.30 in the kitchen. "Would you like some smoked salmon?" (I only later realised that he first tasted smoked salmon when Victor Gollancz took him to lunch to mark his acceptance of *The Outsider*, and his habitual serving of smoked salmon may have perpetuated that moment.) There was avocado as well. Both his boys were around, and Sally. There was nervous talk while he surfaced from writing space vampires. I spoke about Ricks and Eliot. Colin said, "The unpublished poems [of Eliot] are no good." He told me that in the summer of 1956 he went to Eliot's church (St Stephen's, Gloucester Road) to observe Eliot, who was sitting across the aisle in a back pew. Outside a boy was breaking milk bottles and as churchwarden Eliot looked uncomfortable. Seeing he could be of help, Wilson went outside and shouted, "P— off, you —s" (language which could be heard inside the church), and when he returned Eliot nodded approvingly. (As churchwarden he should have gone out and told the yobs off, and not left the task to Wilson.) Two days later he met Eliot to discuss Pound and reminded him of the milk bottles. Eliot said, "I recognised you, no one else would go to church in a polo-necked sweater."

I filled him in on the Universalist Philosophy Group. He tensed. I told him Ricks had listened to my ideas on the epic and written on Beckett. Wilson said: "Beckett's a c—. I met him at the Royal Court, he had nothing to say, there was no communication." He told me: "You've written more poems than Wordsworth." (He meant that I had written too many poems.) I told him I had been asked to lecture at the College of Psychic Studies. He said he had given five lectures there and said, "I go to a hotel near South Ken station and go to the wine bar and have a bottle of wine and then I go in and talk." He told me that, not knowing what to talk about at a lecture in Penzance, he had talked about a certain part of his anatomy.

We were alone now and, perhaps presumptuously, I said: "I hope to get you back to more philosophical work. You'll be remembered in the next century for *The Outsider* and *Religion and the Rebel*."[34] I got no further. Seething with indignation and resentment, he heatedly denied that I knew what he was "about" or that we had even communicated. I had obviously touched a sensitive spot, and although I soothed him down and reassured him while Joy came in and flashed him a disapproving look, it was clear that our difference of approach had widened, and that there could be no formal alliance between us.

Three days later I visited Fowey and at the second-hand bookshop found the only books by him on display: copies of *The Outsider* and *Religion and the Rebel* – as I predicted he would be remembered.[35] I did not see Colin Wilson again, and in June 2012 was sad to learn that he had had a stroke during an operation on his back and had lost his ability to speak. He died in December 2013, aged 82. (His obituary in *The Guardian* was under the byline of John Ezard, who sent me a draft some years before his own death in 2010. I was responsible for the reference to smoked salmon and fine wine.)

Elemental poems

Poems continued to come. The next night I took a late-night walk. I saw the Milky Way as a lobster and wrote a poem, 'Milky Way: Lobster and Sauce'. The following night I went for a walk at 11.45 p.m. with Anthony in a sea-mist, and wrote a poem, 'Mist: Bat and Walls'. We crossed by ferry to Polruan and walked to the Castle and then to the Singing Kettle for a cream tea. I spent the evening dictating the morning's work and some recent poems, including 'Stillness' ("which I wrote today about three swans and three Red Admirals"). I walked late as a storm approached like a distant war over the sea and sketched out a poem, 'Storm'.

The next morning I got the papers and saw the "guests" of 'Guests' and wrote the poem. I wrote the lecture I had to give to the College of Psychic Studies in October and revised 'The Crack in the Earth'. I went for a late walk under a cloudless, moonless night with very clear stars and wrote five quatrains, all separate, on the night sky with effortless energy: five images for the stars, the best being a fountain, the most original being a peacock's tail. The next day: "Aug. 24. All morning, a sea with jumping lights and a fishing boat surrounded by the splashing. Sat and watched spellbound." I wrote several poems: 'Downpour of Light'; 'Light like Mackerel'; and (having seen a greenfinch on the front lawn) 'Greenfinch with Worm'; and (after sunbathing) 'Trodden Daisies'.

A few days later I wrote:

> The youthful poet dazzles with surface imagery but is less good in depth. The mature poet dispenses with some of the imagery and emphasises structure.... Poetry is discourse (conversation) in images, in a regular meeting with naturalness of the spoken word pulling against the line (and rhyme every second and fourth lines in lyric stanzas). Donne on how a poem batters out gold and the last clause puts on the stamp and gives it currency.[36]

Unruly Universalist philosophers

While I was approaching the end of my autobiographical work I had continued to attend meetings of the Universalist philosophers. There was a meeting at the end of August 1993 which I chaired. I gave a *resumé* of the papers inspired by Universalism, including papers by Geoffrey Read and Alan Mayne that were very supportive of me. Read said perceptively that I had deliberately left Universalism vague. I was aware that there were many definitions of Existentialism and did not want to tie Universalism down to one definition. Chris Macann explained his four-volume unification of the transcendent phenomenology of Husserl and the ontological phenomenology of Heidegger. He had just returned from Freiburg, where he visited both their houses, and he said he had met a château-owner in France, near Bordeaux.

I said that the philosopher is no longer a man in a room imprisoned by walls and fiddling about with language; that he has got outside and is describing the universe from the One down, through all its levels, and is making a coherent statement of everything. Again and again I used the analogy of the Existentialists, saying that six Existentialists all disagreed but all subscribed to the umbrella term. I said that our unified view – our unifying world vision, our attempt to see unity behind multiplicity – is our umbrella. I spoke of the historical perspective, of undoing the Enlightenment, the early Newton and the work of the Royal Society, of going back to 1659, the time of the last Metaphysical poems, and of getting back from words to the universe. I said Existentialism is dead and its demise had left a void which Universalism is filling.

But keeping the philosophers from squabbling was wearying. That evening I wrote: "I am tired, having kept order among the unruly philosophers who often all want to talk at the same time, from 10.30 to 5. I feel as if I have taught all day. I am slightly giddy.... The philosophers are like another staff. Peter Stewart to me: 'You're not so much a philosopher as a visionary.' I: 'A mystic. I think of Whitehead: "The purpose of philosophy is to rationalize mysticism."' I am a mystic and visionary who rationalises mysticism – and am therefore a philosopher who reflects the vision of the Light."[37]

Angel poems

At the beginning of September I had the idea for a sequence of Angel poems. I would go back to *Beauty and Angelhood* and draw on Donne's 'Aire and Angels' and Rilke's 'Every Angel is terrible'. To me, the Angel was the perfected, illumined human being who has transcended man, a kind of Superman who has a unitive vision, understands the Theory of Everything and channels knowledge of spiritual beauty. While unwell, giddy, I drafted six Angel poems for a new post-Muse sequence. "Too tired to polish them tonight. Have taken a second 75mg aspirin today, which has slightly eased my giddiness." Now Angel poems came to me unbidden. I had an appointment with my bank manager, Ken Jones:

Parked at 10.55 in Monkhams Avenue opposite Hutton Close [for a meeting at 11 a.m.], just before the bend to the right, and 'Dark Angel' came to me in the car. I can't even be left alone to park my car without a poem coming. (*See* pp.136–137.) Scribbled it on a piece of paper on my knee, and arrived only slightly late at my meeting.

(Later I lunched with Ken at the Adriatico.)

Two days later I reflected: "4 Sep. Got up at 6 and dictated the first 11 poems of *Angel of Vertical Vision* by 7.30." In my poems I looked back to Spenser's 'Epithalamion' and Donne's 'Aire and Angels', the poems I read at Oxford. Reading these poems then had made them part of my internal system so they became points of reference. I was now reaping the true benefits of that Oxford time. These poems had lived within me and attracted complementary images for 35 years. Reading the poetic tradition of English Literature is a very necessary part of a young poet's preparation.[38]

Revising poems

In early September I began a punishing regime to get my autobiographical writings finished. Very often I worked until 1 a.m. and sometimes later. Each week I covered a year of my autobiography and every Monday and Tuesday I revised about 20 draft poems. Some weeks I achieved finished revisions of 400 lines. I did not calculate the number of poems I had to revise each week to be finished in time, but I just knew that that quantity was right – and it was. My health held.

Marion Lord next door had not been well. She had been sick for two months and lost two stone. She was dehydrated, and tests showed her kidneys were not functioning properly and she had cancer of the pleura. She was told to go to the Cancer Ward at St Bartholomew's Hospital as soon as possible. I had found her tearful, helped her into a taxi with her luggage and waved her off, half knowing that she would never return. She died soon afterwards. As a result of the vomiting and lack of eating the lining of her stomach broke away and she asphyxiated – drowned in her own blood, which came through her mouth and nose.

Her funeral was at St Mary's, Loughton. We then drove to Parndon Wood for the cremation: a few prayers, then the shock of the curtains drawing. Standing at the foot of the chimney near our flowers, I smelt the smoke as Marion burned.

Meanwhile I battled on with my poetic work: "Have been giddy on and off for 6 weeks.... Felt below par: lethargic, sore back, incipient cramp in right leg, lungs congested, health poor. Went to the Light. Felt a tremendous surge at 9.40 and another one at 9.55.... I am trying to work while feeling ill." A couple of days later I wrote:

Poets do their best and present material they have in felicitous rhythms and rhymes. The poet receives from beyond and then presents.... There are therefore two processes in getting a metaphysical poem across.... How do I choose my rhymes? I look at which of two end-words is essential and which more decorative, and change the decorative one. That way the meaning carries on through the rhymes – a trick I have taught myself. Am now revising 'Counter-Renaissance'. Yesterday revised 'Copped Hall'.

Towards the end of September I wrote:

Tackled the first six stanzas of 'In Périgord',... and then did another four stanzas. Sep. 27. Finished 'In Périgord' (18 stanzas),... and then did 'At Penquite House'. In both the poems I start with a place and establish a type of man – St Bernard, St Sampson – and generalise into the soul or the universe, *universalise* the situation. The hallmark of a Universalist poem is this universalisation from a specific local beginning. Sept. 28. Finished 'Clouds Hill' about action and reflection. I know – how do I know? – that T.E. Lawrence thought of the name 'Clouds Hill' in terms of anonymity – he would wrap himself in clouds and hide, like Yahweh – but I see him as a failed mystic who turned away from the world but never found the Light, and lived in perpetual cloud.... Pushed on and finished 'In Shakespeare's Stratford: The Nature of Art'.

At the end of September I was rung by the *West Essex Gazette* and asked where Vicky Norris was. I rang Steve at the Ministry of Transport, and eventually he rang back and said: "Sadly I have to tell you it's true. Vicky's in Berkshire, I'm in London." They had separated following an article in *The Daily Mail* about his association with another woman. I was very sad for both of them, and said so in the *Gazette*, and in the ensuing weeks saw the constituency divide in its attitude. I knew that Norris would not remain our tenant for much longer.

I was still deriving inspiration from sleep. At the beginning of October I

woke and wrote 'After the Fracture, Growth'.... [It] expresses my view of Modernism in just 12 lines. Immediately afterwards I went to the bathroom, did my Canadian 5BX exercises, then, wearing just white pants, went to the bathroom again to wash and saw my eyes and nipples balance in the mirror – was caught off guard by them and remembered Shelley thinking the nipples were eyes – and returned to my study and wrote 'Man (Or: God the Artist)'. Am trying not to write new poems, but these two have just come.

I had to speak to a group at St Albans, Paths of Wisdom. "About 35 casually-dressed middle-aged men and women filed into a kind of drill hall and sat in silence. I spoke from 7.45 to 8.45 about the Fire or Light and showed eight transparencies about my history theory. After tea from 9.10 I asked, "Why see the Light?" I included in my answer: "Because you're not depressed any more. You know the peace that passeth understanding. It is like a still sea and you are on it like a calm boat." I held a meditation in which the Light came down. In the meditation I spoke of a still water-lily on a pond. I finished the meditation at 9.40 and said: "It is so simple. You open your soul to the Light. That is all. But it is the essence of the paths of wisdom." I refused to accept any money from the organiser. She said: "We like having you, you are so sincere, unlike some." I replied: "I don't charge for the Light."

I was distracted from poems again by another meeting of the philosophers at which Macann presented his work. Peter Welsford wanted to build a temple to the new Universalist religion in Glastonbury. I was still revising poems hard:

A day of tremendous risk. All day the typist... sat downstairs while I tried to keep ahead of her, rhyming unrhymed poems. Completed 'At Dark Age Jorvik: The Light of Civilisation' and the sonnet 'Fountain of Stars: The Universe in Love' while she waited for me. Literally kept just ahead of her. 114 lines at least today, over 100 on Monday evening, and the Wordsworth and Potter poems on Sunday. A good three days. Have already done three more Flo poems. The isolation of the poet. I am completely isolated while I plough through these old poems and lick them into shape. The isolation of those who are given the image.

I battled on through a chest infection, and as a result of it fell asleep between 1.30 and 3.15 two afternoons running. I observed: "The copper beech outside my window has been a companion: a fountain of gold and copper leaves, a fire against a blue sky."[39]

I had to break off from my poems to give my lecture to the College of Psychic Studies. I wrote: "19 Oct. All day, poems – 'At Blea Tarn House', 'At Cartmel Priory: Taming the Unicorn' and other Lake-District ones, then focused on my lecture at 4 and drove to Queensborough Place in time for 6.40." I set up slides and transparencies and had coffee with Dudley Poplak, the President of the College of Psychic Studies, who asked, "Would you like to tune in?" I sat on my own for a while. Then I walked to the front of the hall where there was a lectern and desk, and addressed 100 people who had paid £5 a head. The lecture went well. I followed a plan and stopped and ad-libbed, then resumed my plan. There was a line of people at the end. Then Poplak took me to dinner in Brompton Road, a walk through mewses, with the editor of *Mind*. There was talk of Colin Wilson. Poplak said: "It was evident he'd been drinking. He had 70 in the audience." The editor of *Mind* said: "He doesn't say anything new, he's generous and likeable and has a following, but it's superficial, *Reader's-Digest* stuff."

She was friendly with Kathleen Raine, and said that *Temenos*, like the monasteries, is keeping alive the tradition for a future generation. I told how Raine severed her connection with me because I had linked the Royal family to the House of David. Poplak said: "I know the Prince of Wales very well, he wouldn't go along with that, her attitude was rubbish. He believes in the Divine Right of Kings but he isn't ready for the Light yet. He will be. Kathleen Raine is the past, élitist, not concerned with living. You are the future."[40]

New poems kept coming. We spent half-term in Cornwall. I wrote: "Arrived just before 2 a.m. All lights out – and brilliant stars which took my breath away…. Went for a walk and at 2.15 a.m. wrote two poems: on the stars as shingle, and on a tree ['The Shingle of the Stars', and 'Invisible Tree'] – the sense of a living universe." The next morning I

went out to get the papers, returned by the Hotel and crossed the bridge and lingered near the Roundhouse, looking down at the beach below our house, and I could not believe my eyes. The wet shingle where each wave had been was alive, jumping and dancing, glinting in the sun. I stood transfixed, spell-bound, in a trance and watched and watched and watched and felt the 'livingness' of the whole universe. Returned and wrote a poem straightaway, 'Moist', and then 'Peering Face' about the moon I saw on the way down yesterday. And tidied up the [two poems about] vivid stars I saw after 2 a.m. this morning. Four poems since 2 a.m., and I have slept six-and-a-half hours! Down here in Cornwall everything is more intense: moon, stars and waves, all aspects of being seen with being, so that one is in a one-relationship with each one of Nature's phenomena. The more I write poems, the more I find I am absorbed – spellbound – by things I see, which will find their way into poems. It is strange because in a sense I have seen it all before, the more one travels down the Mystic Way into being, the more one responds as being to being – hence the poetic trance. Got logs from outside for the fire and again gazed in wonder at the fire for a very long time and wrote 'Fire'.

I was pondering my "uniting Classical and Romantic in the Baroque" and I wrote:

A symbol of the unification of action and contemplation: the Harbour-master's House. It is at the end of a social village and gazes at the sea of contemplation. The Harbour-master acts by controlling the lock-gates and bringing the boats in, but is also a man of the sea [, i.e. of contemplation].

I noted Auden's envy of Eliot: "Eliot was so damn lucky, he had the mystic vision." A man of contemplation, blessed like Eliot with the mystic vision, I worked on in the Harbour-master's House: I "finished 'Question Mark over the West'," and "worked on getting a good text of the autobiography".

I carried on revising my poems. I wrote: "Nov. 2. All day, numerous sonnets. *The Wind and the Earth* is now up to 30. Was doing a sonnet every half hour or less, with [the typist] sitting waiting for each one to finish. The phone kept going. Steve Norris rang. You can't say to a Government Minister, 'Push off, I'm in the middle of a sonnet.'... Ovid and Milton were pretty full-time but they did not write several sonnets or equivalent a day. Since September – after the Muse poems and my 'American Quintet' – I have been able to tackle all poems put in front of me."

I had been thinking again about my epic:

All my development from now on will be further into the unitive way. The crowning glory of my unitive vision will be my epic. I have held off the epic until I am ready. I have waited for my development to arrive at the start point for the epic. It will express Universalism, the philosophy of the unitive vision.... The unitive vision: Universalism (the philosophy); the Grand Unified Theory in history and world religion; the Fire being behind the universe of science. All these to be reconciled in the epic.... The summit is within reach.

In connection with my epic I had noted that another prediction in *The Fire and the Stones* had come true: "Tomorrow the European Union comes into force. I was born at the height of Britain's imperial power and tomorrow will live in a state in a union – a tangible measure of Britain's decline."

I finished my sequence of sonnets. I wrote:

Nov. 8. Wrote two sonnets last night and four today.... *My Wind and the Earth* sequence has caught a new theme in poetry: the practical clearing up after a death. It is so obvious, but no one else seems to have done it.... Wrote 'Head-Scarf', which I wrote down on a shopping list.... In 200 years' time people will be able to see how we really lived, among mundane things like buying black bags for rubbish.... Artists work hard and sweat to produce their inspired visions. I am like a potter. I fire my pots and then potter about, making tea, getting my vision into shapes."[41]

International politics: exploring the New World Order

My epic poem would include a unitive view of how the world is run. I had learned enough about the New World Order to grasp that during the Second World War there had been powerful influences who may have pushed Hitler into war. I was on a fact-finding mission to unearth these hidden influences.

Alexander King and the New World Order
David Lorimer of the Universalist philosophers arranged for me to hear Dr Alexander King (a Scottish scientist, founder member of NATO and co-founder in 1968 of the global think-tank, the Club of Rome). He had been invited to speak to the Scientific and Medical Network, and I went because I knew King had attended the Bilderberg Group and was an eyewitness of attempts to create a New World Order I would need for my epic.

I drove to the Royal Overseas League in Park Street, off St James's Street, and went up to the India Room. David Lorimer was at the door and he introduced me immediately to King, a smallish, elderly, bespectacled man in a collar and tie and blazer who was drinking Scotch with Peter Fenwick. Fenwick immediately left and King led me to an area where we were by ourselves. I had not expected King to be waiting for me and to ask me to have a drink with him while a roomful of people sat waiting for his talk to begin. I asked him, "Is there going to be a New World Order?" He said, "No." I showed him Stan Deyo's *Cosmic Conspiracy* which contains a map issued by the Club of Rome splitting the world into 10 global groups, and a chart of 9 "interlocked Illuminati fronts" with "the Round Table of the Nine" in the centre and six satellites round it: The Club of Rome, The Bilderberg Group, the UN, The Council on Foreign Relations, The Trilaterial Commission and The Royal Institute of International Affairs. I asked him: "Are you in the Illuminati?" He said: "They call us all sorts of names." I asked: "Are there 9 leaders of the world?" He said: "More." I said: "99?" He said: "More likely 999, but all insignificant, no leaders."

His reply was unsatisfactory. I had hoped he would tell me how many were running the world, but he had not told me anything new. It is likely that he was referring to the "Committee of 300" for he was listed as a member in Dr John Coleman's *Conspirators' Hierarchy: The Story of the Committee of 300*.

Fenwick introduced him in glowing terms, saying how much the Club of Rome had meant to the Scientific and Medical Network and to him personally. King's talk was curiously pessimistic. He said that governments form short-term solutions and few are concerned with the long term. He declared the problems and left us to come up with the solutions in question time. I raised world government. He said it was not feasible. I asked the question to check that I had not misunderstood his dismissal of the New World Order.

I chatted to him afterwards. He said: "I've been to some of the Bilderberg meetings, you know. They might just be able to bring about a world government. We don't want America ruling the world, it's not practical." He spoke as if he and I were on the same side within a British perspective, and in view of his eagerness to speak with me, I wondered if he had links with the intelligence world. He left to spend the night at David Lorimer's.

Offered a Hungarian castle

International politics lured me into Europe. Paul Gorka had rung me from Hungary and told me he was now in a position of influence. He had been made Head of Privatisation in West Hungary, based in Sopron, and had the task of privatising all West Hungary's castles. He had earmarked a 140-room Renaissance castle with Baroque features, which would be freehold in my name, for me to set up a privatised Universalist academy. All the expenses would be covered by the locality in return for the benefits I could bring to the region. This was Gorka saying "thank you" to me for publishing his book and for employing him as my architect.[42] I had to make a formal application for the Castle, which was just 40 kms from Vienna, in the centre of the old Austro-Hungarian empire that had produced Margaret Riley's Light.

I could see a time ahead when this Castle would be the European headquarters of Universalism. But at the present time it was a distraction. It would take me away from my autobiographical writing and epic for like Coopersale Hall it would involve me in renovation and management and take time away from my writing. I knew I would not make the formal application.

Lord Roding and the 'Heroes of the West'

I was now able to confirm some of the discoveries of the 'Heroes of the West'. Ann had been ill with flu. (I had "worked until 1 a.m. and then [gone] to the Light and, standing in our bedroom, pulled a cloak of Light around me to protect me from the flu Ann has got…. A massive inflow of the Light.") As Ann was still unwell I went alone to a reception at Vernon Davies's house for Lord Roding (formerly Patrick Jenkin and a former Government Minister). I found myself talking to Jenkin, who mistook me for a colleague. He said: "Do you remember when we were waiting outside the door to go into a Cabinet meeting and Mrs. Thatcher…." He interrupted himself and said, "Oh, no, it wasn't you, you weren't there then, were you?"

I saw an opportunity to run information past him to see if he agreed. I told him: "I was one of a group – we called ourselves the 'Heroes of the West' – who brought out books about Scargill, Gaddafi and Philby. The USSR was savage just before Communism ended, it wanted to have a *Blitzkrieg* across Western Europe in 35 days." Jenkin nodded and said "35 days", confirming what I had said. I continued, "It was planning a nuclear strike against Western Europe in 1988." Again he nodded. "And it wanted to liquidate the Cabinet through the Brighton bomb. Were you on the receiving end of that?" He said, "Yes." I said. "It was a Soviet–Gaddafi plot. The Soviets wanted to get rid of the British Government and establish a pro-Soviet dictatorship. The IRA were training the NUM and Frank Watters was organising the miners to go from pit to pit." He nodded. "And the USSR had sent in £48 million to [the miners] through Prague and through Gaddafi's students. What I can't understand," I said, "is that bearing all this in mind, how did this information not get used during the 1987 election campaign? You had a privileged seat on the Cabinet table at the time, why not?" "I don't know," Jenkin said, "I just don't know. I felt the same." "And," I said, "projecting it forward, why has it not been mentioned recently?" "Again, I don't know," he said. "It's got to be to do with protecting people. I remember when Ted Rowlands made a speech in the House of Commons saying as much, Mrs. Thatcher was white with fury and said, 'That's completely blown it now.' There is something we don't know."

Jenkin made a speech about hospital trusts. Afterwards I spoke with him again. I explained how I published a book on terrorism. He said, "I remember that book." "*The World Held Hostage*," I said. "Another thing I would like to know," I said, "is when it can be revealed that the raid on Libya – " "I was out by then," he interrupted, "I watched it on the television and wondered like everyone else." "When it can be revealed," I continued, "that 55 planes took part in the raid on Libya, 20 went to Tripoli, 20 to Benghazi and 15 to Sebha to take out Gaddafi's nuclear rockets there which were threatening London, Paris and Bonn." Jenkin nodded. "Built by ex-Nazi Argentinians," I said. He said: "Again, it was to protect sources. And Mrs. Thatcher said that the French refusal to let the planes fly over their territory did wonders for the Anglo-American relationship." "And at the launch," I said, "I spoke about the author's revelation that Operation Babysitter was supplying Gaddafi and the international terrorist movement with arms through Heathrow. Through Heathrow! Madam [i.e. Mrs. Thatcher] would have been horrified." He grinned. Norris came over and the three of us stood together, chatting freely.

I was interested my view of events – the 'Heroes of the West's' view of events – had been confirmed by an ex-Minister who had had a privileged seat at the Cabinet table as Secretary of State for the Environment, and I realised I could have become a politician and shared in such moments of camaraderie.[43]

The philosophers polarised, David Lorimer engaged to Norris McWhirter's daughter
The next meeting of the Universalist philosophers at David Lorimer's house

in Uxbridge ended in controversy. Geoffrey Read greeted me, "I see you've been declaring war, Nicholas." He produced *Psychic News* with a heading about me: "Ex-Professor declares war on Materialists." My lecture at the College of Psychic Studies had been carried on the front page.

Chris Thomson began his presentation and ended at the lack of confidence we can have in the perceiver's perception of the universe. I asked him to answer the question, "What is the universe? What is your view of the universe?" He saw the universe like me as energy that is interconnected, but my question caused a furore and polarised the philosophers into two camps based on their way of seeing the universe. Geoffrey Read took issue with Max Payne. I said to Max, "We are against the philosophers of the last 90 years, we are against the Vienna Circle." I reconciled the polarised positions: "The Mystic Way is a growth from the perception of the rational social ego to the perception of the unitive centre after the transformational shift, so that in his unitive view at the end of the Mystic Way the philosopher perceives the universe with instinctive unity, the vision of the poet. Self and the universe are aspects of one universal whole. We must develop ourselves, but we must also [understand] the universe." However, my reconciliation only lasted for a while and polarisation would split the Universalist philosophers.

David Lorimer had hosted the meetings of philosophers which were now labelled the Universalist Philosophy Group. Norris McWhirter had been my link with the intelligence service while I published books. Until now Lorimer and McWhirter had been in separate compartments of my life. But there was a card on the mantelpiece congratulating David Lorimer on his engagement to Norris McWhirter's daughter, Jane.[44]

The revelation made me wonder whether my path is Providential rather than fortuitous. There again seemed to be an underlying order in the coming-together of two strands in my life: the 'Heroes of the West' with which Norris McWhirter was associated, and the Universalist philosophers with which David Lorimer was associated. First Alexander King, now this engagement – the philosophers were somehow mixed up with international politics and the New World Order.

Metaphysical Centre – Red Mercury, Raina Haig, choosing work over life; end of Fourth Mystic Life
While I pressed on with my autobiographical writing and *Collected Poems: A White Radiance* – on 16 November alone I had written ten sonnets – practical mysticism returned, drawn to my Universalism. Heather Dobbs arranged for me to meet a German lady who had introduced *The Fire and the Stones* to a university in Düsseldorf and who had told Heather that her way of looking was transformed by my Universalism. At the same time I met a

Polish girl with whom Heather was opening a Centre for Practical Metaphysics, a Metaphysical Centre, at a temporary address in Old Street, London.

Agnieszka Milewska was a very strong Polish ex-Catholic girl of 24 with very long hair. She had read philosophy and the history of art at Warsaw University, and she and Heather were Directors of the Centre. She had great confidence and delighted in challenging people's assumptions. She was iconoclastic and favoured fundamental solutions, recommending that members of her audiences should give up their jobs or their partners and turn their backs on the illusory world. She told me she had memories of a previous life as Violette Szabo, who with Madeleine (Noor Inayat Khan, sister of Pir Vilayat Inayat Khan) was awarded the George Cross posthumously after the war. From the age of three she had said to her parents, "I don't want to go back to the concentration camp," and she saw Violette's end, by gas, not shooting. "No," she said to me, "she was not shot…. There were many in the room, trying to get out. I thought, 'Why can't they sit quietly and accept it and not struggle for life outside, which is nothing?' There were many moving bodies, like something out of Dante." She also remembered Violette's haunting poem, written as a code by a cryptographer who worked with SOE (Special Operations Executive) in Bletchley Park, which she had taken into France. It contained a very important message, possibly about the date of D-Day. I chanted:

The life that I have
Is all that I have
And the life that I have
Is yours.

The love that I have
Of the life that I have
Is yours and yours and yours.

Agnieszka thought and said: "It was a number code, each letter was a number." She recalled glimpsing the man who wrote the poem (Leo Marks) through a cattle-wagon window on her way to the camp.

Agnieszka had lived in a flat in Warsaw three years previously with some samples of Red Mercury, a new weapon discovered by the Russians which a Filipino, Alan, had first mentioned to me. (Heather Dobbs had arranged for me to meet him. He had begun by saying he liked my poem 'Sea Force'. "It catches the force of the sea very powerfully. I recite it to myself." He had predicted that London would be a nuclear desert as a result of Red Mercury.)

Red Mercury is a chemical detonator which disturbs the molecules of any element, and can therefore be seen as the philosopher's stone. The Russians had sold it to the Chinese who sold it to an American Jew, who may then have supplied the international terrorist network. The American Jew had Agnieszka guarding this Red Mercury in a rent-free flat in Warsaw for six months. She said, "It was like living with an atom bomb in the bathroom." She supplied me with the formula and other details of Red Mercury. As one last act 'Heroes of the West' took steps to neutralise this dangerous substance, one pinch of which could wipe out a swathe of the population of London. The formula can be found buried in one of my books.

It was now apparent to me that the Metaphysical Centre was the concept of the school for self-realisation I had dreamt of in Japan, and that Agnieszka was a Director who could run it for cells of 10 and spread the Light nationwide. Heather Dobbs and Agnieszka adopted my idea of cells of 10 and asked if I would join them and give occasional talks about my perspective of the Light and my work. A medium Agnieszka was introduced to spoke of a "Nicholas – who is he? Three books will come out. He will be famous.... He is the highest consciousness in the world.... He is combining the High Intelligence of the Light with practical metaphysics."

Agnieszka was now implementing groups of 10. She told me: "It is not lectures but everyday life we should focus on.... Look at yourself without your fame, your books and your schools and see yourself as a failure – *that* is the being who is divine." She listened to a voice within her which said: "A stream in a mountain can be hidden but when it flows down, it cannot be hidden." The context was the spread of Universalism and the Metaphysical Revolution. I was amazed at the clarity of view and authoritative confidence of this 24-year-old, and knew she would go far.

On 4 December I

went to the Light. Surges came in.... Am at the end of a long haul and am tired but still write with a lightness of being. A Lightness of Being. All my works have the massiveness of a mountain about them. I am a mountain-peak writer, not a foothill writer. I write about the summit, where the best glimpses of the sun and the light are to be had.

And yet I was fundamentally very simple: Ernie said at 8 a.m., "There's a huge red sun, you can see it from the landing." And like a little boy I went upstairs and gazed at it for a long time in wonder and went and wrote a poem, 'Red Sun'. I have retained my sense of wonder.

I was determined to reflect the process of the events of my life in my autobiography: "By quoting from my *Diaries*, I can stick close to what happened without imposing an artificial construct on the process." This principle lies behind this work.

Agnieszka again expounded her teaching to me: "We create our own reality from within… [By] the power of inner thought. No one can harm you if you are at a spiritual level. We attract burglars and assaults by psychological worry. You align yourself with the infinite power. I re-invent myself every day." Her teaching was similar to that of New Thought, and Heather Dobbs's Thomas Troward Society. I added to this:

We are existentialising the perceptions of the metaphysical knowledge. Just as Existentialism spoke of freedom that can be acted out, so we enable [people] to create [their] reality, being in touch with the Light within and learning the laws that relate to it…. Universalism: seeking the universal within us, that which is universal within us, the Fire or Light. A school for self-realisation in which to work out the practical Existentialism as Universalism.

The Metaphysical Centre opened on 6 December as a concept rather than as a place. During the day I revised "16 poems in a day, a record" and still found time to attend an Oaklands nativity play (and talk with Vicki Michelle, the comedy actress who was a parent). In the evening I went to the East-West Centre in Old Street.

Before my talk I met Anya, a friend of Agnieszka who had just arrived from Poland. I had shown Agnieszka a leaflet about "the International Society for Universalists" at Warsaw University, and she had asked Anya, a former *New York Times* journalist, to investigate. Anya had visited Professor Kuczynski and had cross-examined him very vigorously. She reported to me that they were "one-world" universalists who were completely non-metaphysical. Anya had handed over the Red Mercury after Agnieszka had left for England, and I was able to question her about her view of the threat it presented.

About 30 attended the opening of the Metaphysical Centre. I talked about the Fire or Light and showed my books, then Heather spoke, then Agnieszka, passionate and weighing into the audience, spirited like a Dostoevskian character – Dostoevsky, Joyce and Proust were her favourite authors – and showing the rebelliousness that impelled her to ask her professors about their sexual performance in question time at Warsaw University, scathingly debunking what they stood for. I spoke again about Universalism, then there was a meditation in which I brought down the Light – it poured through me, purging the room – and then there were questions and answers. Afterwards no one wanted to leave.

This experience of the Light ended my Fourth Mystic Life.

The next day Geoffrey Read expounded his philosophy to the philosophers. He said the universe is emanating. Time began with the first qualification or event. (How? Why? Not explained.) Since then, for the last 4.5 billion years there have been 10^{-23} events or qualifications per second, i.e. 10 thousand million million million events per second. The primordial simplicity has become a multiplicity. "Nothing endures through time, time is derived from a succession of events." (There is a unified diversity. We are all part of the One.) Memories are in the past. A memory is not in the brain cells; rather events are associated. A GCSE exam does not test memory in cells; it tests sympathetic associations. Read said of me (echoing what had been said at a previous meeting): "You're not a systematic thinker, you're a visionary." I retorted: " I give systematic thought to my vision. Substance is one, and is a manifestation of the Fire or Light." (During our break for lunch I spoke to McWhirter's daughter, a brisk woman who told me her father had remarried and was 68.)

There was much in Read's theory that interested me, but he was too reductionist for my metaphysical taste in insisting that there could not be latent movement of a non-physical, metaphysical Fire *before* the beginning of time. However his view of events *after* the beginning of time coincided with my own thinking, and I could see how a pre-existing moving Fire/Absolute could be qualified into a succession of events. Read had in effect defined a position that was distinct from Universalism, even though he had much in common with the Universalism I had stated.

I relayed some of this to Agnieszka, who was predictably scathing: "The only important thing is how to live, how to run your life. Philosophers build pyramids of words, whole libraries. I am in a state of living, not learning. There is only one important thing: to enjoy yourself, to be happy, to be at peace. I live out what the philosopher is saying."

Again I was aware of two polarities in myself: the Hebraistic way (in Matthew Arnold's terminology) of schools of self-realisation and Heather and Agnieszka; and the Hellenistic way (in Arnold's terminology) of my epic and art, which is made out of the quarrel with oneself. *A Mystic Way* was about the persistent tension between the mystic of the Light and the describer of the experience in art, which I like to think I have been able to reconcile and unify in terms of a universe of Fire or Light: action and contemplation.

I expressed some of this tension in poems. I wrote 'Philosopher's Stone: Soul and Golden Flower', a highly metaphysical poem. Earlier I revised 'Sea Rescues: Death Like a Cormorant'. "Today some effective images. A tough metaphysical poetry in which meaning and image wrestle and unify. The first poem draws together the Red Mercury episode, Agnieszka and Geoffrey Read's 'qualifications'."

The Metaphysical Centre held a reception, which I did not attend. Some of those there had never heard of metaphysics. I wrote: "I am not an evangelical getting in people who have not heard of metaphysics...; I am a describer in books and have the intention of writing an epic."

Agnieszka rang, full of Taoist wisdom, being contrary and rebellious, putting the opposite. "Teaching and learning are illusions, go for darkness. Empty, everyone is the same. Enjoy yourself, there are no levels, no differences. Just be in silence." I said: "Very Taoist. $+A + -A = 0$. Silence + words = 0." She said: "Yes, we reconcile through opposites." She insisted: "We can't change others, only ourselves." But, I commented, "Disturb the molecules of another, and then they can change themselves." And I added a stanza to 'Philosopher's Stone: Soul and Golden Flower' to this effect.

I thought of Yeats's words: "The intellect of man is forced to choose/Perfection of the life, or of the work." The Metaphysical Centre and its cells of 10, which I had aspired to in Japan, involved perfecting the life, the only thing Agnieszka felt important. But my autobiographical writing and my coming epic – implementing my Pisan revelation – involved perfecting my work. I wrote: "I have a choice: to choose myself as an artist or as [an Existentialist] philosopher: work or life. I must choose work, and be a describer, not a changer of men. It is the same dilemma I faced in the mid-1960s, only now it is crystalised into: runner of a Metaphysical Centre or writer of an epic? I must reconcile these two polarities in myself: $+A + -A = 0$. It can be both, but not exclusively the first. Life + work = 0." And, of course, one example of this process of reconciliation was *A Mystic Way* and also my synthesis in *My Double Life*.

After completing 22 poems in two days I went to Old Street and met a friend of Agnieszka's, Raina Haig, the granddaughter of Earl Haig, commander of the British Expeditionary Force in France and Belgium during the First World War and a friend of Princess Margaret's. She was nearly blind and after I explained my Theory of Everything in metaphysical terms based on the Fire or Light and the growth of civilizations she said she would like to make a film about my life. It would include my outlook and work, the Fire and my view of history.

The film was to be about my life and the Metaphysical Centre. But I had already chosen work and did not want to be spending time, making a film about perfecting life, which was not what I was trying to do.

The next evening I dined at the House of Commons with Steve Norris. He had not been to bed the previous night, a Tuesday, and would not sleep until the following Friday he was so busy handling work for the Government. We discussed the New World Order and Red Mercury. He said again, looking hard at me, "The MI5 reports would surprise *you* – the details on *certain* people."[45] I left Norris confirmed in my choice of work over life.

Two visits to Mary Seal on the New World Order

With the coming epic in mind I wanted to do research into the New World Order and contacted Mary Seal, who had put on the Global Deception conference (*see* p.426). She invited me to visit her in Walsall, near where a college friend of Ann's lived. On 27 February 1994 I arrived at her house at 12.30. She had long ragged blonde hair and the bungalow was full of cigarette smoke. I wanted to know to what extent the New World Order was involved in the Second World War for my poetic epic.

She handed me *The Executive Intelligence Review*'s report on the *Global 2000 Report* – the New World Order's plan for population reduction – but first needed to explain that "much history is false, it didn't happen". She told me the New World Order would exercise "mind-control", turn all humans into slaves and cause dreadful explosions on the planet. She explained that the New World Order worshipped Lucifer. I found much of what she said far-fetched and unsubstantiated, but was interested in her analysis of who had influenced the *Global 2000 Report*. I agreed with her that there was a good New World Order and a bad New World Order of occultists and Freemasons who had fomented the American and French revolutions. She spoke of John Coleman's *Conspirators' Hierarchy: The Story of the Committee of 300* and said she would send me a package of useful material. We talked until 6 and half-way through her boyfriend Keith came in, ate and went.

In the next few weeks she rang me about the New World Order, but I found what she said far-fetched. I focused on the written sources. I discounted all her references to Jupiter and other planets. I followed up by reading Des Griffin's *Fourth Reich of the Rich* and *Descent into Slavery* and began assembling a reading list that would tell me how the New World Order's ambition for a world government that would suit their interests influenced the outbreak and course of the Second World War. I researched the funding of Hitler by a Warburg bank and Schröder Bank. I was getting a feel for the war. I wrote: "In the epic, show Eisenhower as a delayer, Monty and Churchill... champing for Berlin, and Stalin pressing on to be first in Berlin."

Mary Seal rang me and we talked about Coleman's Committee of 300. She said, "Behind the 300 there may be one person." I asked, "Do you know who it is?" "No." Later I asked: "What is an attractive girl like you doing putting on a conference of that kind?" She said: "I've had nameless people covering my back. The security services don't like what's going on and want it to come out, but have no power." I said: "Being intelligent, I might wonder if someone put you up to having the conference, to winkle out people like me and liquidate them." She said: "No, I'm not working with anybody. But you're safe, people will protect you. They are nameless but they are on your side. If you're not working for anyone, you're the only person I've ever met who isn't out for their own agenda. You seem so nice and decent."

Mary had mentioned the Club of Rome, and my research showed that there were 100 members from 53 countries. Alexander King's name kept coming up as its co-founder. I wanted to meet him again. I rang David Lorimer to fix a new meeting. He said, "Alex King is out of town." I said I had his card and Paris address, which I read out over the phone. He said: "I'm away for ten days. I'm getting married to Norris McWhirter's daughter on Saturday." I told him I already knew. "Ring him while I'm away and we'll have lunch when I get back."

My recollection is that I made the call to King but that he would not be in the UK for some months. The meeting did not happen.

When I visited Michael Mann in April he urged me to write a book on international politics and the New World Order, including Red Mercury.[46] It was now known that Red Mercury is a fusion bomb the size of a baseball that can destroy people but not buildings. Apparently one had exploded at Warsaw airport and the buildings were not affected by the explosion. It is not known how many people were killed, if any.

Mary Seal had rung, telling me, "Everyone is deceived, including the Committee of 300." She said she had an Italian temperament and sometimes got worked up, and might come across as too "sharp" with me. I said, "If you become volatile I will say 'Italiano'." I did not realise how quickly I would have to invoke this principle.

I visited her again in Walsall on 16 April. Ann dropped me off and went on to visit her college friend in Birmingham. I arrived at 12.35, early, and saw her hoovering through her picture window. She was not expecting me. She told me she had sent me a letter by recorded delivery which I had not received, saying that she could not work with me as I would get her killed. She said that now I was there I should stay. She made me coffee and showed me a letter she had sent 400 MPs. It was from 'The Supreme Council of the Illuminati', and I thought it might be a forgery. Her boyfriend looked in and left. We talked on. She kept bringing the conversation back to mind-control and UFOs, whereas I kept returning the conversation to the New World Order. Her boyfriend returned and soon afterwards Ann's car arrived and parked outside. She could see me through the picture window.

I had been taking notes, and suddenly Mary became agitated and started walking about. She told me that all books are wrong, they exercise 'mind-control'. "I don't want you to write your book. I want your notes." She swooped and snatched my notes from me and gave them to Keith, her boyfriend, who tore them up into little pieces.

I said, "Italiano, extreme Italiano." I was serious. I said: "That's Nazi

Germany, Hitlerism. Even in Cultural-Revolution China I didn't get my notes torn up. I'm going." I put my sweater on and left, and then discovered I had left my glasses behind. I went back in. Mary said: "You're not going to jeopardise our work for a personal disagreement, surely?" I said: "I don't even get my notes." Now she relented. She got the torn-up fragments and put them in a Safeway bag and gave me a photocopy of the document she had sent the MPs and I left.

Ann said she had watched the whole scene and was very alarmed for my safety. "When they stood over you I thought they were going to attack you." I had gleaned more information about the genocidal plans of the New World Order, the Committee of 300 and the Venetian, Genoan and Black Guelph noble families who had influenced history and planned the population reduction, but only after separating it from her paranoia about mind-control and UFOs. My appetite to find out more about the New World Order had been whetted, but I knew I would not contact Mary Seal again.

I did research into Italy's black nobility and discovered that one of its key members was a young man I knew at Oxford as 'Prince Ozi', a pale-faced, dark-glasses-wearing, shoulder-length-haired fellow whose actual name was Prince Pallavacini-Rostigliosi.[47] I had been rubbing shoulders with the dynastic world-shapers without realising it.

I was researching into Italy on all fronts – Florence, Pisa, now Venice and Genoa – and via Shakespeare. I was reading Stanley Wells on Shakespeare [, *Shakespeare, A Dramatic Life*], how 'Venus and Adonis' and 'The Rape of Lucrece' were based on Ovid's *Metamorphoses*. I wondered whether Shakespeare also came across Venus through Botticelli's *Primavera* (1476–7) and *Birth of Venus* (1485). I wrote: "I am obsessed by Shakespeare. All my bedtime reading is about him. Again and again I feel I know him." The same is true today. I wrote: "I shall write a poem based on 'Venus and Adonis' in which Adonis, the poet and representative of Beauty on earth (and Truth), is killed by the boar of the New World Order which he is hunting, and how he is mourned by Venus/Aphrodite, the goddess of Divine Love and the Light."[48]

I was still researching into world government. I encountered our MEP Patricia Rawlings at Vernon Davies's house and asked her over champagne, "The European Parliament is taking over from the national Parliaments. Any sign of a world government?" She said, "Not yet." Jeffrey Archer came and introduced himself. He extended a hand ("Jeffrey Archer"). I told him I was an author. He asked what books I had written and bristled when I told him, but was courteous.[49] I did not ask his view on a coming world government because I thought he would not be receptive.

Norris ends tenancy

Steve Norris had now terminated our tenancy agreement. He had been behind with his rent, and somehow *The Sunday Times* found out. I had been rung up by two journalists, one after the other, questioning me about the delayed payment. I was supportive of Norris but they had very specific information and later confronted Norris, who rang and said, "Nick, you've just ended my ministerial career." I explained that the journalists seemed to know what the situation was, and I told him to tell John Major I had said he need not pay for a year as I understood he had more than one house to maintain. He was pleased with this.[50] (The next day he was on the televised *Question Time*.) Soon afterwards I attended a gathering at St Stephen's Club, 34 Queen Anne's Gate, at which Norris told me, "We'll do something soon about the money." (I eventually received payment in November 1994.)

Ken Clarke's spreadsheet on the British economy

The Chancellor of the Exchequer Ken Clarke was standing in a doorway: Norris's mother worked for him in Nottingham. I told him, "I have to do figures for my bank manager," and asked: "Do you do a year's figures on one sheet of paper?" He said, "Yes, I do," and produced a sheet of paper from his breast pocket and opened it to show me. He explained he went by 12 indicators – very successfully as the British economy was bearing out. He told me that the inflation figures and exports were in columns on his spreadsheet, and how many of the figures were unreliable and could not be trusted.[51] I told him I had to do more figures for my bank to run two schools than he had to do to run the country, and he laughed. I liked Clarke and thought how unstuffy he was, having reduced the nation's spreadsheet to a sheet of paper. (Was this reductionism in financial management?) I did not then know that Clarke knew more about the annual meetings of the Bilderberg Group than any other politician, and looking back I see a missed opportunity: I should have discussed the world government with him: good and bad political Universalism.

But I was now on the trail of the secret New World Order I would unveil in *The Syndicate*.

End of my autobiographical literature

A Mystic Way; Collected Poems: A White Radiance; Awakening to the Light *– long letter from Ted Hughes*

Meanwhile, I had been writing two books simultaneously by using two computer operators. I had finished *A Mystic Way* (on 31 December 1993). It had been keyed into the computer on the dining-room table and more had been done by the wife of Andrew, the Prontoprint manager in Barking. We all worked incredibly hard. I noted on 30 December that the book had taken

16 months. Andrew printed out work for us to proof-read, and one night Ann and I were at his office with him until 2.45 a.m., and on 5 January until 6.15 a.m. The book went to the designer.

I now began assembling my poems on computer for what would become *Collected Poems: A White Radiance*, revising some as I went along. This work culminated months of putting poems on computer. My *Diaries* are full of specific poems I revised and in January I proof-read. There were frequent problems with our computers. On 30 January I noted that our work on the poems was finished: "1,275 poems in the collection."

Since 8 May 1991 entries in my *Diaries* had been keyed into the computer when there was time. By the end of January 1994 I had begun assembling what would become *Awakening to the Light*: my *Diaries* from 1958 to 1967. On 8 February I packed the manuscripts of *A Mystic Way* and *A White Radiance* away in my loft.

I was looking to make more time for my writing by offloading some of my financial duties. I told the school's bank manager, Ken Jones, I was looking for a bursar. In early February he asked if *he* could become our bursar. He said he had been asked to run a quarter of London for Barclays and he had thought no, he was a people person and would like to be our bursar. He would receive a retirement pension from Barclays, which we would top up. He would therefore be less expensive than many bursars. It would take him many months before he could extricate himself from his bank.

We drove to Cornwall for half-term. There was a great storm: spray fountained over the harbour wall, the wind beat in my face and stung my ears. I noted that Cornwall was like a health farm: "I have slept and eaten well and am full of fresh air." I returned relaxed to Essex. An early copy of *A Mystic Way* was waiting for me. Robin Parfitt, the ex-Chigwell teacher, rang me to say he had found the book in Dillons and bought it, and was enjoying it enormously. Soon afterwards I received an early copy of my first *Collected Poems*, *A White Radiance*.

I finished correcting *Awakening to the Light* on 21 March 1994 at 11.45 p.m. – and then had to proof-read two sets of Oaklands reports. Four days later I received a long typed letter from Ted Hughes, the Poet Laureate: four pages of A4 with 30 or 40 spidery notes in handwriting in the margins. He was very complimentary towards my work, saying that I was right in *The Fire and the Stones*, and asked many questions about the Fire. He said I had learned the language of "the opposition" (the materialists) and so they would listen to me. I reflected: "The poet is central to civilization, not marginal. He channels the Light (or the Fire) and beams it into his civilization." I reflected on the role of the Poet Laureate. Historically the poet laureate was the inspired 'bay-leaf' priest to the monarch. Power has now shifted from the monarch, and while the holder of the laureate post continues with the monarch and injects truth into a secular situation, the actual inspired poet turns to where the power is and addresses world government. Hughes referred to my "raid on the Kremlin" as being like "monsoonal swampings". In my reply I held that the true poet stands firm and resists the decline of the civilization. Hughes's long letter led to a correspondence that lasted until his death.

Down in Cornwall, and thinking of my Pisan vision, I had talked with Ann about the temptation to live in Italy and work in a place that was "a source of inspiration". Ann correctly saw that my writing had come out of my stability, security and infrastructure within the UK. I knew I should not live in exile again. Nadia rang to say she had been reading the books and could not put them down. She asked me about my poems, and I found myself explaining my poetic method to her. I told her:

> They're generalised images of feelings – of joy and suffering – the poems, in the manner of the Roman poets Catullus, Horace and Ovid. A minor poet writes of fish in a pond or a bird in a tree, the major poet writes about the deepest places in the human heart, a spectrum of 60 different feelings and emotions of joy and ecstasy and torment, despair and misery.... My particular image is universalised. I show Grannie dying but it is really man in the universe. Yeats said love and death were the only two things worth writing about in poetry and I show all the feelings about love and death.

I added:

> Shelley wrote out of his life but his feelings, like those towards the Lord Chancellor, are general and universal because everyone experiences such feelings. Rembrandt shows an expression of despair and impending death and bankruptcy in his [most memorable] self-portrait; that is a universal emotion, although it happened on a particular day. Canaletto shows peace in Venice and that becomes peace in all time and timelessness.

A few days later I wrote: "I am against impersonality and so I am against Modernism. I rejected Modernism when I wrote *The Gates of Hell*. I have gone back to Tennyson's *In Memoriam*, by-passed Modernism."

I had the idea of writing a future work, a *Collected Papers* that would include various prose bits and pieces I had written. This is still a project ahead of me, and will be called *Becoming and Being*. While we were in Cornwall Ann had researched into the Egyptian pyramids, and following my explanation for the King's Chamber, where the temple-sleep took place, I had the idea for writing 'The Riddle of the Great Pyramid', Part 2, showing the Great Pyramid as a cathedral for initiation into the Light (*see* p.710).

I finished work on *Awakening to the Light* on 12 April, and on 14 April 1994 handed it over to Michael Mann.

Wales: Beaumaris and Snowdon

At the end of April we drove to Bangor to visit Matthew. He met us at the Bulkeley Hotel, Beaumaris, on Anglesey. In the foyer of dark wooden panelling we checked in and rose to the second floor in the antiquated lift with two crash-gates which did not close properly and ended with a back-jarring jolt. We went for a walk down the pier and looked right towards Bangor under Snowdon, the University on the skyline; straight ahead to purple mountains; and left out to Puffin Island. We dined with Matthew in the hotel. Matthew was very articulate about his course and said: "I might go into teaching." This was the first indication that he might succeed me in the schools. Afterwards we drove to Caernarfon Castle (which was begun by Edward I in 1281), and stood outside the beetling walls. We drove back to his empty house, and saw the sitting-room, kitchen and his basement room. It was cosily furnished with damp patches on the walls (and the hazard of damp spores to his health), many posters and knick-knacks. We saw the peeling bathroom and Dave's upstairs room.

The next day we all had a cooked breakfast. We went up Snowdon on the mountain railway, up from Llanberis station, past the slate quarries, waterfall, green valleys and new-born lambs to Hebron station and then on up (with Glyder Fawr on our left, Arthur's cave where he slumbers). We went up to halfway station and Rocky Valley halt, with Moel Cynghorion on our right, and on to Clogwyn station at 2,556 feet or 779 m and a view up to the snow-streaked Snowdon ridge, down to Llanberis pass and across a hollow with a mere. I took the windy air until I had flushed cheeks and wrote two poems, 'Snow-White' and 'Scale'. We came down, reflecting that England's green and pleasant land was like this in the 18th century. I wrote 'Tiny Flies', 'Togetherness', 'Snowdon' and 'Great Events, Small Things' later in the Capel Curig Pinnacle café, where we had lasagne.

Back at Beaumaris, we saw a boat leaving for Puffin Island and impulsively caught it. As we rounded Puffin Island the shipman pointed out black and white puffins with orange beaks, a colony of razorbills huddling on a ledge, guillemots, cormorants, kittiwakes, a few penguins and some seals. I wrote a poem, 'Puffin Island'. After dinner we returned to our room, which overlooked the Straits of Menai: sea and Snowdon. The hotel was specially built to have a view across the Straits of Menai to Snowdonia and to accommodate Queen Victoria, who, alarmed by rumours of smallpox, did not visit until 1851, when she stayed in room 16, just down the passage from us.

The next morning we all had breakfast at the hotel. An elderly American near us had not been able to unscrew the marmalade jar the previous day and had taken my pre-ordered *Sunday Times* (marked 'Room 50'), requiring someone to go out and buy another one for me. A waitress asked him, "How are you?" He said loudly, "Bacon, eggs, sausage and tomato." I wrote a story of this title.

I was now assembling my short stories. On 21 May 1994 I wrote: "It poured all day. I prepared 32 stories for typing." I then went to St Mary's Loughton where my brother Jonnie took part in a recital for the dedication of the refurbished organ. He played Bach's *Fugue (St Anne)*, Franck's *Pastorale Op. 19* and Louis Vierne's *Finale from Symphony One*.[52]

My forays into autobiography were now over, and my research into international politics and the New World Order gave way to practical tours of European battlefields for my epic. I was already in the throes of a new conflict and new episode.

CHAPTER 4

Hard Slog: Contemplative Works

"Nature, that fram'd us of four elements
Warring within our breasts for regiment,
Doth teach us all to have aspiring minds:
Our souls, whose faculties can comprehend
The wondrous architecture of the world,
And measure every wandering planet's course,
Still climbing after knowledge infinite,
And always moving as the restless spheres,
Will us to wear ourselves, and never rest."

Marlowe, *Tamburlaine the Great*, Part 1, Act 2, Scene 7

I had chosen work and pulled away from the Metaphysical Centre. It was more important to share the experience of Light in works, put it in books, than go on experiencing it in a new mystic life and talking about it to groups. My Fourth Mystic Life now ended and although the Light would appear from time to time as if supporting me I was now in the grip of a great energy that demanded an incessant flow of works. I was like an apple-tree that was bearing a crop of fruit.

In the penultimate phase of the Mystic Way, the climb towards the summits of the seven interconnected hills of the disciplines that bestow knowledge, the spirit is above mist and cloud and instinctively knows the universe is a whole, and not just at the material, physical level. It perceives at the invisible metaphysical level. Feats of great energy become possible and the vision of the One Light is instinctively felt to be a new view of Reality. The spirit instinctively perceives the universe as a unity and a Theory of Everything seems within reach that includes love and beauty, not just the forces that physicists seek to unify.

As I continued my ascent through the disciplines, I created more unifying works that would have been beyond me when I was back in the dark wood.

Episode 10:

Epic and European Culture

Years: 1994–1997
Locations: Essex: Loughton; London: Chingford; Suffolk;
France: D-Day beaches (1994); Europe: Belgium, Germany, Poland, Hungary,
Austria; Germany (1994); Germany (1995); Europe: Holland, Germany,
Belgium, France, Luxembourg (1995); Turkey and Greece (1995); Italy: Bay of
Naples (1995); Russia (1995); Greece (1996); Italy: Rome (1996)
Works: *A Dandelion Clock*; *A Spade Fresh with Mud*; *A Smell of Leaves and Summer*;
The Warlords; *Overlord*
Initiatives: Intuitionist Universalism; revival of verse drama; revival of epic
poem

"The man of letters as such, is not concerned with the political or economic map of Europe; but he should be very much concerned with its cultural map."

T.S. Eliot, *The Man of Letters and the Future of Europe* (1944)

In my new episode I tackled the two books I had seen in Pisa. I was in conflict between my deskbound research for my epic and my latter-day Grand Tour as I captured European classical culture in classical odes. This episode brought the two halves of my Pisan revelation to birth.

Epic and European culture: philosophy of epic, Intuitionist Universalism
Universalist philosophers to contribute to a book
My epic poem *Overlord* had taken shape in my mind for 25 years. (It was now more than 23 years since my visit to Ezra Pound.) My vision in Pisa had spurred me on, as had Ricks's urging me to choose blank verse. I now had freedom from other projects to apply myself to my epic – and to my interest in classical Europe, the other half of my Pisan vision. I was pondering the philosophical background of my epic. I knew my Form from Movement Theory and my Universalism were crucial, but I was seeking to sharpen my Universalism so that I could express 'God's universe' within my epic, and the role of war within it, succinctly. For the next six months a sequence of events I did not seek sharpened and shaped the philosophy of my epic.

The Universalist Group of Philosophers had come up with a project to write essays for a book. A number of us had gone to HarperCollins on 8

February and had met a couple of editors for lunch in a restaurant. David Lorimer had introduced me, and I spoke about the Metaphysical Revolution and Universalism, and proposed a book of essays on science and religion. Geoffrey Read had added, "With you [i.e. me] as leader." The editors had been very interested.

On 16 February I had chaired a meeting for 13 philosophers of the Group, and by lunchtime I had a consensus. The four main contributors would be Chris Macann, Geoffrey Read, Alison Watson and me.

Lecture by John Williamson
There had been another meeting of the philosophers at Peter Hewitt's house in Ham Street, Richmond on 15 March. John Williamson, a 75-year-old white-haired man who had written pamphlets on metaphysics, talked to us. His theme was that everything is a unity. Over lunch he told me that his 16 laws had "come through" in 1944. He had channelled them like automatic writing. He was not used to dealing with philosophers, and said that the Universalist Philosophy Group was "the highest level of meeting he had ever attended in this country". I had said at the meeting that there is a difference between describing the universe in terms of intuitions and scientific evidence, and passing across unevidential channelled materials which beg the question 'Who is the source?' I wanted a metaphysics that could be experienced intuitively rather than one derived from automatic writing.

HarperCollins now asked the four main contributors for their essays. This disappointed Peter Hewitt, who was trying to widen the book to include all the philosophers. Geoffrey Read was then very much on my side. I met with the Universalist philosophers. We decided to hold a conference on 15 October. The four contributors would be the speakers, and their lectures would comprise the essays intended for the book. I was to speak first. I scouted out the venue, Regent's College, Inner Circle, Regent's Park, to hear Mary Midgley – who had flu and could not attend. Her paper was read by Max Payne. Peter Hewitt came up and said he could see the *Temenos* approach was different from our Universalism: "They are traditionalists and go into the Hindu past. They do not come up with ontological theories today."[1] I was interested that he should have detected one of the differences between Kathleen Raine and myself.

At the D-Day beaches with D-Day soldiers for epic.
My epic was set in the last year of the Second World War. I had known for some while that the post-war British predicament could be tracked back to the last year of the war, to the time between D-Day and the aftermath of the fall of Berlin which saw the US replace Britain as world leader, the rise of Stalin's Soviet empire, the birth of the atomic age which meant that we had

to live under the shadow of the atomic bomb, and Britain's imperial and colonial decline.

I now began my programme of visiting places connected with the war and my epic, and places connected with European classical culture. It marked the beginning of a kind of Grand Tour that was split into several journeys rather than undertaken in one go.

At the end of May Ann and I put Anthony on a train to Cornwall (to stay with Ann's mother) and went to Victoria to catch a coach that would begin our tour of the D-Day beaches, to commemorate the 50th anniversary of D-Day. We went to Broadlands, home of Mountbatten, and visited the places in Southwick village associated with Eisenhower, Montgomery and D-Day. We then travelled to Le Havre and toured villages that saw action during the Battle of Normandy. I got to know a D-Day soldier, Robert, now an Aussie, who walked with a swagger. He invited me to drink with him and with other D-Day soldiers that evening. He told me, "I see the faces of my comrades who were killed alongside me every morning." Tearfully he asked me, "Why do you think *I* survived, Nicholas? Why? I can't work it out." I would later base my D-Day soldier in my poetic epic and verse play on his recollections.

We visited Pegasus Bridge, Ouistreham – Le Home-sur-la-Mer was across the estuary and part of Sword – and Arromanches; the British beaches. We then went to the American beaches, to Omaha, Pointe du Hoc and Utah beaches.

On my way back from Cornwall in Ann's car in April I had resolved to write a verse play on the last year of the Second World War before I began my poetic epic:

> I want [my epic] to be accessible and connect with popular culture – so have a theatre version.... This will be a kind of plan for the actual epic, and will be dramatic and in verse, with Shakespearean soliloquies.

My hero for the play would be Montgomery, and for my poetic epic Eisenhower. I now began writing the verse play that would be titled *The Warlords*: "2nd June 1994. I began [it], impulsively, unplanned, determined to take advantage of the perspective I have gained. As with my 'American Liberty Quintet' I am finding the combination of travelling and poetic writing very stimulating."

We visited Falaise and other war villages. On the way home I had the idea for a Chaucerian poem, 'A Modern Pilgrimage' and I wrote the beginning after I arrived home ("by 11 p.m. English time, 12 midnight French time – and I was up at 6.15").[2]

I had been reliving D-Day with the veterans. The Oaklands fête was opened by Vicki Michelle, Yosette in *'Allo 'Allo!* She changed into her character's clothes in the caravan and after I introduced her over the microphone she hung on my arm and said in her French accent, at the end of her speech, "Leesten very carefully, I will say it only once. The fair ees now o-pen." The laughter that followed jarred against my recent encounter with the D-Day veterans. The juxtaposition made me feel uncomfortable: the programme's trivialised take on the war seemed shallow beside Robert's tearful and haunted memories of D-Day and his dead comrades.

I was researching into Auschwitz. I rang to attend a conference and found myself speaking to Ronnie Landau, the author of *The Nazi Holocaust*. We discussed in detail how the holocaust happened. I visited the Imperial War Museum's D-Day exhibition and bought £109 worth of war books and toyed with presenting "the wrath of Monty as he stops Hitler being Overlord and puts an end to the Final Solution".

Ann and I went to Bletchley Park, which had

only opened in 1994 after 30 years of not being mentioned (until 1975).... The ugly house and lake, the huts where the Battle of Britain, Battle of the Atlantic and D-Day were run. Was taken round by Tel Enever, author of the booklet on it all. Took many notes. At the end, an exhibition on Enigma and Lorenz (Hitler's machine); talked to Tony Sale, ex-SIS and assistant to Peter Wright of *Spycatcher*. Also toured the house and the Churchill exhibition in the Mess. The SIS HQ during the war.... Stayed over 4 hours.

The next day Ann and I drove to Duxford

and spent from 3 until 6 on the airfield, mainly seeing Monty's 3 caravans or trailers,... and [I] wrote details in my notebook. Very interesting to see where the war for D-Day was fought – a block at Bletchley Park communicating with Monty's map caravan, where he phoned his subordinates.... Bought £220 worth of war books.[3]

Universalism and the Fire
David Lorimer invited the Universalist Group of Philosophers to state their outlook under bullet points for the Scientific and Medical *Network Review*. On 8 June I had spent the morning with the philosophers agreeing bullet points on 'Universalist philosophy'. Peter Hewitt said he would visit me to get my bullet points on 'Universalism', as if this was different. I did not like the separation between the two and sensed an undercurrent as Geoffrey Read had tackled me on whether my Fire was the same as his One, or a manifestation. I said: "It's an immanent form of what is transcendent. The One becomes the Fire, the One is latent Fire." My *Awakening to the Light* had

been received and was passed round. Peter Hewitt read out a quotation from Whitehead: "Scientists who spend their life with the purpose of proving that it is purposeless constitute an interesting subject of study." David Lorimer said: "I used that in the *Newsletter* two issues ago." Hewitt said: "Nicholas wrote this in 1966." I was astonished at how topical and current the book was: "Besides being process philosophy accumulated each day, it is a young man's journey towards a metaphysical vision."

Debate between Enoch Powell and Roger Scruton; Brian Crozier

I had been invited by Geoffrey Read to attend the *Salisbury Review*'s dinner debate on decadence between Enoch Powell and Roger Scruton at St Columba's church hall, Pont Street. Read had given me Scruton's address and said, "Vision and the philosophical underpinning of a spiritual view, that is what Scruton wants." I had written to Scruton.

Read, bearded and smiling, and I sat near the front. On top table sat Enoch Powell and Scruton, a woman with short bobbed hair between them. On the platform, Scruton, ill at ease, said he was nervous because he was used to opposition and was among friends, a new experience. Powell said he felt uneasy at attributing decay as the observer moves as if on a train. He said the instinctive is beneath the rational, and instinctively we are English, not Continental. We were reacting against decline. Scruton said, "A United Europe is a delusion."

After the question-and-answer session I spoke with Scruton. He asked: "Was it all right? I was very nervous." I reassured him and asked if he had received my books. "Yes." And my letter? "Yes. We'll talk later."

I saw Brian Crozier and tackled him: "Hello Brian." I told him I had two schools now. "Yes, I heard that from someone only three days ago. And three months ago I had to give a radio talk and I used your compilation on Scargill." I wagged my finger at Crozier and told him I was right to see the collapse of Communism as imminent in 1984, and to stand up to the Communists. I said: "1984–86 was the last thrust of hard-line Russia and we stood up to them." "Yes." "For the record, I was right about Russia being ready to fall – one push." "Yes." I told him about the meetings I had with Gorka, "the Iron-Curtain crowd" and Bukovsky at the Free Polish Headquarters in 43 Eaton Place.

I then took Read to Scruton and introduced him. I said that four of us were presenting Universalism on 15 October. He said, "I can't be there, I'll be in Boston." (Where he knew Ricks.) I said, "But you should know what we're doing. We're going back to 1914 and are bringing the universe back into philosophy. William James, Bergson, Husserl, T.E. Hulme." He said: "I know what you're doing, I've read it in your books. Using the index, I've looked up every reference to Universalism in *A Mystic Way*. It's important.

Do keep me informed.'" I reflected that as a nationalist Scruton would not take kindly to Universalism.

The woman with short bobbed hair turned out to be Jessica Douglas-Home. I had not recognised her under her new hairstyle. I went and had a chat, and reminded her of *Budapest Betrayed* and the evening I had had with her. She had a very clear memory of it and said, "The hens." I nodded and talked of my schools. She asked, "What's the philosophy?" She nodded as I explained it was children amid Nature, traditional values and the 3 Rs. I spoke of my books. Then Scruton returned and took her away.

Coalition of philosophers

Peter Hewitt visited me on 23 June and listed the bullet points for 'Universalism'. Again I detected an undercurrent. I disapproved of the splitting of 'Universalism' and 'Universalist philosophy', and sensed that he was up to something. He seemed to be trying to present the Universalist Group of Philosophers as a coalition of separate views. I said that all history was Universalist because it is the "sum total of all the differentiated events from the One". He said: "That's a new idea." But it wasn't, it was in *The Fire and the Stones*.

I went to the philosophers on 7 July. All day Alison Watson read from her thesis at breakneck speed and did not allow any interruption. During the interminable reading, Peter Hewitt fell asleep. In the end I pointed out: "While all these words are happening, there is a perfect rose outside the window." Alison's view boiled down to mine but she referred to No-thing at the beginning rather than the One as a latent Nothingness, a Plenitude. (Like the Existentialists, we all had slightly different emphases – in our case, about the beginning of the universe.)

Four days later Peter Hewitt visited me to rework the bullet points for 'Universalism' and 'Universalist philosophy' and to agree an introduction he was writing for the Scientific and Medical *Network Review*. He saw that empirical Intuitionist metaphysics was a separate way from Rationalist speculative metaphysics. He sent me what he had written up, and I was not pleased. I told him that in his latest version "the Fire or Light had come out in the wash.... The common ground is the tradition of the Fire or Light.... To remove the Fire or Light from Universalism is like removing the Crown from monarchy."[4]

Tony Little

A lot had been happening. Matthew had a vacation job assisting the Deputy Head of Bancroft's in selling computers. He had had to report to Chigwell School to assist his boss in selling a computer to the school. His boss did not turn up, and Matthew demonstrated the computer to his old physics teacher, who agreed to buy enough computers to set up a network.

I had invited Tony Little to give out prizes at Coopersale Hall's prize-giving. "Little spoke at length, mentioning the Hagger family's long association with Chigwell and how Matthew is 'of international standard at *Choi Kwang Do*, and if you're thinking of taking a swipe at Mr Hagger I'd strongly advise against it as his son is of international standard'."

Short stories

I had been compiling my stories and had shown them to Michael Mann. He "agreed 2 volumes (in March and May 1995), one *A Spade Fresh with Mud*, and one *A Smell of Leaves and Summer*". I freewheeled about my epic and the play. Michael "will be prepared to publish [the play] in May together with books 1 and 2 of the epic".

Lunch in the garden with Sebastian Barker

I had visited Sebastian Barker at 70 Wargrave Road, N15 at his request. I wrote: "A cheery bespectacled slightly long-haired Sebastian shaking my hand, open-necked shirt; he led me into the garden where there was a Scotch egg (with a fly sitting on it) and orange juice and water, and we talked from 1 until 7, through a few spots of rain."[5] We had a long talk that ranged from the Fire through physics, philosophy and history to poetry and his reminiscences of his father George Barker, who had learned his trade as a poet (he said) from Eliot. He told me that he had met the daughter of Victor, Lord Rothschild, Victoria, who had been associated with Scruton. (I wondered if Scruton knew that I had identified her father as the fifth man.) He said he would be writing a long review on all my published books and would be sending it to *Acumen*, the *New York Times Review of Books* and perhaps the *Poetry Review*. As he had been chairman of the Poetry Society I was pleased by this development.

I would have to work hard on getting out my stories, verse play and the beginning of my poetic epic.

In wartime Europe for epic: Berlin and Auschwitz

Meanwhile I had been continuing my research into the war for my verse play and poetic epic. I had gone to Harlow and attended a one-man show, *Monty*, by Montgomery's nephew, Gary Montgomery: a very absorbing portrait: Monty in terms of his childhood and parents, his strange putting of people on a pedestal and dropping them when they did not come up to expectations.[6]

In early July we returned to Southwick and we visited places connected with Eisenhower and Montgomery, including the site where Eisenhower had his trailer. We visited Broomfield House. I visited an old soldier in

Blackpool, Paul Huck, and heard his reminiscences on being a wartime chef. He had accompanied Monty to France and back (by small plane) on D-Day, and he had heard the heated words exchanged between Churchill and Monty on 21 July 1944. I was pleased to hear his eyewitness report, and I based a number of situations in *The Warlords* and *Overlord* on his impressions.

To absorb the background for my verse play and epic, I took Ann and our two boys on a two-week coach tour of Europe. We travelled to Calais and Brussels, and visited Aachen. On the coach I read *The Fall of Berlin* by Anthony Read and David Fisher. We passed through Hannover and reached Berlin.

I saw the courtyard where von Stauffenberg was shot and visited the Topography of Terror museum, part of the Gestapo HQ. I found the site of Hitler's Führerbunker in Voss Strasse. With Tony I visited Plotzensee prison, and saw where 5,000 were hanged after Stauffenberg's plot against Hitler. The execution shed was just inside the gate: a room with a black curtain drawn back on two sides, two high-up windows letting in light and a rail from which five heavy steel hooks were suspended. I stood under the right-hand hook and imagined being lifted and my noose slipped over the hook, and "a terrific shudder that was quite involuntary went through me". We visited the Cecilienhof Manor where the Potsdam conference was held. We went to Frederick the Great's Sanssouci and the court where Freisler shouted at those he sentenced to death.

We visited Warsaw and Auschwitz II and saw where the selection was made on the ramp between two railway lines, and the ruins of the gas chamber and crematorium. We went on to Birkenau, Auschwitz I, and visited the killing wall and gallows where the camp commandant was hanged. We visited the gas chamber. Later I wrote a classical ode, 'Auschwitz and Immortality'.

We went to Cracow and saw the ghetto that features in *Schindler's List*. We passed Plaszow, Goeth's camp in *Schindler's List*, now a ruin. We drove via Slovakia to Budapest. I wrote two sonnets: 'Berlin: Von Stauffenberg' and 'Warsaw: Razed, Rebuilt.' In Szentendre we visited a Serbian church, and I wrote a classical ode, 'In the Serbian Orthodox Church of the Annunciation of Szentendre'. I wrote 'On the Danube Frontier', 'Cracow: Ghetto', 'Jasna Gora: Black Madonna', Cracow: Bodily Assumption', 'Potsdam: Frederick's Summer Palace', 'Warsaw: Unknown Soldier' and 'Potsdam: Spokes of Light' – "all at a sitting on my bed between 10.45 and 11.55". The next morning I wrote 'Hannover: *Rathouse*', 'Budapest: Gabriel' and 'Brussels: Quadriga'.

Outside Budapest we met Paul Gorka, who was still in charge of selling privatised castles. He told me I could have a free castle for helping Hungary during the Cold War, but I would have to raise funds to restore it. He offered me a 1580 Jesuit college of 30 rooms, or a 1600 Renaissance building of 48 rooms. I did not want to raise funds to send to Hungary, and nothing came of the offer of a castle.

We went on to Vienna where Tony and I visited the Treasury, *Weltliche Schatzkammer*, and found 'the spear of destiny' reputed to be the spear of Longinus that pierced the side of Christ. There is a legend that whoever owns it rules the world, and Hitler removed it after invading Austria and took it to Nuremberg. I brought this into *Overlord*.

In Vienna we visited the Schloss Schönbrunn, and I wrote a classical ode, 'Summer Palaces' on the Hohenzollerns and Habsburgs, and 'Vienna: Wheel of Fortune' and 'Vienna: History Clock'.

We drove on via Salzburg to Munich, and while the party drank beer in the Hofbräuhaus Ann and I stepped out to a nearby taxi rank, found a driver who spoke English and toured all the Hitler places. We returned to the group in time to catch the coach back to our hotel.

We drove up the Romantic road and caught a boat along the Rhine. I wrote 'Rothenburg: Blood', 'Lorelei: Siren' and 'Berlin: Vibrant East' and reflected: "I like being a poet, sitting on a coach, watching the places drift by and scribbling poems on my knee." We drove to Cologne and through Belgium to Calais. On the journey I began writing *The Warlords* on my knee in the coach and also on the ferry.[7]

I had visited many of the places that would feature in my verse play and poetic epic (see *Selected Diaries* for further details), and I knew I would be writing the verse play throughout August.

Two factions of philosophers: Intuitionist Universalists versus Rationalists following 'New Metaphysics'

I opened the post on 2 August and found two letters from Peter Hewitt. The first enclosed the copy of the statement of bullet points for 'Universalism' and 'Universalist philosophy'. The second said there had been a meeting, that Chris Macann, Geoffrey Read and Alison Watson did not want to go out under a 'Universalist' banner and that David Lorimer and Peter Hewitt thought it a shame. They wanted to call it 'New Metaphysics' philosophy. My feeling was not to go out under a Rationalist 'New Metaphysics' banner. Peter had defined it too precisely to unite. Our presentation now had the flavour of Williamson's 'neo-metaphysics'. The change had been effected in my absence in an underhand way. I said: "I can hardly recognise Universalism in your version of it."

That night I "stayed up until 1.30 a.m. writing the end of my play". (I wanted to know where it would end before I began.) In the few moments I had to think about philosophy, I reflected that they had made a mistake. We had had the discussion in the past, and they were picking over old ground and demonstrating that they did not know their own mind. And the distinction between neo-metaphysics and neo-metaphysical philosophy was not one I could accept. I phoned Peter Hewitt and told him how I felt under three headings. Inconsistency: they were changing their views, weakening their conviction. Neo-metaphysics: the label was wrong. Discourtesy: it was not the way to do it, to wait until I was abroad. I was leaving for Cornwall the next day and let the situation rest there.

Verse play, The Warlords
I was clear that I was "reviving verse drama", and that the epic was "reasserting the metaphysical vision in our time and revealing the essential laws of the universe".

On 4 August Ann, our two boys and I drove down to Cornwall with some 30 books on the war in the boot. It had been muggy in Essex but it was cool in Charlestown. I worked hard writing my verse play and posted what I wrote for typing. I spent "all morning on the play" (7 August); "all morning and afternoon on the play" (8 August); and "wrote from 10 a.m. to 9 p.m." (10 August). "The pentameters are beating in my head, I write quickly." Again: "All day, finishing the quick draft of Act 2 and doing some of Act 1 – Stauffenberg's execution and 2 hangings. Did Monty's closing soliloquy. I have revived the soliloquy and the aside, which go well with verse drama." I "spent the morning... integrating insertions and writing more, e.g. Stalin's soliloquy, and sent two packages". The next day I "wrote until just before midnight, then went for a walk under brilliant stars". I "wrote all morning. D-Day.... Worked till 11, walked with Ann under an umbrella of stars." The next day was "a wonderful summer's day: blue sky, green grass, vivid flowers, many butterflies – as many as 20 on the cornflowers and mauve sea-daisies, mostly cabbage whites with some meadow browns, which prefer the grass". I now realised *The Warlords* was in two parts, like "*Henry IV*, parts 1 and 2 or *Tamburlaine the Great*, parts 1 and 2". (And, indeed, *My Double Life*.) That day I "got up to July 1 1944. Having blitzed Act 2 from Hitler's and Stalin's point of view."

The next day I had a discussion with Michael Mann on the phone: "*A Spade Fresh with Mud* is to come out on 4 April, delivery to Element 1 December. *A Smell of Leaves and Summer* is to come out on 4 June, delivery 1 February. The play and the first two books of the epic are to come out on 4 May, delivery 4 January to Element.... The titles should be different. *Overlord*, the title of the poem, can stay and should stay." I had to come up with a title for the verse play. For the rest of the day I pored over the alternatives. "It suddenly came to me at 8.35. The title should be *The Warlords*. It goes with *Overlord* and is different.... You can't hurry the creative process. It

499

has to take its own time." The next day I rang Michael Mann. "We have got there.... They are clearly cousins now, the two works."

I returned to *The Warlords*. "Wrote an enormous amount... while Ann went to Porthleven." (17 August.) The next day I finished Act 1. I "worked all morning and evening on the Battle of the Bulge" (21 August). I "wrote all day and reached... Eisenhower's telegram to Stalin" (22 August). I "worked to 29 April 1945, Belsen. Got there at 11 p.m. and went for a walk with Anthony. There was a very full moon and the water had flecks of fire in the waves; like a fire flickering on coals in a grate. Or like a shoal of leaping fish." (23 April.) I wrote "from the surrender on Lüneburg Heath... to Churchill's loss of power" (24 August). I dictated from 4 p.m. to midnight (25 August). I "got up at 7.30 and finished dictating to the end of the play by 12.30" (26 August). I posted the package and then began insertions and corrections. The verse play was substantially finished.

On 30 August I "worked all day and finished to within 7 pages of the end: correcting and proof-reading.... Went for a walk late at night and got Burgdorf's final speech on racism. It came to me on Charlestown pier in semi-stormy weather about midnight. I rushed back and wrote it down." The next day I wrote: "It is September tomorrow. I have been down here a month, don't want to go back."[8] I returned to Essex the next day. I had finished *The Warlords* by the end of August, and with the last year of the war in my mind launched straight into the poetic epic, *Overlord*.

Coalition of philosophers: Universalism and New Metaphysics, Intuitionism versus Rationalism

David Lorimer had rung me about the philosophers on 9 August. "There are different camps. Alison has a different agenda. She is a Buddhist and comes from a Buddhist tradition." I asked: "Has she like Scruton read each entry of Universalism mentioned in the index [of *A Mystic Way*]?" David said: "I am sorry they did it without your being there to defend it." He agreed with me that the larger view was better than the narrower. He was going away and wanted to run off leaflets headed 'Universalism and the New Metaphysics'. I agreed to take part on the basis that there was a coalition between my Universalism and their 'New Metaphysics', and that I would go first. I would present Universalism as my Bergsonian Vitalism. For the purposes of 15 October I was in a coalition against materialism. I would not contribute to their book but do my own.

When I returned from Cornwall, my mind full of my poetic epic, Peter Hewitt rang. "Alison is not happy with 'Universalism' in the title, which David has printed, and will not take part on the day." I told Peter that I was not interested in politicking. "Alison wants the bus to have a different designation. She wants it to say 'Hammersmith' instead of 'Shepherd's Bush'. The route isn't going to change. She's got on the wrong bus." I said she had not attended the meetings, and wanted to change everything at the end. I sensed I had given them a problem by not withdrawing from the presentation on 15 October.

Chris Macann rang me on 4 September. He was keen to keep a Universalist broad label because he saw that it would get him a breakthrough. He said that Geoffrey and Alison were afraid of being taken over by me.

Four days later I received my Scientific and Medical *Network Review*. The account of Universalism I had given Hewitt appeared under his name, as *his* initiative. Peter Hewitt rang. I pointed out that it was all under his name and called upon him to tell the truth when he introduced us on 15 October. I said I would not attend his meeting on 16 September.

On 23 September I started work on 'Intuitionist Universalism and the Fire behind the Universe'. I finished it at midnight the following day and combed the work. The others had been meeting, discussing, rehearsing and faffing about, and I had got my contribution done in a day and a half, from start to finish.

Peter Hewitt rang me on 3 October, still trying to integrate me into the group of philosophers under their new banner. I explained that they were from a Rationalist tradition whereas I was from an Intuitionist tradition: "I don't think anyone else is standing for the Intuitionist stream today – [of] Bergson, Whitehead and Sartre." The others had done me a favour. Rather than water myself down so Geoffrey Read would agree, I could be myself and make a statement of what my philosophy is about. I regarded my 15-October lecture as a "platform for the philosophy to go into my epic".[9]

In wartime Germany for epic
I was delving deeper into Germany's role in the Second World War so I could start my poetic epic. I

> researched the atomic origins of the Second World War. We went to war to stop Hitler getting the atomic bomb, which was made possible in December 1938 when Otto Hahn found [nuclear] fission by accident in Berlin. By February 1939 Bohr had fathomed uranium-235, and Einstein wrote to Roosevelt on 2 August 1939 about the military uses, triggering the Second World War.

I was haunted by an image:

> Many spiders' webs outside our front door. Watched several bulbous spiders spinning, going round and round, progressing towards the centre. Many

flies hung still on the webs. Occasionally a midge flew into the net, which trembled; on one occasion the spider ran to it and nipped it dead. On two other occasions it ignored it. The poet is like a spider, going round and round towards the centre, spinning his web [into which images fly] from his own body, a beautiful pattern. The spider's web is a symbol for my epic.

I used this symbol in *Overlord*. I was encouraged in such thinking by a review of *A Mystic Way* in *Communiqué* which said that my work "is of immense importance".[10]

From 6 October Ann and I spent a few days in Germany visiting the main war sites in greater detail than time had permitted in August. We flew to Munich and visited places connected with Hitler. We went on to Berchtesgaden and took a bus and then a lift up to the Eagle's Nest, the tea house built by Bormann. I knew I would have to return for the Berghof. We went on to Dachau and saw the courtyard where prisoners were shot. We visited Ingolstadt where Adam Weishaupt was a Professor of Canon Law. I found a portrait of him in the City Museum. We went on to Nuremberg, where Hitler sought to revive the old German empire.

We took a bus past the Colosseum (Congress Hall), the grandstand of the Zeppelinfeld, where Hitler stood on a podium and addressed 1.6 million people, and saw the 2-kms-long road to the Castle, where Hitler was to have been elected German Emperor, 'Kaiser'. The Märzfeld at Dutzendteich ('dozen ponds'), the Stadium and the New Congress Hall would all make Nuremberg the centre of a new Holy Roman Empire. We passed the Palace of Justice, where the Nazis were tried, and the prison where 10 were executed. We visited the Castle.

I grasped Hitler wanted to revive the Holy Roman Empire and build a world empire stretching from Spain to Russia, and from the British Isles to Egypt. It would include India and the USA. Our visit had deepened my knowledge of contemporary German history.[11] I was getting inside Hitler's mind, but I knew I would have to visit Berchtesgaden again.

Presentation at Regent's College: Intuitionist Universalism as the philosophy of the epic, break with the unenlightened Rationalist philosophers
On 15 October the Group of Philosophers gave four presentations under the banner 'Universalism and the New Metaphysics' at Regent's College in Regent's Park (where Chris Macann was Professor of Philosophy). Anthony and I arrived before 9. Peter Hewitt, his girlfriend and Geoffrey Read arrived with us at the car park; Geoffrey was ingratiating, I cool. We found the room, G08: not a banked, tiered auditorium, but a room with a ring of chairs we arranged into rows. We found a table and a lectern and generally organised.

There were about 40 in the audience. My books were piled on the table

David Lorimer sat at, recording us. Peter Hewitt's introduction used my material without acknowledgement. Alison Watson arrived after I began.

I spoke on 'Intuitionist Universalism and the Fire behind the Universe'. I put up a photocopy of the chart in *The Observer* of 29 June 1958, 'The "Isms" of Philosophy'. It shows the "isms" of philosophy in three generations of pairs: Rationalism and Empiricism (17th to 18th centuries), Idealism and Realism (19th and early 20th centuries) and Intuitionism and Logical Analysis (later 19th and 20th centuries). I said that the first in each descending pair is preoccupied with an invisible Reality (metaphysics); and that the second in each pair is concerned with common sense and experience of the natural world. I said that Intuitionism includes Kierkegaard, Nietzsche, Bergson and Sartre. I held that Universalism is the most recent – indeed, the only recent – flowering of Intuitionism. I spoke for an hour. My contribution was like a hand grenade that went off in different directions.

After coffee Geoffrey Read gave a very simple talk against materialism, flashing up simple statements – particle theory, process theory and the fatal trap (assigning an object to an appearance which is in reality a perception). Anthony found it boring. Heather Dobbs said, "I got nothing from that talk."

We ate a picnic lunch in Regent's Park. Anthony and I sat on the slightly damp grass, "the philosopher on the lawn". I said: "I see +A + –A coming out of zero or Nothingness, a latent Fire, but am not interested in geometric models."

Then the Buddhist Alison Watson spoke, hesitantly, falteringly, using transparencies. The general impression was very bad, to the point of being embarrassing. She said, "Limits of language are limits of thought," and that language fixes reality. She started with "nothing, no-thing in particular", "no structure". She claimed (questionably) that we are co-creating the universe but did not explain how.

Chris Macann, a good person to say that Existentialism has been replaced by Universalism as his *Four Phenomenological Thinkers* is to Phenomenology what H.J. Blackham's *Six Existentialist Thinkers* is to Existentialism, spoke fluently and rapidly, with a diagram on the board. There were labels showing how he was uniting Husserl's transcendental phenomenology and Heidegger's ontological phenomenology.

There was a question-and-answer session. When David Lorimer put up the points about the New Metaphysics, I pointed out that I had written them and that Universalism had been changed to New Metaphysics. Alan Mayne wanted to know if we were influenced by Williamson's neo-metaphysics. I said it was natural he should think that but they had invited this question by calling themselves 'New Metaphysics'. Lorimer and I told Mayne privately, "We can't help you, we don't know why there was a change, ask Alison." Lorimer said to me: "Alison says you begin with the Fire and not 'nothing in particular'." I said: "I begin with Nothingness as a latent Fire. Alison does not say how structure arises from Nothing in particular."

I plan The One and the Many
At the end I slipped away. Peter Hewitt wanted me to stay for a curry with the other speakers, but I said I had to get home to Ann. Chris wanted me to have tea with the speakers at Regent's College, but again I said No, politely. I drove home, cleared up my room and assembled 10 pieces for a new book on Universalism that would present my reconciliation of philosophy and practical mysticism (which became *The One and the Many*). My developing Intuitionism (or Intuitionist Universalism) reconciled my philosophy and practical mysticism.

I spoke with Chris Macann on the telephone. He told me that Read and Watson "feel overshadowed by you. Whatever you do they feel threatened by. Alison has not given a presentation before. It was very abstract and she jumped from the whole to structure and Descartes, yes you are right." Alison Watson rang, hoping I could help organise the four presentations into a book. I said I was busy and put the phone down. Heather rang to tell me that the great-nephew of Evelyn Underhill, author of *Mysticism*, which I was reading moments before my mystical experience of 1971, had been present. She said: "You ought to work with enlightened people now. Those philosophers are not enlightened, and so they are putting themselves forward, taking others' ideas, plagiarising."

To jump forward, on 17 January 1995 I received a letter from Hewitt asking "when I can start my contribution to *his* book". I ignored this letter. Macann told me in mid-April that he had written his contribution, that Hewitt had said it would have to be rewritten and that Watson and Read had written nothing. The book never appeared. Hewitt produced a book about Read's philosophy that alternated turgid passages from Read's papers with his own summarising link passages. He published this himself in 2003 as *The Coherent Universe: An Introduction to Geoffrey Read's New Fundamental Theory of Matter Life and Mind*. The book arrived, and I noted Read's contradiction: "He wants to start the universe with time but writes of the Absolute that enfolds it."[12] Hewitt asked me to review the book for the Scientific and Medical *Network Review*. I declined. He had broken up with his girlfriend who had had his child, and suffered from depression. He died in January 2004 of a combination of alcohol and pills. Macann told me it appeared to be an accident. The exact circumstances are not known. Read died in March 2014.

Back in 1994 I wrote: "I will now go my own way and bring out another book on Universalism." I was relieved that I had finished with the philosophers apart from Chris Macann. I could get on with my literary activities and the 'Grand Tour' of European culture that would underpin my epic and the classical odes that were coming to me increasingly frequently. My Intuitionist Universalism would now express itself through literature, beginning with my epic, rather than philosophy, and its descriptions of the universe would appear in my concrete epic rather than in an abstract work.

Epic and European culture: Overlord
I finish vol. 1 of my Collected Stories, A Spade Fresh with Mud
I was impatient to start my epic, *Overlord*, but first I had to finish assembling the two volumes of stories. These were Universalist stories in the Intuitionist tradition: they reconciled image and statement and approached the truth of the One through intuition rather than reason. I had to cope with a dozen chores in the schools and during the next three days I proof-read 60 stories.

On 20 October 1994 I finished *A Spade Fresh with Mud*, vol. 1 of *Collected Stories*. "By my count there are 220 stories. I have now cleared the backlog hanging over me since the summer."[13]

I begin my epic Overlord, *books 1 and 2*
The next day I

> thought about the poetic epic. My cosmogony comes from my Regent's College lecture. The Fire is a whole principle.... The whole needs division to make a universe – a cosmos – and it needs opposites: Non-Being and Being, chaos and order.

We went down to Charlestown and: "All day, got into the epic, books 1 and 2.... Two universal energies: the Light, and a dark power.... In the evening – 4 till 8.30 – drafted 75 lines of the epic: how God made the universe.... Used the image of the sea which is outside my window." The next day I "drafted the next 75 lines of the epic: Christ speaking in Council. And began the Preface." (Ricks had advised me to have 'Hellish' and 'Heavenly' Councils.) I noted that

> I had to grow and develop Universalism in order to write the epic. That is why I waited 25 years.... Have decided to go to Rome and Sicily and Virgil's tomb, if I can, next April; a cruise of Greece, Troy and Ithaca and other places next July. Possibly another visit to Italy in September?... I am now doing what Milton and Virgil did – and Homer. I am in their footsteps. Later, wrote another 25 or more lines, making 100 today.

We returned from Cornwall. On the journey I wrote on Eisenhower driving to Broomfield House after seeing 'a perfect rainbow', a bow with a great arc:

> As Eisenhower drove through green fields that day,
> Down lanes to Broomfield House, the wind and rain
> Swept through the scent of fresh-cut hay. He stopped
> The car and gazed at a perfect rainbow,
> An arc like a storm-god's bow, one end propped
> By an oak-tree. Swallows skimmed low like planes.
> *Overlord*, book 1, lines 571–576

We got home about 6. Matthew had already arrived from the Continent, having set off at 6.30 a.m. via Bastogne, where he bought me a book on the Ardennes campaign. He was looking better than I had ever seen him, and was fully formed. Perhaps he was now ready to take over what I had been doing in the schools? Again I had him earmarked to succeed me in the schools.

My *Diaries* for October and November reflect the working-out of the ideas I translated into poetic images for the epic. One such idea was to make my Christ 'the Cosmic Christ':

> Ricks advised me to have an avatar, which in Hindu was 'the descent of a deity to earth in incarnate form, incarnate and manifestation', and I can have the descent of 'the Cosmic Christ' to speak to Bonhoeffer and Hitler... and then Stauffenberg.

Now the epic "poured through" (31 October). Two days later:

> On the way to Coopersale Hall saw the laws of the universe, driving my Lexus. Scribbled them on my knee. It is very simple. There are two opposites, the expanding force of Fire... which manifests into existence...; and the contracting force of Darkness.... God holds the two in balance, the cosmological constant, so zero (0) = +A + −A, *yin* and *yang*. The two forces are personified in the Cosmic Christ and Cosmic Satan; Ahura Mazda and Ahriman.

John Ezard rang to say he had been reading *A Mystic Way*. (Ricky had also read it and was now reading all the poems mentioned in the book.) Ezard said I had left a lot of questions unanswered. I was in my poetic self and said: "I am making a statement about man in the universe from every angle – like Donne: philosophy, science, history, religion and social development all interconnected." I said he might recall that I read *The Metaphysical Poets* all through Spain. He said: "What you're doing is the sort of thing that gets written about 20 years afterwards. Your experience is very powerfully written. I was like the person from Porlock [who distracted Coleridge from 'Kubla Khan'] while you were having your mystical experience." On the Oaklands bonfire night, "with Matthew (back from Bangor yesterday and going to France tomorrow) holding the hose very commandingly", I remarked to Anthony (and to Ann) that the sparks from the bonfire, shooting upwards, were like galaxies from the Big Bang, and symbolised our universe. Later I wrote this into *Overlord*. After the fireworks, with many loud bangs seen through rain under the umbrella of the oak-tree, we had soup and hot dogs on the floodlit tennis-court and I felt apart from all, in my poem, set apart from the rest of mankind by my poetic calling and duty, a price I had to pay for keeping alive the vision.

I wrote on into *Overlord*. I passed D-Day and Rommel and tackled the cosmology of Hell. I drew on Universalism on numerous occasions. I was careful to write out of my imagination. I thought of Keats's letter of 1817: "'What the Imagination seizes in Beauty must be Truth', i.e. what the imagination sees is permanent and eternal, what the physical eye sees is transient and ephemeral." I reflected on "the Romantic cult of imagination; the Universalist cult of the Light".

Nadia's note

Caroline shocked me out of poetry. She rang on 26 November to say that Nadia and Sandy had separated. They had visited us a few months back and we had taken them to eat in L'Artista. He wanted to be single and not have the responsibility of planning for the future. She said, "Nadia said to me, if only I'd listened to Dad." I rang Nadia, who was tearful but positive: "He wanted the easy option." I was sad for her, but understood. Two days later Nadia rang again: "He did not like me pressuring him to work." He had written her a note and left while she was at work, and had returned to his own flat. I met her in the Charing Cross Hotel, the former "Oak-Tree office", two days before Christmas. She had short cropped hair, a smile and sad eyes. She told me he had not moved out cleanly and she had had to organise a removal van. He had left her to cope with the bills as he had his own bills now.

Anthony, John Ezard and Richard Norton-Taylor

My intelligence contact had wanted me to sever all connections with Nadia (*see My Double Life 1: This Dark Wood*). Bizarrely, while I was consoling her John Ezard – one of the two I had been asked to tell about my contact with intelligence, now responding to his godson Anthony's approach to talk to the Chigwell sixth form – brought *The Guardian*'s intelligence expert Richard

Norton-Taylor to meet Anthony in the King's Head before taking him across the road to address the Chigwell pupils. Ezard visited me after the event and told me: "It wasn't a good talk, he didn't make contact. They looked bored as if they had to be there." He said Anthony asked two questions. He left. Anthony returned and said: "It was terrible. He was bald with long hair down his back, he looked weird, you couldn't hear him, he looked at his notes, there was no structure, it was disjointed. I asked, 'What difference would it make if there were no intelligence services?' and 'Is it true that the Harvest computers at GCHQ tap 80 million phone calls a day and flag 2.5 million?' He did not reply to the questions, saying people in London send letters by bike rather than use the telephone." The two questions had come from me. I had volunteered to meet Norton-Taylor in the King's Head, but Ezard had said, "He will be nervous and shouldn't meet you before he speaks." Anthony was just finding his feet in the outside world and soon afterwards he told me for the first time that he wished to start his own film company.[14]

At Milton's Cottage, Chalfont St Giles, for epic
By the end of November I was doing "corrections to books 1 and 2 to date". By 6 December I had written 2,000 lines of the epic. I wanted to invoke Milton at the beginning of book 2 and Ann and I went to Chalfont St Giles, where we spent from 2 till 4.30 alone in Milton's Cottage with the new curator. We visited three rooms in the 1580 cottage: the parlour where Milton sat when guests came; the kitchen where they ate; and finally his study, his bedsit where he wrote. I pored over facsimile editions of his workbooks and saw that just before he went blind in 1652 he made a cast list of about 10 for *Paradise Lost*. He is supposed to have begun it in 1655, but "Paradise" – Cromwell's Protectorate – had not been lost by then. I learned that he wrote the whole poem at 50 lines a day in just over six months (200 days for 10,000 lines). The polymath woke at 4 a.m., shuffled blind into the garden, gave dictation to his daughter, wife, two nephews or amanuenses at 12 noon, being "milked" as he called it (there being cows in the next field). After twenty 'wasted' years, Chalfont was the turning-point: he produced the best three-quarters of his work in five years during the last eight years of his life.

The next day I reflected on Milton's grand style. Satan drew on Cromwell's regicide, rising against a King who rules by divine right (which Milton denied). I saw the fallen Angels as Cromwell's Puritans, and Milton was at heart on their side, that was the trouble. So if there is something wrong with Milton's God it is because Milton temperamentally sided with Satan. Milton could only write a poem about rebellion against the King by using the Satan–God idiom. I saw my Satan as seeking to rule the world through a New World Order as a world dictator, the Beast.

I was still attending all the school events. On my return from Milton's Cottage I went to Forest School to see *As You Like It* – I was fascinated by the melancholy Jaques's reference to "stanzas" – and I talked in the interval with Tony Little and Andrew Boggis, the Heads of Chigwell and Forest. At the Oaklands carol service I talked with the vicar, who asked what I was writing. There were banners on either side of St Mary's, one saying "Out of the darkness", the other "Into the Light". I told him, and said, "The epic is on the perennial struggle between Light and darkness – which is experienced in every generation."

On Christmas Day I reflected on similes. I spent all evening on Homer's similes, which describe crowds, not individuals; battle scenes, not travels. I grasped that they drew on the main point out of the poet's experience, and I resolved that all my similes would be out of my experience. I grasped that writing my epic was similar to setting up Coopersale Hall School, when I made my statement in the stone and wood of my building and then saw the public come through the doors. First I had to build my 'palace'; then I could enjoy the rewards.

By the beginning of the new year I had more or less finished the first two books of my epic. I wrote: "The end of a year in which I had three books published – my autobiography, *Collected Poems* and *Diaries* vol. 1 – and wrote a two-part verse play and the first two books of my epic; and delivered a philosophy lecture." The different *genre*s I had been writing in had led me to reflect wryly:

> When I die, I will go into a large room where men sitting at tables will judge my work: Gibbon, Spengler and Toynbee on one table will judge my history; Plato, Whitehead and Hulme (possibly Wittgenstein) my philosophy; Eliot, Yeats and Pound my poetry, along with Milton, Blake and Shelley (especially my epic); Marlowe, Shakespeare and Eliot my verse drama; Somerset Maugham, Greene and Tuohy my stories; Augustine, Hildegard and St John of the Cross my *A Mystic Way*; Augustine, Rilke and Coleridge my *Diaries*. This will be my Last Judgement.

I had worked on assembling my stories in Cornwall, and the first volume, *A Spade Fresh with Mud*, was at last ready on 10 January. The next day I drove with Ann to Shaftesbury, sat with Michael Mann and handed it over. I talked him through *The Warlords* and *Overlord*. I said to him: "Each of my epic books is over 2,000 lines long, twice as long as Virgil's or Milton's. But my theme is huge: it's like the Sistine Chapel, good and evil, war and peace, the opposites in relation to a unity." He was very excited: "Yours are the only books we're doing this year that are any good."

Soon afterwards I was "lungy". It hurt when I breathed. I managed to see my consultant, Dr Hughes, who listened to my chest and tapped on it and heard me breathe. He announced immediately that I had dry pleurisy, which is more painful than wet pleurisy. I was told to rest for three days. The next day I "wrote my Preface to the epic on what epic is and how my poem conforms", and the following day I dictated the Preface and made corrections. I visited David Hughes again and learned I had a patch on my lung last week. I saw the white patch on my X-ray. I carried on researching my epic: "To Coopersale Hall, then back via the bank to watch the Auschwitz ceremony live from Poland. Am still unwell – tired, from the patch on my lung, but was affected."

The schools' bank manager, Ken Jones, had at last agreed to become my Bursar. He would bring with him his excellent funding contacts. I had recently bought the sloping field outside the Coopersale Hall gate from Hammond. (Hammond, of course, had asked to be paid in cash and so I had withdrawn half the purchase price in £50 notes from the bank and walked next door to St Mary's church forecourt where he was waiting for me in a beaten-up red car, looking at a picture of his son Tommy who had committed suicide in one of the two barns opposite Coopersale Hall.) Ken had already secured bank funding for renovating eight new classrooms at Coopersale Hall, and for a bolt-hole, a refuge from the schools where Ann could escape from being Headmistress for an afternoon and early evening, and I could escape the constant phone calls and write in peace. He asked me to look out for such a property.

Stonewell Farm, Peter Bassano and Emilia Lanier; Ted Hughes
We looked at Buckinghamshire, not far down the M25 and had found a small cottage in Wendover that had been given to Anne Boleyn by Henry VIII as a wedding present. It had a large inglenook fireplace and beams but no swimming-pool. Then, on 1 February, after finishing *Overlord*, books 1 and 2, we visited a Tudor farm a few doors down from Milton's Cottage: Stonewell Farm. It was owned by Peter Bassano, a trombone player and conductor descended from the uncle of Emilia Lanier, who had been identified as Shakespeare's Dark Lady by A.L. Rowse (on circumstantial evidence, it has to be said). It was much larger than Anne Boleyn's cottage, also had an inglenook fireplace and ancient stone floor and did not have a swimming-pool.

We returned three days later, and walked round Stonewell Farm again (followed by Bassano's wife, who was breast-feeding her baby). Ann found the main bedroom dark and the atmosphere uncomfortable. I was fascinated by a farmhouse that was c.1450 (or possibly c.1490) and whose well shared the same water supply as Milton's Cottage and past whose front door Milton would have walked many times.

I made an offer. We returned with Argie and the two boys a few days later. Argie was very taken as the farm reminded her of Hill Place and after he had played a Tudor sackbut for us I talked with Peter Bassano about Emilia Lanier and her family and her role in Shakespeare's circle, but remained unconvinced that she was the Dark Lady. My thoughts turned to Milton down the road, and I saw a parallel between his life and mine: "His twenty 'wasted' years writing political pamphlets and his championing of divorce. My time with Scargill, and [coping with] my divorce."

On 17 February I visited Michael Mann in Dorset and handed over *The Warlords* and books 1 and 2 of *Overlord*, which I had now finished. I told him about the parallel between Milton and me, how I waited 25 years until I was 56 to start my epic just like Milton and was about to buy a house just down the road from Milton's Cottage, and how my well and Milton's well shared the same underground water 20 or 30 feet down. He told me: "I've read [an earlier version of] *Overlord* through, it's very easy to get into, and I think it's very good, excellent." I said to Michael: "The way to get an epic [done] is to follow the way of blind Milton and blind Homer: dictate the thing at 50 lines a time, do corrections as you go along, and finish each book as it is done, and don't go back. The way not to get it done is to go back and polish and change and tinker." He said, "I agree."

On 24 February I sent an early copy of *Overlord*, books 1 and 2 to Ted Hughes and had a reply on 23 March: "I started reading with fascination – I rose to it, the omnivorous masterful way you grasp the materials. But same day was swept out of the country on hectic business and got back only last night. Look forward now to reading the rest." Meanwhile on 9 March Michael Mann rang to say he had "had a letter from Iris Murdoch who thanks him for 'Nicholas Hagger's magnificent *Overlord*'".

The same day Peter Bassano rang. He had written and told A.L. Rowse that we had bought his house. He said the Bassanos came from Canareggo in Venice, near the station. However, Bassano kept raising the price, and on 29 March we walked away. (In March 2014 he and his wife were declared bankrupt and forced to leave their house in Great Missenden, Buckinghamshire.)[15]

I work on second volume of Collected Stories, A Smell of Leaves and Summer
Meanwhile, down in Cornwall I had begun to assemble and correct the stories of the second volume, *A Smell of Leaves and Summer*. I broke off to play Matthew chess in the evenings, and to have tea with the owner of the harbour and his wife, Robin and Veronika Davies. They were greatly exercised because the local Ramblers had gone to court to establish a permanent right of way over the bridge across the harbour that was

winched down to admit ships into the inner harbour and to let them back out to sea. A court victory for the Ramblers would prevent Robin from lowering the bridge. He had cordoned off the bridge, denied the local residents access and the village was in turmoil.

I finished correcting the stories of vol. 2 on 1 March. Two days later I "picked up *A Smell of Leaves and Summer*" and thought, "It is a beautiful title." The next day I proof-read the stories. On 17 March I drove to Michael Mann with Ann on a wild March day. There was freezing wind in Shaftesbury. I was in Michael's office by 12.10 and talked until 1.30. I handed over *A Smell of Leaves and Summer*. (I received the first copy on 25 May.) We then discussed *Overlord*: "Vols 3–6 to be in by Christmas 1995, for publication in March 1996 (UK) and May 1996 (US).... I on how *Overlord*... includes the two great events of the century: the Second World War and Communism.... 'The central theme of Western civilization is the struggle between Light and Dark.'" Michael said: "You're outside the poetry world. I can see that they have nothing to say and egg each other on." We discussed Sebastian Barker's review of my work in *Acumen*. Michael had read the review and said, "He hasn't worked out what's going on." He spoke of Barker's ignorance of the Light in my work.[16]

Challenge to Norris

While I was getting my stories, verse play and epic ready Steve Norris's position as our local MP had weakened by the month. In December I had met him at Shepherd's in Marsham Street, London, and he had told me that he might be deselected in March. He said, "You're a good bloke, you helped me and I'm not having you pay the bill, we'll go Dutch." Which we did.

I learned that there would be a move to oust him, and I rang him. He said, "They want me out, as you said in your book [, *A Mystic Way*,] they're Biggs-Davisonites and 'cock-a-hoop' – your word – at what happened to me. I'm not sure that I want to stand again."

The Annual General Meeting at Lopping Hall, Loughton was full on 10 March. Ann and I collected our voting papers and sat in the front row. Norris winked at me from the platform. A report from one of the officers spoke of "ribald" (he pronounced it "rye-bald") "comments" in the press. Norris looked at me and raised his eyebrows. A new President was elected: John Silberrad. Then Norris was called on to speak.

He stood, very relaxed, and spoke about how the Government was full of disagreements over Europe, but how they should unite to block open borders. He got the attention of the audience away from himself. After applause he answered questions. The meeting broke up. The anti-Norrisites had failed to request a vote on the unsuitability of the member.[17]

Hungarian school to be named after me

Gorka had written to say that a millionaire had put up money to buy a school in Hungary that would be named after me. He came on 19 March – "just after I had drafted the next four books of *Overlord* (Falaise–Arnhem–Auschwitz revolt–Ardennes)" – in sleeting snow. Ann served tea and I sat next to Paul. At the end of his two-hour stay he told me that he had lost his job as a Minister; I did not realise he had become a Minister. He returned the next day with a millionaire dentist (Dr Laszlo Szilagyi) and his wife from Sopron, who were allegedly naming a school after me in Hungary as a tribute to my contribution to the liberation of Eastern Europe. They had flown in from Vienna to Heathrow earlier, and they did not speak a word of English. I made them coffee and showed my books at Paul's request. I took them on a tour of Oaklands at lunchtime and then up to Coopersale Hall, where we lunched in the room with the Jacobean frieze. I spoke a few sentences and then waited while Paul interpreted and then spoke more, and so on. We looked round the school.[18] That evening they were my guests for dinner at Cinnamon, an Indian restaurant in Epping. They left in cabs, and I heard no more about the school that was being named after me. In 2003 I heard that Gorka had died in Hungary: his funeral was on 24 April.

In wartime Germany again for epic

Now that I was into the epic I needed to visit places in wartime Germany I had not seen and which I would be writing about in books 3–6. I planned to fly to Munich, hire a car and drive it to Hamburg, stopping off at all the new places.

But first we took a train to Berchtesgaden and then a taxi to the snow-clad Tuerken Hotel in the Bavarian Alps and waded through a foot of settled snow to the site of Hitler's Berghof, now under trees. On our return to the hotel we visited the Berghof's bunker system. Beyond a locked door steps led down to tunnels 200 feet underground, and I saw Hitler's living-room and other rooms. After supper I returned to the Berghof in the dark and stood in the deserted road under the garages (all that was left of Hitler's home) and opened to the Light, which surged into me.

During the night it snowed and we slithered down the mountainside in a taxi and caught a train back to Munich. We hired a car and drove to Flossenbürg, where Bonhoeffer was hanged. We went on to Dresden

Nicholas at Hitler's Berghof on 31 March 1995, while writing *Overlord*

and Colditz and from Wernigerode took a train up the mountain to Brocken. When the sun is low the shadow of anyone standing on the Brocken summit is magnified and thrown across the clouds. The effect is known as 'the Brocken spectre'. I used this image in my poem 'Old Man in a Circle' (and in other poems). On this occasion there was no spectre on the clouds.

We stayed in Goslar (where Wordsworth lived) and next morning drove to Göttingen and saw Buchenwald. We went on to Weimar and saw Goethe's house. I saw the room where he died. I stood in his study and saw where *Faust 2* was found in the cabinet after his death. He had joined the Bavarian Illuminati as Abaris and had recanted. Traces of this youthful folly were in *Faust*.

We went on to Weimar and then Wewelsburg, a triangular 15th-century castle that Himmler had turned into an SS HQ. I visited the hall with 12 pillars and a 12-spoked sun-wheel of 6 swastikas on the floor, and saw the 'Realm of the Dead' underneath, where Himmler had started a cult to the Prince of Darkness. We went on to Externsteine to see the upright rocks where Himmler held ceremonies, and to Paderborn to see the ruins of Charlemagne's Imperial Palace. We visited Hameln (Hamelin) and then went to Sachsenhain, where Himmler held torch-lit ceremonies. We continued to Bergen-Belsen, where traces of the concentration camp had been obliterated under trees and heather.

We drove to Lüneburg and at Deutsch Evern found where Montgomery accepted the Germans' surrender. The place was now in woods within a military base. I asked to see where "General Montgomery's HQ were in 1945", tactfully not mentioning the German 'surrender'. A Hauptmann and two soldiers led the way in a mini-bus up into woods where tanks were being washed. They pointed to two concrete bases, one for the surrender tent and one for a monument. In 1945 there were no trees on this part of the heath. I would use the scene in *The Warlords* and *Overlord*. We drove home via Hamburg.

I would now use these new impressions in books 3–6.[19]

In Holland and France: visiting Matthew in Forbach

From 10 April I worked on book 3 of *Overlord* down in Cornwall, including the invocation to Goethe and the battle of Falaise, breaking off to play Matthew chess in the evenings. There was drama outside my window as the owner of the harbour, Robin Davies, had now sealed off the harbour with gates and was charging for access to the quay and beaches. The local Ramblers were still trying to enforce a permanent right of way across the bridge in the courts and ban the lowering of Robin's bridge. One night the gates were damaged, and the next day they were open as normal.

At the end of April Ann and I visited Matthew, who was spending a year in Forbach in Alsace-Lorraine. We visited wartime battlefields in Holland and France on the way and on the way back. I drove my BMW on to the Harwich car ferry and from Hoek van Holland I drove to Arnhem and ate by the Rijn (Rhine) overlooking the John Frost bridge. We drove to Oosterbeek's Hartenstein Hotel, first the Germans' and then the British HQ, and visited all the places connected with the British and American crossing of the Rhine. We visited Reims' 'Room of Surrender', Eisenhower's map room where Bedell Smith ended the war. We visited places connected with the Battle of the Bulge and then reached our hotel

Nicholas next to picture of Eisenhower in the 'Room of Surrender' in Reims on 29 April 1995

in Saar. Before we could unpack Matthew arrived saying, "Room service."

The next morning we visited Matthew's *lycée* and his room in Forbach, which had spectacular views over the castle (Schlossberg), tower and wooded hills. We walked up to the 13th-century tower above the ruined castle. It had been built to be a watchtower to warn of fires or wars.

I was haunted by the watchtower. The next morning I

woke very early at 4.30 and lay awake until 6 in a half-doze, then got up, took some paper and a pen from my case in the bathroom and sat and wrote out 20 lines of the watchtower image: Christ like a watchman in the ruined tower of the Schlossberg, guarding mankind from puffs of smoke and aghast at the carnage.

In Saar's old town I was full of admiration for the way Matthew had made the best of a difficult situation. We discussed his future and when he might start at Oaklands. I wrote, "I want to groom him for a role that will keep Oaklands and Coopersale Hall on course." I was already looking to replace myself in the schools by a combination of Matthew and our new Bursar.

On the way back we passed through war villages in the eastern Ardennes and drove round Brussels to Calais. I now had to work hard on books 3–6 of the epic.[20]

Overlord, *books 3–6*
By 5 May I was working on book 4, Arnhem. The leaders in *The Times* and

The Daily Telegraph showed my epic was on the national wavelength. *The Times* quoted 'The War of the Sons of Light and the Sons of Darkness', and referred to the evil of Auschwitz, Belsen and tyranny; it quoted Bonhoeffer in Schlossenberg and spoke of finding the right international order. *The Daily Telegraph* focused on extermination. *The Times* dubbed it all demonic. I was in tune with the national soul. I was its mouthpiece, it had the ideas. I was ahead of them for I was asking 'Why were they demonic?' and probing Wewelsburg, Quedlinburg, Verden and the ritualistic cultic side of the SS and the Teutonic Knights. It was interesting that the national papers were all on the same path, although they had not addressed evil in the depth that I had. I noted that I was now "a war poet – a describer of war.... I have many descriptions of appalling, Hellish battles. Man *in extremis*." I had now "written much of bks 3 and 4".

In Cornwall I wrote about the Ardennes. I met Robin Davies's mother-in-law, an 80-year-old German who was in the Hitler Youth and remembered Hitler. She said there was a current of energy from him; he was filled with a power. Her husband was in the Luftwaffe and in 1933 she saw Göring visit to watch little pencils of rockets flying about, and sat with Wernher von Braun, who implemented rocket propulsion and later got a US rocket to the moon. She told me she saw Eisenhower in a castle near Frankfurt in 1945.

On 17 June I completed work on book 5 of the epic: Dorebus's revolt in Auschwitz. Three days later I contrasted my idyllic writing conditions and the horror of Auschwitz: "All round me as I write is Paradise, children running happily in the field and up the path. I am in a world of gassings and executions at Auschwitz as I recreate past agony for bk 5 of my epic. All round me, a sunny warm June day and I am elsewhere, in a torture and agony that has passed. I am with the victims of a time that has passed." A friend of Anthony's reported that he was in France and "at the next table some people were talking about Nicholas Hagger.... This was at Montreuil-sur-Mer, in the Pas-de-Calais, near Le Touquet." It was weird that my writings should be discussed in north France when I had been concentrating so intensely on wartime France, an example of synchronicity. I had a call from Michael Mann, wanting to check the "extent and angle" of books 3–6. "He: 'I told a group it's the greatest poem in the 20th century.' I noted: 'It is at the heart of Europe: of England, France, Germany and Poland. And Italy, Greece, Turkey. And Russia later, and Spain and Portugal. It is a European work.'"[21]

I acquire The Bell, Great Easton; Thaxted Horn Dance
I had turned away from Chalfont St Giles, but we had now found an old timber-framed house in the country village of Great Easton, near Dunmow. The Bell had a date 'circa 1520' on a sign on the front wall, whereas

documentary evidence suggested it was at least as old as 1487.[22] It had a pargeted bell, sun, winged sphinx, sheaves of corn and medieval flowers, "images I can make my own". There was a well-stocked garden, an outdoor swimming-pool and dozens of sheep nuzzled along our fence in the field beyond. The shepherdess lived next door. The 12th-century church across the green had Roman tiles and Saxon stones in its walls, and pealing church bells wafted through the air. I wrote,

> The Bell is a symbol of the poet: the poet's tongue, like the tongue of a bell, rings over the countryside, like the bells from the Norman church, which is 12th-century (1100s).

And of the pargeting:

> The bell represents the tongue of the poet, which rings out over the land; the winged sphinx represents the vision of the poet; the sun represents the Light; the bound sheaf of corn represents the *Collected Poems*; and the floral pargetings represent individual poems.

Nearby Little Easton had a manor house and garden once linked to Henry VIII and Elizabeth I. Daisy, Countess of Warwick, Edward VII's paramour in 1886 and thereafter (while he was Prince of Wales), had lived at Warwick House. H.G. Wells had lived nearby in a Georgian building in the 1930s.

I did not know it but nearby Tilty had literary associations with the 1930s poet George Barker, who was born in Loughton and spent 1939–1940 as a Professor in Japan. His four children by Elizabeth Smart lived in Tilty Mill House, where Dylan Thomas had stayed with its previous owner. The children included Sebastian Barker, who attended the launch of my *Selected Poems* in 1991 and had had me to lunch. (He died of lung cancer on 31 January 2014, having revisited Tilty Mill House the previous day.)

We bought The Bell. Completion was on 26 May. We spent our first night there in early June. There were a hundred sheep baaing in the field, waiting to be sheared. "Am now sitting on the bed in the beamed bedroom. It has a lovely feeling, this home. Very peaceful. I will write some good poems here." The next day I corrected work sitting in front of a log fire in the lion-and-unicorn grate.

That part of Essex was steeped in tradition. Once a year the Dunmow flitch (a side of salted pork) was awarded to a couple deemed not to have had a cross word the previous year. Once a year in nearby Thaxted the Horn Dance was performed. According to tradition the Devil was present during this dance and was received in total silence.

That year the Horn Dance took place on 3 June, and we attended.

A crowd several deep watched and applauded as morris dancers cavorted and leapt. One group had a stag with antlers and no arms, another a crocodile. There were two fools in jester hats and motley. At 10.15 there was silence, and just below the churchyard could be heard a violin. Then came the "horn dancers", in dead silence; six men showing a stag's head with antlers, another four – an archer, who must have been Hern the Hunter; a boy tinkling on a triangle, who followed him; a man on a square horse; and a Chinese with a Chinese umbrella who represented the Devil. They danced in a slow sedate walk, and eventually retired towards the churchyard to loud applause, the violinist still playing. Their hats had symbols, including the rising sun (or Light) and a serpent (the Devil).

I would draw on the Horn Dance in my epic and also in *Classical Odes* (in 'At the Thaxted Horn Dance'). In early July I delighted in sitting near the pond by the sheep and in watching nesting swallows flying in and out of our eaves.[23]

I lecture on Universalism
I had broken off from my epic to write (on 10 April) and deliver (on 18 May) a lecture on Universalism at the Alister Hardy Research Centre in Kensington Square – it was called the Maria Assumpta Centre, a name that evoked the brig *Maria Asumpta*, spelt with one 's', that had often docked in Charlestown. (On 31 May I learned that the *Maria Asumpta* had been smashed to pieces off Padstow the previous day, another instance of synchronicity.) My lecture was entitled 'Universalism and the New Metaphysics: the Fire or Light as common ground for a universal or world-wide civilization and religion' and can be found in *The One and the* Many.

During questions at the end the Chairman said to the audience: "I commend the word 'mosaic' to you: a *mosaic* of different civilizations with different shades and Light." Two days later, on 20 May, I "woke with the idea that Eisenhower sees a mosaic in Versailles… which suggests Christ's unity on earth".

Our two schools were in demand, and I was asked to acquire a school near Brentwood, Bell House, that was closing. I was approached by NatWest, who asked if I would buy it, but the outlay to make it viable would be too great and we declined. Meanwhile Rod Stewart had sought us out. His then wife Rachel Hunter looked at both schools and opted for Oaklands, where his daughter Renee was enrolled.

Steve Norris was too outspoken for his own good. The Prime Minister, John Major, had announced that he would submit himself for re-election, and Norris rang me from his car on his way to vote. He told me, "I shall vote for the least worst option, Major." He then said he had arrived at

Westminster and there was a television crew outside his car. He was on the news that evening repeating that Major was the "least worst option". I later heard that Major changed his mind about reshuffling him to the Department of Trade and Industry after hearing this lukewarm endorsement.[24]

In Turkey and Greece: Troy and Ithaca; St Gerasimos and 'The Warm Glow of the Monastery Courtyard'; Socrates' prison and Plato's Academy
To widen my experience of European culture and to visit Troy for my epic, in mid-July I took Ann and the two boys to Istanbul by air. We hired a car to drive along the coast of Turkey.

We toured Istanbul and then drove to Troy. We entered the enclosed citadel and climbed steps to Cyclopean walls. We walked round the stone ruins of Troy VI and saw the ramp to Troy II (where Priam's old royal palace stood, beside which Schliemann found Helen's treasure), and then I took in the stone ruins of Troy VII and VIIA, Homer's Troy. I stood by the East Gate and was sure the Trojan Horse was left there. I found Paris's house and sat on Helen's terrace and looked across the Scamander plain to where the Greek fleet of 1,000 ships came in. I sat in the hot sun and scribbled out my invocation to Homer in *Overlord*. I could not drag myself away, and by the time I left I had spent four hours there in little shade. I had got Troy in perspective. It was small, with two gates and the war was absurd, a question of honour (and while the Greeks all saved Menelaos's honour the Greek suitors were doing their best to undermine Penelope's on Ithaca). The Greeks skirmished on the plain and were remembered, and Zeus arranged for Troy to fall to curb the overpopulation of the earth.

We drove to Pergamon (Roman Pergamum) and on to Izmir (where Homer is thought to have lived in Bayrakh). We visited Ephesus and drove on to Selçuk and stood over the grave of St John and saw the Artemision, once one of the seven Wonders of the World. We drove on to Didyma and saw the oracle. We took a caique to Samos and walked to the port Polycrates laid out and investigated the ruins of the semicircular mystery school from the time of Pythagoras. We visited the one-kilometre-long tunnel of Eupalinus. We went on to Patmos and visited the Monastery of the Apocalypse, where St John had the visions of *Revelation*. I saw where he lay his head and where Prochorus, his scribe, took dictation.

We flew to Athens and visited the Acropolis. We looked down on the

Nicholas looking at Ithaca on 22 July 1995, while writing *Overlord*

Theatre of Dionysus, where Aeschylus, Sophocles and Euripides appeared and where their works were first performed. We flew to Kefalonia and the next morning crossed to Ithaca. We visited the Cave of the Nymphs where Odysseus hid Alcinous's treasure. I was impressed at Homer's local knowledge of the hole in the roof. We passed the cove of Phorkys where Odysseus landed according to one view (the other being that he landed in Polis Bay) and swam on Phorkys beach, leaving our clothes under one of the olive-trees that lined the shore. We visited Pilikata, the Hill of Hermes, the site of Odysseus's palace from which three seas can be seen (the Ionian and Tyrrhenian seas, and the Gulf of Patras).

We returned to Kefalonia and were met by our taxi-driver John Daphnos, who drove us to Agios Gerasimos, where he insisted we went into the monastery. A service was in progress, and people were gathered round a silver casket which was opened. I looked on the undecomposed, untreated dead body of the patron saint of the island, St Gerasimos, who died in 1579. All kissed the corpse, but we declined, being improperly dressed. I wrote a story about the experience, 'The Warm Glow of the Monastery Courtyard' (the title story of my fourth volume of short stories).

Back in Athens I stood in the Temple of Dionysus under the Acropolis, feeling near Aeschylus, Sophocles and Euripides. We went on to the tradi-tional site of Socrates' prison, which had barred doors, and then went to where an American archaeologist had located the prison: in the Agora, next to the old courthouse. The two rooms to the right of the entrance conform to Plato's description in *Phaedo* of Socrates' quarters in the State prison. They are against the 'drain' (the urinal) and excavations found evidence of poison in the extreme right-hand (inside) room. I stood where, according to the best evidence, Socrates drank hemlock. We went on to Plato's Academy in a garden square, and stood on the floor where Plato worked. We continued to Eleusis and walked through the Greater and Lesser Propylaea to the 'Initiation Hall' (*telesterion*), where during the Greater Mysteries in September an ear of corn was shown, the central image of the Mysteries. We then passed the site of the battle of Salamis in 480BC, where the Greeks defeated the Persians. On the way back we passed Daphne, the grove where I attended a wine festival in 1958.[25]

Many of the places I had visited on this tour would be the subject of classical odes in the coming years.

Finishing Overlord *book 6; Norris discontinuing as MP*
Three days later I left to spend five weeks in Cornwall working on the epic. The weather was good and I balanced writing with time in the sun. By 7 August I reflected that "I must have written more than 13,000 lines since October.... It shows how fluent I am. It would have taken me a morning to

do five lines 40 years ago." The boys came and went and by 19 August I was writing on Arnhem. Anthony had left school and, wanting to become a film director, had chosen to do English and Film Studies at Reading University. Ann returned to Essex briefly to supervise this new arrangement. I noted:

> In my epic, my insistence on human free will, with Providential guidance trying to influence it. My moral universe, Montgomery's haughtiness being repaid with humbling.

By the time Ann returned I had written 15,000 lines of blank verse since October. I "tap-tap-tapped out the metre of my lines with my nail (index finger on either hand) on the wooden desk and Ann said she could hear it downstairs. 'It's like a woodpecker.'" The weather was so good that I was "in shorts [for five weeks], have not worn socks and hardly ever a sweater". I often "walked down to the beach below my window and peered in the rock pools, standing on limpets and barnacles and slippery green seaweed, at shrimps that flicked and hid, at small crabs and fish that looked like bullheads". In early September the boys left and Ann and I drove to Fowey, walked past Quiller-Couch's house, took the ferry to Polruan, and walked past buddleia in which 30 red admirals fluttered to and fro to the Castle and sat on the rocks in bright light.

I had made arrangements for a new Headmistress to replace Ann at Oaklands in January and for our bank manager to begin as Bursar at the two schools in April. Both of them made visits. I was freeing Ann to be a consultant at Coopersale Hall as well as at Oaklands, and I was freeing myself to have more writing time.

I had one last one-to-one meeting with Steve Norris. He had invited me to Brooks's in St James's Street. He was waiting for me in the doorway. We talked at the bar. Over dinner "he told me, 'I'm telling you but no one else knows, not in the constituency, not anywhere. I'm not standing at the next election. I shall resign this week and go into business – run an industry and have a 'one' in front of my salary and write a book for 3 months. I have school fees to provide.... I'm 50 and a Minister of the Crown and I can't make ends meet.'" I talked through the implications. He would see Major first, then write to Di Collins, then have nothing to do with the choice of a replacement. I felt sad and, feeling loyalty towards him as my tenant, empathised.

He described how he gave my books to Major's PPS: "I shall ask him about them. I'm seeing him this week to tell him I'm leaving." He said of his time at Orchard Cottage, "The present President of Albania stayed in Orchard Cottage and slept in the bedroom nearest the school, in 1991." At the end we sat in the library, and a big man wandered about looking at books and peering at me: Michael Bishop of British Midland, Nadia's former boss. Norris talked about the Bilderberg Group: "I still ask Peter Carrington how influential it is." After coffee we left. He said in the street: "You are a friend. You helped me when you didn't need to. I will never forget that, I shall always remember that." He did not contact me again and though I saw him at a couple of social events in the coming weeks our paths have not crossed since that day. He went on to become chairman of Jarvis.

Two days later, on 27 September, I finished book 6. I would work on books 3–6 until December. In quick succession Ann and I visited the boys in their university lodgings. First we went to Reading with Anthony and visited his room at the top of a very cluttered four-storey house, 70 South Street. It was owned by two music teachers who had cleared the top room to let out. They gave us tea.

A few days later we visited Matthew in Bangor with Anthony. We stayed at the Menai Straits Hotel again. In our room there I read an article in *The Times* "saying no one knows what good poetry is today, no one can agree on it" and the next morning I "woke to the thought that I should write an essay 'The End of Culture', on the collapse of standards in the arts". This thought anticipated my 1997 lecture 'Revolution in Thought and Culture'. After breakfast we went to Caernarfon Castle, where Prince Charles was invested. (It had its first Prince of Wales, later Edward II, in 1301.) It was green and open to the rain inside, "but with good battlements, which the boys climbed and I (with much puffing) too". We had a view over Anglesey. Later we celebrated Matthew's birthday in his room. He opened our presents and I reminisced on episodes from his childhood. "He was quite affected." The next day we drove to Capel Curig via Llanberis Pass and had a misty view of Snowdon. Everywhere was green round the rocks. We had coffee at the café at Capel Curig."

The travelling had upset my work rhythm: "I have been operating on my knee in a car and in a hotel room, and my brain is not right and I can barely do it.... Normally, when well, I can hold 500 lines in my mind and make excisions and cut and paste messages higher up or lower down, but the material is so complex that in my present state of mind, with great rings under my eyes denoting lung trouble, I just cannot get on top of it."[26]

In Italy: Cumae and Virgil's tomb
I had been thinking about *The Aeneid*. I had arranged to visit Italian places connected with my epic, particularly Virgil's tomb. In mid-October we flew to Sorrento. We visited the Solfatara volcano in the Phlegraean fields, where bubbling mud and sulphurous steam passed into my description of Hell in *Overlord*. We went to Cumae to see the Sibyl's grotto (whose five openings suggest some of Virgil's '100 mouths'). We looked at Avernus and the curve

of the Bay of Baia (the old Baiae), and later I drafted a "just as Aeneas" passage for book 7 to introduce Eisenhower's descent to the Underworld.

We took a train to Pompeii and also went to Amalfi – I wrote a sonnet, 'Odysseus near Amalfi' – and Paestum. I stood in the Temple of Hera, where I was so ill last time I was there, in 1957. In the museum I saw a Lucanian tomb painting of a diver diving into eternity, and wrote a classical ode, 'A Leaping Diver in Sybarite Paestum'.

We visited Virgil's tomb along the Via Puteolana near Naples. We walked up through a grove to what used to be a tomb by a road, but which was now high up on a cliff, a *columbarium* with weeds growing from the roof, ten niches, a window, three air vents and a sandy floor. I scribbled my invocation to Virgil in *Overlord* and later wrote a classical ode, 'At Virgil's Tomb'.

We went to Herculaneum by train, caught a bus up Vesuvius and looked into the smoking crater. We went to Capri and walked to Tiberius's villa, where he ruled from AD26 or 27 to 36. We visited the Blue Grotto. We visited the villa of Poppaea, Nero's wife.[27]

In the coming years I based several odes on the places I had visited.

In Russia and Crimea: St Petersburg, Yalta, Moscow – books for Solzhenitsyn, KGB

I had arranged to go to St Petersburg, Moscow and Yalta to obtain local colour for my epic, and we left only two days after our return from Italy. We travelled on our own but had Intourist meet us at airports. We flew to St Petersburg and went straight to Dostoevsky's house and arrived as it was closing. We saw all the rooms, and Dostoevsky's study where he wrote *The Brothers Karamazov*, and the divan on which he died. The next morning we toured places associated with Dostoevsky: Nevsky Prospect (where the Underground Man had his quarrel) and the streets where the Underground Man and Raskolnikov lived. We went on to Yusupov Palace, where Rasputin was found and killed. We visited places connected with Pushkin.

We flew to Moscow and early next morning flew on to Simferopol for Yalta. We visited Chekhov's house and the three palaces where Stalin, Roosevelt and Churchill stayed during the Yalta Conference. I took notes on the rooms for book 7. We flew back to Moscow Vnukovo airport. When we landed two ladies in army uniform boarded and lined the passengers into two rows: Ann and me in one row and everyone else in the other. They confiscated our two passports. We had to tour the airport with our luggage to retrieve our passports. No one spoke English and I heard my name broadcast in Russian over the public address system. Ann went to the loo on the first floor and the army lady who took our passports arrived and banged on the loo door saying, "KGB toilet, not for you." The KGB had taken our passports. They were now returned to us.

We reached the Intourist Hotel, Moscow and the phone rang in our room. A lady's voice said: "Aleksandr Solzhenitsyn asked me to ring you. He cannot see you as he is not in Moscow." The caller identified herself as 'Mrs. Bankoul'. She gave me an address where I could leave books for him. I had been interested in Solzhenitsyn's 'Warning to the Western World' since 1976 and had contacted his biographer and been given Mrs. Bankoul's address. I had written offering to bring him four of my books. I had these with me, and the next morning, under the supervision of our Intourist guide, I took them to his apartment at 1 Truzhenikov Pereulda 17, 64 apt, and handed to the concierge *The Fire and the Stones*, *The Universe and the Light*, *The Warlords* and *Overlord* books 1 and 2. We went to the Kremlin and Archangel Cathedral, which had featured in my poem 'Archangel', and to Red Square, and we then went on to Troitse-Lykovo to see Solzhenitsyn's house. We could not find it, but we found the church of the Trinity and crossed the Moskva on a floating bridge: wood planks nailed to rusty fuel cans. I had a good view of the area in which he lived.

Back at the hotel our guide asked where else I would like to visit. I said, thinking of our passports, "The KGB buildings." We walked to Lublyana Square and she pointed out some ten high-rise KGB buildings in a compound and described how prisoners were moved in vans marked 'Bread', 'Milk', 'Butter' so foreign journalists would not think that they contained prisoners. In open defiance after the confiscation of our passports, I stood, legs apart, and took many photos: a shoot-out by camera.[28]

Many of the places we had visited appeared later in my classical odes.

Overlord, book 7

For the rest of the year I wrote the epic in Essex (at 6 Albion Hill and at The Bell, Great Easton) and in Cornwall. I was tap-tap-tapping before announcing fireworks over the microphone at the Oaklands bonfire night (for which Nadia joined us), and "sat in the passenger seat tapping like a woodpecker" on the way to Cornwall. I took time off to visit Anthony at Reading University and saw that he had *A Spade Fresh with Mud* in his room, which he said his friends wanted to read. I was writing summaries of books 3–6 during the schools' end-of-term events, which were affected by snow. The educational charity Gabbitas Educational Consultants had found a Head who would replace Ann at Oaklands and oversee the running of Coopersale Hall, and I took her to watch a Kindergarten concert at Oaklands and sat next to Rod Stewart's wife, Rachel Hunter. She lived in Los Angeles for nine months each year, and was about to return.

I broke off from the epic to attend political events. I encountered John Redwood (who had just stood unsuccessfully against the Prime Minister,

John Major), at the bookless home of Don Lewin, who owned 784 shops in the Clinton Cards chain (that would go into receivership in 2012). When Ann and I had finished our buffet supper Redwood appeared, pulled up a chair and joined us. He seemed to know who I was; perhaps Norris had told him. Aware that he had worked for Rothschilds I ran through the figures for public spending which he said had risen. He told me how he had challenged Major for the leadership: "My influence among MPs is rising.... I have 90 MPs.... I believed I had to do it. The arguments in Cabinet and in private were such that I simply wasn't prepared to go on having them. I thought, 'If you [i.e. Major] want to make it all public, that's up to you.'" Norris joined us and then Redwood made a half-hour speech saying that the Conservatives should be "more conservative". I talked further with him as we waited by the loo. He heaved himself up alongside the recessed basin and sat by the gold taps.

Five days later I was invited to inspect the three candidates to replace Norris as Epping Forest's MP over drinks at Val Metcalfe's house, 56 Station Road. Two of the candidates (one of whom was Caroline Spelman) said they would send their children to one of our schools if elected, and the third, Eleanor Laing, said she would open our fêtes. (Val's husband served drinks without knowing he had ten tumours, eight in his brain, and only eight months to live.) We witnessed the adoption of the new MP at Lopping Hall. The three candidates made speeches and John Silberrad chaired the voting. Eleanor Laing was proclaimed the winner. She was very different from the cultured, well-read Biggs-Davison and the argumentative Norris.

I was drawn back into my cricketing days. I attended a memorial service for my old cricket captain, Alan Lavers, in Chigwell School's chapel. The eulogy dwelt on Alan's time as a Desert Rat at El Alamein and pressing on into Germany. "He never talked about it, but it scarred him." I had not realised that I had been batting with an eyewitness of Montgomery's battle against Rommel. Outside I spoke with Doug Insole, captain of Essex in the 1950s. He introduced me to his wife Rosemary. I went into the dining-hall with him for coffee and food, and he told me that in 1957 I was on his "watch list" of potential county cricketers. I was taken aback as I had been given no inkling. I learned from Jack Watt, who was in my 1957 team, that Tony Durley, with whom I had nearly saved my last game for Buckhurst Hill, had died. Later John Maynard, our opening batsman, told me Durley had died two years previously of cancer of the bowel, aged 60. He and Stella had split up, and two years after the split Stella had married Bill Gilmore, our other opener, who had died of cancer five years previously, at 56. I felt melancholy recalling the faces of our team who were no more.

In Cornwall I finished correcting books 3–6. Anticipating my *Classical Odes*, I reflected: "When I have finished the epic, I will read a lot of Virgil,

Ovid, Catullus and Horace, and return to my roots as a Roman-style poet of country life and satirical observation. Juvenal as well." Back in Essex I noted (after visiting Mabel Reid in Forest Place, her nursing home): "There are two forces in the universe, and will always be. These are in conflict and are held in balance." I drove Anthony to Great Easton – he told me, "I read two or three of your stories each night" – and held the family gathering there with light snow on the ground. I learned that my nephew Charles had "changed his surname to Freeman and that [his closest relatives] have been astonished to read about Freeman in my 'Ancient Mariner poem', i.e. 'The Silence', which is very close to his life." Back in Loughton and combing through my epic I reflected: "I have a European sensibility that straddles England and America and also looks to Russia."

In the New Year I drove to Dorset on a misty day to hand books 3–6 to my publisher, Michael Mann. I was struck by a new seriousness of purpose within the publishing house: the waiting area had been transformed into a production room and I walked through an office that was abustle, everyone working silently, under pressure. Michael was sitting with his production manager, and we were visited by the cover designer and then the new sales and marketing director, who joined us for lunch. Michael explained to her at some length "what Nicholas is about". He said: "What Nicholas is doing is unique. It's magic stuff.... *Overlord* is very exciting, regardless of the metaphysical content.... Nicholas is apart from the poetry world. I under-stand why. If he were in it he would never write what he's writing, and so I'm glad he's apart from it."

I was now forging ahead on books 7–9. I "finished the block on the seven Hells in bk 7" and "worked on Eisenhower's visit to Hell" (13 January). A week later I wrote two passages in book 8 at Great Easton. Back in Loughton I wrote "a bit of bk 12", and two days later "at 11 sat down and wrote two pages straight out of automatic-type writing on the laws of the universe. And did not feel at all tired. I am so creative at present. In fact, creativity was at one time inspiration, i.e. automatic writing." The next day Ann visited Great Easton and "got me to listen to a peal of bells by holding the phone to the window.... I have used this in the last line of the poem. I have ended the poem in Great Easton with Christ coming down and standing on the green and me hearing the bells in The Bell." Three days later I wrote: "The last line of my epic: 'Christ, Paradise is here, in my beamed house.' Compare 'If there is a Paradise on earth, it is this, it is this, it is this.' (The Mughal inscription I saw in New Delhi.)"

I had been looking ahead and resolved to write satires after I had finished the epic, satires "on the follies of our time: royalty and the decline of morals". I would write satirical poems in the manner of Juvenal and Donne about my silver Rome.[29]

I received a letter from Ted Hughes in the form of four sides of card:

> Dear Nicholas – You certainly are industrious. I'm admiring the way you bite off and chew up these great chunks of history in your epic. It's good for verse – to become the workhorse for sheer mass of material. Pressure of the actual – the resources to deal with it drawn from elsewhere.... Keep up the good work – Yours ever, Ted.

It included an interesting passage on his Ovid poems, which were like "a cat pouncing on a mouse".[30]

I pressed on with books 7–9. In early February I "finished most of the bits involving Eisenhower in bk 12, and started on the Satan bits from bk 10". I coped with Steve Norris's moving out of Orchard Cottage, and obtained planning permission to add to the Garden Room at Oaklands (as I learned when John Padfield rang me in Cornwall). Ann and I celebrated our wedding anniversary at the Nare Hotel "just above the Carne beach and looked across to the lights of Portscatho". I observed: "Twenty-two years of generally happy marriage during which I have achieved an enormous amount: ownership of two schools, three houses, a flat and so far ten or eleven books."

In Norwich: Julian of Norwich, Little Walsingham

At the end of February Ann and I spent a long weekend in Norwich researching Julian of Norwich. We started at St Julian's church and found the rebuilt cell on the site of the original cell where Julian lived from 1373 and where she wrote her *Revelations of Divine Love*. I "soaked in the detail for my epic, meditated and let the Light rise". We looked at the Cathedral and drove to Sprowston Manor Hotel, where by 7.30 I "drafted an invocation to Julian of Norwich".

The next day we drove to Little Walsingham, which was very rural. We walked through slight drizzle to the Church of England shrine which recreates the Holy House, England's Nazareth, the house where Gabriel appeared to Mary, as received in a vision of 1061 by Richeldis de Faverches. We found the mound where the shrine of Our Lady stood and the Slipper Chapel, where Henry VIII among pilgrims took off his shoes to walk the Way to Walsingham.

I finished book 7. Our bank manager had started as our Bursar on 26 February and there had been many discussions involving the structure in the schools. School duties cut into my writing time. Tony Little had invited me to be one of the judges of a speech contest. The judges (who included a BBC TV correspondent, John Fryer) had drinks in what was the staff room when I was at school and dined in the Swallow Room before doing the judging in New Hall.[31]

Operation on varicose veins, John Hobbs: antiphospholipid syndrome diagnosed
I now had to cope with an operation. In mid-January I had been referred to John Hobbs of 4 Upper Wimpole Street, a consultant vascular surgeon, who stood me on a stool and fingered the veins in my legs with one hand and drew where they were on paper with the other hand. He worked alongside his wife, a Belgian lady of striking good looks. He told me that I had perforated veins up in my right thigh like a fractured garden hose, and he believed the cause of the perforation could be traced back to the operation I had had in 1985. He had told me that the veins in both legs should come out "or I would get ulcers in future". I had been sent to Prof. Machin of University College Hospital for blood tests to see if there would be a blood clot after an operation.

I had my operation on 21 March at the Fitzroy Nuffield Hospital in Bryanston Square. "Had the anaesthetic. Felt a great wave sweep up and over me as I counted up to 10 and was in mid-thought." I was an hour and a half in theatre and came round in the recovery room. I was wheeled back up where Ann was waiting, having been shopping. I had "two enormous bandages from toe to groin". John Hobbs visited me and told me: "Prof. Machin is very excited about you. He's never had someone like you before. You have a particular condition that explains your thrombophlebitis and TIA (transient ischaemic attack) and there is a real risk of thrombosis.... You are unique, a medical specimen." This was the first diagnosis of my primary antiphospholipid syndrome.

The next day Mrs. Hobbs came by and took off the bandages. She covered about 40 tiny holes with steri-strips and I bled a bit. She said that they X-rayed my right leg first and found the top vein above the knee had not been removed, "although the incision was there". It had been leaking into my foot for 11 years. She said: "You have such good leg muscles, they will help you." They were the result of 25 years of Canadian 5BX exercises. That night I saw how to do Christ's visit to Pope Pius XII and wrote the passage sitting awkwardly in my hospital bed: "Injection in my stomach (heparin) in the middle of it, finished the passage with the stinging." The next day Mr and Mrs. Hobbs visited me. Hobbs said that the technique of operating through tiny holes was pioneered by Mr H. Müller of Neuchâtel Suisse. Marianne Hobbs studied under him and learned the technique.

I limped to attend the last day of term at first Oaklands and then Coopersale Hall, where the Rev. Noakes told a story "about tadpoles in a gloomy pond and one becoming a frog and coming back and saying how good it was in the sunlight". I thought that my works were a report on 'the sunlight'. That evening I was driven to the Royal Albert Hall by Ann to attend a concert entitled 'Classical Spectacular', and afterwards "hobbled to the car, my legs in pain".

The following day I had my stitches removed. I lay on my back on a raised couch while Mr Hobbs tweezered the steri-strips off, cut the threads of stitches, and, dabbing cotton wool in nail-varnish remover, scrubbed away at his blue drawings, the "rivers on my legs". He told me that he and his wife worked two weeks in England and then two weeks in Belgium. His wife's grandfather founded a medical station in the Belgian Congo. "She did the outside of your left leg and the inside of your right, while I did the outside of your right and the inside of your left." They worked by eye. "We just see where the next problem is and make a hole."

I visited Prof. Machin in University College Hospital. He performed extensive tests and told me I had antiphospholipid syndrome. On two occasions

I had anticardiolipin antibodies, which were moderately positive. "Normally people don't have them at all." They target the blood-vessel walls and platelets; are antibodies against lipids which are negatively charged. This shows a predisposition to thrombosis (i.e. clotting). "It's moderate, not at a high level. Why have you got it? I don't know. Will it get better or worse? I don't know. Is it to do with a viral infection? Perhaps. It's acquired, not familial, so it can't be passed on to your children. Keep fit, take exercise. Don't get dehydrated.... There is no drug that wipes them out."... I asked, "Will it result in shortening of life?" He said, "No, not at the present level, but if the level were to rise I would have to revise that reply."[32]

Overlord *books 8–9*

Ann drove me to Cornwall and, "ready to begin a new onslaught on my epic", I "wrote on bridges in bk 8". I saw an eclipse of the moon, "the earth's shape across it, dark, turning the moon blood-red in parts of its obscured orb". I also saw the comet Hyakutake with my naked eye. It would not pass the earth again for 15,000 years. It was "high in the night sky over Charlestown Road, a smudge,... a kind of cocoon with a definite pale white tail". It was rare to see a lunar eclipse, a bloody moon and a comet at the same time. The next day Anthony arrived and we walked at night: "Brilliant moonlight beyond the masts of the ships, a causeway out to sea." Soon afterwards I noted that I had "finished the crossing of the Rhine" and was near the end of book 8.

I gave Anthony some insight into my poetic method. He had asked me to talk about Romantic poetry.

Said Wordsworth was the great poet with realistic images; Coleridge a symbolist with a sparer productivity. I said that Wordsworth responded to the daffodils with an overflow of powerful feelings – 'Aren't they lovely' – and later recollected the emotion in tranquillity. He created out of feelings and emotion.

I said that in my work I too recollect historical emotion in tranquillity (for example at Auschwitz) and that I relive and recreate extremes of emotion in the war situation. I spoke of "my historical event feeling". Milton did this in a sonnet about Piedmont and the Cathars, saying 'how appalling'; and Wordsworth in a sonnet about the French Revolution. I said:

It goes back to Homer. Troy was his historical event, as significant to him as are the Napoleonic wars to us. I look back to Homer, Milton and Wordsworth and find the feeling in the historical event as the basis for my poetic emotion, recollected in the tranquillity of my study.

Back in Essex we went to Great Easton and I wrote into book 9. First thing in the morning I "walked down and communed with the sheep". Two days later I wrote the invocation to Marlowe.

Ann, Matthew and I went to see the house that Nadia had just bought, 21 Chalford Road, West Dulwich. Nadia appeared in the doorway and waved, looking bonny, glowing in her cheeks, very chatty and spontaneous, looking well. We looked round her house and had tea. Her mother, Caroline, now on her own, had been left a half share in the West Dulwich house (following the death of her mother) and legacies (by her aunt and cousin, who had also died). She had bought out the couple her husband had sold a half-share to and had sold the West Dulwich house, 177 South Croxted Road. With the proceeds she had bought 31 Chalford Road to be near Nadia. We visited Caroline at a village shop, Tomlinsons, whose owner she was helping out, and found her poised and assured. In the evening we ate at a local restaurant.[33] The next day Matthew went back to Bangor.

Ann and I spent the weekend at Great Easton. There was a yellowhammer in the blossom by the gate of the church singing "a little bit of bread and no cheese". We went for a drive and from Tilty I had "glimpses of our house across green fields, looking very rural". I wrote about Marshall, Eisenhower and Stalin.

An afternoon with Svetlana Stalin
On the day we left for Cornwall I received a letter from a friend of the Clausons enclosing a letter from Stalin's daughter, Svetlana Alliluyeva: Svetlana Stalin. She had told her about me and my books, and Svetlana had written me a long letter – 10 pages of A4 – about her four books and her wish

to publish material about her mother, who, she said, had shot herself as a courageous protest against Stalin. She had been cold-shouldered by publishers because of her Communist connections and now went under the name of Lana Peters. She lived in Mullion, Cornwall, where I was now heading. It was extraordinary that Stalin's daughter had made contact with me while I was writing *Overlord*. She could provide local colour and share her memories of Stalin in the Kremlin during the Second World War. I believed she had entertained Churchill's and Roosevelt's daughters at Yalta.

Down in Cornwall a film was being made. I walked to buy the papers and heard my name called: "Nicholas." Veronika, the wife of Robin Davies, the harbour-owner, was leaning through a coach window in an 18th-century wig and clothes. I asked what she was doing. "Travelling with Moll Flanders." An actress with ringlets leaned across her and said, "I'm Moll Flanders." Veronika said, "Nicholas, have you met Alex Kingston?" I chatted to her and then there was a call for "action". The coach, pulled by four horses (and controlled by ropes from behind), set off and careered down a ramp towards a tall-masted ship, watched by knots of people. Later the pair were filmed on the quay, walking towards the ship. Later still they stepped onto the ship amongst squawking geese. I wrote a story, 'An Important Star and a Fossil-Lady'.

That afternoon I rang Svetlana. She was very welcoming, and thanked me for ringing. I told her I was in Cornwall quite regularly. I told her Stalin ("your father") was a Martinist Rosicrucian. She said: "I didn't know." "He's thought to have lived with Gurdjieff for a year." "When was that?" "At the Theological Seminary in Tiflis, before 1899." I said what a remarkable lady her mother looked. I told her I had been to Russia in October and had visited Yalta. She said, "Cornwall reminds me of the Crimea." She said Stalin told his mother, "I am like the Tsar." She invited me to visit her.

In the harbour there was more filming the next day: walking on and off the ship, a scene with a chain-gang of convicts. In the evening the harbour was floodlit. There was a storm scene "with boys hauling on a rope to rock the boat, the wind-machine driving rain". The following evening I "went for a long walk... to the end of the pier under a brilliant moon. The water looked like snow."

The next day Ann drove her mother and me to Porthleven, and then took me to Mullion, where Svetlana was standing outside the gate of Melvin House in Mullion Cove Road, waiting for me. She was small with blue eyes (her father's) and browny hair which used to be red, and was now 70. We shook hands and she led me round the back to her bedsit and showed me photos of her late "dear friend from India" (of *Twenty Letters to a Friend*) and of her Russian daughter by him. Incongruously she overlooked a cricket field. We sat in chairs opposite each other. I told her a bit about myself, and then she started talking about herself.

She told me she lived in the Kremlin during the 1930s and of her memories of Stalin during the Second World War. She showed me a picture of her mother taken at Sochi during a picnic in the forest. She opposed Stalin's executions, wrote him a suicide letter and shot herself as a protest. Stalin was devastated and he moved out of the Kremlin apartment that overlooked Alexander Garden in 1932 and built himself a *dacha* at Kuntsevo, 15 miles outside Moscow. She and her half-brother Jacob (by Stalin's first wife) were then looked after in the Kremlin by a housekeeper found by Beria, and Stalin came back to the Kremlin for dinners. She had moved apartments and was now in the Senate building on the first floor. Stalin ran the war on the second floor of the building opposite, which housed the Soviet People's Commissars. He had the whole floor and worked in a large room containing a table with a green cloth, a desk and runner carpets. There were secretaries in the next room. He worked 24 hours at a time. He would go downstairs to the first floor to eat, and Svetlana would sit next to him during dinner. Being Asiatic, during the 1930s he insisted that everyone should eat and drink the best wine. She told me, "I met Churchill in 1942. My father wanted to show off my English. I spoke with him for ten minutes."

She told me how the suicide of her mother had led to Stalin's mistrusting his family during the war. It had turned him against his family. He could not understand the protest: "What did I not give her? She had everything." Svetlana felt: "He grew too quickly into a giant, which she did not like, and she was 22 years younger. She was idealistic and he used to say, 'She was honest, too honest.'" She also criticised collectivization, Trotsky's policy which Stalin inherited, and said Stalin was "unfit to be a leader". The suicide paralysed him for several days, and the family slept in his room to keep an eye on him as he said he wanted to die. It made him distrustful. "If I can't trust her, I can't trust the family." After the purge of the 1930s he started on his family. His wife's brother Alyosha and *his* wife Maria Svanidze were both arrested in 1938 and shot in 1940 after they refused to sign confessions, and others were arrested in the 1940s. Beria had them shot but must have asked Stalin. His brother-in-law, Anna's husband, was also shot. At 16 Svetlana fell in love with a Jew who was put in prison for five years. Stalin did not love his son, Jacob. He refused to swap him for German Generals, and Jacob was shot heading for the electrified wire in his camp to commit suicide.

She spoke of what she had observed of Stalin's conduct of the war. Stalin was paralysed when Hitler invaded Russia on 2 June. He did not broadcast till 2 July but then rallied the country. During the war she saw groups of Generals arrive and he would say to her, "We have some business to discuss, go away now." And he waved her away, very Asian. His mother spoke

Georgian, Svetlana did not. She said, "He was like the Godfather (Al Pacino), gradually getting less innocent and shooting more and more, and everything happening over food. Italians and Georgians are similar. A film should be made of the development of his character." She added, "The family disintegrated and he was not happy at the end of his life."

She spoke of Stalin after the war. He was at the *dacha*. "The Cold War grew out of his mistrust. The war ended and he had to have an enemy to be focused." Stalin died at his *dacha*. He had a stroke, and the Party refused to call a doctor for 16 hours. Beria tried to take over. "He was like Ivan the Terrible and Peter the Great, the sole victor of the war, but he hated the applause and turned pale with anger at 'Glory to Comrade Stalin' – interrupted and said 'No, glory to the army'." His Asiatic roots were in Gori, where, in the museum, there is a photo of Stalin, hair dishevelled, looking down at the body on the bier of his first wife who died in 1907, tears streaming down his cheeks.

She reflected on her father's background and psychology. She did not know if he was a Freemason. (Her father-in-law in America was a 33rd degree Mason and Rosicrucian, and she was encouraged to be Rosicrucian.) He used to say, "The people need a Tsar." He was a peasant from a very poor drunken background. He was relieved when his father was killed in a drunken brawl. He "always needed an angel": his first wife, her mother, and her. But Svetlana became a fallen angel at 16 and after that he did not kiss her or touch her, and was very puritanical. He "hated it when Paulina Molotov got cosmetics and perfumes for Nadya, her mother, and would not have an affair with Paulina". There were "firs at the front of his *dacha*, by the gate, and blossoming trees behind as he loved blossom". He "had a sense of destiny. Being Asian he was both cruel and loving at the same time; typically Georgian."

There was a "demonic side to him: he loved angels because of his demonic side…: the extinction of his family and lack of love for his sons". His son Vassily "trembled, though a General of the Air Force,… he was afraid of him, I wasn't". Stalin told her in 1937, "No one else is left, only you. And I don't need anybody else." She spoke of his "occult power and energy". She said she had not been happy. She had psoriasis on her face "because I am not happy now", having been shunned by two of the seven residents because of who she was, and having been told by the housekeeper, "This was a nice place until you came." I came away at 6.15, having talked with her for four and a half hours. I noted: "The frankness of my questions has reached a new high, even for me; in putting to Svetlana some of the things her father did."[34]

Svetlana left her Mullion bedsit a week later for an Abbeyfield home in Redruth. She sent me material on her mother, and died in 2011. I drew on her eyewitness account of Stalin in *Overlord*.

Earls and endings: at Hay-on-Wye, the Earl of Burford, Asa Briggs, Ted Hughes
Back in Essex we went to Great Easton and before breakfast I sat by the pool: "The birdsong was pure and piping and the sheep were about, the flowers were fresh and vivid in the early morning sun, all hues, and I sat on my seat by the pond with golden water-buttercups and revelled in the paean of praise to the sun." I noted: "I am making literary material out of secret things that have an impact on today. Through my epic I have discovered my literary material: the drive to world government and its background." Anthony rang to say that he had been to the Reading Dillons and on a shelf of books deemed suitable for university courses he had found (alongside Keats, Shelley, Yeats, Pound and Hughes) *Overlord*, books 3–6.

I had a strong feeling I should look in on the literary festival at Hay-on-Wye on our way to Cornwall. I followed my intuition, and we drove to Hay-on-Wye on the day I finished book 9 of *Overlord*. We put up at the Old Black Lion, where Cromwell stayed while his Roundheads attacked the castle. I had not made any arrangements to hear speakers. I saw from the programme that the Earl of Burford was talking on Shakespeare as the 17th Earl of Oxford, and the following morning impulsively paid and sat in the marquee, which was half full.

The bearded Earl came onto the stage and stood at the lectern. He wore a tie and a sports jacket and made his case for 'Shake-spear' being a pseudonym for a man from the upper class whose heroes fell downwards, who knew Greek, who travelled in Italy; a dissident like Solzhenitsyn who had to watch out he did not get killed. He claimed that Shakespeare-Oxford was Queen Elizabeth's lover and was protected, and that Shakespeare's child by the Queen was reared as the Earl of Southampton, so Shakespeare was addressing his son in the sonnets and the Queen was the Dark Lady. I did not believe that Shakespeare was lover of the Queen or that he fathered the heir to the throne, but Burford's sweep, knowledge of Shakespeare and delivery were impressive. We heard Peter Mandelson in discussion with Tony Howard and then walked down to look at the Wye and after a candlelit dinner took a look at Offa's Dyke across the bridge.

Christopher Logue had translated Homer, and I thought I should hear him. The next morning he was reading with Craig Raine. Raine's poems made no impact on me at all, and were not to do with European culture or epic. The poems Logue read, including a passage from his translation of Homer, were entirely unmemorable, unlike his scowling, angry face. During question time he did memorably ask, 'What is the *Zeitgeist*?' I knew that the Romantic *Zeitgeist* was of "feeling and challenging authority", that the Roman Augustan *Zeitgeist* was of urbanity; and that the spirit of the Age in the 1950s was a questioning one. And the next day I wrote a *"Zeitgeist block"* into my epic.

Outside the marquee I encountered the Earl of Burford and I asked him to write down the best edition of *Oxford's Letters*. We discussed the evidence behind his theme, and I said there must be a trunk of Shakespeare's papers somewhere, as Edmund Blunden had told me. He told me: "I'm a direct descendant of the 17th Earl of Oxford on both sides and a direct descendant of the Earl of Southampton." I was interested to hear the Oxfordian case without departing from my belief that Shakespeare was the Stratfordian of traditional literary criticism. I had a long chat with him, not realising that he would ask to work with me, that I would get to know him extremely well and that to meet him was the reason I had visited Hay on an intuitional whim.

We resumed our journey to Cornwall via Tintern Abbey, the subject of Wordsworth's poem. It was surrounded by wooded hills and its arched windows were open and frequented by cooing doves. The Wye slid by, very brown and green, in a very atmospheric romantic chasm. We drove on towards Cornwall, "kestrels fluttering overhead", and had tea at the mill house at Bovey Tracy.

I had seen that Ted Hughes was reading and Asa Briggs speaking at Hay at the end of the week, and we arranged to return from Cornwall via Hay. We drove to the Severn Bridge and stopped at Tintern Abbey again for coffee. We checked in at Hay's Brookfield guest-house, and heard Asa Briggs speak about *History's Turning Points*, to which he had written a Foreword and acted as a consultant. He spoke of not imposing modern morality on the past. I had a chat with him after his lecture.

At six we heard Ted Hughes in a marquee. Some 400 were in the audience, not every seat was filled. He came on from the back, grey-haired, spectacles hanging round his neck over a bluish shirt and red tie, brownish crumpled sports jacket, grey trousers and black shoes. He stood back clutching a book while the Literary Editor of *The Sunday Times* reported that he had been awarded a prize for literary excellence as he had been such a force in English Literature. Hughes delivered an hour's reading (billed as 35 minutes) without moving his feet or looking at the audience, mumbling about the poems to begin with – Ovid, one about his father, then some about Sylvia Plath. The wind wapped the awning of the marquee and flapped and the frame creaked and the spotlights above us danced up and down. It came in gusts and almost drowned out the words, and at the end one of the security guards reported, "Half the marquee's blown away."

Hughes was applauded after each poem but appeared not to notice, and retreated to the applause at the end round to the back. Everyone went to the bookshop expecting to meet him, but he was by the back entrance to the marquee being photographed. He got in a green car and sped away. It was an inglorious ending to his reading. I overheard criticisms of Hughes: "He didn't seem to put himself out, he didn't throw himself into it. I heard him some years ago and he was dynamic. Now he seems to have lost his energy." It was not known that he had cancer. He had been cordoned off from the audience, and when he learned that I was present he sent me a card about the gale that had rocked the marquee.

I saw Hughes as a minor-Georgian poet writing of birds and beasts (like Blunden's 'Pike') but with a major vision, the van-Goghian energy of the animal kingdom. He was in the tradition of D.H. Lawrence's poetry (such as 'Snake'). I noted his shamanic control over animals, interest in sympathetic magic and Graves's goddess. The next day we drove home via Shaftesbury, where I spent a couple of hours discussing *Overlord* with Michael Mann.

Apart from my contact with the Earl of Burford Hay had not touched me. The speakers and readers had removed me from my own experience, taken me out of my life. Back in Essex I plunged back into direct experience.

We went to Great Easton and on to Thaxted for another look at the annual Horn Dance in which (as we saw on p.518) the Devil parades through the crowded main street at dusk, to complete silence. We arrived about 9.30. There were several morris displays under a full moon before silence was called for and from the churchyard came a violinist playing haunting music and ten Chinese-clad dancers, six showing stag's horns, three carrying an umbrella, a bow and arrow and a triangle and one riding a home-made horse. The umbrella-carrier was meant to be the Devil. The crowd were silent until they had left, and then there was loud cheering, everyone smiling. I drew on the appearance of Lucifer, the Devil, as a violinist playing haunting music, in *Overlord* and later in my classical ode, 'At the Thaxted Horn Dance'.

I asked myself what I was trying to do in my epic:

Tell the hidden history of the 20th century and its myths, and relate it to the Light. I asked myself: 'Why have I written the epic?' Because there has not been a major epic in the 20th century.... To get inside Hitler and Stalin, but also inside Eisenhower and Montgomery. Also to show a unitive vision in which an important event, the most important in the 20th century, is related to Nature, Heaven, Hell and intellectual history – the invocations play a part. Also to create a work that towers above the 20th century like a mountain and which contains truth. I am trying to tell the true story of the war, how a modern *Iliad* took place. And at the same time to reveal the workings of the Light and the workings of the universe.

I pondered why my vision had taken so long to take shape:

I thought I had spent 25 years getting my history theory right – from 1966 to 1991 – but in fact I was getting the epic out, from 1969 to 1994, for 25 years. Two major ideas I had in the 1960s.

From Great Easton I went to Tilty church to see the re-enactment of the battle between the Royalist rebels and the Parliamentarians on the field strewn with the Abbey ruins. I watched the Royalist camp of Sir George Lisle; the advance of Fairfax in a royal blue sash, parleying; the Royalist refusal of terms; and an inconclusive battle in which muskets were fired. The Parliamentarians won and executed the last Royalist survivors, ending the Civil War. I later wrote 'At Tilty Battlefield', a classical ode.

Our schools had been feeder schools for Chigwell, and now Tony Little was leaving to become Head of Oakham. I attended his farewell party at the back of Haylands under a marquee in slight drizzle. All the Chigwell staff were present and I was one of two parents and represented the two schools.

The next day, following up the Earl of Burford's urging, Ann and I visited Castle Hedingham, the seat of the de Veres, the Earls of Oxford. We entered the basement of the Norman keep, climbed the spiral staircase to the guardroom and went on up to the Banqueting Hall and up to the minstrels' gallery. A fellow was sweeping, raising a cloud of dust. He was the Hon. Tom Lindsay, descendant from the Earls of Oxford, and current owner. He had never met Burford, his cousin, but knew of him. We discussed the possibility (from the Oxfordian point of view) that this was the castle of Hamlet and Macbeth. I did not believe this but was interested to hear the arguments he advanced. He led Ann and me down the steps, pointing out the foundations of the houses, and took us into the 18th-century Castle House and to the drawing-room and the library. As we left we passed his wife sweeping a path. *Noblesse oblige*. I pondered the obligations of being born to a pile. Ironically, within seven months I would own a historic house and have similar obligations. I would later write a classical ode about Castle Hedingham, and I wrote a tongue-in-cheek invocation to Shakespeare as Oxford two days later in *Overlord*.

I had heard that Mabel Reid had died. She had been barely conscious and was turned two-hourly and did not want visitors. I attended her memorial service at St Mary's. Some of my Oaklands contemporaries were present. Hail rattled and jumped on the church roof, and there was a growl of thunder. There was tea in the parish hall. Afterwards I rang the local paper and talked to them about Mabel Reid whose Nature walks were legendary and who along with Miss Lord had agreed to hand Oaklands on to Ann and me.

We drove to Bangor for Matthew's graduation. We stayed at the Menai Court Hotel. Early the next morning we took our seats for the packed ceremony. Matthew beamed in his blue-greeny sheened gown and mortar-board with his peers, glad to be photographed. An organ played in the parade of dons and played them out. I spoke with his friend Dave's father, who was retiring from GCHQ, Cheltenham. He told me he could not go to Russia.

Oaklands broke up. Ann was retiring from 14 years as Headmistress. Her last long assembly was in two parts: poetry and songs, then the presentation of cups. Ann was almost tearful at the end. Later I made a speech at the staff lunch, and after saying farewell to leavers and retiring staff, pointed out that Ann had been a brilliant Head and was taking a step back, that there was no severance but she would get a kiss (loudly applauded).[35]

In Greece: Helen of Troy's palace and Kazantzakis's house
Having been shown a work in Pisa that would draw on the classical tradition in verse and European culture, which would become my *Classical Odes*, I wanted to tour Greece for this work as much as for my epic. In mid-July I took my family to Greece for a couple of weeks.

We arrived in Athens and were taken out to Sounion, where in wind I found Byron's signature on a marble block and wrote a few lines looking across to the silver mines of Laurion. I wrote a passage on Byron into *Overlord*. We went to the Acropolis and looked down on the seven hills: the Acropolis itself, Pnyx, Mars Hill, Lycabettus, Philopappos (or Hill of the Muses), the Hill of the Nymphs and Strefi. We headed for Thebes, and I saw the crossroads where Oedipus killed Laius. We arrived in Delphi past the Valley of the Muses and visited the Delphic Oracle where the priestess of Apollo, empowered by volcanic fumes, spoke the words of the god that were recorded by priests in hexameters. I wrote a passage on Delphi for *Overlord*.

We visited Olympia's Temple of Zeus and, near the stadium where the first Olympics were held in 776BC (where Themistocles was given a standing ovation in 476BC) I found Pheidias's workshop, and in the museum a cup on which Pheidias had carved 'I am Pheidias's' on the bottom. I wrote a classical ode, 'In Pheidias's Workshop'.

We visited Nestor's palace at Pylos and took a boat to Sphacteria under the Spartan walls. We visited Mystras and then Sparta. In the *Blue Guide* I read about the palace of Menelaos, where Paris ran off with Helen of Troy, and took Anthony in a taxi to find it. We climbed a mountain through long grass and, after being dive-bombed by huge cicadas and bees the size of small birds we found it, an overgrown ruin looking across the river to Mount Taygetos. Nearly five years later I wrote a classical ode, 'At Menelaos's Palace, Sparta'.

We drove to Mycenae and climbed to the acropolis through the Lion Gate and found the *megaron* with the round hearths and the bathroom next door where Agamemnon was murdered with Cassandra. We went on to Argos, past Tiryns and reached Epidavros, and I stood on the centre stone of the ancient theatre and declaimed the first four lines of Euripides *Alcestis* in Greek to my boys, who were among the seats.

Back in Athens, we caught a hydrofoil to Aigina, where we were spending three nights. Next morning we walked to the Temple of Aphaia Aigina, which together with the Parthenon and Sounion formed a triangle that symbolised Athenian power ruling the waves. We visited the old harbour and saw two moles and sunken berths for triremes and bits of 5th-century wall, pulled down in the siege by Athens of 458 or when Athens expelled the population to prevent it from aiding Sparta in 431. In the bus on the way back, scribbling on my knee, I wrote a chunk of poetry about Aegina and Hitler's deportation.

We cruised through the Greek islands for a week. We visited Mykonos, and as in 1958 the sea was rough, with sea-horses racing in. We returned to Ephesus and I found the inscription on the Fountain of Trajan referring to "the whole of the round world", showing knowledge from the Greek-Roman time that the earth was round as sculptors of Atlas knew (*see* p.v). We revisited Patmos's Cave of the Apocalypse. We went to Rhodes and saw where the Colossus (Helios) stood in Mandraki harbour. We visited Lindos and Mussolini's summer residence.

We visited Crete and returned to Knossos. In Iraklion I looked for the house where Kazantzakis last lived, where I slept in 1958, and found it. It had green Venetian blinds and had a plaque over the door saying he was 'born' there ('*gennikos*'). Our guide confirmed that he last lived in the house where he was born.

We sailed to Santorini and visited the caldera and the Admiral's house in Akrotiri, which was in a town of streets and houses on the cliffs, c.1600–1500BC. A fresco showed Mycenaeans visiting the Minoans shortly before the eruption that destroyed Atlantis. There was a body of opinion that the Admiral's house was an Atlantean house, and I later drafted a classical ode, 'The Admiral's House in Atlantis'. Back on the mainland we visited Dafni, the garden where I attended the wine festival in 1958.

I returned with images for my epic and a number of classical odes.[36]

Overlord, *books 10–12*
I had started book 10 on 15 June. We left for Cornwall at the end of July. I wrote the epic every day. On 17 August filming began on *Rebecca* in the harbour. I watched by the far beach, which was floodlit. A boat with two white sails was sunk. The tide went out and it lay on its side. Ann and I watched Charles Dance half-heartedly rowing. He could not manage the oars, and so Tony, the local fisherman, and a friend were paid to swim in

front of his rowing-boat and pull ropes tied to the oars. On screen Dance seems to be rowing unaided. There were lorries and cranes on the harbour, a crane with a great searchlight on top; rain-sprinklers down on the beach.

The next day I noted: "My epic seems to be writing itself. Sat down without any clear idea as to how to do the Potsdam conference, and it is somehow writing itself, as though I am being sent the ideas from beyond." As I wrote I was kept company by a cormorant which stood on the break-water above the sea under my window. "A cormorant sitting on the water, diving to fish; fishing the waters of the ocean. An image for the poet coming up with the poem." I later wrote two poems, 'Cormorant Fishing' and 'Cormorant'.

I took time off from my epic to visit an exhibition on the *Mary Rose* at the Visitors Centre and saw a picture that provided a date for our Harbour-master's House. The caption said it was built between 1792 (when it did not exist) and 1796 (when it did) – two years before the Romantic revolution of 1798, of Wordsworth and Coleridge's *Lyrical Ballads*.[37]

I am asked to acquire Normanhurst School
We returned to Essex. In Cornwall I had had a call from our well-informed accountant, Martin Anderson, saying that we might be offered Normanhurst School. He would not say more. Our Bursar Ken Jones rang two days later to say that Normanhurst was going under, that we would hear this from the local paper and could proceed with a receiver if we were interested. I put these conversations out of my mind as we did not especially want a third school. I had forgotten them when on 9 September after addressing the Oaklands staff and visiting the Head at Coopersale Hall I was given a message that the Headmaster of Normanhurst, Jeremy Leyland had rung, wanting to visit me that afternoon. I returned to our house next to Oaklands (now Oak House).

He came at 2.30 and stayed until 4 and told me in the conservatory that his daughter had recently died, aged 25; and that he had not been doing well and had had to have five or six parents as investors following Inland-Revenue problems. He would like me to be an investor and to have all the financial side, leaving him the educational side. His father, Eric Leyland, a children's author I had read as a boy and editor of the *Children's Newspaper*, now had Parkinson's disease. He proposed that I should buy the four properties, pay an amount into the cash flow, pay him and his parents money that they were owed and take over the running of the school.

He meant that he wanted me to buy Normanhurst as he would be unable to pay the staff's salaries at the end of September and had called a meeting of the parents on Thursday 12 September to announce that the School was being placed in the hands of a receiver. News would be across the front page of the local paper, and parents would start withdrawing children immediately. We would have to buy Normanhurst within three days: four large side-by-side Victorian houses that formed the bulk of the School, three of which were registered in Denmark.

I combed the figures and concluded that the School was viable and that things had slid following the death of the Head's 25-year-old daughter. I was conscious that the entire staff would be made redundant if I did not act by the coming Thursday, and that Ann and I were the only available rescuers who could take over the School in time. The purchase had to be made by Thursday as the roll would start falling away and there would soon be no School left. The next day I sent Ken and one of the accountants to Normanhurst "to ferret and be whippets". They reported back favourably.

I visited Normanhurst that evening. It had four turrets and a central porch, and was a short walk from Chingford station. The classrooms were well-stocked and the School's catchment area extended westward as far as Bethnal Green and the City of London.

We agreed to buy the School and I set up a base in the accountants' boardroom for three days. Advisers came and went and calls to and from the bank, Denmark and institutions were heard by all on speaker-phone. We put together a proposal to the receiver. We then discovered that the Normanhurst staff had not been paid at the end of August, and we would have to take on this additional expense.

On the morning of Thursday 12 September we heard from Copenhagen that the properties had been secured. That evening Ken Jones met the Normanhurst parents and announced that Normanhurst would now be a member of the Oak-Tree Group of Schools. All listened in attentive silence and when he said "Oaklands and Coopersale Hall" there was vigorous nodding all round the hall. There was applause and he was surrounded by staff and parents eager to be reassured. We had rescued the staff and announced our rescue to the parents before any withdrawals.

The day after the public announcement that we had taken on Normanhurst Ann and I escaped the financial discussions to research Marlowe for an invocation in my epic. Ann drove me to Scadbury Manor House, near Chislehurst in Kent, where a messenger sent by the Privy Council came to arrest Marlowe in mid-May 1593. The moated ruin had been owned by Thomas Walsingham IV, Marlowe's patron and cousin of Elizabeth's spymaster Sir Francis Walsingham. Marlowe saw the horseman across the moat and thought about hiding, but presented himself to the Privy Council to clear his name of blasphemy. We went on to Borthwick Street, where Eleanor Bull's victualling house may have stood – where Marlowe was murdered by Ingram Frizer. I later wrote a classical ode, 'At

Scadbury'.

The next day we escaped the financial deliberations again, this time to Hill Hall, near Theydon Mount, Essex, the home of the Elizabethan Secretary of State and Ambassador, Sir Thomas Smith, tutor to the young Edward de Vere, the 17th Earl of Oxford. It had been turned into a prison and been burnt down in 1969 after Christine Keeler was a prisoner. It was in a ruinous condition but there were interesting late-16th-century wall-paintings. We went to St Michael's church (early 17th century) across the green sward and saw the tombs of four Smiths. I later wrote a classical ode, 'At Hill Hall, Theydon Mount: Mind and Soul'.

I was heartened by a call from Peter Donebauer, who told me that *The Warlords* had been at his bedside for more than two months. He read a passage or two every night before going to sleep, and found the two verse plays "'compelling' and 'compulsive'", and thought it could go on at the Globe in a cut form. (He knew the Artistic Director, then Mark Rylance.)

The following day I dictated letters to the parents of all three schools about our acquisition of Normanhurst, and then had another session with John Hobbs in 4 Upper Wimpole Street. There was still a problem with surviving varicose veins in my right leg. I stood up on the blue stool before the long strip light without my trousers, and I had my leg marked in felt pen while he whipped my veins with his fingers. I then lay back on the torture bed and had some 15 or 20 injections into the varicose veins that had survived in my right leg. It was agony. It burnt like acid and stung within and each time I groaned "Aa-aah" and bit my hand. Hobbs asked questions, injecting me and stopping me in mid-sentence. He told me, "People with blue eyes feel less pain. The Russians feel less pain." (I did not believe that and thought he was brainwashing me.) I limped out and walked home from the station. I was heavily bandaged from above the knee to the base of the toes of my right leg and could only just get my shoe on.

The next day I carried forward the purchase of Normanhurst. "Ken negotiated terms for us with the bank." I reflected on the triangle I was creating: "Normanhurst, Oaklands, Coopersale Hall – Chingford, Loughton, Epping; Queen Elizabeth's hunting lodge, Loughton Hall, Epping's Copped Hall." The following day Ken and I parked and walked on Chingford Plain between Rangers Road and Sewardstone Road, and took our place at the front of the tiered staging for the Normanhurst School photo.

The Oak-Tree Group of Schools stabilised Normanhurst, and applications from potential parents increased. I visited the School regularly and got to know all the staff. My aged aunt Argie, hearing some of this through her elderly friends, said, "Nick buys schools like hats."[38]

In Rome: drinking from the spring at Horace's Sabine farm
I needed to visit Rome for the epic and for my accumulating classical odes, and I had booked to take Ann to Rome before Normanhurst was offered to us. The timing was not brilliant.

We flew to Rome and stayed at the magnificent Hotel Columbus, a c.1500 Renaissance building. We walked to Trevi Fountain and the Pantheon (which has a bronze Augustan door and a hole in the dome to let smoke out), originally dedicated to all the gods and now a church, a symbol of universalism. We went to St Peter's and I was taken by the papal canopy of Bernini over the tomb of St Peter, and had my Christ meet the Pope in *Overlord* under the dove in Light and sunburst.

We drove round Rome and saw many landmarks and monuments, including the Capitoline and Forum, the Circus Maximus and Palatine Hill. We visited the Colosseum and found the Mausoleum of Augustus. I studied the Ara Pacis, Augustus's Altar of Peace.

We drove to Licenza to revisit Horace's Sabine farm. Its two-foot-high walls were set out in grass and wild flowers. I found Horace's bedroom and, looking at the sloping mountains above, thought of his *Odes* and of my classical odes. We walked to the spring, the *'fons Bandusiae'* I drank from 39 years previously and became a poet, my Muse's water. I drank from the same spot as it gushed from underground. Later I wrote a classical ode, 'At Horace's Sabine Farm'. We then drove back to Hadrian's Villa at Tivoli. I wrote a classical ode, 'At Hadrian's Villa, Tivoli'.

We were dropped off at the Palatine and visited the House of Livia, Augustus's wife. We walked down the ramp and saw rooms with mosaics, one of fruit-trees. We passed the houses of Tiberius and Caligula and visited the Temple of the Divine Julius, where Caesar was cremated; the Rostra where Antony stirred the crowd; and the Curia (Senate). We went to the Theatre of Pompey, where Caesar was murdered, and to the Spanish Steps and Keats's house. I wrote a classical ode, 'In Keats's House, Rome'. We saw Pope John Paul II in the Vatican's main square, unsmiling and frail, and went on to Hadrian's mausoleum. We found the Papal apartments and walked from room to room, taking in the erotic paintings on the Pope's walls. (This Papal home, not Avignon, was where Buchanan worked as a guide and told me about Alexander VI's room, *see My Double Life 1: This Dark Wood*, p.166.)

We visited churches, including St John Lateran, whose front door came from the Roman Senate. We went to the old Lateran Palace and saw the Holy Staircase which Christ ascended on the day of his crucifixion (so it is said). We went to the Catacombs of St Domitilla and wandered in semi-darkness by skeletons. I wrote a classical ode, 'In Domitilla's Catacomb, Rome.' We visited the Sistine Chapel, and I wrote a classical ode, 'In the

Sistine Chapel'.[39]
Many of the places we had seen appeared in *Overlord*.

Finishing Overlord; *Normanhurst's Founders Day, Nasser Hussain*
I worked on the epic when I could. I was still suffering from the after-effects of the removal of my varicose veins. I had a bandaged right leg while in Rome and I returned to John Hobbs to have my bandage removed. I lay on the couch without my trousers. "Mr Hobbs, 'Get the stabber.' The New-Zealand assistant, who was learning: 'This one?' 'No, that's too blunt, a sharp one. That's it. What you do is you get the blood out when it's like this.' He stabbed me with the stabber. Waves of pain went up my leg as he squeezed out the blood. I: 'In the 18th century at least they gave you a tot of brandy first.' He: 'And the Pantheon was open, you say? What was closed in Rome?' Trying to invite me to have a normal social conversation while I was beside myself with pain from 'the stabber'. A pool of blood lay on the paper sheet. 'Right, now get a puncture plaster.' She: 'This one?' 'No, one of those.' I: 'I've certainly got a puncture.'" Hobbs grinned at me while she looked rather doubtful about the whole situation. The squeezing out of my blood from the crevices of my leg was like the squeezing out of images from the crevices of my mind as I checked the similes in my epic.

The next day I tap-tapped 30 pages of book 8. I had to see the staff at the schools individually about their salary increases, and there were many details about Normanhurst to be discussed in the accountants' boardroom. I fixed up for a country cousin to live with Argie. (Aged 93, she had had an operation to remove an abscess on her sigmoid colon which could have caused peritonitis, and had convalesced in Willow Ward, Forest Place, Buckhurst Hill.) We had been to Cornwall for half-term and I was now adding finishing touches. I leafed through books 7–12 and "wrote in one or two more bits".

While I squeezed out more images I had to return to London for more 'stabbing'. I sat on Hobbs's slim examination couch and was stabbed with the stabber a good six times. Painful squeezing of the blood followed as he tried to get fluid out of my right ankle. I was back with plasters and had to wear my stocking.

The next time I met Michael Mann for lunch in Shaftesbury I discovered that he had teamed up with Penguin and that my two volumes of short stories, along with *The Universe and the Light* and *Overlord* were on the internet as being published by Penguin. The first two volumes of my epic were now being worked on by many hands.

There was a lull in my writing while I coped with an inspection at Normanhurst. Soon afterwards Normanhurst held its Founders Day (prize day) at the Chingford Assembly Hall. I stood with the Head and greeted

Nasser Hussain, the Essex cricketer, who was giving out the prizes. He arrived in an old pullover and baggy trousers. We were in suits. I led him on to the platform under glaring, blinding spotlights. The Head spoke first and (as part of our agreement to take the school over) I made the keynote speech to a sea of faces below in the half-dark, the staff behind me on the platform. I said I was a local boy and had played cricket for Buckhurst Hill. I spoke about standards, self-motivation, goals and setting an example, and set out our educational philosophy. I brought in being an author. This was the first time I had been able to present the Oak-Tree Schools philosophy to the parents. Nasser then presented the prizes.

We sat down in the hall for a display of the children's musical talents and I asked him, "Is it tense in a Test when you come out to bat?" He said: "It is, you're playing for England and there's a big crowd. You've got to keep your limbs relaxed. No, physios don't help. Each individual has to handle it in his own way." On his future, Nasser said: "I'm looking to be a commentator or a writer. I might like to work in a school. I'll stay in touch." Then we watched 'The Pied Piper of Hamelin'. The Pied Piper led the children of Normanhurst into the mountain in what seemed a parable about our rescue of the School. Following the inspection at Normanhurst I made structural changes to the School and held meetings with the staff to explain them. I set up an Improvement Committee to raise standards, and it functioned like a senior management team.

I attended a reception given at St John's Farm in Abridge for Sir Marcus Fox, who was compiling a list of candidates for the European elections. Both Steve Norris and his successor Eleanor Laing were present. Bizarrely, I was asked to take a photo of Norris, Laing and Fox, and I found myself rearranging them: "Eleanor, you're overshadowed by Steve, can you step forward? Steve, you're putting her in the shade, can you step back?" My directions inadvertently caught the feeling of an outgoing MP making way for his successor. I did not encounter Steve Norris again after that evening.

I finished writing the epic once-through on 23 November 1996 (having begun it on 2 June 1994). I wrote that day: "Technically I have finished the epic, though there is still much tinkering to do."

There were staff meetings about the Oaklands ethos. I said: "Oaklands is about fields and atmosphere, about Nature – buttercups, squirrels and magpies, newts; hedgerows." I said, "There is a oneness between the soul and Nature. The children are souls we get forward. Children need to relate to Nature and do exams within that larger context. Children are like plants that grow organically, not machines that function mechanically." I spoke about the unity in the universe. I organised the Oaklands Christmas party for the smallest children. I had Father Christmas clambering up onto a chair outside the Hall window and ringing the School handbell.

I had a meeting with counsel in Bedford Row, and wandered in the daylight and early dusk past 1 Bedford Row, where I was an articled clerk. The gloomy interior had been modernised – I could see fire notices and computers through the windows – but the blackened brick shell round the Georgian windows remained forbidding and alienating. Forty years on, I reflected I could now be a partner there and could have done nothing else with my life. I could have become a thin, worried man bustling to the courts and back, and on to counsel, where I had just been.

I had to go back for more treatment by Mr and Mrs. Hobbs on my right leg. I sat on the examination couch without my trousers. First Mr Hobbs picked up the scab on my left leg with his forceps, then he got the stabber, cradled it in his hand, kept his body between me and it, wiped a red solution on the inside of my right leg with cotton wool, asked "What school events have you got at Christmas time?" and stabbed me and squeezed out the blood. He stabbed and squeezed again. The pain went as soon as he stopped squeezing. He said: "The body is very efficient, it collects blood and waits for the skin to pop as it comes out. You can't remember pain." I did not believe this. The nurse came in. I said to her: "I'm not out of the wood yet, he's got the outside of the leg to do." Then he stabbed me on the outside of the leg and squeezed the blood. There were several piles of bloodstained cotton wool when he had finished and I had three plasters on my leg.

While I was proof-reading book 8 "with a windy sea foaming in under my window" down in Cornwall news came through that Laurens van der Post had died at the age of 90. The papers were full of his obituaries. I reflected on his amazing life. He had known T.E. Lawrence (who introduced him to E.M. Forster), and the Woolfs, who published his first novel. He had had extreme experiences in the war and was anti-socialist; and had had a house in Aldeburgh and played tennis with Britten and Pears. He had known the Prince of Wales through Mountbatten, on whose staff he had served. He had worked with Montgomery. He had known Jung.

Shortly after his death van der Post was the subject of a hostile biography that suggested he had embellished some accounts of his life. There was a rebuttal, and although his prisoner-of-war experiences were untouched his reputation suffered. Thinking back to my visit to his Chelsea apartment (*see* pp.311–312) I had been struck by his attentiveness towards me and his patient caring for his wife. The man I sat with that afternoon was not a charlatan but on the topics we discussed very genuine.

Van der Post's sense of true values made me take a step back and revalue myself and my own writing:

I am groping towards my writing future… as a man of letters…. There can be verse plays, poems, stories, novels and essays or reflections that grow out of place. I need to engage my whole self in my writing at all times.... A work of art reveals truth. I must, as a man of letters, continue to reveal truth in my works of art, but on to verse plays now. Solitude and Nature give one the opportunity to rediscover oneself.... I need to withdraw from the schools and live more fully as a writer.[40]

On 19 December I heard that we had at last completed the purchase of Normanhurst. (It took me three days to announce that we would buy it and more than three months to resolve the legal complexities involving Denmark.) That day and the next day I finished proof-reading books 11 and 12 of *Overlord*. Further proof-reading took me until 30 December. Four days later, on 3 January 1997, I drove to Dorset, saw Michael Mann and handed over the last three books *Overlord*.

This episode was now over. I had completed 41,000 lines of blank verse (over a third of Shakespeare's total of 118,406 lines) in just under two and a half years while visiting places of European culture that would be reflected in my *Classical Odes* and while running two schools and buying a third.

Episode 11:

Verse Plays and Tudor Knots

Years: 1997–2000
Locations: Essex: Loughton; Suffolk; Italy (1998); USA (1998)
Works: *Wheeling Bats and a Harvest Moon*; *The Warm Glow of the Monastery Courtyard*; *A Dandelion Clock*; odes in *Classical Odes*; *The Tragedy of Prince Tudor*
Initiatives: renovation of Normanhurst School; renovation of Otley Hall;
Bartholomew Gosnold

"During my tenure of Otley Hall the Tudor knot of the knot-garden was a symbol for the One."

Nicholas Hagger,
Preface to *A Tudor Knot*, 'Poems on England',
book 1 of *Classical Odes*

In my next episode I bought a moated Tudor Hall and there was a conflict between 'Tudor knots' – the first volume of my classical odes, *A Tudor Knot*, and tangled Suffolk 'knots' – and my next three verse plays, the first of which was called *The Tragedy of Prince Tudor*, which were spurred on by four casts of visiting Globe actors.

Tudor knots: Otley Hall and European culture

The schools' new Bursar had said that he could persuade the bank to fund new projects. He had communicated this to our accountant and I had been urged to buy a largish property as a new project. Sitting on the *chaise longue* in 6 Albion Hill I turned a page of *Country Life* and saw a picture of a many-gabled Tudor Hall with tall chimneys in Suffolk, and was instantly smitten. I showed the picture to Ann and her mother. It was as though I already had a connection with the house, it would have an income. Before Christmas Ann and I agreed to sell the investment apartment near Marble Arch which an earlier accountant had urged us to buy against a rainy day, and look towards Suffolk.[1] It seemed Providential that I should have seen the property so soon after being urged to look.

On 28 December I finished doing my bank projections – forecasts for the coming year's finances in all three schools – and we went to drinks at Arabin House, High Beach, where Tennyson is said to have stayed with Judge Arabin in December 1861.[2] Our host and hostess had split the large Victorian house in two and retained the older part that looks across Beech Hill House to Waltham Abbey, whose spire could be seen from the dining-room. Tennyson, who wrote 'Ring out Wild Bells' in Beech Hill House, walked up the path to visit Mrs. Arabin, passing the circular wall where Judge Arabin sat before going to work and putting on his black cap to sentence miscreants to death.[3]

Purchase of Tudor Otley Hall

Visiting Arabin House confirmed me in my plan to buy a large house, and I arranged to visit the Suffolk house, Otley Hall. Ann, Matthew and I drove through snow the next day, slithering and sliding along the seven-mile-long narrow approach road. We arrived just after 12, not over-impressed by Otley village as it looked a bit new.

I was very taken with the Hall. We drove past a long hedge in Hall Lane to gates and in up the drive into 10 acres of garden and the moat. We parked in front of a brick-and-timber-framed building. The wide front door opened as we crunched through snow and Mrs. Mosesson greeted us, straight-haired with a smiling face and outstretched hand. She was Swedish, like her husband. She took us on a tour of the inside of the house, which is on the front cover of Eric Sandon's *Suffolk Houses*: its Great Hall, linenfold panelling and huge kitchen with minstrels' gallery. I noted bare floors and draughty, leaded-light windows. In one attic room there was a dead pigeon. It was –4°C. We walked through snow past the moat to outhouses, a wood, a henhouse, log cabin, swimming-pool and tennis-court, and back along a nut walk, rose garden and many ducks on the H-shaped lake.

We went back to the kitchen. We got out of wellies, and revived our numb fingers clasping hot coffee round the Aga. We were asked if we would be prepared to open the stately home three weekends a year, and I could see myself living there, writing by the moat, people coming to my door. Mosesson named a price for which I could buy much of the furniture and we inspected what he would leave. We drove back to Great Easton on frozen snow.

Otley Hall from front showing chimneys (left) and from back showing the moat (right)

As I read leaflets he had given me it dawned on me that this historic house was very historical. The Gosnold family had been associated with some of the key figures of the 16th century, including their cousin Edward de Vere. Francis Bacon was related to them. Bartholomew Gosnold had made voyages to the US in 1602, when he named Martha's Vineyard after his daughter Martha, and in 1607, when he founded the North-American colony at Jamestown. The first of these voyages had reputedly been funded by the Earl of Southampton, Shakespeare's patron, while he was in the Tower; and Sir Walter Raleigh had put in funds in return for owning the cargo they brought back. The United States of America based its own founding on the founding of the Jamestown settlement in 1607, and arguably Gosnold was one of the first founders. I said it was like Yeats's Tower – draughty. But I remarked, "If I do it, my writing will include a swathe from Chingford to Aldeburgh; Essex and (later on) Suffolk."

I was advised what to offer by the bank, and phoned a low offer through. The estate agent said there would be no response for a week. We drove to Great Easton and were aware we did not want to lose "the view round the green, the pargeting, the sun-trap at the back and the view of the sheep". We drove to Aldeburgh and looked at the pale green, rolling North Sea. We went on to Wickham Market and Otley village, stopped at Otley church and went on past the Hall. We saw 15 pheasants by the road and looked at Helmingham Hall. We returned convinced that we should keep Great

Easton *and* acquire Otley Hall.

The schools restarted and I had to address the staff at each school. We attended the funeral of the ex-Oaklands teacher, Mrs. Macy at the Unitarian meeting house in Ipswich. Her eldest son told me he had sung 13 of Tennyson's 'Maud' songs at Harrington Hall, after the Maitlands had sold it to the Prices. It had burnt down while the new owners were away and had been restored. We took the opportunity to familiarise ourselves with Suffolk villages: we returned through Kersey, Lindsey, Bildeston, Stowmarket, Monks Eleigh and Lavenham, where we had tea, and then through Long Melford, Cavendish, Clare and Stoke-by-Clare.

I saw ourselves restoring Otley Hall and putting the grounds in order for our retirement. I wrote, as it turned out prophetically: "Perhaps I shall sit in my Elizabethan Hall and write verse plays in the idiom of Marlowe and Shakespeare with a link to the modern Globe." Intuitively I knew even then that there would be a link with the Globe.

On 15 January the estate agent rang to say that 15 had viewed and six were interested. The six should put in their best offer and say what costs they had borne. Otley would be awarded to one of the six on 24 January.

While I coped with running the schools Ann made her own visit to Woodbridge, Wickham Market and then Otley. She rang and asked if I could get her into the Hall. I rang the Mosessons and she toured again. She reported she found it comfortable and warm with old-world faded decadence; but that it was an oasis as she did not like Otley. We had an existential choice: "There are financial, prestige-related, literary, aesthetic, historical and social aspects." I felt the pressure of my coming *Classical Odes*, reflective poems set in country houses: "I may go and live in a house that reflects the English tradition from... the second half of the 12th century for its ownership is recorded in the reign of Richard I. Otley symbolises the Tudor and Elizabethan way of life and Merrie England." But I still felt the pull of Essex: "My reality is in Essex.... Should I not stay in Essex?... Am I an Essex (Epping Forest-Great Easton) writer and poet, or am I an East Anglian poet?"

We went for another drive into Suffolk via Lavenham. We drove several times up and down Hall Lane, looking at Otley Hall over the roadside hedge. We noted the cows and hay bales next door and bought eggs. We drove round and thought Otley not that bad. We had tea in the Swan at Lavenham. We returned to Great Easton for the night and next morning I saw two sheep at the bottom of my garden and felt joy. I was aware of my 'double life', torn between Great Easton and Otley Hall. I had two tangled Tudor knots.

We had been let down by our managing Head who, having had two terms' salary to learn the job in the schools, now wanted to push off to work in the Gulf on the strength of our training without delivering any policies. We initiated the search for a replacement, and Ann and I took our Bursar to Great Easton to view The Bell and then on to Otley Hall, which we saw in late sunlight. It looked magical. Mosesson greeted us and we toured the Hall. We counted five upstairs bedrooms and seven attic bedrooms. We toured the grounds and walked round the moat. We went up on the mound and sat on the seat and, the H-shaped water-garden below us, looked over the fields to Otley church. Ken said: "It's better than I thought." On the way home he went through the possible drawbacks. What if we failed to find an honest housekeeper? Two days later I went up to London and had a medical for life insurance for Otley Hall.

The day of decision arrived when sealed bids would be opened. The estate agent rang me. Otley Hall was offered to us so long as we exchanged contracts that night. I rang our bank manager, who said we could exchange. I rang our solicitor, who said, "Oh God, I've had an awful day." Nevertheless, Ann and I drove to his office in Epping and made phone calls to advance towards an exchange. Now a call came through to his desk from the estate agent saying that one of the others had offered more than us for the house only, with exchange on Monday evening. I told the estate agent, "My wife's interested in the house near Lavenham.... She'll look at it over the weekend. It's a wobble, they need to think it through." The estate agent told us that, contrary to the Mosessons' wishes, our rival did not want the furniture and would not open the Hall to the public.

The solicitor's switchboard was now off so we rang back by arrangement. The estate agent said, "No decision, they say they're leaving it till Monday." I said: "We'll offer another £5,000 for exchange now. It will be withdrawn on Monday, and we won't be around. We've been messed about. We've done everything asked of us." There was a pause. Then the estate agent said, "Ring back in ten minutes." I duly rang back. "Give us another five minutes, we're nearly there. It would be worth your while hanging on for five minutes." We waited five minutes. "We're there. Exchange contracts now. Let the solicitors speak." We signed and rang again. Contracts were deemed exchanged.

As we left we inadvertently set off the burglar alarm. The staff had gone home and set the alarm, not realising we were still there. Later I heard there were two other bids, one from the City and one from an American banker, a senior partner of Morgan Stanley.[4]

Transforming Otley Hall: classical odes
There was a lot to do before we moved in. We advertised in *The Lady* for a couple who would be cook-housekeeper and front-of-house caretaker. I returned to Otley Hall. I met the gardener, who agreed to continue working

under us. We interviewed seven couples for cook-housekeeper and front-of-house caretaker and we appointed a couple who had a home in Devon. They would live in the flat over the kitchen. I was interviewed by *The Times*, *The Daily Mail* and *The East Anglian Daily Times*.

We moved into Otley Hall on 21 February. Ann, Matthew and I arrived in separate cars – Anthony came with us – at 9.45 to find Anna Mosesson among the hens saying, "We're running late," and moving out still happening. While young people went to and fro carrying possessions I walked round with John ticking off the contents so we could complete. At around 11.30 I rang our solicitor and said he could complete, but the carrying backwards and forwards went on until 4 or 5 while our rat-catcher laid rat poison round the house and our electrician and plumber checked the systems. Eventually Matthew returned home and Ann and I made up our bed in the old Banqueting Room and slept. I felt deeply peaceful.

The next morning we had breakfast in the huge kitchen. The couple arrived and prepared lunch. Many photos were taken by *The Times* photographers. We now discovered that the light fittings for the conference kitchen had been stripped out, and the gardener told us that anything not on our list had been thrown in a skip. The next few days were filled with visits by a locksmith, burglar alarm vendor, BT, and more electrical and plumbing work, and the rat-catcher returned to deal with seven wasps' nests and six birds' nests in the loft. One wasps' nest was as big as a fridge-freezer. I met a secretary who had previously worked at Otley Hall, who agreed to be Administrator. We planned to raise revenue from Otley Hall from Open Days, guided tours, conferences, corporate entertaining and films.

I had a long meeting with the new Administrator, and in the evening I held a dinner for half a dozen tour guides she had rounded up. Sitting at the end of the kitchen table with the log fire burning in the grate I talked about the history of Otley Hall and we discussed the dating and Bartholomew Gosnold's role in the founding of America. I enthused them, and four of the six became permanent tour guides who would see through a coach tour or group of visitors on an hourly rate.

Very quickly we put a new system in place. The couple shopped and provided coffee and food when needed; the Administrator advertised and booked tours; there was a 'garden open' day each week when the public could walk round the grounds; and I aimed to be down at the beginning and end of each week.

We announced eight Open Days a year to coincide with bank holidays, the first two to be at the end of March. To get ready for these I needed to buy prints and Persian carpets. I drove to a warehouse between Frinton and Walton and bought a couple of dozen historical prints that would resonate with the public. Argie brought the warming-pan first owned by Hannah

Comfort (*see My Double Life 1: This Dark Wood*, p.6), which we hung on a kitchen wall. My cousin Jill and her husband arrived with more prints. A photocopier was installed and the four guides returned for a training afternoon, so we could all agree the dates of rooms they would be describing. Ann and I attended a carpet auction in Copdock and bought 14 Persian carpets which covered bare floors in the Great Hall, Linenfold Room, bedrooms and passages. I was interviewed by *The East Anglian Daily Times* (Cathy Brown) and a two-page spread appeared, 'Overlord of the Manor'. I was interviewed by the BBC Radio Suffolk (John Eley) in the Hall's grounds: two half-hour programmes that went out on 25 and 27 March. Nadia came for a night, sleeping in the Solar (which had the feel of being the oldest room in Otley Hall, part of the first build) and made signs to hang round the grounds and label the toilets. A local one-man builder painted outside gables from the top of a ladder. The gardener and front-of-house/caretaker worked frantically in the grounds. In a month we transformed the inside and outside of Otley Hall to get it ready for the first public viewings.

The weather was fine for our first Open Day. We opened at 1.30. Some 250 people came through, slowly at first. They parked by the bottom gate and walked round the moat. I addressed them in the Great Hall and Linenfold Room and shot upstairs to the main bedroom and sometimes addressed them there. They had a cream tea afterwards, and spent time poring over my books by the souvenir stall. Matthew manned the gates and his friend Dave patrolled the upstairs corridors along with Anthony. The next day brought a cloudless blue sky. We had 300 through. We talked to groups of 15 or 20 in the Great Hall.

Our front-of-house caretaker reported a conversation he had in the car park: "'Is the man of letters here?' 'Yes, he's here.' 'But can we see him?' 'Yes, you go up to the Hall and you'll see him.' 'But will we be able to speak to him?' 'He won't bite.'"

Dave's father came to collect Dave. He worked in GCHQ and told me: "I've been trying to work out who's behind the CIA. I don't think it's the American Government." I said it was 'Rockefellers' and expanded. He said: "They are the upper echelon, but they haven't got lower down, and they will fail." Later I pointed out that the M25 is a tank corridor and a ring that can besiege London, and he said; "It's obvious, everyone can see it."

We now prepared for the next Open Days on 4 and 5 May. I bought five peacocks, including a two-year-old blue with a wonderful tail and his mate, and two whites to bond them in. At night they roosted in trees near the Hall. I returned to Frinton and bought 87 more prints to distribute round the passages in Otley Hall. I had the chart of 25 civilizations that came with *The Fire and the Stones* framed and hung on the upstairs wall outside the Solar. I drafted a poem on Otley Hall, 'At Otley: Timber-Framed Tradition', which became the first classical ode in *Classical Odes*. (I then revised another ode, 'In Pheidias's Workshop'.) A group of twenty from Cambridge had a tour, and then dinner in the Linenfold Room (served by our front-of-house caretaker as butler and an Open-Day tea lady as maid), and though one of our guides had told them about the Hall they seemed more interested in my writing:

> They sent for me halfway through and asked me questions about *Overlord*. I stood by the fireplace, near [the portrait of] Robert [Gosnold] III, and answered a dozen questions.... I had much to tell them about Otley Hall and Bartholomew Gosnold but still the questions came: "What are you writing now?" It was me they wanted, not the past.

I was down in Suffolk a lot as it was the school holidays. The insurance company which insured Otley Hall sent their representative to interview me: the son of R.W.V. Robins, the captain of Middlesex cricket team in 1947. The interview was about cricket: how Robins Senior stood with folded arms glaring at Compton for being late, how Bradman became his godfather and how he has the cap Bradman wore on his 1948 tour as a memento. He left with only half the insurance questions properly answered.

We were back in Epping Forest for Anthony's birthday, and the family ate at a local Loughton restaurant, Wo Fat (which means 'Harmony and Prosperity'). That day Matthew had run to the Wake Arms and back via the two Forest ponds and Loughton Camp, and again I grasped that

> I can never escape the woodlands and want to write more about Epping Forest and Suffolk. My next project is to write poems that straddle the two.... When in Essex I can write about Suffolk; when in Suffolk, about Essex. I have to be away from the places I write about.

Again I was between opposites in my 'double life'.

I was being drawn deeper into Suffolk life. We looked in at the Otley Show to a see a friend's ram, a Shetland sheep that was black curly-horned, woolly, short-tailed and refined, win the 'Rare Breed' category. At Framsden, near Otley Hall, a meadow was filled with the rare snake's-head fritillary plant one weekend each year. Ann and I went to view on a Sunday: hundreds of purple mottled bells, drooping, hanging down, speckled like orchids, and many white – 300,000 in all according to *The Times*, and many cowslips. That evening I went out for a walk at twilight, loitered outside the Great Hall and heard the cuckoo from beyond the viewing mound, very clear. I had just dictated the first three stanzas of 'In Sybarite Paestum', a classical ode. I noted: "Blair is a cuckoo, pushing Major out of his nest."

On 1 May, Election Day, I voted. The Head of Coopersale Hall, Mrs. Best, was leaving and I appointed Sue Bowdler (who had been coming to Oaklands) to replace her under our managing Head. I then drove to Otley Hall and arrived for supper and watched the first returns from the election, which indicated a Labour landslide. I woke to news of a huge Labour majority next morning. I reflected on its true long-term significance:

> The break-up of the UK.... It is the end of the old Britain. From now on we are a European state.

(Labour devolution would lead to a Scottish vote for independence.) Later that day I drafted "a poem about the General Election", which during the next three-and-a-half weeks became my classical ode, 'Pastoral Ode: Landslide, The End of Great Britain'. Each stanza is connected with an aspect of Otley Hall or its grounds.

The next Open Day we had 234 visitors. I talked to groups in the Great Hall until 4.15 and then had tea. A swarm of bees gathered on a white post. I called a beekeeper, and he lifted them off with his bare hands, put them in a hive and gave me two jars of honey. The next day, also an Open Day, I worked on my 'Pastoral Ode':

> Images of Great Britain's pastoral life as found at Otley Hall, but reconciled with the political theme as in Virgil. Virgil is the model for my new eclogue-y, pastoral Georgics.... I now call it 'Pastoral Ode'.

Once again I addressed groups downstairs and upstairs.

During May I produced an outline for a film on Gosnold's voyages. On 17 February the owner of Charlestown harbour, Robin Davies, had arrived at my house down in Cornwall in a peaked cap with, in a brown wide-brimmed hat, Jack McAdam, General Manager at Mediterranean Film Studies in Malta, a screenwriter well connected in Los Angeles. I gave them coffee, showed them pictures of Gosnold's house and discussed the possibility of a film using the archives at Otley Hall. McAdam asked: "Could you send me a 30-page synopsis for a screenplay – on the circumstances and their lives." On 8 May McAdam proposed that we should work together. I posted my outline on 23 May. Writing the film script (later entitled *Gosnold's Hope* and subsequently entitled *The Founding of America*) would spur me into historical research that I could share with the guides and our visitors.

At another Open Day on 25 May we had 500 visitors. I went to court in Felixstowe to obtain a licence that allowed us to serve alcohol, and the next day two of the guides came to investigate the outside pillars under the

Banqueting Room, which they thought might be ships' masts from the *Concord* (Gosnold's ship during the 1602 voyage) or the *Godspeed* (his ship during the 1606–1607 voyage). We put together a narrative of the historical events involving Otley Hall. This would pass into booklets that we sold to the public, and eventually into a guidebook. A neighbour held another drinks gathering for us. I researched the wall-paintings in our bedroom (the Banqueting Room), which seemed to present members of the Gosnold family as busts on turf-altars to Roman gods in Ovid. (Arthur Golding, translator of Ovid's *Metamorphoses* in 1567, was doubly related to the Gosnolds.) Our one-man builder confirmed a theory of mine that the original front door into the screens passage of the Tudor Otley Hall had been relocated to the side of the 'Playhouse' (my ground-floor study). The measurements of the bolt-holes corresponded exactly.[5]

Death of John Broadley V

May was clouded by news of the terminal illness of John Broadley V, George II's son. I spoke to him over the phone. He told me he had cancer of the liver. I told him, "You're very philosophical." He said, "I've got to be, I can't be anything else." I told him, "There is an invisible body in the visible body," and "Things are worse in the imagination – the dreading – than in reality." He asked me to visit him, and I went on 21 May. I drove to Plumpton, where he had a view over the Downs. The hospice had said he was terrified of dying. His wife had avoided talking to him about death.

I sat with John. After we had talked for a bit I told him: "You will get drowsier and drift and come to and drift and come to and drift and go to sleep. Either there's nothing, in which case you are asleep; or there is something, in which case you will be an invisible body and there may be relatives at the ticket barrier." He smiled. He told me about his morphine pills and how he woke at 6 with pain in his liver. I said, "It's a wretched, wretched business." He said, "Yes, it's a wretched, wretched business. Goodbye, Nick." He was in tears. I was affected and later wrote a short story, 'Morphine and Tears'.[6] A week later, on 28 May, he was found lying dead.

The pro-Nazi Sherstons and Mrs. Schofield, Godolphin House

Our next Open Day, a fine, sunny day, brought 336 visitors. We had found more wall-paintings inside a bathroom cupboard, but we did not show these. An ex-Coopersale Hall parent was among the visitors. He said to me, "Such energy. Three schools and this house. You have done so much since February. And now more books. Such energy."

The next day was also an Open Day. We had 420. They included a man who had heard my lecture to the Quaker Universalists and a man who thought the gates Mrs. Sherston brought from Italy were baroque –

reflecting my neo-Baroque Age.

Two days later, on our way to Cornwall, I visited Mrs. Sherston's son and his wife in a nursing home in Sherborne, Dorset. Edric Sherston was sitting in a chair with his legs out, 85, white-haired. He had been an eyewitness of how all the rooms at Otley Hall were used and what happened in the grounds. He and his mother had been pro-Nazi in the 1930s and had been interned. He said that Sir Oswald Mosley stayed the night at Otley Hall just once, in 1937 (after the Blackshirts rally at Ipswich), sleeping in the Oak Room; whereas the evidence of others who worked at the Hall was that he frequently slept in the Banqueting Room, our bedroom. (Mrs. Sherston's room was the Solar.) Seven weeks later I read an obituary and learned that he had died. Later I wrote a short story, 'An Internee and Dribbled Chocolate'.

At Edric's suggestion I rang Mrs. Schofield, widow of Mrs. Sherston's architect in the 1930s. She and her husband had lived in Otley High House and she was now the owner of Godolphin House in Cornwall. She told me she had an Open Day the next day and would be pleased to see us. We drove to Godolphin House, a 15th-century building made into an ornamental, arched *façade* in the 17th century when it was the home of the poet Sidney Godolphin.

We were greeted imperiously by Mrs. Schofield, who was sitting in a chair at the top of the stairs, slight, grey-haired with firm eyes. We discussed Otley High House and Edric Sherston – everyone could hear what she said, both upstairs and downstairs – and then found Sidney Godolphin's room with an Elizabethan four-poster of 1590; and the King's Room, where Prince Charles (later Charles II) stayed after the battle of Naseby, and the King's gardens. Later I wrote a short story, 'The Lady Who Sat Upstairs'.

In the bookstore downstairs we met Angela Evans, who had bought Pengersick Castle from Mrs. Schofield's son. It had a Tudor garden and herbs – and Tudor ghosts. She invited us to visit her the next day.

Pengersick Castle, Praa Sands was a 13th-century grey castle and tall tower in a state of neglect. We started among the gigantic cobwebs in the cluttered kitchen (empty egg cartons, crumbs, dogs and cats everywhere, a filthy cooker and oven) and climbed from the Gun Room up the unswept spiral staircase to the haunted bedroom with a 17th-century four-poster bed, a faded bedcover in tatters and a musty smell, on to the library, and then to the battlemented turret at the top of the tower. There was a good view to the sea. On the way down I turned off the winding stair into the stone bedroom and felt uneasy: prickles up my spine, a sense that I was not alone. Nothing would have induced me to spend the night in that room.

Pengersick Castle is now regarded as one of the most haunted places in England, and has featured in many programmes on ghosts. Angela was very welcoming and well-informed, but we were glad to leave without eating anything. She died in 2008. I wrote a short story, 'A Tower and Cobwebs like Fishermen's Nets'.

On our way back to Essex we stopped again at Sherborne and visited Sherborne Castle. I managed to persuade a guide to take us to the third floor, which is not open to the public, to Sir Walter Raleigh's study and bedroom, where the School of Night met and Dee's black magic took place. I wrote a classical ode, 'At Raleigh's Sherborne'.

Now Otley Hall had to be got ready for a special Open Day for *Daily Telegraph* readers. A thousand bees had come down the chimney into our bedroom and were swarming on the window-ledge round the queen. I found bees dying on our bedroom floor, and more buzzing outside to get in and surround the queen. Soon afterwards a bat flew backwards and forwards in the passage between our bedroom and the stairs. It dipped and darted like a bird. I opened a diamond-lead window, rolled a copy of *The Sunday Times* and, batting left-handed, swatted it clean out of the window in mid-flight. A *Telegraph* photographer took a hundred pictures of me in different parts of the Hall to accompany an article by Anne Campbell Dixon, who had interviewed me on 5 June. (Her article appeared on 21 June with a picture of me sitting by the rose garden.)

Back in Loughton Argie invited a few friends, including Lord Murray, ex-General-Secretary of the TUC, the former Methodist minister Geoffrey Ainger and me, to a birthday tea, and I called all to order, asked if they were in good voice and led the singing of 'Happy Birthday'.

A few days later Lord and Lady Tollemache, friends of the Royal family, came to tea at Otley Hall. The Tollemaches lived two miles away in Helmingham and came as neighbours. We toured the Hall and the grounds and then we had tea and cakes in the Great Hall. I told them about our coming *Telegraph* day and asked whether we could collaborate by sharing coach tours. Tollemache said he only wanted a limited number of visitors each year. Lady Tollemache, once considered one of the most beautiful women in England, was now a garden designer, and she asked if she could take on our garden. However, she favoured informal gardens whereas I wanted Tudor areas: Tudor roses in our rose garden, a herb-and-knot garden and other Tudor re-creations.

The juxtaposition of tea with the ex-General-Secretary of the TUC and tea with the aristocratic Deputy Lieutenant of Suffolk within a few days contrasted two poles in British society, and my declining of the Tollemaches' garden design encapsulated the English aristocracy's loss of influence over the commercially-driven middle class.

Otley Hall: knot-garden

At Pengersick Castle Angela had sold me a book by Sylvia Landsberg, *The Medieval Garden*. She had told me that Sylvia had created five of the six medieval gardens in English institutions, and that she had studied the flowers in the illuminations (ornamental initial letters) of medieval manuscripts and was the leading authority in the country on what was grown in a medieval garden. I had contacted her on 10 June, three days before the visit of the Tollemaches, and she had agreed to come to Otley to plan a knot-garden and medieval herb-garden. I took Otley Hall's grounds in a Landsberg rather than a Tollemache direction.

Sylvia came on 23 June, and I spent the morning walking with her, identifying areas for different gardens, giving her the feel of the house and of my work. She had lunch in the kitchen with Ann and me, and the gardener joined us. We agreed there should be a herber by the barn, with a turf seat, and her response to my 'knot of Fire': a herb-and-knot garden with 25 beds and a central knot. She wanted the knot-garden to reflect my work and saw 25 beds of herbs as reflecting the 25 civilizations in *The Fire and the Stones*. The central knot would suggest the oneness of the universe which includes all civilizations. We chose the endless knot Elizabeth I embroidered on her prayer-book in 1544 when an innocent girl of 11, unaware that the hand doing the stitching would one day rule the rainbow (*see* p.xxii). Within it were two '8's, a double infinity symbol.

Elizabeth I's embroidered prayer-book of six knots, on one of which Sylvia Landsberg based her design for the knot-garden

It took us more meetings to create a metaphysical herb-and-knot garden: a Tudor knot. In addition to the herber she would design a vine-and-rose tunnel; an orchard; a *parterre*; and medieval areas within the herbaceous border. The rose garden would be reinforced with Tudor roses: *rosa mundi* and *rosa gallica*.

In January 1998 I phoned Sylvia Landsberg and discussed the knot-garden for an hour and a half. I gave her the philosophical picture: how it symbolised the universe. In the centre was a sphere, the great zero, a cosmic egg, the One or Nothing, eternal emptiness that is endlessly round. From it manifested eternity: Non-Being as Princess Elizabeth's endless knot; and Being or time, the *fleurs-de-lis* of history. From it came existence, outside the border. The knot-garden was about time and eternity, the One becoming the many, and the seeds or ingredients of the One. It could be seen as the world

Nicholas with Sylvia Landsberg. Middle: Otley knot-garden drawing, 25 civilizations. Right: Otley knot-garden

of physics emerging from the metaphysical, and all history coming out of the first civilization, the 25 flower-beds within the herb-and-knot garden being the 25 civilizations in my study of history, the early dead civilizations being in the centre, the most recent on the outside. It could also be literature, with poems showing the One and poems, stories and other works showing the many.

Getting the intricate 1544 knot to suggest all these resonances would not be easy, and I said in jest, "We have an intractable knot like the one Alexander the Great encountered. If we can't untie it we need drastic action, we may have to cut the Gordian knot." She said smilingly, "I want to sign your copy of *The Medieval Garden* saying we have unravelled or untied the Gordian knot, not cut it." When she visited Otley Hall on 29 July 1999 to look at her finished work she wrote in the front of my copy of *The Medieval Garden*, "Together we have explored the Gordian knot."

Otley Hall: more transforming and delving
I was transforming Otley Hall in many different ways. On 16 June I hosted lunch for a group from Richmond, Virginia, which included the curator of the museum, Dr Charlie Bryan, who invited me to visit Richmond the following year. I would have a platform to promote Gosnold's role in founding America. A week later, I attended an auction in Felixstowe and bought a longcase clock with a moon face, *fleurs-de-lis* on top and a pleasant 'ting-ting' chime. (The 'ting-ting' was caused by a cracked bell, and the clock was said to be c.1790.) This would stand at the bottom of the stairs and be inspected by hundreds of visitors to Otley Hall.

John Mosesson took me to the Jubilee Hall, Aldeburgh to hear an Aldeburgh-Festival lecture by Prof. Sayeed on colonialism. (Jeremy Thorpe was sitting in the front row, an old man with Parkinson's disease.) I saw that I could give a lecture on European culture from the same stage, and focus the audience on Otley Hall. I raised the idea with him over lunch at his new home in Crag Walk, and through Mosesson, the Head of the Aldeburgh

Foundation and the Mayor of Aldeburgh I arranged to give a lecture on the Revolution in philosophy, history and literature on 3 October.

Two days later I swapped our two black swans for two white cygnets at a bird farm in Copdock. (Swans are royal birds and cannot be bought, but in certain circumstances they can be swapped.) Our two white swans would attract great interest among visitors to Otley Hall.

The Daily Telegraph Open Day on 28 June was for *Telegraph* readers only, who had to carry a copy of *The Telegraph* to be admitted. We had 150 between 10.30 and 6, against 500 between 2 and 6 at our last Open Day. However some visitors booked future tours. All these developments combined to further the transformation of Otley Hall.

The mid-summer Open Days were disappointing. We agreed to open on a weekend that was not a bank holiday. There were many other competing events, and too few heard about the new pattern. Two days later we let a group of student actors put on *The Tempest* on the rose-garden lawn. About 100 came, and after dusk the shadows of the actors fell across the floodlit *façade* of the back (once the front) of Otley Hall. Four days later Otley Hall's insurer, Richard Robins, invited me to Lord's along with a dozen others (including the High Sheriff of Suffolk) to watch Middlesex play the Australian touring team. We had lunch in a hospitality room watching the cricket on the ground where his father R.W.V. Robins had played so often. I wrote a short story, 'A Ghost at Lord's'.

On 1 August we were visited by Michael Godsel, who was 14 when Mrs. Sherston left him Otley Hall in 1950. He was Edric's godson, and told me that Mrs. Sherston had fallen out with Edric over his farm failures. As Michael was a minor, advisers ran Otley Hall. They let it out as an old people's home and to Suffolk County Council, and eventually sold it and all the contents at auction in 1959. Michael told me that at Hampton Court he was told, "If you want to see the finest linenfold in England, go to Otley Hall. It is finer than Hampton Court's Wolsey Rooms." As he owned Otley in 1528, the year his school in Ipswich was opened, it is possible that Wolsey had his eye on Otley Hall and had a hand in installing its linenfold panelling.

We went to Cornwall for a fortnight. I had found a sundial with a motto in Elizabethan English: "Amyddst ye fflowres I tell ye houres." I drafted my classical ode, 'Contemplations by a Sundial'. We picked the sundial up from Dorset on our way to Cornwall, and drove it back via the Secretary of the British Sundial Society in an (unsuccessful) attempt to date it from Mrs. Gatty's 1880 *The Book of Sun-Dials*. I eventually installed it in a meadow of wild flowers between the vine-and-rose tunnel and the H-shaped lake.

At the last Open Day a visitor had given me the telephone number of Mrs. Wells, who was undermaid at Otley Hall from 1936 to 1940 and therefore an eyewitness of the Sherstons' pro-Nazi activities. She told me over the phone: "I have taken Mosley his cup of tea in the morning. Many, many times. Mrs. Sherston and Edric clicked their heels and 'Heil-Hitlered' him. I wouldn't do that, I knew it wasn't right." She was also in Otley Hall the day the maid Annie Self drowned herself in the moat. Edric had told me he had found her under the weeping willow. She told me that she had heard Annie walk past her door on her way to drowning herself from the steps the cat fished from.

Winnie Wells visited Otley Hall at my invitation on 23 August. She was now a little old lady in glasses, virtually blind with a stick. She had memories of the kitchen and the servants' hall which extended from the kitchen wall to the Linenfold chimney. As we walked round she remembered where all the steps were. She was a 'between maid' – between kitchen and scullery – but she doubled up as housemaid and parlourmaid (serving at dinner). She had many stories about Mrs. Sherston's tyrannical outlook towards the staff. She said she had to serve Sir Oswald Mosley at least 50 times. He called her 'Winnie' at the end. She had to go round and put the tea tray on the table beyond his bed in the Banqueting Room, where I now slept. He would playfully tug her apron strings, so she got the butler to take the tea. At table Mosley sat in the Moat Room, his back to the moat. Mrs. Sherston wanted to be 'Heil-Hitlered' by anyone who entered her business room, my Playhouse study. She said there was never anything between him and Mrs. Sherston, it was only political. She saw Mrs. Sherston and Edric driven away in a car to be interned. They were expecting internment and did not say goodbye. The police gave the maids half a crown each to say nothing. I wrote a short story, 'A Drowning and Tugged Apron Strings.'

The next day was Open Day and we had nearly 400 visitors. The following day we had 305. The next day I was visited by Jocelyn Wingfield, a descendant of Edward-Maria Wingfield who was in charge of the Jamestown Fort in early 1607.

I had spent the summer making a selection from my two volumes of short stories and a selection from *Overlord*. I had been revising some of my classical odes, drafted during my travels; for example, 'In the Serbian Orthodox Church at Szentendre' and 'Summer Palaces'. I finished the structure for the film on Gosnold's voyage. McAdam had told me to put the structure on cards, each 10 minutes: 3 for set-up, 6 for confrontation and 3 for resolution. Down in Cornwall I had completed the cards:

The set-up is the failure of the 1602 colony; then there is the confrontation of trying to get another journey going and reaching Virginia; and then there is the answer to the question, will the colony survive?

On our return we went to a pageant in King's Lynn, Norfolk: *Pocahontas*. There were scenes from 1606, and before. I had a fax from Jack McAdam. He said that my outline was "very good" so far, and that I should now write it. Dr Charlie Bryan of the Virginia Historical Society had tea at Otley Hall, and again invited me to Richmond, Virginia. He promised that I would see parts of the stockade at Jamestown that the public cannot see.

During that summer our housekeeper and front-of-house caretaker had caused some concern. They accepted a dinner invitation from a neighbour and agreed to take part in the village's play, which would require daily rehearsals during lunchtimes. The two helpers in our Tea Room, who also wore black and white at more formal events, asked to see us. They reported that our caretaker had claimed to members of the public at our last Open Day to have bought Otley Hall from the sale of his ten-acre farm in Devon. They said he was posing as me, greeting the public as the owner as they parked their cars. They reported that there had been indiscreet talking that could bring the Hall into disrepute. We needed our housekeeper to stay until the end of the season so I had a chat with the couple. When we returned from Cornwall they were still talking indiscreetly in the village, and they resigned on 24 September, blaming a personality clash with our Administrator.[7] Another knot was untangled.

My lecture at Aldeburgh, 'Revolution in Thought and Culture', and The One and the Many
I spent three months reflecting on and writing the lecture I was to give at Aldeburgh on 3 October. I was clear that my lecture could declare a revolution against secular culture and restore the metaphysical perspective. I knew it would be a section in a forthcoming book. (It appeared in *The One and the Many*, and its main idea passed into *A New Philosophy of Literature*.)
I had written:

The Revolution's aims are to reconnect philosophy, history and literature..., to enhance a sense of the One. Its antecedent is the Baroque.... Universalism emphasises the oneness of all.

It was "about a philosophical return to traditional metaphysics and global history and a poetry of search for truth". I reflected wryly: "It is like standing on the barricades in *Les Miserables*.... Someone has to, and I am calling for support.... The Revolution is a crusade to make the culture better." I discussed the Revolution with Michael Mann on my way to Cornwall.

Down in Cornwall I worked on my lecture late at night and wrote: "I am talking about... a movement to restore cultural unity." The next day I "wrote on and off in the evening and finished my lecture". Two days later I finished combing my lecture: "Universalism is a movement listed in stage 44 of Europe's civilization.... I am on the side of Matthew Arnold, really.... I am... a cultural observer."

Back in Essex I was clear about my role in society:

The only way for the artist to recover contact with his culture's roots is to go back to the past and reflect its vitality in images. In a healthy culture, cultural vitality is reflected in creative vitality.... In an unhealthy culture the artist has to go back into the past and rediscover his roots – and then the cultural vitality of the past makes for creative vitality, makes the artist have creative vitality, and it can transform European culture. Yeats, Eliot and Pound all recoiled from the... "heap of broken images" which made them "grimace". They pined for the "ceremonies of innocence" which had been drowned in the blood of the First World War. Pound hankered for the ceremonies of Eleusis. He makes an epic journey into the past to ransack it and "shore his ruins" with fragments.... Eliot asks, "What are the roots that clutch, what branches grow/Out of this stony rubbish?" meaning his culture, which has collapsed.... The only way for an artist in an unhealthy culture to recover contact with his culture's roots is to go back to the past and reflect its vitality in images.

That was what I was doing in my classical odes – visiting places of past vitality and reflecting their vitality in images to perpetuate them in the present.

I linked my preoccupation with culture to the work of the 'Heroes of the West':

The 'Heroes of the West' stood up to Communism, in the West's best interests. The 'Heroes of the West' are now... engineering a metaphysical, much-needed cultural movement, a Revolution. Universalism is a project of the 'Heroes of the West'.

The Otley Hall Administrator spread word of my lecture. She spoke to John Ezard. To Crozier she said: "I believe you spoke with Nicholas at the Enoch Powell evening". Leaflets were sent out. The first paragraph of the press release said:

Today we have branches of secular, Humanistic, cultural diversity and multi-culturalism, but we have lost the sap of the essentially European vision that gave Europe its stupendous works of art.

I came down to Suffolk and at midnight found a warm letter from Asa Briggs. Also, a letter from John Ezard who read *Overlord* for four days in the Isle of Wight recently and discussed it with Sebastian Barker at the funeral of Jeffrey Barnard. I was interviewed by *The East Anglian Daily Times* (Cathy Brown) and a two-page spread about my Revolution appeared on 1 October 1997, 'Bridging the cultural divide'.

In the early evening Lady Bronwen Astor rang: "Hello Nicholas, it's Bronwen." In the course of our talk she said: "If you're ahead of your time it takes time for your time to catch up. What wonderful things you're doing. Providence has plans for you, it will just happen." We spoke of my presence at Cliveden before the Profumo affair. "If it's an accident, you were there by chance. If not an accident, there's a different significance to it." A few days later I learned that the Prince of Wales had asked to see a transcript or text of my lecture. The next day there was a short article in *The Sunday Times* mentioning my "titanic work *Overlord*".

I visited Aldeburgh with the Administrator. Various shops agreed to take posters about my lecture. We visited the Aldeburgh Bookshop and van der Post's house. (The lady who had bought from him told me that five years previously he was too "poorly" to come down.) I was interviewed on Suffolk Radio in Ipswich by John Eley, a roly-poly priest, very Chaucerian, round and bald with twinkling eyes like Hubert. We talked as we walked through his studio and he sat me at a microphone. I had to express the Revolution in half an hour of live interview without using long words, so all could understand – and did so. At the end he said, "You have the gift of making it understandable. You didn't lose me once." Graeme Fletcher, Valerie Eliot's nephew, rang to say that Valerie had returned from a celebration of the parish of East Coker's 700 years of unbroken adminis-tration the previous day and did not seem to have received details of my lecture.

On the day of my lecture Ann and I arrived at the Jubilee Hall before 5. I walked by the North Sea while the sound engineer set up, then sat in a little room at the back while people came in. I emerged from behind a curtain and spoke at the spotlit lectern. I delivered my 'Revolution in Thought and Culture' and made my declaration challenging the present state of European culture. I spoke for an hour and a half and there was half an hour of questions. After that Ricky Herbert turned up, having missed the lecture, taking four and a half hours from London on a Friday night.

Ricky stayed the night at Otley Hall and asked me many questions about the house. He had somehow organised my Oxford acquaintance David Sladen into ringing me. I said: "Not *the* David Sladen?" He said: "Yes." I said: "The David Sladen who dropped his cigarette in a chair while talking about solipsism and leapt off with great alacrity?" (*See My Double Life 1: This*

Dark Wood, p.96.) He said: "Yes, it proved the point I expect." In fact it defeated his solipsistic argument as it proved the existence of something other than himself that was real enough to cause him to flee. He had read *A Mystic Way* and said he was "very impressed" and would like to discuss metaphysics. He said: "I went wrong, I followed the Beats: there wasn't much metaphysics around at Oxford in our day. I wasted time." I said: "At the best the Beats stood for Beatitude and were neo-Blakean. At the worst they were neo-layabouts." I walked with Ricky. He said: "I'm sorry I missed your lecture but I've read your books." That was all. I saw myself as having delivered a lecture in the tradition of Arnold's 'Culture and Anarchy', but he did not take this up. I found I had moved on from how he thought. Some of those who attended the lecture visited Otley Hall that afternoon. Soon afterwards Ricky wrote that he was reading my poems and liked some of the sonnets.

A week later I sent off texts of my address, revised it into book form and chose pieces for a book – "to be called what? Part One is 'The Metaphysical Universe'; Part Two: 'Universalism'; and Part Three, 'Civilization and Culture'". My lecture took me straight to the three-part structure of *The One and the Many* (the only change being that Part Two would be 'Universalism in Philosophy').

I worked on *The One and the Many* from 15 October, throughout November and December, on and off. I was referring to the book as *The One and the Many* by the end of November.

My talk in Cambridge, 'In the Garden of the One'
I had been asked by fax to speak at a literary lunch in Cambridge, after a speaker on European garden architecture, and on the last day of December I spent much of the day writing 'In the Garden of the One', drawing on Parmenides and Goethe but also Marvell, deriving my tradition from the Metaphysicals, Romantics and Zen and referring to our knot-garden and Universalism. I did more work on this on 20 January, and a week later drove to Cambridge and in the Garden House Moat Hotel, Mill Street I sat on top table while May Woods gave a slide show on Renaissance gardens. Over coffee I gave a half-hour address, 'In the Garden of the One', from a lectern at my place. It was well received.[8]

Screenplay about Bartholomew Gosnold, Gosnold's Hope (*later* The Founding of America)
I spent eight months writing the screenplay for Jack McAdam. I had heard that he was leaving Malta to go to Los Angeles the following June, to be Director and Producer of MFS (Mediterranean Film Studios). Through Angela Evans I arranged to visit Compton Castle just outside Torquay on

our way home from Cornwall. It had been the home of Sir Humphrey Gilbert, half-brother of Sir Walter Raleigh and voyager to Newfoundland, which he annexed. He was the first pioneer of empire (and gave John Dee the rights to all American produce north of the 50° parallel). The Castle was now owned by his descendant Geoffrey Gilbert. Gilbert, who had gentle eyes, showed me the Solar, where the two half-brothers would have sat, and we pored over Raleigh's family tree.

I did three-quarters of the first draft by 31 December and, with suggestions from Jack McAdam and my younger son Tony Hagger (who was on his way to becoming a film director) set about turning it from a documentary into "a gripping, ripping yarn". McAdam faxed to say that my new approach was exactly what was needed and was giving it momentum. I finished *Gosnold's Hope* at Great Easton towards the end of March. I wrote the speech Gosnold makes from the pulpit while 20 sheep watched me from the field. I was still amending the script in early August when McAdam took up his new position in Los Angeles.[9] The screenplay is now titled *The Founding of America*.

Death of Ann's mother

Meanwhile, down in Cornwall Ann's mother had been found to be terminally ill, with suspected cancer of the oesophagus (or gullet). On 16 October she rang me to say she had had a letter telling her to go to Royal Cornwall Hospital, Truro for tests the following Monday. Ann found a nursing home for her while investigations continued. We visited her consultant and surgeon at St Austell Community Hospital and heard him confirm that she had cancer and that it was spreading into her lungs. She wanted to go home, so we found a local country cousin. A week later Ann returned to Cornwall.

On the morning of Monday 10 November, Ann's mother had an appointment with the consultant to be told that she had cancer. At 8.30 a.m. she had a heart attack while drinking a cup of tea in bed and died. The timing of her departure was perfect as she was never told of the seriousness of her condition, she had been saved a lot of suffering and had died at home. The coroner told us that an autopsy had established that she also had cancer of the stomach and round her kidneys, and had died of heart failure caused by stomach cancer.

Anthony and I joined Ann in Cornwall and visited her in the chapel of rest (which was manned by our Charlestown neighbour). The next day, the day of the funeral, I returned with Matthew and her sister Pat. The funeral was in St Austell. We followed the coffin down the aisle. The vicar said in his eulogy that she had been the daughter of a tin-miner who grew up in Pendeen and left for Northern Rhodesia, returned to Cornwall when her father was killed, was a Waaf in the war, married in that church, went to

Huddersfield and then returned to Cornwall for the last 30 years of her life. After the lowering of the coffin into the grave in the cemetery Ann went forward first and threw in her flowers, and then I threw earth. There was a buffet lunch back at her house for family and friends. I felt a heaviness in my heart. Now there were no grandparents for the boys. It was just us. And I had learned that Ann's creeping osteoarthritis was a family condition on her father's side.[10]

Collected Stories, *vol. 3*, Wheeling Bats and a Harvest Moon
I had begun compiling my third volume of short stories, *Wheeling Bats and a Harvest Moon* on 18 July 1987, and had nearly reached halfway. I had been encouraged by a call from Graeme Fletcher saying that he had found *A Spade Fresh with Mud* in the Sunderland library and that it had been well stamped and read; and by a letter from Asa Briggs praising the "imaginative power" of my "achievement" in *Overlord* and *The Warlords*.

Down in Cornwall we went to St Benets Abbey, and I wrote 'Love Like a Cheek-Warming Log-Burner'. Three days later, on 17 February 1998, I finished my third volume of stories, *Wheeling Bats and a Harvest Moon*: "I now have my third book of stories."[11]

Otley Hall and Tudor knots; deaths of A.L. Rowse and Frank Tuohy
At Otley Hall the housekeeper and her husband had left on October 21 after working their notice. They went on to look after a housemaster at Eton. We conducted interviews and found a new couple. In November the TV programme *Collector's Lot* came to Otley Hall. On the first day I was filmed giving a guided tour of Otley Hall. A young director (Emma Hallett) came with a presenter (Helen Atkinson-Wood). They had filmed outside and in the Great Hall. I had to 'voice-over', which meant imagining I was standing outside and describing the gables, Elizabethan chimneys and the moat. It is hard to describe to camera what you cannot see but have to recall and imagine. We then went from room to room with me detailing the history.

On 18 and 19 November there was a film crew of 20 and collectors laid out their collections throughout the ground floor. Sue Cook was the presenter, and on the second day I was interviewed describing the main historical events during Otley Hall's history and showing my Roman coins and coins of English monarchs from Richard I to Charles II. Eric Bristow, ex-world darts champion, was a guest. The programme was shown on channel 4 on 8 December.

That winter we found out more about Otley Hall. An 'expert' came to look at the wall-paintings we had discovered in a bathroom cupboard. (They had been painted over and were revealed when our odd-job builder was redecorating.) Sylvia Landsberg came and we discussed the herb-garden and focused on Princess Elizabeth's knot. Aware that Hadrian's garden at Tivoli represented the Roman Empire, I reflected that the centre of my knot-garden at Otley Hall represented my empire: three schools and Otley Hall, four properties in Princess Elizabeth's endless knot, as in my ring. (I had long worn a puzzle ring on the fourth finger of my left hand.) I was very aware that in the centre there were two '8's on their sides, a double infinity symbol, and I wrote: "My garden at Otley should represent my life's effort in relation to the One." I told myself: "Somewhere an 'N' and an 'A'." (The 'N' and 'A', for 'Nicholas' and 'Ann', would later be woven into the top of the thatch on the summer-house.)

A leading expert on wood, Professor Oliver Rackham of Cambridge University, came, a man with shock-white hair and a white beard. He identified a first phase which included the letters on either side of the old door to the Great Hall, 'RC', as standing for Robert Cressener, c.1450. The beams in the Great Hall and *fleurs-de-lis*, he said, were of the same time. The second phase included the windows of the Great Hall, c.1510. During the day he identified later phases. We hosted groups and a lunch for 40. I went to Ipswich Museum for drinks and visited the Tudor and Stuart Gallery, where the curator told me: "The lion and the unicorn is a Stuart symbol – the unicorn symbolised the Stuarts and Scotland." I reflected that "the lion fought the unicorn" referred to England fighting Scotland.

We went to Cornwall and learned that A.L. Rowse had died. A neighbour told me, "I often used to see him in Charlestown. He'd come in to get his hair cut, and then go again. He wouldn't speak to anyone. He was a snob. He was Labour but he wouldn't speak to you." We returned via Frank Tuohy in Yarlington. At Shatwell Farm Tuohy came to the door, shuffling and stooping and jowly, holding – tipping – a glass of red wine at a spillable angle and speaking in breathless sentences. He looked unwell. We sat in his upstairs room and I tried to hear what he was saying. His dog was incontinent and the room smelt. We had lunch downstairs. Anthony, who was with us and questioned him about Henry James's *The Turn of the Screw*, later remarked: "I learned nothing new. I know more about it than he does." When I asked Tuohy, "Do you read?" he replied: "No, only my own books." At 72 Tuohy had grown old, and this was the last time I saw him.

In April 1999, Nadia rang to tell me that Frank Tuohy's obituary was in *The Times*. I did not know he had died of a heart attack the previous Sunday. The obituary said he had a niche in English literature which he made his own: psychological insecurities and embarrassments, the difficulty of communication across cultures and the web of deceit in which we entrap ourselves. He was compared to E.M. Forster.

We spent Christmas in Essex. The husband of our new housekeeper rang from Otley to say that the female swan had died in the H-shaped lake that morning. It was later found to have died of lead poisoning after shovelling up lead shot from the bottom of the lake. We all drove to Otley Hall for Boxing Day and ate in the linenfold room by candlelight. I sat under the portrait of Robert III at one end of the table and Ann at the other end, the boys in the middle on each side, and our caretaker waited on us as butler. Three days later our most handsome blue peacock, which had gone missing, was discovered dead in an orchard near the White Hart.

I was still writing poems and stories. On 1 January we went to Boulge's tiny church and found the grave of the poet Edward Fitzgerald, whose *Rubaiyat* I had taught in Baghdad. I later wrote a poem, 'In Boulge Churchyard'. (On the way back I visited Letheringham Priory, the church of the Wingfields and Nauntons of Otley Hall.) Valerie Eliot's nephew rang. He had read my stories. He agreed they were in the Eliotian imagistic tradition – epiphanies in language like 'The Waste Land'. He liked their metaphysical flavour.

The schools were stable. The consolidation of Normanhurst was continuing. Sue Bowdler had begun as Head at Coopersale Hall. Our managing Head at Oaklands had resigned due to personal difficulties and Ann had stood in. We had had to underpin Oaklands during the summer holidays. We had interviewed and appointed a new Head, who started at Oaklands in January.

I attended a reception at Winterstoke, Bury Road, Sewardstonebury at which Chingford's MP Iain Duncan Smith spoke at length. Derek Higgins, the local builder and property developer, was standing next to me. He caught my eye and then leaned back against the light switch and 'accidentally' plunged the room into darkness. The speech came to an abrupt end. When the lights came back on I asked him, "Did you mean to do that?" He looked at me mischievously. Two days later I "woke with a story in mind, 'A Broken Arm and Flickering Lights'."

I had set out my 'Garden of the One'. I reflected that if my work were set in the Roman times

> it would all fit together like pieces of a jigsaw. We would have portraits of the villa-owners, scenes from the wars and interpretations of history, philosophy and religion. The poems are about everyday life in relation to the One.

Oliver Rackham returned to Otley Hall. We had coffee in the Linenfold Room. He said the linenfold panelling would have come on a horse and cart. I took him to Otley church and he found many tons of stones from Normandy, c.1500. I took him to the Mount, which is near Netherhall field and pottery. He said: "This would have been the original Netherhall."[12]

At Bourn Hall, seat of Haggers
I had traced the name 'Hagger' back to the 'Hacgards' of Suffolk and also to the 'Hagars' of Bourn, Cambridgeshire. I had made a note to visit Bourn at the next opportunity.

On my return from speaking about the 'Garden of the One' in Cambridge, I had visited the church of Bourn, where the Haggers were lords of the manor between the 16th and 18th centuries. I looked at the mizmaze and spoke to a white-haired man who showed me four Hagger graves in the church floor. It was like seeing myself and my family buried there. I took away some pamphlets on the Haggers by a local author, Margaret Greenwood. They told how John Hagger had bought the lordship of the manor of Rigglesby-Bourn during the reign of Elizabeth I, and how Bourn Hall had become an infertility clinic. I took Ann to Bourn a week later and we had lunch in the Golden Lion and visited Margaret Greenwood.

She took us through her lists of the Haggers at Bourn. We visited the church with her and "found the four tombstones in the south-transept floor, two and a half of which were readable". (*See* chapter 1 of *My Double Life 1: This Dark Wood.*) We walked to Bourn Hall where the Medical Director, Peter Brinsden, was waiting. He showed us the outside: guttering dated 1607 marked H with I F beneath it ('Hagar'/'Hagger', 'Iohannes'/'John' and 'Frances'). He showed us the Tudor door and dry moat and we toured the inside – the entrance hall, study, wine cellar and long room – and admired the many fine Tudor features. We visited the Tudor stable block, and had tea in the long room. We returned to Margaret Greenwood who showed us a paten – a shallow dish for communion bread – inscribed: 'The Gift of Frances Hagar to the Church of Bourn 1694/5.' Was I descended from the Bourn Haggers? That was another Tudor knot.

Through Angela Evans I had been put in touch with a heraldic 'expert' and researcher who sent me copies of fines in Latin for the Haggers from 1550 to 1591. (A 'fine' was 'money paid by an incoming tenant in return for the rents being small'.) In 1550 John Hagger was listed as "John Hagger gent". Later he sent me information showing that my great-grandfather was born in Therfield, 10 miles south of Bourn.

In July I visited Bourn again with Ann and Anthony to see a performance of *Twelfth Night* to the side of Bourn Hall, the house the Haggers built. The actors performed in the open air with the house sometimes behind them. We sat on the sloping bank and afterwards Peter Brinsden pointed out floodlit features on the outside of the Hall.[13]

Verse plays: **The Tragedy of Prince Tudor** *and theme of government*
At the Globe: Mark Rylance, Derek Jacobi
I believed (as I had been taught by Ricks) that Shakespeare's works had been

written by Shakespeare of Stratford, but I was interested in listening to the arguments of those who championed other playwrights as Shakespeare. Anthony I had visited the Globe theatre, where Oxfordians were holding a meeting. There were talks on the dating of Shakespeare's plays and on the dedication to the sonnets. Over coffee I spoke to the Earl of Burford, who I had heard at Hay. He told me he was now living in South Woodford, not far from Oaklands. He reminded me he was directly descended from both Edward de Vere and the Earl of Southampton, Shakespeare's patron, who had reputedly funded Gosnold's 1602 voyage. During lunch in the Globe restaurant I spoke with Derek Jacobi. We all sat in the Globe theatre and Mark Rylance (Artistic Director) addressed us for an hour, wearing a brown hat and standing where the groundlings stand. We were then invited to climb onto the stage to get the feel, and, standing on the Globe stage, I asked Rylance if he was interested in modern verse plays and produced *The Warlords*. He said: "Oh, it's Nicholas. I've got this." Peter Donebauer had given him a copy.

Afterwards Anthony and I walked past the sites of the Rose theatre and of the old Globe. Rylance had said that all actors have a secret place within them they can only unlock by "lying to tell the truth". I wrote a story, 'Prancing Truth-Tellers at the Globe'.

The Earl of Burford asks to work at Otley Hall
A few days I received a letter from the Earl of Burford asking if he could work with me. I thought he might have a money-generating role at Otley Hall and be my Literary Secretary. I rang him and he said he might move to Suffolk and rent.

The next day there was a phone call from a lady at the Globe. Could the cast of *The Merchant of Venice* come for three days to Otley Hall and live there and get the feeling of an authentic Elizabethan house? And could the cast of *As You Like It* do the same in the woods at Otley Hall? I detected Rylance's hand behind the call. (In the event, the cast of *The Merchant of Venice* never came.)

The next day the Earl of Burford, Charles, a brown-haired man with a Tudor-style beard, came to 6 Albion Hill. We talked for three hours. He told me he would inherit the Dukedom of St Albans on his father's death, and said of my books: "Your work is like a cathedral amid modern buildings." He came down to Otley Hall and spoke of Shakespeare's metaphysical outlook. He came again and spoke of getting *The Warlords* on stage as a verse play by selecting from the two Parts to make one performable play. This we eventually did.

A week later he told me that Jacobi wanted to read *The Warlords* and that two specialist Shakespearean libraries could be housed at Otley Hall. I said

I would shelve the Literary Room to accommodate the books.

At the beginning of March Charles moved to a rented house in Martlesham and soon afterwards brought his wife, the Countess, to Otley Hall: a long-haired woman in tight legwear with a Canadian accent. Charles started as my Literary Secretary at Otley Hall on 9 March. I talked with him in my study about my work and goals.

Two days later he took me to meet Gillon Aitken, the literary agent, in the World's End area of Chelsea. Gillon greeted us in shirtsleeves and a red waistcoat and gave us coffee in a large booklined room. I freewheeled, and Gillon distinguished my past work from my future work. He wanted to discuss my new work. It was difficult as I had a publisher who was planning to publish future books.

At the end of March Charles and I were interviewed by Cathy Brown of *The East Anglian Daily Times*. She focused on Shakespeare and our literary efforts, and Charles told her that "the problem facing Shakespeare was 'Should society be built on metaphysical or secular foundations?'" A week later the newspaper sent a photographer to take our photo, and the article appeared on 13 May 1998.

I am asked to house Shakespearean Authorship Trust and De Vere Society libraries at Otley Hall and to be a trustee of the SAT

The specialist Shakespearean libraries turned out to be the De Vere Society library – three of the Society's committee members came to Otley Hall and agreed to hand the books over for shelving in our Literary Room, where Charles had a desk – and the library of the Shakespearean Authorship Trust (SAT), which began in 1922 as the Shakespeare Fellowship. The SAT library consisted of some 3,000 books on Shakespeare and the authorship question, many of which were published in the 19th and early 20th centuries and were now out of print. In Loughton I was rung by John Silberrad (the Chairman of the Conservatives who had moved to oust Norris). He was a trustee of the Shakespearean Authorship Trust and would be happy to put the books into Otley Hall. (He said, "I got a letter from the Earl of Burford this morning, saying that you own Otley Hall and that he's working for you." I said: "It's true.") As the two libraries would be put together in one room, I would be able to delve into Edmund Blunden's question: "Where is the trunk containing Shakespeare's last papers?"

On 15 May Dr Ware and John Silberrad, the two surviving trustees of the SAT, came to lunch at Otley Hall. Ware was 90 and made a big impression over lunch when he wrapped the uneaten half of his cheese roll in a paper napkin and put it in his pocket "because it is so tasty". (Perhaps he would eat it with his supper.) Afterwards they toured the Hall and saw where the books would be shelved. Ware and Silberrad asked me if I would join them as a trustee. I saw it would give me a good window on Shakespeare: I would continue to believe that Shakespeare of Stratford wrote Shakespeare unless there was hard evidence elevating one of the 60–70 proposed alternatives, and if there *was* such evidence, all except one of the alternatives had to be pretenders. I agreed to become a trustee. In June I suggested that Charles, the Earl, would be a fourth trustee. There was opposition from the other two, and I had to be very persuasive to get Charles made a trustee.[14]

The Tragedy of Prince Tudor
The Globe's contact with Otley Hall inspired me to return to verse plays. With Charles I discussed a new philosophical work which we thought might be called *The Knot-Garden*. "The Gordian knot echoes [i.e. resonates]… but it is about the tangled knot, cf chains of events, and civilizations, that emerge from the eternal…. I have a poetic collection on the same theme." *Classical Odes*, book one, was called 'A Tudor Knot'. I had thought in February that I should write a verse play about England.[15]

I told Charles that I would write a verse play on the international situation and current affairs, which I would present in terms of the syndicate behind the New World Order, influential families – notably 'Rothschilds' and 'Rockefellers' – that sought world rule so they could increase their billions by profiting from the earth's natural resources. I would show the increasing powerlessness of the UK under its machinations, and would present a prince whose kingdom might disappear before he came to the throne. My Prince Tudor would be a philosophical Prince with a dwindling kingdom before the increasing power of a United States of Europe, itself a creation of the Treaty of Rome, a project of the Bilderberg Group formed from the dynastic 'Rothschild' and 'Rockefeller' families.

Such a scenario would later be familiar to supporters of the United Kingdom Independence Party (UKIP) and of Scottish independence, but in 1998 the suspicious death of Princess Diana and other events were too close and I had to use unfamiliar names in the 1999 version. The 2007 edition of the play would remove what in the Preface I called "the obfuscating names". I wrote: "The Prince is frustrated and marginalised, he wants the Crown to have impact…. He is marginalised, a Montgomery figure looking in distaste at a world that is changing,… and is struggling to preserve the future of the Crown."

The next day I wrote out the main events. "Prince Tudor in shock as he realises that Britain is controlled (sudden revelation), that there will be a loss of sovereignty…. He resolves to tell the nation." That evening I drafted 45 scenes. In April I "wrote Prince Tudor's soliloquy in his garden about the Crown". During a meeting shortly afterwards Charles digressed to *Overlord* and said: "I've been reading your piece on Purgatory." I had described four contemporary writers suffering in Purgatory for their secular works. He said, "I think the writers are John Osborne, Philip Larkin, Kingsley Amis and Salman Rushdie." I said, "Quite right. Four out of four." I reached the end of *Prince Tudor* at the end of May, and Charles sent me a thoughtful fax saying that I had left the poetic "imagery of Chaucer, Spenser and Ben Jonson for the auditory path of Shakespeare, Marlowe and Milton". He said I was healthy for combining imagistic Pound with the grand themes and developing the philosophy of Shakespeare. Although Prince Tudor focused on his kingdom in Britain, I had always seen Britain as part of Europe, as a subdivision of Europe.

I worked on *The Tragedy of Prince Tudor* throughout June. I finished the play once through on 28 June and observed, "Prince Tudor is a Universalist like Stauffenberg, who opposes universal evil in a cause that will help millions of people."[16]

In the Lake District

My Uncle Reg had rung to say he wanted me to have my grandmother's silver teapots, which had passed to his late wife, Aunt Flo, and could I collect them? We had driven to the Lake District on our way back from Cornwall in February. We had tea with Reg in High Newton and found him shuffling and stooping, but otherwise well. He took us to eat in Bardsea, and the restaurant owner brought his wine in a silver goblet and a napkin in a ring, which she tucked under his chin as he peered at the menu through his monocle. Back at home he told us about his Freemasonry. He showed us his set square and Pythagoras's triangle in which the hypotenuse is equal to the square of the two sides. He told me: "It's a lot of nonsense." He had stopped being a Templar because it was not him to be dressing up.

The next morning we drove to Grange and visited a couple he knew who lived in a house with a wonderful view over the sands. They rang the legendary guide Cedric Robinson to arrange a walk so that we could see the oyster-catchers and eider duck. We went on to Cartmel Priory church, and then to Esthwaite Water and Hawkshead, where I visited the church which Wordsworth saw as 'snow-white' and looked in through the schoolroom window. We drove to Blea Tarn and stopped briefly at Blea Tarn House, the Solitary's house. We then drove up Great Langdale, over the top and down the other side, which was very steep. We went on to Grasmere and I looked in on the 14th-century Grasmere church and saw Wordsworth's grave by the clear Rothay.

We went on to Dove Cottage, and had a tour from the houseplace (or kitchen-parlour) to the bedroom of Dorothy (and later William and Mary). We went to the kitchen, parlour and buttery and then up to Wordsworth's sitting-room where I had a good look at his couch and cutlass chair with pink seat. We went on to his bedroom and saw William and Mary's bed, and to the guest bedroom where Coleridge stayed, and (for seven years) de Quincey; and the children's room. In this cottage Wordsworth lived from 1799 to 1808 on Raisley Calvert's legacy which brought in £70 a year, and wrote his best poetry. We went on to the Leech-gatherer's pond up the road, a small tarn under a fell, and then on to Rydal Water, past Nab Cottage (where de Quincey lived), and on to Ambleside, where I saw the house where Wordsworth was Distributor of Stamps for Westmoreland from March 1813 to 1843, when he became Poet Laureate. I gazed at the stepping-stones over the River Rothay which Wordsworth crossed on his way to work. We returned via Windermere.

Back at the house Reg gave us several pieces of silver, which we packed. He was closing down the house and wanted us to take them away. On our return we visited Argie to show her the silver teapots. She said they were her mother's wedding present in 1898 and pointed out a 'B'. She thought the engraving said 'GHB' (George Herbert Broadley). I thought it said 'EB' (Elsie Broadley), or 'G' and 'EB' (George and Elsie Broadley).[17]

Cast of the Globe's As You Like It *stay and rehearse at Otley Hall; Jonathan Cecil* Business was up. The Administrator said that we had 30 bookings, against 14 the same time the previous year. Sylvia Landsberg had now designed our knot-garden, the beds had been laid out with brick surrounds. It contained a border of cotton lavender, *fleurs-de-lis* of wall germander and an endless knot of box with infills of pansies. I collected 120 'Johnny Jump-Up' pansies from the Walled Garden in Saxmundham to speed up the opening of the garden. The 24 other beds contained an array of medieval herbs. We prepared a series of booklet guides on aspects of Otley Hall: on the history, the house and the gardens; and Charles wrote one on me as a man of letters.

The couple had not been coping. The housekeeper had a bad leg which required frequent rest, and her husband constantly complained that there was too much to do. Just as the new season was about to start they shocked us by giving in their notice. There were Open Days. An agency found us applicants, and we appointed our third couple on 24 April. They had worked for Lord Tollemache at Helmingham Hall, and I rang him as he was a referee. (I asked, "What was the cook like?" He replied, "Moody and irritating." I was taken aback, but still appointed the couple. The cook later volunteered that they had been given Christmas Day off and were cooking their own turkey in their oven when they were rung up and asked to serve drinks in the Hall immediately as other staff had not turned up. Their consternation had proved "irritating".)

The cast of the Globe's production of *As You Like It* arrived during the interviews. (The lady from the Globe had visited us on 6 February.) About

20 actors got off the coach, and I took them for a tour outside and inside and ended up talking about Shakespeare and detail of *As You Like It*. Jaques spoke to me outside and said, "I can't find any redeeming features in his character." I said I would find a redeeming feature for him. He wandered round the house in role. I heard him growl at another actor, "You nasty piece of work." Two actors were in the boat on the moat, many actors were in costume, wrestling on the lawn or cooking venison over a fire in the copse where some lamented their banishment. They had dinner in the conference room.

Jonathan Cecil said to me: "You have a picture of my ancestor, Lord William Cecil Burghley. I'm a direct descendant." I told him I would like him to meet Charles. "Your ancestors drove his out of Castle Hedingham in 1591." He smiled and blew cigarette smoke in my face.

The next morning was wet and the actors watched a video in the Great Hall. Eventually I talked to them, and I talked to Jaques several times. I told him he was the focus of the play, the lens that queried the illusion of Arcadia with town disillusion, along with Touchstone (who slept in the log cabin). In the afternoon Jaques caught me after sitting in the boat on the moat to feel melancholy. Together with the assistant producer I devised the view that the play satirised Sidney's *Arcadia*. The old *Arcadia* was written in 1580 in Wilton House (Pembroke's home), and just as Shakespeare satirised Sidney in *Twelfth Night* as Aguecheek, so he satirised Sidney's *Arcadia* in *As You Like It*. Jaques said he would work with that.

The actors took part in more role-play on the stairs. Some of the actors spent the night in the woods, where again they lit a fire and roasted venison. Each had his or her own space. That night they bonded in the conference room till 1 a.m., singing to the guitar.

The new couple started at the end of April. We had more Open Days on 3 and 4 May, and it was soon apparent that the new couple were struggling even more than their predecessors. They had not experienced people in such numbers, and the caretaker had a bad knee which needed frequent resting. In mid-May the previous couple (presumably having heard this) asked to come back. But they had not been able to cope. A week later I had to see the new couple and point out that they were not coping. They reluctantly accepted that this was true and agreed to make way for a younger couple.

There were two more Open Days towards the end of May. Matthew and I travelled down to Otley Hall and rowed on the moat in the boat. The first Open Day was rounded off with a family game of croquet. Laughter rang out over the croquet lawn, and there were groans each time one of us was roqueted into the herbaceous borders. During the second Open Day, when we had 355 visitors, I was given the 1912 sale catalogue which stated that

Otley Hall was a 14th-century house. At the end of May there was a lucrative wedding at which 180 guests were wined in the rose-garden lawn to a string quartet. There was a loud disco and there were complaints from the village.

The cast of *As You Like It* invited Ann and me to the Globe to see a *matinée* of their play. I could see the Otley-Hall influence on the production: wrestlings and Jaques's disillusion. At the end there was thunderous applause and I went to the foyer and telephoned the Green Room and the cast said they would come and see us: John McEnery in his motorcycle leathers – I complimented him on his positioning; the Duke, Amiens, Oliver, Touchstone and Audrey. Rosalind – Anastasia Hille, the tall star – floated down the stairs and came to give me a big kiss, and chat, lithe and composed but without the current of energy that brought her alive on stage. I was taken aback by their warmth. They all said they had pictures of Otley Hall in the dressing-room and how their time there had helped and got them forward, how they bonded and got to know each other. One of them said, "You've a done a lot for the Globe." Jonathan Cecil, Lord Burghley's descendant, came and gave me his phone number.

Visitors to Otley Hall

At Otley Hall, Charles and I lunched with the Oxfordian author Verily Anderson. The village Friendship Club then had tea in the kitchen and a tour of the ground floor. They were all elderly and remembered Otley Hall from the old days. There was a power cut at 11 p.m. and we lit our way to bed with nightlights, which flickered on the Tudor walls and beams as in the 16th century. Two days later a lecturer in Renaissance poetry from Saxmundham lunched with Charles and me. She claimed to be a dancing partner of Prince Charles, and tried very hard to get me to show her a copy of *The Tragedy of Prince Tudor*. She said that Shakespeare was "soliciting virtue", and I put a line in the mouth of the Fool at the end of the play, "I solicit virtue and berate vice." We had a visit from the designer and embroiderers of the New World Tapestry, 24 panels in the tradition of the Bayeux Tapestry, which they unrolled on the kitchen table.

We interviewed our new housekeeper, whose husband was looking after Lord Swinton, an invalid. He was dresser and carer, cook, housekeeper, caretaker, butler and chauffeur, and she said she had to get him away before he had a nervous breakdown. The next day we held a party for Argie who celebrated her 95th birthday. About 50 family and friends came to Otley Hall, including Lord Murray who spent time handling my books. He said he had not realised I was so prolific. He asked me, "What's the point of *The Warlords*?" meaning 'What's the theme?' I described my Shakespearean theme of power, the rivalry for power over Europe, and how I tried to catch the year of Britain's decline but also reveal the world government. I spoke to the throng and Argie's oldest friend, Joyce Westcott, who had worked with Montgomery during the war and had had links with intelligence, embarrassed me by saying publicly at the end, "I had a friend who met you in 1970 and has never forgotten it. You are a very clever man."

I met the new housekeeper's husband, Giovanni Bisoffi, a grave, besuited Italian who would do everything – he would be butler, chauffeur, valet, handyman, gardener, caterer and would lift the standard of the grounds: get the grass growing greener, make everything look tidy, paint the seats, edge and keep the weeds down. We went on to the Maritime Exhibition near the port of Ipswich. Charles arrived with his Canadian wife, who, spotting one of our guides, asked if they could rent a vacant property of his in Hadleigh.

Overlord was still being read with approval. The Oxfordian Elizabeth Imlay of the De Vere Society Committee wrote in a letter that she had become more and more impressed by book 11 of *Overlord*, "I was much tickled by the democratic proceedings in Heaven, 'a grand project.' [You] avoided the reader siding with Satan as in *Paradise Lost* by showing evil in graphic and pathetic details. I feel that the great problem with justifying the ways of God to men is that by God's own design it cannot be done. But, as an overview of historical experience, your poem is just magnificent. With sincere admiration."

Second operation for varicose veins

I had just had another operation to remove more varicose veins. Back in February I had stood on a stool before Mrs. Hobbs, who told me I had a leak in both legs. No groins were involved this time. Tests at the Middlesex Hospital confirmed that. I was a rarity: only one in a hundred has two sets of mid-thigh veins. Had they known, they could have taken them out the first time. I had no leaks in my deep veins, only in my pathological veins.

And so on 18 June I booked in at the Wellington Hospital, St John's Wood. I could see part of the Lord's cricket ground from my window. It was the first day of a test match against South Africa. It was a grey, drizzly day and there was no cricket before lunch, and I watched the South African team practising below me. I was given a heparin injection, again stood on a stool in a gown so that Mr Hobbs could draw the veins he was going to remove. Then there was a knock on the door and one of two men said, "We've come for you."

In the anaesthetic room everyone was in green. I was put out very quickly. Back in my room I had had painkillers and my legs were bandaged. By 4.15 I was watching the cricket on TV and hearing the applause through the window. At 11 that evening I was got up to go to the loo and tore a wound. Scarlet blood spurted over my bandages and sheets as I returned to bed. Next day Mrs. Hobbs took off my bandages and put little steri-strips over the holes she had made – about 40 on each leg. Then she put stockings on my legs. The next day I took off my blood-stained stockings and saw I had large bruises on my upper legs. When I had my stitches removed Mrs. Hobbs told me my lesions were caused by "venous pressure", my varicose veins had been caused by standing while teaching in early years, valve failure, and by my writing. "You need to wear these socks while you're writing."

John Southworth and Fools

I met Charles and told him: "*The Warlords* and *Prince Tudor* are both about sovereignty; they are *Henry V* in modern form – Agincourt and Prince Hal in his garden becoming King. *Prince Tudor* is a warning against the break-up of the UK." I had written quite a large part for the Fool.

Charles invited John Southworth, author of *Fools and Jesters at the English Court*, to lunch. A thin man of about 70 in a suit that hung on his bones, with a creased face, long grey hair and spectacles, he identified the fool on a beam in our Great Hall as 15th-century, about 1450, like the Dutch fool in his book. We talked at length about Shakespeare's fools. Southworth told me: "Eliot was on the verge of creating a new unnaturalistic theatre in *Murder in the Cathedral* and *Family Reunion*, but Martin Browne convinced him to be naturalistic in *The Cocktail Party* and *The Confidential Clerk* and the Erinyes don't work behind the drawing-room curtain, they're ridiculous." I completely agreed.

Opening Otley village fête, John Michell

On 4 July I opened the Otley village fête. I spoke into a microphone at 2 p.m. and then toured stalls and chatted. A week later there was a student production of *As You Like It* on Otley Hall's rose-garden lawn. It was soon wet. I sat under an umbrella but was absorbed. The actors were soaked and all slept in the log cabin.

The next day (arranged by Charles) 58 members of the De Vere Society had their annual conference at Otley Hall. There were lectures on Shakespeare's Italian sources and after lunch Charles lectured "on sovereignty". John Michell, author of *Who Wrote Shakespeare?*, was present and visited the Shakespeare library with me. I had a chat with him about the authorship question. Like me, he distanced himself from all the claimants and wanted to know more about the Stratfordian Shakespeare's life.

Afterwards Ann and I hurried to Ipswich station and attended a concert at the Royal Albert Hall in which Vivaldi's *Four Seasons* was played by candlelight in 18th-century costume, with wigs and breeches. I listened for the cuckoo, a storm, wind and sleeping.[18]

Robert Gosnold III secretary to the Earl of Essex
Through his reading of Diarmaid MacCulloch's *Suffolk and the Tudors*,[19] Charles discovered that Robert Gosnold III had been secretary to the Earl of Essex. I could now understand how Southampton, a great friend of the Earl of Essex, had funded Bartholomew Gosnold's 1602 voyage. The Gosnolds were members of the Essex faction in Tudor life. We spread news of Robert III at the next two Open Days.[20]

I had done further work on *The Tragedy of Prince Tudor* throughout July, but I was also preparing for my verse play, *Ovid Banished*. On 18 July of the first of our two Open Days, I "put up the signs quickly and then worked all afternoon on *Ovid* as only 110 people came through. Got the order of events for what happens in *Ovid Banished*."

In Italy: Verona and Venice – Catullus, Dante and Shakespeare
As preparation for *Ovid Banished* I had arranged to visit Italy – not Rome, but Verona and Venice, which I knew would feature in my classical odes.

In Verona we sat in the Piazza del Erbe, the old Roman Forum, and then walked round the old city monuments with our own guide, focusing on Catullus, Dante and Shakespeare. We tracked Dante's three visits to Verona: in 1303 when he visited the Scalas; in 1312-1318, when he lived in Verona and visited Cangrande I; and in 1320 when he debated on "whether water runs anywhere higher than earth" at the church of Sant' Elena.

We stood where Dante saw Cangrande I, the ruler's brother, aged 12 from a stone staircase in the Scaligeri palace in 1303, and reflected his encounter in the 17th canto of *Paradiso*. We saw where Dante researched in the library and based the Paladins (Twelve Peers) on the statues outside the Cathedral, and where he stood in the cloister and saw the Piazza del Erbe. We saw the palace where Dante stayed with Bartolomeo della Scala (now a police station); and then where he stayed with the Cangrandes in the Castle, opposite the Scala and Cangrande tombs. We went on to the Basilica of San Zeno where Dante saw "the sempiternal rose" in the rose-window of the Wheel of Fortune. It is not golden but white and mauve. I looked at the tower he brought into *Purgatorio*. It was Dante who first reported the Montagues and Capulets, and we saw Juliet's balcony, Romeo's house and Juliet's tomb. We saw the Roman theatre across the Adige river and the arena. Later I wrote a classical ode, 'In Dante's Verona'.

We took a taxi along Lake Garda to Sirmione, walked through narrow streets and took a small train up to the Roman villa, the largest in North Italy, where allegedly Catullus's father lived and entertained Julius Caesar, where Catullus himself often visited and where he died. There were cicadas in the olives and swans on the blue lake. I was very uplifted and during the walk down from the villa I redefined Universalism... as one flowing tradition of poetry and history in which Catullus, Virgil, Horace and Ovid have a place and must be honoured.

Later I wrote a classical ode, 'At Catullus's Sirmione'.

On impulse I asked the taxi-driver to divert to the region between Carpenedolo and Calvisano where Virgil was born in view of the Alps. We went round Calvisano. I found rice and maize but no livestock and no sign of Amaryllis, Virgil's shepherdess, in the cool of the shade. I nevertheless got a feeling for the place of the *Eclogues*. We went on into Mantua and saw the statue of Virgil before heroic and pastoral symbols, with quotations from his work. We also visited the Ducal palace and Castiglione's house, where *The Courtier* must have been written.

Back in Verona I reflected:

I am Universalist in linking myself to all art everywhere and the flow of metaphysical poetry, but I am a nationalist in seeing each locality as important, its own sovereignty and nation-statism. Universalism is not everythingism, it is the flow of metaphysical poetry and knowledge in all cultures, whose history is also a flow in civilizations.

We took a train to Venice and then a water-taxi to San Zaccaria. We passed Venetian houses with water lapping near their ground floor and booked in at the Danieli Hotel with a view across the Laguna. We ate in a little street off St Mark's Square by a bridge. Water lapped onto stone walkways, gondolas bobbed up and down, and gondoliers in boaters with ribbons sang as they propelled their fares under low bridges.

The next day we walked round the Doge's palace and on the Bridge of Sighs where prisoners took their last look at the world. We visited St Mark's church and took a water-bus to Cannaregio and walked across the bridge to St Jeremiah, and in the square found no trace of where Virginia Paduana (the Paduan) lived with the 17th Earl of Oxford. We walked back past the Jewish Ghetto to the Rialto Bridge. We were handed a leaflet about a small concert in the 13th-century Scuola Grande di San Giovanni Evangelista, and between Tintorettos on the walls watched stately dancers with wigs and buckle shoes and, most memorably, heard an achingly sad *adagio* by Albinoni. It was "about making sense of one's life", and was "sombre but also ennobling and arguably triumphant as death takes control". I wrote: "Music puts you in touch with your deeper feelings and takes you out of yourself – and that should be the effect of my poems, a language of the soul."

The next morning, sitting on the 4th-floor terrace of the Danieli having breakfast and watching ships plying to and fro, I was sure that during his lost years Shakespeare took a Venetian ship down the stormy Illyrian coast to Sicily, Athens and Ephesus, and returned via Naples, Rome and Genoa, and that he travelled back via Milan, Mantua, Verona and Padua.

We drove to Padua past Venetian villas along the Brenta canal and visited St Anthony's church and the tomb of Antenor. At the university we saw the colonnaded courtyard and coats of arms where Galileo taught, and the house nearby where Dante stayed while in exile, in 1306. On the way back our driver pointed out a Venetian villa at Belmont on the Brenta canal that was traditionally known as Portia's.

Back in Venice we lunched at Harry's Bar, where Hemingway, a regular, is said to have based the title of the book he was writing in Venice, *Across the River and into the Trees*, on the view across the street and into the trees. Later we glided in a gondola under the Rialto and passed the houses of Casanova and Marco Polo (Venetian ambassador to China), and of Napoleon and Byron. The next morning we walked in St Mark's Square, took a boat to Murano Isle and then tore in a speedboat across open sea to the airport. I sat up on the back, the wind tugging at my hair, and felt exhilarated and well.[21]

I had absorbed the Roman countryside Ovid knew, had advanced my knowledge of the Universalist roles of Catullus and Dante and had visited places known to Shakespeare.

Six forthcoming works: Collected Stories, *vol. 4,* The Warm Glow of the Monastery Courtyard; Ovid Banished; The Warlords *abridged;* Gosnold's Hope; The One and the Many; The New Philosophy of Universalism

Back in England I visited my publisher on 27 July and agreed a timetable of four forthcoming books: *The One and the Many*; then *Wheeling Bats and a Harvest Moon*; *The Tragedy of Prince Tudor*; and *The Warm Glow of the Monastery Courtyard*. I had lunch with Michael Mann and at the end of the afternoon he put on the test cricket. "I spent Saturday at Trent Bridge," he said. I should have guessed that the nephew of F.G. Mann of Middlesex was an avid cricket-watcher.

I now began assembling stories for *The Warm Glow of the Monastery Courtyard*. I wanted to make a start on my next verse play, *Ovid Banished*. I talked with Charles about the story of Ovid's banishment and speculated as to what 'error' caused Augustus to banish him. I thought he criticised Augustus's *imperium* and his treatment of barbarians. He may have supported the Julian line of succession that challenged Augustus's. I pointed out that I had opposed the New World Order's *imperium* by opposing the pro-Soviet Scargill and the break-up of the UK with nation-state patriotism. I knew it was possible to make a stance without fully understanding how it would be interpreted by the administrators of the *imperium*. Ovid had criticised Roman civilization and he was made to live beyond the *limes*, the frontier. He had burned a copy of *Metamorphoses* before going into exile – that was the *carmen* that caused his problem. His adulation of Julius Caesar at the end might suggest support for the Julian line that Augustus's wife Livia and her descendants opposed.

I instinctively identified with Ovid's challenge to Augustus's *imperium* and world government, which was similar to my challenge to the self-interested New World Order in our time. My verse play would be about the New World Order's censorship of the independent-minded artist. I combed Ovid's *Tristia* and *Pontic Epistles*, book 4 (AD14–17) and delved into Ovid's state of mind after Augustus's death in AD14. I reflected, "My verse is heroic and nationalistic, but… I have told the truth about the [New World Order's] world government."[22]

My delving into Roman poetry took me back into Horace, and I saw my *Classical Odes* as being the first four books of odes since Horace's four:

Resolved to write a sequence of poems which reflect on human life as do Horace's *Odes*…. Read several pages [in Karl Galinsky's *Augustan Culture*] on the 'universalism' of Augustan poetry[23] – how the themes are universally human: "the threat of death, freedom from difficulties, material security, inner peace, the fleeting nature of our existence, coming to terms with ourselves, the impossibility of perfect bliss, wealth, contentment with less than wealth or because of less than wealth, the active choice of the kind of life that can minimise anxiety."

I reflected that Virgil aimed for universality by writing an epic that was both historical and mythological. I needed "to evoke rural Suffolk in latter-day eclogues and georgics". I read Catullus, "half his work".

While I was researching Roman verse I was (with Charles) producing a shortened version of the two Parts of *The Warlords*. By the end of August I had agreed a version that 26 actors could perform, and had reduced the play to 120 pages. At the same time I was putting the finishing touches to *The Tragedy of Prince Tudor*, which I sent to my publisher in early September.

I had been working on *Gosnold's Hope* during the summer. I revised it in Cornwall. I was responding to points made by Jack McAdam and Anthony, I sharpened Bartholomew Gosnold's role as the key decision-maker who embodied vision and persuasion, whereas Wingfield, the military man, embodied force and command. I finished *Gosnold's Hope* on 1 September and sent it to Jack McAdam. He replied that the screenplay was now "excellent" and "a property of importance".

Throughout August and September I was working on *The One and the Many*. I wrote the *Preface*, and then started revising it. I focused on

Universalism and edited the magazine articles and lectures into a coherent, sequential text. I realised I could make a clear statement of "how everything is", "a philosophy of Universalism". My research took me into Greek philosophy, and I "ordered four translations of Heracleitus's *Fragments* (all by different people)". The book went to the designer on 7 October. I finished assembling *The Warm Glow of the Monastery Courtyard* on 23 November.

Meanwhile I wrote an outline for the work of philosophy I had provisionally called *The Knot-Garden*. I now felt the book should be called *The End of the Universe* for behind Princess Elizabeth's knot was the 1268 pavement at Westminster Abbey with its Latin inscription which begins, "If the reader wittingly reflects upon all that is laid down, he will discover here the end (*finem*) of the universe." The 'end' of the universe has the meaning 'what the universe seeks to attain'. The idea for this book eventually became *The New Philosophy of Universalism*.

I was still being made a trustee of the Shakespearean Authorship Trust. John Silberrad rang me in Cornwall to say that the deed was being prepared and that he wanted Mark Rylance as fourth trustee. I requested again that the Earl should be a fifth trustee. He was still not keen. Silberrad then said, "The books could go to Southwark in future." He meant that if Rylance was a trustee the Globe could have them. Having installed expensive wooden shelves in the Literary Room to take the books, I was not impressed by this suggestion.[24]

Each of Otley Hall's Open Days at the end of August brought in 250 visitors, and journalists from *The Observer* and *The Daily Telegraph* who wanted to write articles. There was an intense debate among the guides as to the oldest part of Otley Hall, and I knew I would have to sponsor some 'expert' dating. I brought to their attention that Bartholomew Gosnold had been lampooned in Jonson, Marston and Chapman's *Eastward Ho!*

Tudor knots: Otley Hall and Virginia
Asked to arrange twinning between Jamestown and Ipswich

I met James Hehir, the Chief Executive of Ipswich Borough Council on the *Amuda*, a restaurant ship moored in Ipswich dock. He agreed with me that there should be a statue to Gosnold in Ipswich, and that there should be replicas of the *Concord* and *Godspeed*, Gosnold's two ships, at Ipswich. I was due to visit America in October to present Bartholomew Gosnold as the founder of America for having organised the 1606/7 Jamestown voyage, and he asked me to obtain twinning between Ipswich and Jamestown on the strength of Gosnold. To brief me a council official drove me round historic Ipswich: past Wolsey's Gate to the Merchant's House and the timbered building on the corner opposite where Wolsey was brought up by an Ipswich butcher.

I returned to the *Amuda* to meet a leading figure of the Ipswich Historical Society and heard how Gipeswich was founded by Angles c.AD700, was the first Anglian village and gave rise to English. He said there were hundreds of Anglian artefacts in store, and he wondered if I could display some of them at Otley Hall. The Angles had come from Jutland and the Rhine – from Hemsby in Jutland and from Flensburg and Dorstadt in Germany – and *Beowulf* may have been written by East-Anglian Angles in their language, Anglo-Saxon. The next day I wrote a classical ode, 'In Dark Age Angle-Land'.

Down in Cornwall I briefed Robin Davies on these developments. He hoped to build replica ships in Charlestown and sail them to Ipswich. He had been marine co-ordinator during the filming of Spielberg's *Saving Private Ryan*, in charge of a flotilla of more than 80 landing-craft and ships for the film.[25] He said he would send *Gosnold's Hope* to Spielberg, and urged me to ask Jamestown for funding.

In the USA: my lecture in Richmond on Bartholomew Gosnold – Norman Beatty, Bill Kelso, Elizabethan values
I flew to America on 9 October with Ann to introduce Bartholomew Gosnold and Otley Hall to Martha's Vineyard and Virginia, to tackle the Tudor knot of twinning and to write some classical odes. From Boston a car took us through autumn leaves to New Bedford, where we found the airport closed. We could only reach Martha's Vineyard by ferry. Our driver did not know the way, and I spotted the ferry in the distance. We caught it with ten seconds to spare as the gangway was being taken up.

Foul weather closed in and we chugged through thick fog to the murky, dusky lights of Vineyard Haven where Charles's friend Joe Eldridge met us as we staggered with our luggage across mud through driving rain. He drove us to Edgartown's Point Way Inn, an 1851 Greek-Revival sea captain's house, where we had a room in the grounds. He took us to dinner in the Harbour View Hotel.

The next day he took us for a drive around Martha's Vineyard through rain. We saw Edgartown's lighthouse, where Gosnold might have landed, and sea captains' houses, and drove to Oak Bluff, East Chop, Vineyard Haven, Lake Tashmoo and Lambert's Cove. We got out to see the ocean, then drove on to Menemsha, the Gay Head Cliffs, Chilmark and West Tisbury. We lunched at the Black Dog, Vineyard Haven, and were joined by Roger Stritmatter, an Oxfordian friend of Charles's, a thin 30ish man with a goat beard. He had studied the handwriting in the 17th Earl of Oxford's Geneva Bible in the Folger Shakespeare Library whose marked passages – under-lining and marginal comments – could be found in Shakespeare's works, and told me the handwriting was Oxford's "though no reputable handwriter analyser would say that". Joe took us all on to the Edgartown Historical Society's reception for its 76th birthday in a tent in the museum grounds. Afterwards Joe, Roger, Ann and I walked on a nearby beach and saw little sandpipers pecking bugs in the wet sand and running at the movement of each wave, cormorants and a blue eagle.

The weather was too bad for our plane to fly to Cuttyhunk the next day, so Joe took us on a tour of houses in Martha's Vineyard. We passed Chappaquiddick and Dike Bridge, where Mary Jo Kopechne drowned in an upside-down car. The next morning Joe took us to Vineyard Haven to catch the ferry for Cape Cod. He gave us a tiny sapling of a sassafras tree. (Sassafras had been part of Gosnold's cargo in 1602.) The crossing was short. We passed a tolling bell on a buoy.

We landed on Cape Cod at Woods Hole and were driven to Craigville Beach and, near Hyannis, the Kennedy compound of white-slatted houses where JFK, Jackie, Robert and Ethel lived, and (now) Senator Edward Kennedy. We set off for Provincetown via Pleasant Bay, Orleans and Chatham and when we arrived headed straight to Race Point, where Gosnold is thought to have landed and off which he named Cape Cod. We reached the airport where a small twelve-seater Cape Air plane was waiting. Our heavy suitcases were loaded in the nose, our hand luggage in the wings. Four of us flew. A pilot and a woman who sat beside him; and Ann and I, who sat at the back to balance the weight. From the air we had a good view of the end of the Cape, where Gosnold found cod. Half an hour later we came out of cloud and hung over Boston and landed with a bump on Boston airport's runway. We flew from Boston to New York, changed planes, flew on to Richmond and were driven to the Jefferson Hotel.

The next morning we were driven to Jamestown through misty trees and at the Visitor Centre I was introduced to Bill Kelso, the white-haired, white-moustached archaeologist, America's Schliemann: just as Schliemann had discovered Troy, so Kelso had discovered Jamestown Fort and 350,000 artefacts. Both Troy and Jamestown were thought to be legendary rather than historical before they were rediscovered. He had "found a cellar filled with armour from the 1610 extension of the Fort. The 1607 Fort was little excavated, but Kelso had found a skeleton he thought was Stephen Calthorpe's one of Gosnold's settlers." I noted: "The calm River James, very wide."

We were driven to Williamsburg via Archer's Hope (now named College Creek), where the Indians attacked and Gosnold's *Godspeed* fired its cannon. The director of the Raleigh Tavern Society took us for lunch at the Williamsburg Inn and round Colonial Williamsburg, in which John D. Rockefeller Jr had invested $68million – and bought the Williamsburg Inn. We went on to the reconstructed Jamestown Settlement and toured the museum. There were pictures of the Earl of Southampton, who funded Gosnold's 1602 voyage, and of Sir Thomas Smythe, who helped organise Gosnold's 1607 voyage. We walked through the Indian settlement to two reconstructed ships: the *Susan Constant* and *Discovery*. (The *Godspeed* was in Tunisia.) We returned through the reconstructed palisade, and talked to Norman Beatty (formerly a Colonel in the Pentagon) who controlled the funding for the coming 2007 celebration of the 400th anniversary of America's founding, which President Clinton had based on the 1607 Jamestown Settlement. Beatty agreed that the voyage to Jamestown had originated in the neighbourhood of Ipswich and Otley Hall, and I explained Gosnold's role and asked for twinning. He said, "We're very interested in John Smith." John Smith's statue stood by the River James and dominated Jamestown, but he arrived long after Bartholomew Gosnold had died in the Jamestown Fort.

The next day Charlie Bryan, the curator of the Richmond Museum who had visited Otley Hall, came to the Jefferson Hotel with his wife and drove us to the museum. He too was looking ahead to the celebration of the 400th anniversary of America's founding. He gave us a tour, taking us through the history of Virginia and how Clinton invited them both to the White House. Upstairs in the boardroom I attended the meeting of the Celebration 2007 Progress and Events Sub-Committee of the Virginia Historical Society, under the aegis of the Jamestown-Yorktown Foundation. I sat through nearly two hours of presentations about contacting US schools, and then gave my presentation: what Bartholomew Gosnold did at Jamestown, how Ipswich planned to celebrate with a statue, and what Martha's Vineyard were doing. I said there was a three-legged stool: Jamestown, Ipswich/Otley Hall and Martha's Vineyard. I again asked for twinning. At the end I was given a picture of the *Susan Constant* (the main 1607 ship, not Gosnold's) by Norman Beatty. They had their narrative of the founding of Jamestown, and I was challenging it by focusing on the role of Gosnold and Otley Hall.

In the evening we attended a buffet dinner held in our honour in Richmond. Some 30 attended. I met Mrs. Hager, the Lieutenant-Governor's wife; and Tad Thompson, who lived in Jefferson's boyhood home at Tuckahoe Plantation. Also present were Anthony Pelling, former Under-Secretary at Environment in Wilson's UK Government, who went to live in Richmond with his American wife; and Professor Ken Haas.

The next morning Ken Haas took us to the Pamplin Park Civil War site to see where the Unionists broke the Confederates' line on 2 April 1865 to end the Civil War. We walked through woods looking at lines, and ended in McGowan's house. All this time Ken talked about the parallels with my *Overlord* 1 and 2, which he had read and liked. He suggested "that there is a parallel between the Confederacy and Arthurian romance: Tennyson's *Idylls of the King*. Lee is the Eisenhower, Grant the Rommel, Lincoln the Hitler.... The end of an order." I had been subconsciously looking for an Anglo-American theme about the unification of America that could accommodate the founding of America. Eventually I put this theme in my second poetic epic, *Armageddon*. After lunch we went to Drewry's Bluff and saw the Fort that overlooks the James River.

My lecture took place at St Stephen's church that evening. I addressed the English-Speaking Union. I was introduced by the ex-Under-Secretary Tony Pelling, now Chairman of the English-Speaking Union at Richmond. I spoke on Otley Hall to about 50, showed slides, and told the story of Bartholomew Gosnold from 1571 to 1607: how he used his connections to settle Cuttyhunk and was the first mover in settling Jamestown. I ran through what Ipswich and Martha's Vineyard had planned in 2007. Many came and said how much they had enjoyed my talk.

We were driven to Yorktown and visited the battlefield, the surrender field and Moore House, where the surrender was signed. We went on to the Victory Centre and Yorktown village, lunched at the Williamsburg Inn and walked to the Raleigh Tavern and the Governor's House.

Bill Kelso had rung to say he wanted to see me. We drove to Jamestown. Kelso was tied up, so I sat by the River James and mused and wrote a poem that became 'At Jamestown, with the Founder of America'. I reached stanza 7 before Kelso came. He wanted background on my sources. I grasped that Jamestown-Yorktown stood for the British settlement and British defeat, and that Colonial Williamsburg stood for the 1699 American Revolution. The Jamestown-Yorktown Foundation was a pre-Revolutionary set-up that was working for the reunification of Britain and America.

The next morning we toured historic Richmond. We stopped at the Capitol, which Jefferson designed, modelling it on a Roman temple at Nimes. (He was Ambassador to France.) We sat in the old Senate chamber. We went to the Houdon statue of Washington, above which was the Governor's office where every Governor has worked since 1788, and then to the Old Hall of Delegates (where Lee accepted his command), and the Museum of Heroes (including Lee). We went to the Governor's house, drove up and down Monument Avenue looking at the statues of Davis, Jackson, Lee and Maury and visited the Confederacy White House and Jefferson Davis's rooms, including his study and bedroom. We entered St John's church, which had a sunburst on the 18th-century sounding-board over the pulpit and among pews with doors I worked out where Patrick Henry said, "Give me liberty or give me death."

I reflected that the southern landowners belonged to an aristocratic caste system based on Utopian chivalry to those of lower caste. An old patrician order of plantation-owners had had to give way to a new industrial consumer order, and with the change died the old values. The southern landowners were children of the Gosnolds and Wingfields.

The next morning, a Sunday, I dictated an outline of my lecture onto tape in the Hotel lobby, and at 12 we drove to Monticello and took a bus up the mountain to Jefferson's house, where we had a guided tour. I was struck by strange mouldings, an ox's skull and a chrysanthemum, in his study/cabinet and bedroom.

We were driven on to Tuckahoe Plantation. We arrived at 7 and were greeted by Tad and Susan Thompson, he in shorts and relishing the chill breeze through the mosquito-nets. We met their two daughters and son and toured the 1730s wood-panelled house where Jefferson lived from the ages of two to seven and was educated on his own in the schoolroom. We sat in their main room with a view over a bend of the River James and chatted about Virginia, and it dawned on me that the agrarian Virginian life was Elizabethan British. Gosnold brought over the Elizabethan agrarian system and based it not on aristocracy, but rather on land. England had moved on after Gosnold into the Industrial Revolution, but Virginia had remained the same, a landed 'aristocracy' that was threatened and destroyed by the industrial revolutionary north (which had kept up with England). Elizabethan England lived on in Virginia, thanks to Gosnold, for a while. Virginia was vanished England.

The next day we drove to North Carolina. On the way I wrote a 12-stanza poem on Jefferson, 'On Top of Jefferson's Mountain', for which I had made notes for the previous day. We visited the Roanoke Fort that Raleigh had colonised. Walking through woods I savoured the atmosphere of the Lost Colony and saw that the settlers' ideal was agrarian: they were each to be given 500 acres, just under Tad's 600 acres. The Elizabethan agrarian ideal had been continued by the North Carolinians and Virginians. On the way back I wrote a 12-stanza classical ode, 'The Lost Colony at Roanoke', retitled 'On Roanoke Island'), "making 24 stanzas in all today, some 240 lines".

I had greatly enjoyed Virginia and understood it. The southerners took the Elizabethan ideal of land and agrarian values and continued it at Roanoke and Jamestown and this was the ideal that was challenged during the Civil War: the southern pro-British ideal.

Back in Richmond we dined in the hotel's Lemaire restaurant (named after Jefferson's cook) and were unexpectedly joined by Tony Pelling and his wife. He told me he was disillusioned with Richmond and had not made the money he wanted to. He asked whether my promotion of Otley Hall, Gosnold, twinning and *Gosnold's Hope* had translated into any funding, and I had to admit that despite intense interest it had not. He told me that he had fed the writer of the British television series *Yes, Minister* with story-lines while he was Under-Secretary. Our last dinner in Richmond was full of laughter.

The next morning we were taken to Agecroft Hall, which had been shipped in crates from Lancashire in 1925 and rebuilt in Virginia in 1928. I wondered if Otley Hall should be dismantled, crated and exported to America. We flew to New York, the picture I had been given stowed in a rear 'closet'.[26]

My visit put Otley Hall and Bartholomew Gosnold on the Virginia map, and Jamestown Virginians would make several visits to Ipswich, go along with twinning and be entrammelled in Suffolk's Tudor knots.

Mark Rylance visits Otley Hall

I returned to Otley Hall to find the vine-and-rose tunnel up and the knot-garden being set out. The old thatch was off the summer-house, which was being rethatched. (Without my knowing, the thatcher was weaving an entwined 'N' and 'A' into the ridge of the thatch.) The couple shocked me by telling me they would be leaving to operate the family hotel in Italy. Our Administrator would also be leaving to go on maternity leave. Charles, faced with the Blair Government's abolition of hereditary peers, had written a pamphlet 'In Defence of Hereditary Peers'. I worked on the classical odes about Jamestown and Roanoke during a short visit to Cornwall.

The following week Mark Rylance, Artistic Director of the Globe, came to lunch at Otley Hall with his wife, Claire van Kampen, a blonde with hair back in a pony-tail. He wore a brown hat, which he took off for our tour of the Hall and grounds. Over lunch in the Linenfold Room, which Charles attended, Rylance said he wanted to have more Globe actors rehearsing with us. He wanted to be a trustee of the Shakespearean Authorship Trust.

We discussed my verse plays. He asked me what I was doing with the verse. I told him. He asked me why I had a cinematic form in *The Warlords*, and I explained Universalism's dynamic flow and flux as I tell the story. He said, "I tell a story and commercially sell seats." I said: "My play is nothing if it doesn't do that." He raised the problems of stagecraft – an actor would have to perform more than one role – and the isolation of the characters. I said the characters *are* isolated and spoke of their disharmony until final harmony. He said *The Tragedy of Prince Tudor* was "too daring": the Royal family had a good relationship with the Globe. Charles said that I was making a mythology of contemporary events. I said I was within the paradigm of the New World Order. Rylance said it would be better to set it back in time, in Abyssinia. He also said he was very interested in *Ovid Banished* and in my "theme of government". He left with a clearer idea of what I was trying to do in my verse plays.

After he went I heard that Ted Hughes had died of cancer. I now understood his dedication to me in the front of a copy of *Birthday Letters*, which had arrived through the post in March 1998: "Before us stands yesterday."

I did not then know that Rylance was a Baconian. A few days later I received a letter from him: "You remind me of Bacon at times with your love for gardens, history and philosophy. Claire and I came away brimming with resonances. Your vision of present-day history, your house, Charles's work on the authorship, and introduction of you and the Globe, through us. Very interesting. We had a strong feeling that parts of *Hamlet* were written in the Linenfold Parlour."

I thought that the only way *Hamlet* could have been written in the Linenfold Room was if Shakespeare had come to the private theatre at Otley Hall with a group of actors when the Chamberlain's Men were in Ipswich on their way to a great East Anglian house in 1602–1603; or if 'Shakespeare' was a pseudonym for the Earl of Oxford and he had come to live at Otley Hall with his cousin Robert Gosnold III, Secretary to the Earl of Essex, after he was thrown out of Castle Hedingham in 1591 and had later stayed at Otley Hall during the writing of *Hamlet*. However, there was no evidence for any of this.[27]

Tebbit and the New World Order

Lord Tebbit had been invited to Normanhurst's Founders Day prize-giving at the Chingford Assembly Hall. There was no sign of him at 3 o'clock, so I told the Head to start. Tebbit arrived at 3.10, having been held up by traffic as a result of the Lord Mayor's Show. I led him down an aisle and onto the platform, and after he had distributed the prizes I took him down to the first row of the audience to watch a play put on by the pupils. Over a cup of tea while we waited for it to begin I spoke of the plan to break Britain up into eight regions. I asked, "Is Blair naïve or acting out someone's agenda?" He said: "He's acting out someone's agenda." At the end I escorted him out into the dark to his Range Rover. He put his hand on the ignition and I said through the window, "England's in a parlous state." We talked for 45 minutes, during which Iain Duncan Smith, whose constituency he was visiting, joined us. He stood by the other window while Tebbit and I talked. I said, "There needs to be an organisation to stop England breaking into eight regions and Kent being grouped with Picardy and Normandy." He said: "Yes. It should be called the ELF, the English Liberation Front." I said the breaking-up of England was a stepping-stone towards the New World Order's world government. "We know who's doing it." He said: "'Rockefellers'." He added: "Bilderberg are a pressure group." I pointed out that they had been responsible for creating the Treaty of Rome. He said: "They're not all powerful. Let them sort out Africa, then I'll believe they can run the world."

Tebbit left, and his "'Rockefellers'" led to my exposure of the self-interested New World Order in *The Syndicate*. Three months later I received a letter from Tebbit describing *The Warlords* as a remarkable piece of work, and commenting on the break-up of the United Kingdom: "How right you are."

I had had some moles removed from my neck, stomach and left shin. The receptionist at Holly House was ex-chairman of the Oaklands Parents' Association, I was greeted by another parent, another was in X-ray and another in the pharmacy. A nurse said, "You're very well known. When the list went up, so many said, 'Oh, I know Mr Hagger.'"[28]

Twinning: Ipswich and Jamestown, Lord Belstead and Bill Kelso

I told representatives of Ipswich Borough Council and Suffolk County Council that twinning with Jamestown was a possibility, and an arrangement was made for me to speak to a group of sculptors about a statue to Bartholomew Gosnold at a function at St Edmundsbury Cathedral. I met the Lord Lieutenant of Suffolk, Lord Belstead, once Leader of the House of Lords and a Minister under Thatcher, a tall, gangling ex-Etonian with a soft voice and royal demeanour, and explained the American interest to him. He agreed to come to Otley Hall. I addressed the Otley Friendship Club in the village hall about my visit to Jamestown.

Bill Kelso, the Jamestown archaeologist, came to Otley Hall with his blonde wife. We spent the morning touring the Hall and grounds, and then I took them to Letheringham, up a bumpy lane and into the church with Wingfield brasses and plaques, and then to Wetheringsett to see the Rectory where Hakluyt wrote his *Principall Navigations*.[29] I was struck by the

Nicholas with Bill Kelso, the rediscoverer of Jamestown Fort, in Otley Hall's Great Hall on 23 November 1998

many ploughed fields between the houses. In the Tudor time these nearby villages were the Gosnolds' nearest neighbours. On the way back we visited Otley High House. Kelso asked me to send him a copy of my screenplay.[30] Jack McAdam had resigned to take up his new position, and communicating with him was now more difficult.

UK to be split into 8 regions

Mike Weidman of the Borough Council, who had met me with James Hehir, visited Otley Hall to debrief me on twinning. I said: "England is to be split into eight regions – what's our region?" He said: "Six counties: Suffolk, Essex, Norfolk, Cambridgeshire, Bedfordshire and Hertfordshire. We were expecting an announcement in the Queen's Speech but nothing happened. It was just the hereditary peers."[31] He later gave me a document the Council had received about the regionalising break-up of England which I had put to Tebbit, corroborating my view in *The Tragedy of Prince Tudor* (which I was still revising during the following January and February).

Martin Taylor and the earth-dollar

Weirdly I now, on 9 December 1998, had a long telephone conversation with the Secretary of the Bilderberg Group. I had been invited to my bank's branch managers' annual November dinner at Grosvenor House. Martin Taylor, the bank's Chief Executive, addressed the 1,500 guests. He talked too far back from the microphone and could not be heard. Consequently people talked and the hubbub made it even harder to hear. He said that the bank had contributed to a fund to bail out Russia. At the end I told my table that I was going to ask him what he had said, but by the time I reached the microphone Taylor had left. The managers on my table told me I should write to him, and an address was supplied. In due course I received a letter from him saying I should ring, but when I did he was on answerphone. I left a message and then discovered he had resigned as Chief Executive of the bank allegedly over the bail-out for Russia.

A few days later Martin Taylor rang me. "Martin Taylor here. I'm sorry you weren't able to reach me earlier." I thanked him for his letter and said how good it was of him to speak in view of his impending resignation. He said: "There was a certain dramatic irony about that evening." I did not know he had made his speech after resigning. I asked him if the globalist scenario was on course He said: "Yes, that's right. That's what we all hope." I wanted to know if there was to be a single earth currency and said: "As I see it, there will be a United States of the World with an earth dollar or an earth single currency, and the United States of Europe is a stepping-stone to it with its single currency." He said: "That's right." I asked: "What time scale? 2002?" He said: "More likely 20 years." So that was the plan! He had attended Bilderberg three times. I had heard it from the horse's mouth.

I said that America had been founded from Otley Hall, and explained how. I invited him: "Come and see it." He said: "I'd love to, it sounds fascinating." I said: "You may find you're in charge of defending the euro or sterling, and if that appointment happens and you're looking for a quiet place to have a small conference, come to Otley Hall." He said: "I need some time on my own first." It was a good interview full of laughter and urbane, academic good humour – and the assumption that world rule and globalism is the agenda we should all be working on.[32] The coming benevolent World State will need the earth-dollar.

'Plahouse'

Our couple left (the housekeeper in tears). From a poor field we appointed my childhood doctor's son and his wife. At interview he asked, "Where are your schools?" I said: "One is in Loughton." He said: "I was born there." I said: "It's Oaklands." He said: "I went there. I lived in Albion Hill." He told me his father's name. I said: "He was my doctor." Now I could see who he was. I had an image of him in short trousers, aged about four.

The appointment proved to be a disappointment. The new couple did not want to work as many hours as our previous couple. They wanted to retitle the position 'Events Co-ordinator/Property Manager' and 'Hospitality Manager' and wanted to take over the booking and running of conferences from the Administrator, who, they said, should make her computer available to them and take their letters. They retained their local cottage, to which they disappeared when we were in Essex, and there were tales of lights being left on in outbuildings, the back door being left open all night and the grass being left uncut until I reappeared. There were tales of empty bottles of wine being removed before I came down, of curries being cooked in the kitchen and of the village store selling take-away curries while we were away. I wanted Otley Hall to cover its own costs and our new Administrator was chosen to keep an eye on in-house expenditure and to increase the number of conferences being held in our conference room.

I was thinking about the 'Plahouse' at Otley Hall: now my study. It had always been referred to in Otley Hall documents as 'the Plahouse'. I found in the *Shorter Oxford English Dictionary*: "Playhouse. 1599. A building in which plays are acted; a theatre." Oliver Rackham had said that the columns outside, once red, were like those at the Globe. He thought my study was a 'tiring-room' ('attiring' room or changing-room). There would have been no wall behind the columns, and the actors would have sat behind a curtain and emerged between two columns left open. There would have been no raised stage. The audience would have sat on benches in the rose garden or stood. Travelling actors had passed near Otley: the Chamberlain's Men in 1595 and 1602–1603; and again after they became the King's Men in 1609. When the theatres were closed during the Civil War the 'Plahouse' was turned into a cockpit or bowls alley, documents suggested. I was writing verse plays in the 'Plahouse'.

Rackham came again and we had coffee in the 'Plahouse'. He confirmed that the window behind where I sat dated to the 1580s. I explained that in 1829 there had been a painting of Curtius leaping into the chasm on an inside wall of the 'Plahouse', and that this may have referred to the sacrifice of the Earl of Essex. (In 1829 there was an inscription on a quarry in the Great Hall, "*Rob. Gosnold, nemo mortalium omnibus horis sapit*", attributing to Essex's Secretary the sad reflection, "No mortal knows what all the hours will bring.") A few days later I wrote a classical ode, 'On Curtius Leaping into the Earth'. Charles was making a selection of my English poems, which we would call *Poems for England*.[33]

Twinning with Jamestown, Lord Belstead, Gen. Knapp; sculpture of Gosnold
In early January I briefed seven guides, Charles, the couple and Ann about America and gave out a new pamphlet that would be for sale, 'Bartholomew Gosnold'. I told them about our new researcher's work on the dating of the Hall. I brought them up to date on developments in the grounds, including the knot-garden.

The Lord Lieutenant of Suffolk, Lord Belstead, visited Otley Hall. We sat in the Great Hall over coffee and he discussed the possibility of a Royal visit so I could brief the Queen on the US plan to base its 400th anniversary on its founding from the Ipswich neighbourhood in 1607 and about Jamestown's possibly twinning with Ipswich. Charles walked in and raised his pamphlet. Belstead said that the hereditary peers' opposition was over as they could not win. I asked: "Is the UK breaking up as an accident because of Blair's devolution policies, or is he doing it deliberately because 'Rockefellers' have told him to do it?" He said: "I don't know, that's what we all want to know. As you know from your study [*The Fire and the Stones*], empires break up." After Charles left Belstead got back to Jamestown 2007 and wanted to know what Norman Beatty had said. I told him Beatty envisaged the Queen and the President of the US of the day being there with 100,000 people. I said, returning the conversation to a Royal visit: "I may be speaking out of turn but the Queen needs to be briefed if she is going to be meeting Americans." He said: "I agree, and you're not speaking out of turn. Leave it with me. But it may be that it will have to be a secret meeting."

The 'secret meeting' would be overtaken by events. After lunch Charles told me of his plan to disrupt the Lords from the throne, and how Black Rod would fall on him. And he mentioned his concern that *Prince Tudor* would leave me in a bad position with the Royal family.

I spoke to the Sculpture Working Party in the Civic Centre. Ten committee members agreed to a sculpture of Bartholomew Gosnold, provided funding could be raised from public subscription or from America. I visited Butley Priory, an Augustinian monastery gatehouse of c.1320 run by Frances Cavendish, and later wrote a classical ode, 'At Butley Priory Gatehouse'. When I returned Mike Weidman rang. He had received two letters from Norman Beatty to James Hehir approving my scheme and a maritime museum, statue and replica boats. In his first letter Beatty said:

It was clear from your letter that you have caught the vision that Nicholas Hagger so eloquently conveyed in England and in America. We were very impressed with his presentations here last fall.... I personally believe only imaginative and large-scale ideas such as those suggested by Mr Hagger will have any chance of attracting major international funding, especially from key organisations and individuals in America and England.

His second letter introduced General John Knapp, his ambassador, who would be coming in a week's time. Weidman agreed to send copies of these letters to Lord Belstead.

I installed a dovecote at Otley Hall and attended a lecture on peers and Shakespeare by Charles at Hadleigh Town Hall. Then I joined a group (consisting of the ex-Head of Ipswich School, Mike Weidman and Robin Davies, who had come up from Cornwall specially) to receive General John Knapp and his son Major John Knapp. They had come to see what Ipswich was doing for the 400th anniversary of the founding of the United States by Bartholomew Gosnold and others in 2007, and the Ipswich end were agog that there might be US funding. We showed them maps of historic Ipswich and unsuccessfully hunted for their ancestors' tomb in St Peter's church. We dined them on the *Amuda* and expressed the hope that Jamestown would twin with Ipswich and fund several projects. General Knapp later wrote to Robin Davies from the US suggesting there would be Anglo-American co-operation and that he would be reporting favourably.

Timothy Easton, the artist, who doubled up as a Tudor 'expert', came to Otley Hall and declared that there was a symbol of the universe on a panel in the centre of the fireplace. He said it had been moved from the screen passage and contained pitted stars. There were 'M's (Maria or Mary), and 'AM' (*Ave Maria*); and the black 'VV' in brick on the outside of the chimneys was to ward off evil spirits.[34]

Death of Argie

I arranged for a new country cousin to live with Argie, who was now 95, for one week a month. With prescience Argie told her that she would die in 1999. On 27 January a friend who lived nearby rang me at 8 a.m. to say that Argie was feeling terrible. I went round and Argie confirmed this but said she did not want to go into hospital. I said she must have a doctor's visit to establish how serious her condition was. The doctor came at 11.45 and said she must go to Princess Alexandra Hospital, Harlow. As she got into the ambulance she asked her friend, "Is this the end?" Ann travelled with Argie and stayed with her.

I arrived that evening and found Nightingale Ward. She looked frail, gaunt and wild. The doctor told her, "You've got heart failure caused by congestion in both lungs. If we get rid of the congestion, there won't be heart failure." The next day she was looking less wild. The wild look was caused by lack of oxygen as her lungs filled with fluid. She said to me, "I've had as near as damn it double pneumonia."

A few days later she was moved to St Margaret's Hospital, Epping. I visited her in Plane Ward. David Hoppit's mother was in the same ward, having had a stroke. Mrs. Bonner, who had for years attended local functions dressed as 'Queen Victoria', was visiting her husband. They had been guests at Coopersale Hall functions. I asked if I could do anything for him. He told me, "You can't do anything for me, no one can do anything for me." (He died a few days later.) Argie's X-ray showed that her lungs were nearly clear. She was lucid with me. As I left I turned and waved. She waved feebly back, sitting in bed in spectacles, frail and thin like a Belsen victim.

The next day Ann visited her with my sister Frances. They found her worse: nodding off to sleep and "talking scribble". When I arrived she was bleary-eyed. She was given a drink and kept nodding off, nearly spilling the liquid. I watched her chest. She did not breathe while I slowly counted up to 7. Had she taken her last breath? Then there was a breath, then another. Then no breathing for another count of 7. She slept much. I visited her at 6 and sat with her. She was taking a breath every second in little pants, her mouth open. She said, "I feel terribly hot." She was dry and her pneumonia had given her a fever. I got a fan and arranged for the blanket to be removed. She tried to get out of her nightie and then out of bed. She said, "Please let me get out." As I sat with her she raised her arms, her hands up as if clinging to a precipice, her fingers like claws. Her mouth was open, her false teeth were falling across her tongue. I could see that she was sinking.

The next day Ann sat with Argie, covering for me during the day while I kept appointments at Otley Hall. She rang from her car in the afternoon and said: "Argie died ten minutes ago. She went at 3.30."

She had been distressed and said she felt unwell. Then she had settled down into a rhythmic sleep, 30 breaths a minute. She was unconscious, her eyes were closed. Her breathing grew shallower and shallower and then stopped. The curtains were drawn round her, and the nurses came and did things without saying anything. They gave Ann a procedural letter. It was a merciful release.

I wished I could have been there for the end. But we had done everything we could. She had told the country cousin that she would die that year and she was right.[35]

The next day my brother Jonathan gave a pre-arranged organ recital, at which the family gathered in Tunbridge Wells. We stayed the night. The following morning I produced Argie's wishes and we planned the funeral. On my return to Loughton I visited Argie's flat and found her birth certificate and pension book, which would be needed for a death certificate to be issued. I found a copy of her will and rang her solicitor. Her will stated that her father, George Broadley I, was "a just and upright man" and favoured the feminine line, and that Frances would get the flat; I was to get the furniture. There were bequests to great-nephews and great-nieces and the Broadleys were to get two-sixths of the residue, the Haggers four-sixths (of which I was to receive one-sixth, less bequests and inheritance tax). There was a note in her handwriting by the will: "Nick gets nothing." She evidently went back on that idea, but I had no problem with the concept, being in the fortunate position of owning schools and properties. I did not mind Argie leaving to the 'feminine line', but I had to disagree with her: George I had *ignored* the feminine line, and had *not* properly provided for Argie and her sisters as his will made clear.

Three days later I rang Frances. I said, "Are you sitting down? You've got 28 Valley Close." She burst into tears and said, "That's not fair." She was upset, feeling that it should have been equally divided. Then my brother Jonathan rang, having received a copy of the will. "I'm appalled. It's a stupid will. Fran gets it all and we get nothing as we have to pay inheritance tax. She could have had our esteem by a fair division. Now, for all time, the division is tainted, and she will be a byword down here for unfairness."

It seemed less than fair that the descendants of George II, who had benefited from the family business to the exclusion of Argie, my mother and Flo, should have two-sixths of Argie's estate. But as the estate was eaten up by inheritance tax on the flat and capital, the shares were academic, and there would be no sixths for anybody. One-sixth of nothing was nothing, and everybody apart from my sister had nothing, though I did benefit from some furniture.

The truth was, Argie was looking at the family from her father's perspective, which is why she had wanted the Broadleys to benefit, and, being medical, she wanted her flat to go to my medical sister, two of whose immediate family were also medical. She had grown up in the time of the suffragettes, for whom 'the feminine line' would have been an attractive ideal. She had joined the Salvation Army at one point in her life, had beaten a drum on the streets of London and had wanted to go to Africa to save the Africans. She had been fiercely idealistic, and her will had to be understood in this light. Frances sold the flat and invested the proceeds for her children.

I went to see Argie in the Chapel of Rest at the undertaker's. I was shocked by how masculine she looked. I could have been looking at a man's face. It was longer than the face I knew, less round. I said a few words to her – "You *are* dead and will shortly be going on a journey, thank you for all you did for us" – and opened my hands and went to the Light and felt a terrific surge come through me and go down my legs, as though she were welcoming me warmly, greeting me. I said, "You have survived, there is a life after this one," and there were many surges. She lay in a white gown with embroidered suns, her hands folded together in prayer, her thin fingers interlocked, all coming out of a white coffin cover in the Balmoral coffin I had chosen with a brass name inscription. Later I reflected that I had seen an ugliness, a manliness, in her I had not seen before.

Argie's funeral took place a week later. The family gathered at our Loughton house in Albion Hill. My brother Robert was too ill to come. I gave Jonathan (as executor) a pile of bills and Frances a pile of letters for her to reply to. The hearse drew up at 9.15 with two limousines. We drove to the crematorium at Parndon Wood. The coffin came in to shouted words. During the address a blue tit clung to the window, trying to look in. The story was told again of Argie witnessing her father dying: he had sat up and cried out "Tom", suggesting that his eldest son Tom had come to meet him.

After the cremation we drove back to the Methodist church in Loughton. A congregation of about 85 was waiting for us. Lord Murray and I performed the readings, and Dame Phyllis Friend, formerly matron of the London Hospital, gave the address. My reading (chosen by Argie) was *Philippians* 4, verses 6–9. "Think on these things." Through the reading Argie seemed to be justifying her controversial will, but I widened the message by pausing after the words "true", "just" and "of good report" to suggest fairness. Her previous Methodist minister gave his personal reflections and spoke of her decision to have open-heart surgery at 80. He reminded us that her date of birth was under the foundation-stone of the church hall in which her memorial service was taking place.[36]

Otley Hall and ghosts

Down in Charlestown the artist Kerris of Polkerris visited us. He produced a long picture of the Harbour-master's House in a storm, snuggling on land against an aggressive sea as water broke over the pier and fountained up under a dark, stormy, cloudy sky. I said: "It catches the energy in the sea and the wind and shows our domesticity huddling under the cliff. I like it." It hung over our hearth, and I reflected it caught the elemental forces in Charlestown – the energies of storm and calm. I now needed him to paint the sunlight on the sea and, suggest the mystic One. The next day Kerris came for his money. He told me he was in the tradition of Constable and Turner and showed the symmetry and beauty in Nature. He could not understand why, from paintings of landscapes submitted by Cornish artists, the Tate had selected just one painting: a large blank canvas with a red dot in its centre.

I talked on BBC Radio Suffolk for 3½ minutes on the founding of America from Otley Hall. The next day a writer and photographer from *OK!* magazine came to write about the founding of the US from Otley Hall and to interview our family. I took Ann out in the boat on the moat and a wind blew us towards the bank. There was an outside shot by the cornucopia. We were photographed in the Great Hall having tea at the fireside, and then I was photographed in the screen passage.

The following day there was more filming. In the Linenfold Room there was a strange incident. The photographer set up an umbrella that reflects light, and briefly left the room. I was standing by the window. As I turned, the open umbrella closed violently down onto the bulb, which flashed and went out. The photographer, Roger Allston, rushed back into the room and discovered that the umbrella's handle, which he had encased in a straight steel tube, was bent. He said, "I've never known this happen anywhere despite 30 years in the business. It must have been a terrific force that closed it and bent the handle within this steel tube – a paranormal force. Your ghost." He replaced the bulb and that too failed. He replaced that and the third bulb failed. He said he had never known that during his career, "Not three bulbs failing, one after the other." I said to the picture of Robert Gosnold III, "It's all right, it's all right to let the filming continue," and after that there were no hitches. I wondered if the ghost of Robert Gosnold III had been active. Later all my family were filmed sitting round the Linenfold Room table and then I had to sit in the rose garden in the big oak chair that had floral decoration on its back (c.1600). Filming ended at 6.45 and I took the family to eat at Seckford Hall.

I received an early copy of *The One and the Many* in early March, and was now correcting the proofs of *The Warm Glow of the Monastery Courtyard*. The next day I finished *Ovid Banished*, but was still revising it on 19 April.

I booked a survey by Philip Aitken of the dating of Otley Hall and then a geophysical survey to probe the Tudor courtyard under the rose garden. I gave an interview on the gardens to *The East Anglian Daily Times*. Our new researcher had discovered that Robert Gosnold I leased Otley Hall to Robert III in 1566 and lived upstairs. I attended the opening of Christchurch Mansion, where Mike Weidman told me that Beatty had written asking for costings and what Ipswich would do in 2007. US funding was a possibility but it seemed that Ipswich was expected to contribute although it was short of money.

We had an Open Day. I was sent for as a white-haired old man was telling a packed Linenfold Room that there was a ghost in the corner. I saw him pointing at the old man in the picture, Robert Gosnold III, who had leased the downstairs, including this room, from 1566 and had featured in the collapsing umbrella. He was saying that Robert III's ghost was in the corner opposite the door, an old man of 80. (Robert III died in 1615 at the age of 80.) All listened in tense silence. I walked to the corner and said, "Where's the ghost?" "No, no, you're standing on his feet," the old man, who told me his name was Mr Forsdock, said. "There's no one here," I declared to defuse the situation, and everyone laughed. Mr Forsdock then walked to the window and pointed up at the Banqueting Room: "There's another one waving through the window up there, a little girl." "Thank you very much," I said, "That's where I'm sleeping tonight," and again everyone laughed.

In fact there was a tradition at Otley Hall that in the 17th century a 14-year-old girl was locked up in the garderobe cupboard by my bed, clamoured to be released and died of starvation. I had heard the story on a previous Open Day from a former owner of Otley Hall, Lady Foster. I took Mr Forsdock up to my bedroom, and he said the girl was following us around the room. If he was a genuine clairvoyant then I had been sleeping in the company of a ghost, and would continue to do so.

The following week I visited Hedingham Castle with Charles. We had tea in the guide Charles Bird's cottage. Bird believed that Shakespeare's works were written by the 17th Earl of Oxford, who was based at the castle. He took us up a lane across fields to Kirby Hall, where the 17th Earl of Oxford spent much time and where Gen. Fairfax came – his wife was Ann Vere. The Fairfax campaign was planned under a 600-year-old oak nearby, which I saw. The eight dogs that killed Actaeon in Arthur Golding's translation of Ovid were named after the surrounding woods, for example Hunter's, according to Bird. Golding tutored his nephew, the 17th Earl of Oxford, but the naming of the dogs after local woods tells us about Golding's knowledge of the locality rather than about Shakespeare's. Bird took us to Rushley Green and pronounced it the flat heath King Lear wandered on during his madness. There was no evidence that this was so, or that Oxford was Shakespeare.[37]

Our latest couple had continued to cause concern and to everyone's relief they resigned. They served out their notice and then changed their minds. They wanted to come back on a different basis: running courses in the conference room. They were supposed to be our housekeeper and caretaker who would feed the many groups the guides addressed, not additional Administrators. We then heard that our previous couple, the Bisoffis, had returned from Italy and were working in England. I contacted them and learned that they might come back if I found them a home outside Otley Hall where they could receive their three grown-up children and their families. I proposed to buy an investment property they could live in for a while.

St Osyth Priory

Towards the end of March I became interested in St Osyth Priory, a walled property within 383 acres resembling an Oxford college: a 1475 Gatehouse, monastic ruins, a 13th-century chapel, a 16th-century tower and buildings over many centuries providing more than 100 rooms. It had been owned by

Thomas Cromwell and the Earl of Rochford, and was in general disrepair. It was 12 miles from Rochester and near the sea, and I could see it as a staging post between Loughton and Otley. I would run it with staff who would hold Open Days, conferences and weddings. The original St Osyth had links to the East Anglians and the East Saxons, and was martyred in 653 by marauding Danes.

I took the family to visit the Priory, whose walls and tower dominated the tiny village by St Osyth beach. The estate agent said, "I know you own Otley Hall and Coopersale Hall," and showed me round with the security guard who also ran conferences and weddings. (He told me he had been in the SAS and military intelligence.) Parts of the property were 12th-century and there was an old tithe barn and bailiff's cottage. The rose-garden was very formal, within box hedges. I was very taken with the image of St George and the Dragon on the outside of the Gatehouse. (I had slain dragons – the hydra, gorgon and chimera – during my winning of my independence.) All periods in English history were in this place: the East Anglians, Saxons and Danes, the Anarchy, Magna Carta, Chaucer, the Wars of the Roses, the Tudor line, the Renaissance, the Georgian time and the Victorian Gothic. The whole history of English literature could be found among the monastic ruins and monks' graves. I wrote a classical ode, 'At St Osyth's Priory'.

Ann and I made a second visit to St Osyth. We identified an apartment with good views, and an exhibition area, and we drove round the 383 acres with the agent and security guard, noting the many pheasants and deer. Three days later we were told we could have the Anglian artefacts on loan from Ipswich to form a museum there. I made a third visit with Ann, Matthew and Ken, our Bursar, and looked round every room, climbed the tower and identified the kitchen to be used for conferences and weddings. I returned with Ann, Ken and an accountant and met a Planning official. I told him I wanted to keep the estate as a whole and outlined some plans, which he liked. The estate agent said that the Priory was second only to Audley End in the county of Essex.

The accountant wanted me to go ahead. I was objective: "The 1120s are... in historic houses, and need not be bought. I can visit and write poems about the places.... I am stepping back from St Osyth's, from all the conversion work that will be required to make it work."

A few days later Ken, our Bursar, reported that he had contacted the building engineer who had surveyed the Priory two years previously. The engineer had dug out his report and read it to Ken from his car phone. There was £954,000 worth of remedial work to do, including £85,000 on the Gatehouse and £150,000 on the boundary wall. The engineer shared the conclusions of the survey report, which had cost tens of thousands of pounds. We learned that spending £484,000 had been deemed urgent two years previously, and that the Gatehouse had been deemed too dangerous for the public to enter as there was dilapidation just inside the main entrance.

I reacted to this news by reflecting: "What is at stake, is the next ten years. My priority is to get my writing done – finish my poems and verse plays. My remedial work must be done on my writing…. St Osyth… [is] just a poem." The next day I wrote to the estate agent setting out the expenditure needed before the public could enter and walked away from St Osyth's.[38]

The Priory was bought by the Sargeant family. Soon after their purchase the boundary wall was deemed dangerous and they had to outlay £1m to make it safe. In 2013 they needed to raise £22million to renovate the unsafe buildings.

Anglo-Saxon Suffolk
My dealings with the Anglian artefacts led to our joining a weekend visiting Anglo-Saxon Suffolk. There was a reception at the Novotel, Ipswich and a talk on Gipeswich (Anglo-Saxon Ipswich). The next morning the group visited West Stow, a reconstructed Anglo-Saxon village, c.420–650, that housed the rural new people after the Romans left. I noted the ventilation under the floors, the central fire under thatch and the sack beds. We went on to Grime's Graves, flint mines from c.1000BC. I climbed down a ladder through a chalk seam to 30 feet below ground level and saw the black flint in the rock and the lit chambers of ancient mines. We went on to Lavenham and then Kersey, where we had tea at The Bell and walked down to the water-splash. There was then a reception in the Anglo-Saxon room of the Ipswich Museum.

The next day we went to Sutton Hoo and looked at the pillow mounds, Raedwald's tomb and long ship. We saw the large white house where a clair-voyant saw soldiers circling the mound from a second-floor window; a glimpse that led to the discovery of Anglo-Saxon Sutton Hoo. Later I drafted two classical odes, 'At Royal Sutton Hoo: Raedwald and the End of England' and 'In Anglo-Saxon Suffolk'. "Fell asleep before I completed stanza 7 (of 8) of the first poem – I wrote the Sutton Hoo poem first to get it out of the way before I did the more universal one." I also wrote a poem, 'Flint'.[39]

Tudor houses: The Thatch, South Wraxall Manor
I visited The Thatch in Otley village, a Tudor property that would house our excellent couple. The Bisoffis came, viewed the property, agreed to join us and went off to work their notice. We had more Open Days. (The visitors included Ed Hutton who under my captaincy at Chigwell, playing for the Under-15, took 10 wickets in an innings against another school. It was

strange to be discussing my cricketing youth at Otley Hall.)

I was visited by a writer from *The Suffolk Journal* who wanted to write an article on Otley Hall's gardens. Two days later I wrote a poem, 'In an English Garden, True to Nature'. Iris Murdoch died. She had written to me, exhorting me "Onward!", and I reflected that three of my correspondents – Ted Hughes, Frank Tuohy and Iris Murdoch had died within a few weeks of each other.

We tried once again to unravel the Tudor knot of the dating of Otley Hall. Philip Aitken came, looked at the various wings and declared that in his view Robert Gosnold I pulled down the old Otley Hall and built a new building alongside it c.1520. Thinking of Oliver Rackham's view that parts dated back to at least c.1450, I said: "But we know the Gosnolds rented from 1401 to 1542 – is it likely he'd pull down his house as a tenant in 1520?" The knot seemed unravellable. Jocelyn Wingfield brought 35 Americans from his extended family and I spoke to them about the dating one lunchtime.

For my 60th birthday Ann took me to the Priory, Lavenham, and a 1540ish room, the Great Chamber, with a four-poster. We ate in the Great House in Market Place, where all my children were sitting waiting as a surprise. I wrote a classical ode, 'Sixty in Lavenham Priory'.

On 27 May 1999 I visited our Essex solicitor and signed contracts for The Thatch, Otley and for 6 Quay Road, Charlestown, which had been owned by a German housewife from Hamburg who had just died. Her widower was living at Lake Como and wanted to sell. He had asked me if we would consider taking it on as a 'buy to let' investment, and the bank had agreed. It was four doors down from our Charlestown property, and with a letting agency finding weekly 'holiday' tenants we found a housekeeper and ran it from our Charlestown house.

We had two more Open Days, during which Matthew reported that he had got engaged to Melanie in Plymouth. In due course we booked his wedding at Otley church in August 2000.

I found it hard to resist looking at Tudor houses that came on the market. The latest had leapt out at me: a large stone manor house in Wiltshire that had been connected with Sir Walter Raleigh. We viewed it on our way to Cornwall. It was near Bradford-upon-Avon: South Wraxall Manor, a serene, grey stone building with a gatehouse (1399), Great Hall fireplace (1598), a Solar with sculpted stone figures and a 'Raleigh room' where Raleigh and Sir Walter Long smoked. There was a view over the surrounding countryside. It had its own cricket field across a (not too busy) road that divided the estate. I drafted a classical ode, 'South Wraxall Manor, Wiltshire'. Once again my excitement and yearning for a Tudor property was mixed up with poetic inspiration. It was as if I had to adopt the posture of a passionate buyer to research my poem.

'A Defence of Traditional Poetic Method'
While down in Cornwall I wrote 'A Defence of Traditional Poetic Method or: Poking the Hornets' Nest', extracts from which would appear in the Appendix of my *Collected Poems*. I wrote a classical ode, 'A Tudor Youth'[40] and monitored the dendrochronology (dating by the number of tree-rings) that Philip Aitken had organised, which was disappointing: the 'expert' had only been able to take half a dozen cores, and had not been able to unravel, or cut, the dating knot.

Verse plays: Ovid Banished, The Rise of Oliver Cromwell
Ovid Banished
Down in Cornwall before Christmas 1998 I had got stuck into *Ovid Banished*:

> Had a phenomenal day. *Ovid Banished* flowed through so easily. I wrote as if automatically, not thinking, gazing at the sea, seeing words appear on the end of my biro. By 6 I had reached Act 2, scene 7, a massive amount, and barely a muffed line.... I have yanked *Ovid Banished* forward. As usual I come to Cornwall run down, tired, overworked; and I get beneath myself, sleep off my tiredness, get my energy flowing again, locate my creative self – which is what I have done today.

Five days later I "dashed off two soliloquies in which Augustus brings himself to a choice between the Julians and the Claudians". By the end of the year I was "three-fifths through" the play. In January I was thinking about Acts 4 and 5.[41]

The Rise of Oliver Cromwell
I had resolved to write a new verse play on Cromwell's rise to power, *The Rise of Oliver Cromwell*. On 29 March 1999 I "drafted 85 scenes in 5 Acts and have the skeleton of [the] verse play". At Otley Hall I wondered: "Did Cromwell act alone?"[42]

Charles and I found out that Dutch Rosicrucians in Amsterdam sent funds for his New Model Army on the understanding that he would remove Charles I and admit Jews into England. We had been researching into revolutions further to the article 'Old Regimes' I wrote immediately after the Libyan revolution[43] and found an exchange of letters between Oliver Cromwell and Ebenezer Pratt of the Mulheim Synagogue, Amsterdam: on 16 June 1647 Cromwell promised to kill Charles I; and on 12 July 1647 Pratt urged that Charles I should be tried and then executed. These two letters can be read in my book *The Secret History of the West*.[44] The Dutch Rosicrucians dreamt of a universal empire that in those days amounted to a world government. Charles I, in his speech before his execution, referred to "conquests by forces of world imperialism" and seemed to understand that he was a victim of international Rosicrucian Freemasonry.[45]

I started writing *The Rise of Oliver Cromwell* on 24 April. I worked on it for the rest of the year, along with *The Secret History of the West*.

Cast of the Globe's Julius Caesar *stay and rehearse at Otley Hall*
The Globe cast arrived to rehearse *Julius Caesar* quite late in the evening. I showed the actors to their rooms and we had a glass of wine in the Great Hall. Mark Rylance, who was directing the play, arrived after midnight, and I took him for a walk to show him where the actors could go. I offered him the double bed in the Literary Room, thinking that he might like to browse in the Shakespeare library before going to bed, but he announced that he had brought a tent, which he and his wife pitched near the woods. He did not seem to be interested in the books.

The next morning I took the group for a tour. John McEnery, who had played Jaques, was one of the actors. I was shocked that his flat in Shoreditch had burnt down when a candle overbalanced and that he had been in hospital for several weeks with a burnt arm.

The actors spent the next day rehearsing and I was invited to join them in the evening in the conference room for a dinner they prepared. I sat next to Caesar and discussed how to play a dictator. Then Mark spoke to all. He proposed getting up at 4 a.m. to re-enact conspirators making their way to the thatched summer-house, and revellers intercepting them. The sooth-sayer, a little old man with a beard, asked me for a three-pin plug. Everyone had a glass of champagne and the company were very together.

The next morning Mark called on me and said we would be starting in ten minutes, would I join him. I joined the actors. It was another glorious day. I sat with Mark on the stairs outside the Oak Room and heard Caesar talking with Calpurnia. They went downstairs, Caesar in dressing-gown and bare feet, and played a scene outside the front door while we watched. We then went to the Linenfold Room to listen while Caesar entertained all the conspirators he had welcomed with open arms. He gave them a glass of wine. I had to stand in for a player and say: "Lord Caesar, the Senate awaits you."

They left and walked round the moat to the rose-garden lawn where the soothsayer spoke. Caesar received 33 cuts on the croquet lawn, and fell before the newly-thatched summer-house. Mark said that the ungram-matical "the most unkindest cut" should be said "the most..., unkindest cut". (Caesar changes his sentence construction as he staggers before he falls.)

We went with the plebs to the mound. "What's happened, we need to know." Brutus spoke to the crowd from the mound. Then Antony spoke, very "honourable" in a straight way. Mark said to me, "He's a friend of

Brutus, they don't realise he's going to turn it." Cinna the poet was killed and we broke for lunch.

At 5 an 'expert' on Tudor music and weapons demonstrated the longbow, musket, pike, halberd, sword and buckler, and 12 actors paraded as pikemen. The cast were shown how to bow to an officer in the Elizabethan time: "Take hat off, step back and elegant bow."

A pig roast was ready at 8. A local fellow who helped in the grounds had arrived with the skinned pig and had mounted it on a spit. A fire had been lit and corrugated-iron guards placed round it to reflect the heat. The roasted pig was carried to the conference room by two of the actors while drummers beat drums and flautists played pipes. The carcass was put on a table and the spit was drawn. The roast was then carved.

That evening I sat with the actors in the conference room as they ate. Antony told me he loved Caesar *and* Brutus. I spoke with Brutus about his nobility: he was a stoic who did not believe in murder or suicide but committed both – because he saw that Caesar had to be deposed. I sat with Caesar and discussed how his attitude caused the conspirators to conspire. We talked about Caesar's greatness. I said: "He held Italy together, he's a centre, as constant as the northern star. *Après moi le déluge. L'État, c'est moi.*" I asked Caesar who had taken over from Richard Burton. He said: "Mark Rylance."

The next morning the actors proscribed the senators in the Great Hall and executed five, who had earlier been led, hands behind backs, to the peacock cage. ("Don't talk.") They were lain flat and then Antony personally executed them, exploring his sense of power. They had swords thrust into their stomachs, and cuts were made on their upper legs, arms and throats.

The actors spent the rest of the morning and part of the afternoon on the field that adjoins Otley Hall. (A neighbouring farmer had given them permission.) Mark Rylance asked me to arm myself to take part in the final battle. I went to the kitchen and came out with a meat cleaver, which I brandished at Cassius's troops. Mark banned this on health and safety grounds and recast me as an ensign-bearer. I had 30 seconds to find an ensign, and seized a broom from the conference-room kitchen. I tied a tea-towel to it and covered the brush part with another tea-towel, and bore it behind Antony as a kind of canopy. We marched across the field to Cassius's camp and fought a pitched battle. We were outnumbered four against 25, but yelled, "Death to traitors, we kill all traitors, death to them." *They* chanted, making cuts with their swords. We won. Cassius committed suicide on the mound, Brutus by the field's small moat (which in Tudor times protected animal feed). I looked across the field from the mayhem of Brutus's camp and saw a rural scene – a barn and our house.

We said our goodbyes. In my speech to the actors I said how much I had enjoyed working with them and how impressed I was by the production. I said that if they were a pleb or an ensign-carrier short, they should not ring around but should ask me. Everyone laughed. Mark said to me after the actors had gone, "Everyone was impressed by your knowledge of the play." He asked for a copy of *Ovid Banished,* which I gave him together with a signed copy of *The Tragedy of Prince Tudor.*

After he left with his wife, Charles presented me with his 'Earl of Oxford concord' (an agreement involving land, 1580): "I thought you might like it in return for all you've done for me. I think the Earl of Oxford signed it." It was his most treasured possession and I was very touched.

Ann and I went to the Globe to see *Julius Caesar.* I was disappointed. The play lacked energy, and no actor dominated the audience. Caesar and Antony were laid back. I thought Mark was an inexperienced director. We were asked to go to the restaurant and I sat with Cassius and heard how tired he was, and ill. Mark and Claire found us, and Mark explained that Caesar is 'father' to three sons: Cassius, Brutus and Antony. I reflected on Mark's definition of 'eloquence' in his programme note: "Speaking with force, fluency and appropriateness to move the emotions and affect the reason." He had not succeeded in moving the emotions. I had enjoyed participating in the rehearsals at Otley Hall, but much of the zest and banter had evaporated in the stage performance.

We were invited back to the Globe to see *The Comedy of Errors,* "a romp on a silly theme – two twin brothers of the same name with two twin servants of the same name. Too far-fetched to take seriously…. I was not engaged or involved."[46]

Next works

I had spoken to my publisher, Michael Mann. On 9 June he told me that he was prepared to publish my "two [next] verse plays (*Ovid Banished* and *The Rise of Oliver Cromwell*); and two books of poems – *Poems for England* and the most recent poems, [my classical odes]". He asked me to visit him on 24 June.

But by then everything had changed. He told me he had been in a partnership with Penguin for the last year, and Penguin had just been taken over by Putnams and were more sales conscious. He wanted me to produce some big books that would go down well with Putnams. He added an updating of Part Two of *The Fire and the Stones,* which would become *The Rise and Fall of Civilizations;* a book on revolutions, *The Secret History of the West;* and *The End of the Universe* (which would become *The New Philosophy of Universalism*). He now asked me to write the books in a new order: *The Rise and Fall of Civilizations,* which I should begin immediately and finish by the end of November for publication in August 2000; *Ovid Banished; Poems for England*, which might be retitled *Visions of England*; *The Secret History of Revolutions*, which would become *The Secret History of the West*; *The Rise of Oliver Cromwell*; and *The End of the Universe*; the classical odes would be entitled *A Tudor Knot* (now the title of book 1 of *Classical Odes*).

I got straight on with *The Rise and Fall of Civilizations* and produced an opening chapter within a few days. But then Michael's secretary rang, asking if I would meet him at his publicity company, Midas, at 7–8 Kendrick Mews, London SW7 at 7 a.m. the next day. I reported to Midas (via 33 Stanhope Gardens, where I looked up at the two front windows I had occupied). Michael Mann arrived "fresh from receiving the Queen's Award yesterday". There had been another meeting and now *The Secret History of the West* (as *The Secret History of Revolutions* was now referred to) had been fast-tracked. I should abandon work on *The Rise and Fall of Civilizations* and forge ahead on *The Secret History of the West*.[47]

I was now beginning to unravel the Tudor knots, and with the handing-over of *The Rise of Oliver Cromwell* my verse plays had come to an end, and a new episode was beginning.

Episode 12:

Classical Odes and Utopianism

Years: 1999–2003
Locations: Loughton, Buckhurst Hill: Carcassonne, Montségur; Rennes-le-Château; Iceland; Sicily; Turin; Rome; Lisbon; Spain; Mediterranean; Cyprus; Bordeaux; Heidelberg; Freiburg; China
Works: *Classical Odes*; *The Secret History of the West*; *The Syndicate*
Initiatives: Shakespearean authorship; dating by dendrochronology; four-book volume of odes; New World Order

"My classical approach seeks an ordered, controlled, serene view of a time when there is as much of a split or schism in the English soul as there was during the Civil War. The anguish caused by this schism is experienced Romantically. The blend of a Romantic agony and Classical treatment is Universalist, and these Odes are fundamentally Universalist despite their classical style."

Nicholas Hagger,
Preface to *A Tudor Knot*, 'Poems on England',
book 1 of *Classical Odes*

In my next episode my examination of utopianism – dreams of a perfect society – within Western civilization was in conflict with my presentation of the imperfect world in my classical odes.

Utopianism: The Secret History of the West *and the Lords*

Perfect utopias, and the classical tradition in Classical Odes

A 'Utopia' (like Sir Thomas More's *Utopia* of 1516) is "an imagined perfect place or state of things" (*Concise Oxford Dictionary*) and a utopian "an idealistic reformer" who dreams of making the world perfect. In *The Secret History of the West* I set out the Western occultist tradition since 1453, and the roots within it of all utopian Western revolutions and of the New World Order.

At the same time I was widening my classical odes into a presentation of the classical tradition that has been the backbone of the West. My *Classical Odes*, the finished book I had glimpsed in Pisa along with the one-volume *Overlord*, consists of reflective poems, Universalist fusions of thinking and feeling in the long tradition of odes that began with Pindar, passed through Horace and took in Marvell, Milton, Wordsworth and Keats. They are classical in following the principles held to be of permanent value by the authors of classical antiquity, and in their restrained style. As the Preface says, they emphasise "proportion, balance, formal harmony, control, order, serenity, clarity and submitting to rules". Each ode is a sustained meditation or objective reflection that fuses place and idea. I reflect with dismay on the decline of the Great Britain of Churchill and Montgomery, focus on the transition to living in the coming United States of Europe and under a New World Order, and my reflections are imbued with a sense that the universe is One.

Work on The Secret History of the West

I intended *The Secret History of the West* to be a secret history of all the revolutions since 1453. At Otley Hall (on 7 June 1999 and again on 25 June) I told Charles we were researching the Protestant Revolution, beginning with the Cathar Revolution within the Reformation Revolution, and then the Puritan Revolution, which would be background for *The Rise of Oliver Cromwell*. We would then be researching the Glorious Revolution, the American Revolution, the French Revolution, the Imperialist Revolution in Britain and Germany and the Russian Revolution. We would come up with a new model for how revolutions operate.

The Reformation Revolution featured Philip Sidney and I took Ann to Montacute House to look at a portrait of Sidney, c.1588. I was startled to read on it one of his favourite quotations, Hannibal's, *'Inveniam viam aut faciam'*, 'I shall find a way or make a way' – a possible origin for Samuel

Harsnett's Chigwell School motto of 1629 ('*Aut inveniam viam aut faciam*'). In strange synchronicity, in July 1999 the ex-Head of Chigwell School, Tony Little, returned from Oakham School to distribute the Oaklands prizes at Woodford's Hawkey Hall. Sitting next to him waiting for a concert to begin I whispered, "There's a vacancy at Eton. You went there, you could apply." He smirked and said nothing. I persisted. "Eton next?" He: "It's in some disarray." I: "It needs you to sort it out?" A few years later he returned to Chigwell as Head Master of Eton, having started there in 2002, and told me on the call-over steps, "I'd just had the interview and had been told I'd got it and that I should keep quiet and not tell anyone until an announcement was made, and you came out with what I was trying to keep secret. I wondered if you are a mind-reader."

The Reformation Revolution also featured Lord Burghley and the 17th Earl of Oxford, and after having 40 from Otley village to tea at Otley Hall I received a party from the Earl of Oxford's Castle Hedingham. Their leader, Charles Bird, told me he believed that Shakespeare's papers are in the 15th Earl of Oxford's tomb in the Hedingham church. He took me to the SAT library, found the First Folio of 1623, explained the colophons and told me two hares were 'leverets', and that the first three letters of 'leveret' ('lev') indicated that the First Folio contained the works of 'Lord Edward Vere'. I did not believe this. He spoke of the Latin *Chronicles* of Ralph de Coggeshall, who from 1207 to 1218 was an Abbot at the Cistercian Coggeshall Abbey.

While I pondered Western civilization's utopian revolutions I was very aware that Otley Hall covered the period from 1453 and began probing the dating of Otley Hall. I got Philip Aitken and Oliver Rackham to take off the linenfold panelling to look at the posts behind it, the Solar panelling and the panelling in the Great Hall, which showed a stud sporting 16th-century yellow-ochre. In conjunction with Philip Aitken and Edward Martin I asked our gardener to dig a hole in the rose-garden lawn, and we found the old flint courtyard a metre down. In Tudor times the present rear of Otley Hall was its front, and it would have been approached on this flint courtyard. At the beginning of the summer holidays I cleared my study in Albion Hill and moved its contents, including all my material for *The Secret History of the West*, to Otley Hall. On the first night I heard a pair of nightjars in the wood magically squawking, 'churr' and 'hooick'.

Thinking about revolutions, I went back to my article, 'Old Regimes' which I had written in the days following Gaddafi's *coup*. I reflected that my experience of revolution in Libya had led me to *The Anatomy of Revolution* for my article and prepared me for *The Secret History of the West*. The very same day I was thinking about Libya Nadia rang to say that Caroline had had a stroke: she had blacked out in a bathroom, banged her head and cut her nose, and her balance had gone. Two days later she had been on jury service, and at 4 p.m. when all were commanded "All rise" she keeled over to the left and was caught.[1] Once again I pondered synchronicity. There seemed to be an inevitable progression from my experiencing revolution in Libya to my writing about all the revolutions since 1453 in *The Secret History of the West*.

In Cathar country: Carcassonne, Rennes-le-Château, Montségur
Needing to visit Cathar country in Southern France for the Cathar Revolution, I flew to Carcassonne airport with Ann, hired a car and drove to our hotel. We walked to the nearby 12th-14th-century walled city and that night ate in the open air in the square where the Crusaders assembled for the Albigensian Crusade against the Montségur Cathars (who had murdered the Catholic Inquisitors).

We drove up a mountain to Rennes-le-Château, admired the Pyrenees in the distance and entered the church of Saint Mary Magdalene, which had been rebuilt by the local priest Bérenger Saunière in the 19th century. The authors of *The Holy Blood and the Holy Grail* claimed that Saunière had stumbled on evidence that Jesus survived the crucifixion, married Mary Magdalene and had children, and that his descendants were the Frankish Merovingian kings of the 5th century, knowledge guarded by the Priory of Sion from the 11th century. The authors claimed that Saunière had built the church from money given him by the Vatican to keep silent.

In the church I saw the figure of Asmodeus, guardian of the treasure of Solomon, horned like the Devil. The stations of the cross had roses on them. In the museum I saw an 8th-century pillar which was inscribed 'Mission 1891'. 'Mission' included the word 'Sion'. The lettering over the door said: '*Regnum Mundi*' ('the Kingdom of the World'), '*Lumen in Coeli*' ('Light in Heaven'). I wrote a classical ode, 'At Rennes-le-Château: Mission 1891'.

We drove through mountain passes to a car park below Montségur. I left Ann and walked into the Field of the Burned, where 205 Cathars threw themselves on flames. I climbed through woods up steep steps, sleeper after sleeper, to the fortress, which was over 1,200 metres high. The original *château* was razed after the siege of 1244 and, breathless, I stood within the ruined walls and gazed at the tower that by tradition was the Grail chapel where the Cathar sacrament, the *consolamentum*, was taken. I saw the two slits in the wall on the first floor between which the Grail was, by tradition, located. I descended back to Ann, my legs nearly going (as after the descent of Ben Nevis) and arrived just as a sheet of rain approached. I later wrote a classical ode, 'At Carcassonne and Montségur: Castles of Light'.

We visited Narbonne and Beziers, and saw where 20,000 Cathars were slaughtered and burned. We celebrated Ann's birthday in a restaurant, L'Ostal des Troubadours, in the medieval streets of Carcassonne, near the 12th-century Château Comtal. We also walked to the Museum of Torture and saw torture instruments used by the Inquisition, and saw the Crusaders' HQ: the courtyard where they assembled and their dining-room. I returned with a clear view of the Cathars.[2]

The Secret History of the West *and revolutions; Nasser Hussain's dinner at Lord's*

Back in England we went to Otley Hall and I wrote my Preface to *The Secret History of the West*. I also spoke to visitors under the Council's 'Invitation to View' scheme and later played croquet on the croquet lawn with my sons before the couple served formal dinner in the Linenfold Room.

We went to Cornwall at the end of July and I wrote into the Reformation and Puritan Revolutions. I stopped working to witness a total solar eclipse. A row of people sat on canvas chairs with picnics along the wall outside our window, looking out to sea. ("It... was almost as dark as midnight. No stars. Silence. No birds.") I wrote a classical ode, 'The Eclipse of Reason (Or: Totality)'. I had to return to Essex to supervise building work. Back in Cornwall I noted that I had completed 29 sections of *The Secret History of the West* "and have 94 to do". I narrated the rise of Oliver Cromwell and Rosicrucianism from a historical point of view. The chapter provided a historical account of the events covered in my verse play, *The Rise of Oliver Cromwell*.

I carried on with *The Secret History of the West*, and wrote on utopianism, Cromwell, Hartlib, and the Glorious Revolution. Back in Suffolk the summer season at Otley Hall was over, and there were few bookings for the autumn. I held a meeting with the staff and urged them to mount a telephone campaign and follow-ups to start filling the order books for the next six months. The new school year started, and the Normanhurst GCSE results were greatly improved, 80 per cent receiving A–C in 5 subjects.

We returned to Cornwall and encountered a gale. I stood outside, leaning over the wall, and wrote a poem, 'Sea-Gale and the One' "to catch the energy of this creature [the sea] that keeps me company, whose mood is so readily roused by the wind".

Back in Essex I wrote the pattern of revolutions. I worked on the Renaissance and Reformation, and on the American Revolution. At Otley Hall BBC Radio Suffolk interviewed me live on Bartholomew Gosnold's founding of America in 1607.[3] In October I was working on the Boston Tea Party and the American War of Independence.

I took time off to attend a dinner in the Long Room at Lord's. Nasser Hussain had asked if I would support his Benefit Year and I took a party of family members and school advisers. There was a raffle, and Ken's wife won a cricket bat signed by the Indian team, which she gave me. After dinner I took my two sons up to the dressing-room used by the England team, took my stance at an imaginary wicket, tapped my bat against my right foot and executed a perfect cover-drive – and nearly beheaded Nasser, who, wearing DJ, had come in unobserved to look at his name on the board of centurions. He ducked, and I said, "Just coming to the attention of the England captain." Everyone laughed, including Nasser.[4]

In November I was writing about the First World War, and about civilizations and revolutions:

> Civilizations are driven by visions of the Light, the transformational stages by revolutions, which... secularise and break civilizations down, and get human rights at the expense of civilizations. There are two opposite tendencies.... Civilizations are noble ideas of good. Revolutions are violent ways of making things better – at the expense of civilizations.

As if by synchronicity I was rung by an Australian reader who told me he read my work on civilizations every day: "'Every day I read Gibbon.' I: 'Good.' He: 'And Spengler's *Decline of the West*.' I: 'Good.' He: 'And *The Fire and the Stones* and *The Universe and the Light* which came before it.' I: 'It came after it, but *very* good. Well done, in fact.'"

In mid-November I wrote on the Russian Revolution in Cornwall, kept company by the cormorant on the breakwater below my window. On the way back we stopped for tea at Bovey Tracey. We sat by the river, and I felt the peace as I looked at the river life: "the swarm of gnats, dancing, all of one mind; the hawfinch (or crossbill), yellow wagtail. The peace as the water-wheel turned, sheep in the background."

Peace was not what my publisher was experiencing. I rang him, and "he suddenly opened up: 'It's been terrible.... Penguin England has dumped Penguin America.... We've got Penguin, Harper, Perseus trying to buy us out. The investors want to sell.'" It dawned on me that my publisher might not be in existence by the time I had finished *The Secret History of the West*.

I was approaching the end of my study of utopianism. Towards the end of January I finished a chapter on the New World Order. I wondered if I had "a 2-parter. Part 1: The Revolutions. Part 2: The New World Order." Michael Mann had told me a fortnight earlier that "he may be bankrupt within 7 days". He had raised $15million but it would not be with him for 60 days. I pressed on and "wrote in a bit on the Bilderberg Group". I was for a virtuous world government but opposed to a self-interested one. "Universalism is right – intellectually and emotionally" but I opposed the self-interested New World Order.

On 29 March I was at last able to hand the book over. Michael wanted it to be called *The Secret History of the West* (and not *The Secret History of Revolution*, as I had proposed). He agreed that my next project should be a revision and update of *The Fire and the Stones,* to be titled *The Rise and Fall of Civilizations.*

Two days later I "combed half of *The Rise of Oliver Cromwell*" to make sure that the history tallied with chapter 2 of *The Secret History of the West.* Michael recommended that the book should be edited.[5] I revised *The Secret History of the West* chapter by chapter in conjunction with John Baldock.

The Earl of Burford's protest: leap onto woolsack
My work on utopianism was interrupted by publicity surrounding a utopian protest by my Literary Secretary, Charles, who opposed the Labour Government's (and European Union's) plan to abolish the Lords' hereditary peers. Charles and I had had many conversations about the House of Lords' Third Reading of the bill to abolish hereditary peers. He was waiting to inherit the Dukedom of St Albans – like Prospero waiting to be restored as the rightful Duke of Milan – and had a personal stake in opposing the bill. We agreed that the bill was linked to the European Union's plan to split the UK into eight regions – Scotland, Wales, London and five regions of England, grouping some parts of southern England with parts of France – as it would remove the peers most likely to block the plan, a theme I had put into *The Tragedy of Prince Tudor.* Charles was mindful that his ancestor the 3rd Earl of Southampton, Shakespeare's patron, had joined Essex's rebellion in 1601 and marched through London calling "For the Queen".

Charles was determined to denounce the bill in the Lords, and accuse its Labour supporters of treason. He resisted change, wanting to keep the Lords as it was, rather than abolish 700 years of tradition that would worsen the UK. As the son of a Duke he was allowed to sit on the raised step near the throne, and he had told me on 16 July that he would interrupt the Third Reading from there by leaping onto the throne and addressing the House of Lords. I talked him out of standing on the throne, which, I said, would be interpreted as being disrespectful to the Queen. He then fixed on the Speaker's seat: the woolsack. His intervention would a "beautiful act" that would speak down the centuries and be remembered in 400 years' time like Essex's protest. Ann and I went to Cornwall for half-term and he rang me there the day before the Third Reading to confirm that he was going ahead.

Sky News was the first to report what happened on 26 October 1999. Charles had rushed forward from the steps near the throne, climbed on the woolsack and harangued MPs to left and right. Many called out "Sit down", but he continued. Some peers called, "Get him out." Having denounced the bringers of the bill as traitors and the presentation of the bill as treason, Charles was dragged out of the chamber and banned from the Palace of Westminster by Black Rod. The Third Reading was passed by 221 votes to 81. Charles was the lead item in all the news programmes. He rang me from

Brooks's at 5.30.

Charles's courageous exploit can be relived on YouTube.[6] The House of Lords was packed, with past Prime Ministers and Government Ministers, including Tebbit. Charles's distant figure on the woolsack shouting to left and right reminded me of Lenin. I told him, "It *was* a beautiful act that will be remembered for 400 years." He said: "My second sentence was 'They're breaking up Britain.' Conrad Russell was yelling at me to get down." Bertrand Russell's grandson was a contemporary of mine at Oxford and a frequent debater at the Oxford Union. Charles told me: "When I left, after a reprimand by Black Rod, all the press ran after me and I gave out my leaflets. Outside they pushed a microphone in my face. I didn't have time to collect my thoughts. I was asked, 'Where do you work, Lord Burford?' I replied, 'At Otley Hall, I'm helping Nicholas Hagger to write a book on revolutions.'"

I was now implicated. There was something very splendid about his leap onto the woolsack and his haranguing of so many distinguished people, and I admired his spirit and courage, but I was glad to be down in Cornwall and out of reach of the press. *The Daily Telegraph* tracked him down to Otley Hall, and interviewed and photographed him in the Great Hall. The Suffolk TV programme *Look East* broadcast a report mentioning me and showing archive film of Otley Hall.

Charles's "beautiful act" did not go down well with his father. Charles later told me that the Duke of St Albans had sent him a letter and added a PS: "The above was written before your disgusting behaviour in the House."

The abolition of the hereditary peers' voting rights was in the tradition of the abandoned Liberal Reforms of 1911. In the first stage of this new reform 600 of Britain's hereditary peers would lose their 700-year-old right to sit and vote in the House of Lords, while 92 would continue to sit and vote in the Lords until the long-term reform was completed. Completion had not happened by 2014, and Charles's leap may have delayed its implementation and prolonged the sitting rights of the 92. Charles was praised for his spirit. I told Lord Murray in Loughton's Bookshop, "One of our employees disturbed your peace, I'm afraid." Murray said: "Oh, I wasn't there. A spirited young man. The Lords could do with waking up."

A consequence of Charles's protest became apparent on our return from Cornwall. There was a by-election in Kensington and Chelsea, and on 3 November Charles was asked to stand as an independent by the little-known Democratic Party. (It had been founded in November 1998 by a Malvern businessman, who also funded the party.) Charles had agreed to stand, seeing a platform for his views and realising that if he won, he would set Black Rod a problem, for how could he be banned from the Palace of

Westminster if he were an elected MP? The next day he held a press conference in Abbey Gardens, which was broken up by Black Rod after ten minutes because he was on Palace-of-Westminster premises. Black Rod's aide had entered and said, "Lord Burford, out," and Charles had continued the conference on the green. A leading figure of the Democratic Party, the shadowy John Gouriet – who had a military background in Sandhurst, the Ministry of Defence, NATO and intelligence according to his CV, and had asked Charles to stand – accused Black Rod of bullying. (It was a Nazi tactic to provoke a fight with authority and then claim victimisation.) The Democratic Party regarded the House of Lords as preventing Britain from becoming an elected dictatorship. I could see that Charles had been "carried away by an extremist".

Charles was left to campaign against Michael Portillo of the Conservatives on his own. The founder of the Democratic Party was not interested in votes, according to Charles, and refused to pay him any expenses. When Charles said he would not attend the count unless he was paid John Gouriet made a small payment. Charles reported that he was questioned about me and my work.[7] The votes were counted and Portillo was easily elected.

The truth was, the British Establishment was losing its power to Europe, which controlled between 15 and 50 per cent of its legislation (depending on what laws are included), and would soon be struggling to avert the break-up of the United Kingdom. The UK was caught between its old imperial nationalist identity and its new role as a state within a European superstate, and Charles's leap reflected the dwindling power of the Lords in this transitional time. Charles was unhappy at the aristocracy's loss of influence and at the prospect that he might be a Duke without a voice, and his frustration was evident in his protest. I was an eyewitness of these constitutional strains.

Classical odes on England and Europe
My classical odes, which I had glimpsed in Pisa, took root in Otley Hall's Tudor ambience and emerged from the conflict between the UK, the EU and New World Order, which had already thrown up *The Tragedy of Prince Tudor*. Many of my classical odes were shaped by events surrounding Otley Hall.

North Tawton: Ted Hughes's house
Odes were never far away. The immediate family were together at Anthony's degree ceremony at Reading University, at which, after a fanfare, Ant, in a gown with a blue hood and mortarboard, shook hands with the white-gloved Vice-Chancellor; and again to see in the millennium at Coombe House, near Crediton, Devon, an 18th-century mansion on the side of a

small valley.

The next morning we drove to North Tawton. We passed the entrance to Ted Hughes's home, Court Green, and in the churchyard I peeped through a gap in a Leylandii hedge at the back of the house from which he wrote to me and sent me *Birthday Letters*, and saw where he and Sylvia Plath picked daffodils and sold them. During a medieval banquet in Coombe House's cellars that evening I reflected that his ashes were scattered within the restricted zone of an army rifle-range on Dartmoor so he could be at one with the moor he loved without being trampled on by the vengeful feet of pro-Plath fanatics. Later I wrote two classical odes, 'At Coombe House, Devon: A New Millennium' and 'In North Tawton Churchyard'.

Otley Hall and the media; digging up rose-garden lawn, Jon Ronson and New World Order

A team of 18 'experts' round Philip Aitken and the artist Timothy Easton began dating Otley Hall from the wood panelling and challenging all previous datings to provide data for an authoritative guidebook. Otley Hall was the first Hall of its age to be dated by dendrochronology. Two archaeologists dug another trench in the rose-garden lawn to examine the flint-and-clay courtyard.

I was interviewed at Otley Hall by David Webb of BBC Radio Suffolk, who made four tapes of seven minutes each about the Linenfold Room, the Great Hall, upstairs and the Literary Room. I visited James Hehir, the Chief Executive of Ipswich Borough Council with a couple of advisers and persuaded him to agree to all our plans for the 400th anniversary of the founding of the US.

Charles invited Jon Ronson, who worked for Channel 4 and had a column in *The Guardian*, to lunch. He specialised in how groups are demonised and had links with Jim Tucker, who for years had investigated the Bilderberg Group. He described how he had investigated the New World Order and met David Rockefeller (a story he later told in *Them*). A few days later Lord Somerleyton of Somerleyton Hall came to lunch among 'Invitation to View' visitors. Somerleyton told me he had hoped to speak to Charles about his protest but Charles was self-conscious about his new notoriety and absented himself. (I sat with Somerleyton and David Sheepshanks, the Chairman of Ipswich Town Football Club.)

During an interlude in Cornwall we visited St Mawes Castle, which had been begun by Henry VIII, and saw choughs. I wrote a classical ode, 'At St Mawes Castle: The Defence of England' during the journey back to Essex.

A team from Anglia TV arrived to film Otley Hall. The presenter was Vicky Kimm. The next day Marie Norton of BBC Radio Suffolk visited Otley Hall, and I had to talk for three programmes about the garden, the Great

Hall and Literary Room. After talking on television and radio about the founding of America, I reflected that I could have been more specific about the origins of the North-American civilization in *The Fire and the Stones*, and that I had been "guided into having Otley Hall so that I could learn about the origins of the American civilization". I was interviewed by *The East Anglian Daily Times* (Cathy Brown) on the dating of Otley Hall, America, my writing, the gardens and the TV programme.

I was organising the coming wedding, and there had to be fittings for morning suits and a visit to Otley church and a discussion of the service. I was helping Anthony choose a flat near us, which he secured. Further to the publicity surrounding his protest Charles had been asked to write a book on his ancestor Nell Gwyn: a 'royal book', which would focus on his family. He handed me a letter of resignation so that he could leave and write his book. He told me in my study at Otley Hall that he would write under the name Charles Beauclerk, and would not be known any more as the Earl of Burford. I was taken aback, but was pleased for him.[8]

Cast of the Globe's The Tempest *stay and rehearse at Otley Hall – Vanessa Redgrave, Tim Carroll*
The Globe's cast for *The Tempest* had arrived the previous day at Otley Hall. I had been in Cornwall. I had found a housekeeper to look after our new property in Charlestown, 6 Quay Road, and I arrived in time to greet the coach: 25 actors including Vanessa Redgrave, who I found charming. I took them for a tour and they invited me to their banquet. I sat next to Vanessa and later Antonio, who said, "You are a very prolific writer, you've written masses. Your theme is abuse of power. The abuse of power." He was right. All my verse plays – *The Warlords, The Tragedy of Prince Tudor, Ovid Banished* and *The Rise of Oliver Cromwell*, and of course *Overlord* – are about the abuse of power. After the banquet the actors all came into the Great Hall and warmed themselves before the log fire, then went out to a camp-fire in the woods.

Next morning I talked with Tim Carroll, Master of Verse for *The Tempest*. He said, "There is 'a disjunction between the verse and what the audience hears'. Verse has been revived after 300 years and a time when the verse had to be concealed (as in Eliot). The 'verse plays' of the last 300 years such as Shelley's and Yeats's have not worked well as drama. Shakespeare achieved a natural effect.... Imagery heightens the language. There has been a feeling that the iambic pentameter destroys the sense, but that's a red herring. Once you write faultless iambics, you have to vary them – as Shakespeare does." He said that sometimes the feeling stresses the unstressed word, and an iambic line can often sound a 4-stressed line.

Over lunch I sat by Vanessa and told her about my discussion with Tim and said I had revived the verse play. We got on to the theme of the epic and of *Overlord* – and the world government; the billionaires. She said she was still unsure how to play Prospero. I took her up to the Literary Room and showed her the SAT library, and she selected a dozen books. On the wall was a framed article saying that according to Everett Hale the island of *The Tempest* was Martha's Vineyard as there are similarities between the phraseology in accounts of Bartholomew Gosnold's 1602 voyage and the language of *The Tempest*. (There are also claims that the island was Bermuda and, more plausibly as the ship in *The Tempest* set sail from Carthage, either Pantelleria or Vulcano, islands off Sicily.) She said, "The island is the world, and Prospero is manipulating the bad people so he can seek revenge, but that means he is bad."

Charles joined us and said, "All Shakespeare's plays are about giving up a temporal crown for a spiritual crown," and "As in *Hamlet*, Prospero uses a play to touch the conscience of the King." I suggested that Prospero is temporal and power-struck until a pivotal turning-point turns him spiritual – Vanessa said the turning-point is when Ariel questions him – and that he should then renounce the world with "I'll drown my book", which he is forcing himself to do. I said to her: "The book is very important. You must have it with you. It contains your spells. Prospero's final speech must be moving; [you] must sob, 'I'll drown my book.'"

Later I took Anthony to see her in the summer-house and she said she would be happy to act in his graduate film or contact someone for him if she wasn't suitable. I asked her about John Lennon's alleged gift of £45,000 to the Workers Revolutionary Party. She said, "It never happened. He was contract-killed." She said of John Osborne, a friend of her first husband Tony Richardson: "He was the opposite of the Angry Young Men. He released his emotion and energy by creating an opposite, something actors do."

That evening I ate with the actors. I sat with Caliban and Trinculo. We talked about the colonialist and subhuman layers of Caliban's servitude. Caliban felt he owned the island and resented having to work and live there.[9]

The next morning I told the staff that Charles was leaving. I gave Vanessa an inscribed copy of *The Warlords* and made a speech to the assembled company at lunch, saying that I had to leave for Iceland at 4 p.m., a journey that was more appropriate to *The Ancient Mariner* than *The Tempest*. There was a thunderous round of applause and the cast waved us off.

In Iceland: whales and volcanoes

I was aware that Icelandic sagas were part of the classical tradition of

Western civilization, and I had wanted to set a couple of classical odes in Iceland, a country Ann had long wanted to visit.

We flew to Reykjavik and toured the city. The open-air Laugardalur 'swimming-pool' was in fact in a volcanic crater with thermal, hot-spring water of 27°C. We visited the Golden Circle. We were driven through icy snow to Thingvellir National Park and saw where the Icelandic Parliament first met in 960. The Eurasian continental plates meet on a fault line that is full of geo-thermal activity. We went to Geysir, and to Strokkur hot spring which fountained 25 metres. We passed steaming holes and reached Gullfoss waterfall. At Helles Haeda near Mt Hengill we put on orange uniforms and I drove Ann on a snow-scooter across laval snowfields under a blue sky. Throughout the Golden Circle the ground was in turmoil and (we were told) could have erupted at any time.

We visited the Keflavik Whaling Centre, where whaling ships had harpoons on a rear platform. We took a whaling boat towards Snæfellsjökull glacier, and saw ten minke whales and more than ten Atlantic white-sided dolphins. We passed colonies of fulmers, kittiwakes, gannets and puffins. On the way back we bathed in four hot pools, the hottest being 39–40°C. The next day we were driven by coach through *Njal's Saga* country to Skogafoss, a high waterfall. I wrote a classical ode, 'Whale-Watching under Snæfellsjökull'.

We flew to the Westman Islands, where the Eldfell volcano on Heimaey erupted in 1973, burying the town (a latter-day Pompeii). We were driven round Heimaey past golden plovers to Eldfell, the new volcano, and Helgafell, the ancient volcano which erupted 5,000 years ago, and saw houses under lava. We took a tiny boat to the cave of Klettshellir and saw guillemots, razorbills, fulmars and kittiwakes. I wrote another classical ode, 'In the Westman Islands off Iceland'.

We flew to Akureyri and drove round the fjord, which had Arctic terns on it and on to Godafoss waterfall and the settlement of Reykjahlid, on whose lunar landscape of lava dunes Neil Armstrong trained for his moon journey in 1969. We saw sulphur pits and a huge glacier's ice-cap. On our last day we drove to Hafnarfördur's Blue Lagoon and waded out in waist-deep water that steamed blue and in some hot spots was almost scalding. We were in fact bathing in the crater of an active volcano with sand and rocks at the bottom that could have blown while we were there.[10]

My two Icelandic odes captured the island's culture to my satisfaction.

Cast of the Globe's Hamlet *stay and rehearse at Otley Hall – Mark Rylance, Richard Olivier, Giles Block*
The cast of the Globe's *Hamlet* arrived while I was addressing Normanhurst and then Coopersale Hall on the day before the beginning of the summer

term. I met up with Richard Olivier, Larry's director son, and Giles Block, the director. I gave them a tour and was invited to give Hamlet (Mark Rylance) and Horatio a philosophy class as Doctor of Philosophy at Wittenberg. I sat in the Literary Room with Hamlet and Horatio as my pupils and with Giles Block lying on his back behind the bed, knees up, to be out of sight. I talked about Renaissance Humanism in Wittenberg and the Reformation that had eroded the Christian cosmology of the Catholics. I mentioned Neoplatonism, and before I could get to Rosicrucianism a messenger burst in with news that Hamlet's father had died. Mark Rylance "hung his head". Over supper I spoke with Olivier and Rylance – with Mark about Wittenberg, Rosicrucianism, Bacon, the Knights of the Helmet and Pallas Athene's spear.

After supper I was asked to be a priest. I was dressed in a frock coat with a high collar and stood before the entire cast in the summer-house where there was now an altar. I had to improvise the wedding of Gertrude and Claudius, and read from the prayer-book. I said that my master, the Pope, would not be happy about the speed of the wedding. The bride and groom urged me to "hurry up". I read out the marriage service while Hamlet sulked. I married them before the candles on the altar, and several of the cast commented afterwards, "A beautiful service." We all attended the wedding breakfast, carousing in the Great Hall while the ghost appeared to Hamlet on the mound.

The next morning I encountered Gertrude sitting by the moat. She told me she really felt married to Claudius. Later she told our new caretaker that she was on her honeymoon and that she would rather have married the priest than Claudius. Rylance behaved madly – lying on the rose-garden lawn and kicking, taking off his shirt (in lieu of his doublet).

In the afternoon I attended the play scene in the Linenfold Room. The entire cast sat round the walls – the furniture had been removed, the table had been carried through into the Great Hall – and Rylance organised the players, laughing bizarrely. The dumb show re-enacted the scene of Hamlet's father's murder to his uncle Claudius in a confined space. Rylance had told me he felt the play scene had been written in the Linenfold Room, and he demonstrated that it could be played in a very confined space. The stabbing of Polonius took place in the Oak Room; the near-murder of Claudius in the Solar.

After the dumb show I sat with Giles Block. We discussed verse. Speaking with a quiet, academic manner, he said Shakespeare is 25-per-cent prose. "In verse, people fully express their feelings, and they conceal their feelings in prose. In prose we speak to conceal our feelings rather than reveal them." He showed me a quotation from Goldsmith in a pamphlet. I scribbled it down: "We speak to conceal rather than reveal our feelings." He went on: "The mind censors the heart, prose is a vehicle for concealment. As Master of Verse of *Julius Caesar* I tried to hear the human voice and catch it – as did Shakespeare. People speak in iambic pentameters." I said that Byron and Shelley wrote dramatic poems rather than poetic dramas. He agreed.

Around 8 Hamlet disappeared. I did not know it, but the gravedigger had dug a grave in the woods near our main gate, and Rylance had lain in the grave and had it filled in with earth, leaving only his head exposed, so he could learn what it was like to be dead. He was buried alive, up to his neck with a foot of clay on him. Only Horatio was allowed near him. It was a form of method-acting, which Olivier did not like. Rylance found that he could hardly breathe due to the pressure of the earth on his chest. He could have died, and Otley Hall's insurance would have been liable.

I had been invited to eat with the actors about 9.15. Rylance was still missing. After dark he entered the Conference Room in his hat, wearing a blanket and looking very pale. I greeted him with, "It's a ghost." He smiled. I had just been poured wine by Claudius, and I sat beside Rylance. He was almost shivering from being under the soil in the dark. He said he felt "free". It was "an ordeal" and he did not want a hot bath. He spoke of the weight of the earth on his chest.

I had told Gertrude about the maid Annie Self, who drowned herself in the moat. She and the director, Giles Block, both said that Ophelia should go into the moat. Next morning I found Ophelia lying back with her hair in the moat, being supervised by Giles and watched by Gertrude, from an upstairs window. I immediately put a stop to what they were doing and explained that she could catch Weil's disease, which is transmitted by rats' urine in water coming into contact with the eyes (or cuts, grazes, the lining of the nose, the mouth and throat). Giles took my point and Ophelia was banned from getting the water of the moat into her eyes. Ophelia then asked me to accompany her into the herb-and-knot garden so she could pick flowers to hand out on the stage at the Globe. I found all the flowers she needed. (Rue was in a pot, separated from the other herbs as its leaves can burn.) The herbs Ophelia picked were used throughout the entire season at the Globe.

Meanwhile pirates took over the boat on the moat and Hamlet was captured. Elsewhere soldiers took part in Fortinbras's battle. Before the actors left around 5 Giles Block asked me why I thought verse plays are worth doing and listened while I talked about the theme of world government.

The cast of *The Tempest* invited us to the Globe to see a *matinée*. Vanessa Redgrave was a human Prospero with some self-division. We went round to the stage door and had tea in the Green Room with the master of the ship, Ferdinand. Vanessa took us out onto the balcony, and we sat while she smoked between performances. She talked about how tiring she found the run, how she did not go out but just paced herself; how she now had to rest. We chatted at some length about Otley Hall. I wrote a short story, 'Two Metres Down Inside a Male Imperialist'.

A week later we returned to the Globe to watch *Hamlet*. Mark Rylance's Hamlet carried the performance, which had pace. Mark started with his back to the audience, who did not see his face for five minutes; and he wore black. Again we went to the stage door and I met Polonius, Claudius and Horatio. We went to the Green Room and talked with Rosencrantz and then Mark came in. He left us with Claire, then returned with a large brown parcel with my name on it (written by him) and a green card. I opened it. It was a Globe cushion with quotations from Shakespeare's plays, which we put in the Great Hall at Otley. The card had a quotation from *Antony and Cleopatra* ("I dreamt there was an Emperor Antony") and a message from Mark. Mark showed no sign of being tired even though he had done a rehearsal, a performance and photo shoot that day. Claire told Ann, "Mark controls the groundlings in character. Caliban comes out of character to control them and then goes back into character. It's better to do it from within character." Both Mark and Horatio told me, "I saw you sitting up there." They told me the actors are always looking to see who is in the audience, and behind the scenes they whisper to each other, "Did you see so-and-so in the audience?"[11]

Dating project from dendrochronology – Philip Aitken, Timothy Easton; Charlie Bryan; the Earl of Burford leaves and is now known as Charles Beauclerk
The 'experts' moved on to Great Easton. Adrian Gibson, who had worked with Cecil Hewett, author of *English Historic Carpentry*, found central tenons with soffit spurs, which were first known in 1363. He found a soffit tenon diminished haunch joint over the dining-room table, a joint Hewett had dated to c.1510–1512. He and Philip Aitken identified phase 1 as my study and the bedroom across the corridor from it, and the half end of the sitting-room below, which was a screens passage. Phase 2 was the dining-room and the other end of the sitting-room. Phase 3 was the addition of the long room that served as the local mortuary. A few days later Ann and I went to Tilty Abbey and "looked round the chapel without the gate", and I wrote a classical ode, 'Sheep at Tilty Abbey'.

The Virginia Historical Society came to lunch at Otley Hall, including Charlie Bryan, the curator of the Richmond Museum. Charlie sat next to me with his assistant curator, Jim Kelly. Kelly had been looking at my *Overlord* and suggested I should write an epic about the American Civil War. He said: "Lincoln should be the hero." I did not like the idea of writing from the point of view of the trusting, coarse northerners rather than the grave, patrician southerners. I told him that I would write an epic that included

American history. *Armageddon*, which would be about Bush's hunting down of bin Laden after 9/11, would include passages on the American Civil War (e.g. book 12, lines 350–565).

I was too busy meeting existing writing commitments to think about a new epic. I had begun a revision of *The Secret History of the West*. I was also working on classical odes. I had been polishing 'The Eclipse of Reason (Or: Totality)' and 'At St Mawes Castle: The Defence of England', and was polishing my classical odes on Tudor dating and joints. I was still putting the finishing touches to *The Rise of Oliver Cromwell*. I spoke with Michael Mann, who told me that the future of Element would be guaranteed within a fortnight and that there would be a one-volume paperback edition of *Ovid Banished* and *The Rise of Oliver Cromwell*, so I had to finish work on both plays.

Charles had been working his notice. After two more Open Days – the first of which was affected by local flooding, providing a paltry 45 visitors, the second 232 – we exchanged gifts. He gave me two books on Elizabethan poetry, suggesting a tradition I am continuing. I gave him two Charles II coins, marking his descent from Nell Gwyn. (I had been reflecting on Charles II as for my birthday Ann had given me a Charles II low wooden chair, c.1670.) Charles told me that Norris McWhirter, who had taken up my cause in 1986, had invited him to address an audience of 20 in Winchester, having latched on to his protest on the woolsack as an act of freedom to be taken up by his Freedom Association. He now wished to be known as Charles Beauclerk.

There were strains among the 'experts' at Otley Hall but several beams were dated by dendrochronology. Our dendrochronologist Martin Bridge had dated the screen passage in the Great Hall to 1498–1509, and the Banqueting Room and Playhouse to 1588. It was established that the Playhouse contained trees felled in the spring of 1588, Armada year. I read about the Elizabethan 'square playhouse', which had dimensions similar to those in the Playhouse. The tiring-house always had glazed windows, like those at the end of my study. I wrote a classical ode, 'Imagining Tudor Players in the Plahouse' – "my 'Circus Animals' Desertion'".

The four main 'experts' gathered at Otley Hall: Gibson, Bridge, Aitken and Easton. A few days later Bridge reported that he had dated the screen passage to "1511 winter, i.e. 1512" but he did not "want to contradict 1498–1509, his earlier findings". The kitchen was 1518–1538, "his gut instinct is 1518". Meanwhile Victor Chinnery found the staircase to be mid-17th century. We had been enormously successful in dating Otley Hall from its wood.

The 'experts' returned to Great Easton. Martin Bridge, had dated the Bell. The trees were felled in the winter of 1527/8, confirming that the Bell was used as Tilty Abbey's house for the last eight years of its monastic life. Bridge sent Aitken an email asking, "What is it about this man Hagger that makes him so lucky? An exact date doesn't happen, and he's had it twice." First the beams in the Great Hall and Banqueting Room at Otley Hall, now Great Easton. Later Aitken rang to say that Great Easton had a phase 1 which included smoke-blackening, to which an extension was added in 1528.[12]

While all this was going on I had, since April, been losing weight to return to my body mass index. My method was to insist on smaller portions – no food on the rim of my plate – and no butter, cheese, cream or chocolate. More than three months later, on 9 July, the day 85 staff from the three schools came down to Otley Hall for a guided tour and tea, I had shed 32 lbs, getting on for 2½ stone. (I was 12 stone 13 lbs from 15 stone 3 lbs.) My new leanness was accompanied by new writing energies.

'Zeus's Ass'

I had followed the British Prime Minister Blair's attitude towards the New World Order, and I saw him as a mouthpiece for their agenda, which included taming the House of Lords and condemning Charles's protest. Blair addressed 10,000 ladies of the Women's Institute at Wembley Arena on 7 June 2000. His speech was slow-handclapped. I saw that I could write "a mock-heroic poem about Blair's failure at the Women's Institute" which would be "in the tradition of Pope's 'Rape of the Lock' and Dryden's 'Mac Flecknoe'". The next day, 10 June, I drafted an outline, and I wrote the seven cantos by 31 July.

In 'Zeus's Ass', Zeus is alarmed that Britain is being slow to enter a United States of Europe, a stepping-stone to world government, and intrigues the advent of a leader who will win support by charming Little Britain with vacuousness and then dismantle the UK's constitutional structures. Zeus is alarmed that the Women's Institute have seen through the charm. Edward Garnier (later the UK's Solicitor-General) read the poem and made some observations. While I was writing 'Zeus's Ass' I was revising *The Secret History of the West* chapter by chapter.[13]

Opening fête at Bourn, seat of Haggers

A visit to Bourn inspired a classical ode. Margaret Greenwood and other villagers were convinced that I was a descendant of the Bourn Haggers, and I had been invited to open the Bourn Millennium fête on 1 July to raise funds for the church. Ann and I had lunch in the Golden Lion and met Margaret's husband outside the front door of Bourn Hall. We walked round to the microphone and he introduced me to a crowd of several hundred on the back lawn. I spoke of John Hagger's coming to Bourn in c.1550 and building the Hall, how there are Haggers buried in the church and what a worthy cause the church was. I declared the fête open, toured the stalls, chatted to about 20 villagers, judged a contest and drew the raffle. Margaret Greenwood asked, "Would Nicholas like to buy the Hall back?" I was told the villagers would prefer Bourn Hall to be privately owned rather than a centre for the testing of drugs.[14] The next day there was a family gathering at Biddenham, at which I made a speech and briefed my side of the family on Bourn. I wrote a classical ode, 'At the Bourn Fête: Ancestors'.

In Sicily: Motya and Syracuse – quarry where Athenians were imprisoned
My visit to Sicily inspired several classical odes and advanced my Universalism. I had read about the exploits of the Greeks and the Carthaginians there in Ancient History at school.

We landed at Palermo and hired a car. We made our way to Agrigento and visited the Valley of the Temples. We walked in the Temple of Olympian Zeus and three other Greek temples (of Castor and Pollux, Heracles and Concord). Back in our hotel I plotted a poem on the Greeks and Carthaginians.

We went to Motya, a tiny island from which the Carthaginians tried to conquer Sicily. The island was full of firs, myrtles and cicadas, and surrounded by walls within which was a Punic city, only 4 per cent of which had been excavated. We visited the House of Amphoras and the *tophet*, the ruined stone sanctuary where children were sacrificed to the goddess Tanit and her consort Baal Hammon. We saw the inner harbour (*cothon*) for Carthaginian ships. I began writing a classical ode, 'On Motya and the Ephemerality of Nationalism'.

We visited the temple at Segesta and the complex of Greek temples at Selinunte. We swam on the beach below the acropolis where the Carthaginians stormed ashore.

In Syracuse we stayed in the Grand Hotel Villa Politi, where Churchill used to stay. I wandered out to the hotel pool and looked down over a wall on the Latomia dei Cappucchini. To my astonishment this was the very lime stone quarry where (according to Cicero in *Verres*) the 7,000 Athenian prisoners were held by the Spartans when Syracuse was a battleground between the Athenians and the Spartans towards the end of the Peloponnesian War (as described in Thucydides's books 6 and 7). Among the prisoners were Nicias and Demonsthenes, who were put to death. We drove round to the entrance to the quarry and, wandering between cliff walls 45 metres high, I knew I had a classical ode linking the collapse of Nicias's expedition and the end of the British Empire.

The next morning I revisited the limestone quarry and absorbed what had been a 5th-century-BC concentration camp. Each of the 7,000 had one square yard and slept in his own defecation from lack of space, and so died of disease. We drove to Noto, and 3 kms out on the road to Pachino found the bridge over the Asinaro that was the site of Nicias's final land defeat and capture, where the Greeks were slaughtered drinking water after their retreat. Later I wrote 'In Syracuse: The End of Empires'. I wrote of my poems on Motya and Syracuse, "I have moved against nationalism.... These are Universalist poems."

The next morning I woke at 6.45 with a poem, 'Quarry', latently in my mind, and "half-pulled back the curtain and wrote it without being able to see the page". This poem disappeared into my papers and missed being included in my *Collected Poems*. It reappeared in 2014. It refers to "a quarry in my mind". In my *Diary* I wrote: "I must get every poem out of my 'quarry in my mind' during the next decade. My ambition is to gather all my poems about the ancient world – collect them." Part Two of *Classical Odes*, *In Europe's Ruins*, was taking shape in my mind.

We continued to a hotel, the Villa Paradiso dell'Etna in San Giovanni La Punta, which Rommel used as his headquarters for the Sicily campaign. We had a good view of Etna. We took a cable car, then a Jeep to the top of Etna and looked down into the old crater where Empedocles is said to have leapt. Back at the hotel we celebrated Ann's 50th birthday over dinner. I wrote a classical ode, 'Etna: Eruption of Intense Power'. We flew home past Etna and had a clear view of the crater, which was not in cloud.[15]

The artist Timothy Easton was waiting to give Ann a picture he had painted of Otley Hall, which I had commissioned for her birthday. He had put his easel up on the croquet lawn near the summer-house and the painting looked across the rose garden to the back of Otley Hall, showing the 'A' of the linked 'N' and 'A' woven into the thatched roof of the summer-house, the Elizabethan 'Plahouse' and Globe actors rehearsing *Hamlet* in its vicinity, suggesting modern actors continuing the Elizabethan tradition that had so exercised the 'experts'.

Element go into receivership

The editing of *The Secret History of the West* was like cooking a meal, my editor, John Baldock, told me over the phone: "You need to get the ingredients and then determine the quantities – a little more of this, or less of that, to get a tasty dish." He quoted Yeats, "We make out of the quarrel with others, rhetoric, but of the quarrel with ourselves, poetry." Ricks had quoted this as we walked round Oxford discussing *Overlord* (*see* p.457) and had said, "You must find the quarrel with yourself." I told Baldock that my quarrel with myself was between the nobleness of the Utopian vision and the way tyrants have imposed it, "mucked it up with guillotines and firing-squads, which are wrong".

I had devised a four-part revolutionary dynamic that could be found in all revolutions and which my book applied to each revolution I discussed: first there was a heretical occult inspiration; then an intellectual expression; then a political expression; then a physical consolidation. The inspiration of revolutions was often Freemasonic (Weishaupt in the Russian revolution). Their intellectual expression promoted the idea (Marx and Engels in the Russian Revolution). The political expression was of a tyrant (Lenin in the Russian Revolution). The physical consolidation consolidated the political expression (Stalin in the Russian Revolution).

Baldock was in favour of non-duality. To him, as to me, there were no dualisms. Revolutions were in conflict with civilizations but changed society just as Satan brought about necessary changes while being in conflict with God's work, a theme in *Overlord*. Similarly, the choice between two New World Orders was not dualistic but furthered the One – the self-interested New World Order prepared the way for the World State's world government which would solve the world's problems altruistically.

The two opposites were aspects of one process. I had seen pairs of opposites reconciled by the One, and very often one of the pair of opposites prepared the way for the second. My double life was not a duality, and my work in intelligence seemed to have been used by the One to bring me to the Light and advance my metaphysical perspective. The social was in conflict with the deeper view of the universe, but it too prepared the way for the soul to unfold and blossom.

Baldock told me he was impressed by *The Secret History of the West* and that the book "would do" at its present length; but his brief was to make it shorter. He sent me notes on each chapter, which I implemented. I worked down in Cornwall, kept company by my cormorant.

On 1 August Michael Mann rang: "Element is on the brink of extinction. All three plans have collapsed." He was looking for someone to put in at least £3.5million.

Michael Mann had kept going for 23 years; surely he would find a way out? He had been given the Queen's Award a year back; surely he could not go under? I now wrote as an act of faith.

On 17 August there was a phone call from Michael Mann. I asked him, "How have you done?" He replied: "I haven't done particularly well. In fact, we're in receivership." He said that his bank had called in the receiver. He was calm and said it was a relief. "No one can take away the last 23 years, they are there."

I said I was sorry and disappointed for him, and thanked him for all he had done. He said, "We'll stay in touch, I'll help you."

The next day I rang Baldock. He was philosophical, pointing out how developments in publishing had not helped. He had finished his lists of questions. I would complete my implementing so I would have a book ready to present to a new publisher. I finished work on *The Secret History of the West* on 19 September. I then turned my attention more fully to my classical odes.

The receiver had camped in Element's headquarters in Shaftesbury to wind up its affairs. I had a call from one of the ex-Element staff who was helping the receiver. He said, "I've worked in books all my life and I just cannot see books being sent to be pulped. Can you give me the address of a warehouse by tomorrow, and I will divert the lorry that collects your books to that address. It won't cost you anything." I found an advert in *The Bookseller*, gave him an address near Rochester and took delivery of all the copies of my titles that had been held in Element's warehouse.

Chrysalis had bought a large slice of Element, and without warning I received a wadge of 17 contracts for all my past books, which they said they would re-issue within six months to a year. I had got to know Mark Barty-King, Managing Director of Transworld until he fell ill, and later Chairman. (He also served on the Council of the Publishers' Association.) He was very sympathetic and commented, "It's not usual to send 17 contracts through the post like that, they must have researched you and decided they want you." He said, "You have to do it. If someone's bringing out all your past books, you have to do it. But it's not an ordinary thing to happen."[16]

Chrysalis brought out all my past books as promised, but seemed to have no plans for any new books.

Matthew's wedding

Matthew's wedding took place at Otley church. Mr Fosdyke, who had seen a German spy put off a plane in a local field during the war, collected the family, wearing morning dress. Three of his Rolls-Royces drove us to the church. Melanie was led down the aisle by her father. Canon Lunney in his address spoke of Bartholomew Gosnold setting out from Otley Hall to America in the *Godspeed* and said, "And Godspeed to Matthew." Outside there were photos before the ancient door.

We all returned in the Rolls-Royces to Otley Hall for champagne on the croquet lawn while a string quartet played in the rose garden. In the marquee 170 stood and applauded the arrival of the bride and groom, and after the toastmaster's announcement I spoke into the microphone, recalling the 1506 wedding at Otley Hall and the 1607 voyage. The Canon said grace. After the breakfast there were speeches from the bride's father, Matthew ("well organised and fluent") and Anthony, whose witty and humorous speech was much praised. The cake was cut, there was coffee in the conference room and we chatted outside until the band struck up. I spoke to all members of our wide family in the early dark, under the stars. There was dancing. The bride and groom left up a corridor of arched hands and slept in the Oak Room. The next morning they joined the house party for breakfast and left for their honeymoon in Egypt. It was a very memorable wedding. I wrote a classical ode, 'Wedding at Otley Hall'.

We missed Matthew – and also our younger son Tony, who had left Loughton to live in Covent Garden near his film friends for six months. After completing his MA he had been accepted as a student at the London International Film School (now known as the London Film School) with a view to becoming a film director. At Normanhurst School there was another upheaval as the Head announced that he was leaving to live in Nottingham, too far for him to commute every day to school.

On Dartmoor: Bronze Age stones

We went down to Cornwall for a couple of weeks. We were taken to Dartmoor by Ann's cousin and her husband, frequent visitors there as they helped to maintain a system of hikers' 'letter-boxes'. From Tavistock we drove to Pew Tor and had a picnic lunch overlooking Moortown Farm, where Ted Hughes farmed. I saw the grey stone house and the sloping sheepfield from the winding road beyond bracken. It was a black, granity, windy landscape among sheep.

We drove past tors and Merrivale Quarry (which, I had been told, had supplied the pink granite of our Cornish front steps), parked and walked to the Merrivale Bronze Age stone rows and circle. In the centre of rows of stones the kistvean (grave) of the chieftain was aligned east-west so that the sun's rays fell on it at dawn and sunset. There was a stone circle of 11 stones, which I thought reflected the 11 surrounding tors; and a nearby menhir. The circle was connected with sun-worship: the Indo-European Kurgans who migrated from the steppes of Russia c.4400/4300–3500BC brought sun-worship with them. There were hut circles with doorways, and cairns.

We went on to Dunnabridge sheep pound and the Stannary parliament, and on to Dartmeet, Princetown and Tor Royal. We returned to Leedon Tor, sat among piled boulders and sheltered from the wind near sheep and a dozen still horses. I accompanied Ann's cousin's husband on foot to the Tor and while he went off to hunt for a stolen hikers' 'letter-box' I sat and reflected. The next day I drafted and polished a classical ode, 'Stone Circle: Reflections on Leedon Tor, Dartmoor'. "It is 11 stanzas long, the same number as the eleven stones of the Merrivale stone circle. I have tapped into the crags of Dartmoor."

Three television programmes on Otley Hall

Back in Suffolk, I made three television programmes on Otley Hall in two days. One of our guides, Kay Pratt, acted as interviewer and asked me 70 questions, and my son Tony and his business partner John (a Sicilian New-Yorker) did the filming. The first half-hour programme took a morning. The second programme took only two hours. The third programme "was after tea and overtaken by rain and shortage of film" and was completed the following day. (Tony and John slept in an attic bedroom and John was awoken by a terrifying ghostly presence that, he claimed, brushed against his face.) We then watched the rushes. Some of Kay's questions had to be refilmed. As there was no script I could not remember what my original answers had been, but we coped.

The three television programmes were requested by a station on Cape Cod and were shown on American television. Tony's name as director was deleted from the credits and replaced by the name of an American director who had not been to Otley Hall or done any filming, and we received no payment. Suing was not an option as it would have left us even more out of pocket.

Shakespearean Authorship Trust meeting

At Silberrad's insistence, there had been a first meeting of the newly-revived Shakespearean Authorship Trust (SAT) at the Globe. Silberrad, Charles and I met in the foyer and were taken by Mark Rylance (wearing his brown hat and green shirt) up to his room. Silberrad distributed the official positions of the four trustees: Mark would be Chairman, Silberrad Treasurer, Charles Librarian and I would be Secretary. Silberrad proposed that the two collections of books at Otley Hall should be unified and centralised at the Globe. Having funded shelving in the Literary Room, I was not impressed. There were to be lectures on the authorship question at the Globe. Mark, a Baconian, wanted Peter Dawkins, a fellow-Baconian, to be a trustee.

Afterwards Charles and I found a "noisy restaurant opposite Cannon Street". He told me that his agent was not interested in discussing anything except *Nell Gwyn*. Somehow our collaborative research had been brought to an end by the agent. His leap onto the woolsack had resulted in his confinement within the 17th century and silence on anything 'modern'.

Holcombe Court

Once again my imagination was seized by a stone historic house. I saw that Holcombe Court in Holcombe Rogus, Devon was for sale. I remarked on this to my bank manager, who said he could offer me a cheap-rate mortgage if I wanted it. Ann and I took a train to Tiverton Parkway, where we were met and driven to a stone walled building with a tower. King John had stayed there in King John's Room in the early 13th century, but Victorian rebuilding made it hard to work out how much was medieval or Tudor. I loved the tower, but the windows were too high for me to have a study in one of its rooms. The Great Hall looked Victorian. There were no formal gardens, just four lakes and green fields; and a 14th-century dovehouse.[17] Later I looked at pictures of Thor Ballylee, Yeats's tower, and decided: "I am obsessed with towers, which is why I was after Holcombe Hall." I wrote a classical ode, 'At Holcombe Court, Devon: Tower'. And having written the poem and assuaged my imagination, I was no longer interested in buying the historic house. It was as though my imagination had thrust me into a viewing to bring the ode to birth.

In Italy: Turin and Rome – the Turin Shroud and the Fall of Rome
I knew a visit to Turin and Rome would inspire some classical odes. We flew to Turin and toured the Roman and Savoy sites.

We visited the Duomo to see the Turin Shroud, which has haunted Western civilization's utopianism. The queue had to keep moving, but I spent three minutes gazing at the bloodstains: the wounds on the pale, elongated cloth, the thorns in the head and the wounds in the side, hands and feet. Having weighed all the evidence, I felt there was a good chance that it was not a forgery but an actual relic from the time of Christ. Later I drafted a classical ode, 'At the Turin Shroud: The Face of Christ'.

We went on to the Egyptian museum and found the Tomb of Kha: the mummy of an architect from 1400 BC surrounded by his possessions. Later I wrote a classical ode, 'At the Tomb of Kha: On the Transcendence of Mortality'. We went on to the Royal Palace and toured the sumptuous baroque Savoy rooms. The Savoyards had displayed the Shroud to subdue the masses, and I wrote a classical ode, 'In the Baroque Royal Palace of the Defunct House of Savoy, Turin: On the Ephemerality of Monarchs'.

In Rome we visited Nero's Golden Palace, underground arches covered in Fabullus's wall-paintings which began the Renaissance. I noted the paintings of Ulysses, Achilles and Hector which Nero knew: an epic theme. Later I wrote a classical ode, 'In Nero's Golden Palace'.

We visited an exhibition of Botticelli's illustrations of Dante in the Piazza del Quirinale, and I wrote a classical ode, 'Among Botticelli's Rediscovered Illustrations of Dante'. We walked on the Palatine Hill in rain and I later wrote a classical ode, 'A Walk through the Palatine into Julian Rome'.

We drove to Bracciano, the castle of the Duke Orsini and his wife Isabella, the real-life characters in Webster's *The White Devil*, and I photographed paintings of Orsini and a smirking Isabella. I wrote a classical ode, 'At Bracciano Castle, Near Rome' on the return journey, "and just scribbled out the last line, car swaying, writing jerking, as the car swung into the hotel". We ate in the Pancrazio restaurant, which was in a cellar under the exact spot where Julius Caesar was stabbed to death, and I included a stanza about the Pancrazio in 'A Walk through the Palatine into Julian Rome'.

On our way to the airport we went through the Porta San Sebastiano: the walls Honorius fortified before the Fall of Rome. They witnessed the sack of Rome. I scribbled out a classical ode on the Fall of Rome, 'At the Gates of San Sebastian: The Fall of Rome', which I would position at the beginning of book 2, *In Europe's Ruins*, of *Classical Odes*. On the flight home I added finishing touches to the eight poems I had written in Italy. I polished these poems until early December.[18]

History projects

While we were in Italy the Administrator and gardener left Otley Hall, and I returned to problems that had to be resolved.

I was confronted by my screenplay *Gosnold's Hope*. Jack McAdam could not be contacted at any of the addresses or phone numbers, and Robin Davies had completely lost touch with him. I had been too busy to contact producers. Now a slim paperback arrived in the post, pinching the screenplay's title: *Gosnold's Hope* by Harold Wilson, an American who had researched Bartholomew Gosnold and visited Otley Hall during our time there. I wondered if one of our guides had mentioned my *Gosnold's Hope*, and if he had heard my lecture in Richmond, Virginia.

I skimmed through his book. There was a lot he did not know and there were two or three howlers, but two-thirds of the story was there in minimal treatment. One good thing about the book was that someone else, not me, was saying that Bartholomew Gosnold had a claim to be the founder of the United States. I was now interviewed on the book by *The East Anglian Daily Times* (Cathy Brown). The two-page spread brought the television cameras of *Look East* back. They captured Otley Hall in a lyrical piece about Englishness with a couple of snippets on me, "an important person not included in the portraits".

My cousin Jill's husband Roger had been very interested in Otley Hall. He had visited to supply prints and had asked many questions. They had now bought Little Coggeshall Abbey, which had been founded by King Stephen c.1140 and was made Cistercian in 1148. The Abbot's Lodging and Guest House were c.1185–1190. Ann and I were invited to lunch in the 1581 Manor House, which backed onto the Blackwater, a diverted strip of the river, with 60 acres and a quay house for mooring and a boat. We had champagne in the Great Hall and toured the 12th-century part. We lunched in the dining-room, then walked with Roger across the mound and planked bridge to look back at the house as a whole. My distant relatives, the Sibrees were present. (Margaret Sibree was the daughter of John Broadley III.) I wrote a classical ode, 'At Little Coggeshall Abbey'.

We went to Cornwall the next day. I met a planning appeals inspector and appealed against a ruling that we should not be allowed to install Velox windows in our roof. I took him to the top of the harbour and invited him to count the number of houses that had roof lights. He counted 10 and agreed that I had been discriminated against. While in Cornwall I dictated Prefaces to *The Rise of Oliver Cromwell* and *Ovid Banished*.

My younger son Tony had gone to the US to further the short film he was making, *Desperately Seeking Spielberg*. He rang to say that he had got into the BAFTA LA awards as film crew and filmed Spielberg, and took other film as well. He spoke to Spielberg's no. 2, Gerry Lewis, who said, "That's what Spielberg would have done at your age." His short film would be an ironic take on the search for fame in the celebrity culture. ("Fame is a means, not an end; a means of getting a message across to millions of people. Spielberg is an image or symbol of that communication.")

Later Matthew and Melanie came by. Matthew announced: "You are going to be a grandfather on 6 July." We were all delighted.

Order was restored at Normanhurst with the appointment of the popular science teacher as the new Head. I unveiled him in my Founders Day speech to 500 people at the Chingford Assembly Hall. There was "a cheer" when I made the announcement. Our ISA (Independent Schools Association) contact gave out the prizes. One of the staff had apparently incurable leukaemia. He had elected to go on working and was on the microphone introducing the concert. The children sang out 'I'm gonna live forever' (a line from the musical *Fame*): a moving gesture of support. Eleven years later, in 2013, I met him at Normanhurst's 90th anniversary, and he told me that he had been selected to take part in an experiment, had taken tablets worth £24,000 and had ever since been in remission.[19]

Ann and I attended the Historic Houses Association AGM at the Queen Elizabeth II Conference Centre in London. The Association represented 2,000 historic houses, many of medieval origins. The Earl of Leicester spoke, and the Chairman of English Heritage. I talked with both of them, and Lord Somerleyton and Sir Nicholas Bacon, a descendant from the nephew of Sir Francis Bacon. My cousin Jill and Roger were present (Roger in a khaki corduroy suit), and we lunched with them at a large round table.

We returned by tube and caught a taxi from Loughton station to take us home. It stopped to turn right into Albion Hill. A car turned across the traffic in front of us, and an oncoming motorcyclist hit its wing. The bike fell, he was propelled through the air, hit the top of the car and fell in the road in front of us, writhing in pain. I got out and knelt by his side and held his hands to stop him rolling about. He was barely 16 and was clutching a kneecap. The driver of the car, a local doctor, was standing miserably in shock by the road. Ann called an ambulance, which came very quickly, and I stayed with the boy until it arrived, assuring him he would be all right.

Death had invaded my life, and historic houses, the Earl of Leicester and the medieval phase of Western civilization had paled to insignificance. The boy's father rang me the next day to thank me. The boy's knee was smashed in ten places, some bits too tiny to piece together. The hospital had wired it up, but he would have to learn to walk again. He would not be able to join the fire service as he had planned. I was interviewed by the police and absolved the doctor, who had often opposed Oaklands School. He showed no gratitude and in 2009 he spoke in the Council Chamber for three minutes against us in an unsuccessful attempt to oppose a planning application. I wrote a classical ode, 'Accident'.

Peter Donebauer and world history website – Bamber Gascoigne, Michael Frayn
I had become associated with a project to make world history accessible through the internet. Peter Donebauer had worked with Bamber Gascoigne, presenter of University Challenge, to create HistoryWorld. Peter had asked me to join a group of investors. I had agreed as *The Fire and the Stones* had set out the 25 civilizations of world history and had attended a reception at the National Gallery. I encountered the quizmaster by the cloakroom, and I accompanied him upstairs to the reception. I saw Michael Frayn standing erect and dignified. He said, wizened, hook-nosed and bespectacled as I approached him: "Michael Frayn." I said: "Nicholas Hagger." We discussed world history, Otley Hall, Bartholomew Gosnold, verse plays and publishers. Gascoigne then gave a short presentation and demonstrated his website. I sipped wine while he showed us how to get to the Fall of Constantinople and see it in terms of the Byzantine as well as the Roman Empire. Afterwards he asked me about Richmond, Virginia and if I could give him an introduction to the museum. I wrote a classical ode, 'In the National Gallery'.[20]

Bill Kelso and Patricia Cornwell lunch at Otley Hall
Bill Kelso, the Jamestown archaeologist, came to lunch on a Sunday at Otley Hall with seven other Americans, including Patricia Cornwell, writer of thrillers about serial killers. I gave them a tour of the Hall and answered many questions over lunch, sitting at the end of the long kitchen table. Patricia wrote many things I said into her large notebook and invited me to her house in Richmond: "It's a 1950s house, but I'll ply you with good white wine so you won't notice it." I walked with her across the croquet lawn to look at the summer-house, and she told me, "I'm more interested in Shakespeare than in my own books. I wanted to be a poet. I reckoned no one would pay me anything if I wrote poetry, so I write crime." I told her that the quest for Reality is not motivated by money. She seemed slightly ashamed of her work. She asked if I would like her to put Otley Hall and my books on her website. Her helper trotted nearby and told me, "My job is to

keep Miss Cornwell happy." She told me she employed eight people to help create her output.

That day I told Bill Kelso he should dig in the Jamestown Fort for Bartholomew Gosnold's body. He told me he felt that Gosnold might be buried outside the walls of the Fort. I said, "No, he will be in the dead centre of the Fort. All the ordnance was fired when he was buried – the three cannons in each corner of the triangular Fort – and out of courtesy to the dead man he would have been equidistant from each cannon, in the centre." Kelso nodded and told me he would work with that theory and look for the centre, which would be difficult as one corner of the Fort was submerged in the River James. "If I can find all three corners, I can calculate the centre of the triangle."

Structure of Classical Odes
Throughout December I worked on classical odes. I reworked a poem about the visit by the Globe cast of *Hamlet*, 'Imagination and Reality: The Globe Actors Search for Realism'. I worked on two classical odes on the Christmas events at the schools: 'At Coopersale Hall's Christmas Concert: Education' and 'At the Chingford Carol Service: Christian Religion'. I followed the Nice Summit, which was enlarging Europe to 25 members and eventually a superstate and embryonic United States of Europe, and down in Cornwall wrote 'Reflections on the Nice Summit'. I worked on 'At Coombe House, Devon: A New Millennium' and on 'In Otley Hall's Medieval Gardens'. (I reckoned I must have put it down unfinished when Michael Mann appealed to me to get *The Secret History of the West* out as soon as possible.) I knew I was making a statement of Western civilization: "When I have finished my poems [, *Classical Odes*], I will have put down on paper all I want to say about English, European and American culture – and the interaction between the three." I did more work on 'In Boulge Churchyard', 'Petrol Blockade' and 'Among Brueghel's Peasants: On the Artist as Truth-Teller'. I worked on 'At Theydon Garnon Church', 'At Hadrian's Villa, Tivoli', 'At the Bell: The Past', 'A Tudor Youth' and 'At the Start of a New Millennium, the Sun Rising against Aquarius'. (I had celebrated the new millennium on 31 December 1999 but another school of thought held that the new millennium began on 31 December 2000.)

My classical odes were taking shape. There would be four books, each with a different focus. Book One, *A Tudor Knot*, would focus on the nation-state: England. Book Two, *In Europe's Ruins*, would focus on Europe. Book Three, *A Global Sway*, would focus on globalism. Book Four, *The Western Universe*, would focus on a metaphysical approach to the One in everyday life. I was trying to catch the passing of England into a European state under the global sway of American globalism and the New World Order. England was in a time of transition, and loyalties to the nation-state were mixed with England's cultural roots in Europe – and in the wider world. There was a widespread feeling that Englishness was being superseded by Europeanness and globalism.

My everyday life threw up new odes. I had a consultation with Professor Machin about my primary antiphospholipid syndrome. Sitting under a huge Japanese poster headlined 'Antiphospholipid Conference, 1998', he said, "There shouldn't be *any* antiphospholipids. Yours are weakly positive, you shouldn't have any." I asked, "What happens if they begin to become *strongly* positive?" He said, "You die, Mr Hagger. You die." "Oh, I see," I said. I wrote a classical ode, 'Blood Test: Anti-Phospholipids'.

I went to my osteopath and on to meet Donebauer. Sitting in his waiting-room I scribbled eight stanzas on my 'fibrous knot', for an ode entitled 'At the Osteopath: Soul and Body'.

Virginian Governor's representative

America's global sway intruded into my classic odes. Governor Gilmore of Virginia sent a consultant, Will Connors, "to fact-find". Connors lunched with me at Otley Hall, a thinnish, bespectacled young man in a dark grey suit. He told me the Governor or his wife would be coming to Otley Hall in early May to further the 2007 US celebration of its 400th anniversary and to carry forward Jamestown's twinning with Ipswich, which I had started in 1998. He asked if I would hold a reception. He told me that the Gilmores were very close to the Bushes, and that President Bush would be aware of the visit. He knew of my study of 25 civilizations and asked if he could take away a copy of *The Fire and the Stones* to pass to Governor Gilmore and perhaps President Bush. I wrote letters informing Lord Belstead, the Lord Lieutenant of Suffolk, and James Hehir, the Chief Executive of Ipswich Borough Council. I was now the link between Jamestown and Ipswich.

I put finishing touches to *The Secret History of the West* knowing it would be published elsewhere. I had visited Chrysalis in Brewery Road, opposite Pentonville Prison, and found the building in chaos with files stacked round computers and no Managing Editor expected until June.[21]

Every day I worked on a classical ode. I overhauled the odes I had drafted in America and in Italy.

In Portugal: navigators

I knew I had a classical ode about Portugal. Ann and I flew to Lisbon. We visited the Maritime Museum and spent a good hour in the Room of the Discoveries, soaking in Henry the Navigator, Diogo Cao's visit to Africa and Vasco da Gama's discovery of India. I saw da Gama's mobile altar and 'archangel' and went on to the Castelo de Sao Jorge where he visited Manuel

I after his voyage of 1497/8. I visited his tomb, which has ropes carved in stone, in the church of the Hieronymite convent. I drafted a classical ode that was eventually titled 'Among Lisbon's Discoverers'.

Back in England I wrote more classical odes. I attended a lunch Mark Rylance gave for the SAT trustees and Christopher Dams of the de Vere Society. His aim was to get agreement for all the Shakespeare books at Otley Hall to go to the Globe, but Dams said he was happy with the present arrangement and Rylance had to back down.

Ann and I went to Cornwall, where I worked on odes and wrote 'On Trilobites and Asteroids'. On our return I was again invited by Bird to visit the surroundings of Hedingham Castle. I wrote another classical ode about de Vere, 'Round Hedingham Castle'.

I went to Chigwell School for the annual Shrove Tuesday dinner and sat opposite the younger brother of a contemporary of mine based in Cyprus whose plane had been blown up on the order of Col. Grivas (who I had encountered in Greece in 1960). I wrote a classical ode, 'At the Old Chigwellians' Shrove-Tuesday Dinner'.[22]

In Spain: El Escorial library, unity of knowledge and disciplines; Paradise
I knew that I had classical odes to write about Spain, and had arranged to take Ann on a coach tour of Andalucia. We flew to Madrid and toured the city. We visited the palace and I later wrote a classical ode, 'At the Bourbon Royal Palace, Madrid'.

We broke away from the group at the Prado, were collected by car and sped to Philip II's palace at El Escorial. We arrived by 3.50 – it closed at 5 p.m. – and toured the apartments of first the Queen, then of Philip II. I saw the long strolling room of maps, where the Armada decision was taken; the bedroom where he died; and his study next door, where he wrote out the order for the Armada to invade.

We visited the royal pantheon of all the Spanish kings and eventually arrived at the library: up stairs to a long room with a barrel ceiling covered in frescoes, all pre-1584, representing all the seven medieval disciplines, the seven Liberal Arts or Sciences – grammar, rhetoric, dialectics, arithmetic, music, geometry and astrology – with philosophy and theology at each end. There were 45,000 books on the shelves, and there was a model of the earth-centred universe with the sun outside. The library showed a unity of 16th-century knowledge and all disciplines, and made a Universalist statement. It was equivalent to the unity of 20th- and 21st century knowledge and all disciplines I am endeavouring to show in this work. I wrote a classical ode, 'At Philip the Second's El Escorial: The Unity of Knowledge'.

We went to Toledo and visited the El Greco museum. I wrote 'In El Greco's Toledo'. We were taken to Cordoba and visited the Alcazar de los

Reyes Cristianos, a late-13th-century palace where Columbus was received in 1486 by Isabella and Ferdinand before he went to America. I drafted 'In Moorish Cordoba: An Orange Tree' with a stork in a nest.

We visited Granada. In the Alhambra I began a discussion with our guide on Oneness and Paradise that continued throughout the afternoon. We visited the sultan's palace and *harem*, and saw the four rivers of Paradise from the fountain. We walked to the garden of Generalife, a copy of Paradise going back to the 13th and 14th centuries. In the coach on the way back I drafted a classical ode, 'In the Moorish Alhambra, Granada: Paradise, Oneness'.

We visited Seville and made two visits to the Alcazar. I saw the two rooms associated with Columbus and visited the royal apartments, including the suite Isabella occupied. On the ground floor of the white courtyard near the arms of Isabella and Ferdinand I read *'Non Plus Ultra'*: 'No farther.' Isabella and Ferdinand were saying, "We can ease up now we've taken Granada. No more expansion." On the balcony of the same courtyard and on his summer pavilion Charles V contradicted their message with a call to expand the Spanish Empire: *'Plus Ultra'*: 'Farther!' I wrote another classical ode, 'At the Moorish Alcazar, Seville'.[23]

Utopianism: Jamestown and Ipswich
Dating project ended: I write a guidebook to Otley Hall
Jamestown's interest in twinning with Ipswich had meant that writing a guidebook to Otley Hall had become urgent. I told Timothy Easton that the dating project now had to end as I had to write the guidebook on the basis of the dendrochronology we had already done. The same day a Suffolk printer sent a photographer to take photos for the guidebook.

Virginian deputation from Jamestown to Ipswich Borough Council, and lunch at Otley Hall; no twinning in prospect
Governor Gilmore's representative, Boyd S. Richardson Jr, came to Ipswich to visit James Hehir at the Chief Executive's office and propose that Jamestown and Ipswich should have "sister-city status". He was accompanied by a Tourism Marketing Manager of the Virginia Tourism Corporation and two other Americans. I met them outside Hehir's door along with a Manager from the Suffolk Tourist Board and two Council officials. We all trooped in to the office where the Leader of the Council and the Mayor were seated at a long table. The Mayor made a speech of welcome. The Leader then said it would affect the 3-May election and he might be accused of spending taxpayers' money on "junkets".

There was an awkward silence. It was evident that the Mayor and Leader had only just heard about the sister-city proposal and had not been briefed.

I had to speak. Addressing the Mayor and Leader, I explained that the Americans' visit was connected with their celebration of the 400th anniversary of the founding of America in 1607, a date based on the voyage to Jamestown which had been planned at Otley Hall. I said that the Americans' sister-city proposal was based on the origin of the 1607 voyage's being near Ipswich. I said that Ipswich should feel honoured to be requested to be a sister city of Jamestown. The Tourism Marketing Manager said that Governor and Mrs. Gilmore would be coming on 2 May to carry the sister-city idea forward.

When the meeting ended the four Americans (feeling deflated and humiliated) and my two Council contacts came to Otley Hall in their cars and lunched in the Linenfold Room. We British were appalled at the lack of preparation, grasp and vision of the Leader and Mayor. We told the Americans that there *would* be support for their proposal. A few days later I was interviewed by *The East Anglian Daily Times* (Cathy Brown) on 2007, and in due course her article appeared, 'Raising the star-spangled banner for a Suffolk hero'.[24]

Down in Cornwall I polished the Spanish poems. We attended a special opening of the Eden Project and visited the two large greenhouses (or biomes), one clammy, the other dry. I wrote a classical ode, 'At the Eden Project: Paradise'. The guidebook – my reconciliation of the conflicting opinions of 18 'experts' or 'enthusiasts' – arrived by courier.[25]

We were now informed that Virginia's First Lady, Roxane Gilmore, not her husband, would be leading the delegation on 2 May, and the local police visited Otley Hall to discuss security.

Another Virginian deputation under Roxane Gilmore, First Lady, at Christchurch Mansion, televised speeches and lunch at Otley Hall; Lord Tollemache
The day of the Americans' visit began early. A television crew arrived at 7.45. I was interviewed on BBC Radio Suffolk while they set up. Then I was interviewed from 8 until 8.40 in the Great Hall by the American History channel for a programme about the 400th anniversary in 2007 which would be seen in most American schools. I answered Tim Nolan's questions on Jamestown and Bartholomew Gosnold. Four times he asked me, "What is the significance of that fireplace?" and I replied, using different words each time, that the voyage to Jamestown was thought to have been planned before it and so it could be said that in 1606 it witnessed the founding of the United States.

I was then taken to Civic Drive and waited with Council officials for the American coach to arrive. When it came I climbed on board and greeted and welcomed the many familiar faces and went down and sat near Bill Kelso and Norman Beatty. I was introduced to the First Lady, Roxane Gilmore, "a well-groomed lady in a trouser suit, bejewelled and shortish-blonde-haired". More than two dozen distinguished Americans had made the journey to England to call for Jamestown and Ipswich to be sister cities.

The coach took us to Christchurch Mansion, which dated back to Tudor times. I had to do another radio interview alongside the First Lady. Eventually we assembled for televised speeches. The Mayor spoke. There was then an unscheduled speech by one of the American visitors, who introduced a colleague to read a "proclamation" that Jamestown and Ipswich should be "potential partners". The First Lady spoke very fluently. Then I spoke.

I had been asked to present the historical connection between Ipswich and Jamestown, and covered Otley Hall, Bartholomew Gosnold and details of the 1606/7 voyage. I pointed out that this took place "13 years before the *Mayflower* arrived" and there was a roar of approval from the Virginians. After the speeches there was a photo of the speakers and more television. Then the First Lady and I left very publicly to ride to Otley Hall in an American limousine with an American flag flying over one wing.

When we reached Otley Hall for the reception there was a line and we shook hands with some 50 guests. Lord Tollemache arrived last. I explained to the First Lady within his earshot: "As Deputy Lieutenant, Lord Tollemache will be reporting to the Queen." "That's more or less it," Lord Tollemache agreed. Lunch was in different rooms.

At the US Embassy – Governor Gilmore, Patricia Cornwell
Before her official departure the First Lady presented me with a small round silver tray with the Great Seal of Virginia engraved in the centre. Governor Gilmore had not been able to come to Ipswich as he had another engagement in London – I wondered if he was put out by Ipswich's rebuff – but I was to join him at an event at the US Embassy that evening. By arrangement I travelled with the departing Americans on their coach.

We had tea at the Churchill Hotel under old masters. There I signed a copy of *The Fire and the Stones* for President Bush. We travelled by coach to the US Embassy and having passed through airport-style security and electronic surveillance we were greeted by the First Lady, Roxane, who thanked me for my hospitality. She asked, "Have you met my husband?" He was shaking hands further down the line, and she withdrew him and brought him to me and we chatted about Otley Hall. I told him I had brought a book for him and would look for him at the end. I added, "I know you have direct access to President Bush. I've signed another book for him. Could I ask you to deliver it?" He said, "I'll do it, I'm seeing him on our return. I'll make sure he has it." Their black bodyguard came and said to me, "The Governor and his wife are like that" – he put his two forefingers side by side – "with the Bushes."

There were a couple of hundred in the large embassy reception room. I spoke briefly to Patricia Cornwell who was clearly put out by Ipswich's rebuff. She had heard about the humiliation of the American deputation in Ipswich and clearly took a dim view of it. Governor Gilmore made a speech in which he recognised various people, including Patricia Cornwell. Months later, I wrote a classical ode, 'At the American Embassy, London'.[26]

The American delegation felt disappointed and let down by the Ipswich Borough Council's unwillingness to implement sister-city status or make any commitment to celebrate in 2007 the 400th anniversary of the founding of the US from Suffolk at Jamestown in 1607. Although Ipswich's decision was largely financial, it may have also been to some extent ideological – opposed to the American invasion of Afghanistan. I also felt let down, by the Chief Executive who had asked me to arrange twinning when I went to Virginia, and by all the Suffolk officials, including the Lord Lieutenant and his Deputy. I had made it all happen, but they had not followed up with financial support. They had exercised no leadership. That evening I decided to wash my hands of Suffolk officialdom, which had proved completely and utterly useless.

Classical odes on Mediterranean

Mediterranean cruise – Roger Bannister and return to Libya
I knew I would have many classical odes from the shore excursions from a cruise round the Mediterranean in the *Minerva*. There was a discount for alumni of Worcester College, and the ports of call included Tripoli in Libya. Having fled Libya under threat of imminent arrest in 1970, I could make a safe return among a faceless horde disembarking from a ship.

Ann and I flew to Athens and joined the *Minerva* in Piraeus. Before sailing we were taken by coach (via the Corinthian Canal, past Eleusis, Salamis, Megara and Argos) to Mycenae. From the Lion Gate we made our way up to the *megaron*, and I fell into step with an elderly doctor who had had a hip replacement. I was striding up to the Acropolis but restrained my speed to walk at his pace. We looked at the throne room of Agamemnon and the bathroom where he was murdered. We lunched at the Agamemnon Palace at one long table, and the elderly doctor talked loudly and admiringly about Norris McWhirter. I was sitting a few places further down and said I had known Norris. We went on past Tiryns and Nauplion to Epidavros, and in the theatre I stood with the doctor and pondered that all the Greek plays used the Agamemnon story as their plot: a blending of history and verse drama.

Back on the *Minerva* there was a champagne reception in DJ. I came down in the lift with the elderly doctor, who asked my name. In return, I asked his. "Roger Bannister." Now I looked carefully I realised that under his years was my boyhood athletics hero who ran the first four-minute mile on 6 May 1954

(3 minutes 59.4 seconds), a record he held for 46 days. I said, "I looked up to you when I was at school, we all talked about your feat. You hardly did any training because you were studying to be a doctor." "That's right," he said. He had become Master of Pembroke College, Oxford. I had struck up a friendship without knowing who he was. I wrote two classical odes, 'At Agamemnon's Mycenae and Epidavros: Justice' and 'At Epidavros: Temple-Sleep'.

We disembarked in Crete's Souda Bay and visited the British and German Second World War cemeteries. We stood on Hill 107, where the Germans won the battle for Crete, and were addressed by the crippled *Daily Telegraph* defence editor, Sir John Keegan. As we walked back to the coach Bannister fell into step with me. We returned to Chania. I wrote a classical ode, 'At Chania's Hill 107'.

We had a day at sea. We quickly settled into the ship's routine: dining in the formal dining-room or on the informal Bridge Deck, using the stairs or the lift, attending lectures and strolling or sunbathing on the topmost, Promenade Deck. We headed for Libya and passed near Leptis Magna. I drafted a classical ode, 'Near Leptis Magna'. We docked in Benghazi and were taken by coach into the desert past palms and over the Green Mountain, escorted by two police cars with hazard lights flashing. I relished the irony that I, who had fled Libya in 1970 after an attempt to arrest me, should be welcomed on my return by a VIP escort.

At Cyrene we walked down a slope to the Temple of Zeus (c.525BC) and the forum-agora complex. We saw the fountain of Apollo where Battus and his friends founded Cyrene; and the tomb of Battus. On the way back I wrote a classical ode, 'At Cyrene: Apollo's Bride'.

We docked in Tripoli. I breakfasted on the Bridge Deck in the open air, looking at the Phoenician settlement I had visited in 1969, and realised that a new promenade had been built out towards the sea. Beneath us secret policemen stood as still as lampposts, blatantly watching us.

We disembarked and were driven by coach through Giorgimpopoli. The sandy lanes had gone and I absorbed the villages and people we passed and relived my time in Libya with fascination and a fixed grimace. We toured Sabratha with a guide: the theatre, the site of Apuleius's trial, the forum, the baths, the latrines and the mosaics by the sea. In the museum I saw the mosaic of Neptune, taken from the baths of Oceanus, his eyes towards Carthage and full of foreboding. I wrote a classical ode, 'At Sabratha'.

After lunch on the Bridge Deck we were driven by coach round the Italian port of Tripoli. I was struck by the huge portraits of Gaddafi dressed in traditional Libyan dress that hung on the fronts of buildings, making out that Gaddafi was a man of the people. We went up to Garden City and returned along the waterfront to the Castle, passing landmarks I remembered. We walked round the Caramanlis' Castle as I did so often in 1969 and then into the Old City.

From the Old City we emerged into Castle Square, and I was stopped by the driver of a limousine: "Mr Hagger? Get in." He said that the hire of the limousine had already been paid for and we could go wherever we wanted. I was amazed at our apparent good fortune. I had told one of the cruise lecturers, a former UK Ambassador to Malta, that I had had to flee Libya in 1970 and that I would be taking a taxi from Castle Square to revisit my old haunts in Tripoli. I said, "I'm telling you this in case I don't return." He had pleaded with me to reconsider, but I was adamant. I had tipped him off about my intentions, and I was sure some organisation had arranged the car, perhaps as a way of saying 'Thank you' for past favours.

We spent the rest of the afternoon looking for places in Tripoli I had always wanted to revisit. We drove to Garden City and looked for the sandy lane opposite Ben Ashur mosque where I had lived from 1968 to 1970, but was unable to find it: the sandy lanes had been replaced by roads and the buildings seemed to have been renewed. I could find no trace of Mohammed's greengrocer's stall or of Ben Nagy's apartment block. We tried to find the gated University campus. It seemed to have been replaced by half a dozen new campuses. Where I taught seemed to be a field. We drove on to Giorgimpopoli. Again the sandy lanes had gone and I could find no trace of the water-tower. I thought I found the hardware shop, but I could not be certain. The open view from the road to the sea had been blocked by a wall. The changes to the Tripoli I had known had been extensive. Much of the Tripoli I had known was now a region of the mind.

The driver asked me if I thought that Libyans were responsible for the Lockerbie bombing over Scotland. I said, "No, I think it was an Iranian operation, revenge for the US Navy's accidental downing of an Iranian commercial jet in 1988." In March 2014 it was revealed by a defector that Iran ordered the Lockerbie bombing and that it was carried out by Syrian-based extremists, including an ex-Iranian intelligence officer.

Back on board the *Minerva* I found the ex-Ambassador and thanked him for supplying the limousine. He nodded, looked at me quizzically and remained silent. There was no doubt about it, some organisation had assisted my return to Tripoli without revealing its identity. I had managed to revisit the environs of my old haunts without being arrested. I wrote a classical ode, 'Return to Tripoli'.

At Sousse we visited El Djem amphitheatre. In the coach on the way back to the ship I wrote a classical ode, 'At El Djem Amphitheatre: Desert Rose'. We docked at Tunis and visited Carthage, which fought two Punic wars against Rome in the 3rd century BC. We viewed the 7th-century ruins from Byrsa Hill, went to the museum and then to the ruined amphitheatre where

Churchill spoke to the troops after the Battle of Tunis in 1943. We went to the Tophet, the sacred enclosure to Baal Hammon where Dido was burned. We then drove to the round harbour to see the military port and the Admiral's island with tunnel-like berths for 300 ships. I stood in awe of Carthaginian sea power. I bought a poster of Virgil with the muses of tragedy and history, which I framed and hung near my study. I wrote a classical ode, 'At Carthage'.

We moved on to Sicily, and returned to the temples of Selinunte. I wrote a classical ode, 'In Selinunte's Carthaginian Settlement'. We docked at Trapani and visited Erice, which is on top of a mountain. According to tradition Erice was founded by Trojans under Aeneas who settled there after the Trojan War, and Aeneas founded the Temple of Venus and dedicated it to his mother, Venus. Virgil wrote of Aeneas's party "on the crest of Eryx" (*Aeneid* 5.759 ff). I saw the Temple of Venus on a podium, broken columns and a well above a precipitous drop. Here the cult of Venus was kept by 1,000 sacred prostitutes in the 5th century BC (and by 5,000 in the 3rd century BC), who lived in the town and, acting on behalf of Venus, by their sacred act of love brought rain and made the earth fertile. I went back to Segesta, which had also been settled by Elymnians, descendants of Trojans, and the guide said that the temple was founded by Aeneas and may have been dedicated *to* Aeneas. I wrote a classical ode, 'Among Aeneas's Trojans'.

We sailed on to Sardinia and visited Su Nuraxi at Barumini, a *nuraghi* (round fortress with a central tower) of c.1470BC. Nearby there were houses of c.800BC. On the way back to the ship I wrote a classical ode, 'At Su Nuraxi, in Sardinia'.

We sailed on to Menorca and entered the long deep harbour of Mahon. We went to Ciudadela and I asked the guide if she knew Manuel Saurina, the psychiatrist in Tripoli. "Oh yes, he died about three years ago. Of alcohol-cirrhosis. He's buried in the cemetery. The service was in his local church. Near where he practised." I reflected that the atheist and sensualist who proclaimed that the way to live was to live in the moment, drink, make money and have pleasure, had re-entered the Christian fold in death. On the coach back to the ship I wrote a classical ode, 'In Colonial Menorca'.

We concluded our voyage at Barcelona. There was a tour of the city, which ended at a viewing-platform with Barcelona spread beneath us. Over coffee Bannister told me about his running career. He ran at the Athens stadium in 1948 and became interested in the classical Greek view of the body and of athletes, in Hippocrates and in becoming a doctor. He told me he had "failed" by not winning a medal in 1952 and gave himself two more years to break the four-minute barrier. He ran 4 minutes 3 seconds and 4 minutes 2 seconds. On 6 May 1954 he only decided to try and break the barrier half an hour before the race began as the weather was so bad. He had to run 4 seconds faster than normal to make up for the weather. "I was more interested in qualifying, the public were more interested in the barrier." I left the cruise feeling I had got to know him well.[27]

Election, 'Pastoral Ode: Landslide, The End of Great Britain'
I spent the rest of the year reworking the first drafts of my European classical odes. I went to Cornwall and reworked the odes I had written during the cruise. On 8 June news came through while I was at Otley Hall that Blair's New Labour had won a landslide victory in the British General Election, and I wrote 'Pastoral Ode: Landslide, The End of Great Britain'. I had a clear sense that a thousand years of English tradition were at an end as we passed into a European superstate, and in each stanza I contrasted the political news with the beauty of Otley Hall's medieval- and Tudor-style grounds.

Heaven and Earth Show, gym
The television cameras returned to Otley Hall: I was interviewed by Diarmuid Gavin for the *Heaven and Earth Show* sitting on the garden wall and talking about the knot-garden and the history of the Hall. Chris Macann came down to Otley Hall and we lunched on the rose-garden lawn at a table with a blue-and-white tablecloth.

As part of my weight reduction I had joined the gym at Repton Park, and walked, cycled, cross-trained, and pulled light weights in what used to be the assembly hall of the old Claybury Psychiatric Hospital. When I was a boy my father used to say to me, "Don't work too hard or you'll end up in Claybury." My father was right, in a sense I *had* ended up in Claybury. I wrote a classical ode, 'In Claybury Gym: Cult of the Body'.

Matthew now Managing Principal
Everything had gone well in the schools. At Oaklands the Headmistress had been replaced by a more consensual Head, a relative by marriage of Robin Parfitt, ex-Head of the Junior School at Chigwell. She did not consider that any staff who had a different view from hers should leave. Coopersale Hall was found to be 'above average' at an inspection, and I took over Nick's Bistro in Epping to thank 45 staff over dinner. Matthew had given notice to his school, West Hatch, and would be starting as Managing Principal in early September, allowing me to retire from the day-to-day running of the schools. I reflected, "I am like Ulysses (in Tennyson's poem), putting my son Telemachus into my kingdom and leaving myself free to go beyond the baths of all the Western stars and breast new experience." Matthew had sold his townhouse and then its replacement near a railway line and was buying Miss Lord's old house.

Birth of grandson, Ben

On 12 July our grandson was born. We had a call and went to Whipps Cross Hospital. Matthew met us inside the door and said, full of emotion, "It's a boy, Ben. Ventouse and forceps. Seven and a half pounds." We had to wait an hour, and went up to the ward. Melanie was nursing the baby in a blanket. She offered him to me. I had a biro in my breast-pocket and as I nursed him his tiny one-hour-old fingernails reached out to hold the pen, and I wondered if he would be a writer one day. At Coopersale Hall's prize-giving the previous day, the guest speaker had asked me to light a candle to illustrate her talk. A new life had been lit, Ben was a new person in our family. I was now a grandfather, 'Grandpa'. Later I wrote a classical ode, 'Breathing Air: Mystery'.

Nicholas writing 'At Ambresbury Banks', Epping on 21 July 2001

I had been working on classical odes set in Greece when Nadia came to see Ben. We went to Ambresbury Banks, a local Iron-Age fort, where staff from the museum in Waltham Abbey were dressed as Iron-Age peasants, one as Boudicca. Nadia took a photo of me writing a classical ode, 'At Ambresbury Banks, Epping', standing by an earth wall.

Tony Blair in Charlestown

Ann and I went down to Cornwall and I moved on to odes written in Italy and Germany, polishing an ode every day. Up the road in Charlestown a neighbour was dying of cancer behind the open windows and drawn curtains of his first-floor bedroom. He had asked, "When can I have chemotherapy?" and had been told, "When you're strong enough to walk round the harbour." Cream teas were being sold nearby for Regatta Week, and a band was playing. Very softly the band played 'Walk On'. He died the next day. Later I wrote a short story, 'Walking on from the Harbour'.

In August little Ben joined us in Cornwall. I walked with Matthew to the rocks near Gull Island, and wrote a classical ode, 'At Charlestown: Among Rock Pools'. I worked on classical odes set in Italy and Germany.

I was revising my ode, 'In Obersalzberg' when I heard on the lunchtime news that the British Prime Minister Tony Blair and his wife would be visiting Charlestown. A crowd gathered outside the Pier House Hotel on the other side of the narrow inner harbour, and a van with a satellite dish parked outside our house. The driver told me that Blair was at the Visitors Centre just up the road. I wandered up with Matthew. We stood on a grassy knoll with our heads under a tree as there were television cameras. Blair emerged with his wife, grinning in a blue shirt, looking sun-tanned and holding her hand. He saw me and stopped. He stared at me, and I stared back. He seemed to know who I was, and I wondered in what connection: 'Zeus's Ass'? Charles's leap onto the woolsack? He took up a position by the wall overlooking the harbour and tall-masted ships, so that the crowd outside the hotel was in the background. Thirty cameramen took photos. The Blairs then left Charlestown. The crowd had been waiting more than two hours, and the local vicar was standing on the hotel steps to welcome the couple – in vain.

The next day the photos were on the front pages of all the newspapers as evidence that Cornish resorts were crowded despite the economic conditions. The crowd had been set up to be a backdrop for Blair's spin on sparsely-attended holiday resorts. I wrote a classical ode, 'In Cornwall: A New Renaissance'.[28]

New gardener joins from Sir Evelyn de Rothschild's Ascott House

Back at Otley Hall, we had an Open Day. In the morning I met with our brilliant new gardener, Steve Tett. He had not started yet but had come to observe. We sat on chairs at a table on the croquet lawn. He had worked at Hampton Court, Hever Castle, Peter de Savary's Littlecote House and other historic sites, and most recently at Ascott House, the home of Sir Evelyn de Rothschild (who was worth at least $20billion).[29] He told me that on one particular day at Ascott House Sir Evelyn de Rothschild told the staff to finish at 11. One gardener was slow in finishing. Suddenly President Clinton appeared from behind a hedge and said, "Hello, how's it going?" Clinton was supposed to be in the US, not in the UK. He had secretly come to visit Rothschild. Steve added, "Blair was there the week before." Ascott House was a base for the English end of the New World Order, and I found it weird that our gardener had applied to come to us from there.

Somehow I had acquired Rothschild's gardener, who was still in touch with his friends at Ascott House. He knew all the Latin names of all the plants and was soon giving advice on Garden Open Days, when gardeners came from far and wide to consult him about their plants. I could not believe we had such an expert gardener.

Wine-tasting at Helmingham Hall: Lord Tollemache's 34 generations and anapaest

I was invited by an estate agent to a sponsored wine-tasting at Helmingham Hall, the seat of the Tollemaches. The guests stood on the lawn in front of the 16th-century Hall, and I tippled as dusk fell and the gnats danced. Lord Tollemache came and stood modestly at my elbow. We went for a walk round the redbrick, turreted Helmingham Hall: along the front to the formal gardens, through gates with horses' heads, past flower-beds with many blooms, down to another gate that looked onto a tennis-court and back to a white urn. We had walked alongside the moat and were now by a herb-and-knot garden with union-jack designs. Lord Tollemache told me that two Tollemaches had fought in the Battle of Crécy in 1346.

I wrote a classical ode, 'At Helmingham Hall'. I sent it to Lord Tollemache, who wrote back pointing out that my line "O thirty-generationed Tollemaches" was inaccurate as it should say "thirty-four-generationed". His letter plunged me into crisis. I had a perfect pentameter, and Tollemache was, perhaps hubristically, asking me to add a syllable. My classical odes were all written in perfect pentameters, and unless I dropped the word 'O' (which I was not prepared to do) this line would be the only exception in *Classical Odes*. I resolved to make the change in the interests of historical accuracy, but, aware that I had compromised the precision and purity of my scansion, I wrote to Christopher Ricks explaining that there was now a blemish in my book, and that I had designated the first three syllables of 'generationed' as the only anapaest in *Classical Odes*.

Next time I saw him Ricks told me he had found it highly amusing that I had jibbed at putting in the actual number of Tollemaches' generations on metrical grounds. I told him I was sure that Virgil, Horace or Ovid would have done the same.

Lord Braybrooke

I was now focusing on Essex. I wrote two classical odes, 'In Addison's Essex', and 'At Colchester Keep'. I had invited the Lord Lieutenant of Essex, Lord Robin Braybrooke, to Coopersale Hall, and on 11 September I gave him a tour and we then had lunch in the small room with the Jacobean frieze round the upper wall (grimacing figures and a Green Man). He told me that his family had had 10 Earls of Suffolk and that he was the 10th Braybrooke. We discussed Otley Hall, the founding of America, sister-city status, my literature, Lord Cornwallis, President Bush and the Queen's reaction to Blair. He raised royal visits. He told me, "The Queen's difficult. She's only been four times in the 10 years I've been Lord Lieutenant of Essex." He asked for a prospectus to forward to a royal.

I escorted him to his car and waved him off. He later told me that he turned on his car radio down Coopersale Hall's private drive and heard that the Twin Towers had been attacked. I went back to the Head's room and Ken, our Bursar, told me that his wife had rung his mobile with the same news. I later wrote a stanza about this visit in a classical ode, 'In the Lord Lieutenant of Essex's Yorktown'.[30]

Utopianism: New World Order
9/11, 'Attack on America'

America was under attack from utopian Jihadists. I knew immediately that there had been a clash of civilizations, that Jihadists within the Arab civilization were challenging the North-American civilization and the American *imperium*. Osama bin Laden was named as number-one suspect. The question in many minds was, how could he have organised such an attack from a cave in Afghanistan? It seemed that some within America's hidden State had found out that the attack was coming and had stood down America's fighter-aircraft defence. The New World Order seemed to be involved as the Twin Towers were unofficially named after David and Nelson Rockefeller, and the attack was used to mobilise American public support for a retaliatory invasion of Afghanistan. The US had oil pipelines there which had been molested by the Taliban, who were protecting bin Laden.

I was reflecting the Age, and the next day I began a long poem, 'Attack on America'. I was interested to read on 16 December that Paul Kennedy, who had argued in *The Rise and Fall of the Great Powers* that America was in a decline due to "imperial overstretch", had taken issue with me for saying in *The Fire and the Stones* that (as I wrote on the flyleaf of the book I presented to President George W. Bush) "the 21st century is the American century".

I knew from the Global Deception conference that the New World Order had a programme for population reduction, which was set out in *The Global 2000 Report*, which had been written for President Carter. This had been a Penguin paperback, but for some reason was completely unobtainable. I went to the British Library and ordered it on computer, and it came within half an hour. I spent the day combing through it and took over 80 pages of photocopies. I returned three days later and tried to order the second volume, *Global Future; A Time to Act*, but it was only available in Lincolnshire and would have to be sent specially to London. I did more work on the first volume, probing the population estimates which seemed to assume a reduction in the world's population of 2 billion, presumably as a result of local wars, famines and disease. I returned three days later and spent the morning on what seemed to be the only copy of *Global Future* in the UK. Chris Macann arrived at lunchtime in a hat and coat, and we lunched in the restaurant. Later I wrote two classical odes: 'At the British Library: Universalism is an Existentialism',[31] and 'In the British Library: Proofs of Genocide'.

The American-led Coalition attacked Afghanistan on 7 October. In 'Attack on America' I reflected the campaign in Afghanistan until the fall of Tora Bora, and finished the poem on 17 December. I was trying to convey the truth about the invasion of Afghanistan.

Early version of The Syndicate: 11 September and the New World Order – *Edward Garnier, Iain Duncan Smith*
I began writing the Postscript to *The Secret History of the West* in the days

following 9/11. It was soon clear that I had a sequel to *The Secret History of the West*, not a Postscript, and I thought of it as *11 September and the New World Order*. It eventually became *The Syndicate*. I visited the chambers of my libel lawyer, Edward (later Sir Edward) Garnier at 1 Brick Court and at his request spent three hours 40 minutes explaining the background, during which he sent out for sandwiches. As well as being an MP he had been Shadow Attorney General since 1997. Iain Duncan Smith had just become Leader of the Opposition, and to his evident resentment had removed him from that position, as he lamented.

I found it very valuable to talk through the New World Order with a Parliamentarian of his standing, and he confirmed much of what I had found out, and asked me many questions. A month later he sent me a list of points. I returned to Brick Court and spent two hours discussing the New World Order and how to present it.

Duncan Smith then gave out prizes at Normanhurst's Founders Day. I introduced him on the platform and we sang the school song, 'He Who Would Valiant Be' together, sharing a hymn sheet. (I said to him, "We've got to sing from the same hymn sheet." He whispered, "That's what I'm telling my party we must do.") I asked him what it was like being Leader of the Opposition. He told me, "There are so many meetings, arranged by my Chief of Staff. I'm trying to cut them down. Prime Minister's Questions takes the whole of Wednesday. I wish it could be once a fortnight. It makes a great hole in the week."

Nicholas Hagger and Iain Duncan Smith singing the School song at Normanhurst Founders' Day, 2001

Two days later I was back in Brick Court going through the orange and green markings on my typescript (orange, my proposed solutions; green, new queries). At the end we talked about Duncan Smith. Garnier said, "He makes people hold his cup and saucer.... He has no intellectual enquiry.... He's given all us backbenchers half an hour a week." I asked, "What, 160 of you are vying for one half-hour slot?" "Yes. He shuts himself away in his room and we don't see him. His PPS is supposed to liaise with us in the tearoom but he's spying on us, and we don't talk to him.... There will be a *putsch*. It's a question of timing. It can't be now because a divided party will mean another lost election. The time will come." I could see trouble ahead.

Down in Cornwall I wrote a new beginning for *11 September and the New*

World Order, which was now a separate volume. We had consented to have the Harbour-master's House turned into a film set for *Two Men Went to War*. The front had been painted black and a sign proclaiming 'The Ship Inn' had been hung above our front door. While I worked on amending the two books the two main actors came in and out of the front door, doing many takes. Later I was invited to join their open-air banquet on tables overlooking the inner harbour. I wrote a classical ode, 'On The Film Set: Home Truths'. I finished the new book on 8 December.[32]

Classical odes on English and European history
Historic houses: Titchfield, Sandringham
I was still carrying forward my classical odes.

We drove to Titchfield, the seat of the 3rd Earl of Southampton, Shakespeare's patron, and stayed at the Bugle Hotel. We looked in on the church of St Peter's and found the Wriothesley tomb, which has a relief showing the 3rd Earl as a boy of eight, kneeling hands-together. (This tomb may be referred to in Shakespeare's sonnet 4: "Thy unused beauty must be tombed with thee.") We walked to the 13th-century Abbey, now a ruin: a greyish sandstone building with no roof, two Tudor chimneys and a Playhouse open to the sky on the first floor with an open hearth and brick surround. There was a corner pillar in the room, which Shakespeare would have known and where some of his early plays may have been first performed. Later I wrote a classical ode, 'At the Earl of Southampton's Titchfield'.

We went to the Mansion House as guests of Worcester College for a Worcester College fund-raising event. I shook hands with the Lord Mayor, the Provost, Tim Sainsbury and Lord Faulkner, and over champagne chatted to my contemporary Sir John Weston, ex-Ambassador to the UN and NATO, and another contemporary of mine, the Appeal Court Judge Sir Simon Brown (later Lord Brown). I talked to my moral tutor Alec Graham, who remembered me; to Professor Jim Campbell, who had climbed in and was admonished by O'Toole, "I hate thee for thou art a Christian," and who I had told I would write a play on the 'Holy Brotherhood' – I told him, "It's now *The Rise of Oliver Cromwell*"; and Ricks's successor, David Bradshaw. We dined in the Egyptian Room, and at the end I talked with Francis Reynolds, my old Law tutor, who said, "I saw your name and wondered if I'd recognise you. I remember you came and saw me and said you didn't like Law and I said 'In that case, you must change.'" Later I wrote a classical ode, 'At the Mansion House'.

Three days later I returned to Worcester College, Oxford, for a Gaudy. I was allocated a room in the Sainsbury building and after a service in the newly-restored, 'Neronian' chapel with incense and many anthems, and then a group photo, I sat again at the long tables in hall. I was opposite Sir John Weston, who said of David Rockefeller, "He's a sweet, sweet man." I sat next to Alan Magnus, with whom I had travelled to Greece and who told me he had spent a year at Normanhurst as a boy, and Jim Morgan, another contemporary of mine who had worked for the BBC and defiantly smoked a pipe after the meal. Morgan died shortly afterwards. Later I wrote a classical ode, 'At Worcester College, Oxford: Gaudy'.

Alan Magnus told me at the Gaudy that he had a film of our visit to Greece. He invited me to see it in Hendon, and he projected his home movie on his sitting-room wall. It showed me at the age of 19 tugging a fig and leaping back as a green beetle fell on my bare arm. Later I wrote a classical ode, 'A Teenager in Greece: Youth and Age'.

Ann and I went to Sandringham to attend the East of England Tourist Board's Annual General Meeting chaired by Lord Somerleyton in the Visitors Centre. Afterwards we walked round the church, which was full of silver and gold, and then rode on a kind of train, sitting sideways, drawn by a tractor, to the House. We walked through six rooms on the ground floor and I was struck by the family feeling within the many framed photos. We had tea, and I had thoughts on sovereignty and national independence. On the way home I wrote a classical ode, 'At Sandringham'.

Christening of Ben

Our grandson Ben was baptised at St Mary's church, Loughton, in the christening shawl I had worn in July 1939 and there was a reception in Coopersale Hall's assembly hall, where our family sat at a central table. Later I wrote a classical ode, 'At St Mary's, Loughton: Christening'.

Historic houses: Somerleyton, Spains Hall

Lord Somerleyton had invited us to the Annual General Meeting of the East Anglian Region of the Historic Houses Association at Somerleyton Hall, a huge Victorian Hall built in Jacobean-Italianate style on his 5,000-acre estate at Lovingland, near Lowestoft. Coffee was in the Loggia, the meeting in the ballroom. As we queued for lunch I encountered my cousin Jill on sticks. I had not realised she had had a stroke on Easter Sunday. I chatted at length to Eddie Leicester, and Lord Somerleyton gave us a tour. He was a confident speaker and raised many laughs. Later I wrote a classical ode, 'At and With Somerleyton'.

We went to a Magistrates court to support Tony. While he was waiting for traffic-lights to turn green in a film van after dark an old lady crossing the road behind him stumbled into his rear wing. She fell. Tony got out, covered her with his coat and called for help, like the Good Samaritan. Now she had alleged that she was on the pedestrian crossing and was knocked down, and was claiming compensation for a broken arm, which turned into a broken shoulder, but would not say what doctor had diagnosed a fracture. There were many inconsistencies in her story, and in the court the two policemen refused to give evidence against Tony and turned defence witnesses, saying that the case should never have been brought. The case was dismissed. Her turning on a Good Samaritan to extract compensation resonated within me, and I wrote a classical ode, 'At Redbridge Magistrates Court'.

I went to see the ancient library in Spains Hall, Finchingfield. Col. Sir John Ruggles-Brise, Lord Lieutenant of Essex until 1978 and a Governor at Chigwell when I was there, now 93, was waiting for me at the door, bald and bearded. He took me on a tour of the 1570 Hall and asked me to find a long ladder, carry it into the library and lean it at an angle of 45 degrees while he put his frail foot on the bottom rung to stop it from sliding. He told me that the oldest books, some of which were pre-1760s, were on the top shelf. I clambered up the ladder and peered for books connected with Shakespeare, but did not find any. Ruggles-Brise told his daughter, who looked in, that I was his newest friend. He died soon afterwards. Later I wrote a classical ode, 'At Spains Hall, Finchingfield'.

I went to the Annual General Meeting of the Historic Houses Association at Queen Elizabeth II Hall, Westminster. Eddie Leicester seemed to be in charge. We had lunch at a round table near the Earl of Carnarvon and his wife, and when they left a youngish, portly man in his early forties waved us over to join him. He turned out to be the Duke of Rutland. I talked to him about his ancestor Roger Manners, 5th Earl of Rutland, who was thought by some to have written Shakespeare's works. He told me, "We've got a picture of the Earl of Southampton, full length, eight-foot long." I told him that Manners and the 3rd Earl of Southampton were friends and attended theatres together. I invited him to bring all the evidence he had in Belvoir Castle to a meeting of the Shakespearean Authorship Trust and present it. He said, "I'll come." Later I wrote a classical ode, 'In Rutland's England'.

It proved to be the last Historic Houses Association's AGM I would attend. During my time with the HHA I had got to know the descendants of all the key Elizabethan figures: of Lord Burghley, Sir Francis Bacon, Sir Edward Coke, the Earl of Southampton, the Earl of Oxford and the Earl of Rutland (Roger Manners). Talking to these descendants had helped me form my view of Shakespeare and of the Tudor time.

I revisited Copped Hall's racquets court to attend an exhibition of Eric Dawson's water-colour cartoons. I wandered in the Yew Walk where Henry VIII is thought to have strolled on 19 May 1536 till he heard a cannon signify the beheading of Anne Boleyn. Later I wrote a classical ode, 'Copped Hall Revisited'.

Before Christmas I worked on five English classical odes and three Russian odes. Then I drafted another five Russian odes, a Hungarian ode and two Polish odes. I wrote 'In Habsburg Prague, with Knights and King of Jerusalem'. After Christmas I went to Westminster Abbey to view the sanctuary pavement. The spheres on the pavement, which represent the medieval *primum mobile,* are covered by a carpet all the year round, but can be viewed on the day I went. Coronations take place amid these uncovered spheres. I reflected on the medieval and modern views of the universe, and saw where the haunting quotation about "the end (*finem*) of the universe" (*see* p.585) was originally located. Later I wrote a classical ode, 'In Westminster Abbey: Sanctuary Pavement'.[33]

Middle Temple Hall and Twelfth Night
I continued my effort on *Classical Odes.*

At Mark Rylance's invitation Ann and I went to the Middle Temple Hall to see the Quatercentenary production of *Twelfth Night*, a historical creation in the same place (little changed) where the play was first performed 400 years back on 2 February 1602. We entered through the 'Tiring- (attiring-) room' where Mark came and shook my hand wearing the white make-up of an old lady. He was playing Olivia in an all-male cast, but I immediately saw he had based himself on Elizabeth I. We went beyond the screen into the Hall for mulled wine. We sat on banked seats. I could imagine Shakespeare in the corner. I wrote a classical ode, 'At Middle Temple Hall'.

Lord Braybrooke and Cornwallis's surrender sword
Lord Braybrooke invited us to dinner at Abbey House, across the road from Audley End which his family used to own. He and his wife received us with champagne, and Richard Robins was present. We ate near a roaring fire. Robin Braybrooke complained that the Queen did not answer his handwritten letters and he did not know if she had seen them. His wife Corinna was Rab Butler's stepdaughter, and her mother used to play with Ruggles-Brise at Spains Hall. Robin declared himself a "rake": "I was good with an oar. I didn't say 'whore'."

Our dinner conversation led to the British surrender in America by his ancestor, Cornwallis. Robin left the round table and fetched Cornwallis's sword. It was in a thin cardboard hollow tube. Standing in front of the round dinner table he drew the sword and handed it to me. I stood, held the hilt of rolled steel and swished the blade about. It was very light. I did some good fencing parries near the round table where the other four were sitting over coffee.

Cornwallis surrendered America by surrendering the sword to his American counterpart, Washington. (His deputy, O'Hara, offered the sword to Rochambeau, who pointed to Washington, who indicated Lincoln, his number 2.) The sword said 'Gen. Cornwallis 1750'. Cornwallis had died childless, and Robin surmised that the sword had passed to his nephew, the Marquess. Robin found it in Audley End in the 1970s and had tried to sell it to America, without success. I contacted Charlie Bryan of the Richmond Museum. However, the sword's pedigree was questioned and the Americans would not buy it. Later I wrote a classical ode, 'In the Lord Lieutenant of Essex's Yorktown'.

We went to Cornwall for half-term. I had bought 3 Quay Road as a buy-to-let and the land in front of 3 and 4 Quay Road. We got the new house ready to let. I made trips backwards and forwards, took delivery of mattresses, hung pictures and washed down the outside. I wrote two classical odes, 'Home-Making in Charlestown' and 'In Loughton, within Western Civilization'.

Duke of Rutland and SAT

Charles had sent me a card saying he could not attend the coming SAT meeting. He had now renounced his courtesy title of the Earl of Burford and was calling himself Charles Beauclerk. He told me of his title, "It's like a rusty suit of armour. It's a bar to self-knowledge." His family title went back to 1676, and I could see he did not want to explain the issue of his title to the Duke of Rutland.

The Duke of Rutland talked to the SAT in a London apartment. He grasped my hand with his left hand as his right hand was turned back in a claw. He was in a suit and very at ease. He announced that he had received a letter from the Queen's Private Secretary, Sir Robin Janvrin, saying that the Queen would implement the Nice Treaty. He had the letter in his pocket and I asked to see it. (He was like one of the barons at the time of Magna Carta, only his communication from the monarch concerned the surrender of British sovereignty to Europe rather than democratic rights for the people.) Mark Rylance, chairing the meeting holding his brown hat and sitting in an open-necked shirt, kept the Duke waiting for an hour and a half by sticking to the agenda and having him in 'Any other business'. Eventually after 9 the Duke handed out packs his archivist had assembled, and focused on his portrait of the 3rd Earl of Southampton at Belvoir Castle. I said that Roger Manners would have been 15½ when *Venus and Adonis* came out. The Duke pointed out that 'Rosencrantz' and 'Guildenstern' (characters in *Hamlet*) were classmates of Manners at Padua University and that Manners was King James's ambassador at a royal christening at Elsinore in 1603.

The Duke had a chauffeur waiting for him and left. I walked to Warren Street station with Mark (who was now wearing his brown hat). He asked me what I was writing. I told him about my classical odes: "I am writing poems about the enmeshing of idea and place." I said they were innovatory poems and reflected the two halves of the British national psyche: our Englishness and Europeanness. I told him I had seen his Olivia as Elizabeth I grieving for Essex. He nodded and said I was right, and that no other critic had seen this. I wrote a classical ode, 'In Rutland's England'.

The SAT had arranged for me to be interviewed on the Shakespearean authorship question for a television programme. A presenter came with a camera girl to Otley Hall and I spoke in the Great Hall for three-quarters of an hour. When I finished she told me it would be going all round the world, to hundreds of millions of people. I had chattered away one to one without being aware of those listening. She told me she had worked at Faber for two years, and had been Ted Hughes's publicist. "I often met him. I miss him very much."[34]

In Cyprus: Othello's Castle and Grivas's bungalow
We landed in Larnaca and were driven to Paphos's Hotel Annabelle, where there were orange, lemon and tangerine trees outside my window. We took a taxi to the Rock of Aphrodite, where Aphrodite was born out of sea-foam and blown spume. I found the base of the Sanctuary of Aphrodite, c.1200BC, where there was temple-prostitution: virgins gave their virginity to strangers and donated the proceeds to the priests of Aphrodite. We went to Kolossi (a castle given by the Franks to the Knights of St John) and to Kourion. Back in Paphos we sauntered along the waterfront to the Venetian castle. I wrote a classical ode, 'In Aphrodite's Cyprus: Bodily and Spiritual Beauty'.

We visited North Cyprus. We were driven to Nicosia and walked between rows of barbed wire to the Turkish checkpoint. We found a taxi on the Turkish side and drove to Famagusta's old city. We eventually reached the Sea-Gate Citadel, a massive stone shell overlooking the harbour, where Christopher Moro (the Moor) ruled the island between 1506 and 1508. This was Othello's Castle. Both Christopher Moro and his successor Francesco de Sessa were Moors and were regarded as 'Moors of Venice'. We drove on to the ruins of Salamis, one column of the Temple of Zeus and royal tombs of the 8th–7th centuries BC poking through grass.

We drove to Kyrenia and sat on the harbour wall. We then went to Bellapais and saw the Tree of Idleness, "whose shadow," Lawrence Durrell wrote, "incapacitates one for serious work", and the restaurant nearby where Durrell lunched. We climbed a steep narrow street between white houses to Bitter Lemons, the house Durrell restored. We returned to Nicosia and were met by our driver and returned to Paphos. I wrote a classical ode, 'In Turkish Cyprus'.

In Paphos we visited the mosaics of Dionysus, Theseus, Orpheus and

Aion. We found the agora and took a taxi to the Tombs of the Kings: Egyptianised tombs built under the Ptolemies who ruled from Alexandria from the 3rd century BC. They all had courtyards and were houses for the dead to occupy in the Underworld. People were expected to live their after-life in the same way that they lived this life. I wrote a classical ode, 'In Paphos's City of the Dead'.

I had driven past Baia, the Roman Baiae, in 1995, but did not know that the gateway to the Underworld had been discovered there: the Oracle of the Dead. In the first half of March I wrote a classical ode, 'Near Baiae's Oracle of the Dead: Gateway to the Underworld'. I thought of Baiae in Paphos.

We visited Makarios's grave in the Troodos Mountains: a grotto with a marble slab. We entered the nearby Kykkos monastery with gaudy frescoes. It had been EOKA's headquarters, and Grivas and senior EOKA figures came as refugees and attended meetings there dressed as monks.

In Limassol we visited the tomb and enclosure of Grivas, the founder of EOKA in 1951 who I found in Porto Cheli in Greece in 1960. There was a statue of him in battledress and a saluting enclosure with a roof. Nearby, under a Greek flag, was the bungalow that Grivas used when he was in Limassol. The kitchen had a stone trapdoor and stone steps that led down to a cellar, where there was a bed, chair, table and carpet. I wrote a classical ode, 'In EOKA's Cyprus: End of Empire'. Sitting on our Hotel Annabelle veranda and gazing at the sea, I reflected, "I am so conditioned to be a poet now, that I cannot lie still for two hours without lines, or even stanzas, rising."[35]

Davenport's funeral and memorial service

Practically every day for the next nine months I wrote a classical ode. My English teacher, Parry Davenport, who had arrived at Chigwell in May 1947, had died in Wales. His Parkinson's disease had deteriorated and he had been in a coma for a week. The Chigwell master David Ballance rang and asked if I could attend the funeral in Brecon Cathedral. Ann and I made a detour to Brecon on our way to Cornwall, passing the Black Mountains and the Brecon Beacons.

We spent the night in Brecon and next morning walked to the Cathedral. It was deserted, and Davenport (into whose matins I had strayed on my first day) was lying in a banner-draped coffin in the choir, under a candle. We sauntered to the car park to look for Old Chigwellians, and I encountered Donald Thompson, my old Headmaster, grey-haired and round-spectacled, now 91 but looking 60. We chatted and walked to the Cathedral and I sat next to him and his wife in a pew. He told me, "I'm in my penultimate." He was certain he would die the following year. (In fact, he died in March 2006 at the age of 93.) His wife told me how hard the fuses were to find in 1947.

Only four of Davenport's thousands of pupils were present. There was no eulogy on principle as flattering references to his life would conflict with his Christian beliefs.

After the coffin had been carried out we wandered round the Cathedral and in its heritage centre Ann found a stand wired for sound and pushed a button. A voice rasped from beyond the dead: "I'm Parry Davenport, I was ordained in 1939 in Brecon Cathedral." I stood transfixed, listening to the biographical details of the man we had just sent to be cremated. The Chigwell party were nearby, and I beckoned them over and pushed the button again. I wrote a classical ode, 'At Brecon Cathedral'.

In due course I attended Parry Davenport's memorial service in the Chigwell School chapel, and read the passage on the parson in Chaucer's *Prologue* at David Ballance's request, pitching the medieval English between those who knew the text and those who required Anglicisation. Ballance read from Donne's *Sermons*, and David Senton (an actor at school) closed the service by reciting Prospero's burying of his staff. I wandered down the aisle greeting fellow Old Chigwellians and I was approached by Colin Wilcoxon, who asked plaintively why he had not been booked to read Chaucer as he had taught Chaucer for 35 years at Pembroke, Cambridge (where I had visited him to press him to select Tony Little) and had translated his works. I brought the memorial service into a classical ode, 'In Loughton, Impersonating'.[36]

Odes on English cultural history
Down in Cornwall I watched the procession that took the body of Queen Elizabeth the Queen Mother from Clarence House to her lying-in-state in Westminster Hall on television. The crown she wore at her coronation was on the draped coffin, and I was fascinated by its Koh-i-noor diamond, of which a Hindu text said, "He who owns this diamond will own the world." I later wrote a classical ode, 'In the Empress of India's London'.

Back in Suffolk I pondered on the roots of the English sonnet and blank verse. I drove to Framlingham's St Michael's church and visited the coloured alabaster tomb of the Earl of Surrey, the man who 'invented' the English sonnet and blank verse, two stupendous achievements. I had followed his tradition of blank verse in *Overlord*. A statue of him, eyes closed with black hair and a beard, lay on his tomb, and as he was beheaded in 1547 on the orders of Henry VIII (for siding against his successor Edward) his coronet was by his side to symbolise his disgrace. I wrote a classical ode, 'At Surrey's Tomb, Framlingham'.

The next day I joined a tour of the London places associated with Edward de Vere. We began in the Tudor Sutton House, Hackney and then visited St Augustine's Tower. The 17th Earl of Oxford's marble tomb may have stood in front of the tower inside the church that was now no more. We then went by coach (a bizarre tour through Hackney's housing estates and ugly flats) to the site of King's Place, where de Vere lived from 1596 until his death in 1604; to the site of the house de Vere moved to in 1591 after losing Hedingham Castle to Lord Burghley; to St Mary's old church where his new son Henry was baptised; and to the site of the Theatre in Curtain Road, Shoreditch. I wrote a classical ode, 'In De Vere's Hackney'.

There was a conjunction of planets – Jupiter, Saturn, Mars, Venus and Mercury in a near-diagonal line – as had happened in April 2BC, perhaps explaining the bright Star of Bethlehem. I drove from Great Easton to a high country lane near Tilty and spent some time studying the planets through binoculars from a dark barleyfield. I wrote a classical ode, 'In Tilty: Star of Bethlehem'.

The Queen, celebrating her 50th Jubilee, declared in Westminster Hall that she would not abdicate. The following day I began a classical ode, 'In Jubilee London on May Day: Stability and Order', "linking the Queen refusing to abdicate, or stability; developments in the universe; and demonstrations". I commented:

> Poetic logic is one of association. It's like moving from five planets to the Star of Bethlehem to the siege in the Church of the Nativity, Bethlehem. It is not rational logic. It is esemplastic, shaping into One – assembling potsherds into a jar; not fancy saying one thing is like another. Poetry is a means of approaching the unitive vision in 160 lines – through economy and rigorous use of language; stating the One in verse.

I was invited to cricket at Chelmsford by HSBC, who insured part of our schools. I took Matthew with me, and our host told him: "I remember your Dad. He said 'Just come'. It was difficult, I came and we talked an hour and did the business for two schools. It was great." He told me, "You were a Tartar in those days." (Meaning that I drove a hard bargain and wanted things done yesterday.) He gave me a penknife as a memento (perhaps of Oaklands' cut-throat business in those intractable days).

At Otley Hall we had two more Open Days. A member of the public asked the housekeeper of me, "Excuse me, is that Bartholomew Gosnold over there?" I saw a yellowhammer, brilliant yellow with brown wings, and heard owls hooting at night round our window. I reflected that I had admitted high culture and history into my poetry by taking on Otley Hall, "my Yeatsian tower". I worked on a succession of classical odes: 'In Somerset's Avalon'; 'At and With Somerleyton'; 'At the British Library: Universalism is an Existentialism'; and 'At Chingford Assembly Hall: Leaders after Laeken'. I worked on 'In Potsdam' and a satirical ode on the celebrity culture, 'At Beckingham Palace: Talents of a Meritocracy'.

The next day I finished the poem and then gave a 15-minute interview to BBC Radio Suffolk on Bartholomew Gosnold's naming of Cape Cod exactly 400 years previously. They rang three and a half hours later to say that the tape had either been lost or deleted, could I do it again? Which I did. The next day I gave an interview to *Look East* on Gosnold's naming of Cape Cod, during which our front-of-house caretaker caught a swan and held it under his arm for the camera.[37]

In Bordeaux: Comte Hagger

Chris Macann invited us to his château near Bordeaux. He met us at the airport and drove us back to Passirac, near Brossac in Aquitaine. We slept in a neo-Gothic turret. We breakfasted with Chris's wife, Béatrice de Castelbajac, a dark-haired French lady to whom I spoke in French. We drove to Saint-Émilion and lunched in the main square, where Chris ordered Comte Hagger wine. He insisted that there was a Comte Hagger who left Aquitaine when the English were expelled in 1453. We drove to Castillon-la-Bataille and found the monument that commemorated the English defeat in Guyenne.

We dined with Chris, Béatrice and her son and daughter-in-law. The next morning I talked philosophy with Chris in his study, "the window framing the universe", and I explained my view of Being and the universe. I said that the scientist explains the universe, whereas the philosopher describes it and explains all levels.

We visited Béatrice's brother, an unofficial viscount as titles were abolished in France in 1870. He was in a wheelchair. He made it clear that the château would remain within the family. On the way to the airport we visited Saint-Loubès, allegedly the home of Comte Hagger wine. At the hotel there I was told that the wine was sent to Libourne nearby, and I was given an address that enabled me to order Comte Hagger wine, which in due course arrived at Otley Hall. I would serve Comte Hagger Bordeaux at family gatherings. I wrote a classical ode, 'In Aquitaine'.[38]

Odes on traditions: Thaxted, Sulgrave Manor

Back at Otley Hall I found a carving, a signature, on a panel in the Oak Room: 'Barthy Gosno 28½.' Bartholomew Gosnold had been 28½ in 1599, and I wondered if *he* had signed the panelling in that year while staying in the Oak Room.

I had a sandstone statue of an eagle at Great Easton, which adorns our present garden. I wrote: "The orange eagle is a symbol of the poet, who hunts images (voles, mice) from vision high in the sky." At Otley Hall I revived the pumping up of water through the borehole, and wrote, "The pump is a symbol for pumping the waters of poetry from the depths of the underground/unconscious." Such musings came from my daily classical odes: 'At the American Embassy, London', 'At the Pantheon', 'At Castel Sant' Angelo, Rome', 'At the *Ara Pacis*' and 'In Domitilla's Catacomb, Rome'. I worked on a classical ode, 'In Keats' House, Rome'. I had followed the Queen's Golden Jubilee on television, and I wrote a classical ode, 'At the Queen's Golden Jubilee, London: The End of a Golden Age'.

At Thaxted, I was once again fascinated by the 13th-century Horn Dance, which featured the Devil. A troubadour with a violin came mysteriously out of the darkness, playing in ten dancers – six priests of the Devil wearing hats with magic symbols – sun, serpent, eagle or griffin, a ram's head, and two mirrors; a rider on horseback; an archer with a bow and arrow; a tinkler on a triangle; and the Devil under a black umbrella and canopy. To the violinist's eerie music they snaked in silence in a serpentine dance, showing the Devil's horns, returned and faded back into the silence of the churchyard from which they had come. No applause was allowed. It was very haunting: a rite, an occult black mass. Later I wrote a classical ode, 'At the Thaxted Horn Dance'.

I had been told that the Colonial Dames of America, who made an annual donation to Sulgrave Manor, the home of George Washington's ancestors in Northamptonshire, might make a donation to Otley Hall. I drove to Sulgrave Manor, attended their meeting and spoke to the incoming Chairman of the Dames. At lunch in the conference hall, I sat next to the Virginian head of the Delawares, whose English branch of the family, the De La Warrs, had owned Bourn Hall after Admiral Haggar sold it in 1733. She told me 7,000 Colonial Dames paid subscriptions or levies to Head Office. We were addressed by Lord Howe, the assassin of Baroness Thatcher, grey-haired and pot-bellied, jowly, stooping, who said that the US have an imperial role, that the British had done it before, that the *pax Americana* continued the *pax Britannica*; and that the role brings unpopularity.

The Virginian and her husband visited me at Otley Hall – we toured the gardens and identified flowers in the meadow (bee, marsh and purple-spotted orchids, yellow loosestrife and hawkbit) – and said they would recommend the Hall to the Colonial Dames. However, I received a strong letter from Sulgrave Manor's solicitors warning me to have nothing to do with the Colonial Dames. I wrote a classical ode, 'At Sulgrave Manor'.[39]

In Heidelberg and Freiburg: Rosicrucians and philosophers
Chris Macann had told me that he modelled himself on Heidegger. We had arranged to visit all the houses connected with Heidegger and Husserl, and in mid-June I flew to Frankfurt, met Chris (who wore a cloth cap) at the arrival gate, hired a car and drove to Heidelberg. We booked in at Novotel

and went by funicular straight to the castle: a rose-red sandstone ruin with a spectacular view across the Neckar.

The castle was the home of Rosicrucianism. Frederick V of the Wittelsbach family, Elector Palatine of the Rhine and Elector Prince at the age of 15 in 1610, married the daughter of the English King James I, Elizabeth Stuart, in London in 1613. *The Tempest* was performed at the wedding. The 3rd Earl of Southampton, Shakespeare's patron, attended the wedding and escorted Elizabeth to Heidelberg. In 1615 Frederick built Elizabeth an arch (in one night), an 'English palace' and a theatre in the Thick Tower which replicated the Globe. The Rosicrucian Johann Valentin Andreae used the library and wrote the first Rosicrucian texts there. Frederick V presided over a Rosicrucian State in the Palatinate.

We toured the castle and the English palace, and I looked down from the top of the Thick Tower at where the Globe-like theatre had been. I wondered at Southampton's connection with Rosicrucianism, and Rosicrucianism's connection with Shakespeare and the Globe. I wrote a classical ode, 'In Heidelberg's Rosicrucian Castle'.

The next day Chris drove me to Freiburg. We entered Freiburg University and found Room 1010, where Heidegger lectured. We drove to see Heidegger's house from 1928 in Rötebuckweg 47: a white, round-tiled house with white-framed windows, shutters and roses in the front. I rang the bell, (which said 'Heidegger') and spoke to a youngish woman with black hair (Heidegger's granddaughter), who spoke of a house at the back where he died. We went round the back to a white house, Fillibachstrasse 25. I returned and I rang the doorbell again. Chris hid out of embarrassment, and I spoke to the dark lady's husband. No, we could not see Heidegger's study, it was as it was when he used it but was private to the family. No, he did not write any of *Being and Time* there, but in a farmhouse below his hut at Todtnauberg: "He lived there away from his family who were up at the top, he wanted peace to work. He had some problem with Hitler and did not want his children arrested with him." He said Heidegger moved into the house in the garden, which he took me to see. He showed me the downstairs window where Heidegger died, and the study windows on the first floor at the back and side, looking over the garden.

Edmund Husserl, the founder of the Phenomenological movement, was a Professor at Freiburg University. We drove to Günterstal and visited Husserl's grave in a churchyard opposite a tram station. We went on to Lorettostrasse 40 to see Husserl's home from 1916 to 1937 (a huge house, now in flats). We drove to see where Husserl died, at Schöneckstrasse 6. In the cobbled square of Münsterplatz Chris explained how Heidegger reacted against Husserl just as Aristotle did against Plato: pupil against master.

Over breakfast the next morning Chris asked me about the experience of the Light and how it influenced rational theories of a world beyond the physical. I said I was in the intuitionist line, and that rational projections must be grounded in existential experience. Taking Hadrian's pantheon as an example, I said that in that poem I begin in a grounded place, take it forward to physical light on 8 altars and then on to metaphysical penetration of the universe from outside. I said that logic can posit many universes; I am only interested in the one universe I know.

We drove to Heidegger's two houses in Todtnauberg. We got into the Brender house at 20 Martin Heideggerweg off Rüttestrasse, in a green valley. We were shown the space where Heidegger wrote *Being and Time* some time between 1922 when the hut was built and 1927. We then climbed up to the hut on the edge of the Black Forest: a small wood-tiled house with green shutters, a green front door and side door. In this mountain retreat he received Heisenberg. There was a view across wild flowers of timeless mountains, and I felt that Heidegger's writings in such surroundings should have been *more* Wordsworthian and more alert to the One.

On the way back we drove to Plöck 66 where the Existentialist philosopher Karl Jaspers lived from January 1923 to March 1948. There he wrote *Philosophie* and *Existenzphilosophie* before going to Switzerland.

That evening we met Reiner Wiehl, Professor Emeritus of Philosophy at Heidelberg University, at the Palatinate museum restaurant. He was very interested in my work. Wiehl declared that "all philosophies are failures – Heidegger's theory of time, analytical philosophy and Whitehead's process philosophy (which contradicts maths)". I recalled Ricks telling me, "Every epic is a failure. Homer failed, Virgil, Milton, Pound all failed. And you will fail too." According to the Ricks-Wiehl doctrine, no epic poem or philosophy has ever succeeded.

Macann took Wiehl's words to heart and told me later: "Don't be a philosopher. Be a poet and historian.... Professors won't welcome something new and will put it down." Later I wrote a classical ode, 'In Freiburg: Husserl and Heidegger'. (Wiehl died in December 2010.)

We drove back to Frankfurt, returned the car and sat in the airport. Macann told me he did not want to give any philosophical lectures: "I don't want disappointments. I'm happy in the *château*." I was clear that I would bring out my own work on Universalist philosophy, which would become *The New Philosophy of Universalism*, and my book on the New World Order, which would become *The Syndicate*.[40]

Marlowe's window
There had been an SAT lunch at the Globe, followed by a meeting in the Theatre downstairs. Mark Rylance distributed copies of my classical ode, 'At Middle Temple Hall' with approval. He said he wanted a Marlovian trustee.

Mike Frohnsdorff of the Marlowe Society joined us at the end of the meeting and I talked with him at some length. I had been impressed by a paper he had sent me, saying there was a Marlowe Renaissance from 1598 to 1622, that Marlowe was alive for much of this period, that his survival was an open secret with allusions hidden in literature. Marlowe had four literary disguises: Ovid, Musaeus, the Marigold and the Bee. He claimed that Ovid is Marlowe in Jonson's play *The Poetaster* (first performed in 1601). (Jonson is Horace.) The play contains the line: "Or like the Bee, the Marigold's darling." He claimed that in 1622 Donne was alluding to Marlowe in: "The marigold opens to the sunne, though it have no tongue to say so." (Sermon CXII.) He spoke of marigolds in Shakespeare's sonnet 25 ("But as the marigold at the sun's eye") and *Winter's Tale* ("The marigold, that goes to bed wi' the sun"). He claimed that in '*Caltha Poetarum* [meaning 'Marigold of the Poets'] or, The Bumble Bee' by Thomas Cutwode (meaning 'woodcut'), the Bee is the author, Marlowe. Frohnsdorff did not believe that Marlowe wrote Shakespeare's works, but he did believe that Marlowe survived 1593 and wrote some of the sonnets. Was this conclusive proof that Marlowe survived? No. But it was very interesting, and I looked at references to marigolds and bees in Renaissance literature in a new light. The title page of Marlowe's poem 'Hero and Leander' (completed by Chapman and published in 1598) shows a woodcut of two marigolds, one open to the sun, one closed under the moon and a star, and the legend "*Ut Nectar, Ingenium*": "Genius is like Nectar".

Back in England, Mike Frohnsdorff appeared before the SAT committee to discuss his paper, 'The Marigold'. He claimed that Marlowe escaped England in 1593 but condemned himself to longer exile than necessary by insulting the Queen in 'Caltha', which was by Marlowe. Mark Rylance chaired the meeting (in a green shirt and brown hat) and he later walked with me to see Virginia Woolf's house from 1908 to 1911, which Shaw had occupied from 1897 to 1898.

Soon afterwards I attended the unveiling of a stained-glass window to Marlowe in Westminster Abbey that gave his last date as '1593?', the question mark suggesting that he may not have died in 1593. During evensong I sat next to Mike Frohnsdorff, and then we all moved our seats to sit in front of Chaucer's tomb and the covered window. Mike addressed us on 'The Muses' Darling' and there was a song, 'Come live with me and be my love'. Sir Anthony Sher recited a speech from *Tamburlaine*, 'Now clear the triple region of the air.' The window was unveiled and seen to be mauve, and a girl recited a translation from Ovid's *Elegies* (1.15), "Therefore when flint and iron wear away,/Verse is immortal, and shall ne'er decay."

At the end I encountered Mark Rylance clutching ten red roses. He laid four on Chaucer's tomb round the marigold wreath laid earlier for Marlowe;

and the other six at Shakespeare's statue, which was constructed in marble in 1740 and has Shakespeare pointing to a scroll with a garbled quotation from part of Prospero's last speech. Mark pointed out to me its hidden Templar symbolism. "See," he said to me, "he's pointing to the word 'Temple'. His legs are crossed in the Hermetic '8'." (The '8' was a mathematical sign for infinity turned upright, and suggesting eternity.) Mark told me, "I cross my own legs on stage if I feel like it." I asked him if his roses were supposed to be Rosicrucian, from early Freemasonry. He nodded. He was claiming both Marlowe and Shakespeare as Rosicrucians. Not realising that he was a Rosicrucian Baconian, the Marlovians invited Mark Rylance to be President of the Marlowe Society and he accepted. On the tube on the way home I "scribbled out" a classical ode, 'In Poets' Corner with Marlowe: Marigold', oblivious to the looks I was getting.[41]

Odes on affairs of State

I was invited to a barbecue in the American Ambassador's garden in Winfield House, Regent's Park. I chatted to Ambassador Farish, who asked me several questions about Otley Hall. There were 2,000 there: it was like a Royal Garden Party, and the Ambassador had the strut and swagger of a Roman. It was how the British were a hundred years ago. Later I wrote a story, 'In the American Ambassador's Back Garden'.

The Head of Coopersale Hall left to accompany her husband to his new job in Kuwait. For her farewell prize-giving she invited Anna Raeburn, an agony aunt, to give out the prizes. She was quick-talking, and in conversation with me quick to run down the press that gave her her living: "The papers aren't making money, so I work for the internet and radio." I spoke at the end and engineered a standing ovation for the Head, who was in tears as I gave her a picture.

The Queen's long-planned visit to Ipswich took place on 25 July. The Labour Council, having rejected sister-city status, had also moved away from unveiling a statue to Bartholomew Gosnold. The project had been cancelled. (Instead, at the direction of the Council, she unveiled a street sign which turned out to be illegal, and later had to be taken down.) The news was full of the acquittal of Princess Diana's butler, who had been accused of stealing 310 of Diana's possessions. The Queen was alleged to have told him, "Be careful. There are powers at work in this country about which we have no knowledge." Musing on the Secret State and the New World Order, I wrote a classical ode, 'Outside the Old Bailey: A Ruthless Queen?' Down in Cornwall I wrote a classical ode, 'On the Queen's Visit to Ipswich: Dissident'.

I had earlier written 'In the Sistine Chapel', 'In the British Library: Proof of Genocide' and 'By the Arno, Pisa', 'At Tudor Otley Hall: The End of

England' (out of a quarrel with myself), 'At Virgil's Tomb' and 'At Horace's Sabine Farm'. I now worked on 'At the Grotto of the Sybil, Cumae', 'At Poppaea's Villa, Oplontis', 'At Herculaneum' (in which "Ennychelus" in line 59 puns with 'Nicholas'), 'At Pompeii', 'In the Vatican' and 'At Troy VI'. I was consciously following a Roman tradition but adapting it: "I have followed Keats, Shelley and Byron in love for classical ruins, but have replaced mythology with history."

I pressed on with more classical odes: 'In Pergamum', 'In Global Eden', 'At Didyma's Oracle', 'On St John's Patmos', 'At Daphni', 'In Porto Cheli', 'On Sciathos', 'Commonwealth Games: Peace through War', 'On Skiros', 'In Hitler's Nuremberg', 'At Jasna Gora', 'In Cracow', 'In Old Buda', 'In Habsburg Prague, with Knights and King of Jerusalem' and 'In the Kremlin'.

I wrote of a "third group of poems" which "need to express anti-Americanism" from the point of view of "a dissident". I noted that Otley Hall had taken me closer to those running the world and had helped to give me a window on events. I worked on 'At the Winter Palace, St Petersburg', 'At Dostoevsky's Apartment, St Petersburg', 'At the Yusupov Palace, St Petersburg', 'At Chekhov's House, Yalta' and 'In Conference Yalta'. By now I had "virtually finished *In Europe's Ruins*". I had finished Italy, Greece, Turkey, E. Europe, Russia and "may have some more Germany to do, and Austria and Belgium".

Before I left Cornwall I saw Arthur Hosegood being wheelchaired into the back of an ambulance from 4 Quay Road, watched by his neighbours. He had cancer of the bowel, and we all knew he would not return. I spoke to him as he sat in the ambulance. The bins were out, and I said with a black humour I knew he would appreciate, "At least you're not being taken by the binmen." He chuckled and said, "I might as well be taken by them." He declined an operation and died a month later.

We returned for Otley Hall's next Open Days. I worked on more classical odes: 'The Chapel of the Holy Blood, Bruges' (Bruges being the seat of the Bourn Haggers in the 14th century), 'In the De Vere Society Library, Otley Hall: Caleygreyhound', 'At Dickens' House' and 'At Caernarvon Castle'.[42]

English historic houses: Coggeshall Abbey, Horham Hall
I returned a picture to my cousin Jill at Coggeshall Abbey, and found her shuffling around with her stick in a kitchen full of grime, the cat on the table near the opened cheese. Roger came in, slower and frailer, at 67. He took me to see the 68 acres he had bought, the pure spring water he was pumping for their use and the barns he wanted to restore. I had already written a classical ode, 'At Little Coggeshall Abbey'. I worked on 'At St Mary's, Loughton: Christening', 'Copped Hall Revisited', 'At Spain's Hall,

Finchingfield', 'At the London Independent Hospital, Whitechapel', 'At Holly House', 'Home-making in Charlestown', 'At the Prince Regent Budget Seminar: Advisers and Clients' and 'At the Bank Managers' Dinner, Grosvenor House Hotel'.

Down in Cornwall we lunched at the Carlyon Bay Hotel, "where the Head Waiter told us he had been talking to the Brokenshires. 'They come from your village [Loughton], they've had a holiday home down here for years. She worked in the Bookshop when you owned a school. Your mother taught James the violin.'" My mother's violin pupil James Brokenshire MP went on to become Parliamentary Under-Secretary of State for Crime and Security and later Minister for Immigration and Security. That afternoon, with "lashing rain, the sea up over the pier", I wrote my poem 'Sea Energy'.

At the end of October I attended the Annual General Meeting of the East Anglian Region of the Historic Houses Association at Horham Hall, near Thaxted, the home of the historical novelist Evelyn Anthony (then 74) and her husband Michael Ward-Thomas. Elizabeth I stayed there with her court for nine days in 1571 and for five days in 1578, when she received an envoy of the Duke of Anjou who was seeking her hand in marriage. I parked on grass, walked into the porch and Great Hall with a high, coved ceiling and went through to the dining-room for coffee. I stood in the parlour where Elizabeth I received Anjou's envoy. I had a chat with Evelyn Anthony and Ward-Thomas. I wrote a classical ode, 'At Horham Hall'.

I was rung by Mark Barty-King. He said he was retiring from the chairmanship of Transworld in June and looking to start a small publishing firm. He asked if I would join him. The arrangement was overtaken by events and did not happen: he was asked to be Chairman of a newly-formed literary agency.[43]

Utopianism: China
In China: the Humble Administrator's garden and Mao's mausoleum, Chinese classical odes
I had long wanted to revisit China following my discovery of the Cultural Revolution in March 1966. (*See My Double Life 1: This Dark Wood.*) Then China was a 'perfect society' under the tyranny of Chairman Mao. I wanted to look at the new China and determine how far it was still Communist.

We flew to China via Frankfurt (above which I "scribbled out" a classical ode, 'Above Frankfurt: Brain and Soul'). We were met at Shanghai Airport and driven straight to the Jade Buddha temple built in 1882, which immediately signified that Buddhism was being practised openly and not suppressed. We lunched at the Dragon Boat restaurant and then went up the Shanghai Oriental Pearl. We stood 264 metres above Shanghai, and I was struck by the transformation of the city: in 1966 buildings were all low, but now it seemed as if I were in Manhattan. Later I wrote a classical ode, 'In Shanghai's New Manhattan'.

I calculated that only an injection of American or European money could have funded such massive building. We travelled down the river Huangpu (Yellow river), and I had a good view of the Bund, the old British concession quarter in the 1840s which I remembered so clearly from 1966. Later we walked in Nanjing Road and back to the Bund's Peace Hotel. There were framed photos on a first-floor wall of Kissinger meeting the Mayor of Shanghai at the Peace Hotel on 12 September 1996; of Clinton there on 30 June 1998; and of Bush Sr there on 16 October 1998. I was sure they negotiated the funding of the building. In the evening we went to the Grand Opera House to see acrobats, and our guide, who had been a Red Guard in 1969 and escorted those sentenced to death to their execution, holding one arm, told me that the new Shanghai had been built from local taxation. The Chinese of Shanghai could not have afforded building on that scale.

We went by train to Suzhou and visited the Humble Administrator's garden, where the imperial inspector Wang Xianchen built a garden that reflected the Taoist universe for his retirement in 1509. There were rocks, flowers, water and pavilions with poems engraved on their walls, and symbols of abundance and longevity. I walked across bridges and experienced the harmony, and saw the Humble Administrator's rule as symbolic of the world government. We went on to a silk-moth factory. There were jars with worms, cocoons and silk moths at different stages of their life cycle. We went on to the Lingering Garden where, again, pavilions had been constructed in accordance with displayed poetic lines. It was a poet's Paradise. The next day, during a flight, I wrote these three visits into a classical ode, 'In the Humble Administrator's Garden'.

We flew to Yichang and stayed in 'Peach Blossom Hotel'. At the museum the director gave us a stern lecture on how foreigners had looted Chinese museums – and then invited us to buy some treasures. We bought a 400-year-old dragon holding a bell with sun on it – *yang* and *yin*, heaven and earth, the One. I wrote a classical ode, 'Among Yichang museum's Ming Treasures'.

The Three Gorges Dam was built to divert the Yangtse to the north to create a pond the size of Wales and generate electricity. It was expected to displace a million people, who would have to be rehoused, and to disturb ecology. We visited the observatory above the misty Yangtse and viewed the spillway, power plants, shiplocks and gates. We were driven to our ship, the *East Queen*, which would take us through the Three Gorges.

We boarded in rain clutching our heavy luggage, clambering down steps and crossing another ship to reach our ship. We left at 6 a.m. and approached the first gorge. A line 185-metres high was visible in the vegetation on the towering cliffs on either side of us. Everything below that line would be flooded. We passed through the Xiling gorge and entered the Wu gorge. After lunch we entered the Qutang gorge. I drafted a classical ode, 'In the Yangtze's Three Gorges'.

We took a ferry to Baidi Cheng ('White Emperor City'), which flooding would make into an island. We climbed over 200 steps and took a chair-lift to the 'memory pavilion' to the Tang poet Du Fu and the 'memory temple' to the Emperor Liu Bei. The next morning we visited Shibao village, which was on top of a steep hill. There were sedan chairs for hire, carried by two strapping local women. The chair-carriers implored our custom. I was carried over demolished houses and up a muddy track between stalls, uncomfortable at being transported like a 19th-century imperialist but glad to be providing work. I visited the Taoist temple to Guanu Yu and walked through halls devoted to Earth, Man and lastly Heaven. In the afternoon I wrote my visits to Baidi Cheng and Shibao into 'In the Yangtze's Three Gorges'.

We disembarked and drove through Chongqing, which had a population of 32 million (the size of Ireland's). We drove out to the 10,000 12th- and 13th-century stone sculptures carved out of rock at the foot of Baoding mountain, near Dazu: Buddhist scenes to explain the scriptures to the illiterate, including scenes from the life of the Buddha and the Buddha's nirvana. I saw the wheel of life, buffaloes trying to drink (representing desire) and the goddess of mercy, shown with 1,007 hands with eyes in them. All suffering was illustrated. Later I wrote a classical ode, 'At the Foot of Baoding Mountain', about the co-existence of Tantric Buddhism, Confucianism and Taoism (to counterbalance a classical ode I wrote in Spain about Christianity, Islam and Judaism, 'In Moorish Cordoba: An Orange Tree').

In Chongqing we saw where the Yangtze joins the Jialing, and were taken to the main square which was filled with Chinese, who were (bizarrely) ballroom-dancing. Ann and I joined in. We walked to Chiang Kai-shek's house. Later I wrote a classical ode, 'In People's Hall Square, Chongqing'. The next day we were taken for a foot massage in a 'hall of grasses', meaning 'herbs', and I wrote a classical ode, 'In the Hall of a Hundred Grasses, Chongqing'.

We flew to Xian and visited the Terracotta Army. Emperor Qin Shihuangdi, or Qin Shi Huang Di, the first Qin Emperor who unified China in 221BC, began his mausoleum in 246BC. He wanted his army in the after-life and (perhaps influenced by the Egyptian practice of making images of the dead (news of which arrived along the Silk Route) gave orders that his army should be replicated in terracotta. We started at pit 1, where the majority of the figures were found. Only a sixth had been excavated. We went on to pit 2 (the reserve army) and then on to pit 3 (the headquarters). I wrote a classical ode, 'With Xi'an's Terracotta Army'.

We attended a Tang evening at the Shaanxi Grand Opera House, Xian. The Tang had a high culture in 9th-century China at a time when in England Angles and Saxons were living in huts. There was a dumpling banquet at which 20 musicians in gold Tang costumes played on whistling pipes and danced elegantly for the Emperor, with grace and poise. I wrote a classical ode, 'With the Tang Court Musicians'.

We flew to Beijing. We were taken by coach to Tiananmen Square. Our guide pointed out a long queue to go into Mao's mausoleum. He said we had free time and should meet him at the flag at the end of the Square in 45 minutes' time. I was determined to try to see Mao, whose regime I had questioned between 1966 and 1973. At great pace, holding our bags, Ann and I strode to the front of the queue and looked for an attendant to ask how long the wait would be. A young man in mufti shouted to me through a megaphone: "No, no, you over there, security check." A round lady in her fifties in a padded jacket bustled up. "Who are you? Why are you here?" I explained that we were on a tour and wanted to see Mao. "OK, security, you put one bag inside the other and follow me." I pointed out we only had until 9.55. "No problem."

Wondering if we were under arrest, I put Ann's handbag inside my bag and followed her as she bustled across a pedestrian crossing to an office with a window. She pushed in front of the queue, passed our bags through the window and took a counterfoil. "You pay 40 yuan each." I gave her 100 yuan and she pocketed the change. Then she rushed us back through the traffic (where a tank had trundled towards a lone protester in 1989) and pushed into the queue for Mao's tomb and after several movements forward and stops we were admitted to the huge Mao Hall where there was a large seated statue of the Chairman. We filed round the back and ahead saw the Chairman lying on his back in a floodlit crystal coffin filled with helium, a flag below his chin. He was very yellow and stern. There was a snarl on his face.

I stood transfixed. Ann, who was ahead of me, followed the line and left the room. I was in a dialogue with him. I told him that history had moved on, that he had lost and been dumped. I told him my way had triumphed and all he had stood for was being swept aside. I told him, "You were a tyrant, you killed 45 million at least. You should have been overthrown in 1966. Your way has not prevailed." Then I became aware that I had held up the line, and that two soldiers of 8341 Corps (Special Regiment) were glaring at me. Reluctantly I moved on.

The security lady took us to retrieve our bags and I tipped her 70 yuan (£5.50 then). We rejoined the others, who were astonished we had seen Mao.

We made our way to Tiananmen gate, under the rostrum where the Chairman spoke. A huge banner said: "Socialism in China's way." It was spin for 'Chinese Communism has admitted capitalism'. I wrote a classical ode, 'In the Mausoleum of Mao Zedong'.

We went on to the Forbidden City, the residence of the emperors begun by the Mongolian Yuan Dynasty of the 13th–14th centuries. (The first Mongol Yuan Emperor, Kubla Khan, written about by Coleridge, founded Xanadu – now Shang-Tu – 320 miles north of Beijing in 1256.) We walked through courtyards and past marble bridges until we came to the Hall of Supreme Harmony, where, above ramps, Heaven was above clouds in Taoist symbolism. I saw the Emperor's bedroom and where the favourite concubines lived. Later I wrote a classical ode, 'In the Forbidden City'.

We went on to the Temple of Heaven and walked to the Hall of Prayer for Good Harvests where rites took place. Later I wrote a classical ode, 'In the Taoist Temple of Heaven, Beijing'.

We went on to the Summer Palace, which was twice rebuilt by the Empress Cixi. We walked through the courtyard garden to a frozen lake with a view across a bridge to an island and reached the marble boat. I wrote a classical ode, 'In Cixi's Summer Palace'. That evening we went to the Beijing Opera, and I wrote a classical ode, 'At the Beijing Opera: Moving Boat'.

We visited the Great Wall of China. We made a steep ascent with powdery snow and ice underfoot to a watchtower high in the sky. I wrote a classical ode, 'On the Great Wall of China'. We went on to the Emperor Yongle's Ming Tomb at nearby Changling. Thirteen Ming Emperors are buried in a 25-square-mile valley. We walked nearly a mile along the Sacred Way between statues of officials, generals and pairs of animals: horses, xiezhis (fabulous animals with the head of a dragon, the rear of a deer and the tail of a lion), elephants, camels, unicorns and lions. I wrote a classical ode, 'At Yongle's Tomb, Changling'.

I reviewed our visit with our guide who had been a Red Guard. I told him about the security lady in Tiananmen Square. He said, "Police, undercover police. Tiananmen Square is full of police. They have white vans there. They take away people to the police stations." I could see that it was less free in China than he had made out. I asked, "How many students were killed in 1989?" "We don't know. Our number is about 100. Yours about 2,000. We don't know which is the truth. It's not discussed. It's unhelpful even to discuss it." Chairman Mao had gone, and Chinese Communism had admitted capitalism. However, huge schemes like the Three Gorges could displace and destroy the livelihoods of millions of Chinese citizens, who had no redress. Communist China was still a utopian society suppressing vast numbers of Chinese for the greater good of all Chinese. China was still aiming for a perfect society at the expense of vast numbers of its own people.[44]

Classical odes: nearing the end of Classical Odes
Taking stock of Otley Hall, Connaught House

We now looked on Otley Hall as our home. The public were not allowed into our private areas: the Moat Room (our sitting-room), my study, the boys' bedroom and the entire top floor. It was never more of a home, and a wonderfully warm family house, than when we held our winter family gathering there at the end of December. There was sparkling wine in the fire-lit Great Hall and then lunch in the Linenfold Room at a long table with a white tablecloth before a log fire. After lunch all changed places so everyone spoke to everyone. We went out for a walk round the grounds and returned for tea in front of the Linenfold Room log fire, cheeks glowing. It grew dark, but we did not put the lights on. The floodlights outside threw diamond patterns on the Linenfold walls, giving the room a very cosy effect. Then it began snowing. Snowflakes fell between the floodlights and the diamond-led windows, and there was an atmospheric snowing effect on the linenfold wall. The heavy snow outside, the log fire and the flecking on the walls were magical.

Our intention to retire to Otley Hall was well known. Hence our involvement in the planning to celebrate America's 400th anniversary in 2007. From time to time I had found aspects of the public presence in Otley Hall slightly irksome – especially when I was sued for compensation by an old lady who disobeyed the guide's instructions, opened a door above a step and broke her ankle – and the length of the 82-mile journey between Otley Hall and Loughton tiresome; and we had been through a bad patch with some of our staff. But it never crossed my mind that Otley Hall would not be our retirement home. In March I had a profound sense that all life is in a flux and that Otley Hall would be taken from me. My *Classical Odes* needed a poem reflecting this feeling as a contrast to 'In Otley Hall's Medieval Gardens'. I wrote a classical ode 'Farewell to my Tudor Knot', as much a poetic device or literary exercise as a treatment of a real feeling of 'farewell'. The narrative in my odes required me to imagine myself retreating from Otley Hall to Great Easton but I did not feel that I was actually close to leaving.[45]

We had done an enormous amount of work in the course of renovating Otley Hall, a grade-1 building. We had dated every room through dendrochronology, and our innovatory programme came to the attention of, and was spoken about at, the annual meetings of the Historic Houses Association. We had renovated the conference centre and turned the garden shed into a sturdier tiled building; both buildings had been in disrepair when we arrived. We had done a vast amount in the grounds, clearing overgrown woodland, putting in paths and a car-parking area, turning a dilapidated swimming-pool into a large fishpond and commissioning Sylvia Landsberg, designer of five of the six medieval gardens in the UK, to install a new herb-and-knot garden, medieval herber and a vine-and-rose tunnel. There were special areas designed by experts for hebes, hollies, hostas and asters. (We had 75 varieties of holly, 103 of hosta, 40 of aster.) We had introduced many medieval roses into the rose-garden, and now had 75 varieties of rose. Two mosaics had been installed in the grounds. Our excellent gardener Steve, seeing our housekeeper and caretaker go while we were in China, had given notice and left for a large estate near the M25. The gardens had reached a high point under Steve, and it would be hard to maintain his high standard. We still had more to do and funds were now tight.

To embark on the next phase of our renovating – renewing the roof, strengthening the minstrel's gallery, improving the perimeter fencing and gates and upgrading the cooking base – we would have to borrow against Otley Hall's equity. This would mean paying for new bank valuations and collecting views on the market value of our retirement home. In the end we decided that raising funds on equity to pay for these projects should be postponed.

By the time our grandson was over one, Ann was enjoying her role as a grandmother. Both Ben's parents worked – Melanie had just joined the Normanhurst staff – and Ann was in increasing demand to look after him most afternoons. Ann wanted to spend more time in Loughton to be near Ben and be of use to Matthew. The talk of valuations had confronted us with the possibility of selling Otley Hall and retiring near our schools. Much of 6 Albion Hill had been turned over for school administrative use. (It is now known as Oak House and is fully used by Oaklands School.) Ann had looked around for a suitable property that would be near Ben.

Very few suitable properties were available but she found Connaught House, which was just over a mile away from Albion Hill. It was a time of property shortage in Essex and other buyers were after it. Our business manager advised that we should buy it out of bank funds he could arrange and leave it empty as an investment while we decided what to do. Connaught House had a good view at the back over Epping Forest to Queen Elizabeth's hunting lodge and to the spire of High Beach church. It had over four acres of grounds and an indoor swimming-pool. I viewed it and worked out that we would have to add a study for me over the swimming-pool. I met the owner. I made arrangements to buy the property. There would be an early exchange and a delayed completion, and we would upgrade it and sell at a small profit if we were remaining at Otley Hall. Otherwise I would be "a woodlander again, and watch the weather coming in, the bats, listen to the owls and hear the geese flying overhead to Connaught Water".

We completed our purchase of Connaught House on 28 February 2003. Our architect had met with the planners and reported that I might be allowed to build a large study over the swimming-pool, where I could write books with a good view of Epping Forest.

Until the late spring of 2003 we continued to regard Otley Hall as our retirement home. By now our grandson was approaching two and it had been clear for a while that there might be a problem with his parents' marriage. Ann became more insistent that we should relocate to Connaught House. If the situation deteriorated further she would be ahead of things and would act as a stabilising influence. She anticipated helping with our grandson every day and being on hand in case she was needed. I saw the merit of her argument and reluctantly acceded, putting the interests of our son and grandson above my love for Otley Hall. In June we submitted a planning application to enlarge Connaught House. Planning permission for Connaught House was granted on 4 July 2003, and we began making arrangements to hire a builder.

Quay Road, Charlestown

At the same time I agreed to buy 4 Quay Road, Charlestown (Arthur Hosegood's house) as a buy-to-let. I completed the purchase at the end of January 2003. We now had 3, 4 and 6 Quay Road as short-let properties, and I bought the remaining green frontage from Robin Davies. Our visits to Cornwall involved supervising remedial work and refurbishing the properties. We now called the three properties: Quay Cottage, Boatwatch Cottage and Harbourside. We appointed Cornish Traditional Holidays to find weekly tenants and run the properties, and we kept an eye on their general state of repair during our stays in the Harbour-master's House.

'Petals like Snowflakes'

Anthony moved to Highgate to be nearer his Film School. We lunched with him and passed Highgate cemetery (where Marx is buried) and the site of Marvell's cottage. We drove to Hampstead and passed Keats House.

Little Ben was fascinated by Nature, though still only one. I took him into the Oaklands playground on Anthony's birthday and carried him back under a cherry-tree in blossom. "A gust of wind blew petals like snowflakes round our heads and Ben squealed with delight and we were all happy." I wrote a poem, 'Petals like Snowflakes' and a story of the same title about this moment, which I shall never forget.[46]

Discovery of Bartholomew Gosnold's skeleton

On 6 February 2003 I was rung by Bill Kelso, the archaeologist of Jamestown. I had told him to dig in the centre of the triangular Jamestown Fort. I asked: "Have you found Bartholomew yet?" He said: "That's what I'm ringing about. We've found the skeleton of a man in his mid-to-late thirties, all alone, on a high place, about 50 feet from where we were sitting by the River James. He's buried with an object." I asked: "Was he buried with a flag?" He said: "Are you psychic? The object's a flagstaff. Why is that significant?" I said that a military funeral would have included the burial of a flag. He told me: "The skeleton is within a shroud. His skull is perfectly preserved, so his face can be reconstructed. He was five foot one inch in height. He had a back injury which would have given him arthritis and he died of disease. It's an exciting development." I was exhilarated. I had always said Bartholomew Gosnold would be found within the triangle.

I had been asked to take part in a long discussion on Iraq, on BBC Radio Suffolk. I was supposed to be talking with three MPs and Terry Waite, the ex-hostage, and I was supposed to speak for the people of Iraq, side against America. The discovery of Bartholomew cut across this, and I did not want to come across as anti-American at this time. I cancelled my appearance on the radio, and withdrew from an SAT meeting at the Globe. The day Kelso announced his discovery in America I had to sit by a telephone to give interviews to the world's press, including *The Daily Mail*, the *Eastern Daily News* and the *Cape Cod Times*. The skeleton would be displayed at the Smithsonian National Museum of Natural History,[47] but there would have to be DNA corroboration from Bartholomew Gosnold's sister's skeleton to put the identification beyond all doubt.

Bill Kelso rang me again. He told me that an 'expert' had identified the flagstaff as a "leader's staff", "which means it is Gosnold – he was the leader". He told me that the skeleton was in "the dead centre" of the Fort "because of the alignment". He told me, "You were right. And it's been confirmed by our 'expert', we've definitely got Gosnold." I said, "You are the Schliemann of America. When did you discover the Fort, which month in 1996?" "August or September. We found it the first day. When did you come to America?" I said, "October 1998. I gave the lecture in Richmond when I said, 'You've got the wrong man, [John Smith]' and we talked two years and a month after you found Jamestown, and now you've found Achilles. Books will be written about this." "They will." "I hope the story will be told how we sat together and dreamt of finding Gosnold." "It will. It will be told. Your dead-centre theory was right." I said they were never going to bury him outside the Fort because of the Indian attacks. "No, I agree. He's inside. You were right." Bill Kelso and Roxane Gilmore asked me to send them copies of my film script, *Gosnold's Hope*. No funding was ever found for the project. I wrote a classical ode, 'In the Jamestown Fort: The Discovery of Bartholomew Gosnold'.

I spoke at length to Cathy Brown of *The East Anglian Daily Times* about the discovery of Bartholomew Gosnold's skeleton. Her story omitted all mention of Otley Hall. I said to her wryly: "I've given Suffolk this gift of Bartholomew Gosnold and am airbrushed out of it. Like the sister-city status." She said: "Yes, it's bizarre. I was instructed not to proceed by my editor." Weirdly, Otley Hall was not to be written about in Suffolk in connection with the founding of America. I wondered if the council was suppressing news of Otley Hall to avoid expenditure in the run-in to the 2007 anniversary, or whether the suppressal went deeper. (In 2013 Cathy won £6million in the National Lottery.)

The then Group Finance Director (later Executive Director) of N.M. Rothschild & Sons, Andrew Didham, now viewed Otley Hall, a charming man who looked round with his wife, sat over tea at the kitchen table and asked me many detailed questions about the business side, the events and maintenance costs. He interviewed *me*, and did not ask about the history. Sir Evelyn de Rothschild, from whom Steve joined us, though co-chairman of Rothschild Bank A.G., Zurich, was still non-executive chairman of N.M. Rothschild & Sons. I realised the Rothschilds had been so successful over two centuries because they were so nice and had perfect manners. I included his visit in my classical ode, 'In the Houses of Parliament'.[48]

Structuring Classical Odes: *"three of space and one of time"*
Until the end of January I polished my Chinese classical odes. I thought about the structure of the four books, and dictated, "almost guided from beyond", a paragraph for the Preface about the relativity theory in relation to my four books of classical odes. I explained this to Macann as "four books of odes, three of space and one of time": the three of space from the point of view of England, Europe and globalism; the one of time focusing on the approach to eternity, the One, the reality behind the universe. (I told him, "Existentialism is a ladder to the One, Being. It can be thrown aside once you have climbed there." I pointed out that "linguistic analysis has no 'word' for 'Being' or 'Existence'".) Macann told me: "I understand your poems. I can't understand modern poetry like Mallarmé, I need a guide and I haven't got the time. It's not sufficiently rewarding. But I can understand yours."

I got back to European poems in early February: 'With Munich's Wittelsbachs'; 'At Waterloo'; 'At Queen Elizabeth's Hunting Lodge'; 'At Harold's Waltham Abbey'; 'At Coopersale Hall: Founder's Day'; and 'At Mozart's Salzburg'. I pressed on and worked on: 'At Reims' Jerusalem'; 'In the Jamestown Fort: The Discovery of Bartholomew Gosnold'; 'Among

Loughton's Sacred Houses'; and 'At Oaklands'.

I was living in a time there would be a sensational 'proof' that materialism is wrong, both about the beginning of the universe – which began with infinite temperature and density according to the Hubble Space telescope launched in 1990 – and about the end of the universe. According to NASA's 'Map' (Microwave Anistropy Probe) satellite of 2012 the universe is 13.7 billion years old, and according to the European Space Agency's Planck space telescope of 2013 the universe is 13.84 billion years old. A 2014 calculation taking account of the all the information puts the age of the universe as 13.978 billion years (with an uncertainty of plus or minus 37 million years). The new information shows that the universe is expanding forever as a result of the inflation caused by the Big Bang's first split second: so Hawking's Big Crunch is wrong. Infinity was present at the beginning of the universe and will be at the end. This is established because it has been found that dark matter fills 23% of the universe and dark energy 73%, and atoms only 4%. Excited by the potential findings of probes, I drafted a classical ode, 'On Charlestown Pier: The Infinite Universe; The End of Materialism'. I followed this up with another classical ode, 'Among Life's Structures in the West: Against Scientific Materialism'.

After sweeping leaves I structured each book of my *Classical Odes* into two parts, both begun by Otley Hall. Each book focused on classical culture from the perspective of England, Europe, a globalist view of the world and the One. Each reflected on the fall of leaders, global administrators and observation of the universe. The titles of the four books were now in poems asterisked in the Contents. I worked on more classical odes: 'At Beethoven's Birthplace, Bonn'; 'At Chartwell with Churchill'; 'At Connaught House'; 'An Acre on the Moon' (about an acre plot, lot 119/1262, on the moon I had been given by Anthony the previous Christmas); 'The End of Otley Hall'; 'Reflections on the Nice Summit'; and 'On the Enlargement of Europe: A New Constitution'.

While in Cornwall, my attention was struck by a dandelion growing at the top of the harbour. I had the idea of calling my next volume of poems *A Dandelion Clock*. The next day was "gusty and squally" and "the dandelion clock I saw yesterday had been blown away in the night's storm. Wrote a poem about this, seeing it as the universe/my works." I also had the idea for calling a volume of my poems *Summoned by Truth*: three political poems ('Zeus's Ass', 'Attack on America' and 'Shock and Awe'). Meanwhile I had written a philosophical essay, 'A Fourfold Approach to the Fire', for Chris Macann's internet journal at his urging: approaches to the Fire through science, philosophy, history and literature.

I visited a podiatrist and discovered that all my structural problems came from having flat feet and lack of arches: my leg muscles, my snapping tendon by a kneecap, my back problems that had required an osteopath, my varicose veins, the wrecked blood vessels in my right foot and my traumatised toenail. The podiatrist made me fibre-glass orthotics that raised my heels, twisted my feet back into shape, made me use the correct muscles, improved my posture and my back, and alleviated my problems to delay arthritis.

Down in Cornwall, I wrote that "outside my window as light fades the sea is indistinguishable from the sky. It's one. Earlier the terns were diving again." I also wrote: "A full moon and the evening star and nothing else in the sky – visible outside the front door, unlike elsewhere. I like it down here." Earlier the same day, a hot Good Friday, I looked back on my writing life and reflected that I swam against the tide – in the style of my poems, their metaphysical content, my outlook, what I had to say. I was a lone voice crying in a wilderness. But I did what I felt was right, and could have no regrets. Out there was a sceptical society that had not had inner experiences and therefore disparaged them from a norm of social living.[49]

My classical odes were nearly finished. I would write another 29 by March 2005, but they were now sporadic, and an episode had come to an end. *Classical Odes* were no longer at the forefront of my consciousness, and I was no longer reflecting the utopian ambitions of humankind.

CHAPTER 5

Final Ascent: Unitive Vision

"All are but parts of one stupendous whole,
Whose body Nature is, and God the soul."

Pope, 'An Essay on Criticism', lines 267–8

"Behind each shadow reigns a glorious Sun."

Nicholas Hagger, 'Epitaphs', in Collected Poems

The final ascent is always the hardest. Though the end is in sight the last stage of the climb can be arduous and gruelling. But actually the hard work has already been done. The climber has a momentum and is spurred on by the proximity of the end. The last part of the Mystic Way can be the most inspiring part of the journey.

In the final ascent of the Unitive Way, the soul – with unitive vision – sees the universe as a unity and expresses it in unifying works. The Light seen in the mystic life and the shadowy forms of Nature are reconciled in the harmony of $+A + -A = 0$. The wayfarer sees the unity of the universe and of his many-layered self. Unifying vision is seen through the eyes of the Shadow, the white-haired old man I glimpsed in 'The Silence', who I have now become. All my experience, research and writing have brought my Shadow to birth within my self.

The view from the ridge that connects the summits of the hills is breathtaking. With instinctive unitive vision the wayfarer perceives the oneness of all the many phenomena, and the unity of knowledge. The One Light can now be seen to be shining through philosophy, history, literature and all disciplines. The barriers between subjects are broken down, everything is seen to be connected. In the contemplative gaze all Nature is One and all aspects of it are interdisciplinary. The perception of the Seeker who has travelled along the Mystic Way has been transformed. All disciplines appear to be interconnected parts of a universal whole. My unifying works appear to be interlocking pieces of a jigsaw that present an image of a continuum: a rainbow.

In the image a rainbow looms diaphanous out of distant cloud and straddles seven hills, illumined by the sun. It shines above the Seeker's soul and from near the end of his journey he surveys his lifetime's achievements.

Episode 13:

Collected Literature and Secret History

Years: 2003–2006

Locations: Loughton; Buckhurst Hill; Gran Canaria; Scilly Isles; Egypt; Dartmoor

Works: *The Syndicate*; *The Secret History of the West*; *Classical Odes*; *Overlord*, one-volume edition; *Collected Poems 1958–2005*; *The Rise and Fall of Civilizations*; *Collected Verse Plays*; *Collected Stories*; *The Light of Civilization*; *The Secret Founding of America*;

Initiative: focus on founding of America

"It will be enough for me... if these words of mine are judged useful by those who want to understand clearly the events which happened in the past and which (human nature being what it is) will, at some time or other and in much the same ways, be repeated in the future. My work is not a piece of writing designed to meet the taste of an immediate public; but was done to last for ever."

Thucydides, *History of the Peloponnesian War*, book 1.22 (c.410BC), trans. by Rex Warner

In the next episode, acting as a man of letters, I gathered together my stories, poetic output and verse plays into collected volumes and, acting as a historian, delved into secret history to throw light on the growing presence of the New World Order. My role as a sober editor of my own work was in conflict with my inquiring probing of hidden influence and power.

Secret history: The Syndicate *and last classical odes*
US invasion of Iraq: 'Shock and Awe'
The US invasion of Iraq had been building for weeks. I had viewed the increasing war fever with misgivings. I still had clear memories of walking through Baghdad, and did not want to see it bombed back into the Dark Ages. I said to Ann, "For the first time since the Second World War,... we are not on the side of the goodies against the baddies (Russia), blocking aggression in the Cold War; we are on the side of the aggressors who are after oil,... sending in tanks and troops for self-interest, and the trouble is, we need the oil for Western civilization, and we have to go along with it –

pretend that aggression is really self-defence against terrorism when privately we know it isn't. This is not a moral or just war, but smash-and-grab.... And Britain's role is as the 51st American state." Ann agreed: "I'm not in favour of this war, I don't think we should go and fight Iraq." I wrote again: "America and Europe need the oil, so action against Iraq is in our aggressive self-interest.... We must do it without causing civilian deaths, and liberate Iraq from the dictator – to bring a democratic government.... Yet I am reluctant to go to war, and to ally with hegemonists. It's about oil, and we're deceiving ourselves if we think otherwise."

I wrote a classical ode I conceived after being invited to appear on the BBC Radio Suffolk programme on Iraq: 'On Iraq: Peace or War?' I collected two books on Iraq from the local bookshop, read about the streets of Baghdad and compared their maps with the map I had used 40 years previously. I reached stanza 16 of the poem. On 10 March the news reported that Britain and the US might attack Iraq without a second UN resolution, "meaning that American superpower overrides the UN". Thinking of the secret history involved, I asked, "What do Bilderberg want?" I sensed that "invasion will take place very soon". On 20 March news came through of an attempted 'decapitation' strike on Saddam Hussein. I "scribbled stanzas for a poem on Iraq", which passed into 'Shock and Awe'. I noted: "I am a poet of warfare as well as a poet of the peaceful life..., like Virgil."

The next day I watched Shock and Awe, an awesome live transmission of 30 missiles bombarding Baghdad and creating a fire-storm over Saddam's palaces. Tears came into my eyes, I was so sad for the Baghdad I knew. There was a new American doctrine: the power and reach of the American military. I was very upset. I had written 41,000 lines of blank verse on the Second World War, but I was not battle-hardened in my soul. I was still sensitive to the killing of the innocent. By the next day I had written to stanza 57 of 'Shock and Awe'. I was watching the war on television and on 24 March, with the troops 60 miles from Baghdad, I had done more than 60 stanzas of 'Shock and Awe', which counterbalanced 'Attack on America'.

I watched Saddam's last brave appearance on the streets and was distressed that the museum in Baghdad had been ransacked, and that 170,000 artefacts had vanished: pots and statues from several civilizations. The Oil Ministry was ringed with US troops, but not the museum; a vivid revelation of American priorities. I supported the role of the US as an "exporter of democracy and driver of global liberty", but could see that Bilderberg's New World Order was exercising this role selectively, creating global liberty in organisations that suited them. I wrote a classical ode, 'After the Iraq War: Reflections on the Fall of Baghdad'. I finished this on 19 April. The next day I read about the pipeline from Iraq to Israel that would reduce Israel's oil bill and supply the US with cheap oil. I wrote: "The war was about oil. The rest was deception."[1]

Writing The Syndicate: *John Hunt*
One afternoon I answered the telephone. "Nicholas? It's Michael Mann. I'm wondering what you're doing." He told me that he had been helping O-Books – the 'O' stood for the global but also for 'zero' or infinity – and that my name had come up in his discussions with John Hunt. He told me, "I want to help you." He wanted to read my two books on revolutions, *The Secret History of the West* and the book that would become *The Syndicate*. I invited him to lunch.

I met Michael Mann in the entrance of De Vere Cavendish Hotel in Jermyn Street, London SW1, which acted as his London base. We had lunch in the Green's restaurant, Duke Street. We sat in a snug walled off from the other diners, and he told me that his Element investors were driven down by their pension funds and were shattered at not being able to meet their commitments to him. Looking less stressed than when I last saw him, he told me that a key figure in Chrysalis had left the company with a pay-off of £7million, which meant that there could be no funding for new books. He told me that he had reread all my books, that I had outstanding talent and ability and that he wanted to place me with a new publisher to make up for the Element debacle. He asked for copies of my new books.

I was still working on *The Secret History of the West* (at that time titled *Utopias and Massacres*) and on *The Syndicate* (at that time titled as two volumes, *World Peace through War* and *The New World Order and the Third World War*). A week later he rang saying he had a list of points, that he wanted me to explain what *The Syndicate* are doing in a couple of paragraphs; and that he would like to reinvolve John Baldock, who had been preparing *The Secret History of the West* when Element went into receivership. I spoke to Baldock over the telephone. He was still very sore at the demise of Element. I said that Michael "should be forgiven": "He did not want to go under, he ducked and dived to resist it. He published for 25 years when Routledge and others in the *genre* were dwindling. He must be respected for that."

I addressed Michael's questions from mid-May to mid-July, and met them both at The Beckford Arms in Fonthill Gifford, Tisbury in Wiltshire, which had '*De Dieu Tout*' on its sign. Michael was in a blue shirt and blue jeans. He was a Spencer, and was therefore distantly related to Winston Churchill and Princess Diana. He told me that he knew Lord Carrington. ("I used to have dinner with Peter Carrington, I know him.") John Baldock was a slightly-stooping ex-teacher with wavy hair and a gentle smile in brown eyes. He lived in a chapel with a view of green fields and was a volunteer guide at Wilton, whose guidebook he had written. We sat in the garden at an old table and I handed over copies of the books.

Michael said that *The Syndicate* was the hottest book in town, and that I would require careful handling. In mid-September he told me, "The mainstream houses do not take risks, they are entertainment providers. The risks are taken by the small independent houses." He told me: "You are drilling far deeper than anyone else." I told him that Reality is multi-layered and that I had communicated another level of Reality to a lot of people, and that I was reflecting the dissolving structures of the Age.

It had taken six months to reshape the two books. In mid-October Michael wrote to me to say that John Hunt of O-Books wanted to publish *The Syndicate*. There would be further work to do on the book with him. He rang three days later to say that it would be out the following autumn. Editing should be finished by the end of January. In early November Michael invited me to the De Vere Cavendish to meet John Hunt. Michael arrived flustered and hot, having been re-routed via Southampton as there was a car on the line. The roads were congested and John Hunt gave up after four and a half hours, and the meeting was rearranged for a few days later.

On 11 November I finally met John Hunt, a tall, quietly-spoken, pleasant man who had been in publishing since reading English Literature at Oxford in the early 1970s. He had a very sharp mind and saw to the heart of what I was trying to say in *The Syndicate*. We had a long talk over sandwiches in the first-floor lounge of the De Vere Cavendish. I presented the two new books in terms of *The Fire and the Stones* and my study of 25 civilizations, and spoke of the New World Order's dream of uniting all civilizations under their control. John asked me probing questions about the Syndicate and produced three or four sheets of typed notes. He saw "alternate chapters: one on evidence, the next on motives". Like me, he wanted to make the scenario understandable. He told me he would do *The Syndicate* first, and would follow up with *The Secret History of the West*. He wanted to read my classical odes. Michael left at 3 and we sat on. He told me he published 50 books a year and wanted to expand. He described himself as a "Unitarian Universalist". Two days later John sent me a fax saying he would bring out *The Secret History of the West* at the same time as *The Syndicate*. A contract for *The Syndicate* arrived the next day.[2]

Disillusion with the Shakespearean Authorship Trust
The secret history of Shakespeare now occupied my thoughts. There was a two-day SAT conference at the Globe. On the first day four speakers presented the case for four authorship candidates. Mark Rylance chaired the occasion and presented the speakers to about 100 who had paid to sit in a long, narrow upstairs room overlooking the Thames.

Professor William Rubinstein presented the case for the Stratfordian

Shakespeare. He did not believe in his case and was acting as an attorney, representing Stratfordian points of view. Charles had been down to speak on Edward de Vere, the 17th Earl of Oxford, but he had cried off as he was behind on his book, and had asked me to take his place. I, also acting as an attorney, represented the main Oxfordian points. I competed with the river traffic of noisy barges through the open window. After lunch Peter Dawkins, a Baconian, presented the case for Bacon and Mike Frohnsdorff presented the case for Marlowe. At supper there was a speakers' table. Mark Rylance told me that he had a photographic memory and used to be able to see the words as on an autocue in his mind. He said he had a short-term memory and could go straight into his current play, *Richard II*, but could not remember a recent play, *Antony and Cleopatra*.

On the second day there was a question-and-answer session in which the four speakers answered questions. A lady in the audience said she knew who Shakespeare was, and it transpired that Rubinstein had collaborated with an author, Brenda James, to present a new candidate, Sir Henry Neville (an ancestor of Lord Braybrooke, the Lord Lieutenant of Essex), whose name could not be mentioned as Rubinstein had signed a confidentiality agreement. Over lunch there was considerable indignation that the spirit of enquiry had been suppressed. After lunch Robin Williams presented the case for Mary Sidney. At the end there was discussion as to who the unknown candidate might be. In due course the book was published, *The Truth Will Out*, and the new candidate proved to be a former Ambassador to France. Charles and Frohnsdorff sent me long lists of errors, and it was swiftly agreed that Neville did not write Shakespeare's works. I wrote a classical ode, 'Tracking Shake-speare'.

The conference left a sour taste in my mouth. I had joined the SAT so I could calmly review the evidence regarding the authorship objectively, and the SAT had become factional. My ex-solicitor, Ian Hawthorne, had been in the audience and he had raised whether the trustees had been insured for the conference. He pointed out that if someone had fallen down the stairs and been paralysed, the trustees could personally face a large claim for life-long care. I raised this point with Silberrad, who confirmed that all trustees would be liable for any loss. At the next meeting of the trustees while we waited for Mark, who was talking to the Prince's Trust rehabilitated criminals, I led a discussion on what a trustee does, and whether we were all covered for every eventuality.

Mark walked in as we were discussing the possibility of a claim against trustees. We were having a pre-meeting conversation that was not on the agenda – I was taking the minutes – but Mark overreacted and threatened to resign unless he could chair the meeting, which had not yet started. All the speakers at the conference were entitled to £200. I waived my fee in the interests of the SAT. I was surprised that the other speakers did not follow suite and had a discussion about spending surplus money on going to the Ukraine, where there had been interest in the SAT. I had not waived my fee to fund SAT trustees to go to the Ukraine. Then Mark told us that he had been to see the Duke of Rutland (my contact) at Belvoir Castle, and that the Duke had no recollection of coming to the SAT despite his presentation on Roger Manners. Mark said that the insurance of trustees was not necessary.

The insurance question rumbled on all summer. Running schools, I knew about public liability insurance. On 24 September Mark invited me to lunch at the Globe restaurant. He had received a letter from me setting out the insurance problem, but he told me he did not want the SAT to bear the cost of a premium.

At the next meeting on 8 October the question of insurance came up again, and Mark brought in the Globe's Business Manager and asked, "Were we insured for our conference?" He said, "It's a grey area, probably not." I said: "It's like a Parent Association having to insure for a fête, which may not be on the schools' insurance." "Yes." The Business Manager had taken my side. Mark protested, "But we only have one conference a year." I said: "That's time for a person to fall downstairs and break their neck and be in a wheelchair, with a settlement for £10million, with each trustee paying one-seventh each, and anyone here who can't pay has his contribution rolled on to those who can – which may involve some in selling a house or, in my case, schools." Mark said, "You're covered." I said: "Not as a trustee." Peter Dawkins said that we should be covered, and Mark then asked for quotations from the Globe's broker.

At last there was general understanding, but I was not sure that I wanted to remain a trustee among such an unbusiness-like group who were so unalert to potential hazards. Disenchanted with the SAT, I had obtained a quotation for sending the books of both Shakespearean libraries from Otley Hall to the Globe, and I reported this. Mark immediately said that to save money the Globe staff would undertake the packing and transportation. (In the event, the books ended up in a warehouse near the Globe and eventually found their way to Brunel University library, Uxbridge.)[3]

At the schools

While I worked on my secret history I was coping with events at the schools, some of which yielded classical odes. Normanhurst was inspected by Ofsted. On the third day the inspectors reported on their findings to Ann, me and the senior management team. By 10.30 Ann and I were ready for a break and we crossed the road and sat in her parked car. As I relaxed I saw Doug Insole, the former Essex and England cricketer, making his way towards me, stooping. I opened the door and said, "Hello, Doug." We chatted on the pavement. Ann went into a shoe shop. I took Insole in, introduced him – she was examining an insole – and described how I watched him run down to where I was sitting on the boundary at Ilford, pick up the ball and throw it back." He said, "And I expect it bounced three times." I also described how he always gave us his autograph. The inspection went well and a few days later we took over a Chingford restaurant and gave the staff a champagne reception and meal, after which we drove down to Cornwall, arriving at 3.30 a.m. I wrote a classical ode, 'With the Ofsted Inspectors'.

My classics teacher David Horton retired after 50 years in the classroom at Chigwell School. I was invited to a barbecue held out of doors in the Head's garden, Haylands. As Horton's oldest pupil present I was seated next to him among staff who had taught me. In fading light past classics teachers made speeches. It was dark by the time Horton stood to respond, too dark for him to read his notes. He handed them to me and asked me to read them. Squinting in the dark, I fed him one-liners. He thanked everyone for coming, said he had to "cheat" a bit to get to 50 years as he had already retired once, in 1991, then sat down to applause and studied his notes. He said to me, "I forgot to thank those who made speeches." I said, "Stand up and thank them now." Reluctantly, he stood again and gave his thanks. Soon afterwards he came out of retirement and taught at Chigwell for another ten years.

At Coopersale Hall the roll had dropped, and the new Head announced that her husband's job required him to move and she would be going with him. The previous Head, Sue Bowdler, had returned early from Kuwait, having weathered the invasion of Iraq and fierce playground temperatures of 48 degrees. She contacted us before we could hold interviews and asked if she could return. She had been invited to give out the prizes – a longstanding arrangement – and (having told the staff minutes before the prize-giving) I announced her reappointment at the end of prize-giving. There was a cheer from the seated parents, and at the end they crowded round her in delight.

During the summer one of the Normanhurst staff (who had also taught at Coopersale Hall) ran in the South African marathon in heat, had a massive heart attack and died. His body was flown home and Ann and I attended his funeral at Roxwell church (where our domestic help's father had been vicar). The present vicar shouted words from the porch and the coffin was borne by four pallbearers. His family walked behind, and I was startled as *he* seemed to be among them: his twin brother. I wrote a classical ode, 'At Roxwell Church'.

Ernie, the ex-school keeper at Oaklands, underwent an angioplasty. He had an angina attack, was given diamorphine, closed his eyes and died. Ann and I drove to his bungalow near Hitchin and met his family, and I saw where the ex-sentry in the Second World War who had been one of the first to enter Belsen with his Crocodile flame-thrower sat in the garden during his retirement guarding his bird feeder from the squirrels with an air rifle. We went on to his funeral at a nearby crematorium. There was a eulogy which mentioned us, and each of his eleven grandchildren put a rose on his flower-clad wicker coffin: his nickname for his wife was 'Rosie' – who collapsed during the last line of the last song ('The Power of Love'): 'You're my lady'. The mourning of his family was very affecting.

At the Oaklands prize-giving (at which a British athlete, Liz Yelling, gave out the prizes), the Oaklands Head invited Ann and me to meet her relative Robin Parfitt, the former Head of the Junior School at Chigwell, and his wife, who were visiting. Robin was terminally ill. He had not seen us for six years, and wanted to talk education. He said that his brother Tudor was writing on al-Qaeda in the Sudan on a Fulbright scholarship. He told me: "I greatly admire and respect what you've done, you've taken a risk." In August 2006 I heard that he been paralysed down one side and had died.

I was taken back to my early television viewing. Anthony, who had been keen on drama at Chigwell, directed a play, *Hurlyburly*, in the Riverside Studio 3, Hammersmith, where television was based from 1956 to 1970. I sat among banked seats, looking down on the stage where Huw Weldon went out with *Monitor* and Robin Day with *Panorama*, and where the BBC Newses in black and white I used to watch were read. Now it was Tony's turn. Soon afterwards we attended the opening of a new theatre at Chigwell School and inspected a window which bore the name of "the Hagger family".[4]

Finishing Classical Odes

I at last brought my classical odes to a conclusion. I had continued working on the remaining classical odes, many of which were on government: 'At Chartwell with Churchill'; 'The Conquest of England' (on the enlargement of the EU and a gathering European Superstate); 'On Harrowdown Hill' (on the death of the weapons inspector in Iraq, David Kelly); 'In Old Charlestown'; 'In Moonlit Charlestown: The Bright Shadow of Dark Energy'; 'The *Tek Sing*'s Cargo and the Sea'; 'On Martha's Vineyard'; and 'On Montgomery's Lüneburg Heath'.

Many of the classical odes emerged from events I attended. I was invited to a dinner at Chigwell School for the Heads of 'feeder' schools and wrote 'At Chigwell School'. I went to the House of Commons and dined in Dining-Room 'A', and was addressed by Oliver Letwin. Later I wrote 'In the Houses of Parliament'.

I went to the Carlton Club with John Silberrad and shook hands with Boris Johnson. He made an anti-bureaucratic speech: "I was walking in the corridors of the Palace of Westminster minding my own business when a Whip called 'Oy, Boris' and told me to go to Committee Room 14 and read the file there. It turned out to be several inches thick and took me an hour and a half to get the gist. It was all about how there was to be an 'Inspector of Windows'. The European Union had also decreed that there should be an Inspector, or 'Picker-upper', of Dead Sheep." I wrote 'In the Carlton Club'.

I went to Tilty Abbey and heard a lecture on the Cistercians. I wrote 'In Cistercian Tilty Abbey'. I went to Buckingham Palace, which was allowing timed visits, and wandered round the main State rooms feeling at ease because of the spaciousness. I wrote 'In Buckingham Palace's State Rooms'.

Down in Cornwall Ann and I visited the Bernard Leach Pottery at St Ives, named after the most famous British potter since Josiah Wedgewood, who had died in 1979. Ann bought one of his pots. We went on to Talland House, where Virginia Woolf spent twelve summers at St Ives from 1883 to 1895. It looked out to sea to the white lighthouse on Godrevy, which she brought into *To the Lighthouse*. On the way back we stopped at a shop that sold stones and bought a stromatolite fossil of a log which is 4 billion years old and is now outside my front door. I wrote a classical ode, 'At St Ives'.

On our way back to Essex we visited Lowerdown Pottery, Bovey Tracey. David Leach, Bernard Leach's 92-year-old son, himself a famous British potter, hobbled round and shook my hand. He had been born in Tokyo and I told him I had been in Japan. I asked if his father had met Virginia Woolf at Draycott Terrace, where in the 1920s Bernard Leach lived at first 6, then 14, and Woolf stayed at Trevose House. He did not answer my question. We bought two small dishes with lids bearing willow and foxglove designs.

At Great Easton our gardener took me for a drive to show me the site of Stansted's second runway. I wrote a classical ode, 'On Stansted's Second Runway'. Pondering on how I received an image of the finished *Classical Odes* in Pisa, I wrote a classical ode, 'After the Pisan Arno'.

Michael Mann sent me a fax saying he had agreed with John Hunt that John would publish *The Syndicate* and *The Secret History of the West* in autumn 2004, and then *Classical Odes*, followed by *Overlord* in a one-volume edition. I really felt that the end of *Classical Odes* was now in sight and I started to assemble the book. I proof-read the book in November 2005[5] and approved the index on 27 April 2006. I received my first copies on 8 June 2006.

Fall of Iain Duncan Smith

While I was immersed in my secret history I became a witness to the secret history of how Iain Duncan Smith, our local MP for Chingford and Woodford Green, ceased to be the Leader of the Opposition. We had built a new building at the back of Normanhurst, and Duncan Smith had agreed to declare it open by unveiling a plaque. I agreed the wording with his constituency agent (and spindoctor). There were public moves to replace Duncan Smith as Leader of the Opposition, and he was being followed around by television cameras.

On 16 October "the Light poured into me as it hasn't for months". Early next morning I greeted Duncan Smith outside Normanhurst and led him to the library. I showed where we would be speaking and how the curtain worked. I told him that 67 constituency chairmen out of 80 in marginal seats were supporting him. He said, "Oh, yes." We were joined by the Mayor, the Head and some of the Silvester family who had built the new building; and by Ann, Matthew and Ken, our Bursar. I then made a speech outside the library to parents who had gathered in the playground. I commented on the recent inspection, the high pass rate of A–C at GCSE, our new Head and now our new building. I reminded them that Duncan Smith had given out the prizes two years previously and spoke of his high profile. Then Duncan Smith spoke, humorously and self-deprecatingly about the press he was getting and praising the parents for making sacrifices to send their children to a good school. He unveiled the plaque and we had refreshments in the hall where he told me: "I don't read any papers. They're opinions, the journalists writing about themselves, and opinions change. I just carry on doing it. I live each day as it comes." We then toured the school so he could see all the new rooms. I began writing a classical ode, 'At Normanhurst School: A Lost Leader'.

On 23 October Duncan Smith launched a nationwide campaign for a referendum on the European constitution. The Bilderberg Group and Rothschilds wanted the European constitution and could not tolerate Duncan Smith's initiative. Within days he faced a 'no confidence' vote. On 28 October he was replaced as Leader by Michael Howard, who would accept the new European constitution.

On 12 November Duncan Smith spoke at a dinner held in the Great Hall of Bancroft's School. He was escorted by Letwin, who worked for Rothschilds every morning. I asked Letwin if he was going to stay on at Rothschilds. He said, "Yes. I spend the mornings in the real world." He introduced Duncan Smith, stressing the good legacy he had left the party. Duncan Smith in his speech described what had happened as "like a car crash – only you can't walk away from it". He rousingly said that Conservatism meant "taking control of your own lives to make a better economy for your family" and called on everyone to support Howard. He received a standing ovation. I wrote a classical ode, 'At Bancroft's with the Conservatives: Plots and England's Decadence'.

I was reflecting the Age, and the Age in England was one of decay. After a nationalist rally under Thatcher the UK was being pulled apart by the New

World Order, levelled into a state within a coming United States of Europe and struggling to maintain the union of the four territories that made up the United Kingdom. The New World Order and 'Rothschilds' had contributed to this decay.

Two weeks later Ann and I were invited to a dinner in the Commons' Dining-Room 'A', which Duncan Smith was providing. Rikki Radford (who had rung me three days before to discuss his boss's fall) came and told me, "You'll find two chairs tilted forward. They're yours. You can ask him about 'internationalism'. He'll react favourably, that it's being forced on Europe."

I went to the table and found that the two tilted chairs were directly opposite Duncan Smith. Duncan Smith arrived during the starter, toured the table shaking hands and took his seat. No one was talking to Duncan Smith as we ate, so I leaned forward and said that when I heard the words "centrist" and "internationalist" at the Saatchi adoption meeting of Howard, I knew they meant "pro-European constitution". He said, "You're right." I said of Howard, "It would have been over your dead body, but this lot may oppose it with words and let it happen." "It will be over my dead body." I pointed out that Straw had said that the European constitution "is desirable but not necessary". "It's not desirable. They always do that – it's to make us think it's not important, so we'll sign it." There was talk of the plotters. He said: "There's been a *coup*." I said quietly, "It was a Bilderberg Group *coup*." "Oh, you know who they are." I said: "Yes. Clarke would have known about it, but it wasn't Clarke. Perhaps we can talk about this at greater length on a one-to-one some time." "I'd like that." I said of the plotters: "There are 75 positions out of 160 MPs, there are going to be some who are passed over." He agreed that some of the plotters were among the 85 disaffected politicians.

He said, "Howard's ten points behind me. They already know they've made a mistake, my colleagues. We've dropped ten points, I had 6,000 letters. I was five ahead, he's five behind, he's got to make that up. We'll lose, Blair will get in with a reduced majority. The Hutton Inquiry could be serious for Blair, but I don't think he'll have to resign. He'll win the next election." Which is what happened. On Howard, he began: "He's...." He checked himself. I helped him: "He's sold out to Europe." "Yes." He told me, "We in Westminster are important, but the country isn't listening. You have to get out there to the inner cities, where family structure has collapsed and they're on heroin and there's no hope." I pointed out that Gaitskell and Eden had tea after Question Time. "Did Blair invite you?" "No. I don't like Blair. It's Conservatives who do that – Major had drinks with Smith. It's not the other way round." I asked, "Does Blair regard the Queen as a tiresome old lady and do his visit by phone? Or does he respect her wisdom?" He looked at me and took some time to reply. "He has respect but for the person, not the institution. Blair and Prince Charles don't get on at all. There's a serious problem there." I wrote a classical ode, 'In the Commons: *Coup*'.

Rikki Radford visited me and told me, "I'm just going to Central Office and will hear that my contract's been rescinded." He wanted me to employ him. So began the idea that he would use his contacts as Duncan Smith's spindoctor to put *The Syndicate* on the right desks. I reported the possibility to O-Books and put him in touch with John at New Alresford.

In January 2005 Duncan Smith invited me to a gathering in his large room at the House of Commons. Drinks were laid out on a table, doughnuts on a desk, and there were pictures of IDS with Bush and Cheney. Several young men who would join his Centre for Social Justice were present and I chatted to them, and to Nick Wood, Stefan Shakespeare (the co-founder of YouGov) and Melanie Phillips of *The Daily Mail*, who nodded in agreement with what I had to say about the Syndicate's plan to depopulate the earth. Later I received a letter from Duncan Smith asking me to support the Centre for Social Justice.[6]

In Gran Canaria: Fortunate Isles
We had some winter sun in Gran Canaria. We were met and driven to the Grand Hotel Residencia, Maspalomas, where we had a garden apartment. We sat by a pool near palm-trees filled with green parakeets and had dinner on a balcony overlooking the pool. The next day we walked to a lighthouse by a lagoon and ate out. The following day we took a bus to Las Palmas and visited the Governor's house where Columbus is thought to have stayed in 1492 while a rudder was repaired on one of his ships. Columbus would only have known the entrance, the two courtyards and the wall. There was a reconstruction of his cabin. I "scribbled in each room and sketched out a poem on my way back". Excited that the Canary Islands were described on medieval maps as Fortunatae Insulae ('Fortunate Islands'), and that they were also the Isles of the Blessed, the Elysian Fields, I wrote a classical ode, 'In the Fortunate Isles with Columbus'.

The next day we took a taxi to Puerto Rico and took a boat to Puerto de Mogan. There we took a yellow submarine for a 40-minute journey round three wrecks. We climbed down a steel ladder, sat in seats before windows and saw shoals of fish, including trumpet fish. We walked through Mogan's pretty alleyways and returned on a glass-bottomed boat.

We went to the hotel's Wellness Centre and had salt-water therapy in the sea pool, then a Rasul bath, a mud bath first used in Ionian Greece in the 9th century BC, and then by Hippocrates of Kos, Cleopatra in Egypt and the Ottomans. We were coated in black mud, had our pores opened by steam and were wrapped in muslin spread with milk, oil, vanilla, coconut and spices like Cleopatra. We lay mummified for 20 minutes, and I reflected on the Universalist nature of the treatment which spanned Greek, Egyptian and Turkish times and was administered by a Venezuelan. I wrote a classical ode, 'In Maspalomas' Wellness Centre', which I finished during the flight home.[7]

Finishing The Syndicate, *radio*
In those days, when he was bringing out 50 books a year, John Hunt was directly involved in shaping books. *The Syndicate* continued my rereading of secret history. I had found that from the Russian Revolution to the present, money and oil drove events through commercial *élites*: a group of families I called 'the Syndicate' who have dynastically sought to create a self-interested New World Order and take possession of the world's resources. I had found that globalisation, the EEC and the war in Iraq were all means to this end.

From January to March 2004 I worked every day on *The Syndicate*, and sent John many emails containing my changes. I visited John on 10 March, driving down to New Alresford to start work at 8.40 a.m. and finishing at 6.30 p.m., with one brief break to buy sandwiches from the delicatessen. I went again on 12 March. John asked me many questions, and we built in amendments and insertions. I appreciated the intense discussion about passages and his sharp mind, and our collaboration cemented a publisher-author relationship in the one-to-one tradition of the 1930s, which has been eroded by the purely commercial approach. John was interested in the ideas for themselves and did not regard books solely as commercial packs of butter. I worked on the Notes/Sources, and by June the book was ready to be read by Edward Garnier. I proof-read in July and received an early copy in September.

I was interviewed on the Syndicate and oil on Radio Solent in October 2004: a twenty-minute chat in a cupboard of a room with a glass panel in the door, a table with a microphone, a console with red wire and earphones at Broadcasting House in Portland Place. The book came out in early November. Rikki, Duncan Smith's spindoctor, had been promoting the book. He reported that *The Times* and several other newspapers were extremely interested and said they wanted to interview me. They all mysteriously changed their mind. Rikki spoke to Frederick Forsyth and arranged for me to meet him at an event at the Marriott. I duly met him and Duncan Smith joined our conversation.

In April 2005 I was rung by the radio station at Denver, Colorado, and interviewed on *The Syndicate* for an hour. In November I was interviewed on *The Syndicate* live for 53 minutes by Chuck Harder on a radio station in Florida. He asked, "What's worrying you, Nick?" I said: "That a world government's being created and our leaders are pretending it's not happening, and all nation-states are being subsumed into it." "Oh, I agree." He said, "You and I know there are 3,000 people who are running the world, and they control the media and if you break through they marginalise you, ridicule you and eliminate you." I did not comment, but talked of being evidential. He ran past me the idea that al-Qaeda are anti-Syndicate, and that one should be pro-al-Qaeda. I was not having that. I said there was a clash of civilizations, the North-American and Arab civilizations, and that al-Qaeda were extreme Arabs.

In early January 2009 I heard that *The Syndicate* was out in Polish and several months later in Portuguese and Russian.[8]

Sale of Otley Hall

After much agonising and reviewing of personal considerations we had decided to sell Otley Hall for an amount that would reflect our repairs and improvements and the planting we had done in anticipation of our retiring there. The main reason for this decision concerned our family in Essex. There would be side benefits. I would cease to be a curator-guide repeating the same spiel to each group of visitors and escape from sleeping in a creepy, haunted bedroom where after 'lights out' orbs, sometimes white, sometimes red, floated round the dark room at eye-height. Sometimes I hid under the covers.

The property market in Suffolk for a house as large as Otley Hall was far from brisk. After a few unsuitable, unhistorically-minded viewers, the Beaumonts spent four hours viewing the property. Mrs. Beaumont rang Ken and spoke of her intention to buy Otley Hall out of the sale of a business, but said she would not be able to complete until July. She was a solicitor and trained witnesses; her husband had grown up in the Ipswich area and managed a supermarket. The next day, unable to reach the estate agent, she rang Ken and made an offer, which Ken said she would have to increase. She rang him the next day and agreed his figure. Ken said he would recommend acceptance to me and the estate agent. She then rang me, delighted, and assured me that the Hall would remain open to the public who wanted to absorb its history. She said, "I want to assure you, you'll be taking part in 2007. You can come and film with your son when you want. You're part of the story now."

Exchange took place in early April. I received her family and in-laws and gave them a tour. Mrs. Beaumont told our Administrator that she wanted as much business on the books from July onwards as possible. I did all I could to help her in this, by agreeing to leave furniture, accept bookings and pass on unsold copies of my guidebook. I sold The Thatch separately in June 2004.[9] I got on with meeting my architect and builder at Connaught House to begin the building work there.[10]

Then on Saturday 15 May the Beaumonts were waiting for me in the car park when I arrived, and at their request we toured the gardens for a couple of hours. They asked me to identify dozens of shrubs and plants. They said they wanted to reduce the Open Days and coach tours which impacted on the inside of the Hall, and have silent retreats in the grounds. Our tour took us back towards the Hall, and I took the opportunity to say hello to the housekeeper, report my arrival and go to the loo. I resumed our tour.

Three weeks later Beaumont rang Ken and accused me of "serious non-disclosure" regarding the medieval footpath outside our fence, which had always been on Otley Hall's deeds but over which the public had always had a right of way. A previous owner had extended the pond into the footpath, and our insurer had asked us to fence the pond in as a safety measure to prevent village children from drowning. At the same time I had restored a viable footpath to the satisfaction of the Council.[11] Ken said there must have been a misunderstanding. There was then an issue over the employment rights they might inherit. My solicitor was told that I had been "evasive" by disappearing into the kitchen on 15 May. In a further call to Ken, Beaumont said he wanted to pursue my non-disclosure in the courts.

I visited my solicitor and wrote a three-page letter[12] setting out the historical position regarding the footpath. But the damage was now done. The good feeling that had led me to help ease the Beaumonts into a furnished home with conference bookings evaporated, and I was now waiting to be taken to court. On 15 July we handed Otley Hall over to a couple who we hoped would continue to hold Open Days to show the Hall's history.

Soon afterwards there were further changes. The historic Linenfold Room was decorated with modern art. The Administrator was placed on a new hourly-rate contract as a consultant for three months, and she then left. Most of our guides resigned. The housekeeper and gardener were now Eastern-Europeans. Slovakians ran the Hall and grounds. There was a large event with a marquee at the end of August, at which "the previous owners were blessed". (Ann said: "I didn't want to be blessed.") Having attended Otley church's Bible-reading group, Mrs. Beaumont became the local vicar. The retreats in the grounds were linked to functional Christianity rather than history.[13]

We calculated that we had received 40,000 people in the course of seven years (in coach tours, Open Days, garden Open Days, conferences and dinners). I had become knowledgeable on Tudor architecture, early American history and the Virginian *élite*.

At Cliveden
For my 65th birthday in May Ann took me, as a surprise, to Cliveden, where

Bronwen Astor was chatelaine at the time of the Profumo Affair in 1963. We booked in at the Shrewsbury suite, named after the Countess of Shrewsbury who eloped with George Villiers, 2nd Duke of Buckingham, in 1668. Villiers killed her husband in a duel and later bought Cliveden, where they lived together. We went down to tea before the huge fireplace in the Great Hall and then walked to the clock tower. As we returned a little boy ran towards me who looked like Ben – and it was Ben. Behind him were Matthew, Melanie, Nadia and Anthony. We continued our walk and found the pool in which Christine Keeler, invited by Stephen Ward along with the Russian Ivanov, an intelligence officer in the Soviet GRU, met Profumo, the British Secretary of State for War who had been invited by Lord Astor, Bronwen's husband. Back at the entrance (near George Bernard Shaw's stick, which was in a glass case) I was shown the post table where, according to Bronwen, Ward removed the Skybolt plans addressed to Astor by *The Observer*, photo-copied them and then replaced them. The photocopies were apparently passed on to the Russians.

We dined in the dining-room by the terrace where I stood with Bill Astor in 1960 (before the theft of the Skybolt plans), and I thought of the 1930s intellectuals of the Cliveden Set, including the Editor of *The Times*, who dined here while meeting to avoid war and perpetuate the British Empire (which Churchill, in the opposite camp, bargained away to defeat Hitler).

The next morning, my birthday, after presents in our sitting-room (which included a caligraphied poem of mine Ann had done, 'Sea Force', over a picture of Porthleven), we swam in the pool and sunbathed beside it. Later most of us (but not Melanie) walked down past the 1565 statue of Pluto and Persephone through woods to the river and to Spring Cottage, where Profumo stayed with Ward. The butler let us look round. I wandered into the hall, a downstairs bedroom and then upstairs into a sitting-room with a picture of Christine Keeler, signed by Ward, and to the main bedroom, and then downstairs to the kitchen, dining-room and study. Outside a roof terrace was reached by steps.

For tea I had champagne and cake with the first two lines of 'Sea Force' in icing. Matthew's card was headed 'Not Quite Shakespeare: A Most Sillie Birthday Ode': "Egad! Gadzooks and by my troth,/Forsooth methinks, thou may,/Perchance be not as sprightly young,/As thou wert yesterday!" We dined, walked under the stars and sat in front of the fireplace in the Great Hall. I wrote a classical ode, 'In Stephen Ward's Web'.[14]

Upheaval

The main reason for our sale of Otley Hall was the break-up of Matthew's marriage and our need to be on hand for our grandson Ben. I must skate over the details, but having gathered that all was not well for some while we had been considering what we should do to be ahead of the situation regarding caring for Ben. Melanie had urged Matthew to sell their house as "it's not working". Now she told him that she wanted to end the marriage, and could not be dissuaded by her shocked mother and stepfather. Matthew had a wretched summer during which he acted maturely and sensibly, and established all the facts. They went to Ibiza in July, and on the second day Melanie again urged him to sell their house. Matthew brought Ben down to Cornwall in August, and there was discussion in Charlestown. Melanie had had a wedding at Otley Hall, a job at Normanhurst, a good life-style and had been treated as a member of the family, but (advised by a 'friend' who had not met any of us) she wanted a different life-style and to leave the marriage. There was no evidence that she was suffering from post-natal depression, and her wishes had to be accepted at face value and respected. Having grappled with the situation for months, Matthew no longer wished to be with her.

There was an agreement that under a divorce settlement she would have a small house a mile or so away and that Matthew and she would share custody. Ben would stay at Oaklands until he was seven, and then go to Chigwell School, like the rest of us. Matthew could see Ben almost daily. Melanie would leave Normanhurst and find work at another local school. It was heartbreaking for Matthew to steer all this through in Ben's best interests, and it was heartbreaking for Ann and me as we looked after Ben while Matthew was at work. We were, however, pleased that we had returned from Otley Hall to Connaught House and could be on hand to provide the emotional and logistical support that grandparents provide in such situations: collecting Ben from school and contributing to new stability. Ann was now in place to be an active grandmother, giving our grandson security at a difficult time on a daily basis. Melanie lived on the top floor of their house as a lodger until Christmas while a house was bought for her and she could find a new school. Bemused by the development, her mother and stepfather moved her out in silence. By then Matthew had met Kate, a solicitor, and the day after the move-out they went to Barcelona together to discuss their new life.[15]

I had walked away from my intelligence work disenchanted to help look after my daughter, who I had been told I should never see again (*see My Double Life 1: This Dark Wood*), and now I had walked away from Otley Hall disenchanted to help look after my grandson. Sometimes family come before work and property.

Our attempt to retire to Otley Hall had been overtaken by family events. A utopian experiment had come to an end. Our decision to sell Otley Hall was largely forced on us by circumstances. Looking back I wonder if Providence had arranged for me to absorb Tudor architecture and historical knowledge in 1997 as I would need them for coming books. I wondered if it had then wanted me to turn my back on Otley Hall to give me time to fulfil my coming writing commitments and become a full-time author. Certainly *My Double Life* would not have been written had we retained Otley Hall.

Travellers next to Coopersale Hall

While Matthew was in Ibiza travellers arrived on the field next to our football field adjoining Coopersale Hall on a Friday evening. Residents alerted me. I organised them into blocking the private road we owned and turning back lorries carrying concrete. The next morning I bought a sturdy chain and tied it to two trees at the bottom of the road, and residents manned our roadblock. Police did not interfere. On the Sunday all the councillors and our new MP Eleanor Laing visited the private road to assess the situation.

Eventually I decided to confront the travellers. As I opened the high gate a little girl ran to her father and handed him a knife with a long blade. He told me the travellers owned the field. I explained that they had no access onto my private road.[16] My strategy was to display strength and negotiate, and I was relieved when the high gate shut behind me. One of the residents knew a fellow who had an East-End gang of fearsome Bosnians. He visited the travellers and said with great authority, "These people are *friends* of mine." "Oh, I'm sorry, I didn't know." An arrangement was made to sell the field to a resident, and (after Ann and I spent a night at Maryland Manor, near Brentwood, to celebrate her birthday), the travellers were out by Wednesday afternoon.

Later the big fellow arrived by the chain to collect his 'earnings' from the grateful residents. He sat in an open-topped red sports car while we heaped pre-arranged wads of banknotes onto the passenger seat. Then he opened the glove compartment, and with his left hand scooped up the mound of banknotes and shoved it into the glove compartment. I asked if we could be photographed together, and he leapt out of his car and put an arm round my shoulder. Later he took up with a parent at one of our schools and in March 2009 visited Ken, our Bursar, and Matthew to discuss delaying payment of some fees. They worked out who he was and humoured him. At the end of their meeting the big fellow said, "If you've got anyone who hasn't paid, I'll collect the money for you." He meant, 'I'll visit your late payers with my Bosnians and come back with your fees.' We hastily assured him that we did not need his help.[17]

The Secret History of the West

In July 2004 I began further work on *The Secret History of the West*. It focused on the influence secret organisations have had on the main revolutions in the

West since 1453 and showed how Utopian visions of ideal revolutionary societies end in massacres and guillotinings. I had firmed up my new view of why revolutions happen: an idealist has a vision which is then corrupted by a political regime and results in physical repression. John wanted to know how many of the idealists who had the vision belonged to 'the hidden hand'. Clarity has always been a goal of mine, and I made clarifying amendments until September. I then worked through the Notes/Sources again. I was still working on the book in November. The proofs arrived on 18 March, and I was still reading a second set of proofs on 1 May. I received early copies of *The Secret History of the West* in mid-November 2005.[18]

Medical

There were deaths, some of which were reflected in my *Collected Stories*. Alan Lavers's daughter Jenny Murrant, who I employed at Coopersale Hall, died after her fourth stroke. In January Tony Egan, a nuclear physicist with whom I was at school (who gave me a completely wrong explanation of the facts of life as we walked down Chigwell High Road and had a wooden board rubber flung at his head by fiery Davenport), was travelling in South Africa in a minibus that overturned. Lying in a pool of oil, with a crushed inside, the bus having rolled over him, he whispered, "I would like to see my lovely wife just one last time." They put her hand in his. He looked at her without saying anything and died.

In April the husband of Ann's friend Avril, Stuart, had a massive brain haemorrhage in their beamed sitting-room in their Suffolk cottage with honeysuckle round the door and died. We attended the funeral with Anthony in a Tudor church up the lane where Anne Boleyn's heart is said to be buried. The church was packed with his work colleagues – he had been Deputy Education Officer for Suffolk – and Avril lay bluebells on his coffin.[19]

My sister Frances had received a nursing degree – BSc (Hons) Nurse Practitioner Primary Healthcare – at the Royal Festival Hall. I sat with Richard as several hundred students in gowns, blue hoods and mortarboards filed before the News presenter Trevor Macdonald to cheers and hollers from their supporters.

At the end of July my Uncle Reg died at a home in the Lake District, aged 92. And in September my god-daughter Elizabeth, a GP, was married in Oxford at St Ebbe's church. I read a lesson from *Ephesians* 5, 21–33.

Ann had been coping with osteoarthritis and problems in her carpal tunnels and hips. She countered constriction in her fingers and wrists by attending classes on pottery, calligraphy and art, and constriction in her knees and ankles by walking and swimming.[20] One of her paintings was of a pair of battered walking boots, one holding two rulers, the other three paintbrushes, symbolising her mathematical and creative sides but also her domination of her feet and her hands. I was full of admiration at her determination.

In the Scilly Isles: 'In the Brilliant Autumn Sunshine, Among a Thousand Islands'
Near the start of the summer holidays we went to Cornwall. In warm, dry weather (with green and red six-spot burnets crawling in our lavender) we drove from Charlestown to Penzance heliport and flew by helicopter over Land's End and then St Mary's to Tresco, over round seaweedy shapes under shallow water: ancient huts. We were tractored on a trailer with seats to New Grimsby and the Island Hotel, from where we had stunning views across light-blue agapanthus and water of some 20 islands. After lunch we walked to the Abbey Gardens, then got a lift back on a trailer, sat on rocks below our balcony and watched a stormy petrel, a fulmar and a seal. I learned that in the Dark Ages, Tresco, Bryher and Samson were all part of Renteman; that Tresco separated from St Martin's and St Mary's by AD500 following a tidal surge caused by volcanic activity; and that Samson separated from Renteman by 1016.

The next morning we drove to New Grimsby quay and were greeted by a bearded man on the *Fieldore*, which hove off. He agreed to take us on a tour of the islands, but said the tides were against visiting St Agnes and the Western Rocks. We climbed aboard and passed old yacht moorings, Charles's and Cromwell's castles and then St Helier, Tean, White Island, and St Martin's. We reached the Eastern Islands, where two dozen seals basked on rocks and we saw cormorants, shags, a northern diver, fulmars and three oyster-catchers. We chugged on past St Mary's to Samson, saw its ruined houses, passed the Northern Rocks and had a view of the beach in Appletree Bay whence Arthur left for Avalon (which was Great Arthur of the Eastern Islands, according to Scilly lore). We continued to Hell Bay and through a swell to within sight of the quay where we started. We clambered down into a dinghy that was on a mooring, and were taken ashore.

I had been out among a thousand islands, the boatman told me, and that afternoon I wrote a story, 'In the Brilliant Autumn Sunshine, Among a Thousand Islands', the first story for volume 5 of my *Collected Stories*, a wry account of the boat trip and of scepticism and mysticism. When I wrote of a thousand islands I was aware that I would complete a thousand stories.

The next day we caught the *Firethorn* via Bryher to St Mary's. We left our luggage in the unattended waiting-room and made our way to Porthcressa Beach, under Buzza Tower, and looked across lovely yellow sand, a curved bay and islands. We lunched by the Old Fire Station, got on a bus and toured the island. We stopped at the Western Rocks where Sir Cloudesley Shovell was wrecked. Later we collected our luggage and persuaded a Skybus driver to take us to the heliport.[21]

In Brussels: "a top-down organisation"
I had long wanted to probe the secret history of the 1950s Common-Market buildings in Brussels, and I arranged to meet Geoffrey Van Orden, our MEP, at the European Parliament. We caught the Eurostar to Brussels, checked in at our hotel and booked a city tour. We drove to the Palais de Justice (in whose 27 courts and 245 other rooms Orson Wells wanted to film Kafka's *Trial*), the Colonne du Congrès, the Royal Palace, the Belgian Parliament, the house where Byron stayed for 10 days after Waterloo and the royal castle at Laeken. We passed the Council of Ministers' building, the European Parliament and the European Commission building, and later ate near the Grand Place.

We visited the vast brick house where Erasmus lived for several months in 1521. It had diamond-lead windows and beeswax walls, and Erasmus's study had a sloping desk with a lip at the bottom. We visited the chapter room, the White Room and the library, and I noticed an hourglass topped with a death's-head skull. I noted: "The Renaissance began in Italy with Plethon and Ficino, but began in Northern Europe here." I pondered on Erasmus and considered writing my own *In Praise of Folly*.

We drove to the new Commission building in Avenue du President Robert Schuman opposite the old Palais Berlaymont (abandoned because of asbestos) and the Council of Ministers (Charlemagne building) in Rue de la Loi. We were dropped off at the European Parliament and were greeted by Geoffrey Van Orden, who was wearing a dark suit and mauve tie, and by his assistant, who took us on a tour. We surrendered our passports and went to the first-floor Committee Room where the Conservatives' group were meeting and where Geoffrey now sat on a platform as Vice-Chairman of the Foreign Affairs Committee. We went up to the larger Parliament Chamber, where the President sat and then to Geoffrey's room on the 14th floor.

Geoffrey was waiting for us and showed us to chairs. *The Syndicate* was on his desk. He talked about the prospects of the European Constitution, which he believed would not happen, and said that the admission of Turkey would undermine the superstate. We discussed how the EC came into being: the Council on Foreign Relations, Monnet and the Marshall Plan. I put it to him "that a world government is the context for Europe". He said: "It's definitely a top-down organisation, not a bottom-up one. It's being imposed." I said I wanted to know if the Syndicate's hand could be detected in the early purchases of buildings and asked him to investigate who built the original buildings, including the Berlaymont. He said he would try and find out.

We went on to the 18th-century palace of Charles de Lorraine, who features in *The Secret History of the West*. The marble staircase displayed images from alchemy. We had tea at the Hotel Metropole, a haunt of many writers, and dinner at The Swan, a restaurant in the house where the *Communist Manifesto* was written, where Marx lived and he and Engels wrote before and during 1848. We ate in a warm, panelled room before a fireplace decorated with swans, and I was struck by the incongruity of Marx writing about workers and the poor in an elegant house that now contained Brussels' most expensive restaurant. We visited the house where Pieter Bruegel the Elder died in 1569.

We visited the NATO building in Boulevard Leopold III, and then (again) the Château de Laeken, a distant dome by a statue against the skyline. I was struck by the flimsiness of the New World Order's buildings in contrast to the solidness of the old monarchical buildings. The monarchy was on the side of the New World Order: the King of Belgium must have approved of the Laeken conference of 2000, otherwise he would not have opened his home for it.[22] I wrote a classical ode, 'In Euro-City, Brussels'.

Leaving the Shakespearean Authorship Trust

I was becoming more and more disenchanted with the SAT. At their January meeting Mark Rylance rang John Shahan in the US to learn more about his 'Declaration of reasonable doubt about the identity of William Shakespeare'. He proposed that 'anti-Stratfordians' should sign it under the SAT umbrella on the Globe's stage along with "star-studded" actors. I knew I would never sign this Declaration (which Stratfordians would later describe as 'anti-Shakespearean').

I did not attend the February meeting and I declined to attend the launch of Dawkins's book claiming that Bacon was Shakespeare, *The Shakespeare Enigma*. Rylance rang me on 2 July and spoke to me for 50 minutes. Initially he wanted me to explain Elizabeth of Bohemia, but then wanted to know: "Are you happy the books have gone? How are you?" I told him I was busy coping with my move from Otley Hall. He said, "I hope you'll still come to Trustee meetings."

In December I received a letter from Rylance saying that (the financially wise) Silberrad was relinquishing the post of Treasurer following an operation, and was to be replaced by a less experienced man. As I, was liable for at least one-seventh of any SAT shortfall as a Trustee, careful Silberrad's relinquishing of the purse strings made me think it was now time to leave.

I was too immersed in amending books to attend the next SAT meeting. In early February 2005 I had another letter from Mark Rylance, full of admiration for my writing and all I had done but saying anyone who cannot attend meetings should walk away. Two weeks later I wrote to Rylance and my Fellow Trustees resigning as SAT Trustee. I gave multiple reasons, including my unlimited liability over claims, which was never addressed; and my independence and reluctance to be identified with any point of view.[23]

In Stratford-upon-Avon

Two days later I visited Stratford-upon-Avon with Ann, to reaffirm my roots in the Stratfordian Shakespeare. We booked in at the 15th–16th century Shakespeare Hotel in the High Street, near New Place and the local school, the College, where the Headmaster was paid twice as much as the Head of Eton by the woolmen and is said to have possessed a copy of Ovid's *Metamorphoses*, on whose Diana Shakespeare is thought to have based Titania. We went straight to Shakespeare's Birthplace. Shakespeare inherited the house in 1603, but, having lived in New Place since 1597, allowed his sister Joan Hart to live there. An exhibition stressed that Shakespeare left 26s.8d. each to John Heming and Henry Cordell, his two fellow actors who edited the First Folio that was published seven years after his death, in 1623. The guide in the room where Shakespeare's parents lived pointed out that Shakespeare was mentioned in 1656 in Dugdale's *The History and Antiquities of Warwickshire*. It was said that his nieces showed visitors round the Birthplace in the 1670s, while the landlord of the Swan and Maidenhead Inn took people to see New Place.

We went on to Judith's house (now a café/restaurant) and then Nash's house, where Shakespeare's granddaughter Elizabeth lived after marrying Nash in 1626 at the age of 15 (having grown up in New Place). I looked out of the window at New Place where Shakespeare lived from 1610 to 1616 and wrote *Cymbeline*, *The Winter's Tale*, *The Tempest*, and perhaps *Henry VIII* and *Two Noble Kinsmen*. I saw the four cellars, the base of the hearth and the knot-garden where Shakespeare is alleged to have written *The Tempest*. It was pointed out that 25 people believed Shakespeare of Stratford wrote Shakespeare's works because they paid him. After Nash's death, Elizabeth married John Bernard and lived in Abington manor house, Northampton, with Shakespeare's last papers until she died in 1670. The wooden trunk (or chest) may then have been in Northampton. The guide at Nash's house told me that when John Bernard died in 1674 the trunk went to the eldest of her three daughters, Eleanor, whose husband Henry Gilbert got administration papers for John Bernard's death and lived in Warwick. The guide told me that the trunk was left above a butcher's shop in Warwick that burned down in the early 1690s. The trunk is thought to have been destroyed in the fire.

However, there was another story that the trunk remained at New Place, which Susanna, Shakespeare's daughter, took over when Shakespeare died in 1616, and had then gone to Bearley Grange and finally to Kingsthorpe, north of Stratford, in the 19th century.

We went on to Hall's Croft, Susanna's previous house. The lady guide said, "This was the third biggest house in Stratford. The College was the biggest, and New Place the second biggest. The Shakespeare family owned two of the top three."

The next day we walked to Holy Trinity church and Shakespeare's grave (which is between the graves of Anne Hathaway, Nash, Hall and Susanna Hall, Shakespeare's daughter). A helpful churchwarden brought me an 1836 plan of the chancel showing the graves are 7 ft 6 inches x 3 foot 7 inches. There were changes to the church in 1842, when the rail was pulled back outside the graves, and the floor was raised in 1896. The churchwarden told me that Shakespeare's purchase of land brought with it the position of lay Rector: "He's not there because of his writing but because he was lay Rector."

We went on to Anne Hathaway's cottage in Shottery. The courting settle, on which (according to the tradition in the Hathaway family) William and Anne sat, has been dated by dendrochronology as c.1609, too late for it to be Shakespeare's courting settle. As I left Anne Hathaway's cottage I jotted down, "Do a poem – 'Return to Stratford', on Stratfordianism – after a nightmare of blind alleys." We went on to Wilmcote, where Shakespeare's mother Mary Arden left to marry John Shakespeare in 1557.

I reflected on the two actors who edited the First Folio, the 1656 mention of Shakespeare, the Shakespeares' prominent position in the community and ownership of the second- and third-largest houses in Stratford and the land that gave Shakespeare a lay rectorship, and I connected the money that made all this possible with his plays and his investment in the Globe. As Andrew Gurr points out in *The Shakespeare Company 1594–1642*, under James Burbage of the Chamberlain's Men, owner of The Theatre, from 1599 actors including Shakespeare became managers and made a profit.

That afternoon we walked to the Swan Theatre via Shakespeare's garden at the back of New Place, and saw *Julius Caesar*. Antony was played by Gary Oliver (the son-in-law of Ann's secretary at Oaklands). Afterwards he came to our hotel, shook my hand and over a cream tea discussed Caesar's will and whether his bequest to all Romans was in the will or made up by Mark Antony. After dinner we walked across the road to the Falcon ("a pub by 1660") and I pondered the night Shakespeare spent drinking in 1616 that led to his catching a chill and early death. Was he drinking in the New Place garden or in a local tavern?

I had previously visited Stratford in 1954; 1969 (when I stayed in the Falcon); and 1986. I thought my poem, 'In Shakespeare's Stratford: The Nature of Art', written in 1986, got him right. Like John Osborne he was a dramatist who got a job as an actor. He pillaged Plutarch and other sources, and regarded his plays as plagiarised and their manuscripts as not worth keeping.

On the way home we visited Alveston Manor and again looked at the cedar in the garden where *A Midsummer Night's Dream* was allegedly first performed. We drove to Charlecote and looked through the gates at the home of Sir Thomas Lucy (Justice Shallow), where allegedly Shakespeare was caught poaching. I had become a writer sitting by the Avon in the summer of 1954. I had looked at the evidence for the main claimants to the authorship of Shakespeare's plays and had found none of it compelling. I was therefore still with the evidence for the Stratfordian Shakespeare as the author of the plays, as historical tradition had always maintained.[24] Later I wrote a classical ode, 'Return to Stratford', a title that also suggested 'Return to Stratfordianism'.

I had made sense of Shakespeare of Stratford and I now genuinely felt that I did not want to be associated with the questioners of the authorship.

The Light of Civilization

At the end of 2004 I began work on *The Light of Civilization*, my updating of Part One of *The Fire and the Stones*. In January 2005 I was editing *The Light of Civilization* for John Hunt. It updated Part One of *The Fire and the Stones*. I saw the mystic vision that was later expressed in all the religions as the basis for civilization, and I showed that all religions share the common vision of the Light. I connected the Light-inspired religions to their civilizations and cultures, and showed that the religions and civilizations decline when the original Light is lost. I stated the tradition of the Light which has inspired the civilizations, and a sub-tradition: the heretical Light in Western civilization, whose future I considered. I revised the section on the Egyptian Light in January and finished work on the book on 28 January. I revised the Notes and References to Sources in June and July and sent the book off in early August. I was still tinkering with the Appendix in November 2005.

I was still proof-reading *The Light of Civilization* during the first half of January 2006. I finished reading the final proofs between 23 April and 3 May 2006. In August there was a very favourable review in *Nexus*, verbally playing on 'Light' in the title: "Brilliant."[25]

In Egypt: charnel-house in Sinai, Bedouin and the universe

I had wanted to return to Egypt to probe the secret history of the Great Pyramid and of the Sphinx for *The Light of Civilization*, for *The Rise and Fall of Civilizations*, for my story 'The Riddle of the Great Pyramid' and for *Classical Odes*. But first I wanted to absorb Luxor and Sinai.

At the end of January we flew to Luxor and drove to Western Thebes. We crossed the Nile and drove through palms to the Colossi of Memnon, gigantic statues of Amenhotep III and his wife round which the wind whistled. We drove on to the Valley of the Nobles and the tombs of Rahmose (governor of Thebes during the reigns of Amenhotep III and his son Akhenaton), Userhet (a royal scribe) and Khaemhet (Amenhotep III's royal inspector of granaries, and scribe). We reached the Ramesseum and saw fragments of the huge statue of Ramesses II, the transliteration of whose throne name into Greek was 'Ozymandias' and whose imminent arrival at the British Museum in 1818 inspired Shelley's poem. Shelley's "legs of stone" were in fact feet, and his "lone and level sands stretched far away" had a Theban mountain range behind them. Bones – of men as old as Ramesses II – and fragments of wine cups lay nearby on the surface of the sand.

We went on to Hatshepsut's tomb, where wall paintings and carvings showed an obelisk being brought by ships, and to the tomb of Ay, according to one view the killer of Tutankhamen. We walked to the tomb of Tutankhamen (the boy king who continued his father Akhenaton's worship of the Aton, then changed back to Amon) and peered into the chambers where gold was found.

In the afternoon we visited the Karnak temple, which had columns 22 metres high, obelisks – Cleopatra's Needle came from this temple – and statues of Ramesses II. In the Temple of Luxor there were columns and a huge sitting statue or Colossus of Ramesses II. I wondered if this was where in a former life (according to my regression) I laid a garland. We took a gharry back. Later we went to the *Son et Lumière* at the temple of Karnak, where I learned that Ramesses II (perhaps my boyfriend in a past life, according to my regression) ruled 67 years and fathered 92 boys and 106 girls.

The next day we travelled in convoy to Abydos and Hurghada. We drove past mud-huts where the men were in *jellabiya*s, and donkeys laden with sugar cane, white ibises and herons, a hoopoe and cattle. At every town or road junction two armed security men saw our convoy safely through. There was a dug-in machine-gun post by the entrance at Abydos and at the back an armed man on a camel watched us from a ridge. Abydos contained an empty tomb that had been built by Seti I as a tomb for Osiris. The convoy moved on to Dendara's temple of Hathor, some of which was after 250BC, and on an outside wall there was a larger-than-life-size outline of Cleopatra (c.32BC).

We flew to Sharm el-Sheikh and were taken to the Four Seasons Hotel, a Moorish palace with many courtyards, and escorted to a bungalow in the grounds. I was struck by the air. I remember Marjorie Coates telling me in Baghdad that the air of Upper Egypt was like wine, and I understood what she meant, for the air slowed me down and made me sleepy. We were driven to Naama Bay to go on the *Seascope*, which took us underwater to view barracudas and purple jellyfish. We returned for a Pharaonic massage from toes to scalp: we had a round muslin poultice – of camomile and mint dipped in a hot oil of sweet almond and wheat germ mixed with jasmine and rose – raked over our bodies.

We crossed Sinai, a bleak, rugged landscape of volcanic rock, passing Bedouin and Bedouin settlements (at one of which 25 Bedouin sold beads, stones, fossils and crystals spread out on a wall), to the 6th-century St Catherine's monastery, which lay under a towering hill. The Egyptians round it were from the Romany tribe descended from 200 families of Roman slaves brought from the north shore of Anatolia and from Alexandria that Justinian settled there to guard the monastery (as stated in the 9th-century *Chronicles* of Eutychios, Patriarch of Alexandria. (Our 'Romany gypsies' are supposed to have originated in Egypt.) We entered by a path between the 6th-century walls and looked inside the 6th-century church, which was festooned with hanging chandeliers and censers. We passed Catherine's wrist bone in a glass case. We passed through the Chapel of the Transfiguration and went on to the Chapel of the Burning Bush (which had a 4th-century doorway) inside which the burning bush used to stand. Now the burning bush was outside, with trailing strands. In the museum we saw the original of my icon Christ Pantocrator (presumably painted on Justinian's orders).

We went to the charnel-house. From the entrance we saw the robed skeleton (in a glass case) of Stephanos, the 6th-century architect; and behind him the piled bones of all the monks since then, heaped together in an ossuary. The monks had all been buried for a couple of years so their flesh could decay and had then been dug up so their bones could join those of the other monks. There was a mound of 200 or 300 skulls: all the monks. The practice continues, and a bearded, bespectacled Greek-Orthodox monk in a long black hat told me in perfect English that his skull would join them one day.

On the way back we passed Bedouin tombs of stones. Bedouin cannot read or write and so their lives are commemorated by a heap of stones. We stopped to have tea with roadside Bedouin. A young Bedouin in a *jellabiya* and his cousin wearing a black veil brought tea containing *shih*, which they find in the mountains around Sinai, a plant or herb that is good for flu or colds. I asked the young fellow, "Do you feel at one with the universe?" He said, "Yes, and I feel part of this place." He told me the Bedouin secret of happiness is not to be attached to possessions and to treasure the universe. Ann had bought a crystal from an old Bedouin during our morning journey, and he had told her it was called "The Secret of the Desert". Later I wrote a story, 'The Secret of the Desert'.

We flew to Cairo and drove to the Great Pyramid (passing the balcony of the Mena House Hotel where visitors gathered for the opening of the Suez

Canal in 1869 and where Churchill met Roosevelt). We entered the Great Pyramid and, with Ann behind me, I crouch-walked through the early tunnelled walls to the steps and crouch-climbed until we could stand and ascend the steep wooden ramp with iron steps to the King's Chamber. I stood before the empty granite sarcophagus that had presumably contained Khufu's body and studied the two airholes. The other rooms, including the Queen's Chamber, were closed, so we retraced our steps, first with plenty of headroom and then crouch-advancing, crab-like, sideways to avoid splitting our heads open on the cave roof.

We went on to the Valley Temple of Khufu's son Chephren, where Chephren's body was brought to be mummified; and then on to the Sphinx. Dismissing the view that the Sphinx goes back to c.12,000BC, I studied the face and was sure it was the face of Khufu rather than of Chephren: the causeway of Chephren's Valley Temple skirts the Sphinx, which preceded it. In bitter cold we returned to see three pyramids, the Sphinx, *mastabas* and the Valley Temple lit up for *Son et Lumière*. I wrote a classical ode, 'In Egypt: Tyranny and Armageddon'.

I asked the guide Ahmad ten questions about the Great Pyramid, and his answers were illuminating. He thought it was a cenotaph, an empty tomb, as the massively heavy sarcophagus would have to have been installed while the pyramid was being built and Khufu did not worship Ra. Khufu was supreme ruler and wanted everyone to worship him, not Ra, the morning sun (or the scarab, the midday sun, or Atum, the evening sun). He did not take the name Ra as did his son Khafra (or Chephren). There was a tradition that the Great Pyramid was a place of initiation in which initiates lay for whole nights in the empty sarcophagi in the Queen's Chamber and King's Chamber to relive successive stages of the Mystic Life, dying away from their self in darkness during their 'temple-sleep'.

While I waited to board to fly home, in the café area in front of Gate 3, at the extreme-left front table facing the Gate, I scribbled the first two pages of 'The Solution to the Mystery of the Great Pyramid' (later titled 'The Meaning and Purpose of the Great Pyramid'), the sequel (42 years later) to 'The Riddle of the Great Pyramid'. (*See* p.487.) During the flight I revised 'The Riddle of the Great Pyramid' and the Egyptian section of *The Light of Civilization*. I finished the last words as the plane doors opened.[26]

Collected literature: **Classical Odes, Collected Poems**
I had long thought of bringing out my collected literary works. During the spring and summer of 2005 Michael Mann had meetings with John Hunt in the course of which he established timetables for volumes of my collected works. I had had the idea in mid-April of bringing out, in addition to *Classical Odes*, a one-volume edition of *Overlord* and an updated *Collected*

Poems 1958–2005; also *Collected Short Stories* and *Collected Verse Plays*. I put the idea to Mann, and he met me in the Cavendish on 27 April with a suggested timetable. (I said he was my Max Brod, who was behind Kafka's works.) He rang me on 11 May to say that John had told him, "I want to do all Nicholas's books." In July I learned that I should deliver *Overlord* in November (for publication in June 2006) and *Collected Poems* on 1 January (for publication in October 2006).[27]

Classical Odes

In *Classical Odes*, the first four-book Odes since Horace, as we have seen I tried to catch the elegiac feeling that Englishness is being superseded by Europeanism and globalism. I tried to capture the English and European cultural traditions by rooting poems in their iconic places.

I was now near the end of the classical odes I had been writing on and off since 1994. I had written an ode, 'On Harrowdown Hill', about the alleged suicide of David Kelly, the weapons inspector in Iraq, a verdict that left me "stirred up, seething". I had written the last ode, 'At Connaught House', in early February 2004. I recorded on 9 February that I had "finished the odes... and with them, ten years' work (1994–2004) and have fulfilled my vision by the Pisan Arno when I glimpsed both my epic and my odes in one instant". I had worked on assembling *Classical Odes* since October 2004. I was preparing *Classical Odes* throughout February and early March 2005, not realising that I would write a few more odes, including three more odes in a year's time. I revised 'In Egypt: Tyranny and Armageddon' between 30 March and 2 April 2005, when I noted: "I've done 100 stanzas in nine days (800 lines of poetry)." I wrote the Preface. Throughout April I wrote stanzas into existing classical odes, expanding several poems, and I finished work on the book on 30 April.

I had now fulfilled the last half of my Pisan vision. John Hunt commented of my classical odes: "Your strength is moving from the particular to the universal."[28]

Collected Poems 1958–2005

Collected Poems was harder to do. Adding the last three volumes involved assembling all the poems I had written since 1993, and in many cases reworking them. This involved regular driving to and from Chigwell Row, a 4-mile drive, where my computer operator lived. I was always dropping in tapes and collecting her print-out, a method I had devised to increase my productivity.

I had to rework my political poems. In November 2004, having researched the invasion of Iraq for *The Syndicate*, I revised 'Shock and Awe', my poem about the invasion. *Summoned by Truth, Three Political Poems expressing Humanitarian Concerns*, contained 'Zeus's Ass', 'Attack on America' and 'Shock and Awe'. I first of all had the idea of calling this volume 'Summoned by Lies', having receiving the words on waking, but two days later, on 24 January 2005, I "woke with the correct title… in my mind…. It is more positive."

I had to add some new works, including 'Groans of the Muses'. In May 2003 I had had the idea of calling volume 30 of my *Collected Poems Sighs of the Muses*, and of beginning it with 'Groans of the Muses'. It was inspired by Spenser's 'Tears of the Muses'. I wrote:

Reflected on 'Tears of the Muses', the Muses' sorrow at the poor state of the arts; the 'Dunciad' is in that tradition – only scathing and satirical. I have a 'Tears of the Muses'. Now it's 'The Despair of the Muses', or rather 'Groans of the Muses': groans at all the rubbish that masquerades as art.

It would be "a blistering attack on publishers, producers, directors, the media, the BBC, poets and philosophers, all of whom had gone materialist".[29] On 28 May I wrote: "Should my poem be 'Groans of the Muses'?... Yes, 'Groans of the Muses'. The Tears of 1590 have become Groans in 2005." I wrote the poem by 30 May 2005.

I was reading through the first 27 volumes at the end of July. In mid-August I realised that the "hundred billion stars" in our galaxy in 'The Silence' was now, following unmanned spacecraft, "two hundred billion stars", and I observed that our galaxy had doubled in known size since I wrote the poem in the mid-1960s. Since 2005 new data from the Kepler Space Telescope suggests our galaxy, the Milky Way, contains 300 billion and perhaps as many as 500 billion stars, and a German supercomputer has calculated that the universe contains as many as 500 billion galaxies. Some 20 billion of the stars in the Milky Way are earth-like planets.[30] The universe has trebled or even quintupled in known size since the mid-1960s in my adult lifetime, and I have had to hone my view of the universe against an ever-changing background of scientific knowledge and data. I wrote my Preface to *Collected Poems*, but there was still much more to do.[31]

It took me until mid-December to finish my new work, my revisions and the Notes. In the course of moving all my work from Otley Hall, Great Easton and 6 Albion Hill to Connaught House, I discovered 55 'lost' poems I did not know that I had, and I worked on these and included them. In December I wrote 'Authorship Question in a Dumbed-Down Time'. I finally sent *Collected Poems* off on 15 December 2005.

The 30 volumes of *Collected Poems 1958–2005* follow my journey along the Mystic Way – my descent through the Dark Night to my centre, my experience of illumination and my ascent to a unitive vision of the One – and reflect the Age through reactions to Communism, the decline of Europe, America and the invasions of Afghanistan and Iraq.

Having combed through *Collected Poems*, I was struck that "my myth is Orpheus: the poet who lost his Eurydice, went down into the Underworld to retrieve her, looked back and lost her again; who was torn apart by Maenads and whose head goes on singing posthumously, as mine will". I noted that I could "call my *Collected Poems* 'Orpheus Singing'". In view of my dream I could have called it 'Orpheus among Green Apples'.

I was now convinced that the summer of 1966 was crucial in turning me into a regular, self-disciplined poet in England. I had disciplined myself to write every morning in my brother's house at 57 High Beach Road, Loughton.

In January 2006 I discovered four more poems, and then a hoard of 42 more, caught up in press cuttings I was sorting. These were included in *Collected Poems*; between 22 and 29 January I polished 48 poems I had rounded up following our move into Connaught House. I finished reading the final proofs between 14 April and 3 May 2006. There were more proofs to read in the course of May.[32]

The Rise and Fall of Civilizations
In October 2004 I began work on *The Rise and Fall of Civilizations*, which had been timetabled to appear in March 2007. I was working on this book in February 2005.

The sequel to *The Light of Civilization*, the book updated the patterns of civilizations in Part 2 of *The Fire and the Stones* and interpreted the dynamics of their origin, rise and collapse and how one civilization leads to the next. It showed where our civilization is heading today.

I had completed the work once-through by 19 August. I was still proof-reading the book in November and finished my work on it on 18 December 2005. I was still proof-reading it on 31 January 2006. I had final proofs to read at the end of August and polished a chart in September. I received an early proof on 29 October 2007. I was still working on proofs in February 2008.

I now associated my history with my classical education. I reflected that

> my history came from Tacitus (*Germania*) and Thucydides (*The Peloponnesian War*); also Livy. Those class translations and homeworks.... I developed a sense of history from my classical mentors.[33]

Christopher Ricks, Professor of Poetry
In July 2004 Christopher Ricks had sent me a 1944 first edition of *Horizon* (in itself a collector's item) with an article in it by T.S. Eliot, 'The Man of Letters

and the Future of Europe'. He wrote, "Apt to your thinking, no?" It was extremely apt as one of my roles as a man of letters was to reconnect the English to the European tradition, and I drew on this rare work in an epigraph in *Classical Odes* and in *My Double Life 2: A Rainbow over the Hills*.

Christopher Ricks was now Professor of Poetry at Oxford. I had been unable to attend his first lecture – I rang the University and enquired but no one seemed to be able to tell me a date. Ricks sent a copy of the *Times Literary Supplement* which reproduced his drift on the difference between prose and poetry. (His Neoclassical view was that poetry had a different scheme of punctuation from that of prose, both being written by the rational, social ego.) I arranged to stay at the Eastgate Hotel with Ann for his May lecture. We walked up the High past Schools to the 18th-century Radcliffe Camera (now part of the Bodleian) where I used to spend my mornings, and as usual stood in the Bodleian courtyard and looked at the 'schools' labelled over the doorways. There was no 'Literature' in 1602, when it was built. We walked back to the Queen's Lane coffee-house (opened by Cirques Jobson in 1654) and had tea.

We found our way across the road to Examination Schools South, where Ricks, balding, chubby, rosy-cheeked, bespectacled, smiling, was tinkering with equipment. He greeted me very warmly – he came down the aisle saying, "Nice to see you, thank you for coming" – and soon after came and had another chat. The hall filled up and at 5 he stood at the lectern, discarded the microphone, which boomed and echoed, and spoke in a flow of effortlessly structured argument without notes, very impressively. (Professor John Carey, asked on the radio who was the best lecturer he had ever heard, said, "'Christopher Ricks. He is so intelligent, he radiates energy. He is very very good. The best lectures are about pace.'")[34] His theme was unconventional: a study of Bob Dylan as being in the tradition of poets and translators he mentioned, and of the word-play in his songs.

At the end the audience slowly dispersed. A few went up to the front and were hugged. He beamed. I went and shook him by the hand, and he invited Ann and me to have a drink with him at Balliol. He set a scampering pace up the High. Others who had been invited fell back. I caught him and chatted about Empson and Irie (his pupil in Japan as mentioned in Haffenden's book, who later looked after me). I told him that when I was an undergraduate Auden was Professor of Poetry and I had listened to him standing outside the hall, looking over shoulders, as the crush was so great.

In the Buttery he bought us all drinks and we went out into the quad and stood in the evening sun. He had been an undergraduate at Balliol. He asked an academic who joined us of his lecture, "Was it scruffy?" "No, it wasn't scruffy." At 7 he shook hands all round and scurried off to collect his gown to dine in Balliol hall.

Shakespeare's bedchamber

The next morning Ann and I walked to 3 Cornmarket Street, climbed the winding stairs and entered the 'Painted Room', whose panelling had an orange and scarlet tracery of flowers and vines with bunches of grapes and IHS over the chimney-breast. Here, according to *Aubrey's Brief Lives*,[35] Shakespeare broke his journey between London and Stratford and lodged with John Davenant,[36] who was vintner (wine-merchant) at the Tavern (later the Crown) at this address. In this bedchamber, between 1592 and 1614 (when Davenant owned it) Shakespeare looked at the lettering on the frieze above the panelling: "And last of the rest be thou/gods servant for that hold i best/In the mornynge earlye/serve god devoutlye/Fear god above allthynge."[37] According to Aubrey Shakespeare was "exceedingly respected", and he stood as godfather for Davenant's son William in St Martin's church, near Carfax, nearby. There was a tradition that he had a relationship with Jane Davenant and was William's father. While I absorbed Shakespeare's presence in this room, Ann talked to the lady who received us, who had once been her boss, for when studying just outside Oxford she and Avril had had a holiday job with Oxford Aunts before the firm moved to this room. Her former boss said, "I remember your face."

We toured the Bodleian, the world's oldest library: the 1602 room of Bodley and the 1610 extension; Duke Humfrey's library upstairs (the original medieval section completed in 1487, rededicated in 1602); the Divinity room; the Convocation House (a Jacobean replica of Parliament); and then the court room. We returned to the silence of the library: vertical shelving, some chained books. We stood again in the 1602 courtyard near the 1630 statue of the 3rd Earl of Pembroke. We went on to St Mary's church, which had accommodated the University until 1320 and then visited the Sheldonian (which is based on the theatre of Marcellus in Rome).

The next day we saw *Henry IV*, parts 1 and 2 at the National Theatre – I engaged with the usurping King and the rebels in the Eastcheap tavern – and the following day we were back in Oxford at Ricks's invitation to a poetry reading at Balliol. Ricks had said, "I'm host, I introduce everyone and pay for the wine." I sat in the sun outside Lecture Room 23 and Ricks called out, "Hello Nicholas," and came and shook my hand. I could not say that I was impressed by the two poets who read, but it was a pleasant occasion and at the end he said, an excellent host, "Goodbye Nick."

Earlier we had driven round my old haunts at Oxford: 10 Walton Well Road, 57 Southmoor Road, Jericho, the bridge to Port Meadow and the towpath by the Thames.[38] Later I wrote a poem, 'Return to Oxford'.

Shakespeare's trunk

Ten days later I took time off from working on my collected volumes to renew my Stratfordian roots. I delved into Shakespeare's relatives with a view to establishing the trail for his trunk. We drove to Snitterfield and were directed to an old timber-framed, dilapidated barn of a house which had allegedly once belonged to Shakespeare's grandfather, Richard Shakespeare, and where Shakespeare's father John was brought up, although evidence is scanty. I was also shown to a timber-framed house in Bell Lane, near a hollow and sheep, which, it was said, had also belonged to Shakespeare's family. I found Bearley Grange, which was across fields at the back of Mary Arden's Farm in Wilmcote. We went to *Twelfth Night* and stayed the night at Alveston Manor Hotel.

The next morning we went to Northampton Museum and Art Galley to research the Bernards of Abington and Lady Bernard's co-heiresses: Elizabeth (who married Henry Gilbert); Mary (who married Thomas Higgs); and Eleanor (who married Samuel Cotton). I wondered if the contents of Shakespeare's trunk or chest were in a Records Office in Derbyshire, Gloucestershire or Bedfordshire, in which their three husbands resided.

We returned to the Shakespeare Centre, next to the Birthplace, and I chatted to the Head of the International Shakespeare Association, who told me I should ask Kelso to dig up Shakespeare's body in Stratford church, as this had never happened. I visited the church the next day and the helpful churchwarden I had met previously confirmed that no one had ever tried to dig up the grave of Shakespeare or Anne Hathaway, and there had been no use of subground radar.

I looked in at the Falcon and studied the panelling in the coffee-room that (according to *Old Houses of Stratford-upon-Avon*) had come from New Place. It was plain, like the panelling in the Otley Hall Solar. We drove to Tiddington and found the ford in the River Avon where cattle could wade through, where Shakespeare's son Hamnet drowned. I noted the willows.[39]

I left Stratford-upon-Avon with a hunch that on Elizabeth Hall's death Shakespeare's last papers passed to Edward Nash, cousin of Thomas Nash and a Trustee of Lady Bernard's estate, which he sold to Sir Edward Walker (who left them to his son-in-law Sir John Clopton). That was the trail I now had to pursue when I could make time, in response to Edmund Blunden's request.

Charles Beauclerk and Nell Gwyn

Charles's book *Nell Gwyn: A Biography* had just come out. Charles sent me a copy inscribed to "my erstwhile employer and mentor". There was a gathering in the State Apartments at the Royal Hospital Chelsea for his family and immediate circle. When I arrived Charles was standing alone in the middle of a vast room with huge paintings on the walls, and he and I talked while more came. I spoke to John Gouriet, who had persuaded him to stand as MP and initiated the severance of his connection with Otley Hall.

Mark Rylance (wearing a red open-necked shirt when the rest of us were in suits) came and asked, "Did you receive my letter?" He had asked me to be an associate of the SAT, but I was determined to sever all links with questioning the authorship of Shakespeare's works. I told him I did not like the confrontational 'Declaration of Doubt' document. I told him about my visits to Snitterfield and Tiddington. He said he felt the SAT should be a quest for Shakespeare, and not confrontational. I said I had done far more outside the SAT in pursuing this quest than in it. He told me, "You're an independent mind, you are independent." He said, "John Silberrad said that he and you were the only two who kept the SAT alive – couldn't you be an associate?" But I had heard the evidence for the alternatives and found it unpersuasive.

I spoke to Charles's father, the Duke of St Albans, and told him that I was aware there had been a family rift and that I had urged Charles to return to his family. I said I hoped his book on his ancestor Nell Gwyn symbolised that. He nodded but said very little, and grinned.

There were speeches: by the publisher; by John Gouriet, who poked fun like a best man, saying that Charles had been fined for speaking while at Eton and that his career then went into a nosedive and how he leapt on the woolsack; and then Charles himself, who spoke of the love between an orange-seller and the King. He said that Nell's ordinariness brought the people to the monarch, and that she thus represented sovereignty.[40]

Otley Hall top private garden in UK
Otley Hall was in the news. A national poll in *The Independent* had voted Otley Hall, during our tenure, as the top privately-owned garden in the UK. It came sixth of all the UK's gardens, but the five above it were State-owned. It was clearly Steve's work in the grounds under us that achieved this verdict: Ann, lunching at Dickins & Jones in London after shopping, encountered our guide Kay, joined her table and was told, "I'm down to do a garden tour but I'm worried as the garden is awful." She said that parts of the garden that we had created had been dismantled.[41]

Bill Kelso, Gosnold DNA and Shelley church
Just before I sold Otley Hall, Bill Kelso, convinced he had discovered Bartholomew Gosnold's skeleton, had visited me to delve into Gosnold's boyhood. He told me over lunch in the kitchen of Otley Hall that Bartholomew led a rough-and-tumble life. He had a broken nose, two broken ribs, two broken vertebrae, a damaged wrist and a very bad right ankle. We discussed where he lived as a boy, and I drove him to Rouse Hall housing estate (where Rouse Hall stood before it was pulled down); Manor

Farm; Clopton Hall; Grundisburgh Manor, which Bartholomew's father acquired in 1589; and Otley High House, where his father lived until 1589. Benedicta Chamberlain gave us tea and told us about the ghosts her children had seen there. She showed us the Roman road that Bartholomew would have taken to walk to the manorial school at Otley Hall.

Kelso had told me he wanted to dig up Gosnold's sister, who was buried before the altar of Shelley church. He had visited Timothy Easton and Philip Aitken that morning to try to arrange this. I warned him that they were "fabric men rather than document men" who disregarded documents: "It's like saying Bill Kelso never existed because the beams are 2020 rather 1996." That went home: "I was having that discussion in Jamestown." Later I wrote a classical ode, 'In Search of Bartholomew Gosnold's Boyhood Home'.[42]

Bill Kelso came to Shelley, near Hadleigh, in June 2005 to collect DNA from Bartholomew Gosnold's sister and prove that the skeleton in the US was Bartholomew's. I drove to the hamlet down a country lane among poppies and joined the exclusive group of a dozen people inside the medieval church. Kelso greeted me with a friendly smile and pointed to a tombstone before the altar, which his 'experts' had identified as Bartholomew's sister's tomb. "They're going to take the bricks up round the slab, then lift the slab." More than 20 TV cameras homed in on two fellows knocking on bricks with hammers and chisels. Kelso 'introduced' me to the 'expert' Edward Martin (who had dug up Otley Hall's rose-garden lawn).

David Webb approached and interviewed me for Radio 4 for nearly 20 minutes on how I went to America and, in a minority of one, campaigned to have Gosnold given his full due. I then asked Edward how he knew the slab was Gosnold's sister's when there was no writing on it. "There used to be a brass plate, see here. We know she was buried in the church, and by a process of elimination it's this one." "So if the DNA doesn't match, we may have picked on the wrong tomb?" "Yes." There was soon a heap of rubble before the altar of the medieval church, and at that point we were all asked to leave.

I later heard that there was no DNA match and 'the expert' had got the wrong tomb. ('The expert' maintained that it was the right tomb and that the skeleton Kelso found was not Bartholomew's.) Kelso was no nearer to authenticating the skeleton as being Bartholomew Gosnold's.

Family events
Events unfolded within the family. In November 2005 Nadia told me that she had met Ian Gibbons, a keyboard player for the Kinks and other groups, who often played with Ray Davies and lived at Rochford in Essex. She had met his five-year-old son. In January, during a phonecall he made lasting 3 hours 40 minutes, Ian agreed they would be together in the future.

As she was spending a lot of time travelling between Essex and West Dulwich, Nadia agreed that her Dulwich house should be sold. The plan was that Caroline would also sell hers, and they would move within reach of each other. Caroline sold hers first and found a house in Saxmundham, Suffolk. Nadia's sale was slower. I met Ian on my birthday at our local Marriott and found him likeable with short back and sides and a lot of common sense. A few days later Nadia rang me to say she had sold and was looking at buying in Coggeshall, which was an hour from Ian in Rochford and an hour from Caroline in her new house. Ann and I met Nadia in Coggeshall and helped her choose one of the four houses she was shown: the most manageable for her, 62 Stoneham Street with a long garden. She was able to complete on the Coggeshall house in mid-August and exchanged on her Dulwich house a week later. Nadia told me she "just knows" that Ian was going to be with her for a very long time. In December 2005 she told me that his brother-in-law had offered them a house in a small Essex village and, after a visit to Goa, they decided to buy it.

Anthony was selling his Essex flat and leaving his Highgate flat for another Highgate property. He had been casting for his student film and as she had promised Vanessa Redgrave tried to help. She could not act herself but she rang Tony and offered her daughter Joely. Tony had already cast the younger part, and so had to decline. His film school nominated him to be interviewed on the BBC World Service as a British director. On the strength of going out before the world as a British director, he was asked to direct a couple of short films in Birmingham. When in due course he showed his student film, it was graded among the top nine out of 80.

Tony started a film company and made a film, *Half-Term*, in Charlestown. It was chosen from 2,000 films to be shown at the Tirana Film Festival in Albania in December 2005, where Tony saw the screening, which was well received. In January *Half-Term* was shortlisted out of thousands for the Bermuda Film Festival, where he met Michael Douglas, and also for the Festival at Sacramento, where it won 'Best International Film' and he met Arnold Schwarzenegger in his office. It also won first prize at the Rhode Island Film Festival and the 'Best Student Film Award' at the Falmouth Film Festival. In February 2006 Tony made a documentary on Pineapple.

People we knew had fallen ill. Our builder in Cornwall had a heart attack. Our former neighbour in Cornwall, Ken Gowsell, had lung cancer. He had been a ship's captain and thought his cancer was caused by the ships' boilers. He died in a hospice on 4 December 2005. His widow told me when we went down to Cornwall that he was cremated in a wicker basket. David Hoppit, with whom I went to Italy in 1957, had throat cancer and survived. I learned in October that he was in remission, having lost three stone and having a burnt, scarred throat. Our gardener at Great Easton had cancer of the stomach. I sent him a card showing invasive bracken in a garden. He told me that the card was "inspired" and was by his bed for the 15 weeks of his chemotherapy. Some of these conditions were reflected in my stories.

Ben was sometimes left to play with us before and after school to allow Matthew to visit Heads in the three schools, and I often read to him. He loved Beatrix Potter's books, particularly *The Tale of Mr Jeremy Fisher* and *The Tale of Peter Rabbit*. He was learning to cope with bigger boys in the playground, and now and again he would tell me about his worries.

In December he came in one morning and said to me, aged four, having worked it out, "The universe is in infinity, and infinity is in itself." I talked of walking along a road without end: "Infinity is here where we are and is all round us." Ben said: "It's everywhere, all round us." He said it with such conviction and was so right that he seemed to be a philosopher at four.

My brother Jonnie rang me and said he had had lunch with Jacob Rothschild, who "is not completely out of it", and that he would soon be having lunch with Sir Evelyn de Rothschild through Eddie George, former Governor of the Bank of England, who was a director on "our board".[43] (I had heard Eddie George begin a speech at the Grosvenor House Hotel, where I was a guest of my bank again in November 1999: "Hands up who likes bank managers. That's 600 hands – 300 bank managers voting with both hands.")

Connaught House
We had been given planning permission to extend Connaught House. Our builder, Gordon Silvester, had invited us to his 65th birthday party 13 September 2003, which was billed as celebrating 40 years of Silvesters' trading, in a marquee in his field near Takeley. He was joined by many of his clients and their advisers, and after lunch Gordon made a speech, reading from his notes, losing his place and hilariously muttering ad-lib comments. ("What's that word? I can't read this.") An electrician spoke: "I met Gordon when, as a baby, I threw his teddy out of his pram." There was dancing to Ray Davies's 'Sunny Afternoon': 'The taxman's taken all my dough' (his protest against Harold Wilson's mid-1960s reforms). I spoke with the electrician, Gordon's son Andrew and a quantitative surveyor and organised coming building work at Connaught House.[44] To the background music of Ray Davies, with whom Nadia was now connected, I met the builder, electrician and architect who would work on the upgrading and expansion of Connaught House.

Work on Connaught House had progressed since then. There had been numerous meetings between the architect, builder, planner and others, and the extensions at the back (to the kitchen, dining-room and sitting-room) and the addition of my study area over the swimming-pool were sufficiently advanced by the following August 2005 for me to be introducing filing cabinets and other furniture. All the possessions we had brought from Otley Hall had been stored in Great Easton, and these were moved on 1 September 2005. Two Hungarian painters began painting upstairs. My library was now assembled on oak shelves: all four walls filled with my books, and two bookcases in the centre. One of the Hungarian painters spotted Gorka's *Budapest Betrayed*. He said he had read it in Budapest and recalled that it contained a picture of me. (The Hungarian painters were teachers supplementing their income by painting 16 hours a day during the school holidays and sleeping on site in sleeping-bags.) He asked how I thought Gorka had died. I said he might have been murdered for being anti-Russian. He said, "We have a lot of mysterious things like that in Hungary."

During this building work I had come across Pythagoras's *Tetraktys* (1 + 2 + 3 + 4 = 10, = 1 + 0): a triangle with a central point that makes three more triangles, a diagram for how One (the point) becomes Many. I saw Connaught House as the central point between the three schools. Connaught House *was* geographically between the three schools, equidistant from Oaklands and Normanhurst, with Coopersale Hall farther away, and the four triangles were: the outer triangle between the three schools and, within it, the three inner triangles that met at the central point of Connaught House.

A stony paddock between the house and the Forest gate was large enough to replicate Sylvia Landsberg's Otley Hall knot-garden with a herbaceous border along a hedge. Outside chairs and tables and a bust of Apollo arrived from Cornwall, where we had found them. Our cannon on wheels also arrived. (We had bought this in Cornwall some years previously and it had guarded 6 Albion Hill.) The heating was improved. Work continued throughout October, and in November computers were fitted, and a lightning conductor. We slept at Connaught House for the first time on 29 November. There were still workmen on the top floor throughout December, and we moved in properly on 23 December 2005. We held the Christmas gathering for our family there. We could accommodate 30 for lunch in different rooms, and the family gathering took place at Connaught House for the next eight years. At the end of December I was sorting the library and the upper archives room. The work inside the house was substantially done.

Matthew Hagger speaking at Normanhurst School's Founders Day

Converting a dilapidated brick stable into an annexe would take until April 2006.[45]

As I had planned, I had pulled away from the schools and had placed them in the care of Matthew while I began a new bout of writing. Like Tennyson's Ulysses I had left my kingdom in the hands of my son Telemachus and was sailing "beyond the sunset, and the baths/Of all the Western stars", "to strive, to seek, to find, and not to yield".

John Silberrad and Sisyphus

Silberrad had a view on my collected literature. In April 2005 I rang him to check the boundaries of Churchill's constituency. He said that during the war it covered Chigwell Urban District Council, Chingford, Waltham Abbey, Epping and Harlow. In 1945 this was split into Woodford division and Epping division. In 1952, Woodford and Wanstead became separate, and Chigwell UDC and Ongar went to Biggs-Davison. In 1971 Chigwell split from Epping, which went to Tebbit. We discussed the bombing of Churchill's constituency, especially Loughton as stocks of coal at the new station were a target. Lord Haw-Haw, he said, announced that Loughton would be bombed, and in autumn 1940 several were killed near Loughton station.

Shortly afterwards I met him in the cut-through between Brook Road and Loughton High Road. He asked me about my writing and I told him about the books I had to get ready: my collected literature. He said: "You'll never finish your work. You'll be like Sisyphus who rolled his boulder up to the top of the hill – and was fated to have it fall down again and go back to the beginning."

Silberrad's words rang in my ears. In one sense he was right: each new work was a boulder that started at the bottom of the hill. In another sense he was wrong. My boulders did not roll back down the hill. I would continue to deliver each boulder to the top of the hill and then go down to start pushing my next boulder. Over time they would form a cairn, a landmark, like the Bedouins' heap of stones. Later I put a couple of framed pictures on my study wall of Sisyphus pushing a large boulder up a hill.

Death of Silberrad

Those were the last words Silberrad spoke to me: his comparison of me to Sisyphus. I did not see him in the summer. In September Ann read in the local paper that he had died. I found out that he had been in hospital for two weeks with a mild heart attack. He was transferred to St Bartholomew's Hospital and died there on 9 September, aged 77.

Silberrad's funeral took place at St John's church, Loughton on 26 September 2005. Mark Rylance rang and asked if I would represent the SAT even though I had severed my links. The church was packed: Silberrad had been a churchwarden there for many years. He had prepared the service, including the address, which told how he was a member of the Cambridge Footlights; hence his interest in drama. I shared a service sheet with the Chairman of Trustees of Copped Hall (later President), Denys Favre, who was at the end of my pew. Near the end of the service a ladybird landed on our sheet and dropped on the pew as we stood. Favre carded it onto the floor, where it crawled to the centre of the aisle. The coffin was being hoisted unto the pallbearers' shoulders. I nudged Favre and pointed. Favre, who was well over 90, scuttled out into the aisle, crouched, made swiping movements with the service sheet and saved the ladybird from being crushed under the pallbearers' feet – and was nearly himself run down in the process. Later I wrote a short story, 'A Coffin and a Ladybird'.

It was brought to my attention that the green walk down to the Ching alongside Connaught House belonged to an old medieval meadow of 200 old plants, which may have included our new garden. Henry VIII may have processed down it to hunt from Queen Elizabeth's hunting lodge while staying at his palace at King's Place in Buckhurst Hill. I discovered that the site of Henry VIII's palace in King's Place had formed part of Silberrad's father's garden.[46]

Paul Doherty and Faustian striving

Our guest speaker for 2005 at the Normanhurst Founders Day was Paul Doherty, the Head of Trinity, Woodford and the author of (then) 80 books (later 100), mostly historical fiction set in ancient Egypt and the Middle Ages. He was a priest and a classicist, and he told me as I greeted him and chatted, "I love telling stories." Swarthy, slightly stout and short with grey hair, he cut an impressive figure on the platform. Not speaking from notes, he told a story, spoke of Aristotle and urged our pupils to do their best. His punchline was, "You must keep striving, you may not make it but you must keep striving." I completely agreed with his Faustian message, which reflected my editing in my collected literature.[47]

Christopher Ricks and plagiarism

Ann and I attended Ricks's next Professor of Poetry lecture, which took place in the Examination Schools' East School on 21 November 2005. I had written asking him to source a quotation from Eliot, and he appeared at my elbow, shook me by the hand and said: "I've answered your letter. The quotation is from the conclusion of *The Use of Poetry and the Use of Criticism*." I had not yet received the letter.

His subject was Geoffrey Hill, a fellow expatriate in Boston. He dwelt on how Hill had ransacked Eliot's work for words such as 'haruspicate', which he then used in his own work. I reminded him at the end that Eliot was accused of plagiarism by quoting others in 'The Waste Land', and now Hill was doing the same: plagiarism had reached a second generation. He said, "I haven't an issue with plagiarism, have you?" And then, "I haven't given plagiarism a thought, I'll think about it." Neoclassical critics approve of such copying. I later wrote to him saying that in my view a poet should reflect the universe in his own words, not in the words of his predecessors. I was stating a Universalist point of view which included the Romantic perspective along with the Neoclassical.

David Cameron

Ann felt that I should attend a debate between the two contenders for the Conservative leadership, David Cameron and David Davis, in Methodist Central Hall, Westminster. We had tea in the London Marriott County Hall hotel, the ex-headquarters of my former employers the Inner London Education Authority, which had been abolished under Thatcher. It was now a hotel with a library restaurant, and we sat among busts of Milton, Shakespeare, Agrippa and Plato. Then we walked across the river to the Hall, showed our passports and the secret number we had been sent, and sat three or four rows back. Davis and Cameron made statements, answered questions and then summed up. I was struck by how clear Davis was. There were cries from the audience at Cameron, "Stick to the point," "Don't waffle". Cameron, of course, was chosen. I wrote a poem for *Collected Poems*, 'Hustings: Raw'.[48]

Secret history: towards The Secret Founding of America
Harry Beckhough, Montgomery and Ultra

I had long wanted to delve into the secret history of El Alamein. Did Montgomery win the battle on his own merit or was he following instructions from Bletchley Park? I had written to Montgomery to ask him a couple of weeks before he died.

I had been written to by Harry Beckhough, who had worked with Montgomery during the war and described himself as "the ancient warrior". He told me in his letter he had conveyed Ultra transcripts to Montgomery before El Alamein. He had heard about me from Duncan Smith and wanted me to speak at a symposium in Marlborough. Having made Montgomery the hero of *The Warlords* I was keen to talk with him. (In another letter he told me that the Conservatives had received EU money to be more pro-European after the fall of Duncan Smith, as I had suspected.)

Ann and I checked in at the Castle and Ball, Marlborough, and met Harry, a smallish man with a moustache who hailed from Harrogate and had moved to Marlborough eight years previously to be near his daughter. We talked from 5.45 to 7.15 at a downstairs table, where food was also served. He told me he had been a code-breaker at Bletchley Park and was one of two out of more than 20 selected to work with Montgomery in Egypt. His job was to hand him information from Ultra. He approached Montgomery and tried to give him a message, which was printed on edible rice paper. Montgomery said, "No, you must give it to my Liaison Officer." Thereafter Harry gave the Ultra information, written on rice-paper so it could be chewed and swallowed as it was so secret, to Montgomery's assistant. Montgomery could then look at the rice-paper in private and in public claim his decisions were based on his own judgement. He made speeches to the troops saying, "I can read Rommel's mind," and claimed that his strategy at El Alamein came from his own assessment even though it was based on Enigma intercepts. I had tried to visit Montgomery on this very point, and now I had an answer that was more truthful than the answer Montgomery would have given me had I seen him.

Having been anti-German during the war, Harry was convinced that Germany, rather than the American-European network I had revealed, was running the world today. On 6 October 2010 at the Conservative Party Conference David Cameron called for a standing ovation for Harry Beckhough, then 96, and, believing they were honouring his great age, the audience duly stood and applauded. I suspect that the applause was a secret recognition of his wartime service in supplying Montgomery with crucial information.

The next morning I held my seminar in St Mary's church hall, Marlborough. Trestle-tables had been arranged in a square. Harry introduced me and chaired the meeting, mentally agile despite his years. I spoke for 40 minutes and then took part in a discussion for another two hours. The 30 or so present had all been involved in intelligence in some way, Harry told me. They were very well-informed, and we had a high level of analysis. Several of the ex-intelligence men asked if I would be their leader. I said: "I'm just putting the information out. I'm not trying to overthrow the Government. If we were now in Russia in Dostoevsky's time, the Tsarist police would burst in and arrest us." Robert Francis, Harry's assistant, said helpfully: "The group is not seditious and Nicholas is not trying to be a leader." We had lunch at the Bear, where there was an afternoon session on the managerial organisation, Common Purpose.

I received a letter from Harry: "Your visit was an outstanding success. Almost all had been well briefed in advance, so you were addressing an already convinced audience. But they especially enjoyed your informal manner... and frank, natural presentation. They expected a kind of lecture from the voice of authority, but instead had the pleasure of listening to the experiences of a fellow-seeker.... So once again, many thanks and well done – you certainly had an intelligent, captivated audience."[49]

Lindsay Jenkins and Germany

The following February Ann and I returned to Marlborough on our way to Cornwall, to hear Lindsay Jenkins's eurosceptical view of the EU and its secret history. I was greeted warmly by Robert Francis, who told me the fifth man was definitely Victor, Lord Rothschild. He said that another speaker had dropped out because of the strength of my research in *The Syndicate*, which had made him lose confidence in seeing Germany as running the world. Jenkins, when I asked her, told me that Germany was behind the Treaty of Rome, and she was surprised when I contradicted her and said it was the Syndicate. I noted: "Lindsay Jenkins has not understood her own research. She has facts but she has missed the pattern: the Syndicate thesis."[50]

Hernia operation

At the end of October I began to feel pain in the region of my stomach, and I found a lump in my upper groin. My doctor's surgery diagnosed a hernia, and I was referred to Mr Machesney at Holly House. He examined me and said I had *two* hernias, one umbilical and one abdominal. Further tests established that there might be three hernias. I had a colonoscopy at the Roding Hospital. I remember turning sideways to look at a screen, and then hearing a nurse saying in recovery, "Nicholas, wake up, you've had your colonoscopy." I had been given an amnesia drug which wiped my recollection. Machesney then appeared and told, "You have diverticular disease and need to be on a high-fibre diet." He said there was no trace of cancer.

I had my operation a few days later. The anaesthetist injected the back of my left hand. It felt "like three bee stings and went on for two minutes". He said, "You'll be out in a minute." I said, "It's reached my neck." I felt a wave of numbness, and that was the last I knew until I woke up in the recovery room. A nurse said, "You had three hernias done." I was wheeled out and up in the lift and encountered Ann in the corridor.

Later that night I was told to walk down the corridor to avoid thrombosis. In my gown, which was tied at the back of my neck, and stockings, I saw 'Andrew Boggis' on a door which was ajar, and put my head round and greeted the Head of Forest School ("Good evening Mr Boggis"). He told me he was in with gallstones. He was sitting in bed in his gown working on papers, and told me he was writing a speech.

In January 2006 he made the speech, as Chairman to the Headmasters' and the Headmistresses' Conference, defending independent education against Government interference. The national newspapers had headlines quoting him as urging: "Mr Blair, kindly get your tanks off our quadrangles."[51]

The next morning the surgeon visited me. I had had a laproscopic hernia repair through my belly button. He repaired two hernias on either side of the abdomen, put in two 10 x 15 cm gauzes, sewed up the umbilical rupture with stitches and repaired a third hernia near my belly button on the way out. I saw him four days later and he told me: "I blew you up like a balloon." "And inserted the gauzes rolled up so they sprang open inside directed by camera?" "Exactly that." He told me that the sedative I had had for my colonoscopy was Midazolam, which has the effect of amnesia. "Is it like a date rape drug?" "Yes."[52]

The Secret Founding of America *and steroids for insect bite*
I had now plunged into *The Secret Founding of America*. When Michael Mann met me at the Cavendish on 27 April 2005, he had shared with me an idea for a book that he had had for many years. He said it should be called *The Secret Founding of America* and would cover how Freemasonry affected the Founding Fathers. He said he would like to entrust the idea to me because of my knowledge of the founding of America in 1607, and that either Watkins (with whom he was now associated) or John Hunt would publish it.

Michael approached John, and there was an exchange of emails to arrive at a synopsis. With his usual sharpness, John advised me to start with the received story of the founding of America and then proceed to who really founded the US. I said that Gosnold was the planting father of rural Elizabethan values, which John Smith blended with his Freemasonry, which passed to the Founding Fathers. Michael saw the emails and now wanted Watkins to publish the book, and John graciously took a step back as the book had been Michael's idea. Michael presented my synopsis to a publishers meeting. I had a contract in mid-August to complete the book by July 2006, for publication in April 2007. Because I was working simultaneously on four other books (*Collected Poems*, *The Rise and Fall of Civilizations*, *The Light of Civilization* and *Collected Verse Plays*) I could not think about *The Secret Founding of America* until the end of the year. In December 2005 I "got the story straight and worked out the chapters". I worked out that I needed to do 5,000 words a week to complete the book in 16 weeks, four months, by the end of April, leaving two months for revision. By early January I had established myself in Connaught House and was ready to begin in February 2006.[53]

In *The Secret Founding of America*, another secret history, I narrated the founding of the US at Jamestown in 1607. I wrote that America is widely thought to have been founded by English Separatists, English Anglicans and Spanish Catholics, but that it was really founded by Freemasons in Virginia and Massachusetts who were followed by Enlightenment Deists and the German Illuminati. As a result America became a Freemasonic State under George Washington; the geography and architecture of Washington DC are Freemasonic, the Freemasons battled for America, and America is substantially a Freemasonic State today. I worked every day on the text for two and a half months and finished my initial work on the book on 20 April 2006.

Down in Cornwall I noticed a red rose on the inside of my left shin, which itched. When I returned to Essex I visited my doctor's surgery and was referred to a vascular consultant on 27 April. He called in a skin specialist, Dr Bewley, who immediately said I had Lyme disease, which is caused by a tick bite. It is a bacterial disease borne by a deer tick that lives near forests, and within a month comes out in a 'bull's eye' rash, which is what I had. My leg had a bull's eye, its pupil in the centre. My consultant said that if it was ignored all my organs would shut down and death would follow within two years.

The disease was not known until 1975, and surfaced in Connecticut. Ironically, while writing *The Secret Founding of America* I had apparently acquired an American disease. Doubly ironically, Ann went for walks in Epping Forest with a walking group and often brushed against bracken that might hold deer ticks, and I who just sat in my study writing on America had the disease and she did not. Whether the strain of thinking about ten books simultaneously had lowered my resistance and left my immune system open to it, or whether I would have contracted it anyway even if I were thinking about no books, I did not know.

I had had a blood test for Lyme disease at my doctor's surgery, and my doctor told me it was negative. "I don't think you've got Lyme disease. You've had a broken vein." So I went back to the consultant and had a skin biopsy, which involved a local anaesthetic and stitches. Assuming I had been bitten by an insect, the insect had injected its poison which was circulating in my blood, and I would have to take steroids to counteract it. My consultant said that in addition to my antibiotic (Doxycycline) I must be on a steroid, Prednisolone.[54] Though my biopsy result would not be back for a while I was immediately placed on five tablets each morning for the next week, then four, then three, then two, then one, reducing. He said the tablets would "get everything", that nothing would survive them, and that a future blood test would show my blood was all clear.

The medication made concentration extremely difficult. Making a simple journey to the local shops which would normally be instinctive had to be approached as a military operation and split into stages as I could not see the way to my destination in my mind. I was having to write with this handicap, and it required all my powers of concentration to get my work done. I suffered from aphasia: I forgot words. I was washed through with feelings. I forgot appointments. My head was clouded with tablets.

Eventually I had a message from the consultant's secretary: "The biopsy showed a profound reaction to an insect bite – insect unknown." I reflected that Lord Carnarvon died of an insect bite after the discovery of Tutankhamen's tomb. I might not have had Lyme disease after all. But the experience echoed one of the last lines in 'Epitaphs' in *Collected Poems*: "Listen beneath the breeze and tick of time...."

I got the book away to Watkins on 18 May. Throughout June and July there was a flow of questions and recommendations from an editor, requiring minor amendments. I was told that the cover would be a Freemasonic staircase, but I insisted that as the founding took place in the 17th century it should show a ship, suggesting the voyage to Jamestown or the *Mayflower*. My idea prevailed. I was told that I should rewrite chapter 9 as Duncan Baird, the owner of Watkins, was nervous about some of the things I had said involving the New World Order. Baird's PA rang me on 18 October 2006 to say that he would ring me in five minutes: "Your book is so high-profile in America we've got to get the last chapter right." I was on the phone for three hours ten minutes (6–9.10 p.m.). He went through the chapter line by line and we made a few small changes to ensure a neutral tone. He, rightly, said that the last chapter should not differ in tone from the rest of the book, and the differences in tone he had spotted required changing a word here and there. I complied up to a point. I corrected proofs in Cornwall at the end of October.

In late November Duncan Baird invited me to lunch at the Camerino (now Chettinad) in Percy Street. Duncan was a pleasant, precise, balding fellow with small spectacles who was already sitting at a table. He told me had been a Reader at All Souls before working for OUP. He talked fluently and precisely, and we got on to the book towards the end of the first course. He took three pages of detailed notes on A4 to take to his sales team in the US the following week. Apart from a session on captions for the illustrations, the book was now finished. I received my first copy in March 2007.[55]

Collected literature: **Collected Verse Plays,** *one-volume* **Overlord, Collected Stories**
Collected Verse Plays
In November 2005 Michael Mann had said that he was establishing a date for *Collected Verse Plays*, and that I should begin work. In mid-January I combed through *The Tragedy of Prince Tudor*, changing the names of some of the characters to the more recognisable names (such as Rockefeller and Rothschild) that my made-up names had masked. I also wrote a Preface to *Collected Verse Plays*. I then turned to *The Warlords* and made some changes. I assembled all my Prefaces of my individual verse plays.

In January 2006 I had put the finishing touches to three books (*Collected*

Poems, The Rise and Fall of Civilizations and *The Light of Civilization*) as well as working on *Collected Verse Plays* and *The Secret Founding of America*. I could only maintain such an intensive work programme by having two people working for me, one at her home some evenings and one at my home during the mornings. In early January my evening secretary told me she would have to discontinue working for me later in the year. Her husband's franchise in Prontaprint would not be renewed in September, and the business might then close. His health had been poor, and they would retire to the south coast. In a few months' time I would have to have a new secretarial arrangement based on Connaught House that would replace both these secretaries.

Collected Verse Plays collected *The Warlords*, parts 1 and 2, *The Tragedy of Prince Tudor, Ovid Banished* and *The Rise of Oliver Cromwell* in one volume. I had revived verse drama, which had declined c.1640, and all my verse plays could now be seen to deal with the tyrannical impact of imperialist states: the impact on Montgomery, who the New World Order marginalised; on Prince Tudor's struggle to preserve the culture and identity of his kingdom against the New World Order and Europe; on Ovid, banished for life by Augustus; and on Charles I, beheaded, following a financial deal between Cromwell and the Jews of Amsterdam that led to the return of Jews to England. In early April I included *Ovid Banished* and *The Rise of Oliver Cromwell*, and I finished my initial work on the book on 27 April 2006. I proof-read the book at the end of October. I was reading further proofs in January and February 2007. I received the first copy at the end of April 2007.[56]

Working on ten books simultaneously
In March 2006 John Hunt sent me an email saying he wanted to bring out my five literary books in two-monthly intervals between May 2006 and January 2007 in the following order: *Classical Odes; Collected Poems; Overlord; Collected Verse Plays;* and *Collected Short Stories*. He would later change the order of *Collected Verse Plays* and *Overlord*, but, with *The Light of Civilization* in and *The Secret Founding of America* and *The Rise and Fall of Civilizations* still being worked on, I was working on eight books in the present round almost simultaneously.[57] Thinking about all these at the same time, and seeing through *The Syndicate* and *The Secret History of the West* brought the tally I was working on simultaneously up to ten while supervising the building work at Connaught House and being a figurehead at the three schools. I had been overworking and had jeopardised my health.

I had generated my classical odes afresh, but *Overlord* and *Collected Poems* had been saved on floppy discs which had been superseded by CDs. An ex-Zimbabwean soldier and computer troubleshooter and wizard, Rob

Learmonth, salvaged my earlier work using antiquated equipment, and presented me with up-to-date CDs. On some pages he had lost line breaks, and the entire books had to be proof-read. There was extra work to be done involving Prefaces and Appendices.

One-volume Overlord

The one-volume edition of *Overlord* was straightforward. Rob gave me a CD in early May. I assembled the one-volume *Overlord* during May and sent it to the publisher on 5 June 2006. Proofs arrived at the beginning of August and I finished proof-reading on 15 August.

My first poetic epic of 41,000 lines of blank verse (the first major English-language poetic epic in the tradition of Homer's *Iliad* and Virgil's *Aeneid* since Milton's *Paradise Lost*) follows Eisenhower's pursuit of Hitler from D-Day to the Fall of Berlin (our Troy) and narrates the battles and suffering – and the hidden conflicts between Stalin, Roosevelt and Churchill; Eisenhower and Montgomery; and Hitler and his generals.[58]

Connaught House grounds, sale of The Bell

At Connaught House, where I was now preparing my collected literature, the improvements had been in the annexe and the grounds. The brick base for the knot-garden was completed, and in February the staircase to the new floor in the annexe was finished. Electronic gates were installed, along with new pumps for the fountain and pond. The grounds were turfed and security lights installed. In April 2006 I noted, "We have doubled the size of Connaught House." The statues I had brought from Otley Hall were cemented in: two on either side of the knot-garden, the rest in the grounds. Some 200 fish arrived from a lake that was being drained elsewhere. There were several *koi* carp and a golden orfe. Alongside the bust of Apollo that had been placed at the foot of the spiral staircase to my study I fixed plaques bearing two Latin inscriptions: "*Initium est dimidium facti*", "To begin is the hardest thing" (a Latin proverb); and "*Quem fors dierum cumque dabit lucro appone*", "Take as a gift whatever the day brings forth" or "Count the present as one of life's treasures" (from Horace *Odes* 1.9). Rabbits invaded the garden and ate plants, so we fixed discreet rabbit-netting to keep them out. A heron speared one of our *koi* and we installed netting to safeguard the fish. Many varieties of birds flocked to our bird feeders, including goldfinches.

Connaught House had turned into a Paradise, and we visited Great Easton less often. The proposed second runway at Stansted airport would be within view at the back, and the new perimeter fence might be sited across the water-splash further down our road. We put The Bell on the market once we had moved our Otley Hall furniture to Connaught House.

I cleared The Bell in early January 2007 and we exchanged contracts in mid-February, and completed a week later.[59]

Schools

The schools flourished. In January 2006 our Head at Coopersale Hall gave two terms' notice as her husband had been found to have Parkinson's disease and she decided to look after him full-time. At Prize Day in July she tearfully bowed out in the marquee a second time, sitting next to her successor.

An Oaklands teacher Ros Ingram was found to have cancer in her lymph nodes, breast, pelvis and femur. She visited us during her nine weeks of chemotherapy. In October 2007 there was a message that Ros was going into a hospice. The next morning her husband rang and said she had just died. The funeral was arranged for a day we were away. Ann was to give the address, so she wrote it and Matthew delivered it on her behalf. In the same month, October, there was an Oaklands inspection which reported the school as being outstanding, in particular the management; a tribute to Matthew.

There were sporadic events at Chigwell School. At the Old Chigwellians' Shrove Tuesday supper I talked with Col. Bob Stewart MP, who immediately placed me: "You have schools." I attended an Archbishop Harsnett symposium at Chigwell School, which involved lectures on the founder of Chigwell School. We crossed Roding Lane to go to the church and Lord Sugar swept by in his chauffeur-driven blue limousine as the bell-ringers rang a carillon of six bells in our honour. A couple of weeks later Donald Thompson's memorial service took place at Chigwell School. One of the speakers was my contemporary David Senton, who spoke of Thompson's sense of humour. Thompson had asked him to disguise himself as an Indian potentate and open a school fête. He was greeted on arrival by Thompson and distributed shillings to the boys as he walked about. It gave Thompson great satisfaction that no one saw through the deception. I also spoke to Colin Wilcoxon, the Cambridge Chaucer don.

Loredana Morrison interviewed me for the Old Chigwellians' *Mitre* magazine, and there was a page about me in the next issue under the heading 'Distinguished Contemporary Thinker'.[60]

Ricks's lectures

In 2006 I attended three Professor-of-Poetry lectures by Christopher Ricks, who had been an early witness of my collected poetic works.

In February Ann and I had made our way to Examination Schools' East School and encountered Ricks alone in the hall. "Good, you can check the sound for me, I was about to run down and hear my own voice." When he had sorted out the sound system I ran a punctuation question by him: "The title of a poem has single inverted commas round it, but Americans put double. I'm a stickler for accuracy, it's like using someone else's toothbrush if you get inverted commas wrong. What do you do in the US?" He grimaced "Urghh" when I mentioned the toothbrush and gave a huge shudder. He then said, "But double inverted commas are better when there's an apostrophe. For example Dylan's 'The times they are a-changin'", the single at the end looks like double. A-changin' single and then double is better." In these two volumes I have stuck with single and English tradition.

Much of his lecture was again on Geoffrey Hill. In the course of it he said that Eliot looks to Tennyson, and (as in Neoclassical criticism) every poet looks back to a previous poet. At the end I joined him at the front and after he had shaken my hand and thanked me for "coming from so far" I said to him, "I'm thinking of Tuohy, who told me *not* to be influenced by Eliot to allow my own voice to come through." He said, "And that's what you've done, Eliot doesn't like narrative. You've gone back to Tennyson." "'Morte d'Arthur'," I said. He said, "Yes." I came away convinced that a poet should not be rearranging the words of Yeats or another dead poet "to make a copied or cribbed poem that has nothing to do with direct experience – it's pallid academicism". I felt, "A poet should look at the universe and respond, as Tennyson did." I took a dim view of poets plagiarising other poems and did not want them to be reworking poems within the literary tradition. Yet on the way home I thought "my *Idylls of the King* is *Overlord;*... my Tennysonian *Collected Poems* is my *Collected Poems;*... my *Gates of Hell* [is] like *In Memoriam*", and that perhaps Ricks was right: I look back to Tennyson. (Perhaps I was merely quarrelling with myself.)

In May Ann and I again sat in the East School and Ricks appeared from the back in a dark suit and white shirt. Again there was interference from the sound system, and this time he ditched the microphone and gave a lecture on how Lowell was the American heir to Eliot and Pound, but more Pound, and how both related to Dante. All were expatriates. He said, "Intellectuals argue without quarrelling."

He spoke of the "arguing" between Eliot and Pound in endnotes. He mentioned that Eliot's *After Strange Gods* in the 1930s was taken up by Pound in his radio broadcast against Jews, and said that Eliot's "familiar compound ghost" was Pound ('com-Pound'). It now seemed so obvious, but no one had said it before. He found a reference to the *Book of Ezra* ("to beautify the house of the Lord"). He described how Lowell wrote to Pound on 2 May 1936, asking to work under him and saying he was a relative of Amy Lowell. He said Lowell's Brunetto looked to Pound as his guide. He said Pound's withdrawal into silence was from guilt at the harm he had done, which at the time he had taken for virtue. He said that Pound was set to raise money under a 'Bel Esprit' scheme to get Eliot out of his bank so that he could write poetry, but that Eliot did not want to leave the bank. Pound was furious at Eliot's 'defection' to Milton, and he wrote in the *Sewanee Review* after Eliot died that Eliot's was "the true Dantescan voice". (In 1918 Eliot had praised Pound for being Dantesque.) Both were plagued by remorse. Pound wrote, "I should have listened to Possum." Eliot's remorse was for having written *After Strange Gods*.

At the end of his stunning lecture Ricks played a 1964 recording of Pound reading Lowell's 'Brunetto' canto – "about son, guide, lost path, journey home and friend". This recording had been sent to Lowell by Olga Rudge (who I met). Reading Lowell's poem Pound accepted his role as Lowell's guide – and I thought of how "he [, Pound,] acted as my guide: 'If you can see it, then you've already done it. Seeing it's half the battle.'" I saw that Pound's "encouragement of me from a remorseful silence at the harm he had done" was encouragement from a guide who had come to doubt – indeed, disbelieve – himself. I was opened up. Ricks said, "I find that very moving," and ended.

There was long and deafening applause while Ricks said "Thank you" many times and held up a hand. I stumbled to the front and thanked him and said I would be reflecting on that reading of Pound's for the next three months. "Thank you for coming." It was not the time to talk or socialise. Under the influence of the steroids I was taking for my insect bite I was opened up and was wet-eyed from inside Schools back to the car park by Worcester College. I had felt Pound's predicament intensely, and had mixed Ricks's lecture about Pound with my own memories of meeting him.

I wrote:

I was lost in a wood and was turned round by a guide like Lowell and Eliot encountering the 'familiar compound ghost' (Pound) – for all of us the guide was Pound. And he was in agony at the harm he did which resulted in the death sentence for treason, his 'insanity' (in an insane asylum) and his silence. And he was Eliot's guide, [like] Virgil in Dante. And I thought of my guides: Colin Wilson, who got me started as a writer; Donald Thompson and Horton, who had [already] introduced me to Homer, Virgil, Horace and the [other] Roman poets; Ricks who came in on p.2 of my *Collected Poems* and taught me to appreciate poetry…; Fitzsimmons, briefly, was my Brunetto…; Tomlin in philosophy; Tuohy in prose; Pound, [who] got me to start my epic, encouraged me. I outgrew most of them, but Ricks had read more than I had, for example, Lowell's letters, and transmitted the American end of culture without writing a word [of poetry] – he was still my guide, more than anyone. And the guides had failed in different ways…. Pound, who guided me to my epic, had been anti-Jew, but I had turned his atmosphere around by writing about Auschwitz.

Then I thought

> how I had an argument with Ricks, always have. He had taught me social satire and I had written 'Zeus's Ass', but I had stuck to being a mystic. At my first meeting with him I said, "I prefer mystical poetry, Wordsworth and the One." Tuohy had enjoined, 'Find your voice, there should be no resonance of Eliot.'… In Ricks's view, everyone is out of someone…, and if you echo someone – crib from someone – you get in the team…. He guards the Tree of Tradition, and poets feed off mulberry leaves, spin their cocoons hanging onto the leaves – which he, as the new Q [, Quiller-Couch], guards.

I was aware that there was

> an argument between poet and critic. This poet acknowledges that the critic has read more interestingly and incisively than any other critic he has encountered and in a way more relevant to his work, and looks on him as a guide out of the dark wood into Light (Pound's statement as to what the true terrain of poetry is [, *see My Double Life 1, This Dark Wood*, p.vi]). But at the same time he demands the right to experience life and Nature at first hand, as Wordsworth did, and not through a maze of references to dead poets…. You can continue their tradition without academic references. The Neoclassical and the Baroque, the difference. Direct contact with life as opposed to words that conjure dead masters who they're cribbing.

There was Raphael and the School of Raphael – Eliot and the School of Eliot. It was better to be a Raphael than an imitator in an academic school. It was better to be, like Wordsworth, a man speaking to men. Hill and Lowell were

> like painters of Raphael's School who paint with Raphael's style and not their own. They sit in solitude and refer to dead writers in their crossword activities, and do not make fresh contact with life.

Ricks had

> delivered an earthquake of a lecture which touched the fundamental conception of myself and my guides, past and present, and the direction of my poetry, which I assert is right for me. He mentioned Kathleen Raine, his elder and better by more than 20 years, as saying that Lowell is Eliot's heir.

I wrote on 5 June 2006 to thank Ricks for his stunning lecture, and took up with him the "cribbing" tradition that substituted references to other poems in place of direct poetic experience.

In November Ann and I again went to the East School and after microphone testing Ricks sat in the chair in front of me and shook my hand: "You've got all your hair and you look well." I said, "I haven't worked as hard as you have." "But you have, what you've done is very impressive, a great tribute to your energy." I asked him, of Empson's 1942 'Sonnet', "Who are 'the loony hooters'? Chinese? British? Churchill and the war leaders?" "I don't know." "And do they jeer or make hooting noises?" "Both, I should think. I'll send you Haffenden's notes on the poem. He knows more about it than anyone else. Have you seen his edition of Empson? I'll send you a photocopy. I'll put it in my diary. If I write 'Loony Hooters to NH' you won't get alarmed." I watched as he wrote me in his diary as 'NH'.

His lecture was on Eliot's view (in one long paragraph) of Othello, demonstrating that, as Eliot argued, Othello self-dramatises. Ricks spoke of "thinking well of oneself" and I noted: "Behind Ricks's criticism is a human trait, which his criticism illustrates."[61]

Stories for In the Brilliant Autumn Sunshine
I was still finishing my fifth volume of short stories, *In the Brilliant Autumn Sunshine*.

Ann took me to the bittern hide in Fishers Green. We did not see any bitterns, but there were golden eye, pochards, great-crested grebe, flocks of lapwings and siskins. I wrote a short story, 'A Study like a Bittern-Hide'.

In March we booked in at the Housel Bay Hotel at the Lizard, Cornwall, above a lighthouse with a revolving light that sent a beam into our window and above stormy petrels. The next day we picked Ann's 80-year-old aunt up from Porthleven "to stay with us for a night", drove to Kynance Cove and then to Pendeen to see the lighthouse and coastguard's cottage nearby where she had lived, Geevor mine and then Cape Cornwall, Sennen Cove and Land's End. We returned with her to our hotel and without her seeing, keeping it secret, I put her suitcase in her room. We took her upstairs to have a better view and surprised her: "That's my case." Ann's Cornish family gathered for dinner downstairs to celebrate her 80th birthday. I wrote a story, 'A Lighthouse and a Surprise'.

In Charlestown I was visited by Valerie Jacob, who had been A.L. Rowse's housekeeper on the Trenarren headland from 1996 to 1997 (when he was 93). She talked for an hour over coffee about his home life. She confirmed Rowse used to get his hair cut in Charlestown. I wrote a short story, 'A Bed Surrounded by Papers'.

For my birthday Ann gave me a framed, elaborately decorated letter 'N' which she had worked on in her calligraphy class. It had been done while it seemed that I had Lyme disease, and the endurance of the gold letter against the decorative transient foliage I found very beautiful. It stands in an alcove in my study. On the same day, to celebrate my birthday, my immediate family took me to a champagne reception in a marquee at Garnish Hall, which David Cameron attended. I was by the entrance when Eleanor Laing brought Cameron in, spotted me and introduced him to me first. Eleanor said, "Nick Hagger has three schools and does lots of interesting things." She did not mention my books. He said, "Really?" and looked around the marquee as I chatted. I noticed he did the same with all those he met. They did not engage his full attention because he was glancing around to see who was nearby and elsewhere. But to give him his due, he later came to my table and stood beside me for a photo-graph. (There were 200 Oak-Tree-Schools promotional leaflets bearing the three schools' oak-tree logo on a table for people to help themselves that day, 22 May 2006. Our beautiful oak-tree logo, which had graced Oak-Tree Books before passing to the schools, was almost immediately adopted by the Conservative Party. Central office announced to the press on 10 August 2006 that an oak-tree would be their new logo, and their oak-tree only later became squiggly.)

Nicholas and David Cameron MP with Ann on 22 May 2006

I spoke with James Brokenshire, my mother's violin pupil, who would be Minister for Immigration and Security in Cameron's Coalition Government. (His first speech controversially condemned the metropolitan *élite* for employing "migrants", as distinct from illegal immigrants, and several ministers had to defend their own employment of non-British domestic staff.) After Cameron left there was an auction and then a speech by Eleanor Laing who, faced with widespread pent-up chattering after the auction, called her constituents to order and when they were slow to respond memorably shouted, "Shut up." (In 2013 she became Deputy Speaker and regularly kept order by shouting at MPs, "Order, order.") I wrote a story, 'A Shrill "Shut Up" and Shambles'.

In July, Ann and I received an invitation to a garden party at Buckingham Palace. We spent a summer afternoon strolling in the grounds among 8,500 guests and having tea and cakes. At 4 the Queen and Duke of Edinburgh emerged. We waited near the Royal Tea Tent for the Queen to pass. She was surrounded by men carrying furled umbrellas. I wrote a story, 'An Awesome Queen and Umbrella-ed Flunkeys'.

In August on the way home from Cornwall we visited Dartmoor. From Tavistock we drove to Merrivale Prehistoric Settlement, on which I wrote a short story, 'Stone Rows and the One'. We drove to Princetown and on to

Two Bridges Hotel, which stands in a dell amid hills. The next day we drove via Dartmeet to Widecombe village and then on to Buckland Abbey, home of Sir Richard Grenville and later Sir Francis Drake, who spent his last 15 years there. I stood in Drake's study, a panelled room where his resistance to the Spanish Armada was discussed. I also stood in his bedroom. I was struck by how much had survived from Drake's time. I wrote a story, 'Seven Riding on the Mare'.

We went on to Endsleigh House, c.1810 with gardens from the Romantic time, including chasms. We waited in the library to be called to dine, and I was greeted by the owner's daughter, Alex Polizzi (who would later present the television series, *The Hotel Inspector*). We chatted. The next morning Ann and I walked round the picturesque garden, and I wrote a short story, 'A Shell House and Plunging Gorges'.

A few days later Matthew took me to the Oval to watch England v. Pakistan as a delayed birthday present. The match was controversial as an umpire awarded 5 penalty runs against Pakistan for cheating by ball-tampering. The Pakistani team protested by not coming out after tea – we in the crowd had no idea what was happening – and they were deemed to have forfeited the match. I wrote a short story, 'A Changed Ball and Western Rules'.

Ann and I went to the Cheltenham literary festival. Stanley Wells gave a presentation on the facial images of Shakespeare. Afterwards I asked him if he had heard that Shakespeare was a schoolmaster at Titchfield and that a Warwick butcher had held his last trunk, aspects of Shakespeare's secret history, and he replied, "No" to both questions. We then heard Christopher Tyerman on the crusades, Holy War and bin Laden, on which I took notes for my forthcoming *Crusaders* (which would become *Armageddon*).

And then – the reason I went to Cheltenham – I heard Paul Davies on 'The Goldilocks Enigma': on why, rather than how, the conditions in the universe are just right for human life. He stopped short of saying why existence is as it is, and left us with options. But I took notes for what would become *The New Philosophy of Universalism*.

In October 2006 Richard Larn, his wife and her son came to Charlestown to catalogue the bits and pieces salvaged from shipwrecks displayed in the Shipwreck Centre. We sat at a table in the Carlyon Bay Hotel's restaurant and talked about his six-volume Lloyds work on shipwrecks, which took him nine years to assemble. He had written many local books including *Charlestown*, to which I had contributed a dedicatory poem at his request, and he later became a Gorsedh Bard.

At Barclays' dinner at Grosvenor House Hotel the highest manager I had contact with told me, "I have been hearing within the bank details of megabillionaires and the Bilderberg Group running the world – you were right, and over Iraq."[62] Secret history was pervasive and infiltrated the conversation at my bank's dinner.

I received a card from John Ezard offering to put me in the *Dictionary of National Biography*, to which he contributed entries. "The catch is, you have to be dead. I'll do you now if you're planning to die quickly." I rang him and learned that he was increasingly immobile. He had ulcers on his feet and had to have dressings and ice-packs to cope with their weepings. (I had no immediate plans to die, and his offer was never implemented. He predeceased me.)

I also received a letter from Bill Kelso regarding the 400th anniversary of the founding of America, lamenting: "I have absolutely nothing to do with any of the events in 2007. Actually the 1607 Fort, the very thing being commemorated, will play a miniscule role in all the pomp and circumstance. Hard to believe." I found out that Colonial Williamsburg was the main funder for 2007, and that the organisation of the anniversary had been removed from Jamestown to Rockefeller-built Colonial Williamsburg. (In the event, the Queen visited Jamestown in 2007 and Kelso showed her round.)

Collected Stories, *including* In the Brilliant Autumn Sunshine

Collected Stories collected five volumes (each covering a decade, starting with the 1960s) totalling 1,001 very short stories (the same number as in *Arabian Nights Entertainments* or *The Thousand and One Nights*). The last volume was *In the Brilliant Autumn Sunshine*. The book demonstrated that I had created a new genre: a miniature story that conveys a truth through an image and can provide a complete literary experience in a few minutes. I was struck by my titles: the great majority of the titles of my stories contained and reconciled a pair of opposites, as did each of the 30 episodes of *My Double Life 1* and 2.

I had received a CD from Rob on 18 April 2006. Because I was involved in other books I did not begin assembling the book until 21 July 2006, when I was in Cornwall. I proof-read the five volumes throughout August and finished on 24 September 2006, when all 1,001 stories were in. I corrected the text until 13 October, when it was sent to the publisher. I made further amendments between 8 November and 3 December, and handed the book over when I met John Hunt on 4 December. I noted I had put in 90 hours' work on the stories in the three previous weeks. I read proofs in January and February 2007. I received the first copy at the end of April 2007.[63]

Another episode had now come to an end. I had finished my collected literature and my secret history, and was already embroiled in a new episode.

Episode 14:

Order and Terror

Years: 2007–2009
Locations: Buckhurst Hill; Iran; Austria; Ecuador; Galapagos Islands;
Antarctica; Paris; North Norway
Works: *The Last Tourist in Iran*; *The New Philosophy of Universalism*; *The Revolution That Didn't Happen*; *The Libyan Revolution*; *Armageddon*
Initiatives: philosophy of Universalism; poetic epic on War on Terror

"We find in the objective world a high degree of order."

Albert Einstein

A new episode began in which I caught the order within the universe in a philosophical work and reflected the War on Terror and its allies which undermined the harmony of that order in our daily lives. I reflected the conflict between order and terror in travelogues and another poetic epic, and focused on the culture of Muslim countries blighted by terror: Iran, Libya, Afghanistan and Iraq.

Terror: **Armageddon** *and Iran*
Beginning of Armageddon *as* Crusaders
I had had the idea of writing a second poetic epic on 21 May 2006 when under steroids, the day after Ricks's "earthquake of a lecture". I thought of the title as *Crusaders*. It would be about "Bush bringing liberty and democracy to the world" and "bin Laden, a new Saladin," seeking to establish a new caliphate based in Baghdad. Both were crusaders in different ways. At the end of May I drafted an outline for the 12 books for *Crusaders* and turned it into a synopsis. In mid-June I saw that the epic was about the transformations of Bush (both inner and outer), and the clash between the North-American and the Arab civilization, between Christendom and Islam. I envisaged a narrative poem in the tradition of Tennyson's *Idylls of the King*. I explored the myth of Armageddon in early October.

I wanted to visit Iraq and asked both my MP and MEP if I could be attached to a delegation. But Iraq was considered unsafe. In early November I switched my focus to Iran, which was intriguing a Greater Shiite Empire at the expense of the Sunnis and had nuclear ambitions. In mid-November, ignoring the risk, I impulsively made arrangements to visit Iran.

On 4 December John Hunt invited me to meet him in the Charing Cross Hotel in London, in the first-floor coffee area that had been "the Oak-Tree office". John, in an open-necked shirt and jacket and looking distinguished, went straight into my books. We had lunch in the adjoining Betjeman restaurant overlooking the Strand, and I talked about *Crusaders*. He asked me to write a "travelogue" on my coming visit to Iran. I also talked about the book that would become *The New Philosophy of Universalism*. The four hours I spent with him were very productive.

On 18 December I noted, "Worked on *Crusaders*, which I have now decided to call *Armageddon*".[1]

In Iran: machine-guns at Natanz and the Hidden Imam's well
In January with some apprehension I flew on my own to Tehran to absorb the Shiite response to the War on Terror. I was met by a car and driven to Rey. We passed the American Embassy where the American kidnapees were held. There were still anti-American slogans on the wall. We walked through the bazaar and visited the Archaeological Museum and Khomeini mosque.

We flew to Shiraz and drove through green vegetation to Hafez's garden and tomb among orange-trees, and to Sadi's tomb, where I encountered a dervish.

The next day we drove through a gorge in the mountains to Persepolis, which was full of broken columns and doorways and which I had to myself. It was now clear that I was the only Westerner touring Iran. I studied the Persian carvings on some of the buildings and realised that they had influenced Pheidias.

We went on to Pasargadae to see the Palace of Cyrus the Great, c.546BC, and his huge tomb, which Alexander the Great visited. We went on to Yazd, passing a cypress tree that was 4,500–5,000 years old, older than the Great Pyramid. I spoke to the guardian of the tree. We stayed in a garden hotel. I breakfasted before a picture of Sohrab and Rostam from the *Shahnameh*. We visited the Friday mosque, the Zoroastrian fire-temple and then the Towers of Silence, circular stone walls on hills where the bodies of dead Zoroastrians were laid out on stones for vultures to pick them clean. We lunched at a *caravanserai* at Meynob and drove on to Isfahan, where I walked to Imam Square through snow and saw the mosques.

I was the only visitor to the Shah mosque the next morning. We went to the Sheikh Lotfollah mosque, and on to the royal palace, where Shah Abbas I watched polo from the balcony upstairs. We drove on to Natanz through flurries of snow and looked in on a Husaynieh, where villagers huddled round a fire.

We headed out through snow-covered mountains, and approached the nuclear site. I was watching the milometer and when we were a kilometre away I pointed my camera and clicked. My guide, who was sitting in the front seat, became agitated. He turned and said, "This is a restricted zone. It's very dangerous. They are watching cars and have machine-guns. Look, there are machine-guns trained on us on the right now. Put the camera away."

Was there a nuclear programme at Natanz behind the enclosed two-kilometre-long fence on my left? If there wasn't, why were machine-guns trained on our car? We passed at least ten anti-aircraft guns near the perimeter fence.

We stayed the night in Kashan. The next morning we visited a Safavid pavilion in an earthly 'Paradise' with four water-channels that met. We drove on to Jamkaran well just before Qom. Until 1970 this was a small desert well beside a mosque built by a man to whom the Hidden *Imam* appeared in a dream 300 years previously. The stone well had a waist-high cover round it topped with a steel grille. The Hidden *Imam* is supposed to live down the well, and a queue of people dropped messages through the grille. Shiites believe that after a period of anarchy the Hidden Imam will return up the well in a Second Coming. I was photographed peering through the grille for signs of life at the bottom of the well.

I went to the Jamkaran mosque nearby. I took off my shoes and sat cross-legged among 50 Iranians, many of whom were *mullah*s (some with black turbans signifying that they were descended from the Prophet). Because I was intensely aware that I was at the heart of Iran's opposition to the West I meditated and asked the Light to prevent a nuclear conflict. The Light shone brightly into my soul.

In Qom I visited Ayatollah Khomeini's low house behind a wall. I took off my shoes, climbed a few steps and turned right into Khomeini's living-room, where a *mullah* sat over the *Koran*. We drove to the burial shrine for Fatemah, and then through the Zagros mountains to Hamadan. There we visited the 14th-century mausoleum of Esther (author of a book in the *Old Testament*) and Mordecai. We went on to the Achaemenian Ganjnameh outside Hamadan, climbed impacted snow and ice and found on rock inscriptions by Darius and Xerxes I.

The next morning I visited Avicenna's tomb in a temperature of minus 20°C. We went on to Ecbatana, and visited the museum. This area had belonged to the Medes. We returned to Tehran and toured the Shah's French-styled White Palace.

We went to Ayatollah Khomeini's Tehran house and I looked through glass at his living-room and paltry possessions. From his living-room a raised walkway led into a Husaynieh, where on a raised platform he could speak to a television camera. The faithful gathered below to sit on carpets and hear his decrees after the revolution, and announcements of executions.[2]

The danger I was in when I passed Natanz was soon apparent. Six weeks after I returned, on 9 March 2007 an American, Robert Levinson, was arrested in Iran for allegedly gathering intelligence on the nuclear program for the CIA. He then vanished. A video of him was released in 2011, and in 2014 he was still being held in Iran.

The Last Tourist in Iran

I wrote *The Last Tourist in Iran* in three weeks and four days (23 January–16 February 2007). I combined the form of a travelogue with in-depth historical reflection in an attempt to get to the heart of the Iranian Islamic mind. I contrasted Iran's cultural heritage and the nuclear crisis which might trigger international intervention. Having visited the Hidden *Imam*'s well, Ayatollah Khomeini's living-rooms in Qom and Tehran and the Shah's Winter Palace, and having driven past the nuclear site at Natanz, I had formed a rounded view of Iran's confrontational nuclear policy. The book narrates my tour round Iran. I made corrections and assembled the Appendix and sent the book off on 23 March 2007. The text was copy-edited by a Professor in California and I was reading proofs in June and July.[3] I received the first copy in mid-January 2008.

In the Jamkaran mosque I had asked the Light to prevent a nuclear conflict and bring peace, and there were US-Iran peace talks in 2013. In January 2014, seven years after my visit, I received an email from my guide (Farhad in the book) addressed to me as "UK author", wishing me a happy and peaceful new year.

In Austria: Waterloo ball, The Lost Englishman

In August 2006 Anthony had introduced us to an Albanian diplomat who had deputised for the Ambassador in Austria. (She had been secretary to the Prime Minister, who, facing a *coup*, had sent her to the Embassy in Austria and had then lost his job.) He had brought her to meet us, and in February 2007 she had asked if we would attend a UN ball in Vienna in the room in the Hofburg Imperial Palace where the ball was held in 1815 to celebrate the Duke of Wellington's victory over Napoleon at Waterloo. I was very interested in attending a ball in the 1815 setting.

We flew to Vienna in early March 2007 and took a taxi through rain to the Graben Hotel. It had been a regular haunt of Franz Kafka's, and there were letters by Max Brod, Kafka's literary friend, on a downstairs wall. The four of us went out to eat through rain, and walked back past the floodlit Hofburg. We toured the Hofburg the next morning. I had seen six rooms in 1967. Now 75 rooms were on show, including Franz Joseph's study where he heard news of the suicide of Crown Prince Rudolf in Mayerling. We were in the headquarters of the Holy Roman Empire.

We took the train to the UN's OSCE (Organization for Security and Co-operation in Europe) building, which stood next to the IAEA building. We went up to the conference room and the board room, and visited other rooms, including the library. I had the idea of making my fictional 'lost Englishman' a UN technical expert on nuclear weapons who lives in Vienna and is kidnapped to Iran.

In the evening we were taken to the Hofburg Imperial Palace's Congress Centre (Heldenplatz). We queued, men in DJs, women in long gowns, and took champagne. We went up to the crowded ballroom with three Baroque paintings on the ceiling, marble surrounds with columns and six enormous chandeliers. There were 1,280 guests in the ballroom and two adjoining rooms. We assembled our buffet dinners in a side room, and ate to dancing: Viennese waltzes and military music that allowed men wearing military jackets with many medals to strut. There was a display of Spanish flamenco dancing after midnight. We left at 3 a.m.

The next morning we went to St Stephen's Cathedral. I visited the catacombs that included the ossuaries: the bones of 500 victims of the Black Death in a room off a brick tunnel. In the afternoon we went to the Schönbrunn Palace, which I barely recollected from 1994, and had a guided tour.

The next morning we had coffee in the square opposite the Cathedral. We then took a taxi to the Albanian diplomat's apartment and left our cases. We walked past the road containing the Albanian Embassy to the Belvedere, Prince Eugene of Savoy's palace. There was an exhibition of Austrian art, and we lunched in a German beer-cellar and restaurant nearby, the Salmbräu. Then we collected our cases and headed for the airport.[4]

Three novellas

In August 2004 I had worked on two of my three novellas (*Juben* and *The Eternicide*). By January 2007 their titles had changed and I was working on the same two novellas, now called *The Tree of Knowledge* and *The Soul-Destroyer*. In February I had noted that they represent "a negative way. They arrive at truth through its opposite, define good in terms of evil." I now turned to *The Lost Englishman* and wrote in my experience of Vienna.

I carried on my work on *The Tree of Knowledge*, *The Soul-Destroyer* and *The Lost Englishman* into July. In mid-June I recorded the mythical basis of each book: in each, a hero goes down to the Underworld. *The Tree of Knowledge* (previously *Juben*) reworked the myth of Tammuz and Inanna. *The Soul-Destroyer* reworked the myth of the Golden Bough which stood near the entrance to the Underworld by Lake Avernus. It was guarded by a King of the Wood who was slain by his successor, who became the new King of the Wood. *The Lost Englishman* reworked Orpheus's descent to the Underworld. I had a trilogy of three novellas I had attempted in my youth about the destructiveness of materialism and they were novellas rather than realistic novels.

I did more work on *The Lost Englishman* in May 2008.[5]

Death of Ricky Herbert

In April I received an email from Ricky's wife Marie: "Some of you already know my bad news, that my beloved husband Ricky died yesterday [9 April] suddenly, of a heart attack...." I could see his life clearly as an Underground Man's rejection of the System, having turned his back on a career, looked to the East and lived in a drug-dream. I felt sad at his unfulfilled promise.

I attended his funeral at Mortlake crematorium. I was greeted by a Polish contemporary of mine at Oxford, Ilona Halberstadt, who was with Glenn, one of the Randolph Set. I did not recognise her and said, "Nicholas." She said, "I know." She pointed out Quintin Hoare (who had worked with Perry Anderson on the *New Left Review* and had been general editor of the eight-volume Pelican Marx library). Looking fatter and greyer than when I last saw him, he said to me: "You became a legend by becoming a Professor at 24." I smiled, "Same age as Nietzsche." He grinned and told me of his Bosnian connection through his wife. He asked of Masterman, our Provost, "He was in intelligence, wasn't he?" Then the coffin arrived in a hearse and we went into the chapel, 22 in all. There were words from the lame vicar, and a prayer. Ricky's actress sister (who was on sticks with a twisted hip) read from a *logion* ('saying') by Oxyrhynchus: "Raise the stone and thou shalt find me, cleave the wood and there am I. Let not him who seeks cease from seeking until he finds. When he finds, he shall be astonished. Astonished, he shall reach the Kingdom and there he shall rest." She said that Ricky had inscribed the reading on the flyleaf of his partner Marie's Bible in 1970. There was a psalm, then a tribute by John Howe, who had supplied him with drugs at Oxford. He described Ricky as a teacher who was interested in Eastern religions.

I was indignant that he was giving the tribute. His actions had led to Ricky's addiction to drugs. We filed out after the coffin slid behind the doors on rollers, and stood awkwardly in the corridor near a couple of garlands.

We went back to Ricky's house in Burlington Avenue, and I stood in his elegant sitting-room with books on either side of the fireplace. I went out into the garden where Glenn told me he was sent down from Oxford for selling a stolen car. Ilona came up and said that David Sladen had been very enthusiastic about *A Mystic Way* and would like to meet me. Then Rachel came out and sat on a chair on the lawn and invited me to sit beside her. She told me: "Ricky did a bit of this" – she jabbed herself with an imaginary needle – "and that was sorted out by the mid-1960s. Then he smoked it all to the stars. He was an academic. I went to India but he did not go. You went to Japan and China but he did not go. He was sceptical of everything. And his philosophy of inaction was a cover for something else: he had things in his mind but he didn't do anything with it, he smoked it to the stars." I asked: "When did that stop?" She did not answer, indicating that it was continuing when he died.

She told me the circumstances of his death. "He went to get a paper. He walked very slowly because of the arthritis in his leg. He returned with his paper and a roll for breakfast, and sat upstairs in his study and did the crossword. Marie called up to him to bring a packet of washing-powder down. There was no reply, so she went up and found him sitting over his crossword. A lovely way to go."

I found Marie and asked when we had last met. She said, "It was in 1971." I said, "I can see you, with blonde hair and dark glasses. Where was it?" "In my Notting-Hill flat in Linden Gardens." She told me she had met Ricky in 1966 and lived with him from 1969 and except for two months apart in 1971 they had been together ever since. "I was with him for 38 years."

I went out into the garden to say goodbye to some of my contemporaries. John Howe was smoking. I asked, "What's that?" "It's hash, man." "Where from?" "South Africa. It's South African skunk, man. You don't do it?" "No," I said firmly, and again I was indignant. He had ruined Ricky's life by introducing him to drugs, and he was openly and unrepentantly smoking hashish at his funeral, having given his tribute.[6]

25 radio broadcasts to USA on The Secret Founding of America

The American publicists had arranged for me to make 25 live radio broadcasts to the US on *The Secret Founding of America*. Each radio company was to ring me at an agreed time, and I would do the interview from my study desk.

The first broadcast was to St Louis (10 mins). I talked about the planting and like a butterfly alighted on dates – 1607, 1565 – and then was off again to 1933 and how the Seal was Weishaupt's. The next day I had three radio slots: at 2.10 to the west coast, Cable Radio Network; at 3.05 to Iowa – the first question was "Were you offended that our President winked at your Queen?", and there were questions about the Civil War and Lincoln; and then to Milwaukee in Wisconsin (20 mins), when I was asked to explain how the Founding Fathers used Christianity as a veneer. Each interviewer had a different angle.

The next day there were three more broadcasts: to Connecticut (10 mins);

to San Francisco; and to Arizona. The following day I made four broadcasts: to Cincinnati; to Mayville, Wisconsin; to Oregon, which included a surprise phone-in; and to Texas (30 mins, which boiled down to a quarter of an hour because of all the adverts). The next day there were three more broadcasts: to Detroit; to Phoenix, Arizona; and to Huntington, West Virginia (15 mins).

Five days later I made a broadcast that was syndicated throughout America. I was asked questions about the East India Company, Hitler's Thule Society, Bush Sr and Skull and Bones. The interviewer was all over the place. I was sent a round robin to three coast-to-coast radio presenters saying that I should be compared to Da Vinci, Solomon and Moses, and a book collector announced that he would save any of my books before anyone else's except Adam Smith's. Michael Mann wrote that I was becoming famous and that he was the dervish who opened the door.

I broadcast to Boston, Massachusetts (25 mins): a good, lively discussion with no break for adverts. On my birthday I made a global broadcast on Fox Radio News. I went out to every country in the world. From my point of view it was less than satisfactory: there was a screaming siren, the title of my book was read out and there were a couple of zany questions, and that was all. There was no real discussion, just publicity for the book. Nevertheless, I had gone out live to the world. Two days later I broadcast to West Virginia, on 1607; and to Colorado, where the interviewer was "very obsequious". I had a break in Cornwall and immediately on my return broadcast to Brownsville, Texas (35 mins on 'Good Books'). The next day I was supposed to broadcast to Philadelphia, but their call never came. I spoke to Philadelphia (5 mins) a week later.

On 15 July I made my twenty-fifth broadcast, live to Hawaii (one hour). It was scheduled for 3 a.m. to 4 a.m., British time. I slept from 10 p.m. to 1.45 a.m., had a cup of tea and tried to stay awake. The interviewer said he did not want to discuss America, he would ask me questions on things that had interested him in my book. His first question was "What is the Merovingian dynasty and the Kingship of Jerusalem?" His second question was "How did Alaska join the US?" And so it went on: a glorified test of my general knowledge. There was a lot on the New World Order and the US. I talked for an hour and went back to bed soon after 4 a.m.

I pondered the anti-social hours of that scheduling and the semi-irrelevance of the questions in relation to my book, and decided I would not be doing any more live broadcasts to America for a while.

I relented less than a year later. I was booked to do a global broadcast for an hour on my writings, particularly *The Syndicate*. The radio station[7] tried to send me a list of questions, but being an old hand now at radio broadcasts, I told my PA, "No, I'll just do it." I was introduced from Rome and the interviewer was in the US. I said I had stumbled across the Syndicate while researching into civilizations, and had discovered that it was trying to subsume all civilizations. I said that the Syndicate was within the North-American civilization just as the Round Table had been within the British Empire. I said their New World Order might not happen.

Aware that I was going out throughout the world, I tried to mention each continent. I discussed the birth rate in China; 9/11 in the US; Islamic extremists; and Afghanistan. I spoke of Russia and Iran opposing the New World Order. I brought in South America, Africa, India and Pakistan and of course Europe so that individuals listening could hear reference to their own continent or region and feel involved. My broadcast lasted 56 minutes in all, and went out (I was told) "to every country in the world".

Christopher Ricks

Two days before his May Professor-of-Poetry lecture, Ricks rang me: "It's Christopher Ricks here. It's very good of you to be travelling so far to come to my lecture on Monday, and I wonder if you'd have tea with me, at 4 o'clock, in the little tea bar just across the road from Examination Schools. It's the road that goes up to Teddy Hall." I said that my second son Tony would be driving me. He went on, "I'm sorry I've been so negligent but I'm an old man in a hurry." I told him that I had had to make 25 live broadcasts to the States and had done 14 this last week, and he said, "You are doing well." Ricks said of finding the tea bar, "It will be an intelligence test."

Tony and I were in Cirques Jobson's 1654 Queen's Lane coffee-house when Ricks came in at 4, shook hands and sat in the window. He talked to Tony about films until we had ordered – he had cappuccino, I had tea and Tony latte – and then he said to me: "You're a phenomenon." I said, "I take it all in my stride." He laughed and said, "Seven-league boots." He wanted to know what questions I had been asked in my radio interviews. I told him the farther east in the US I addressed, the more interested they were in 1607.

I asked if he had another book of essays coming out. He said, "Perhaps. I had to give lectures for Kermode. They asked him first, he's ten years older than me, and he couldn't do them. They rather cut across what I was doing but you would have liked them. They were about Pound and Eliot." He said he was running out of ideas for Professor-of-Poetry lectures. "I've got two more years to do. What should I do next year?" I said, "You don't like people after the 1930s." He said, "I can't hear them." He asked where I go for my research. I said: "I have a library." He showed an interest, so I said, "Come and stay." "I don't travel. When I go to London it's to stay with my children. I'm here for five weeks in the summer. I know you like Oxford." I told him about *Crusaders* (later *Armageddon*) and he said he would talk me through it in July or August. He said, "I'm giving my [library] books away to make friends with the necessity of dying."

He asked Tony, "Have you read Colin MacCabe's book on Godard?" I eventually said, "He split the Cambridge faculty with semiotics, a brand of structuralism, and went off into film, paring down the syllabus like Danny the Red." Ricks said: "I don't like him because he told me a word I'd used of Eliot isn't in the dictionary, and I found it with 'after' in front. He'd bet me a pint, and I waited but it never happened. He looked up the wrong word, but he said he was right."

He asked me: "Why do you write history?" I said, "It gives the publishers something to sell so they're more likely to do what I'm really interested in." He said, "Like Robert Graves." I said, "Yes, *I, Claudius*." There was talk of philosophy and Universalism. He said to Anthony, "Don't worry about philosophy and Universalism," jokingly. He left at 4.40, shaking hands outside after paying, and crossing the road on his own to organise his lecture.

I remarked to Tony that I had seen Auden's Professor-of-Poetry lecture on *The Tempest* over several shoulders at the back of a crowd, and now the Professor of Poetry invited me to have tea with him before the lecture.

Ricks's lecture in the East School, a long room with old masters, was on Empson's treatment of Shakespeare's sonnets. He spoke of the eternal triangle of Empson's marriage which Empson had encouraged, and held that Joyce had a similar view of his marriage. Empson believed that there was a similar triangle in Shakespeare's sonnets (Southampton – the Dark Lady – Shakespeare). I did not believe that Shakespeare had a similar view of his triangle. (I have since half-wondered if Shakespeare's triangle was Pembroke – Lady Mary Wroth – Shakespeare, but there is no evidence for this.) Ricks spoke kind words on Haffenden's biography of Empson. I thanked Ricks at the end and as we shook hands I asked, "Is Haffenden here?" Yes, he's at the back on the left with grey hair."

I went to the back and spoke to Haffenden, who was in a jacket and tie and stockily built. I told him, "I'm a pupil of Christopher Ricks, and he brought Empson to Worcester probably in 1960, and in 1963 I became a Professor in Japan, doing what Empson did, under Yukio Irie. And I was under Professor Narita as well." Haffenden said, "Irie showed me some photos of Empson in his garden that were taken in the 1970s." I had not realised that Irie, who had looked after me in Japan, had kept in touch with Empson.

Afterwards Tony picked up on Ricks's saying that Motion was "not much good as a poet". Tony said, "I don't think he thinks anyone's much good." He pointed out, "Ricks said people say they're going to write things and they don't do them." I pointed out that there was a gulf between his Neoclassical and my Universalist principles, but said I appreciated his sharing of his immense reading with me. I recalled Tony telling me one

Saturday in March: "You did excellently. You wanted to write and you had an expanding business and your family, you did it all." Tony was good at putting things in perspective.[8]

Eternity and Providence

For my birthday Ann gave me a magnified paperweight with a beautiful gold-leaf 'N', a subtle blending of green, blue and gold, to go with the decorated letter she had given me. I saw the green as Nature, the blue as eternity and the gold my Light-filled works.

My view of eternity was strained when my nephew Andrew married a junior doctor at St Andrew's church, Oxford. The vicar said, "God knew about this marriage before the universe was created." I had pondered the workings of Providence with some profundity, but even I could not accept that. His wife could have chosen to remain on her path and not join his. After the service we walked to Wolfson College for the reception. We queued to be received and I was next to Sir Philip Mawer. He told me he would cease to be Parliamentary Commissioner for Standards at the end of the year, but said that Gordon Brown, then our Prime Minister, had asked him to work in 10 Downing Street, anticipating scandals. I said, "You'll be Minister of Banana Skins." He laughed. We left the reception before midnight and had a final family chat at the Cotswold Lodge Hotel in the Banbury Road.[9]

Order: The New Philosophy of Universalism *and the order in the universe*
Beginning of The New Philosophy of Universalism

In November 1993 Mark Barty-King, then Managing Director of Transworld and publisher of Stephen Hawking's best-selling *A Brief History of Time*, had met me over a drink. He had read some of my work and asked if I would consider writing a book that would counterbalance Hawking's materialistic outlook with a more metaphysical approach. He told me it was ironical that he was Hawking's publisher as he was on the metaphysical, not the materialistic, side. I had to get clear of my many other projects before I could think deeply about this book, and Barty-King died before I could make a start.

I was brought back to the book Barty-King had proposed by Ann's card for our wedding anniversary on 22 February. With it were details of a cruise on the *Minerva* to Antarctica via the Falklands and South Georgia. I had to book within six days. I had always linked the book with a visit to the Galapagos Islands, which inspired Darwin's theory of evolution. I checked to see if we could visit the Galapagos Islands before joining the ship in Argentina. It was logistically impossible. The only way to visit both was to go to the Galapagos Islands in July and Antarctica in November. Needing to confront evolution and climate change for *The New Philosophy of Universalism*, I booked both, including a visit to Peru after the Galapagos

Islands.

I sent John Hunt an email about Universalism, and spoke of a coming work that would be a *"prolegomena* to reconnecting philosophy to the natural world and the universe (and to the One)". A week later I received a contract. For large parts of April and May I worked on a synopsis, which went through several versions and amendments. John (setting admirably high standards as usual) wanted the scientific presentation to be "testable", and, having always been evidential, I made sure I would deliver testability.[10]

In the Galapagos Islands: 13 species of finches, turtles' instincts and Darwinist evolution

On 23 July we left to confront Darwinian evolution in the Galapagos Islands. We flew to Madrid and caught another flight to Quito, Ecuador, which looked run-down and in need of a coat of paint as we drove from the airport to our hotel. From our room we had a view of mountains.

The next day we flew to Baltra, or South Seymour, in the Galapagos Islands. I wandered out of the tiny airport and found a large iguana near my feet. Ignoring seven seals sleeping in the bus shelter, we took a bus to the port and caught an inflatable to the small ship, *Galaven* ('Galapagos Adventurer' in Spanish). We were allocated a teak-wood cabin.

We set off by inflatable for a beach on Santa Cruz (Playa Las Bachas): a flat, sandy, coral beach with black laval rocks and low scrub that included prickly pear. A flock of blue-tailed boobies swept overhead, and grinning brown pelicans flew by. We saw blue herons and brown noddies silhouetted against Daphne Major and Minor, and Bartolomé. We walked past large red Sally Lightfoot crabs and a blue crab, and passed a turtle's nest, eggs covered by sand, and saw pink flamingos. Iguanas crawled to swim in the warm water. In the scrub were yellow mangrove warblers.

We dined at one of three tables that accommodated nine couples. The others were not interested in digesting what we had seen; they wanted to drink wine and talk from topic to topic as if in a pub. Later an enormous locust flew onto the deck: black with grasshopper legs and green on its side. It was larger than my camera, and must have come from the mangroves of Bartolomé. I described it to two naturalists accompanying our voyage, who were mystified. So I claimed it as a new species: 'Hagger's locust'.

The next morning we went by inflatable to Pinnacle Rock and saw penguin nest holes and three tiny Galapagos penguins, and brown pelicans. One of our naturalists said that the Galapagos Islands were only between 3 and 8 million years old, the minimum length of time required for evolution to deliver the Galapagos effects. We had a view over the bay between Bartolomé and Santiago, where Darwin's *Beagle* put in. Frigate-birds circled.

Yellow mangrove warblers and small-ground and medium-ground finches flitted in red mangroves. I sat on the landing-beach and watched a lava lizard climb onto a sleeping sea lion and lick flies, an example of symbiosis.

We sailed to Sullivan Bay and walked on 120-year-old black lava shaped like ropes. I sat by the escutia (Galapagos pine) and watched a Galapagos mockingbird fly by, sea lions and iguanas eat algae, stormy petrels skim low over the water.

The next morning we went out early and crossed by inflatable to Puerto Egas, Santiago, in St James Bay. We wet-landed where (according to his great-grandson) Darwin camped. Sea lions were barking and sleeping on black volcanic sand. I walked on the Darwin trail that Darwin took to climb the misty volcano and passed a Galapagos hawk. I saw a semipalmated plover, an oystercatcher and a whimbrel. Boobies dived for black-tailed mullet fish. There was a smell of breeding snakes in the wind. We passed a wandering tattler bird. Two noddies sat on a brown pelican's head and picked food out of its mouth. I saw a yellow-crowned night heron with a gold-crested crown.

I walked with our naturalist Gino and asked what is behind the instinctive behaviour of sea lions and iguanas, of animals and reptiles, what drives evolution. He said, "Self-improvement." I asked, "But how do new creatures know how to improve themselves? How do creatures get born knowing they have to improve themselves?" He went very quiet and agreed that there was a mystery for which science has no answers. But where science ends, philosophy begins. I said, "There is an orderly system, it's not chaos. Lizards lay eggs and depart and some hatch and survive, some hatch and die – but the system is kept going and all creatures keep the system going." I was in the Galapagos Islands to absorb Darwin and evolution in living terms, and to understand what impels it. I questioned why there are 13 species of Galapagos finch and only one species of human.

We returned to Sombrero Chino ('Chinese hat', i.e. 'coolie hat') where Ann had swum from the beach while I trekked up the mountain. I walked among sea lions and saw a mother lying on her back on the tideline giving the pup her milk. Red rock supported candelabra cactus and red sesuvium. We returned to our small ship for lunch. There was a big swell, and the ship dipped and rolled as we made our way to Santa Cruz. The passengers were too seasick to eat that evening.

I drafted the idea for a poem on evolution, 'An Evolution Quartet'. It would focus on the "Galapagos/Peruvian experiences of creation (laval rock); evolution (Darwin on Santiago); consciousness (Incas and the sun); and orderly systems (the Inca view) – moving beyond Darwinism to trans-mutation by the Light". I also drafted the idea for a poem on Antarctica: "Falklands (war/birds); South Georgia and polar exploration; Antarctica and melting ice, global warming, floods." Then I drafted a poem on Iran: "Old Persia – Persepolis; old Iran – Isfahan architecture; the Revolution; and nuclear Natanz." These three poems still remain to be written, and I intend to write them.

The next morning we walked from the port, Puerto Ayora, through candelabra and prickly-pear (*opuntia*) cactus to the Darwin Research Station, which had escutia and mangroves round the entrance. It was to visit this Research Station that I had come to the Galapagos Islands. There we saw some of the 11 species of old tortoises, thought to date back 3–4 million years. We saw six saddleback tortoises that were each 140–150 years old. We went to a pen of dome-shaped tortoises and then on through prickly pears to Lonesome George, the last of his species and the model for ET in Spielberg's film. He posed with his neck in the air.

We walked to the Van Straelen Centre and were eventually introduced to Luis Alfonso Perez, the Centre's Tourist and Administration Manager, who, when I asked him about "the self-organising principle in biology" and said I wanted to discuss evolution, left and returned with an Ecuadorian botanist, Daniel Segura. He showed us a DVD on the work of the Centre in the cinema, and with Ann sitting next to me, Segura standing (a youngish, serious fellow) and Perez interpreting, I asked some 30 questions in the course of an hour and a half about "the secret of life".

At first Segura's answers were Darwinist: "Some creatures die because they don't adapt, if they change to adapt to their environment they survive like Darwin's finches." I asked what made the cactus finch adapt? Starvation. Eventually I asked, "What is the self-improving principle that drives finches and tortoises to improve themselves and adapt?" We spoke of animals, plants and insects developing to a new species and passing on their adaption in DNA. I pressed him on the inheritance of acquired character- istics (Darwin's Lamarckian principle, derided by neo-Darwinists and now back following the discovery of DNA). He did not give me a satisfactory answer. I asked him what life is and pressed him on evolution. He said, "Evolution is something in the genes. Self-organising in the genes." Eventually I asked, "If the St Lucia finch was first and arrived from Costa Rica and caused variation, does *opuntia* obey the same principle?" He said, "Yes." He told me, "Botanists want to discover the secret of life." I said: "Physicists believe they can discover the Theory of Everything, but even if they do they can't include the biological secret of life." He agreed.

I summed up: "The self-organising, self-imposing mitochondrial principle in the genes, which contain a plan for growth, a blueprint of a human-to-be, mammal-to-be, reptile-to-be, plant-to-be, organises adaptions and varieties, and transmutations are conveyed to their successors, even a new species." He said: "Yes." Perez added: "That's what I think."

Walking back, I said to Ann: "The universe came from a point (as we know from Hubble's inflation), and all species came from one cell. So what caused that one cell to split?" Ann said: "Need for survival, like the turtles leaving the sea and crawling up the beach to bury their eggs and then going back down the beach, the young being picked off by frigate-birds." I said: "What causes the instinct for survival?" And I was back to Creation.

I had done what I set out to do, to ask many questions of the Darwin Research Station. We returned to Puerto Ayora to pick up the bus and see large tortoises in their natural habitats in the highlands. We passed cattle egrets on cattle and a black ani bird pecking off a tortoise. There were three water-basking tortoises, one of which was 160 years old. It was alive in 1847. We went on to look at the last lava flow. Back on board we slept with a rough sea slooshing the portholes.

We woke by Floreana. Both Drake and the *Beagle* had moored there before we had. We went ashore to Post Office cove, whose post-office box or letter drop had been used by pirates from c.1600. I fell into conversation with Mary Morrison, a youngish Assistant Professor in cell biology at Lycoming College, Williamsport, Pennsylvania, a reductionist, who (when I asked her) during a chat, said, "Life is an electrical activity across a membrane." She told me that acquired characteristics can be passed on through the culture. "So Darwin and Lamarck were both right; but baseball or cricketing skills can't be passed on."

In the afternoon we went to a beach (Punta Cormorant) and saw a yellow-crowned night heron, shearwaters and a Nazca booby; and on a nearby lake more flamingos. We walked to a bay the other side of the island where thousands of stingrays come to feed on ghost crabs, which bury themselves. There were turtle nests in the upper sand and a frigate-bird made low dives, looking for hatched turtles. The turtles' instinctive behaviour amazed me. They hatch below sand and stop if it is too hot and wait for the cool at night so they do not get eaten by frigates as they crawl towards the sea. Mary told me that instructions to hatched turtles to remain under sand until dark can be transmitted in the cells, and do not need DNA. She agreed that if a machine like the one at CERN could replicate the first cell, then we would be close to the secret of life.

The next day we were on Espanola. We made a wet landing by inflatable on a deserted coral strip (Gardner Bay). Mockingbirds scuttled round our feet and hopped on our bags looking for water. Groups of sea lions lay along the sand. I encountered another, more high-grade naturalist, Samuel Quiroz, talking to another group, who told me that acquired characteristics *can* be inherited and passed on in genes: "Primary genes are about specifics, skills are more behavioural but can be inherited. Cell information becomes a genotype over a generation." Samuel came into conflict with Mary, who had said of turtle-hatching, "Turtles have a concept of hot and cold, they have no concept of frigate-birds." Samuel told her, "They *have* a concept of a frigate-bird, an instinct." It was clear that the scientists I had approached disagreed among themselves.

Back on the boat I asked Mary how many cells there had been since the first cell. She said it takes 10^{16} cell divisions to go from one cell to a human being, and that there is a 10^{-6} (one in a million) chance of error, of a mistake being made. There are 10^{10} mutations during the normal development of a human being. If a cell does not get the right instructions it commits suicide. I calculated that the number of human cell divisions ever, since the first cell, is 10^{16} (for one human) x 7 billion (the number of humans alive) x 100 billion (the estimated number of humans before those alive today). That did not take account of mutations and did not include mammals, reptiles, insects and plants.

In the afternoon we went to Punta Suarez and walked among red iguanas (which faced the sun in the afternoon to reduce the heat on their backs) and tame mockingbirds. One perched on my sleeve, and then my wrist, looking for water. We walked inland, past salt bushes, stepping across rugged boulders. On 19 April Ann had had an operation on an ankle at Holly House which had required her to sleep in an aircast boot, and she gamely did her best on the uneven terrain to reach two dozen waved albatrosses that waddled on their 'airstrip'. They had thick white necks, yellow beaks and grey-black wings, and they ran to take off. We saw a mating dance: two albatrosses clacked beaks. A red Hood lava lizard (named after the Galapagos Hood Island) picked grubs from an albatross's back. We walked on across a rocky cliff above the sea under soaring albatrosses, boobies and swallow-tailed gulls and reached a blowhole, where crashing waves, with a roar, fountained spray 30 or 40 feet into the air. We passed a Galapagos hawk and a bush with 20 or 30 finches. We passed a Galapagos fly-catcher.

After dinner, sitting on the deck, Mary gave me a class in Darwinism and the origin of life. She spoke of the Oparin/Miller primordial soup that created molecular activity. She described how cells divide and copy DNA and how there is a chance of error each time. Her view was a reductionist, biochemical view that did not satisfactorily explain how the 'soup' existed in the first place, or how the first cell arose. I pointed out there was also an *expansionist* view, that we are products of the universe, the One. To the reductionists, as she pointed out, the One is irrelevant as we are all cells, and that is the end of it.

The next day we were off San Cristóbal. We took the inflatable to a beach on Lobos Island, passing frigates with red pouches, sea lions, stingrays in clear water, lava gulls and yellow warblers. I sat on black laval rocks near a laval gull, a Sally Lightfoot crab and a yellow wagtail, and was joined by a bull sea lion. I wrote a draft poem but had to evacuate my rock to flee dive-bomb attacks by two yellow paper-wasps. Back on board I asked Mary about the link between atoms and cells. She told me again about the 'soup' but admitted that no one knows how atoms came to exist.

We went to Puerto Baquerizo Moreno where sea splashed on rocks and we saw leaping seals and diving boobies. We took a bus to the highlands, up into cloud, and arrived at La Galapaguera, where an exhibition showed that we are distant cousins of tortoises, descending from mammals as opposed to reptiles. Many finches appeared, responding to our naturalist's "call" made through a clenched fist. I saw a black vegetarian finch and a woodpecker finch. I had now seen 11 of Darwin's 13 finches.

The next day we were off North Seymour. Frigates flew over rocks that were one million years old. After lunch we left the small ship on an inflatable and landed on Baltra, or South Seymour, in a choppy sea. A bus took us to the airport, and we flew back to Ecuador, waved goodbye to the party and headed for the Hotel Quito with my biology section in my forthcoming book clear in my mind. I had acquired many biological details from my observation and research into the instinctive behaviour of the mammals and reptiles I had encountered on the Galapagos Islands, which coloured my Universalist thinking in my coming book.[11]

In Peru: sun-centred Incas and Machu Picchu's Temple of the Sun

We were going to Peru to get to the bottom of the Incas' view of the sun, and whether they believed in a round earth revolving round the sun. The next morning we approached the Incas in Quito, which was named after the pre-Inca tribe. The Incas ruled Ecuador from 1492 to 1534, when 300 Spanish Conquistadors arrived and ruled through 3,000 Indians. We went to the site of Huayna Capac's Inca palace, which was turned into a monastery, and to the site of an Inca temple, where there was now a huge statue of the Virgin Mary. We toured the Old Town and saw the Cathedral and several churches, and in the main square, the Presidential house.

We flew to Lima in Peru. We were driven round Lima and saw how a 1535 Spanish conquest obliterated the Incas and erected a Cathedral and St Francis's monastery and church, which we visited along with a 5th–8th-century temple built by the Lima culture (the Huaca Pucllana).

The next day we flew to Cusco, which is in a valley surrounded by mountains at 3,300 metres. Some visitors suffer from altitude sickness, but we were unaffected. We checked in at the Hotel Ruinas, and then walked to Plaza de Annas. We were close to the base of the palace of the Inca king Pachacuti (or Pachacutec). We went on to the Inca Museum, which is in an 18th-century colonial Spanish house.

We toured Cusco. We started at Qurikancha, the most important temple in the Inca Empire, bits of which survived obliteration by the church of Santa Dominga: traces of the Temples of the Rainbow, Three Worlds (the upper world, the present world and the underworld), Venus and the Stars, Lightning and the Moon. We saw the Inca altar. On the outside of the altar was fixed the golden 'sun of Inti' that went missing after the arrival of the Spanish. It was 2 metres by 2 metres, with closed eyes, mouth and rays. (It was reputedly removed by the Spanish and lost at gambling by Mancio de Leguisamo, and I wondered if the winning Spanish gambler had sent Inti to the Vatican. John Henning's *The Conquest of the Incas* states that the face of Inti, the Punchau, was taken and hidden by the Incas, not the Spanish; and that the story of the gambling was boastful.)

We went on to Saksaywaman, a Temple of the Sun on three levels representing the upper world, this world and the underworld, and on to Puka Pukara, a 'red fortress' on a high plateau commanding a view of four valleys which lead to the Four Quarters of the Inca Kingdom. It was called the Inca Empire's 'navel' (the navel being at the centre of four human limbs, two legs and two arms).

We went on to Qenqo, a rocky cleft with a path through it which seems to have symbolised the Underworld. In the middle there was a granite slab on which mummification took place, and where there were animal and human sacrifices. (The common people went past a snake to the underworld, the nobles past a condor to the upper world, where they carried on living.) We later visited the Museum of Pre-Columbian Arts (covering the Moche, Masca, Huari, Chin and Inca cultures).

We visited an Indian community 3,700 metres (nearly 12,000 feet) up in the Andes. It was in a tiny place, Ccaccaccollo, and to reach it our minibus drove along mud paths with precipices and drops of a thousand feet. Under wooden houses perched on the side of a mountain two dozen Indian ladies were weaving. They were cut off from the outside world, and all the men were away, working as cooks or baggage handlers, except for one, Rufino, who was 100 years old and sat between two sticks. He told me that the secret of a long life was to avoid alcohol and eat food without chemicals. He cupped his hand and I gave him a sol for being 100. He looked at it and seemed pleased enough. We went on to a small farm for llamas and alpacas, which we fed with alfalfa.

Our minibus took us on to the Sacred River, the Urubamba, which wound through a green valley where the Incas came for fruit. We went on to an Inca neighbourhood at Pisac, 3,500 metres above the valley. I visited an Inca cemetery: inaccessible holes in a cliff face reached by rope. There were stone outlines of abandoned houses, a Temple of the Sun and an observatory. We drove on to Ollantaytambo, where there is a Temple of the Moon with windows, and Temple of the Sun high up on tiers. Across the valley on another mountain were four tiers of buildings, near which the god Tunupa, protector of harvests carved by Incas on the slope of the rock, looked down on us with massive eyes and mouth. Every 21 June (the winter solstice) at 9 a.m. the sun moves from the Temple of the Sun to Tunupa's eyes, and every 22 December (the summer solstice) at 11 or 12 a shadow fills a gullied-out hole in the rock-face.

We went on to the Temple of the Condor where the outline of a condor at rest with a bill is carved on the mountain. On 22 December a shadow is cast on a table where there was an animal or human sacrifice by nobles. We went on to our hotel, San Augustin, in Urubamba, which had opened as a monastery in 1630.

We took a glass-topped train that trundled on a single track through towering crags to Aguas Calientes. A porter wheeled our luggage through a market to the Machu Picchu Hotel and our room had a balcony above the rapids of the boulder-strewn Urubamba, plunging mountains and gorges.

We visited Machu Picchu. We left at 6.15 a.m. the next morning on a bus that climbed through the Amazon jungle, up zigzag bends past orchids to the top of a crag. By 7 we were looking down on green-grey semi-circular Machu Picchu's terraces with mountains all round, wooded slopes, chasms and gorges. I spotted the Temple of the Sun. I left Ann to sit at a lower level, which she had to herself, and climbed to the very top. The sun had broken over the top of a range and its rays shone out across the misty mountains. I understood why Inti is rayed. Swifts darted around us above steepling rocks. There were already 100 young people on the plateau of the top, vying to have their pictures taken and receiving certificates to cheers and claps. Awe at the numinous disappeared into the social *mêlée*, and I rejoined Ann.

We walked with our guide to Machu Picchu and looked down on 274 buildings that had been inhabited by more than 1,000 people in its agricultural, industrial, religious and urban districts. It had been built from c.1430 to 1530, and was abandoned in 1542 and covered in jungle until it was rediscovered in 1911. We went to the Mother Earth Temple below the Temple of the Sun, a cave with sculpted steps where llama sacrifices were made, and to the Inca Princess's residence. The Temple of the Sun above it had two windows. The guide showed us a diagram from *The Astronomy of the Incas* by Tom Zuidema. It showed the sun on 21 June (at 7.21 a.m.) and 22 December (at 6.18 a.m.) striking the same point inside the Temple, with an angle between the June and December lines of 46.9°, and a line bisecting this angle at 23.45° linked the sun to the axis of the earth. He said that the Inca engineers and astronomers knew how the universe ran. He said that the Incas had worked out that the earth is moving round the sun, as can be established by these angles, before Copernicus (1473–1543) and Galileo

(1564–1642). The Incas knew about equinoxes and solstices and could predict when crops should be sown and amendments to the calendar. Pachacuti (1438–1471) had his court at Cusco near the Temple of the Sun there so he could project himself as master of the universe.

History was being stood on its head. The Greeks and Romans had known that the earth is round, as can be seen from ancient statues of Atlas holding up the globe (*see* p.v). Columbus came to believe in 1483 that the earth is round and that the East Indies could be reached by sailing west. In 1492 Columbus thought he had found American natives who were ignorant of the universe. However if our guide was right, in some respects the American Incas were superior to Spanish Christians for they believed the earth went round the sun whereas the Spanish believed that the sun revolved around the earth and that Jerusalem was the centre of the universe. Did the Incas worship the sun because they had worked out that the earth moved round the sun, and were the Nazca lines, figures when seen from the air, communications with the sun?

We went on to the religious district and stood by Intihuatana, a sundial – a place where the sun is tethered to the earth, a tethering point where Incas would have felt closest to Inti. If the sun was tethered to the earth, it was likely that the earth was preventing the sun from floating away by the tether. Both were static in the Incas' minds. Or could the earth's orbit round the sun be kept regular and held in place by the tether? We went on to the industrial district, and then on to the Temple of Condor in the lower urban district. I found the Royal Palace near the Temple of the Sun, where Pachacuti is thought to have stayed when he came to review the works.

I had been tipped off as to where I could find original Inca treasures and was offered a wooden cup with a yellow plant colouring, which, I was told, represented the sun (Inti) on a 'lake' ('*cocha*'). On another interpretation it showed the sun rising (Inti) and the sun setting, and the meeting of the Four Quarters, and so was post-1440, of the time (and style) of Pachacuti. It was used for corn drinks or sacrifices to Mother Earth. I bought it. The Incas were still around: in a shop that sold pyramids I was assisted by a descendant of an old Inca family, a swarthy girl with slit brown eyes and the elegance of a princess, who was very proud of her Inca roots.

Back in Lima and at sea level we made our way to the National Museum's Inca Room. The first object in a case that I saw was a replica of my '*quero*' (cup of wood). I found a museum official who spoke English, showed him and said I had a similar cup. He said it would be Inca and of the time of Pachacuti, that the diamond within a diamond can often represent 'lake' ('*cocha*'), but it can also be Inti setting as the same symbol with rays on all four sides represents Inti rising. Without doubt, I had an interesting Inca cup.

We flew back to London. I had deepened my thinking about the Incas' view of the earth's relationship with the sun, which they thought was tethered to the earth. I researched astronomy in the Inca time – the solstices and equinoxes – and concluded that there was no academic evidence that the Incas knew they lived in a heliocentric universe.[12] However, to my surprise the Incas had given me a number of insights into the medieval view of the running of the universe, which would stand me in good stead in *The New Philosophy of Universalism*.

The New Philosophy of Universalism
Towards the end of August I began work on the biology section of *The New Philosophy of Universalism*. In June my PA had resigned on learning that her father had terminal cancer. The temporary replacement had a day-time job in a recruitment agency. She came at 7 a.m. and left at 8 a.m. to go to work, and returned at 4.30 p.m. on her way home. There were regular early-morning sessions throughout September.

On 20 September I met John Hunt in the Charing Cross Hotel coffee lounge. Much of our conversation was on aspects of the book though mostly on biology and cosmology. We agreed that man is not a finished form, that evolution is continuing, including the evolution of consciousness. Again, we had lunch in the dining area ten yards away. The next day he emailed, asking if I could finish the book in six months. He asked for a new synopsis that would reflect the detailed points in our discussion, including the universal principle of order. A few days later I noted:

The Law of Order and the Law of Randomness, a philosophical *yin* and *yang* = Being + Existence; Being's Order + Existence's Randomness.

Order and Randomness were another +A and –A, which together equalled 0, the One.

In October I completed my treatment of biology, which included evidential lists, and turned to cosmology and physics. I worked on the biocosmology, ecology and physiology chapters, and was ready to consider Ice Ages and the creation of continents as I left for Antarctica.[13]

In Argentina, Falkland Islands, South Georgia, Antarctica: Ice Ages and global warming
It was now time to absorb the ecology of the Southern Ocean and confront climate change. We flew to Buenos Aires on 5 November, and the next afternoon drove through the city to Tigre and saw the 20-mile-wide River Plate (the scene of Admiral Woodhouse's naval battle, *see My Double Life 1: This Dark Wood*, p.121). We toured Buenos Aires: the train station, the British

built in 1850 and most memorably La Recoleta cemetery, which was opened in the 1870s for yellow-fever victims. It was a City of the Dead: streets with mausoleums as large as houses, with front doors. The dead had been laid to rest above ground on shelves that could be seen through glass along with photos and busts; past generations still venerated. The tomb of the Duarte family included the future First Lady of Argentina, Eva Peron (one of three illegitimate children). We passed the Malvinas memorial and reached the Pink House, and saw the balcony from which Eva and Galtieri spoke. We arrived at the port that was ravaged by yellow fever.

We set off for Antarctica. We flew to Ushaia and again boarded the *Minerva* (renamed *Explorer II* for this voyage). We immediately grasped that there were fewer passengers than usual. The passenger list had been restricted to 120, and on health-and-safety grounds there were more than 240 crew, a ratio of two crew to each passenger. We dined as the ship left Ushaia (gulls feeding and settling in our wake) for the notorious Drake's Passage and I made contact with the very experienced speakers: natural historians, a geologist and experts on global warming and Ice Ages.

The next day was at sea. We walked on deck in our new red parka jackets, which were very warm, and saw two fin whales (a mother and baby) alongside the ship. The next morning we went by Zodiac to West Falklands New Island. We landed near the woolshed where shortly before the Falklands War Argentinians landed and daubed 'Viva Argentina'. We hiked half a mile up a slope to where a colony of rockhopper penguins stood on cliffs that sloped down to the sea. We also saw a colony of black-bowed albatrosses and, over a hill, penguin cormorants. I walked back with a Falklander who had seen two headless Argentinian corpses in the street in 1982, and we returned to the ship through stinging rain.

After lunch we landed on Carcass Island in a slight swell. We walked up from a sandy cove to the McGills's house, had tea and cakes and returned past gorse to the Zodiac. There was now a swell which brought huge waves. We made unsuccessful approaches to the platform at the foot of the steps up into the ship, and with the Zodiac rising and plunging like a lift below the steps we were grabbed one at a time and bundled onto the platform to climb aboard.

We landed at Stanley the next morning and toured the Falklands battle-fields. We drove through open, craggy terrain, alongside minefields, past Wireless Range, Mount Longdon, Mount Tumbledown, Mount Harriet and Two Sisters, past Bluff Cove to Fitzroy Farm, which the British captured. After coffee in the community centre we walked to the uninhabited Port Pleasant to see where the *Sir Galahad* was sunk. At 11 a.m. near the war memorials a two-minute silence was observed. We all stood in silence in a hailstorm that stung our cheeks. We returned to Stanley and saw the

Governor's House, Victory Green and Margaret Thatcher Drive. There was a snowstorm in mid-afternoon. Stanley was tiny, more like a remote English village than an island capital.

We spent two days at sea during which I spoke at length with the geologist, Patrick Abbott, Professor Emeritus in Geological Sciences at San Diego University. He showed me his laptop data on Ice-Age cycles, and agreed that we are in a glacial period, that global warming is within an Ice Age. (In 2013 the global cooling increased the Arctic Ice Cap by 920,000 square miles in a year.) We watched the birds follow our wake, and saw a royal albatross, a southern giant petrel, many cape petrels, a black-browed albatross, prions and two wandering albatrosses. A naturalist told me that the Ancient Mariner had shot a wandering albatross, and that the sailors had hung it round his neck on his back, which was what sailors did if anyone killed a wandering albatross. I lunched with a marine biologist and dined with a microbiologist. On the second day we encountered icebergs and our speed slowed. I drafted paragraphs on plate tectonics and was able to discuss them with our geologist, Pat Abbott.

We wet-landed on South Georgia off a Zodiac, swinging our legs over the side between breakers. Along the beach of Salisbury Plain, before white mountains and glaciers on a stretch of stones, stood tens of thousands of king penguins. They covered the huge plain and stretched up the distant mountainside, many with food in their bellies to regurgitate for their chicks. Among them, brown chicks flapped their flippers. Skuas flew low, looking for scraps of food and wounded penguins. A Darwinist naturalist told us they only thought of survival and food and had no social interaction. However, they were all in tiny groups and I could detect social interaction within their groups and with the many thousands of their species. Fur seals and huge elephant seals lay on the beach and flopped aggressively towards rivals that had encroached on their territory. After lunch on the ship a Zodiac took us to inaccessible coves, and we saw gentoo and macaroni penguins, grey-headed and sooty albatrosses and big petrels. When I took my gloves off to cope with my camera the cold numbed my fingers.

The next morning we moored at Grytviken on the other side of South Georgia in a lagoon-like sea under snow-white mountains. We made a wet landing near Shackleton's grave, where there was an oration on how 'the Boss' brought all his men back safely, a feat that precipitated his heart attack on *Quest* in this beautiful bay. We all toasted him from cartons of white wine. As a boy I had read of Shackleton's legendary rescue of his men stranded on Elephant Island in 1916 by rowing the 800 nautical miles to South Georgia and traversing the mountainous island on foot to raise the alarm. During the final, gruelling march to the whaling station at Grytviken with his two companions (Crean and Worsley) he reported that he was aware of a mysterious presence at his elbow, giving rise to Eliot's line in 'The Waste Land' "Who is the third who walks always beside you?" (As Shackleton had two companions during the march, Eliot should have written "fourth", not "third".) We walked down over uneven grass and patches of snow past basking seals and penguins to the now derelict whaling station and noted rusting, decaying equipment near a couple of decaying whaling-boats.

We replicated the last two miles of Shackleton's heroic rescue that afternoon. We landed on a beach in Stromness Bay, collected pebbles to frighten off aggressive fur and elephant seals and route-marched two miles to the waterfall Shackleton and his two men had lowered themselves down by rope at the end of their crossing of South Georgia. During our march back we walked through sloping scree and shallow streams and were dive-bombed by Antarctic terns until we were clear of their eggs. It was a gruelling hike for us, and all the more so for Shackleton's men as they were already exhausted and starving.

At 4 a.m. the next morning we went by Zodiac to South Georgia's Gold Harbour under the Bertrab glacier. On the long beach, beyond elephant seals, were many king and gentoo penguins. Skuas were eating a downy penguin chick. We sailed on to Drygalski fjord, where we saw a bit of Gondwanaland (the southern supercontinent that separated from Laurasia 200–180 million years ago when rocks speared up from the earth's crust by the Scotia plate). I had a lengthy discussion on Ice Ages and climate change with our geologist, Pat Abbott.

We had two more days at sea. There was a storm and the ship rolled from sea to sky. At lunch the tablecloths were wetted to stop plates sliding about. At one point everyone rushed to one side of the ship to watch a pod of orcas – several killer whales and calves – attack a minke whale while a huge flock of birds flapped on the water, sensing food. It was announced that this was only the third time that such an attack had been seen in the waters of the Southern Ocean.

Pat Abbott advanced the idea that DNA only goes back around 75,000 years as a volcanic eruption about that time that wiped out the dinosaurs reduced humankind to a few people There was no evidence for this. I lunched with Pat and his wife and discussed geology and global warming. In the afternoon I wrote much of my book's sections on plate tectonics and Ice Ages.

We reached the South Shetland Islands. We landed by Zodiac on Penguin Island – boulders, pebbles and ice – and trudged through deep snow past Adélie penguins to a colony of chinstrap penguins. I talked to two naturalists about instincts to return to old breeding-grounds and later wrote four paragraphs into the book. After lunch we landed on King George Island, the largest of the South Shetland Islands. We found a colony of

Adélie penguins in thick snow, and trudged to Henryk Arctowski Polish Antarctic Station. I asked a Polish girl selling postcards who owned the island (named after George III), and she replied, "Argentina." Argentina claims ownership of the island but it is part of the British Antarctic territory.

Early next morning we reached another South Shetland Island, Deception Island. We entered the gap in the caldera, Neptune's Bellows, in a temperature of zero and a windchill that froze the nose. We walked to the old British base hut, which had been abandoned after a volcanic eruption. The beach was black volcanic ash, and the steaming waters smelt of sulphur which seemed to suit the cape penguins. The snow was knee-deep in some places, and I saw Neptune's Window high up on a ridge.

We now approached our objective: a landing on the Antarctic Peninsula in Paradise Bay. In the evening we were in the Gerlache Strait between Brabant Island and Graham Land on the Peninsula. There were stunning views and the sun seemed to set but did not set. It was very windy – there was a force 11 wind – and icebergs flowed past us. We sheltered for the night out of the wind at anchor near Brabant Island. The sun and the moon on the ice gave a magical, wonderful light. At 3.30 a.m. next morning we had spectacular views of Anvers Island, Wiencke Island and Bryde Island. We entered Paradise Bay on the Antarctic Peninsula, a 'lagoon' surrounded by towering white mountains and glaciers. We saw a disused Argentinian station (Almirante Brown) and beside it a colony of gentoos and on the black water under the white mountain peaks there was pack ice, a glacier having calved an hour previously. There were a few blue-eyed shags, but otherwise there was an eerie stillness.

We clambered down into a Zodiac and slowly made our way through the ice. The stillness was uncanny. There were small icebergs and bits of the broken-away glacier around us, and the surrounding mountain peaks contained glaciers that would soon calve. We wet-landed on a tiny stony shelf on the Antarctic Peninsula, and I climbed ten feet onto a rock and stood, out of sight of everyone else, briefly alone on Antarctica.

After lunch in the open air on the Bridge deck, the sun warm on our cheeks through the hole in the ozone layer, we were allowed to visit the captain on the bridge. The captain told us as we steered through the Neumayer Channel that an iceberg had calved and spread pack ice up one end of Paradise Bay while we were standing on the stones and rocks of Antarctica. We had not heard the distant roar.

We reached Port Lockroy on Wiencke Island in mid-afternoon. We visited the British Base A (1944–1952), a large hut surrounded by gentoo penguins and thick snow. We went on a Zodiac tour of the bay and saw Weddell seals and Dominican gulls. The ship continued along the Neumayer Channel to Dallmann Bay.

We entered the notorious Drake's Passage on our way back to Ushaia. The ship rolled and creaked. The next morning the tannoy woke us early: "Good morning, ladies and gentlemen. Sadly, I have to tell you that our sister ship, *Explorer I*, has sunk in the Antarctic Sound. Our thoughts go out to the passengers and crew." BBC television carried a report that "*The Explorer*" had sunk, and showed a picture of our ship, *Explorer II* (as the *Minerva* was known for this voyage). Our son Matthew was opening a newly-astroturfed tennis-court at Coopersale Hall with Ray Clemence, the former Spurs and England goalkeeper. He received a message from one of the staff, who had seen an early news, that his parents might be at the bottom of the Antarctic Sound, and carried on with the opening. It those days there was no signal between Ushaia and Antarctica, and so no mobile or email messages were possible. All passengers were asked to queue at the ship's reception to send a fax, and eventually Matthew received a fax from the ship confirming that we were safe. A later announcement confirmed that *Explorer I* had hit a small iceberg and been holed, and that the passengers and crew were safe although their luggage was under the sea.

We returned across Drake's Passage to Cape Horn. In former days, seeing Cape Horn entitled sailors to put one foot on the table and wear an earring without being punished. We disembarked at Ushaia amid snow-streaked mountains. A notice said: "Ushaia, the end of the world – the beginning of everything." After we had our passports stamped 'The End of the World' I thought how I had returned from a remote universal 'everything' that had been beyond the social world. We were taken to a lake to see where Yamanas (native Indians) lived before white settlers wiped them out, and beavers' colonies. We flew back to Buenos Aires, and on the television in our hotel room we saw pictures of *Explorer I* listing, holed by a submerged iceberg like the *Titanic*.

My observation of wildlife in the Southern Ocean and my research into Ice Ages, global warming and plate tectonics had carried forward my thinking regarding the order within the universe.[14]

The New Philosophy of Universalism *continued: synthetic method*
My temporary PA had left to oversee branches of her recruitment agency and she had put me in touch with Ingrid Kirk, a highly competent, multi-lingual Dutch secretary with legal and medical experience who had become my permanent PA. She had worked a couple of mornings before I left for Antarctica. She worked with me every morning and took away tapes to key in at home, and I now made good progress on *The New Philosophy of Universalism*. In December I moved from biology to the Presocratics, and by mid-December I was working on the Big Bang (chapter 3), and then the 40 conditions that are just right for human life (chapter 5). I then moved on to

the quantum vacuum (chapter 4).

In January I worked on the decline of Western philosophy (chapter 2). I was opposed to linguistic analysis. Analysis breaks down into differing components, like breaking a vase into potsherds, whereas its opposite, synthesis, reassembles the differing components or bits into a unity, pieces the bits back together. Analytical philosophy reduces language, and with it the universe, to bits whereas synthetic philosophy esemplastically reassembles the universe into a unity. *The New Philosophy of Universalism* is a rare example of synthetic philosophy, and the synthetic method can be found in *My Double Life 1* and *2*.

I then completed the sections on ecology and physiology (chs.7 and 8) and moved on to my metaphysical review of the universe (chs.9 and 10). On 1 February I finished the applications of Universalist thinking (chs.11 and 12). Throughout February I combed through, making amendments and adjustments, and in March compiled the Notes and References about sources. In April I compiled the philosophical families and the timeline. I made sure that the cover would show the shuttlecock-shaped expanding universe with a surfer crouched on the edge of surging expansion, his feet in space-time, his body and head in the surrounding infinite. The surfer is my image for the man who lives in both the finite and the infinite.

In Parts One and Two of *The New Philosophy of Universalism* I focus on the universe known to contemporary scientists. The biology and geology section evaluates evolution and draws on my visits to the Galapagos Islands and Antarctica. In Part Three I show that Universalism is a systematic philosophy of the expanding universe, Nature and man, and how a Law of Order counterbalances a Law of Randomness. In Part Four I present its global applications. In a time when philosophy has preferred to focus on logic and language and has become increasingly irrelevant, I show Universalism reconnecting philosophy to Nature and the thinking of the Presocratic Greeks, and reunifying the universe and scientific disciplines so philosophy can once again consider the whole of reality. I show how the new philosophy restates the order within the universe, the oneness of humankind and an infinite Reality perceived as Light. The subtitle of the book is: *The Infinite and the Law of Order*.

At the end of March I wrote: "In my philosophy I aim to be magisterial – masterly in the sense of dominating material." At the end of April I wrote: "I am near the end of the book. The immensity of the task I have just completed is now dawning on me." (Interestingly, David Lorimer used the word "magisterial" and Chris Macann "immense" in their public comments.) The day before I sent the book off I wrote: "I am in a passive, fallow mode after so much effort." The sustained thinking had drained me, but I had got the book done in just over five months after returning from

Antarctica (to which just over two months should be added to cover my work before Antarctica).[15]

Ken Campbell: reading of The Warlords, *death and funeral*
My philosophy of Universalism combined all pairs of opposites in accordance with $+A + -A = 0$, including war and peace, which I had reconciled in *The Warlords*.

In January 2007 I had attended a one-man show by my contemporary Old Chigwellian Ken Campbell in the drama theatre at Chigwell School. He was known as a dramatist of surrealistic, anarchic plays and as an actor. He was bald with huge eyebrows, and as I sat in the front row and listened to his zany monologue, at one point his eyes fixed on mine. After the interval he came out holding *The Syndicate*. He began the second half by saying to me, "I've read your books. Here, sign this." To mirth from the audience I duly signed and wrote above my signature, thinking back to 1957, "Do you remember visiting Jimmy in his signal-box?" He read what I had written and said, "Yes, I do." After the show I chatted to some of my contemporaries, and he joined me and gave me his address and phone number. He had moved to 40 Baldwin's Hill, Loughton with his three dogs. He had had to leave his previous address because his pit-bull terrier had bitten a policeman.

I next encountered him at my local garage as I was filling my car. We chatted. Two days later I visited him and talked through the wrought-iron lattice across his open front door. I handed him *Collected Verse Plays*. He was wearing a blue sweater with epaulettes and with his bald head and bushy eyebrows looked gnome-like in his small house with a protruding gable that was down steep steps from the road. Later he rang to say that he wanted to organise a reading of *The Warlords* in Hampstead in the late autumn. He asked if he could have one or two more of my books which he had not read, and the next day I took them to him.

This time the iron lattice was open. He sat me in a chair in a cluttered room at the back. It was full of African masques and a ventriloquist's dummy of Campbell. He stood and did a one-man show in a loud voice. He said he was in the tradition of the long-dead Jimmy Cooper, who lived out of the box office of a small theatre in Ilford. He painted the sets, directed and acted, and kept himself in his signal-box. Ken wanted Oliver Senton (the son of David Senton, my contemporary at Chigwell) to be at the reading, along with Campbell's "epic man" who spoke in iambic pentameters. He told me he had visited one of my Latin teachers, Webb (who gave me my Tutankhamen figurine), in a hospice. Webb was in a coma, and Campbell had talked about Newfoundland, where he had just been. Webb sat up and said, "Newfoundland? That's where I came from."

Campbell described a walk through St John's up to the citadel. When he reached the top, Webb lapsed back into his coma and died. Campbell asked if I would like a cup of tea and cast around for a cup that was not awaiting the washing-up, but I declined.

In September he sent me a postcard telling me that the reading would take place at midday on 16 December. In early December he told me I had disregarded everything that happened at the Royal Court and had gone back to Eliot, Fry and Ronald Duncan. I said: "Back to Sophocles and Shakespeare, no scenery, words replacing scenery. It's a poetic form." He said the reading would be from 12.30 to 8. He asked if Tony could be present and bring his camera.

Two days before the reading he invited me to the Foresters Arms, across the road from him. We spent two hours discussing *The Warlords*, Montgomery, Eisenhower and the Syndicate's plans. He was extremely eager to hear about 'secret information' which he could pass on at the reading. He told me his group of actors was known as his 'School of Night' (a name he had taken from Raleigh's 'School of Night' which Shakespeare satirised in *Love's Labour's Lost*).

On 16 December Tony drove me to 12 Buckland Crescent, NW3. We found at least a dozen actors in a large room sharing broken rolls, cheese, wine and juice and talking in small groups. Dark-haired, dark-eyed Sue Rose owned the house and acted as hostess. Campbell called everyone to order and we sat on chairs in a circle. He introduced me, and with Tony filming (and with David and Oliver Senton present) I spoke about the verse and a little bit about the play. Campbell said that five should audition for Montgomery, and I whittled them down to the last two, one of whom, Oliver Senton, proposed the other, Chris Fairbank, who had acted in *Auf Wiedersehen, Pet* in the 1980s. He read brilliantly. We stopped periodically, and I fast-forwarded them to speed things up. Campbell said that the reduced version of *The Warlords* form should be produced with some further cuts, and built round Chris Fairbank's Montgomery.[16]

On the way home Tony said he would produce a further reduced version that would be acceptable to all. And in early August 2008 he finished a draft entitled *Montgomery*.[17] He brought a print-out round on 2 September. The intention was that I should give it to Ken Campbell but later that same day Campbell's death was announced – on the very day that *Montgomery* was finished. The obituaries in *The Times* and *The Guardian* dwelt on his anarchic humour which was in the tradition of the French surrealists, of Ionesco and N.F. Simpson. Like them he developed absurd logic, suggesting that an African tribe's English should be the international language.

His daughter rang with details of his funeral. She told me she had bought a caravan and, excited, her father had invited her to Sunday lunch. When she arrived he was lying on the dog cushions on the floor looking very peaceful with his eyes closed, "perfectly arranged". "He hadn't fallen, and his box with his passport was nearby, next to him." She said he must have felt a heart attack coming on, and instead of ringing 999 had got his important box which he kept hidden, lain down and meditated, and been taken. She said, "I am very proud that he was my father." I told her that I was there at the start, and had met Jimmy. She said, "He was very excited about your play at the studio."

I attended his funeral at Epping Forest Burial Park, North Weald. Between two and three hundred drank coffee at the Gathering Centre near pictures on a board of Campbell in his productions and albums of photos. I was the only Old Chigwellian. I came across Warren Mitchell, sitting in a wheelchair on his own at 82 – he had starred with Campbell in *Art* in 1999 – and told him I had seen the beginning of Campbell's career at school. I spoke to one or two of the 'School of Night', including Chris Fairbank. We sat in rows of chairs for a humanist service (no hymns or prayers), and from a screen at the front came Campbell's voice: "'Funeral' is an anagram for 'Real fun'." There was loud laughter. A kind of memorial service followed: an appreciation of his life by three actors who had known him. There was a song, a snippet from one of his productions, and words from his ex-wife (an actress, Prunella Gee, who had briefly been a Bond girl – a masseuse in *Thunderball*) and his daughter. Then a young man in his thirties wearing a T-shirt rushed to the front, shouting, and tried to open the coffin, which was pushed off its holder and nearly fell to the ground. He shouted, "I am so sorry, I didn't want him to die." I wondered what he had done. He was wrestled away and hustled out. There were impromptu contributions from others, including a tearful Warren Mitchell. There were stories. Campbell had been asked, "What's your opinion of the after-life?" "I'm for it." The proceedings ended with Campbell's voice talking about the universe.

We followed the coffin into the Forest around a stony path, his three dogs on leashes, led by actors playing a clarinet and violin. There was a green carpet round the grave, and six actors lowered the coffin. We lined up to throw a handful of earth onto the coffin. On the way back I fell into step with his ex-wife, Pru, who had been educated at Benenden and had been on the road with him. I said his improvisations undermined all forms, and she said, "He had no taste." I said, "But he had good taste in finding you," and she flashed me an appreciative glance. I encountered Warren Mitchell and at his request gave him directions as to how to find Campbell's house in Loughton. Later I walked with Sue Rose. She told me that the disturber had quarrelled with Ken and felt responsible for his death. I said that Campbell's daughter said he had had a heart attack. She said doubtfully, "Mmm." I wondered if she had another explanation for his being beautifully arranged by his box.

I reflected that Campbell was an anarchist who had blown up everything: scripts, dramatic form, the English language, the sonnet – one of his turns was to get a performer to recite a sonnet counting from 100 to 0 backwards to blow up all feeling – and I wondered if he found a kindred spirit in me because I had blown up nationalism and also the New World Order. But I was not an anarchist. I saw traditional forms dissolving into new schemes. I was not blowing up Western civilization, merely presenting its next stage.[18]

I saw him as a rebel against all conventions. He was an artistic terrorist who blew up the stage. He blew up being a director of a provincial theatre and went roadshow to take theatre to people. He blew up Shakespeare by translating him into pidgin English. He blew up dialogue and put in its place monologue. He blew up the audience by putting on a 22-hour play which was performed at the National Theatre. One of the speakers at his funeral said: "He is in Heaven, and God's been pushed off his throne." He would be finding a way to blow up God.

He had sacked the old theatre and literature. Being innovatory is good, but sacking the old and not putting anything in its place is like destroying the garden and leaving it a waste land. One should not blow things up without putting an improvement in their place. I did not want to blow up the feeling behind the sonnet by obliterating it through counting but add to it and try to reach the standard of the past, of Milton and Wordsworth. I did not want to blow up Shakespeare for pidgin English but to enhance understanding of Shakespeare (via the SAT in my case). Like the anti-Roman barbarians, Campbell had sacked the world and put nothing in its place. The 1860 Nihilists had been destructive. I wondered whether Campbell's destruction had led to self-destruction.

Shoulder operation

I had visited an osteopath for preventative treatment, and was astonished to be told that my pelvis had been out for perhaps 35 years, making one leg longer than the other and causing back problems. He manoeuvred my pelvis back into position, and then found that I only had a 70% ability to hold my right arm up straight, which had probably affected my handwriting. The problem was in my shoulder.

Twenty years of hard writing had taken their toll on my right shoulder. I had felt pain in my right shoulder in Peru and had seen a consultant at Holly House, who believed I had rotator cuff tendons rubbing against a bone. I was given a steroid injection 2 cms (three-quarters of an inch) into my shoulder a few days later, but whereas before I could not move my right arm above 45 degrees I could now only move it to 60 degrees. In January another consultant said (after an MRI) I had a bone spur digging into a tendon, and I needed a small operation. Otherwise my tendon would go on fraying and I would end up unable to use my right hand or write. He said, "This has gone on for over five or ten years. It's wear and tear. All the writing you've been doing has caught up with you." In mid-February I went into the London Independent Hospital. I was given an injection, and the next thing I knew was waking back in my room, having had a keyhole removal of the bone spur. The muscles and tendons of my shoulder had been raked out.[19]

Ann and I spent the night of our wedding anniversary at Down Hall Country House Hotel, whose monastic 14th-century buildings had been bought by Matthew Prior in 1720 just before he died. That building had been pulled down and rebuilt in 1870–1873. We dined in great chairs before a leaping fire in the Ibbetson Room, and my shoulder was getting back to normal.

Ben and Chigwell

Ben came to lunch with Matthew and Kate and said, "I've got into Chigwell," meaning he had passed the entrance exam to Chigwell School. Over lunch I made a little speech: "Grandpa went to Chigwell and wrote about newts and they said, 'Yes, you can come here.' Daddy went and wrote about a lifeboat and they said, 'Yes, you can come here.' Uncle Tony went and wrote about flapjack and they said, 'Yes, you can come here.' And now Ben has gone and written about a castle and they said, 'Yes, you can come here.' I think that calls for a family clap." So, to his delight, we all clapped Ben, who came and held my arm, looking pleased. I was pleased that Ben had found his path and that a family tradition was being continued. To help encourage this had been one of my reasons for leaving Otley Hall.[20]

Matthew's wedding

We had returned from Peru to learn that Matthew and Kate had become engaged on their last night in Tunisia. Over champagne Kate showed us her diamond ring. The talk was of wedding venues and wedding dresses.

Matthew and Kate were married in the chapel at Chigwell School on 22 March. Matthew and his best man, Tony, left in mauve frilly cravats and tails to prepare the reception in cold sleety snow. Ian and Nadia arrived. Ann's relatives from Cornwall had stayed overnight. Cars transported us all and we greeted the assembling guests. The bride appeared out of a blizzard, tall, **Matthew and Kate**

elegant in white and a veil, led by her father. The marriage service was taken by Father Johnston (who had passed on his '*Choi* school' to Matthew) and Father Chris Collingwood. There were readings. I read at the end 'A Wedding Poem' (chosen by Matthew, not one of mine), which contained the line "A wedding is a fusion of two souls".

The reception was in New Hall. We returned to the chapel for photos because of the snowy conditions, and there were more photos in the old staff room under pictures of four Heads I had known (James, Thompson, Wilson and Little). The wedding breakfast was in the dining-hall. I sat on top table, which was adorned with flowers and ivy, between Kate and Ann. Between courses I left the platform and circulated among the guests. There was a short speech from Kate's father and then speeches from Matthew and Tony, which were both witty and well-received. We then returned to New Hall for the rest of the evening, and I stood in the semi-dark near where I sat to take my entrance exam in 1946 and where I sat, lost, on my first day in 1947 and observed the cavorting under flashing lights and wondered where 60 years had gone. Ann looked after Ben while I spoke to a succession of guests. Ben came back and slept at Connaught House. Matthew and Kate left for a honeymoon in Dubai and the Maldives.[21]

There was another wedding at the beginning of May, in Cheshire. My nephew William married Rachel at the 15th-century St Oswald's church, Malpas. The reception was at Wrenbury Hall, where we met the family. I was seated at a table opposite Martin Neary, who had been Organist and Master of the Choristers at Westminster Abbey for ten years. We returned to our hotel in Nantwich and could understand why it was in an enclosed, gated alley: there was massive yobbery in the street outside as a couple of hundred youths shouted, retched and fought at 12.45 a.m.[22]

Wilton House
For a surprise birthday outing, Ann took me from Victoria to Salisbury on the old Venice-Simplon Orient Express. We had breakfast on the train and were driven to Salisbury Cathedral where I stood by the grave in the floor of Edward Heath whose cause I had advanced in Tanzania, and later passed his house. We went on to Wilton House, the seat of the Earls of Pembroke and of Mary Sidney, Countess of Pembroke, a low stone building by the River Nadder. The guide told me that in his opinion Shakespeare's first 17 sonnets were written for the 3rd Earl, William Herbert (whose statue stands in the Bodleian quadrangle). We toured the building. We passed the 1743 copy of the Westminster-Abbey statue of Shakespeare and walked past dozens of Roman and Greek busts and fronts of tombs and the internal courtyard (now a knot-garden) where *As You Like It* was allegedly first performed. Little of the Tudor building survived the fire of 1647. I passed 17th-century illustra-

tions of Arcadia, and through the stairwell on the way out I noticed a picture on the wall, high up, 'The Harmony of History and Poetry', an image of which I arranged to be sent to me. Back on the coach we passed the tiny stone church at Bemerton where George Herbert was vicar, and drove into Arcadia, the green fields and water-meadows along the River Nadder which flows into the Avon. We passed Stonehenge before returning to the station for dinner on the train on the way home.[23]

Opening bank branch
Towards the end of February Barclays had Matthew, Ken and me for lunch in a private room on the 31st floor of their skyscraper in the Docklands with four of their management team, who asked when my connection with my branch started. I described how I had been to tea with the manager's daughter in 1944 and had been allowed to take away two handfuls of foreign coins brought back by servicemen, and said I might be the branch's oldest customer. We were shown oak-panelling from David Barclay's house, c.1733 and the art collection worth £30million, and we ended looking down from a great height on the Pool of London at St Katherine's Dock.

In early May two of the managers invited Matthew and me to cricket at Chelmsford, and sitting by the boundary I was told, "You're going to be asked to open the refurbished Loughton branch, cut the ribbon. We'll have the press there. We took on board what you were saying about the coins, being Barclays' oldest customer at that branch." And so I was rung by the Barclays press officer, who established that my connection with the bank went back to 1944 and that I had had an account there since 1958. On 19 May I went to the bank at 9.30 with Ken and Matthew. We toured the rooms behind the counter and I revisited, and pointed out, where my heap of coins had formed a hill. Then I stood before a ribbon held across the outside of the open doors and I proclaimed to those who were queuing inside, the cashiers and a few passers-by, "I have great pleasure in declaring Barclays' Loughton branch open," and ceremonially cut the ribbon. There was applause and we went inside for Buck's Fizz.[24] (In 2014 the branch became digital, and the cashier-related operation I had unveiled was reduced.)

Tony's award: Young Filmmaker of the Year
Tony had been making progress as a film director. Following *Half-Term* he was shortlisted out of hundreds into the last five for the Brabourne prize, which funded a young director to make a film. He gave his presentation before the judging panel. The next day he heard that the judges had been split and he had come second to a more experienced director. A fortnight later he had breakfast with Stephen Fry, and on the strength of *Half-Term* he acquired the rights to *The Liar* on condition that he was personally involved

in writing the full script. Tony gave Fry a copy of my *Classical Odes*. Ricks's name had come up, and Fry told Tony that he had been under Ricks at Cambridge. On 30 May the Brabourne Trust rang Tony and told him he had  been adjudged the Young Filmmaker of the Year and that he would receive £1,000. On 25 June he received his award at the BAFTA Awards ceremony in the presence of Princess Anne, who spoke to him for several minutes. The Master of Ceremonies was Stephen Fry, who gave him the longest build-up of the evening and announced, to great applause, that Tony would be directing *The Liar*. At the same time the award for the winner of the Brabourne Prize was reduced to £1,000, the same as Tony's.[25]

Tony Hagger, filmmaker

Duke of Gloucester, Nicholas Soames

I was unable to attend the BAFTA Awards because I had accepted an invitation stating that I would be presented to the Duke of Gloucester at a dinner for the Epping Forest Centenary Trust at The Warren. About 50 gathered on the lawn on a warm summer evening, and the Duke of Gloucester arrived late with Lord Petre, the Lord-Lieutenant of Essex (who I had met at Otley Hall) and stood apart. Half a dozen full-time Forest worthies were taken to meet him. Then, as dinner was already late, we took our seats at dining-tables in the conference room, while the Duke sat in a corner. Speaking quietly, he made a short speech and left before the end of the meal. I chatted to Lord Petre about Otley Hall. (He was descended from Robert, Lord Petre who in 1711 snipped a lock from the coiffed head of Arabella Fermor at his home in Ingatestone Hall and inspired Pope's 'The Rape of the Lock'.)[26]

I fared better at a 'Churchill evening' at the home of John Padfield in Theydon Bois. My admiration for Churchill had been behind my links with John Biggs-Davison, then Steve Norris and Lord Tebbit, and over champagne in the garden I spoke with the guest of honour, Nicholas Soames, Churchill's grandson. I told him that I had heard Churchill in 1945, that I had welded Sunnis, Shiites and Kurds in Baghdad, and that Churchill's creation of Iraq had not been a folly. After dinner Soames read a long speech about Churchill's many-sided career as a soldier, craftsman, painter and writer of war memoirs (for which he was awarded a Nobel Prize). I spoke with Van Orden and James Brokenshire before I left.[27]

Nadia's wedding

In early February 2008 Nadia had rung and said that she and Ian wanted to get married in July, after Ian's high-profile concert with Ray Davies at

Hampton Court at the end of May. I was delighted for her.

In July Nadia was married at Leez Priory, near Felsted, Essex: two 16th-century crenellated gatehouses with later additions. Nadia had booked Ann and me into the Granary. We changed and chatted to a few who had assembled, and then Nadia and I were called away and led to the back of the ruined gatehouse. We emerged from under its 16th-century arch (Nadia very elegant in a full-length white wedding dress, I now wearing a maroon tie to go with Ian's cravat) and walked across the lawn to the red carpet between chairs filled with guests and headed past cameras and up steps to the proscenium arch within the main building. I was asked, "Who gives this bride to be married?" I said loudly, "I do." I sat while Ian and Nadia made their responses under the arch. Then Ian led her down the steps and along the red carpet to trays of pink champagne.

Our family converged on us and I chatted to Caroline, still tall with considerable bearing, who had been a witness in the ceremony. My sister said she had a timeless face. Her brother John questioned me about my books and her son Damian told me he would be leading a tank squadron in Basra in November. I also spoke at some length with Caroline's nephew on Damian's side, Simon, who

Nicholas gives Nadia away at her marriage to Ian (see *My Double Life 1: This Dark Wood*, p.460, "Never see your daughter again")

had worked in publishing and was about to start at the British Library. I spoke to musician friends of Ian's, and then we climbed the stairs by the main arch to the Great Hall, where I was shown to top table and seated between Nadia and Ann and opposite Caroline.

The organiser announced, "The father of the bride, Nicholas," and I rose. I spoke about Ian and then dwelt on Nadia, and read a short poem of eight lines I had written in May, 'Two in One'. I produced from my pocket two halves of a polished ammonite 165 million years old, older than human love, and presented the two halves to the couple. I toasted the bride and groom and sat down to thunderous applause. Ian spoke humorously, and then Nadia spoke very warmly, describing me as a tower of strength. She gave me a framed text of 'Sunny Afternoon' ('The taxman's taken all my dough'), signed (at Hampton Court) 'To Nicholas, Ray Davies'. I chatted with Caroline's older brother, Richard, who was now in his eighties and frail, but recalled attending the demonstration in Grosvenor Square 40 years previously.

We went downstairs to the disco room and I danced with Nadia. We then went out into the warm floodlit night and played croquet with Matthew, Tony and Ben, roqueting our opponents' croquet balls into the illumined gatehouse. Many more guests had arrived after the meal.

In a room off the main arch the wedding cake was cut. We took our plates out to chairs in the warm floodlit dark and sat in a group, and Caroline came and sat beside me. She talked about the War on Terror, and, apprehensively, about Damian's posting to Iraq, which was no longer the peaceful country we had known.

Next morning breakfast was at large round tables. Ann and I, Tony and Matthew, Kate and Ben sat at one. Caroline arrived after us with Damian, his wife and three children, and I invited them to join us, which they did. Nadia and Ian then came, and we squeezed them in. We had a harmonious breakfast, chatting freely with each other across the two sides of our families, that purged the atmosphere and brought a belated reconciliation to the discord of over 38 years previously.

Later I sent Damian *The Last Tourist in Iran*, which contained details of a factory in Tehran that produced IEDs (Improvised Explosive Devices) of the kind being sent into Iraq.

I sat and reflected that Damian's father had not been invited, and that I had mounted a wedding that could not have happened if I had gone along with the SIS's ban on my having any further contact with Nadia. Nadia later told me, "Thursday was the best day of my life. It went too quickly. Lots of people have rung and said how lovely it was."[28] I reflected it was the happiest day in her life first because she was overjoyed to be marrying Ian, and because her family was happily reunited and she was the centre of loving attention from all she knew. She and Ian left to spend a few days in Mykonos.

Terror: **Armageddon** *and revolutions*
At Tennyson's Farringford

The day after Ann's birthday I took her to the Isle of Wight to stay at Farringford, once Tennyson's house. I had asked Ricks if he could meet us there, but he wrote that it was impossible. (Tony had taken me to hear his Professor-of-Poetry lecture on 12 May, in which Ricks asked why Graves ended 134 of his poems with question marks, whereas Yeats ended with statements. He had said that he preferred Graves to Yeats, and spoke warmly of Yvor Winters, the Neoclassical critic whose *In Defense of Reason* I had attacked in the essay I wrote in Japan, 'In Defence of the Sequence of Images'.)

We caught the car ferry from Lymington and crossed the harbour bar (now bits of old breakwater) as Tennyson did with his pilot and landed at Yarmouth. We drove to Farringford, an ivied, grand 19th-century house with crenellations on the crest of a hill. We were shown to room 3, 'A.T's Room', Tennyson's bedroom, which had varnished floorboards and a four-poster. We were told that much of the furniture had remained since Tennyson's time. Next door was his wife's room, 'E.T's Room'.

We went down to the new drawing-room for a cream tea. The doors were open and the view of the distant sea was mostly obscured by trees that were not there in Tennyson's day. We went up and found the library on the first floor, Tennyson's new study. Then we went up to Room 17, Tennyson's old attic study, now a bedroom, only the window-frames of which had survived from Tennyson's time. But here he wrote 'Maud', the first four Idylls and 'The Charge of the Light Brigade'. There was a view to the hollow beneath the wood which I was sure was the hollow that the 'I' of 'Maud' hated. The same view could be seen from the library, Tennyson's large new study (c.1861), to which I returned. Here he wrote the last Idylls and 'Locksley Hall' and copied out 'Crossing the Bar' in the fading light and showed Nurse Durham, who had come in to light candles. I looked at his cape, pipes and smoking-hat in a glass display case. Then we took a 'secret staircase', winding down to the conservatory by the old drawing-room, and sat on Tennyson's red settee. I took the path by the roses that led to the summer-house where he escaped visitors and wrote 'Enoch Arden'.

Although Tennyson left this magical, Victorian house for Blackdown, near Haslemere, and died there, I felt his presence as I reconstructed all the places where he wrote poems and received visitors. I noted the mirror and cabinet in the new drawing-room, and reckoned the new dining-room stood on what had been the hollow beneath the wood. I reflected that Tennyson came here to be near Osborne House and Queen Victoria, but also to be out of the limelight as he was naturally shy. I returned to the library. The electric light was not working, but I saw from a sketch in the half-light exactly where Tennyson sat, looking out at the wood of 'Maud'.

After sleeping well, the next morning I sat in the window of Tennyson's bedroom and eventually walked to a gate with a latch, which Tennyson may have been thinking of in 'Maud'. We spent the day driving round the Isle of Wight: to Freshwater Bay, Hanover Point, the Dinosaur Farm Museum (which had dinosaur bones), Ventnor and Shanklin, where we lunched and looked at the Crab Inn where Longfellow stayed. We went on to Sandown, Bembridge and Ryde. We visited Brading Roman villa. We returned to Farringford and dined. I was told that the nursery was in Room 8, which Emily now haunts.

In the fading light I returned to the library, Tennyson's new study, and began making a fair copy of a poem I had scribbled in Ryde (some lines to

Tennyson). Suddenly I felt my spine tingle and my hair prickle, at first as I used to feel when approaching my bedroom at Otley Hall, but then much stronger. The feeling became invasive, it was huge. I felt Tennyson's presence behind me but was not frightened at all. I sat on until it was dark and the light was fading, and I found myself speaking aloud to Tennyson. I said I respected him and asked him to help me in my second epic. 'He' sent me terrific surges as I wrote. It became too dark to see what I was writing and as there was no electric light I asked him to follow me to Room 3, his bedroom.

I returned to Room 3, where Ann was reading in silence. I sat at the small table in the window and there was another terrific surge. He had followed me. He was with me for half an hour. I had written an invocation to Tennyson in draft (*Armageddon*, book 4, 625ff) and at the end, he was "still with me and will be my guide".

The next morning I sat in the library, Tennyson's new study, in broad daylight without any dramatic effects. We toured the Isle of Wight during the day. We went to Carisbrooke Castle and saw the room above the Great Hall where Charles I was imprisoned for five months. (The fireplace and squint were still intact.) There I saw an old photograph of Tennyson's new study in the 1870s. I found Princess Elizabeth's 'prison' and death room, and Charles I's second prison, of which only the window he tried to escape through and a fireplace survive. We went on to Newport Roman villa and Arreton Manor. We then went to Brook Chine where a dozen had met to go fossil-hunting for we might find sponges, fool's gold, fossilised wood and dinosaur's bones and teeth. We would have to walk over slippery rocks, and we returned to Farringford.

After dinner I sat again in Tennyson's new study, at the table (his 'desk') in twilight. I instantly felt my hair prickle and my spine tingle, very strongly. I spoke to Tennyson again, "Alfred, I was here yesterday, I'm writing my second epic poem. Please help me." A tremendous surge came through. Again I said I was going to Room 3, his bedroom, and again within a minute of my sitting down there I was 'invaded' by energy up my neck that made my hair stand on end and raised the hairs on my arms and fingers.

I again slept soundly and next day we visited Osborne House. It was quite crowded. I dwelt on Queen Victoria's family life and her sea view from the upper terrace. I saw the room where she died, the bed still in it. I visited the audience room where Tennyson met her. We lunched on the lower terrace and then crossed by chain-ferry to West Cowes. We went on to the Needles. We caught a bus up to the Old and New Batteries, where rockets were tested during the Cold War. I sat among yellow daisies, six-spot burnets and azure blues.

Back at Farringford I tried to find the site of the old summer-house, but the field of long grass where it was supposed to have been was enclosed in barbed wire. After dinner I returned to Tennyson's new study and began to correct my invocation to Tennyson. Again there were very strong surges. I spoke to him in the gloomy room, saying I had to reconcile my view of Armageddon with the view of St John's *Revelation* and the myth of the Holy Grail, and I asked him to help me. There was a terrific surge up my back and scalp and all over me, and I scribbled own seven points in the margin of the topmost sheet, all pointing to the fact that the Grail should not be found, though all want to find it. This achieved the reconciliation I wanted. I said he was sitting in the chair to the left of the fire or standing over me, and again there was massive power and I felt enfolded. I noted: "I, Nicholas Faust, was as far out as thought can reach, in dialogue with a former Poet Laureate about my forthcoming work – and receiving answers. How well I understand Marlowe's Faustus." I told Alfred again that I was returning to Room 3, his former bedroom, and he came with me. A minute after I began scribbling there, there was a strong invasive surge. I felt warmed through and through.

The next day we went to Dimbola and saw the photos taken by Mrs. Cameron. We went on to Shanklin and found Keats Cottage. It was closed, but I rang the bell next door and a lady took us in. A gift shop was being opened at the front. At the back was Keats's landlady Mrs. Williams's kitchen with an original window, and the office next door where she slept. Upstairs I was shown Keats's small room with a fireplace and saw his bedroom next door. His study – his writing-room – overlooked Shanklin Chine and perhaps the sea. (Keats says so, though I was told the view in his day was to a cliff.) I stood in Keats's writing-room and reflected that after the great odes of May 1819, in July and August, he wrote parts of 'Lamia' and 'Endymion' there, and four Acts of *Otto the Great*. Also, 'The Pot of Basil' and 'The Eve of St Agnes'. I reflected that in 1819 he wrote of this writing-room as his "little coffin of a room". He also had a room at Carisbrooke with Mrs. Cook, where he wrote the first line of 'Endymion' after looking at Carisbrooke Castle.

We walked down the Shanklin Chine through flora and fauna and trees clinging to the ravine's steep sides, through a narrow valley with water at the bottom and stood before the sea. I reflected that Keats first came to Shanklin in April 1817 and wrote 'It keeps eternal whisperings' after walking down the ravine of the Shanklin Chine and encountering the sea from the very spot where I stood. The "desolate shore" was the sandy beach I could see with breakwaters to the right, and the 10,000-year-old cliffs of the chine.

We went on to Bonchurch, the village Tennyson was staying in when he heard about Farringford, and on to Godshill, and then returned to

Farringford, where I had one more look for the summer-house. I let myself out of the picket gate with the latch and managed to climb into the field, which had now been half-cut for hay. Treading on the cut stalks I looked for the base of the summer-house. I had with me a map in Emily Tennyson's *Farringford Journal*, and I stood on what I reckoned was the spot. But there was no trace of any foundation. I had to content myself with the unchanged view that he would have had while writing 'The Holy Grail': cornfields and blue sea in the distant Freshwater Bay.

I returned one final time to Tennyson's new study in fading light. Again I felt a presence. I asked it if it would help me in the coming months. There was a surge (answering Yes). I asked, "Are you pleased I am in this room?" There was a warm surge. I asked, "Are you standing?" There was a strong surge. "Are you standing next to me?" A strong surge. I called him "Alfred". A strong surge. I asked, "Will you help me in my next project?" A strong surge. Our dialogue continued for about 20 minutes as dusk fell. It was as though I had said "Goodbye from me at Farringford" for I was not aware of any presence in Room 3.

We checked out the next morning. The girl on Reception said there had been a plaque on a post in the field giving the location of the summer-house, but that the owner of the farm where we had had a cream tea had removed it as he now owned the field. On the way to the ferry we stopped at All Saints' church to see where Tennyson worshipped and the box tomb in the churchyard where the family, excluding Alfred, were buried. We had a misty crossing back to the Lymington harbour bar.

A few days later I wrote Ricks a full account of my experiences in Tennyson's new study.[29]

Armageddon

I was already immersed in my second poetic epic, *Armageddon*, when I visited Farringford. I had had the idea for some while of writing a long poem about Bush bringing liberty and democracy to the world. I still thought of this work as *Crusaders* as Bush and bin Laden were both crusaders. I had worked on the story and myth, and had drafted a synopsis of the twelve books. I was aware that I was following in Tennyson's footsteps: his long narrative poem, *Idylls of the King*. At the end of September I wrote: "If Tennyson were alive today he would do *Crusaders* as an *Idylls of the King*." (I wrote an invocation to Tennyson as the poet of *Idylls of the King* in *Armageddon*, book 2, 139ff.) I was involved in other works in 2006, but there are several entries in my *Diaries* between September and December as the epic took shape in my mind.

I had gone to Iran to deepen my knowledge of the Shiites. In February 2007 I again mulled over *Armageddon* (as this epic poem had now become).

At the end of March I printed out a synopsis and (between other works) worked on it towards the end of April. I discussed this epic with John Hunt when I met him on 20 September 2007 on my return from the Galapagos Islands and Peru, and he asked as we "staggered ten yards from coffee to the dining area to eat" whether the poem should be called *Holy War*.

On 12 May I had told Ricks that I had finished my philosophy book and was now starting the epic. He had said: "You are fecund." I began thinking about *Armageddon* as soon as *The New Philosophy of Universalism* had been sent off in early May 2008. I began writing the new work on 8 June and wrote 675 lines in four days. I reached the end of book one on 29 June. In early July I was thinking about the clash of civilizations between the North-American and Arab civilizations, and I was teaching Ben to play chess on "our Christians v. Muslims set". (One side was dressed in Crusaders' armour, the other in the armour of the forces of Saladin.) By mid-July I could see where the new epic was going.

Christopher Ricks had kindly said he would discuss *Armageddon* with me in August. On my return from the Galapagos Islands and Peru I found a letter from him saying he regretted he would not be able to meet me as he had had to return to the US on 31 July. He had written his letter on the back of the translation of a poem by Petrarch about Laura's death of the plague, the Black Death, on 6 April 1348. I had already decided to write in blank verse again, and did not have any technical issues to discuss. (I was inspired by Petrarch's poem to write a sonnet seeing Death as a 'terrorist', 'Death the Terrorist'.)

In *Armageddon*'s 26,000 lines of blank verse I follow the War on Terror: George W. Bush's struggle against the Islamic extremism of Osama bin Laden and al-Qaeda. I show bin Laden as possessing at least 20 nuclear suitcase-bombs (a purchase confirmed by Hans Blix of the IAEA in 2004), some of which he planned to explode simultaneously in 10 American cities – hence the title. Through his response to September 11 2001 and the wars of Afghanistan and Iraq Bush transforms himself, the US and the world. The poem reflects the Age and tries to make sense of the first decade of the 21st century.

I worked on the epic down in Cornwall and was researching the invasion of Iraq when I realised I needed material that was in Essex. On our way back from Cornwall we drove to Totnes and stayed in the Daniel Defoe room of the Royal Seven Stars Hotel (an old 1666 coaching-inn where Defoe stayed in 1720), and walked up to the Brutus Stone, an old polished granite rock where, according to medieval legend, the son of Aeneas got off his boat in c.1170BC when there was water there, called the place 'Totnes' and founded Britain. I wrote invocations to Brutus and Defoe which went into book nine of *Armageddon*.[30] I got back to the epic briefly at the end of August, but then other projects intervened (*see* below) and I could not return to *Armageddon* until after Christmas.

The Revolution That Didn't Happen

As far back as 3 December 2007 I had been emailed by a Malcolm Lister, who had written on the British miners' strike, saying he had read my *Scargill the Stalinist?* and asking if I would like to collaborate on a new book on the 1984 miners' strike. He wrote again in April, proposing that we should write different chapters. However, I had my own view of the miners' strike and replied that we should write separate books.

I wrote *The Revolution That Didn't Happen* intending that it should be published in time for the 25th anniversary of the 1984 British miners' strike and Brighton bombing. The main reason I stopped work on *Armageddon* in August was to dash off this book, which would be an eyewitness historical record. I drafted an outline of 12 chapters, and completed chapters 1 and 2, and 11 and 12, by the end of August. I worked on the book from 21 September and much of October. It was finished on 25 October but I continued to add bits throughout November and up to 18 December. By then I had switched to *The Libyan Revolution*.[31]

The book has not yet appeared, but the intention is that it will be published when I have found time to do some further amending.

The Libyan Revolution

Asa Briggs had told me in the Buttery at Worcester College in 1978 that I should write a memoir of the Libyan Revolution, setting out the Muntasser *coup* that Gaddafi stole. On 8 June 2008 it dawned on me that the 40th anniversary of the Gaddafi *coup* would be marked in just over a year's time, on 1 September 2009. I wrote: "I should write a short memoir of Libya and have my newspaper articles at the end." In Cornwall I planned this book's chapter scheme while writing on the miners' strike. In early September I was working on five books simultaneously: *Armageddon*; *The Revolution That Didn't Happen*; *The Libyan Revolution*; *Montgomery* and *The New Philosophy of Universalism*, for whose index I highlighted words I wanted to include which would go to the indexer.

I wrote *The Libyan Revolution* all through November and into mid-December and I finished the book on 11 January. I returned to *Armageddon* but continued occasional work on Libya until early February.[32]

The Libyan Revolution appeared in time for the 40th anniversary of the 1969 revolution. It tells the story of Gaddafi's *coup* (and of the rival *coup* of which I was an eyewitness), and then follows the development of the Libyan Revolution, which it assesses. It presents a portrait of Western Libya to 2009, and my Barbary Gipsy articles are in an Appendix.

Order and Terror: paths, invocations and **Armageddon**
Matthew's path

Matthew's *Choi Kwang Do* had taught him self-defence and had withstood an attempted mugging in August 2004. Matthew had been talking on his mobile while walking to Loughton station along a footpath with high netting on either side when three muscular youths made the mistake of demanding his phone. Matthew scythed into them with high Choi kicks and karate-like chops and left all three lying dazed on the ground. He then hurried to Loughton Police Station to explain what he had done, and why. The policeman said, "You should have killed them."

The wear-and-tear of the *Choi* kicks (which in training can sever a block of wood) had jarred a knee, and on 20 August Matthew had an operation for a 'sports injury' that involved accessing the cartilage behind his kneecap. The operation was not wholly successful. Three weeks before, Kate had returned from a visit to relatives in Canada with news that she was pregnant.[33]

Caroline's path

Just before Matthew's operation Nadia rang me: "I am afraid I've got some bad news. Mum's got breast cancer." It had been revealed after a routine scan, and an operation had been pencilled in for early October. I rang Caroline and said how sorry I was, and urged her to be positive. Ann had long collected stones: every window-ledge of our house had stones with healing properties and fossils, and for her last birthday I had given her a meteorite pendant, two bits of moon and Mars rock that came from NASA and an amber fossil with a prehistoric dragonfly inside it. From a shop in St Albans she bought a green crystal, a peridot stone that is held to heal breast cancer.

In early October Ann and I visited Caroline in Saxmundham. She was in a terraced house with a small garden crammed with potted plants and bird feeders crowded with birds, including goldfinches. I recognised forgotten, familiar paintings on the walls and rugs on the floor that had once been within our house. I gave her an aloe vera plant held to have healing properties. Caroline unwrapped the peridot stone and was touched. Ann chatted and left to shop.

I asked Caroline about the practicalities of her operation on 21 October. Nadia would be on hand to take her in and collect her. She was afraid that the cancer may have spread, but I said there was no evidence yet and that she should be optimistic and be determined to make a full recovery. She told me of her despair in the nights, and that her Hindu philosophy course had taught her that she had a path to follow. She said, "Our paths were different. You followed a different path from mine. I was lost in Libya, it was the wrong place. You went on and met Ann and wrote books. I'm not sure of my purpose." She said that, looking back she could see she had been "naïve" in her youth. Ann returned and we all had a cup of tea at a round table that had belonged to Caroline's parents and had witnessed my first wedding reception, sitting on the spoked chairs we sat on during my first visit to meet Caroline's parents. There were many books in the sitting-room and in other rooms, including her bedroom, as we saw when she showed us round.

On the way back Ann and I discussed purpose and paths. Ann said: "We are born on our paths and then make choices, and a branch leads to other choices. We have to be true to ourselves, and there is more than one path for us. You could have been a writer had you not gone to Oxford, you could have done it from Law and then left Law to be a full-time writer. I could have gone to college to be an almoner within the Welfare State (a position now abolished) rather than become a teacher. I wanted to be a counsellor to put people on the right path. Our paths coincided, we walked beside each other as our paths joined. Paths are not predestined or random-haphazard, but chosen in accordance with our nature and our skills and inheritance (our genes). Sometimes people make a wrong choice against their natures, like Ricky choosing drugs. It's anodyne, a self-justification that 'our paths had to diverge so we both benefited'. There are different choices for different routes, they go well if it's within you."

I thought this a very wise statement of our paths. Ann had been attending weekly art classes, and a room at Connaught House was filled with her canvases, each of which made a telling point. A boot with three paintbrushes propped inside (*see* pp.701–702) told of her love of walking and painting. A teapot and cups showed her love of family tea. But her work was also universal: an egg the size of the Earth with sperm swimming round it like comets evoked with great simplicity the very heart of life. The same true eye had made a very definite statement about paths, while she was concentrating on driving back to Essex.

I reflected that by and large I had made right choices. I suffered a defection. Was Caroline's defecting choice right for her? It had led to Damian, who was now in Iraq (where we had been). When she moved from 177 South Croxted Road she had allegedly destroyed the canvas she had painted of me in Japan, which showed me in a fisherman's polo-necked sweater, that had hung on my study wall. (I could not understand that decision, just as I could not understand how she could have pawned her engagement ring and not reclaimed it by the due date.) I thought her purpose was to be creative through her paintings, to be a mother for her children and a grandmother. At night she chewed over her achievement, but I could see the path she was on. She had said, "Our paths were always going to be different." She meant that our separation was inevitable, but I was not sure that anything is inevitable.

Ann and I visited Caroline again two weeks later, to wish her well for her coming operation. Ann went shopping in Woodbridge, and I had lunch with Caroline on her parents' round table. She told me how her father was in Holtzminden prisoner-of-war camp during the First World War with Leonard Pearson, and that during an escape down a tunnel the Germans had arrived and kicked the tunnel in, and that Pearson had been trapped for seven hours and lost his reason. She showed me Barry Winchester's two books about the time, *Beyond the Tumult* and *84 Days*, the first of which mentioned her father – indeed he had written the introduction to the book in July 1971. She told me that Pearson's wife had "cursed" her father and his family (her mother, brothers and her) for causing Pearson to be in the tunnel. She told me she only "jokingly believed in" this curse, and said she sometimes felt it "was behind what happened to our marriage". She said, "In Japan I was diverted, and it did me no good. But I knew from Japan that it wasn't right. I kept being interfered with, diverted. It wasn't your fault. Our marriage was doomed." She did not believe in the curse but was talking as if our separation was inevitable. She was from a military family, and somehow accepted the Pearson rage. She was adamant that she and I were doomed from Japan. "It felt wrong. We were always going to split."

The idea shocked me. Had I really been on a doomed path without really knowing it for most of the 1960s? Had she been sent to help me start my quest abroad, and had she almost immediately known she should leave for another path? If so, the wood I was in had been dark indeed. I thought of my efforts to save our marriage on Malta. Were they doomed from the outset? Not by a curse, but by her having made her mind up that our paths would diverge very early on? Had my marriage died in the course of the events covered in *Awakening to the Light* (which ends in 1967) without my knowing it? I realised I did not know much about her path, and that all I could know was my own path, and that I was right to be on it.

Ann returned and stayed an hour. The talk was of raw food and Suffolk places with occasional forays into cancer: the food that homeopaths say is good for cancer-sufferers. We left and drove back through early dark.

In due course Nadia rang to tell me that Caroline had had her operation and was comfortable. A fortnight later Nadia rang again. Caroline had been upset. She felt she was not in control of events but at the mercy of them. News that Damian was not within the security of the airport at Basra but in the more exposed Shatt al-Arab region on the Iran border (where we had once spent an idyllic day) had not helped. Damian was in charge of 90 men, the only tank squadron there. Nadia's role was to shore Caroline up.

In early December we took presents to Nadia's twee house in a terraced row with a garden and a view from upstairs across fields to the River

Crouch. (My poem 'At Colinton' was framed, on a wall, and bricks I gave her in Japan were on a floor.) We had lunch, during which Ian rang from Germany, where he was performing. I learned that Caroline's dog had fallen on the pavement and her vet found and removed a melon-sized lump on its spleen that was cancerous. And Caroline's eldest brother had been found to have cancer of the bowel.

The last time I saw her I had said, "Promise you'll be positive." A few days later I received a haunting Christmas card from Caroline. The picture showed a rider leading a horse into a wood and lines from Robert Frost's 'Stopping by Woods on a Snowy Evening' were printed:

> The woods are lovely, dark and deep
> But I have promises to keep,
> And miles to go before I sleep,
> And miles to go before I sleep.

Caroline's path had led into her own dark wood.[34]

Oxford paths

A fortnight previously I had been back to Oxford for a Gaudy, a reunion for my year (whose 50th – 'quinquagesimal' – anniversary of matriculation we were marking) and for another year. We stood in the Lower Senior Common Room at Worcester College, a panelled medieval room with a picture of five of the nine Fellows in 1936–7, including Bryan-Brown. The current Provost was unable to attend as he had just had an operation on a knee, and the Vice-Provost told us in front of the painting that in 1958, our year, there were a Provost and 15 Fellows and an intake of 90. There were 302 in the college that year, whereas now there were 604 with 50 staff, 34 Junior Fellows and 35 lecturers. I chatted to contemporaries with whom I had been especially friendly, and to Sir John Weston, who loomed in the Fellows' Garden. I asked him, "Do you keep in touch with the Foreign Office?" He said, "I've retired. I stopped in 1998. I wrote articles in the first five years, but the only people I see now I see as friends. There's more to life than that." Alan Magnus, who accompanied me to Greece in 1958, came and talked coal. David Oxley reminded me that we shared a tutorial and I had had to make excuses for his absences playing Rugby League. He was now Chief Executive of the Rugby League (and in 2013 would become its President). Judge John Weeks QC, who shared a Law tutorial with me, sidled up for a chat. Another in my Law set, Jonathan Watt, had played cricket for Sussex. There was a group photo on the steps, in which we all wore black DJ except for Weston, who wore a burgundy dinner-jacket that drew attention to himself.

We dined in the dining-hall (where I took my entrance exam), and it was said that Worcester College was now the most thriving Oxford College in terms of academic and sporting results, and demand for places. I looked at the two sconces which were near me. One, in front of me, was dated 1719, five years after the founding of Worcester College. The other, a flagon or silver goblet, was dated 1863. (In my day an undergraduate could be made to drink a sconce filled with beer if he talked about religion, politics or sex in hall. Everyone did, but sconcing was rare.) Then there were speeches. Weston read a long grace in Latin and made a speech in his burgundy jacket. There was a list of college members who had recently died. We repaired to the Buttery, and Piers Harford confirmed to me that Charles Nunn (who had shared a room with Ricky and made me coffee so many times, and had learned Italian to read Dante in the original) had committed suicide shortly after leaving Oxford, and that talk of his being in Alaska or Baffin Island had been an elaborate cover-up. He said, "His address is Heaven, or Hell."

That night I slept in an undergraduate room on staircase 24, overlooking 20 Worcester Place where I began my Oxford career, and I reflected that we had all known our paths. Weston had known that he should go into the Foreign Office, Oxley had known that he had to play Rugby League, Weeks had known that he had to persevere with Law and I had known that I had to steep myself in literature. The Vice-Provost had said that Masterman had chosen Ricks, and once again I had a sense of Masterman's brooding Edwardian presence behind my path from a time when the British Empire bestrode the world. I was struck by the way we all found our way during those three years we were together, and of the profound difference the College had made to all of us as it encouraged us on our true paths.[35]

John le Carré
Tony and I met at Queen Elizabeth Hall to hear John le Carré speak about his path and his work. A white-haired man in a brown sports jacket, he had a softness despite his piercing eyes. He spoke of his progress since childhood: his con-man father, his time in Berne and his love of the Germans. He said he was attracted and repelled by the secret world he was sucked into at a young age, and what it does to the self. He said it makes for a lack of spontaneity and interferes with emotions. He said he wrote to convey a feeling, which seemed to question the system and America's role in the world. He spoke of the emotional involvement needed to get suspense; of the art of story-telling; and of the similarity between researching as a writer and being a spy. He took some questions from the audience of a thousand, and at the end nodded and bowed to the applause and walked off. It was announced that he would not be signing books but that there were pre-signed copies on a table. I had thought I might meet him

as our paths had been similar, but, having heard him, I saw him as being stuck in his secret world. He wanted to "make the secret world speak for the overt world", and our aims were completely different, as were our paths, and meeting him was no longer a necessity.[36]

Ben and history

At half-term Ann and I took Ben to St Albans to see the Roman remains. We went to the theatre, which has one column standing, and I showed him where the actors emerged from their dressing-rooms. We visited the mosaic in a house in a park, and walked through the museum. Ben was interested in history, and we devised a story about a father who was pro-Celtic and a son who was pro-Roman, which he could act out in solitary play among his lego.

In February 2009 we took Ben to West Stow to see the Anglo-Saxon settlement of some eight reconstructed round huts that were thatched or covered with tree branches, and we agreed that the primitive farmers who lived there were way behind the cultured Romans, who had built in stone.

For successive birthdays I had given him a tarantula and a large scorpion in glass boxes he had hung on his wall, but now he was looking for monsters in history and beginning to find them.[37]

Ricks's path

There was a telephone call. "It's Christopher Ricks. Are you coming to my lecture? There's a reception afterwards, not held by me, but have you heard tell of it? I'd like you and your nearest and dearest to come. It's in the North School. It'll be after my lecture so I'll be able to talk to you rather than see your attentive face looking at me." I mentioned my letter about Tennyson. He said, "Oh, you're a mystic, but I'm like H.G. Wells and don't believe in an after-life. Well goodbye."

Ann and I duly drove to Oxford and settled in the café opposite Schools. Ricks came in with a fellow in a sweater and sat where he and I had sat with Tony. On our way out I shook him by the hand. He said, "I'm in another performance now. See you later."

His lecture was on ghosts and Anthony Hecht, an American poet about whom he was writing. There were many rapid points, taking in Arnold, Eliot, *Hamlet* and so on. He spoke for exactly an hour. I complimented him afterwards on the timing. "No, it should be 53 minutes. I was seven minutes too long."

We walked from Examination Schools' East School to the North School, a wide examination room where there were glasses of wine. Ricks came and stood by my side and explained that the wife of Sir Anthony Kenny, ex-Master of Balliol had invited alumni, who were all labelled. The reception was for them. Alumni converged on us, and Ricks introduced me as "a poet". He said, "I must introduce you to Judith", his wife, and I chatted to her: an American woman of statuesque beauty. She told me she was an academic in graphic art: photography. "I've taken so many pictures of poets through Christopher, for example Lowell." She told me that Christopher had agreed with Boston that for the next three years he would not grade papers but would lecture and write his book on Eliot, which Valerie, Eliot's widow, had asked him to do. She had Alzheimer's disease – "She drifts in and out" – and, aware of what had happened to her, had offloaded Eliot's letters to John Haffenden and his unpublished poems to Christopher. Christopher had told Judith, "I'm 75 and I've done everything I've wanted to do." Then the Eliot book turned up. He had trodden a fulfilling path.

Judith pointed out Jon Stallworthy, a poet and former publisher who was now Master of Wolfson College. I chatted to him, and he lamented the slowness within the publishing process. We were then joined by Sir Anthony Kenny who had written a four-volume *New History of Western Philosophy*. I told him about *A New Philosophy of Universalism* and he asked me to send him a copy.

I talked with Ricks further, and gave him an account of what it felt like to be alone in Tennyson's study at dusk. He listened with interest. On our way out, and knowing that Tennyson was dear to his heart, I thanked Ricks and said, with a twinkle in my eye, "A suggestion for your next lecture, 'Ghosts I believe in, by Christopher Ricks.'" He said, "Go on," slapping me with his hand and laughing.[38]

Individual paths
At her Cornish cousin Diane's 40th wedding anniversary lunch for about 25 in Cornwall in the Pier House, Charlestown, Ann made a speech in which she said, "The secret of the survival of their relationship is that they both respect each other's areas of interest. This is true of the survival of all relationships." She meant that both respect each other's individual paths. It was certainly true of our marriage. She respected my right to research and write – she had given me a small statue of Rodin's *The Thinker* the previous Christmas – and go to the gym, and I respected her various activities: her art (in the past her pottery, calligraphy, walking and counselling), her bridge, her pilates, NADFAS, the University of the Third Age, WI, her monthly gathering of local ladies, lunches with her former staff, and her days out with her elderly aunt and her college friends, including annual visits to Christmas markets.

We again hosted the family gathering the day after Boxing Day. My brother Rob said how lucky we were in our parents. They gave us culture and attention, and, I said, independence to cycle to school and roam

London. They had placed all their four children on their individual paths.[39]

That winter Ann and I did many things together. We went to the annual Epping Forest Friends Dinner (when Judge Gerald Butler again alleged that Blair had leaned on Goldsmith to pronounce on the legality of the war in Iraq). We attended the Annual Advent Procession at Chigwell church, the candlelit service when the congregation hold candles in the dark. (Collingwood, who had taken the service at Matthew's wedding, had written in the introduction on the service sheet: "God, the Light, is never, and can never be, absent.") We went to *Blood Wedding* at the Chigwell Drama Centre, where Ken Campbell's daughter came and spoke to me, saying that my books were in her toilet, where her father had shelved them. (John Ezard rang to say he had visited Campbell's grave twice.) We went to Nottingham to witness my god-daughter's total-immersion baptism in an exposed font in the aisle which was like a small swimming-pool. She waded six steps down and lay back to be dunked under the waist-deep water by her vicar in a second baptism that cleansed her from the intervening years and made a public statement about her path.

Sale of 10 Crescent View with sitting tenant
My mother's investment flat, 10 Crescent View, had had a sitting tenant since her death in 1981. He had been to court to get the rent reduced to "what he could afford" and under British law had the right to remain there on that basis for the rest of his life. We all knew he worked from home while being on benefit. For 30 years he had complained that the four of us who inherited the property had not commissioned extensive building, reroofing and refurbishing work way in excess of the controlled rent we received to maintain him in the style to which he aspired. We had collectively come to the view that if we could find a buyer, we should sell the property with the sitting tenant in it and save ourselves huge bills for building work. Through my bank's dinners at Grosvenor House Hotel I had met John Maidman, who managed 17,000 properties, of which he owned 3,600. To my astonishment he volunteered to be our consultant. Having considered all the options, he confirmed that our plan was the best solution. My brother Rob found a buyer, and the flat was sold by the end of January along with our whining tenant. The four of us had a quarter each of the modest proceeds, but we were glad to be shot of the property and the potential financial liability.[40]

Recital in Saint-Sulpice: two invocations
My younger brother Jonnie was retiring at 60 from running the Grosvenor Estate (worth around £7 billion) for the Duke of Westminster. To celebrate his 60th birthday and his retirement he invited us to France to hear him give a recital on the organ at Saint-Sulpice where his boyhood hero, Marcel

Dupré, had played. A framed photo of the organ had hung in the Journey's End nursery when he was a boy. He issued invitations to his generation of our family and to friends, and on 6 February we all made our way by Eurostar to Paris. He had booked us into the Citidanes Hotel on the Quai des Grands Augustins opposite the Île-de-France, and we had a large air-conditioned apartment each.

The next morning I wrote an invocation to Robespierre for *Armageddon* (book 6, 117ff). We then walked through the Conciergerie and found the guardroom where Robespierre conducted the Revolutionary Tribunal and where Marie Antoinette was sentenced. We went to the prisoners' gallery and looked at the reconstructed cells and the Girondins' and Marie Antoinette's chapels. We went to the women's courtyard and saw the fountain in which prisoners washed their clothes. I looked at the reconstruction of Marie Antoinette's cell. I worked some of these details into my invocation to Robespierre.

We then walked to the Louvre, wandered through the first-floor paintings, including the Mona Lisa, and lunched by a high-up window in the Café Richelieu, which had a view across the glass pyramid. It began to snow and we travelled by taxi back to our hotel in a blizzard. After the snow I wandered outside along the quai beyond Notre Dame to the Île Saint-Louis and revisited the spot where I sat and read *Paradise Lost* in 1959 and the seat I sometimes sat on at the foot of the steps leading down from the Pont Saint-Michel. Here I had learned to be an epic poet, reading among trees. Here I had begun my true path.

In the early evening we found our way to Saint-Sulpice and looked at the gnomon in the floor and the 'P' and 'S' in one of the round transept windows, officially 'Pierre' and 'Sulpice', but perhaps 'Priory of Sion'. I absorbed the statues and barrel-vaulting, and the sunbursts and candles on the altar. The organ loft was very high up.

The recital began with Martin Neary, who played an improvisation by Sophie-Véronique with 'Happy Birthday' in the music, and then Jonnie took over. He played two pieces by Dupré and was applauded. He waved, a tiny figure up in the loft. I wrote this experience into my invocation to Marcel Dupré in book 12 of *Armageddon*.

We returned to our hotel, changed and went to a champagne reception in a packed restaurant. Jonnie's eldest son greeted me and said, "Two minutes, we've been waiting for you." I fought my way through the throng and found a glass of champagne and had a quick sip. Then I was speaking – standing up steps, addressing a packed restaurant, all standing – as Jonnie's eldest brother on the weekend after his 60th birthday and retirement. I expressed the thanks of the guests for our accommodation, for his recital and for organising the dinner, and said that Dupré had been his hero since he was 15. I said he had hated ticking as an accountant, but had persevered and had had a very successful career, he had found his path. I said he was a bit like Blair. Jonnie said indignantly, "What?" To laughter I explained that he resembled Blair not in spinning but in timing. Blair had got out before the credit crunch was mentioned, and Jonnie had *nearly* got out before the credit crunch was mentioned. I talked of his six retirement jobs, most of which seemed to be in Bermuda. I said that Henri Mulet, the composer, had burned all his works and gone into a monastery for 30 years. I said this was not going to happen to Jonnie. I called for a toast and the singing of 'Happy Birthday'. Everyone had had two glasses of champagne to my one sip, and they laughed a lot even though I was sober.

There was a sit-down supper at which the closest Hagger relatives were separated so one could be on each table. Martin Neary sat by me. Afterwards we walked back. The next day I wrote my invocation to Dupré. Neary was about, and he said to Ann: "The Haggers are all real and really nice people. They're all talented." (He had rebuilt the Duke of Westminster's organ at Eaton Hall, and he and Jonnie had given a recital for the Duke and Duchess to christen the rebuilt organ.) He asked Ann, "Did you have the best of the bunch?" Ann would not tell me what she replied.

We walked to Notre Dame for Martin Neary's recital, and I found the north window, which is on the front cover of *The Fire and the Stones*. I stood with Neary at the front looking at the organ with a great crowd in front of us before he started playing. He duly gave his recital, and there was a service. I listened to the heavenly voices of sopranos in the choir and watched the swinging of the smoking censer. We left and had *café au lait* in the street near the hotel, and Neary and his wife walked by. He stopped and had another chat by our table. We then headed back to our hotel to prepare for the return journey.[41] I reflected that Jonnie's path had led him through the Duke's billions to the organ loft high up in Saint-Sulpice, a framed photo of which he had looked at every day from the nursery dining-table when he was a boy.

Armageddon *continued*

Having abandoned *Armageddon* to write books on the events of 1984 and on Libya I now returned to my second epic poem. I had written bits in November, and in December "dictated the grasshopper clock and bees bits and reviewed bks 7–11 in the light of world events and the tribulation". I polished my plan in mid-January, but then broke off to have an operation.

At the beginning of December I had gone to my doctor with a urinary infection. This was cleared up, but further tests showed that my prostate was interfering with my urine flow, which pooled back into my bladder and became infected. I was advised to have a TURP (transurethral resection of the prostate), and I went into Holly House under Mr Hines on 15 January. I had my usual heparin injection, had a mask placed over my nose and knew no more. I had an epidural when I was asleep and woke in the recovery room among half a dozen nurses in shower hats. I was back in my room two hours after I went down, at 12.30. I had a bag, which was inconvenient, but the next two days I was able to lie in bed reading Tudor Parfitt's *The Lost Ark of the Covenant*, wondering if I could use the Ark in *Armageddon*.

Back home I got back into *Armageddon*. I worked on the Timeline, on the Antichrist and on Bush's roadmap. By the beginning of February I was working on book 4.

In February I looked ahead to books 7–12. I read Tillyard's *The English Epic and Its Background*. I wrote of his

four epic requirements: high quality and high seriousness; amplitude, breadth; control and structure; and a choric element – ability to reach a large group of people living near my time. I believe I have all these.

On 7 March I wrote "the Hell piece in book 4". I noted: "Satan symbolises the disorder element, Christ the order element." On 17 March I "watched the video of the Berg beheading and wrote about it all afternoon" for book 6. By the end of March I had finished book 7 and much of book 8.[42]

North Norway: Vikings and Northern Lights, invocations
I had always known that I should visit North Norway to see the Northern Lights and absorb a land from which the Haggers may have originated. ('*Hagr*' means 'fit' or 'ready' in Old Norse, and the same homing instinct had sent me to Denmark.) I knew I had a passage or two waiting to be written for *Armageddon*. Towards the end of February Ann and I flew to Oslo and then on to Tromso. We landed on an ice-covered runway and wheeled our luggage through thick snow to a coach that drove us to the port. We boarded our ship, the *Trollfjord*, in freezing wind. It was –3 or –4°C and that night would be –6 or –7°C. We made our way to our cabin and sailed for Honningsvag. We toasted our wedding anniversary over dinner.

The next morning we stopped at Havoysund and looked down on little dolls' houses under snow. We continued on black waves and entered a blizzard, and the bleakness of the sea reminded me of the Anglo-Saxon poems 'The Seafarer' and 'The Wanderer', whose narrators yearned in freezing weather for the warmth of their lord's home. I grasped how relieved the Vikings would have been to land on the temperate shores of England and escape the hardship of the northern winter back home.

We landed at Honningsvag, a small town with snow-impacted roads, and we sped by coach, following a fast snow-plough, through mountains to

North Cape, Europe's most northerly point, which is in the Arctic Circle. We were in the land of the Sami people, the original Norwegians who arrived from Asia from c.9000BC, and had slit eyes (as had our Sami guide). We returned through Sami encampments to our hotel in Honningsvag near the water and, having left our bags, were driven to a wooden jetty where king crabs were being lifted from the sea in a net. We saw five crabs killed and were taken into a room heated by a birchwood stove where their legs and claws were boiled. We were then fed them on pine platters. The fisherman who presided told me of his Viking origins.

Next morning we had breakfast by Honningvag harbour: pretty houses, a small boat, calm water. We then made a four-hour coach journey through three long tunnels by a fjord and through birch-trees against snow to the seat of Altaic culture associated with shamanism, whose rock carvings predate c.7000BC. We stopped at the Alta Igloo Hotel 20 kms outside Alta among pines, had a quick lunch of reindeer burgers and did a 10-km run in a dog sleigh. Ann sat in the sleigh and I drove from the back, steering and braking be standing on the footbrake.

We then had hot currant juice in a Sami tepee constructed of 22 poles that met at the top in a hole to let out smoke from a gigantic fire of birchwood below. It was how the Altaians lived c.7000BC. This tepee was based on a design 9,000 years old, taken from rock carvings. The hole allowed spirits to come and go, and the structure was a kind of World Tree, Yggdrasil.

We returned to our hotel and had a tour of the igloo outside in which we would be sleeping. The hall had sculptures in ice and there was a corridor with rooms to left and right, all in ice. The door was a curtain, and the large double icebed in each room had reindeer skins. The floor was ice. The temperature outside was −14°C and inside it was only −7.

We left our sleeping quarters with some relief and drove on a horse sleigh along a track between pines to an open field where there was a cloudless, pollution-free night sky with very bright stars, but no Northern Lights. The driver, a wizened old man swathed in skins said gravely with great dignity, "Listen to the silence, it is beautiful." This was how Altaic man saw the stars. We had supper in the hotel and before pudding someone called out, "Something's happening." We put on our coats and rushed out.

The Northern Lights were gathering. There were glimmers. It was now −20°C outside, and the strength of the Northern Lights intensified slowly. There was a horizontal green band on the left and then vertical drapes of a curtain with a hem that rippled in the solar wind and moved slowly from right to left, predominantly green with bits of pale blue and brightest above distant woods. I was looking at the Aurora Borealis, the heavenly curtain. I saw the Aurora as symbolising the veil between Being and Existence, and knew I would invoke the Northern Lights in book 11 of *Armageddon*. The hem of the curtain began to fade, and soon there were only glimmerings. I stayed out until 11.30 (going in at regular intervals to get warm) but there was no further activity.

We went to the igloo to sleep. I cleaned my teeth in the shower area in the hotel, locked our luggage away, collected two sleeping-bags and pillows and carried them out into the open air (–20°C) and for ten yards into the igloo and went straight to our room. I sat on the reindeer skins on the icebed and took my boots off. I wriggled into a sleeping-bag, wearing my hat. Ann did the same. We went to sleep on the reindeer skins fairly rapidly. We woke at 5.45 a.m., and agreed it was time to go back into the warm hotel. There I wrote my invocation to the Northern Lights for *Armageddon*, book 11, lines 372–444 in the sitting-room with three tables to the left of the main entrance of the Alta Igloo Hotel. There I had the idea of Christ creeping like a vicar and wrote book 11, lines 445–448.

We left under a clear blue sky and drove through spruce on white snow to Lake Alta, which was now blue, and from a nearby tiny, two-roomed airport flew back to Oslo and from there back home. I had confronted my Viking roots and would write an invocation to Snorri Sturluson about them in book 5 of *Armageddon*.[43]

Birth of grandson, Alex

Our second grandson was born on 1 April at Princess Alexandra Hospital, Harlow. Kate went in for 8 and Alex (as Alexander was immediately known) was born by Caesarean section later that morning. Matthew sent us a text with a picture: "Hello, my name is Alex…. And Mummy is doing well." We went to Chamberlan Ward with Ben, and with Kate lying with a drip in her arm, drowsy under morphine, we took turns in holding the new arrival: "eyes screwn up, hands and feet inside a swaddling babygrow to protect his face against his nails". (He had scratched his face with his nails during the birth.)

He quickly grew into an affectionate toddler with a great sense of fun. Almost as soon as he could speak he called me "Conker", a retaliation for my calling him "Acorn" (the offspring of an oak-tree) rather than because 'Nicholas' in Greek means 'conqueror of the people'.

Coopersale Hall's 20th anniversary

The schools had continued to thrive. The new Normanhurst Head had looked out of her window and seen Boris Johnson, Mayor of London, giving a TV interview outside our gate. She rushed downstairs and barged in on the interview, said, "Mr Johnson, welcome to Chingford on behalf of Normanhurst School. You will come and meet pupils, won't you?" She hijacked him from the interview to a nursery class, and he gave her a florid quote: "Normanhurst is the future of Chingford." He then went back out and resumed his interview. The episode was photographed for the local paper.

At Oaklands Jade Goody, a 'Reality TV celebrity' (who revealed that she thought East Anglia was a country), was now one of our parents, and we were doing our best for her two boys, which included shielding them from publicity. Her cervical cancer had spread to her liver and bowel, and elsewhere, and she died towards the end of March. At her funeral, which was at St John's, Buckhurst Hill, people lined the streets and threw flowers. (The boys' father took them away from Oaklands soon afterwards and put them into a school nearer where he lived. One of them returned to Coopersale Hall.)

To celebrate the 20th anniversary of my founding of Coopersale Hall every past pupil and staff member was invited to lunch at the school on Sunday, 3 May 2009. We calculated that there would be no more than 200 (rather than several thousand), and under that number turned up. Our first two Heads were present, and several past staff. There were tours of the school, Orchard Cottage and the Studio, and there was an exhibition of past cuttings and photographs.

There were speeches, which Matthew compèred. The first two Heads both spoke and then Matthew introduced me, saying that it had been a gamble to buy Coopersale Hall and open a school at the beginning of a recession, and that few could have pulled it off – "but my father did". Then I spoke about the founding, telling the story of 1989–1990, bringing in Steve Norris and David Seaman. Ann Miller, former Chairman of Epping Forest District Council and a past teacher of the oldest pupils, told me later: "You've got something here that works."

After the formalities I slipped away and visited the room Churchill slept in upstairs. I stood quietly looking out at Epping, and I was suddenly aware that I was not alone, and felt a strong presence that (in view of my time in Farringford) I thought was Tennyson. The next day I described the experience in book 12 of *Armageddon* (lines 3263–3330).[44]

Ricks and Neoclassical principles

I was not able to attend Ricks's Professor-of-Poetry lecture in February as I was returning from Paris. The last lecture of his five-year 'term of office' took place on 11 May. Tony drove me to Oxford, and I showed him the Painted Room of Sir William Davenant and the Bodleian on our way to the South School, the largest lecture room so far. Ricks greeted us in a suit and introduced me to David Womersley, who wrote an introduction to Gibbon's *Decline and Fall*. Ricks's talk seemed to take up my playful suggestion ('ghosts I believe in'), for it was titled 'Eliot and the Ghost of Coleridge', a look at Eliot's *The Use of Poetry and the Use of Criticism*.

His lecture was a Neoclassical onslaught on metaphysics. He said that poets should have 'negative capability', Keats's ability to lose himself and imagine himself into the being of the sparrow on the lawn. He said there should be no reaching after fact or reason. Coleridge had to step back from theory and a system of German metaphysics, which had had a stultifying effect on his verse. Coleridge subdued his desire for a theory. He said that a poet should have a credo round certain principles. He was haunted by the Muse. Eliot was not seeking a system of metaphysics. He said that genius takes from high talents and improves. This was the Neoclassical view, that poets copy poems from the past and express their genius by improving them. (I had to admit to myself that I had taken Dante's view of Hell and Heaven in both *Overlord* and *Armageddon* and had tried to improve them.) He spoke of Pound's 1918 credo, that the imperfect symbol is the natural object. He said that to a poet intelligence should not be at the mercy of the emotions – a Neoclassical, anti-Romantic view. He held that poetry and prose are different systems of punctuation. (This was a Neoclassical view: to a Neoclassical critic poetry, like prose, comes from the rational, social ego, and poetry is not received from the beyond.) He said that intelligence is the discernment of exactly what and how much you feel in a situation. He laid out unstructured principles to guide a poet, and what stood out was that "genius is improving other people's work".

There was a reception in the North School, where there was an end-of-term atmosphere. I congratulated him and said he must feel a sense of relief at completing his five years. "Yes, it's a bit like that." I agreed with him that one should step back from a system after seeing what the universe is. I said I too operate from principles. Tony took a photo on his phone of us holding glasses of wine and talking. David Womersley came and chatted. He told me, "Gibbon doesn't advance theories, just principles: religion

Nicholas with Christopher Ricks on 11 May 2009

and barbarism." (Where do principles of religion and barbarism end and a theory that civilizations fall through religion and barbarism begin?) Both Ricks and his wife spoke at some length to Tony – his wife was very interested in film and Tony's impending visit to Cannes – and Ricks told me that he had found two early poems of Eliot so far. He did not know if Eliot wrote any poems *after* his 'retirement'.

On the way back I mulled over Ricks's beliefs – principles – that inspiration and genius do not come from the beyond; that the Muse is social; and that everything applies to this life. He was a sceptical critic for a sceptical time, and the 'imagination' was social rather than an unveiler of the One. The next day I wrote apostrophising Pound in book 12 and included Ricks's "definition of genius" (book 12, lines 3331–3430). (Ricks was made a Knight Bachelor in the June Birthday Honours.)[45]

70th birthday and return to Otley Hall

On my 70th birthday Ann drove me towards Suffolk for two nights away at a surprise destination. On the way Matthew rang to say that we had sold 3, 4 and 6 Quay Road, Charlestown, leaving us with just our own house in Cornwall. Renting out the three properties had not covered their costs, and with banks having stopped lending because of the banking crisis and increased demand at Coopersale Hall requiring a new building of four class-rooms, it made sense to move our money from holiday lets to school expansion. We had decided to sell at the end of January and be clear of the properties by my 70th birthday, and we had sold for our asking price on our target date.

(Ann had given me a card of Abu Simbel, showing three seated kings who were submerged by the sea. They represented the three Cornish properties by the sea, drowned by rising waters, of course, but they also, very appropriately, represented the three schools that would survive the rising waters, and more specifically the three in charge: Matthew, her and me.)

After a journey through Suffolk lanes we arrived at Hintlesham Hall, a 1720s Georgian façade concealing the remnants of a 1565–1595 building with chimneys, visited by Elizabeth I in 1579. We had tea in the garden outside the old part in warm sunshine and I was joined by the immediate family: Tony and his German girlfriend; Matthew, Kate, Ben and Alex; and finally Nadia, without Ian who was recovering from having his appendix removed in Germany. We moved to a corner of the ancient drawing-room, dined in the dining-room and then sat in the library with our wine.

The next morning we went to Sutton Hoo, and after lunch heard how the ship burial thought to be of King Raedwald was discovered. We returned to our hotel and I sat in the sun while Ben swam in the pool. After dinner I quoted Housman to the family: "Loveliest of trees, the cherry now...." When I reached

Now, of my threescore years and ten,
Twenty will not come again,

I did not say

And take from seventy springs a score,
It only leaves me fifty more.

I said: "And take from seventy springs seventy,/It only leaves me...." I pulled a face and grimaced with my bottom lip out and my eyes looking down in their corners, and all laughed.

Next morning after breakfast I sat in the sun. Nadia had to leave as Ian had had a relapse. Matthew then announced that it was Open Day at Otley Hall, and that we were all going to try to visit. He said that as the new owners had threatened to take us to court regarding the public right of way in the green lane since medieval times (a fact of life that could not be changed), we would just turn up as members of the public and not declare who we were.

We entered the familiar Otley Hall grounds by the bottom gate and parked near the barn. We walked past the herber along the bottom of the H-shaped lake, through the vine-and-rose tunnel and the small wood, into the knot-garden – few of our plants and plant names had survived – and round the croquet lawn past the summer-house to the lilac walk, past the moat and the aster garden, along the moat walk, round past invasive slides of a children's playground to the tea-room. We sat outside at one of our old tables. Matthew brought out tea, and when an owner appeared I bent down and retied my shoelace. Tudor dancing began outside the front door and, knowing the owners would be distracted, we approached the front door through the rose-garden and walked in. We all stood in the Great Hall and I was able to absorb the many pieces of furniture and framed documents that I had left.

One of the new owners appeared and said to Matthew, "I am the owner, have you come a long way? Where are you from?" Matthew, holding Alex, smiled at her and said, "Essex." (I never said, "I am the owner." I always presented Otley Hall in terms of the Gosnolds.) Ann and I discreetly went into the Linenfold Room, and again I stood and absorbed the familiar furniture. I could hear "the owner's" voice, and so we climbed the creaky staircase and went to the Banqueting Room, our former bedroom. Then a voice said, "Hello, Nicholas." It was the only guide from my day who was still guiding for the new owners. Unmasked, I chatted, and realised that Ben was trying to get into the gardrobe, the cupboard where a little girl had been locked and died within reach of where I used to go to sleep, and I knew I had to be out within minutes. We walked to the Solar and then the Oak Room and through to the minstrels' gallery, and down into the kitchen. We returned to the front door and collectively made our escape.

The dancing had finished, and we walked briskly across the lawn between the H-shaped lake and the large wood. The peacock pen and fishpool had been returned to a tennis-court and swimming-pool, and the greenhouse we had stored plants in during the cold weather was derelict and overgrown. I had noticed that many areas of what, as a result of our tenure, had been voted the best private garden in the UK were unweeded. But the maze on the front cover of my *Selected Poems, A Metaphysical's Way of Fire* had now been laid in the lawn: the Chartres maze I had told the new owners I would have created if I had stayed. I had read Sam Newton's *The Origins of Beowulf*, which locates *Beowulf* in East Anglia, among Danish exiles, and in particular the area of the River Deben near Helmingham, which was a couple of miles from Otley Hall. If this view is true, then Otley Hall was in the setting of *Beowulf*. We reached our car and left.

It was a pleasant surprise to walk round the Hall and grounds once again, but I did not regret having left. I did not want to address groups of visitors on the Gosnolds repetitively any more. Connaught House was more comfortable and had enabled me to collect all my books into one library and all my archives into two archive rooms; and my study was now a media studio that provided administrative support for me to produce my books. I was clear that I was on the right path.

I had two more birthday presents. A week later Tony took me to see the last night of a musical based on Wedekind's *Spring Awakening*, which was written in 1890–1891 and set in a school. In early July Matthew took Tony and me to Lord's for a champagne reception among 23 cricketers. I spoke to John Emburey and James Foster (the Essex wicket-keeper), who told me he lived in Loughton. We dined alongside Martin Bicknall, who told me how hard it had been to adjust to retirement after the adulation of the crowds. A panel of four (Gillespie, Jeff Thompson, Thorpe and Alec Stewart) answered questions, and there was much mirth.

Ann had ten of her paintings – seven acrylic and three water colours – on display at an exhibition in Bedford House, and I photographed her beside them. She had had to attend the funeral of a college friend, who was found dead in bed, and as a birthday present I took her to the south coast.[46]

In Eastbourne

Ann and I spent three days in Eastbourne, staying at the Grand Hotel, a solid Victorian Belgravian-style building with a side view to the sea off Beachy Head. We walked along the Grand Parade past the Wish Martello tower to the pier, alongside empty stony beaches with breakwaters. We dined in the formal dining-room.

The next day we drove to Bexhill and St Leonards, and the Royal Victoria Hotel where we spent our wedding night. It had been taken over and the standard had dropped, but we had a sandwich lunch in the recognisable first-floor lounge. Thirty-five years had passed, and my new family and my books had happened since I was last there.

We went on to Rye. We parked and walked and found the Elizabethan dramatist John Fletcher's house, now a tea-room. He was born in 1579 and collaborated with Shakespeare on *The Two Noble Kinsmen,* and the front door he went in and out of as a toddler was still there. We returned via Pevensey Castle, which William I built c.1080 in the Bay where he landed between Bexhill cliffs and Beachy Head.

The next day we drove to Beachy Head and went west instead of east, to Seaford and then to Brighton. We stopped at 3 Sussex Square to remember Tuohy and look up at the first-floor apartment where I stayed. We passed the rebuilt Grand Hotel, blown up by the IRA. The Lawns Hotel, Hove, I stayed in as a boy had disappeared. We went to Portslade and on to Worthing, which was very crowded, and then on to Littlehampton. We made our way to Felpham, where Blake attacked a soldier, and reached Bognor. We had tea at the Royal Norfolk Hotel and found 26 Glamis Street, where I stayed as a boy in 1945 and 1946. The door I came out of all those years ago was still there. My father would have taken a day off work to come down and find and inspect our lodgings. We returned to Eastbourne and left the next morning.[47]

We had driven along the south coast from Bognor to Rye and revisited places I remembered, but nowhere was a patch on the sea view at Charlestown in Cornwall for unspoilt quietness and closeness to the sea – and for having the conditions that had chunks of books flowing into my head, as had *Armageddon.*

The end of Armageddon

In April I pressed on into books 9 and 10. On 7 April I was in Cornwall: "Wind roaring in the chimney, ribbons of surf out to sea in the dark at low tide, rain lashing against the panes as I worked on. Had to have the window closed, but most of the day had both windows open, working in sweater and body-warmer to keep warm while I oxygenated." And on 9 April: "I can think so clearly in the Cornish fresh air, and the work is effortless." The next day: "A lovely moon. Am in a state of collapse having finished the Gaza bits in one day."

In the second half of April I had a very painful left knee, which was diagnosed as a torn cartilage. I had several sessions of physiotherapy and averted an operation. Towards the end of April I was working on books 11 and 12. Back at Connaught House I "worked on Christ's visit to Bush and Obama" and a day later "Christ's visit to David Rockefeller, all afternoon (after feeding the fish)".

At the beginning of May the end was in sight. On 2 May I wrote "Christ speaking to Heaven and visiting Connaught House". A few days later I "worked on the Museum of Monstrous Dunces". On 9 May I began writing "7 Heavens and to the end of Christ's speech inaugurating his Kingdom in Heaven". Ann arrived with shopping, and in the course of carrying it in, my arms full of bags, I tripped on the front step and cracked my head above my right eye on the four-billion-year-old stromatolite log by the front door. I resumed with ice round the lump on my forehead.

Chris Macann had sent me a leaflet about his life's work, a phenomenological philosophy in the tradition of Heidegger (1700 pages), which begins with being (titled *Being and Becoming*). On 16 May he emailed me, saying that he was "still trying to reconcile his starting with Being and my starting with Nothingness". (My Emptiness is also a plenitude, as I had learned in the Far East, and my Nothingness has the potentiality to become Being in a process of manifestation.) That afternoon I "wrote the last block of *Armageddon*, on the knot-garden". And noted: "Have now finished the first draft."

The next few weeks I spent checking what I had written. I did the Timeline. I noted on 10 June:

> I have a vocabulary count of 50,394 words in my collected poetic works (*Collected Poems*, *Overlord*, *Classical Odes*, *Collected Verse Plays* and *Armageddon*). This is some 20,000 words more than Shakespeare's count (around 31,000). To put it in perspective, there are 1–1.5 million words in English. The main dictionary has 650,000 words.

I had used one in 13 words in the main dictionary. I wrote the Preface. I had taken issue with Neoclassical 'copying' of past works, and, tongue-in-cheek, I compared Lowell's 'Brunetto Latini' and Dante's canto 15 version, his source, and on 18 June "did my own version of Brunetto and slipped it into *Armageddon* book 4". I worked on the Appendix, including al-Qaeda's historical attempts to acquire weapons of mass destruction, and prepared the summaries of each book. On 3 July I wrote: "My long haul on *Armageddon* is approaching an end."

For a couple of weeks I read through *Armageddon* to make sure I was happy with the final text. We went down to Cornwall and, having sold the three cottages nearby, took the good-quality table and chairs from next door and installed them in our breakfast room. We did a lot of clearing up and took bags to the dump. Back in Essex Matthew secured a planning change of use for our old house, which could now be absorbed into Oaklands. The local consultant who I helped when a motorcyclist collided with his car had spoken against us in the Council Chamber for the second time, but this time he had been defeated 17–1.

I travelled back to Essex by train and made final corrections to *Armageddon*. The book was sent to the publisher on 11 August. I was reading proofs at the end of August and again in early October.

I had taken stock of my works. I wrote:

Camus was a model of mine. He wrote history (*The Rebel*), philosophy (*The Myth of Sisyphus*) and literature (*The Plague* and *The Outsider*). That combination I have taken over, in a different way. Instead of the history of revolution I have shifted to the history of [civilizations, revolutions and] the New World Order. Instead of the philosophy of absurd Existentialism I have shifted to Universalism and the universe. And instead of fiction I have shifted to poetry. But Camus is a forerunner".[48]

With the ending of *Armageddon* the current episode ended. I had already moved on from reflecting universal order and War on Terror. I was already immersed in a new episode and a new pair of conflicting opposites.

Episode 15:

Internationalism and Localism

Years: 2009-2013
Locations: Buckhurst Hill; Mediterranean cruise; India, Sri Lanka and Arabia
Works: *The World Government, The Secret American Dream, A New Philosophy of Literature, A View of Epping Forest, My Double Life 1: This Dark Wood, My Double Life 2: A Rainbow over the Hills, Selected Poems: Quest for the One; Selected Stories: Follies and Vices of the Modern Elizabethan Age*
Initiative: statecraft for a World State

"Unless we establish some form of world government, it will not be possible for us to avert a World War III in the future."
Winston Churchill, Prime Minister of Great Britain (1945)

"Human society can be saved only by Universalism."
Emery Reves, *The Anatomy of Peace* (1945)

"One must wait until the evening to see how splendid the day has been."
Sophocles, *Oedipus at Colonus*

In my next episode the internationalism of a coming World State, an ideal form of government that would abolish war, famine and disease and implement universal order in a political Universalism, was in conflict with localism.

Internationalism: The World Government *and* The Secret American Dream

The World Government, *other books and radio*

The *Concise Oxford Dictionary* defines the global perspective of internationalism as "the advocacy of a community of interests among nations", and localism as "a preference for what is local".

I had planned *The World Government* since October 2008. John Hunt had questioned me on the argument of the book in November and at the end of December had requested a synopsis. He later said that the book "should be like *The New Philosophy of Universalism* – a political Universalism – rather than a sequel to *The Syndicate*". I sent him a new outline in early January 2009. In August I sketched a 9-chapter synopsis for the book, and on the train back to Cornwall I read all the material and was ready to make a start. The next morning, on 13 August 2009, "the Light came through unbidden for about a minute as I lay awake. Four surges and shines in me, not from a deep level but more surface." I saw it as an encouragement for "*Armageddon* and my plans for a new World State in *The World Government*".

I started writing the book on 17 August. I was in chapter 3 on 1 September, and the next day wrote:

> Thoughts on the World State. My challenge, to come up with a State that solves all our problems. Norris asked me to devise a plan to control R & R [, 'Rockefellers' and 'Rothschilds'], and this I have done.

The way to control the New World Order was to make the world government an elected body. I wrote on through September and finished chapter 7 on 4 October, and chapter 8 on 11 October, when I wrote:

> I am a sorter-out of problems among other things. I sorted out history and now I have sorted out philosophy. I am sorting out the world government. And I have sorted out local education. What I take on I sort out. Have I sorted out literature? In a way. The epic poem, yes. *Collected Poems*, yes. Stories, yes.

I reached the end of chapter 9 on 15 October, and reached the end of the Epilogue and the end of the book on 17 October. I then spent another five weeks combing through and making adjustments. The book was sent off on 23 November.

The World Government, a work of political Universalism, takes up my philosophy of the oneness of the universe and humankind and its application in many disciplines, including international relations, and presents the long-yearned-for human dream of world government and a World State that will enforce peace. In the hands of self-interested commercial *élites* – the Syndicate – concerned to loot the earth's resources to enrich themselves a world government could be disastrous. In the hands of a philanthropic body of experts and elected representatives a world government could benefit humankind by legislating to abolish war, famine, disease and poverty.

In *The World Government* I state the ideal view of a democratic world government that is voted in by the world's citizens as opposed to the self-interested version the Syndicate want to bring in as an imposed New World Order. I detail the future structures of global governance and offer a philosophical vision of a better future in the tradition of Plato and Kant. (Such a world government harks back to a mythical original Universalist time when all humankind spoke a common language, before overreachers built the Tower of Babel too high in the hope of reaching Heaven and humankind was condemned to babble in many tongues. King Solomon was one of the first to work for a world government: he united the tribes he ruled into one central kingdom, and today would be regarded as a one-worlder.)

While I worked on *The World Government* I had to service my other books. There were proofs of *Armageddon* to correct. Anthony Kenny sent me a card saying that *The New Philosophy of Universalism* was a substantial work. The card showed Ktisis, the Libyan Isis, beside a tree. I thought he saw me as Isis in Libyan garb and holding a new tree of philosophy – mine. Ricks wrote of *The New Philosophy of Universalism* that he had been "magnuming your opus, oeuvre, achievement". (There was a verbal play on *magnum opus*, a 'magnum' being a wine bottle of twice the standard size; and he had invented a verb suggesting 'sipping from a magnum of champagne'.)

The next day I received a letter from Asa Briggs warmly welcoming *The Libyan Revolution* and mentioning my "prodigious" output. He described his ailments (including DVT and an eye problem). Eleanor Laing wrote that she was showing *The Libyan Revolution* to Liam Fox, Shadow Secretary of State for Defence. Sir Philip Mawer wanted me to send to David Miliband, the Foreign Secretary, and to William Hague, the Shadow Foreign Secretary, which I duly did. (Hague sent me a letter and I understood that my Barbary Gipsy articles were being combed through by the Ministry of Defence during the Anglo-French bombing of Libya in 2011.) At the Chigwell School Advent Service Tony Brooker, an adviser to Sheikh Hamad bin Jassim Al Thani, then Prime Minister and Foreign Minister of Qatar, had asked me to sign a copy of *The Last Tourist in Iran* to Sheikh Hamad, and now he asked me to sign a copy of *The Libyan Revolution* to him.

I had to make more global radio broadcasts on *The Secret Founding of America*: in November I was interviewed by Jay Weidner for an hour from 2 a.m. GMT. The interview was chopped up into four 15-minute programmes dealing with the planting of America, the founding of the United States, the Freemasonry behind the Civil War and the Freemasonic State today (and its links to the New World Order). They went out at peak time in the US, between 6 and 7 p.m.

I was still working on *The World Government* during the first half of 2010. I read two sets of proofs in March,[1] and did further proof-reading in May and June 2010.

The Secret American Dream

Michael Mann had lamented earlier in 2009 that he needed a "global book" for Watkins, and my global broadcast spurred him to ask me to send him a proposal for a global book in September. I knew that President Obama was a spokesman for the New World Order, with a brief to calm feeling in the Middle East and consolidate the gains under Bush, and I was researching his step-by-step attempts to improve the standard of living of the peoples of the world. I believed he wanted the American Dream to be shared by all humankind. Michael's request was a golden opportunity to assemble the evidence for this scenario. I sent him my Proposal, tweaked the book's global and present perspective and reduced the book's length at his urging. On 2 October Michael emailed me that Watkins were very keen to publish, and that I should hand the book in by 1 May. I had to finish *The World Government* before I could start writing. I did research and improved my plan until the end of November, when I noted: "Am in a fallow period... as I get ready for the next exertion."

Then I had an idea in my sleep. On 3 December I noted:

After a fallow period yesterday, slept, and woke with an instruction from beyond to follow the pattern of *The Secret Founding of America*. Dressed and sat at my desk and drafted the structure for *The Secret American Dream*. Have The Real Story of Liberty's Empire in the title. Part One: When Liberty's Empire Apparently Began. The Colonial Empire, Foreign Interventions, Imperial Hegemony. Part Two: When Liberty's Empire Really Began: Federal Expansion (and Freemasonry), Regional Expansion. Part Three: Liberty's Empire Now: Globalisation, New World Order. Part Four: The Secret American Dream: Liberty's World State: The Rise of a World State, Universal Peace.

I had been taken by surprise by this sudden influx of inspired structure, to which the book adheres.

The Secret American Dream is about the exporting of the American Dream to all humankind. The American empire began with the rise of the United States, the US's federal unification and expansion westwards, and continued with the colonial empire and, after US interventions in two European wars, with imperial hegemony. This expansion turned into US world supremacy and superpowerdom, and gave rise to the commercial *élites* who gave birth to the New World Order. I provide evidence for Obama's secret plan to create a benign world government that will have the power to abolish war, famine, disease and poverty and establish a universal peace that will extend the American Dream to everyone on Earth. I show that Liberty has a Universalist destiny.

I reflected that in my writing one focus of research had led to another. I had chosen Eisenhower to focus on in the mid-1990s and George W. Bush in the late 2000s, and the work I had done on them helped me write *The Secret American Dream*. It was as though my earlier work had prepared me to write my later work, and increasingly I saw myself as "a mere amanuensis", being guided step by step towards a mosaic of interconnecting works.

By 15 December I had finished chapter 3, and recorded that Part One had been finished in 12 days. By Christmas Eve I had reached the end of chapter 5. In the new year, 2010, I pushed on and finished chapter 6 on 7 January. I. There was heavy snow and I had a lung infection that was debilitating. I was going very slowly: I was without a PA for six weeks, and had no internet for ten days.

Ann's right hip had given her shooting pains. An X-ray showed that her hip was knobbled with osteophytes, arthritic bone spurs that grated when she moved and protruded into a nerve, causing pain. A hip replacement at Holly House was fixed for 3 February. There were many arrangements to make. She would need a 'grabber' (like a litter-picker) for picking things up off the floor as she would not be able to bend. She would need a shower-stool, a handrail. Much of January was spent in getting ready. The operation seemed to go well. She was away from her hospital bed for five hours and regained consciousness to find her legs wedged apart and strapped, numb from the epidural. I visited her four times a day – at breakfast, lunch, tea and supper time – for the week she was in hospital. When I collected her I got her into the passenger seat of my car by sitting her on a round swivel-seat and swivelling her legs into the car. I drove her home. After that I was her carer, taking her breakfast, helping her out of bed to go to the bathroom, creaming her legs, rolling on her surgical stockings and bringing a flow of drinks, Rich Tea biscuits and soup on a tray at regular intervals. On 16 February I reckoned I had shed half a stone from the to-ing and fro-ing.

Somehow I kept the book going, and finished the first draft on 24

February, three months after I began. I then spent three weeks reading it through, making amendments and working on the Appendix. I sent the book off on 19 April. Michael Mann emailed that it was "astounding" and that he was riveted. It went to an editor, who sent me lists of points I had to answer between 14 June and 14 July. There were more proofs to read in August.

Watkins changed 'World State' on the cover to 'New World Order', making me out to be on the side of the New World Order. Someone in Watkins had not appreciated the distinction. I tried to get it changed back, but it was too late. So I placed definitions of the World State and the New World Order on a page near the Contents.[2]

Lisbon Treaty

In early November 2009 the Lisbon Treaty had been in the news. It would become law on 1 December, after which the UK would be under a super-state. I wrote, "So my writing took place against the long extinction of the UK under the EU, a State with legal personality." I approved of an elected, benevolent World State, but had doubts about the devious way in which the EU was being imposed on between 15 and 50 per cent of the UK's law-making (depending on which UK laws are included). I "drafted a 14-stanza ode, 'The End of Great Britain: the Demise of a Nation-State'". UK MPs now had little power, but when Eleanor Laing, Steve Norris's replacement, was being scrutinised as to which of her two properties was her main one, Ann and I attended a meeting at Roding Valley High School and supported her – she owned her Westminster property before she came to our constituency and acquired a base there – and helped to see off an attempt to deselect her. At the next Friends of Epping Forest dinner Judge Gerald Butler "took my arm and said I was sitting next to him", and scurrilously told me a very senior member of the Government had received £12million for going along with the Lisbon Treaty. He would not give me his evidence, but talked of speaking with Peter Goldsmith, the ex-Attorney General, and lunching with Derry Irvine, the ex-Lord Chancellor.

In March 2010 I heard that Judge Gerald Butler had died of a heart attack in a Salisbury restaurant en route to Cornwall. It was thought he was having an asthmatic attack. His ashes were scattered in the River Fowey, beneath his home there.[3]

Reading of Overlord: Eric Galati

As usual I had to service my other books, and in particular *Overlord*. Before Ann went into hospital Eric Galati, an American actor who was 25 stone and had been in a short film, *The Hit*, a contact of Eustace Mullins and devotee of Ezra Pound, asked to meet me in London. He lived on Long Island like

Gatsby. He said he wanted to give a reading from *Overlord*, which he had read along with others of my books. I had met him at the Charing Cross Hotel. He asked me to select some passages, but made it clear that he would make the final choice.

He rang me in November 2008 to say that he had met John Calder, a British publisher, who had suggested he gave his reading at the Calder Bookshop Theatre on 28 January. He said that he needed to find a theme. In due course he rang me to say that he had found his theme in the pebble and the orange. I had forgotten that I had written about a pebble or an orange in *Overlord* (book 11, 3683 and 3687). Eric was trying to present the integrity and inviolability of the earth and the loving provision of food for humans. He added, "*Overlord* is so rich."

In January he rang me to say that he thought *Overlord* is Manichaean. I disagreed. I said: "Iranian Manichaeism is Light versus Darkness, a perpetual dualism without a reconciliation, war between Ahura Mazda and Ahriman (Light versus Darkness). But in my work I apply [the algebraic] +A + −A = 0. The opposites are reconciled. It's Manichaeistic Gnosticism reconciled with theology – St Clement of Alexandria's reconciliation." Eric was very interested in *Overlord*'s view of the New World Order, and he asked me whether "Rockefeller is Overlord".

On 28 January 2010 Tony and I arrived at John Calder's Bookshop Theatre at 51 The Cut in heavy rain. According to two demoralised staff, Calder's Bookshop had just been sold and as John Calder had not confirmed the booking to Eric, the staff had not advertised beyond placing a board with my name and *Overlord* written in chalk out in the street in the rain. There was an audience, but the impending sale had undermined the occasion. Eric read well and gave a good performance. He read with great feeling, and my evocation of Dresden moved him to tears, as did my account of Hiroshima. He deftly wove passages into a mini-narrative, and he and I answered questions at the end about my vision and his interpretation. I talked about the narrative tradition, how poetry's mansion has many rooms, how a poet can be mythological as well as historical (as in *Armageddon*) and how opposites are reconciled by a unity that is behind dualism.[4]

Localism: archives and occasions

Localism, "a preference for what is local", is an attitude or state of mind that grows out of attachment to a particular locality or place. I was attached to the Epping Forest locality, and to Charlestown in Cornwall. While I wrote my Universalist works, which relate to the universe and the whole world, I was also overseeing the running of local schools and being a carer in Connaught House on the verge of Epping Forest. Every day I walked in the grounds, related to the shrubs and plants, and carried on my work in my study. Localists are more interested in the work of their gardens and councils than in national, international or global politics.

Archives

My archives kept me local. As soon as I sent off *The Secret American Dream* I turned to my archives, and every day from 19 April to 14 June 2010, with help from my PA, I assembled all the papers relating to each book of mine in a separate plastic storage box, sorted them into bundles, arranged them in chronological order and catalogued each folder on computer. There were now 75 allocated boxes of my Works archives. I had joined the Shakespearean Authorship Trust to listen to evidence that might take me to "Shakespeare's trunk" (Edmund Blunden's words to describe a wooden chest holding Shakespeare's last papers), and now I was assembling my own system of trunks or chests, cataloguing my past papers, doing the sorting myself as only I knew what the papers were. I made contact with the British Library, the Bodleian and other bodies that hold papers of dead authors, and was encouraged to continue. By 4 May I had "23 boxes done". By 2014 I had completed 55 Works and 5 Life boxes.

Orpheus

As I sorted my life's writings, I was struck by how "my writing pattern has followed a solitary path in isolation". I could see Universalism as being the philosophy of a coming World State. I was particularly struck by how I settled on the myth of Orpheus for the early part of my life, and the myth of the Grail that blended with it. I wrote:

> Combing my old poems I noticed how I am dominated by the myth of Orpheus, who worshipped Apollo and Dionysus…. Orpheus appears several times in my poetic works…. I went down to the Underworld… and looked back…, and was torn to pieces by the Maenads – but came alive again and lived a disembodied life making poems and doing writings…. The Muses buried [Orpheus] at the foot of Mount Olympus, and his head carried on prophesying.[5]

Ray Davies

In May 2010 Ann and I went to Ipswich to attend a concert that Ian was playing in. We booked into the Salthouse Harbour Hotel overlooking the crowded marina and had tea with Ian and Nadia in the foyer. Ray Davies, wearing tight trousers, Bohemian-looking, aloof, waved to us through the window while on his mobile. We took our seats in the balcony of the Regent Theatre. There was a massive amount of equipment on stage. Ray Davies compèred the numbers, and with Ian on the keyboard sang 'Sunny Afternoon' and 'Waterloo Sunset'. I was struck by how many lines in the songs could be taken as mild social comment ("Where have all the good times gone?") but also by the thinness of the offerings. Many of the songs were just one line with elaborations and could not stand up to scrutiny like poetry. Towards the end the music became very loud.

Back at our hotel we sat in the foyer with Nadia and Ian, and Ray Davies came by. I stood to have a chat with him, and thanked him for sending the signed 'Sunny Afternoon' for Nadia's wedding. I said I remembered him lying in a boat singing the song on Top of the Pops in the mid-1960s, and asked where the boat was. He said, "Hertfordshire." I did not ask him if the taxman had really taken all his dough in the mid-1960s. I found him quiet and retiring, slightly reticent; an outsider. One of his band said, "Ray keeps himself apart from us. He's the boss." When he appeared it was like a Head going into the staff room. Later, he asked Nadia if I would sign *Collected Poems* to him. Later still Nadia told me he carried my *Collected Poems* around with him. He said the book is "heavy" (in weight). It was on the floor by his bed, and I heard that he had tripped over the book and nearly broken his neck.[6]

Local politics and Coalition

Ann and I attended a Garden Party at Valerie Metcalfe's for her MP son Stephen. I expected to hear the latest news on local issues, but the talk was of the Coalition between the Conservatives and Liberal Democrats nationally and locally. Stephen told me the Coalition was actual and working at the bottom, not just at the top. He said he had no office or desk in Westminster and was operating on the floor with a laptop. James Brokenshire MP told me there had to be an agreed position with the Liberal Democrats on everything, and the Conservatives had to stick to it. He said, "The Coalition's working and it's genuine." Eleanor Laing MP had been Shadow Minister for Constitutional Affairs and had been told she would have the portfolio in Government. The post had gone to the Liberal Democrats when the Coalition was formed. She naturally had reservations about the Coalition.

I spoke to several local politicians and with David Collischon, the creator of Filofax, who told me, sitting at the bottom of the garden with a stick, "I've got Parkinson's disease. I've had it for six years. It's been dormant but this year it's come on quite badly. I can't walk in a straight line or balance. It's a downward curve."[7]

The Oxford Playhouse and Jonathan Bate

When I am in Oxford Worcester College is local. Ann's birthday present was tickets for Simon Callow's one-man show on Shakespeare, *The Man from Stratford*, at the Oxford Playhouse in June 2010. We checked in at the Randolph Hotel (where my parents stayed and had me to dinner on my 21st birthday) during the afternoon and walked in the grounds of Worcester College. We sat on the seat with two sphinxes and griffins by the arch near the lake where I sat on the morning I gave up Law for English Literature and changed my direction fifty-one years previously. I suddenly felt that my autobiographical poem on direction and destiny (whose title I had received in the air over Iraq), 'Life Cycle', should begin there, and I scribbled notes for the opening passage. We wandered back past my medieval tutor room to the Provost's Yard, where Blackham spoke to us about Existentialism on a hot summer evening, and on to the climb-in gate I pushed Peter O'Toole over. We returned past staircase 5 and found that my room and Ricky's were now occupied by dons as teaching rooms. We returned to the Randolph for tea, walked to the Bodleian quadrangle to say 'hello' to the Earl of Pembroke, walked back to the Randolph for an early supper and then took our seats in the Playhouse for a portrait of Shakespeare written by Jonathan Bate before *The Soul of the Age*, which I had been reading at bedtime. We heard that Shakespeare's best friend was Richard Burbage, and that he reworked old stories and shared the takings and so was known in Stratford for property and land rather than plays.

In the interval Ann asked me to buy two mint-choc ice-creams. I said I was going to have a word with Jonathan Bate. She said there was no evidence that he was present. Following my intuition, I walked to the back of the theatre and looked at the coffee-bar lounge. The counter had gone along with the carpet, but I could see where I sat and read 'Medusa' during Horovitz's poetry session. I returned to the top of the stairs, looked down on the foyer and recognised Bate standing alone by the road. (It was stiflingly hot, all the front doors had been opened to let in air.) I made my way down, pushed through the throng towards Bate's cream summer jacket and asked, "Are you Jonathan Bate?" Tall, sharp-eyed with a vigorous face, he said, "Yes." He said how hot it was in the auditorium and how cool it was where he was standing. I told him I had been at Worcester College just down the road and had often been to the Playhouse more than 50 years ago. He looked down and said nothing. I told him that I had been, and was no longer, a Trustee of the Shakespearean Authorship Trust and that I had wanted him to be a trustee to represent Shakespeare of Stratford. He said that he had given up debating with the SAT as the representatives he had met lacked scholarship. I told him that I had been looking for evidence of 'Shakespeare's trunk' and asked if we could talk further. He gave me his card and asked me to send him an email. He signed my copy of his book, which I had with me.

I was the only member of the packed audience who had confronted Bate.

I returned to Ann with two mint-choc ice-creams and ten minutes of the interval still remaining. She found it hard to believe that I had spoken with Bate en route to finding ice-creams.

On 23 June I sent Bate an email on 'Blunden's trunk' and on 28 June another email wondering what scroll the Earl of Pembroke was holding in the 1630 statue of him at the Bodleian. Had the sculptor linked him to Shakespeare's works through the scroll? Was he Mr W.H. (William Herbert)? On 5 July Coleen Day, the Director of Development and Alumni Relations of Worcester College, sent me an email saying that the new Provost of Worcester College was: Jonathan Bate. I was astonished. He had already been appointed when I told him I had been at Worcester College. My next email congratulated him on his appointment.

Bate replied thanking me. He said that all Shakespeare's foul papers and prompt-book copies would have been recycled as that was the practice of the time. (I distinguished between Shakespeare's foul papers and prompt-book copies and his last papers relating to New Place, Stratford. Blunden had told me, "I don't believe that Shakespeare could have retired to Stratford and not written anything in the last four years of his life. No writer could give up writing completely like that.") Bate steered me towards Fulke Greville – Shakespeare's "master" – as being responsible for a school that Shakespeare taught in under Greville family patronage.

Later I found out that Bate had been a pupil at Sevenoaks School of Alan Hurd (in whose cricket team I had played at Chigwell, with whom I had visited Lord's and sat near the boundary one long summer's day, and who had himself played for the Gentlemen of England at Lord's in 1959–60 and taken five wickets). He later told me that Hurd was his mentor.

So it was that I met the successor to Sir John Masterman and Asa Briggs standing in Beaumont Street on a hot evening, keeping quiet about his appointment (like Tony Little at my prize day after being appointed to Eton).[8]

John Hunt's expansion

John Hunt invited me to Hampshire. He told me he had published 105 books in the current year and wanted to publish 240 in the following year, signalling that he was preparing to sign me up for future books that would help him achieve this expansion.

Ann dropped me off at Deershot Lodge in rural Hampshire on 6 July. It was very hot and John was in shorts. He led me to the outbuilding that housed his publishing administration and I said hello to a couple of his staff, who were bent over screens. We had coffee in his house, in the elegant sitting-room, and I talked about the books I saw ahead. After an hour and a quarter we adjourned to the garden and sat in the shade of an apple-tree near his pond, and I carried on talking. There was a field beyond the hedge that still had deer, and there were bees in the lavender. It was very summery, and after another hour John went indoors and returned with crab soup and toast. He talked about his plans to expand, and after lunch asked if I would join him in his office upstairs, where he posted the forthcoming books I had talked about on his publishing database, for which I should now write Proposals. His computer showed that he had 775 authors, and he told me that within a year he would have 1,500 (which he achieved). It was an excellent session, and (as in Pisa) I could see a decade ahead. Ann collected me (having visited Jane Austen's and Gilbert White's houses), and took a picture of me with John at his gate. I left seeing long local writing days ahead.[9]

Three generations

There were local family events. A few days later Ben collected a prize at Chigwell School's Speech Day. Ann and I sat in the vast marquee in great heat, and later Ann took a photograph of Matthew, Ben and me with the marquee in the background: three generations.

Three generations, Nicholas, Matthew, Ben on 10 July 2010

For a school project Ben had had to interview "an old person" about the bombing of London during the Second World War. He chose to interview me for my childhood memories of doodle-bugs. (I was not too "old" to beat him at table-tennis and chess after the interview.) Soon afterwards we took him to Butterfly World in Hertfordshire and stood among the tropical plants while owl butterflies and swallow-tails wheeled round our heads and settled on our chests and our fingers.[10]

Matthew took Ann and me to see the changes he had made at 6 Albion Hill. Our bedroom had been knocked through into Tony's bedroom to make one long computer room with more than 20 screens round its walls. I stood where I had so often climbed into bed, my head full of *Overlord*, elegiac that a familiar place with so many memories had passed to a new generation (Matthew's) to communicate new technological knowledge to the next generation (Ben's).

Raymond Blanc

Ann spent her 60th birthday at Le Manoir aux Quat'Saisons, near Oxford. A waistcoated porter with a trolley led us from the car park. We walked between two rows of lavender to reception and were escorted to our 15th-century beamy suite, Eugenie, where champagne was delivered. Later we walked to the Japanese water-garden and back past a large lake-like stewpond with ducks and had tea. We returned to our room and then had a nine-course meal of Raymond Blanc recipes.

The next morning after breakfast Ann joined her all-day cooking course (part of her present). I visited the medieval parish church of St Mary's, Great Milton. I sat in a pew, scribbled lines for a poem, 'At Le Manoir aux Quat'Saisons', and rediscovered my poetic self (after working on *The Secret American Dream*).

Matthew arrived with his family mid-morning and drove me to Oxford. We visited some shops and walked by the River Cherwell. We lunched in the High, walked through the Bodleian quadrangle, greeted the Earl of Pembroke and I showed Ben the cross outside Balliol where the three martyrs were burnt. We looked in at Worcester College. Ben and I walked to the lake and sat on the seat with sphinxes and griffins. We looked in at staircase 7 and up at Ricks's window, and then across to staircase 5.

Back at the Manoir we had tea on the lawn. Tony joined us and then Ann, who was surprised to see her family waiting for her. We all had dinner.

After breakfast the next morning Matthew walked with Alex on the croquet lawn. Raymond Blanc hobbled up on crutches, grey-haired and bearded. I joined Matthew and found myself talking to Raymond Blanc. He shook my hand and told me how he fell down the stairs and broke his leg in three or four places, and his foot. We discussed his Japanese garden. I explained the significance of the lantern (*ishidoro*, 'stone torch-basket') and the *yugen*. Tony joined us. He knew Raymond's son and had been in a Manchester United hospitality suite with both of them. There was an arrangement for Raymond's son to be in a film Tony would make.

Birthday presents were handed over in Matthew's room. We had a final walk. We looked at the armillary sphere – the celestial globe (constructed from metal rings) and showing the equator – that had been devised by Ptolemy and had the earth at the centre of the universe, not the sun – and passed the Japanese tea-house by the stone torch-basket and stewpond. As we drove home I drafted Part 3 of my poem on the Manoir on my knee.[11]

More than three years later we returned to the Manoir and made an out-of-hours visit to the Ashmolean, where we wandered round works of Bacon and Moore – it was weird to see paintings by a man I had known exhibited with such adulation when he saw so little meaning in life – and we met Prof. Chris Howgego, Keeper of the Heberden Coin Room. He identified the head on the coin I found in 1946 as belonging to Elagabalus rather than Caracalla, and came back and dined with us. I was interested to see that the Manoir's 'Garden Notes' now included reference to the *yugen*, which I had explained to Blanc during my last visit.

Cornwall damp and William Golding

Matthew had had an operation on a knee at a small hospital specialising in sports injuries in Kent on 1 April to put right the earlier operation he had had. When we went round to wish Alex a happy first birthday the next day he was lying back in shorts with a heavily bandaged knee and a crutch propped against his couch, in some pain. He still needed another remedial operation on the cartilage behind his kneecap.

Kate drove Ann (still recovering from her hip operation), Alex and me to Cornwall. Matthew and Ben followed by train two days later, Matthew hobbling in on his crutch. The next day, sitting over supper, Matthew had pointed his crutch at a skirting-board that was rotten, suggesting damp.[12]

When we were down in Cornwall at the beginning of June 2010, Larry (our all-purpose builder) took the skirting-board off and said there was wet rot. He brought in a specialist, who took damp readings and found a very high level of damp. Plaster needed to be hacked off, walls injected in some places and there should be some tanking. The house was due for internal decoration. I rang the specialist company and agreed that work should start on 28 July and last till 18 August.

Ann and I drove to Cornwall on 21 July. Matthew, Kate, Ben and Alex arrived the next day and enjoyed a few days' holiday. I took Ben down to the beach below my window. We walked carefully on the bladderwrack, limpets and green slime on the rocks surrounding the deeper pools and caught a crab. I looked back up at our house from our beach 'front garden' and it seemed an integral part of the cliff wall and Smeaton's harbour. Matthew and his family left on 28 July just after 7 a.m.

The specialist firm arrived within an hour and rolled back or removed all carpets, piled furniture in the sitting-room and covered it with polythene sheeting. They surrounded the stairwell with sheeting to prevent dust from rising upstairs and we had to lift a flap to go up and down the stairs. Masking tape sealed some doors. Then men drilled into the cob walls and exposed brickwork. Rubble lay on floors, dust hung in the air. In the dining-room Rodney (a vivid man) found a timber with a fruiting-body on it: wet rot just turning to dry rot. The specialist company recommended that some areas should be treated for dry rot.

In our breakfast-room Rodney disclosed the original entrance to one of two houses built from granite blocks the pier had been built from in 1791. When Joseph Smeaton, the Georgian engineer, built Charlestown pier there were reputedly seven tiny houses in Charlestown. These had since disappeared, and two had turned up within the thick inner wall of our house. The back part of our house had originally been a shed, and there were cobbles under our kitchen floor, suggesting it was originally outside our house. Larry suggested that we should preserve glimpses of the stone blocks within our wall, and that is what happened. Three-inch-long nails from the early 1790s were found.

I returned to Connaught House for a week to carry books forward. It was now so dusty in the Harbour-master's House that Ann stayed with her aunt in Porthleven that week (having taken Ben to Bude, where he was spending a week with his mother). We both returned to find the rooms coated with a dark cement plaster. There was a cement mixer in the dining-room. The kitchen had been found to be damp and needed clearing, and we cleared the cupboards and packed our crockery and saucepans in plastic boxes. We then had to choose new tiles for the kitchen and curtains and carpets for most rooms.

On 9 August, his work finished, Rodney casually said, "I used to work for Sir William Golding. He lived on the road from Truro to Falmouth, up a lane before the Norway Inn, in a house called Talimar. The first time I saw him I thought he was the gardener. Once, I was up steps and I fell off onto Sir William's *chaise longue*. He didn't seem to mind, he was very good about it. Whenever he had a slate missing he used to ring me and I'd go up and fit it for him. He wrote *Lord of the*...." He was trying to remember the title. "He had another cottage nearby and I used to look after that. Just alongside his property, it was."

We returned to Essex on 12 August. Later Larry, who was overseeing the work, told me that the kitchen sea-wall was saturated as a result of a leaking pipe. The house was put back together by our Cornish team.[13]

Internationalism: **A New Philosophy of Literature, Selected Stories** *and global media*

A New Philosophy of Literature: *Copped Hall, Light and Shadow*

To me it has always been axiomatic that there are two quite different literary sensibilities, and two quite different uses of the imagination. One sensibility is social and classical, and the writer uses his imagination to transmute his personal experience into creating other social characters. The other sensibility is more individual, and, like Coleridge and Wordsworth (as presented in Maurice Bowra's *The Romantic Imagination*) the writer uses the imagination to see beyond the social to the metaphysical One. I had assumed that everyone was aware of these two sensibilities, and was shocked that during our occasional correspondence Gillon Aitken seemed only aware of the first sensibility in an email in October 2009. I resolved to write a book that would set out the two sensibilities so clearly that they would be axiomatic to everybody. (Later I sent him a copy, making it clear that our exchange had inspired the book.)

In October 2009 I thought of this book as a work of literary Universalism. I thought its subtitle might be 'The Vision of the Infinite and the Universalist

Literary Tradition'. I wrote to John Hunt about the book on 22 October. I referred to the book many times in the course of November.

By April 2010 I thought of the book as *The Light and the Shadow*. In May I was invited to a VIP reception at Copped Hall, which was being restored after a disastrous fire in 1917. Ann and I entered a bare-brick 'building site' of a hallway, climbed upstairs and entered the bare-brick, dilapidated saloon where thirty people talked over wine. I encountered Alan Cox, a shortish man of 67, the driving force behind the restoration, an architect who had organised bank borrowing to buy the property and restore it to the condition and décor it was in c.1750, after John Conyers I demolished Heneage's Elizabethan Copped Hall and rebuilt it.

He took me down steps to look at the 1928 Rolls-Royce of Mrs. Wythes. I looked back up at the pediment and saw a sundial with two figures on either side. I asked him what they were. Cox said, "Light and Shadow." Squinting I could make out the Latin *'Umbra'* for 'Shadow'. I was electrified, thinking of the working-title of my next book. I asked him if he could send me a close-up image for me to use on the front cover. Later he took us on a tour of bare, sometimes smoke-black rooms, but my thoughts were of the 1895 figures of Light and Shadow (*Lumen* and *Umbra*) on either side of the sundial. A week later I received a picture with the motto: *'Me umbra regit vos lumen'*, 'The shadow rules me [i.e. the sundial], the light you'. The image spurred me to think deeply about my coming literary book.[14]

I pondered *The Light and the Shadow* from April to July 2010. I knew I had two threads, social literature and metaphysical literature, but was not sure how far back to take them. On 12 July I shared my dilemma in an email to John Hunt. He replied on 21 July (with his special gift for detecting the true start of a book), suggesting that the title should be *A New Philosophy of Literature*. (I preserved my working title, 'The Light and the Shadow', as the title of Part One.) I immediately saw that I should start with the *Epic of Gilgamesh*, c.2600BC. I "got stuck into chapter 1" the next day and finished chapter 1 on 27 July. The next day I talked with John on the phone. He said, "I can't recall a philosophy of literature." I said, "We might have a new discipline." Coping with the damp in Cornwall slowed me down, but I worked on the book during my visit to Essex, and again during the week after our departure from Charlestown.[15]

A New Philosophy of Literature, a statement of literary Universalism, traces the fundamental theme of world literature. It shows it has alternating metaphysical and secular aspects: a quest for Reality and immortality that began with the *Epic of Gilgamesh*; and condemnation of social vices in relation to an implied virtue. It sets out to show that since classical times these two antithetical traditions have periodically been synthesised by Universalists. It aims to set out the world Universalist literary tradition: the writers who from ancient times have based their work on the fundamental Universalist theme – from the Graeco-Roman world, the Middle Ages, Renaissance, Baroque Age and Neoclassical, Romantic, Victorian and Modernist periods to the modern time.

Mediterranean cruise: 'The Way to Rome', Peter O'Toole
Ann had spotted a cruise that would follow by sea the spirit of the 18th-century Grand Tour across land (which was inspired by interest in Pope's Augustan writings): the journey by coach and on foot from Paris, across the Swiss Alps to Turin, Rome and Naples; and back through Germany and Holland. The *Minerva* would sail round Spain and end visiting Rome and Naples. I agreed to go, thinking that some of the historical places would inspire *A New Philosophy of Literature*. I was also deeply interested in Europe. We would be visiting eurozone countries affected by the financial crisis, and I had planned to write a poetic mini-epic, a choric verse play, celebrating the growth of Europe: *The Dream of Europa*. The European Agency for Fundamental Rights had put out an appeal for a creative work on Europe, and I was ready to begin writing when the project was cancelled in May due to the euro crisis. I still plan to write *The Dream of Europa*.

We were driven to Dover by Kate, boarded the *Minerva*, had tea, were addressed by all the speakers and then dined. The next day we were off St Peter Port, Guernsey. We landed by tender and toured the island, and later attended the captain's reception.

After a day at sea we docked in Spain. We drove to Santiago de Compostela, a place of medieval pilgrimage. We had coffee in a 15th-century hostelry, a convent of St Francis, and entered the Cathedral, where a service was in progress. We walked down a side aisle to the 12th-century Romanesque end where early Gothic began, stepping round people kneeling at confessionals, their heads held by priests. We saw the Holy Door outside, which is only open during Holy Year. That afternoon I began a poem about Grand Tours, 'The Way to Rome'.

I had read on the list of guests 'P.J. O'Toole'. Everyone else was listed by their first name and then surname. I said to Ann, "That's Peter O'Toole." She was sceptical but that evening I saw him dining with a nurse. I could not get across to speak to him then, but later that evening I attended a lecture on Nelson in the Darwin Lounge and at the end saw him in a pink jacket being helped by his nurse to a comfortable chair. I saw him put a small silver flask into his pocket. He was 78 years old, grey-haired and wore tinted glasses.

He was alone, so I went and said, "Peter, may I say hello from 50 years ago." (*See My Double Life 1: This Dark Wood*, pp.104–105.) I could smell alcohol on him, and remembered he was an alcoholic. I told him how he came back to my room in Oxford and we discussed *The Merchant of Venice*, and how at midnight I had helped him climb out over a 10-foot-high gate with his chauffeur. I said, "I can't remember the chauffeur's name." He smiled, "Lionel?" "Yes, Lionel." I told him, "I said, 'You must be quiet,' but you tried to set fire to the Law library, and then near the gate in the dark the History tutor climbed in. I got you behind a bush, and you shouted out, 'I hate thee for thou art a Christian,' and the tutor ran off, terrified." He laughed and asked, "What was I doing in Oxford?" "Waiting for Sian Phillips to finish playing at the Oxford Playhouse. You were in the Gloucester Arms." "Oh yes, *The Taming of the Shrew*." "Yes, that's right." I said, "You drank a bottle of vodka while you were in my room. A year later you made *Lawrence of Arabia* with pretend Arabs while I was working in Baghdad with real Arabs." He laughed again. I told him my son Tony was a film director. I said that in Rome I wanted to see Augustus's frescoes, which had been restored after 40 years, and would be hiring a car. I would be pleased if he would come with me. "Think about it." He thanked me.

I was now aware that a crowd had gathered round us in the half-lit Darwin Lounge. He stood and said, "Shake hands." We shook hands. He said, "I didn't grasp your hand properly, do it again, a good firm handshake." We shook hands again. He said, "Thank you, Nicholas, for telling me these things that happened so long ago, and for making me laugh." Then his nurse took over. She said to me, "I'm Lucy, I look after Mr O'Toole." And she helped him up and led him away from the crowd back to his cabin, which was next to the captain's bridge.

There (one of the *Minerva* staff told me) she was helping him with some research into his career. He would not go ashore. I sadly contrasted his frail unsteadiness on his feet with his nimble strutting on top of a railway carriage in *Lawrence of Arabia*. (I did not see him after the cruise, and he died in December 2013, aged 81, after a long illness – hence his nurse.)

The next day we berthed in Oporto. We visited the Cathedral and saw how barrels of port were produced. After another day at sea we landed at Cadiz. We were driven by coach and I saw the beach – now full of turnstones – where Drake landed.

The following day we again visited the Alhambra, near Granada. (*See* p.641.) I again mused on the 14th-century Moorish power and Paradise. The next two days were at sea.

We then went to Siena by coach. We walked to St Domenico's church, and I saw the dead head of the 14th-century mystic St Catherine of Siena, who died in 1387: wimpled, eyes closed, petite, demure behind glass. In a case next to it was a finger from her right hand.

We walked down to the cobbles of the Piazza del Campo, where twice a year ten horses race in the inter-district Palio di Siena. We reached the Duomo, which has 56 images on the marble floor dating from 1372 to 1562:

sibyls, pagan philosophers including Socrates, and *Old Testament* images. There were statues of Plato and Aristotle outside dating from 1290, long before Ficino. Returning crusaders had brought Plato to Siena.

We went on to a farm, where we had lunch looking across a valley at the distant town of San Gimignano. We went on to the town and visited the Town Hall, and I saw the room where Dante came as an Ambassador in 1299. On the wall was a picture of Dante standing under the same frescoes that I was standing under. There were more medieval frescoes and scenes in a nearby 12th-century Romanesque church.

The next morning we were off Corsica, which we reached by tender. We toured the north-west. We passed where a bullet struck a rock and sent splinters into Nelson's temple, blinding him. We visited the church of Our Lady of the Hillside, which overlooked it. That evening there was another captain's reception.[16]

The next day the ship docked at Cittavecchio, and Ann and I travelled by car to Rome. (O'Toole did not join us. He had sent me a note: "Dear NH, Am myself doing a work of writing, hence the six-week cruise. Lucy V my PA. Away from all. At it most days. Mountain of research to collate. Thanks for the thought…. Reclusively yours, P.") We entered the Forum about 9.30 and walked to the Palatine. Disappointingly, the House of Augustus was closed, and so was the House of Livia. I got my bearings and did useful research. Then we walked back to the Temple of Divine Julius, and lingered at the Caesar and Augustus forums, and by the Rostrum. We left at 11.30, and our driver took us past Mussolini's palace, the Trevi fountain and the Spanish steps.

We returned to the ship for lunch and then set off by coach for Tarquinia, seat of the Etruscans and early kings of Rome. There was a tradition that Aeneas founded Etruria. We began in the museum, where there were sarcophagi, and then toured the Necropolis, going down flights of steps into individual shaft tombs, mostly c.6th–4th-centuries BC. We returned to the ship for dinner.

The next day we docked at Naples and were taken by coach to Pompeii. (*See also* p.523.) We walked from the theatre via the baths, shops and a fountain and looked at the lead-pipe system and the stepping-stones across roads and sewage effluent when the drains overflowed, allowing a chariot through between the first and third of the three stepping-stones. We noted the polygonal stones of a road with bits of marble between them, which acted like Cat's-eyes in moonlight. We went on to the Forum and saw the plaster casts of people who had choked to death from volcanic fumes.

On the last day I finished my 40-stanza poem on the Grand Tour, 'The Way to Rome'. From Naples we flew home.

Finishing A New Philosophy of Literature
I returned to *A New Philosophy of Literature* on 20 September. Towards the end of October I reached chapter 5 and in mid-November chapter 8. By 20 December I had reached chapter 10. I had virtually finished the book at the end of March 2011, and combed it for another three weeks before sending it off on 21 April.[17] I wrote: "The eight-month haul is over, nearer nine months." I read proofs in May and June 2011.

Ricks and the Triton
I sent a copy of *A New Philosophy of Literature* to Christopher Ricks in the US. In March 2012 a copy of the first edition of a finely produced 1962 book, *The Victoria and the Triton*, arrived through the post. It was about two round-the-world voyages, one by the Portuguese navigator Ferdinand Magellan and the other, retracing his route, by the US nuclear submarine the *Triton*. There was a note: "For Nicholas, who travels imaginatively. With thanks for *A New Philosophy of Literature* and with good wishes, Christopher. 50 years on [from 1962]." Magellan organised the first circumnavigation of the globe in 1519–1522, and the *Triton* had been the first to circumnavigate the earth underwater in 1960.

I saw the book as a symbol of my distinction between inspiration and Neoclassical imitation. The *Victoria* was dependent on wind and slow. The *Triton* imitated the *Victoria*'s route but did it in a new way and more quickly. I saw it as "a profound Vorticist symbol with rushes of ideas in all directions". It was about pioneering and better technique – a Neoclassical riposte to my contrast between the metaphysical and the social, the Romantic and Neoclassical in my statement of the fundamental theme of world literature. It did not change my view of the fundamental theme, but I was full of admiration at the brilliance and neatness of the image. I reflected that I was a pioneer who had depended on inspiration and had circumnavigated the globe to bring back Universalism, and that he was an ultra-modern, high-tech imitator who covered the ground more effectively. I widened his symbol to the contrast between poet and critic: the poet was blown by the wind whereas the critic functioned with nuclear power and instruments.[18]

'Hermitage'
I was receiving inspiration from the grounds at Connaught House. At night there were hooting owls. I loved the bees in the lavender of the knot-garden. I listened to the clear piping of the song-thrush most mornings. I watched a ladybird on a leaf. I drafted poems: 'Owl', 'Honey-bees', 'Song-Thrush' and 'Ladybird'. To my dismay three days later I found two song-thrushes lying dead near each other, and buried them. I wrote two more poems: 'Song-Thrush II' and 'Pine Cone'. I still had many poems to write. I had listed all

the poems I planned to do: about 40.

Connaught House had become a 'hermitage'. I had withdrawn from society to write books in my study and like Chaucer's reeve lived near a heath and behind trees. Coleridge wrote, "This Hermit good lives in that wood", and that was what I did: for parts of each day I lived like a solitary hermit on the edge of Epping Forest.[19]

Hermitage viewed from near Connaught Water

Xing and Ovid Banished

Over the years I had been associated with numerous people within the schools and the book trade, including a number of publishers, editors, publicity specialists and other marketeers, and for a long while my own website had listed and described my books. Three Wikipedia pages had grown up higgledy-piggledy. A Normanhurst parent later told me that he had posted the first entry about *Overlord*. My own website, which I had had for about ten years, was more accurate, but I noted that foreign bookshops and Ebay sellers frequently added a snippet from my Wikipedia entry to details of the books they were selling online. Someone acting under the name 'Hagger' was reported to Wikipedia by an unknown person for vandalising other Wikipedia entries over several months, and the Wikipedia administrators had been notified that I was the main suspect. My PA told them the vandalising 'Hagger' was not me. It looked as if I was being framed for deletion.

I was a bemused bystander when (according to a warning tab) "Chinese agent, Xing", who had in 2008 deleted a Nigerian poet who supported Tibet, now proposed me for deletion. It was like living under the French Revolution and being proscribed for the guillotine. For a month (4 January–9 February 2011) there was a battle of opinion out there, in the course of which it was bizarrely asserted by Xing that O-Books was another name for Oak-Tree Books (defunct for more than 25 years). It was asserted that there was no evidence that I had been tutor to Prince Hitachi. My higgledy-piggledy entries had more than 50 sources, but "insufficient sources" was given as a reason for deletion. Xing wanted me out. I was aware that there are 250,000 Chinese agents on retainers to carry out China's cyber-wishes. It must be borne in mind that *The Syndicate* and now *The World Government* had been selling round the world, and that the Chinese regime does not want China to be subordinated to a New World Order or world government. First the entries on *Overlord* and *Armageddon*, and finally the entry on me, were guillotined.

All this happened while I was writing *A New Philosophy of Literature*. What was happening out there was illusory – error, *Maya* – and I did not want to waste a moment of my writing time reflecting on it. I got on with the task in hand. Tony arranged for my website to be redesigned so that a secret state (through one of 250,000 retained operatives) could not completely airbrush me out of cyber-existence.

I had written about the *"error"* that resulted in Ovid's banishment, and I wondered if the modern equivalent of Roman banishment was banishment from the internet. Ovid's books were removed from Roman libraries, and now my books had been removed from Wikipedia's screens. Had I, though living in a 'hermitage', suffered a similar fate to Ovid's? Was I treading in Ovid's footsteps and on a path I had already charted in *Ovid Banished*? It seemed I was now living another pair of opposites: +A (writing) + –A (banishment) = 0 (the One experienced through the solitude of enforced obscurity); another twist to 'my double life'.

So far as I am aware Xing's opposition and suppressing activities have not impeded me: weeks later Michael Mann asked me to send a copy of *The Secret American Dream* to President Obama, and when I went to the White House's website to leave a message on a contact page that a book was in the post I was startled to see my personal details and address come up, and in the 'Telephone' slot, weirdly and encouragingly wrongly, was my PA's mobile number.

Selected Stories: Follies and Vices of the Modern Elizabethan Age

I had long wanted to select the best of my 1,001 stories, and now wanted my selection to reflect the fundamental theme of world literature I had outlined in *A New Philosophy of Literature*. Part One would be on the social follies and vices; Part Two on the quest for the One: the quest for Reality and approaches to the One. I wanted my selection to be called *Selected Stories: Follies and Vices of the Modern Elizabethan Age* and to be no longer than 200 pages. I worked on a selection when I was down in Cornwall in February 2011 – while taking Ben to see owls and to the smugglers' Jamaica Inn – and I worked on the selection again in April. By 22 April I had whittled the stories down to 55 in each of the two Parts, and two days later I had them down to 43 stories in each Part. On 26 April I had finished my selection.[20] I listed the vices in October 2012.

Libya: Adam Boulton and BBC Radio 5

In March I received an email from *Sky News* asking if they could interview me on Libya. I rang and was told that Adam Boulton and Sarah Hughes would interview me at 1.45 p.m. that day on the lunchtime *Boulton & Co.*

Gaddafi's fall seemed imminent, and having survived his intimidation in 1970 I was delighted to be able to go out on a global network he might be watching and let him know that I had outlasted him. A car collected me and dropped me in Millbank. I passed Sir Christopher Meyer, the UK's ex-Ambassador to the US. He stopped and stared at me in the doorway. I took the lift to the second floor lobby and buzzed at the door of the Sky suite. I reported in and was waved to a seat. I realised that Sarah was talking to the world with her back to me ten yards away, and that I was on TV in the background. Others joined me: an anti-Gaddafi Libyan, a pro-Government Bahraini and Richard Ottaway MP. I said to him, "You're Chairman of the Foreign Affairs Select Committee and you were Chairman of the 1922 Committee." He looked astonished. "Yes I was." Jeremy Corbyn MP entered, and Ottaway immediately began to negotiate with our handler to be interviewed separately from Corbyn.

Eventually it was my turn. I was led in to a cordoned-off area within the open-plan suite and invited to sit at a table. Adam Boulton was sitting reading notes. I nodded to him. Sarah came and chatted. She asked where I had been and about my schools. Adam said, "You've written a lot of books." I gave him a signed copy of *The Libyan Revolution*. Someone said, "Three minutes." We sat in darkness, facing a distant camera with a light. "Two minutes." "One minute." "Ten seconds." "Five seconds." "Now." Adam read from an autocue. He and Sarah had typed questions in front of them. I had nothing. Adam said that I had predicted in 1970 that Gaddafi would last 40 years. "You were right then, so you may be right about now." He asked me about my memories of Gaddafi.

I spoke for eight minutes on the *coup* I was involved in, how Gaddafi stole it, my memories of his visits to the University, and how I had nearly been executed. (Two weeks previously Gaddafi's men had beaten up three BBC journalists and threatened them with execution, 41 years after they had done the same to me.) I was asked about Gaddafi's eccentricity, and said he was true to his Berber roots. I was asked about his hats and spoke of their tribal significance in Libya. Then suddenly it was all over. "Good to meet you," Adam said, and I was off. From the car, which had been waiting for me, I saw Vince Cable walking along the street.

I made another broadcast on Libya for BBC Radio 5 *Live Drive* in February 2012. It marked the first anniversary of the fall of Gaddafi. I had to listen at my desk around 6.45 p.m. while a euphoric Libyan teacher of English spoke from Tripoli's Martyrs' Square. He said that everyone was cheering and crying, and was overcome by the crowds and the occasion. I was then asked for my view. It fell to me to be realistic. I said there was no stability or central control in Libya: 250 militias were arresting people and holding 8,000 pro-Gaddafi prisoners, and there was little sign of a national security force. I wondered how parliamentary and presidential elections could take place when the country was in anarchy, indeed chaos. Gaddafi had been a ruthless tyrant, but at least there had been central control, and the cheering, tearful crowds in Tripoli were masking the passing of Libya into the hands of 250 separate and skirmishing militias. (By 2014 there were 1,700 out-of-control militias.)[21]

War in the Middle East, death of bin Laden
An article in the *American Free Press* revealed that the Bilderberg Group was pushing the US into a war in the Middle East, which would begin with the civil war in Libya and was intended to result in the overthrow of the Iranian regime. Events in Egypt and Syria had to be seen within the context of the New World Order – and therefore of the World State.[22] On 2 May there were reports of the death of bin Laden, which would enrage al-Qaeda. In due course I wrote the killing of bin Laden as an Epilogue to go into a future edition of *Armageddon*.

Philosophy lecture on internet
I was invited to address the London branch of the Scientific and Medical Network in a converted chapel in Hampstead on *The New Philosophy of Universalism*: a PowerPoint presentation with slides. My talk could be listened to simultaneously on the internet and it would then be available online. I spoke for an hour and ten minutes about the universe and Universalism, and then there were questions. Several in the audience had heard me before, and their questions included questions about the Syndicate, notably by a former employee of Rothschilds. There was no escaping the New World Order, and therefore the World State, even when I was talking about the universe.[23]

Localism: A View of Epping Forest

While I was approaching literature from the perspective of a World State, seeing all world literature as a unity, and pronouncing on events in Libya, I was at the same time continuing to lead a local life, as I had always done. Within my current pair of opposites there was a localist eye that was in conflict with my global preoccupations.

Schools
The schools had been going very well. The Heads of Normanhurst and Coopersale Hall had left at the end of the previous summer term – the Coopersale Hall Head was half-Canadian and had emigrated to Canada – and their replacements (Claire Osborn at Normanhurst and Kaye Lovejoy at Coopersale Hall) had brought new enthusiasm and skill. Oaklands had had

a successful inspection and we thanked the staff by taking over the upper room at the local Café Rouge. At Oaklands too, there was a change of Head, the previous Head retiring after ten years of great success. She was replaced internally (by Cheryl Macnair). We were getting ready to build a new block of four classrooms at Coopersale Hall to add to a new classroom already opened. We had delayed applying the proceeds of the three Cornish cottages to this building programme until we had weathered the worst of the recession.

Birth of granddaughter, Olivia

In June 2010 Kate had revealed that she was four weeks' pregnant with our third grandchild. At the end of September she rang to say that she was having a daughter, our first granddaughter. A fortnight later she told us that she and Matthew would be calling the new baby Olivia. I said, "Ollie?" And that was how it proved to be. Ollie was born on 9 February 2011 at Princess Alexandra Hospital, Harlow, and I observed her little formed fingers and exposed toes until Sister came and told us off for being there: "Partners only on the first day." The next day I drafted a poem, 'A Wish for my Granddaughter'.

There were family events at the O2. Our bank arranged for Ben to have a day of playing tennis with Boris Becker there, a long coaching session. And in November (a late birthday present) we all accompanied Ann to hear the blind tenor, Andrea Bocelli at the O2.

In Gloucestershire: Roman culture

A fortnight later Ann and I drove to Painswick in Gloucestershire to use a voucher (given us by Nadia) for an overnight stay at Cardynham House, which had been built in 1489. We were in a room with beeswaxed walls, a four-poster bed and a stone fireplace over which was inscribed the epitaph of Tiberius Claudius Secundus taken from Rome's Baths of Caracalla: "*Balnea, vina, Venus corrumpunt corpora nostra, sed vitam faciunt*": "Baths, wine and love corrupt our bodies but make up life." Between the windows was inscribed an epigram by Martial (4.24): "*Omnes quas habuit, Fabiane, Lycoris amicas/extulit;uxori fiat amica meae*": "Fabianus, Lycoris has buried all the female friends she had. May she make friends with my wife." Both melancholy Roman messages were universal: the local medieval folk of Painswick who put them up felt connected to universal Roman culture, and I wrote a story, 'Lycoris Buries her Friends'. The next morning we visited the Slimbridge Wildfowl and Wetlands Centre, which had been associated with Peter Scott. On the way back we looked at Berkeley Castle, having sat with the owners on the *Minerva*, and we had tea at Tetbury.[24]

We attended the annual dinner of the local Friends of Epping Forest, and learned from a neighbour of the Balls family who had lived in Albion Hill, Loughton for many years that their business, Balls Brothers, had gone into administration after more than 50 years of trading. The business had run off-licences selling *vina*, but they had expanded too quickly into City restaurants and their bank had demanded repayment. My sister Frances had been friendly with a daughter of Derek Balls and had stayed with her when our father died, and been taken to the Lord Mayor's Show. Fifty years ago the family was a byword for stability, and it was a melancholy measure of the financial crisis that such a solid family business should have gone under.[25] Talking about Epping Forest with Tricia Moxey and Ken Hoy at the Friends' dinner strengthened my resolve to start *A View of Epping Forest*.

Death of John Ezard

In October 2010 I learned from the Rev. Richard Wallace (an Old Chigwellian contemporary of mine I met at a Chigwell gathering) that John Ezard was in King George V Hospital, near Gants Hill, on account of his lungs and was waiting to go into a nursing home. In December I sent John a Christmas card there. On 14 December Wallace rang to say that Ezard had died the previous Saturday. He had broken his leg in June or July and was in plaster, and it did not heal. He could not hear well. He had been on a life-support machine for a while. I reckoned that my card arrived the day before he died.

I attended John's funeral with Tony, his godson. I picked up Wallace on the way, and we drove to a small church beyond Brentwood where some 20 *Guardian* journalists were standing round. The vicar arrived and handed out orders of service, and the coffin was borne in. There was a hymn and a psalm, and then Alan Smith gave a tribute. John's career in journalism had progressed alongside his, and he said that John was always "contrary". I knew what he meant: John had a gift for taking the opposite point of view to stimulate a discussion. Living through episodes dominated by pairs of opposites, I took his "contrariness" in my stride, but I could see that it might irk others.

The vicar spoke, picking out features of John. He invited his god-daughter to light a candle, but she said, "No." The coffin was carried out and we stood outside. I spoke to his wife and daughter (a blonde of 37), to his brother and the only other Old Chigwellian present, Nicky Macy (the youngest son of the Oaklands teacher under Miss Lord) who told me, "He shouldn't die at 71." (In December 2011 he himself died in hospital at 71.)

I drove the vicar to John's local, the Tower Arms, South Weald, where there were refreshments. I spoke with John's widow, who had disapproved of independent schools and therefore me when she was younger, but was now courteous and charming. She told me that he had had pneumonia but would not stop smoking, that he had smoked himself to death while insisting, "My lungs are made of leather." She shook her head. I spoke to Alan Smith and recalled meeting him 41 years previously in John's company, when the three of us talked in a pub near *The Guardian*. Tony was being pestered inappropriately by an inebriated elderly man, who then came to me and asked if I would give him a lift to a station. Tony had a word with me and said, "It's Eddie Linden, I recognise him from the launch of *The Fire and the Stones*." I realised that I had met him 41 years before, in the company of John Heath-Stubbs and his hangers-on. Linden edited *Aquarius*, a poetry magazine, and under normal circumstances we would have had a conversation. We made a bland excuse and left.

First Ricky, now Ezard. I had been left high and dry by those I associated with when I chose to be a writer – and an intelligence agent. John had been good value in those early days, and his 'contrariness' had got worse while I was in Japan.[26]

Charles Beauclerk and Shakespeare
Charles's second book, *Shakespeare's Lost Kingdom* had split Oxfordians. The Americans had taken to his 'Prince Tudor theory' (that Shakespeare was both the son and lover of Elizabeth I) and it had influenced *Anonymous*, a film starring Vanessa Redgrave that had seen Shakespeare as the 17th Earl of Oxford in that dual relationship with the Queen. Charles had been cold-shouldered by the British De Vere Society and he had been deselected as President, as he had told me over the phone in January. Derek Jacobi had resigned from the De Vere Society in protest. Charles complained that the SAT was now dominated by Baconians, and he could not see himself staying much longer.

He visited me a fortnight later. We talked in my study. He was toying with starting an independent Free school. He told me his landlord, a former guide at Otley Hall, now had Parkinson's disease. I drove him back to Buckhurst Hill station, aware that he was trying to find a new direction.[27]

Garden and Bellerophon
I revelled in being localist and out of the reach of the world's noticeboard. I often thought of Marvell's lines at the beginning of 'The Garden': "How vainly men themselves amaze/To win the Palm, the Oke, the Bayes." The garden was a depository of true values. Winning garlands was not the way to live. I believed in keeping both feet on the ground in the garden and being content within the moment, not hankering after distant longings or attachments. We were fortunate in our choice of a new gardener, Gerry, who maintained a slow rhythm during his time with us and, having green fingers, made everything burgeon and grow.

The Old Chigwellians' annual magazine, *The OC Mitre*, came out in

December with excerpts from my two poetic epics and a classical ode. This issue gave me a local audience and confirmed my resolve to write a local book next.

On the roof of the annexe at Connaught House was a weathervane: Bellerophon riding to Heaven on a winged horse (Pegasus), pennant streaming, having slain the chimera. Wandering about the grounds, feeding the large *koi* in their pool, looking at nuthatches and long-tailed tits on the bird feeders and watching a fox slink across the lawn, standing by Apollo and listening to a song-thrush, I sometimes felt my immortal soul rise like Bellerophon on the wings of poetic inspiration.[28]

A View of Epping Forest
Ann and I made two visits to Waltham Abbey. We had tea outside the Welsh Harp in warm summer weather and walked by the weir to Harold's bridge and the 14th-century gateway. We returned a week later to visit the Abbey (and had tea inside the church at Upshire on the way back). Both visits spurred me on towards my next, local book.

I had long wanted to write a book about Epping Forest that would bring together its history, its places and the spirit that inspired my Forest poems. As I had lived there since 1943 it would have the flavour of a personal memoir while being objective. The Olympic Games of 2012 would be taking place in Stratford, near one end of the Forest, and my book would have to be out by May 2012 to be in bookshops near the Olympics. I would have to write the book in six months, between May and October.

I was planning the book in April as I finished *A New Philosophy of Literature*. I wrote the first paragraph about the River Roding on 4 May. My working title was 'A Portrait of Epping Forest', but I knew I could not use that as Sir William Addison had used it. I found my title on 24 May: "Changed the title of the Epping Forest book to *A View of Epping Forest*." Part One would present a history of the Forest from the Ice Age to 1878. Part Two would dwell on Forest places: my own Loughton; Chigwell, Woodford and my own Buckhurst Hill; Waltham Abbey, High Beach and Upshire; Epping and the Theydons; and Chingford Plain. The book would cover the local area that inspired my growth as a poet and was the cradle of my Universalism.

I fleshed out the history section in June, and finished writing on the places in draft on 4 August. (I had had to cope with reading two sets of proofs of *A New Philosophy of Literature* in May and June.)

Departures
While I was writing I coped with local events. Our accountants celebrated their 60th anniversary at the Tower of London towards the end of June. In the New Armouries banqueting suite we sat on the round table presided

over by Martin Anderson, who had done much for our schools and had had a long spell away with cancer of his oesophagus. He came and sat next to me and told me he had been reading *The World Government*. This was the last time I saw him: he died of cancer in November 2012.

In June Ann exhibited her tulip and freesia paintings at Bedford House. A few days later we hosted a dinner for 68 Coopersale Hall staff at Unico restaurant, Epping following the school's latest inspection. The following month Matthew holidayed in Florida with Ben. Tony had moved out of his local flat in Buckhurst Hill and had bought a house in nearby Leytonstone to be nearer London. He spent time with us while work took place on his new property, and would move in on 1 November.

Cornwall: hermit
Down in Cornwall I wrote:

> I am like a hermit or anchorite down here. I sit in my cell (my room overlooking the sea) and contemplate as did the hermits on the cliffs of Tintagel, and understand my past, find the patterns in my past that give me understanding of the present. I am in harmony with the waves and the sky. [As well as Connaught House,] Cornwall is my hermitage.

On 8 August I wrote: "The lights are leaping on the sea, splashes of light, a thundershower of sunshine, each splash mirror-white, flurries of wind, small icebergs scudding across the water. Stopped my combing... to write 'Splashes of Light'." Again: "Brilliant stars. Wished I could capture their rawness.... My perspective shattered and changed. Little 'I', great stars. Epping Forest seemed very small."[29]

On the Isle of Man: Great Laxey wheel
I took Ann to the Isle of Man to rediscover her father's roots. To her, the Isle of Man was local. We flew to Douglas and stayed in the Sefton, where Norman Wisdom had been a regular visitor. (There was a statue of him, sitting on his bench with his cap tilted jauntily outside one of the doors.) Ann's paternal grandmother had owned several houses in the Isle of Man and Liverpool, and the next morning we visited the family homes at 3 Woodville Crescent (which Ann's grandmother had run as a guest-house) and at 13 Empire Terrace (where Ann worked one summer vacation when she was 19). We went on to Pretoria, Sea View Road, Onchan (where Ann's father lived and Ann was photographed as a bridesmaid when she was four) and to Sundown, Lower Ballanard Road (where her aunt had lived). We then visited King William's College, Castletown (the independent school where Ann's father was educated). All these places were local to Ann's

family.

We visited King Orry's grave, a megalith 5,000 years old, and then the Great Laxey wheel, which pumped water from the deepest mine to reveal lead and zinc. I immediately saw the mine as a symbol of artistic depths and the wheel as the circular, repetitive round of my daily pumping out of distracting thoughts to reveal the lead-and-zinc-like images I mine. I wrote a poem, 'The Wheel of Creation'.

We were driven to Bride and Point of Ayre, and up under Snaefell to Peel. We went on to St John's and the Tynewald, to the Calf of Man and then to Cregneash, Port St Mary and Castletown. The next day we went to Port Erin by single-track steam train. We walked to the beach and then caught another train to Castletown and visited the 1570 school room.

Back in Douglas we took a horse tram along by the sea. From a local shop Ann bought a gold 'three-legs', perhaps recognising her Manx links to her father, her grandmother and aunt.[30]

Christening of Alex and Ollie

In early September there was a combined christening for Alex and Ollie in the chapel at Chigwell School. As we all stood waiting in groups in the courtyard where we used to have call-over, Alex arrived, saw me and ran the entire length of the chapel to the call-over steps for me to lift him up, and then he put his head on my shoulder. Little Ollie was baptised first, and Alex, having seen that water was splashed on her head, leaned his head back to co-operate, to general amusement.

Finishing A View of Epping Forest

I spent much of August, September and October combing the text of *A View of Epping Forest* and doing preparatory work on the index. During this time I extracted the section on Chigwell School and edited it for the December issue of *The OC Mitre*. I added my poems about Epping Forest in an Appendix that also included Lidar images (which show land without vegetation) of the ancient Forest settlements. (Loughton Camp, Ambresbury Banks and the High Beach pillow mounds). The book was sent off on 8 November.

Jonathan Bate

That evening I went to the Oxford and Cambridge Club in Pall Mall and attended a meeting of the Worcester Society in the Marlborough Room. Jonathan Bate, wearing black-rimmed spectacles and sitting behind a table, had things to say. We all went upstairs to a large room of Palmerston's era and stood with champagne in a horseshoe until Bate joined us. He walked down to the end of the horseshoe without acknowledging anybody and when he reached me said, "Hello, Nick," and we talked about his one-man show on Shakespeare. I told him I had just finished *A View of Epping Forest* and talked of Fairmead Cottage's links with Clare, whose biography he had written. He had visited Epping Forest for local colour on Clare, but no, he did not get there.

At the end of dinner Bate made a speech urging everyone to make endowments to the College in their wills. Aware that Fulke Greville's monument had been endoscoped in May and been found to contain rubble and no last papers of Shakespeare's, I later asked what he knew about the connection between Lady Mary Wroth of Loughton Hall, the 3rd Earl of Pembroke (William Herbert, possibly the dedicatee of Shakespeare's *Sonnets*, "Mr W.H.", who had two children by her) and Ben Jonson (who had stayed with her at Loughton Hall): "What was going on? Was Shakespeare involved?" He said, "I don't know. It would be worth researching."

I had finished *A View of Epping Forest*, but had left unanswered one of the main local literary questions: did the 3rd Earl of Pembroke visit Loughton Hall to see his children along with Ben Jonson and (if Pembroke was his patron) Shakespeare?[31] I corrected proofs at the end of November 2011 and received my first copy of the book at the end of April 2012.

Internationalism: My Double Life 1: This Dark Wood *and radio*

Bronwen Astor and Skybolt

The châtelaine of Cliveden, Bronwen Astor, the best-known model of the late 1950s whose account of the Light can be found in her biography,[32] had attended my Winchester lecture and told me I was 20 years ahead of my time. I thought she would be interested in new information regarding the Soviet spy ring at Cliveden in the early 1960s, and emailed her. She suggested that we should meet in Starbucks, Pimlico Road on 12 May. I found a table inside the door, and a few minutes later she sailed in, tall and elegant. I reminded her that I had first visited Cliveden in 1960, and had spoken to her husband, Lord Astor, on the terrace. She told me she had experienced the Light once, in 1959. She said, "I haven't experienced the Light since 1959." (I noted: "I experienced it last night, was overtaken on my way to the dishwasher and sat and let it in." It was as if the Light was letting me know that it approved of my forthcoming visit to Lady Astor.) She told me it was "a watery" Light rather than a blinding inner sun, and that she had become a spiritual director to look after the soul rather than a psychotherapist to look after the ego.

We got on to the Soviet ring. I showed her Christine Keeler's *The Truth at Last*, p.106: "While Bill [, Bronwen's husband, Lord Astor,] was changing, Stephen [Ward] stole some letters which he later handed over to Eugene [Ivanov]. The letters were useful information about the Skybolt missiles which were to be Britain's nuclear weaponry." She told me that Stephen Ward stole the plans sent to her husband by *The Observer* (*see* p.698) while she was talking to Christine Keeler in the hall. Her husband and Ward went to his ground-floor study, where the post was. Her husband went upstairs to change. Ward would follow to give him a massage. "Ward turned back as if to go to the loo, which was next door to Bill's study." He had re-entered the study.

I asked her to read the next bit: "Stephen [Ward] was a happy and busy man when we got back to Wimpole Mews. He phoned Roger Hollis while I started to make some lunch." Hollis was then Head of MI5, and I showed her an article with extracts from Chapman Pincher's book *Treachery*, which claimed that Hollis (who had been at Worcester College, Oxford), Ward and Ivanov were a Soviet ring that was seeking to obtain the Skybolt plans and the date when missiles were being sent to Germany. She read on in Keeler's book: "I was to find out, through pillow talk, from Jack Profumo when nuclear warheads were being moved to Germany" (p.107). I told Bronwen, "You were present when Ward stole the Skybolt plans from Bill's study to pass to the Soviet Union. That was what the Profumo Affair was about." She was thoughtful and told me, "We knew the Kennedys." At that moment a robin with a red breast flew into Starbucks and sat on the second stair, waiting to be fed. I thought that Ward had flown into Cliveden like a robin redbreast.

We walked back to her house in Ranelagh Grove. Her walls were covered with photographs from the Cliveden time and of her grandchildren. Her PA took a copy of the article on *Treachery*. She said, "Ward used to say he was a spy." I said: "What better cover than to tell the truth?"[33]

Hadrian's Wall

Ann and I had visited Hadrian's Wall, a boundary of the Roman World State. We stayed in a hotel just outside Newcastle.

We were taken through green countryside, past farms and large estates, to the Birdoswald Roman fort (which had a 7th-century addition built in the Dark Ages) and then to Vindolanda, a flat frontier town under a quarry on a hill. The museum had writing on birch bark. We went on to Housesteads and then to the Temple of Mithras. There were holes round Mithras's head for a lamp to shine through the dark, suggesting the Light of Mithras.

The next day we visited Segedunum, a fort, and went on to Arbeia, where there was a reconstruction of a barracks. The next day we drove to Chesters, walked across fields to the River Tyne and looked at the ruins of a fort, part of a Roman bridge and a bathhouse. Later I wrote a poem, 'On Hadrian's Wall', with sections on the places I had visited.[34]

Gidleigh Park: episodes and beginning of This Dark Wood, *a bowl of fir-cones*
I had had the idea of writing an autobiography about how my works emerged from my entire life for some years. I had thought of it as *The Seven Hills* in December 2006 and in Cusco in 2007, and again around Christmas 2007. I had raised it with John Hunt in April 2008. I had still thought of this work as *The Seven Hills* in December 2009 and in March 2010, but by 19 September 2010 it had become *This Dark Wood*. In May 2011 I began an outline for the book, but was immediately diverted by having to begin *A View of Epping Forest*. I referred to *This Dark Wood* in July and August.

We went to Cornwall and on our way back, on 19–20 August 2011, we spent a couple of days at Gidleigh Park, Dartmoor. We drove to Two Bridges and then on past bracken, heather and gorse, past settlements, cairns, black-headed sheep and bullfinches to a narrow lane that took us to the four timber-framed gables of the house Bartholomew Gidleigh bought in 1660. We were greeted by ten staff in black and white, and tails, and were escorted to our first-floor room (named after Huccalby Tor), where I sat in the window and watched a river, the North Teign, plashing over boulders with Dartmoor in the distance. That evening we sampled the 'fine dining'.

The next morning was wet. Ann decided to sit downstairs. I went to my room and sat in the window overlooking the river, which was narrow enough to leap across, and received from beyond the paragraphs about Gidleigh Park that appear in the Prologue of *This Dark Wood*. The haunting image of the river rushing by suggested my life and all life, and a bowl of fir-cones in my window suggested episodes from my life and all lives. I had thought about *This Dark Wood* on and off for some while, and only two days before coming to Gidleigh Park I had asked in my *Diary* what the theme would be. The paragraphs I received were an answer to my question.

Now I sat like a hermit, contemplating the river and the distant moors and reflecting on the pattern of my life and of all lives, and of the meaning of my life and of all lives. I reflected on the connection of my life and of all lives with order in the universe, and the connection between the situations in my life and in all lives and notions of accident, design and destiny. I pondered my Universalism. I asked myself, 'Where did my life go and what did I do with it?' Looking at the bowl of fir-cones I saw my life as a number of self-contained but related episodes that should be treated as a whole, like a bowl of fir-cones. And suddenly I grasped that my new work would avoid conventional autobiography and chronological narrative of events for episodes.

The rain lifted and we took our packed lunch, supplied by the hotel as two backpacks, to the water-garden and ate on some steps. Brown trout rose for flies in the narrow river near my feet, a buzzard called and hovered overhead, there were a couple of dippers. We sat alone, red wine in fluted glasses, tablecloth laid out on the ground and ate among the dragonflies and trout ripples in a mossy glade. We then packed lunch into our backpacks and walked to a humped-back bridge and returned through a bluebell wood. All round us were Bronze-Age settlements, stone circles, cairns, stone rows, hut circles. The North Teign river rises among cairns and settlements on Bronze-Age Dartmoor.

I arrived back in Essex the next day with my structure of episodes firmly in my mind.[35]

I returned to the outline of *This Dark Wood* in November 2011. On 22 November I visited John Hunt in Hampshire. I arrived at 10.15 and sat in his kitchen while he finished making turnip soup. We then went upstairs and checked my entries on screen. We discussed *A View of Epping Forest* and we agreed that *This Dark Wood* would be my next work. At 12.40 we sat

in his dining-room and ate our turnip soup. When Ann arrived at the gate, John came to the car and chatted briefly. Ann took our picture.

On 27 January 2012 Tricia Moxey came to lunch and mentioned Fibonacci spirals. (*See My Double Life 1: This Dark Wood*, p.xxvii.) By mid-February I had reached episode 5 and mid March episode 9; by mid April episode 12.[36]

Nicholas with John Hunt on 22 November 2011

Bletchley Park

At the end of September 2011 Ann took me for a weekend in the Northampton Marriott Hotel to absorb Bletchley Park. The first evening our group was shown an Enigma machine identical to the one on which the Bletchley Park decoders had worked. Its owner demonstrated its 10^{114} ways of changing a message to encrypt it. I was allowed to handle it and operate it, and later began a poem on code-breaking, 'Enigma'. The next day we visited the military intelligence museum at Chicksands. There was much on the Intelligence Corps – case histories of retrievable names – and a section on the First World War, and on the role of pilots who were shot down over enemy lines while on 'a reconnaissance sortie': taking photographs of military positions from the air. I raised my uncle Tom, who had been shot down while on 'a reconnaissance sortie' over enemy lines, with an expert there, and was told that he was almost certainly on a spying mission. I had followed in the 'reconnaissance' genetic footsteps of my uncle Tom.

We went on to Bletchley Park and lunched in Hut 12. Our guide told me that Sir John Masterman had to leave Bletchley Park out of *The Double-Cross System*. We walked to see where Code and Cryptic was first housed: on an upper floor under the SIS. We visited the stables occupied by Turing early on. We saw the British Bombe, a code-breaker that had 1.5×10^{20} variations before it repeated itself. (There are 9×10^{21} stars in the universe.) We visited the National Museum of Computing to see the Turing machine and 'Heath Robinson', and finally the Colossus, an electronic machine. We went to Block C and saw Enigma machines downstairs. We went to Hut 8 and found Turing's reconstructed room, his mug chained to the radiator. We went to Hut 4 for tea, then went to the mansion.

I visited the bookshop and was stunned to see Asa Briggs's *Secret Days* (published when he was 90) about his time working in Hut 6 deciphering Enigma machine messages from the German Army and Air Force from 1943 to 1945. Without hesitation I bought the book. He had not even told his wife that he had worked at Bletchley Park until he wrote the book. I now grasped why Sir John Masterman had been pro-Briggs, who had been a Fellow at Worcester College, Oxford from 1945 to 1955. Later I did further work on 'Enigma', on "the necessity for nationalism against Hitler but the necessity for being one with all humankind".

The next day we visited Milton Hall where the Jeds had trained. I met an American lieutenant-colonel just back from Afghanistan who told me that the US anti-terrorist warfare near Kabul that he had been involved in was based on the Jeds. I met the last of the Jeds, Harry Verlander, who told me he had been trained to kill in many ways. He had killed hundreds in France (stretching wire between trees to behead German motorcyclists) and in Burma, where he spent six months behind enemy lines. We visited the Carpetbagger Museum, Harrington on our way home.[37]

Libya: Shukri Ghanem and Gaddafi, BBC Radio 5
Gaddafi was being toppled by the NATO air attacks on Libya to protect the people of Benghazi from his threatened genocide. Shukri Ghanem (who had fixed up my Barbary-Gipsy articles) had gone on to become Libya's oil minister and had become Gaddafi's General Secretary of the General People's Committee (Prime Minister) from June 2003 to March 2006. In May 2011 it was announced that Shukri had fled to Tunisia. He then surfaced in Italy. I was approached by a filmmaker for Channel 4 to take part in a film on the fall of Gaddafi and was asked to contact Shukri. I began trying to find his new address. The film never happened.

On 22 August 2011 I was asked to take part in a broadcast on BBC Radio 5 *Live Drive* with a Libyan lawyer who had worked with Gaddafi, who was in the studio. I spoke from my desk around 6.40 p.m. I was asked, "Where's Gaddafi?" I said, "He's in Libya, organising an insurgency." The lawyer agreed. I asked if al-Qaeda were among the rebels, and said that if Gaddafi had not taken over, Libya would now have democracy, freedom and prosperity instead of wasting its money on terrorism.

On 30 September I dreamt that I found Gaddafi's hiding-place, in a "hole, with shallow water". I saw Gaddafi's "bare head and untidy hair". I "got a head-and-shoulders [i.e. took a photo] of Gaddafi going down into this hole, with shallow water".

On 20 October 2011 television showed an amateur video of Gaddafi being captured – he was dragged out from his hiding-place in a storm drain in which there was shallow water – and shot. I was rung up by BBC Radio 5 *Live Drive* and asked if I would talk for five minutes about how I was nearly executed. In the event they were late in ringing me, and I only had two minutes before they cut me off. But I was on the air waves, talking about my 'execution' on the day Gaddafi was 'executed', having survived him.[38]

Human Rights Watch reported that Gaddafi had tried to escape from Sirte with 250 men in a 50-car convoy, which was hit by two NATO missiles. He sheltered in a drainage pipe with his defence minister and a guard who tried to throw a grenade at rebel attackers. It bounced back into the pipe and blew up, killing the defence minister. Shrapnel wounded Gaddafi in his head. Rebels seized him and as they led him out, filmed on a mobile phone, they assaulted him and one of them thrust a bayonet between his buttocks. There was a massive loss of blood, and Gaddafi may have been dead by the time another rebel fired a bullet into his head. His body was loaded nearly naked in an ambulance and taken to Misurata, whose inhabitants queued to file past and look at him.[39]

Gaddafi's death affected Shukri. He had defected to Vienna in May 2011 and in June confirmed that he had joined the opposition to Gaddafi. He was found dead in Vienna's Danube on 29 April 2012, days after – in exchange for immunity from prosecution – he had offered to tell two Libyan officials what he knew about suspect oil deals: vast sums of money skimmed from Libya's oil wealth and lodged in Gaddafi bank accounts under innocuous names. A Libyan banker advising the Government on assets recovery said, "A lot of Shukri Ghanem's partners who did corrupt deals with him wanted him to stay quiet,"[40] and it is possible that Shukri was silenced by the long arm of Gaddafi's family interests.

Localism: operations and ceremonies
Ann's hip
Meanwhile, down in Cornwall at the end of October 2011 Ann's hip had dislocated as she got out of her car in front of our house in the dark after visiting her aunt in Porthleven. I went out to give her a hand with bags and found her lying in agony on wet grass in drizzle. Her leg bone had come out

of her socket and gone into the surrounding tissue, and she could not move. I rang 999 and an ambulance arrived. Paramedics gave her morphine and it took half an hour to get her onto a stretcher and into the ambulance. I packed an overnight bag for her and followed the ambulance in Ann's car (which had brought us down) to the Royal Cornwall Hospital, Truro. I stayed with her while she was admitted to a ward and pressed for an immediate operation. An X-ray showed the ball way above the socket, and after I left, soon after 2 a.m. the surgeon manipulated it back without breaking her skin. She stayed in hospital the next day, and the following day I collected her, wheelchaired her to her car and drove her back to Essex.

She dislocated again five weeks later in Aachen, Germany. She had just begun a visit to Christmas markets in three countries when she fell back in a shop while standing talking. The pain was excruciating. Within an hour she had been driven to Aachen University Hospital and operated on. Again, the skin was not broken. She woke up with plaster to her knee round a broom handle, which meant she could not move. I had to repatriate her. Our health insurance company wanted to find a flight with eight adjacent seats for a stretcher. Flights were fully booked, and there was no prospect of a quick return this way. I persuaded them to send an ambulance, which left Kent at 4 a.m., collected her midday and returned her around 8 p.m.

I was clear that two really painful dislocations within five weeks meant that the original fitting had not been done correctly, and I promised to find the most expert remedial surgeon who would correct her new hip so it would never dislocate again. Within three days of her return, after researching and consulting hip surgeons (including Germany's leading hip surgeon) I found Sarah Muirhead-Allwood, who had operated on the Queen Mother and ran the London Hip Unit.

On 13 December I sat in on Ann's consultation with Sarah at the London Hip Unit in Devonshire Street. She wore spectacles and fiddled with a row of plastic bones and sockets spread out on her wide desk, trying to get a match. On the wall was a huge X-ray of Ann's right hip, and she ruled a diagonal line across the hip and measured it with her ruler. She asked questions and said she suspected that the head that fits into the socket was too small. On 10 January 2012 Ann returned for a pre-op.

Ann had her remedial operation at Princess Grace Hospital on 27 February. I rang and was put through to her in the afternoon. Sarah had looked in and said, "I changed the socket and the ball, it was to do with the angles." She had had a new metal tantalum cup and a ceramic ball that was 36mm instead of 29mm, and a polyurethane lining. There would now be no more dislocations. The original replacement had been fitted at the wrong angle. Her first replacement was 'off the peg' – a choice of three sizes, large, medium or small – whereas her latest hip was bespoke tailored: made-to-measure.

I took Ann home four days later. We had bought an electric height-adjustable bed. Once again I was a carer. I shopped, cooked and carried cups, plates and glasses to and fro on a tray. Quite soon she was hobbling on crutches. On 24 March I drove her in her car to White Roding. She dismounted onto a soapbox I placed in the car park, and we had tea. A few days later we returned to the London Hip Unit and were told she could now drive. She had a course of physiotherapy at St Margaret's Hospital during April.[41]

Rod Stewart at Coopersale Hall

At Coopersale Hall we had built a classroom in 2010 as infill in the classrooms we had built in 1996–1997, and a block of four classrooms, including a lift in 2011.

On 30 November 2011 the block of four classrooms was formally opened by Rod Stewart and Penny Lancaster, whose young son, a pupil, had been video-linked to his classroom and had downloaded classwork while spending three months with his parents in Las Vegas. There was a reception in the library for local VIPs, into which they walked. Rod had wavy hair in all directions, and wore a sweater and leopard shoes, and Penny was very at ease, tall and blonde. I explained to them that Churchill had stayed at their house, Wood House, while fighting the 1924 by-election and had come to this room to meet Lord Lyle, who he was to succeed as MP for Epping. We discussed our sharing of Churchill. We then walked to the new building in blinding sunshine and stood on the raised walkway looking into the tennis-court below where the school and parents were standing (including Brad Friedel, the Spurs goalie and a parent). I stood next to them while first Matthew, then the Head spoke.

Rod then performed the opening, drawing small curtains to unveil a plaque. On the way back I explained that my son-in-law played with Ray Davies, with whom Rod was at school. Rod told me how much he paid for Wood House in 1986 and asked how much I had paid for Coopersale Hall in 1988, wanting to be reassured that he had not been overcharged.

Nicholas with Rod Stewart and Penny Lancaster at the opening of a new building at Coopersale Hall School on 30 November 2011

10 Downing Street's perspective

Wherever family events take place, they have the feel of local events. My sister's 60th birthday was celebrated in the village hall at Biddenham on a Sunday. I spoke with her husband Richard's brother-in-law Sir Philip Mawer, who had worked for Gordon Brown in 10 Downing Street, in the heart of the British Establishment. We talked about my probing books, and I was interested to hear number 10's tolerant perspective on my books: he told me, "You are allowed to operate." Again I thought of Elizabeth I holding the rainbow and keeping it under her control (*see* p.xxii).

Russian-Bulgarian wedding

My brother Jonnie's second son James married his Bulgarian girlfriend who had won her country's top scholarship to study in the US. Ann and I drove to Eastbourne and had tea with a view of the pier, green sea and gulls "hindward hovering" (as I put it in my early poem, 'The Oceanographer at Night'). We then drove to Fletching and stayed at the 16th-century Griffin Inn in deep countryside.

The next day we attended the service in Tunbridge Wells, which included a prayer in Bulgarian. Martin Neary, the organist, played a trumpet call on the organ during the return down the aisle. We drove to Horsted Place for the reception, and I chatted to the bride's mother, who was Russian (and told me she supported Putin). Out in the garden the bride and groom re-enacted traditional Bulgarian wedding customs: they sat back-to-back and broke a round loaf of bread over their heads to see who would be the breadwinner; and then the bride and her mother fed both with the bread, covering the crusts first with salt and then with honey (to suggest life's plenty, bitterness and sweetness). Then a long sheet was laid out on the lawn, and a bucket with red and white carnations in water was placed on it. The bride kicked it. The carnation that flew the farthest was red, meaning that their first child would be a boy. Later there were speeches and toasts. James read a speech in Bulgarian without any idea of what he was saying, which caused mirth among the Bulgarians.

East Grinstead, Snowdonia

On the way back the next day we drove through East Grinstead and 'by chance' found ourselves in Cranston Road. I stopped at Beecholme, a red semi-detached house without a hedge (which had been cut down). I saw the window I stood in near the road during the war. There was no sign of the pine in the back garden. We drove on and found ourselves in Maypole Road 'by accident'. I saw the site of my grandmother's house and garden. Our direction took us onto Crescent Road and Aunt Maude's house. Without trying, I saw Moat Road and Mount Noddy playground. I had 'coincidentally' revisited some of the locations connected with my grandmother and my early life in East Grinstead, and I reflected that I was a Sussex person then.

Soon after he moved into Leytonstone, Tony had invited Ann and me to dinner, and we spoke with his German girlfriend. He had a dog, a cross between a Jack Russell and a Bichon Frisé. We had gone to dinner again in early April, and walked in his immaculate garden. On 18 April he came round and read us an email from Stephen Fry about his most recent script for *The Liar*. Fry said he was overwhelmed, had not thought it would be one-tenth as good and laughed out loud twelve times. However, the opinion of others in the business was that the script still needed further drafts.

Tony's girlfriend's family were visiting England, and they had booked Pengwern Old Hall in Snowdonia Park for a long weekend. Ann and I were invited to join them. We drove to Wales via Capel Curig (where we had tea) and Bangor (passing the University and the house where Matthew had lived), and found the mid-15th-century Hall down a lane, over a bridge and near a field of black sheep surrounded by mountains. We ate venison, before a log fire, and the conversation was mostly in English, with some German and French. The next day we returned via Shrewsbury and Ironbridge, and had tea in the historic Madeley Court Hotel, which had a fine sundial. I wrote a poem, 'Time II'.

For my birthday in May Ann gave me an elm, one of 300 that had been grown near Dunmow to be planted all round Britain to perpetuate the survival of the elm after Dutch elm disease. I planted it on the other side of our main lawn. All my children and grandchildren gathered for birthday tea, and Alex, now three, helped me blow out my candles while all sang "Happy birthday".[42]

Oaklands' 75th anniversary, the Haggers' 30th anniversary at Oaklands.
The summer of 2012 marked anniversaries. The first was the Queen's Diamond Jubilee on television. I watched the flotilla approach the standing Queen, the biggest spectacle on the Thames since 1652 when Charles II returned with Catherine of Braganza and 10,000 ships. I wrote a poem, 'Changelessness like a Fanfare: Trumpeting a Jubilee'. With wind gusting I wrote its counterpart, 'Wind: Change'.[43]

Oaklands' 75th anniversary coincided with the 30th anniversary of our taking over the school in 1982, and there was an event in a marquee on Sunday 1 July 2012 to mark the occasion. Some 350 past pupils and staff came from far and wide, and there were exhibitions of old registers and photos in the assembly hall and studio. Matthew had gone through the format of the day with me at the Oval as we watched England play West Indies in a one-dayer (his birthday present to me).

I greeted a queue of Old Oaklandians after they had registered on the field under the oak-tree of the school badge. Some had been at the school at the same time as me. Many came and told me about their time at the school. There were some members of the Parents' Association when we had arrived. My two brothers and sister had been at Oaklands, and they came. The Mayor of Loughton was present. A buffet lunch was eaten at tables within the long marquee.

The speeches began after lunch. I had been asked to make two speeches, one sharing memories of being a pupil and the other sharing memories of our take-over in 1982.[44] I spoke for ten minutes about the school's opening in 1937 and my recollections as a boy. Miss Lord's secretary, who had been at school 45 years, spoke next. I then spoke again and recounted the events from 1977 to 1982. The ex-Head, Pam Simmonds, spoke last. Tony filmed the speeches from the front row. Later *West Essex Life* requested a photo of the entire Hagger family present (getting on for more than a dozen). That Sunday marked a high point in our life at the schools. All round the main field and the school animated conversations were taking place as past pupils caught up and shared memories.[45]

Two days later the Coopersale Hall prizes were given out by Brad Friedel, the Spurs goalie, and two days after that the Oaklands prizes were given out by Eleanor Laing. The next day Iain Duncan Smith, now Secretary of State for Work and Pensions, gave out the prizes for Normanhurst at the Chingford Assembly Hall and volunteered to be photographed with each prize-winner on the stage.

Sports

Matthew was now running the schools with a painful knee from *Choi*. Towards the end of July 2012 he had another remedial operation on his knee in the small hospital in Kent that specialised in sports injuries (Spire Alexandra Hospital, Chatham). The operation was only partly successful as the surgeon could not probe behind his kneecap into an area that had not shown up on his scan and he would have to have yet another operation to have a cartilage graft. With two small children and huge demands on his time, and to-ing and fro-ing between the schools, Matthew elected not to have yet another operation for the time being and to put up with the pain for the next few years.

Two days later, Kate brought the children to swim in our pool. Matthew, in shorts, came too. He hobbled in, his knee heavily bandaged, and sat and watched with his leg up. We learned that Kate's father, who had been on dialysis, had been chosen to have a kidney transplant as a perfect match had been found.

My PA Ingrid was dancing with her zumba group in the forecourt of St

Mary's, Loughton to raise funds for charity. I stood in a small crowd in the High Road and watched, and found myself near our domestic help, Christine, and her friend, the sister of Winston Ramsey, whose *Epping Forest Then and Now* I had consulted during my writing of *A View of Epping Forest*. Soon afterwards Ramsey emailed me welcoming *A View of Epping Forest*.

The Olympic Games' opening ceremony presented a Labour view of Britain: 19th-century bosses in stove-pipe hats, NHS patients dancing on their beds and no mention of Churchill or of standing up to Hitler. I drafted a poem, 'Isle of Wonder'. Tony had Olympic tickets for soccer at Wembley, and asked me to join his party. We saw Mexico beat Japan. (Tony handed out Zapata moustaches for us all to wear as it had been agreed we would support Mexico.)

Three days later I visited John Dutchman at his home in Buckhurst Hill. The ex-footballer was suffering from Alzheimer's disease and prostate cancer, and was in a fragile condition. I presented him with a copy of *A View of Epping Forest* which I had signed for him. He was overcome and collapsed into tears: "I think of you every day." He gripped my hand, struggling for words. "This means a lot to me." I looked through his 'memory book' of old photos which his wife had put together of old photos, including some of Corinthian Casuals at the Oval, showing Doggart and Insole. At King's College, Cambridge he had lived near E.M. Forster, and had often seen him.[46] In December 2012 I learned that he had been moved to a local nursing home, Forest Place.

Internationalism: A Rainbow over the Hills, Selected Poems, *India, and Arabia*

A Rainbow over the Hills

On 1 June 2012 I had come to the conclusion that my account of my life should be in two volumes. We went down to Cornwall and, having finished amendments to *This Dark Wood* on 14 August, on 19 August I began *A Rainbow over the Hills*. The title had suggested itself from an email Charles Beauclerk sent me regarding *A New Philosophy of Literature*: "I can't think of any other person on this earth who could take nearly 5,000 years of writing and unite it with a single overarching vision, like a perfect rainbow." I arrived at the subtitle three days later. I planned volume 2 down in Cornwall in August.

Because I was working on *Selected Poems: Quest for the One* I could not get into the new book until 28 October. Then I was able to work on it every day. The combined title, *My Double Life*, 1 and 2, emerged in the course of a discussion with Tony on Christmas Day 2012, in the late afternoon. I saw my double life as my everyday, social, working life and my writing and metaphysical life, but I was also thinking of the pairs of opposites in each episode. I worked on the book for the next seven months and took it to Cornwall, from 3 to 26 August 2013. Working like a hermit in my 'cell' (my upstairs room overlooking St Austell Bay), feeling I was in a cliff-top beach-hut, oxygenated by the pure air coming off the Atlantic Ocean, looking down on the sand and sparkling sea and pondering international themes, I wrote episodes 13 and 14 and much of episode 15, which I finished on 7 September 2013.

I had taken just over eleven months to cover 40 years.[47] I took a further seven-and-a-half months (until 25 April 2014) to amend *My Double Life, 1* and *2*, and on 17 March 2014 received in sleep specific instructions as to how to amend the Table of Contents of both books, which I implemented throughout that day.

Selected Poems: Quest for the One
My *Selected Stories: Follies and Vices of the Modern Elizabethan Age* illustrates the fundamental theme of world literature I set out in *A New Philosophy of Literature*. Part One is titled 'Follies and Vices', and Part Two 'Quest for the One'. At the end of May I began a comparable selection of my poems, *Selected Poems: Quest for the One*. This book also illustrates the fundamental theme's pair of opposites, only Part One is titled 'Quest for the One' and Part Two 'Follies and Vices'. On 4 June I made a selection from *Overlord* and *Armageddon* to be included in this volume.[48]

Down in Cornwall I wrote the Preface, and back in Essex, as details emerged, a belated Epilogue for *Armageddon* on the death of bin Laden. I worked on my selection of poems and excerpts all though September and finished on 27 October 2012.

Both my *Selected Stories: Follies and Vices of the Modern Elizabethan Age* and my *Selected Poems: Quest for the One* were now ready to be published after *My Double Life 1* and *2*.

Beverley Minster and The First Dazzling Chill of Winter
David Hoppit had emailed me in early November 2012 asking me to write a piece for *The OC Mitre*'s next issue on a life-changing event. In October I wrote about his Corinthian coin which I believe got me into Oxford. (*See My Double Life 1: This Dark Wood*, pp.71–72.) I received *The OC Mitre* in December.[49]

Writing the piece took me back to stories. As a Christmas present Ann had booked a rail excursion to Beverley Minster in South Yorkshire. We had an elaborate breakfast in an old, elegant carriage among some of 400 modern pilgrims attending a carol concert. The Minster was packed and afterwards there were tours of the medieval stained glass, the Percy canopy and 68 misericords. There was a tour of the roof space. I climbed 113 steep steps up a 1220 spiral staircase and saw the treadwheel which had raised the oak roof trusses from near the altar below. We walked through gloom to a round glass rose window, from which we looked down on Beverley from a height of 200 feet. I stood with a group of elderly pilgrims who had been dazzled by the choristers and medieval music. I was dazzled by the light from the window. I was electrified by the situation and knew that it was significant. I climbed another 30 feet up nearly perpendicular steps, and then another 20 feet up another ladder to the walkway along the top of the Minster's ceiling. I returned down another spiral staircase.

We walked back to the station and sat on the train with (from the sound of them) some very heathen modern pilgrims. The next day I wrote a story, 'The First Dazzling Chill of Winter'. I realised it was the title story of my sixth volume of stories, *The First Dazzling Chill of Winter*, which would further illustrate the fundamental theme of world literature. Two days later I drafted a poem, 'At Beverley Minster'.[50]

Change

An old order was changing. My accounting assistant, Jeremy Miller, who had spent a day a week with me for the best part of twenty years, had retired in his early seventies in 2010, and had soon after successfully recovered from prostate cancer. Now my Bursar, Ken Jones, my former bank manager, retired after more than 17 years. The main 130 staff from the three schools crowded into the Coopersale Hall assembly hall for a buffet lunch at circular tables, and there were speeches by Matthew and three Heads, and presentations. Then Ken made a long, emotional speech in the course of which he demonstrated his multi-tasking by juggling balls. Both men were replaced by highly computer-experienced staff chosen by Matthew who were more at home in the digital age.

The next day we met Nadia and Ian at the 16th-century Barn Brasserie at Great Tey to celebrate Nadia's 50th birthday. They had just returned from a night in The Swan, Lavenham, and told me they had visited the Priory and

Nadia with her husband Ian Gibbons

seen the sofas where we celebrated my 60th birthday before a fire. They had elected to have half a dozen events with different branches of the family and their friends, and had wanted to have a small lunch with us so we could all talk. Eleven days later they took us out to another lunch at the Bluebell, Chigwell.[51]

In the new year we held the last of eight successive family gatherings at Connaught House. Ann's other hip (which would be replaced in March

2014), Matthew's knee and my worsening umbilical hernia all meant that we were participating in the event against doctors' advice. We knew there could be no more for a while as none of us could lift the furniture and crockery we brought in from the schools to seat more than thirty guests. There was an elegiac mood as the guests sensed this, and many tried to lighten our load by mucking in.

In India, Sri Lanka and Arabia: 'Revisiting the British Raj', 'Reflections in Arabia' – Paradise is 'here and now', Gandhi, pirates and frankincense
As an internationalist, I had long wanted to revisit India to reflect on the British Raj, our Indian Empire, and see whether claims that India would be world's number-2 economy by 2030 were realistic. I wanted to feel the plight of one-seventh of humankind. We booked to tour the Golden Triangle (Delhi, Agra and Jaipur) and then cruise up the west coast on the *Minerva*. I knew our visit would yield a poem.

Ann and I flew to Delhi in February 2013 and landed in fog at 4 a.m. Indian time. As we were coached to the Taj Palace Hotel, our guide, Dinesh Kapoor, said wisely: "India is so diverse that of anything you say about it, the opposite is also true." I was reconciling opposites again. After a short sleep our group toured Old Delhi. We went to the Raj Ghat (Gandhi's crematorium site) and to the Jama Masjid (where I climbed steps to the courtyard of the mosque built by Shah Jahan, the fifth Mughal Emperor who also built the nearby Red Fort). At the entrance to the mosque I bought Dinesh's book, *Delhi down the Ages*. We were then pedalled by rickshaw through the narrow streets of the 17th-century old market, past spices, silver, lace, wedding dresses and books.

The next day we toured New Delhi: the Government quarter, Parliament and the Viceroy's palace near Nehru's Presidential palace. We stopped at the sandstone canopy from which George V's statue was removed at the end of the Raj. The British had built New Delhi from 1912 to 1932, and it had merely been foundations in 1921 when the Amritsar massacre began the disturbances that would culminate in independence. I was struck by the British confidence (or folly) in carrying on building throughout the 1920s despite the disturbances.

We went on to the tomb of Humayun, the 16th-century Mughal Emperor, where the four rivers of Paradise formed a cross, and then to the Qutal tower, a 12th–13th-century minaret. Back at the hotel a receptionist told me that the British Prime Minister David Cameron had stayed at our hotel with 200 businessmen the day before we arrived.

We were up at 3.45 a.m. to take the train to Agra. We left our luggage at our hotel and were taken by coach to rickshaws, which pedalled us to the Taj Mahal. Again, the four rivers of Paradise crossed beyond the gateway to

Heaven. The white domes reflected the order within the universe against distant thunderclouds. We walked to the chamber room above the subterraenean tomb of Shah Jahan and his wife Mumtaz. Our guide reckoned that Shah Jahan shifted his capital to Delhi before the tomb was finished, and that he therefore built the Taj Mahal because he wanted to leave behind a perfect monument of architecture, an architectural work of perfection.

We were taken to Agra's Red Fort and I walked up a slope to a Hall of Audience where Emperor Shah Jahan made proclamations to the assembled people through a Prime Minister, who stood below him on a marble platform. I walked to the *harem* for 5,000 women and to the royal palace of Shah Jahan, who in 1658 was imprisoned there by a son and waved to crowds below from a balcony from which he could see the finished Taj Mahal across the River Yamuna.

We were driven to Fatehpur Sikri, Akbar's red sandstone fort and capital from 1569 to 1585. I stood under the balcony of the Hall of Audience where Akbar sat invisible and spoke to his people below. We walked to the Muslim Turkish Sultana's house, and in different courtyards saw the quarters of Akbar's Christian and Hindu queens. We went on to the Keoladeo Ghana National Park, a Maharaja's hunting-ground until the 1950s, where a wizened, bearded, turbaned Indian pedalled us in his rickshaw and pointed out green bee-eaters, spot-billed ducks and (near rhesus monkeys and an antelope) tailorbirds and snakebirds. We saw treepies, white-breasted kingfishers, glossy ibis, whistling and laughing ducks, black-headed ibis, jungler babblers and painted storks.

We drove to Jaipur and checked in at the Jai Mahal palace, the house of the Prime Minister of Jaipur from the 1860s. In the dark we watched Indian dancing: three men on rhythmic drums and a woman in North-Indian dress with a bowl of fire on her head, a symbol for illumination. She danced, swaying, adding bowls until she had a pile of four on her head that did not tumble down.

The next day we went to Jaipur's Amber Fort. We queued for an elephant on a high platform, sat back on the railed box which was at knee-height and with our legs hanging down rode up the steep ramp to the Fort's first courtyard. We walked through the elephant gate to the Hall of Glasses and the *harem*, and returned by Jeep. After lunch we drove past the Water Palace, a summer palace in the middle of a lake, and I saw redshank, black-winged stilts, Indian pond herons and cattle egrets.

We visited the Jantar Mantar observatory. Jai Singh, who ruled the state of Jaipur, used astronomy for astrological purposes, and was told to move his capital on 18 November 1727. We saw his 18th-century astronomical instruments. We went on to the City palace, where there were displays of maharajas' robes. The next day we drove back to Delhi, stopping at the

Palace of Glass on the way out. I worked on my poem, 'Revisiting the British Raj'. By now more than half our party had been ill. We had been warned about eating water-based food or food that was not piping hot, and those of us (like ourselves) who avoided being ill dry-washed our hands several times a day with anti-bacterial hand gel.

The next morning we had time to ourselves and I visited Delhi's Red Fort, which made a great impact on me in 1967. I was dropped off by car, entered near the Lahore Gate, walked to the Hall of Public Audience, which had a throne and canopy, and on to the Rang Mahal (the women's chambers) and the Khas Mahal (the royal apartments), through which ran the 'stream of Paradise'. There I saw the Emperor's prayer-room, bedroom, sitting-room and balcony all built between 1639 and 1648, which replicated the rooms in Agra's Red Fort that had been vacated for here.

Beyond these two buildings, across a small white courtyard of marble, was the Diwan-i-Khas. In its centre (surrounded by 4 inner rows of 4 columns and beyond it 6 outer rows of 6 columns) had stood the Peacock Throne that was taken to Persia in 1739, one of Shah Jahan's seven jewelled thrones. Over the inside corner arches of two of the inner columns on the north and south side was inscribed the verse by the Persian Sufi poet Amir Khusraw I had found in 1967, which can be translated: "If there be Paradise on the earth, it is this, it is this, it is this." (Or "It is here, it is here, it is here.") The verse could be seen from the Peacock Throne and reminded Shah Jahan that Paradise was in Delhi, not Agra with its Taj Mahal. The verse had haunted me for more than 45 years. I spoke to a soldier who was guarding the place, and with his approval climbed over a rope so I could take a photo. I walked back, having seen what I had come to see, and on the way out looked in on the Museum on India's Struggle for Freedom.

As I was driven back to our hotel, I was full of admiration for the young man I had been who had got himself to this place on public transport in 1967 and had noted the Persian verse. My life was then ahead of me, my dark wood was about to intensify and I would soon be in the chaos of Libya. Shah Jahan had moved on from Mumtaz and the Taj Mahal, and I now grasped that Paradise is in the 'here and now', not in the 'then'. I thought of the British who during the 1920s and 1930s had thought that Paradise was here, in a new city they were building to be a showcase of the Empire, ignoring the swelling independence movement outside Delhi. Biggs-Davison was among the last to come out to this Paradise, in 1946–1947. I grasped that Paradise was in one's locality, a local order from which one could create the order of an Empire, or a World State.

That afternoon we flew to Sri Lanka. We joined the *Minerva* in Colombo well after midnight. We unpacked in our cabin, had two or three hours sleep and left early for Kandy along a road beside a railway, both built by the

British, hundreds of whom had died from malaria. At Kandy we lunched in the Hotel Suisse where Mountbatten had stayed when Viceroy of Ceylon. I found his suite (in room 204): a bedroom with a 1930s bed and chairs, and a sitting-room with four chairs. We left a display of drumming and a whirling dervish and were driven to the Buddhist Temple of the Tooth. We walked past the spot where a suicide truck had killed 20, passed through two court-yards and reached a long wooden hall where a golden door hid the seven temple-shaped containers that concealed the tooth of the Buddha few living people had seen. (The tooth was rumoured to be a 3-inches-long animal's fang.) On the way back we stopped at a spice grove run by devotees of Ayurvedic medicine, who matched herbs from their garden to our ailments.

The *Minerva* began her journey up the west coast of India. We stopped at Tuticorin and drove to Christ Church where there was an *impromptu* service. We had to stand and sing a hymn, 'Eternal Father, strong to save', whose refrain is 'Oh, hear us when we cry to Thee,/For those in peril on the sea.' The hymn drew our attention to our plight. We had not realised that for the next ten days we would be in peril – from pirates. The churchyard contained graves of British missionaries after 1856 and of an English civil servant who had been assassinated in 1911 by pro-independence Indians. We walked through the 16th-century Temple of Vishnu at Krishnapuram in our socks.

That evening at the captain's reception I encountered Sir Anthony Kenny, the ex-Master of Balliol who I had met in the company of Ricks and who had sent me a card of Ktisis, the Libyan Isis. He told me his four volumes on past philosophy (covering the ground of Tomlin's *Philosophers of East and West*) were now out as one volume, and he had no plans to write a fifth about new directions in philosophy. He had difficulty in walking, and our paths did not often cross.

We sailed on into pirate waters, and there was a drill. We had to stand in the cabin corridors with our life-jackets and keep clear of all portholes and windows. Razor wire was fastened to the sides of the ship to prevent boarding. After lunch we landed in Kochi and visited a 16th-century Dutch palace that had been built by the Portuguese and saw the Chinese fishing-nets suspended from poles and operated by levers and weights that had been introduced by traders from the court of Kubla Khan. We went on to St Francis church, the first built by Europeans in India, and saw the vacated grave of Vasco da Gama, Viceroy of Portugal, who was buried there until his body was removed to Lisbon. Above the pews were *punkhas*, gently-swinging cloth fans on frames operated by a *punkah-wallah*. Next door was the 1506 building where Da Gama lived in the 1520s and where St Francis Xavier stayed when he was a parish priest. There was an evening perfor-mance on the ship of a Kathakali dance of a scene from the *Ramayana*, to an hour of drum-rolling and chanting.

We went to the Alleppey Backwaters and, sitting on chairs on the upper deck of a local boat, toured canals built by the Dutch and saw the paddy-fields farmed by the British. Above our heads among the trees were white-throated kingfishers, bee-eaters and black drongos with forked tails. We returned to Fort Kochi. The following day at sea I sunbathed on the Promenade Deck in a hazy sun and noticed lesions on my back in the bathroom mirror.

The next day we visited Old Goa. We drove through palms and bougainvillea to St Catherine's Cathedral, and found a 17th-century mural of the Garden of Paradise showing Adam and Eve among flowers and birds. We went on to the Basilica of Bom Jesus and saw the tomb of St Francis Xavier, who had arrived in Goa in 1552. His head showed distantly through the crystal side of his high-up coffin. On the way back we walked in the old Portuguese quarter between brightly-coloured Portuguese houses with balconies and exotic trees.

After lunch the next day we visited Mumbai (formerly known as Bombay). We sauntered round the Gateway of India which commemorated the visit of George V, Emperor of India. We then drove through the commercial centre and visited the Prince of Wales Museum (subsequently renamed). We passed Victoria Terminal, an elaborate building with Indian-Gothic arcades. We passed three Parsee fire temples and Chowpatty beach and arrived at Mani Bhavan, the Gandhi memorial museum in Mumbai. I visited Gandhi's room on the second floor where he stayed when in Bombay: on the mosaic was a spinning-wheel (to keep in touch with the poor), a simple mattress and a pillow. There was a balcony outside, where he pitched a tent in which he prayed and slept, and where he was arrested in 1932. From his room he issued his call to strike in April 1919, which resulted in the massacre at Amritsar, which he arguably provoked.

The next morning we drove through Mumbai again and visited an open-air laundry under skyscrapers and the Ishkon temple to Krishna (of the Hare Krishna sect). We were driven to the Hanging Gardens, where an elderly Indian told me: "People are saying it was better under the British Raj." (He meant that for him there was no unemployment or retirement benefit, and that the political leaders were corrupt.) We passed the Parsee Towers of Silence, which peeped through trees.

The next day we went to Porbandar. We drove past pelicans and flamingos to the Sudama Temple where idols within were said to date back 5,000 years. I was electrified by the stone maze, which could be walked, a symbol for the cycle of births and deaths, liberation from which could be found in its central *nirvana*. I reflected on the wheel of time and the transmigration of souls. We went on to Gandhi's birthplace, Kirti Mandir, a 1710 house on three floors with steep staircases. The room of Gandhi's birth was on the ground floor, the spot marked by a swastika in the mosaic. Further up was the reading-room where Gandhi did his homework.

The next two days we were at sea, ploughing through waters close to past pirate attacks. We woke in Fujairah and drove through oases with palms to Dubai, which we toured: first Old Dubai (1970s–1990s) and its royal palaces; and then New Dubai, where we saw the Burj al-Arabi, a hotel shaped like a sail. We went on to Burj Khalifa, the tallest building in the world, 828 metres. We queued and went up by fast lift to the observation platform at 454 metres and looked down on modern buildings on hazy sand.

The next day we were in Oman. We toured Muscat city, the new Grand Mosque built Sultan Qaboos and his low, white palace in Old Muscat. I bought bags of frankincense, which smelt of Eastern mystery and promise. In the afternoon we went to the 17th-century Nakhl Fort. We passed Bedouin. On the way back I wrote a poem, 'Reflections in Arabia', about Dubai and Oman. The following day we flew home from Oman airport and I put the finishing touches to my poem 'Revisiting the British Raj'.[52]

I had seen enough of India's poor to convince me that the country had a long way to go before becoming the number–2 economy in the world, but I could see India taking her place in a world government. I had seen Arabia as a materialistic place, trying to emulate the West within inhospitable desert. My reflections on both India and Arabia had advanced my internationalism.

Hernia operation and removal of carcinomas: Icarus

I had an operation after my return from India. Mr Machesney, who had repaired my three hernias in 2005, operated on me again in Holly House on 22 March. The anaesthetist placed a mask over my nose and said, "You're going to have a nice sleep. Tell me when you're asleep." I told him, "I'm not asleep yet." And then I was coming to in recovery. I was wheeled back to my room. Mr Machesney visited and explained my plasters. He said he had pumped me up. My feet were attached to an SCD Express machine that monitored my blood flow and squeezed my calves when it detected blood returning up my legs. I stayed on the machine a day to reduce the chances of thrombosis, and then began 28 days of injecting myself with heparin in my abdomen.

I had noticed lesions in India. I visited my doctor on 25 April, and he diagnosed a form of skin cancer. He said I had been exposed to the sun over the years and that my sunbathing had caught up with me. He referred me to the consultant who had identified my 'Lyme disease'. On 2 May he examined me and said I had three basal cell carcinomas on my back. He took me to a nearby room, lay me face down, gave me three local anaesthetics, scraped off each carcinoma and put it in a pot to send for analysis. My back was raw in three places. He told me, "You aren't going to die of this." He said there was no reason why I should have any more problems with my skin. A fortnight later the results of the biopsies were known. I had indeed had three basal cell carcinomas.[53]

I thought of Icarus, who flew too near the sun and fell into the sea and drowned. I had exposed myself to the life-giving sun and had found its rays destructive. I thought of my poem 'Sunbathing', which is about basking in the Light. I thought that in future my sunbathing should be under the Light, not the sun.

End of a nationalist era: Thatcher's funeral, New World Order – The Grove
All had not been well in the UK. The 2008 banking crisis had plunged the country into recession. Labour had left the country with a huge deficit and a legacy of austerity, cuts, a squeeze on welfare and accelerated urban decay. For several years immigrants had been pouring in, and schools and hospitals were full. Society was fracturing and the social classes were fractious. The British Establishment had lost power to a growing United States of Europe, which controlled between 15 and 50 per cent of its legislation (depending on what laws are included), and the unity of the UK was under threat: ahead was the prospect of Scottish independence. It was clear that the way of life of the British nation-state was coming to an end, and with it the nationalist and imperial era that had built the British Empire, won two world wars in the 20th century and contributed to winning the Cold War, an effort I had served. It was a miracle that our schools were thriving amid the national demoralisation.

Down in Cornwall in April Ann and I had tea (on a voucher given us by Nadia) at Fowey Hall Hotel. We sat high above the river in the large Victorian house and looked beyond wide steps across to Polruan. Kenneth Grahame, author of *The Wind in the Willows*, had first visited Fowey in 1899 and had spotted the Hall from the river. He had stayed there, and it was supposed to have inspired Toad Hall. I sat and thought wistfully of the Edwardian Age, when Great Britain had ruled a quarter of the world and the British way of life had a stable social structure and oozed confidence and certainties.

Two days earlier Margaret Thatcher had died in the Ritz Hotel in London. I watched her funeral on television. Crowds lined the streets and the spectacle was reminiscent of Churchill's funeral. I grasped that we were witnessing the end of an assertive nationalist – indeed, national – era. She had put Britain's interests above all other considerations in taking back the Falklands, defeating the miners and standing up to Europe. That assertive nationalism had now ended, and Britain was dwindling from a nation-state into a state in a coming United States of Europe. Between 15 and 17 April I wrote a poem, 'Ceremonial: On the End of a National Era, The Funeral of

Margaret Thatcher'.

For my birthday Ann surprised me by taking me to The Grove, Watford, a luxurious hotel in 300 acres that offered Ayurvedic treatments in its spa. Coincidentally the 2013 Bilderberg Group meeting was scheduled to take place there in June. I had met Iain Duncan Smith again on 10 May and over drinks had told him that the New World Order was coming to England shortly, and asked him to keep an eye on the plutocrats who had an agenda for international events. He asked me to send him details. I was delighted to be spending a night at the venue of the Bilderberg Group just a fortnight before their conference there.

We arrived at the gates and were interrogated by a woman police constable who wanted to know our business. She relaxed when we said we were staying a night. We drove down into a valley and up a hill the other side to the distant mansion. A man in a hat took our bags and another drove our car away. We were checked in by staff who reminded me of immigration controllers. We lunched in the glasshouse bar and then I walked from the old Elizabethan Hall, once the seat of the Earls of Clarendon where Queen Victoria created 'the weekend break', alongside the new building begun in 2005 to the large conference room with wisteria round the glass windows. A Russian in the housekeeping department spoke to me and volunteered to show me inside. He took me through a door into a large room that could seat 600 and which could be partitioned into three rooms. This was where the Bilderberg Group would meet on 6 June. The organisers of the New World Order who intrigued the appointments of Presidents and Prime Ministers and then influenced them were hiring this space, and while they were in residence there would be a half-mile exclusion zone round the perimeter and helicopters would fly overhead.

We had our Ayurvedic treatment with hot stones and later ate in Colette's restaurant, and spent a very comfortable night. After breakfast the next morning I wandered in the grounds, looked through the windows into the conference hall and mused on the conference agenda and the speakers who would be delivering it. Syria would be prominent, and there would be a discussion on supporting the rebels and weakening the Shiite crescent round Iran, whose central bank (along with Cuba's and North Korea's) was one of only three in the world not controlled by 'Rothschilds'. A nationalist era had ended and Britain would now be expected to advance the New World Order's interests. Britain's international influence was now linked to the interests of the New World Order.[54]

Incidents and retirements
We celebrated Tony's birthday in Wo Fat ('Harmony and Prosperity'). Nadia and Ian joined us. I knew that Nadia had tripped over packing boxes in a

recording studio while Ian was recording two days before I had left for India. She had told me that she had had concussion and made light of the incident. Now she told me she had suffered a depressed fracture of her skull near her right eye socket, which had given her headaches. The healing process was well underway and (having sold her house in Coggeshall earlier in the year), she was planning her husband's musical tours and engagements, as his PA and agent.

I had been playing chess with Ben and had taught him fool's mate. He told me he had fool's-mated a boy in the school chess club, played him again, and fool's-mated him a second time. Ben joined Matthew, Tony and me at Lord's to watch a one-dayer, England v. New Zealand (Matthew's birthday present to me). Soon afterwards we celebrated Ben's 11th birthday. He had turned into a lovely boy who was very good with Alex and Ollie. Shortly afterwards, he left for a holiday on the American west coast with his mother.

Under Matthew's supervision, the schools had prospered. The last Oaklands inspection (for the younger years, in March 2013) had resulted in 17 'outstandings' out of 17, a really impressive result as the inspectors were constantly raising the bar and had only given notice on a Friday that they were coming the following Monday. I had always intended that Oaklands should become a Centre of Excellence, and this was now being confirmed. Matthew found a Latin motto for the Oak-Tree Group of Schools, *'Excellentia et Sapientia'* ('Excellence and Wisdom'), which he had checked with Horton's successor at Chigwell and which now appeared on events programmes, and I thought how appropriately it reflected the concept of a Centre of Excellence in a Group motto (the individual schools retaining their own mottos and identities). In September 2013 Ollie joined her brother at Oaklands. Building improvements were ongoing. The new Coopersale Hall building was in full use. There were 150 on the Oaklands waiting-list in 1988 before I opened Coopersale Hall School, and now, 25 years later, after all our building and expansion (and despite Chigwell's opening a new pre-prep school), there were 150 on the Oaklands waiting-list.

The Coopersale Hall prize-giving was performed by the former world triple-jump champion, Phillips Idowu, a parent. Matthew said in his intro-duction that he could jump the width of our marquee. One of our staff at Coopersale Hall told me she had seen a ghost outside the Churchill room a year previously, and she, I, and other staff climbed the stairs after the prize-giving and stood so that she could describe the incident. She had come out of her room on a dark winter evening about 6 p.m. and a hooded monk in brown had materialised out of the loo wall next to the Churchill room, stared at her and gone back into the wall. The land on which Coopersale Hall now stood had reverted to the Crown in 1120, and I did not know if monks had lived there during the Middle Ages. I received her account without probing its objectivity.

There were retirement gatherings. Miss Lord's secretary at Oaklands, and subsequently Ann's, Carol Norris retired after 45 years service. On the last day of term we gave her an 1840 glass Victorian vase decorated with oak leaves (only three years younger than the Oaklands building according to the received view). A week earlier I attended the farewell gathering for my dentist Norman Roback, who had learned to extract teeth in Glasgow by putting a knee on the patient's throat to get leverage and then yanking. He had worked for 50 years in the same room.

Shortly afterwards I attended the second retirement of David Horton, my Classics master, who had served 60 years at Chigwell School. (*See* p.689 for his previous retirement.) There was tea on the dining-hall lawn on a hot July afternoon, and I told him that my literature, history and philosophy had come from what I had learned in his classes about the ancient Greeks and Romans: my literature from Homer, Aeschylus, Sophocles, Euripides, Virgil, Catullus, Horace and Ovid; my history from Herodotus, Thucydides, Livy and Tacitus; and my philosophy from Socrates, Plato, Aristotle, Cicero, Seneca and Plotinus. I gave him a card with Latin verses from Horace's second epode:

> Libet iacere modo sub antiqua ilice,
> Modo in tenaci gramine;
> Labuntur altis interim ripis aquae,
> Queruntur in silvis aves.

They can be translated:

> It is pleasing now to lie under an old oak-tree,
> Now in the clingy grass;
> And meanwhile waters flow into full streams,
> The birds are complaining in the woods.

Mary Rose

I took Ann to Portsmouth for her birthday to see the recently opened exhibition about the *Mary Rose*. The starboard half of the ship was now under cover, and some of the 19,000 artefacts retrieved from it were on display, including the cannons that had been in the lower gun ports that were open when wind caught her sails on 19 July 1545 and caused her to heel over and sink in the Solent. Most of the Tudor crockery and chests that sank had been retrieved, making the exhibition a 1545 time capsule: our equivalent to Pompeii. We looked at the skulls and the reconstructed faces of some of the crew and related to a time when under Henry VIII England was both anti-European and anti-Scot. Ahead of us were referenda on Europe and Scotland, and our nationalist era, which had just ended, reflected the nationalism of Henry's time. I mused on 'Little England's isolationism' and our new regional, more international outlook. I drove Ann on to Sandbanks, home to many millionaires, and we stayed a night at the Haven Hotel, dining on the terrace by the water while the chain ferry went backwards and forwards to and from the Isle of Purbeck. Two days later we flew in a helicopter across London and I saw the seat of our nation-state's nationalist Government laid out beneath me along the Thames. Later I wrote a poem, 'Reflections by the *Mary Rose*'.

Cornwall and the universe

In early August we went to Cornwall for three weeks and I worked on the last episodes of this book. A chimney in our house had been rebuilt as its defective mortar had made a bedroom wall damp. (Larry, who had looked after us for 20 years and had overseen the rebuilding, had just been diagnosed with inoperable cancer of his lungs and brain, but insisted on seeing our chimney through.) I sat in my window overlooking the sparkling sea, and poems came to me, including 'One: Reflection'.

Matthew came down with Kate and the three children. He and I walked late at night and looked up at the stars from the harbour wall. We noted the seven pulses, the last one long, of the light from the Cannis Lighthouse and the two flashes and after a pause of nine seconds another two from the Eddystone Lighthouse. It was the dog days when there were supposed to be shooting-stars every minute. I reminded him that when he was a boy I had put a groundsheet in our back garden and he, Tony and I had lain on our backs and looked up at the stars while I pointed out the main constellations. When we returned we all went into the back garden, and he and Kate lay on their backs on the wooden decking at the bottom of our lawn while Ann and I sat in chairs. The universe I had written about in *The Universe and the Light* and *The New Philosophy of Universalism* was suspended above some of my family, and we all related to it. To them, I believe, as to me, the more recognisable constellations such as the Plough and the 'W' of Cassiopeia were like old friends. I was in harmony – indeed, in friendship – with the universe, and I had taught my family to be in their own harmony.[55]

The word and the Light

Ben went on to stay with his mother in Sunderland. They visited Durham and went to an exhibition on the Lindisfarne and St Cuthbert Gospels at the Wolfson Gallery. In the gift shop Ben said he wanted to buy me a cork-based stone mat inscribed with the opening of St John's Gospel in Latin from St

Cuthbert's 698 Gospel. He gave this to me at Matthew's at the end of August. The Latin could be translated: "In the beginning was the Word, and the Word was with God, and the Word was God.... And the light shineth in darkness; and the darkness comprehended it not. There was a man sent from God.... The same came for a witness, to bear witness of the Light."

The focus on 'the word' in combination with 'the Light' impressed me. Ben had heard enough of my work to know that the stone mat contained my main theme. I was greatly touched I now had a reminder of my life's mission on my desk: to reconnect the word and the Light, the social and the metaphysical: my double life. In *My Double Life 1* and 2 I had borne witness to the Light.[56]

International affairs: Syria, Iran, Crimea and reconciling opposites in a World State
In May the *American Free Press* had stated that pro-Israel representatives in Congress had seized on reports of sarin nerve gas by the Israeli Brigadier-General Itai Brun and had pressed John Kerry, US Secretary of State, to urge a military attack on Syria.[57] Obama had visited Israel on 20 March, and the Bilderberg Group, meeting at The Grove from 6 to 9 June discussed Syria and urged military action. Towards the end of August Obama rang the British Prime Minister Cameron and asked him to support a US military strike against Syria without going to the UN. The pro-Rothschild interventionist Blair, Middle East envoy for the UN, EU, US and Russia, supported a US strike. Recalled from holiday, the majority of British MPs refused to support US military action against Syria. Some MPs were unconvinced as there was no credible plan for what would happen after a military attack. There was little doubt that sarin nerve gas had been used in Syria, but many wondered if the Assad regime had been framed by Israeli-infiltrating rebels to expedite a US attack on Assad.

At first it seemed that the British had plunged into isolationism, but their stance had the effect of blocking the New World Order's plan for a military strike. I was a 'conviction writer' in the sense that Thatcher had been a 'conviction politician', only my conviction as a 'World State' internationalist reflecting the Age was very different from her exclusively nationalist and local conviction. I wanted Britain to be involved in shaping the world in the image of the ideal World State rather than be a bystander. Being an internationalist, I deplored isolationism and was keen to uphold international law on chemical weapons – provided international law was not being abused by a New World Order "false flag" manoeuvre. Obama felt he had been elected to stop the wars in Iraq and Afghanistan, not start a new one, and he had led the Western world from behind. In Congress his reluctance to attack Syria seemed at best weak leadership and at worst a wriggling out of upholding a US 'red line'.

I had charted Britain's post-imperial decline in my poems with a heavy heart, and I wanted Britain to continue her role in the world. I wanted Britain to work to bring in a World State that would abolish war, famine, disease and poverty throughout the world. The New World Order's wars in Iraq and Afghanistan had much to do with oil, and the central banks in those two countries were now controlled by 'Rothschilds' Moving towards a new war in Syria was part of a process to effect the new regime change in Iran and the New World Order's control of Iranian oil and central bank. I wanted an internationalist solution that would reverse the flow of refugees, stop the suffering and bring stability to the Middle East. I wanted international order to be upheld in Syria, and was pleased when Assad agreed to surrender his chemical weapons to UN inspectors, and Iran, under a new President, began talks with the US.

I supported the 'special relationship' between the US and the UK as the best means of bringing about a UN-created World State and as a brake on unilateral New-World-Order-inspired, self-interested military acts. I was keen that Universalist principles should triumph: that +A (the US and allies) + −A (the Assad regime, Iran and Russia) should be harmonised in the One (the World State), that the two opposites should be reconciled; that the international double life should be unified in a World State.

In early September the G20 meeting took place in St Petersburg. The US President and Russian President hardly spoke to each other, and sat as far apart as possible. It seemed there was a return to the politics of the Cold War, with Russia guarding her satellite Syria and being in open contest with the West. Russia would reinforce this impression in March 2014 by annexing Crimea. (The unipolar world in which there was one superpower, the US, had gone; and once again there was a bipolar world in which the US was challenged by an expansionist, neo-colonial Russia.) A Russian official was reported to have said that Britain was "a small island no one listens to".

Nationalism was apparent in Cameron's retort. He said the British had cleared the European continent of Fascism and had abolished slavery. (In 1808 Parliament passed the Slave Trade Act 1807.) He said that Britain had invented every sport currently played around the world, and has been responsible for art, literature, music and philosophy that delights the entire world and for scientific discoveries that gave the world the Industrial Revolution, television and the world-wide web. (It could be maintained that the innovation was a collective process and joint international – it could be said 'Universalist' – effort.) He said that Britain had the sixth-largest economy, the fourth-best-funded military and effective diplomats, and had contributed hugely to world civilization. All this was true.

The UK has made a phenomenal contribution to world civilization. But I want to see things from the perspective of world civilization rather than from the perspective of an individual country. The truest perspective is that seen from a Universalist World State under which all opposites are reconciled: +A (nations) + −A (failing states) = 0 (World State).

Internationalism and localism: universal reflections in a local garden

The view out of my window is of Epping Forest. We all live locally, in a locality. I grew up there and have described in *My Double Life 1* and *2* how I went away to understand the world and reflect the Age, how I let the world into my soul and became an internationalist; how I absorbed the wisdom of the Far East (+A + −A = 0), and saw how all opposites are reconciled. I saw that Britain was European and had a global role, and reflected this perspective in my two poetic epics, *Overlord* and *Armageddon*, and in my *Classical Odes*. My history and philosophy, like my literature, reflect this global perspective. While I was away I discovered that in my work, as Yeats put it of his work in 1892: "The mystical life is at the centre of all that I do and all that I think and all that I write." I was not interested in 'Little Englanders' like Larkin, who despised 'abroad'. I knew there was more to reflecting the universe than the farmland memories and re-creations in the verse of Hughes and Heaney.

I brought what I had found back to my locality and researched it in *A View of Epping Forest*, so I could say like Eliot in 'Little Gidding':

We shall not cease from exploration
And the end of all our exploring
Will be to arrive where we started
And know the place for the first time.

Every day I went about my local business, and internationalism and localism were woven together in my life and in my work as well as in this, my most recent episode.

My story

From my window I look across my garden at the dark wood on the skyline and reflect. The story I have told in Part Two of *My Double Life* is about my journey from history and poetry through philosophy and practical mysticism into international politics, epic, classical odes, European culture, literature, statecraft, travelogues and local history. It is a story of transformation, and of how I put my vision of unity in my books.

I began as a published author while developing Oaklands into Oak-Tree Schools by founding Coopersale Hall. I acquired a harbour property in Cornwall where I could turn my reflections into books. Two prominent poets and a historian spoke at my launch and I was known for world history and poetry. I turned to philosophy after being invited to lecture at Winchester and grounded my philosophy in my 'practical mysticism' meetings. As I developed Universalism the philosophers placed themselves under me. I wrote autobiography and researched into international politics. In Pisa I had a vision of my next two books: an epic poem and odes on European culture. I withdrew from the philosophers and finished these two works. I acquired a third school, Normanhurst, and with three thriving schools and more than 245 teachers, classroom assistants, support and ancillary staff I had 'got back' the family business that had been taken away from my mother. I also acquired Tudor Otley Hall, and, spurred on by my contact with the Globe, wrote verse plays while finishing my odes. I researched the New World Order and investigated utopian societies and secret history. I sold Otley Hall and in my 'hermitage' by Epping Forest made collections of my literature. I wrote a philosophical work that caught the order of the universe, and in a second poetic epic captured the rampaging Muslim terror. I had a vision of world government and produced works of statecraft, and a local history – I was both global and local.

I had been a man of property and in my philosophy I had set out the manifestation of the One. For much of this time I had worn a puzzle ring on the ring finger of my left hand: four interlocked rings that at the social level represented three schools and Otley Hall, now Connaught House, but at the metaphysical level symbolised the manifestation of the One from Nothing to Non-Being, Being and Existence – the union of time and eternity. As an author I put my vision of unity in my books, and in my double life I lived at one with the universe close to my garden on the edge of Epping Forest.

The face within the stone
From my balcony I wandered down my spiral staircase and stood near my bust of Apollo and reflected that this has been a Univeralist work: an attempt to catch a life as a whole along with its work, in a national, international and local setting and reflecting the causes, influences and beliefs of the Age.

My hewing of my story out of a mass of material in this work resembles Michelangelo's hewing a face out of stone. Michelangelo is reputed to have claimed, "I saw the angel in the marble and carved until I set him free," and, "Every block of stone has a statue inside it and it is the task of the sculptor to discover it." He chiselled at a block of marble to reveal the face within. The face in this work, furrowed by my double life, was always within the material and I have hewn it out.

It is a face transformed by time, and I have probed for the origins of its growth. I wandered through an open door to our hall and stood by my

French clock of c.1860: a statue of a boy holding a book and leaning on a bookcase near a globe. He is reading about the world. The clock displays unified knowledge, and is a Universalist symbol. I look on that boy as my younger self. That boy grew up to be me.

Universal myth: Odysseus, Philoctetes, Jason, Orpheus, Tammuz, Faust, Prometheus, Heracles, Perseus, Bellerophon, Sisyphus, Icarus, Paradise, transforming Mystic Way

Looking back on my journey and my quest I see I acted out several of the Greek myths which are still potent in our time: the heroic journey of Odysseus (or Ulysses) round the Mediterranean; the quest of Jason to find the golden fleece; the quest of Orpheus to and from the Underworld, and his loss of Eurydice; the adventurous quest for Fire of Prometheus; the ordeals of Heracles, Perseus and Bellerophon (slayers of the hydra, gorgon and chimera); and the daily toil of Sisyphus pushing his boulder up a hill and then having to start all over again. These Greek myths that lurk behind my story are all aspects of one underlying proto-myth of transformation, or metamorphosis, that includes Philoctetes's wound that would not heal and his mastery of Heracles's bow, Tammuz's descent into the Underworld, Faust's deal with Mephistopheles to acquire knowledge, Dante's journey from Hell to Paradise and all progress along the Mystic Way, including Icarus's flight too near the sun: a composite Universalist myth. This includes the common language of humankind before the building of the Tower of Babel. The individual myths and the universal mythical journey they illustrate can be found in my story: my quest through loss, the Underworld and knowledge to Fire (the Light), ordeals and then my works, like pushing boulders uphill.

Similarly, my journey belongs to a universal Mystic Way that is shared by all the religions and traditions in *The Light of Civilization*. It has aspects that are Christian, Buddhist, Hindu, Taoist and from other traditions, all of which are themselves aspects of one underlying proto-quest whose traces can be found in all civilizations and cultures at all times during the last 5,000 years.

Acceptance of the transforming past and the present

The past is ever with me. Every week I park near the house in Brooklyn Avenue where I lay awake as a boy and listened for doodle-bugs, and drive past Journey's End where I was living when I heard my call to be a poet and set out on my journey. Looking back I see the past as a transforming process that led to my present predicament and carries me towards the future. I accept all that happened to me in the past, and my narrative – my record – presents my understanding of the process of transformation that led to my present situation.

Connaught House, my 'hermitage', measures out my remaining time and reconciles me to the past. In our hall, where hang two barometers my great-grandfather used when writing about the weather for *The Times*, can be heard the tick and chime of three clocks which tell the hours: the quick, high-pitched tinkle of the French clock; the slower ting-ting-ting of the moon-faced longcase clock; and the rich Westminster chimes of the American Ansonia wall clock that stood in my grandmother's hall, of which I wrote in 'The Silence':

> A quarter stirs and musically resounds
> With a lost century's languor,
> The echoes curl with soporific yawns
> And relapse in slumber....

Its chimes were heard by my grandfather, who was named after the Metaphysical poet George Herbert, and by his son Tom (soon to be killed on a 'reconnaissance' mission at 19) during the heyday of the family business before the First World War, and now billow through the downstairs rooms of the seat of the new family business I created. The tick-tick-tick of time above the silence concentrates my mind on the present, draws me back to my grandparents, reconciles me to the past and points me towards the liberating causeway of my future.

Universal intelligence

Looking back at my transformation I can see how my choices – to acquire Oaklands, contact my first publisher and replace Otley Hall with my 'hermitage'– led to my present situation and that I was living within an immense intelligence that inspired my daily work. Again and again as I worked on a problem spontaneous flashes came through, sometimes in sleep, suggesting that (like Michelangelo's statues) my works were already within this intelligence and just had to be hewn out. I am astonished at the ease with which I revealed my unseen works and made them manifest. I wonder if the artist opens to the universal intelligence of a field that surrounds us like the Higgs field, and is inspired and guided by its 'Divine Mind' whose Light wants him to complete his work.

Distilling: Golden Age

In my lifetime I have lived through immense changes, scientific discoveries, advancement of knowledge and globalisation: the splitting of the atom and the discovery of computers and DNA. Spacecraft have landed on the moon and flown past planets, the Higgs-boson field has given matter mass and the cooling cosmic background radiation has been found to echo the Big Bang. In 2014 came confirmation of inflation in the first 100 million billion billion billionth of a second in space-time 13.978 billion years ago (plus or minus 37 million years) and of Einstein's gravitational waves. Also during my lifetime humankind has tripled from 2.3 billion in 1939 to more than 7 billion. My outlook on the universe, both as a philosopher and as a man of letters, has embraced these discoveries and changes. The younger generation has a massive challenge to distil, refine and make sense of all the new knowledge and computerised information in a way that is meaningful to young lives, and only a Universalist approach – with the perspective of a World State – can undertake such a major act of distilling.

Having reached this point in my double life I look back at the electronic world into which my grandchildren are growing: portable tablet computers that give instant access to libraries, news coverage, the most complex travel, billing and banking transactions, social networking and the ubiquitous 'popular' culture I looked down on when I aspired to achieve. In my grand-children's new electronic world, schools may one day be replaced by internet-learning, books by more developed tablets and our thriving family business may one day be superseded. My grandchildren may be unable to retire until they are 70 or older and may lack time to distil their lives from the vast complex of information on the internet. They may look back on my generation's distilling – and on my distilling in *My Double Life 1* and *2* – with wonder that we had the time to do it and regard the years I have described in my story as a Golden Age.

'Intellect'

In early September 2013[58] I drove to Oaklands to see the improvements Matthew had made during the summer holidays: raised paths, a new Garden Room floor and a newly-equipped medical room. I sat with my grandson Alex (nearly four and a half) in his Transition classroom. Oaklands had been 'brought up' in the summer holidays. The schools flourished through our policy of perpetual improvement, thanks to Matthew's efforts. My birthday present to Matthew in October would be a small Greek-Roman statue of the Titan Atlas on bended knee, bearing our globe on his back (with a misshapen Greek-Roman outline of Africa, *see* p.v). I had borne the weight of three schools on my shoulders, and I, more than anyone, realised the burden that had now passed to him.

Over the years my works had found their way into a number of interna-tional compendia: *International Who's Who of Authors and Writers*, *International Who's Who of Poetry*, *The Cambridge Blue Book*, *The Writers Directory* and the *Dictionary of International Biography*. In my postbox by the front gates I found a letter saying that I had been selected "on merit" to be in the 8th edition of *2000 Outstanding Intellectuals of the 21st Century*. The letter (citing the *Oxford English Dictionary*) defined 'intellectualism' as the "doctrine that knowledge is wholly or mainly derived from the actions of the intellect, i.e. pure reason", and an 'intellectual' as a "person possessing a good understanding, enlightened person". It was ironic that I had stood up for enlightenment – illumination – among the philosophers by opposing rationalism with intuitionism.

At the very beginning of my authorial career I announced (on p.6 of *The Fire and the Stones*) that to me the 'intellect' (Latin *'intellectus'*, 'perception' and therefore 'understanding') is a perceptive faculty. I had held off authorship until I had achieved clarity on this from my own living, and this was the starting-point of my 40 books. It is the intellect that perceives the Light. It is the intuitive faculty that perceives universals, meaning and the unity of the universe (as in Shelley's "Intellectual Beauty"). It is to be distinguished from the 'reason'. The 'reason' is a logical faculty that analyses particulars and makes distinctions, and often sees meaninglessness and disunity. I have employed the reason in my books in the service of clarity, of getting across ideas as clearly as possible. But I have always tried to convey understanding that comes from enlightenment. If 'pure reason' is (as in Coleridge's *Biographia Literaria*) what the faculty of the 'intellect' perceives, illuminated thinking, then my work may merit inclusion in this compendium. If, however, it is what drives the rational, logical faculty, then I am surprised, for my use of 'reason' in this sense has been a means to an end rather than an end in itself, a means of writing with clarity about my intuition regarding a Reality beyond it: the One. But I was pleased that I was being read attentively out there.

Soon afterwards I was told that I had been selected to appear in *Outstanding People in the Arts Today*, a publication listing biographies of the world's most prominent artists, musicians, writers and all connected with the arts.

Unified view of health

I wandered past my statue of Venus de Milo to the bird feeders under the apple-trees and gazed at the herb-and-knot garden. I thought of a herb-garden's healing properties. My unitive way of looking intuitively sees into the underlying unity of things. I look back on my health issues and wonder if they display a pattern and were all interconnected if not symptoms of a primary cause.

I had a structural problem: my flat feet and lack of arches impacted on my leg muscles, out-of-true pelvis and posture and resulted in my back problems. Outside influences contributed to the TB I had as a boy (acquired from cows' milk), my varicose veins (too much occupational standing as a lecturer), and my hernias (too much heavy lifting with an unstable back). I also had a blood problem: my neutropenia (too few white blood cells, diagnosed in 1975) may have led to my antiphospholipid syndrome, which made my blood sticky, and the stickiness of my blood may also have contributed to my bronchiectasis which developed from my TB and left me with a deficiency of oxygen and a lifelong need for fresh air to combat drowsiness; my thrombophlebitis; and perhaps even my TIA (transient ischaemic attack). (Medical research has found that neutropenia can be seen in patients with antiphospholipid syndrome, which is itself linked to bronchiectasis in many patients.)

Did my sticky blood flow cause my ankle valves to fail and the wrecked blood vessels in my right foot? And did it cause a lethargic blood flow in the muscles round my lower back and waist and so contribute to my back problems and hernias? And if it could be established that inadequate blood flow and valve use also contributed to the development of my feet as an infant and to my flat feet as a child, and therefore to my structural problem, then all my symptoms could be related to a primary cause.

Unified perception looks for the unifying factor behind health as well as the unity within life's journey and quest.

My garden and Paradise
At the end of *Candide* Voltaire wrote, *"Il faut cultiver le jardin,"* and has been understood to mean that one should live close to one's garden, that the philosopher should live locally in a daily relationship with his garden.

I took a tub of fish food down to our fishpond, which would have been within Henry VIII's Fairmead during the time of the *Mary Rose*. Knowing I would finish *My Double Life 2: A Rainbow over the Hills* in draft that evening, I thought (like Empson on his return from Japan), *"Nunc dimittis"* (loosely 'Now I can die', *see* p.456). I stood at peace near my carp, goldfish and rudd on the outside slope of the crater whose rim joined the seven hills of Loughton into a ridge. Here I often saw squirrels, rabbits, sometimes a fox and occasionally a snake. Ten parakeets often squawked in the large oak-tree, green woodpeckers pecked on the lawn, great- and lesser-spotted woodpeckers came to the nut-feeders along with nuthatches, great tits, blue tits and long-tailed tits and, sometimes, a kestrel (pink chest, hooked bill and talons). Meadow browns and cabbage whites fluttered in the knot-garden, and bees crawled in the lavender. Apple-trees ripened different varieties of apple: Crispin, Lane's Prince Albert, Wisley Crab, Dumelow's Seedling, Newton Wonder, King of the Pippins and Warner's King. I walked back through the rose-garden and surveyed my shrubs and plants. I admired the water-lilies in the pond and fountain. I relished the abundance of wild flowers: the stitchwort and purple vetch on the lawn, buttercups in the field, daisies.

Behind the bust of Apollo on a brick wall were the inscriptions I had fixed: one from Horace (*Odes* 1.9) – "*Quem fors dierum cumque dabit lucro appone*" ("Take as a gift whatever the day brings forth"), and the other of a Latin proverb: "*Initium est dimidium facti.*" ("To begin is the hardest thing," literally "The beginning is half the deed." The idea was: "Once you've started, you're halfway there.") People I knew well often became ill or died – Frank Tuohy, Ricky Herbert and John Ezard – and I knew I had been right to start writing down my double life while I was well rather than leave it until (overtaken by one of my interconnected health issues) I might be too infirm to make a start. The proverb had told me that it was important to make a start while I was in good health.

I had made choices – to save Normanhurst, to set up at Otley Hall – and these choices had determined the allocation of my time. If I had not made these choices I would have had more time for my writing but would not have encountered the situations and met the people that deepened my writing and led to my vision. Had Ann not said, "Go and ask Miss Lord if you can have Oaklands" I might still be living in Wandsworth, having taught all my life and not had the time to write any works. If I had not made my decision to leave Law by Worcester College's lake and my decision on Gorran Haven's pier to go abroad for ten years, I might not have begun my journey. Several paths branched off my main path, and had I followed any one of them I could have taken a path that was not the path I took, not my intended or true path, and could have become an archaeologist, a cricketer, a solicitor, a mass marketer of satellite dishes or an MP.

My decision to start had led to my journey through all the disciplines and I had left behind a statement of my way of looking, my vision of unity, not just in my works but also within my knot-gardens: at Otley Hall, which had been voted the number-one private garden in the UK, and my replication of it here in my Forest garden.

From the terrace by Apollo I looked back at my garden. I was in the 'here and now', in a harmonious Paradise of 'here and now', not in a Hell of anguish. In the course of my story I had progressed from Hell to Paradise. All round me was a local Paradise, a Paradisal locality, and I could say with Shah Jahan and Amir Khusraw, "If there is Paradise on earth, it is here, it is here, it is here."

Paradise is in the 'here and now', in the moment. Paradise can be glimpsed when the soul is in harmony with the universe in the moment as in the harmony in the Humble Administrator's garden. Paradise is local, and the responsible soul wants to extend the harmony of the local vision worldwide so it can be shared by all humankind within the harmony of the coming World State, which reconciles internationalism and localism. The

Light in one's locality is the Light of humankind, and addresses internationalist concerns. The wisdom regarding harmony that I brought back from the Far East – the underlying order of reconciled opposites – can be applied to the Middle East, which sorely needs reconciliation. And so for me, Paradise was in Connaught House in the 'here and now' *and* in the harmonious universe. Localism and internationalism are reconciled in the underlying pattern and unity of the soul's simultaneous engagement with its locality and the universe.

I put down my fish food, sauntered through my knot-garden and slipped out of the gate to the Forest. Standing on the sloping green ride known as Warren Hill that runs down to the Ching Brook, I had a clear view up the outside of the crater across which runs the Epping New Road which traverses the full length of the ridge of the seven hills. I reflected that I had had four 'Mystic Lives' and numerous experiences of the Light, and that my experiences of the Light were fundamental to the thinking in my works. I reflected that I had started writing as a poet, had widened to include short stories, verse plays and other literary forms and had widened further to include history and philosophy in my search for the One. In the course of my journey I had witnessed many follies and vices of our time. Now I had completed 40 books.

For 25 years I had been busy turning out books in my 'hermitages' in Essex, Cornwall and Suffolk. I had been too busy finishing new works to promote my past works, and with single-mindedness I had produced a large body of work. I had ignored the received view of our intellectual and political leaders, who had drawn their curtains on the universe and Europe, shut out the Milky Way's 500 billion stars and Europe's control of between 15 and 50 per cent of the UK's legislation (depending on what laws are included). I had not drawn my curtains across my window, I had let in the universe and the reality of Europe.

In the course of being prolific I had looked at the state of modern literature, been dismayed by its secular horizons and had got on with reflecting the universe more truly. I had been independent. I had done my own metaphysical thing, woven my own rainbow out of dark clouds and sunshine. (On an upstairs wall in Connaught House was the Rainbow portrait of Elizabeth I, showing her holding a rainbow beneath a Latin inscription, '*Non sine sole iris*', 'No rainbow without the sun', *see* p.xxii).

During the last 25 years I had withdrawn from active involvement in the world step by step to give myself time and devote myself to writing my 40 books, which were like children. They had gone out into the world and found their own feet: this one was reprinting in the US, that one had passed a landmark number of sales. Was it worth all the non-stop effort and striving? Sophocles reputedly wrote, "One must wait until the evening to know how splendid the day has been." It was what I had within myself to do, and I followed my inner drive and calling. So, yes, although a new electronic age has reduced the demand for books, it has to have been worth the effort.

I knew the Light of my four 'Mystic Lives', and from time to time I saw the forms of Nature as its shadows. The Light shines through my works, which are also shadows. And I have become the Shadow I encountered in 'The Silence'. In the unitive vision the two opposites of the Light and the Shadow (*Lumen* and *Umbra*) are reconciled in harmony. And the Light and the Shadow (Nature's forms) are united in the rainbow, which is both Light and form and now and again shines out my works. As the portrait of Elizabeth I proclaims, "No rainbow without sun, the Light."

On this day of short downpours and sunshine above the rim of the crater, the ridge that connects the seven hills of Loughton, hung a Paradisal rainbow that harmoniously united sunshine and showers, happiness and sorrow in an arc of great beauty. With the dark wood behind me I stood on the approach to the ridge, having finished the narrative of *My Double Life 2: A Rainbow over the Hills*. I would soon be celebrating my 40th wedding anniversary, 40 years of marriage during which I had written 40 books: I would soon be carrying in my breast pocket a pinkish rough-hewn hexagonal ruby, a gift from Ann. I would soon be celebrating my 75th birthday and Coopersale Hall's 25th anniversary. I was pleased with the way things had gone with my writing – my works that all related to the One – and the three schools that huddled, along with Connaught House, beneath the arch of the glistening rainbow. I had found my way, I had completed my quest for the One. Paradise was here, near the unifying top of the seven hills. Paradise was beneath the rainbow over the hills.

*

Rainbow: vision of unity and unification, the One

I knew that the rainbow presented (and represented) the One. It gathered over the hills, its seven bands glowing in the sky, calling all to the vision of unity. It shone out. Each of its seven bands reflected one of the seven hills in which all can toil upwards. Collectively its bands proclaimed a goal, a reminder of what is available to all. It was a universal rainbow to which all could aspire and interpret the bands in ways that suited their bent.

At the social level the seven disciplines I had followed were followed under the watchful eye of the State in the tradition of the Rainbow portrait (*see* p.xxii), in which the rainbow is in the grip of Elizabeth I who is cloaked in eyes, ears and mouths. At the metaphysical level, and to me, the rainbow was beyond the reach of the secret State, independent of its controlling hand, and soared above the seven hills.

I had sensed that each of the seven hills offered a different insight. By toiling up each it was possible to achieve: personal growth; knowledge of truth (amid the errors of the Age); knowledge of the order within the universe; perception of the pattern within world history; understanding of how there could be a political World State; perception of the unity of world religions; and perception of how the culture of the Age should be renewed.

Each discipline invited a separate trek to the One: achieving personal growth involved a trek up transpersonal psychology and mysticism; knowing truth, a trek up literature; knowing the order within the universe, a trek up science and philosophy (including cosmology); seeing the pattern within world history, a trek up world history; understanding how there could be a political World State, a trek up international politics and state-craft; perceiving the unity of world religions, a trek up comparative religion; and seeing how the culture of the Age should be renewed, a trek up world culture.

Now I saw that each of the seven bands of the rainbow expressed a different Universalism, *which my books reflected* (see p.873). Between them my books expressed seven Universalisms within seven disciplines and hills. (*See* pp.xxvi, 260.)

The rainbow I sometimes saw out there came and went, and for long spells – several months or even a year – it was not visible. It was out of mind. Like the Light, it was always there even though it remained unseen. When it appeared its seven bands shone out, proclaiming an overarching vision of unity.

The rainbow came and went as my books came and went. The rainbow was universal and proclaimed a vision for *all* to achieve, but in a sense *a* rainbow came and went with each of my books. Each of my books heralded the vision of unity, of oneness, in one of the seven disciplines. Each described a toiling up one of the seven hills and reflected one band of the rainbow. It shone out a message of unity and then disappeared. My next book reappeared to blazon out the vision of unity again. Looking at the 40 rainbows thrown from the crystal that hangs in my study window by the setting sun, I felt that each rainbow represents one of my books, that in a sense each of my books is a rainbow. Each of my books shone out when published, like the universal rainbow, and was blazoned before the world for a short while and then faded, although it was still there.

Now I understood that in my double life I could view the whole rainbow simultaneously from opposite perspectives: first as *all* the seven hills and disciplines, each of which corresponds to one band; and secondly as just *one* of the seven hills and disciplines, its bands being subsets of just one disci-pline. Each of my books shone out one discipline and at least one of the seven sub-bands within that discipline. Thirdly the rainbow's seven bands could be seen as a blend or reconciliation of these two opposites, in seven different ways: seven bands for each discipline, each of which has seven bands (or sub-bands) making 49 different bands (or sub-bands) in all.

The seven bands of transpersonal psychology and mysticism reflected: the individual; awakening; purgation; illumination; a centre-shift; transformation; and the unitive way. The whole rainbow expressed the vision of Oneness of transpersonal psychology and mysticism.

Literature's seven bands reflected: lyric poetry; odes; epic; verse drama; short stories; autobiography; and travelogues. The whole rainbow expressed the vision of Oneness of literature, and in all literary experience.

The seven bands of science – all the sciences – and philosophy reflected: scepticism; rationalist hypothesis; empirical evidence; linguistic analysis; a phenomenological centre-shift; transformation; and intuitional truth. The whole rainbow expressed the vision of Oneness of the universe of science and philosophy, and the experience of Reality as the One.

World history's seven bands reflected: locality; nation-states; cultures; civilizations; pattern; the élitist New World Order; and the unification of all civilizations in a World State. The whole rainbow expressed the vision of Oneness of world history, and the oneness of human history.

The seven bands of international politics and statecraft reflected: party; bureaucracy; nation-states; regions (such as the unification of Europe); a divided world; unifying statecraft; and the unification of all countries in a World State. The whole rainbow expressed the vision of Oneness of international politics and statecraft, and the international, political oneness of all humankind.

The seven bands of comparative religion reflected: leader (for example, the Buddha, Christ); Light; sect; national religion; regional religion; interfaith policy; and the process of the unification of all religions. (I could also see a separate band for each of seven religions: Christianity; Islam; Hinduism; Buddhism; Sikhism; Judaism; and Taoism.) The whole rainbow expressed the vision of Oneness of comparative religion, and the oneness of all religions.

World culture's seven bands reflected: locality; national culture; regional culture; civilization (for example, the culture of Western civilization); secular culture; metaphysical culture; and unified, balanced world culture. The whole rainbow expressed the vision of Oneness of world culture, and the oneness of all cultures.

Now I saw that the rainbow also represented a unification of the seven visions of unity within the seven separate disciplines which all led to the vision of the One. The rainbow proclaimed the oneness: of human beings in relation to the universe via transpersonal psychology and mysticism; of all experience via literature; of the universe via science and philosophy (including cosmology); of human history via world history; of all humankind via international politics and statecraft, and a World State; of all religions via comparative religion; of all cultures via world culture. The unified vision of all the onenesses was Universalist. My vision of Universalism in seven disciplines resembled an intermittent rainbow whose seven bands overarch seven hills and reconcile all opposites under its unity.

The unification of the seven visions of unity was like the unification of the seven hills of Loughton, which are separate from one angle and integrated from another. From Loughton seven clearly-discernible and separate hills lead up to the rim of the crater that curves round the village on three sides. But from the other side of the crater, high up on the rim round the slope overlooking Henry VIII's Fairmead deer park in my Buckhurst Hill, the hills disappear and there is only one ridge, curved like a bow: like a rainbow lying on its side as if it were a shadow thrown by the rainbow arched above The seven hills of achievement are perceived as one unified, integrated ridge.

I recalled that down in the crater during air raids my mother read me her story about my brother and me climbing up a rainbow and speaking to Thor on his thundercloud, and now I wondered if my seven-banded rainbow had formed in my mind from the seed she sowed in my soul during those dangerous wartime nights.

The one rainbow shone out for all humankind, calling tiny humans below to toil among the hills and reflect some of the 49 individual bands within the seven ways of viewing the seven-banded rainbow. It spoke directly to each individual who answered its call to climb for achievements. All who responded left traces of their toil behind, like cairns on a mountainside: books like mounds of stones that were monuments as well as landmarks. The rainbow proclaimed a life of purpose to all who had eyes to see and were prepared to give a lifetime's work to mirror its vision of unity.

Rainbow
Seven disciplines and Universalisms
How the bands of the rainbow reflect Nicholas Hagger's works

Band of rainbow	Works	Discipline and Universalism
Red	Personal growth/transformation, mysticism and religion: *The Fire and the Stones*; *A Mystic Way*; *The Light of Civilization*; *My Double Life 1: This Dark Wood*.	Mystical Universalism
Orange	Truth: the Age, lyric poetry, verse drama, epic, short stories, diaries, autobiography, travel, letters (man of letters): *Selected Poems*; *Collected Poems: A White Radiance*; *A Mystic Way*; *Awakening to the Light*; *A Spade Fresh with Mud*; *The Warlords*; *The Sweet Smell of Summer*; *Wheeling Bats and a Harvest Moon*; *The Warm Glow of the Monastery Courtyard*; *The Tragedy of Prince Tudor*; *Classical Odes*; *Overlord*, one-volume edition; *Collected Poems 1958–2005*; *Collected Verse Plays*; *Collected Stories*; *The Last Tourist in Iran*; *The Libyan Revolution*; *Armageddon*; *A New Philosophy of Literature*; *My Double Life 1: This Dark Wood*; *My Double Life 2: A Rainbow over the Hills*; *Selected Poems: Quest for the One*; *Selected Stories: Follies and Vices of the Elizabethan Age*.	Literary Universalism
Yellow	Order of universe, science and philosophy: *The Universe and the Light*; *The One and the Many*; *The New Philosophy of Universalism*.	Philosophical Universalism
Green	Pattern of world history: *The Fire and the Stones*; *The Syndicate*; *The Secret History of the West*; *The Light of Civilization*; *The Rise and Fall of Civilizations*; *The World Government*; *The Secret American Dream*; *The Syndicate*; *A View of Epping Forest* (local history).	Historical Universalism
Blue	International politics and statecraft towards a World State: *The Fire and the Stones*; *Scargill the Stalinist?*; FREE; *The Syndicate*; *The Secret History of the West*; *The Secret Founding of America*; *The Rise and Fall of Civilizations*; *The World Government*; *The Secret American Dream*.	Political Universalism
Indigo	Unity of world religions/comparative religion: *The Fire and the Stones*; *The Light of Civilization*.	Religious Universalism
Violet	Unified culture of Age, Metaphysical Revolution: *The Fire and the Stones*; *The Light of Civilization*; *The One and the Many*.	Cultural Universalism

Epilogue:

Rainbow over Hills

Episodes, structure, pattern and unity in double lives

"Exegi monumentum aere perennius"
"My work is done, the memorial more enduring than brass."

Horace, Odes, 3.30.1

We have seen in *My Double Life 1: This Dark Wood* that my double life was split between my everyday, social working life (in universities, intelligence work, journalism and teaching) and my more metaphysical writing life (poems and stories); and in *My Double Life 2: A Rainbow over the Hills* that my double life was also split between my everyday, social working life (running schools, small publishing and a historic house) and my more metaphysical writing life (bringing out 40 books).

My double life and episodes
Working and writing lives
In my double life I had a working life in which I earned a living and engaged with normal social life, and a more metaphysical writing life in which I also lived intensely in my imagination and inner vision while composing works. I lived in the social world and opened to inner metaphysical inklings in my writings: I removed myself from the social ego of my working life to write in the solitude of my soul at my writer's desk and state the One in seven disciplines.

Brain physiologists deny that the soul exists as it cannot be found within the brain or brain function. By 'soul' I refer to the complex of intuitional feelings I contact in my writing that are open to and fed by metaphysical influences beyond the more superficial rational, social ego. Such an Intuitionist view is confirmed by the dictionary definitions of 'soul': "the spiritual or immaterial part of a human being, often regarded as immortal", "the moral or emotional or intellectual nature of a person" (*Concise Oxford Dictionary*); "the principle of thought and action in man, commonly regarded as an entity distinct from the body"; "the spiritual part of man in contrast to the purely physical"; "the seat of the emotions, feelings or sentiments, the emotional part of man's nature", "intellectual or spiritual power, high development of mental faculties"; "the spiritual part of man considered in its moral aspect or in relation to God", "the spiritual part of man regarded

874

as surviving after death", "the disembodied spirit of a (deceased) person regarded as a separate entity" (*Shorter Oxford English Dictionary*).

In truth, the writer operates under cover in his working life, which gives him material. Angus Wilson told me in Libya that a writer is a like a spy. He goes about his everyday life in the social world in disguise and takes bits of information back to his writing-desk. Graham Greene said something similar: "The great advantage of being a writer is that you can spy on people. You're there, listening to every word, but part of you is observing. Everything is useful to a writer, you see – every scrap, even the longest and most boring of luncheon parties." (Both Wilson and Greene worked in intelligence.) Chekhov, who also led a double life, went about his working life as a low-paid physician treating the poor for free and took back to his desk observations he put in his stories and plays.

As an educator I too have operated as a kind of spy, jotting observations on folded paper I keep in the breast pocket of my shirt to take back to my writing-desk. In my double life I have alternated between my working life and my writing life, which have appeared to be in contradiction. I seem to have alternated between opposites in my living.

Social and metaphysical worlds

Throughout my life I have been aware of two worlds. The first was social: the world of my childhood homes and education, and of my later employment, my working life. But within my historical and social setting I had glimpses of another, higher world: the metaphysical world I contacted during my writing life and perceived as the source of the social world. I contacted a Reality quite different from everyday social Reality. Within it was a world of intense consciousness, gleams from the beyond and awareness of meaning I have been able to locate during my writing life. Return from this higher world made the everyday world seem trivial, but the two complemented each other.

My double life is with me every waking moment for I exist between the social and the metaphysical worlds in my working and writing lives, and I move backwards and forwards between the two every hour. My double life has held both these worlds in balance.

My turbulent time: from post-imperial nationhood to Universalism

My double life has been lived between the local environment of my Essex childhood and England, and a global setting involving both West and East. Looking back I see that I have lived through a turbulent time.

I was shaped by a United Kingdom that has undergone a profound transformation during my lifetime. I lived through Churchill's saving of Britain from Hitler. I lived through Atlee's founding of the National Health

Service and the Welfare State, and through socialism. I lived through Britain's imperial and colonial decline after Suez and contributed to resisting it in my intelligence work. I lived through an anti-Communist time and helped prevent Europe from being overrun by Soviet power. I lived through a time when Britain was in decline, her finances controlled by the International Monetary Fund and the trade unions. I lived through the Thatcherite revolution: the eclipsing of trade-union power, privatisation, the restoration of Britain's military reputation after the Falklands war and victory in the Cold War. I contributed by my deeds and writing: I opposed Scargill, ran privatised schools, and campaigned for FREE to end the Cold War. I lived through a time of rule by lesser men who ran up a deficit and weakened Britain. I helped draw attention to this in my satirical verse. I lived under the passing of Britain into a new state, the European Union. I lived through a time of terrorism and of the New World Order's response in Afghanistan and Iraq, and reflected this in my writings. In my writings I correctly predicted the end of Soviet Communism, the advent of a United States of Europe and the jihadist attempt to establish a new caliphate based in Baghdad. I have seen the future: a World State; and have reflected it in my writings. I reflected the Age in my life and work, and so this account of my life and work reflects my Age, the Age into which I was born and through which I lived.

In *My Double Life* I have shown why I turned my back on nationhood for Universalism (and its regional, internationalist and globalist forms) and how I exposed the corrupt, tyrannical, self-interested New World Order which was blocking a genuine democratic world government and World State that would benefit all humankind.

In my double life I was fortunate to meet many of our Age's leading educators, academics, literary critics, publishers, journalists, businessmen, lawyers, judges, terrorists, military leaders, courtiers, diplomats, ambassadors, civil servants, spies, poets, writers, dramatists, actors and actresses, directors, filmmakers, television presenters, musicians, scientists, biologists, physicists, cosmologists, philosophers, historians, politicians, ministers, trade union leaders, bankers, financiers, peers, aristocrats, archaeologists, dendrochronological 'experts', footballers, cricketers, athletes, religious leaders, gurus and healers, as a glance through the Table of Contents (*see* **p.ix**) will bear out. I was able to observe at first hand and get a handle on the workings of the British *élite* as it slid from nationhood into European union within our struggling Western civilization.

Now I am surrounded by the faces of those I used to know in this turbulent time, who are no more: my parents and grandparents, aunts and uncles; Thompson, my Head at Chigwell; A.B. Brown, my Law tutor; Ricky Herbert, who jumped into the canal outside college to prove he was free;

John Ezard, with whom I discussed so many writers; Tomlin, philosopher and my boss in Japan; Tuohy, writer and my fellow traveller in China; Buchanan, my colleague in Tokyo; Gaddafi, whose head lolled on my shoulder before I shrugged his cap off; Gorka, Hungarian spy who leaked intelligence comments to me; Krassó, who took up my idea to petition for a Soviet withdrawal from Europe; Biggs-Davison, who backed FREE and died mysteriously after a visit to Angola; Gascoyne and Kathleen Raine who spoke at my launch. All who made an impact on me and are now dead, who I portrayed in these two volumes – they crowd round me in my study at night, faces I used to know that are no more, once warm and friendly and now pale and vaporous from beyond the grave in my sorrowful imagination.

Looking back I see that the England I have tried to describe has largely vanished. I have tried to recapture my homeland and my young self by an imaginative recreation of my lost past. I retrieved my lost world to some extent by buying my old school. The post-war, post-imperial England in my mind could be a bleak place, a place of cold, ration books and Cold War as an imperial, colonial role was abandoned and a new role, eventually linked to a United States of Europe, hard to accept.

My task and mission?
Looking back, I am amazed that I found my way to Universalism through the personal difficulties I encountered. In *My Double Life 1: This Dark Wood* I described how I lived through a traumatic time. There were days when I felt completely abandoned. I did not want to be a lawyer and was not sure that I was on the right path. Yet things turned out all right for me. I could not have imagined as I emerged from the dark wood that I would own three schools, have 245 staff and write 40 books that (judging from the emails I receive) are thoughtfully and carefully read. I could not have dreamt of writing nearly 1,500 poems, more than 300 classical odes, 2 poetic epics, 5 verse plays and over 1,000 short stories. Even in our darkest days there is hope, for we cannot know what is about to unfold. We must have faith that the future will improve, and continue resolutely with steadfastness.

Looking back it seems that this outcome was always meant to be, and that I *had* to enter the dark wood to develop the qualities I would need to undertake the works that would be woven into my rainbow. There seems to be an inevitability about the outcome. So *was* it always meant to be? *Was* it Providential, not an accident?

At the beginning of *My Double Life I: This Dark Wood* I said it can be estimated that I was conceived around 29 August 1938, a month before Chamberlain waved a piece of paper and said "Peace in our time" when the truth (according to Goebbels' diaries) was that Hitler had already planned the Second World War and a time of universal war was about to begin. Was I conceived shortly before the Munich agreement and born into the time of Hitler's bellicosity to understand the traumatic events that followed by writing *Overlord* and to fashion and convey a vision of Universalism, of international order and world peace? Was this my task? Was I sent down from another realm to put together from my experience, and leave behind, a vision of a better future?

Whether I was born with a mission or circumstantially, accidentally, developed a vision in the course of emerging from my dark wood, the fact remains that in my 30 episodes I journeyed from experience of wartime bombing to a vision our blind time needs. Quite simply, I saw the future and laid out how it is going to be: a benevolent world government with a Universalist outlook. I wrote it down and therefore brought it in.

My ordinary and extraordinary double life

In *My Double Life 1* and *2* I have tried to reflect how ordinary experiences threw up my works. At the same time, I am clear that something extraordinary happened to me in 1971. I have never lost sight of how extremely important my experience in 13 Egerton Gardens on Friday 10 September 1971 has been for my double life, and I have remained faithful to it for more than 40 years. I have regarded this experience as fundamentally universal: everyone can know the Light, the sun that shines from within when all else is dark and gives the world meaning with its rays.

Nevertheless, though universal, mine was not an experience that is universally known and I have sometimes felt like Nunez in H.G. Wells's short story 'The Country of the Blind',[1] a parable on the solitude of the artist. A mountaineer in Ecuador's Andes falls over a precipice into the legendary, cut-off 'Country of the Blind' where all the inhabitants have been blind for 14 generations due to a strange disease. He is found by blind people who cannot see what he can see. He tells them, "In the Country of the Blind the One-eyed Man is King," and proclaims himself King of the Blind. The blind have no word for 'see' and think him mad. They do not believe in sight and put him down for an operation to raise him to the level of a blind citizen. He flees.

Like the man in Wells's story I reported a sun I had seen and attempted to describe it to people who did not understand. I experienced the Light known to mystics for thousands of years and described my experience to people who did not believe in its existence. I have come to the conclusion that it is best not to proselytise about its existence, but to record the facts and put them into literary works (as Eliot did), and "those who have eyes to see, let them see".

It would have been so much easier if I had remained an anti-metaphysical Neoclassical poet operating within Ricks's principles rather than become an innovator, but I had the experience of the 'sun' – 93 experiences in all (*see* Appendix 1, p.903) – and I had to be true to what I had seen even though this lost me the support of influential sceptics.

It is true to say that my double life has been lived between the ordinary and the extraordinary.

No duality

The two halves of my double life, my working life and my writing life, have always been interconnected, and although they appear opposed within a dialectic they are essentially aspects of one process. Many of my poems and stories, and my historical and philosophical insights, have been inspired by my working life of teaching books to students and running staff.

I always had a +A and a –A in my double life, a *yin* and a *yang*, as befits a Gemini, but there was always an = 0 that perpetually reconciled the contradictions and opposites I experienced. Although my life was lived between opposites I believe there is no duality in the universe, and that there are no dualisms as each opposite is contained within a greater unity, like the pairs of scales in a fir cone. My double life has essentially been one life in which the social ego or persona of my working life has operated within, and as an extension of, the inner vision of the soul in which I have spent my writing life. In my single life it can be said that +A (soul) and –A (social ego) are harmonised within the One (unified living): a Universalist reconciliation.

Episodes

In both volumes of *My Double Life* each episode is governed by a pair of opposites in accordance with the dialectic: +A + –A = 0. I must point out that most of my episodes did not begin and end abruptly. Each episode was rooted in, and grew out of, the previous episode, and faded in the next episode. In each episode can be found the seeds of the opposites of the next episode and the fading of the opposites found within the previous episode. To a small extent episodes overlap.

The contradictions between my working and writing lives are reconciled within an underlying and unfolding unity (+A + –A = 0) in which one energy and pattern of transformation works through conflicting pairs of apparent opposites within my episodes.

Pattern of transformation in 30 episodes and pairs of opposites

In the Epilogue of *My Double Life 1: This Dark Wood* I said that a full life may have 42 episodes, and I set out the first 15 episodes of my double life to show a pattern of transformation within their pairs of opposites that resemble a double helix:

episode 1: family–war
episode 2: Nature–school
episode 3: archaeology–politics
episode 4: literature–law
episode 5: wisdom–intelligence
episode 6: marriage–dictatorship
episode 7: vitalism–mechanism
episode 8: the Absolute–scepticism
episode 9: civilizations–Communism
episode 10: Establishment–revolution
episode 11: liberation–tyranny
episode 12: purgation–separation
episode 13: Ambassador–journalism
episode 14: illumination–nationalism
episode 15: meaning–disenchantment

I showed that the first of each pair belongs to a helix (or spiral curve) that has a positive progression, a transformation in the soul towards a vision of the unity of the universe. I showed that the second of each pair belongs to a helix (or spiral curve) that has a negative aspect that returns the soul to the social world of the rational, social ego, thereby restraining the transformation. In each pair the positive aspect is Intuitionist, *yin*, and the negative aspect is Rationalist, *yang*, the two conflicting aspects reconciled within Universalism. To state this another way, +A (Intuitionism) + –A (Rationalism) = 0 (Universalism).

So have the second 15 of my episodes and pairs of opposites, 'doubles' I lived through in my double life, followed the same pattern? To recap, these were:

episode 1: remarriage–comprehensive education
episode 2: lyric poetry–administration
episode 3: new powers–dogmatic authority
episode 4: Baroque–egalitarian socialism
episode 5: vision–subversion
episode 6: Universalism–expansionism
episode 7: metaphysical poetry–world history
episode 8: philosophy–practical mysticism
episode 9: autobiography–international politics
episode 10: epic–European culture
episode 11: verse plays–Tudor knots
episode 12: classical odes–utopianism
episode 13: collected literature–secret history

episode 14: order–terror
episode 15: internationalism–localism

The second 15 episodes in my life continue to show a progression or trans-formation, or inner development, in a continuation of the 'double helix'. In each episode there is a conflict – a push-pull tug of war – between a positive aspect (the first in each pair in the above list) which impels the transforming soul and advances the transformation; and a negative aspect (the second in each pair in the above list) which impels the social ego that pulls against and restrains the transformation. The transformation continues the progression towards a vision of the unity of the universe through a working-out of +A + −A = 0, in which the +A represents the positive aspect of each episode (the transforming power of the soul) and the −A the negative aspect of each episode (the anti-transforming pull of the social ego). The transformation involves a tussle between Intuitionist *yin* and Rationalist *yang*, the two conflicting aspects reconciled within Universalism.

The positive aspects (+A) of the second 15 episodes reflect the soul's inner development. They have the following sequence within one helix:

remarriage; lyric poetry; new powers; Baroque; vision; Universalism; metaphysical poetry; philosophy; autobiography; epic; verse plays; classical odes; collected literature; order; internationalism.

In all the above there is a positive progression from my remarriage to my presentation of a Universalist World State, thereby advancing the transfor-mation.

The negative aspects (−A) reflect the social ego's involvement in the outer world. They have the following sequence within the other helix:

comprehensive education; administration; dogmatic authority; egalitarian socialism; subversion; expansionism; world history; practical mysticism; international politics; European culture; Tudor knots; utopianism; secret history; terror; localism.

In all of these episodes there is a regressive tendency in relation to the positive progression – from comprehensive education to localism. Within the transformation, all these negative aspects pull against the soul's devel-oping sense of the unity of the universe and return it to the social world of the rational, social ego, thereby restraining the transformation.

In the second 15 episodes as in the first the positive and negative aspects are held in balance within episodes and the pairs of opposites, and within the reconciling power of memory. The deeper soul and social ego have to be held in balance.

The episodes, then, continue to have a pattern: a transformation in terms of the conflicting opposites of $+A + -A = 0$. The progression on the positive (or 'soul') side or helix is balanced on the negative (or 'social ego') side or helix by a regression back to the outer world.

As I look at my double-helix-like life I see a pattern in the succession of episodes, which reveal "a repeated decorative design" (my definition of 'pattern' in the Epilogue of *My Double Life 1: This Dark Wood*). This is like the pattern on a carpet, wallpaper or dress; and I see symmetrical intervals in the "correct proportion of parts of an equal shape and size" in relation to the structure of the whole (my definition of 'symmetry' in the Epilogue of *My Double Life 1: This Dark Wood*). The same is true of the pairs of opposites. I also see a pattern in linked pairs of events, in the similarities between events within different episodes.

Nodal points in 30 episodes

I said in the Epilogue of *My Double Life 1: This Dark Wood* that I would list these linked pairs of events. Because in botany the knob "on a plant stem from which one or more leaves emerge" is called a 'node' (*Concise Oxford Dictionary*), I think of the first of these linked events as 'nodal points'. In the first of the linked events there is a knob, and in the second of the linked events there is a leaf which has grown from it (as it were). 'Nodal points' do not relate to the structure of a spruce cone, but both are images from within botany.

The main linked events, the nodal points, in the pattern of my life are:

My Double Life 1: This Dark Wood
- 1944. German bombs on the Loughton cricket field – would use bombing in *Overlord*.
- 1944. My mother read me her typed-out bedtime story 'The Rainbow Children' many times – would write *A Rainbow over the Hills*.
- 1944. Was sent to Oaklands School, Albion Hill – it would provide my livelihood while I wrote my books and developed my world vision (*Weltanschauung*).
- 1945. Spilt damson jam at sixth birthday party – was offered Oaklands near this spot by Miss Lord.
- 1945. My father was a tenant of the Maitlands – focused on the Maitlands in *A View of Epping Forest* (after my daughter knew them in Harrington Hall).
- 1945/1951/1953. Met Churchill and Montgomery – would write about them in *The Warlords* and *Overlord*.
- 1947. Saw Middlesex play cricket – the nephew and son of two of the

Middlesex cricketers (Mann and Robins) would be my publisher and insurer.

- 1951–1955. Was captain of cricket and football teams – a preparation for leading school staff.
- 1953. Visited D-Day beaches from Le Home – a preparation for writing about the D-Day beaches in *Overlord*.
- 1956. Read *Tradition and Design in the Iliad* – needed for *Overlord* and *Armageddon*.
- 1956. Excavated a *cloaca* (sewer) in Chester – put me off archaeology and guided me into literature.
- 1956. Hungarian refugees came to Grange Farm and one gave me all his Hungarian coins – focused on Hungary in the 1980s (FREE).
- 1956. Swapped a Greek coin with Hoppit at school – was questioned on it in my interview to enter Worcester College, Oxford and it furthered my admission.
- 1957. Read Chester Wilmot, *The Struggle for Europe*, in solicitor's office – would need it for *Overlord*.
- 1957. Read 'The Wreck of the Deutschland' – *Overlord* would be about the wreck of Deutschland.
- 1957. Played cricket on Buckhurst Hill's top ground – was introduced to forest Buckhurst Hill and would live within walking distance of the ground.
- 1958. Trust Accounts and Bookkeeping – needed for bookkeeping at Oaklands.
- 1958. Slept on the floor of Kazantzakis's study in Crete – a nudge that I should leave Law for Literature.
- 1959. Chose to change from Law to English by the Worcester College lake – my choice led to the founding of my poetic *oeuvre* and to Ricks's advice on my choice of verse for *Overlord*.
- 1960 and 1961. Shown St Austell while visiting/staying with Colin Wilson – Ann came from there and I would own 'a house by a harbour' I had seen in my mind near there.
- 1960. Found Col. Grivas in Greece – led to sherry with my Provost, Sir John Masterman, and eventual entrée into the intelligence service.
- 1961. Visited Colin Wilson – on Gorran Haven harbour chose to spend ten years abroad questing for the One.
- 1961. Worked as debt collector – needed this skill when running schools.
- 1961. Went to Iraq – would need to write about the American invasion of Iraq in *Armageddon*.
- 1961–1962. Travelled from work to Sheikh Omar al-Suhrawardi's tomb – was shown the nephew of the leading figure of the illumina-

tionist school, Shahab al-Din Suhrawardi, who would be significant after 1971.

- 1963. Gardened before going to Japan – needed for supervising gardeners at schools, Otley Hall and Connaught House.
- 1963. Gardened in three schools before going to Japan – was shown three schools, would eventually own and run three schools.
- 1963. Shown a comprehensive school – became a Senior Teacher in one.
- 1963. Worked in library placing books on shelves – would be writing books that would have their own places on shelves.
- 1963–1967. Taught Contemporary English Poetry to Japanese students – would need it for my poetry.
- 1964. Met Frank Tuohy – needed his training in writing stories and focusing on places.
- 1964–1977. Taught Gibbon, Spengler and Toynbee to Japanese PhD students – would need them for my view of civilizations.
- 1969. Wrote articles in Libya (organised by future prime minister) – would need them for the Appendix of *The Libyan Revolution*.
- 1971. Met Ann among her schoolchildren – in retrospect, would need a wife who was a trained teacher to share the enterprise of Oaklands.

My Double Life 2: A Rainbow over the Hills
- 1973–1985. Wrote short essays on 'A'-level books – would need them for Appendix of *A New Philosophy of Literature*.
- 1977. My mother invited Miss Lord to Tony's christening – Miss Lord, offered Oaklands, which would allow me to write my world vision.
- 1980s. Went to lectures in Winchester – was invited to lecture there in 1992 and my lecture formed the first third of *The Universe and the Light*.
- 1987. Attended the Frankfurt Book Fair for Oak-Tree Books – was told by a German that I had a new Universalist view of world history.
- 1990 (November). Attended the Frankfurt Book Fair for Oak-Tree Books – met two Mainstream publishers, one of whom recommended me to my first publisher.
- 1997. Bought Otley Hall – and wrote *The Secret Founding of America* and *The Secret American Dream* out of what it helped me glean about the US.
- 2006. My grandfather lived at Fairmead in 1898 – I lived at a different Fairmead from 2006.
- 2010 (May). Visited Copped Hall and saw the pediment – used it in *A New Philosophy of Literature*.

Again and again, in many episodes, something has happened in one episode that would be of use in a later episode, like a leaf growing from a plant's knob, suggesting a law by which transformation works, showing growth within the soul in action. The event in the first episode is linked to, and similar to, the event in a later episode which it has helped, suggesting a repetitive decorative design. Pattern, we have seen in the Epilogue of *My Double Life 1: This Dark Wood*, is "repeated decorative design", and the nodal points may indicate a further decorative *motif* at symmetrical intervals. Such linked events may repeat at symmetrical intervals like episodes and pairs of opposites. Nodal points do not seem accidental when viewed within their pattern and when one instance is set alongside many other instances.

Each of the nodal points shown above may be one of a succession of nodal points that are in "correct proportion" to the whole. As each episode and event is unified in relation to my whole life as are individual scales in a whole cone, the pattern of episodes and events reveals the unity of my life.

In all, 42 episodes and over 50 works

I have said that a full life may have 42 episodes. Many will not live to experience all their potential episodes. I write with the skull I bought at auction in an alcove near my writing hand as a *memento mori*, a reminder of my impending death and that I may not live to see all my 42 episodes. I am about to enter a new episode that will usher in a new pair of opposites. It has not happened yet, and what form it will take will depend on my next projects. I have not chosen the order in which these will happen, but ahead of me are the following works and impending pairs of opposites:

Becoming and Being
Selected Letters
Life Cycle and Other Poems
The First Dazzling Chill of Winter, vol. 6 of Collected Stories
Three novellas, a trilogy:
    The Tree of Knowledge
    The Soul-Destroyer
    The Lost Englishman
What Does it Mean to Be English?
Shakespeare's Trunk, A Quest for Shakespeare
Memoir of a Tudor Hall
A Cornish Memoir
Selected Diaries, on works
The Revolution That Didn't Happen
The Essential Hagger

If I am given time, this programme will bring the tally of my works to well over 50.

Assuming that I work down this list from the top, my next episode will involve a clear split between supporting material (unpublished papers and letters) and creative material (poems and stories). But life has a strange way of throwing up new situations, and my next episode may include a *motif* I have not considered. The true nature of an episode is best seen retrospectively.

A new situation has already been thrown up. In 2014 while planning my poem 'Life Cycle', my *Prelude* along with 'The Silence', I outlined a human life-cycle pattern of 12 seven-year cycles that reflect the renewal cycles of the body cells and hair every seven years and complement, without contradicting, the life cycle of 42 episodes I have presented in *My Double Life 1* and *2*.

Universal double lives and the Universalist rainbow
Structure, pattern and unity in all double lives

In the Epilogue of *My Double Life 1: This Dark Wood* I said that the underlying structure of the episodes and layered pairs of opposites in my life can be found in the underlying structure of the episodes and layered pairs of opposites in all lives. I said that the structure, pattern and unity of my life is an example, even a template, of the structure, pattern and unity that can be found in all lives. I have uncovered a universal pattern. The unifying pattern of all 30 episodes of my life reflects the pattern and unity of all lives.

Everyone has different careers, episodes, pairs of opposites and nodal points, but the underlying principle of these is present in all lives. All lives obey the $+A + -A = 0$ of the pairs of opposites and nodal points. Human beings from all the different walks of life – scientists, mathematicians, engineers – can find a similar pattern in their own lives. They have all transformed themselves in some way. Their early efforts have contributed to how they have ended up: what we sow we reap. They have all been on a quest for knowledge of some sort. This may have resulted in their acquiring practical skills which have earned their living, or positions of management responsibility, but the same principles apply to their pattern as apply to mine. Some pursue active living and self-transformation, others live within the social ego and lack self-transformation. The archetypal pattern of human lives is of progress to a unitive vision, which is ahead of everyone even though many opt not to follow it. Lives led for purpose and achievement and lives led for hedonistic enjoyment have the same structure, pattern and unity. They are all a succession of episodes with pairs of opposites and nodal points. Each life has its own pattern whose structure is recognisably similar – indeed, identical – to the pattern of others just as the structure of a spruce cone is identical to the structure of all other spruce cones. All human beings therefore have double lives.

The structure, pattern and unity of the double life of all human beings is a double spiral, a double helix, pairs of opposites which contain nodal points.

Free will, chance and Providence in all double lives

As the expanding universe is surrounded by the infinite and has a law of order, and the Light conveys spiritual powers, it is possible that we each have a pre-ordained task that is contained in our genes at birth, and that we have to find our rightful path in the experiences we encounter in this dark wood. If so, we can speak of destiny, a pre-determined, or pre-allotted task. It may be that our paths are not chosen by accident, but by our free will which is driven by an instinctive knowledge of what path we aim to be on to fulfil our destiny. The concept of destiny is credible because the infinite surrounds our shuttlecock-shaped universe.

Do we have a pre-ordained, pre-determined or pre-allotted task to fulfil on earth, a destiny? Are the paths of our lives chosen by accident – by chance – or by our free will? Do we have an instinctive knowledge of the Providential path we should follow to fulfil our destiny?

My Double Life shows that free will and chance both have a part in our +A + −A = 0, and may be reconciled in an underlying Providential destiny (0). I chose some events and some events happened by chance, accident and coincidence. Similarly I chose the opposites in some episodes. But some events and episodes happened to me or were chosen for me (for example my study of Law). And some events – for example my attending Oaklands as a boy and then owning it for more than 30 years while I wrote my 40 books – seem to point to a Providential destiny. My works – which grew beneath my episodes like the seeds beneath the scales of a spruce cone – seem to fulfil a Providential destiny. There seems to be a Providential aspect to my double life. Unlike the ego, which is buffeted by accident, the soul seems to be guided by destiny. We have a path and our free will may make choices to keep us on our predestined path.

As it was for me, so it is for all humankind. All have double lives and are on a journey, whether or not they recognise it, and have conflicts within each episode. All are a mixture of choosing some events (+A) and of having some events happen to them by chance, accident or coincidence (−A). If there has been an underlying Providential destiny (0) behind my double life, then the same must be true of the double lives of all other human beings.

Rainbow over the hills: visible and invisible rainbow in all double lives

I have said that I emerged from dark post-imperial England into the sunshine of a universal vision of all nations, that I moved beyond nationhood to a Universalist perspective. And it is with this vision that I want to close my book.

My double life was, in one sense, a progression, a development, a transformation from a view of post-imperial nationhood to a view of the world and the universe that now embraces all humankind: the new outlook of a future time to which, after years of observation, study and reflection, I have with some difficulty given birth. All double lives have progressed from nationhood to this Universalist perspective in their own ways. The rainbow is above all a Universalist symbol.

As if sensing that I might have a Providential destiny, on my christening the artist Gwen Broad (a mystic in her own right) wrote to me, "May the eventide have just sufficient clouds to make a glorious sunset!" Her wish, beautifully expressed, conjured the prospect of a life of achievement deepened by suffering and a serene eventide that will slowly fade and disappear for ever.

Now that I am in my eventide I have a different perspective. I think of my illumined works that, from time to time, shine out over the hills like a rainbow and remind all of the vision of unity in which seven disciplines are banded together by metaphysical experience. During my double life my rainbow was permanently present though mostly invisible, and occasionally bestrode the hills in public view. I expect my rainbow to continue to come and go.

As I stood on the green ride on the sloping crater the rainbow gathered and manifested in the still air and I was pleased I had completed my unifying work. I knew the rainbow that had hung above my double life and reconciled and united my opposites was a *universal* rainbow that hangs above *all* double lives and reconciles and unites *their* opposites. It proclaims that all opposites are reconciled and that all double lives are therefore unified lives in harmony with the One.

The rainbow shone out over the hills calling all to achieve and all double lives to a vision of unity. It proclaimed the union of rain and sun, suffering and joy, the ephemeral and the infinite, time and eternity. It straddled the natural world and unified the seven hills of achievement. My soul leapt as if greeting its faintly-remembered invisible home.

The rainbow gleamed and all looked up in wonder from the hills in which they toiled. The iridescent rainbow straddled the hills, joined earth and heaven and called all souls to admire its beauty and reflect it in their lives: shimmer with unifying Light, glisten from their dewy Paradise and shine the wisdom of the One into the contradictory world.

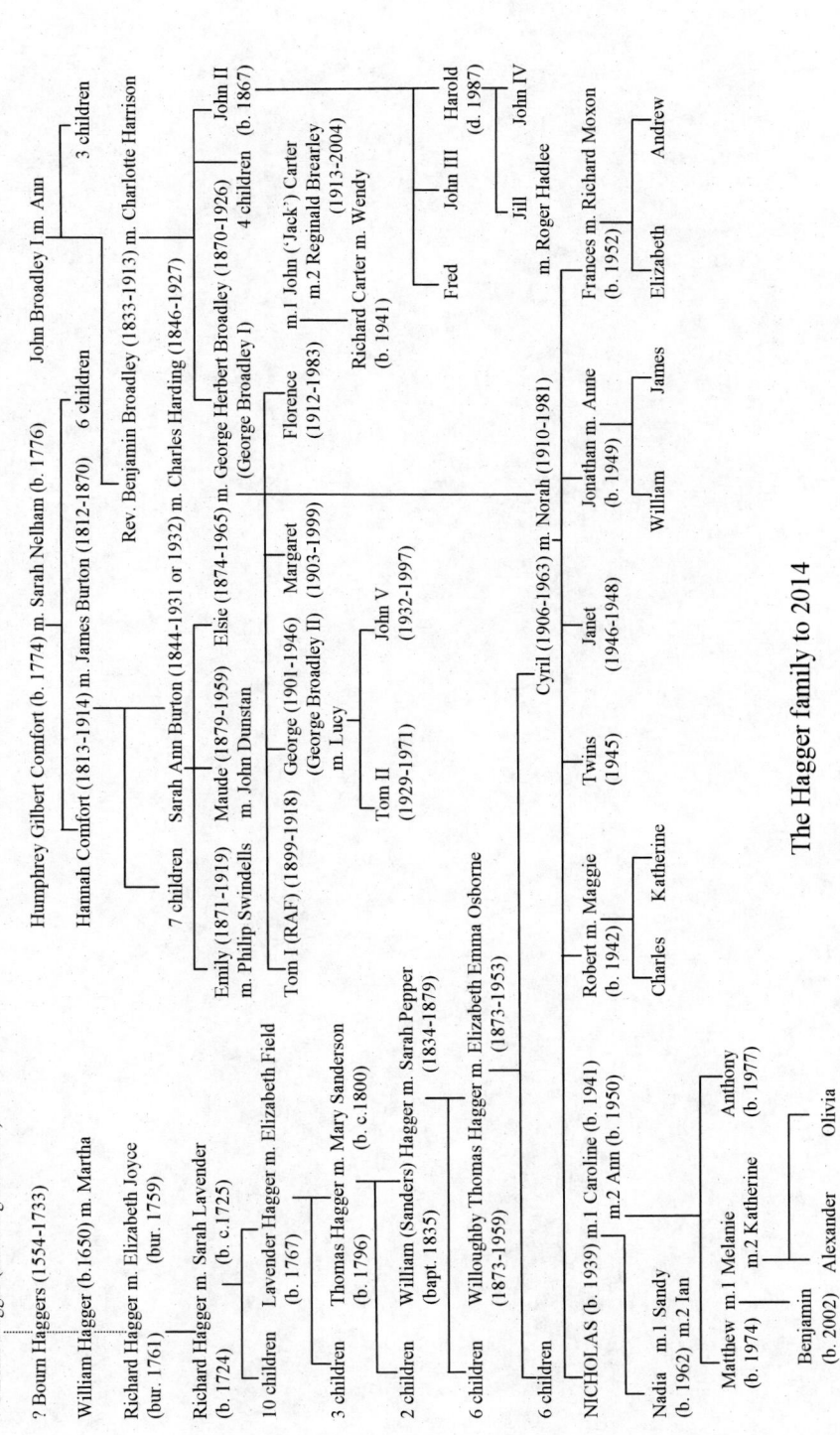

The Hagger family to 2014

Timeline

List of dates of key events in Nicholas Hagger's life
referred to in *My Double Life 2: A Rainbow over the Hills*

29 Apr 1972–12 May 1979	Dark Night of the Spirit: new powers.
31 Aug 1973	Leaves Riverway School.
1 Sep 1973–31 Aug 1974	Second-in-command in the English Department, Henry Thornton School.
24, 28–29 Oct 1973	Writes 'In Marvell's Garden, at Nun Appleton', reworked in 1980 as 'A Metaphysical in Marvell's Garden'.
24 Dec 1973	Agrees sale of 9 Crescent View, Loughton to tenant.
1974–1975	Writes *Visions near the Gates of Paradise*.
22 Feb 1974	Marriage to Ann.
20 Mar 1974	Moves out of newly-sold flat 6 in 33 Stanhope Gardens.
4 Apr 1974	Moves into newly-purchased flat 5 in 10 Brechin Place.
1 Sep 1974–31 Dec 1985	Head of English and Senior Teacher, Garratt Green School.
3 Oct 1974	Birth of Matthew.
27 Oct 1975	Matthew's christening.
1976–1979	Writes *Whispers from the West*.
6–7 Nov 1976	Writes 'The European Resurgence'.
24 Nov 1976	Tells Margaret Thatcher face-to-face in the Waldorf Hotel that East-European nations should be liberated from the Soviet Union.
4 Feb 1977	Moves to 100A Stapleton Road.
5 Apr 1977	Dinner with Philby's son-in-law, Donald Maclean's son.
26 Apr 1977	Birth of Anthony.
25 Sep 1977	Anthony's christening, Miss Lord offers Oaklands School.
undated 13–26 Nov 1977	Attends poetry reading by David Gascoyne and Kathleen Raine with Frank Tuohy.
25 Apr 1978	Moves out of newly-sold flat in 10 Brechin Place.
15 Aug 1978	Moves into newly-purchased 46 Ritherdon Road.
undated 25–30 Sep 1978	Encounters Colin Wilson.
7, 20 Oct 1978	Asa Briggs urges the writing of this account.
18–20 Feb 1979	Christopher Ricks considers as Metaphysical poet.

13 May 1979–31 Oct 1981	Third Mystic Life.
24 Aug 1979	Idea of *The Fire and the Stones* received in sleep.
Oct 1979–Apr 1980	Revises Elegies for *The Fire-Flower*.
Sep 1980–Jul 1981	Discussions with Tom Dyer, Brain of Britain.
1981–1985	Writes *A Rainbow in the Spray*.
14 Apr 1981	Miss Lord agrees to sell Oaklands School.
1 Nov 1981–7 Apr 1990	Dark Night of the Spirit: ordeals.
1 May 1982	Christopher Ricks considers as Romantic poet.
1 Sep 1982	Principal of Oaklands School, with Ann as Headmistress.
17–29 Oct 1982	Christopher Ricks considers as Baroque poet.
1 Nov 1982	Death of mother.
12 Feb 1983	ILEA inspectors ban marking.
Apr–Jun 1983	Sells 46 Ritherdon Road to Norman Rodway.
11 Nov 1983	Explains FREE (Freedom for the Republics of Eastern Europe) to Lord Whitelaw.
12 Nov 1983–May 1984	FREE.
21, 22 Feb 1984	Meets Brian Crozier and Josef Josten through John Biggs-Davison.
Mar 1984	Miners' strike begins.
4 Jun 1984	Diagnosed with bronchiectasis.
15 Jun–2 Jul 1984	Subversion of FREE by Josten.
12 Jul 1984	Receives material on Scargill.
18–19 Jul 1984	Writes article on the miners' strike for *The Times* at the invitation of the Editor, Charlie Douglas-Home.
29 Jul–11 Aug 1984	Visit to Lake District and Scotland.
9 Aug 1984	Josten blocks article.
22–23 Sep 1984	Writes *Scargill the Stalinist?*
12 Oct 1984	Brighton bomb injures Tebbit.
15 Nov 1984	Scargill at Soviet Embassy.
23 Nov 1984	Invited to meet Peter Walker, Secretary of State for Energy.
29 Nov 1984	Launch of *Scargill the Stalinist?*
13 Dec 1984	NUM sit-in in Foyles.
Feb 1985	Founding of the 'Heroes of the West'.
22–26 Feb, 11 May, 14 June, 19–30 July 1985	Visits to France.
3 Mar 1985	End of miners' strike.
15–29 Apr 1985	Five neo-Baroque Universalist poems.
12 Aug 1985	Idea for *The Fire and the Stones* again received in sleep.
12 Aug 1985	Death of John Cameron.

11–13 October 1985	Visit to Frankfurt.
29 Oct 1985	Death of Charlie Douglas-Home.
29 Nov 1985	Death of Josten.
Dec 1985	Voluntary severance from ILEA.
1986–1988	Writes *Question Mark over the West*.
27 Feb 1986	Meets Lord Whitelaw.
24 Mar, 7 May 1986	Meetings at Swiss Cottage Holiday Inn, operation to eliminate Gaddafi's missiles near Sebha.
14 Apr 1986	News of operation to eliminate Gaddafi's missiles near Sebha.
30 Apr 1986	Meets Lord Whitelaw in Lord Privy Seal's Council office about Victor, Lord Rothschild and terrorism. Recommendations photocopied.
5 May 1986	Thatcher uses Recommendations to end Soviet terrorism at Tokyo Summit, 4–6 May 1986.
1 Jul 1986	Launch of McForan's *The World Held Hostage*.
8–16 Jul 1986	Norris McWhirter's investigation.
1–7 Aug 1986	Tour of Europe.
2 Sep 1986	Launch of Tomlin's *Philosophers of East and West*.
1–5 Oct 1986	Visit to Frankfurt.
21 Oct 1986	News of Krassó's petition for democracy in Eastern Europe, inspired by FREE.
4 Nov 1986	Launch of Gorka's *Budapest Betrayed*, broadcast behind Iron Curtain and challenge to Soviet sphere of influence agreed at 1943 Tehran Conference.
7 Dec 1986–11 May 1989	Writes *The Fire and the Stones*.
21 Jan 1987	At 10 Downing Street.
22 Jul, 7 Aug 1987	Asked to export satellite dishes behind the Iron Curtain.
31 Jul–4 Aug 1987	Visit to Denmark.
7–11 Oct 1987	Visit to Frankfurt.
15 Dec 1987	Acquires Harbour-master's House, Charlestown.
16 Jan, 25 Feb 1988	Death and memorial service of Tomlin.
26 Jan 1988	Kathleen Raine consults about obituary.
17 Feb 1988	Suspected TIA.
26 Feb 1988	Declines to be considered to replace Biggs-Davison as MP.
17 Sep, 4 Nov 1988	Death and memorial service of John Biggs-Davison.
26 Sep 1988	Eliot's centenary service, meets Laurens van der Post.
3 Nov 1988–9 Mar 1989	Founds Coopersale Hall School.
19 Apr 1989	Coopersale Hall School opens.

2 Jun 1989–6 Oct 1990	Writes *Selected Poems: A Metaphysical's Way of Fire*.
7 Sep 1989	Full opening of Coopersale Hall School.
1 Sep 1989–31 May 1994	Steve Norris MP lives at Coopersale Hall School as tenant.
28 Oct 1989	Visit to Laurens van der Post.
28 Oct 1989, 13, 21 Sep 1990	Visits to Kathleen Raine.
1990–1992	Building of Coopersale Hall extension.
Feb 1990	Gorka becomes Coopersale Hall School's architect.
8 Apr 1990–6 Dec 1993	Fourth Mystic Life.
23–30 Apr 1990	Visit to Hungary.
9 Jul 1990	Lord Tebbit formally opens Coopersale Hall School.
10 Aug 1990	Visit to Kathleen Raine.
7–9 Dec 1990	Visit to Prague.
27 Mar 1991	Death of David Bohm.
22 Apr 1991	Launch of *The Fire and the Stones* and *Selected Poems, A Metaphysical's Way of Fire*. Speakers Asa Briggs, Kathleen Raine, David Gascoyne.
1, 12 May 1991	Asked to lecture at *Temenos* Academy by Kathleen Raine.
8 May 1991–17 Aug 1992	Writes *Awakening to the Light*.
31 May 1991	Break with Kathleen Raine.
6, 14, 22 Aug, 22 Oct, 18, 20 Dec 1991	Visits to Colin Wilson.
27 Sep, 2 Oct 1991	Establishes Foundation of the Light.
9–12 Oct 1991	Visit to Frankfurt.
31 Dec 1991–9 Sep 1992	Writes *The Universe and the Light*.
27 Mar 1992	Visit to David Bohm.
10 Apr 1992	Winchester lecture, 'The Nature of Light'.
14 Apr 1992	Visit to Colin Wilson.
9, 17 May, 7, 14, 21 Jun 1992	Mystery school.
31 Aug 1992–30 Dec 1993	Writes *A Mystic Way*.
1–5 Sep 1992	Conference on reductionism at Jesus College, Cambridge.
4 Sep 1992	Form from Movement Theory drafted in Jesus College's hall.
2 Jan 1993	Death of Miss Lord.
9–10 Jan 1993	Global Deception Conference, meets Eustace Mullins.
27 Jan 1993	Meets Christopher Ricks.
27 Jan 1993–2 Feb 1994	Assembles *Collected Poems: A White Radiance*.
7, 10, 13 Apr 1993	Visits to Colin Wilson.

14 Apr 1993	Visit to Frank Tuohy.
16–18 Apr 1993	Addresses Quaker Universalists in Birmingham.
27 Apr 1993	Metaphysical Research Group retitled Universalist Group of Philosophers.
29 Apr–4 May 1993	Conference on Ficino in Florence.
3 May 1993	'Sees' finished *Overlord* and *Classical Odes* in Pisa.
21 Jun 1993	Decision to use blank verse for *Overlord*, made with Christopher Ricks.
8–29 Jul 1993	Visit to USA.
5 Aug 1993	Nadia's marriage.
18 Aug 1993	Last visit to Colin Wilson.
6 Dec 1993	Metaphysical Centre opens.
7 Dec 1993 to date	Unitive Life.
1994–2004	Writes *A Dandelion Clock*.
7 Feb–14 April 1994	Assembles *Awakening to the Light*.
27 Feb, 16 Apr 1994	Visits to Mary Seal.
14 May 1994–10 Jan 1995	Assembles *A Spade Fresh with Mud*.
28 May–4 Jun 1994	Visit to France.
2 Jun 1994–23 Nov 1996	Writes *Overlord*.
2 Jun 1994–17 Feb 1995	Writes *Overlord* books 1 and 2.
18 Jul–1 Aug 1994	Tour of Europe.
26 Jul 1994–3 Mar 2005	Writes classical odes.
1–31 Aug 1994	Writes *The Warlords*.
6–9 Oct 1994	Visit to Germany.
15 Oct 1994	Lecture on Intuitionist Universalism at Regent's College.
15 Oct 1994	Break with philosophers.
8 Feb–17 Mar 1995	Assembles *A Smell of Leaves and Summer*.
31 Mar–6 Apr 1995	Tour of Germany.
10 Apr–27 Sep 1995	Writes *Overlord* books 3–6.
27 Apr–1 May 1995	Tour of Europe.
18 May 1995	Lecture on Universalism at Alister Hardy Research Centre.
26 May 1995	Purchases The Bell, Great Easton.
14–25 Jul 1995	Tour of Turkey and Greece.
22 Jul 1995	Sees undecomposed body of St Gerasimos in Kefalonia.
25 Sep 1995	Steve Norris reveals he is discontinuing as MP.
14–21 Oct 1995	Tour of Bay of Naples.
24–28 Oct 1995	Tour of Russia and Crimea.
13 Jan–4 Jun 1996	Writes *Overlord* books 7-9.
4 May 1996	Visit to Svetlana Stalin.

24–26 May 1996	Visit to Hay-on-Wye
25 May 1996	Meets Charles Beauclerk, Earl of Burford.
6 Jun, 1 Jul 1996	Death and memorial service of Mabel Reid.
15 Jun–23 Nov 1996	Writes *Overlord* books 10–12.
12–27 Jul 1996	Tour of Greece and Turkey.
9–12, 19 Sep 1996	Acquires Normanhurst School, forms the Oak-Tree Group of Schools (Oaklands, Coopersale Hall and Normanhurst).
24–26 Sep 1996	Visit to Rome.
20 Jan 1997–7 Oct 1998	Assembles *The One and the Many*.
24 Jan 1997	Acquires Otley Hall.
6 Jul 1997	Opens Otley village fête.
18 Jul 1997–17 Feb 1998	Assembles *Wheeling Bats and a Harvest Moon*.
3 Aug 1997–22 Mar 1998	Writes screenplay, *Gosnold's Hope* (retitled *The Founding of America*).
3 Oct 1997	Lecture at Aldeburgh, 'Revolution in Thought and Culture'.
10 Nov 1997	Death of Ann's mother.
24 Jan 1998	Meets Mark Rylance at the Globe.
28 Jan 1998	Lecture on 'The Garden of the One', Cambridge.
28 Jan 1998	Visit to Bourn Hall, seat of the Haggers.
5, 18 Feb 1998	Death and funeral of Argie.
9 Mar 1998	Charles Beauclerk becomes Literary Secretary.
3 Apr–28 Jun 1998	Writes *The Tragedy of Prince Tudor*.
24–25 April 1998	Globe cast of *As You Like It* stay and rehearse at Otley Hall.
28–30 Apr 1998	Globe cast of *Julius Caesar* stay and rehearse at Otley Hall.
15–31 May 1998	Becomes a trustee of SAT, houses Shakespearean Authorship Trust library.
4 Jul 1998	Opens Otley village fête.
20–24 Jul 1998	Visit to Venice.
27 Jul–23 Nov 1998	Assembles *The Warm Glow of the Monastery Courtyard*.
4–28 Aug 1998	Assembles reduced version of *The Warlords*.
9–21 Oct 1998	Tour of USA's east coast.
15 Oct 1998	Lecture on Bartholomew Gosnold in Richmond, Virginia.
29 Oct 1998	Mark Rylance lunches at Otley Hall.
Nov 1998	Lord Tebbit distributes Normanhurst prizes.
9 Dec 1998	Questions Martin Taylor about earth-dollar.
13 Dec 1998–3 April 1999	Writes *Ovid Banished*.

29 Mar, 24 Apr 1999– 9 Jun 2000	Writes *The Rise of Oliver Cromwell*.
30 Jun 1999–29 Mar 2000	Writes *The Secret History of the West*.
13 Jul 1999	Tony Little, later Head Master of Eton, distributes Oaklands prizes.
17–20 Jul 1999	Tour of Cathar France.
26 Oct 1999	Charles Beauclerk, the Earl of Burford, leaps onto the woolsack in the Lords.
2000–2005	Writes *Summoned by Truth*.
12–14 Apr 2000	Globe cast of *The Tempest* including Vanessa Redgrave stay and rehearse at Otley Hall.
14–21 Apr 2000	Tour of Iceland.
26–28 Apr 2000	Globe cast of *Hamlet* stay and rehearse at Otley Hall.
28 Apr 2000	Charles Beauclerk leaves Otley Hall.
1 Jul 2000	Opens fête at Bourn Hall.
14–20 Jul 2000	Tour of Sicily.
5 Aug 2000	Matthew's marriage to Melanie.
28 Sep–5 Oct 2000	Visit to Turin and Rome.
19 Nov 2000	Patricia Cornwell lunches at Otley Hall.
13–15 Feb 2001	Visit to Lisbon.
14 Mar 2001	Jamestown deputation to twin with Ipswich lunch at Otley Hall.
30 Mar–6 Apr 2001	Visit to Spain.
2 May 2001	Virginia's First Lady and twinning deputation at Christchurch Mansion and Otley Hall.
2 May 2001	Visits US Embassy and Governor Gilmore.
6–20 May 2001	Mediterranean cruise.
10–12 May 2001	Revisits Libya.
Jul 2001	Matthew Hagger becomes Managing Principal of Oak-Tree Group of Schools.
12 Jul 2001	Birth of Ben, first grandson.
6 Sep 2001	With "thirty-four generationed" Lord Tollemache at Helmingham Hall.
24 Nov 2001	Iain Duncan Smith MP distributes Normanhurst prizes.
7 Feb 2002	Lord Braybrooke shows Cornwallis's surrender sword over lunch.
23–28 Mar 2002	Visit to Cyprus.
21–24 Jun 2002	Visit to Heidelberg and Freiburg, Heidegger and Husserl places, with Christopher Macann.
9–23 Nov 2002	Visit to China.

6 Feb 2003	Kelso claims to have discovered Bartholomew Gosnold's skeleton in Jamestown Fort.
28 Feb 2003	Acquires Connaught House.
17 Oct 2003	Iain Duncan Smith MP opens new block at Normanhurst School.
11 Nov 2003	Meets John Hunt.
17–22 Nov 2003	Visit to Gran Canaria.
Jan–Mar 2004	Assembles *The Syndicate*.
Jul–Nov 2004	Assembles *The Secret History of the West*.
15 Jul 2004	Sells Otley Hall.
2–4 Aug 2004	Visit to Scilly Isles.
Aug 2004	Works on first two of trilogy of novellas.
Oct 2004–19 Aug 2005	Assembles *The Rise and Fall of Civilizations*.
Nov 2004–15 Dec 2005	Assembles *Collected Poems 1958–2005*.
30 Nov–2 Dec 2004	Visit to Brussels.
1 Jan 2005–16 July 2005	Assembles *The Light of Civilization*.
31 Jan–8 Feb 2005	Visit to Egypt.
9 Feb–30 Apr 2005	Assembles *Classical Odes*.
20 Feb, 9 May, 20 Nov 2005	Attends Christopher Ricks's Professor-of-Poetry lectures at Oxford.
23 Feb 2005	Leaves the Shakespearean Authorship Trust.
13 Jun 2005	Kelso digs up Shelley church for Gosnold DNA.
9, 26 Sep 2005	Death and funeral of John Silberrad.
19 Dec 2005–18 May 2006	Writes *The Secret Founding of America*.
4 Dec 2005	Addresses Harry Beckhough's intelligence group.
15 Jan–27 Apr 2006	Assembles *Collected Verse Plays*.
27 Apr 2006	Lyme disease suspected.
5 May–5 Jun 2006	Assembles one-volume *Overlord*.
21 Jul–13 Oct 2006	Assembles *Collected Stories*.
12–14 Aug 2006	Visit to Dartmoor.
18 Feb 2007	Sells The Bell.
13–20 Jan 2007	Visit to Iran.
23 Jan–16 Feb 2007	Writes *The Last Tourist in Iran*.
Jan–Aug 2007, May 2008	Works on trilogy of novellas.
8–11 Mar 2007	Visit to Vienna.
9, 17 Apr 2007	Death and funeral of Ricky Herbert.
8 May–15 Jul 2007	25 radio broadcasts to USA.
14 May 2007	Attends Christopher Ricks's Professor-of-Poetry lecture at Oxford.
23 Jul–11 Aug 2007	Visit to Galapagos Islands and Peru.
27 Aug–4 Nov, 27 Nov 2007–1 May 2008	Writes *The New Philosophy of Universalism*.

5–26 Nov 2007	Visit to Argentina, Falkland Islands, South Georgia and Antarctica.
16 Dec 2007	Ken Campbell's 'School of Night' actors read *The Warlords*.
22 Mar 2008	Matthew's marriage to Kate.
22 May–5 Sep 2008, 21 Jan–22 Jul 2009	Writes *Armageddon*.
12 May, 24 Nov 2008	Attends Christopher Ricks's Professor-of-Poetry lectures at Oxford.
14 May 2008	Visit to Wilton House.
15 Jun 2008	Tony Hagger, Young Filmmaker of the Year.
10 Jul 2008	Nadia's marriage to Ian.
20–25 Jul 2008	Stays at Tennyson's Farringford.
26–28 Aug 2008	Visit to Totnes.
31 Aug, 8 Sep 2008	Death and funeral of Ken Campbell.
21 Sep–18 Dec 2008	Writes *The Revolution That Didn't Happen*.
1 Sep 2008–5 Feb 2009	Writes *The Libyan Revolution*.
28 Jan 2009	Eric Galati reads from *Overlord* in London.
6–8 Feb 2009	Visit to Paris, recital in Saint-Sulpice.
26 Feb–1 Mar 2009	Visit to North Norway.
28 Feb 2009	Sees Northern Lights.
1 Apr 2009	Birth of Alex, second grandson.
3 May 2009	Coopersale Hall School's 20th anniversary.
11 May 2009	Attends Christopher Ricks's Professor-of-Poetry lecture at Oxford.
24 May 2009	Revisits Otley Hall.
23–26 Jul 2009	Visit to Eastbourne.
17 Aug–23 Nov 2009	Writes *The World Government*.
3 Dec 2009–19 Apr 2010	Writes *The Secret American Dream*.
20 May 2010	Sees the sundial at Copped Hall.
18–19 Jul 2010	Ann's 60th birthday at Le Manoir aux Quat'Saisons.
22 Jul 2010–31 Mar 2011	Writes *A New Philosophy of Literature*.
26 Aug–10 Sep 2010	Mediterranean cruise, encounters Peter O'Toole.
11 Dec 2010, 6 Jan 2011	Death and funeral of John Ezard.
9 Feb 2011	Birth of Olivia, first granddaughter.
21 Mar 2011	Interviewed on Gaddafi by Adam Boulton.
13–26 Apr 2011	Assembles *Selected Stories: Follies and Vices of the Modern Elizabethan Age*.
19 Apr 2011	Lecture on *The New Philosophy of Universalism* for internet.
4 May–8 Nov 2011	Writes *A View of Epping Forest*.
1–4 Jul 2011	Visit to Hadrian's Wall.

19–21 Aug 2011	Visit to Gidleigh Park.
31 Aug–3 Sep 2011	Visit to Isle of Man.
30 Nov 2011	Rod Stewart opens new building at Coopersale Hall School.
14 Jan–14 Aug 2012	Writes *My Double Life 1: This Dark Wood*.
7 Mar 2012	Receives *The Victoria and the Triton* from Ricks.
1 Jul 2012	Oaklands 75th anniversary, Haggers' 30th anniversary at Oak-Tree Group of Schools.
19 Aug 2012–7 Sep 2013	Writes *My Double Life 2: A Rainbow over the Hills*.
7 September–27 Oct 2012	Assembles *Selected Poems: Quest for the One*.
20 Feb–13 Mar 2013	Visit to India, Sri Lanka and Arabia.
22–23 May 2013	Visit to the Grove before Bilderberg Group meeting.
Apr 2014	25th anniversary of Coopersale Hall School.
22 May 2014	75th birthday.

APPENDIX

1

Light

77 experiences of the metaphysical Light or Fire, 2 Mystic Lives, a Dark Night, Unitive Life: with interconnected visions, surges, sleep inspiration and Oneness ('showings') in *My Double Life 2: A Rainbow over the Hills*

Page	Date	Experience
		Dark Night of the Spirit, new powers: 29 April 1972–12 May 1979
12	24 Jan 1974	Fire and vision: great fire in a grate.
12	27 Jan 1974	Blue Light.
21	4 Aug 1974	Experiences the Oneness of the universe in the fusion of clouds and ground in Earl's Path pond on Strawberry Hill.
22–23	28 Aug 1974	Light.
25	13 Oct 1974	Blue Light.
28	1 Dec 1974	Blue Light.
30	2 Mar 1975	Sleep inspiration: vision of ecumenical unity, union of sects and religions, religious Universalism.
31	9 Mar 1975	Blue Light.
32	11 May 1975	Blue Light.
44	21 Dec 1975	Blue Light.
45	18 Apr 1976	Light and rose Light.
47	30 May 1976	Red Light, "the other day" for second time.
53	16 Oct 1976	Visions "two nights ago": fine old masters, patterns, richly-domed Cathedral (Heaven).
54	5 May 1976	Surge.
58	4 May 1977	Blue Light.
62	1, 2, 3, 4, 5, 6, 7 Aug 1977	Surges (healing).
63	13 Aug 1977	Light and visions: glimmerings, celestial curtain, the star, the dawning (Light), imagination: carpet full of colours, perfect pattern, stained-glass window, red saint, cloud over a sun.
65	12 Oct 1977	Blue Light.
65	27 Oct 1977	Gold Light, visions: Kandinsky scrivenings (*sic*), floating through patterns towards a sunrise, golden 'cauliflower', gold light with a gold coin of an emperor on it, beautiful Tibetan-like monsters.

70	14 May 1978	Light.
72	11 Jul 1978	Light and surges (healing).
78	18 Oct 1978	Light: blue diamond.

Third Mystic Life: 13 May 1979–31 October 1981

83	13 May 1979	Light.
84	12 Jul 1979	Surges (healing).
86	24 Aug 1979	Sleep inspiration: idea of *The Fire and the Stones*, civilizations as 'Light-bearers', first metaphysical, then secular.
88	23 Dec 1979	Surges (healing).
91	29 Jan 1980	Silver Light, also Fire, also surges (healing).
93	30 Mar 1980	Light, also Fire.
95	2 Jul 1980	Blue Light and vision: elaborate blue light with sparkling 'beads' across it, heavenly vision.
107	10 May 1981	Light.
108	31 May 1981	Golden Light, rose Light, also Fire.
112	21 Aug 1981	Sleep inspiration: two images, crab-pots and lighthouse.
114	31 Oct 1981	Surge (healing).

Dark Night of the Spirit, ordeals: 1 November 1981–7 April 1990

126	25 Aug 1982	Light.
136	6 Aug 1983	Sleep inspiration: poem, 12 stanzas of 'Night Visions in Charlestown'.
138	11 Aug 1983	Sleep inspiration: poem, 'Crab-Fishing on a Boundless Deep'.
144	31 Dec 1983	Light.
161	7 Aug 1984	Light.
185	30 Mar 1985	'Heard' 12 seconds of an unwritten majestic symphony.
189–190	16 Apr 1985	Light. 'Saw' art exhibition.
195	3 Jun 1985	Surge (healing).
200	12 Aug 1985	Light, sleep inspiration: idea for a book showing that the Light makes civilizations grow (reinforcing idea of *The Fire and the Stones*).
260–261	7 Dec 1986	Fire and surges.
263	Undated 22–26 Mar 1987	Surges (healing).
264	4 Apr 1987	Fire.
277	28 Feb 1988	Sleep inspiration: problem of Israelite civilization's expansion solved in sleep.

281	11 Dec 1987	Light.
281	13 Dec 1987	Light and Fire.
297	29 Apr 1989	Sleep inspiration: beginning of 'Introduction to the New Universalism', and therefore Universalism, received in sleep.

Fourth Mystic Life: 8 April 1990–6 December 1993

317	8 Apr 1990	Light.
317	9 Apr 1990	Light.
317	10 Apr 1990	Light.
317	11 Apr 1990	Light (and surge).
317	12 Apr 1990	Surge.
331	14 Nov 1990	Light.
334	19 Dec 1990	Light (and surges).
334	24 Dec 1990	Light (and surges).
341	5 Apr 1991	Fire.
341	6 Apr 1991	Light (and surges).
341–342	7 Apr 1991	Light.
343	20 Apr 1991	Light.
346	6 May 1991	Fire (and surges).
351	25 Jun 1991	Light.
363	2 Sep 1991	Sleep inspiration: a dream showing 20–30 lines of 'Reflection and Reality: Peak Experiences and Tidal Consciousness', Shadow on the clouds.
367	11 Dec 1991	Light.
368	26 Sep 1991	Sleep inspiration: a haunting dream, large face of Orpheus, tall as orchard trees, with dozens of green apples in front of it (perhaps symbolising poems).
373	13 Nov 1991	Light.
375	28 Nov 1991	Light.
383	3 Feb 1992	Light.
387	7 Apr 1992	Sleep inspiration: idea that the Light is a fifth, expanding force and responsible for early inflation.
386–387	25 Jan 1992	Sleep inspiration: a long dream, watching John Major, computer, date of early UK general election on 9 April 1992, red line moved: growth! Prime Minister Major benefiting from growth. Prophesies Major's 1992 election victory.
394	1 May 1992	Light.
396	9 May 1992	Light.
396	13 May 1992	Light.
397	17 May 1992	Light (healing).

403	21 Jun 1992	Light.
408	20 Jul 1992	Light (and surge).
416	9 Sep 1992	Surges (healing).
430	9 Dec 1992	Light.
431	2 Jan 1993	Light.
435	9 Feb 1993	Sleep inspiration: idea that Hitler was an Illuminatist.
435	11 Feb 1993	Light.
436	23 Feb 1993	Light.
439	3 Apr 1993	Light.
439	5 Apr 1993	Light.
445	17 Apr 1993	Light.
450	2 May 1993	Light.
451	3 May 1993	Revelation/vision in Pisa: 'saw' two vast finished works – *Overlord* and *Classical Odes* (not yet written) – in ten seconds.
455	2 Jun 1993	Light.
460	11 Jul 1993	Sleep inspiration: two American Liberty Quintets, 'New York' and 'Boston'.
463	9 Aug 1993	Light.
467	20 Sep 1993	Light (and surges).
469	8 Oct 1993	Light.
473	2 Nov 1993	Light.
477	4 Dec 1993	Light (and surges).
478	6 Dec 1993	Light.

Unitive Life: 7 December 1993 to date

513	31 Mar 1995	Light.
527	29 Feb 1996	Light.
599	11 Feb 1999	Light (and surges).
692	16 Oct 2003	Light.
712	24 Jan 2005	Sleep inspiration: title of *Summoned by Truth*.
742	18 Jan 2007	Light.
778	21 Jul 2008	Surges.
778	22 Jul 2008	Surges.
779	23 Jul 2008	Surges.
780	24 Jul 2008	Surges.
804	13 Aug 2009	Light (and surges).
806	3 Dec 2009	Sleep inspiration: structure of *The Secret American Dream* to be similar to the structure of *The Secret Founding of America*.
833	11 May 2011	Light.

| 838 | 30 Sep 2011 | Dream: 'saw' Gaddafi's last hiding-place on 20 October, a hole with shallow water. |
| 845 | 17 Mar 2014 | Sleep inspiration: specific details within the Table of Contents in *My Double Life 1* and *2* that needed amending, e.g. order of entries. |

Whole life: extracts from *My Double Life 1* and *2*

Light

93 experiences extracted from Light appendices of *My Double Life 1* and *2*, which show experiences of the Light in both volumes

16 experiences in *My Double Life 1: This Dark Wood*

185	11 Sep 1965	First experience of Light as orb of Fire. Visions: scrivenings in foreign language, corn stalks, whirlpool.
187	11 Oct 1965	Golden Light.
187–188	18 Oct 1965	Round white Light, dazzling like a white sun.
373	10 Sep 1971	Light. Visions: white light, bare winter tree of white fire, flowing, rippling (Flowing Light), white flower like chrysanthemum (Golden Flower), sun, stars, fountain of white light, white point, circle of light.
375–376	11 Sep 1971	Light. Visions: dome of light, yellow and purple tomb, old gold death mask, filigree light, face of God, point of white light, egg, Christ on the cross, devil, saint, crown of thorns, Roman robe, yellow rose, black thorns, child, death-mask, frost, white flower, suns, shafts of light, long white-hot line like trunk of tree.
377–378	12 Sep 1971	Light. Visions: (morning) red flower, streaks of white, red lights, prison gates, egg, face of God, white wheel, white light, yellow mountain range, stars with rings, blob of moon, blobs, thorns with light behind, Greek theatre; (afternoon) golden star, golden rays, silver star.
379	24 Sep 1971	Visions: streaks of white light, golden (white) flower like dahlia.
389–390	21 Nov 1971	Visions: Diamond. Fire, golden glow, laurel wreath.
391	3 Jan 1972	Light. Visions: snowflakes, Saints, Pope's head, monk, altar, Cathedral, white light.
401	3 Apr 1972	Visions: Flowing Light, golden head of Christ, crown of thorns in golden light, Roman effigy of

		God, white sun, two stars, white ageless face.
402	8 Apr 1972	Visions: golden furniture, temple columns, brown statue head, celestial curtain, diamond in luminous blue light (first experience of blue Light), Golden Flower, light flashing up.
403	17 Apr 1972	Visions: possessed, in union with the Light, aglow with the mystic Fire.
403	22 Apr 1972	Visions: pale blue light that blended with dazzling white light like a diamond shining in the sun.
404	28 Apr 1972	Visions: white light with blue tints, hoop of light like sun-halo.
443	3–4 Dec 1972	White light, white sun, dim.
468	31 Jul 1973	Visions: Greek temples, African mask, light nearly breaking.

77 experiences in *My Double Life 2: A Rainbow over the Hills*

12	24 Jan 1974	Fire and vision: great fire in a grate.
12	27 Jan 1974	Blue Light.
22–23	28 Aug 1974	Light.
25	13 Oct 1974	Blue Light.
28	1 Dec 1974	Blue Light.
31	9 Mar 1975	Blue Light.
32	11 May 1975	Blue Light.
44	21 Dec 1975	Blue Light.
45	18 Apr 1976	Light and rose Light.
47	30 May 1976	Red Light, "the other day" for second time.
58	4 May 1977	Blue Light.
63	13 Aug 1977	Light and visions: glimmerings, celestial curtain, the star, the dawning (Light), imagination: carpet full of colours, perfect pattern, stained-glass window, red saint, cloud over a sun.
65	12 Oct 1977	Blue Light.
65	27 Oct 1977	Gold Light, visions: Kandinsky scrivenings (*sic*) , floating through patterns towards a sunrise, golden 'cauliflower', gold light with a gold coin of an emperor on it, beautiful Tibetan-like monsters.
70	14 May 1978	Light.
72	11 Jul 1978	Light and surges (healing).
78	18 Oct 1978	Light: blue diamond.
83	13 May 1979	Light.
91	29 Jan 1980	Silver Light, also Fire, also surges (healing).
93	30 Mar 1980	Light, also Fire.

95	2 Jul 1980	Blue Light and vision: elaborate blue light with sparkling 'beads' across it, heavenly vision.
107	10 May 1981	Light.
108	31 May 1981	Golden Light, rose Light, also Fire.
126	25 Aug 1982	Light.
144	31 Dec 1983	Light.
161	7 Aug 1984	Light.
189–190	16 Apr 1985	Light.
200	12 Aug 1985	Light, sleep inspiration: idea for a book showing that the Light makes civilizations grow (reinforcing idea of *The Fire and the Stones*).
260–261	7 Dec 1986	Fire and surges.
264	4 Apr 1987	Fire.
281	11 Dec 1987	Light.
281	13 Dec 1987	Light and Fire.
317	8 Apr 1990	Light.
317	9 Apr 1990	Light.
317	10 Apr 1990	Light.
317	11 Apr 1990	Light (and surge).
331	14 Nov 1990	Light.
334	19 Dec 1990	Light (and surges).
334	24 Dec 1990	Light (and surges).
341	5 Apr 1991	Fire.
341	6 Apr 1991	Light (and surges).
341	7 Apr 1991	Light.
343	20 Apr 1991	Light.
346	6 May 1991	Fire (and surges).
351	25 Jun 1991	Light.
367	11 Dec 1991	Light.
373	13 Nov 1991	Light.
375	28 Nov 1991	Light.
383	3 Feb 1992	Light.
394	1 May 1992	Light.
396	9 May 1992	Light.
396	13 May 1992	Light.
397	17 May 1992	Light.
403	21 Jun 1992	Light.
408	20 Jul 1992	Light (and surge).
430	9 Dec 1992	Light.
431	2 Jan 1993	Light.
435	11 Feb 1993	Light.
436	23 Feb 1993	Light.

439	3 Apr 1993	Light.
439	5 Apr 1993	Light.
445	17 Apr 1993	Light.
450	2 May 1993	Light.
455	2 Jun 1993	Light.
463	9 Aug 1993	Light.
467	20 Sep 1993	Light (and surges).
469	8 Oct 1993	Light.
473	2 Nov 1993	Light.
477	4 Dec 1993	Light (and surges).
478	6 Dec 1993	Light.
513	31 Mar 1995	Light.
527	29 Feb 1996	Light.
599	11 Feb 1999	Light (and surges).
692	16 Oct 2003	Light.
742	18 Jan 2007	Light.
804	13 Aug 2009	Light (and surges).
833	11 May 2011	Light.

Sleep inspiration

20 experiences extracted from Light appendices of *My Double Life 1* and *2*, which show Nicholas Hagger received some of his most fundamental ideas (asterisked) in sleep

3 experiences in *My Double Life 1: This Dark Wood*

60	Jun 1954	Sleep inspiration: in a dream 'saw' the 'O' level Greek set-books exam paper with four passages to translate.
142	18 Jan 1962	Inspiration: received 'Life Cycle' on a plane above Ur while sitting with eyes closed, anticipated life cycle of 25 civilizations and universal pattern of life.
185	13 Sep 1965	Sleep inspiration: centre-shift – in a dream 'saw' an earthquake, falling masonry, ruins, corpses dancing.

17 experiences in *My Double Life 2: A Rainbow over the Hills*

30	2 Mar 1975	Sleep inspiration: vision of ecumenical unity, union of sects and religions, religious Universalism.
86	24 Aug 1979	Sleep inspiration: idea of *The Fire and the Stones*, civilizations as 'Light-bearers', first metaphysical, then secular. *
112	21 Aug 1981	Sleep inspiration: two images, crab-pots and light-

		house.
136	6 Aug 1983	Sleep inspiration: poem, 12 stanzas of 'Night Visions in Charlestown'.
138	11 Aug 1983	Sleep inspiration: poem, 'Crab-Fishing on a Boundless Deep'.
200	12 Aug 1985	Light, sleep inspiration: idea for a book showing that the Light makes civilizations grow (reinforcing idea of *The Fire and the Stones*). *
277	28 Feb 1988	Sleep inspiration: problem of Israelite civilization's expansion solved in sleep.
297	29 Apr 1989	Sleep inspiration: beginning of 'Introduction to the New Universalism', and therefore Universalism, received in sleep. *
363	2 Sep 1991	Sleep inspiration: dream showing 20–30 lines of 'Reflection and Reality: Peak Experiences and Tidal Consciousness', Shadow on the clouds.
368	26 Sep 1991	Sleep inspiration: dream, large face of Orpheus, tall as orchard trees, with dozens of green apples in front of it (perhaps symbolising poems). *
386–387	7 Apr 1992	Sleep inspiration: idea that the Light is a fifth, expanding force and responsible for early inflation.
387	25 Jan 1992	Sleep inspiration: received date of UK general election, 9 April 1992 while observing British Prime Minister John Major by a computer showing growth. Prophesies Major's 1992 election victory.
435	9 Feb 1993	Sleep inspiration: idea that Hitler was an Illuminatist.
460	11 Jul 1993	Sleep inspiration: two American Liberty Quintets, 'New York' and 'Boston'.
712	24 Jan 2005	Sleep inspiration: title of *Summoned by Truth*.
806	3 Dec 2009	Sleep inspiration: structure of *The Secret American Dream* to be similar to the structure of *The Secret Founding of America*.
845	17 Mar 2014	Sleep inspiration: specific details within the Table of Contents in *My Double Life 1* and *2* that needed amending, e.g. order of entries.

Experiences of Oneness
6 experiences extracted from Light appendices of *My Double Life 1* and *2*,
which highlight Nicholas Hagger's early awareness of the One

5 experiences in *My Double Life 1: This Dark Wood*

60–61	Jul/Aug 1954	Experiences the Oneness of the universe on Merrow golf course.
92	Mar 1959	Experiences the Oneness of the universe by Worcester College lake.
160–161	13 Nov 1963	Experiences the Oneness of the universe by Strawberry Hill pond.
177	5–6 Jan 1965	Experience of the Oneness of the universe at Kyoto's Ryoanji Stone Garden.
184	11–12 Aug 1965	Second experience of the Oneness of the universe at Kyoto's Ryoanji Stone Garden.

1 experience in *My Double Life 2: A Rainbow over the Hills*

21	4 Aug 1974	Experiences the Oneness of the universe in the fusion of clouds and ground in Earl's Path pond on Strawberry Hill.

Mystic Way behind Works

4 Mystic Lives, Dark Night of the Soul, Dark Night of the Spirit (new powers/ordeals) and Unitive Life extracted from Light appendices of *My Double Life 1* and *2*, which show Nicholas Hagger's Mystic Way as a whole

My Double Life 1: This Dark Wood
First Mystic Life: 20 July 1964–18 October 1965
Dark Night of the Soul: 19 October 1965–2 September 1971
Second Mystic Life: 3 September 1971–28 April 1972
Dark Night of the Spirit, new powers: 29 April 1972–12 May 1979

My Double Life 2: A Rainbow over the Hills
Dark Night of the Spirit, new powers: 29 April 1972–12 May 1979 (continued)
Third Mystic Life: 13 May 1979–31 October 1981
Dark Night of the Spirit, ordeals: 1 November 1981–7 April 1990
Fourth Mystic Life: 8 April 1990–6 December 1993
Unitive Life: 7 December 1993 to date

2

Collected Works

Nicholas Hagger's Collected Works

Literature
Poetry volumes
- *Selected Poems: A Metaphysical's Way of Fire* (1991)
- *Collected Poems: A White Radiance*, 1958–1993 (1994) which includes:
  - A Well of Truth, 1958–1963
  - A Stone Torch-Basket, 1963–1965
  - The Early Education and Making of a Mystic, 1965–1966
  - The Silence, 1965–1966
  - The Wings and the Sword, 1966–1969
  - Old Man in a Circle, 1967
  - The Gates of Hell, 1969–1972
  - The Flight, 1970
  - Bulb in Winter, 1972–1974
  - A Pilgrim in the Garden, 1973–1974
  - The Night-Sea Crossing, 1974
  - Visions Near the Gates of Paradise, 1974–1975
  - The Four Seasons, 1975
  - Lighthouse, 1975
  - The Weed-Garden, 1975
  - The Labyrinth, 1976
  - Whispers from the West, 1976–1979
  - Lady of the Lamp, 1979
  - The Fire-Flower, 1980
  - Beauty and Angelhood, 1981
  - The Wind and the Earth, 1981
  - A Rainbow in the Spray, 1981–1985
  - Question Mark over the West, 1986–1988
  - A Sneeze in the Universe, 1989–1992
  - A Flirtation with the Muse, 1992–1993
  - Sojourns, 1993
  - Angel of Vertical Vision, 1993
- *Collected Poems, 1958–2005* (2006), which includes the above and also:
  - A Dandelion Clock, 1994–2004
  - Summoned by Truth, 2000–2005
  - Sighs of the Muses, 2005

- *Classical Odes*: Poems on England, Europe and a Global Theme, and of Everyday Life in the One, 1994–2005 (2006), which includes:
  - Book One, A Tudor Knot
  - Book Two, In Europe's Ruins
  - Book Three, A Global Sway
  - Book Four, The Western Universe
- *Selected Poems: Quest for the One* (2015)

Epic Poems

- *Overlord: The Triumph of Light*, 1944–1945 (published in four separate volumes 1995–1997)
  - *Overlord*, books 1–2 (1995)
  - *Overlord*, books 3–6 (1996)
  - *Overlord*, books 7–9 (1997)
  - *Overlord*, books 10–12 (1997)
- *Overlord: The Triumph of Light, 1944–1945* (one-volume edition, 2006)
- *Armageddon*: The Triumph of Universal Order, An Epic Poem on the War on Terror and of Holy-War Crusaders (2010)

Verse Plays

- *The Warlords: From D-Day to Berlin, Parts 1 and 2* (1995)
- *The Tragedy of Prince Tudor: A Nightmare* (1999)
- *Collected Verse Plays* (2007), which includes the above and also:
  - *Ovid Banished* (1999)
  - *The Rise of Oliver Cromwell* (2000)
  - *The Warlords*, abridged version of Parts 1 and 2 (2000)

Short Stories

- *A Spade Fresh with Mud, Collected Stories*, volume 1 (1995)
- *A Smell of Leaves and Summer: Collected Stories*, volume 2 (1995)
- *Wheeling Bats and a Harvest Moon: Collected Stories*, volume 3 (1999)
- *The Warm Glow of the Monastery Courtyard: Collected Stories*, volume 4 (1999)
- *Collected Stories: A Thousand and One Mini-Stories or Verbal Paintings* (2007), which includes:
  - *In the Brilliant Autumn Sunshine: Collected Stories*, volume 5 (2007)
- *Selected Stories: Follies and Vices of the Modern Elizabethan Age* (2015)

Autobiographical

- *Awakening to the Light*: Diaries, volume 1, 1958–1967 (1994)
- *A Mystic Way*: A Spiritual Autobiography (1994)
- *My Double Life 1: This Dark Wood*, A Journey into Light, Episodes and Pattern in a Writer's Life (2015)
- *My Double Life 2: A Rainbow over the Hills*, The Vision of Unity, Episodes and Pattern in a Writer's Life (2015)

Literary Investigations

- 'In Defence of the Sequence of Images', in T.S. Eliot, *A Tribute from Japan*, ed.

by Masao Hirai & E.W.F. Tomlin, Kenkyusha Press, Tokyo, 1966
- *A New Philosophy of Literature*: The Fundamental Theme and Unity of World Literature, The Vision of the Infinite and the Universalist Literary Tradition (2012)

Literary Travelogues/Eyewitness History
- *Scargill the Stalinist?*, The Communist Role in the 1984 Miners' Strike (1984)
- *The Last Tourist in Iran*, From Persepolis to Nuclear Natanz (2008)
- *The Libyan Revolution*: Its Origins and Legacy, A Memoir and Assessment (2009)
- *A View of Epping Forest* (2012)

History

Universalist Cultural History
- *The Fire and the Stones*: A Grand Unified Theory of World History and Religion (1991)
- *The Light of Civilization*: How the Vision of God has Inspired All the Great Civilizations (2006)
- *The Rise and Fall of Civilizations*: Why Civilizations Rise and Fall and What Happens When They End (2008)

Historical Investigations
- *The Syndicate*: The Story of the Coming World Government (2004)
- *The Secret History of the West*: The influence of Secret Organisations on Western History from the Renaissance to the 20th Century (2005)
- *The Secret Founding of America*: The Real Story of Freemasons, Puritans and the Battle for the New World (2007)
- *The Secret American Dream*: The Real Story of Liberty's Empire and the Rise of a World State (2011)

Philosophy

Universalist Philosophy
- *The Universe and the Light*: A New View of the Universe and Reality (1993)
- *The One and the Many*: Universalism and the Vision of Unity (1999)
- *The New Philosophy of Universalism*: The Infinite and the Law of Order (2009)

Universalist Political Philosophy
- *The World Government*: A Blueprint for a Universal World State (2010)

3

Innovations

Nicholas Hagger's works contain 54 innovations.
These throw light on the originality of his method and *oeuvre*.

Innovations in his literary works include:

- presenting a new Universalist, neo-Baroque approach in his poems (*Collected Poems, Classical Odes, Overlord, Armageddon*);
- writing the first poetic epics in English since *Paradise Lost* (*Overlord* and *Armageddon*);
- writing the first epic poems based on contemporary history (*Overlord* and *Armageddon*);
- writing the first two national epic poems completed since Homer (*Overlord* and *Armageddon*);
- writing the first two British poetic epics with American heroes, qualifying both works as American as well as British epics (*Overlord* and *Armageddon*);
- writing the first four-books-of-odes since the Roman Horace and French Ronsard (*Classical Odes*);
- writing the first work to contrast and reconcile in depth both insular British Eurosceptical and pro-European views in verse (*Classical Odes*);
- writing more poems/poetic lines than Wordsworth or Tennyson, the first poet since the 19th century to do so (*Collected Poems, Classical Odes, Overlord* and *Armageddon*);
- mounting a new revival of verse plays (*Collected Verse Plays*);
- devising a new form of miniature stories (*Collected Stories*);
- writing the first collection of more than 1,000 short stories (*Collected Stories*);
- writing the first mystical autobiography to see life as a progress along the Mystic Way (*A Mystic Way*);
- writing the first autobiography to describe 93 documented experiences of the metaphysical Light first glimpsed during intelligence work and 40 books within 7 disciplines as expressions of the unified vision (*My Double Life 1: This Dark Wood, My Double Life 2: A Rainbow over the Hills*);
- writing the first autobiography to narrate a life as a succession of episodes with pairs of opposites (*My Double Life 1: This Dark Wood, My Double Life 2: A Rainbow over the Hills*);
- writing a new form of objective narrative memoir or literary travelogue, eliminating personal detail to focus on a country objectively in narrative

(*The Last Tourist in Iran, The Libyan Revolution*);

- writing a new form of personal memoir on Epping Forest that includes objective narrative (*A View of Epping Forest*);
- writing the first statement of the fundamental theme of world literature (*A New Philosophy of Literature*); and
- writing the first statement of the Universalist tradition in literature (*A New Philosophy of Literature*).

Innovations in his historical works include:

- presenting a new Universalist view of world history as indivisible (*The Fire and the Stones, The Light of Civilization, The Rise and Fall of Civilizations*);
- making the first identification of a common inspiration for all civilizations (*The Light of Civilization*);
- presenting a new 61-stage rising/falling pattern of civilizations (*The Fire and the Stones, The Rise and Fall of Civilizations*);
- discovering a new law of history – Ted Hughes wrote (see *Letters of Ted Hughes*) that Hagger has discovered "a genuine historical pattern and law" (*The Light of Civilization, The Rise and Fall of Civilizations*);
- presenting the first grand unified theory of history and religion (*The Light of Civilization, The Rise and Fall of Civilizations*);
- discovering the 1966 Chinese Cultural Revolution during a visit to China (*Awakening to the Light*);
- anticipating the course of European history ('The European Resurgence', 1976, *see* Appendix 5);
- suggesting that ancient Persia inspired classical Greek art/Pheidias (*The Last Tourist in Iran*);
- giving the first eyewitness description of the attempted *coup*/revolution in Libya that immediately preceded Gaddafi's *coup*/revolution (*The Libyan Revolution*);
- providing a new explanation for all post-1453 revolutions with a four-part revolutionary dynamic (*Secret History of the West*);
- providing a new explanation for the impact of secret societies on post-Renaissance history (*The Secret History of the West, The Syndicate*); and
- providing a new explanation for the history of Epping Forest in a 'whole sweep' view of its evolution and places (*A View of Epping Forest*).

Innovations in his focus on American and contemporary global history:

- providing a new explanation for the founding of America (*The Secret Founding of America*);
- providing the first detailed coverage of the élitist attempt to form a world government and break the mould of rising/falling civilizations (*The*

Syndicate);

- using the name "The Syndicate" to denote the network of families and commercial firms that runs the world (*The Syndicate*);
- proposing a partial, supranational World State that would replace the United Nations, abolish war, poverty, disease and famine and control the Syndicate (*The World Government, The Secret American Dream*);
- detailing America's ambition to export the American dream to all humankind (*The Secret American Dream*);
- probing of the future political, military, commercial, ethical, and philo-sophical role of the world's biggest superpower (*The Secret American Dream*); and
- pioneering the identification of Bartholomew Gosnold as the founder of America and via a lecture in Richmond, Virginia advising American archaeologist Bill Kelso where to unearth Gosnold's skeleton (*The Secret Founding of America*).

Innovations in his philosophical works include:
- returning Western philosophy to its Presocratic roots (*The New Philosophy of Universalism*);
- detailing the significance in philosophy of the Light reported by mystics (*The Fire and the Stones, The Universe and the Light* and *The New Philosophy of Universalism*);
- stating a new Universalist philosophy of the universe (*The Universe and the Light, The New Philosophy of Universalism*);
- proposing a new law of order (*The New Philosophy of Universalism*);
- proposing a detailed blueprint for a new World State as an expression of political Universalism (*The World Government*).
- calling for a new Metaphysical Revolution (*The Universe and the Light, The One and the Many, The New Philosophy of Universalism*);
- calling for a new revolution in thought and culture (*The One and the Many, The New Philosophy of Universalism*);
- describing the experience of the infinite in terms of an astronaut-surfer on the edge of our expanding universe (*The New Philosophy of Universalism*);
- predicting a new science of photonology and biophotonology (*The New Philosophy of Universalism*); and
- proposing a detailed blueprint for a new World State as an expression of political Universalism (*The World Government*).

His presentation of Universalism as one outlook within different disciplines is innovatory. He has established an original and alternative approach in seven fields (*see* p.873):
1 Mystical Universalism, in personal growth and transformation which

leads to a perception of the unity of the universe;

2 Literary Universalism, combining sense and spirit, Classicism and Romanticism both in content and method, perceiving all the world's literature as a unity;

3 Philosophical Universalism (which extends to the philosophy of science), investigating the order and unity of the universe;

4 Historical Universalism, perceiving all world history as a unity via the patterns of 25 civilizations;

5 Political Universalism, focusing (in international politics and statecraft) on the world unity of a coming World State that would control the Syndicate;

6 Religious Universalism, identifying the common essence of all religions in comparative religion; and

7 Cultural Universalism, identifying a unified world culture.

His literary, historical and philosophical works are interconnected through his Universalist approach. They interlock like pieces *of* a jigsaw puzzle which combine to show a picture. Like a jigsaw piece, an individual work can take on added meaning when it is slotted into, and related to, his complete *oeuvre*. Thus, particular poems, stories and verse plays can be connected to particular chapters in his historical and philosophical works which deepen their background. When it is finally finished, his ambitious *oeuvre* promises to present a picture of almost every aspect of the Age, Western civilization and its roots.

4

Visits

Visits by Nicholas Hagger to countries/places
touched on in *My Double Life 2: A Rainbow over the Hills*
(For details see *Selected Diaries*)

1976	12–15 April	France – D-Day beaches: Cherbourg, Valognes, Ste Mère-Eglise, Utah/Omaha beaches, Bayeux, Arromanches, Juno/Sword beaches, Pegasus Bridge, Cabourg, Deauville, Trouville, Caen, Ouistreham; Hill 112, Falaise; Chartres; Versailles, Paris, Rouen.
1985	22–26 February	France: Boulogne, Paris (Conciergerie), Versailles, Caen, Rouen.
	11 May	France: Paris.
	14 June	France: Rouen via Normandy.
	19–30 July	France – Dordogne: Orleans, Blois, Périgueux, Les Eyzies, Sarlat, St Cyprian, Beynac, La Roque, Domme, Gourdon, Rocamadour, Padirac, Souillac, La Madeleine, Les Combarelles, Cap Blanc, St Emilion, Bordeaux, La Rochelle, Nantes, Mont St Michel, Rouen, Boulogne.
	11–13 October	Germany: Frankfurt.
1986	1–7 August	Europe. Belgium: Dunkirk, Bruges, Ghent, Antwerp, Waterloo, Brussels. Holland: Amsterdam. Germany: Bonn. Luxembourg: Echternach, Luxembourg City, Bourscheid (Ardennes). France: Lille.
	1–5 October	Germany: Frankfurt.
1987	31 July–4 August	Denmark: Esbjerg, Rynkeby, Ladby, Kertminde, Svendborg, Trelleborg, Fyrkat, Nodebo, Gilleleje, Helsingor (Elsinor), Kobenhavn (Copenhagen), Odense, Jelling.
	7–11 October	Germany: Frankfurt.
1990	23–30 April	Hungary: Budapest, Szentendre, Visegrad, Esztergon, Tura, Kocskemet.
	7–9 December	Czechoslovakia: Prague.
1991	9–12 October	Germany: Frankfurt.

1993	29 April–3 May	Italy: Florence, Pisa.
	8–29 July	USA: New York, Boston, Niagara Falls, Washington, Philadelphia, Florida (Orlando, St Petersburg, Daytona).
1994	28 May–4 June	France – D-Day beaches via Southwick House, Broomfield House, Fort Southwick, Fort Nelson: Caen, Villers-Bocage, Banville, Pegasus Bridge, Ouistreham, Sword and Juno beaches, Arromanches (Gold), Mulberries, Bayeux, American beaches (Omaha, Pointe du Hoc), Colleville, Lisieux, Falaise, Chambois, Montormel (Falaise Gap), St Foy de Montgommery, Rouen, Atlantic Wall, Calais.
	2 July	Southwick
	18 July–1 August	Europe. Belgium: Brussels. Germany: Hannover, Berlin. Poland: Poznan, Warsaw, Auschwitz, Cracow. Hungary: Budapest via Slovakia. Austria: Vienna, Salzburg. Germany: Munich, Cologne via Rothenburg, Rhine. France: Moselle, Meuse.
	6–9 October	Germany: Munich, Berchtesgaden, Dachau, Ingoldstadt, Nuremberg.
1995	31 March–6 April	Germany: Obersalzburg/Berghof, Dresden, Goslar via Colditz, Brocken, Gottingen, Flossenberg, Weimar, Buchenwald, Wewelsburg, Externsteine, Hermannsdenkel, Padeborn, Verden, Sachsenhain, Belsen, Luneburg, Deutsch Evern.
	27 April–1 May	Europe. Holland: Hoek van Holland, Arnhem, Oosterbeek, Nijmegen. Germany: Rheinberg, Büderich, Wesel, Straelen. Holland: Venlo, Maastricht. Belgium: Bastogne. France: Reims. Luxembourg: Clervaux. Germany: Saar. France: Forbach. Germany: Trier. Belgium: Ardennes. Luxembourg: Echternach. Belgium: Oûr, St Vith. Germany: Losheim. Belgium: Elsenborn, Malmédy, Stavelot. France: Calais
	14–25 July	Turkey: Istanbul, Troy, Guzelyali, Kusadasi, Ephesus, Selçuk, Didyma. Greece: Samos, Patmos, Athens, Kefalonia, Ithaca, Athens, Eleusis.
	14–21 October	Italy: Sorrento, Mount Vesuvius, Solfatara, Cumae, Avernus, Pompeii, Herculaneum, Oplontis, Amalfi, Paestum, Capri, Naples.
	24–28 October	Russia: St Petersburg, Moscow, Yalta.

1996	24–26 May	Herefordshire: Hay-on-Wye
	12–27 July	Greece: Athens, Sunion, Thebes, Delphi, Naupactus, Patras, Olympia, Pylos, Sphacteria, Mistras, Sparta, Mycenae, Epidavros (Epidaurus), Peiraeus. Greek islands: Aigina (Aegina), Mykonos. Turkey: Ephesus. Greek Islands: Patmos, Rhodes. Crete (Knossos). Santorini (Akrotiri). Greece: Dafni (Daphnae), Athens.
	22–26 September	Italy: Rome, Licenza (Horace's villa), Tivoli, Vatican.
1998	20–24 July	Italy: Verona, Mantua, Sirmione, Venice, Padua.
	9–21 October	USA: Boston, New Bedford, Martha's Vineyard, Virginia (Richmond, Jamestown, Pamplin Park civil war site, Yorktown, Monticello, Tuckahoe plantation), New York.
1999	17–20 July	France: Carcassone, Rennes-le-Château, Montségur, Narbonne, Béziers.
2000	14–21 April	Iceland: Reykjavik, Golden Circle, Thingvellir, South Shore whale-watching, Westman Isles, Heimaey, Lake Myvatn, Reykjanes (Blue Lagoon).
	14–20 July	Sicily: Palermo, Agrigento, Marsala, Motya, Segesta, Selinunte, Syracuse, Etna, Taormina, Catania.
	28 September–2 October	Italy: Turin, Rome.
2001	13–15 February	Portugal: Lisbon.
2001	30 March–6 April	Spain – Andalusia: Madrid, Toledo, La Carlota, Cordoba, Grenada, Seville, Malaga.
	6–20 May	Mediterranean. Greece: Athens. Crete: Chania. Libya: Benghazi, Cyrene, Tripoli, Sabratha. Tunisia: Sousse/El Djem, Tunis, Carthage. Sicily: Selinunte, Agrigento, Trapani, Erice, Segesta. Sardinia: Barumini. Minorca: Mahon. Spain: Barcelona.
2002	23–28 March	Cyprus: Pafos (Ptolemaic tombs, Temple of Aphrodite), Nicosia, Famagusta, Salamis, Kirenia, Bellapais, Troodos mountains (Makarios's monastery).
	17–19 May	France: Bordeaux.
	21–24 June	Germany: Heidelberg, Freiburg.
	9–23 November	China: Shanghai, Suzhou, Yichang, Yangtze's Three Gorges, Shibaozhai, Chongqing, Xian (terracotta army), Beijing (Temple of Heaven, Forbidden City).

2003	17–22 November	Gran Canaria: Maspalomas.
2004	2–4 August	Scilly Isles.
	30 November–	
	2 December	Belgium: Brussels.
2005	31 January–	
	8 February	Egypt: Luxor, Karnak, Sharm El Sheikh, St Catherine's monastery (Mount Sinai), Cairo (Pyramids).
2006	12–14 August	Devon: Dartmoor.
2007	13–20 January	Iran: Tehran, Shiraz, Persepolis, Yazd, Nain, Isfahan, Natanz, Kashan, Qom, Saveh, Hamadan, Malayer, Arak.
	8–11 March	Austria: Vienna.
	23 July–11 August	Ecuador: Quito. Galapagos Islands: Baltra (South Seymour), Bartolomé, Santiago, Santa Cruz, Floreana, Espanola, San Cristobel, North Seymour. Peru: Lima, Cuzco, Urubamba, Ccaccakoyllo, Machu Picchu.
	5–26 November	Antarctica. Argentina: Buenos Aires, Ushuaia. Falkland Islands: Port Stanley. South Georgia: Salisbury Plain, Elsehul, Grytviken, Stromness. Penguin Island. King George Island: Arctowski station. Deception Island. Goudier Island: Port Lockroy. Antarctic Peninsula: Paradise Bay.
2008	22–23 February	Essex: Down Hall.
	14 May	Wiltshire: Wilton, Salisbury.
	20–25 July	Isle of Wight: Farringford.
	26–28 August	Devon: Totnes.
	22 October	Hertfordshire: St Albans.
2009	6–8 February	France: Paris.
	26 February–	
	1 March	North Norway: Tromso, Honingsvag, North Cape, Alta.
	23–26 July	Sussex: Eastbourne.
2010	26 August–	
	10 September	Mediterranean via Guernsey. Spain: Santiago de Compostela. Portugal: Oporto. Spain: Cadiz, Granada (Alhambra). Italy: Siena, San Gimignano. Corsica: Calvi. Italy: Rome, Tarquinia, Naples, Pompeii.
	26–27 November	Gloucestershire: Painswick, Slimbridge, Tetbury.
2011	1–4 July	Northumberland: Hadrian's Wall.

	19–21 August	Devon: Gidleigh Park.
	31 August– 3 September	Isle of Man.
2013	20 February– 13 March	India, Sri Lanka and Arabia. India, Golden Triangle: Old and New Delhi, Agra, Bharatpur, Jaipur. Sri Lanka: Colombo, Kandy. India: Tuticorin, Kochi, Old Goa, Mumbai (Bombay), Porbandar. United Arab Emirates: Fujairah. Dubai. Oman: Muscat.

5

Europe

'The European Resurgence'
November 1976
Paper by Nicholas Hagger

1. Definition of Europe

According to European (including Soviet) geographers, Europe, the homeland of the white peoples, stretches from the Atlantic to the Urals, and runs South to the Caspian and then West to the Black Sea. It includes the island groups of Svalbard (Norway), the British Isles, the Faeroes (Denmark), Iceland, the Madeira Islands (Portugal) and the Canary Islands (Spain). As such, Europe has an area of 4,100,000 square miles and a population, on 1971 estimates, of 640 million. "Europe" therefore includes all the territories behind the European Iron Curtain which are under Soviet occupation: East Germany, Poland, Czechoslovakia, Hungary, Yugoslavia, Romania and Bulgaria. "Europe" includes a number of other territories that have been occupied by the Soviet Union: Estonia, Latvia, Lithuania, East Prussia; Belorussia, the Ukraine; and Moldavia; all of which have linguistic and cultural differences from the rest of the Soviet Union.

2. The Political Resurgence

Europe has declined in the twentieth century as a result of two civil wars, the loss of all the European empires (the British, the French, the German, the Belgian, the Dutch, the Italian, the Spanish and the Portuguese empires), and the advance of Soviet totalitarianism. Now Free Europe is expanding through the European Community. Solzhenitsyn is wrong in fearing the imminent fall of the West, and Toynbee is right in predicting that a "Universal State" is ahead for Europe; the European Community *is* the Universal State and this will expand at the Soviet Union's expense rather than fall to the Soviet Union. This expansion, which Churchill was the first to see, is the political Resurgence. The European Community will expand to include Spain, Portugal, Greece, Norway, Sweden, Switzerland and Austria. It will then attract factions from the part of Europe that is illegally occupied by the Soviet Union, factions that will argue that their territories have as much right as the Western European ones to belong to a free Europe.

3. *The Liberation of Occupied Europe*

Occupied Europe should be given the opportunity to leave the Soviet bloc and join the European Community. This opportunity will only arise if the Soviet Union weakens its grip on the occupied territories. There is a chance that this will happen during the next 20 years; see Amalrik's *Will the Soviet Union Survive Until 1984?*. The experience of Hungary (1956) and of Czechoslovakia (1968) should not lead us to believe that the Soviet Union will *always* send in tanks. There will come a time when she will not. There are signs of weakening in the concessions to world Communist parties last June. There must be a European Foreign Policy that helps occupied Europe to de-Sovietise itself. Radio broadcasts, propaganda and help for dissidents have their place, but European MPs have a part to play. Conservative MPs in the European Parliament should therefore press for the withdrawal of Soviet imperialism from occupied Europe. They should say loud and clear that all imperialism has contracted except for Soviet imperialism, and that it is now only just for Soviet imperialism to follow suit. This should be a daily theme in a concerted European Foreign Policy. Europe must belong to Europe and not to any occupying power. This is a great historical idea which can rouse the silent majority of Europe to voice, and inspire electorates in Britain. All Europe (as she is geographically defined) must be free.

4. *Union with Christian Democrats*

To achieve such a Foreign Policy, the Conservatives need to have a majority in the European Parliament. They should unite with the Christian Democrats in Europe as Mrs. Thatcher has said, and secure a majority over the Social Democrats and Communists without depending on Liberal support.

5. *The Christian Democratic Ideology*

Such an alliance means that Conservatives should be reasonably happy with the Christian Democratic ideology. This goes back to the Catholic confessional parties which existed in Germany from the 1870s and in Italy from 1918, and in both countries there was an anti-Fascist impetus in 1945. Geoffrey Pridham analyses Christian Democracy in Italy and West Germany in a contribution to *Social and Political Movements in Western Europe* (ed Kolinsky and Paterson), and his conclusion is: "There is much similarity between the CDU/CSU and the DC to justify talking of a clear Christian Democratic stream in West European politics", a stream which represents a "merger between Christian values in politics and the concept of democracy". Pridham defines the Christian Democratic ideology under the headings of: Anti-Communism; the Concept of Democracy; European Unity; Traditional Roman Catholic values; Social Progress; and Economic Liberalism. (See "Ideology" attached.) Conservatives have been unhappy about the commitment to federalism and the "confessional" background of the Christian Democrats, and so they have not joined the

European People's Party which all the Christian Democrats of the Community (from Ireland, Belgium, France, Luxembourg and the Netherlands as well as from Germany and Italy) formed in 1976, and which is now under the Chairmanship of the Belgian Prime Minister, Mr Leo Tindemans. The Conservatives should join the E.P.P. The majority parties (the Conservatives and the Christian Democrats) will then be able to co-ordinate their efforts.

6. The Ideology of Europe
The Christian Democratic ideology forms the basis of the European ideology. European civilization grew out of the idea of Christendom. British Parliamentary democracy has Christian roots (Stephen Langton), and the economic freedom of capitalism grew out of the Reformation. The freedom and dignity and value of the individual is a Christian concept. The European ideology is founded on traditional values, and it has been weakened by socialism and political liberalism, and so-called modern values. The conflict between Free Europe and Occupied Europe is the conflict between Christendom, democracy and capitalism on the one hand, and totalitarian Communism and socialism on the other hand. It is therefore nonsense for people to say, "The West has no ideology." Under socialism and modern values, the West may appear not to have a distinctive ideology, but that is because the true ideology of Europe has been buried. It needs to be unearthed.

7. The Religious Resurgence
Because the idea of Christendom opposes the idea of Communism, as the Russian Baptists know, and is at the roots of the European ideology, it is to the advantage of Europe that Christendom should be reunited through the Ecumenical Movement so that the one Church can play a role in the new Europe. The reunification of the Church – the religious Resurgence – will reconcile Catholic confessional and Protestant groups within the E.P.P., and it will help to unite and integrate the Catholic, Protestant and Orthodox communities in Europe. The Ecumenical Movement should therefore be given every support.

8. The New "Empire" Concept
Europe is heading for a Resurgence that is political (through the European Community), religious (through the Ecumenical Movement) and artistic (through the Golden Age of Classicism that always accompanies Universal States, see Toynbee). As the nation-states unite into an expanding Universal State, and the Christian sects unite into one Church, there can be an effective restoration of the Holy Roman Empire of Charlemagne under the Conservatives and Christian Democrats. The revival of the idea of the Holy Roman Empire of the eighth century takes us back to the vitality at the source of European civilization. The new concept of "empire" is defined in the *Shorter Oxford English*

Dictionary: "an extensive territory (especially an aggregate of many states) ruled over by an emperor, or by a sovereign state." The "sovereign state" in the case of Europe will be the European superstructure of government, of which the European Parliament forms a part. The perpetuation of the idea of "empire", in a totally different sense from the sense in which the British Empire was an "empire", will have emotive appeal to an electorate.

9. *The United States of Europe*
The Churchillian vision was of "a kind of United States of Europe" (Zürich, 19 September 1946). It is one of the ideals of the European Movement that there should be political and monetary union in Europe rather than an alliance of nation-states. If this happens, then Europe will be like the United States. England, Scotland and Wales will be like California, Texas or Pennsylvania; they will either form one state or (if devolution leads to developments) three states, their Prime Ministers having the force of State Governors. The "United States" concept is but an extension of the "empire" concept.

10. *The Global Perspective*
Looking a very long way ahead, one can see the possibility that a United States of Europe will unite with the United States of America to form a United States of the West. In algebraic terms, USE + USA = USW. Electorates are inspired by possibilities, and so this possibility can lurk in the background: that the European Resurgence is a first step towards a political unification of the West, which may in turn one day lead to some sort of world government. Such a concept is the result of the conquest of space. We can see the earth as a ball on film, and it seems ridiculous that such a tiny ball should not be unified. This shift in our perspective is as major as the shift from the perspective of the Middle Ages to the perspective of the Renaissance. The Resurgence perspective, indeed, is the Renaissance of our time. Bearing these future possibilities in mind, we can see how imperative it is for future generations that Europe should now oppose Communism rather than condone it; that Europe should rise above Communism to a new moral greatness, just as Churchill rose above Fascism to moral greatness. The anti-Communist mission of Europe is a worldwide one, and Europe should work to free her former colonies from Communist influence, so that they can enjoy their rightful inheritance of freedom.

6

The New Baroque Vision

1979, 1982

Nicholas Hagger introduced the Baroque principle in his poem 'The Silence' (1966–1967) – "While, naked on the petalled lawn,/A new Baroque age is born" – and wrote a neo-Baroque manifesto in 1973 (*see My Double Life 1: This Dark Wood*, p.469). He was thinking about the neo-Baroque in November 1977. He firmed up the Baroque principle in the course of three letters he wrote to Christopher Ricks in 1979 and 1982.

Extracts from letter written by Nicholas Hagger to Christopher Ricks on 18 February 1979:

"Dear Christopher,
I feel I may have resolved some of the difficulties I expressed in my last letter.... As a slight change of focus is involved, I would like to set it down on paper before we meet.

I now feel that I am, perhaps, above all a *Metaphysical* poet. My strengths may be metaphor, verbal play, and possibly (in some of my work) wit, and these are blended with a Metaphysical subject matter, a search for reality, i.e. enlightenment. A Metaphysical poet must have a metaphysic to be metaphysical about, and the background to mine is in the synopsis [of what would become *The Fire and the Stones*] I sent you. Being a Metaphysical, I: start naturally with personal situations; am interested in the theme of love; am fairly learned and certainly interested in 'the new philosophy'; am fascinated by the relation between the spirit and the senses (e.g. in *The Gates of Hell*); tend to compress and fuse thought and image; and am interested in the way symbols reflect my metaphysic. My present tendency towards Symbolism, which I referred to in my last letter, can, perhaps, be partly seen in terms of layers of ambiguity, a Metaphysical fascination with poems that move at two or more different levels at the same time.

If all this is so, then the relationship between my mysticism and verbal play becomes understandable. The mysticism is but one part of my Metaphysical sensibility and outlook, the other part being the verbal play and ambiguity (the part that Kathleen Raine would be against). This part surely originates with the Metaphysicals, but more recently it goes back to Empson (your ancestor, some say) and *Seven Types of Ambiguity*. Empson absorbed the East when he was a predecessor of mine at my University in Tokyo – I was told by a contemporary

929

that he was sacked in 1934, I believe, for sitting nude in a taxi after some nude bathing spree – and he was an admirer of Marvell's 'Garden' ('There is something very Far-Eastern about this'). He surely goes back to the Metaphysicals, whereas so many of his Movement followers only go back to the 18th century. In so far as you have carried forward the Empson tradition, my verbal play is very definitely Ricksite. A selection or anthology of my poems should therefore aim to reveal its Metaphysical qualities, which include both the mysticism and the verbal play.

I have said that the background of my metaphysic is in the synopsis.... This partly deals with how the new science (subatomic physics and biology) has debunked the old philosophies and made a metaphysics of enlightenment possible again.... Such a book... could resemble a book by Donne or Marvell about the new ideas of the Age of the Metaphysicals.... I regard such a book as a background to the Metaphysical outlook of these poems, and I am all the more convinced that there should be a selection or anthology of my poems.

This letter is really an attempt at self-definition. You may disagree and have another definition, change the focus. It will be interesting to hear. Understanding (as opposed to knowing) oneself is a terrible problem when one has written so many different things, and I am reminded of Eliot's remark about Tennyson: 'He was capable of illumination which he was incapable of understanding.' I am not sure that this definition would have taken place had we not arranged to meet, so I am already grateful to you for sharpening the focus.

I hope to appear soon after midday on Tuesday.

Yours, Nicholas."

Extracts from letter written by Nicholas Hagger to Christopher Ricks on 1 May 1982:

"Dear Christopher,
First, many congratulations on becoming King Edward VII Professor of English. I always knew you would sooner or later succeed Leavis as the major literary influence at Cambridge, so I am not surprised. I have long thought of you as the curator of the tradition; hence my use of the term 'Ricksite'.

Secondly... I would be very interested in your reaction to a new *perspective*, if you could find the time to give it. I have spent over three years pondering the anthology of thirty poems, which you suggested. The trouble was, if I discounted the longer works and merely chose 30 of the smaller ones, I did not even touch on the main theme of my work. As I pondered, it slowly dawned on me that the 'Metaphysical' model I proposed three years ago is incomplete, and that I have in fact all along been continuing the *Romantic tradition* of Blake, Wordsworth, Coleridge and Shelley, albeit as a pretty Metaphysical Romantic. I have now written a *Preface* to this effect. It appears at the beginning of the accompanying selection, and I would be very interested in your opinion, if you could spare the time to read it.

It seems to me that seeing my poems in a Romantic perspective accounts for many of the things that made you uneasy when we last met, and solves a number of the problems. You found my poems: (1) ruminative instead of immediate – ruminative like Wordsworth instead of Metaphysical; (2) personal rather than individual – a Romantic trait; (3) explicit in places – again a Romantic feature; (4) sometimes arbitrary as to what appears in the next line – explained by Romantic organic form dressed as musical form, and by post-Romantic emotional linking or juxtaposition of images. You disliked (5) some of the 19th-century diction – an extension of the Romantic tone; and (6) the ending of some poems with a question – which is allowed in Romantic poems, e.g. 'Ode to the West Wind', 'Ode to a Nightingale', 'Grantchester'. Romantic and post-Romantic criticism are very different from Neoclassical criticism, and allow many things (e.g. organic form, and a freer line as in 'Christabel') that Neoclassical 'statement' criticism cannot allow, and I would like to know if you agree that relating my poems to their correct *genre* clears up some of the difficulties.

I have been reticent about *The Gates of Hell* till now, allowing it to gather dust on a shelf for ten years, as many of the poems in it were written in the sort of pain Shelley must have felt when he wrote 'To the Lord Chancellor'; but they certainly fit in with a Romantic view of my work, as outlined in the *Preface*, and may even be among my best works in terms of Romantic (as opposed to Neoclassical) principles. The emotional Romantic approach explains some of the relationships between things; for example, 'child's balloon' in 'Flow: Moon and Sea', which you commented on, is now appropriate as it suggests a fear of making the girl pregnant and creating a child who will have a balloon.

In this selection I have included whole works rather than excerpts you have so far seen, so that the organic form can show itself to best advantage. (Imagine an anthology of any Romantic without some of the longer works.) I have concentrated on the longer works which illustrate the theme of the *Preface*, rather than on the hundreds of short poems. *The Fire-Flower* you have not seen at all as these poems were all written since we last met (although some are rewrites), and you will see that 'The Tree of Imagination' is partly about you and our last meeting. I don't know how it reads, but it is meant to be complimentary in making you the number-one critic and guardian of the Tree of Tradition.

I am aware that you are on the Neoclassical rather than the Romantic side – you were very interested in social satire in the early 1960s and have approached Keats from the viewpoint of social embarrassment, and have championed Mary Douglas – but on the other hand the subjects of your books are all on the Romantic side, and I know from our tutorials that you like Wordsworth. I know you will take a fair and balanced view, and will judge Romantic poetry by Romantic standards and not by the hostile Neoclassical standards Yvor Winters used in *In Defense of Reason*....

Your ever devoted, Nicholas."

Extracts from letter written by Nicholas Hagger to Christopher Ricks on 17 October 1982:

"Dear Christopher,

As promised, I enclose version 4, the last version, of my Preface. It is well over double the length of version 3. You will see that there is a considerable shift of ground from a Romantic position to what I call a 'Baroque' position (i.e. Classicism plus Romanticism, sense plus spirit). The word appears in the dedication to 'The Silence' (1965–6), and in line 1332 of that work. Version 3 was but another stepping-stone to the finished idea, which was there as long ago as 1965 if I could but have grasped it.

I have tried to define myself – retrospectively – in terms of first the Metaphysicals and then the Romantics, but each time I have been unable to explain the distinct *Classical* elements in my work, e.g. the 'Ricksite' verbal play and the fact that much of what I have written is actually from the 'social ego' (although admittedly it generally opens to 'the beyond'). In what must be seen as a significant development, I have now faced the fact that though my work obviously draws on the Metaphysicals and the Romantics – I was clearly right in seeing my roots as immediately being in Romantic Idealism – it also has a Classical element, to which your remark about W. Jackson Bate indirectly drew my attention, and that in art a combination of Classicism and Romanticism is 'baroque'. (See pages 23–29 for a deepened view of this term and recurring cycles in art.) I have – seriously! – in all modesty and humility – of the kind I learned from you! – tried to relate myself to the past, to place myself somewhere within the great tradition. The attempt has not worked. No matter how hard I tried, I could not 'fit my work in' with what is already there. I was telling half the truth about my work but I was not doing justice to the whole of it. Therefore I have (almost reluctantly) been forced to consider that I am doing something *new*, that I have been somewhat original and innovative all along in creating a new 'baroque' poetry which shares some of the assumptions of the Metaphysicals and the Romantics and blends with the New Age consciousness of Sir George Trevelyan and others. I am sure I have now come to rest and have finally achieved my 'public stance', and that there will be no more developments, only modifications. I am sure you will not receive a letter next year putting forward another view!

Of course, it will now be even harder for me to get the poems across to the public. Like a third political party, I would be attacked from both sides: by the Neoclassicals like Larkin for being too Romantic and mystical in my subject matter, and by Neo-romantics like Kathleen Raine for being too concerned with the classical social ego as opposed to the Platonist 'other mind'. Nevertheless, my primary concern is not getting the work across, but correctly identifying what it is (as if I were writing an essay for you), and the getting it across is secondary. Wordsworth wrote that 'every great and original writer, in proportion as he is great or original, must create the taste by which he is to be relished; he must teach the art by which he is to be seen'. In so far as I *have* been original in writing 'baroque' poetry, the onus has been on me to create a taste for it, and now that I know the taste, I can set about creating it. The *Preface* is a start, and I now have an 'ideological' basis for an anthology, if I can get round to the agonising business of making a very small selection.

I think this definition of my work allows me more latitude in the future. The 'price' you spoke of in your letter was presumably a price in human terms, and Baroque poetry, which allows the social ego in in a way that Neo-romantic poetry does not, affords more human scope, and accounts for the considerable human interest in my many short poems; and therefore reduces 'the price'. I am also now set to embark on the 12-book epic which I have had in mind for 20 years, and which I consulted Ezra Pound about in Rapallo in 1970. (Pound gave me his blessing, saying, 'T. E. Hulme said to me in 1914, "Everything a writer has to say can be put on half a side of a postcard, and all the rest is application and elaboration." Have you got that? If you have, then two ends of the twentieth century are now meeting.') This epic will draw heavily on the external world and the human Classical side, and it is itself a Baroque conception. (Milton, after all, lived in the original Baroque Age.)

My life has undergone a dramatic change within the last year, as if in preparation for this enterprise. In July I exchanged contracts on the private Essex day preparatory school (3–11) which I attended from 1944–1947, and have installed my wife as Headmistress. We are sole owners.... I will soon be able to retire from teaching in Marxist ILEA..., and I will be able to spend the mornings writing my epic in the midst of Nature. The time, in the sense of leisure, and the freedom for which I have long yearned are now within my grasp. I will be able to reread many of the books I read for you at Oxford. Meanwhile the local community will come to my door. Yes, the Baroque is a very appropriate reconciliation between the social and contemplative forces I will meet during the next two or three decades.

As a result of this latest and *last* development, I do not now need to see Kermode or any of the Romantic specialists at Cambridge. I have thought my way out of my quandary on my own, despite all the hectic Essex activity and commuting. I think you will welcome my development as it includes rather than excludes the Classical. I think you will regard it as a step in the right direction, even though, while I acknowledge the continuity of Augustan into Romantic (largely thanks to your last letter, your tutor's knack of opening up new vistas with a phrase), there is still some tension as the Romantic part of the Baroque synthesis pulls against the Augustan; and you will probably still withhold appreciation....

With very many thanks for bearing with me and helping me in labour, and of course looking forward to hearing your reaction to version 4 of the *Preface*,

Your ever devoted, Nicholas."

7

FREE

1983–1984

Shortened version of paper by Nicholas Hagger on FREE
(Freedom for the Republics of Eastern Europe),
Proposals for assertive statecraft
(Version 5 of the paper on FREE)

Highly Confidential
**The FREE (Freedom for the Republics of
Eastern Europe) Movement**
(Western policies towards the countries of East-Central Europe)

1. Most of East-Central Europe has been under Soviet *occupation* since World War Two, and as a result the peoples of East-Central Europe are not free.

2. The East-Central European peoples yearn to be free, as is evidenced by the revolts in East Germany, Hungary, Czechoslovakia and Poland, and public opinion is currently expressing itself *in demonstrations* against the siting of SS-22s on Czech and East German soil.

3. The *Brezhnev Doctrine* (that the Soviet Union and Warsaw Pact nations have the right to intervene if in their judgement one of them pursues policies that threaten the common interests of the others) looks as if it will be continued now that the Brezhnevites are back in power under Chernenko, and any further revolts can be expected to be crushed.

4. The East-Central European countries face further Sovietisation and isolation from the West, and their peoples will feel progressively abandoned. Their desperate and frustrated desire for self-determination may turn bloody and endanger world peace unless a *peaceful outlet* can be found for their hopes, a campaign of an overt political nature which will focus attention on their plight.

5. Such a campaign would call for the *peaceful withdrawal* of the imperialistic Soviet occupying forces, so that the East-Central European countries could join the Western democracies in an enlarged, Greater Europe, and affirm the values of their European cultures against Communist values, which destroy all cultures.

6. The Western democracies are now threatened by Communism, which has made advances, either by direct aggression or by Cuban proxy, in Asia, the Middle East, Africa and Central America, and which has used *détente* as part of its strategy. Any peaceful change in East-Central Europe will relieve the pressure on the threatened Western countries, and it will be *in the interests of the Western alliance* as well as the occupied nations.

7. It is proposed that there should be London-based anti-Soviet freedom-fighting *liberation movements* for all the East-Central European countries now under the Soviet yoke. These would be non-violent, peaceful organisations, and would not represent armies, as did the African liberation movements, but they would have clandestine contacts in their own countries.

8. Exile representatives would open propaganda *offices* in London for Free Latvia, Free Lithuania, Free Estonia, Free Poland, Free Czechoslovakia, Free Hungary, Free Romania, Free Bulgaria, Free Yugoslavia, Free East Germany, Free Albania, Free Byelorussia (Belarus), Free Georgia, Free Ukraine, and for Free Russia; for a Free Russia would grant the East-Central European peoples their freedom and adopt a safer policy regarding nuclear weapons.

9. *A British Advisory Committee* composed of suitable British people would co-ordinate the publicity of the offices to maximise the impression that there is widespread disaffection within the decaying Soviet empire. This British-exile movement would be called the FREE (Freedom for the Republics of Eastern Europe) Movement.

10. The *aims and objectives* of the offices and the British Advisory Committee would be to draw attention to the Soviet occupation of East-Central Europe, to report specific incidents of protest against it (e.g. the protests against the instal-lation of SS-22s on East-Central European soil), and to continue to draw attention to it; to provide news and information and lobby people; and to change public opinion, so that a climate is created in which politicians and others can speak of "the anti-Soviet liberation movements".

11. The *legal basis* of the FREE Movement's campaign would be the Soviet Constitution of 1977, which guarantees all its republics the right to secession, their own diplomacy and even their own army; and certain UN resolutions (of SWAPO's case against South Africa's occupation of Namibia). The campaign would insist on self-determination for the various countries within their pre-World-War-Two or post-World-War-Two boundaries, and it would call for the abrogation of the Yalta Treaty, which the Soviet Union has broken.

12. *American support* for this idea is more likely now, under Reagan, than at any time since World War Two, as the US no longer regards the Soviet presence in East-Central Europe as permanent.

13. The *Soviet Union* should not object to the presence of these offices as London is a traditional host for exiles and is already host to the European Liaison Group, a Free Polish Government, and the PLO. The situation would be similar to that in World War Two when countries under Nazi occupation were represented in the UK.

14. The offices and British Advisory Committee should surface in the autumn of this year to capitalise on the feeling in Czechoslovakia and East Germany regarding the installation of SS-22s. They should qualify for *funding*.

15. Some suitable person should be given the task of *co-ordinating* first the establishment, and then the work and operations, of the offices and the British Advisory Committee.

8

Warning

1984

Times leader of 29 November 1984
based on *Scargill the Stalinist?*
(which was subtitled *A Warning to the British People*)

WE HAVE BEEN WARNED

When is a communist not a communist? It is possible in this country to call somebody a fascist as a term of general abuse but it is less easy to call somebody a communist without running the risk of libel. Mr Arthur Scargill is not now a member of the Communist Party though he was in his youth and early manhood. He is a member of the Labour Party but everything he says and does is consistent with a certain kind of communism and receives the full and open support from many close colleagues who are themselves formal members of the Communist Party of Great Britain.

There are basically three kinds of communists in this country: those who inhabit the Communist Party to maintain it as a tightly disciplined and cohesive body; those who inhabit the Labour Party on the grounds that the long-term communist interest is best served by working through the Labour Party which has more opportunities for exercising political power; and those who actually conceal their inner convictions by inhabiting other groups or communities such as the Tory or Alliance parties, the media, the universities, teacher training colleges and any useful institution which can be subverted and manipulated by a communist agent of influence.

Mr Scargill belongs clearly to the second category and on his own admission. He left the Communist Party, in his own words, because he objected to its policy of de-Stalinisation and because he wanted to join a political organization, the Labour Party, where there was real power. But the singular characteristic about this year's miners' strike is that for the first time for many years, the communist element is so overt, even triumphalist, that the Labour Party and its leadership has been cowed into following the communist lead.

It is this communist presence, coupled with Mr Scargill's predominant role in the leadership and orchestration of the strike with a permanent coterie of communist colleagues, that makes it legitimate to examine his origins in the Communist Party and the consistency with which he has pursued his political objectives even after his departure from the Communist Party.

An examination of Mr Scargill's record, ably presented in a booklet published yesterday (i.e. 28 November 1984), shows no evidence that his formal departure from the Communist Party caused any change in his belief in the need to wage a class war in Britain to bring about a totally socialist society. His declared tactics have been first to change the Labour Party from within by removing all bans and proscriptions on far-left groups including the Communist Party. Having created such a "broad left" coalition, the leadership of each trade union would be packed with communists who would use their block votes to change Party policy and enforce such change. They would then proceed to discard what was left of the old social democratic ethos of the right wing of the Labour Party. It would by then have "completely served its purpose".

Such a party, containing all the far-left organizations but clearly run by a nucleus of communists or communist sympathisers as the NUM is now run, would take its struggle repeatedly to the streets. As Mr Scargill described it in the columns of the *Morning Star*, which has given him emphatic and sustained support throughout this strike, his view of the class war would involve "every sinew in every factory, office, dole queue, docks, railway, plant and mill" to be strained to the maximum. "Waiting in the wings are four million unemployed whose numbers could swell the picket line at any time. What is urgently needed is the rapid and total mobilization of the trade union and labour movements to take positive advantage of a unique opportunity to defend our class and roll back the machinery of oppression, exploitation and deep-seated human misery."

This strategy is spelt out in the Communist Party' official manifesto "The British Road to Socialism". It is thus hardly surprising that Mr Scargill and his lieutenants find it so easy to enlist the support of the Soviet and Libyan authorities. What is more surprising, however, is that such support has been given when there is so little evidence that the country is anywhere near the pre-revolutionary condition in which Mr Scargill would like it to be. The refusal of trade unionists to be dragooned as class warriors is reassuring. Less reassuring is the ambivalence shown to Mr Scargill and the communists by the leadership of the TUC, many elements in the Labour Party, and all those people in the country who seem to have reached some personal accommodation with the ugly violence and class war rhetoric of Scargillism.

So the conditions of a successful revolution have eluded Mr Scargill. Nevertheless he will surely continue to work for these objectives within the Labour Party. We must expect him to be able to mobilise strong-arm groups forged in the crucible of picket violence and loyal only to his bidding in further industrial or political thuggery. He will exploit the stab-in-the back theory to explain the reluctance of the Labour movement to support his insurrection. Sadly those sentiments will be echoed in many a sectarian Labour committee room which is hostile to Mr Kinnock's leadership.

However, perhaps Mr Scargill has ultimately done Britain a service. One consequence of the coal strike is that Britain has woken up to the much wider involvement of formal and informal communists in industrial and political life than most people realised. The reds are not under the bed. They are on the television screen, or the radio. They share Labour platforms. They patronise the TUC. They intimidate Mr Kinnock. They are feted at rallies. They are cheered when they abuse the police. Their parliamentary allies endorse their defiance of the law. Does this suggest that they have become respectable? Emphatically not. We have been warned.

Scargill the Stalinist?, discussed in the leading article on this page, is published by Oak-Tree Books Ltd., 11 Rosemont Road, London NW3, price £2.50.

9

World Anti-Terror Summit

1986

Nicholas Hagger met Desmond McForan in the Charing Cross Hotel on 20 February 1986 and dictated the Recommendations to end Soviet-based terrorism (below) to go into an Appendix in *The World Held Hostage*; a 'Heroes of the West' operation. On 30 April Lord Whitelaw, Margaret Thatcher's number 2, asked Nicholas Hagger if he could photocopy the Recommendations from an early proof of the book to hand to Margaret Thatcher, who would be attending a World Anti-Terror Summit in Tokyo a few days later. On 5 May the World Anti-Terror Summit accepted a British plan to end terrorism and effectively ended Soviet-based terrorism. *The World Held Hostage* was published on 1 July 1986.

The Recommendations, which were taken to the Summit, and the Summit's Statement, which was based on a British plan to end terrorism, can be compared below.

1. Nicholas Hagger's Recommendations to end terrorism, dictated to Desmond McForan and in *The World Held Hostage*

1. Airports
Airports in all Western countries should up-grade their security by using 3-dimensional scanners along with systematic baggage and personal searches, particularly at airports operating international flights. Only passengers should be allowed to enter any waiting area, thus reducing the possibility of further attacks such as those at Vienna and Rome airports in late December 1985. All airport personnel should undergo security clearance checks. On-board searches of ALL hand luggage would reduce the risk of an airport worker assisting terrorists to smuggle weaponry aboard.

2. Airlines
Western airlines who insist on flying to dangerous airports such as Beirut, Athens, Karachi, Manila, New Delhi and Tripoli, should be ordered by the airlines' own Government to effect adequate high-risk insurance for each passenger carried on any part of that flight. Similarly, the airlines' own Government should exact a levy from such airlines in order to underwrite such insurance in case the airlines themselves are unable to find insurers. This may have the effect of raising the cost of tickets to dangerous airports.

3. Exit visas

These should be introduced for all those individuals wishing to visit states such as Libya, Lebanon, Cuba, Iran, USSR and the Eastern *Bloc* and all countries involved in terrorism. Western nationals arriving back from those countries should be personally screened and nationals of those countries should undergo questioning.

4. Skymarshals

All flights should have skymarshals to increase on-board security. They should be armed with disabling darts which could be fired inside the planes without endangering the pressure level. Low velocity, small hand guns could also be considered for use.

5. Safeguarding of targets

All Western embassies, consulates, trade, cultural and other centres should, where appropriate, have barriers against car bombers erected. There should be a substantial increase in the installation of detection devices and, where necessary, an increase in military and/or security personnel.

6. The Hague Treaty of 1970

The reaffirmation of the Hague Treaty concerning the apprehension and extradition of aeroplane hijackers should be extended to include other hijackers of trains, buses, cars and ships. Those countries reaffirming the treaty must comply with its provisions and begin to isolate others which do not. Western governments should review their own policies towards terrorism and actively expose leaders of terrorist states who lie and protest their non-involvement.

7. Retaliatory action

All Western governments should seriously consider retaliatory action in order to intensify pressure upon the terrorists. In cases where specific countries such as Libya can be clearly identified as instigators of specific terrorist acts, Western governments should consider bombing specific military targets in those countries as both a reprisal and a deterrent. They should not be dissuaded by Gaddafi's[1] threats of "interminable war" made at the beginning of January 1986, and consideration should be given to toppling Gaddafi. All Palestinians, Shiites or Sikhs should, when a terrorist act is perpetrated by any of these factions against a Western democracy, stand guarantor and undergo thorough security screening. No funds from any of these nationals should be allowed to be transferred abroad until prior permission has been granted. All vehicles and all personnel should be searched and identified at each border crossing of each subscribing Western democracy. Capital Punishment should be reintroduced for all perpetrators of terrorist acts, involving loss of life. Security forces should be placed on a "search and destroy" footing regarding known terrorists who refuse to give themselves up, and there should be a system of rewards for information provided.

8. Diplomatic and other government personnel
Any country which supports terrorism should have its diplomatic missions reduced or recalled. The same should apply to other government personnel. Similar reductions should also take place in the diplomatic personnel representing those countries in the West. Since Robert Kennedy's assassination in 1968 by the Palestinian Sirhan Sirhan, world leaders have been imperilled, a process that culminated in Olaf Palme's murder on 28 February 1986. This was ordered by Abu Nidal and the Rejection Front to curtail Palme's Middle East peace-making.

9. Trade: economic sanctions
Western Governments should cut trade to those countries who aid and abet terrorism. Export grants should be withdrawn from companies trading with the USSR, Eastern *Bloc* countries, North Korea, Vietnam and Libya. Companies continuing to trade in violation of a Government directive should be fined a total of ten times the value of the order. A total Western ban should be placed on the issue of certificates of origin and any company found supplying them should be wholly investigated and fined.

10. Security liaison
A central national databank on terrorism should be created with an international link between countries mutually agreeing the extradition of terrorists for offences in any of the Pact countries. There should be a greater flow of information between the security forces of the West, and in turn these security forces should increase attempts at infiltration of terrorist organisations. At the same time increased security screening should be employed by the services in order to root out those who collaborate with known terrorists. There should also be a significant increase in the use of the "military option" where a successful operation is thought to be possible such as that carried out in December 1985 by Egypt in Malta. Crack Western military units should increase the amount of joint operation exercises undertaken, in order to present a co-ordinated anti-terrorist front.

11. The Press
Where terrorism is concerned, the press should be restricted in their reporting. It is simply not good enough for journalists to argue that censorship is being employed where terrorism is encouraged by free publicity. No one argues that news must be reported: it is the often hysterical way in which it is reported that

fuels the terror of acts committed in the hope that democracy will be destroyed. Simple, factual reported – restricted in length, and giving the minimum of facts – in the newspapers, with a partial television and radio blackout, only while negotiations are taking place, is not too much to ask of journalists when the very fabric of the society they supposedly avow is under critical threat. Procedures on the present UK system of the D-notice should work effectively. Offending newspapers and journalists should be reprimanded and their reporting rights curtailed.

12. Most importantly, Western Governments must act consistently and in concert. They must organise an Anti-Terror Summit of world Pact leaders in order to agree firstly, that hijackers will be extradited to their country of origin or tried in the country of arrival; secondly, that individual governments will not enter into agreements or accommodations with terrorists; thirdly, that no policy is enacted that will encourage terrorists, for example those convicted and imprisoned for terrorist crimes should *not* be considered for remission of sentence.

A firm policy regarding criminal acts linked to terrorism (bank robberies to acquire money to purchase weapons) should be formulated. Searches should also be continuously made to track the funding arrangements of terrorist groups and, where specific bank accounts can be traced, these should be seized.

If the USSR and other Third World countries continue to use the UN and its agencies in an improper fashion, then the Western democracies should reduce their contribution. In addition, they should give notice of withdrawal from those agencies most abused. The USA should assert its sovereignty over the New York UN Headquarters and should warn the KGB that spying and disinformation activities will not be tolerated. On 7 March 1986 the US finally made a start by ordering the Soviet Union to cut its diplomatic mission to the UN from 275 people to 170 by April 1988. If necessary, the West should withdraw *en bloc* from the UN or, at the very least, give notice that such a decision is on the table for serious consideration.

These proposals, enforced together, would reduce the terrorist menace to little more than the harmless baying of caged wolves and yet they represent the minimum level acceptable to all truly democratic societies and as such are easily attainable. To this end, I charge the leaders of each Western Government to begin their response to the terrorist threat by implementing these twelve points. It is their elected duty to protect us: it is unacceptable that they should not know how.

Unless these points are implemented leaders of the world's democracies will be directly responsible for the entire collapse of Western civilization at the hands of some 50 centrally co-ordinated anti-Western terrorist movements with their 2 million trained and armed destabilisers. The gravity of the situation cannot be emphasised too strongly, particularly since more than 2,000 Soviet military advisers have been sent by Gorbachev to bolster Gaddafi's *régime* since Gaddafi met Gorbachev in Moscow in October 1985. Some of the things this book warns against have come to pass since the book was finished: how much more will come to pass? Now that the facts have been clearly stated, and the many foregoing revelations show a pattern, the West must stand up to the anti-Western terrorists.

2. The World Anti-Terror Summit's Statement on International Terrorism, 5 May 1986 (based on British plan)

(Numbers in brackets refer to numbered points in Recommendations. The only point not included was 4, Skymarshals, which had cost and safety implications for airlines.)

Statement on International Terrorism, Tokyo Summit

1. We, the Heads of State or Government of seven major democracies and the representatives of the European Community, assembled here in Tokyo, strongly reaffirm our condemnation of international terrorism in all its forms, of its accomplices and of those, including governments, who sponsor or support it. We abhor the increase in the level of such terrorism since our last meeting, and in particular its blatant and cynical use as an instrument of Government policy. Terrorism has no justification. It spreads only by the use of contemptible means, ignoring the values of human life, freedom and dignity. It must be fought relentlessly and without compromise.

2. Recognizing that the continuing fight against terrorism is a task which the international community as a whole (12) has to undertake, we pledge ourselves to make maximum efforts to fight against the source. Terrorism must be fought effectively through determined, tenacious, discreet and patient action (5) combining national measures with international co-operation (10). Therefore, we urge all like-minded nations to collaborate with us, particularly in such international for as the United Nations, the International Civil Aviation Organization and the International Maritime Organization, drawing on their expertise to improve and extend countermeasures (5) against terrorism and those who sponsor or support it.

3. We, the Heads of State or Government, agree to intensify the exchange of information (10) in relevant *fora* on threat and potential threats (5) emanating from terrorist activities and those who sponsor or support them, and on ways to prevent them.

4. We specify the following as measures open to any government concerned to deny to international terrorists the opportunity and the means to carry out their aims (11), and to identify and deter those who perpetrate such terrorism. We have decided to apply these measures within the framework of international law (12) and in our own jurisdiction (12) in respect of any state which is clearly involved in sponsoring or supporting international terrorism, and in particular of Libya (7, 9, end),* until such time as the state concerned abandons its complicity in, or support for, such terrorism. These measures are:

- refusal to export arms (9) to states which sponsor or support terrorism;
- strict limits on the size of the diplomatic and consular missions (8) and other official bodies abroad of states which engage in such activities, control of travel of members of such missions and bodies, and, where appropriate, radical reductions in, or even the closure of, such missions and bodies;
- denial of entry (6) to all persons, including diplomatic personnel, who have been expelled or expelled or excluded from one of our states on suspicion of involvement in international terrorism or who have been convicted of such a terrorist offense;
- improved extradition (6) procedures within due process of domestic law for bringing to trial those who have perpetrated such acts of terrorism;
- stricter immigration and visa requirements (3) and procedures in respect of nationals of states which sponsor or support terrorism;
- the closest possible bilateral and multilateral co-operation between police and security (1, 3, 10) organizations and other relevant authorities in the fight against terrorism.

Each of us is committed to work in the appropriate international bodies to which we belong to ensure that similar measures are accepted and acted upon by as many other governments as possible.

5. We will maintain close co-operation in furthering the objectives of this statement and in considering further measures. We agree to make the 1978 Bonn Declaration more effective in dealing with all forms of terrorism affecting civil aviation (1, 2). We are ready to promote bilaterally and multilaterally further actions to be taken in international organizations or *fora* competent to fight against international terrorism in any of its forms.

*Retaliation against Libya (7) took place with the bombing on 15 April 1986, shortly before the Summit.

10

International Politics

Nicholas Hagger championed patriotic British causes, freeing Europe from Soviet occupation and delivering a Universalist World State. His initiatives and pro-Western, Churchillian principles and stance in international politics (encapsulated in 'The Heroes of the West') were 'behind the scenes' and spread out over 50 years, but when drawn together are seen to have advanced the British cause, defended the West against Soviet expansionism during the Cold War and shaped the post-1991 world and a coming World State.

Aug 1960	Located the UK's most wanted enemy, Col. Grivas, in Greece.
Nov 1961–Jun 1962	Implemented Churchill's policy of reconciling Sunnis, Shiites and Kurds in Iraq.
Nov 1961–Jan 1962	Helped monitor Kaseem's military movements in Baghdad.
Jul 1965	Clinched Japanese loan to Bank of England.
Oct 1965	Helped plan Prince and Princess Hitachi's State visit to UK.
19 Jun 1966	Received a vision of enlightened world leaders in a World State's world government in the Cathedral of the Archangel in Moscow (described in 'Archangel'); now stood for a World State.
Nov–Dec 1966	Pressed for increase in Japanese funding of Asian Development Bank.
31 Oct 1966, 9 Jan 1967	Called for the removal of Mao.
19 Mar 1967	Discovered the Chinese Cultural Revolution while interrogating the Vice-President of Peking University.
3, 15 Nov 1968, 1969	Inspired a *coup* to keep Libya pro-Western after King Idris and was set to control Libyan oil.
24 Aug 1969	Wrote an article on the closeness of Libyan-British relations that appeared in English and Arabic in Libya – and triggered Gaddafi's 1–September Revolution.
5 Sep 1969	Planned date for pro-Western *coup* to be carried out by Col. Saad eddin Bushwerib and Ben Nagy for Muntassers.
Oct–Nov 1969	Arranged the defection to the UK of Viktor and his

	nuclear secrets, fending off attempt by the CIA to persuade Viktor to defect to the US.
1 Jan 1970	Knocked off Col. Gaddafi's peaked hat in defiance of Gaddafi's Revolution.
19 Feb 1970	First to locate Soviet SAM-3 missile transporter, near El Alamein.
27–28 May 1970	Defied Mohammed Barassi's terror-state threats of execution on behalf of Gaddafi.
24 Aug 1970–	
17 May 1973	Appointed as Edward Heath's 'unofficial Ambassador' to the African liberation movements and Chinese.
12 Sep 1972	Persuaded Tanzanian Minister of Foreign Affairs to move Tanzania away from the Chinese and back towards British and Western influence, and to invite Sir Alec Douglas-Home and Edward Heath to visit Dar and offer British aid.
20 Sep 1972	Outmanoeuvred the entire Tanzanian state to access restricted area of Chinese Tanzam railway by appealing to President Nyerere.
6–7 Nov 1976	Wrote 'The European Resurgence' about the coming expansion of Europe.
24 Nov 1976	Told Thatcher at the Waldorf Hotel that East-European nations should be liberated from the Soviet Union.
11 Nov 1983	Explained FREE (Freedom for the Republics of Eastern Europe) to Lord Whitelaw, Thatcher's no. 2.
12 Nov 1983–May 1984	Wrote papers on FREE.
20 Feb 1984	Spoke to Brian Crozier about a new group, 'The Heroes of the West'.
15 Nov 1984	Exposed anti-Western Communist influence on the British miners' strike, sending Scargill to the Soviet Embassy.
20 Feb 1986	Spoke to McForan about 'The Heroes of the West'.
24 Mar 1986	Meeting at Swiss Cottage Holiday Inn to eliminate Gaddafi's anti-Western missiles near Sebha.
30 Apr 1986	Identified Victor, Lord Rothschild to Lord Whitelaw as fifth man, triggering Rothschild's appeal to Thatcher.
30 Apr 1986	Permitted Lord Whitelaw to photocopy Recommendations, Soviet-based terrorism ended at Tokyo Summit of 4–6 May which implemented

	Recommendations.
1 Jul 1986	Drew attention to the Babysitter who was supplying Gaddafi with arms through Heathrow.
Oct 1986	Inspired Krassó to petition for democracy in four East-European countries.
4 Nov 1986	Exposed anti-Western Philby's betrayal of 45 British agents in Hungary, all of whom were executed.
4 Nov 1986	Broadcast on FREE behind Iron Curtain and into USSR and challenged Soviet sphere of influence agreed at 1943 Tehran Conference.
27 Nov 1986	Inspired Bukovsky's Resistance International to include FREE aims.
22 Jul–7 Aug 1987	Planned to export satellite dishes behind Iron Curtain to counter Soviet propaganda.
1987–1988	FREE implemented in monthly meetings of Committee of Captive Nations.
26 Feb 1988	Declined to be considered to replace Biggs-Davison as MP.
9–10 Jan 1993, 27 Feb, 16 Apr 1994	Delved into the New World Order at conference on Global Deception and visited the organiser.
28 Oct 1995	Delivered four of his books to Solzhenitsyn in Moscow.
9 Dec 1998	Spoke to Martin Taylor, Secretary of the Bilderberg Group, about the timing of the New World Order and the earth-dollar.
3 Apr–28 Jun 1999	Exposed plan to break UK into 8 regions in *The Tragedy of Prince Tudor*.
26 Oct 1999	Involved in defending the House of Lords when his Literary Secretary, the Earl of Burford, leapt onto the woolsack to protest at the abolition of the hereditary peers' 700-year-old voting rights in the Lords.
2004	Exposed the self-interested New World Order of the Syndicate.
17 Jan 2007	Drove past Natanz nuclear site in Iran, machine-guns trained on his car proved that Iran had something to hide in Natanz.
18 Jan 2007	Contemplated an end to Iran's nuclear program at Jamkaran mosque, near the Hidden Imam's well.
22 May–5 Sep 2008, 21 Jan–22 Jul 2009	Exposed al-Qaeda's plan to explode 20 nuclear-suitcase bombs in 10 US cities (confirmed by Hans

Blix in 2004) in *Armageddon,* his second poetic epic on the War on Terror.

17 Aug–23 Nov 2009   Set out the World State in *The World Government.*

Notes and References

The narrative draws on files, letters, notes, diaries, pocket diaries, newspaper articles, booklets and other autobiographical material. These sources, including the *Diaries,* are in the Hagger archive. The notes are numbered within episodes rather than chapters.

Most of the quotations in the narrative are from Nicholas Hagger's *Diaries,* 1963–2013. To avoid overuse of notes there is often only one note in each headed section. (In long sections there will be more than one note.) This note will list a succession of dates relating to *Diary* entries in the order in which they appear within the section. Some listings will therefore not be in strict chronological order. The important thing is that there is a source, written on the day on which they happened, for most of the events and reflections in the text, which do not just depend on my memory. Almost every word in every section can therefore be sourced and verified by referring to the dates listed in each note. Ideally, every sentence would have a sourcing note, but this is clearly impractical and the above solution is the best alternative.

There are separate notes within a paragraph for dates of more significant or evidential quotations, and for sources other than the *Diaries.*

Epigraphs
1.   *The Times,* 'Have found secret of DNA, love Daddy', 23 March 2013, p.3.

Prologue: The Path

PART ONE
Towards the Shimmering Rainbow
1.   Through a Mist of Unknowing: Dark Night of the Spirit and Infused Powers
1.   Nicholas Hagger, *A View of Epping Forest,* p.101.

Episode 1: Remarriage and Comprehensive Education
1.   *The autobiography of William Butler Yeats,* p.128.
2.   Hagger, *Diaries,* 7, 11, 20 October 1973.
3.   Hagger, *Diaries,* 22–24 October 1973; 21 August 1984; 2, 3, 6, 8 November 1973.
4.   Hagger, *Diaries,* 16, 18, 22, 23, 30, 31 December 1973.
5.   Hagger, *Diaries,* 18, 24, 26–28 January 1974.
6.   Hagger, *Diaries,* 29 January, 3, 5, 7, 8 February 1974.
7.   Hagger, *Diaries,* 9, 17, 23 February 1974.
8.   Hagger, *Diaries,* 12 April 1974.

9.   Hagger, *Diaries*, 23, 29, 30 April, 6, 5, 10, 13 May 1974.

10.   Hagger, *Diaries*, 31 May, 1, 2, 11, 14, 18, 21 June 1974.

11.   Hagger, *Diaries*, 5 July 1974.

12.   Hagger, *Diaries*, 17 July 1974.

13.   Hagger, *Diaries*, 18 July 1974.

Episode 2: Lyric Poetry and Administration

1.   Hagger, *Diaries*, 20 July 1974.

2.   Hagger, *Diaries*, 24, 25 July, 2 August, 29 July 1974.

3.   Hagger, *Diaries*, 4, 5, 7, 10, 11 August 1974.

4.   Hagger, *Diaries*, 14, 15, 25, 28 August, 2 September 1974.

5.   Hagger, *Diaries*, 28 August 1974.

6.   Hagger, *Diaries*, 7, 27, 29 September 1974.

7.   Hagger, *Diaries*, 3 October 1974.

8.   Hagger, *Diaries*, 3, 13, 26 October 1974.

9.   Hagger, *Diaries*, 26 October 1974.

10.   Hagger, *Diaries*, 2–4, 6, 9, 10, 25, 27 November 1974.

11.   Hagger, *Diaries*, 29 November, 14, 4, 7, 1 December 1974.

12.   Hagger, *Diaries*, 21, 26, 28 December 1974; 1 January 1975.

13.   Hagger, *Diaries*, 31 January, 8, 9, 14, 16, 23 February, 1, 2 March 1975.

14.   Hagger, *Diaries*, 9, 12, 21, 26 March, 1, 5, 12 April 1975.

15.   Hagger, *Diaries*, 13, 19, 21 April, 12 May, 11 June 1975.

16.   Hagger, *Diaries*, 12–28 June, 8, 9 July 1975.

17.   Hagger, *Diaries*, 3– 7 July 1975.

18.   Hagger, *Diaries*, 2 August 1975.

19.   Hagger, *Diaries*, 2 August 1975.

20.   Hagger, *Diaries*, 2 August 1975.

21.   Hagger, *Diaries*, 4–6 August 1975. See photo in *A Summary of King Arthur in Cornwall*, Tintagel, 1936, 1974, p.27.

22.   Hagger, *Diaries*, 7, 8, 10 August 1975.

23.   Hagger, *Diaries*, 10, 11 August 1975.

24.   Hagger, *Diaries*, 12, 13–17, 19, 18, 21, 30 August 1975.

25.   Hagger, *Diaries*, 14, 16, 19 September, 9, 18 October 1975.

26.   Hagger, *Diaries*, 23 October 1975.

27.   Hagger, *Diaries*, 26 October 1975.

28.   Card from Frank Tuohy, 31 October 1975; in the Hagger archive.

29.   Hagger, *Diaries*, 30 October 1975.

30.   Hagger, *Diaries*, 2, 4–5, 5, 30 November, 2, 6, 13, 20, 22 December 1975.

31.   Hagger, *Diaries*, 6, 7–12, 28, 31 December 1975.

32.   Hagger, *Diaries*, 9 November 1975; 21 February 1976; 11 November 1975.

33.   Hagger, *Diaries*, 26, 27 February, 13, 27 March, 4 April 1976; 21 December 1975; 11 April 1976.

34. Hagger, *Diaries*, 13–15, 18, 19 April 1976.
35. Hagger, *Diaries*, 26, 28 April, 5, 6 May 1976.
36. Hagger, *Diaries*, 10, 15, 30 May, 5 June 1976.
37. Hagger, *A New Philosophy of Literature*, pp.415–421.
38. Hagger, *Diaries*, 22 June 1976.
39. Hagger, *Diaries*, 23 June 1976.
40. Hagger, *Diaries*, 1, 4, 13, 16, 29, 30 August 1976.
41. Hagger, *Diaries*, 30 August, 18 September, 5 October 1976.
42. Hagger, *Diaries*, 5, 17–24 October, 6 November 1976.
43. Hagger, *Diaries*, 24 November 1976.
44. Hagger, *Diaries*, 15, 16 October, 6 November, 29 October 1976.
45. Hagger, *Diaries*, 27 September, 13, 14 November 1976.
46. Frank Tuohy, *Yeats: An Illustrated Biography*, Herbert Press, 1976, 1991.
47. Hagger, *Diaries*, 5 December 1976.
48. Hagger, *Diaries*, 20, 30 December 1976.
49. Hagger, *Diaries*, 16–22 April 1977.
50. Hagger, *Diaries*, 5 April 1977.
51. Hagger, *Diaries*, 26 April, 4 May 1977.
52. Hagger, *Diaries*, 9 March 1977.
53. Hagger, *Diaries*, 6, 15, 18 May 1977.
54. Hagger, *Diaries*, 26 May–8 June, 25 June, 1 July 1977.
55. Hagger, *Diaries*, 27, 28 July 1977.

Episode 3: New Powers and Dogmatic Authority
1. Hagger, *Diaries*, 31 July, 1–4 August 1977.
2. Hagger, *Diaries*, 13, 18, 21 August 1977.
3. Hagger, *Diaries*, 25 September, 12, 27, 31 October 1977.
4. Letter from Nicholas Hagger to Frank Tuohy, 26 November 1977; in the Hagger archive.
5. Hagger, *Diaries*, undated 13–26 November 1977.
6. Card from Frank Tuohy to Nicholas Hagger, 20 July 1974; in the Hagger archive.
7. Hagger, *Diaries*, undated 13–26 November, 10, 17, 18, 22, 28 December 1977; 2 April 1978.
8. Hagger, *Diaries*, 16, 18 April, 1, 14, undated after 14 May 1978.
9. Hagger, *Diaries*, 21 January 1978.
10. Hagger, *Diaries*, 20, 24, 28 August 1978.
11. Hagger, *Diaries*, 12, 26 May, 11 June, 11, 21 July 1978.
12. Hagger, *Diaries*, 23 July 1978.
13. Hagger, *Diaries*, 3, 5 August 1978.
14. Hagger, *Diaries*, 16 September 1978.
15. Letter from Asa Briggs to Nicholas Hagger, 20 October 1978, following

Gaudy; in the Hagger archive.

16. Hagger, *Diaries*, 18, 20 October 1978.
17. Hagger, *Diaries*, 5, 10 November 1978.
18. Hagger, *Diaries*, 15, 18 November, 13 December 1978.
19. Hagger, *Diaries*, 1, 4 February 1979.
20. Hagger, *Diaries*, 17 February 1979. *See* also letter from Nicholas Hagger to Christopher Ricks, 18 February 1979. (Appendix 6, p.929)
21. Hagger, *Diaries*, 17, 20 February 1979.
22. For details of this conversation, *see* Hagger, *Collected Poems 1958–2005*, p.873.
23. Hagger, *Diaries*, 11, 12 March 1979.
24. Hagger, *Diaries*, 14 April 1979.
25. Hagger, *Diaries*, 13, 26 May, 11 June 1979.
26. Hagger, *Diaries*, 17 June, 6, 18 July 1979.
27. Hagger, *Diaries*, 8 June 1979.
28. Hagger, *Diaries*, 8, 12, 13, 15, 17 August 1979.
29. Hagger, *Diaries*, 24, 28 August 1979.
30. Hagger, *Diaries*, 8, 18 September, 8–10, 19 October 1979.
31. Hagger, *Diaries*, 7, 27 October, 10, 11 November, 22, 23 December 1979.
32. Hagger, *Diaries*, 23, 24, 26 December 1979; 3, 12, 14 January 1980.
33. Hagger, *Diaries*, 19 January 1980.
34. Hagger, *Diaries*, 21 January 1980.
35. Hagger, *Diaries*, 27 January, 12 February 1980.
36. Hagger, *Diaries*, 29 January, 10 February 1980.
37. Hagger, *Diaries*, 19, after 22 February, 21–24, 28, 30 March, 10 April, 30 March 1980.
38. Hagger, *Diaries*, 9, 17 April, 3, 5, 11, 16 May, undated 31 May–7 June 1980.
39. Hagger, *Diaries*, 21, 28–29, 30 May, 7 June, 21 May 1980.
40. Hagger, *Diaries*, undated 7–20 June, 21 May, 20, 28–29, 22 June 1980.
41. Hagger, *Diaries*, 2, 5, 11 July, 7, 26 August 1980.
42. Hagger, *Diaries*, 20, 27 September, 1 October, 19 September, 3, 10, 11 October 1980.
43. Hagger, *Diaries*, 14, 30 October 1980.
44. Hagger, *Diaries*, 20, 22, 23, 30 November 1980.
45. Hagger, *Diaries*, 21, 14 December 1980; 3, 5 January 1981.
46. Hagger, *Diaries*, 25 November 1980; 11 January, 10, 22 February, 4 March 1981.
47. Hagger, *Diaries*, 14, 15 March, 12, undated 14–20 April 1981.

2. Ordeals of Independence: Trials of the Dark Night, Battles against Communism

Episode 4: Baroque and Egalitarian Socialism

1. Hagger, *Diaries*, undated after 21, 29 March, 14 April 1981.
2. Hagger, *Diaries*, undated 14–20 April, 2 May, 22, 25 April 1981.
3. Hagger, *Diaries*, 8, 10, 11, 16, 24 May 1981.
4. Hagger, *Diaries*, 29–31 May, 8, 14 June 1981.
5. Hagger, *Diaries*, 21 June 1981.
6. Hagger, *Diaries*, 18 July 1981.
7. Hagger, *Diaries*, 20 April, 11, 12, 20, 26 July 1981.
8. Hagger, *Diaries*, 30, 31 July, 1–3, 8, 9 August 1981.
9. Hardwicke Drummond Rawnsley, *Reminiscences of Wordsworth among the Peasantry of Westmoreland*, p.13.
10. Hagger, *Diaries*, 11, 13, 21 August 1981.
11. Hagger, *Diaries*, 5, 13, 20 August, 4 September 1981.
12. Hagger, *Diaries*, 1, 2, 4, 9 November 1981; 12 July 1983; 14 February 1988.
13. Hagger, *Diaries*, 21, 23 November, 19 December 1981; 2, 9, 12 January 1982.
14. Hagger, *Diaries*, 17, 24, 30, 31 January 1982.
15. Hagger, *Diaries*, 5, 21, 22 February, 4 March 1982.
16. Hagger, *Diaries*, 7, 4, 7, 10, 15, 17, 24 April, undated 25 April–2 May 1982.
17. Hagger, *Diaries*, 2, 27 May, 12, 14, 15 June, 29 May 1982.
18. Hagger, *Diaries*, 12 February, 10 May, 8 April, 11 July, 11, 16 August 1982.
19. Hagger, *Diaries*, 19, 20–22, 25 August 1982.
20. Hagger, *Diaries*, 29 October, 23 December 1982.
21. Hagger, *Diaries*, 3, 5 October, 7, 26 November 1982.
22. Hagger, *Diaries*, 25–27 February 1983.
23. Hagger, *Diaries*, 3 April, undated 20 May–10 June 1983.
24. Hagger, *Diaries*, 6, undated 6–20 May, 12 February 1983.
25. Hagger, *Diaries*, undated 27 January–12 February, 19 June, 6 July 1983.
26. Hagger, *Diaries*, 2, 4–8, 10 August 1983.
27. Hagger, *Diaries*, 24, 25 July, 2, 9, 11, 12 August 1983.
28. Hagger, *Diaries*, 13, 16, 17 August, 13 September 1983.
29. Hagger, *Diaries*, 18 August, 3 September 1983.

Episode 5: Vision and Subversion
1. Hagger, *Diaries*, 20 September 1983.
2. Hagger, *Diaries*, 25 September 1983.
3. Letter from Prof. C.B. Cox to Nicholas Hagger, 20 January 1984; in the Hagger archive.
4. Hagger, *Diaries*, 1, 2, 5, 7, 15 October 1983.
5. Hagger, *Diaries*, 12, undated 12–22 November 1983.
6. Hagger, *Diaries*, undated 17–25, 31 December 1983; 1, 2, 6, 27 January 1984.
7. Letter from Sir John Biggs-Davison MP to Nicholas Hagger, 19 January 1984; in the Hagger archive.
8. Letter from Josef Josten to Sir John Biggs-Davison MP, 4 January 1984; in

the Hagger archive.

9. Letter from Nicholas Hagger to Sir John Biggs-Davison MP, 22 January 1984; in the Hagger archive.

10. Letter from Nicholas Hagger to Sir John Biggs-Davison MP, 23 January 1984; in the Hagger archive.

11. Letter from Sir John Biggs-Davison MP to Nicholas Hagger, 26 January 1984; in the Hagger archive

12. Letter from Nicholas Hagger to Sir John Biggs-Davison MP, 29 January 1984; in the Hagger archive.

13. Letters from Sir John Biggs-Davison MP to Josef Josten and Brian Crozier, 31 January 1984; in the Hagger archive.

14. Brian Crozier, *Free Agent: The Unseen War 1941–1991*, p.31.

15. *Guinness Book of World Records*, 1988.

16. The FREE (Freedom for the Republics of Eastern Europe) Movement, full-length version, paragraph 50; in the Hagger archive.

17. Letter from George Miller to Nicholas Hagger, 22 February 1984; in the Hagger archive.

18. Invitation and compliments card; in the Hagger archive.

19. Letter from Nicholas Hagger to Sir John Biggs-Davison MP, 23 February 1984; in the Hagger archive.

20. Hagger, *Diaries*, 19 March, 27 April 1984.

21. Letter from Nicholas Hagger to Sir John Biggs-Davison MP, 23 March 1984; in the Hagger archive.

22. Hagger, *Diaries*, undated 19 March–9 April 1984.

23. Letter from Sir John Biggs-Davison MP to Nicholas Hagger, 26 March 1984; in the Hagger archive.

24. Letter from Nicholas Hagger to Sir John Biggs-Davison MP, 29 March 1984; in the Hagger archive.

25. Letter from Sir John Biggs-Davison MP to Nicholas Hagger, 3 April 1984; in the Hagger archive.

26. Letter from Nicholas Hagger to Brian Crozier, 2 April 1984; in the Hagger archive.

27. Hagger, *Diaries*, 17 May 1984.

28. Letter from Nicholas Hagger to Jeremy Mitchell, 13 April 1984; in the Hagger archive.

29. Hagger, *Diaries*, undated 9–17 April 1984.

30. Letter from Brian Crozier to Nicholas Hagger, 3 April 1984; in the Hagger archive.

31. Hagger, *Diaries*, 17 April 1984.

32. Letter from Josef Josten to Nicholas Hagger, 18 April 1984; in the Hagger archive.

33. Letter from Sir John Biggs-Davison's Private Secretary to Nicholas Hagger,

19 April 1984; in the Hagger archive.

34. Letter from Nicholas Hagger to Brian Crozier, 24 April 1984; in the Hagger archive.

35. Letter from Josef Josten to Nicholas Hagger, 15 June 1984; in the Hagger archive.

36. Letter from Nicholas Hagger to Josef Josten, 24 June 1984; in the Hagger archive.

37. Letter from Josef Josten to Nicholas Hagger, 2 July 1984.

38. Letter from Nicholas Hagger to Josef Josten, 4 July 1984.

39. Hagger, *Diaries*, undated 27–31, 31 May, 12 June 1984.

40. Letter from Nicholas Hagger to Charlie-Douglas Home, 16 July 1984; in the Hagger archive.

41. Hagger, *Diaries*, 20, 26 July, 12 May, undated 28 June–14 July 1984.

42. Hagger, *Diaries*, 30 July 1984.

43. Hagger, *Diaries*, 31 July, 1, 5, 6 August 1984.

44. Hagger, *Diaries*, 7, 8 August 1984.

45. Hagger, *Diaries*, 9 August 1984.

46. Letter from John Keats to his brother Tom, 6 August 1818.

47. Hagger, *Diaries*, 10, 11 August 1984.

48. Letter from Nicholas Hagger to William Deedes, 13 August 1984; in the Hagger archive.

49. Hagger, *Diaries*, 17, 18, 19 August 1984.

50. Letters from Nicholas Hagger to Charlie Douglas-Home, Bill Deedes and Josef Josten, 19 August 1984; in the Hagger archive.

51. Hagger, *Diaries*, 5, 21–23, 26 August 1984.

52. Letter from Peter Stothard to Nicholas Hagger, 10 August 1984; in the Hagger archive.

53. Hagger, *Diaries*, 1, 13, 20, 8, 12, 15, 12, 17 September 1984.

54. Hagger, *Diaries*, 29 January 1985; 15, 25 September 1984.

55. Bishop of Durham, *The Daily Telegraph*, 9 October 1984.

56. Hagger, *Diaries*, 30 September 1984.

57. Letters from Josef Josten to Nicholas Hagger, 17 September, 9 October 1984; in the Hagger archive.

58. Letter from Josef Josten to Nicholas Hagger, 31 October 1984; in the Hagger archive.

59. Hagger, *Diaries*, 4 November, 16 October 1984.

60. Letter from Josef Josten to Nicholas Hagger, 9 November 1984; in the Hagger archive.

61. *The Times Diary*, 15 November 1984; in the Hagger archive.

62. *Daily Mail*, 16 November 1984; in the Hagger archive.

63. Hagger, *Diaries*, 17 November 1984.

64. Seumas Milne, *The Enemy Within*, p.275.

65. *The Daily Mail*, 3 January 2014, pp.12–13, 'Maggie plan to put Army on streets'.
66. Hagger, *Diaries*, 23 November 1984.
67. Nicholas Hagger's typed speech for the launch, 29 November 1984; in the Hagger archive.
68. Hagger, *Diaries*, 1 December 1984.
69. Draft typed agreement, undated; in the Hagger archive.
70. Letter from Nicholas Hagger to Josef Josten, 2 December 1984; in the Hagger archive.
71. *The Times Diary*, 'Book Marx', 14 December 1984; in the Hagger archive.
72. Hagger, *Diaries*, 22 December 1984.
73. Letter from Nicholas Hagger to Brian Crozier, 6 January 1985; in the Hagger archive.
74. Letter from Brian Crozier to Nicholas Hagger, 9 January 1985; in the Hagger archive.
75. '*Scargill the Stalinist?* – second edition', accompanying Brian Crozier's letter to Nicholas Hagger of 5 January 1985; in the Hagger archive.
76. Hagger, *Diaries*, 18, 22 January, 10, undated 15–23, 15 February 1985.
77. Hagger, *Diaries*, 23, 24 February 1985.
78. Hagger, *Diaries*, 6 March 1985.
79. Letter from John Cameron to Nicholas Hagger; in the Hagger archive.
80. Letter from John Cameron to Nicholas Hagger, 12 August 1985; in the Hagger archive.
81. Hagger, *Diaries*, 27 September 1985.
82. Jessica Douglas-Home in conversation with Nicholas Hagger, 28 September 1986.

Episode 6: Universalism and Expansionism
1. Hagger, *Diaries*, 30 March 1985.
2. Hagger, *Diaries*, 6, 7 April 1985.
3. Hagger, *Diaries*, 8–9 April 1985.
4. Hagger, *Diaries*, 9–11 April 1985.
5. Hagger, *Diaries*, 15 April 1985.
6. Hagger, *Diaries*, 17, 18 April 1985.
7. Hagger, *Diaries*, 18, 19 April 1985.
8. Hagger, *Diaries*, 20 April 1985.
9. Hagger, *Diaries*, 20–24, 29 April 1985.
10. Hagger, *Diaries*, 26, 28 April, 2, 5, 6, 12 1985.
11. Hagger, *Diaries*, 11 May 1985; visit to Shoreham on 30 May, recorded in Hagger, *Diaries*, 2 June 1985.
12. Hagger, *Diaries*, 1–3 June 1985.
13. Hagger, *Diaries*, 14, 21 June, 2 (dancers), 13, 14, 17 July 1985.

14. Hagger, *Diaries*, 19–22, 23, 24, 27 July 1985.

15. Hagger, *Diaries*, 9, 11 August 1985.

16. Hagger, *Diaries*, 12 August 1985.

17. Hagger, *Diaries*, 16, 17, 19, 20–22 August 1985.

18. Hagger, *Diaries*, undated 9–23 November 1985.

19. Hagger, *Diaries*, 25, 26, undated 23–30 August (order and harmony), undated 1–7, 9 September 1985.

20. Hagger, *Diaries*, 21, 25 September, 3, 19 October 1985.

21. Hagger, *Diaries*, 2 October 1985 (and letter from Caroline Wilson to Nicholas Hagger; in the Hagger archive), undated 8–13 December 1985.

22. Also *see* Christine Toomey, 'Revealed: Pact's Blitzkrieg Plan to Invade West', *Sunday Times*, 28 March 1993.

23. This view of Philby was repeated in February 1986, *see* Hagger *Diaries*, undated 22 February–16 March 1986.

24. Christopher Wilson, *The Daily Telegraph*, 22 November 2009; *Daily Mail*, 1 June 2013.

25. Hagger, *Diaries*, 3 November 1985.

26. *The Spectator*, 21 September 2002.

27. Hagger, *Diaries*, 3, 9, 23 November, 6 December 1985.

28. Hagger, *Diaries*, 7 December 1985.

29. Hagger, *Diaries*, 20 December 1985.

30. Hagger, *Diaries*, 14, undated 14–21 January 1986.

31. Hagger, *Diaries*, 21 January, 20 February 1986.

32. Desmond McForan, *The World Held Hostage, The War Waged by International Terrorism*, pp.133–134.

33. McForan, *op. cit.*, pp.229–233.

34. Hagger, *Diaries*, 25 January, 26 February, undated 26 January–2 February, 4 February 1986.

35. Hagger, *Diaries*, 21–22 February 1986.

36. Hagger, *Diaries*, undated 22 February–16 March 1986.

37. Hagger, *Diaries*, undated 22 February–16 March 1986.

38. Hagger, *Diaries*, 24, 26 May 1986.

39. Nicholas Hagger, *Scargill the Stalinist?*, p.127.

40. McForan, *op. cit.*, pp.146, 150–153, 124, 144–145, 234.

41. Hagger, *Diaries*, 30 March, 5, undated 5–10 April 1986.

42. Letter from Sir George Trevelyan to Nicholas Hagger, 12 April 1986.

43. Hagger, *Diaries*, 14, 15 April 1986.

44. Hagger, *Diaries*, 15–18 April, 17 May 1986.

45. Hagger, *Diaries*, undated 19–23, 26 April 1986.

46. Hagger, *Diaries*, 30 April 1986.

47. McForan, *op. cit.*, pp.229–233.

48. Hagger, *Diaries*, 1 May 1986.

49. Hagger, *Diaries*, 3 May 1986.
50. Hagger, *Diaries*, 4 May 1986.
51. Hagger, *Diaries*, undated 3–17 May 1986.
52. Hagger, *Diaries*, undated 18–24, 31 May, 6 June 1986.
53. Hagger, *Diaries*, 21, 27 June, undated 27 June–6 July 1986.
54. Hagger, *Diaries*, 7 July 1986.
55. Hagger, *Diaries*, 8, 16 July 1986.
56. *The Times*, 21 April 1988.
57. Hagger, *Diaries*, 17, 19, 26 July 1986.
58. Hagger, *Diaries*, 26 July 1986.
59. Hagger, *Diaries*, 30 July 1986.
60. Hagger, *Diaries*, 2–6 August 1986.
61. Hagger, *Diaries*, 12–14 August 1986.
62. Hagger, *Diaries*, 16, 17, 19, 21, 22, 21, 23, 25 August 1986.
63. Hagger, *Diaries*, 3, 6 September 1986.
64. Hagger, *Diaries*, 14, 28 September 1986.
65. Hagger, *Diaries*, 10, 17, 21, 22, 25–27 October 1986.
66. Hagger, *Diaries*, 2, 3 November 1986.
67. Hagger, *Diaries*, 2, 12 November 1986.
68. Karen de Young, in 'Bin Laden Took Part in 1986 Arms Deal, Book Says', http://www.washingtonpost.com/wp-dyn/content/story/2008/03/31/ST2008033102952.html, states that Osama bin Laden flew to London in 1986 to help negotiate the purchase of Russian-made surface-to-air missiles to be used by Arab fighters battling the Soviet military in Afghanistan, according to Steve Coll's *The Bin Ladens: An Arabian Family in the American Century*, Penguin Press, 2008. The deal for Russian SA-7 missiles was arranged via contacts with the German arms manufacturer Heckler & Koch through an associate of Salem bin Laden. Osama bin Laden and his half-brother Salem bin Laden met the contacts several times at the Dorchester Hotel, London. According to 'Context of (Early-Mid 1986): Salem Bin Laden Asks Pentagon to Supply Missiles to Arab Afghans, Receives No Reply', sub-heading 'Mid-1986: Osama and Salem Bin Laden Purchase Anti-Aircraft Missiles in London', http://www.historycommons.org/context.jsp?item=aearlymid86salempentagon, the bin Ladens were in London in mid-1986 buying anti-aircraft missiles, and in late 1986 Osama bin Laden was establishing the first training camp in Afghanistan for Arabs fighting in the Soviet-Afghan war. They apparently flew from London to America. They may have stopped in London in early November during their return to Afghanistan.
69. Hagger, *Diaries*, 4 November 1986.
70. Hagger, *Diaries*, 17, 27 November, 3 December 1986.
71. *The Times* and *The Daily Telegraph*, 3 December 1986.

72. Hagger, *Diaries*, 6, undated 7–15 December 1986.
73. Roland Perry, *The Fifth Man*, p.89.
74. Hagger, *Diaries*, 31 December 1986; 13 January 1987.
75. Hagger, *Diaries*, 21 January 1987.
76. Hagger, *Diaries*, 18 February 1987.

PART TWO
The Unitive Way: the Seven Hills of Achievement
3. Arrival in the Hills
Episode 7: Metaphysical Poetry and World History

1. Hagger, *Diaries*, 7, undated 7–15, undated 19–23, 23, 27, 28 December 1986; 9 January, undated 3–9, 14 February 1987.
2. Hagger, *Diaries*, undated 22–26 March, 1, 3, 4, 19 20, 26 April, 15 June, 4 May, 22 June, 18 May, 2 June, 4 May 1987.
3. Jack Straw, *Last Man Standing, Memoirs of a Political Survivor*, Macmillan, 2012, chapter 1.
4. Hagger, *Diaries*, 11–13 April 1987.
5. Hagger, *Diaries*, 15–16 July 1987.
6. Hagger, *Diaries*, 30 July 1987.
7. Hagger, *Diaries*, 1–4 August 1987.
8. Letter from Kathleen Raine to Nicholas Hagger; in the Hagger archive.
9. Hagger, *Diaries*, 14, 15, 17, 18, 27 August 1987.
10. Hagger, *Diaries*, 22 July, 7 August 1987.
11. Hagger, *Diaries*, 14, 24 September 1987; undated 3–8 April 1988.
12. Hagger, *Diaries*, 10, 14 October, 3, undated 10–23, 24 November, 25, 27, 29, 30 December 1987; 2, 18, 24 January, 28 February, 27 March 1988.
13. Hagger, *Diaries*, 27 November 1987.
14. Hagger, *Diaries*, 1 December 1987; 3, 11 January 1988.
15. Hagger, *Diaries*, 7, 24, 27 August 1987; 26 January, 25 February 1988.
16. Card from Kathleen Raine to Nicholas Hagger, 4 March 1988; in the Hagger archive.
17. Hagger, *Diaries*, 25 February 1988; 16 September, 27 November, 11, 13 December 1987; 3, 17, 18, 24, 17–18, 24, 18 February 1988.
18. Hagger, *Diaries*, undated 3–10 February 1988.
19. Hagger, Diaries, 8–9, 10–11, 21 April 1988.
20. Hagger, *Diaries*, 18–19 May, 6, 18 June, 3, undated 5–9 July 1988.
21. Hagger, *Diaries*, 28 May, undated 30 May–2 June, 26 July, 4, 7, 12 August, undated 28 August–8 September 1988.
22. Hagger, *Diaries*, 26 February 1988, undated 23–26 September, 6 October 1988; 3 February 1989.
23. E.F.W. Tomlin, *T.S. Eliot: A Friendship*, pp.232–233.
24. Hagger, *Diaries*, 26, 27 September 1988.

25. Hagger, *Diaries*, 20, 12, 25–27 October 1988.
26. Hagger, *Diaries*, 3, 8 November, 23 December 1988; 12, 14, 13 February, 26 March 1989.
27. Hagger, *Diaries*, 26 March, 1–3 April 1989.
28. Hagger, *Diaries*, 4 March, 28 April 1989.
29. Hagger, *Diaries*, 29 April, 11 May 1989
30. Hagger, *Diaries*, 9 June 1989.
31. Hagger, *Diaries*, 30 May, 1, 29 June, 13, 20–21 July 1989.
32. Hagger, *Diaries*, 19 July 1989
33. Hagger, *Diaries*, 23–27 July 1989.
34. Hagger, *Diaries*, 1, 6, 8, 10, 13, 14, 10, 15 August 1989.
35. Hagger, *Diaries*, 12, 13, 16–19, 25 August, undated 2–16 September, 20, 23, undated 20–24, 24, 26 October 1989.
36. Hagger, *Diaries*, 10, 22 September, 4, 25 November 1989.
37. Hagger, *Diaries*, 29 December 1989; 25–26 January, 4, 10, 11, 15, 20 February, 7, 8, March, 28 January, 9 March 1990.
38. Hagger, *Diaries*, 28 October, undated 28 October–1 November, 28 October 1989.
39. Hagger, *Diaries*, 28, 30 October 1989.
40. Hagger, *Diaries*, 21 November, 3, 18–20 December 1989.
41. Hagger, *Diaries*, 22, 25–27, 31 December 1989.
42. Hagger, *Diaries*, 18, 19 March 1990.
43. Hagger, *Diaries*, 20, 23–25, 25 March, 4 February, 28 March, 1, 2, 6–13, 21 April 1990.
44. Hagger, Diaries, 21, 24, 25, 16, 28, 29 April 1990.
45. Hagger, *Diaries*, 14, 20, 26, 31 May, 12, 20, 24 June, undated 28 June–2 July 1990.
46. Hagger, *Diaries*, 9 July 1990.
47. Hagger, *Diaries*, 25–27, 29, 30 July, 6, 10, 11 August 1990.
48. Hagger, *Diaries*, 14, 19–20, 26, 28, 29 August 1990.
49. Hagger, *Diaries*, 2, 4, 13, 20–22, 21, 22, 28, 29 September, 2–4, 6, 15, 25 October, 9, 16, 14, 20 November 1990.
50. Hagger, *Diaries*, 7–9 December 1990.
51. Hagger, *Diaries*, 10, 19, 24, 25 December 1990.
52. Hagger, *Diaries*, 14, 22, 29 January, 3, 8, 25 February, 4, 8, 11, 21, 22 March 1991.
53. Letters from Kathleen Raine to Nicholas Hagger, 21, 25 March 1991; in the Hagger archive.
54. Hagger, *Diaries*, 27, 29, 30 March, 2–4 April 1991.
55. Hagger, *Diaries*, 5–7 April 1991.
56. Hagger, *Diaries*, 10, 12, 16–19, 18–21 April 1991.
57. Hagger, *Diaries*, 22 April 1991.

58. David Gascoyne, *Journal 1937–1939*, p.141.
59. Hagger, *Diaries*, 22 April, undated 2–6 May, 25 April 1991.
60. Leaflet, '*Temenos* Academy of Integral Studies', "Part-time teaching posts and duties would be offered to... Nicholas Hagger, Philosophy of History (taught from the Integral standpoint)".
61. Hagger, *Diaries*, 28 April 1991.
62. Letter from Sebastian Barker to Nicholas Hagger, 28 April 1991; in the Hagger archive.
63. Hagger, *Diaries*, 28 April, 6, 11 May 1991.
64. Letter from Frank Kermode to Nicholas Hagger, 11 May 1991; in the Hagger archive.
65. Hagger, *Diaries*, 14, 17 May 1991.
66. Letter from Kathleen Raine to Nicholas Hagger, 12 May 1991; in the Hagger archive.
67. Hagger, *Diaries*, 15, 23, 25, 28 May 1991.
68. Hagger, *Diaries*, 28–30 May 1991.
69. Letter from Kathleen Raine to Nicholas Hagger, 1 May 1991; in the Hagger archive.
70. Letter from Kathleen Raine to Nicholas Hagger, 12 May 1991; in the Hagger archive.
71. Letter from Nicholas Hagger to Kathleen Raine, 4 June 1991; in the Hagger archive.
72. Letter from Nicholas Hagger to Kathleen Raine, 9 June 1991; in the Hagger archive.
73. Letter from Nicholas Hagger to Kathleen Raine, 14 June 1991; in the Hagger archive.
74. Hagger, *Diaries*, 5, 10, 23, 25, 26, 29 June, 7, 19–22, 24, 25, 27–29, 31 July 1991.
75. Hagger, *Diaries*, 3 August 1991.

Episode 8: Philosophy and Practical Mysticism
1. Hagger, *Diaries*, 25 July 1991.
2. Letter from Colin Wilson to Nicholas Hagger; in the Hagger archive.
3. Hagger, *Diaries*, 5 August 1991.
4. Hagger, *Diaries*, 6, 7, 9 August 1991.
5. Hagger, *Diaries*, 27 March, 4 June, 13, 14 August 1991.
6. Hagger, *Diaries*, 15 August 1991.
7. Hagger, *Diaries*, 15–18, 20, 19–22 August 1991.
8. Hagger, *Diaries*, 22–24, 29 August 1991.
9. Hagger, *Diaries*, 2, 17 September 1991.
10. Hagger, *Diaries*, 3, 8 September 1991.
11. Hagger, *Diaries*, 17 September, 3, 5, 9, 12, 23–24, 28, 27–28 October, 10, 11, 15, 16 November, 6, 10–12 December 1991; 26–27 March 1992; 20, 21

September 1991.

12. Hagger, *Diaries*, 22 September 1991.

13. Letter from T.S. Eliot to Colin Wilson; quoted in Hagger, *Diaries*, 18 December 1991; in the Hagger archive.

14. Hagger, *Diaries*, 26, 29 September 1991.

15. Hagger, *Diaries*, 1–2 October 1991.

16. Hagger, *Diaries*, 19–22 October 1991.

17. Hagger, *Diaries*, 7, 10, 17 November 1991.

18. Hagger, *Diaries*, 27 September, 1, 4 October, 10, 13, 14, 16, 21 November 1991.

19. Hagger, *Diaries*, 26–28 November, 5, 7, 27 December 1991.

20. Hagger, *Diaries*, 16, 18 December 1991.

21. A.N. Whitehead, *Modes of Thought*; in *Alfred North Whitehead, An Anthology*, p.924.

22. Hagger, *Diaries*, 18–20, 23–25 December 1991.

23. Hagger, *Diaries*, 3 January 1992; 30, 31 December 1991; 5, 9, 5, 8 January 1992.

24. Hagger, *Diaries*, 16 January 1992.

25. Nicholas Hagger, *The Universe and the Light*, pp.121–161.

26. Hagger, *Diaries*, 27 February 1992.

27. Hagger, *Diaries*, 23, 24 August, 26 December 1991; 30, 31 January, 7, 8 February, 31 January 1992.

28. Hagger, *Diaries*, 11 February 1992.

29. Hagger, *Diaries*, 17 February, 5 March, 12 August 1992.

30. Hagger, *Diaries*, 3, 10 February 1992.

31. Hagger, *Diaries*, 15–20, 29 February, 9, 13, 18, 28, 15, 23 March, 1, 2, 4, 5, 7, 8 April 1992.

32. Hagger, *Diaries*, 25 January, 12, 15 February 1992.

33. Hagger, *Diaries*, 10, 12, 10–12, 14, 16, 19 April 1992. For the *Diary* entry of 7 September 1963 *see* Nicholas Hagger, *Awakening to the Light*, p.43.

34. Hagger, *Diaries*, 16–18, 23, 25, 26, 28, 30 April, 2, 1, 3, 10 May 1992.

35. Hagger, *Diaries*, 23 March, 2, 3, 5, 9, 10, 16, 13, 15 May, 28 August, 17, 18 May 1992.

36. Hagger, *Diaries*, 19, 24, 26, 27, 25–29 May 1992.

37. Hagger, *Diaries*, 30, 26 May, 2, 1, 5–7, 11–14, 16–18 June 1992.

38. Hagger, *Diaries*, 20–22 June 1992.

39. Hagger, *Diaries*, 19, 22, 23 June, 5 July, 24, 29 June, 1 July, 30 June, 1–3, 8, 6, 12, 10, 12, 15, 13, 15–20, 22, 27, 30, 31 July, 3–5, 7, 9 August 1992.

40. Hagger, *Diaries*, 1 September 1992.

41. Hagger, *Diaries*, 1–4 September 1992.

42. Hagger, *Diaries*, 4, 5, 8–10, 12, 15–17, 19 September 1992.

43. Hagger, *Diaries*, 19 September, 3 November, 21, 22, 26, 27 September, 3, 8

October, 24 August, 8, 13, 14 October 1992.

Episode 9: Autobiography and International Politics
1. Hagger, *Diaries*, 8–11 August 1992.
2. Letter from Sir Laurens van der Post to Nicholas Hagger, 5 August 1992; in the Hagger archive.
3. Hagger, *Diaries*, 12, 14, 15, 17, 18, 21, 27, 30, 31 August 1992.
4. Hagger, *Diaries*, 24 December, 15, 16 October 1992; 4, 8, 9, 12 January 1993.
5. Hagger, *Diaries*, 22, 25, 28 October, 1, 15, 16 November, 26 October, 26 November, 27 October, 1 December 1992.
6. Hagger, *Diaries*, 9–11, 24 December 1992
7. Hagger, *Diaries*, 2, 12 January 1993.
8. Hagger, *Diaries*, 17–19 December 1992; 2, 26 January 1993.
9. Hagger, *Diaries*, 24, 27 January 1993.
10. Hagger, *Diaries*, 28 January–1 February, 9, 11, 14, 23–26 February, 9, 13, 24, 25 March, 28 February, 21, 29 March 1993.
11. Hagger, *Diaries*, 2–6, 5 April 1993.
12. Hagger, *Diaries*, 6, 7 April 1993.
13. Hagger, *Diaries*, 9, 10, 12 April 1993.
14. Hagger, *Diaries*, 13 April 1993.
15. Hagger, *Diaries*, 14 April 1993.
16. Hagger, *Diaries*, 16–19, 21–24 April 1993.
17. Hagger, *Diaries*, 27 April 1993.
18. Hagger, *Diaries*, 30 March, 29 April–2 May 1993.
19. Hagger, *Diaries*, 3 May 1993.
20. Nicholas Hagger, *A New Philosophy of Literature*, pp.336–371.
21. Hagger, *Diaries*, 3 May 1993.
22. Hagger, *Diaries*, 4 May 1993.
23. Hagger, *Diaries*, 5, 6 May 1993.
24. Hagger, *Diaries*, 9, 11 May 1993.
25. Hagger, *Diaries*, 9–10 May 1993.
26. Hagger, *Diaries*, 11–12 May 1993.
27. Hagger, *Diaries*, 6, 16, 17 May 1993.
28. Hagger, *Diaries*, 19, 22, 25 May 1993.
29. Hagger, *Diaries*, 2, 5, 7, 8 June 1993.
30. Hagger, *Diaries*, 14, 21 June 1993.
31. Hagger, *Diaries*, 8–10, 12–14, 16, 20, 28 July 1993.
32. Hagger, *Diaries*, 4 August 1993.
33. Hagger, *Diaries*, 9, 13–16 August 1993.
34. Hagger, *Diaries*, 18 August 1993.
35. Hagger, *Diaries*, 21 August 1993.
36. Hagger, *Diaries*, 20–25, 28 August 1993.

37. Hagger, *Diaries*, 31 August 1993.
38. Hagger, *Diaries*, 1, 2, 4 September 1993.
39. Hagger, *Diaries*, 17 September, 1 October, 18, 20, 26–28 September, 3, 8, 12, 13, 17 October 1993.
40. Hagger, *Diaries*, 19 October 1993.
41. Hagger, *Diaries*, 22–24 October, 2 November, 31 October, 8 November 1993.
42. Hagger, *Diaries*, 14 June, 27 October, 25 September 1993.
43. Hagger, *Diaries*, 2, 5 November 1993.
44. Hagger, *Diaries*, 11 November 1993.
45. Hagger, *Diaries*, 3 October, 19 November, 1, 3, 2, 4, 6–9, 12, 14, 15 December 1993.
46. Hagger, *Diaries*, 27 February, 12, 19, 23 March, 14 April 1994.
47. Hagger, *Diaries*, 9, 16 April, 10 May 1994.
48. Hagger, *Diaries*, 20, 22 April 1994.
49. Hagger, *Diaries*, 22 April 1994.
50. Hagger, *Diaries*, 14 May 1994.
51. Hagger, *Diaries*, 19 May 1994.
52. Hagger, *Diaries*, 30 December 1993; 30 January, 5, 19–20 February, 25 March, 4 April, 31 March, 5, 30 April, 21 May 1994.

4. Hard Slog: Contemplative Works
Episode 10: Epic and European Culture

1. Hagger, *Diaries*, 8 February, 15 March, 7 May 1994.
2. Hagger, Diaries, 29–31 May, 1, 2 June, 7 April, 2–4 June 1994.
3. Hagger, *Diaries*, 11, 17–19 June 1994.
4. Hagger, *Diaries*, 8 June, 29 March, 2, 9 August, 20, 23 June, 7, 11, 16 July 1994.
5. Hagger, *Diaries*, 29 June, 4 July 1994.
6. Hagger, *Diaries*, 27 June 1994.
7. Hagger, *Diaries*, 2, 9, 18–30, 31 July 1994.
8. Hagger, *Diaries*, 10, 12–17, 30, 31 August 1994.
9. Hagger, *Diaries*, 2, 3, 9, 26 August, 4, 8, 24 September, 3, 6 October 1994.
10. Hagger, *Diaries*, 10, 26 September, 6 October 1994.
11. Hagger, *Diaries*, 6–9 October 1994.
12. Hagger, *Diaries*, 15, 16, 19 October 1994; 17 January 1995; 31 October 1994; 22 March 2003.
13. Hagger, *Diaries*, 11–14, 20 October 1994.
14. Hagger, *Diaries*, 21, 23, 24, 26, 30 October, 2, 5, 18, 26, 28, 29 November, 3, 23, 5, 6 December 1994; 7 January 1995.
15. Hagger, *Diaries*, 29 November, 9, 10, 9, 13, 25, 27 December 1994; 1 January 1995; 4 December 1994; 13, 18, 19–21, 26, 27, 31 January, 1, 4, 11, 12, 17, 19 February, 9 March 1995; *The Mail on Sunday*, 9 March 2014.

16. Hagger, *Diaries*, 3, 17 March 1995.
17. Hagger, *Diaries*, 21 December 1994; 24 January, 10 March 1995.
18. Hagger, *Diaries*, 19, 20 March 1995.
19. Hagger, *Diaries*, 25, 31 March–6 April 1995.
20. Hagger, *Diaries*, 27 April–1 May 1995.
21. Hagger, *Diaries*, 8, 13, 28 May, 20, 24, 30 June 1995.
22. According to Tilty Public Records, Hagger, *Diaries*, 17 June 1995.
23. Hagger, *Diaries*, 20, 22, 23 April, 2, 3 June, 2 July 1995.
24. Hagger, *Diaries*, 18 May, 14, 8, 25 June, 4, 5 July 1995.
25. Hagger, *Diaries*, 14–25 July 1995.
26. Hagger, *Diaries*, 22, 26, 30, 31 August, 1, 25, 30 September, 1 October 1995.
27. Hagger, *Diaries*, 15–20 October 1995.
28. Hagger, *Diaries*, 24–27 October, 10 April, 16 September, 8, 9, 28 October 1995.
29. Hagger, *Diaries*, 10 November, 11, 7, 14–16, 23, 19, 23, 30, 31 December 1995; 5, 20, 21, 23, 25, 28, 23 January 1996.
30. Letter from Ted Hughes to Nicholas Hagger, 28 January 1996; in the Hagger archive.
31. Hagger, *Diaries*, 21, 22, 29 February, 1, 12 March 1996.
32. Hagger, *Diaries*, 19 January, 16 February, 21–23, 29 March, 1 April 1996.
33. Hagger, *Diaries*, 3, 4, 6, 9, 10, 17, 30 April 1996.
34. Hagger, *Diaries*, 30 April–4 May 1996.
35. Hagger, *Diaries*, 12–14, 24–27, 30 May, 1, 2, 1, 5, 6, 12, 28, 29, 7 June, 1, 8–10 July 1996.
36. Hagger, *Diaries*, 12–26 July 1996.
37. Hagger, *Diaries*, 17, 18, 25, 29 August 1996.
38. Hagger, *Diaries*, 13, 15 August, 9, 10, 12, 14, 15, 21, 17–21 September 1996.
39. Hagger, *Diaries*, 22–25 September 1996.
40. Hagger, *Diaries*, 7 October, 23, 10 November, 24, 26 October, 4 November, 24 December, 8, 16, 21 November, 2, 5, 9, 17 December 1996.

Episode 11: Verse Plays and Tudor Knots
1. Hagger, *Diaries*, 20 December 1996; 25 January 1997; 24 December 1996.
2. Nicholas Hagger, *A View of Epping Forest*, pp.197–199.
3. Hagger, *Diaries*, 29 December 1996.
4. Hagger, *Diaries*, 1, 3, 4, 6, 11, 15, 18, 19, 21–24 January, 20 March 1997.
5. Hagger, *Diaries*, 21, 22 February, 17, 26, 15, 22 March, 8–11, 23, 25–27 April, 1, 2, 5, 9–11, 16, 17 May 1997.
6. Hagger, *Diaries*, 14, 21 May 1997.
7. Hagger, *Diaries*, 25–27, 29, 30 May, 1, 5, 21, 13, 14, 10, 23 June 1997; 30 January 1998; 16, 25, 27 June, 1 August, 30 July, 20, 5, 23 August, 1, 21, 22, 28 July, 24, 25 September 1997.

8. Hagger, *Diaries*, 2, 18, 23, 3–5, 26, 31 July, 18 August, 3, 7 September, 7, 14, 27 July, 1, 4, 7–10, 12, 21, 28 August, 8, 13, 18, 22, 27–30 September, 2– 4 October, 21 December, 30, 28 November, 31 December 1997; 20, 28 January 1998.

9. Hagger, *Diaries*, 13 October, 1 November 1997; 5, 11, 16 January, 22 March, 30 July–1 August 1998.

10. Hagger, *Diaries*, 26, 28 October, 9, 10, 15, 16, 25 November 1997.

11. Hagger, *Diaries*, 15, 17 October 1997; 14, 17 February 1998.

12. Hagger, *Diaries*, 4, 18, 19 November, 8 December, 28 November, 6, 1, 15, 18, 19 December 1997; 15 April 1999; 25, 30, 26, 29 December 1997; 1, 16, 18 January, 6 February 1998.

13. Hagger, *Diaries*, 28 January, 7 February, 13 March, 11 May, 18 July 1998.

14. Hagger, *Diaries*, 24, 25, 29, 31 January, 1–3, 9, 12, 17, 18 February, 2, 6, 11, 30 March, 6 April, 30 January, 6 April, 15 May, 16 June 1998.

15. Hagger, *Diaries*, 31 March, 10, 14 February 1998.

16. Hagger, *Diaries*, 2, 3, 11 April, 31 May, 29 June 1998.

17. Hagger, *Diaries*, 19, 20, 22 February 1998.

18. Hagger, *Diaries*, 13, 29, 31 March, 24, 25 April, 3, 4, 15, 21, 23–25 May, 2, 5, 7–9, 12, 14, 17 June, 23 February, 18, 19 March, 18–20 June, 3, 4, 11, 12 July 1998.

19. Diarmaid MacCulloch, *Suffolk and the Tudors: Politics and Religion in an English County, 1500–1600*.

20. Hagger, *Diaries*, 16, 18, 19 July 1998.

21. Hagger, *Diaries*, 20–24 July 1998.

22. Hagger, *Diaries*, 27, 29 July, 13, 15, 16, 22 August 1998.

23. Karl Galinsky's *Augustan Culture*, p.242. (For universalism in Augustan poetry, *see* pp.237–244.)

24. Hagger, *Diaries*, 23 August, 13 September, 24, 4–6, 19, 28, 15, 26, 27 August, 3 September, 30, 31 July, 1–3, 13, 18, 26 August, 1 September, 13 October, 7, 18–20 August, 23, 13 September, 5 August 1998.

25. Hagger, *Diaries*, 14 September 1998, 2 October 1998, 25 July 1997.

26. Hagger, *Diaries*, 9–18 October 1998.

27. Hagger, *Diaries*, 23, 29 October, 6, 8 November 1998.

28. Hagger, *Diaries*, 14 November 1998; 23 February 1999; 10 November 1998.

29. Richard Hakluyt, *The Principall Navigations*, in Hakluyt, *Voyages*, vols 1–8.

30. Hagger, *Diaries*, 23 November 1998.

31. Hagger, *Diaries*, 30 November 1998.

32. Hagger, *Diaries*, 25 November, 4, 9 December 1998.

33. Hagger, *Diaries*, 28 November 1998; 30 May 1999; 30 November, 2 December 1998; 11 January 1999; 21, 15 December 1998.

34. Hagger, *Diaries*, 8, 15, 19, 24, 25, 29 January, 15, 6 February 1999.

35. Hagger, *Diaries*, 2, 27, 28 January, 2–5 February 1999.

36. Hagger, *Diaries*, 7, 10, 11, 18 February 1999.
37. Hagger, *Diaries*, 15, 16, 24, 26, 27 February, 2, 6, 9, 10, 12, 13, 15, 16, 19 March, 3, 4, 13 April 1999.
38. Hagger, *Diaries*, 18, 20, 26 March, 2, 5, 8, 15, 16, 28 April, 4, 5 May 1999.
39. Hagger, *Diaries*, 7–9 May 1999.
40. Hagger, *Diaries*, 14, 16, 21 May, 29 March, 27 May, 1, 4, 3 June 1999.
41. Hagger, *Diaries*, 15, 20, 31 December 1998; 9 January 1999.
42. Hagger, *Diaries*, 29 March, 2 April 1999.
43. Nicholas Hagger, *The Libyan Revolution*, p.275, 'Old Regimes', 14 September 1969.
44. Nicholas Hagger, *The Secret History of the West*, pp.125–126.
45. Nicholas Hagger, *The Secret History of the West*, p.131.
46. Hagger, *Diaries*, 28–30 April, 19 May, 10 June 1999.
47. Hagger, *Diaries*, 10, 25, 27, 28, 30 June, 1 July 1999.

Episode 12: Classical Odes and utopianism

1. Hagger, *Diaries*, 24, 12 June, 13 July, 14 June, 5, 11, 15, 9 July 1999.
2. Hagger, *Diaries*, 17–20 July 1999.
3. Hagger, *Diaries*, 24 July, 17, 21, 24 August, 7, 11, 12, 17, 18, 20, 30 September 1999.
4. Hagger, *Diaries*, 12 October 1999; Nicholas Hagger, *A View of Epping Forest*, p.265.
5. Hagger, *Diaries*, 10, 11, 18, 19, 22 November 1999; 11, 29 March, 5 April 2000.
6. *See* http://www.youtube.com/watch?v=tx2wmZUUc88&list=PL51462CE4 3DDD3BDB&index=7
7. Hagger, *Diaries*, 26 October, 26 November 1999, 26, 27 October, 9 December, 29 October, 1, 3–6, 26, 29 November 1999.
8. Hagger, *Diaries*, 31 December 1999; 1, 2, 27, 28, 31 January, 14 February 2000; 5 October 1999; 18, 25, 26 February, 2, 4, 16–18 March, 16, 19, 20 February, 21 March, 13 April 2000. For 15–50 per cent, *see* 'UK law: What proportion is influenced by the EU?', https://fullfact.org/europe/eu_make_ uk_law-29587.
9. Hagger, *Diaries*, 12, 13 April 2000.
10. Hagger, *Diaries*, 14–21 April 2000.
11. Hagger, *Diaries*, 26–28 April, 21, 28 June 2000.
12. Hagger, *Diaries*, 3, 6, 7, 9, 10 May, 30 April, 13, 14, 21, 23, 27, 31, 28, 29 May, 4, 9, 14, 16, 17, 21, 27 June, 6, 12, 13 July 2000.
13. Hagger, *Diaries*, 10–13, 18, 19, 22, 24, 25 June, 8, 19, 29, 31 July, 1, 2 August, 9, 22 September 2000.
14. Hagger, *Diaries*, 1 July 2000.
15. Hagger, *Diaries*, 14–20 July 2000.

16. Hagger, *Diaries*, 26 July, 1, 8, 9, 11,12, 14, 17–20 August, 9, 19 September, 5 October, 12, 13, 15 December 2000.

17. Hagger, *Diaries*, 4, 5 August, 23 July, 14, 23, 24, 26, 31 August, 1, 2 September, 24 July, 30, 31 August, 16, 21, 22, 24 September 2000.

18. Hagger, *Diaries*, 28 September–2 October, 4, 21, 26 October, 8, 18, 24, 26, 29 November, 2, 3 December 2000.

19. Hagger, *Diaries*, 10, 15, 20, 22 October, 4 November, 24, 25, 27 October, 13 September, 7 November, 13, 18 October, 2, 9, 11 November 2000.

20. Hagger, *Diaries*, 14, 15 November 2000; 5 August 2009.

21. Hagger, *Diaries*, 19 November, 6, 7, 12, 17, 19, 22, 28–31 December 2000; 3, 4, 11, 17 January, 8 March, 7 June 2001.

22. Hagger, *Diaries*, 13–15 February, 19, 23, 25, 27 February 2001

23. Hagger, *Diaries*, 30 March–6 April 2001.

24. Hagger, *Diaries*, 5, 14, 22 March 2001.

25. Nicholas Hagger, Guidebook, *Otley Hall*, 2001.

26. Hagger, *Diaries*, 8, 23, 27 April, 2 May, 17 December 2001.

27. Hagger, *Diaries*, 6–20 May 2001; for Lockerbie, *see The Daily Telegraph*, 'Iran's Lockerbie bombers', 10 March 2014 .

28. Hagger, *Diaries*, 27 May, 8, 13, 17, 25 June, 11 July, 27 June, 11 July, 9 August, 11, 12, 15 July, 11, 15, 16 August 2001.

29. *See* http://www.celebritynetworth.com/richest-businessmen.

30. Hagger, *Diaries*, 6, 8, 10–12 September 2001.

31. Hagger, *Diaries*, 2, 5, 8 October 2001.

32. Hagger, *Diaries*, 27 September, 25 October, 1, 24, 26, 7, 8, 10–12, 24 November, 8, 12 December 2001.

33. Hagger, *Diaries*, 22, 26, 29 September, 4, 29–31 October, 30 November, 2, 27 December 2001.

34. Hagger, *Diaries*, 30 January, 7, 21, 26 February 2002; 6 December 2001; 27, 28 February, 3, 16 March 2002.

35. Hagger, *Diaries*, 23–28 March 2002.

36. Hagger, *Diaries*, 29 March, 2, 3, 28 April, 5 July 2002.

37. Hagger, *Diaries*, 5, 12, 13, 25, 26, 19, 20, 22, 24 April, 1, 2, 5, 6, 8, 9, 13 May 2002.

38. Hagger, *Diaries*, 17–20 May 2002.

39. Hagger, *Diaries*, 21, 25–27, 30 May, 1, 3, 5, 8, 15, 20, 16, 17 June 2002.

40. Hagger, *Diaries*, 1 May, 21–24, 29, 30 June 2002.

41. Hagger, *Diaries*, 11, 23 May, 5 September, 1, 11, 13, 14 July 2002.

42. Hagger, *Diaries*, 7, 10, 17–30 July, 31 July–13 August, 14–22, 16, 19 August, 29, 1, 12, 18, 28 September, 2 October 2002.

43. Hagger, *Diaries*, 4, 5, 11, 15–17, 19, 20 October, 2, 5 November, 5, 8 December 2002.

44. Hagger, *Diaries*, 9–22 November 2002.

45. Hagger, *Diaries*, 30, 31 December 2001; 5, 6 March 2002.
46. Hagger, *Diaries*, 12, 19, 27 September, 1, 8, 10 October 2002, 16, 31 December 2002; 31 January, 1, 3 March, 13, 18 January, 2 February, 26 April 2003; 15 December 2002; 28 January 2003.
47. For pictures of Bartholomew Gosnold's skeleton, *see* http://anthropology.si.edu/writteninbone/unusual_case.html.
48. Hagger, *Diaries*, 12 February, 6 March, 18 February, 13 September 2003.
49. Hagger, *Diaries*, 21, 26, 5, 20 January, 3–5, 7, 10, 11, 18–21, 21, 28 February, 31 March, 5, 10, 11, 15, 12, 13 April, 21, 25 January, 19, 27 February, 2, 4, 17, 18 March, 25, 16, 18 April 2003.

5. Final Ascent: Unitive Vision
Episode 13: Collected Literature and Secret History
1. Hagger, *Diaries*, 16, 19 February, 14, 23, 10, 20–24 March, 4, 13, 14, 19, 20 April 2003.
2. Hagger, *Diaries*, 8, 16, 20 May, 11, 12 July, 9, 11 September, 17, 20 October, 4, 6, 11–14 November 2003.
3. Hagger, *Diaries*, 14, 15, 17, 27 June, 9, 24 September, 8 October 2003.
4. Hagger, *Diaries*, 12, 14, 16, 21 May, 7 July, 4, 18 June, 1, 4, 8 July, 27 August, 19 September, 17, 24 October, 21 September, 6 December, 13 October 2003.
5. Hagger, *Diaries*, 17, 18–21 July, 9, 13, 25 August, 6, 16, 17, 19, 20, 24 September, 13, 18, 30, 9 December 2003; 7, 10, 12, 14 November 2005.
6. Hagger, *Diaries*, 4, 16 September, 9, 16, 17, 29, 30 October, 12, 27 November, 2 December 2003; 17 January 2005.
7. Hagger, *Diaries*, 17–21 November 2003.
8. Hagger, *Diaries*, 10, 12 March, 24 June, 7, 8 July, 19 October, 3 November, 13 August, 15, 25, 27 October, 1, 7, 29 January, 3, 9 February, 19–23, 25 November, 28, 29 December 2004; 26 April, 10, 11 November 2005; 5 January, 24 August, 24 September 2009.
9. Completion was on 23 June 2004.
10. Hagger, *Diaries*, 13, 15–18, 20 March, 6, 13 April, 4, 7, 15 May 2004.
11. Letter between solicitors of 22 June 2004, enclosing a letter from Suffolk County Council of 17 June 2004; in the Hagger archive.
12. Letter from Nicholas Hagger to John Jones of 28 June 2004; in the Hagger archive.
13. Hagger, *Diaries*, 11, 14, 29 June, 12, 14, 20, 15, 29 July, 16, 19, 29, 31 August 2004.
14. Hagger, *Diaries*, 21–23 May 2004.
15. Hagger, *Diaries*, 13, 15, 19, 21, 22, 24 August, 8, 9, 28 September, 23, 24, 26 December 2004.
16. Nicholas Hagger, *A View of Epping Forest*, pp.240–241.
17. Hagger, *Diaries*, 16–21 July 2004; 9 March 2009.

18. Hagger, *Diaries*, 8, 25 July, 7, 27–30 August, 7 September, 3, 8 November 2004; 21 November 2005.

19. Hagger, *Diaries*, 2–5 January, 25 April, 1, 4 May 2004.

20. Hagger, *Diaries*, 26 April, 13, 30 July, 23 August, 4, 28 September, 3 October 2004.

21. Hagger, *Diaries*, 2–4 August 2004.

22. Hagger, *Diaries*, 3 November, 30 November–2 December 2004.

23. Hagger, *Diaries*, 20 January, 4 March, 2 July, 8 December 2004; 26 January, 9, 23 February 2005.

24. Hagger, *Diaries*, 11, 16 March, 25, 26 February 2005.

25. Hagger, *Diaries*, 26 July, 19, 28 November, 22, 24 January, 4 June, 4, 14 July, 5 August 2005; 9, 10, 12, 13, 16 January, 9, 12, 13 August 2006.

26. Hagger, *Diaries*, 1–8 December 2005. For the Sphinx as Khufu, *see* Nicholas Hagger, *The Light of Civilization*, pp.62–63.

27. Hagger, *Diaries*, 13, 20, 27, 29 April, 11 May, 9 July 2005.

28. Hagger, *Diaries*, 8 February 2006.

29. Hagger, *Diaries*, 3, 4 May 2003.

30. For 300 billion stars and 20 billion earth-like planets, *see* http://science.time.com/2013/11/04/so-much-for-earth-being-special-there-could-be-20-billion-just-like-it/. For 500 billion stars *see* http://www.daily-galaxy.com/my_weblog/2013/06/500-billion-a-universe-of-galaxies-some-older-than-milky-way.html.

31. Hagger, *Diaries*, 5, 8, 16, 26–31 July, 17, 19, 20 August 2005.

32. Hagger, *Diaries*, 27 November, 8, 15 December, 5 November, 30 March–5April, 8–10, 30 April 2005; 21–30 January, 11–19, 23 May 2006.

33. Hagger, *Diaries*, 2–5, 7, 8, 11, 12, 15, 16, 24, 28 January, 15, 16 February, 26 July, 5–7, 14, 17, 22, 24, 29, 31 May, 4 June, 19 August, 5, 8 November, 18 December 2005; 7, 13, 14, 16, 29, 31 January 2006; 17–20 August, 13–19 September, 29 October 2007; 4–8, 18 February 2008; 1 June 2005.

34. Hagger, *Diaries*, 29 July 2004; 14 April 1998.

35. *See* http://andromeda.rutgers.edu/~jlynch/Texts/aubrey-shakespeare.html.

36. *See* http://www.oxfordhistory.org.uk/mayors/1603_1714/davenant_john_16 21.html.

37. *See* http://www.headington.org.uk/oxon/cornmarket/east/03_painted_roo m.html.

38. Hagger, *Diaries*, 1, 9–12 May 2005.

39. Hagger, *Diaries*, 19–21 May 2005.

40. Hagger, *Diaries*, 1, 3, 6 June 2005.

41. Hagger, *Diaries*, 25 January, 13 June 2005.

42. Hagger, *Diaries*, 8, 9, 13 May 2003.

43. Hagger, *Diaries*, 13 June, 15 March, 22, 25 May, 11 June, 10, 19 August, 23 September, 26 October, 30 December 2005; 6, 9, 27 March, 28 April 2006; 4,

14 January, 24 February, 14, 24, 30 March, 20, 21 July, 6 October, 11 November, 7, 8 December 2005; 10, 24 January, 3, 23 March, 3 April, 11, 14 August, 17, 19 November 2006; 29 March, 5, 26 April, 30 May, 1, 2, 10, 12, 16 June, 4, 12, 19, 25 August, 18 October, 5, 18 December 2005; 26 January, 30 April 2006; 19 July, 5 December, 12 October 2005.

44. Hagger, *Diaries*, 9 July, 13 September 2003.

45. Hagger, *Diaries*, 21 August, 26 June, 15, 17, 22, 29, 30 September, 14, 16, 29 November, 23, 27 December 2005.

46. Hagger, *Diaries*, 24 April, 15, 17 September 2005.

47. Hagger, *Diaries*, 12, 14 November 2005.

48. Hagger, *Diaries*, 22 November 2005.

49. Hagger, *Diaries*, 11 July, 19 September, 27 October, 3, 20 December 2005.

50. Hagger, *Diaries*, 12 February 2006.

51. Nicholas Hagger, *A View of Epping Forest*, p.166.

52. Hagger, *Diaries*, 29–31 October, 9, 15, 26 November, 2, 9, 10, 14 December 2005.

53. Hagger, *Diaries*, 4 February 2006.

54. Hagger, *Diaries*, 14, 15, 24, 27, 28 April, 11, 17 May 2006.

55. Hagger, *Diaries*, 27 April, 25 May, 7, 11, 14, 15, 20 June, 4, 5, 15 August, 1 September, 18 October, 19 December 2005; 18 May 2006; 27, 28 November 2008; 16, 19, 22, 23, 25 June, 12, 13, 25 July, 6, 8, 9 September, 18, 21, 26, 30 October, 22 November, 21 December 2006.

56. Hagger, *Diaries*, 22 November 2005; 14–19, 25 January, 1, 2 February, 23–27, 30 October 2006; 23, 25–26, 29–30 January, 5, 19, 20, 22–23 February, 30 April 2007.

57. Hagger, *Diaries*, 24 March, 18 April, 3 May 2006.

58. Hagger, *Diaries*, 16, 17, 20–25 July, 5–7, 21, 23 August 2005; 5, 6, 9, 20, 24–31 May, 1–5 June 2006.

59. Hagger, *Diaries*, 5 January, 8, 10, 18 February, 5, 15 March, 15, 25 April, 4, 14, 17, 27 May, 7, 9 June, 2 July, 3 November, 7 December, 9, 11, 20, 26 January, 28 April, 3, 7, 10 November 2006; 6 January, 16, 23 February 2007.

60. Hagger, *Diaries*, 5 January, 3, 9, 22, 28 February, 8, 10 March, 11 July 2006; 25–26 October 2007; 13 June, 1 July, 5, 20 October, 8 December 2006.

61. Hagger, *Diaries*, 20 February, 15 May, 20 November 2006.

62. Hagger, *Diaries*, 19 February, 17, 18 March, 2 April, 22 May, 2006; 16 October 2013; 13 July, 12–14 August, 20 August, 9–11, 28 October, 29 November, 22, 23, 28, 29 December 2006.

63. Hagger, *Diaries*, 23 January, 23, 27 February 2007; 18 April, 21 July–9 August, 17 September, 13 October, 4, 29 December 2006; 30 April 2007.

Episode 14: Order and Terror

1. Hagger, *Diaries*, 21, 25–27, 30, 31 May, 16, 18, 30 June, 29, 30 September, 2,

28 October, 1, 15–18, 20, 21 November, 25, 26, 30, 31 December 2006.

2. Hagger, *Diaries*, 14–20 January 2007.

3. Hagger, *Diaries*, 22 January, 23 March, 24, 18 April, 26–27 June, 4, 16 July 2007.

4. Hagger, *Diaries*, 21, 23 August, 5 December 2006; 9 February, 6, 8–11 March 2007.

5. Hagger, *Diaries*, 1–4, 8–11 January, 10 February, 19 March, 1–5, 8, 19–24, 27, 29 April, 4, 19–20, 26–31 May, 1, 4, 9–15, 18–21, 23 June, 6, 8–9, 14–17 July, 17, 21–23 August, 7–15 September 2007; 5–7, 10–11, 13, 17, 19–20, 23–25, 28, 30 May, 3 June 2008.

6. Hagger, *Diaries*, 13–14, 17 April 2007.

7. Hagger, *Diaries*, 5, 7–11, 16–17, 21–22, 24, 29, 30 May, 8 June, 15 July 2007. Full list of broadcasts in May–July 2007:

   • Jack Roberts of Cable Radio Network – CRN National National, 10 mins (8 May);
   • Jan Mickelson of WHO-AM Des Moines, 25 mins (8 May);
   • Greg Berg of WGTD-FM Milwaukee WI, 30 mins (8 May);
   • Brad Davis of Talk of Connecticut Hartford Regionally Syndicated CT, 10 mins (9 May);
   • Jeff Schectman of KVON-AM San Francisco, 30 mins (9 May);
   • Pat McMahon of KTAR-AM Phoenix AZ, 30 mins (9 May);
   • Brian Thomas/John of WKRC-AM Cincinnati, 15 mins (10 May);
   • Mike "Silk" Casper of WMDC Mayville WI, 10 mins (10 May);
   • Bill Meyer of KMED-AM Medford OR, 20 mins (10 May);
   • Eric Von Wade of KEYS-AM Corpus Christi, 30 mins (10 May);
   • Paul Miller of WPHM-AM, Detroit MI, 10 mins (11 May);
   • Charles Goyette of KFNX-AM Phoenix AR, 25 mins (11 May);
   • Jean Dean of WRVC-AM, Huntington, 30 mins (11 May);
   • Peter Solomon of WIP-AM Philadelphia PA, 30 mins (13 May);
   • Thom Hartmann of Eastern Air America Radio, The Thom Hartmann Show, National Syndicated, 15 mins (16 May);
   • Quinn of WHJY-WWDG-WHEP-WGIR-FM Providence, 15 mins (17 May);
   • Tommy B of KBUL-AM Billings MT, 30 mins (21 May);
   • Mancow of Fox Radio News Network, 20 mins (22 May);
   • Tron Simpson of KCMN-AM Colorado, 10 mins (24 May);
   • Mike & Amanda of WKWS-FM, Charleston WV, 10 mins (24 May);
   • John Cook of KMBH-FM Brownsville, 30 mins (29 May);
   • Sonja Harju & Fred Bremner of Lifeline Universal Media Statewide Oregon, 60 mins (4 June);
   • Don Lancer of KYW-AM Philadelphia PA, 10 mins (8 June);
   • Sharmai & Keith Amber of Hawaii Radio, 60 mins (15 July).

See http://www.bbsradio.com/beyondthematrix/, Patricia Cori, 24 February 2008.

8. Hagger, *Diaries*, 12, 14 May, 24 March 2007.

9. Hagger, *Diaries*, 7 February, 22 May, 4, 13 June, 7–8, 11 July 2007.

10. Hagger, *Diaries*, 22, 24, 26, 28 February, 5, 24, 26, 28–29 March, 4, 6, 18 April, 1–2, 4,12–13, 15 May 2007.

11. Hagger, *Diaries*, 19, 27 April, 23–31 July 2007.

12. Hagger, *Diaries*, 1–9 August, 1 September 2007.

13. Hagger, *Diaries*, 27–29 August, 3–7, 11, 15, 18–19, 20–21, 23–25, 27–28 September, 4–17, 20, 22–23, 27–28, 30 October, 1, 4 November 2007.

14. Hagger, *Diaries*, 5–26 November 2007; 8 September 2013.

15. Hagger, *Diaries*, 12, 24, 26 October, 1 November, 5, 9–10, 18, 22, 28 December 2007; 2, 3, 10, 12, 14, 17, 30 January, 1, 12, 18, 20, 24, 29 February, 3, 9–16, 18–19, 24, 29 March, 2, 5–25, 30 April 2008; 27 June, 12 July 2007; 31 March, 27, 30 April 2008.

16. Hagger, *Diaries*, 29 January, 8, 10–11 July, 14 September, 2, 14, 16 December 2008.

17. *Montgomery*, 26 December 2007; 6 January, 29 May 2008; in the Hagger archive.

18. Hagger, *Diaries*, 26 December 2007; 6 January, 3 August, 2, 4, 6, 8–10 September 2008.

19. Hagger, *Diaries*, 12, 15, 21, 22 September, 1 November 2007; 22, 24, 29 January, 8, 13–15, 22 February 2008.

20. Hagger, *Diaries*, 24 February 2008.

21. Hagger, *Diaries*, 22 March 2008.

22. Hagger, *Diaries*, 3 May 2008.

23. Hagger, *Diaries*, 14 May 2008.

24. Hagger, *Diaries*, 20 February, 2, 9, 19 May 2008.

25. Hagger, *Diaries*, 14, 27, 29 April, 14, 30 May, 5, 25 June 2008.

26. Hagger, *Diaries*, 25 June 2008.

27. Hagger, *Diaries*, 23 June 2008.

28. Hagger, *Diaries*, 10–12, 28 July 2008.

29. Hagger, *Diaries*, 20–25, 29 July 2008.

30. Hagger, *Diaries*, 16 February, 28–30 March, 7, 23 April, 10 June, 20 September 2007; 1, 3, 12, 22–23, 26–27, 29 May, 8–15, 20, 24, 28 June, 2, 3, 6, 16 July 2008; 12 August, 15–16 September 2007; 27, 29 July, 2–3, 5, 8, 10–12, 23, 26–27, 29–30 August, 2 September 2008.

31. Hagger, *Diaries*, 3 December 2007; 17, 19, 21 April, 16, 18, 20–23, 29 August, 5, 7, 11, 21–23, 26, 28, 30 September, 3, 8, 10–13, 18–19, 25, 27, 29 October, 2–4, 11, 28, 29 November, 2, 3, 10, 11, 17, 18, 20, 22 December 2008.

32. Hagger, *Diaries*, 8 June, 22, 23, 25 August, 5 September, 30–31 October, 2–4, 6, 8, 15–16, 21–25, 29 November, 9, 15–18, 20, 24, 29–30 December 2008; 3, 5,

9, 11, 13, 21 January, 4, 5 February 2009.

33. Hagger, *Diaries*, 6, 7, 9, 20 August 2008.
34. Hagger, *Diaries*, 11, 12, 14, 30 September, 2, 15, 21 October, 17, 20 November, 6, 8, 16 December 2008.
35. Hagger, *Diaries*, 18 September 2008.
36. Hagger, *Diaries*, 1 October 2008.
37. Hagger, *Diaries*, 7 August, 22 October 2008; 20 February 2009.
38. Hagger, *Diaries*, 18, 24 November 2008.
39. Hagger, *Diaries*, 21 December 2008; 26 December 2007; 20 November, 1, 5, 14, 21, 27 December 2008.
40. Hagger, *Diaries*, 1, 29 February 2008; 9, 13, 23, 30 January 2009.
41. Hagger, *Diaries*, 7–8 February 2009.
42. Hagger, *Diaries*, 9, 13 November, 19 December 2008; 12, 13 January 2009; 3, 10, 13, 23 December 2008; 8, 15–18, 19–21, 24–27, 29 January, 1, 9, 12, 16, 24 February, 2, 6–7, 17, 21, 27–30 March 2009.
43. Hagger, *Diaries*, 26 February–1 March 2009.
44. Hagger, *Diaries*, 3–4 May 2009.
45. Hagger, *Diaries*, 11–12 May, 15 June 2009.
46. Hagger, *Diaries*, 16 June, 28 January, 19 March, 20, 24 April, 17–18, 20, 22–24, 10, 30 May, 4, 26 June, 2 July 2009.
47. Hagger, *Diaries*, 23, 24, 25–26 July 2009.
48. Hagger, *Diaries*, 9, 12, 16, 24 February, 2, 6–7, 17, 21, 26–30 March, 2, 7, 9–15, 18, 20, 24–26, 28–30 April, 2–4, 6, 9, 15–16, 19, 27, 29–31 May, 4, 8, 9–10, 12–14, 18–20, 23–24, 26–27, 29–30 June, 3, 28, 30 July, 1, 4, 10–11 August, 2, 7, 9 April, 21, 26–28 August, 5–6, 8, 10 October, 12 July 2009.

Episode 15: Internationalism and Localism
1. Hagger, *Diaries*, 24 October, 12–13 November, 29, 31 December 2008; 2 January, 11–13, 14, 16, 17–19, 26, 29 August, 1–2, 5, 10, 16–18 September, 4, 11–20, 28, 30 October, 1–4, 6, 10–11, 13, 18–21, 23 November 2009; 23 March 2011; 21, 26–28 August, 13, 30 September, 1, 5–6, 8, 10, 29 October, 16 November 2009; 5–12, 14–18, 25–26, 31 March, 1 April 2010.
2. Hagger, *Diaries*, 20, 30 September, 2, 9, 11–12, 14, 16, 25, 28–30 November, 1–3 December, 24 November, 15–16, 19, 24, 29 December 2009; 4–5, 7, 9–11, 17 January, 1, 3–11, 16–17, 22, 24 February, 2–3, 12, 17, 30 March, 3, 7, 10–11, 15–16, 19, 27 April, 14–18, 28, 30 June, 1, 5, 7, 12–14 July, 13–17, 12 August 2010.
3. Hagger, *Diaries*, 20 November 2008; 26 October, 3, 5, 19 November 2009; 15 March 2010. For 15–50 per cent, *see* 'UK law: What proportion is influenced by the EU?', https://fullfact.org/europe/eu_make_uk_law-29587.
4. Hagger, *Diaries*, 29 September, 5, 13–15, 18, 20–21, 30 November, 3, 15 December 2008; 16, 23, 28, 30 January, 2, 7 February 2010.

5. Hagger, *Diaries*, 19 April–14 June, 23 January, 28 February, 26 March, 24 April 2010.

6. Hagger, *Diaries*, 22 May, 27 June 2010.

7. Hagger, *Diaries*, 6 June 2010.

8. Hagger, *Diaries*, 21, 23, 27 June 2010; Nicholas Hagger's email to Jonathan Bate, 5 July 2010.

9. Hagger, *Diaries*, 6 July 2010.

10. Hagger, *Diaries*, 23, 27 January, 16 July 2010.

11. Hagger, *Diaries*, 17–19 July 2010.

12. Hagger, *Diaries*, 20 March, 2, 11 April 2010.

13. Hagger, *Diaries*, 2, 18 June, 27–30 July, 6–10, 12, 19 August 2010.

14. Hagger, *Diaries*, 20, 26, 30 May 2010.

15. Hagger, *Diaries*, 6–8, 17, 18, 20–22 October, 9, 11,14, 15, 19, 21–23 November, 17 December 2009; 14 April, 30, 31 May, 2, 18–20 June, 9, 11, 12, 15, 21, 23–30 July, 7, 8, 10, 19–21, 25 August 2010.

16. Hagger, *Diaries*, 2, 5 April, 5 May, 26–27, 29, 31 August, 1–6 September 2010; 20 September 2010–21 April 2011.

17. Hagger, *Diaries*, 20 September 2010–21 April 2011 for "eight-month haul".

18. Hagger, *Diaries*, 7, 8 March, 2012.

19. Hagger, *Diaries*, 27, 29 March, 1 April 2012; 11 December 2011.

20. Hagger, *Diaries*, 19, 26 November 2010; 22 February, 6, 13–15, 21–24, 26 April 2011; 19, 26–27 October, 2012.

21. Hagger, *Diaries*, 24, 25 February, 21 March 2011; 17 February 2012. For 1,700 militias, *see* http://www.bbc.co.uk/news/world-africa-25701470.

22. Hagger, *Diaries*, 15 March 2011.

23. Hagger, *Diaries*, 19 April 2011.

24. Hagger, *Diaries*, 12, 26–27 November 2010.

25. Hagger, *Diaries*, 11 June, 30 September, 16 October, 24, 25, 30 November 2010.

26. Hagger, *Diaries*, 9 October, 14 December 2010; 4, 6, 7 January 2011.

27. Hagger, *Diaries*, 13, 26 January 2011.

28. Hagger, *Diaries*, 11, 15 November, 7 December 2010; 22 January 2011.

29. Hagger, *Diaries*, 25 April, 2, 21 May, 24, 29 June, 28 July, 8 August, 27 October, 6 April–8 November 2011.

30. Hagger, *Diaries*, 31 August, 1, 2 September 2011.

31. Hagger, *Diaries*, 16 September, 8 November 2011.

32. Peter Stanford, *Bronwen Astor, Her Life and Times*, p.135.

33. Hagger, *Diaries*, 12 May 2011.

34. Hagger, *Diaries*, 1–5 July 2011.

35. Hagger, *Diaries*, 19–20 August 2011.

36. Hagger, *Diaries*, 28, 31 December 2006; 15 March, 27, 31 December 2007; 19 January, 19, 29 April 2008; 2, 4 December 2009; 13, 14 March, 19 September

2010; 1 January, 1 July, 13, 17 August, 13, 15–17, 19–20 November 2011; 2 December 2011–19 April 2012.

37. Hagger, *Diaries*, 30 September–2 October 2011.

38. Hagger, *Diaries*, 30 September, 17 May, 1, 5 June, 16, 22, 23 August, 20 October 2011.

39. Damian McElroy, 'Gaddafi died after being stabbed with bayonet, says report,' *The Daily Telegraph*, 17 October 2012; Martin Fletcher, 'Revealed, the final desperate days of Gaddafi and loyalists', *The Times*, 17 October 2012.

40. The *New York Times*, articles selected in association with the *Observer*, 17 June 2012, pp.1, 4. The Libyan banker was Abdelhamid el-Jadi.

41. Hagger, *Diaries*, 28–31 October, 2–6 December 2011; 10 January, 26–28 February, 1–2, 23–24, 29 March 2012.

42. Hagger, *Diaries*, 18 March 2012; 13 November 2011; 8 April, 6 May, 26–28 April, 16, 20 May 2012.

43. Hagger, Diaries, 3, 6–7, 10 June 2012.

44. *See* http://www.oaklandsschool.co.uk/75th-anniversary-celebration.

45. Hagger, *Diaries*, 19 June, 1, 2 July 2012.

46. Hagger, *Diaries*, 10 August 2012.

47. Hagger, *Diaries*, 26 May, 4, 7–9, 11 June, 13, 16–19 August 2012; 28 October 2012–7 September 2013 (*The Rise and Fall of Civilizations*).

48. Hagger, *Diaries*, 31 May, 1, 3–4 June 2011.

49. Hagger, *Diaries*, 24 February, 26 October, 1, 2 November, 10 December 2012.

50. Hagger, *Diaries*, 22–24 December 2012.

51. Hagger, *Diaries*, 14, 23 December 2012.

52. Hagger, *Diaries*, 20, 21, 23, 22, 24 February–8 March, 11–13 March 2013.

53. Hagger, *Diaries*, 16, 17, 23 January, 22–23 March, 25 April, 2, 16 May 2013.

54. Hagger, *Diaries*, 10, 15, 17 April, 22 May 2013. For 15–50 per cent, *see* 'UK law: What proportion is influenced by the EU?', https://fullfact.org/europe/eu_make_uk_law-29587.

55. Hagger, *Diaries*, 19 February, 26 April, 21, 31 May, 3 June, 2 July, 27 June, 3, 5, 19–21 July, 7, 12 August 2013.

56. Hagger, *Diaries*, 29 August 2013.

57. *See American Free Press*, 13 May 2013, p.15, 'US Makes Case For Wrecking Syria Like It Has Iraq, Afghanistan, Libya'.

58. Hagger, *Diaries*, 7 September 2013.

Epilogue: Rainbow over Hills
Episodes, structure, pattern and unity in double lives

1. H.G. Wells, *Selected Short Stories*, pp.123–146.

Bibliography/Reading List

Anderson, William, *Dante the Maker*, Hutchinson, 1983.

Bohm, David, *A Suggest Interpretation of the Quantum Theory Hidden under Variables, Physical Review,* vol. 85, No. 2, 15 January 1952.

Bohm, David, *Wholeness and the Implicate Order*, Routledge, London, 1980.

Crozier, Brian, *Free Agent: The Unseen War 1941–1991*, HarperCollins, 1993.

Galinsky, Karl, *Augustan Culture*, Princeton University Press, 1996.

Gascoyne, David, *Journal 1937–1939*, Enitharmon Press, 1978.

Global 2000 Report to the President, Penguin, London, 1982.

Global Future: Time to Act, Report to the President on Global Resources, Environment and Population, Council on Environmental Quality, Department of State, January 1981.

Hagger, Nicholas, *A New Philosophy of Literature*, O-Books, 2012.

Hagger, Nicholas, *A View of Epping Forest*, O-Books, 2012.

Hagger, Nicholas, *Awakening to the Light*, Element, 1994.

Hagger, Nicholas, *Collected Poems 1958–2005*, O-Books, 2006.

Hagger, Nicholas, *My Double Life 1: This Dark Wood*, O-Books, 2015.

Hagger, Nicholas, *Scargill the Stalinist?*, Oak-Tree Books, 1984.

Hagger, Nicholas, *The Libyan Revolution* , O-Books, 2009.

Hagger, Nicholas, *The Secret History of the West*, O-Books, 2005.

Hagger, Nicholas, *The Universe and the Light*, Element, 1993.

Hakluyt, *Voyages*, vols 1–8, Everyman's Library, 1907, 1962.

Keeler, Christine, with Douglas Thompson, *The Truth at Last, My Story*, Sidgwick & Jackson, 2001.

MacCulloch, Diarmaid, *Suffolk and the Tudors: Politics and Religion in an English County, 1500–1600*, Oxford University Press, 1986.

McForan, Desmond, *The World Held Hostage, The War Waged by International Terrorism*, Oak-Tree Books, 1986.

Milne, Seumas, *The Enemy Within, The Secret War Against the Miners*, Verso, 1994.

Perry, Roland, *The Fifth Man*, Sedgwick and Jackson, 1994.

Rawnsley, Hardwicke Drummond, *Reminiscences of Wordsworth among the Peasantry of Westmoreland*, Dillon's, 1968.

Roberts, Michael, ed. *Faber Book of Modern Verse*, Faber & Faber, 1951.

Stanford, Peter, *Bronwen Astor, Her Life and Times*, HarperCollins, 2001.

Tillyard, E.M.W., *The English Epic and Its Background*, Oxford University Press, 1966.

Tomlin, E.W.F., *T.S. Eliot: A Friendship*, Routledge, 1988.

Wells, H.G., *Selected Short Stories*, Penguin, 1958.

Whitehead, Alfred North, *An Anthology selected by F.S.C. Northrop & Mason W. Gross*, Cambridge University Press, 1953.

Index

Note: Page numbers for illustrations appear in italics. Titles of books where the author is not indicated are by Nicholas Hagger. Entries are mainly in alphabetical order but in some cases, where they describe a narrative, in chronological or page order.

birthday tea 558
95th birthday 578
death of 597–8, 896
funeral 598–600
Broadley, Tom I 196, 863, *889*
killed on spying mission 836
the Brocken spectre 514
Brod, Max 711, 743
Brokenshire, James 670, 737, 774, 811
Brooke, Rupert 128
Brooklyn Avenue 862
Broten, Henning 413–14, 415, 417
Brown, A.B. 77
Bruce MacManaway's healing centre
78–9
Brugge (Bruges) 252
and Holy Blood; and Grail cup 236
Bryan-Brown, A.N. 786
Bryan, Charlie 563, 588, 625
curator Richmond Museum 560
Buchan, John 208
Buckingham Palace garden party 737
Budapest Betrayed (Gorka) 318, 721
decision to end publishing 252,
254
finished with State education and
publishing 256
launch 246–9, 893
challenges post-war British
foreign policy 248
calls for a free Eastern Europe
247
Communism seems unassailable
249
denounces Philby 248
live broadcast into the USSR on
FREE 247, *247*
Sabbat on Nicholas's challenge
to 1943 Tehran Agreement 248
silence 249
Thatcher sends best wishes 248
wounds the chimera 248

and Philby's betrayal 45, 242
publishers' dinner 254
silence round 251
Bukovsky, Vladimir 244, 250, 494
founds Resistance International
incorporating FREE 246, 250
Bulganin, Nikolay Aleksandrovich
253
Bullock, Larry 857
Bunyan, John 60
Burford, Charles, Earl of (later
Charles Beauclerk) 536, 577, 896
asks to work at Otley Hall 572–3
book on Nell Gwyn 620
brings SAT and de Vere Society
libraries 572–3
changes name to Charles Beauclerk
620
and Dukedom of St Albans 572,
616
gift of 'Earl of Oxford concord' 609
Nicholas's Literary Secretary 572–3
plan to disrupt the Lords 596
protest: leap onto woolsack
616–17, 897
resigns from Otley Hall 620, 621,
626
stands in by-election 617–18
and transition from nation-state to
European state 618
view of Shakespeare as 17th Earl of
Oxford 534–5
"Your work is like a cathedral
amid modern buildings" 572
Bushwerib, Col. Saad eddin 77
Butler, Judge Gerald 790, 808
Byron, Lord George Gordon 22, 457,
624
'Byzantium' (Yeats) 458

Caesar, Julius 582
calm and unitive life 26

Index

Index

BOOKS

O is a symbol of the world, of oneness and unity. In different cultures it also means the "eye," symbolizing knowledge and insight. We aim to publish books that are accessible, constructive and that challenge accepted opinion, both that of academia and the "moral majority."

Our books are available in all good English language bookstores worldwide. If you don't see the book on the shelves ask the bookstore to order it for you, quoting the ISBN number and title. Alternatively you can order online (all major online retail sites carry our titles) or contact the distributor in the relevant country, listed on the copyright page.

See our website www.o-books.com for a full list of over 500 titles, growing by 100 a year.

And tune in to myspiritradio.com for our book review radio show, hosted by June-Elleni Laine, where you can listen to the authors discussing their books.

MySpiritRadio